Canadian Cataloguing in Publication Data

Lefton, Lester A., 1946–
  Psychology

Canadian ed.
Includes bibliographical references and index
ISBN 0-205-30493-1

1. Psychology. I. Boyes, Michael Clifford, 1955– . II. Ogden, Nancy Anne,
1958– . III. Title.

BF121.L43 2000   150   C99-931626-5

Allyn and Bacon, Inc., Needham Heights, MA
Prentice-Hall, Inc., Upper Saddle River, New Jersey
Prentice-Hall International (UK) Limited, London
Prentice-Hall of Australia, Pty. Limited, Sydney
Prentice-Hall Hispanoamericana, S.A., Mexico City
Prentice-Hall of India Private Limited, New Delhi
Prentice-Hall of Japan, Inc., Tokyo
Simon & Schuster Southeast Asia Private Limited, Singapore
Editora Prentice-Hall do Brasil, Ltda., Rio de Janeiro

ISBN 0-205-30493-1

Vice President, Editorial Director: Laura Pearson
Acquisitions Editor: Nicole Lukach
Signing Representative: Colleen Henderson
Marketing Manager: Kathleen McGill
Developmental Editor: Dawn du Quesnay
Production Editor: Andrew Winton
Copy Editor: Susan Broadhurst
Production Coordinator: Wendy Moran
Photo Research: Susan Wallace-Cox
Art Director: Mary Opper
Cover Design: Alex Li
Cover Image: Yukimasa Hirota/Photonica
Page Layout: Debbie Kumpf

Original English Language edition published by Allyn and Bacon, Inc., Needham Heights, MA.
Copyright © 2000, 1997, 1994, 1991, 1985, 1982, 1979.

1 2 3 4 5   04 03 02 01 00

Printed and bound in the United States of America.

Visit the Prentice Hall Canada web site! Send us your comments, browse our catalogues, and more at
www.phcanada.com. Or reach us through e-mail at **phabinfo_pubcanada@prenhall.com**.

www.prenticehall.ca/lefton

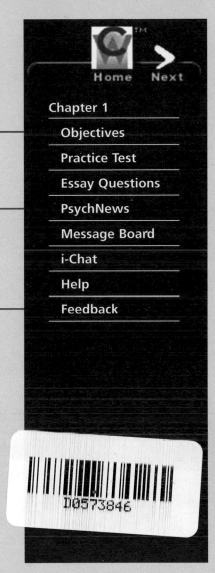

2) Online Study Guide

Interactive Study Guide modules form the core of the student learning experience in the Companion Website. These modules are categorized according to their functionality:

- Learning Objectives
- Practice Tests
- Essay questions
- FAQ's

The Practice Test modules provide students with the ability to send answers to our grader and receive instant feedback on their progress through our Results Reporter. Coaching comments and references back to the textbook ensure that students take advantage of all resources available to enhance their learning experience.

3) Reference Material

New material from the field broadens the coverage in the text. The **PsychNews** module contains regularly updated articles from every area of psychology, relevant to each chapter. Students can check in here to see what's happening in the world of psychology.

4) Communication

Companion Websites contain the communication tools necessary to deliver courses in a **Distance Learning** environment. **Message Board** allows users to post messages and check back periodically for responses. **i-Chat** allows users to discuss course topics in real time, and enables professors to host on-line classes.

Communication facilities of Companion Websites provide a key element for distributed learning environments. There are two types of communication facilities currently in use in Companion Websites:

- **Message Board** – this module takes advantage of browser technology providing the users of each Companion Website with a national newsgroup to post and reply to relevant course topics.

- **i-Chat** – enables instructor-led group activities in real time. Using our chat client, instructors can display Website content while students participate in the discussion.

Note: Companion Website content will vary slightly from site to site depending on discipline requirements.

The Companion Website for this text can be found at:
www.prenticehall.ca/lefton

**ALLYN AND
BACON CANADA**

1870 Birchmount Road
Scarborough, Ontario M1P 2J7

To order:
Call: 1-800-567-3800
Fax: 1-800-263-7733

For samples:
Call: 1-800-850-5813
Fax: (416) 299-2539
E-mail:
phcinfo_pubcanada@pearsoned.com

Psychology

CANADIAN EDITION

Lester A. Lefton
The George Washington University

Michael C. Boyes
University of Calgary

Nancy A. Ogden
Mount Royal College

Allyn and Bacon Canada
Toronto

To my wife, Linda,
a woman of great beauty,
courage, strength, and sensitivity.
Linda is my wife, my partner,
and, especially, my friend.

— L.A.L

For our children: Michael, Daniel, Danielle,
David, Kathryn, Emily

— M.C.B., N.A.O.

Brief Contents

Contents

Chapter 4
Consciousness   114

Chapter 5
Learning   150

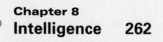

To the Student

Welcome to the Lefton learning experience! No matter who you are, this book will have meaning for you because it deals with everyday issues of human thought and behaviour.

- If you are having difficulty with your roommate . . .
- If the adjustment to college or university was more difficult than you thought it would be . . .
- If you become stressed out over exams and papers . . .
- If you argue with your parents . . .
- If a friend has been depressed for a long time . . .
- If you have difficulty retaining information for tests . . .

then reading this book will give you insights. We believe very strongly in helping students retain all of the insights they can from a book; therefore, we have made a special effort to make psychology both understandable and interesting.

Be an Active Learner

The following important study tips will increase your effectiveness as a student and help to reduce your stress level as you study:

- Become actively involved in the learning process.
- Make new information meaningful by linking information that you are learning for the first time to your life experiences and knowledge.
- Be responsible for your own learning.

Use the Study Skills Guide

One way to really improve your studying and to be an active learner is to use the SQ3R system, which reminds learners to *survey, question, read, recite,* and *review* when reading textbooks (Robinson, 1970). Students have used SQ3R effectively and successfully for over 50 years. It is a tried-and-true active study method, which is why it is the strategy most recommended by psychology professors. The original SQ3R method has been modified slightly to "SQ3R plus": *survey, question, read, recite, review*—plus *write* and *reflect*. To be an effective learner of psychology, follow the steps on pages xvii–xviii of this preface to apply the SQ3R plus system.

Use the Pedagogical Features

Pedagogical features are integrated in *Psychology, Canadian Edition* to stimulate your active involvement with and critical thinking about issues, as well as to help you learn more efficiently and effectively.

Brain and Behaviour. *Psychology* particularly emphasizes the relationship between biology and the environment. Psychologists now recognize that people are influenced by both genetics and the environment. We have integrated biological concepts and neuropsychology throughout the text and have focused on high-interest topics in special sections called "Brain and Behaviour." Topics include plasticity of the brain, perceiving faces, melatonin, the biology behind learning, and study techniques that can help you take advantage of how the brain functions so you will remember more effectively. A full-colour two-page spread in Chapter 2 (see pages 52 and 53) with graphic representations of the brain will help you locate the parts of the brain as you read about them in the text. We suggest you flag this page right away for easy reference as you progress through the text.

◀

InterActivities. The icon in the margin of the text indicates a link to a relevant Web site on the Internet. Links to the sites can be found at the Lefton Web site at *http://www.prenticehall.ca/lefton*. The icons indicate topics that will be updated at the Web site so that you will have access to the most recent events and research in the field of psychology.

Study Skills Guide. At the end of this section is a guide full of learning tips (see pages xv and xvi). Once you have read it over, you may want to flag the list of SQ3R learning steps so that you can keep them in mind as you study.

Critical Thinking. Learning about psychology means learning about the thinking process itself. Developing critical thinking skills is thus a major theme—from Chapter 1's introduction to the scientific method and critical thinking (on pp. 6 and 12), to Think Critically questions at the end of major sections, to questions within the text that model critical thinking. In addition, special sections called *The Research Process* show you how psychologists use (and sometimes abuse) the scientific method.

◀

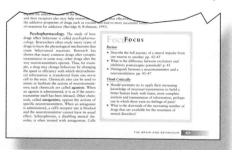

◀

Focus. According to learning theory, retention improves if you review and rethink what you have read. Throughout the text, short review sections called *Focus* will remind you to pause, answer questions, and think about what you have just learned. Some questions will review what you have learned; others will encourage you to think critically—to go beyond what you have read to form new connections. The *Focus* boxes are conveniently placed and include page references to show where topics are discussed in the text. Answers to the questions in the *Focus* sections are available from your instructor, if you need to check your answers.

Key Terms. Key terms appear in boldface type in the text and are defined in the margin as well as in the end-of-book *Glossary*, with a pronunciation guide where appropriate. In addition, the key terms are listed with page references within each chapter's *Summary and Review*, to provide you with an additional opportunity to review key concepts after you have finished the chapter.

Building Tables. Presenting important theories and concepts in a way that shows the development of ideas is a major pedagogical element in this text. Widely applauded by students and instructors in the United States, the *Building Tables* have remained a key part of this Canadian edition. As you master a set of concepts, it is added to a Building Table that lists related concepts. These tables allow you to compare, contrast, and integrate concepts. They, too, are an excellent study and review aid.

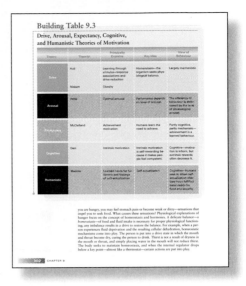

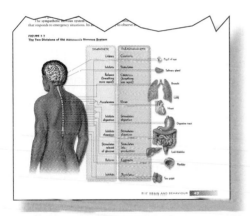

Art. A picture can be worth a thousand words, especially if you are a visual learner. Inspired by the look of the World Wide Web, the art in *Psychology* has been designed with a three-dimensional look. The anatomical and brain art was rendered by a studio specializing in medical illustrations to ensure greater accuracy and pedagogical value.

Diversity. A goal of the text is to introduce you to the growing diversity of Canadian culture and to show you how multicultural factors must be taken into account when viewing psychological data. This means thinking critically about issues such as gender, ethnicity, age, and socioeconomic status. Multicultural topics are featured in special *Diversity* sections throughout the text.

Experiencing Psychology. Featuring interesting topics such as left-handedness, tickling, happiness, and proactive coping, the *Experiencing Psychology* sections focus on how psychology can be applied to everyday life. The goal is to show how psychologists build bridges between research and application. Experiencing psychology is also a recurring theme throughout the text.

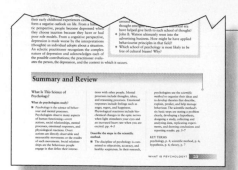

Chapter Summary and Review. Every chapter ends with a carefully structured *Summary and Review*. The summary is organized by section headings and includes page references to relevant portions of the text. The review is set up in a question-and-answer format and includes a list of key terms.

Use the Supplements

 ou can further reinforce your learning by making use of a variety of supplements that are designed to enhance the Lefton learning experience. These supplements are available from Allyn and Bacon Canada.

Keeping Pace Plus. *Keeping Pace Plus* is an active reading study guide. This carefully structured study guide helps you participate actively in learning about psychology. It contains book-specific exercises, learning objectives, review sections, and a language enrichment section for students who need help with vocabulary. With page-referenced reviews, *Keeping Pace Plus* guarantees a total learning experience for anyone who uses it.

Allyn and Bacon Canada Interactive Web site. The purchase of a new book provides you with a direct connection to Peregrine Publisher's *Psychology Place*, which offers users of this text a variety of exercises to enhance the total learning experience. The *Psychology Place* includes practice tests, learning objectives, chapter summaries, and links to relevant Internet sites, as well as a wealth of activities and simulations. It provides access to an abundance of timely and highly interesting material, which will be updated and often and will evolve continually.

Allyn and Bacon PSYCH-ED!: Core Concepts in Psychology Interactive CD-ROM. This interactive CD-ROM covers 14 core psychology topics. Through a central Resource Centre, you can access the following features:

- *Guided Tour*, a brief tutorial
- *Topic Exploration*, the heart of the program, is designed to enhance your understanding of the 14 core concepts. Each topic includes a Video Focus, which offers related video features with critical thinking questions; a Guided Review, which offers summaries, definitions, and animations to enhance your understanding of psychology's major themes and concepts; Try It! Activities, which engage you in hands-on activities to let you experience psychology yourself; and Test Your Knowledge, which are multiple-choice questions with feedback on right and wrong answers.
- The *Library* provides another rich resource of reference materials. It contains indexes of figures, videos, and key terms, and it allows you to browse these at will. The Library also contains a special section on improving study skills.

Evaluating Psychological Information: Sharpening Your Critical Thinking Skills, Third Edition. Developed by James Bell, this workbook focuses on helping you evaluate psychological research systematically and improve your critical thinking skills.

Tools of Critical Thinking. This critical thinking text by David A. Levy provides tools and skills for approaching all forms of problem solving, particularly in psychology.

Psychologically Speaking: A Self-Assessment. Craig Poulenez Donovan and Peter C. Rosato have prepared a workbook of enjoyable self-assessment exercises paralleling the chapters in the text.

The SQ3R Plus System

One way to really improve your studying and to be an active learner is to use the SQ3R system, which reminds learners to *survey, question, read, recite, and review* when reading textbooks (Robinson, 1970). Students have used SQ3R effectively and successfully for over fifty years. It is a tried-and-true active study method, which is why it is the reading strategy most recommended by psychology professors. We have modified the original SQ3R method slightly to SQ3R plus: survey, question, read, recite, review, plus write and reflect. To be an effective learner, use the SQ3R plus system when studying psychology.

To use SQ3R plus, follow the steps outlined below:

Review. Before you begin studying:

■ Read the outline at the beginning of the chapter and the chapter's opening paragraphs; this will provide a brief overview of the chapter.

■ Scan topic headings and examine the *Focus* questions that appear throughout the chapter in order to further refine your overview of the chapter's goals.

■ Look at the photos, art, tables, and graphs to get a visual idea of what you will be studying.

■ Scan the tables, especially the Building Tables, for a preview of the concepts that you will want to compare and contrast as you read. By doing so, you can learn the similarities and differences among various theories presented.

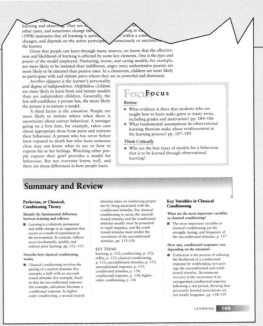

■ Pay attention to other special features, such as print styles, the use of color in the text, and the *Summary and Review* sections.

■ You may also want to plan a brief study break at the end of each major section in the chapter.

Question. Develop questions based on the topic headings within the chapter. Examine the *Focus* questions that appear every few pages. This step will increase your involvement, interest, and concentration because each question you ask gives you the goal of finding the answers.

Read. Read the text and answer the questions you've asked. Focus on making the material you are reading personally relevant.

Recite. Recite means saying things from memory. You can also be an active learner by putting concepts in your own words.

Review. Double-check the accuracy of your recall and your understanding of the material to be learned. Try to pull together key terms and concepts. You may wish to use one of the many Allyn and Bacon supplements. The supplements include a study guide, practice tests, an on-line study guide, and an interactive CD-ROM, all designed specifically to enhance your learning experience. You can also visit the Psychology Place learning site via *www.prenticehall.ca/lefton*.

Write and **reflect**. Write a summary of key points to increase the quality and quantity of your learning. When you reflect on your own learning, you are not only an active learner but also a critical thinker—a person able to make good use of newly learned information.

Improve Your Memory

Rehearse! If you want to remember something, there's no substitute for rehearsal. If you really want to remember ideas for a long time, you need to understand them; and this requires the use of elaborative rehearsal. With elaborative rehearsal, you generate meaning as you repeat and think about the information.

Be an active learner. By simply using your own thoughts, asking and answering your own questions, and organizing information in ways that make sense to you, you become an active learner.

Generate personal meaning. Find ways to connect yourself and your experiences to the material you are studying.

Practice over time. Study a particular subject for a relatively short time every day or every other day, rather than trying to cram it all into one session.

Plan on relearning. Most forgetting occurs right after something has been learned. If you go back and relearn the same material, you will learn it more quickly and forget less of it.

Take advantage of the primacy and recency effects. You are most likely to remember information received at the beginning and at the end of a study session or lecture. So, instead of forcing yourself to have long, drawn-out study sessions, take a short (5- to 10-minute) break after you have studied for 20 to 30 minutes.

Focus to prevent interference. When studying, focus on one course or learning task at a time. Make use of chunking. Break up or group ideas together in an organized way in order to memorize them.

Use mnemonics. Use memory aids such as acronyms, slogans, or jingles to help you remember.

Use mediation. Mediation is a bridging technique that allows you to link two items to be remembered with a third item or image that ties them together and serves as a cue for retrieval.

Use the von Restorff effect. Make one item in a group of things to be learned stand out; it will be easier to remember. Exaggerate the meaning of the idea you want to remember by making the idea seem funny or bizarre.

Review in different contexts or modalities. Try to review and rehearse in different settings or through more than one sense. For example, if you first hear the information, also write it down.

Prepare the environment. Study in a quiet place and limit distractions.

SQ3R Plus Keys to Studying

SURVEY

- Read the outline and the chapter's opening paragraphs.
- Scan topic headings and examine the *Focus* questions.
- Look at the photos, art, tables, and graphs for a visual overview.
- Scan the tables, especially the Building Tables, for a preview of the concepts that you will want to compare and contrast.
- Pay attention to other special features, such as print styles, the use of colour in the text, and the *Summary and Review* sections.
- Plan a brief study break at the end of each major section.

QUESTION

- Develop questions based on the topic headings within the chapter.
- Examine the *Focus* questions.

READ

- Read the text carefully and answer the questions you've asked. Make the material personally relevant.

RECITE

- Say things from memory, putting concepts in your own words.

REVIEW

- Double-check the accuracy of your recall.
- Try to pull together key terms and concepts.

WRITE AND REFLECT

- Write a summary of key points in your own words and think about how they relate to your life.

To the Instructor

Writing this book was both an adventure and a challenge. Six strategic goals guided our work on *Psychology, Canadian Edition*. First and foremost, we wanted to keep current with the new directions in psychology, so we have written many sections of the book to reflect the new explosion of information on neuropsychology. We also have emphasized the coverage of evolutionary psychology and behavioural genetics. Second, we wanted to stress diversity and sensitivity to culture and gender; we were particularly interested in showing that psychologists must consider the wide range of participants in research. To make reasonable generalizations about human behaviour they must consider ethnic, cultural, age, and gender bias. Third, we wanted to show that research is a cornerstone of psychology; *Psychology, Canadian Edition*, reflects an emphasis on the role of research in psychology, highlighting important Canadian contributions. In emphasizing the importance of research, we especially wanted to focus on critical thinking as a key to good scientific thought and research—our fourth goal. Fifth, we wanted to focus on how applications grow from research and how psychologists build conceptual bridges between research and applications. Last, we wanted to be sure to sustain student interest and understanding. It can sometimes be difficult to blend three authorial voices, but to help accomplish this last goal, we have tried to harmonize three distinct voices into one highly personable, reader-friendly style.

Psychology, Canadian Edition: Content and Organization

Content. *Psychology, Canadian Edition*, covers the core concepts of psychology in addition to emerging trends and topics. The chapters on the biological bases of behaviour, memory, and cognition have received particular attention, to ensure that they reflect the most current thinking and research available. In addition, the chapters on intelligence, development, psychological disorders, treatment, and social psychology were thoroughly scrutinized and revised. Current data and theories on neuropsychology, behavioural genetics, and evolutionary psychology are presented. The applied fields are similarly represented, with complete coverage of topics such as child development, gender differences, performance appraisal, and testing issues. The text covers high-interest topics including therapy, codependence, substance abuse, brain plasticity, and Alzheimer's disease. These topics are presented in an integrated manner, bringing science and application together and showing how they flow directly from traditional psychology. The content of the text reflects the current status of psychological science without being trendy or neglecting the classics.

Canadian Content. *Psychology, Canadian Edition* was conceived out of the need for more textbooks that provide a familiar, Canadian context for our students. Canadian places and cultural icons, sports heroes and entertainers, demographics, census data, and laws are woven throughout the text to help students feel at home, and to give them a truer picture of the society in which they are studying psychology.

This text attempts to enhance that picture in two additional ways. First, significant Canadian research is highlighted where it is relevant and illustrates important psychological concepts. This alerts students to the fact that important psychological research has been done in the past and is being done now in this country, and it sets an encouraging example for those who want to go on in the study of psychology. Students will read about classic and contemporary Canadian research such as the sensory deprivation experiments at McGill in the 1950s, the work of Seudfeld and Coren at UBC on Restricted Environmental Stimulation, the pioneering work of Hebb on human memory and thinking, and Ames's work at Simon Fraser University on the adjustment of Romanian orphans adopted by Canadian parents.

Second, this text reflects the ethnic diversity of Canadian society, which is obviously very different from that of American society and, in fact, unique in the world. Diversity topics covered include psychology that is uniquely Canadian, ethnic youth gangs in Manitoba and Toronto, self-perception in Canadians versus Japanese, the effects of stress on recent immigrants and Canadian farmers, Asian Canadians and mental health, and suicide in aboriginal communities, to name just a few.

Brain and Behaviour. *Psychology, Canadian Edition* particularly emphasizes the relationship between biology and the environment. Psychologists now recognize that people are influenced by both genetics and the environment. We have integrated biology and neuropsychology throughout the text and have focused on high-interest topics in special sections called *Brain and Behaviour*. Topics include plastic reorganization of the somatosensory areas of the brain, prosopagnosia, melatonin, the biological underpinnings of learning, and the neurochemistry of schizophrenia.

Organization. We talked with hundreds of psychology teachers to determine the most logical and sought-after chapter sequence and internal chapter structure. You will notice that the social psychology chapter follows the chapter on personality, with its focus on the individual; this seemed to us the most logical placement. This decision was also a response to professors who preferred to see the growth of social psychology acknowledged by placing the chapter earlier in the text than is usual. Still, every chapter is written so that it can either stand alone or be read in sequence with others. Also, every chapter has been written with the aim of providing a structured approach, with a smooth, cohesive flow of information. The internal structure of each chapter attempts to match the way teachers present material.

Supplements for Instructors

The *Instructor's Resource Manual* contains a wealth of classroom activities, demonstrations and handouts, and numerous additional teaching aids, including learning objectives, annotated lecture outlines, lecture examples, and suggestions for using other supplements.

A lengthy *Test Item File* has been developed, and is also available in *computerized format* (in Macintosh or Windows platforms). Many of the items have been classroom-tested and validated. Over 3000 multiple-choice questions are available on the test bank.

A full set of colour acetate *transparencies* is available to enhance classroom lectures and discussions, along with a supplemental set of 60 acetates newly rendered for the U.S. Seventh Edition.

An interactive *video*, with on-screen critical thinking questions and a video user's guide, has been developed to accompany *Psychology*; the video segments illustrate real-life applications of the textbook topics and provide a springboard for initiating classroom discussions. The accompanying video user's guide offers suggestions for how to use the video in class and contains a summary of each video segment.

The *Digital Media Archive* is a CD-ROM that contains hundreds of full-colour digitized images, audio, video, and lecture outlines to enhance introductory psychology lectures. The Digital Media Archive contains digitized images of some of the upgraded art in this edition.

A *PowerPoint presentation*, for Windows, is also available to accompany the text.

Allyn and Bacon Canada also makes available to instructors an extensive *videotape library*. Please see your local sales representative for details regarding the video policy.

Acknowledgements

While writing may be a solitary enterprise, getting something published is a profoundly social event. We must thank our research assistant, Kevin Wills, for his superb reference-chasing skills and his willingness to fit yet one more library trip into his busy schedule. The many people in agencies and organizations such as the Canadian Psychological Association, Statistics Canada, and Health Canada who happily provided information are also to be thanked. Most importantly, we must thank the elite crew at Prentice Hall Canada for the unflappable way that they smoothly guided the editorial process. Especially worthy of thanks are Laura Pearson, Nicole Lukach, Dawn du Quesnay, Andrew Winton, and Susan Broadhurst for their professionalism and the gentle nature of their requests for clarification. Finally, we owe respectful thanks to those of our colleagues who reviewed versions of this manuscript with Canadian adaptation in mind. They included:

Christopher Burris
St. Jerome's University

William Clemens
University College of Cape Breton

Dianne Crisp
Kwantlen University College

Hank Davis
University of Guelph

Nancy Digdon
Grant MacEwan Community College

Thom Herrmann
University of Guelph

Paul Hillock
Algonquin College

Val Howard
Medicine Hat College

James Mottin
University of Guelph

Gary Poole
Simon Fraser University

Mardy Roberts
Mount Royal College

Harry Strub
University of Winnipeg

C. Scott Wilson
Douglas College

Pat Wolfe
Algonquin College

Their insightful comments, observations, and constructive criticism gave us much to think about and made this a better book.

It goes without saying that we are indebted to the many reviewers who contributed to the U.S. Seventh Edition of *Psychology*, on which the Canadian edition was based:

Bill Adler,
Collin County Community College

Michael Bergmire,
Jefferson College

Michele Y. Breault,
Truman State University

Frederick Brown,
Penn State University

Dennis Cogan,
Texas Technical University

John Creech,
Collin County Community College

Martha Ellis,
Collin County Community College

Paul W. Foos,
University of North Carolina at
Charlotte

Carie Forden,
Clarion University

Thomas Gerry,
Columbia-Greene Community College

Marjorie Hardy,
Muhlenberg College

Judith Jankowski,
Grand Rapids Community College

Don C. Johnson,
West Texas A&M University

James J. Johnson,
Illinois State University

Jerwen Jou,
University of Texas–Pan American

Allen Keniston,
University of Wisconsin–Eau Claire

Wayne Lesko,
Marymount University

Gary T. Montgomery,
University of Texas–Pan American

Nancy Simpson,
Trident Technical College

Peggy Skinner,
South Plains College

Michael Spiegler,
Providence College

Kevin Sumrall,
Montgomery College

Nancy Simpson,
Trident Technical College

Peggy Skinner,
South Plains College

Michael Spiegler,
Providence College

Kevin Sumrall,
Montgomery College

For all of your help, we are deeply grateful.

— *Lester A. Lefton*
— *Michael C. Boyes*
— *Nancy A. Ogden*

Credits

Figures and Tables

Statistics Canada information is used with permission of the Minister of Industry, as Minister responsible for Statistics Canada. Information on the availability of the wide range of data from Statistics Canada can be obtained from Statistics Canada's Offices, its World Wide Web site at www.statcan.ca, and its toll-free access number 1-800-263-1136.

Chapter 3: Figure 3.2, p. 82: From Dowling, J. E., & Boycott, B. B. (1966). *Proceedings of the Royal Society* (London), B166, 80–111, Figure 7. Reprinted by permission. Figure 3.3, p. 83: From Pirenne, M. H. (1967). *Vision and the eye*, 32. London: Chapman and Hall, Ltd. Reprianted by permission. Figure 3.10, p. 89: Reprinted from *Vision Research*, 4, MacNichol, Edward F. Jr., Retinal mechanisms of color vision, 119–133, Copyright 1964, with permission from Elsevier Science. Figure 3.14, p. 95: M. C. Escher's "Relativity" © 1998 Cordon Art B.V.—Baarn—Holland. All rights reserved. Figure 3.15, p. 97: From Beck, Jacob (1966). Effects of orientation and of shpae similarity on perceptual grouping. *Perception and Psychophysics*, 1, 300–302. Reprinted by permission Psychonomic Society, Inc.

Chapter 4: Figure 4.1, p. 123: From *Some must watch while some must sleep* by Dement, William C., Copyright © 1972 by William C. Dement. Used by permission of the Stanford Alumni Association and William C. Dement. Figure 4.2, p. 124: Reprinted with permission from Roffwarg, H. P., Muzio, & Dement, W. C. Ontogenetic development of human sleep-dream cycle. *Science, 152*, 604–609. Copyright 1966 by American Association for the Advancement of Science. Figure 4.3, p. 140: From Ray, Oakley, & Ksir, Charles (1993). *Drugs, society, and human behavior*, ed. 6, 1993, 194. St. Louis, MO: Mosby-Year Book, Inc. Reprinted by permission.

Chapter 6: Figure 6.6, p. 212: From Kosslyn, Stephen, M. (1975). Information representation in visual images. *Cognitive Psychology, 7*, 341–370. Reprinted by permission of Academic Press, Inc. Figure 6.7, p. 212: Reprinted with permission of Shepard, R. N., & Metzler, J. Mental rotation of three-dimensional objects. *Science, 171*, 701–703. Copyright 1971 by American Association for the Advancement of Science.

Chapter 8: Table 8.1, p. 266: H. Gardner & T. Hatch, Multiple intelligences go to school: Educational implications of the theory of multiple intelligences, *Educational Researcher, 18 (8)* 1989, 6; with adaptation based on personal communication from H. Gardner (1996). Table 8.6, p. 281: Adapted from Sattler, Jerome M. (1992). *Assessment of children*, revised and updated, 3rd Edition, 79. San Diego: Sattler. Reprinted by permission.

Chapter 9: Figure 9.6, p. 320: Copyright David Matsumoto and Paul Ekman. Figure 9.7, p. 321: From *Emotion: A psychoevolutionary synthesis* by Robert Plutchik. Copyright 1980 by Robert Plutchik. Reprinted by permission of Addison-Wesley Educational Publishers, Inc.

Chapter 10: Figure 10.2, p. 339: From Berk, Laura (1993). *Infants, children, and adolescents.*, 166. Copyright © 1993 by Allyn and Bacon. Reprinted by permission. Figure 10.3, p. 340: From Frankenberg, W. K. & Dobbs, J. B. (1967). The Denver Developmental Screening Tests. *Journal of Pediatrics, 71*, 191. Reprinted by permission of Mosby-Yearbook, Inc. Figure 10.5, p. 344: From Clarke-Stewart, A., Friedman, S., & Koch, J. *Child development: A topical approach,* 191. Copyright © 1985. Reprinted by permission of John Wiley & Sons, Inc. Figure 10.6, p. 347: © 1995 Susan Avishai. Reprinted by permission.

Chapter 11: Figure 11.2, p. 397: Adapted from Statistics Canada, Catalogue No. 93-310, 1971, 1981, 1991.

Chapter 12: Figure 12.5, p. 439: From the *Minnesota Multiphase Personality Inventory*. Copyright © the University of Minnesota 1942, 1943 (renewed 1970). MMPI scale names reproduced by permission of the publisher. Figure 12.4, p. 442: From Cohen, R. J., Montague, P., Nathanson, L., & Swerdik, M. E. (1998). *Psychological testing*. Mountainview, CA: Mayfield Publishing Co. Reprinted by permission.

Chapter 13: Figure 13.7, p. 471: From Milgram, S. Behavioral study of obedience. *Journal of Abnormal and Social Psychology, 67*, 371–378. Copyright 1963. Used with permission. Table 13.4, p. 490: From Hendrick, C., & Hendrick, S. A theory and method of love. *Journal of Personality and Social Psychology, 50*, 392–402. Copyright © 1986 by the American Psychological Association. Reprinted with permission.

Chapter 14: Table 14.1, p. 499: From Kanner, A. D., Coyne, J. C., Schaefer, C., & Lazarus, R. S. (1981). Comparison of two modes of stress measurement: Daily hassles and uplifts versus major life events. *Journal of Behavioral Medicine, 4*, 1–39. Reprinted by permission of Plenum Publishing Corp. Figure 14.4, p. 501: Figure from Selye, Hans (1978). *The stress of life*, Second Edition. Copyright 1976. Reproduced with permission of The McGraw-Hill Companies. Table 14.2, p. 503: Reprinted from *Journal of Psychosomatic Research, II*, Holmes, T. H., & Rahe, R. H., Social readjustment rating scale, 213–218. Copyright 1967, with permission from Elsevier Science.

Chapter 15: Table 15.5, p. 550: From Meyer, Robert G., & Salmon, Paul. *Abnormal psychology,* 2nd ed., p. 333 and the work of Edwin Shneidman and Norman Farberow. Copyright © 1988 by Allyn and Bacon. Reprinted by permission. Figure 15.2, p. 565: From Tsaung, M. T., & Vandermey, R. (1980). *Genes and the mind.* Oxford, England: Oxford University Press. Reprinted by permission.

Chapter 16: Table 16.1, p. 567: From Mahrer, A. R., & Nadler, W. p. Good moments in psychotherapy: A preliminary review, a list, and some promising research avenues. *Journal of Consulting and Clinical Psychology, 54,* 10–15. Copyright © 1986 by the American Psychological Association. Reprinted with permission. Figure 16.3, p. 579: Reprinted from *Behavior Research and Therapy, 2,* Ayllon, T., & Haughton, T., Modification of symptomatic verbal behavior of mental patients, 87–97. Copyright 1964, with permission from Elsevier Science. Figure 16.4, p. 580: From Ayllon, T., & Azrin, N. H. The measurement and reinforcement of behaviour of psychotics. *Journal of the Experimental Analysis of Behavior, 8,* 357–383. Copyright 1965 by the Society for the Experimental Analysis of Behavior, Inc. Reprinted by permission. Table 16.4, p. 586: From Ellis, Albert, Ph.D., & Harper, Robert A., Ph.D. *A guide to rational living.* © 1989, 1961. Reprinted by permission.

Chapter 17: Figure 17.4, p. 614: From Locke, E. A., & Schweiger, D. M. (1979). Participation in decision-making: One more look. In B. M. Staw (Ed.), *Research in organizational behavior, 1.* Greenwich, CT: JAI Press. Reprinted by permission. Figure 17.5, p. 626: From Baum, A., & Valins, S. (1977). Suite-style dorm and traditional corridor dorm figure, *Architecture and Social Behavior.* Mahwah, NJ: Lawrence Erlbaum Assoc., Inc. Reprinted by permission. Figure 17.6, p. 628: From Altman, I. & Vinsel, A. M. (1977). Personal space: An analysis of E. T. Hall's proxemics framework. In I. Altman, A. Rapoport, & J. F. Wohlwill (Eds.), *Human behavior and environment: Vol. 2. Advances in theory and research.* New York: Plenum Press. Reprinted by permission.

Photo Credits

Box icons: *Diversity,* Brian Smith; *Research Process,* PhotoDisc, Inc.

Chapter 1: p. 3, Corbis/Digital Stock; p. 6, Brian Smith; p. 8, Courtesy of Neal E. Miller/Yale University; p. 14, Will Hart; p. 16, Canapress/Regina Leader-Post/Pat Pettit; p. 18, Steve Winter/Black Star; p. 23, Canapress/Paul Chiasson; p. 25, Will Faller; p. 29 (top), National Library of Medicine; p. 29 (bottom), Corbis/Bettmann; p. 30, Ken Heyman/Woodfin Camp & Associates.

Chapter 2: p. 37, Custom Medical; p. 39, CNRI/SPL/Science Source/Photo Researchers; p. 41, Charlyn Zlotnick/Woodfin Camp & Associates; p. 44 (middle), Andrew Leonard/Science Source/Photo Researchers; p. 44 (bottom), Omikron/Science Source/Photo Researchers; p. 47, Canapress/Frank Gunn; p. 48, Photo Researchers/Brian Yarvin; p. 51, Brad Markel/Gamma Liaison; p. 54, A. Glauberman/Science Source/Photo Researchers; p. 58 (top), Brooks/Brown/Science Source/Photo Researchers; p. 58 (bottom), Robert Holmgren/Peter Arnold Inc.; p. 59, Wellcome Dept. of Cognitive Neurology/SPL/Science Source/Photo Researchers; p. 60, Prof. K. Ugurbil/Peter Arnold Inc.; p. 65, Corbis/Digital Stock; p. 69, Michel Gouverneur/Gamma Liaison.

Chapter 3: p. 75, Will Hart; p. 77, PhotoDisc, Inc.; p. 79, David Harvey/Woodfin Camp & Associates; p. 80 (top), PhotoDisc, Inc.; p. 80 (bottom), Benjamin Ailes; p. 83, Ralph C. Eagle, Jr., MD/Science Source/Photo Researchers; p. 85, Alain Morvan/Gamma Liaison; p. 91 (bottom), Mike Yamashita/Woodfin Camp & Associates; p. 93 (middle), Corbis/Digital Stock; p. 93 (bottom), Corbis/Bettmann; p. 94, Ron Pretzer/Luxe; p. 96, Richard Lord/The Image Works; p. 103, Omikron/Science Source/Photo Researchers; p. 110, Michael Justice/The Image Works.

Chapter 4: p. 115, PhotoDisc, Inc.; p. 119, Corbis/UPI; p. 121, HMS/Index Stock Imagery; p. 123, Will and Deni McIntyre/Science Source/Photo Researchers; p. 124, Ted Spagna/Science Source/Photo Researchers; p. 128, Bonnie Kamin; p. 131, The Granger Collection, New York; p. 133, David H. Wells/The Image Works; p. 134, Bob Daemmrich/Stock, Boston; p. 135, Brian Phillips/The Image Works; p. 137, Ed Kashi; p. 140 (top), A. Lichtenstein/The Image Works; p. 140 (middle), First Light/T & D. McCarthy; p. 145, James Prince/Science Source/Photo Researchers

Chapter 5: p. 151, PhotoDisc, Inc.; p. 153, Blair Seitz/Science Source/Photo Researchers; p. 155, Archives of the History of American Psychology/The University of Akron; p. 162, Stan Wayman/Science Source/Photo Researchers; p. 165, AP/Wide World Photos; p. 166, Robert Brenner/PhotoEdit; p. 171 (top left), Brian Smith; p. 171 (top right), Omikron/Science Source/Photo Researchers; p. 171 (bottom left), First Light/Jan Milne; p. 171 (bottom right), Jim Pickerell; p. 180, Michael Newman/PhotoEdit; p. 182, Will Faller; p. 185, Will Faller; p. 187, Photosynthesis Archives.

Chapter 6: p. 190, PhotoDisc, Inc.; p. 191, Archive Photos; p. 198, Peter Menzel/Stock, Boston; p. 200, Brian Smith; p. 204 (top), Will Hart; p. 204 (middle), Canapress/Frank Gunn; p. 208, Corbis/Bettmann; p. 209, Canapress; p. 215 (middle), Gunter Ziesler/Peter Arnold, Inc.; p. 215 (bottom), Archives of the History of American Psychology/The University of Akron; p. 217, NASA; p. 219, Progressive Conservative Party of Canada; p. 220, Bob Daemmrich/The Image Works; p. 222, Marley Soltes/*Seattle Times.*

Chapter 7: p. 229, Courtesy of Lester Lefton; p. 231 (left), Stephen J. Krasemann/The National Audubon Society Collection/Photo Researchers; p. 231 (right), Tim Davis/The National Audubon Society Collection/Photo Researchers; p. 233, Corbis/UPI; p. 236, AP/Wide World Photos; p. 238, Robert Ginn/PhotoEdit; p. 245, Jonathan Schaeffer/University of Alberta; p. 248, Kal Muller/Woodfin Camp & Associates; p. 252, The Image Works/John Eastcott.

Chapter 8: p. 263, PhotoDisc, Inc.; p. 268, Stephen Frisch/Stock, Boston; p. 270, Archives of the History of American Psychology/The University of Akron; p. 276, Bob Daemmrich/The Image Works; p. 280, Alan Oddie/PhotoEdit; p. 282, Robert Azzi/Woodfin Camp & Associates; p. 286, Brian Smith; p. 287, Bob Daemmrich/The Image Works.

Chapter 9: p. 288, Brian Smith; p. 299, Ed Lallo/Liaison International; p. 303, Richard Howard; p. 305, Super Stock; p. 306, Jose Galvez/PhotoEdit; p. 307 (left), Jorie Gracen/The Gamma Liaison; p. 307 (right), Brad Markel/Gamma Liaison; p. 308, Index Stock Imagery, Inc./William Thompson; p. 315, Lew Merrim/Monkmeyer; p. 316, AP/Wide World Photos; p. 317, Kathy Ferguson/PhotoEdit; p. 322, Tony Stone Images/Mary Kate Denny.

Chapter 10: p. 331, Brian Smith; p. 333, Minnesota Twins Study; p. 337 (top and middle), Petit Format-Nestle/Science Source/Photo Researchers; p. 337 (bottom), J. Stevenson/SPL/Science Source/Photo Researchers; p. 338, Jean Shifrin/Associated Press/The Atlanta Journal and Constitution; p. 340 (top), Charles Gupton/Stock, Boston; p. 340 (bottom), Spencer Grant/Stock, Boston; p. 341 (top), Courtesy of Dr. David Linton; p. 341 (bottom), From Meltzoff, A.N., and Moore, M.K. "Imitation of facial and manual gestures by human neonates." *Science*, 198, 75. Copyright 1977 by American Association for the Advancement of Science; p. 342, Courtesy of J. Campos, B. Bertenthal, and R. Kermoran; p. 344 (top left), Super Stock; p. 344 (top right), Laura Dwight/Peter Arnold Inc.; p. 344 (middle left), James A. Sugar/Black Star; p. 344 (middle right), Laura Dwight/Peter Arnold Inc.; p. 344 (bottom left), Andy Cox/Tony Stone Images; p. 344 (bottom right), Richard Hutchings/Photo Researchers; p. 349 (top), Courtesy of Shukria Aziz; p. 349 (bottom), John Coletti/Index Stock Imagery; p. 355, Martin Rogers/Stock, Boston; p. 356, Robert Harbison; p. 363, Will Hart; p. 365, Brian Smith; p. 366, Robert Harbison; p. 369, Liane Enkelis/Stock, Boston.

Chapter 11: p. 375, David Young-Wolff/PhotoEdit; p. 377 (top), Strauss/Curtis/Offshoot Stock; p. 377 (bottom), Will Hart; p. 378, Bob Daemmrich/Stock, Boston; p. 379, Bob Daemmrich/The Image Works; p. 383, Canapress/Winnipeg Free Press/Joe Bryksa; p. 387, Brian Smith; p. 389, Spencer Grant/Monkmeyer; p. 391, Zigy Kaluzny/Tony Stone Images; p. 393, Will Faller; p. 397, Tony Stone Images/Donna Day; p. 401, Stephen Marks/Black Star; p. 402, Scott Thode/International Stock.

Chapter 12: p. 407, PhotoDisc, Inc.; p. 408, National Library of Medicine; p. 412, Prettyman/PhotoEdit; p. 416, Alaska Division of Tourism; p. 417 (top), National Library of Medicine; p. 417 (bottom), Allison Wright/Stock, Boston; p. 418, Mary Evans Picture Library; p. 420 (top), Corbis/Bettmann; p. 420 (bottom), Roger Ressmeyer/Corbis; p. 423 (middle), Archives of the History of American Psychology/The University of Akron; p. 423 (bottom), Photofest; p. 424, Will Hart; p. 425, Nova Stock/PhotoEdit; p. 426, Goldberg/Monkmeyer; p. 431, Brian Smith; p. 441, Lew Merrim/Monkmeyer.

Chapter 13: p. 447, Canapress/Mike Ridewood; p. 449, Canapress/Kim Stallknecht; p. 451, MADD Canada; p. 454, Canapress/Rene Johnston; p. 455, Philip G. Zimbardo; p. 459, Brian Smith; p. 460, Tony Stone Images/Charles Gupton; p. 463, First Light/Mark Stephenson; p. 469, William Vandervert/*Scientific American*; p. 470, Courtesy of the Milgram Estate; p. 476, Drew Crawford/The Image Works; p. 477, Napoleon A. Chagnon/Anthro-Photo; p. 480, PhotoDisc, Inc.; p. 481, Michael Newman/PhotoEdit; p. 486, D. Perrett, I. Penton-Voak, M. Burk/University of St. Andrews/SPL/Science Source/Photo Researchers.

Chapter 14: p. 495, N/A/Jasmine/TNI; p. 499 (top), Tony Stone Images/Kaluzny/Thatcher; p. 499 (bottom), Jonathan Nourok/PhotoEdit; p. 501, Courtesy of Hans Selye; p. 504, Tony Stone Images/Kevin Moran; p. 507 (top), Canapress/Paul Chiasson; p. 507 (middle), Michael Newman/PhotoEdit; p. 514, Bob Daemmrich/Stock, Boston; p. 517, Rick Strange/Index Stock Imagery.

Chapter 15: p. 523, Brian Smith; p. 524, Calgary Herald/Peter Brosseau; p. 525, National Library of Medicine; p. 531, Evan Agostini/Gamma Liaison; p. 533, Will Hart; p. 535, Brian Smith; p. 538, Canapress/Phil Snell; p. 542, Will Hart; p. 544, Grantpix/Monkmeyer; p. 547, AP/Wide World Photos; p. 549, Canapress/Brandon Sun/Bruce Bumstead; p. 553, Gregory Rec/Gamma Liaison; p. 556, NIH/Science Source/Photo Researchers; p. 558, Courtesy of the Genain Estate.

Chapter 16: 563, PhotoDisc, Inc.; p. 565, Will Faller; p. 566, Photofest; p. 571, AP/Wide World Photos; p. 574, Michael Rougier/*Life Magazine* © Time Inc.; p. 576, Copyright 1991 by The Estate of Frederick Perls/*The Gestalt Journal Press*; p. 580, Stephen Marks; p. 581, PH Merrill Publishing; p. 582, Lori Adamski Peek/Tony Stone Images; p. 588, Will Hart; p. 589, Will Hart; p. 592, Will and Deni McIntyre/Science Source/Photo Researchers; p. 595, Louisa Preston.

Chapter 17: p. 601, PhotoDisc, Inc.; p. 604, Michael Newman/PhotoEdit; p. 606, Kerbs/Monkmeyer; p. 609, Tony Stone Images/David Young-Wolff; p. 610, Charles Gupton/Stock, Boston; p. 613, Charles Gupton/Tony Stone Images; p. 614, Reuters/Mousse/Archive Photos; p. 619 (all), From Andre, Anthony D., and Segal, Leon D. (April 1993). Design Functions. *Ergonomics in Design, 5*. Copyright 1993 by the Human Factors and Ergonomics Society. All rights reserved; p. 625, Rod Rolle/Gamma Liaison; p. 627, Brian Smith; p. 631, Brian Smith; p. 635, Will Faller; p. 637, Canapress/AP Photo/Chris Gardner.

Chapter 1

What Is Psychology?

Michele Cooper knew that her friend Janet was on the edge of something disastrous. "On the edge" is what Michele kept thinking, "on the edge." Michele and Janet had been close friends since first year. They had met at frosh orientation and had been roommates since. But Janet's recent history was perplexing. With each passing month she seemed more moody. At first, she passed it off as homesickness, later as exam stress, and recently as "winter blues." Her ups and downs were making her very hard to live with at times. Michele never knew what to expect, and she felt as if she was always walking on eggshells. And then, one Saturday evening, Janet made an attempt at suicide.

Michele was an active problem solver, not a passive worrier. She could not control Janet's moods or her actions and she was desperately seeking some insight into what was going on so as to know how she could best help. She sought that help through the Internet. Michele clicked on her Web browser, went to a well-known search engine, and typed in "Psychology." Click. She received 4 200 756 "hits" or likely sites with information. She knew she would have to refine her search. "Depression." Click. There were still 4400 hits. "Suicide." Click. "Behaviour." Click "Lethargy." Click. "Depressive." Click. Fifteen minutes and many leads later, Michele had learned that there was an enormous volume of research on depression, suicide, and therapy. She found that the American National Institutes of Health have a major information site on depression, that millions of dollars each year are spent trying to the find its causes, and that millions more are spent on its treatment. Michele explored a particular site in detail—it announced that depression is the psychiatric equivalent of the common cold and that it may precede a suicide attempt. It went on to say that nearly 15 percent of the population will suffer from depression at some time in their lives and that the rate may be nearly twice as high among women as it is among men. Michele decided that Janet was becoming a statistic. And she wasn't going to let that happen. ■

Michele could not cure Janet. But helping Janet realize that she needed professional help was a beginning, and Michele could certainly help provide her friend with compassion and emotional support. Millions of men and women each year seek out help for a complex array of disorders and symptoms and much help is available. You may have a friend or family member who has had a problem and perhaps you have done an Internet search similar to the one Michele did, or perhaps you went to a library or bookstore. If you did, you discovered that there is a whole array of therapeutic techniques, drugs, and combination treatments—and the good news is that these help many people.

Psychologists study and try to help people like Michele and Janet. Sometimes they have to refer clients to practitioners who can prescribe medications; in addition, they work with whole families to restore them to balance. Perhaps this story about Janet will help you understand why we consider psychology, the science of human behaviour and mental processes, so moving, fascinating, and exciting. Psychology helps us understand the nature of human interactions—how individuals grow up and grow independent, how people make their way in the world, form relationships with others, and lead fulfilling lives. It also addresses issues such as the abuse of women, children, and the elderly and drug abuse. We began and continue to study psychology because people fascinate us. You may be taking this course for the same reason.

Before we begin to explore psychology, it is important to carefully define and describe it. Many students assume that psychology uses Freud's theories to provide therapy to clients reclining on couches. Although psychology does explore personality, maladjustment, and therapy, it encompasses far more. You will see that psychologists, whether practitioners or researchers, tend to be investigators who carefully and systematically attempt to discover the underpinnings of human behaviour and mental processes. Similarly, many students think of psychology as the science of the mind. It is that, of course, but—as this text emphasizes so strongly—it is also a biological science, and one that is increasingly interdisciplinary. Lastly, some casual observers think of psychology as common sense; but the truth is that the hindsight of common sense, which explains past events so well, rarely allows people to make predictions about future behaviour and events—and this is a key goal of psychological inquiry. Students of psychology often think of themselves as psychological detectives, sifting through facts and theories in an orderly way, attempting to uncover the many causes of behaviour, so as ultimately to help individuals or organizations become everything they wish to be. Let's begin our exploration with a definition of the science that we find so exciting and that we believe ultimately will help Janet.

What Is This Science of Psychology?

W hat exactly is psychology? It is as difficult for us to provide a definition of psychology that includes all of its elements as it would be for you to list all of the reasons why you might want to study it. We'll begin with a simple definition and gradually expand on it. Broadly defined, **psychology** is the science of behaviour and mental processes.

Let's look at the first part of this definition, because it is key to understanding what sets real psychology apart from the popular psychology of talk shows and tabloids. Psychology is a *science*. Because psychology is a science, psychologists use scientific principles, carefully defined methods, and precise procedures to present an organized body of knowledge and to draw inferences, or make predictions, about how people will behave in the future. Predicting behaviour is important, for it enables psychologists to help people anticipate their reactions to certain situations and learn how to express themselves in manageable and reasonable ways. For example, because excessive stress can cause anxiety, depression, and even heart

Psychology: The science of behaviour and mental processes.

attacks, psychologists use theories about stress to devise therapies to help people handle it more effectively.

Interestingly, there remain some who claim that psychology is not a science, who see human behaviour as either fixed or subject to little change, and who think that people should rely on self-direction rather than on the help of psychologists to reach their potential. These divergent views exist cross-culturally as well; there is not the same degree of consensus about the usefulness of psychology around the world. Former Soviet bloc nations take a dim view of therapy, and as in some Asian cultures, people are expected to be self-reliant—accordingly, they are less likely to seek help from psychologists than are Canadians.

Now for the second part of the definition: psychology as the science of *behaviour and mental processes*. Psychologists observe many aspects of human functioning—overt actions or behaviours, social relationships, mental processes, emotional responses, and physiological reactions. In cultures outside North America, especially former Soviet bloc nations, psychology also embraces paranormal phenomena such as telepathy and clairvoyance.

Overt actions are directly observable and measurable movements or the results of such movements. Walking, talking, playing, kissing, gestures, and expressions are examples of overt actions. Results or products of overt actions might be the papers you write, the piles of unsorted laundry in your bedroom, or the body you have kept in shape through regular exercise. *Social relationships* are the behaviours we engage in that define our interactions with other people. We make assumptions about the causes of other people's behaviours; we try to change their attitudes; we avoid them or engage them; we date, marry, and have children with them. *Mental processes*, which most of us consider the main grist for the psychological mill, include thoughts and ideas as well as more complex reasoning processes. *Emotional responses* basically are feelings such as anger, regret, lust, happiness, and depression. *Physiological reactions* are closely associated with emotional responses. They include an increased heart rate when you are excited, biochemical changes when light stimulates your eyes, and high blood pressure in response to stress. All of these are fair game for psychological scientists.

Psychology is considered a social and behavioural science because it deals with behaviour and mental process. In recent years the Canadian Psychological Association has focused attention on the contributions of the behavioural and social sciences, which address many of our society's daunting challenges, and on the critical importance of psychology, which improves our country's health by eliminating child abuse and neglect and violence against women, and by increasing the safety and security of our communities. Psychology also contributes by helping educate our society to learn and think critically, training workers to be more efficient and productive, and sensitizing people to diversity—the broad range of customs and lifestyles we find within our borders and those we see in the world beyond. With these themes in mind, and because psychology is a science, it is crucial that we follow some key principles of science as we evaluate research and the applications of research. These are considered next.

Three Principles of Scientific Endeavour

As a science, psychology is committed to objectivity, accuracy, and healthy scepticism about the study of behaviour and mental processes. These three basic principles are the very core of what makes psychology a science. These basic principles can help you, too, be a critical thinker in your day-to-day life.

Objectivity. For psychologists, objectivity means evaluating research and theory on their merits, without preconceived ideas. For example, when scientists challenged the validity of lie detector tests both believers and sceptics stepped up offering case studies, as well as anecdotal experiences, that supported or discounted their usefulness. Psychologists attempt to bring scientific objectivity to the research arena; they know that common-sense approaches to phenomena often are anecdotal and can explain events that may have happened, but that such approaches can rarely predict behaviour or mental processes in the future. Remember, as a science we want to describe *and* predict—common sense relies heavily on looking backwards—having hindsight—but is not very objective or reliable in making predictions about behaviour.

Accuracy. Psychologists are concerned with gathering data from the laboratory and the real world in precise ways—that is, with accuracy. For instance, to conclude from a small number of eyewitness accounts that large numbers of people have been abducted by aliens falls considerably short of scientific accuracy. Might there be other plausible explanations for why a number of people have told very similar accounts of small, ghostly figures levitating people to flying-saucer laboratories? Might those reporting such incidents suffer from similar psychological disorders? Rather than relying on limited samples and immediate impressions, psychologists base their thinking on detailed and thorough study that is as precise as possible.

Healthy Scepticism. One needn't be a scientific researcher to realize that in science, and in life, we observe many amazing events and so a careful approach to reports of strange events and phenomena is necessary. Many people think twice when they hear stories about people charged with serious crimes claiming that voices or other personalities were responsible for the crimes with which they are charged. Appealing as it may be to believe accounts of alien abductions or criminal multiple personalities, psychologists maintain a healthy scepticism: a cautious view of data, hypotheses, and theories until results are repeated, verified, and established over time.

The Scientific Method in Psychology

Like other scientists, psychologists use the scientific method in developing theories that describe, explain, predict, and help change behaviour. The **scientific method** in psychology is the technique used to discover knowledge about human behaviour and mental processes; in experimentation, it involves *stating the problem, developing hypotheses, designing a study, collecting and analyzing data* (which often includes manipulating some part of the environment to better understand what conditions can lead to a behaviour or phenomenon), *replicating results,* and *drawing conclusions and reporting results.*

Let's break down the scientific method into its six basic steps, so that you can have an overview of how psychologists do their work. There will be more to say about the research process very shortly.

Stating the Problem. The question a psychologist asks must be stated in such a way that it can be answered; that is, it must be stated in a way that lends itself to investigation. For instance, if you ask the question "What is the mind?" little headway can be made even through rigorous techniques. But if you ask "To what extent is zinc effective in alleviating cold symptoms?" or "Does St. John's Wort work better than Prozac in treating depression?" the question can be tested with some degree of clarity.

Developing Hypotheses. In the next step of the scientific method, psychologists form educated guesses about how people are likely to react. Such a formulation is called a **hypothesis**—a tentative statement or idea expressing a causal relationship between two events or variables that are to be evaluated in a research study. A hypothesis might be that a specific diet—perhaps one low in refined sugar—is more effective than any other diet in controlling or reducing hyperactive behaviour in 10-year-old boys; further, the hypothesis might assert that such a diet will be 10 percent more effective than another diet or no special diet at all.

Scientific method: In psychology, the techniques used to discover knowledge about human behaviour and mental processes; in experimentation, the scientific method involves stating the problem, developing hypotheses, designing a study, collecting and analyzing data (which often includes manipulating some part of the environment to better understand what conditions can lead to a behaviour or phenomenon), replicating results, and drawing conclusions and reporting results.

Hypothesis: A tentative statement or idea expressing a causal relationship between two events or variables that are to be evaluated in a research study.

After stating the problem and developing a hypothesis, psychologists sometimes develop a theory from their current knowledge and past research. A **theory** is a collection of interrelated ideas and facts put forward to describe, explain, and predict behaviour and mental processes. For example, a theory that parental neglect, poverty, and a bad peer group contribute to delinquency might put together related facts about personality, gender differences, cultural differences, and the demographics of delinquency. Such a theory must organize data well and must create testable predictions to check the theory. Such testing usually occurs within the context of a well-designed research study.

Theory: In psychology, a collection of interrelated ideas and facts put forward to describe, explain, and predict behaviour and mental processes.

Designing a Study. Researchers next have to develop an approach to studying a problem, which will test a hypothesis or theory. They identify key variables, responses, and techniques that will help them understand the issue at hand. At the outset, the key elements of the study must be defined. The behaviours to be examined have to be carefully specified: How are they to be measured, with what instruments, how frequently, and by whom? In children who are identified as delinquents, some behaviours are fairly easily specified—for example, criminal behaviour. Other behaviours, such as anxiety and lack of self-esteem, which may be related to delinquency, are more difficult to define precisely—in delinquent children, or in anyone else for that matter.

Collecting and Analyzing Data. After researchers have specified the key elements and chosen the participants for an experiment, they conduct the experiment, hoping it will yield interpretable, meaningful results. This requires carefully designed techniques for data collection so as not to bias the results in favour of one hypothesis or another. The data also must be collected, organized, coded, and simplified in a way that allows for a reasonable set of conclusions to be drawn. For example if a researcher has 10 000 observations of 300 participants, something must be done to make sense of all this information. Statistical techniques usually are called upon to help summarize and condense the data.

Replicating Results. Most researchers are aware of their own all-too-human tendency to *bias*, or subtly predetermine, the outcomes of their research so that they obtain precisely the results they expected. One way to control such bias is to *replicate*, or repeat the experiment, or to have another researcher try to reproduce the same results. If the results of a replicated experiment are the same, a researcher generally will say that the results are reliable and are likely to occur again given the same set of circumstances.

Drawing Conclusions and Reporting Results. When results are organized and statistics are calculated, researchers try to organize ideas and observations to make predictions about behaviour. They begin to draw conclusions about results and relate those conclusions to the data that they have collected. Ultimately, researchers report their results to the scientific community by publishing their study—they report their findings as well as their interpretations of what they think the results mean.

Now that we have a general overview of the research process, let's go into more detail, to examine how psychologists go about the process of scientific inquiry.

Focus

Review

- Why might thought be considered behaviour? p. 5
- Identify three key principles of scientific endeavour to which scientists must be committed. pp. 5–6
- Describe the steps followed when using the scientific method. pp. 6–7
- Why would successfully replicating a research study be so important to scientists? p. 7

Think Critically

- You may have read that scientists have theorized that for women, estrogen replacement therapy may reduce the incidence of Alzheimer's disease, a progressive degenerative disorder affecting memory. What questions would you ask, and what issues would you be concerned with, in attempting to test this hypothesis?

The Research Process

I f you ever have the opportunity to tour a psychologist's laboratory, you should do so. Even better, if you ever have the opportunity to assist a psychologist in research, take advantage of it. Although psychologists use most of the techniques other scientists use, they adapt these techniques to deal with the uncertainties of human behaviour. The typical research process in psychology is quite systematic and begins with a specific question—the "stating the problem" step of the scientific method. The process usually takes the form of an **experiment**—a procedure in which a researcher systematically manipulates and observes elements of a situation in order to answer a question and, usually, to establish causality. For example, if a researcher wants to determine the relationship between an animal's eating behaviour and its weight, the researcher could systematically vary (manipulate) how much the animal ate and then weigh (observe) the animal each day to infer that eating behaviour and weight are causally related.

Variables, Hypotheses, and Experimental and Control Groups

Variables. A **variable** is a condition or a characteristic of a situation or person that is subject to change (that varies) either within or across situations or individuals. Researchers manipulate some variables in order to measure how the changes in them affect other variables. There are two types of variables in any experiment: independent and dependent variables. The **independent variable** is the variable in a controlled experiment that the experimenter directly and purposely manipulated. The **dependent variable** is the variable that is expected to change as a result of manipulation of the independent variable. For example, a researcher might hypothesize that increases in temperature would adversely affect behaviour. The researcher therefore might raise the temperature in a room and measure whether a person's activity level is increased or decreased by the manipulation of the temperature.

Or imagine a simple reaction-time experiment intended to determine the effects of sleep loss on behaviour. The participants in the study might be a large group of university students who normally sleep about seven hours a night. The independent (manipulated) variable might be the number of hours university students are allowed to sleep. The dependent variable could be the students' reaction times to a stimulus—for example, how quickly they push a button when a light is flashed.

Hypotheses. As we saw earlier, a *hypothesis* is a tentative statement or idea expressing a causal relationship between two events or variables that are to be evaluated in a research study. The hypothesis of the sleep loss experiment might be that students deprived of sleep will react more slowly to a stimulus than will students allowed to sleep their regular seven hours. Suppose the participants sleep in the laboratory on four successive nights and are tested each morning on a reaction-time task. The participants sleep seven hours on each of three nights but sleep only four hours on the fourth night. If the response times after the first three nights are constant and if all other factors are held equal, any observed differences in reaction times on the fourth test (following the night of four hours of sleep) can be attributed to the number of hours of sleep. That is, changes in the independent variable (numbers of hours of sleep) will produce changes in the dependent variable (reaction time). If the results show that students deprived of sleep respond on the reaction-time task a half-second slower than they did after normal sleep, the researcher could feel justified in concluding that sleep deprivation acts to slow down reaction time. The researcher's hypothesis would have been supported by the experiment.

Experimental and Control Groups. Researchers must determine whether it is actually the changes in the manipulated variable, and not some unknown extraneous factor, that cause a change in the dependent variable. One way to do this is to

Experiment: A procedure in which a researcher systematically manipulates and observes elements of a situation in order to answer a question and, usually, to test hyphotheses and make inferences about cause and effect.

Variable: A condition or characteristic of a situation or a person that is subject to change (that varies) within or across situations or individuals.

Independent variable: The variable in a controlled experiment that the experimenter directly and purposely manipulates to see how the other variables under study will be affected.

Dependent variable: The variable in a controlled experiment that is expected to change because of the manipulation of the independent variable.

set up at the start of the experiment at least two groups of participants who are identical in important ways. **Participants** are individuals who take part in experiments and whose behaviour is observed for research data collection (previously referred to as *subjects*, this term was changed to reflect the fact that people actively and voluntarily participate in experiments). The attributes participants must have in common will depend on what the experimenter is testing. For example, because reflexes slow down as a person grows older, the researcher in the reaction-time experiment would want to ensure that the two groups were composed of participants of the same or nearly the same age.

Once the participants are known to be similar on important attributes, they are assigned randomly to either the experimental or the control group. *Random assignment* means that the participants are assigned by lottery rather than on the basis of any particular characteristic, preference, or situation that might have even a remote possibility of influencing the outcome. The **experimental group** is the group of participants to whom a treatment is given. Some psychologists even refer to the experimental group as the *treatment group*. The **control group** is the comparison group—the group of participants tested on the dependent variable in the same way as the experimental group but for whom the treatment is not given. In the reaction-time experiment, the students who sleep a full seven hours on all four nights are the control group. Those who are allowed to sleep only four hours on the last night are the experimental group. Their treatment was being deprived of sleep; of course, in other research studies, their treatment may be being allowed more sleep, a drug, or perhaps some special sleep techniques. By comparing the reaction times (the dependent variable) for the experimental and control groups, the researcher can determine whether the independent variable is responsible for any differences in the dependent variable between the groups.

If the researcher is confident that all of the participants responded with the same reaction time before the experiment—that is, that the two groups are truly comparable—then the researcher can conclude that sleep deprivation is the cause of the experimental group's decreased performance. Without comparable groups, the effect of the treatment variable is not clear, and few real conclusions can be drawn from the data.

Of course, extraneous, or irrelevant, variables can also make interpretation difficult. *Extraneous variables* are factors that affect the results of an experiment but that are not of interest to the experimenter. An example of an extraneous variable is a thunderstorm that occurs during an experiment in which anxiety is being measured through a physical response such as rises in skin conductivity. It would be difficult or impossible for the researchers to ascertain how much of the increased skin conductivity was due to manipulations they created and how much was due to anxiety about thunder. When extraneous variables occur during an experiment (or just before it), they may *confound results*—make data difficult to interpret.

Operational Definitions, Sample Size, and Significant Differences

Operational Definitions. A key component of successful scientific research is that all terms used in describing the variables and the experimental procedure must be given operational definitions. An **operational definition** is a definition of a variable in terms of a set of the methods or procedures used to measure or study that variable. When a researcher manipulates an organism's state of hunger, the concept *hunger* must be defined in terms of the procedures necessary to produce hunger. For example, a researcher might be interested in the effects of hunger (the independent variable) on exploratory behaviour (the dependent variable) in mice. The researcher might deprive mice of food for 6, 10, 12, or 24 hours and then observe and record their exploratory behaviour. The researcher might operationally define hunger in terms of the number of hours of food deprivation and exploratory behaviour in terms of the number of times the mice walked farther than 60 centimetres down a path.

Participant: An individual who takes part in an experiment and whose behaviour is observed for research data collection; previously known as a *subject*.

Experimental group: In an experiment, a group of participants to whom a treatment is given.

Control group: In an experiment, the comparison group—the group of participants tested on the dependent variable in the same way as the experimental group but for whom the treatment is not given.

Operational definition: Definition of a variable in terms of the set of methods or procedures used to measure or study that variable.

Sample Size. Another important factor in an experiment is the size and representativeness of the sample. A **sample** is a group of participants who are assumed to be representative of the population about which an inference is being made. For example, a researcher studying Canadians' attitudes about mental illness has to put together a sample of people that properly reflects the make-up of the Canadian population.

The number of participants in a sample is very important. If an effect is obtained consistently with a large enough number of participants, the researcher can reasonably rule out individual differences and chance as causes. The key assumption is that a large sample better represents the population to which the researcher wishes to generalize the results.

Significant Differences. Researchers want to be sure that the differences they find are significant. For psychologists, a **significant difference** in an experiment is a difference that is statistically unlikely to have occurred because of chance alone and that is most likely due to the systematic manipulation of the independent variable. For example, when one therapy technique appears to be more effective than another, the researcher wants to be sure that the results with the first technique are significantly different from the results with the second and that the difference is large enough to be important in the outside world. The results are significantly different only if they could not be due to chance, due to the use of only one or two participants, or due to a unique set of participants. Such conclusions can come only from experiments in which participants are randomly assigned to experimental and control groups, an independent variable is systematically manipulated, and attempts are made to control extraneous variables. If experimental results are not statistically significant, they are not considered to have established a finding or confirmed a hypothesis.

Successful Experiments Avoid Pitfalls

Good experiments often involve several experimental groups, each tested under different conditions. Another study of the effects of sleep deprivation might involve a control group and five experimental groups. The participants in each of the experimental groups might be deprived of sleep for a different length of time (sleep deprivation operationally defined in terms of number of hours of sleep lost from the normal number of hours slept). In this way, the researcher could examine the effects of several different degrees of sleep deprivation on reaction time.

In a well-designed experiment, the experimenter also looks closely at the nature of the independent variable. Are there actual values for the independent variable above or below which results will differ markedly? For example, the researcher might find that a one-hour loss of sleep has no effect, that a two-hour deprivation produces only a modest effect, and that every additional hour of deprivation markedly slows reaction time. These results would show that reaction time is dependent on the amount of sleep deprivation. The use of several experimental groups yields better understanding of how the independent variable (sleep deprivation) affects the dependent variable (reaction time).

Expectancy Effects. Frequently, things turn out just the way a researcher expects. Researchers are aware, however, that their *expectancies*, or expectations, about results may influence their findings, particularly where human behaviour is concerned. A researcher may unwittingly create a situation that leads to specific prophesied results—a **self-fulfilling prophecy**. For example, a teacher may develop expectations about a student's performance early in the year, then unconsciously set low (or high) standards for that student. Sensing those standards, the student will often confirm the teacher's expectations, even when the expectations may not reflect the student's potential ability. In these instances, the student's performance has fulfilled the teacher's prophecy, regardless of other factors.

Sample: A group of participants who are assumed to be representative of the population about which an inference is being made.

Significant difference: In an experiment, a difference that is unlikely to have occurred because of chance alone and is most likely due to the systematic manipulation of the independent variable.

Self-fulfilling prophecy: The unwitting creation by a researcher of a situation that leads to specific prophesied results.

To avoid the risk of self-fulfilling prophecies, researchers often use a **double-blind technique**—a research technique in which neither the experimenter nor the participants know who is in the control or the experimental group. In this situation, someone who is not connected with the research project keeps track of which participants are assigned to which group. The double-blind technique minimizes the effect that a researcher's subtle cues might have on participants. (In a single-blind experiment, the researcher knows who is in the experimental group and who is in the control group, but the participants do not know who is assigned to which group or whether they are being presented with a manipulated variable.)

Researchers also try to minimize the demand characteristics of studies. **Demand characteristics** are the elements of a study situation that might direct how things happen or tip off a participant as to the purpose of the study and perhaps thereby elicit specific behaviour from the participant. Participants who even *think* they know the real purpose of a study may try to behave "appropriately" and in so doing may distort the results. Some techniques that minimize the impact of demand characteristics are the use of computers to decrease interaction with people (participants are less likely to want to act appropriately for a computer), of unobtrusive measures such as tape recording rather than note taking, and of deception (concealing the real purpose of the study; see the section on ethics beginning on page 17) until the end of the research session.

Even when a double-blind procedure is used and demand characteristics are minimized, participants often just behave differently when they are in a research study. This finding is known as the **Hawthorne effect**, after some early research studies at the Hawthorne industrial plant that showed that people behave differently (usually better) when they know they are being observed. Researchers therefore attempt to make participants feel comfortable and natural and to create experimental situations that minimize the effects of participation. They often do not collect data until after participants have adapted to the experimental situation and have become less distracted about being part of the research study.

Correlation Is Not Necessarily Causation

Consider this statement: In general, the more education you have, the higher your yearly income. This statement is a true descriptive statement, but only up to a point. After a person receives a college degree, adding a professional degree is less likely to add significant additional income to the person's yearly take-home pay. It is not accurate to say that each unit of education causes income to rise; rather, education allows a person to open new doors and creates opportunities to earn more. At a certain point, another master's degree helps little in increasing opportunities. In short, more education does not directly cause more yearly income.

Only controlled laboratory *experiments* permit researchers to take the next step in the scientific method. They form theories and develop hypotheses in order to make *cause-and-effect statements*— inferences about the causes of behaviour. Here is a key point: *Correlated events are not necessarily causally related.* Two events are *correlated* when the increased presence (or absence) of a particular situation is regularly associated with a high (or low) presence of another situation, event, or situational feature. For example, a researcher who finds that children whose parents are divorced have more emotional problems and commit more crimes than children from intact families can state that there is a correlation. However, the researcher cannot conclude that parental divorce *causes* emotional problems or crime (see Figure 1.1). Events are considered causally

Double-blind technique: A research technique in which neither the experimenter nor the participants know who is in the control and experimental groups.

Demand characteristics: Elements of a study situation that might set things up in a specific way or tip off a participant as to the purpose of the study and perhaps thereby elicit specific behaviour from the participant.

Hawthorne effect: The finding, based on early research studies at the Hawthorne industrial plant, that people behave differently (usually better) when they know they are being observed.

FIGURE 1.1
Correlations Do Not Show Causation
Although research shows that broken homes and crime are correlated, it does not show causation. Poverty, a third variable, may be the cause of both crime and broken homes.

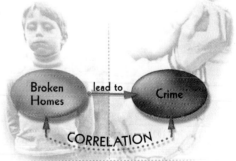

FAULTY ASSUMPTION

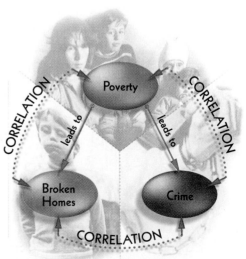

MORE LIKELY ASSUMPTION

related only when one event makes another event occur—when one event or situation is contingent on another.

When psychologists suggest that one situation causes another, they have to be sure that several specific conditions are met. They pay close attention to how the data are collected and to whether the results of the study are replicated in additional experiments. To make meaningful causal inferences, psychologists must create situations in which they can limit the likelihood of obtaining a result that is simply a chance occurrence or due to other irrelevant factors. Only by using carefully formulated experiments can psychologists make sound interpretations of their results and cautiously extend them to other situations. Experiments have specific components and requirements, which we'll examine next. But before we do, it may be helpful for you to see how you can use these same processes to sharpen your own thinking.

Thinking Critically and Evaluating Research

Psychologists, like all scientists, are trained to think, to evaluate research critically, and to put their results into a meaningful framework. Psychologists follow a traditional approach to evaluating research. To benefit from this textbook, you might find it helpful to use the same critical thinking skills and framework in order to follow their logic, to understand their approach, and to evaluate their research.

Critical thinking consists of collecting and evaluating the evidence, sifting through the choices, assessing the outcomes, and deciding whether the conclusions make sense. When you think critically, you are being evaluative. You are not accepting glib generalizations; instead you are determining the relevance of facts and looking for biases and imbalances, as well as for objectivity and testable, repeatable results. A critical thinker identifies central issues and is careful not to draw cause-and-effect conclusions from correlations. A critical thinker also has to tolerate some uncertainty and be patient—all of the answers do not come at once.

When you think critically about research, you become a detective sorting through facts. You look objectively at the facts, question the hypotheses and conclusions, avoid oversimplification, and consider all of the arguments, objections, and counter-arguments. You evaluate all assumptions and assertively seek out conflicting points of view. You revise your opinions when the data and your conclusions call for it. Whenever you have to evaluate a research study in this text, the popular press, or a psychological publication, you will find it helpful to focus on five research criteria: purpose, methodology, participants, repeatability, and conclusions.

Purpose. What is the purpose of this research? What is the researcher trying to test, demonstrate, or prove? Has the problem been clearly defined? Is the researcher qualified to conduct this research? Is the researcher biased?

Methodology. Is the methodology appropriate and carefully executed? Is the method of investigation used (for example, a case study, survey, or experiment) the most appropriate one for the topic? Has the method been utilized properly? Is there a control group? Have variables been carefully (operationally) defined? Has the researcher followed ethical guidelines (a topic considered on p. 17)?

Participants. Was the sample of participants properly chosen and carefully described? How was the sample selected? Does the sample accurately reflect the characteristics of the population of individuals about which the researcher would like to make generalizations? Will any generalizations be possible from this study?

Repeatability. Are the results repeatable? Has the researcher shown the same finding more than once? Have other investigators made similar findings? Are the results clear and unambiguous—that is, not open to criticism based on poor methodology?

Conclusions. How logical are the conclusions, implications, and applications suggested by the study? Does the researcher's data support them? Has the researcher gone beyond the data, drawing conclusions that might fit a predisposed view rather than conclusions that follow logically from the facts of the study? What implications do the data have for psychology as a science and as a profession? What are the potential implications for you as an individual? Has the researcher considered alternative explanations?

Think again about the sleep deprivation experiment described earlier. Use the five criteria to evaluate this research. The participants were college students deprived of sleep and tested on a reaction-time task.

Was the purpose of the study clear? The purpose was to assess the effect of sleep loss on reaction time.

Was the methodology appropriate? The method involved depriving participants of sleep after they had become used to sleeping in a controlled environment; participants were tested each morning. The task was operationally defined.

Was the sample of participants properly chosen? The participants were college students who were in good health. Reasonable generalizations from their reaction times to the reaction times of other similarly aged people might be possible.

Are the results repeatable? If the results were obtained with several groups of participants, and if the results were consistent within each of those groups, the repeatability of the results would seem assured.

How logical are the conclusions? Limited conclusions can be drawn from such a research study. There was only one age group—college students. There were no controls on other factors in the students' environment, such as workloads, school pressure, energy expenditures, and history of sleep loss. A simple conclusion about sleep deprivation could be drawn: In a controlled research study of college students, sleep deprivation tends to slow down reaction time. However, not much more could be said, and no generalizations could be applied to, say, children, older adults, or the chronically mentally ill. The results of the study do not contradict common sense, but they add little to our overall understanding of sleep deprivation.

A key to thinking critically about research is to be evaluative, to question all aspects of the study. Think about the advantages as well as the limitations of the research method used. You can also apply your critical thinking skills to nonacademic material. When a TV commercial tells you that 9 out of 10 doctors recommend Brand X, think critically about that claim. What kind of doctors, for what kind of ailment, for patients of what age, and for what extent of usage?

As you read this text, evaluate research findings. We will present the research to you in ways that allow you to critically evaluate it and to draw your own conclusions. From time to time in each chapter we will also ask you some *Focus* questions, called *Think Critically*. These questions will suggest new ideas and perspectives for you to consider as you evaluate the research studies presented. These are not the only places in the text where you should use your critical thinking skills, but they are specific places where you definitely can be evaluative.

Other Methods of Psychological Inquiry

Experiments, with their focus on cause-and-effect relationships, are not the only way to collect data about human behaviour. Techniques providing descriptive information about behaviour and that capture how well one variable predicts another are also important and useful. These techniques include questionnaires, interviews, naturalistic observation, and case studies.

Questionnaires. A **questionnaire**, or *survey*, is usually a printed form with questions that is given to a large group of people. Researchers use questionnaires to gather a large amount of information from many people in a short time. A questionnaire being used to learn the typical characteristics of psychology students might be distributed to students enrolled in an introductory psychology course. It

Questionnaire: A printed form with questions, usually given to a large group of people; used by researchers to gather a substantial amount of data in a short time; also known as a *survey*.

might ask each student to list age, sex, height, weight, previous courses taken, grades in high school, graduating exam scores, number of brothers and sisters, and parents' financial status. There might also be questions regarding sexual activity, career goals, and personal preferences in TV shows, clothing styles, and music.

One aim of surveys is to discover relationships among variables. For example, a questionnaire designed to assess aggressiveness might ask respondents to list their sex, the number of fights they have had in the past, their feelings of anger, and the sports they enjoy. The researcher who is analyzing the results might use them to determine whether men and women tend to differ in reporting aggressive behaviours.

The strength of the questionnaire is that it gathers a large amount of information in a short time. Its weaknesses are that it is impersonal, it gathers only the information asked by the questions, it limits the participants' range of responses, it cannot prevent respondents from leaving some questions unanswered or from being untruthful in their responses, and it does not provide a structure from which cause-and-effect relationships can be inferred (although correlations may be found).

Interviews. An **interview** is typically a face-to-face meeting in which a researcher (interviewer) asks an individual a series of standardized questions. The interviewer usually tape-records or writes down the participant's responses. The advantage of an interview over a questionnaire is that it allows for a wider range of responses. An interviewer who notes an exaggerated response, for example, might decide to ask related questions and thus explore more fully an area that seems important to the participant. The interview technique is time-consuming, however, and, as with questionnaires, no cause-and-effect relationships can be inferred.

Naturalistic Observation. A seemingly simple way to find out about behaviour is to observe it. As we've discussed, however, people who are told they are going to be observed tend to become self-conscious and alter their natural behaviour. Therefore, psychologists often use the technique of **naturalistic observation**—careful and objective observation of events from a distance, without observer intervention. The intent is to see how people or animals behave in their natural settings.

A psychologist conducting research on persuasion might pretend to be a browsing shopper at car lots, furniture stores, and appliance centres to discover how salespeople convince customers to buy expensive products. For example, the researcher might observe that one particularly successful car salesperson tends to show budget-minded customers the most expensive automobiles first, so that mid-priced models will seem more affordable by comparison. The researcher also might watch a salesperson through a one-way mirror of the kind used to detect thefts in supermarkets.

The strength of naturalistic observation is that the data collected are unaffected by the researcher's presence or by a laboratory setting. Naturalistic observers must take their data where and how they find them. They cannot manipulate the environment, because that might alter the behaviour they are observing. Because variables cannot be manipulated, data from naturalistic observation, like those from questionnaires and interviews, are descriptive and do not permit cause-and-effect conclusions.

A second major weakness is that the behaviour the psychologist may wish to examine is not always exhibited. For example, sometimes groups of people do not act persuasively or become aggressive; sometimes animals do not engage in mating behaviour. For these reasons naturalistic observation is also very time-consuming.

Case Studies. The **case study** is a method of interviewing participants to gain information about their background, including data on factors such as childhood, family, education, and social and sexual interactions. The information in a case

Interview: A face-to-face meeting in which a series of standardized questions are used to gather detailed information.

Naturalistic observation: Careful and objective observation of events from a distance, without observer intervention.

Case study: A method of interviewing participants to gain information about their backgrounds, including data on factors such as childhood, family, education, and social and sexual interactions.

Table 1.1 Five Approaches to Collecting Data

Approach	Strengths	Weaknesses
Experiment	Manipulation of variables to control outside influences; best method for identifying causal relationships.	Laboratory environment is artificial; limited generalizability of findings; manipulation of some variables is unethical or impractical.
Questionnaire	Effective means of measuring actions, attitudes, opinions, preferences, and intentions of large numbers of people.	Lack of explanatory power; validity of findings is limited by sample; reliability is difficult to determine; self-report may be inaccurate or biased.
Interview	Allows a wide range of responses; follow-up questions are possible.	Does not enable researchers to draw conclusions about causal relationships; time-consuming.
Naturalistic observation	Behaviour is unaffected by a researcher's manipulations.	Little opportunity to control variables; time-consuming.
Case study	Extensive evidence is gathered on a single person.	Lack of generalizability of findings; time-consuming.

study describes in detail a specific person's responses to the world; the case study is often used to describe a potential method of treatment.

The strength of the case study is that the information it provides is extensive, for one individual. A weakness is that the information describes only one person's particular situation. Because the behaviour of one person may be like that of others or may be unique, researchers cannot generalize from one individual to an entire population. They must be cautious even when generalizing from a number of case studies.

See Table 1.1 for a summary of the major approaches to data collection.

Avoiding Gender, Ethnicity, and Cultural Bias

Some people argue that human beings are all pretty much the same. But in 1897 William James cleverly wrote, "There is very little difference between one person and another, but what little difference there is, is very important" (pp. 256–257). James's comment reminds us that to ensure good experiments we have to have a large sample of participants who accurately reflect the population. In addition, researchers also must be careful to avoid subtle biases that influence results, such as gender, ethnicity, and cultural bias. At any stage of the research endeavour, an experimenter can influence the results and their interpretation by making assumptions about people, their tendencies, and how they might be affected by the variable under study. Such assumptions often are affected by researchers' attitudes about whether to report findings such as gender or ethnicity differences among participants.

Although many behaviours seem universal, truly universal behaviours are those that occur in all human beings regardless of their culture. When research studies are used to draw conclusions and make generalizations about people, it is important to understand that enormous differences exist among both individuals and groups of people. The young and the old may behave differently under similar conditions; research done only on men may yield different results from research done only on women. People are not all alike and do not all behave in the same way, even when in the same situation. Thus, researchers have become especially sensitive to issues of human diversity.

To do effective research, draw meaningful conclusions, and make generalizations that may be wide-ranging, researchers must recognize and test for elements of diversity, even within one country, such as Canada. A society includes individuals from many different cultures, ethnicities, religions, and so on. Each subgroup has developed its own style of living, which may vary considerably from that of the majority culture and may lead to marked ethnic-related differences in day-to-day behaviour and in mental health (Al-Issa, 1982). Psychologists say that a community, organization, or nation is culturally diverse if it has differences in race, ethnicity, language, nationality, age, and religion within it.

Ethnicity. *Ethnicity* refers to people's common traits, background, and allegiances, which are often cultural, religious, or language-based; ethnicity is learned from family, friends, and experiences. Families of English and French Canadians along with a broad range of other groups bring to the Canadian experience a wealth of different world-views and different ways of raising children, based on their particular heritages. The make-up of the Canadian population is diverse. The 1996 census revealed that French is the first language of about 25 percent of Canadians, about 7 percent of the Canadian population are of Asian descent, and about 3 percent of the population are Aboriginal (Statistics Canada, 1998).

Culture. Culture reflects a person's racial and ethnic background, religious and social values, artistic and musical tastes, and scholarly interests. Culture is the unwritten social and psychological dictionary that each of us has learned and through which we interpret ourselves and others (Landrine, Klonoff, & Brown-Collins, 1992). Various cultural vantage points shape behaviour, values, and even mental health. One such vantage point that must be considered is the difference between individualist and collectivist cultures. Individualist cultures (like Canada's) stress personal rather than group goals, and individual freedom and autonomy are valued; collectivist cultures (like many Asian cultures) stress group needs over individual ones, and a tightly knit social fabric and willingness to go along with the group are highly valued.

Class. Closely tied to culture is a person's class. Although the Canadian class structure is not as rigid as it was in the last century or is in some non-Western countries and although class distinctions are somewhat fuzzy, Canadians do fall into several socioeconomic classes. Among these classes are the economically poor, the disadvantaged, the educated, and the middle class. In different socioeconomic classes (which include individuals of different races and cultures), people may view the world differently and behave differently primarily because of their socioeconomic status. A research study that is not sensitive to such variables may confuse the causes of its results. For example, not considering socioeconomic class as a key variable in a study of drug use may lead to conclusions that are not true or, at a minimum, are not generalizable to all socioeconomic classes.

Gender. Psychologists know that due to both biological and social reasons, women often react differently than men do in psychological situations. This makes it easy to see that the gender of the sample in a research study is crucial (Denmark, 1994). For example, research on morality shows that, in general, women may see moral situations differently than men do; research on brain functions shows differences in brain structure between men and women; research on communication styles, aggression, and love shows sharp differences between men and women. Further, more than half of the people treated by mental health practitioners are women—although this may be because men with mental health problems are less likely to seek therapy. These differences must be examined closely if we are to properly understand them.

Age or Disabilities. The exceptional and the elderly are two other groups that shape research results in distinctive ways. The exceptional include individuals diagnosed with mental retardation, learning disabilities, or physical disabilities. Assessing and assisting exceptional individuals often require a special sensitivity on the part of professionals. In addition, the elderly are a growing percentage of the general population. More than 3.2 million Canadians are age 65 or older (Statistics Canada, 1998), and the aging of the baby boomers means that that number will continue to rise until about 2016. Psychologists are involved in developing programs that focus on the special needs of the exceptional and the elderly for social support, physical and psychological therapy, and continuing education.

Diversity within versus Between Groups. The differing perspectives on day-to-day behaviour that special groups bring to the fabric of society have not always been appreciated, understood, or even recognized in psychological research or theory. For example, psychologists now take Freud to task for developing a personality theory that is seen as clearly gender biased. (We will be evaluating Freud's personality theory in Chapter 12). In Freud's day, however, gender bias was not a matter for concern. Further, minorities and special groups such as the exceptional and the elderly were rarely—if ever—included in psychological research studies intended to represent the general population. Today psychologists seek to study all types of people to make valid conclusions based on scientific evidence. They see cultural diversity as an opportunity for both researchers and practitioners; they also recognize that they must research, learn about, and theorize about this diversity to help individuals optimize their potential (Hall, 1997). It is crucial to realize, though, that *there are usually more differences within a group than between groups*. For example, visual-spatial abilities differ more greatly among women than they do between men and women.

Individual circumstances exist, and people's individual experiences make broad generalizations impossible. Individuals and special populations often act just as the majority population does, but occasionally do so with a slightly different twist or variation. Here is the key point to remember as you read this book: While people are very much alike and share many common, even universal, experiences and behaviours, every individual is unique; each person's behaviour reflects diverse life experiences.

Ethics in Psychological Research

R esearchers must pay special attention to ethical considerations when conducting research with either human beings or animals. **Ethics** in research comprises the rules concerning appropriate and humane conduct that investigators use to guide their research; these rules govern the treatment of animals, the rights of human beings, and the responsibilities of investigators.

Research with Animals

Almost everyone has heard about animal research in psychology and other scientific experiments. Using animals in research studies allows experimenters to isolate simple aspects of behaviour and to eliminate the complex distractions and variables that arise in studies involving human beings. The use of animals also enables researchers to conduct studies that could not be conducted ethically with human

Ethics: Rules of proper and acceptable conduct that investigators use to guide psychological research; these rules concern the treatment of animals, the rights of human beings, and the responsibilities of investigators.

beings. For example, it would be unethical to deprive human infants of visual stimulation to investigate the effects of visual restriction on their perceptual development. Furthermore, because most animals have shorter life spans than human beings, experimenters can observe and control animals' entire life history, perform autopsies to obtain information, and study several generations in a short time. Research with animals has helped psychologists understand many aspects of human health and behaviour (Baldwin, 1993).

Some people object to the use of animals in research, but at present there are no known realistic alternatives (Gallup & Suarez, 1985). For example, experiments on laboratory rats reveal much about the addictive properties of cocaine and its adverse effects on behaviour. Similar experiments with human beings would be unethical. In

addition, many people with diseases, such as multiple sclerosis and Alzheimer's disease, are experiencing breakthroughs on a daily basis and have legitimate hopes for a cure because of animal research and experimentation (Feeney, 1987). Most researchers are aware of and sensitive to the needs of animals (Plous, 1996); furthermore, the Canadian Psychological Association has strict ethical guidelines for the humane and sensitive care and treatment of animals used in research. As well, the agencies that manage research grants, such as the Natural Science and Engineering Research Council (NSERC) and the Medical Research Council (MRC), also demand strict adherence to codes of humane treatment (see also Canadian Council on Animal Care, 1989).

Human Participants

Although animal research is an important part of psychological research, psychologists more often work with human participants. In such research, psychologists investigate many of the same processes they study with animals, as well as design experiments specifically for human participants. A psychologist who wishes to test whether an enhanced environment makes organisms smarter may use both animals and human participants. First, the researcher may train one rat to run complicated mazes while leaving its littermate in a barren environment. Several months later, the researcher, in examining the two animals, may discover that the brain cells of the maze-running rat are larger and have more internal connections. Along the same lines, the psychologist may test whether a decline in IQ scores among nursing home residents can be halted or reversed by enriching their environment with classes and special activities.

The Canadian Psychological Association (CPA, 1991) has strict ethical guidelines for research with human participants. As well, the three major granting agencies in Canada (Medical Research Council, Natural Science and Engineering Research Council, and the Social Sciences and Humanities Research Council) have created a tri-council policy document on research involving humans (MRC, NSERC, & SSHRC, 1998). Participants cannot be coerced to do things that are harmful to them, that could have other negative effects, or that would violate standards of decency. The investigator is responsible for ensuring the ethical treatment of the participants in a research study. In addition, any information gained in an experimental situation is considered strictly confidential. Before a study begins, human participants also must give the researcher their **informed consent**—agreement through a signed document that they understand the nature of their participation in the research and have been fully informed of the general nature of the research, its goals, and its methods. Participants are free to decline to participate or

Informed consent: The agreement of participants expressed through a signed document that indicates that they understand the nature of their participation in upcoming research and have been fully informed of the general nature of the research, its goals, and its methods.

to withdraw at any time without penalty. At the end of the project, participants must be debriefed. A **debriefing** informs participants about the true nature of an experiment, including hypotheses, methods, and expected or potential results. The debriefing is done *after* the experiment so that the validity of the participants' responses is not affected by their knowledge of the experiment's purpose.

Debriefing: A procedure to inform participants about the true nature of an experiment after its completion.

These ethical guidelines also apply to the interactions between clinical psychologists and their clients in therapy. Clients must be fully informed as to the nature of the therapy the psychologist is going to provide and must be assured that what they say to the psychologist will be kept in confidence. They also may need to be informed that psychologists in Canada do not have the same legal protection or "privilege" in their interactions with clients that is afforded to lawyers and priests. For example, if a client confesses a crime to their psychologist or if they state an intention to harm themselves or someone else, the psychologist is bound ethically to both take care that no harm comes to their client but also that no harm comes to others. In such a case the psychologist may seek assistance if the threat of harm seems imminent or may work with the client to help them avoid causing harm or turn themselves in if they have committed a crime.

Deception in Psychological Research

Is it ever acceptable for researchers to deceive human participants in psychological studies? Imagine a situation in which a researcher misleads a person into believing that she is causing another person pain in order to examine the conditions under which she might refuse to continue to harm another. Is this acceptable? Or is it acceptable for a researcher to try to change a human participant's views of social or political issues? The answer to these questions is generally no. Researchers must not use deception unless the study has important scientific, educational, or applied value. And even then, two key procedures must be followed: obtaining informed consent and providing debriefing.

Some psychologists believe that deception is unacceptable under *any* circumstances. They assert that it undermines the public's belief in the integrity of scientists and that its costs outweigh its potential benefits. Most psychologists do not conduct research in which there is deception; those who do are particularly careful to use rigorous informed consent procedures and extensive debriefing to minimize potentially harmful effects. Whenever deception must be used to achieve some legitimate scientific goal, psychologists go to extraordinary lengths to protect the well-being, rights, and dignity of the participants; anything less is considered a violation of CPA guidelines (Canadian Psychological Association, 1991).

You may be wondering what kinds of people actually do this work of psychology. Who are these people handing out questionnaires and depriving students of sleep? Next we'll examine who psychologists are and what they do on a day-by-day basis.

Focus

Review

- Distinguish between the independent and the dependent variable as well as the control and the experimental group. pp. 8, 9
- Identify two elements in the design of an experiment that are especially important to making generalizations about the results. pp. 9–10
- Why is it important for psychologists to consider the cultural context in which behaviour occurs? pp. 15–16

Think Critically

- Imagine a research study testing the effects of a low dosage of a drug that helps relieve anxiety. The participants are a sample of 50 men who suffer from job-related stress. What are the limitations of such a study? Would you say that such a study is poorly designed, or that it has a flawed methodology?
- Why do you think sample size is so important in psychological research?
- As psychologists are increasingly considering themselves biomedical researchers, what kind of special training do you think they need in ethics?

Who Are These People
We Call Psychologists?

S ometimes people mistakenly assume that all psychologists primarily assist those suffering from debilitating mental disorders, such as schizophrenia and severe depression; but psychologists actually do a much broader range of things. Psychologists study nearly every aspect of life, not only to understand how people behave but to help them lead happier, healthier, more productive lives. Some psychologists practise psychology; others teach or do research. Most are involved in a combination of activities.

While some psychologists help people with problems, others help well-adjusted people by providing services such as career counselling and assistance with community projects. Some psychologists seek to provide people with interpersonal skills and knowledge about self-help techniques. And, as *Experiencing Psychology* reveals, some psychologists work with professional athletes and musicians to improve their public performances.

Psychologists, then, are professionals who study behaviour and use behavioural principles in scientific research or in applied settings. Most have an advanced degree, usually a Ph.D. Many psychologists also train for an additional year or two in a specialized area such as mental health, physiology, or child development.

Founded in 1939, the Canadian Psychological Association (CPA) is the largest professional organization for psychologists in Canada. Its purpose is to advance psychology as a science, a profession, and a means of promoting human welfare. The CPA disseminates research publications (e.g., *Canadian Psychology*, *Canadian Journal of Experimental Psychology*, and *Canadian Journal of Behavioural Psychology*) that serve as a primary means for many psychologists to present their research to other professionals. In addition to belonging to the CPA many Canadian psychologists also belong to the American Psychological Association (APA) through a reciprocal arrangement that allows them to become members for a reduced fee if they are already members of the CPA.

The CPA is not the sole voice of psychology within Canada. Many specialty groups have emerged over the years. For example, organizations consisting mainly of developmental, behavioural, cognitive, or neuroscience psychologists have been formed. In 1990 the Canadian Society for Brain, Behaviour, and Cognitive Science (CSBBCS) was founded; it has a membership of about 600 psychologists with academic interests and focuses on scientific research rather than on practice or applied interests. Two of its goals are to preserve the scientific base of psychology and to promote public understanding of psychology as a science. In addition, psychological associations in each province and territory are responsible for overseeing the chartering (or certification) of practising psychologists.

People are often unsure about the differences among clinical psychologists, psychiatrists, and psychoanalysts. All are mental health practitioners who help people with serious emotional and behaviour problems, but each looks at behaviour differently. **Clinical psychologists** usually have a Ph.D. in psychology and view behaviour and emotions from a psychological perspective. In contrast, **psychiatrists** are physicians (medical doctors) who have chosen to specialize in the treatment of emotional disorders. Patients who see psychiatrists often have both physical and emotional problems. As physicians, psychiatrists can prescribe drugs and can admit patients for hospitalization. In 1995 the APA voted to pursue the development of curricula that would prepare psychologists to prescribe drugs.

Clinical psychologists generally have more extensive training than psychiatrists do in research, assessment, and psychological treatment of emotional problems. Their non-medical perspective gives them different roles in hospital settings and encourages them to examine social and interpersonal variables more than psychiatrists do. Psychiatrists are physicians and use a medical approach, which often

Psychologist: Professional who studies behaviour and uses behavioural principles in scientific research or in applied settings.

Clinical psychologist: Mental health practitioner who views behaviour and mental processes from a psychological perspective and who uses research-based knowledge to treat persons with serious emotional or behavioural problems or to do research into the causes of behaviour.

Psychiatrist: Physician (medical doctor) specializing in the treatment of patients with emotional disorders.

experiencing psychology

Using Psychological Knowledge to Improve Performance

You may be wondering what psychology can do for you as you go about your life. Psychology might appear to be just another academic subject, a set of theories and concepts to be learned in order to pass an exam and complete a course requirement. Not so. Psychology can be applied to everyday life in an endless variety of ways, as we'll see throughout this book. Let's look at just one example.

Did you take piano lessons as a child? Do you remember those dreaded days when you and your teacher's other students had to perform in recitals? You froze, staring at the keyboard. The teacher placed the sheet music in front of you, but you had no idea what the notes meant. Somehow you eventually managed to stumble through the performance, all the while saying to yourself, "But I know this piece! Why can't I play it?"

You or a friend of yours may have a similar problem when it comes to writing exams. Despite being well prepared you become so anxious during the exam that you have trouble recalling even the most basic facts correctly.

How can psychological knowledge help in such situations? These episodes stem from a phenomenon called performance anxiety, and they can be avoided, or at least alleviated,

with a little knowledge of psychological processes. In fact, many top athletes are assisted by sport psychologists, who help them maintain their focus and avoid becoming too emotionally involved in their performances. The athlete can then concentrate on the specific actions necessary while still enjoying the experience of competing. The same principles can be applied to other types of performances, including piano recitals and public speaking.

People need to separate the judgmental part of the personality from the part that's performing. The best performances occur when the athlete or musician isn't actually thinking about the performance—not giving the body a lot of instructions, not telling it to correct mistakes, not evaluating the action in any way. Instead, good performances occur when the performer is in a state of effortless concentration. It's a matter of not trying too hard but simply focusing on the action itself. Musicians can achieve this type of concentration by focusing on each measure as it is being played, rather than saying to themselves, "I've got to be careful to hit all the sixteenth notes in that tough section coming up next."

Psychologists offer advice based on well-known psychological

concepts that we will encounter throughout this book (see especially Chapter 17, which deals with applied psychology, including sport psychology). An understanding of the processes of learning and thinking (Chapters 5 and 6) can be helpful in developing ways to mute our judgmental side and allow our natural abilities to come through. Knowledge of the principles of motivation and emotion (Chapter 9) also can be helpful. And while writing exams is not as physically demanding as figure skating or high-jumping, the same issues of concentration and relaxation apply. If you are experiencing serious problems writing exams, especially when you are sure your preparations for them have gone well, you may find that assistance is available through your college's or university's student counselling centre free of charge.

You use psychological principles all the time, and, in truth, all of human behaviour is part of psychology—the subject of this book. You will see that the many subfields of psychology that affect individual performance are related to one another. The way we as individuals can improve our individual performance—indeed, improve our lives—is by understanding basic psychological processes. ■

involves making assumptions about behaviour—for example, that abnormal behaviour is disease-like in nature—that many psychologists do not make. Clinical psychologists and psychiatrists often see a similar mix of clients and often work together as part of a mental health team. Most psychologists and psychiatrists support collaborative efforts.

Psychoanalysts are frequently psychiatrists (as physicians they are able to prescribe medications); they have training in the technique of psychoanalysis and use it to treat people with emotional problems. As we'll soon see, psychoanalysis was originated by Sigmund Freud and includes the study of unconscious motivation and dream analysis. In a strict Freudian psychoanalysis, a course of daily therapy sessions is required; the patient's treatment may last for several years. In the past, psychoanalysts had to be physicians. In 1988, however, Freudian psychoanalytic institutes began to accept non-physicians into their training programs, a practice

Psychoanalyst: Psychiatrist or, occasionally, non-medical practitioner who has studied the technique of psychoanalysis and uses it to treat people with emotional problems.

begun earlier by Jungian institutes. Thus, all practitioners may treat similar clients; but therapists' individual training and assumptions may vary, and this may be reflected in their choice of treatment.

Choosing Psychology as a Career

When we were first attracted to psychology as a career, it was because we had a desire to help others. We recognized that psychology is an optimistic profession—the truth is that psychologists unabashedly admit to this bias. Psychologists generally don't assume that our lives are fixed and instead believe that there is much we can do to make our lives more productive and enjoyable.

Many psychologists help others through the delivery of mental health services. But many psychologists are intrigued by the analysis of data; they focus on research and the discovery of knowledge. These psychologists seek out careers as scientists, practitioners, or consultants because they enjoy the process of searching for and explaining the causes of human behaviour.

Psychology attracts many students who like the idea of understanding human behaviour and helping others. The causes and implications of behaviour intrigue these students; they realize that psychology is part of the fabric of daily life. Psychology is one of the most popular undergraduate majors. Today's psychology students are increasingly female, ethnically diverse, and interested in many of its subspecialties, such as health psychology, child psychology, or social psychology. And there is good news for students who go on to graduate school: Unemployment among psychologists is low. Most experts agree that employment opportunities will continue to be good; psychology is often cited as one of the top 10 growth areas for jobs. Furthermore, compensation for psychologists is good.

Training, of course, is the key to employment. A psychologist who (1) obtains a Ph.D. in clinical psychology, (2) writes a professional practice exam, and (3) completes an approved internship can become chartered by their provincial College of Psychologists and will have a wide variety of job opportunities available in both the private and public sectors. Individuals with a master's degree can function in a variety of settings, and even those with a bachelor's degree can play an important role in delivering psychological services. Salaries, responsibilities, and working conditions tend to be commensurate with level of training in the discipline. Psychologists with Ph.D.s are increasingly filling supervisory roles in the delivery of mental health services (Humphreys, 1996).

Many of the members of the CPA who work in the field of psychology deliver human services. Most of these psychologists work in clinics, community mental health centres, veterans' hospitals, general hospitals, and mental health hospitals. The others are private practitioners who maintain offices and work in schools, universities, business, and numerous other public and private settings.

Most psychologists employed by hospitals spend their time in the direct delivery of human services, including individual and group therapy. Business, government, and industry employ a small percentage of psychologists. Many psychologists are employed by universities, nearly half of them in psychology departments. University psychologists spend most of their time researching and teaching.

Diversity looks at a sampling of the many ways in which Canadian psychologists and psychological research are contributing to the well-being of Canadians and adding to our growing storehouse of psychological knowledge.

FIGURE 1.2
What Psychologists Do

(Based on data from The College of Psychologists of Ontario, May 31, 1999.)

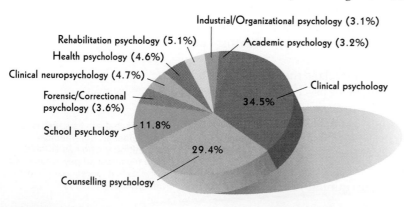

Industrial/Organizational psychology (3.1%)
Rehabilitation psychology (5.1%)
Academic psychology (3.2%)
Health psychology (4.6%)
Clinical neuropsychology (4.7%)
Forensic/Correctional psychology (3.6%)
Clinical psychology 34.5%
School psychology 11.8%
Counselling psychology 29.4%

Psychology That Is Uniquely Canadian

Psychology is a discipline that spans borders and continents. The research of Canadian psychologists contributes not just to Canadian psychological knowledge but to psychological knowledge in general. The work of Canadian psychologists will be highlighted, when and where appropriate in this textbook. On the topic of diversity, however, there are a number of types of psychological research that, while they may not be done only in Canada, Canadian psychologists are either especially well prepared to address or in which the issue is somewhat unique to Canadian society.

Canada is constitutionally a bilingual country. Unlike in the United States where English is the sole language of government and commerce, there are many regions in Canada where bilingual development is the norm. Canadian researchers are in the forefront of studies examining bilingualism and second-language learning. Canadian elementary school immersion programs are considered models for how such programs should be set up and run. As well, Canadian researchers are actively involved in research looking at literacy for children and adults from homes where English or French is not the family's first language.

Canada has a federal policy of multiculturalism, which means that, unlike the American "melting pot" approach to the integration of immigrants into mainstream culture, we in Canada are committed to a distinct approach that blends Canadian citizenship and ethnic heritage. A recent federal survey revealed that 95 percent of Canadians are proud both of being a Canadian and of their ethnic heritage. Psychologists are studying the effects that this general social policy has on the process of acculturation faced by new immigrants to Canada.

A large proportion of Canada is referred to as the North, even by Canadians. There are distinct challenges to living in the sometimes harsh conditions found in northern latitudes. In addition to cold and snow, there is a lack of sunlight in the winter months, which has implications for seasonal affect disorder, a form of depression linked to lack of sunlight. Social issues also have arisen, including the evaluation of decisions to relocate groups of Innu and Inuit living in the North. Canadian psychologists are learning much about the community/social conditions that lead to dramatic increases in the suicide rate among young members of those communities. ■

Applied Research, Human Services, and Experimental Psychology

Applied research, human services, and experimental psychology have much in common. Actually, human services is a subfield of applied research, but it comprises such a large proportion of psychologists that it generally is viewed as a separate field of psychology. All psychologists consider research and theory to be the cornerstones of their approach (Beutler et al., 1995). A human service provider also may do research, and a researcher who works in a university also may provide human services to the university or the community at large. For example, a human service psychologist may help an alcoholic patient by applying learning principles discovered in an experimental laboratory. Similarly, problems discovered by therapists challenge researchers to investigate causes in the laboratory. This cross-fertilization is stimulating. Let's look at each of these areas.

I

Applied Research. Applied psychologists do research and then use that research to solve practical problems. Many use psychological principles in businesses, government, and institutions, such as hospitals.

Engineering psychologists (sometimes called *human factors psychologists*) use psychological principles to help people design machines for safe and efficient use (for example, an easy-to-use ATM machine). We will discuss this field in Chapter 17.

Educational psychologists focus on such topics as how learning occurs in the classroom, how intelligence affects performance, and the relationship between personality and learning. We also will discuss this field in Chapter 17.

Forensic psychologists deal with legal issues, often working in courts and correctional systems. They evaluate whether inmates are ready for parole, whether a rehabilitation program is achieving its goals, or whether an accused criminal has lied, deserves an "insanity defence," or is likely to give false testimony.

Health psychologists determine how lifestyle changes can improve health. They devise techniques for helping people avoid medical and psychological problems. We will discuss this field further in Chapter 14.

Behavioural medicine psychologists help people who suffer from chronic physical problems such as back pain and migraine headaches to learn to cope and develop techniques to manage pain.

Sport psychologists are in an emerging field that focuses on brain–behaviour interactions, the role of sports in healthful lifestyles, and the motivation and preparation of athletes. We will discuss this field in Chapter 17.

Industrial/organizational psychologists help employers evaluate employees; they also focus on personnel selection, employee motivation and training, work behaviour, incentives, and work appraisals. They apply psychological research and theory to organizational problems such as productivity, turnover, absenteeism, and management–labour relations. Working in human resources offices and in other departments at universities and businesses, they also evaluate organizational programs. Industrial/organizational psychologists are discussed in greater detail in Chapter 17.

Human Services. Many human service psychologists use behavioural principles to teach people to cope with life more effectively. They try to help people solve problems and promote well-being. Within the human service area are the subfields of clinical, counselling, community, and school psychology.

Clinical psychologists help clients with personal problems such as anger, shyness, depression, and marital discord. They work either in private practice or at hospitals, mental institutions, or social service agencies. They administer psychological tests, interview potential clients, and use psychological methods to treat emotional problems. Many universities employ psychologists to help students and staff handle the pressures of academic life.

Counselling psychologists, like clinical psychologists, work with people who have personal problems. They also help people handle career planning, adjustment problems such as marriage, family, and parenting problems, and substance abuse. Counselling psychology began in the 1940s, and at first the problems presented by its clients were less serious than those presented by clients of clinical psychologists. However, since the 1980s, the problems of layoffs, spousal abuse, and violence have been addressed for treatment, and counselling psychologists increasingly have used psychotherapy and other therapies that previously were used exclusively by clinical psychologists. According to many practitioners and researchers, counselling and clinical psychology are converging (Fitzgerald & Osipow, 1986).

Counselling psychologists may work for public agencies such as mental health centres, hospitals, and universities. Many work in college or university counselling centres, where they help students adjust to the academic atmosphere and provide them with vocational and educational guidance. Like clinical psychologists, many counselling psychologists research the causes and treatment of maladjustment.

Community psychologists strengthen existing social support networks and stimulate the formation of new networks to meet a variety of challenges (L. R. Gonzales et al., 1983). Their goal is to help individuals and their neighbourhoods or communities to grow, develop, plan for the future, and prevent problems from developing. Community psychology emerged in response to the widespread desire for an action-oriented approach to individual and social adjustment, and one of its key elements is community involvement to effect social change. For example, community psychologists have been instrumental in organizing social support groups that help AIDS patients and their families handle the stress and loss of self-esteem produced by this catastrophic illness. Community psychologists work in mental health agencies, government, and private organizations. We will discuss this field in Chapter 17.

School psychologists help students, teachers, parents, and administrators to communicate effectively with one another and accomplish mutually agreed-upon goals. School psychology began in 1896 at the University of Pennsylvania in a clinic founded to study and treat children considered to be "morally or mentally defective." Early leaders such as G. Stanley Hall and Lightner Witmer were crucial in promoting psychological interventions and techniques in schools (T. K. Fagan, 1992). Today school psychologists administer and interpret tests, help teachers with classroom-related problems, and influence school policies and procedures (Bardon, 1983). They foster communication among parents, teachers, administrators, and other psychologists at schools. They also provide information to teachers and parents about students' progress and advise them on how to help students achieve more.

Experimental Psychology. Experimental psychologists try to identify and understand the basic elements of behaviour and mental processes. Theirs is an approach, not a specific field. That is, experimental psychology involves the use of a set of *techniques*; it is not defined simply by the topics it examines. For example, applied psychologists may be involved in experimental research. However, experimental psychologists focus on understanding basic research issues, whereas applied psychologists generally use experimental techniques to improve a specific situation, help a mental health practitioner, or work with an employer.

Experimental psychology covers many areas of interest, some of which overlap with fields outside psychology. Experimental psychologists may be interested, for example, in visual perception, in how people learn language or solve problems, or in how hormones influence behaviour. *Physiological psychologists* (sometimes called *neuropsychologists*) try to understand the relationship between the brain and behaviour (see *Brain and Behaviour*). They may examine drugs, hormones, and the effects of brain damage caused by strokes. We will discuss some of their explorations in Chapter 2. *Cognitive psychologists* focus on thought processes, especially on the relationships among learning, memory, and perception. They may, for example, examine how organisms process and interpret information on the basis of some internal representation in memory. We will discuss this field further in Chapter 7. *Developmental psychologists* focus on the emotional, physical, and intellectual changes that take place throughout people's lives. We will return to this field in Chapters 10 and 11. *Social psychologists* study how other people affect an individual's behaviour and thoughts and how people interact with

Focus

Review

◆ Identify the focuses of applied research, human services, and experimental psychology. pp. 23–25
◆ What makes experimental psychologists different from applied psychologists? p. 25

Think Critically

◆ Which types of practitioners do you think would be best suited to work with Janet, whose story opened this chapter?
◆ If you were to seek help for marital conflict, what would be the key reason for choosing a psychologist rather than a psychiatrist?

brain and behaviour

We've Come a Long Way

"I couldn't get myself to react. I felt very still and very empty, the way the eye of a tornado must feel, moving dully along in the middle of the surrounding hullabaloo." Like many other well-known writers of the twentieth century, Sylvia Plath, author of those words from *The Bell Jar* (1971, p. 3), felt as though she had spent most of her life in a rarefied atmosphere, as if in a bell jar. Emotionally devastated, depressed, angry, agitated, and sometimes alcoholic, Plath, Zelda Fitzgerald, Robert Lowell, William Styron, and Tennessee Williams were labelled "despondent," "disturbed," or "melancholy." Those of them who were wealthy, and those who did not commit suicide, were sent to sanatoriums for rest and recuperation. In the early part of the twentieth century, the mentally ill were routinely locked up, kept in back rooms, or, at best, shunned by society. The causes of their problems were unknown, and treatments were haphazard. Thousands of them were told to take rest cures and breathe fresh, clean air. Experimental treatments consisted of cold-water baths, special diets, occupational therapy, and exercise. But for the vast majority of individuals, rest and fresh air was not a cure.

Schizophrenia and depression were the real problems these people faced—often made worse by alcoholism and other drug abuse. We will have much to say about schizophrenia, depression, and their causes and treatment in Chapters 15 and 16. For now, from a historical point of view, several key ideas are worth noting. First, disorders like depression, in which a person becomes overwhelmingly sad and dejected and loses interest in most of life's activities, are now considered psychological disorders, not diseases of the blood or kidneys that call for rest and clean air. Second, depression and most other psychological disorders are now considered treatable. Third, and perhaps most important from a psychologist's point of view, we now know that specific brain mechanisms are responsible for many disorders like depression, and that drugs can be part of the treatment.

One technique we use for diagnosis is brain imaging or brain scanning. Brain scans (discussed in Chapter 2) make the examination of the brain easier and more precise, thereby providing detailed information about its workings. For example, research shows that small brain lesions (areas of damaged tissue, often due to disease or injury) are common in the elderly and are a natural part of the aging process. But more importantly, researchers are establishing links among brain lesions, neurochemistry, and depression.

one another. For example, they may examine attitude formation, aggressive versus helping behaviour, or the formation of intimate relationships. We will discuss this field in Chapter 13.

How Have Schools of Psychological Thought Developed?

Psychology as a discipline and a science would not have been recognized as such 200 years ago. The psychological study of human behaviour has evolved over a relatively brief time span, beginning a little more than a century ago. Over that time, psychologists have subscribed to many different perspectives. Once fully developed and presented, these perspectives serve to orient researchers and provide them with a frame of reference in which to do new work. A specific perspective on the study of behaviour is called a *school of psychological thought*. This section discusses the development of schools of psychological thought. You will see that the study of behaviour and mental processes, despite its short life, has had a rich and varied history.

Unlike early twentieth-century practitioners, today's psychologists are combining old-school "talking therapy" with high-tech diagnostic tools and drug therapy. They've learned that people who suffer from depression sometimes have brain lesions but usually have changed levels of substances in the brain called neurotransmitters (we'll have more to say about them later). Whether neurotransmitters cause the depression or whether depression causes such changes in brain chemistry is not yet completely clear. Nevertheless, when people are seriously depressed, certain drug therapies can be effective in altering neurotransmission processes. When they are on drug therapies such as Prozac (Chapter 16), changes in people's thought processes can be tracked (Chapter 7). We can observe the brain in action through various imaging techniques (Chapter 2). And we can help people cope with the stressors in their life (Chapter 14) to better meet the demands of their environments (Chapter 11). All of this has come about because we now better understand the links between brain and behaviour.

The connections between what we feel, think, and do and our biological inheritances are being explored intensively today. Is our eating behaviour, sexuality, or shyness biologically determined? Do we have a predisposition to aggressiveness? Is our genetic heritage our destiny? All these questions, and many more, are being addressed through studies of links between the brain and behaviour. It is easy to see the brain's control over other structures of the body—especially when people take psychoactive drugs (drugs that affect the nervous system and the brain itself). A person takes a drug, which affects the firing of neurons and the flow of neurotransmitters in the brain; these changes make the person feel different. The person responds to the feeling, and further brain changes take place. In other words, the brain affects behaviour, and behaviour in turn affects the brain. Such brain-behaviour connections can be found in other situations as well.

Throughout this book, we will attempt to show you some of these links through special features called *Brain and Behaviour,* which will highlight situations where the connections are especially notable or where research is making important breakthroughs. These connections related to depression are quite dramatic—drugs act on brain substances to help people who are depressed. In other areas of behaviour such connections may be important as well—drugs to help you sleep, adjust to time changes, or remember things better, for example. In still other areas, research on brain-behaviour connections is more tenuous. Changing people's attitudes about safe driving is less about brain-behaviour relations and more about laying out rules and providing motivation. So, we will try to focus on the unique brain-behaviour relationship where it is most appropriate to do so: where psychologists have done solid research on the key relationships.

We've come a long way since the time when people said that a disturbed person was suffering from "the vapours" or was the "the black sheep of the family"—psychologists are now coming to understand the complex and important relationship between our brains and our behaviour. ∎

The Early Traditions

Structuralism—The Contents of Consciousness. Wilhelm Wundt (1832–1920) (pronounced *Voont*) developed the first widely accepted school of psychological thought. In Leipzig, Germany, in 1879, the former medical student and physiologist founded the first psychological laboratory; its focus was the study of mental life (Leahey, 1992). Before Wundt, the field of psychology simply did not exist; what are now considered psychological questions lay in the domains of philosophy, medicine, and theology. Wundt was a formal, humourless man, but his lectures were extremely popular, and his dozens of graduate students were admiring followers. One of Wundt's major contributions was teaching his students to use the scientific method when asking psychological questions (Benjamin et al., 1992). Edward B. Titchener (1867–1927), an Englishman, helped popularize Wundt's ideas, along with his own, in the English-speaking world.

Wundt, Titchener, and others espoused structuralism. **Structuralism** was the school of psychological thought that considered the organized structure of immediate, conscious experience as the proper subject matter of psychology. Instead of looking at the broad range of behaviour and mental processes that psychologists consider today, structuralists tried to observe only the inner workings of the mind to find the elements of conscious experience.

Structuralism: The school of psychological thought that considered the organized structure of immediate, conscious experience to be the proper subject matter of psychology.

To discover these elements of conscious experience, Wundt and Titchener used the technique of **introspection**, or *self-examination*, the systematic description and analysis by a person of what he or she is thinking and feeling. In the process, they also conducted some of the first experiments in psychology. For example, they studied the speed of thought by observing reaction times for simple tasks.

By today's standards, of course, the structuralists focused too narrowly on individuals' conscious experiences. Understanding one person's conscious experience actually reveals little about another's. Thus, though they provided a starting point for psychological research, the structuralists' results allowed for few generalizations and the school made little progress in describing the nature of the mind.

Functionalism—How Does the Mind Work? Before long, a new school developed, bringing with it a new, more active way of thinking about behaviour. Built on the basic concepts of structuralism, **functionalism** was the school of psychological thought that tried to discover not just the mind's structures but how and why the mind *functions* and is related to consciousness. It also sought to understand how people adapted to their environment.

This lively new school of thought, with Harvard University–trained physician and professor of anatomy William James (1842–1910) at its head, argued that knowing only the contents of consciousness (structuralism) was too limited. Unlike Wundt, James was charming, informal, outgoing, and vivacious; especially well liked by his students, James argued that a psychologist also had to know how the contents of consciousness functioned and worked together. Through such knowledge, the psychologist could understand how the mind (consciousness) guided behaviour. In 1890 James published *Principles of Psychology*, in which he described the mind as a dynamic set of continuously evolving elements. In this work he coined the phrase *stream of consciousness*, describing the mind as a river, always flowing, never remaining still.

James broadened the scope of structuralism by studying animals, by applying psychology in practical areas such as education, and by experimenting on overt behaviour, not just mental processes. James's ideas influenced the life and writing of G. Stanley Hall (1844–1924), an American psychologist who was one of Wundt's early students. Hall, as Titchener was for structuralism, was an organizer and promoter of functionalist psychology.

Functionalists continued to use introspection as a technique; for them psychology was still the study of consciousness. For many of the emerging schools of psychology, however, this scope was too limiting. The early schools of psychological thought were soon replaced by different conceptualizations: Gestalt psychology, psychoanalysis, behaviourism, and humanistic and cognitive approaches to psychology.

Gestalt Psychology—Examining Wholes. In the early twentieth century, while some psychologists were feeling their way forward with structuralism and functionalism, others were developing very different approaches. One such approach was **Gestalt psychology** (*Gestalt* means "configuration")—the school of psychological thought that argued that it is necessary to study a person's total experience, not just parts of experience (the mind or behaviour). Gestalt psychologists such as Max Wertheimer (1880–1943) and Kurt Koffka (1886–1941) suggested that conscious experience is more than simply the sum of its individual parts, much as it is hard to fully understand how a car runs by studying all of its parts in detail. Arguing that each mind organizes the elements of experience into something unique, by adding structure and meaning to incoming stimuli, Gestalt psychologists analyzed the world in terms of perceptual frameworks. They proposed that people mold simple sensory elements into patterns through which they then interpret the world. By analyzing the whole experience—the patterns of a person's perceptions and thoughts—one could understand the mind and its workings.

Eventually Gestalt psychology became a major influence in many areas of psychology—for example, in therapy. A Gestalt-oriented therapist dealing with a "problem" family member might try to see how the "part" (the person perceived as the problem) could be better understood in the context of the "whole" (the family configuration). However, as broad as its influence was, Gestalt psychology seemed lacking in scientific rigour and somewhat mystical, and it never achieved as wide a following as did psychoanalysis.

Psychoanalysis—Probing the Unconscious. One of the first researchers to develop a theory about emotional disturbance was Sigmund Freud (1856–1939). Freud grew up during a difficult time in the history of central Europe; he became a dark, brooding, complex, yet charismatic figure. Freud was a physician who was interested in helping people overcome anxiety; he worked in Vienna, Austria, focusing on the causes and treatment of emotional disturbances. Working from the premise that unconscious mental processes direct daily behaviour, he developed techniques to explore those unconscious processes; these techniques include free association and dream interpretation. He emphasized that childhood experiences shape and influence future adult behaviours and that sexual energy fuels day-to-day behaviour.

Freud created the **psychoanalytic approach**—the school of psychological thought that assumes that psychological maladjustment is a consequence of anxiety resulting from unresolved conflicts and forces of which a person generally is unaware. Its therapeutic technique is *psychoanalysis*. The psychoanalytic perspective has undergone many changes since Freud devised it. At times, in fact, it seems only loosely connected to Freud's basic ideas. When this approach was introduced in North America, most psychologists ignored it. But by the 1920s, when intellectual growth caused society to emerge from the repressed Victorian era, the influence of the psychoanalytic approach spread rapidly. Soon it was so influential and widely studied that it threatened to eclipse research-based laboratory psychology (Hornstein, 1992). Chapter 12 discusses Freud's theory of personality, and Chapter 16 discusses psychoanalysis as the therapeutic technique derived from his theory.

Psychological Schools Grow Broader

The early schools of psychology focused on the mind and how it functioned; for example, psychoanalysis examined how the unconscious operated and shaped later development. Yet it was not until the mid-1920s that the influences of learning were stressed, and it was not until the 1940s and 1950s that the roles of free will and self-expression were investigated. The 1970s saw the emergence of cognitive psychology, which stresses thinking processes; psychology in the 1980s and 1990s also has been heavily influenced by studies of the neurological and biological foundations of behaviour. Let's look at these more modern trends in the history of psychology.

Behaviourism—Observable Behaviour. Despite their differences in focus, the structuralists, functionalists, Gestaltists, and psychoanalysts were all concerned with the functioning of the mind. They were all interested in private perceptions and conscious or unconscious activity. In the early twentieth century, however, North American psychology moved from studying the contents of the mind to studying overt behaviour. At the forefront of that movement was John B. Watson (1878–1958), the founder of behaviourism. **Behaviourism** is the school of psychological thought that rejects the study of the contents of consciousness

Psychoanalytic [SYE-ko-an-uh-LIT-ick] approach: The school of psychological thought developed by Freud, which assumes that psychological maladjustment is a consequence of anxiety resulting from unresolved conflicts and forces of which a person may be unaware; includes the therapeutic technique known as *psychoanalysis*.

Behaviourism: The school of psychological thought that rejects the study of the contents of consciousness and focuses on describing and measuring only that which is observable directly or through assessment instruments.

and focuses instead on describing and measuring only behaviour—that which is observable directly through assessment instruments.

Watson was an upstart—clever, brash, and defiant. Trained as a functionalist, he argued forcefully that there was no reasonable, objective way to study the human mind, particularly through introspection. Watson, flamboyantly and with great self-assurance, contended that behaviour, not the private contents of the mind, was the proper subject matter of psychology. According to Watson, psychologists should study only activities that can be objectively observed and measured; prediction and control should be the theoretical goals of psychology. This contention was a major break with previous psychological thought. Watson rejected the work of Wundt and most other early psychologists; he argued that psychologists should put the study of consciousness behind them.

After Watson, other researchers extended and developed behaviourism, so much so that in North America in the 1920s, behaviourism became the dominant and only acceptable view of psychology. Among those supporting the study of behaviourism, and certainly its most widely recognized proponent, was Harvard psychologist B. F. Skinner (1904–1990). In the 1940s Skinner attempted to explain the causes of behaviour by cataloguing and describing the relations among events in the environment (*stimuli*) and a person's or animal's reactions (*responses*). Skinner's behaviourism led the way for thousands of research studies on conditioning and human behaviour, a special focus on stimuli and responses, and the controlling of behaviour through learning principles.

Skinner is arguably the most influential psychologist ever trained in North America. Although he spent his research time studying animals, his writings focus on people. His theories about using principles of operant conditioning to design a utopian society brought him lasting fame. But Skinner was more of an engineer, a behavioural technician, than he was a theorist. Determining the best time to get up in the morning, inventing a better hearing aid, designing a comfortable enclosed crib for his daughters—these were the kinds of tasks he found most rewarding. Skinner's thinking classified him as a behaviourist. He believed that we are what we do—that there is no "self," only a collection of possible behaviours. Skinner was also a determinist. In his view, our actions are more a result of past experiences than genetics. According to Skinner, our environment determines completely what we do. We control our actions about as much as a rock in an avalanche controls its resting-place.

Behaviourists focus on how observable responses are learned, modified, or forgotten. They usually emphasize how current behaviour is acquired or modified rather than examine inherited characteristics or early childhood experiences. One of their fundamental assumptions is that disordered behaviour can be replaced with appropriate, worthwhile behaviour through traditional learning techniques (described in Chapter 5).

Early behaviourists took a relatively unbending view of the scope of psychology by refusing to study mental phenomena. Non-behaviourists of their time argued that not all behaviour can be explained by stimuli and responses alone. They focused instead on such topics as creativity, the origins of thought, and the expression of love. Today behaviourists are beginning to study a wider range of human behaviour, including mental phenomena such as decision making and maladjustment (Rachlin, 1995).

Humanistic Psychology—Free Will. Another important perspective within modern psychology is **humanistic psychology**—the school of psychological thought that emphasizes the uniqueness of each human being's experience and the idea that human beings have free will to determine their destiny. Stressing individual free choice, the humanistic approach arose in the post–Second World War era. It was in part a response to disagreement with aspects of the psychoanalytic and behavioural views. Humanistic psychologists see people as inherently good and as striving to fulfil

Humanistic psychology:
The school of psychological thought that emphasizes the uniqueness of each human being and the idea that human beings have free will to determine their destiny.

themselves; they believe that psychoanalytical theorists are wrong to say that people are fraught with inner conflict and that behaviourists are too narrowly focused on stimulus–response relations. Humanists focus on individual uniqueness and decision-making ability; they assume that subjective experience contributes positively to establishing and maintaining a normal lifestyle.

Humanistic psychologists assert that human beings are conscious, creative, and born with an innate desire to fulfil themselves. They say that psychologists must examine human behaviour as individuals experience it. Proponents of the humanistic view, such as Abraham Maslow and Carl Rogers (both of whom we will study in Chapter 12), believe that human beings have the desire to achieve a state of **self-actualization**. Self-actualization is a final level of psychological development in which a person attempts to minimize ill health, function fully, have a superior perception of reality, and feel a strong sense of self-acceptance. Humanistic psychologists believe that people create their own perceptions of the world, choose their own experiences, and interpret reality in ways that lead towards self-actualization. Thus, for humanists, self-actualization is not only a final state but also an instinctual and motivational need.

Cognitive Psychology—Thinking Again. In the 1960s and 1970s, many psychologists realized that behaviourism in its strict form had limitations, particularly its narrow focus on observable behaviour. As an outgrowth of behaviourism (and as a reaction to it), these psychologists developed **cognitive psychology**—the school of psychological thought that focuses on the mental processes and activities involved in perception, learning, memory, and thinking. In a short period, so many theories developed, and so many psychologists embraced them, that psychologists began to say that a cognitive revolution was taking place within the discipline. This perspective goes beyond behaviourism in considering the mental processes involved in behaviour—for example, how people solve problems and appraise threatening situations and how they acquire, code, store, and retrieve information. Though it is sometimes seen as anti-behaviourist, this perspective is not that. It simply views the strict behavioural approach as missing a key component—mental processes. Cognitive psychology encompasses theories on both symbolic thought processes and the physiological processes that underlie thought; for example, many cognitive theories are put forth to explain how the brain operates. Today cognitive psychology exerts a wide influence on psychological thinking.

The cognitive perspective asserts that human beings engage in behaviours, both worthwhile and maladjusted, because of ideas and thoughts. Cognitive psychologists may be clinicians working with maladjusted clients to help them achieve more realistic ideas about the world; the clients then use these changed thoughts to alter their behaviour and to adjust to the world more effectively. A cognitively oriented clinician might help a client realize that her distorted thoughts about her own importance were interfering with her ability to get along with co-workers, for example. Cognitive psychologists also may be researchers who study intelligence, memory, perception, and the mental processes underlying all thought.

Because cognitive psychology spans many psychological fields and research traditions, it is hard to identify a single person who could be called its leader. However, psychologists Albert Bandura, Albert Ellis, Aaron Beck, George Miller, Ulric Neisser, and Richard Lazarus have all taken a prominent role, and their work will be discussed in later chapters.

Biological Perspective—Predispositions. If you think that people are genetically predisposed to win, lose, be fat, be athletic, or be outgoing you might focus much of your research on the biological basis of behaviour. Indeed, researchers are increasingly turning to biology to explain behaviour. The **biological perspective**, also referred to as the *neuroscience perspective*, is the school of psychological thought that examines psychological issues based on how heredity and biological structures affect mental processes and behaviour and that focuses on how physical mechanisms affect emotions, feelings, thoughts, desires, and sensory experiences.

Self-actualization: The fundamental human need to strive to fulfil one's potential, thus, a state of motivation, according to Maslow; from a humanist's view, a final level of psychological development in which a person attempts to minimize ill health, function fully, have a superior perception of reality, and feel a strong sense of self-acceptance.

Cognitive psychology: The school of psychological thought that focuses on the mental processes and activities involved in perception, learning, memory, and thinking.

Biological perspective: The school of psychological thought that examines psychological issues based on how heredity and biological structures affect mental processes and behaviour and that focuses on how physical mechanisms affect emotions, feelings, thoughts, desires, and sensory experiences; also known as the *neuroscience perspective*.

Researchers with a biological perspective might study genetic abnormalities, central nervous system problems, brain damage, or hormonal changes, for example. Today, exciting research is investigating whether a person's biological heritage leads to depression, learning disabilities, or homosexuality. Each day, groundbreaking research is occurring. Researchers Donald Hebb (memory), Michael Gazzaniga (perception), Noam Chomsky (language), Irving Gottesman (schizophrenia), and Robert Plomin (intelligence) are often cited as leaders of the biological perspective. You'll be hearing more about their work in the chapters to come.

The biological perspective is especially important in studies of sensation and perception, memory, and many types of maladjustment. It is pivotal in research on abnormal behaviour such as schizophrenia, which is linked in part to genetics, or on alcoholism, which in many cases has biological underpinnings. Because of the growing importance of the biological perspective, it has earned a prominent position in psychology—which you will see reflected in this text. We will revisit it many times, on many topics, in later chapters. In addition, most chapters will feature "Brain and Behaviour" boxes, which spotlight the latest breakthroughs in the study of brain-genetics-behaviour interaction.

 Evolutionary Psychology. Is your sense of humour shaped by the same processes that shaped adaptive physical features such as our opposable thumb and erect posture? Did cave men and women laugh at life the way we do? Some psychologists think so; a distinctly psychobiological approach is **evolutionary psychology**—the psychological perspective that seeks to explain and predict behaviours by analyzing how specific behaviours, over the course of many generations, have led to adaptations that allow the species to survive. Evolutionary psychology assumes that behavioural tendencies that help organisms adapt, be fit, and survive will be passed on to successive generations through a greater likelihood of reproduction. Using ideas such as "survival of the fittest," these researchers argue that, in the same way that human beings have evolved physically, they have evolved in other areas that we might say are mental or psychological. Evolutionary psychology argues that significant portions of human behaviours and mental abilities are directly coded in the genome—they are innate. Language is but one example. Human beings may learn language from one another but they do so at about the same rate and the same age in a wide variety of cultures and languages. For this reason, psychologists think that language learning is a universal behaviour and ability that is encoded in the genome (Monaco et al., 1998). Other examples of common human behaviours in which evolutionary psychologists are especially interested are humour, emotions, parenting, and romantic love. In previous years, such behaviours have been called, among other things, "evolved cognitive structures," "special learning mechanisms," and "innate activities." Evolutionary psychologists assert that there is an evolved heredity in certain psychological traits; they argue that these traits were not always what they are today. For example, in the early stages of human evolution, language consisted merely of grunts, groans, and crude gestures. But through the course of generations, those who grunted good directions, warnings, and other communications were more likely to survive difficult circumstances. Those who survived taught their offspring, and over successive generations language developed and ultimately was encoded in the human genome.

It is not a new idea that the development of the brain is sensitive to experience. William James, the first American psychologist and the leader of functionalism, spoke of instincts at length in his classic book *Principles of Psychology*. James referred to instincts as specialized neural circuits that are common to every member of the species and are a product of that species' evolutionary history. Today, cognitive psychologists, evolutionary biologists, and neuroscientists are studying those neural circuits. They investigate how circuits are organized and specialized, and especially how they have evolved. Their approach assumes that the brain is a physical system whose operation is governed by a biochemical process, which can be organized and modified in a regular fashion, and that natural selection and a species' evolutionary history can determine how it currently operates. This means that the history of a species, over centuries, modifies the structure of the species' brain. Evolutionary psychologists argue (and most psychologists agree) that human behaviour and mental processes are *plastic*, or subject to change. The design of the brain and how it operates have been shaped by previous experiences, not only in an individual's lifetime, but also in the lifetime of the species. From an evolutionary perspective this constant change serves as an adaptive mechanism by which individuals, and their brains, are constantly evolving. So, our behaviour is affected not only by what goes on around us, but also by the experiences of our species.

Eclecticism. Psychologists now realize that there are complex relationships among the factors that affect both overt behaviour and mental processes. Therefore, most psychologists involved in applied psychology, especially in clinical and counselling psychology, are eclectic in their perspective. **Eclecticism** is a combination of theories, facts, or techniques. In clinical and counselling psychology, eclecticism means using a variety of approaches to evaluate data, theories, and therapies as appropriate for an individual client, rather than relying exclusively on the techniques of one school of psychology.

Eclecticism allows a researcher or practitioner to view a problem from several orientations. For example, consider depression, the disabling mood disorder that affects 10 to 20 percent of men and women in Canada at some time in their lives (Chapter 15 discusses depression at length). From a biological perspective, people become depressed because of changes in brain chemistry. From a behavioural point of view, people learn to be depressed and sad because of faulty reward systems in their environment. From a psychoanalytic perspective, people become depressed because their early childhood experiences caused them to form a negative outlook on life. From a humanistic perspective, people become depressed when they choose inaction because they have or had poor role models. From a cognitive perspective, depression is made worse by the interpretations (thoughts) an individual adopts about a situation. An eclectic practitioner recognizes the complex nature of depression and acknowledges each of the possible contributions; the practitioner evaluates the person, the depression, and the context in which it occurs.

> **Eclecticism [ek-LECK-ti-sizm]:** In psychology, a combination of theories, facts, or techniques; the practice of using whatever clinical and counselling techniques are appropriate for an individual client rather than relying exclusively on the techniques of one school of psychology.

Focus

Review

◆ Identify the key assumptions underlying each school of psychological thought. pp. 27–33

◆ Why was Watson's behaviourism such a departure from other schools of psychological thought? pp. 29–30

Think Critically

◆ Think about the historical events occurring around the time that each school of psychological thought emerged. How might the historical era have helped give birth to each school of thought?

◆ John B. Watson ultimately went into the advertising business. How might he have applied behaviourist principles in that field?

◆ Which school of psychology is most likely to be free of cultural biases? Why?

Summary and Review

What Is This Science of Psychology?

What do psychologists study?

■ *Psychology* is the science of behaviour and mental processes. Psychologists observe many aspects of human functioning—overt actions, social relationships, mental processes, emotional responses, and physiological reactions. Overt actions are directly observable and measurable movements or the results of such movements. Social relationships are the behaviours people engage in that define their interac-

tions with other people. Mental processes include thoughts, ideas, and reasoning processes. Emotional responses include feelings such as anger, regret, and happiness. Physiological reactions include biochemical changes in the optic nerves when light stimulates your eyes and an increased heart rate when you are excited. pp. 4–5

Describe the steps in the scientific method.

■ The discipline of psychology is committed to objectivity, accuracy, and healthy scepticism. In their research,

psychologists use the *scientific method* to organize their ideas and to develop theories that describe, explain, predict, and help manage behaviour. The scientific method's six basic steps are stating a problem clearly, developing a hypothesis, designing a study, collecting and analyzing data, replicating experiments, and drawing conclusions and reporting results. pp. 5–7

KEY TERMS
psychology, p. 4; scientific method, p. 6; hypothesis, p. 6; theory, p. 7

The Research Process

Describe an experiment and indicate its key components.

■ An *experiment* is a procedure in which a researcher systematically strives to discover and describe the relationship between variables. Only controlled experiments allow for cause-and-effect statements. A *variable* is a characteristic of a situation or person that is subject to change (that varies) either within or across situations or individuals. The experimenter directly and purposely manipulates an independent variable. The *dependent variable* is expected to change because of manipulations of the independent variable. p. 8

■ A *hypothesis* is a tentative statement or idea expressing a causal relationship between two events or variables that are to be evaluated in a research study. p. 8

■ An *operational definition* is a definition of a variable in terms of a set of procedures used to measure or study that variable. A *sample* is a group of participants who are assumed to be representative of the population about which an inference is being made. A *significant difference* means that there is a statistically determined likelihood that a behaviour has not occurred because of chance alone. pp. 9–10

How do researchers ensure objectivity?

■ To ensure objectivity, researchers attempt to minimize *self-fulfilling prophecies* by using carefully controlled situations—for example, the *double-blind technique*, in which neither researcher nor participant knows who is assigned to the *experimental* or *control group*. The double-blind technique helps minimize *demand characteristics*—the elements of a study situation that might clue a participant as to the purpose of the study and thereby might elicit specific behaviour from the participant. It also helps minimize the *Hawthorne effect*—the tendency of people, as shown in early research studies at the Hawthorne industrial plant, to behave differently (usually better) when they know they are being observed. pp. 10–11

■ Critical thinking involves evaluating evidence, sifting through choices, assessing outcomes, and deciding whether conclusions make sense. When evaluating research studies, critical thinkers focus on five research criteria: purpose, methodology, participants, repeatability, and conclusions. pp. 12–13

Aside from experiments, what are the various other methods of research?

■ *Questionnaires*, or surveys, are used by researchers to gather large amounts of information from many people in a short time. *Interviews* typically are face-to-face meetings in which researchers (interviewers) ask individuals series of standardized questions. In *naturalistic observation*, psychologists observe from a distance how people or animals behave in their natural settings. By contrast, *case study* methods involve interviewing participants to gain information concerning their background, including data on such things as childhood, family, education, and social and sexual interactions. pp. 13–15

When is a group considered culturally diverse?

■ Psychologists say that a group—for example, a community, organization, or nation—is culturally diverse if it has within it differences in race, ethnicity, language, nationality, age, and religion. p. 16

KEY TERMS
experiment, p. 8; variable, p. 8; independent variable, p. 8; dependent variable, p. 8; participant, p. 9; experimental group, p. 9; control group, p. 9; operational definition, p. 9; sample, p. 10; significant difference, p. 10; self-fulfilling prophecy, p. 10; double-blind technique, p. 11; demand characteristics, p. 11; Hawthorne effect, p. 11; questionnaire, p. 13; interview, p. 14; naturalistic observation, p. 14; case study, p. 14

Ethics in Psychological Research

Describe the ethical considerations in psychological research.

■ *Ethics* in research comprises the rules of conduct that investigators use to guide their research; these rules concern the treatment of animals, the rights of human beings, and the responsibilities of investigators. The Canadian Psychological Association (CPA) has strict ethical guidelines for animal research. Human participants cannot be coerced to do things that are harmful to themselves, that would have other negative effects, or that would violate standards of decency. In addition, any information gained in an experimental situation is considered to be strictly confidential. Human participants must give *informed consent* to a researcher and must undergo *debriefing* following an experiment so that they understand the true nature of the research. In general, researchers must not use deception unless the study has highly important scientific, educational, or applied value. pp. 17–19

KEY TERMS
ethics, p. 17; informed consent, p. 18; debriefing, p. 19

Who Are These People We Call Psychologists?

Distinguish the various types of psychology professionals.

■ *Psychologists* are professionals who study behaviour and use behavioural principles in scientific research or in applied settings. Most psychologists have an advanced degree, usually a Ph.D. A *psychiatrist* is a medical doctor who has specialized in the treatment of emotional disorders. *Psychoanalysts* are usually psychiatrists; they have training in the specialized Freudian technique of psychoanalysis for treating people with emotional problems. pp. 20–21

KEY TERMS
psychologist, p. 20; clinical psychologist, p. 20; psychiatrist, p. 20; psychoanalyst, p. 21

Choosing Psychology as a Career

In what fields are psychologists likely to be employed?

■ A majority of psychologists are in human service fields such as clinical, counselling, and school psychology. Most others work in universities, business, and government doing research, teaching, and evaluation of programs. Psychology is attracting an increasing number of women. p. 22

Identify the focuses of applied research, human services, and experimental psychology.

- The three main fields of psychology are applied research, human services, and experimental psychology. All three consider research and theory to be the cornerstone of the psychological approach. Applied researchers use research to solve practical problems. Human service psychologists focus on helping individuals solve problems and on promoting their well-being. Experimental psychologists usually focus on teaching and research. pp. 23–25

How Have Schools of Psychological Thought Developed?

Identify the key assumptions underlying each school of psychological thought.

- Psychology became a field of study in the mid-1800s. *Structuralism*, founded by Wundt, focused on the contents of consciousness through *introspection* and was the first true school of psychological thought.

Functionalism, led by James and others, emphasized how and why the mind works. *Gestalt psychology*, in contrast to structuralism and functionalism, focused on perceptual frameworks and suggested that conscious experience is more than simply the sum of its individual parts. Arguing that each mind organizes the elements of experience into something unique, the early Gestalt psychologists studied perceptual phenomena. The *psychoanalytic approach* developed by Freud is the school of psychological thought that assumes that psychological maladjustment is a consequence of anxiety resulting from unresolved conflicts and forces of which a person may be unaware; its therapeutic technique is psychoanalysis. pp. 27–29

- Watson, the founder of *behaviourism*, argued that the proper subject of psychological study was observable behaviour. Skinner took up the behaviourist banner through much of the twentieth century. *Humanistic psychology* arose in response to the psychoanalytic and behavioural views and stresses free

will and *self-actualization*. *Cognitive psychology* focuses on perception, memory, learning, and thinking and asserts that human beings engage in both worthwhile and maladjusted behaviours because of ideas and thoughts. The *biological perspective* examines how heredity and biological structures affect mental processes and behaviour. *Evolutionary psychology* examines behaviours by analyzing how specific behaviours, over the course of many generations, have led to adaptations that allow the species to survive. *Eclecticism* acknowledges the complex relationships among factors affecting behavioural and mental processes and combines theories and techniques as appropriate to the situation. pp. 29–33

KEY TERMS
structuralism, p. 27; introspection, p. 28; functionalism, p. 28; Gestalt psychology, p. 28; psychoanalytic approach, p. 29; behaviourism, p. 29; humanistic psychology, p. 30; self-actualization, p. 31; cognitive psychology, p. 31; biological perspective, p. 31; evolutionary psychology, p. 32; eclecticism, p. 33

Weblinks

Sigmund Freud and the Freud Archives
www.plaza.interport.net/nypsan/freudarc.html
An extensive collection of links to other Internet resources on Freud and his work, including biographical information, libraries, and museums related to Freud.

Critical Thinking in Psychology
www.gateway1.gmcc.ab.ca/~digdonn/psych104/think.htm
This interactive Web page allows you to test your knowledge while learning about critical thinking. Includes quizzes and information on correlational and experimental designs, how to design studies, and asking testable questions.

Canadian Psychological Association (CPA)
www.cpa.ca
This comprehensive bilingual site provides in-depth information about the CPA, as well as links to psychology sites by province, career sites, psychology departments in universities, and other national psychology associations.

Mental Health Net
mentalhelp.net
CMHC Systems sponsors this large mental health resource guide. Links, articles, news, and chat rooms are all accessible from this site.

National Institutes of Health (NIH)
www.nig.gov
This American site provides an overview of the NIH and links to health publications, research news, and funding opportunities.

Code of Ethical Conduct for Research Involving Humans
www.hssfc.ca/gen/CodeContentsEng.html
This site provides the ethical framework for research involving humans set out by the Tri-Council Working Group of Canada. Includes research procedures and practices, as well as sample consent forms.

PsychCrawler
www.psychcrawler.com
This index does your psychological finding for you. Simply enter the term you are researching and it will provide the appropriate links.

The History of Psychology
www.unb.ca/web/units/psych/likely/psyc4053.htm
A chronology of important events in psychology is provided at this University of New Brunswick site. The chronology is an interactive learning experience, containing online quizzes, games, and quotations.

Chapter 2

The Brain and Behaviour

Robert's grandmother had a stroke, or what some doctors were calling a brain attack. The "attack" had made it difficult for her to move the right side of her body and to speak, but she seemed to understand whatever was said to her and could communicate by writing notes.

When he visited her in the hospital and later when he would take her to church Robert noticed that she seemed to be adjusting to her new physical limitations, but that she was most bothered by her inability to sing along with the choir. She, and everyone else in her family, including Robert, could sing beautifully. As he helped his grandmother Robert wondered about his family's singing skills: Did they share a genetic talent for music or did the love of music that his grandmother had shared with her children and grandchildren help them learn to appreciate and produce

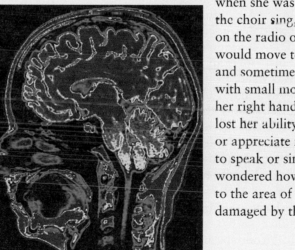

music using their voices? And what had happened to his grandmother? Had she lost the gift because of the brain attack? Over time Robert noticed that his grandmother, while unable to sing along, seemed to be happiest when she was listening to the choir sing, or to music on the radio or stereo. She would move to the music and sometimes conduct with small movements of her right hand. She hadn't lost her ability to listen to or appreciate music, only to speak or sing. Robert wondered how this related to the area of her brain damaged by the stroke. ■

Nature: An individual's genetically inherited characteristics.

Nurture: The sum of the experiences an individual has in the environment.

Today we actually understand quite a lot about what happens when certain areas of the brain are damaged. And we are working to understand more fully the relationships between inherited genes and life experiences. Psychologists know that there is a complex interplay between biology and experience, between inherited traits and encounters in the world—that is, between nature and nurture. **Nature** is a person's inherited characteristics, determined by genetics; **nurture** is the sum of the experiences a person has in the environment. For example, you can lift weights for years trying to build up your physical strength, but your capabilities are limited by your inherited body structure. Similarly, people try to maximize their intellectual skills through education; yet not everyone can become a nuclear physicist. Also, a person's inherited traits may not become evident in behaviour unless the environment supports and encourages those traits. For example, people with special talents must be given opportunities to express and develop them. If Mozart had not had access to musical instruments, his talent might have remained untapped.

In this chapter we first examine the issue of nature versus nurture, in order to lay a strong foundation for studying the biological processes that underlie all human behaviour and mental processes. Beginning with the smallest biological building blocks of behaviour—genetics and neurons—we follow with the structure and functioning of the brain. We then look at how scientists study brain activity and how chemical substances in our bodies affect our behaviour. Remember that our focus will be on how biological processes, especially brain activity, affects behaviour; this focus is coming to dominate much of psychological thinking.

Nature versus Nurture

Imagine that your father always insisted that you were a born athlete. He argued that your sister was the scholar in the family because she began reading at a very early age. He seemed to reason that his children had to be born *either* an athlete *or* a scholar. Your father assumed that what you were like was fixed; he allowed little room for environmental influences. Such beliefs highlight a major question in psychology: What is the relationship between biological mechanisms and environmental mechanisms—between nature and nurture? The debate over what determines abilities and behaviour is often a debate over the relative contributions of these biological and environmental variables. How much of what we are depends on the genes we inherited from our parents? How much is related to the environment in which we are raised—or to our parents' expectations for us? As we shall see, *both* genes and experience are important factors affecting behaviour. In fact, it makes little sense to talk about one without talking about the other.

Your specific genetic make-up is not affected by your day-to-day experiences. Over tens of thousands of years humans have evolved a highly organized brain that allows learning to affect their behaviour. Your brain acts as a library of information. Each new enriching experience affects your later behaviour. Some who consider nurture more important than nature suggest that people are not limited by their genetic heritage, because learning, training, and hard work can stretch their potential. John B. Watson, a pioneer in the field of behaviourism (which we will examine further in Chapter 5), sang the praises of nurture:

> Give me a dozen healthy infants, well-formed, and my own specialized world to bring them up in and I'll guarantee to take any one at random and train him to become any type of specialist I might select—doctor, lawyer, artist, merchant-chief, and, yes, even beggar man and thief, regardless of his talents, penchants, tendencies, abilities, vocations, and race of his ancestors. I am exaggerating, of course, but so have the [proponents of the heredity position] ... (1924, p. 104)

Psychologists know that biological make-up affects people's intelligence. But can the environment interact with and modify biological make-up, as Watson contended? The truth is that genetic traits provide the framework for behaviour; within that framework, experiences ultimately shape what individuals feel, think, and do. Let's take a closer look at the key genetic factors that shape day-to-day behaviour.

The Basics of Genetics

Is it possible that at conception a switch, gate, or hormonal trigger is pulled that determines whether an individual will be outgoing, shy, musical, or happy? Are our sexual urges determined at birth? Does our genetic make-up go so far as to increase our risk of becoming depressed, schizophrenic, or anxious? Biologists began to examine these questions, and many more, by studying genetics, focusing on issues such as how blue eyes, brown hair, height, and a tendency to develop diabetes or high blood pressure are transmitted from one generation to the next. **Genetics** is the study of *heredity*—the biological transmission of traits and characteristics from parents to offspring. Behavioural traits such as temperament and intelligence and disorders such as Alzheimer's disease and schizophrenia also have a genetic basis; this is why psychologists are especially interested in heredity (Chorney et al., 1998; Hammer, 1998). The field of *behavioural genetics* has thus emerged; its focus is on the relationship and influence of genetics on behaviour. It asks questions about whether human characteristics such as shyness, impulsiveness, or intelligence have a genetic, inherited basis. If they have a genetic base, to what extent is the behaviour biological and to what extent is it learned? *Heritability* (Plomin, 1990) refers to the extent that individual differences in such complex traits as intelligence or dancing ability are due to genetic factors. Remember that many characteristics that vary among individuals require a genetic contribution from both parents. For this reason, estimates of how heritable a characteristic is are estimates of how likely a trait or characteristic is *within a group* (not within a specific person). We will take a closer look at heritability in Chapter 8.

Uniqueness of Human Beings. With the exception of identical twins (discussed on page 41), every human being is genetically unique. Although each of us shares traits with our brothers, sisters, and parents, none of us is identical to them or to anyone else. The reason is that a large number of genes determine, or at least influence, each person's cognitive, personality, and emotional characteristics (Reiss, 1995, 1997).

Each human cell, except the sex cells, normally contains 23 pairs of chromosomes (46 chromosomes in all). **Chromosomes** are microscopic strands of a chemical substance called deoxyribonucleic acid (DNA) found in the nucleus (centre) of every body cell (see Figure 2.1). DNA is composed of oxygen, nitrogen, carbon, hydrogen, and phosphorous atoms. Chromosomes carry the self-replicating genetic information in their basic functional units—the genes, thousands of which line up along each chromosome. **Genes** are the units of hereditary transmission, consisting of DNA and protein. Genes control various aspects of a person's physical make-up, including eye colour, hair colour, and height—and perhaps psychological aspects such as basic intellectual abilities as well. Every such trait is determined by a pair of genes located in parallel positions on the paired chromosomes. These corresponding genes influence the same trait, but they often carry a different form of the genetic code for that trait, and one of them may be dominant over the other. For example, if the two genes for eye colour carry the genetic codes for blue and brown eyes, respectively, the individual will be brown-eyed, because the brown gene is *dominant*. Different, alternative forms of a gene that occupy the same position on paired chromosomes are called **alleles.**

Genetics: The study of heredity, the biological transmission of traits and characteristics from parents to offspring.

Chromosome: A strand of DNA in the nuclei of all cells, which carries genetic information.

Gene: The unit of hereditary transmission carried in chromosomes and consisting of DNA and protein.

Allele [A-leel]: Each member of a pair of genes, which occupies a particular place on a paired chromosome.

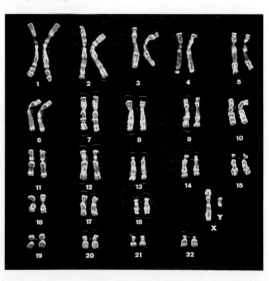

FIGURE 2.1

Building Blocks of Genetics
Each of the trillions of cells in the human body has 23 pairs of chromosomes in its nucleus. Each chromosome is essentially a long, threadlike strand of DNA, a giant molecule consisting of two spiralling and cross-linked chains. Resembling a twisted ladder and referred to as a *double helix*, each DNA molecule carries thousands of genes—the basic building blocks of the genetic code—which direct the synthesis of all the body's proteins.

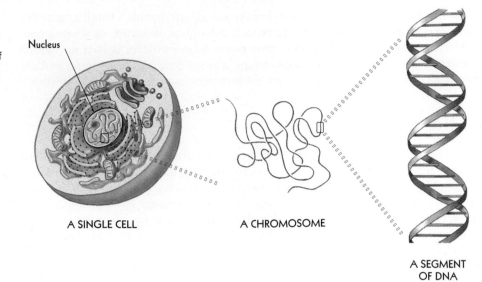

Nucleus

A SINGLE CELL

A CHROMOSOME

A SEGMENT OF DNA

Each allele on a chromosome has a corresponding allele on the other chromosome of the pair; one of the alleles is inherited separately from each parent. Although a pair of genes may control a specific trait, most traits are determined by more than one gene pair.

Each parent's sperm or ovum (egg) contains 23 chromosomes: half of the final 46. The first 22 pairs of chromosomes carry the same types of genetic information in both males and females. The twenty-third pair differs. This pair of chromosomes determines a person's sex. In females, the twenty-third pair contains two X chromosomes; in males, it contains one X and one Y chromosome. At the moment of conception, a sperm and an ovum, each containing half of each parent's chromosomes, combine to form a new organism and the chromosomes recombine to form new pairs. There are 8 388 608 possible combinations of the 23 pairs of chromosomes, with 70 368 744 000 000 possible combinations of genes. Since most traits are determined by multiple gene pairs, you can see that the chance of any two individuals being exactly alike is exceedingly slim.

Mapping the Genome. In an exciting research revolution that has been taking place since the 1980s, biological researchers have been trying to map the specific traits associated with specific chromosomes. That is, they have been trying to map the human *genome*—the total DNA blueprint of heritable traits contained in every cell of the body. This involves dividing the chromosomes into smaller fragments that can be characterized and ordering (mapping) them to correspond to their respective locations on the chromosomes. Researchers have been quite successful in this effort. More than 16 000 of the estimated 100 000 human genes have been mapped. Researchers have identified the exact location of genes contributing to muscular dystrophy, Huntington's disease, some cancers, and some psychological disorders, such as schizophrenia. Some researchers argue that even the nature of family social interactions has a genetic basis, because elements of personality (Bouchard & Hur, 1998), maladjustment (Plomin et al., 1994; Eley, 1997), and language acquisition (Fisher et al., 1998) may be genetically determined. As McClearn (1991) argued, the focus of research has shifted from showing that genetic influences exist to exploring their details and significance.

Of course, researchers must consider what to do with genes once they are identified. When psychologists understand the basic genetic and biological mechanisms and their relationship to behaviour, they will be better able to predict the situations in which maladjustment and behaviour disorders may occur. Yet this creates some interesting ethical dilemmas: What if a particular chromosomal pattern is shown to be associated with antisocial personality disorder? Would it be desirable or ethical to screen newborns to identify those at risk of becoming criminals? Could this information be used to terminate pregnancies? Medical ethicists and psychologists argue that such screening cannot and should not be used for such purposes. Ethical considerations and legislation to guard people's rights are high on the agenda of genetic researchers. A cautionary note: It is important to remember that genetics only lays the framework for our behaviour; so many events, life experiences, and cultural influences affect us that genetic influences must not be considered *the* determiner of behaviour. Genes set the parameters but the environment determines where we end up within an often large range.

Fraternal twins: Double births that occur when two sperm fertilize two ova; fraternal twins are no more or less genetically alike than non-twin siblings.

Identical twins: Double births that occur when a zygote splits into two identical cells, which then separate and develop independently; identical twins have exactly the same genetic make-up.

Twins and the Nature-versus-Nurture Issue

In addition to studying the impact of biological mechanisms on behaviour and mental processes, researchers also examine the contributions of the environment. One of the best ways psychologists have found to do this is to study twins to assess the contributions of nature and nurture. Twins make ideal subjects for these experiments because they begin life in the same uterine environment and share similar patterns of nutrition and other prenatal influences. **Fraternal twins** are double births that occur when two sperm fertilize two ova (eggs) and the two resulting zygotes (fertilized eggs) implant themselves in the uterus and grow alongside each other. The genes of these twins are not identical, so the siblings are only as genetically similar as other brothers and sisters would be (sharing about 50 percent of their genes). Fraternal twins can be the same sex or different sexes. Only about 12 sets of fraternal twins occur in every 1000 births. **Identical twins** are double births that occur when one zygote splits into two identical cells, which then separate and develop independently. The multiplication of these cells proceeds normally, and the cells become two genetically identical organisms, always the same sex. Only 4 sets of identical twins occur in every 1000 births.

Identical twins' genetic factors (nature) are fixed; however, if the twins are reared apart, their environments (nurture) are different—that is, they grow up in different families and homes. By comparing psychological characteristics of identical twins reared apart, researchers can assess the extent to which environment affects behaviour and perhaps unravel a bit more of the nature–nurture fabric. Researchers such as Tony Vernon of the University of Western Ontario have concluded that significant psychological similarities between identical twins are probably due to biological variables, and that significant psychological differences are probably due to environmental variables. They ask the question "How much of the differences or variability between twins (or any individuals, for that matter) is due to inherited characteristics?"

There are striking similarities in identical twins, even in those reared apart all of their lives (Wright, 1977). For example, a long and famous series of studies, called the Minnesota adoption studies, show that young adopted children are similar intellectually and in personality to other children in their adoptive family. This suggests that family environment exerts a great influence on young children. By adolescence, however, there is greater variation. Plomin (1989, 1994b),

Focus

Review

◆ What is the distinction between nature and nurture? p. 38

◆ What fundamental assumption can researchers make about identical twins that causes them to be ideal participants in nature-versus-nurture studies? p. 41

Think Critically

◆ What are potential environmental influences that can alter people's inherited characteristics? What can be done to limit such influences, and should we try to make such changes?

◆ The effort to map the genome and understand the biological characteristics associated with particular gene patterns has ethical implications. What if scientists find genes strongly associated with criminality, for example? What should be done with this knowledge?

Bouchard (Bouchard et al., 1990), and Turkheimer (1991) assert that even though environmental influences, especially on intelligence, are strong, heredity exerts a stronger influence. But psychologists meet this assertion with healthy scepticism, because the whole story is yet to be told. We know, for example, that experiences outside the family exert a powerful influence (Wright, 1997).

Communication in the Nervous System

E ven the simplest tasks require smooth functioning of the communications system that we call the nervous system. When there is a misfire, a glitch, in the communications process, people have trouble. For example, a research study in 1998 showed that people with dyslexia, who have difficulty with reading and who often reverse letters and words, don't use the usual pathways and regions of the brain that non-dyslexics do (Shaywitz et al., 1998). We'll have more to say about dyslexia and this study later, but for now the key idea is that the nervous system underlies all behaviour, including tasks like reading.

Walking, running, or driving a car requires a large number of coordinated movements, and that's without considering the need to pay attention to the surroundings and perhaps carry on a conversation at the same time. In some ways the nervous system acts like the conductor of a symphony orchestra, sending, receiving, processing, interpreting, and storing vital information. Many psychologists study how electrical and chemical signals in the brain represent and process such information. By studying how the nervous system's components work together and how they are integrated, psychologists learn a great deal about the nature and diversity of human behaviour.

The **nervous system** is made up of the structures and organs that allow all behaviour and mental processes to take place. The nervous system consists of two divisions—the *central nervous system* (the brain and spinal cord) and the *peripheral nervous system* (nerves connecting the central nervous system with the rest of the body). We'll examine these two divisions shortly. First, however, you need to understand how communication proceeds within the system as a whole. The nervous system is composed of billions of cells, many of which receive information from thousands of other cells (Nauta & Feirtag, 1986). The most elementary unit in the nervous system is the neuron, the building block of the entire system, which is where we will begin.

The Neuron

The basic unit of the nervous system is a single cell: the **neuron**, or *nerve cell*. There are billions of neurons throughout the body (as many as 100 billion in the brain alone), differing in shape, size, and function. Some neurons operate quickly, others relatively slowly. Some neurons are large; others are extremely small. Often neurons are grouped together in bundles; the bundles of neuron fibres are called *nerves* if they exist in the peripheral nervous system and *tracts* if they are in the central nervous system.

Not all of the neurons in your body are active at once. Nonetheless, they are always on alert, ready to convey information and signals to some part of the nervous system. Nerve pathways allow signals to flow (1) *to* the brain and spinal cord from the sense organs and muscles, and (2) *from* the brain and spinal cord to the sense organs and muscles, carrying messages for initiating new behaviour. Each type of neuron involved in this two-way neuronal firing has a name: **Afferent neurons** (from the Latin *ad*, "to," and *ferre*, "carry") send messages to the spinal cord and brain; **efferent neurons** (from the Latin *ex*, "out of," and *ferre*, "carry") send messages from the brain and spinal cord to other structures in the body (see Figure 2.2).

Nervous system: The structures and organs that act as the communication system for the body allowing all behaviour and mental processes to take place.

Neuron [NYER-on]: The basic unit (a single cell) of the nervous system comprising dendrites, which receive neural signals; a cell body, which generates electrical signals; and an axon, which transmits neural signals. Also known as a *nerve cell.*

Afferent neurons: Neurons that send messages to the spinal cord and brain.

Efferent neurons: Neurons that send messages from the brain and spinal cord to other structures in the body.

FIGURE 2.2
The Action of Afferent and Efferent Neurons

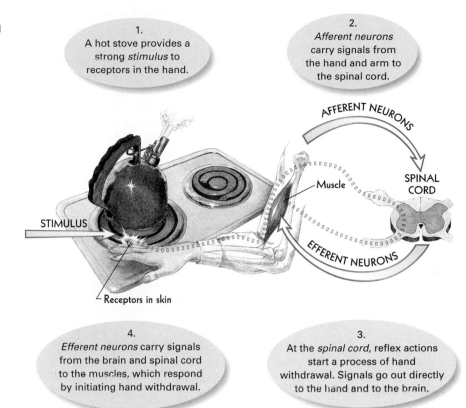

1. A hot stove provides a strong *stimulus* to receptors in the hand.

2. *Afferent neurons* carry signals from the hand and arm to the spinal cord.

AFFERENT NEURONS

SPINAL CORD

EFFERENT NEURONS

Muscle

STIMULUS

Receptors in skin

4. *Efferent neurons* carry signals from the brain and spinal cord to the muscles, which respond by initiating hand withdrawal.

3. At the *spinal cord*, reflex actions start a process of hand withdrawal. Signals go out directly to the hand and to the brain.

Types of Neurons. There are three types of neurons: sensory neurons, motor neurons, and interneurons. *Sensory neurons* are afferent neurons that convey information from the body's sense organs to the brain and spinal cord. *Motor neurons* are efferent neurons that carry information from the brain and spinal cord to the muscles and glands. *Interneurons* connect neurons together and combine the activities of sensory and motor neurons. There are many more interneurons than sensory or motor neurons; the interneurons form a network that allows the other neurons to interact with one another. Neurons are surrounded by *glial cells*, which nourish the neurons and help hold them in place. Glial cells are small—and 10 times more numerous than sensory neurons, motor neurons, or interneurons. They help insulate the brain from toxins, and they are the basis of the neurons' *myelin sheath*. The axons of many neurons, especially the longer ones, are *myelinated*, or covered with a thin white substance (the myelin sheath) that allows them to conduct signals faster than unmyelinated neurons.

Parts of a Neuron. Typically, neurons are composed of four primary parts: dendrites, a cell body, an axon, and axon terminals (see Figure 2.3). **Dendrites** (from the Greek word for "tree," because of their branchlike appearance) are thin, bushy, widely branching fibres that become narrower as they spread away from the cell body. Dendrites receive signals from neighbouring neurons and carry them back to the cell body. At the *cell body*, the signals are transformed and continue to travel along the **axon** to the *axon terminals* (the end points of each neuron). Like dendrites, axons have branches at their endings.

Neuronal Synapses. For almost all neurons, the axon terminals (the button-like structures in the photo at the bottom of page 44) of one neuron lie very close to receptor sites (dendrites, cell body, or axons) of other neurons. The microscopically small space between the axon terminals of one neuron and the receptor sites of another is called a **synapse** (see Figure 2.4). The signal from one neuron may travel across the synapse to another neuron. You can think of many neurons strung together in a long chain as a relay team sending signals, conveying information, or initiating

Dendrites: Thin, bushy, widely branching fibres extending from the neuron cell body that receive signals from neighbouring neurons and carry them back to the cell body.

Axon: A thin, elongated process that leads from the neuron cell body and serves to transmit signals from the cell body through the axon terminal to adjacent neurons, muscles, or glands.

Synapse [SIN-apps]: The microscopically small space between the axon terminals of one neuron and the receptor sites of another neuron.

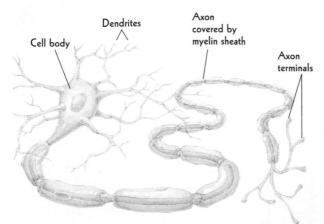

Dendrites

Cell body

Axon covered by myelin sheath

Axon terminals

FIGURE 2.3

The Basic Components of a Neuron

Neurons appear in many forms, but all possess the basic structures shown here: a cell body, an axon (with myelin sheath and axon terminals), and dendrites.

some action in a cell, muscle, or gland. Neurons may receive information from as many as 1000 neighbouring neurons and may "synapse on" (transmit information to) as many as 1000 to 10 000 other neurons (Nauta & Fiertag, 1986).

Electrochemical Processes. How do neurons communicate? What kind of signals do they transmit? Neuroscientists know that nerves are more complex than relay circuits, and are affected by a wide array of electrical and chemical (*electrochemical*) variables. Two types of electrochemical processes take place. The first involves activity within a neuron; the second involves neurotransmitter substances (chemicals) that are released from the axons of one neuron and act on neighbouring neurons.

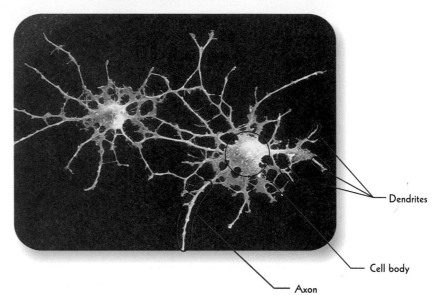

Dendrites

Cell body

Axon

FIGURE 2.4

The Synapse

The synapse is very small. Chemicals released by the axon terminals cross the synapse to stimulate the cell body or the dendrites of another neuron.

Axon terminal

Cell body

Axon

Synapse

Synapse

Understanding how information is transmitted within a neuron involves learning about how electrochemical impulses travel from the dendrites to the axon terminals. A widely accepted explanation of these electrochemical processes is that an extremely thin (less than 0.00001 millimetre thick) membrane surrounds every neuron; and there are channels, or "gates," in this permeable membrane through which electrically charged ions and small particles can pass. Normally the inside of the neuron is in a resting state in which it remains negatively charged, relative to the outside. This resting state is maintained by the cell membrane. The cell membrane is *polarized*; that is, the internal electrical state of the neuron (negatively charged) differs from its external state (positively charged).

Action Potentials. When the neuron has been stimulated (its resting state has been disturbed), the cell membrane's permeability is altered, resulting in a reduced voltage difference (the inside of the cell is less negative), and the cell is said to be *depolarized*. If a sufficient amount of stimulation occurs, the axon reaches its threshold and the sodium "gates" of the cell membrane open, causing a rapid reversal of electrical

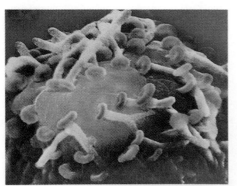

polarity. Positively charged sodium ions rush into the axon. At this point an action potential has been generated (see Figure 2.5). The **action potential**, or *spike discharge*, is an electrical current that is sent down the axon of a neuron and is initiated by a rapid reversal of the electrical balance of the cell membrane. Once the sodium ions reach a concentration that eliminates the negative potential inside the axon, the sodium gates close and a mechanism referred to as the *sodium-potassium pump* ejects sodium ions until the original resting potential is restored.

A neuron does not necessarily fire or produce an action potential every time it is stimulated. If the level of polarization across the cell membrane has not been disturbed enough to generate an action potential—in other words, if the neuron has not reached its threshold (or the level of stimulation intensity that when exceeded causes a stimulus to be effective)—the cell will not fire. Cells that are highly stimulated are more likely to fire than cells that are less stimulated. For example, a bright flash from a camera will stimulate a large number of cells in the visual areas of the brain, but a flicker of a candle may affect far fewer cells. When neurons fire, they generate action potentials in an **all-or-none** fashion—that is, the firing of the neuron, like the firing of a gun, occurs at either full strength or not at all. Action potentials occur in 2 to 4 milliseconds; therefore, neurons normally cannot fire more than 500 times per second. After each firing a neuron needs time to recover; the time needed for recovery is called the **refractory period**. During this period action potentials are much less likely to occur.

Neurotransmitters. When an action potential reaches the end of an axon, it triggers the release of **neurotransmitters**—chemicals that normally reside in the axon terminal within synaptic vesicles (small storage structures in the axon terminal) (Dunant & Israel, 1985). The neurotransmitters that are released into the synapse move across the synaptic space and bind to receptor sites on an adjacent cell, thereby transmitting the impulses to the next neuron (see Figure 2.6). We will examine the various types and effects of neurotransmitters shortly. When a neurotransmitter has affected the adjacent neuron, it has accomplished its main mission; the neurotransmitter is then either neutralized by an enzyme or taken back up by the neuron that released it, in a process called *reuptake*. Sometimes neurotransmitters excite, or cause the receiving neurons to fire more easily (depolarization); sometimes they inhibit, or cause the receiving neurons to fire less easily (hyperpolarization). A change in the membrane potential of a neuron due to the release of neurotransmitters is called a *postsynaptic potential (PSP)*. *Excitatory PSPs* make it easier for the cell to fire; *inhibitory PSPs* make it harder for the cell to fire. Because thousands of neurons may synapse on a single cell, a single neuron can receive both excitatory and inhibitory PSPs at once (Abbott et al., 1997). The neuron then "sums" these inputs and only fires after reaching the threshold.

Action potential: An electrical current sent down the axon of a neuron, initiated in an all-or-none fashion by a rapid reversal of the electrical balance of the cell membrane. Also known as a *spike discharge*.

All-or-none: Either at full strength or not at all; a principle by which neurons fire.

Refractory period: The recovery period of a neuron after it fires, during which it cannot fire again; this period allows the neuron to reestablish electrical balance with its surroundings.

Neurotransmitter [NYER-oh-TRANS-mitt-er]: Chemical substance that resides in the axon terminals and within synaptic vesicles and that, when released, moves across the synaptic space and binds to a receptor site on adjacent neurons.

FIGURE 2.5 Generation of an Action Potential

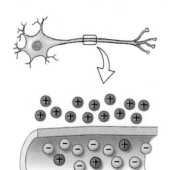

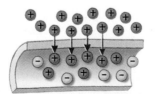

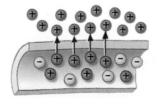

1. When the neuron is at rest, the inside is negatively charged relative to the outside.

2. When the neuron is stimulated, positively charged particles enter. The action potential is initiated—the neuron is *depolarized*.

3. After a brief period, some positively charged particles are pushed outside the neuron, and the neuron moves back towards its polarized state.

4. The neuron has finally returned to its initial polarized resting state.

Neurotransmitters and Behaviour

There are a large number of neurotransmitters; at least 70 have been identified. One of them, gamma-aminobutyric acid (GABA), is involved in virtually every behaviour, including anxiety states. Another important neurotransmitter, *serotonin*, is located throughout the brain, is especially important in sleep (McGinty & Szymusiak, 1988), and has been implicated in depression (Delgado et al., 1990). The most well known neurotransmitter, however, is *acetylcholine*, which is found in neurons throughout the brain and spinal cord. Acetylcholine is crucial to excitation of the skeletal muscles, the muscles that allow you to move. It is also important in such day-to-day functions as memory, learning, and sexual behaviour. The memory problems associated with Alzheimer's disease (discussed in Chapter 11) appear to be related to an inability to produce sufficient amounts of acetylcholine. Table 2.1 describes five key neurotransmitters and their effects.

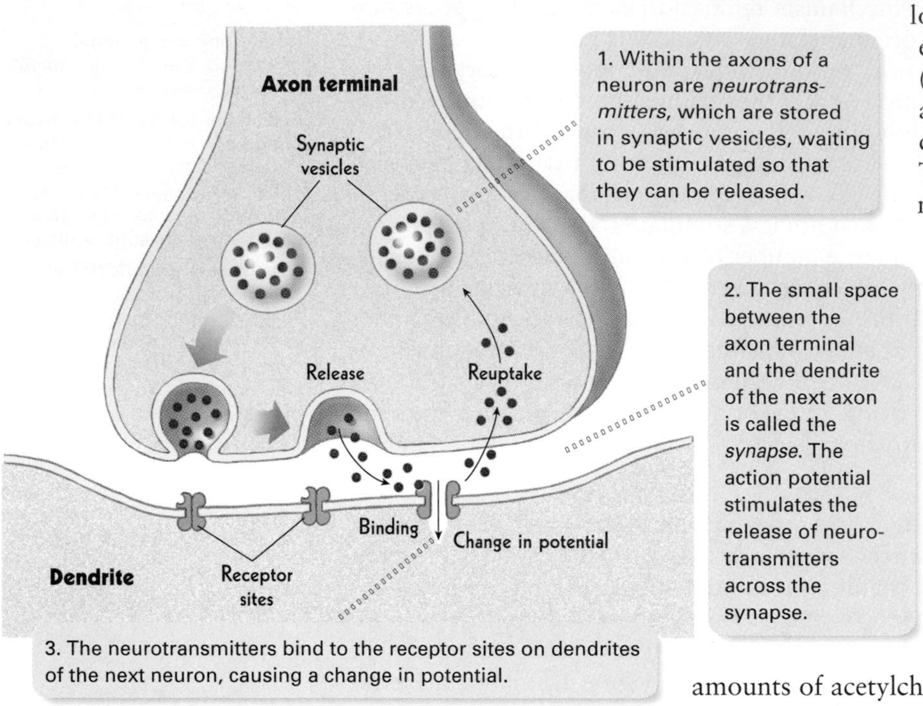

Axon terminal

Synaptic vesicles

1. Within the axons of a neuron are *neurotransmitters*, which are stored in synaptic vesicles, waiting to be stimulated so that they can be released.

Release   Reuptake

2. The small space between the axon terminal and the dendrite of the next axon is called the *synapse*. The action potential stimulates the release of neurotransmitters across the synapse.

Binding   Change in potential

Dendrite   Receptor sites

3. The neurotransmitters bind to the receptor sites on dendrites of the next neuron, causing a change in potential.

FIGURE 2.6
Major Steps in Neuronal Transmission

Research on Neurotransmitters. Although scientists have known about the existence of neurotransmitters for a long time, only recently have they realized the significance of these substances in the study of human behaviour. For example, researchers have found that serotonin affects motivation and mood and that schizophrenia is associated with increased levels of activity in neural circuits that use certain neurotransmitters. Serotonin is implicated in the debilitating disorder of autism. In addition, researchers find that people with Parkinson's disease, whose symptoms include weakness and uncontrollable shaking, have low levels of the neurotransmitter dopamine. When clinicians give these people drugs that have the same effects as dopamine (such as L-dopa), many of their symptoms are alleviated temporarily. Although it is unlikely that one neurotransmitter alone can cause a disorder such as autism, schizophrenia, or Parkinson's disease, a single neurotransmitter may play an important role in the onset or maintenance of such an illness.

Table 2.1 Five Key Neurotransmitters

Neurotransmitter	Location	Functions
Acetylcholine	Brain, spinal cord, autonomic nervous system, selected organs	Released at neuromuscular junctions. Also involved in memory
Norepinephrine	Brain, spinal cord, selected organs	Regulates physical and psychological arousal. Also involved in learning, memory, and emotions
Dopamine	Brain	Linked to muscle activity, emotional arousal, learning, and memory
Serotonin	Brain, spinal cord	Linked to activity level, sleep, appetite, and emotion
GABA	Brain, spinal cord	Involved in motor behaviour and level of arousal

Neuropeptides are chains of amino acids that act much like neurotransmitters, and are, for this reason, sometimes referred to as pseudotransmitters. The effects of endorphins, naturally produced neuropeptides perhaps most well known for inducing "runner's high," are mimicked by the actions of the narcotic morphine. Similar to the ways in which morphine affects hospitalized patients, endorphins inhibit certain synaptic transmissions—particularly those involving pain—and generally make people feel good (e.g., Miller et al., 1993). We will examine pain, endorphins, and pain management in more detail in Chapter 3.

At first, researchers thought that only one type of neurotransmitter existed in each neuron and that each neurotransmitter acted on only one type of receptor. Today researchers know that neurons often hold more than one type of neurotransmitter, and that these may act on more than one receptor, causing different effects. Some neurotransmitters (especially neuropeptides) are released into the bloodstream, so their effects may be far-reaching. Researchers now think of these neurotransmitters as neuromodulators. **Neuromodulators** are chemical substances that function to increase or decrease the sensitivity of widely distributed neurons to the specific effects of other neurotransmitters. A neuropeptide released into the bloodstream, for example, affects not only a single cell's immediate ion transfer but also whole classes, groups, or networks of cells, such as those within the limbic system, a brain structure known to be involved with emotional responses.

The study of neurotransmitters may hold the key to an understanding of drug addiction. It appears that all addictive drugs affect neurotransmitter actions and/or levels (generally linked to particular types of dopamine receptors). Such effects help explain the addictive nature of the drugs themselves. The study of neurotransmitters and their receptors also may help researchers find drugs that effectively will block the addictive properties of drugs such as cocaine and lead to more successful forms of treatment for addiction (Berridge & Robinson, 1995).

Psychopharmacology. The study of how drugs affect behaviour is called *psychopharmacology.* Researchers often study many types of drugs to learn the physiological mechanisms that cause behavioural reactions. Research has shown that many common drugs alter synaptic transmission in some way; other drugs alter the way neurotransmitters operate. Thus, for example, a drug may change behaviour by changing the speed or efficiency with which electrochemical information is transferred from one nerve cell to the next. Chemicals also can be used to mimic or facilitate the actions of neurotransmitters; such chemicals are called **agonists**. When an agonist is administered, it is as if the neurotransmitter itself has been released. Other chemicals, called **antagonists**, oppose the actions of specific neurotransmitters. When an antagonist is administered, a cell's receptor site is blocked and the neurotransmitter cannot have its usual effect. Schizophrenia, a disabling mental disorder, is often treated with antagonists. Cells

Neuromodulator: Chemical substance that functions to increase or decrease the sensitivity of widely distributed neurons to the specific effects of neurotransmitters.

Agonist [AG-oh-nist]: Chemical that mimics the actions of a neurotransmitter, usually by occupying receptor sites and facilitating neurochemical transfers.

Antagonist: Chemical that opposes the actions of a neurotransmitter, usually by preventing the neurotransmitter from occupying a receptor site.

Focus

Review

◆ Describe the full journey of a neural impulse from one neuron to another. pp. 42–45

◆ What is the difference between excitatory and inhibitory postsynaptic potentials? p. 45

◆ Distinguish between a neurotransmitter and a neuromodulator. pp. 45–47

Think Critically

◆ Should scientists try to apply their increasing knowledge of neuronal transmission to build a better human body with faster, more complete analysis and transmission of information, perhaps one in which there exist no feelings of pain?

◆ What is the downside of the increasing number of drugs that are available for the treatment of mental disorders?

that normally respond to dopamine are blocked from doing so by being exposed to certain drugs that act as antagonists, and symptoms of schizophrenia are thereby alleviated. (Dopamine in relation to schizophrenia will be discussed in more detail in Chapter 15.) Some drugs block the reabsorption, or reuptake, of neurotransmitters from their receptor sites. For example, the drug Prozac exerts its effect by blocking the reuptake of serotonin, prolonging the ability of released serotonin to stimulate the postsynaptic cell. This drug has proved highly useful in the treatment of depression (Julien, 1995).

When neurons fire, information is transferred from the sense organs to the brain and from the brain to the muscular system and the glands. If psychologists knew precisely how this transfer occurred, they could more successfully predict and manage the behaviour of people with neurological damage, mood disorders, or epilepsy. However, the firing of neurons and the release of neurotransmitters and neuromodulators do not in themselves completely explain the biological bases of human behaviour. The firing of individual neurons is an incomplete picture because it is the brain as a whole that receives, interprets, and acts on neuronal impulses. It is to the brain and the nervous system that we turn next.

Organization of the Nervous System

I t is a dark, wet evening; you are driving down a deserted road, listening to some 1970s oldies. Though you believe you have had enough sleep you find your eyes getting heavy and eventually are startled when the right tires of your car hit the gravel on the shoulder of the road. Suddenly very alert, you ease off the gas and bring the car to a safe stop. You wait a bit for your breathing and heart rate to return to normal before driving on to look for a safe place to get some rest. On just such a second-by-second basis, the nervous system controls behaviour. It is therefore essential for psychologists to understand the organization and functions of the nervous system and its mutually dependent systems and divisions. Recall that the nervous system is made up of the peripheral nervous system and the central nervous system. The central nervous system consists of the brain and spinal cord; the peripheral nervous system connects the central nervous system to the rest of the body. Let's examine them both in detail.

The Peripheral Nervous System

The **peripheral nervous system** is the part of the nervous system that carries information to and from the spinal cord and the brain through spinal nerves attached to the spinal cord and by a system of 12 cranial nerves, which carry signals directly to and from the brain. The peripheral nervous system contains all of the neurons and nerves (groups of axons) that are not in the central nervous system; its nerves focus on the *periphery*, or outer parts, of the body. Its two major divisions are the somatic nervous system and the autonomic nervous system.

The Somatic Nervous System. The **somatic nervous system** is the part of the peripheral nervous system that both responds to the external senses of sight, hearing, touch, smell, and taste and acts on the outside world. Generally considered under the individual's voluntary control, the somatic nervous system is involved in perceptual processing (processing information gathered through one's senses) and in control of movement and striate muscles. Because it carries information from the sense organs to the brain and from the brain and spinal cord to the consciously controlled muscles, it consists of both sensory (afferent) and motor (efferent) neurons. The somatic system allows you to see an oncoming truck and to get out of its way.

The Autonomic Nervous System. The **autonomic nervous system** is the part of the peripheral nervous system that controls the vital processes of the body, such as heart rate, digestion, blood pressure, and functioning of internal organs. In contrast to the somatic nervous system, it operates continuously and involuntarily (although the technique of biofeedback, discussed in Chapter 4, sometimes has proved to be effective in bringing a few of these processes under partial voluntary control). The system is called "autonomic" because many of its subsystems are self-regulating, focused on the use and conservation of energy resources. The autonomic nervous system is made up of two divisions: the sympathetic nervous system and the parasympathetic nervous system, which work together to control the activities of muscles and glands (see Figure 2.7).

The **sympathetic nervous system** is the part of the autonomic nervous system that responds to emergency situations. Its activities are easy to observe and measure.

Autonomic nervous system [au-toe-NOM-ick]: The part of the peripheral nervous system that controls the vital and automatic processes of the body, such as heart rate, digestion, blood pressure, and functioning of internal organs.

Sympathetic nervous system: The part of the autonomic nervous system that becomes most active in response to emergency situations; it calls up bodily resources as needed for major energy expenditures.

FIGURE 2.7
The Two Divisions of the Autonomic Nervous System

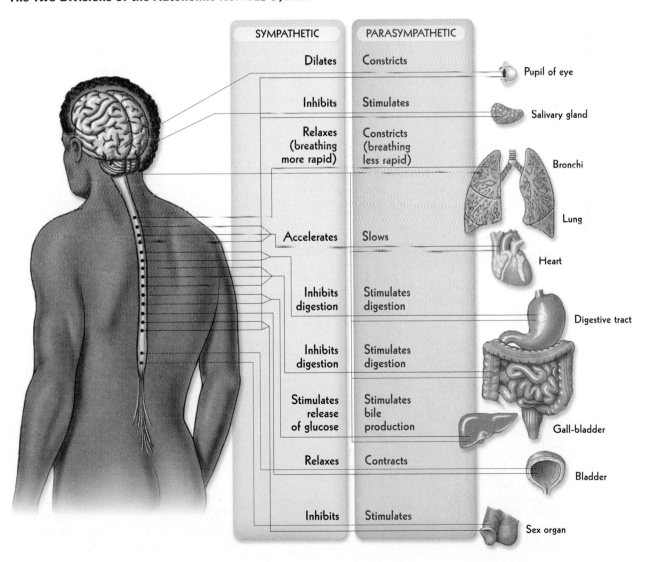

Activation results in a sharp increase in heart rate and blood pressure, slowing of digestion, dilation of the pupils, and general preparation for an emergency—sometimes called the *fight-or-flight response*. These changes usually are accompanied by an increased flow of epinephrine, or adrenalin, which is a substance released by the adrenal gland (to be discussed later in this chapter), and they are regulated by a set of neurons in the hypothalamus and brain stem (to be discussed shortly) (Jansen et al., 1995). Increased activity of the sympathetic nervous system is what makes your heart pound and your mouth go dry when your car drives off of the road.

When the sympathetic nervous system is active and the organism is in a fight-or-flight position, the somatic nervous system also is activated. For example, when a large, snarling dog chases a cyclist, the cyclist's adrenal gland is stimulated by the sympathetic nervous system; the burst of energy produced by epinephrine (released by the adrenal gland) affects the somatic nervous system, making the cyclist's muscles respond strongly and rapidly. Thus, changes in the sympathetic nervous system can produce rapid changes in the organism's somatic nervous system; these changes usually are seen in emotional behaviour and in stress reactions (discussed in detail in Chapters 9 and 14). Even simple responses, such as blushing from embarrassment, are regulated by the sympathetic nervous system.

The **parasympathetic nervous system**, which is active most of the time, is the part of the autonomic nervous system that controls the normal operations of the body, such as digestion, blood pressure, and heart rate. In other words, it keeps the body running smoothly. This system calms everything down and moves the heartbeat back to normal after an emergency. Unlike the sympathetic system, the parasympathetic activity does not show sharp changes on a minute-by-minute basis.

It is important to note that in reality these two systems are not as independent as the previous discussion may suggest. Rather, the overall state of an organism depends on the *balance* between the sympathetic and parasympathetic systems. For example, an increase in heart rate can result from either an increase in sympathetic activity or a decrease in parasympathetic activity. Often, a strong parasympathetic system response occurs following a prolonged period of sympathetic system dominance.

The Central Nervous System

The **central nervous system** is one of the two major parts of the nervous system. Consisting of the brain and the spinal cord, it serves as the main processing system for most information in the body (see Figure 2.8).

FIGURE 2.8
The Basic Divisions of the Nervous System

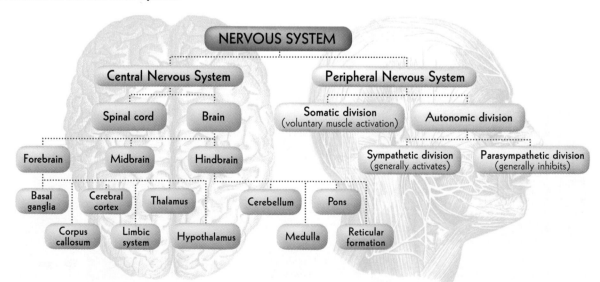

Although exactly how the brain functions remains a mystery that is far from being completely understood, neuroscientists do know that the brain operates through many mutually dependent systems and subsystems to affect and control behaviour. As you've seen in our discussion of neuronal activity, millions of brain cells are involved in the performance of even simple activities. When you walk, for example, the visual areas of the brain are active and your sight guides you, the brain's motor areas help make your legs move, and the cerebellum helps you keep your balance. It is the central nervous system communicating with the muscles and glands, under the control of the brain, that allows all of these things to happen so effortlessly.

The brain is the control centre, but it receives much of its information from the spinal cord, the main communication line to the rest of the body, and from the cranial nerves. The **spinal cord**, contained within the spinal column, receives signals from the sensory organs, muscles, and glands and relays these signals to the brain. Not all behaviours involve the brain directly. Among them are *spinal reflexes*—actions that are controlled almost solely by the spinal cord and a system of neurons that create a reflexive response. The knee jerk, elicited by a tap on the tendon below the kneecap, is one such spinal reflex. A sensory input (the tap) is linked to a motor response (the knee jerk) without first passing through the brain. Most signals eventually make their way up the spinal cord to the brain for further analysis, but the knee jerk response happens at the level of the spinal cord, before the brain has had time to register and act on the tap.

The spinal cord's importance cannot be overstated. When a person's spinal cord is severed the information exchange between the brain and the muscles and glands below the point of damage is halted. Spinal reflexes still operate, and knee jerk responses are evident. However, individuals like actor Christopher Reeve who suffer spinal cord damage lose voluntary control over muscles in the parts of their bodies below the site of the injury. This shows that the spinal cord serves a key communication function between the brain and the rest of the body. Let's turn next to the brain itself.

Brain Structures

Intelligence, personality, memory, and the ability to communicate through language reside in a small organ protected in the skull—the brain. Our brains are highly evolved, complex, and specialized. It is this specialization that allows us to think about the past and the future, to communicate possibilities, and to determine our destiny. Scientists know much about the structure and functions of the brain, yet still have a great deal to learn. They have studied its structure, its functions, its interconnections, and what happens to it when it is damaged. Let's examine the brain structure by structure.

The **brain** is the part of the central nervous system that regulates, monitors, processes, and guides other nervous system activity. Located in the skull, the human brain is an organ weighing about 1.4 kilograms and composed of two large *cerebral hemispheres*, one on the right side and one on the left. More will be said later about what each hemisphere is responsible for. A large bundle of nerve fibres, the *corpus*

THE Human Brain

The human brain is divided into three major sections: the forebrain, the midbrain, and the hindbrain. Each of these is revealed in progressively more detail here.

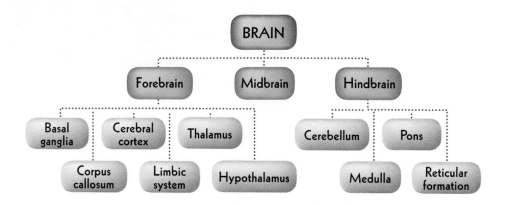

The midbrain, located between the forebrain and the hindbrain, consists of several major structures, as well as a number of smaller but important nuclei (collections of cell bodies). The reticular formation extends from the hindbrain into the midbrain.

The human brain—a cross-section

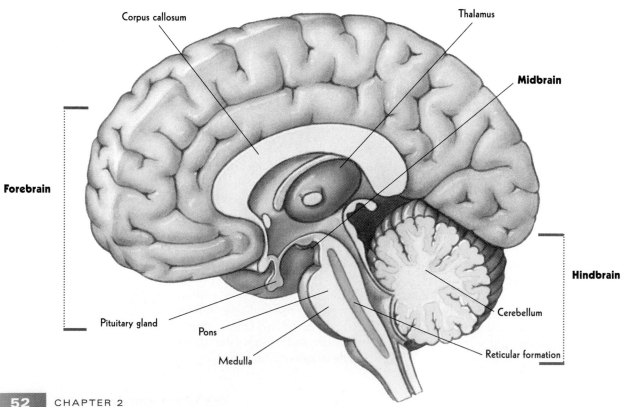

The hindbrain consists of the cerebellum, the medulla, the reticular formation, and the pons.

Structures of the brain

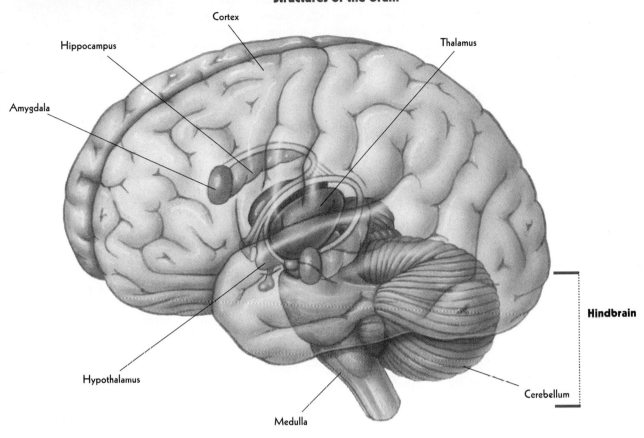

Cortex

Hippocampus

Amygdala

Thalamus

Hypothalamus

Medulla

Cerebellum

Hindbrain

The forebrain is the largest and most complex of the three major sections of the brain. It encompasses the thalamus, the hypothalamus, the hippocampus, the amygdala, the basal ganglia (not shown here), the corpus callosum, and the cortex.

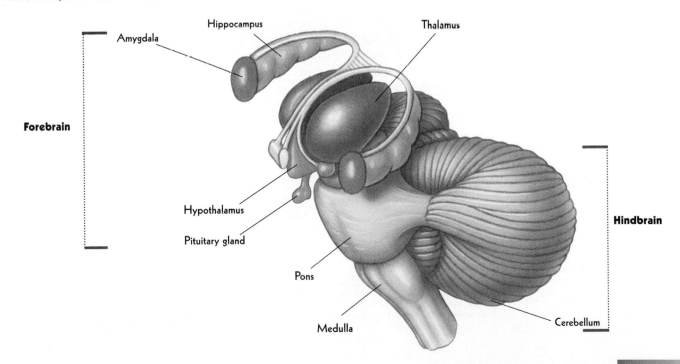

Amygdala

Hippocampus

Thalamus

Forebrain

Hypothalamus

Pituitary gland

Pons

Medulla

Cerebellum

Hindbrain

callosum, connects the two hemispheres and permits the transfer of information between them. Besides being divided into right and left halves, the brain can be divided into areas with special functions. Some parts are specialized for visual activities; others are involved in hearing, sleeping, breathing, eating, and other important functions. Some brain activities are localized. Most speech and language activity, for example, can be pinpointed to a specific area, usually on the left side of the brain. Other activities may occur in both hemispheres. For example, visual activity occurs in the visual cortex, which occupies both sides of the brain. You will see later in this chapter, however, that although some functions are localized, there is disagreement about how widespread this specialization is.

In examining the brain, we begin where the spinal cord and the brain meet. Many structures and functions in this deep portion of the brain are responsible for basic bodily processes, such as breathing, sleeping, and eating. As we move away from the spinal cord towards higher areas of the brain, we find more complicated structures and functions. Both as individual brains grow and as the brain has evolved through history, it has been observed to form organizationally and functionally into three fairly discrete sections: the hindbrain, the midbrain, and the forebrain (which includes the cortex). (Follow along in the figures on pages 52 and 53.) Structures in the hindbrain and midbrain are organizationally more primitive than structures in the forebrain and are responsible for more basic, reflexive actions. Structures in the lower portions of the forebrain are organizationally somewhat more complex and involve higher mental functions. Of still higher levels of functioning is the cortex, the deeply fissured grey surface matter that covers the cerebral hemispheres and serves as the basis for thought processing—one of the most advanced abilities of humans.

Hindbrain

When you watch a hockey team charge gracefully down the ice you probably are not thinking about how well the players' cerebellums are functioning. It turns out that part of the hindbrain, the cerebellum, helps fine-tune the placing of each skate blade on the ice as well as guide the movements needed to make a shot to the upper corner of the net at just the right moment. The four main structures of the hindbrain receive afferent signals from other parts of the brain and from the spinal cord; they interpret the signals and either relay the information to more complex parts of the brain or immediately cause the body to act. The **hindbrain** (refer to pages 52 and 53) contains the oldest parts of the brain, in terms of evolution, and consists of the medulla, the reticular formation, the pons, and the cerebellum.

The **medulla**, through which many afferent and efferent signals pass, is a dense elongated bundle of nerve fibres lying just above the spinal cord and controls heart rate, blood pressure, and breathing. Within the medulla and extending out into the cortex is a latticelike network of nerve cells, the reticular formation, which directly controls a person's state of arousal, waking, and sleeping, as well as responsive bodily functions; damage to it can result in coma and death. The **reticular formation** extends into and through the pons and the midbrain, with projections towards the cortex; without the reticular formation we would not be aware of sensory information. As well, it is involved in muscle tone, cardiac and circulatory reflexes, and attention. The **pons** provides a link between the medulla and the cerebellum and the rest of the brain and spinal cord; portions of the pons affect sleep, dreaming, and respiration.

Hindbrain: The most primitive, organizationally, of the three functional divisions of the brain, consisting of the medulla, reticular formation, pons, and cerebellum.

Medulla [meh-DUH-lah]: The most primitive and lowest portion of the hindbrain; controls basic bodily functions such as breathing.

Reticular formation [reh-TICK-you-lar]: Extending out from the medulla, a latticelike network of neurons that directly controls a person's state of arousal, waking, and sleeping, as well as other bodily functions.

Pons: A structure of the hindbrain that connects with the medulla and the cerebellum, provides a link with the rest of the brain, and is involved in sleep.

The **cerebellum** (or "little brain"), a large structure attached to the back surface of the brain stem, influences balance, coordination, movement, and single joint actions such as the flex of an elbow or knee. It allows you to do such things as walk in a straight line, type accurately on a keyboard, coordinate the many movements involved in dancing—and fire pucks into the back of the net. The cerebellum also is involved in a number of cognitive (thinking) operations, including learning (Daum et al., 1993; Leiner, Leiner, & Dow, 1986).

Midbrain

The **midbrain** (refer to pages 52 and 53) consists of nuclei (collections of cell bodies) that receive afferent signals from other parts of the brain and from the spinal cord. Like the hindbrain, the midbrain interprets the signals and either relays the information to a more complex part of the brain or causes the body to act at once. One portion of the midbrain is involved in smoothness of movement and another is involved in reflexive movement. Movements of the eyeball in its socket, for example, are controlled by the *superior colliculus*, a structure in the midbrain. The reticular formation continues into the midbrain.

Forebrain

The **forebrain** is the most advanced brain structure organizationally and structurally; it is also the largest and most complicated of the brain structures because of its many interrelated parts: the thalamus and hypothalamus, the limbic system, the basal ganglia and corpus callosum, and the cortex.

Thalamus and Hypothalamus. The **thalamus** (refer to pages 52 and 53) acts primarily as a relay station for sensory information. It integrates and analyzes this input and sends the information on to the primary sensory cortex. Therefore, all sensory information (except for olfaction) proceeds through the thalamus before being routed to other areas of the brain. The **hypothalamus**, which is relatively small (the size of a pea) and located just below the thalamus, has numerous connections with the rest of the forebrain and the midbrain and affects many species-specific behaviours, such as eating, drinking, and sexual arousal. It plays a crucial role in regulating the body's internal environment by maintaining homeostatic balance in such areas as blood sugar levels or body temperature. It also is involved in regulating the endocrine system. We will discuss the role of the hypothalamus in more detail in Chapter 9.

Limbic System. One of the most complex and least understood structures of the brain is the **limbic system** (see Figure 2.9). This system is located between the brain stem and the cerebral hemispheres and is an interconnected group of structures (including parts of the cortex, thalamus, and hypothalamus) involved in emotions, memory, social behaviour, and brain disorders such as epilepsy. Within the limbic system are the hippocampus and the amygdala. The *hippocampus* is located deep

Cerebellum [seh-rah-BELL-um]: A large structure that is attached to the back surface of the brain stem and that influences balance, coordination, and movement.

Midbrain: The second level of the three organizational structures of the brain; receives afferent signals from other parts of the brain and from the spinal cord, interprets the signals, and either relays the information to a more complex part of the brain or causes the body to act at once; considered important in the regulation of movement.

Forebrain: The largest, most complicated, and most advanced organizationally and functionally of the three divisions of the brain, with many interrelated parts: the thalamus and hypothalamus, the limbic system, the basal ganglia and corpus callosum, and the cortex.

Thalamus: A large structure of the forebrain that acts primarily as a routing station to send information to other parts of the brain but probably also performs some interpretive functions; nearly all sensory information proceeds through the thalamus.

Hypothalamus: A relatively small structure of the forebrain, lying just below the thalamus, that acts through its connections with the rest of the forebrain and the midbrain and affects many complex behaviours, such as eating, drinking, and sexual activity.

Limbic system: An interconnected group of structures (including parts of the cortex, thalamus, and hypothalamus) located deep within the temporal lobe and involved in emotions, memory, social behaviour, and brain disorders such as epilepsy; within the limbic system are the hippocampus and the amygdala.

FIGURE 2.9
Principal Structures of the Limbic System

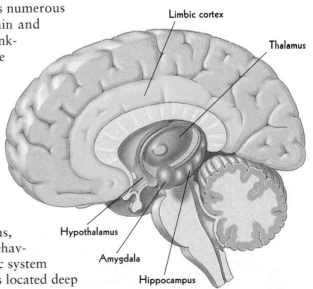

Limbic cortex

Thalamus

Hypothalamus

Amygdala

Hippocampus

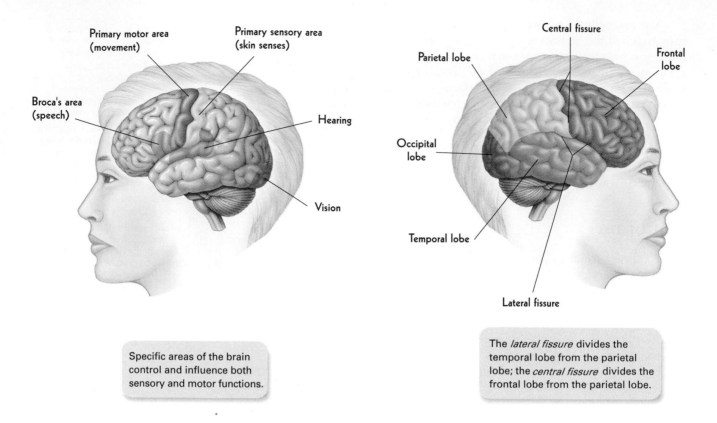

Specific areas of the brain control and influence both sensory and motor functions.

The *lateral fissure* divides the temporal lobe from the parietal lobe; the *central fissure* divides the frontal lobe from the parietal lobe.

	Location	Function
Frontal lobe	In front of the central fissure; contains the motor cortex and Broca's area	Memory Movement Speech and language production
Parietal lobe	Behind frontal lobe	Sense of touch and body position
Temporal lobe	Below lateral fissure and parietal lobe	Speech, hearing, and some visual information processing
Occipital lobe	Back of the brain, next to and behind parietal and temporal lobes	Visual sense
Association cortex	Areas between parietal, temporal, and occipital lobes	Believed to be responsible for complex behaviours that involve thinking and sensory processes

FIGURE 2.10
The Cortex and the Lobes of the Brain
The cortex is the exterior covering of the cerebral hemispheres. It consists of four major lobes and the association cortex. The cortex plays a special role in behaviour because it is directly involved in thought.

within the temporal lobe and is involved in new learning, in encoding and retrieving long-term memories, in navigating about the world, and in some emotional functions (Maguire et al., 1998).

The *amygdala*, a set of cells connected to the hippocampus, is also involved in emotional control and in the formation of emotional memories. Canadian researchers Brian Kolb and Ian Wishaw (1996) indicate that the amygdala is particularly important in directing attention to emotionally salient characteristics of behaviour. Stimulation of the amygdala in animals, for instance, produces attack responses. As another example, rabies leads to the deterioration and eventual destruction of the amygdala. That deterioration is associated with uncontrolled fits of violence. Surgical removal of the amygdala in human beings was once a radical way of treating people who were extremely violent. The amygdala is now considered important in the recognition of fear, in learning, and in a wide range of other emotions (Bechara et al., 1995; Damasio, 1994). Stimulation of several areas of the limbic system in rats also produces what appear to be highly pleasurable sensations. Olds and Milner (1954) discovered that, when given small doses of electrical current in some of the limbic areas as a reward for pressing a bar, rats chose bar pressing over eating, even they had been deprived of food for long periods. The researchers called the areas of the amygdala being stimulated in this experiment *pleasure centres*.

The Basal Ganglia and Corpus Callosum. The *basal ganglia* are a series of nuclei located deep in the forebrain to the left and right of the thalamus. They control movements and posture and are also associated with Parkinson's disease. Parts of the basal ganglia influence muscle tone and initiate commands to the cerebellum and to higher brain centres. Damage to this important neurological centre can have severe behavioural consequences. The *corpus callosum* is a thick band of 200 million or so nerve fibres that provide cross-hemisphere connections that conveys information between the cerebral hemispheres; damage to it results in essentially two separate brains within one skull. We'll return to the corpus callosum shortly.

Cortex. The brain has two major portions, referred to as the left and right cerebral hemispheres (we'll discuss brain specialization in more detail shortly). In terms of evolution, these two hemispheres are the youngest parts of our brains. The exterior covering of these hemispheres, called the **cortex** (or neocortex), is about two millimetres thick and consists of six thin layers of nerve cells. It is *convoluted*, or furrowed. These **convolutions** (called gyri and fissures), folds in the tissue of the cerebral hemispheres and the overlying cortex, create more surface area within a small space. The overall surface area of the cortex is at least 1.5 square feet. A highly developed cortex is evident in human beings, but not all mammals show such specialization, and most other mammals' brains are less deeply fissured. The cortex plays a special role in behaviour because it is intimately involved in thought and reason.

A traditional way to divide the cortex is to consider it to be a series of lobes, or areas, each with characteristic structures and functions. The most prominent structures are two deep fissures (very deep furrows, or folds)—the *lateral fissure* and the *central fissure*—that divide the lobes. These easily recognizable fissures are like deep ravines that run among the convolutions, separating the various lobes; these deep cortical valleys are thought to be especially important in thought (Markowitsch & Tulving, 1994). The *frontal lobe* is in front of the central fissure; the *parietal lobe* is behind it. Below the lateral fissure and the parietal lobe is the *temporal lobe*. And at the back of the head, behind the parietal and temporal lobes, is the *occipital lobe*. Figure 2.10 describes each lobe and its primary functions.

Cortex: The convoluted, or furrowed, exterior covering of the brain's hemispheres, which is about two millimetres thick, consists of six thin layers of nerve cells, and traditionally is divided into a series of lobes, or areas, each with characteristic structures; thought to be involved in both sensory interpretation and complex thought processes.

Convolutions: Characteristic folds in the tissues of the cerebral hemispheres and the overlying cortex.

Studying the Brain

In the eighteenth century, people called "phrenologists" measured the size of heads and examined bumps and prominent features such as a large protruding forehead; their reasoning was that prominent features might be associated with certain kinds of thoughts. Today scientists have come a long way from phrenology. They know that the brain plays a central role in controlling behaviour, and they are continually trying to understand it better, but now they use scientific techniques that go far beyond simple observation. Knowledge of the brain and its relationship to behaviour comes about in part through the study of *neuroanatomy*— the structures of the nervous system. Some neuroanatomists do postmortem (after

Electroencephalogram (EEG)
[eel-ECK-tro-en-SEFF-uh-low-
gram]: Record of electrical
brain-wave patterns obtained
through electrodes placed on
the scalp.

death) studies of the brains of people who have died of tumours, brain diseases, and trauma (injury) to the brain. These researchers are attempting to correlate the type of brain damage or disruption with the loss of specific abilities, such as seeing, reading, and writing. Some brain damage occurs through accidents, strokes, and brain tumours; observing the behaviours and mental processes of individuals with known damage provides further information. Neuroanatomists who study behaviour often

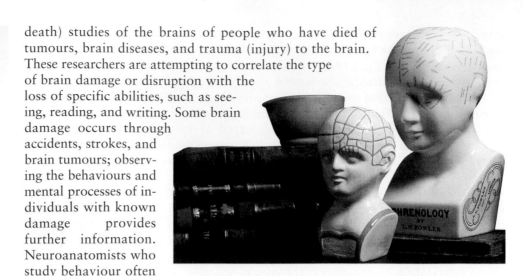

use *ablation* as a principal technique. In ablation researchers remove or destroy a portion of an animal's brain and study the animal to determine which behaviours have been disrupted. Today, ablation studies are complemented by electrical recording techniques such as EEGs, MRIs, and CT and PET scans. Still other researchers study brain–behaviour relationships by watching animals or children as they interact with their environment and solve problems.

Monitoring Neuronal Activity

Though nonliving brains can be dissected, neuroscientists are becoming more interested in exploring the functions and interconnections of the active central nervous system, a more difficult task. Much of what scientists now know about the electrical activity in the nervous system comes from laboratory studies of abnormalities in brain structure and function. In conducting such studies, scientists use several basic procedures to measure the activity of the nervous system.

One technique is *single unit recording*, in which researchers insert a thin wire, needle, or glass tube containing an electrolyte solution into or next to a single neuron to measure its electrical activity. Because neurons fire extremely rapidly, data are often fed into a computer, which averages the number of times the cell fires in one second or one minute. Scientists typically perform this type of recording technique on the neurons of rats, cats, or monkeys. There are widely scattered neural clusters that act together, in synchrony, and identifying them all is a task of Herculean proportion. But synchronized neural firing is very relevant to understanding movement and perception; synchronized output from widely spaced neurons may be at the heart of perception and thought and of consciousness itself (Crick, 1998; Riehle, 1997; Singer, 1995). For example, groups of neurons, called

cell assemblies, probably represent objects in the visual system by firing synchronously and binding separate kinds of information such as motion, colour, and shape together (Engel et al., 1992). Such synchronized firing of diverse cells has allowed specialization to take place in different brain regions and yet combines neural output for higher-order thought.

Another technique, *electroencephalography*, measures electrical activity in the nervous systems of both animals and human beings. It produces a record of brain-wave activity called an **electroencephalogram**, or **EEG** (*electro* means "electrical," *encephalon* means "brain," and *gram* means "record"). A small electrode placed on the scalp records the gross electrical activity of the brain by simultaneously measuring the output of thousands of cells beneath the skull to produce an EEG. EEGs, which generally are computer analyzed, are used for a variety of purposes, including the assessment of brain damage, epilepsy, tumours, and other abnormalities. When brain waves that are normally synchronized become erratic, this is usually evidence of an abnormality requiring further investigation and analysis.

In normal, healthy human beings, EEGs show a variety of characteristic brain-wave patterns, depending on the person's level and kind of mental activity. Researchers usually describe brain waves in terms of their *frequency* (the number of waves in a unit of time) and *amplitude* (the relative height or size of the waves). If people are awake, relaxed, have their eyes closed, and are not engaged in active thinking, their EEGs are predominantly composed of *alpha waves*, which occur at a moderate rate (frequency) of 8 to 12 cycles per second and are of moderate amplitude. When people are excited, their brain waves change dramatically from alpha waves to *beta waves*, which are of high frequency and low amplitude. At different times during sleep, people show varying patterns of high-frequency and low-frequency brain waves correlated with dreaming activity and restorative functions, both of which are discussed in Chapter 4.

Three revolutionary diagnostic techniques for measuring the activity of the nervous system have emerged in the last two decades: CT, PET, and MRI scanning. **CT (computerized tomography) scans** are computer-assisted X-ray images of the brain (or any area of the body) in three dimensions—essentially a computerized series of X-rays that show photographic slices of part of the brain or body. CT scans are particularly helpful in locating tumours or regions destroyed by strokes, accidents, or other brain abnormalities.

PET (positron emission tomography) tracks radioactive markers injected into the bloodstream to enable researchers to observe metabolic activity by recording glucose use taking place in the brain; the scans measure local variations in cerebral blood flow, which is correlated with neural activity. PET scans allow researchers to watch the actual functioning of the brain, to observe how the brain modifies itself as mental activity occurs, and to predict human behaviour from brain functioning. PET scans are relatively new to neuroscientists but research in this area is growing rapidly. For example, Alivisatos and Petrides (1997) traced regional blood flow with PET scans during simple cognitive tasks and found a relationship between blood flow and cognitive activity. Moreover, specific brain regions were found to be associated with specific types of memory or thought processes (Cabeza & Nyberg, 1997; Wagner et al., 1998), and those areas showed more blood flow for particular tasks. For example, recall tasks showed greater blood flow compared to recognition tasks (Cabeza et al., 1997). The potential of PET scans has yet to be fully realized, but researchers are using them to study a wide range of psychological coding processes as well as psychological disorders such as schizophrenia (Andreasasen, 1997). The biggest problem with PET scans is that although they efficiently display cortical function, they lack spatial resolution (resolution is approximately 10 millimetres) and precise anatomical localization of the activated region.

MRI (magnetic resonance imaging) uses magnetic fields instead of X-rays and has far greater clarity and resolution than other currently available techniques. MRIs can distinguish brain areas as small as one or two millimetres. This is useful because although the general locations of brain functions are known, the *exact* locations vary from individual to individual. Because the magnetic fields can penetrate bone, MRIs are particularly useful for diagnosing cartilage and bone marrow problems and tissue damage. Furthermore, because no substance, radioactive or otherwise, needs to be injected to provide results, MRI scans are often preferred to PET scans.

CT (computerized tomography) scans: Computer-assisted X-ray images of the brain (or any area of the body) in three dimensions—essentially a computerized series of X-rays that show photographic slices of part of the brain or body.

PET (positron emission tomography): Imaging technique that uses radioactive markers injected into the bloodstream to enable researchers to observe metabolic activity by recording glucose use taking place in the brain; measures local variations in cerebral blood flow, which is correlated with mental activity.

MRI (magnetic resonance imaging): Imaging technique that uses magnetic fields instead of X-rays and has great clarity and resolution. MRIs can distinguish brain parts as small as one or two millimetres and can penetrate bone, making them particularly useful for diagnosing cartilage and bone marrow problems and tissue damage.

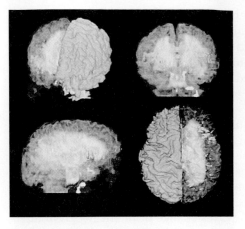

These sorts of imaging tools were only the stuff of science fiction until a few years ago. Imagine observing the brain function as it performs its many tasks. Today, we use the *fMRI* (**functional magnetic resonance imaging**), an imaging technique that can locate where your brain processes certain functions. A patient performs a particular task while the imaging is taking place. The area of the brain responsible for this task will show an increase in metabolism (blood flow) that ultimately will lead to a signal change in the MRI image. By performing specific tasks that correspond to different functions, it is possible to locate the corresponding brain activation. Unlike PET studies, which require a break or time-out between conditions (to allow radioactive traces to leave the system), fMRI studies allow for alternating experimental conditions in the same individual—this is distinct and important advantage of the fMRI.

Typically, an fMRI research study will image the brains of two or more participants in varying experimental conditions and then compare the images and activity of the brains in those two conditions and between the two people (Pugh et al., 1997). Often the participants are healthy individuals (a control group) and those with some type of disorder (an experimental group); often the tasks are cognitive ones that require participants to read, imagine, or perhaps calculate. Research shows that specific brain sites are indeed affected by specific tasks (e.g., Just et al., 1996). For example, one study that used the fMRI technique (Shaywitz et al., 1998) showed that individuals with reading disabilities (dyslexics) use their brains differently than individuals without reading disabilities. They asked participants—normal individuals and dyslexics—to perform reading tasks such as naming letters and identifying words. Among participants without reading disabilities, key areas of the brain became active, notably the visual cortex, the angular gyrus, and the left temporal-parietal area (Wernicke's area). Participants with dyslexia showed little activity in these areas but activity in other areas not typically associated with the reading tasks. These patterns led researchers to state that they had identified a "neural signature" for the impairment. The key point is that the fMRI technique has helped scientists understand when and how the brain operates, and it may allow researchers to develop techniques to help people with various disorders such as dyslexia and to understand and improve normal processes such as memory (Brewer et al., 1998).

Table 2.2 summarizes the four important imaging techniques we have just discussed.

CT, PET, and MRI scans are making the examination of brain tissue and processes easier and more precise, thereby providing more information about the brain and its workings. For example, researchers have been able to show that small *brain lesions* (areas of damaged brain tissue, often due to disease or injury) are common in elderly people and are a natural part of aging. Further, researchers are establishing tentative links among brain lesions and illness, neurochemistry, and depression (Nemeroff et al., 1988).

New techniques are emerging on a regular basis. For example, one new non-invasive technique is called transcranial magnetic stimulation (TMS); it can induce lesion-like disruption of brain activity in animals to investigate attention, discrimination, and plasticity (Walsh & Cowey, 1998).

Brain Specialization—The Left and Right of Things

Did David Helfgott, the sensitive, cigarette-smoking, brilliant pianist with psychiatric problems who overcame adversity, portrayed in the film *Shine*, have a disorder in a particular lobe? Are there specific places in the brain that control specific

fMRI (functional magnetic resonance imaging): Imaging technique that can locate where the brain processes certain functions. A patient performs a particular task while the imaging is taking place. Brain areas responsible for this task will show an increase in metabolism (blood flow) that ultimately will lead to a signal change in the MRI image

Table 2.2 Four Important Imaging Techniques

Technique	Function and Application
CT (computerized tomography)	Produces computer-enhanced, three-dimensional, X-ray images of the brain (or any part of the body), essentially a series of X-rays showing photographic slices of the brain (or other part of the body)
PET (positron emission tomography)	Tracks radioactive markers that were injected into the bloodstream, enabling researchers to monitor marked variations in cerebral activity, which are correlated with mental processes
MRI (magnetic resonance imaging)	Uses magnetic fields instead of X-rays to produce highly detailed images of brain tissue that have far greater clarity and resolution than CT scans; can distinguish brain parts as small as 1 or 2 millimetres
fMRI (functional MRI)	Registers changes in the metabolism (energy consumption) of cells in various regions of the brain and thus allows observation of activity in the brain as it takes place

behaviours and thoughts? Does one side of the brain have more control over certain behaviours than the other side (for example, handedness—see *Experiencing Psychology*)? Is there a gender difference? Some science writers have concluded that brain hemisphere dominance even may affect your choice of occupation, and certainly your world-view. Let's explore the evidence.

Splitting the Brain. Most of our body's organs are represented bilaterally (arms, legs, kidneys) and do the same thing. We know that human beings can lose one of their kidneys and function well. Our general symmetry may be misleading, however. Studies of brain structure show that different areas of the two-sided brain are responsible for different functions. Noted brain and consciousness expert Robert Ornstein (1997) likens the two sides of the brain to a tale of two cities in which complex operations exist in each hemisphere but are often as different as Montreal and Beijing!

Since the early 1970s, Nobel Prize winner Roger Sperry (1913–1994) and Michael Gazzaniga have been at the forefront of research in brain organization. Gazzaniga has concluded that the human brain has a modular organization—that it is divided into discrete units that interact to produce mental activity (Gazzaniga, 1989). Importantly, more recent research suggests that the more experience an organism has with a particular event, situation, or concept, the more specialized the brain becomes (Jacobs, 1997).

Studies by Sperry (1985) and Gazzaniga (1983) show that in most human beings one cerebral hemisphere, usually the left, is specialized for the processing of speech and language; the other, usually the right, appears better able to handle spatial tasks and musical and artistic endeavours. Such hemispheric specialization within the brain frequently is referred to as right or left *brain dominance*. Some of the evidence for such hemispheric specialization comes from studies monitoring brain-wave activity in normal participants exposed to different kinds of stimuli. For example, when normal participants are asked to look at or think about letters, or perhaps to rehearse a speech, some characteristic brain-wave activity can be detected on the left side of the brain. When these participants are asked to perform creative tasks or are told to reorganize some spatial pattern, brain-wave activity is apparent on the right side of the brain. Although studies of brain waves do not yield complete or thoroughly convincing knowledge of brain function or brain structure,

experiencing psychology

Left-handed in a Right-handed World

I n his book *The Left-Hander Syndrome*, Stanley Coren, a well-known psychologist at the University of British Columbia, painfully details the many ways in which a small portion of our population is inconvenienced simply because they prefer to use their left hand for most major tasks. In fact, about 10 percent of the population are left-handed, depending on how you define it. Our handedness—left-handedness especially—affects our lives directly, as well as the lives of those who design machines, automobiles, and the desks in our classrooms.

It is likely that a couple of different genes control whether you use principally your left hand or your right hand—what psychologists call "handedness" (Klar, 1996). One of the genes probably controls whether you are left- or right-hemisphere dominant; the other likely determines whether your brain dominance controls your handedness. Most left-handed people are right-brain dominant, and right-handed people are left-brain dominant. Because handedness is a genetically determined trait, we naturally see a correlation of handedness with biological parents, and not with adoptive parents. Left-handedness is determined before birth, appears in all cultures, and has been around for thousands of years. While 54 percent of animals (cats, mice, and rats at least) have a dominant paw, they are virtually equally divided between whether the right paw or the left paw is dominant (Annet, 1985).

But there also is a strong cultural contribution; parents reinforce right-handed behaviour, and our world is set up in a right-handed way. School desks are made to support your right arm and hand for writing. Computer mice are organized and shaped for people who use their right hand. Safety levers on mechanical equipment are placed for right-handed people to grab. Sitting at a crowded table to eat dinner becomes an elbow-clashing ordeal for those who are left-handed. And until recent decades, lefties were discriminated against and heavily encouraged to switch hands.

Despite such recent accommodations as specially designed, and more expensive, computer mice, which have reversible buttons for lefties, the world is still structured for the right-handed. As a consequence left-handed people are more likely to have accidents (Graham & Cleveland, 1996). Perhaps because their accidents are more frequent and more severe, they also suffer more pain from accidents (Coren & Porac, 1996), and Coren has argued that left-handed people die at a younger age (Halpern & Coren, 1991)—but this is a hotly disputed assertion (Harris, 1993).

The research on left-handedness, especially on accidents and death rates, is controversial for a number of reasons, many of which reflect methodological problems. First, to do good research, we have to separate "strong right-handers" from "strong left-handers"—and this often has not been done. Second,

how does a researcher define people as lefties or righties? By which hand they use for writing? Drawing? Throwing a ball? Perhaps dealing cards? Depending on how one defines left-handedness, it turns out that some people are solely left-handed—they do everything with their left hand. Others are right-handed, and many people are ambidextrous, using both hands. Up to half of left-handed writers throw a ball with their right hand! Furthermore, research shows that most right-handed people (about 95 percent) process speech and language exclusively with the left hemispheres of their brains—they are clearly left-hemisphere dominant for many activities—while only 50 percent of left-handed people process speech and language exclusively in the right hemispheres of their brains—they have a mixed dominance and are more likely to use both hemispheres to process language (Hiscock & Kinsbourne, 1987).

What do we know for sure about handedness? We have learned that handedness is partly, but not solely, biological. We know that since the brain is plastic, those who initially might be solely lefties may learn and modify their behaviour, become ambidextrous, and ultimately modify the workings of their brains. We also know that despite recent accommodations to the lefties of the world, the work and home environments are organized for righties, and this affects the way lefties live and work in both minor and major ways. Lefties of the world, unite! ■

evidence is mounting. For example, research using MRI scans supports a left-right distinction for pitch and music perception and indicates a difference between individuals who have perfect pitch and the rest of us (Schlaug et al., 1995). Similarly, an array of studies asserts a right-brain dominance for men in spatial tasks but a left-brain dominance for women in reading comprehension (Ornstein, 1997).

What happens to behaviour and mental processes when connections between the left and right sides of the brain are cut? Many important studies have involved **split-brain patients**—typically, these are people with uncontrollable, life-threatening epilepsy who have undergone an operation to sever the corpus callosum (the band of fibres that connects the left and right hemispheres of the brain) to prevent seizures from spreading across the hemispheres. Special testing revealed that after the operation there was little or no perceptual or cognitive interaction between the hemispheres; the patients seemed to have two distinct, independent brains, each with its own abilities. Yet these patients appeared unaffected by this procedure and were able to live normal, productive lives. Studies of split-brain patients are invaluable to scientists seeking to understand how the brain works—in particular, how the left and right hemispheres function together (e.g., Blanc-Garin, Fauré, & Sabio, 1993). (See Figure 2.11.)

In a normal brain, each cerebral hemisphere is neurologically connected to the opposite side of the body; thus, the left hemisphere normally controls the right side of the body (Johnson, 1998). Split-brain patients are unable to use the speech and language capabilities located in the left hemisphere to describe activities carried out by the right hemisphere. In experimental conditions, when stimulus information is presented exclusively to their left hemispheres (by presenting it in the right visual

Split-brain patients: People whose corpus callosum, which normally connects the two cerebral hemispheres, has been surgically severed.

FIGURE 2.11
The Effects of Severing the Corpus Callosum

Imagine that a man whose corpus callosum (but not his optic nerves) has been severed is staring directly before him at a screen on either side of which a researcher can flash words or pictures. The researcher flashes a picture of an apple on the right side of the screen. The man is able to name the image because it has been sent via his optic nerves only to his brain's left hemisphere—where verbal processing occurs. When the researcher flashes the word spoon on the left side of the screen, the man's optic nerves send an image exclusively to his right hemisphere—which predominantly processes nonverbal stimuli. Now, because the right hemisphere is nonverbal, when the man is asked to name what he sees on the screen, he is unable to name the image as the word *spoon*. If he is asked to use his right hand, which is controlled by the left hemisphere, to pick out the object named on the screen (a spoon) from several objects, by touch alone, he will not be able to do so. However, if the man is asked to use his left hand to touch the object named on the screen, he can do so. The left hand is controlled by the right hemisphere, which is spatially adept and has been exposed to the word *spoon*.

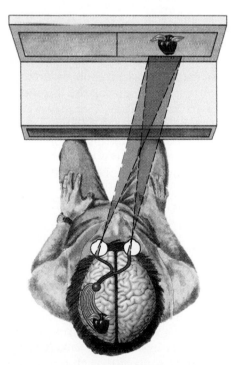

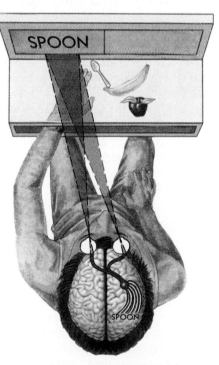

"I see an apple."　　　　　　　"I don't know what the image is."

field while participants stare straight ahead), they can identify the stimulus, describe it, and deal with it in essentially normal ways. But when the same stimulus is presented to their right hemispheres, they can perform matching tasks (saying that two items are identical) but are unable to describe the stimulus verbally (a left-hemisphere task). Such artificial viewing situations must be generated in a laboratory. In day-to-day life split-brain patients encounter stimuli that are presented to both hemispheres and so are able to perform normally.

Studies of split-brain patients show two key concepts: (1) localization of specific functions, and (2) the fact that not every behaviour is traceable to a single structure in the central nervous system. Most behaviours involve the combined work of several areas. Although there seem to be some specifically left-brain and right-brain activities (e.g., Kingstone et al., 1995) and certain key functions associated with one side of the brain (Baynes et al., 1998; Metcalfe, Funnell, & Gazzaniga, 1995), which may have developed early in life (McManus & Bryden, 1991) and may be slightly different for men and women (Zaidel et al., 1995), the two halves of the brain still work together (Banich, 1995).

There is no doubt that lateralization and specificity of functions exist in human beings and animals (Hopkins, 1997; Scalaidhe, Wilson, & Goldman-Rakic, 1997). There also is no doubt that the study of brain functions and the work of Sperry and Gazzaniga have been influential in developing the current understanding of brain specificity. For example, people with a strong right-brain dominance, who are generally left-handed, may develop differently than right-handers, and this may affect a number of important events in their lives (Halpern & Coren, 1993).

Unfortunately, the popular press and TV newscasters oversimplify the specificity of functions, and in some cases overgeneralize their significance to account for school problems, marital problems, artistic abilities, and even baseball batting averages. The full extent of hemispheric specialization is yet to be determined. Although it is recognized that the left side of the brain performs a recognition task and that the right side is necessary to put that recognition into context (Ornstein, 1997), most scientists and critical thinkers maintain a healthy scepticism about the existence of "two minds" in one.

Plasticity and Change

Basic brain organization is established well before birth and does not change in any substantial way after birth; but details of brain structure and functions, particularly in the cerebral cortex, are subject to continued growth and development. What happens in one cell affects what happens in neighbouring cells, so psychologists recognize that the brain is still *malleable* (changeable), especially during the formative years. This ability to change is often referred to as *plasticity*. (See *Brain and Behaviour*.) Within limits, the nervous system can be modified and fine-tuned by experience, which can be acquired over many years (Shatz, 1992), and the brain can be trained to relearn and simulate previous learning that may have been lost through an accident or some other brain trauma (Singer, 1995; Hinton, Plaut, & Shallice, 1993).

Experience with specific stimuli reinforces the development of neural structures (Kilgard & Merzenich, 1998). The developing brain can be likened to a highway system that expands with use. Less travelled roads are abandoned, but popular ones are broadened and new ones are added as needed. When neural structures are used, reused, and constantly updated, they become faster and more easily accessed (Moser et al., 1998; Zhang et al., 1997). During early fetal and infant development, the neural links, connections, and interconnections are embellished (Crair, Gillespie, & Stryker, 1998) and if unused may begin to disappear (Colman, Nabekura, & Lichtman, 1997). Such elaboration and refinement is greater when organisms are placed in complex, super-enriched (e.g., visually stimulating) environments (Chang, Isaacs, & Greenough, 1991). For example, one study showed that children with language-based learning impairments could be taught to use repetitive and adaptive

brain and behaviour
Plasticity—Evidence from Musicians

Our brains are amazingly malleable. For example, at birth, infants' brains are not fully formed; over the ensuing weeks and months, brain organization continues to take place, abilities continue to develop, and significant brain growth occurs. Recent evidence suggests that visual, auditory, and tactile input to the adult brain also changes the central nervous system.

Thomas Elbert led a group of researchers (Elbert et al., 1995) who examined whether there are special populations of individuals whose experiences have resulted in unique brain changes. Reasoning that musicians might be such a group, the researchers decided to examine whether skilled musicians have brains that are specially organized as a result of their musical training.

Elbert and his colleagues specifically examined whether years of practice by violinists and other string players, who perform elaborate fingering with the left hand, produce changes in the brain organization of these musicians. String players use the fingers of their left hand continually. By contrast, the right hand moves the bow but does not require such intricate manual dexterity. Do years of practice and experience have an effect on the brain organization of string players? Do these musicians differ from non-musicians in this regard?

The researchers performed an experiment in which they used MRI scans (which provide records of brain activity) to examine the size and strength of changes in the brains of string players. Nine musicians (six violinists, two cellists, and one guitarist) who had played their instruments on average for over a decade served as participants in the study. They spent an average of 10 hours per week practising. Six non-musicians served as a control group.

The experimenters stimulated the fingers of both the left and the right hands of all participants by applying pressure through a non-painful stimulator. By examining MRIs, the researchers recorded the strength and location of resulting activity in the brain, especially in the somatosensory areas.

The cortical activity of the musicians was stronger than that of the non-musicians. Also important was the finding that the location of the tactile stimulation in the brain was shifted for the musicians. Pressure on the left fingers activated more brain cells in the musicians than in the non-musicians. By contrast, when the right-finger stimulation of the musicians was compared to that of the control subjects, there were no significant differences in brain organization. There also was a correlation between the age at which the string players began studying their instruments and the magnitude in the change due to stimulation. The earlier the string players began studying music, the greater the effect.

Thus, the key finding was that the extent of somatosensory cortical representation of the fingers was greater for musicians than for control subjects, and results of left-finger stimulation were greater than for right-finger stimulation. The researchers concluded that the brain is plastic and continues to be plastic—even in adults the brain continues to modify itself in response to the stimulation brought to it. Other research shows that musicians, unlike the rest of us, are far more likely to have perfect pitch (the ability to distinguish a given pitch without reference to any other pitch). Musicians have developed areas of the brain that are larger than the same areas in non-musicians and are far more likely to have these larger areas if they had music lessons at a young age (Schlaug et al., 1995). In fact, 40 percent of musicians had perfect pitch if they had music lessons before age four, but the percentage of adult musicians who had it dropped to only 4 percent if their musical training began after nine years of age (Schlaug, 1995). This same basic result has been found by other teams of researchers (Pantev et al., 1998).

What does all of this mean? Cortical reorganization allows people who are injured in accidents to recover from brain trauma. The fact that this reorganization occurs at all in adults, whose brains are fully formed, is an important finding. The implication of the work of Elbert and then of Pantev is that there is continuous plastic reorganization of the somatosensory areas of the brain. Is plasticity in response to tactile stimulation an isolated case? Are other parts of the brain also able to change? Does such cortical reorganization occur only in musicians who have been studying for years? These are questions yet to be answered. But this study is an interesting and important beginning. ◼

training exercises to overcome their problems. The exercises are assumed to change neuronal structures and allow improvement in speech and language processing (Merzenich et al., 1996).

Changes in the brain occur not only in young organisms but in aging ones as well. As human beings grow older, their central nervous systems function differently—sometimes not as well as before. There are decreases in the numbers of neurons and receptors, for example. In addition, some learning tasks become more difficult. This does not mean that older organisms do not experience changes in neuronal structuring. Researchers have demonstrated that they can trace changes in brain functioning with changes in learning. McCandliss, Posner, and Givon (1997) traced brain electrophysiological changes that occurred over a five-week period when human beings were asked to learn new language-like nonsense words. Key areas of the brain at first showed little response to the learning task, but after training were more responsive. The researchers concluded that not only is the brain plastic but they had shown physiological evidence of it in merely five weeks.

Research is also focusing on the drug enhancement of learning; finding specific proteins, drugs, and new treatments that alter brain functioning may provide keys to understanding brain development and its effects on behaviour. This understanding is especially important in cases of neural diseases such as Alzheimer's or in cases where there has been trauma to the nervous system. Early trauma can have delayed effects. For example, damage to the frontal lobes early in life can result in effects that are only fully realized later in life when higher cognitive functions normally begin to emerge (Eslinger et al., 1992). Can damage done to the nervous system be repaired? Injury to the brain early in an organism's life can be devastating, but the extent and permanence of the damage depend on the nature of the injury, the age at which it takes place, and the presence of several buffering factors, such as the availability of an enriched environment (Kolb, 1989) and training. Human beings are amazingly adaptable and the brain can adjust to a changing world by reorganizing brain structure and behaviour (Houde & Jordan, 1998; Moser et al., 1998).

Neurotransplants

The idea of replacing body parts is no longer science fiction; physicians routinely conduct kidney and heart transplants. But could the theme of the science-fiction movie *Donovan's Brain* be a reality—could you take a brain or a portion of a brain and transplant it in another organism? Researchers are focusing on this question in an effort to help patients with brain disorders such as Alzheimer's or Parkinson's disease. The outcomes for Parkinson's patients have been mixed, with some enjoying significant improvements and others responding little if at all (Kopyov et al., 1996). The research is complicated, and also has serious ethical implications.

Can brain tissue that is transplanted from one organism to another survive and develop normally? Research shows that the answer depends on the type of tissue and the site where it is transplanted. Some sites prove to be good locations; others are less successful at fostering normal growth. Transplantation is most likely to be successful where cells are clearly organized, as in the visual cortex (Raisman, Morris, & Zhou, 1987). In a series of studies, researchers Fine (1986) and Mikhailova and colleagues (1991) successfully grafted (attached) brain tissue to the central nervous system in rats and other organisms and were able to observe behaviour changes associated with the graft. Yet research with animals, however successful, is not the same as research with human beings. People with Parkinson's disease (in which brain tissue no longer secretes sufficient levels of dopamine, causing muscular rigidity and tremors) have been treated with implants of healthy fetal brain tissue with positive results (Bekhtereva et al., 1990). The implants survive, grow naturally, and secrete dopamine, and the patients' conditions improve (Lindvall, 1991; Lindvall et al., 1990).

Neurotransplants may open up a world of therapeutic possibilities. Victims of head injuries, brain diseases, and birth defects could all benefit. But should the medical and psychological communities be allowed to create a more perfect human being? There are surgical risks; many techniques are dangerous and as yet unproven. Physicians and researchers must establish procedures for selecting the best candidates for such experimentation. And what about the source of the transplanted tissue? Successful implants have used human fetal tissue. Researchers and ethicists alike are unsure under what conditions, if any, fetal tissue should be made available. An alternative that may skirt some of the ethical issues associated with the use of human fetal tissue is the use of fetal tissue from pigs or monkeys. A second alternative is the use of a patient's own dopamine-producing, healthy tissue. This procedure is being explored (Madrazo et al., 1987) but does not seem promising.

Hormones and Glands

I n 1978 Dan White fatally shot both San Francisco mayor George Moscone and city supervisor Harvey Milk. In court, White's attorney successfully argued that a diet of junk food had jumbled his client's brain and reduced his capacity for moral behaviour. White spent only three years in prison for committing the double homicide. Although the "Twinkie defence" is no longer a legal defence in California, White's lawyer capitalized on the fact that a person's body chemistry—even an imbalance in blood sugar levels—can have a dramatic impact on behaviour. It is true that body chemistry, hormones, and learned experiences can work together to influence a person. But does this render people unaccountable for their own actions, as Dan White's lawyer claimed?

Combinations of factors are usually the answer to many complex psychological questions, but research shows that some abilities and behaviours have a direct hormonal link—that is, hormones directly affect the behaviour. For example, in a paper presented at a scientific meeting in 1988, psychologist Doreen Kimura of the University of Western Ontario reported that when some women experience low estrogen levels during and immediately after menstruation, they excel at spatial tasks but perform less well on motor tasks. The differences are small and do not occur in all women. Work in this area is in its early stages, but it is interesting because of the links indicated between hormones and behaviour and because of the differences observed between men and women. The links are mediated by the endocrine glands and show the complexity of the relationship of behaviour, body structures, and hormones and other substances that flow through our bodies.

Endocrine Glands

Throughout each day, glands manufacture and secrete substances that affect many of our behaviours. Psychologists are particularly interested in the **endocrine glands**—ductless glands that secrete hormones directly into the bloodstream, rather than through a specific duct into a target organ. (See Figure 2.12 for the location of several endocrine glands.) **Hormones** are chemicals produced by the endocrine

Endocrine glands [END-oh-krin]: Ductless glands that secrete hormones directly into the bloodstream, rather than through a specific duct, or opening, into a target organ.

Hormones: Chemicals produced by endocrine glands that regulate the activities of specific organs or cells.

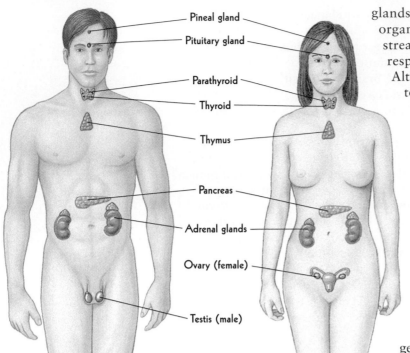

Pineal gland

Pituitary gland

Parathyroid

Thyroid

Thymus

Pancreas

Adrenal glands

Ovary (female)

Testis (male)

FIGURE 2.12
The Endocrine Glands
The endocrine glands are situated throughout the body. Though small in size, they exert enormous influences on behaviour.

glands that regulate the activities of specific organs or cells; they travel through the bloodstream to target organs containing cells that respond specifically to particular hormones. Although researchers do not know the extent to which hormones control people's behaviour, there is no doubt that the glandular system is involved in regulating bodily activities. Each hormone affects behaviour and eventually other glands, which in turn affect other behaviours. A disorder in the thyroid, for example, affects not only the metabolic rate but also the pituitary gland, which in turn regulates many other glands. The glands, hormones, and target organs interact; the brain initiates the release of hormones, which affect the target organs, which in turn affect behaviour, which in turn affects the brain, and so on. *Diversity*, on pages 69 and 70, explores the question of whether gender differences are caused by hormones.

Sexual Behaviour. In newborn animals, hormones have an irreversible effect on sexual behaviour—they set specific behaviour patterns in motion by permanently affecting brain development. In human adults, sexual behaviour is to some extent under hormonal control. One study, for example, showed a significant correlation between married couples' hormone levels and frequency of intercourse (Persky, 1978). Hormones such as testosterone and estrogen, whose release is affected by the pituitary gland, the adrenal gland, the testes, and the ovaries, are certainly involved in sexual activity.

Pituitary Gland. The most important endocrine gland is the **pituitary gland**, which is often called the body's master gland because it regulates the actions of many other endocrine glands (see Figure 2.13). The pituitary gland is located at the

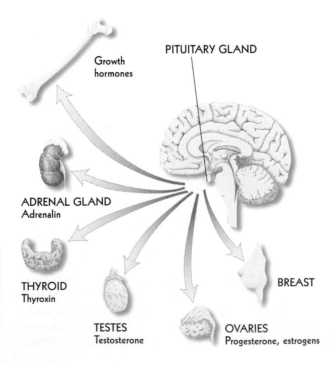

PITUITARY GLAND

Growth hormones

ADRENAL GLAND
Adrenalin

THYROID
Thyroxin

TESTES
Testosterone

OVARIES
Progesterone, estrogens

BREAST

FIGURE 2.13
The Pituitary Gland
The pituitary gland is often called the body's master gland because it regulates many of the other endocrine glands. Located at the base of the brain, the pea-sized pituitary gland affects behaviour indirectly through control of other glands and directly through release of hormones—including growth hormones and sex hormones—into the bloodstream.

Pituitary gland [pit-YOU-ih-tare-ee]: The body's master gland located at the base of the brain and closely linked to the hypothalamus; regulates the actions of other endocrine glands; major function is the control of growth hormones.

diversity

Do Gender Differences Lie in Our Brains or in Our Glands?

Some people believe that men and women are essentially the same; however, research does show some important biological and behavioural differences. In recent years, research on gender differences in brain organization has created a volatile debate.

Let's look at some facts. During fetal development, sex hormones are present in the fetus and help create sexual differentiation. Sex hormones also are thought to create permanent changes in brain development that become evident in later behaviour. Research shows that, on average, men do better than women on some spatial tasks—for example, the mental rotation of objects (Linn & Petersen, 1985). Across numerous research studies, men do better, on average, in mathematical reasoning and in some motor tasks, such as guiding projectiles through space (Halpern, 1986).

By contrast, women do better than men on some perceptual tasks—for example, the rapid matching of items. Women have greater verbal fluency than men and outperform men in some arithmetic calculations (Hyde, Fennema, & Lamon, 1990). They also do better than men at reading emotions from photographs. For other tasks on which both sexes do equally well—for example, rhyming—men and women use different areas of the brain to perform the task (Shaywitz et al., 1995). Women tend to use both sides of the brain in cognitive tasks such as spelling, for example; men use primarily the left side of the brain. While women use both ears equally, men favour the right ear. Not all gender differences appear at all ages and at all phases of learning, however. Gender differences in problem solving, for example, tend to favour females in elementary

school and males after puberty (Hyde, Fennema, & Lamon, 1990).

At birth, human brains are remarkably alike. Doreen Kimura (1992) of the University of Western Ontario asserts that differing patterns of abilities probably reflect different hormonal influences after birth, which result in structural asymmetries. In males, androgens (male hormones) predominate; they may affect the size and function of brain structures such as the hypothalamus. For example, when newborn rats are administered large doses of androgens, their brains develop differently than when they are administered large doses of estrogens (female hormones), and this difference alters their behavioural abilities permanently.

Of course, making the leap to human beings is difficult, because ethics preclude the manipulation of hormone levels of newborns. However, it is possible to make inferences from hormone levels and task performance in humans. Researchers have measured the abilities of human adults while simultaneously measuring their levels of the male hormone testosterone. Testosterone is present in all human beings, although men show significantly higher levels than women do. Valerie Shute measured these levels in men and women and found that women with high levels of testosterone performed better on spatial tasks than

women with low levels; in men, the reverse was true. Shute's conclusion was that testosterone levels in men and women affect performance (Shute et al., 1983).

Are gender differences also influenced by the social environment—by the way in which individuals are raised? The answer to this question is certainly yes. Some gender differences may be biologically based, but Western culture emphasizes and encourages them. Psychologist Sandra Lipsitz Bem (1993) asserts that many traditionally held gender stereotypes are embedded in culture and in social institutions and perpetuate a society that values males more than females. For example, boys traditionally have been encouraged to participate in rough-and-tumble sports, while girls have been encouraged to take part in domestic activities. Men traditionally have been expected to be the providers—the wage earners and problem solvers—whereas women have been expected to be the nurturers—mothers and caregivers.

Today, however, more men and women in Western societies are sharing roles and responsibilities; in raising children, many parents are showing a greater understanding

continued on next page

that boys and girls should have equal opportunities. The effects of changing societal values are becoming more evident in individual behaviour. In some Western cultures, differences between men and women that have long been apparent are diminishing; access to and enrolment in courses where problem solving is encouraged—for example, engineering or physics—are increasing among women. Unfortunately, many girls experience direct and indirect devaluing from peers, parents, and teachers (Reis, 1991) and avoid advanced mathematics and science courses due to diminished self-esteem (Benbow & Arjimand, 1990). This in turn perpetuates stereotypes and in some cases causes discrimination. In Chapter 11 we'll discuss the fact that many of the differences between males and females in mathematical ability are exceedingly small and perhaps social in origin, and that the extent of those differences is shrinking each year.

Most important is the fact that *there are usually more differences within a gender than between genders*. For example, there are greater differences among individual women's spatial abilities than between women's and men's spatial abilities. This idea is especially important to consider when you are trying to determine the relevance of gender differences you may observe. It becomes impossible to generalize results to all people if the data are taken only from a small sample of women or men. ■

Insulin: A hormone produced by the pancreas; facilitates the transport of sugar from the blood into body cells, where it is metabolized.

Diabetes mellitus [mel-LIGHT-us]: A condition in which too little insulin is produced, causing sugar to be insufficiently transported out of the blood and into body cells.

Hypoglycemia [hi-po-gly-SEE-me-uh]: A condition in which overproduction of insulin results in a very low blood sugar level.

base of the brain and is directly controlled by the hypothalamus. One of its major functions is the control of growth hormones.

The pea-sized pituitary gland is divided into two lobes, the anterior and the posterior. Secretions from the lobes produce direct changes in bodily functions, such as growth, and affect other glands. The *anterior lobe* produces a number of hormones—including those that stimulate the thyroid and adrenal glands, each of which controls specific behaviours; growth hormones (called somatotrophins), which control the body's development; and sex hormones (called gonadotrophins), which are involved in sexual behaviour. A person's psychological state influences the secretions from the anterior pituitary; for example, viewing sexually explicit films raises the level of gonadotrophins (LaFerla, Anderson, & Schalch, 1978). The *posterior lobe* of the pituitary gland stores and secretes two major hormones, antidiuretic hormone (ADH) and oxytocin. ADH is a vasopressin, acting on the kidneys to increase fluid absorption and decrease the amount of urine produced by the body as well as constricting blood vessels and hence raising blood pressure. Oxytocin stimulates uterine contractions in pregnant women and causes labour to begin. It also helps nursing mothers release milk.

 Pancreas. Another endocrine gland, the *pancreas*, is involved in regulating the body's sugar levels. Sugar in the blood determines a person's energy level. When blood sugar is high, people are energetic; when it is low, they feel weak and tired. Cells in the pancreas called the *islets of Langerhans* control the production of **insulin**—the pancreatic hormone that facilitates the transport of sugar into body cells, where it is metabolized. Two insulin-related problems are diabetes and hypoglycemia. **Diabetes mellitus** is a condition in which an insufficient amount of insulin is produced, causing sugar to be inefficiently transported out of the bloodstream into the cells and thus allowing too much sugar to accumulate in the blood. Some types of this condition can be treated through diet and weight loss, while other types require regular injections of insulin. If the pancreas errs in the opposite direction, the result is hypoglycemia. **Hypoglycemia** is a very low blood sugar level caused by the overproduction of insulin. Hypoglycemic patients have little energy. The condition usually can be controlled through diet, with careful monitoring of types of food eaten and daily calorie intake.

Focus

Review

◆ What evidence has led researchers to conclude that hormonal differences in development affect behaviour in adulthood? pp. 67–71

◆ Why are researchers justified in concluding that the pituitary gland is the master gland? pp. 68, 70

Think Critically

◆ What are the social implications of the conclusion researchers have reached about gender differences in intellectual and other abilities? Should men and women be expected to do things differently?

Adrenal Glands. The *adrenal glands*, which are also involved in behaviour, are located just above the kidneys and are divided into two parts. The *adrenal medulla*, located deep within each adrenal gland, produces epinephrine (adrenalin), a substance that dramatically alters energy levels and affects a person's reactions to stress through stimulation of the sympathetic nervous system. Imagine that you are being chased through a dark alley. The release of epinephrine makes your heart pound and gives you a burst of energy to help you outdistance your pursuer. The *adrenal cortex*, the outer layer that covers each adrenal gland, secretes a hormone that is involved in growth and development as well as others that are involved in increasing blood sugar levels and boosting energy.

Summary and Review

Nature versus Nurture

What is the distinction between nature and nurture?

■ Psychologists generally assert that human behaviour is influenced by both *nature* (heredity) and *nurture* (environment). Psychologists study the biological bases of behaviour to better understand how these two variables interact. pp. 38–39

What is genetics, and why do psychologists study it?

■ *Genetics* is the study of heredity—the biological transmission of traits and characteristics from parents to offspring. Chromosomes carry the inherited potential of each person. Each chromosome contains thousands of *genes*, made up of DNA. Genes are the basic unit of heredity. The twenty-third pair of chromosomes determines the gender of a fetus. pp. 39–40

■ One goal of genetic research is to help prevent genetic defects such as *muscular dystrophy and Huntington's disease*. pp. 40–41

■ *Identical twins* share exactly the same genetic heritage; they come from one ovum and one sperm and are always the same sex. *Fraternal twins* are produced by two ova and two sperm and therefore can be both males, both females, or one male and one female. They share genetic characteristics to the same degree as other siblings do. Studying twins allows researchers to clarify the effects of nature and nurture on developmental processes. pp. 41–42

KEY TERMS
nature, p. 38; nurture, p. 38; genetics, p. 39; chromosome, p. 39; gene, p. 39; allele, p. 39; fraternal twins, p. 41; identical twins, p. 41

Communication in the Nervous System

Describe the full journey of a neural impulse from one neuron to another.

■ The basic unit of the *nervous system* is the *neuron*, or nerve cell, made up of *dendrites*, a cell body, an *axon*, and axon terminals. The space between the axon terminals and another neuron is the *synapse*. pp. 42–44

■ The *action potential* is caused by the stimulation of the neuron. If there is enough stimulation at the cell body to exceed the threshold, a spike discharge occurs (with a rapid reversal of cell membrane polarity). The neuron fires on an *all-or-none* basis and has a *refractory period*, during which it cannot fire. The action potential propagates down the axon and stimulates the release of *neurotransmitters* that reside in the axon terminal's *synaptic vesicles*. The neurotransmitters move across the synaptic gap and bind to receptor sites on the neighbouring cells, thereby conveying information to other neurons. pp. 44–45

What is the focus of psychopharmacology?

■ Psychopharmacology is the study of how drugs affect behaviour. Research often focuses on *agonists* and *antagonists*. An agonist is a chemical that mimics or facilitates the actions of a neurotransmitter, usually by occupying receptor sites. An antagonist is a chemical that opposes the actions of a neurotransmitter, usually by preventing it from occupying receptor sites. pp. 47–48

KEY TERMS
nervous system, p. 42; neuron, p. 42; afferent neurons, p. 42; efferent neurons, p. 42; dendrites, p. 43; axon, p. 43; synapse, p. 43; action potential, p. 45; all-or-none, p. 45; refractory period, p. 45; neurotransmitter, p. 45; neuromodulator, p. 47; agonist, p. 47; antagonist, p. 47

Organization of the Nervous System

Describe the subdivisions of the nervous system.

■ The nervous system is composed of two subsystems: the central and peripheral nervous systems. The *central nervous system* consists of the brain and the spinal cord. The *peripheral nervous system* carries information to and from the spinal cord and brain through spinal and cranial nerves. The peripheral nervous system is further divided into the *somatic* and *autonomic nervous systems*. The autonomic nervous system is made up of two divisions: the *sympathetic* and *parasympathetic nervous systems*, each having different functions. pp. 48–51

KEY TERMS
peripheral nervous system, p. 48; somatic nervous system, p. 48; autonomic nervous system, p. 49;

sympathetic nervous system, p. 49; parasympathetic nervous system, p. 50; central nervous system, p. 50; spinal cord, p. 51

Brain Structures

What are the major sections of the brain, and what are its structures?

■ The *brain* is divided into three sections: the hindbrain, the midbrain, and the forebrain (which includes the cortex). The *hindbrain* consists of four main structures: the *medulla*, the *reticular formation*, the *pons*, and the *cerebellum*. The *midbrain* is made up of nuclei that receive afferent signals from other parts of the brain and from the spinal cord, interpret them, and either relay the information to other parts of the brain or cause the body to act at once. The *forebrain* is the largest and most complicated brain structure; it comprises the *thalamus* and the *hypothalamus*, the *limbic system*, the *basal ganglia*, the *corpus callosum*, and the *cortex*. Two prominent structures of the cortex are the deep fissures—the lateral fissure and the central fissure—that divide the cortex's lobes. pp. 51–57

KEY TERMS
brain, p. 51; hindbrain, p. 54; medulla, p. 54; reticular formation, p. 54; pons, p. 54; cerebellum, p. 55; midbrain, p. 55; forebrain, p. 55; thalamus, p. 55; hypothalamus, p. 55; limbic system, p. 55; cortex, p. 57; convolutions, p. 57

Studying the Brain

Describe several techniques for studying brain activity and functions.

■ One technique for measuring the electrical activity of the nervous system is single unit recording, through which scientists record activity from single cells by placing an electrode within or next to those cells. Another technique is electroencephalography. Researchers can use records of brain-wave patterns, called *electroencephalograms (EEGs)*, to assess neurological disorders and the types of electrical activity that occur during thought, sleep, and other behaviours. Three significant new techniques for measuring the activity of the nervous system have been developed. *CT (computerized tomography) scans* are created by computer-assisted X-ray procedures. *PET (positron emission tomography)* uses radiochemical procedures and allow researchers to observe metabolic changes in progress. *MRI (magnetic resonance imaging)* is similar to CT scans but is not invasive and does not use radiation. *fMRI (functional magnetic resonance imaging* is an imaging technique that takes place during task performance. pp. 58–60

■ Research shows that in most human beings, one cerebral hemisphere—usually the left—is specialized for processing speech and language; the other—usually the right—appears better able to handle spatial tasks and musical and artistic endeavours. p. 61

■ Normal cerebral hemispheres are neurologically connected to opposite sides of the body. In laboratory studies, *split-brain patients* are unable to use the speech and language capabilities of the left hemisphere to describe activities carried out by the right hemisphere due to the severing of the *corpus callosum*. pp. 63–64

KEY TERMS
electroencephalogram (EEG), p. 58; CT (computerized tomography) scans, p. 59; PET (positron emission tomography), p. 59; MRI (magnetic resonance imaging), p. 59; fMRI (functional magnetic resonance imaging, p. 60; split-brain patients, p. 63

Hormones and Glands

How does the endocrine system affect behaviour?

■ The *endocrine glands* are a group of ductless glands that affect behaviour by secreting *hormones* into the bloodstream. Each gland influences different aspects of behaviour, but all are regulated in one way or another by the *pituitary gland*. The pituitary gland is appropriately referred to as the master gland because of its central role in regulating hormones; another important gland is the *pancreas*, which is involved in regulating the body's sugar levels. pp. 67–70

KEY TERMS
endocrine glands, p. 67; hormones, p. 67; pituitary gland, p. 68; insulin, p. 70; diabetes mellitus, p. 70; hypoglycemia, p. 70

Weblinks

A Brain Anatomy Browser
www.nvl.virginia.edu/javaman
Click on a position of the brain to view the cross-section at that location. This Java-enabled site allows you to explore the anatomy of the brain.

Learning Guide for the Human Brain
www.uta.marmt.edu/~psychol/brain.html
You can test your knowledge of the brain's anatomy at this site. Click your mouse on an area of the brain and the name and explanation of that area will appear.

The Whole Brain Atlas
www.med.harvard.edu/AANLIB
This site provides images of a normal brain, as well as those affected by stroke, multiple sclerosis, tumours, Alzheimer's disease, and Huntington's disease. Time-lapse movies illustrate the gradual changes that occur within one year.

Neurotransmitters and Neuroactive Peptides
weber.u.washington.edu/~chudler/chnt1.html
Diagrams, charts, and links to other sites effectively explain how neurotransmitters function.

Neuropsychology Homepage
www.tbidoc.com
This Web page explains neuropsychology and brain injury. Links and resources are offered to help understand the neuropsychologist's role in dealing with brain injury.

Synaptic Transmissions
www.tc.cornell.edu/er94/ff01winter/ff04a.html
Four three-dimensional diagrams from Cornell University depict how synaptic transmissions function. The rich colour and detail of the illustrations are visually impressive.

Endocrine Disrupters
www3.hmc.edu/~clewis/endocrine/intro.htm
The effects of endocrine disrupters on human and wildlife populations, as well as an explanation of the different types of hormones and which glands secrete them, are detailed at this Web site.

Chapter 3

Sensation and Perception

Jean-Claude is typical of many second-graders—smart, eager, and energetic. He is well loved at home, is provided with lots of stimulation, and has been well nourished and well cared for. But life for Jean-Claude is becoming frustrating. School is difficult; homework is becoming a source of conflict with his parents. Friends are beginning to find his poor abilities, which outside of school are limited to things like playing cards slowly and football fumbles, to be annoying. Jean-Claude is being stereotyped, typecast, and alienated. It is happening slowly, day by day, but nevertheless it is happening. His problem is perceptual, and his teachers are just beginning to see it.

"Bright and intelligent, quick at games, as able in most areas as his or her peers" is a typical prelude of many psychologists before they announce that Jean-Claude has an inability to read—a diagnosis that is often called "reading disability." A reading disability is one of the most common of the various learning disabilities that exist. In some school districts, as many as 15 percent of all children are diagnosed with a learning disability, and many have a reading disability. Children with reading problems have trouble decoding words, distinguishing one syllable from another, and figuring out new and unfamiliar words. They experience difficulty with coding, decoding, and mapping words to letters and sounds. If you or someone you know has such a disability, then you understand some of the real disadvantage faced by Jean-Claude and his family. ■

The causes of reading disability are complex, and no single explanation can account for any particular case. Some researchers assert that far too many have been identified as reading disabled; indeed definitions of learning disabilities are unclear—focusing more on what these individuals can't do than on what they can. Research is being done on various types of processing deficits—processing that takes place with the visual stimulus at the beginning of reading, as well as more complex processing that involves decision making and elaborate perceptual and cognitive coding. For example, some of the newest physiological research shows anatomical differences in brain structure and functioning between readers with disabilities and readers without disabilities (Shaywitz 1996; Shaywitz et al., 1998). Perceptual deficits are at least partly responsible for some types of learning disability. To better understand these and other perceptual problems, it is important to develop an understanding of our perceptual systems and their underlying structures.

The Perceptual Experience

W henever you are exposed to a stimulus in the environment—a word on a page or a breeze through your hair—the stimulus initiates an electrochemical change in the receptors in your body. That change in turn initiates the processes of sensation and perception. Psychologists study sensation and perception because what people sense and perceive determines how they understand and interpret the world. Such understanding depends on a combination of environmental stimulation, past experiences, and current interpretations. Although the relationship between perception and culture has not been extensively researched, it is clear that culture can affect perception—through socialization people learn what to believe, pay attention to, notice, and expect in the environment. For example, composers have long known that a person's experiences with music can make some melodies, especially non-Western ones, sound unfamiliar and dissonant.

Sensation and Perception

Traditionally, psychologists have studied sensation and perception together as closely related—as we do in this chapter. **Sensation** is the process in which the sense organ receptor cells are stimulated and relay their initial information to higher brain centres for further processing. **Perception** is the process whereby an organism selects and interprets sensory input in order to give it meaning. Thus, sensation provides the stimuli for further perceptual processing. For example, when light striking the eyeball initiates electrochemical changes, you experience the sensation of light. But your interpretation of the pattern of light and its resulting neural representation as a specific image are part of perception.

When researchers examine sensation and perception they usually adopt an approach that starts at the most fundamental level of sensation—where the stimulus meets the receptors—and work up to more complex perceptual tasks involving interpretation. This is often called *bottom-up processing*. Bottom-up processing tends to be involuntary, almost automatic, and helps us discern and discriminate fast-changing information that occurs to our sense organs. Other researchers examine complex perceptual phenomena from more complex interpretations or memories— not surprisingly, called *top-down processing*. This type of processing focuses on aspects of the perceptual process such as selective attention and active decision making. For example, when we decide to search for a friend in a crowd, we establish a series of relevant criteria (tall, red-headed, wearing a blue shirt) through a series of decision rules based on our representation of our friend in memory. Top-down processing probably holds the key to our understanding not only of perception,

Sensation: The process in which the sense organ receptor cells are stimulated and relay their initial information to higher brain centres for further processing.

Perception: The process whereby an organism selects and interprets sensory input so that it acquires meaning.

but of consciousness because perception and consciousness are more than reflexive discrimination processes; rather, both perception and consciousness require integration of current sensory experiences (bottom-up analysis) with past experiences and even cultural expectations (top-down analysis).

These two approaches, from the top down and the bottom up, are both necessary and useful because sensation and perception involve whole sets of neurons and previous experiences, as well as stimulation from the environment that occurs at the sense organs. Because of this, perceptual psychologists generally think in terms of *perceptual systems*—the interacting sets of structures, functions, and operations by means of which people perceive the world around them. Sensory and perceptual processes rely so closely on each other that many researchers think of the two processes as being inseparable. So, sensation and perception together form an entire process through which an organism acquires sensory input, converts it into electrochemical energy, and interprets it so that it acquires organization, form, and meaning. It is through such processes that people explore the world and discover its rules. This complex process involves the nervous system in interaction with sensory receptors for vision, hearing, taste, smell, and/or touch.

Psychophysics [SYE-co-FIZ-icks]: The subfield that focuses on the relationship between physical stimuli and people's conscious experience of them.

Absolute threshold: The statistically determined minimum level of stimulation necessary to excite a perceptual system.

Psychophysics

Although perceptual systems are different, they share a common process. In each case, an environmental stimulus creates an initial stimulation of the sensory receptors. Receptor cells translate that form of energy into neuronal impulses, and the impulses are then sent to specific areas of the brain for further processing. Many psychologists who study such relationships use techniques from the area of **psychophysics**—focusing on the relationship between physical stimuli and people's conscious experience of those stimuli.

Psychophysical studies attempt to relate the physical dimension of stimuli to psychological experience. This often begins with studying sensory thresholds. We often speak of a *threshold* as a dividing line, the point at which things become different. In perception, a threshold is the value of a sensory event at the point at which things are perceived as being different. Early researchers, such as Ernst Weber and Gustav Fechner, sought to investigate *absolute thresholds*, the minimum levels of stimulation necessary to excite a perceptual system, such as vision. They asked, for example, what minimum intensity of light is necessary for a person to say, "I see it," or what minimum pressure is necessary to feel something against the skin. It turns out that a simple absolute threshold describing everyone's experiences is impossible to determine, because no two individuals see or feel at exactly the same minimum amount of intensity due to many variables. So, for a psychologist, the **absolute threshold** is the minimum level of stimulation necessary to excite a perceptual system that enables an observer to detect a stimulus 50 percent of the time. Another type of threshold is the *difference threshold*—the amount of change necessary for an observer to report 50 percent of the time that a level of stimulation (say, a sound) has changed or is different from another value (i.e., has gotten louder or softer). For example, how much louder does your CD player have to be for you to notice that it is, in fact, louder? Does it matter how loud it was in the first place?

Psychologists have devised a variety of methods for studying perceptual thresholds. In one—the *method of limits*—various values of a stimulus are presented in ascending or descending order. For example, a psychologist may present lights of very low intensity, then slightly higher intensity, and then higher still. A participant's task is to say when he or she finally sees the light—or, in the case of descending limits, no longer sees it. In another method—the *method of constant stimuli*—values of a signal are presented in random (not ascending or descending) order; the participants' task is to respond "yes" or "no," indicating that they have either detected a stimulus or not.

Both the method of limits and the method of constant stimuli have methodological weaknesses—they do not allow for key factors in the human observer. In the

Signal detection theory: The theory that holds that an observer's perception is dependent on the intensity of a stimulus, on the observer's motivation, on the criteria he or she sets up, and on the "noise" that is present.

Subliminal perception: Perception below the threshold of awareness.

last few decades, researchers studying thresholds have used the method of signal detection theory. **Signal detection theory** holds that an observer's perception is dependent not only on the intensity of a stimulus but on the observer's motivation; for example, when you are worried about a friend being late, you listen especially carefully for cars that may be coming down the street. Your perception also is dependent on the level of auditory stimulation that enables you to state, "Yes, that is enough for me to say that I detect the signal—the sound of a car." Your perception also is dependent on the *noise* (the unstructured, constant background activity) that is present; in our example, the noise of children playing in the street, birds chirping, or the television from the next apartment all make detecting the sound of your friend's automobile more difficult. Therefore, researchers manipulate signal intensity but also manipulate motivation levels (by offering varying rewards for detection), criteria (for example, by telling participants to be *very* sure before they respond, "Yes, I detect the signal"), and levels of noise. It turns out that all four of these variables affect a person's willingness to say, "Yes, I detect the signal." This important finding lends support to the idea that there is no single or absolute threshold—each individual's response will vary from one type of situation to the next.

Subliminal Perception

Subliminal perception is perception below the threshold of awareness. Do subliminal self-help audiotapes do all that they claim? If a visual or auditory stimulus is presented so quickly or at such a low intensity or volume that you cannot consciously perceive it, can it affect your behaviour? Is it affecting your brain organization?

Modern studies of this type of perception began in the 1950s with tales of an innovative advertising ploy. The story was that a marketing executive had superimposed messages on a movie that said, among other things, "Buy popcorn." According to some enterprising advertising agents, movie theatres could induce audiences to buy more popcorn by flashing advertisements on the screen at speeds too fast to be consciously observed. Although psychological research has shown that there are no strong effects of this sort of advertising (Trappey, 1996), other research suggests that a large proportion of the public clearly believes that it works and that it is being used regularly by advertisers (Rogers & Smith, 1993).

Subliminal perception is possible. In fact, many cognitive scientists build theories around it (e.g., Kihlstrom, Barnhardt, & Tataryn, 1992). However, historically the concept of subliminal perception has been controversial. Many of the early studies in the 1960s lacked control groups and did not specify the variables being manipulated. Some did not adjust the presentation duration of the words they used to take individual differences into account. Other studies presented sexual words to see if they affected responses more than neutral or emotionally uncharged words did. Would the sexual words be threatening and emotionally arousing and lead participants to perceptually block out these stimuli? Initial results showed that participants did indeed show increased thresholds and had higher autonomic activity for these words, indicating arousal. Of course it is very likely that, even if detected, some participants were too embarrassed to repeat the noxious words to the experimenter (often a person of the opposite sex) and so denied having seen them.

To avoid some of these methodological problems, later experiments presented participants with both threatening and neutral words for very brief durations. Participants responded by repeating the words or by pressing a button as soon as they saw a word they had been told to look for. In these experiments, threatening words had to be presented for a longer time or at a greater intensity level than nonthreatening words in order to be identified.

Evidence exists for subliminal effects in a variety of experimental settings (Klinger & Greenwald, 1995). The presentation of a threatening message—for example, an aggressive or sexual message—may raise the perceptual threshold above normal levels, making it harder for the participant to perceive subsequent subliminal words. Some researchers suggest that the unconscious mind or some other personality variable acts as a censor (Silverman, 1983). Balay and Shevrin (1988) suggest that a higher processing stage beyond the sensory or perceptual stage affects the perceptual process. They maintain that subliminal perception can be explained in terms of non-perceptual variables such as motivation, previous experience, repetition, and unconscious or critical censoring processes that influence perceptual thresholds.

In some controlled situations, subliminal stimuli can influence perception, attitudes, and behaviour (Greenwald, Klinger, & Schuh, 1995; Krosnick et al., 1992; Underwood, 1994). In the real world, however, we are constantly faced with many competing sensory stimuli. Therefore, what grabs our attention depends on many variables, such as importance, prominence, and interest. Should we fear mind control by advertisers or other unsolicited outside stimuli? The answer is probably no, because such attempts are ineffective (Trappey, 1996). Can backwards speech in rock music be interpreted and understood? Again, the answer is no (Begg, Needham, & Bookbinder, 1993). Can listening to tapes while we are asleep help us learn Greek or Latin? Once more, the answer is no (Moore, 1995). In the end, subliminal perception, and any learning that results from it, is subtle at most (Smith & Rogers, 1994) and greatly affected by such non-perceptual non-biological variables as expectation, motivation, previous experience, personality, and other learned, culturally based behaviours (Pratkanis, Eskenazi, & Greenwald, 1994).

Selective Attention

Have you ever tried to study and listen to quiet music at the same time? You may have thought that the music barely reached your threshold of awareness. Yet you may have found your attention wandering. Did certain melodies or words start to interrupt your studying? Research on attention shows that human beings constantly extract signals from the world around them. Although we receive many different messages at once, we can watch, listen, and attend to only a small number of stimuli at a time.

Because people can pay attention to only one or two things at a time, psychologists sometimes call the study of attention the study of *selective attention*. Early researchers in this area (Broadbent, 1958) described the *cocktail party phenomenon*, whereby a person can hear his or her name spoken across a crowded and noisy room. The person cannot discern the content of conversations across the room under such conditions, but does hear his or her name.

Perceptual psychologists are interested in the complex processes through which people extract information from the environment. These psychologists hope to answer the following question: Which stimuli do people choose to listen to? They study the *allocation* of a person's attention. For example, measuring selective attention in the auditory senses can involve the use of selective-listening tasks in which participants wearing pairs of headphones simultaneously receive different messages in each ear. Their task often is to *shadow*, or repeat, a message heard in one ear. Typically, they report that they are able to listen to a speaker in *either* the left ear or the right ear and can provide information about the content and quality of that speaker's voice but are unable to attend to qualities of the stimuli in both ears at the same time.

There are several theories about how people attend selectively, two of which are the filter theory and the attenuation theory. The *filter theory* states that human

beings possess a limited capacity to process information and that perceptual "filters" screen out or ignore extraneous information. The *attenuation theory* states that all information is analyzed but that intervening factors inhibit (attenuate) attention so that only selected information reaches the highest centres of processing. Hundreds of selective-listening studies have examined the claims of filter theory versus attenuation theory, and recent research favours attenuation theory (Wood & Cowan, 1995). But regardless of whether people filter or attenuate information, selective-attention studies show that human beings must select among available stimuli. It is impossible, for example, to attend to four lectures at once. A listener can extract information from only one speaker at a time. Admittedly, you can do more than one task at a time—for example, you can drive a car and listen to the radio—but you cannot use the same channel (such as vision) or concentrate equally on information from many channels for several tasks simultaneously. For example, you cannot sing along with the radio, study, and identify an odour at the same time.

Clearly, our sensory systems have limited capacities. People have limited ability to divide their attention between tasks and must allocate their perceptual resources for greatest efficiency. But what happens when the need to divide is not necessary? What occurs when there is a restricted environment?

Restricted Environmental Stimulation

Imagine utter loneliness . . . darkness . . . complete lack of light and sound. Imagine being in an isolation tank where you don't have to adapt to the light—because there is absolutely none. This was the case described in a compelling 1978 novel, a page-turner by Paddy Chayefsky entitled *Altered States,* and in its movie version starring William Hurt. It is a great story that raises provocative questions about human perceptual systems and consciousness—and the relationship between the two.

In 1954, at McGill University, neurophysiologist John Lilly enlisted modern technology to find out what would happen if the brain were deprived of all sensory input—he created a situation much like that described in Chayefsky's novel. Lilly constructed an isolation tank that excluded all light and sound and was filled with heavily salted water, which allows for easy floating. In this artificial sea, deprived of all external stimuli, Lilly experienced dreams, reveries, hallucinations, and other altered states.

Psychologists call such a situation one of restricted environmental stimulation. And some researchers argue that psychological benefits can be derived from sensory restriction (deprivation)—isolation from sights, sounds, smells, tastes, and feeling. The current president of the Canadian Psychological Association, Peter Seudfeld, has studied the effects of restricted environmental stimulation therapy (REST) for years at the University of British Columbia. Suedfeld and Coren (1989) have explained that early research participant reports of discomfort and hallucinations likely were due to poor participant selection (some people hallucinate without experiencing a REST situation) and to the stressful way in which those REST experiences were handled (participants were led to believe that they might see things or feel discomfort, and so some participants obliged). Suedfeld and his colleagues have found that spending time in a REST chamber (either lying on a cot in the dark or floating in a bath of epsom salts) can reduce anxiety (Suedfeld & Eich, 1995), enhance sports performance (Suedfeld, Collier, & Harnett, 1993; Suedfeld & Bruno, 1990), reduce the frequency of tension headaches (Wallbaum et al., 1991), help people quit smoking (Suedfeld, 1990), and even improve the functioning of autistic children (Suedfeld & Schwartz, 1981).

There are a number of hypotheses about why REST has such a broad range of effects. These include simple relaxation or becoming "focused" as one might through meditation or concentration. Or it may be that the REST experience allows the non-dominant cerebral hemisphere to exert more influence than usual on functioning. Once fully understood, the range of REST's effects very likely will tell us a great deal about our perceptual systems.

Focus

Review

◆ Why have modern researchers viewed perception as a unitary rather than a two-step (sensation followed by perception) process? pp. 76–77
◆ What evidence exists to show that when a person receives more than one incoming message at the same time, the person can attend to only one? pp. 79–80

Think Critically

◆ How does the culture prime, or pre-cue, individuals to focus their attention in important ways?
◆ What assumptions does a researcher make when depriving an organism of sensory experience and then measuring behaviour?

The Visual System

I magine that you are in an unfamiliar house at night when the power goes out. You hear creaking sounds but have no idea where they are coming from. You stub your toe on the coffee table, then frantically grope along the walls until you reach the kitchen, where you fumble through the drawers in search of a flashlight. You quickly come to appreciate the sense of sight when you are suddenly without it.

Human beings derive more information through sight than through any other sense. By some estimates, the eyes contain 70 percent of the body's sense receptors. Visible light exists as a small band of energy contained within the electromagnetic spectrum. The electromagnetic spectrum includes gamma rays, X-rays, ultraviolet rays, visible light, infrared rays, radar, broadcast bands, and AC currents (see Figure 3.1). Note that the visible **light** that can be seen by the human eye is a very small portion of that spectrum. Light may come directly from a source or may be reflected from an object. We begin our analysis of the visual system in a bottom-up analysis with light and the structure of the eye. Our visual system is exceedingly intricate; although often likened to a camera that records images, our visual system is interpretive, and a top-down analysis, which will be presented later in this section, shows that the camera analogy is a weak one relating in a rudimentary way to certain structures.

Light: The portion of the electromagnetic spectrum visible to the eye.

FIGURE 3.1
The Electromagnetic Spectrum
People can perceive only a small part of the total electromagnetic spectrum.

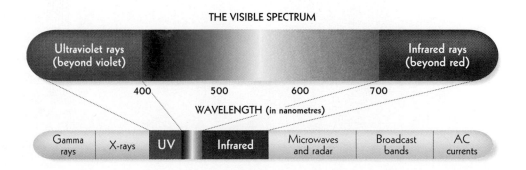

THE VISIBLE SPECTRUM

Ultraviolet rays (beyond violet)

Infrared rays (beyond red)

400   500   600   700

WAVELENGTH (in nanometres)

| Gamma rays | X-rays | UV | Infrared | Microwaves and radar | Broadcast bands | AC currents |

The Structure of the Eye

Figure 3.2 shows the major structures of the human eye. Light first passes through the *cornea*—a small, transparent bulge covering both the *pupil* (the dark opening in the centre of the eye) and the pigmented (coloured) *iris*. Behind the pupil is the *lens*, which is about four millimetres thick. Together, the cornea, the pupil, the iris, and the lens focus images onto the retina. The *retina*, a layer of neurons that lines the back of the eye, captures images and sends them to the brain for processing, which ultimately will produce conscious visual experience. The iris regulates the amount of light entering the eye. Constriction of the iris makes the pupil smaller, letting in less light but creating a more sharply focused image on the retina. Dilation of the iris makes the pupil bigger and allows in more light, but the images produced will appear more blurred.

To form a useful image, it is necessary for light from an object to be focused on the retina. The cornea and the lens both contribute to image formation. If either of these elements is too long or too short, a blurred image is formed. People with elongated eyeballs are **myopic**, or *nearsighted*; they are able to see things that are close to them but have trouble seeing objects at a distance, because the image falls in front of the retina. **Hyperopic**, or *farsighted*, people have shortened eyeballs. They have trouble seeing things up close but are able to see objects at a distance, because the image is focused behind the retina.

The *retina* has a complex multilayered organization consisting of a network of neurons. Of these, the most important are the **photoreceptors** (the light-sensitive cells). After light passes through several layers of other cells it strikes the photoreceptor layer, which consists of *rods* (large, rod-shaped receptors) and *cones* (small, cone-shaped receptors). Here light energy is transformed into electrical energy in a process called **transduction**. This electrical energy is transferred from the more than 120 million rods and 6 million cones to the *bipolar cells*. A set of rods converges onto a single bipolar cell. At the same time, hundreds of cones synapse and converge onto other bipolar cells, as do other sets of rods. From the bipolar cells, electrochemical energy is transferred to the

Myopic [my-OP-ick]: Able to see things that are close but having trouble seeing objects at a distance. Also known as *nearsighted*.

Hyperopic [HY-per-OP-ick]: Having trouble seeing things that are close but able to see objects at a distance. Also known as *farsighted*.

Photoreceptors: The light-sensitive cells in the retina: rods and cones.

Transduction: The process by which a perceptual system analyzes stimuli and converts them into electrical impulses. Also known as *coding*.

Visual cortex: The most important area of the brain's occipital lobe, which receives information from the lateral geniculate nucleus. Also known as the *striate cortex*.

FIGURE 3.2
The Main Structures of the Eye
The photoreceptors of the retina are connected to higher brain pathways through the optic nerve. Light filters through layers of retinal cells before hitting the receptors (rods and cones), located at the back of the eyeball and pointed away from the incoming light. The rods and cones pass an electrical impulse to the bipolar cells, which in turn relay the impulse back out to the ganglion cells. The axons of the ganglion cells form the fibres of the optic nerve.

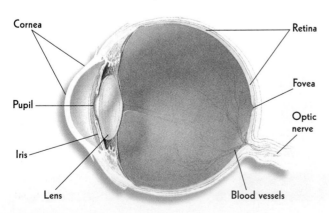

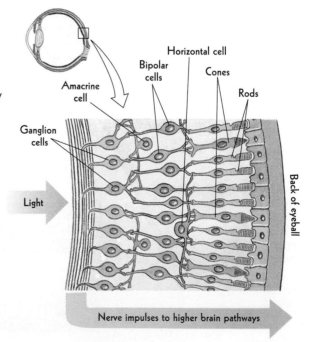

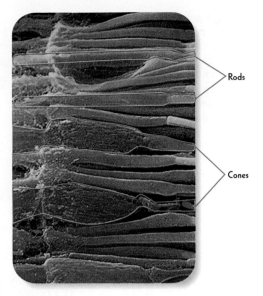

ganglion cell layer of the retina. Dozens of bipolar cells synapse and converge onto each ganglion cell (there are about 1 million in total). The axons of the ganglion cells make up the *optic nerve*, which carries information to higher pathways in the nervous system. Still further coding takes place in the brain's **visual cortex**, or *striate cortex*. The visual cortex is the most important specialized area of the brain's occipital lobe; it is the location at which visual information receives complex analysis.

Rods and Cones. The *duplicity theory of vision* asserts that the two separate receptor systems in the retina, the rods and the cones, are structurally different and are used to accomplish different tasks. For the most part cones are tightly packed in the centre of the retina, at the *fovea*, and are used for day vision, colour vision, and fine visual discrimination. Rods are found on the rest of the retina (the periphery) and are used predominantly for night vision (see Figure 3.3). This means that cones are important for tasks in which resolution of fine details is needed. For example, a standard eye exam measures visual acuity. Rods are needed when light levels are low; for example, when you are looking for something in a darkened room.

FIGURE 3.3
The Distribution of Rods and Cones and the Blind Spot
The centre of the retina (the fovea) contains only cones. At about 18° of visual angle (a measure of the size of images on the retina), there are no receptors at all. This is the place where the optic nerve leaves the eye, called the blind spot. Because the *blind spot* for each eye is on the nasal side of the eyeball, there is no loss of vision; the two blind spots do not overlap.

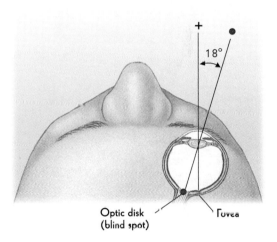

+   ●

Here is a demonstration of the blind spot. Close your left eye. Look at the black plus sign with your right eye and move the page slowly back and forth, towards and away from yourself. The red dot disappears from your vision when its image falls on your blind spot.

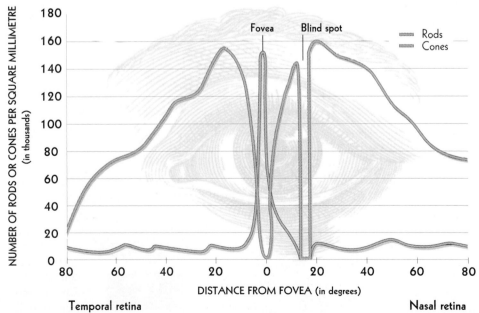

FIGURE 3.4
A Dark Adaptation Curve

The dashed line represents a typical overall dark adaptation curve. The two solid lines represent separate dark adaptation for rods and cones. Most dark adaptation occurs within 10 minutes. Rods, however, continue to adapt for another 20 minutes, reaching greater levels of sensitivity.

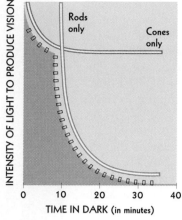

FIGURE 3.5
The Major Components of the Visual System

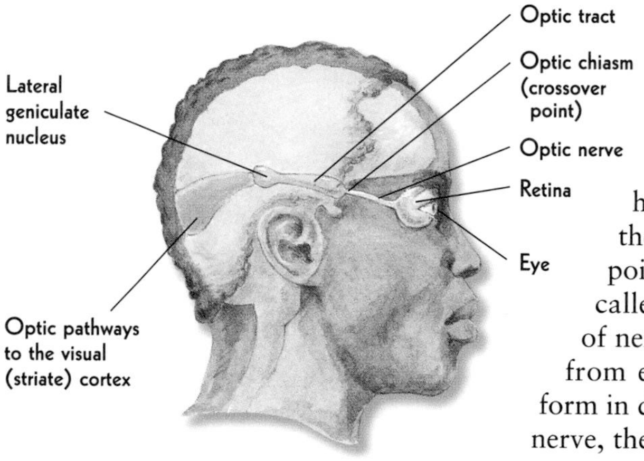

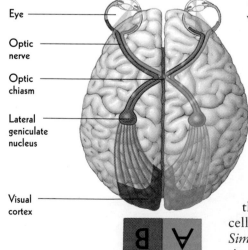

FIGURE 3.6
A Visual Image Is Projected to Both Hemispheres of the Brain

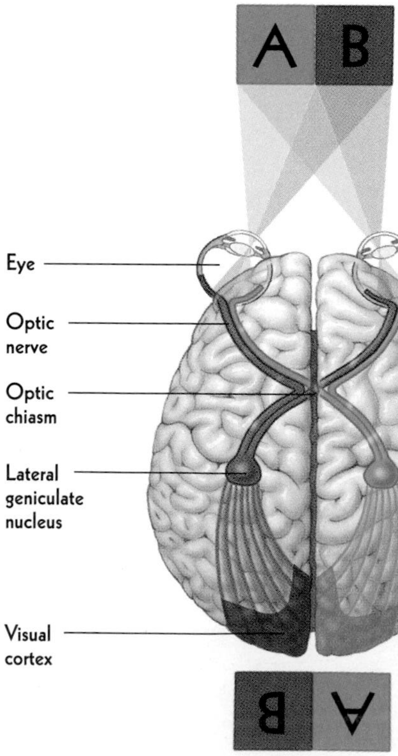

Dark adaptation: Increased sensitivity to light in a dark environment; when a person moves from a light environment to a dark one, chemicals in the rods and cones regenerate and return to their inactive state, and light sensitivity increases.

Optic chiasm [KI-azm]: The point at which half of the optic nerve fibres from each eye cross over and project to the other side of the brain.

Receptive fields: The areas of the retina that, when stimulated, produce a change in the firing of cells in the visual system.

Dark adaptation is the increase in sensitivity that occurs when the illumination level changes from high (bright) to low (dark). In dark adaptation, chemicals in the photoreceptors (rods and cones) regenerate and return to their inactive state and light sensitivity increases. If you go from a well-lit lobby into a dark theatre, for example, you will experience a brief period of low light sensitivity, during which you will be unable to distinguish empty seats. However, this inability to see objects quickly passes and your sensitivity increases. Of course, after leaving a dark theatre and returning to the afternoon sunlight, you must squint or shade your eyes until they become adapted to the light.

Figure 3.4 shows a dark adaptation curve. The first part of the curve is determined by cones, the second part by rods. The speed at which the photochemicals in the rods and cones regenerate determines the shape of the two parts of the curve. Your cones adapt to reduced levels of light in about 7 to 10 minutes. Your rods begin adapting after 10 minutes and are maximally adapted by 30 minutes.

Higher Pathways. Each eye is connected to both sides of the brain; its optic nerve fibres travel in equal halves to each hemisphere of the brain—for example, half of the fibres from the left eye go to the right side of the brain. The point at which the fibres from the right and left eyes cross over is called the **optic chiasm** (see Figures 3.5 and 3.6). This crossover of nerve fibres allows the brain to process two sets of signals (one from each eye) from an image and helps human beings perceive form in depth. As electrical impulses leave the retina through the optic nerve, they proceed to higher centres of the brain, including the lateral geniculate nucleus and the visual cortex, or striate cortex (see Figure 3.5). These connections are quite specific (Mason & Sretavan, 1997).

Knowledge of how electrochemical signals are processed in the striate cortex comes from studies of receptive fields and associated pathways. **Receptive fields** are areas of the retina that, when stimulated, produce a change in the firing of cells higher in the visual system. For example, specific cells will fire, or become active, if a vertical line is presented to the retina but not if a horizontal line is presented. Many perceptual psychologists refer to these stimulated visual system cells as *feature detectors*. David Hubel and Torsten Wiesel (1962) found receptive fields that are sensitive to such features of a stimulus line as its position, length, movement, colour, or intensity. Hubel and Wiesel characterized the responding critical feature-detecting cells as simple, complex, or hypercomplex. *Simple cells* respond to bars of light in a particular orientation. *Complex cells* respond

brain and behaviour
Prosopagnosia—Do I Know You?

Shania Twain, Michael J. Fox, Celine Dion, and Dan Ackroyd all have striking faces. So do Jean Chrétien, Queen Elizabeth, and Pierre Trudeau. Faces define and differentiate people. Whether a person's eyes, teeth, or hair are facial "landmarks" is unclear, but the perception of faces is special. We all engage in the perceptual task of gazing at, discerning, analyzing, remembering, and recognizing faces. Even in the first weeks of life, newborns are able to distinguish faces from other objects, and they quickly develop the ability to recognize their principal caregiver's face (Fantz, 1961).

Research on brain structure shows that there is something special about face perception that distinguishes it from other kinds of perception. Some interesting evidence comes from studies of agnosia. People with **agnosia** have normal, intact perceptual systems—for detecting colours, shape, and motion—and have no verbal, memory, or intellectual impairment. And yet they are unable to recognize things they should be able to. Agnosia usually occurs because of injury to the brain from an accident, or perhaps because of a stroke. A patient with agnosia can see stimuli but cannot name them. When presented with an object—a cup or a candle, for example—an agnosic is not able to name it. Some visual agnosias are very specific—for example, colour agnosia, movement agnosia, and object agnosia.

Ruth M. had a special type of agnosia that prevented her from recognizing people from their facial characteristics. She could identify objects, scenes, and places, but if presented with the face of a friend, she went blank. This kind of agnosia is called prosopagnosia—the inability to recognize faces. When such patients are shown a picture of a spouse, mother, friend, or even themselves, they cannot name the person in the photo.

They know that an image is a face, but they cannot tell one face from another. Research shows that such patients often have other perceptual problems as well, but that their ability to recognize faces is exceptionally impaired (Farah, Levinson, & Klein, 1995).

Is it possible that there are special regions of the brain responsible for prosopagnosia? Are there "face detectors"? Several lines of evidence support this notion. First, research shows that certain brain cells are activated by facial stimuli and not by other stimuli (Renault et al., 1989). Some individual cells (around the temporal lobes) respond best to faces, sometimes even to faces in a particular orientation, such as frontal or profile views. Unfortunately, the appealing idea of "one-face, one-neuron" is somewhat flawed, because it would not be adaptive to rely solely on one neuron to recognize important and familiar people in our lives (neurons die all the time!). We know that people are particularly skilled at recognizing faces, but when faces are distorted, turned upside-down, or otherwise taken out of normal perspective, face recognition is far more difficult (Farah et al., 1998; McNeil & Warrington, 1993), though still possible. The photo shows a sculpture of Prince Charles. Despite the gross exaggeration of his features, you can still tell who he is. This suggests that parts of faces do not make up face recognition—it is the totality of what we see that is important. In the end, this leads some researchers to believe that face perception depends on a specialized, neurophysiologically distinct processing system.

Remember that patients with agnosia have lesions or damage to a specific area of the brain, so the conclusion that specific brain areas are responsible for perceptual abilities is logical. But face perception cannot occur through analysis of perception of specific

features. We know that single features, or even combinations of them, do not allow for any meaningful level of facial recognition (Farah, O'Reilly, & Vecera, 1993). The whole—the face—seems to be more than the sum of its parts. So, prosopagnosics may suffer from such deficits because the visual system is interactive—when one part is not operating well, or is damaged, other parts are affected (Tovee & Cohen, 1993). There are multiple pathways and areas that process visual information, any of which might contribute to prosopagnosia and other agnosias (Wacholtz, 1996). Our ability to recognize faces depends on an ability to recognize components—eyes, ears, teeth, and so on—but it also depends on many systems from both sides of the brain acting together (Rapcsak et al., 1994).

Psychologists study agnosia in general, and prosopagnosia in particular, because it helps them understand the specific areas of the brain. But such study also leads to the conclusion that our visual system is made up of interacting and interdependent parts that create a whole visual experience. Some tasks require very specific object recognition, but other tasks, such as face perception, require a more holistic, interactive analysis that depends on both hemispheres of the brain (Rumiati & Humphreys, 1997) and on the whole brain acting in concert (Farah, 1990). The whole-versus-part distinction as it relates to prosopagnosia continues to be a cutting-edge research issue that ultimately may help determine relationships between the brain and behaviour. ■

Agnosia: An inability to recognize a sensory stimulus that should be recognizable (because all normal perceptual processes are intact and there is no verbal, memory, or intellectual impairment).

most vigorously to a bar of light moving in a particular direction. *Hypercomplex cells* are the most specific; they respond only to a bar of light of a particular length and orientation that moves in a particular direction. The work of Hubel and Wiesel earned them a Nobel Prize in 1981 and has been supported and extended by other noted researchers (e.g., Livingston, 1990; Heeger, 1994). According to Hubel and Wiesel electrical coding moves from simple analysis to more complex analysis as information proceeds through the visual system (Maunsell, 1995; Schiller, 1994).

Psychologists now know that receptive fields also help link visual perception of space to body movements; for example, when you reach over and turn off your alarm clock in the morning. Receptive fields are associated not only with every area of the visual cortex but with some non-visual areas; for example, receptive fields stimulate cells in the parietal cortex, which is associated with spatial orientation (Corbetta et al., 1995; Serno et al., 1995), and in the temporal lobe, which is involved in the recognition of faces and other commonly recognized objects (Allison et al., 1994). Receptive fields may be linked together in complex ways (Zeki, 1992), as it is unlikely that a direct, strong connection exists between individual cells—our perceptual system is just too sophisticated and adaptable (Crick and Koch, 1998) to involve unchangeable, hard-wired connections.

Receptive fields may be a key element in understanding perception, but we also know that the visual system separates processing of an object's form and colour—*what* it is—from its spatial location—*where* it is. Both behavioural and neural evidence exists to support such a distinction. Kirpatrick and Wasserman (1997) found evidence of "what" and "where" information in a visual discrimination task performed with animals. In humans, Mecklinger and Muller (1996) found distinctions in memory stores. Furthermore, prefrontal cortical neurons seem to be tuned to detect either "what" information or "where" information, and some cells seem to respond to *both* "what" and "where" an object is. Rao, Rainer, and Miller (1997) and Kilgard and Merzenich (1998) have found high degrees of specificity for "what" and "where" cells in the prefrontal cortex, and suggest that not only is this area sensitive to experience (plastic) but it may hold the key to understanding how we link objects to places, as when we follow directions according to landmarks ("the park across from the elementary school").

Study of electrochemical changes in the visual system shows that the brain processes many components of a scene—what, where, when, colour, movement—simultaneously. We refer to such simultaneous processing of information as *parallel processing* in contrast to simple step-by-step or *serial processing*. As you think about what happens to visual stimulation as it proceeds to the brain, you can image the multiple types of processing that exist at multiple levels of the brain, all at the same time. Such parallel processing allows for fast recognition of complexities in the world; it also explains how brain-damaged individuals can recognize some elements of a scene and not others. It helps explain why Jean-Claude, the reading disabled boy whose story opened this chapter, can be smart and astute, able to see, play the piano, and draw, but unable to map sounds to letters. Representation and interpretation of the world happens in multiple brain locations, and for Jean-Claude some of those locations are operating differently or less efficiently. The concept of parallel processing is also important to an understanding of a perceptual problem known as prosopagnosia, described in *Brain and Behaviour* on page 85.

Eye Movements

Your eyes can fixate on a target or be in constant motion. They search for familiar faces in a crowded classroom, scan a page of headlines and articles in a newspaper, or follow a baseball hit high into right field for a home run. These eye movements allow us to position our eyes so that an image will fall on the fovea, the area where fine detail is processed. As such, eye movements play an important role in vision. Research on eye movements reveals what people are looking at, how long they look at it, and perhaps where they will look next. The study of eye movements also may contribute to a better understanding of some puzzling research questions, such as the nature of reading disabilities. Abnormal eye movements are commonly observed in poor readers when they encounter difficult text (Rayner, 1985; Schiffman, 1990). However, it is unclear whether these abnormalities are causally related to the reading disability or whether they reflect other underlying neural difficulties (Livingstone et al., 1991; Raymond et al., 1988). There are three different kinds of eye movements. The first, *saccadic eye movements*, involves rapid shifts of gaze from one object to another; the second, *smooth pursuit eye movements*, follows moving targets; and the third, *vestibular eye movements*, allows the eyes to remain steady while the head and body are in motion.

Saccades are the most common type of eye movement—in fact, the eyes make at least 100 000 saccades per day. They are the voluntary eye movements made when the eyes jump from one location to another, such as when you are reading, driving, or looking for an object. The eyes can make only four or five saccades in a second. Each movement takes only about 20 to 50 milliseconds, but there is a delay of about 200 to 250 milliseconds before the next movement can be made. During this delay the eyes fixate on some part of the visual field. People use eye *fixations* to form representations of the visual world, probably by integrating successive glances into memory (Rayner & Pollatsek, 1992). Noton and Stark (1971) have demonstrated that individuals use uniquely characteristic eye movement patterns (see Figure 3.7) when viewing pictures for later identification.

Smooth pursuit movements are automatic, smooth eye movements that follow a moving stimulus. This type of eye movement is used to track a moving object, such as a golf ball rolling (hopefully) towards the hole.

Vestibular eye movements compensate for head or body movement. Whenever the head moves, the eyes reflexively make a compensatory movement so that a stable environment is perceived. Ask a friend to stare at your nose while turning her head from side to side. Observe how her eyes move in relation to her head movements.

When researchers study eye movements they study the process from the bottom up and from the top down, examining the physiology and nature of the actual movements and the reasons those movements might or might not occur.

Colour Vision

Think of all the different shades of blue (navy blue, sky blue, baby blue, royal blue, turquoise, aqua). If you are like most people, you have no trouble discriminating among a wide range of colours. Colour depends on the wavelength of light particles that stimulate the photoreceptors. It has three psychological dimensions: hue, brightness, and saturation. These dimensions correspond to three physical properties of light: wavelength, intensity, and purity.

When people speak of the colour of an object, they are referring to its **hue**—whether the light reflected from the object looks red, blue, orange, or some other colour. *Hue* is a psychological term, because objects themselves do not possess colour. Rather, a person's perception of colour is determined by how the eyes and brain interpret reflected wavelengths. In the visible spectrum, a different hue is associated with each wavelength. Light with a wavelength of 400–450 nanometres looks blue; light with a wavelength of 700 nanometres looks red.

The second psychological dimension of colour is **brightness**—how light or dark the hue of an object appears. Brightness is affected by three variables: (1) The greater the intensity of reflected light, the brighter the object; (2) the shorter the wavelength of reflected light, the brighter the object; (3) the nearer the wavelengths are to being in the 500 to 600 nanometre (yellow) range, the more sensitive the photoreceptors (see Figure 3.8). This is why school buses and fire engines are often painted yellow—they are more visible to motorists.

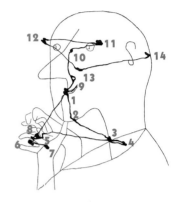

FIGURE 3.7
Scan Paths Are Highly Individual
This scan path shows eye movements made by a person viewing a drawing adapted from Paul Klee's *Old Man Figuring*. The numbers show the order of the visual fixations. Lines between the numbers represent saccades, which occupied about 10% of the viewing time. The remainder of the time was spent fixating.

Saccades [sack-ADZ]: Rapid voluntary movements of the eyes, to focus on different points.

Smooth pursuit movements: Automatic, smooth eye movements that follow a moving stimulus.

Vestibular eye movements: Reflexive eye movements that compensate for head or body movement.

Hue: The psychological property of light referred to as colour and determined by the wavelength reflected from an object.

Brightness: The lightness or darkness of reflected light, determined in large part by the light's intensity.

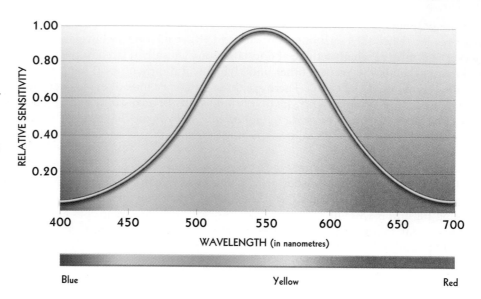

FIGURE 3.8
Human Beings Are More Sensitive to Yellow Than to Any Other Wavelength

The average observer's sensitivity to visible light during daylight reaches a peak at 555 nanometres. Thus, the normal human eye is more sensitive to yellow wavelengths than to red or blue. The curve in the graph is called a *spectral sensitivity curve*.

FIGURE 3.9
Hue, Brightness, and Saturation

These colours have the same dominant wavelength (hue) but different saturation and brightness.

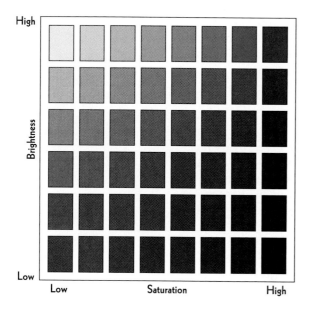

The third psychological dimension of colour is **saturation**, or *purity*—the depth and richness of hue of reflected light, determined by the homogeneity of the wavelengths contained in the light. Few objects reflect light that is totally pure. Usually objects reflect a mixture of wavelengths. Pure, saturated light has a narrow band of wavelengths and, thus, a narrow range of perceived colour. A saturated red light with no blue, yellow, or white in it, for example, appears as a very intense red.

Unsaturated colours are produced by a wider band of wavelengths. Unsaturated red light can appear to be light pink, dark red, or brownish, because its wider range of wavelengths makes it less pure (see Figure 3.9).

Theories of Colour Vision. How does the brain code and process colour? Two nineteenth-century scientists, Thomas Young and Hermann von Helmholtz, working independently, proposed that different types of cones provide the basis for colour coding in the visual system. *Colour coding* is the ability to discriminate among colours on the basis of differences in wavelength. According to the **trichromatic theory**, or the *Young–Helmholtz theory*, mixing three basic colours (red, green, and blue) can make all colours. (*Trichromatic* means "three colours"; *tri* means "three" and *chroma* means "colour.") All cone cells in the retina are assumed to respond to all wavelengths that stimulate them; but there are three types of cones that respond maximally to the red, green, or blue wavelength (see Figure 3.10). The proportional combination of neural output of the red-sensitive, green-sensitive, and blue-sensitive cones provides the information that enables a person to distinguish colour. Because each person's neurons are unique, it is likely that each of us sees colour somewhat differently.

Unfortunately, the trichromatic theory does not explain some specific visual phenomena well. For example, it does not explain why some colours look more vivid when placed next to others (colour contrast). It does not explain why people asked to name the basic colours nearly always name more than three. Further, the trichromatic theory does not do a good job of explaining aspects of **colour blindness**—the inability to perceive different hues. For example, many people with colour deficiencies cannot discriminate colours successfully in two areas of the visual spectrum. In 1887, to resolve some of the problems

Saturation: The depth of hue of reflected light, as determined by the homogeneity of the wavelengths contained in the light. Also known as *purity*.

Trichromatic theory [try-kroe-MAT-ick]: The visual theory, stated by Young and Helmholtz, that all colours can be made by mixing three basic colours: red, green, and blue. Also known as the *Young–Helmholtz theory*.

Colour blindness: The inability to perceive different hues.

left unsolved by the trichromatic theory, Ewald Herring proposed another theory of colour vision—the **opponent-process theory**. This theory assumes that there are six basic colours to which people respond and that there are three types of receptors: red–green, blue–yellow, and black–white. Every receptor fires in response to all wavelengths, but in each pair of receptors, one receptor fires maximally to one wavelength. Maximum firing to red, for example, is accompanied by a low rate of firing to green. Opponent-process theory explains colour contrast and colour blindness better than the trichromatic theory.

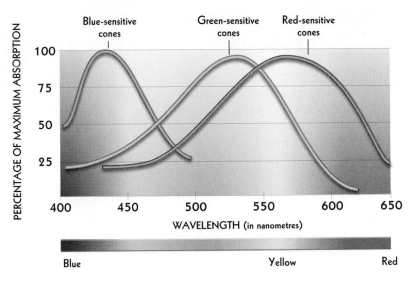

FIGURE 3.10
Three Types of Cones
Each of the three types of cones in the eye has peak sensitivity in a different area of the visible spectrum. Thus, certain cells are more responsive to some wavelengths than to others.

Both the trichromatic theory and the opponent-process theory have received support from research (e.g., Hurvich & Jameson, 1974). Studies of the chemistry and absorptive properties of the retina do show three classes of cones. Thus, the trichromatic theory seems to describe accurately the coding at the retina (Marks, Dobell, & MacNichol, 1964). Support for the opponent-process theory comes from microelectrode studies of the lateral geniculate nucleus in monkeys. Cells in this nucleus respond differently to various wavelengths. When the eye is stimulated with light of a wavelength between 400 and 500 nanometres, some cells in the lateral geniculate nucleus decrease their rate of firing. If the eye is stimulated with a longer-wavelength light, the firing rate increases (DeValois & Jacobs, 1968). This change is predicted by the opponent-process theory. Exactly how colour information is transferred from the retina to the lateral geniculate nucleus remains to be discovered. Some of the data that helped test the trichromatic and opponent-process theories came from people with abnormal colour vision.

Colour Blindness. In 1794, John Dalton, formulator of the atomic theory of matter, believed he had figured out why he couldn't distinguish his red stockings from his green ones. He reasoned that something blue in his eyeball absorbed red light and prevented him from seeing red. Dalton was not the first person to suffer from red–green colour blindness, but he was the first to try to describe it scientifically. In fact, today about 8 percent of males and 0.5 percent of females have some form of colour deficiency (Nathans, 1989).

Most human beings have normal colour vision and can distinguish among about 100 different hues; they are considered trichromats. **Trichromats** are people who can perceive all three primary colours and thus can distinguish any colour. A very few people (less than 1 percent) do not see any colour. These people, known as **monochromats**, are totally colour-blind and cannot discriminate among wavelengths, often because they lack cone receptors in their retinas (Boynton, 1988). The lack of a specific colour-absorbing pigment or chemical in the cones makes accurate colour discriminations impossible. Fortunately, most people with colour vision deficiencies (about 8 percent of men and 1 percent of women) are only partially colour-deficient (Nathans, 1989). **Dichromats** are people who can distinguish only two of the three basic hues; they have deficiencies in either the red–green or the blue–yellow area. About 2 percent of men cannot discriminate between reds and greens (Wyszecki & Stiles, 1967). What does the world look like to a person who is a dichromat? People with a colour deficiency see all of the colours in a range of the electromagnetic spectrum as the same. For example, to a person with a blue–yellow deficiency, all greens, blues, and violets look the same; a person with a red–green deficiency may see red, green, and yellow as yellow. Many colour-blind individuals have distorted colour responses in several areas of the electromagnetic spectrum; that is, they have trouble with several colours.

Opponent-process theory: The theory, proposed by Herring, that colour is coded by stimulation of three types of paired receptors; each pair of receptors is assumed to operate in an antagonistic way so that stimulation by a given wavelength produces excitation of one receptor of the pair and inhibition of the other receptor.

Trichromats [TRY-kroe-MATZ]: People who can perceive all three primary colours and thus who can distinguish any colour.

Monochromats [MON-o-kroe-MATZ]: People who cannot perceive any colour, usually because their retinas contain only rods.

Dichromats [DIE-kroe-MATZ]: People who can distinguish only two of the three basic hues.

Focus

Review

- Describe how the visual system works when light hits the eye. pp. 82–83
- What is the evidence for the duplicity theory of vision? pp. 83–84
- What do receptive fields tell researchers about the perceptual process? p. 84, 86

Think Critically

- Viewing traditional 3-D comics through special glasses creates the perception of depth. Explain how you think this might work.
- Why do you think that psychologists prefer to use the term *colour-deficient* rather than *colour-blind* when describing people who have trouble seeing colours?

The precise role of genetics in colour blindness is not clear, but this deficiency is transmitted genetically from mothers to their male offspring. The high number of men who are colour-blind, compared to women, is due to the way the genetic information is coded and passed on to each generation. The genetic transmission occurs on the twenty-third pair of chromosomes and results from inherited alterations in the genes on the X chromosome that are responsible for cone pigments. Since girls have two X chromosomes and boys have only one, a girl will only be colour-deficient if she inherits the defective gene from both parents.

Visual Perception

As we said at the beginning of this chapter, perceptual experiences use sensory input but also involve past events in addition to current stimulation. Integrating previous experiences with new events makes perceptual encounters more meaningful. For example, it is only with experience that children learn that an object stays the same size and shape when it is moved away from their immediate location. In this section, we will look at a range of visual perceptual phenomena that rely heavily on the integration of past and current experiences.

Perception of Form: Constancy

Perceptual constancy is the maintenance of a stable perception in the presence of continual, substantial variation in physical stimulation. For example, you recognize your dog whether you are viewing it from the side, the front, or the back. You recognize it in low light, whether it is close or far away. Despite variations in size, shape, and luminance you recognize your pet. This ability to perceive enduring qualities in the face of enormous change is impressive. Thus the perceptual constancy task cannot simply rely on sensory stimuli. We must evaluate and interpret the sensory input, relying on our memories of and our experiences with stable objects and a reasonably permanent world.

Size Constancy. People generally can judge the size of an object, even if the size of its image on the retina changes. For example, you can estimate the height of a six-foot man who is standing 15 metres away and who casts a small image on the retina; you can also estimate his height from only two metres away, when he casts a much larger image on the retina. **Size constancy** is the ability of the perceptual system to recognize that an object remains constant in size regardless of its distance from the observer or the size of its image on the retina.

Three variables determine a person's ability to maintain size constancy: (1) experience with the true size of objects, (2) the distance between the object and the person, and (3) the presence of surrounding objects. As an object is moved farther away, the size of its image on the retina decreases and its perceived distance

Size constancy: The ability of the perceptual system to recognize that an object remains constant in size regardless of its distance from the observer or the size of its image on the retina.

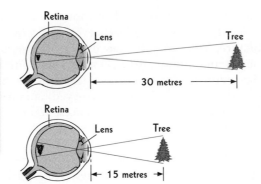

SIZE CONSTANCY: The size of the image on the retina gets larger or smaller as you move closer to or farther away from an object. But thanks to size constancy, you still perceive the object as being the same size.

Retina
Lens
Tree
30 metres

Retina
Lens
Tree
15 metres

FIGURE 3.11
Perceptual Constancies
Size constancy is the perceptual system's ability to recognize that an object remains the same size regardless of its distance from an observer or the size of its image on the retina. *Shape constancy* is the perceptual system's ability to recognize a shape despite changes in the angle or position from which it is viewed.

SHAPE CONSTANCY: A door is a door is a door . . . whether it is open, shut, or viewed at an angle.

increases (see Figure 3.11). These two processes always work together. Moreover, as an object is moved away, its size relative to the objects around it does not change. This is why knowing the size of surrounding objects helps people determine the moved object's distance as well as its actual size.

Researchers have studied how experience helps people establish and maintain size constancy. Bower (1966) trained 50- to 60-day-old infants to look towards a specific object by reinforcing their direction of gaze (the reinforcement was an adult saying "peekaboo"). He then placed other objects of different sizes at various distances from the infants so that the sizes of their retinal images varied. Finally, he arranged the objects so that the small ones were close to the infants and the large ones were farther away, causing the sizes of retinal images to be the same. In all of these situations, the infants showed size constancy. They turned their heads only towards the original reinforced object, not towards the other objects that produced images of the same size on the retina. It is clear that infants attain size constancy by the age of six months and probably as early as four months (Luger, Bower, & Wishart, 1983; McKenzie, Tootell, & Day, 1980).

Shape Constancy. Another important aspect of form perception is **shape constancy**—the ability to recognize a shape despite changes in the angle or position from which it is viewed (see Figure 3.11). For example, even though you usually see trees standing perpendicular to the ground, you can recognize a tree when it has been chopped down and is lying in a horizontal position. Similarly, an ice cream cone looks triangular when you view it from the side; yet you perceive it as an ice cream cone even when you view it from above, where it appears more circular than triangular.

Shape constancy: The ability to recognize a shape despite changes in the orientation or angle from which it is viewed.

Depth Perception

For centuries, Zen landscape artists have used the principles of perception to create seemingly expansive, rugged gardens

out of tiny plots of land. Although a Zen landscape artist can fool the eye, you judge the distance of objects every day when you drive a car, catch a ball, or take a picture. You estimate your distance from an object and the distance between one object and another. Closely associated with these two tasks is the ability to see in three dimensions—that is, in terms of height, width, and depth. Both monocular (one-eyed) and binocular (two-eyed) cues are used in depth perception. Binocular cues predominate at close distances, and monocular cues are used for distant scenes and two-dimensional fields of view, such as paintings.

Monocular Depth Cues. Depth cues that do not depend on the use of both eyes are **monocular depth cues** (see Figure 3.12). There are dynamic and static monocular depth cues. Two important dynamic monocular depth cues relate to the

FIGURE 3.12
Depth Perception
The ability to see in three dimensions—height, width, and depth—depends on both monocular and binocular cues.

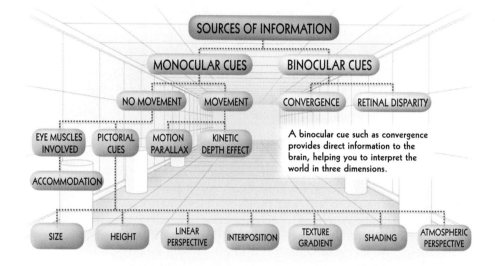

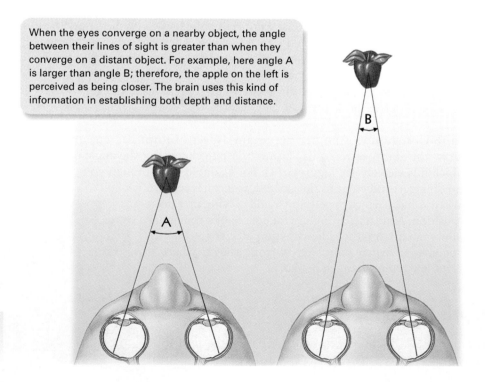

When the eyes converge on a nearby object, the angle between their lines of sight is greater than when they converge on a distant object. For example, here angle A is larger than angle B; therefore, the apple on the left is perceived as being closer. The brain uses this kind of information in establishing both depth and distance.

Monocular depth cues [mah-NAHK-you-ler]: Depth cues that do not depend on the use of both eyes.

effects of motion on perception. The first cue, *motion parallax*, occurs when a moving observer stares at a fixed point. The objects behind that point appear to move in the same direction as the observer; the objects in front of the point appear to move in the opposite direction. For example, if you stare at a fence while riding in a moving car, the trees behind the fence rails seem to move in the same direction as the car (forward) and the bushes in front of the rails seem to move in the opposite direction (backwards). Motion parallax also affects the speed at which objects appear to move. Objects at a greater distance from the moving observer appear to move more slowly than objects that are closer. The second monocular depth cue derived from movement is the *kinetic depth effect*. Objects that look flat when they are stationary appear to be three-dimensional when set in motion. When two-dimensional projections—such as images of squares or rods shown on a computer screen—are rotated, they appear to have three dimensions.

Static monocular depth cues are often seen in photographs and paintings. For example, larger or taller objects usually are perceived to be closer than smaller ones, particularly in relation to surrounding objects. In addition, *linear perspective* affects perception; this cue is based on the principle that distant objects appear to be closer together than nearer objects. For example, a painter shows distance by making parallel lines converge as they recede. Another monocular cue for depth is *interposition*. When one object blocks part of another, the first appears to be closer. A fourth monocular cue is *texture*; surfaces that have little texture or detail seem to be in the distance. Artists often use the additional cues of *highlighting* and *shadowing*. Highlighted (light) objects appear close; shadowed (dark) objects appear to be farther away. In addition, the perceptual system picks up other information from shadowing, including the curvature of surfaces (Cavanagh & Leclerc, 1989). Still another monocular depth cue is *atmospheric perspective*, which relates to light wavelengths themselves. Distant mountains often look blue, for example, because long (red) wavelengths are more easily scattered as they pass through the air, allowing more short (blue) wavelengths to reach our eyes. Leonardo da Vinci used this phenomenon in his paintings; he even developed an equation for how much blue pigment should be mixed with the natural colour of an object so the object would appear as far away as he wished. Michelangelo's angels seem to float off the ceiling of the Sistine Chapel because he used colour so effectively to portray depth.

If a person looks from one object to another one at a different distance, the lenses of the eye will accommodate—that is, change shape to adapt to the depth of focus. This monocular cue is available from each eye separately. **Accommodation** is the change in the shape of the lens that enables the observer to keep an object in focus on the retina when the object is moved or when the choice of objects changes. Muscles attached to the lens control this change, which provides information about the shape of the lens to the higher processing systems in the brain.

Binocular Depth Cues. Most people, even infants, also use **binocular depth cues**—cues requiring the use of both eyes. One important binocular depth cue is **retinal disparity**, which is the slight difference between the visual images projected on the two retinas. Retinal disparity occurs because the eyes are physically five to seven centimetres apart, which causes them to see objects from slightly different angles. To see how retinal disparity works, hold a finger up in front of some distant object. Examine the object first with one eye and then with the other eye. Your finger will appear in different positions relative to the object. The closer objects are to the eyes, the farther apart their images on the retinas will be—and the greater the retinal disparity. Objects at a great distance produce little retinal disparity.

Another binocular depth cue is convergence. **Convergence** is the movement of the eyes towards each other in order to keep visual input at corresponding points on the retinas as an object moves closer to the observer. Like accommodation, convergence is controlled by muscles in the eye that convey information to the brain and thus provide a potent physiological depth cue for stimuli close to observers. When an object is beyond 7 to 10 metres away, the eyes are aimed pretty much in parallel, and the effect of this cue diminishes. When we wish to look at objects further away, our eyes diverge, rotating outward, each moving in an opposite direction.

Illusions

Have you ever seen water ahead on the road, only to find it has disappeared a moment later as you drive by that spot? When the normal visual process and depth cues seem to break down, you experience an optical illusion. An **illusion** is a perception of a physical stimulus that differs from measurable reality and the commonly expected appearance; many consider it a misperception of stimulation.

A common illusion is the *Müller–Lyer illusion*, in which two equal-length lines with arrows attached to their ends appear to be of different lengths. A similar illusion is the *Ponzo illusion* (sometimes called the railroad illusion), in which two horizontal lines of the same length, bracketed by slanted lines, appear to be of different lengths. (See Figure 3.13 for examples of these two illusions and three others. Figure 3.14 presents another perceptual phenomenon.) One natural illusion is the moon illusion. Although the actual size of the moon and the size of its image on the retina do not change, the moon appears about 30 percent larger when it is near the horizon than when it is overhead. The *moon illusion* is quite striking. In just a few minutes, the size of the moon appears to change from quite large to quite small. The moon illusion is even seen in photographs and paintings (Coren & Aks, 1990).

How do visual illusions work? No completely satisfactory explanations have been found. Recent theories account for them in terms of the backgrounds against which the objects are seen.

FIGURE 3.13
Five Well-Known Illusions
In the Müller-Lyer and Ponzo illusions, lines of equal length appear to differ in length. The photos with the Müller-Lyer illusion show how the arrows can represent a "near corner" and a "far corner." In the Zollner illusion, the short lines make the longer ones seem not parallel, even though they are. In the Wundt illusion, the centre horizontal lines are parallel, even though they appear bent. In the Poggendorf illusion, the line disappears behind a solid and reappears in a position that seems wrong.

Ponzo Illusion

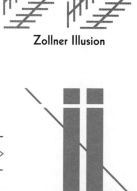

Zollner Illusion

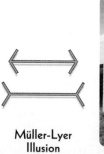

Müller-Lyer
Illusion

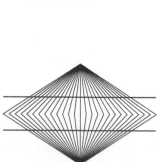

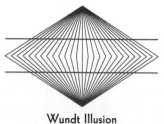

Wundt Illusion

Poggendorf Illusion

These explanations are based on the observer's previous experiences and well-developed perceptual constancies. (*Diversity* on page 96 explores how cultural experiences affect the experience of illusions.) For example, the moon illusion is explained by the fact that, when seen overhead, the moon has a featureless background, whereas at the horizon objects are close to it. Objects in the landscape provide cues about distance that change the observer's perception of the size of the moon (Baird, Wagner, & Fuld, 1990; Restle, 1970). To see how the moon illusion depends on landscape cues, try this: When the moon is at the horizon, bend over and look at it from between your legs. Since that position screens out some of the horizon cues, the magnitude of the illusion will be reduced.

The Ponzo illusion is similarly accounted for by the linear perspective provided by the slanted background lines. The Müller–Lyer illusion occurs because of the angle and shape of the arrows attached to the ends of the lines. Lines angled inwards are often interpreted as far corners—those that are most distant from the observer. Lines angled outwards are commonly interpreted as near corners—those that are closest to the observer. Therefore, lines with far-corner angles attached to them appear longer because their length is judged in a context of distance.

These are not the only ways of explaining illusions. Some researchers assert that people see the moon as having different sizes on the horizon and overhead because they judge it as they judge other moving objects that pass through space. Because the moon does not move closer to them, they assume it is moving away. Objects that move away get smaller; hence the illusion of a change in the size of the moon (Reed, 1984). This explanation focuses on constancies but also takes account of movement, space, and the atmosphere.

FIGURE 3.14
Impossible Figures
Many types of drawings trick the perceiver because they portray *impossible figures*. The longer you stare at this drawing by M. C. Escher, the more visually confusing you'll find the arrangement of its components.

Gestalt Laws of Organization

Gestalt psychologists suggest that conscious experience is more than the sum of its parts. They argue that the mind organizes the elements of experience to form something unique; they thus view the world in terms of perceptual frameworks. Analyzed as a whole experience, the patterns of a person's perceptions make sense. The first Gestalt psychologists—including Max Wertheimer, Kurt Koffka, and Wolfgang Köhler—greatly influenced early theories of form perception. These psychologists assumed (wrongly) that human perceptual processes *solely* reflect brain organization and that they could learn about the workings of the brain by studying perception. Researchers now know, of course, that the relationship between brain structure and function is much more complex—perception is a process that not only represents stimuli but reflects past experiences as well.

The early Gestaltists focused their perceptual studies on the ways in which people experience form and organization. These early researchers believed people organize each complex visual field into a coherent whole rather than seeing individual, unrelated elements. That is, they believed people see groups of elements, not fragmented parts. According to this idea, called the **law of Prägnanz**, items or stimuli that *can* be grouped together and seen as a whole, or a form, *will* be seen that way; people see the simplest shape consistent with available information. So, for example, people tend to see the series of 16 dots in the lower left portion of Figure 3.15 as a square. Not only did the Gestaltists see the world through the lenses of grouping and form but they also felt that retinal stimulation was directly reflected in physiological processing.

Law of Prägnanz [PREG-nants]: The Gestalt principle that when items or stimuli *can* be grouped together and seen as a whole, they *will* be.

Cross-cultural Research on Illusions

If you travel across Canada and take note of the advertisements in the local newspapers and on the local television stations you probably will notice differences in each region or city. As well, if you compare those advertisements to similar ones in the United States you may note a few distinct aspects shared by the Canadian advertisements.

Each person brings a lifetime of experiences to his or her perceptions. This becomes especially clear from research conducted cross-culturally. Cross-cultural research on illusions, for example, shows that the Müller–Lyer and Ponzo illusions are perceived differently by different cultures. Leibowitz (1971) conducted a series of studies on the Ponzo illusion using both American participants and participants from Guam, where there are no railroads and perspective cues are far less prevalent than in the United States. Leibowitz had his participants judge the Ponzo illusion in line drawings and in photographs. He found that the degree of the illusion increased for the American participants as he added more pictorial depth cues. The participants from Guam showed few differences when more pictorial cues were added. Other differences also existed; for example, the participants from Guam viewed depth differently than their American counterparts. The different cultures viewed the world in dissimilar ways.

Other illusions have been investigated with different cultural groups. For example, Pedersen and Wheeler (1983) compared the reactions of two groups of Navajos to the Müller–Lyer illusion. One group lived in rectangular houses, where the individuals had extensive experience with corners, angles, and oblique lines. The other group lived in traditional Navajo round houses, similar to the Zulu roundhouse shown in the photo, where early experiences included far fewer encounters with angles. The researchers found that those who lived in angular houses were more susceptible to the Müller–Lyer illusion, which depends on angles. Some researchers say that such illusions depend on the *carpenter effect*, because in Western cultures carpenters use lines, angles, and geometry to build houses.

Although there is little systematic scientific evidence on the topic, musicians have long known that a person's experiences with Western music make 12-tone music and Indian and Asian melodies sound unfamiliar and dissonant. The perception of music, like the perception of illusions, depends on early experiences. Research shows that people's visual and auditory perceptions are also culturally dependent. Deregowski (1980) asserts that there is a dearth of non-Western studies; yet he is able to conclude in his review of studies of language, pictures, smell, and illusions that there are cross-cultural differences that reflect people's cultures. Individuals from other cultures initially do not see illusions and some features of depth; but when key characteristics of pictures and scenes are pointed out, they often exclaim, "Oh, now I see it!" Yet initially they fail to recognize visual cues that individuals from Western cultures do perceive. Cross-cultural research is exciting and illuminating, though unfortunately limited in its extent. For psychologists to develop truly comprehensive theories of perception, they must incorporate cross-cultural differences into their research. ■

I The law of Prägnanz was based on principles of organization for the perception of figures, especially contours, which help define figure–ground relationships. Gestalt psychologists focused on the nature of *figure–ground relationships*, contending that people perceive *figures* (the main objects of sensory attention—the foregrounds) as distinct from the *grounds* (the backgrounds) on which they are presented (see Figure 3.16). Gestalt psychologists developed the following series of laws, the first three of which are illustrated in the upper part of Figure 3.15, for predicting which areas of an ambiguous pattern would be seen as the figure (foreground) and which would be seen as the ground (background):

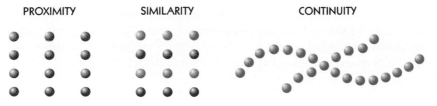

PROXIMITY   SIMILARITY   CONTINUITY

FIGURE 3.15
Gestalt Laws
Gestalt principles are the organizing elements humans use to
group perceptual fragments
into the coherent wholes by
which they perceive the world.

According to the Gestalt law of proximity, the circles on the left appear to be
arranged in vertical columns because items that are close together tend to be
perceived as a unit. According to the law of similarity, the red and blue circles
in the middle appear to be arranged in horizontal rows because similar items tend
to be perceived in groups. According to the law of continuity, an observer can
predict where the next item should occur in the arrangement on the right because
the grouping of items projects lines into space.

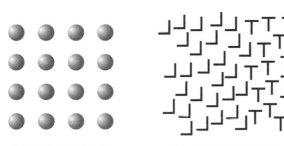

The law of Prägnanz:
Items or stimuli that *can*
be grouped together as
a whole *will* be. These
16 dots are typically
perceived as a square.

In a study asking people to divide these objects into two
groups, Beck (1966) found that participants generally
placed the boundary between upright and tilted *Ts*
rather than between the backward *Ls* and the upright *Ts*
because the latter appear more similar. Beck argued
that this result supports the law of Prägnanz.

FIGURE 3.16
The Figure–Ground
Relationship
Gestalt psychologists studied
the figure–ground relationship.
In this drawing, figure and
ground can be reversed. You
can see either two faces
against a white background or
a goblet against a dark background.

■ *Law of proximity*—elements close to one another in space or time will be
perceived as groups.

■ *Law of similarity*—similar items will be perceived as groups.

■ *Law of continuity*—a string of items will indicate where the next item in the
string will be found.

■ *Common fate principle*—items that move or change together will be
perceived as a whole.

■ *Law of closure*—parts of a figure that are
not presented will be filled in by the
perceptual system.

Beck (1966) conducted a well-known study
that examined Gestalt principles (see the lower
right portion of Figure 3.15). However, Beck's
work showed that Gestalt principles are vague:
They apply whether participants choose orientation or shape to break up the figure, but they do
not explain why orientation predominated in
Beck's study. Gestalt laws are not always
obeyed, nor are they always consistent with current knowledge of brain organization. For
example, when a figure is made up of other figures people are not always consistent in what
they choose to pay attention to, the larger figure
or the embedded smaller ones (Rock & Palmer,

Focus

Review
◆ What are the key variables that allow a person to
maintain size constancy? pp. 90–91
◆ Explain how monocular and binocular depth cues
help people see depth. pp. 92–94
◆ How do perceptual psychologists account for the
moon illusion? pp. 94–95

Think Critically
◆ What do Gestalt researchers mean when they say
that the whole is greater than the sum of its parts?
◆ How do you think culture exerts its influence on
your perceptual systems?

1990). Furthermore, our "what" and "where" processing cells are located in various locations throughout the brain—processing is not merely bottom up but also top down. Nevertheless, these early investigations continue to influence perceptual psychologists as springboards that have some elements of truth.

Hearing

You may have heard the oft-repeated idea that blind people can hear better than sighted individuals; at least with some tasks, it turns out to be true (Lessard et al., 1998). Hearing is taken for granted by most of us, but the ability and task of a listener is exceedingly complex. Consider music. Listening closely to a Beethoven symphony is delightful and intriguing, but it is difficult because so much is going on at once. With more than 20 instruments playing, the listener must process many sounds, rhythms, and intensities simultaneously. Like seeing, hearing is a complex process that involves converting physical stimuli into a psychological experience. For example, suppose that a tuning fork is struck or a stereo system booms out a bass note. In both cases, sound waves are being created and air is being moved. The movement of the air and the accompanying changes in air pressure (physical stimuli) cause your eardrum to move back and forth rapidly. The movement of the eardrum triggers a series of *electromechanical* and *electrochemical* changes that you ultimately experience as sound.

Sound

When a tuning fork, the reed of a clarinet, or a person's vocal cords are set in motion, the resulting vibrations cause sound waves. You can place your hand in front of a stereo speaker and feel the displacement of the sound waves when the volume rises. **Sound** is the psychological experience that occurs when changes in air pressure are transduced to nerve impulses at the receptive organ for hearing. The resulting tones, or sounds, vary in frequency and amplitude. Sound is often thought of in terms of two psychological aspects, pitch and loudness, which are associated with the two physical attributes of frequency and amplitude.

As shown in Figure 3.17, **frequency** is the number of times a complete change in air pressure occurs during a given unit of time. Within one second, for example, there may be 50 complete changes (50 cycles per second) or 10 000 complete changes (10 000 cycles per second). Frequency is usually measured in hertz (Hz); one Hz equals one cycle per second. Frequency determines the pitch, or *tone*, of a sound; **pitch** is the psychological experience that corresponds with the frequency of an auditory stimulus. High-pitched tones usually have high frequencies. When a piano hammer strikes a short string on the right-hand end of a piano, the string vibrates at a high frequency and sounds high in pitch; when a long string (at the left-hand end) is struck, it vibrates less frequently and sounds low in pitch.

Amplitude, or *intensity*, is the total energy of a sound wave, and determines the loudness of a sound. High-amplitude sound waves have more energy than low-amplitude waves; they apply greater force to the ear. Amplitude is measured in *decibels*. Every increase of 20 decibels corresponds to a tenfold increase in intensity. (Decibels are measured on a logarithmic scale, which means that increases are exponential, not linear; thus, increases in sound intensity measured in decibels are quite steep.) As Figure 3.18 shows, normal conversation has an amplitude of about 60 decibels, and sounds at about 120 decibels are painfully loud.

Amplitude and frequency are not correlated. A low-frequency sound can be very loud or very soft; that is, it can have either high or low amplitude. Middle C on a piano, for example, can be loud or soft. The frequency (pitch) of the sound stays the same—it is still middle C—only its amplitude (loudness) varies. The psychological

Sound: The psychological experience that occurs when changes in air pressure take place at the receptive organ for hearing; the resulting tones, or sounds, vary in frequency and amplitude.

Frequency: In sound waves, a measure of the number of times a complete change in air pressure occurs per unit of time; expressed in hertz (Hz), or cycles per second.

Pitch: The psychological experience that corresponds with the frequency of an auditory stimulus. Also known as *tone.*

Amplitude: The total energy of a sound wave, which determines the loudness of a sound. Also known as *intensity.*

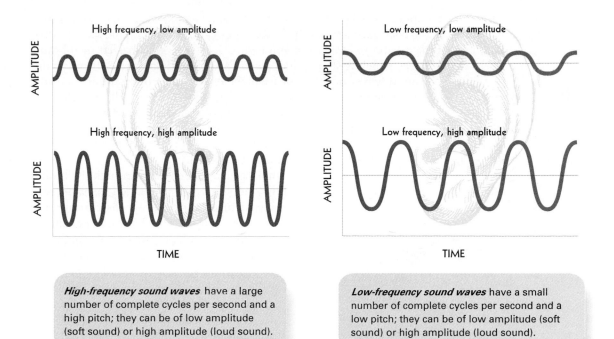

High frequency, low amplitude

AMPLITUDE

High frequency, high amplitude

AMPLITUDE

TIME

Low frequency, low amplitude

AMPLITUDE

Low frequency, high amplitude

AMPLITUDE

TIME

High-frequency sound waves have a large number of complete cycles per second and a high pitch; they can be of low amplitude (soft sound) or high amplitude (loud sound).

Low-frequency sound waves have a small number of complete cycles per second and a low pitch; they can be of low amplitude (soft sound) or high amplitude (loud sound).

FIGURE 3.17
The Frequency and Amplitude of Sound Waves
A person's psychological experience of sound depends on the frequency and amplitude of sound waves.

perception of loudness depends on other factors, such as background noise and whether the person is paying attention to the sound. Another psychological dimension, *timbre*, is the complexity of a sound—the different mixture of amplitudes and frequencies that make up the sound. For example, a piano or guitar produces many harmonics and so has greater timbre than a flute, which produces clear, pure tones. People's perceptions of all of these qualities depend on the physical structure of their ears.

Structure of the Ear

The receptive organ for *audition*, or hearing, is the ear: It translates physical stimuli (sound waves) first into mechanical motion and then into electrical impulses that the brain can interpret. The ear has three major parts: the outer ear, the middle ear, and the inner ear. The tissue on the outside of the head (the pinna) is part of the outer ear. The eardrum (*tympanic membrane*) is the boundary between the outer and middle ear. When sound waves enter the ear, they produce changes in the pressure of the air on the eardrum. The eardrum responds to these changes by vibrating.

The middle ear is quite small. Within it, tiny bones (*ossicles*) known as the *hammer*, *anvil*, and *stirrup*, help convert the large forces striking the eardrum into a small, concentrated force. Two small muscles are attached to the ossicles; these muscles serve a protective function and contract reflexively in response to intense sounds. They help protect the delicate mechanisms of the inner ear from the damaging effects of a loud noise that could overstimulate them (Borg & Counter, 1989).

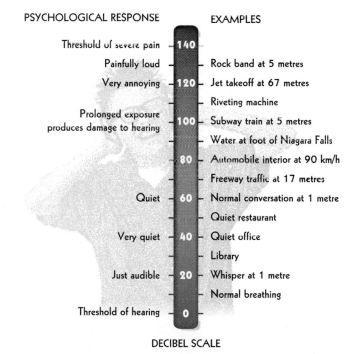

PSYCHOLOGICAL RESPONSE | EXAMPLES

Threshold of severe pain — 140
Painfully loud — | Rock band at 5 metres
Very annoying — 120 | Jet takeoff at 67 metres
| Riveting machine
Prolonged exposure produces damage to hearing — 100 | Subway train at 5 metres
| Water at foot of Niagara Falls
— 80 | Automobile interior at 90 km/h
| Freeway traffic at 17 metres
Quiet — 60 | Normal conversation at 1 metre
| Quiet restaurant
Very quiet — 40 | Quiet office
| Library
Just audible — 20 | Whisper at 1 metre
| Normal breathing
Threshold of hearing — 0

DECIBEL SCALE

FIGURE 3.18
Psychological Responses to Various Sound Intensities
High-amplitude sound waves, such as those generated by a rock band, have greater energy than low-amplitude waves and a greater impact on the sensitive structure of the ears.

Ultimately, the middle ear bones stimulate the *basilar membrane*, which runs down the middle of the *cochlea*, a spiral tube in the inner ear. Figure 3.19 shows the major structures of the middle and inner ear, and Figure 3.20 shows the basilar membrane. In the cochlea, which is shaped like a snail's shell and comprises three chambers, sound waves of different frequencies stimulate different areas of the basilar membrane. These areas, in turn, stimulate hair cells, which bring about the initial electrical coding of sound waves. These hair cells are remarkably sensitive. Hudspeth (1983), for example, found that hair cells respond when they are displaced as little as 100 picometres (trillionths of a metre).

Electrical impulses make their way through the brain's auditory nervous system in much the same way as visual information proceeds through the visual nervous system. The electrochemical neuronal impulses proceed through the auditory nerve to the midbrain and finally to the auditory cortex. Studies of single cells in the auditory areas of the brain show that some cells are more responsive to certain frequencies than to others. Katsuki (1961) found cells that are maximally sensitive to certain narrow frequency ranges; if a frequency is outside their range, these cells might not fire at all. This finding is analogous to the findings reported by Hubel and Wiesel, who discovered receptive visual fields in which proper stimulation brought about dramatic changes in the firing of a cell. Research supports a highly organized columnar organization in the auditory system, much like that of the visual system (deCharms, Blake & Merzenich, 1998).

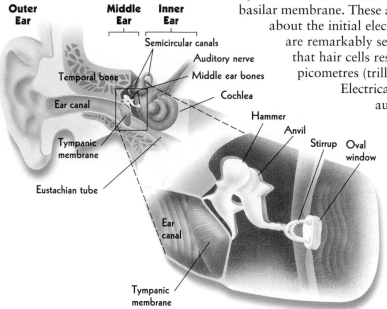

FIGURE 3.19
The Major Structures of the Ear

Outer Ear — Middle Ear — Inner Ear

Semicircular canals
Auditory nerve
Temporal bone
Middle ear bones
Cochlea
Ear canal
Hammer
Anvil
Stirrup
Oval window
Tympanic membrane
Eustachian tube
Ear canal
Tympanic membrane

Theories of Hearing

Most theories of hearing fall into two major classes: place theories and frequency theories. *Place theories* claim that the analysis of sound occurs in the basilar membrane, with different frequencies and intensities affecting different parts (places) of the membrane. These theories assert that each sound wave causes a travelling wave on the basilar membrane, which in turn causes changes in the hair cells on the membrane. These changes then trigger specific information about pitch.

In contrast, *frequency theories* maintain that the analysis of pitch and intensity occurs at higher centres (levels) of processing, perhaps in the auditory area of the cortex, and that the basilar membrane merely transfers information to those centres. These theories suggest that the entire basilar membrane is stimulated and that its overall rate of responding is transferred to the auditory nerve and beyond, where analysis takes place.

FIGURE 3.20
The Basilar Membrane
In this view, the cochlea has been unwound and cut open to reveal the basilar membrane, which is covered with thousands of hair cells. Pressure variations in the fluid that fills the cochlea cause oscillations to travel in waves along the basilar membrane, stimulating the hair cells.

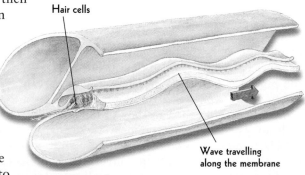

Hair cells

Wave travelling along the membrane

Like theories that attempt to explain colour vision, both place theories and frequency theories present theoretical problems. And neither type of theory explains all of the data about pitch and loudness. For example, hair cells do not act independently (as place theories suggest) but instead act together (as frequency theories suggest). Further, the rate at which hair cells fire is not fast enough to keep up with sound waves (typically having frequencies of 1000 to 10 000 cycles per second), as frequency theories suggest.

To get around these difficulties, modern researchers have developed theories of auditory information processing that attempt to explain pitch in terms of both specific action in parts of the basilar membrane and complex frequency analyses at higher levels. Theories that seem at odds with one another can work together to explain pitch and loudness when the best parts of them are combined. (Does this remind you of the debate over the trichromatic and opponent-process theories of colour vision we discussed earlier?)

Sound Localization

How do you know where to turn when you hear a baby crying? Although not as direction-sensitive as many animals, human beings have amazingly efficient sound localization (direction-determining) abilities. Researchers have learned much about such abilities by presenting sound through headsets, with one sound presented to one ear and another sound presented to the other ear. Such experiments have revealed that there are two key concepts in sound localization: interaural time differences and interaural intensity differences. Because you have two ears, a sound made to the left of your head will arrive at the left ear before the right ear. Thus, you have an *interaural time difference*. In addition, the sound will reach the two ears at different intensities. A sound made at your left will be slightly more intense to the left ear than to the right ear; thus, there is an *interaural intensity difference*. These two pieces of information are analyzed in the brain at nuclei that are especially sensitive to time and intensity differences between the ears.

Some potential ambiguities exist in sound localization, however. What happens when the sound source is just in front of you, and thus is equidistant from your two ears? It turns out that head and body movements help resolve the source of a sound. You rotate your head or move your body when you are unsure of the source of a sound. In addition, the external ear (pinna) has ridges and folds that bounce sounds around a bit. This creates slight delays that help you localize sounds. Finally, sight and past experiences with sounds aid in the task of localizing sounds in space.

Hearing Impairments

Sixteen percent of adults and more than one-third of people over age 60 have a hearing loss. In total, about 4 out of 100 Canadians have a hearing impairment (National Advisory Council on Aging, 1997). Older individuals are often discriminated against because of their hearing problem. The causes of the impairments are numerous and include both environmental and genetic factors, and they lead to varying degrees of conduction deafness, sensorineural deafness, or a combination of the two (Vahava et al., 1998).

Conduction deafness is deafness resulting from interference with the transmission of sound to the neural mechanism of the inner ear. The interference may be caused by something temporary, such as a head cold or a buildup of wax in the outer ear canal. Or it may be caused by something far more serious, such as hardening of the tympanic membrane, destruction of the tiny bones within the ear, or diseases that create pressure in the middle ear. If the affected person can get help with transmission of the sound past the point of the conduction problem, hearing can be improved.

Conduction deafness: Deafness resulting from interference with the transmission of sound to the neural mechanism of the inner ear.

Focus

Review

◆ What is the difference between pitch and frequency? p. 98
◆ How does a person locate a sound in space? p. 101
◆ Distinguish between conduction deafness and sensorineural deafness. pp. 101–102

Think Critically

◆ Why do scientists consider sound a psychological experience rather than a physical one?
◆ Why might an inner ear infection cause light-headedness?

Sensorineural deafness is deafness resulting from damage to the cochlea, the auditory nerve, or higher auditory processing centres. The most common cause of this type of deafness is ongoing exposure to very high-intensity sound, such as that of rock bands or jet planes. Listening to even moderately loud music for longer than 15 minutes a day can cause permanent deafness.

An audiometer, which presents sounds of different frequencies through a headphone, measures hearing loss; results are presented as an *audiogram*, which is a graph showing hearing sensitivity at selected frequencies. The audiogram of the person being tested is compared with that of a person with no known hearing loss. A simpler way to assess and diagnose hearing impairment is to test a person's recognition of spoken words. In a typical test of this sort, a person listens to a tape recording of speech sounds that are standardized in terms of loudness and pitch. Performance is based on the number of words the participant can repeat correctly at various intensity levels. Non-medical personnel, who then refer individuals who may have hearing problems to a physician, often administer this type of test.

You can easily see that hearing and vision have many similarities in their perceptual mechanisms. In both perceptual systems, physical energy is transduced into electrochemical energy. Coding takes place at several locations in the brain, and people can have impairments in either visual or auditory abilities.

Taste and Smell

Try the following experiment. Cut a fresh onion in half and inhale its odour while holding a piece of raw potato in your mouth. Now chew the potato. Does the potato taste like an onion? This experiment demonstrates that taste and smell are closely linked. Food contains substances that act as stimuli for both taste and smell.

There is one taste most people have a special fondness for: sweetness. Babies prefer sweet foods, as do great-grandmothers. But researchers know that a sweet tooth involves a craving for more than the taste of sugar. People with a sweet tooth crave candy, cake, ice cream, and sometimes liquor. Their bodies learn that sweetness is associated with many foods that are high in carbohydrates and fat. Carbohydrates act almost as sedatives. So your cravings for some substances—your desire to taste or smell or eat or drink them—are affected by a number of variables, including the composition of the food, its smells, what it ultimately does to you, and your previous experiences with it.

Taste

Try to think back to some memorable taste experiences you had recently or remember having had as a child. How about the first time you remember eating Brussels sprouts (if you have ever tried them). How about your first cup of coffee? Can you remember ever being very surprised by the taste of something? Perhaps biting into a lemon wedge while thinking it was an orange? Taste sensations are very powerful.

Sensorineural deafness [sen-so-ree-NEW-ruhl]: Deafness resulting from damage to the cochlea, the auditory nerve, or higher auditory processing centres.

Taste is so complex that it is usually studied from the bottom up. Taste is a chemical sense; food placed in the mouth is partially dissolved in saliva and stimulates the *taste buds*, the primary receptors for taste stimuli (see Figure 3.21). When substances contact the taste buds, you experience taste. The taste buds are found on small bumps on the tongue—papillae. Each hill-like papilla is separated from the next by a trenchlike moat; on the walls of this moat are the taste buds, which can be seen only under a microscope. Each taste bud (human beings have about 10 000 of them) consists of 5 to 150 *taste cells*. These cells last for only 10 to 14 days and are constantly renewed.

Although psychologists do not know exactly how many tastes there are, most agree that there are four basic ones: sweet, sour, salty, and bitter. Most foods contain more than one primary taste; Hawaiian pizza, for example, offers a complicated taste stimulus and also stimulates the sense of smell. All taste cells are sensitive to all taste stimuli, but some cells are more sensitive to some stimuli than to others. (In this regard, they are much like the cones in the retina, which are sensitive to all wavelengths but are especially sensitive to a specific range of wavelengths.) By isolating stimuli that initiate only one taste sensation, psychologists have found that some regions of the tongue seem to be more sensitive to particular taste stimuli than others. The tip of the tongue, for example, is more sensitive to sweet tastes than the back of the tongue, and the sides of the tongue are especially sensitive to sour tastes (see Figure 3.21).

Some people are more sensitive to taste than others, and this seems to be genetically determined. In fact, there are vast differences in sensitivity among people. Some individuals are considered non-tasters, most are considered medium tasters, and some are considered supertasters. Well-known taste researcher Linda Bartoshuk and her colleagues (1996) found that non-tasters had as few as 11 buds per square centimetre on the tip of the tongue, whereas supertasters had as many as 1100 taste buds per square centimetre. Supertasters taste sweet foods as too sweet, bitter foods as too bitter, and so forth, while non-tasters cannot distinguish among basic tastes and require additional samples of food to discern flavour. Interesting, and not yet explained, is the finding that women are more likely to be supertasters (Bartoshuk, Duffy, & Miller, 1994).

The taste of a particular food depends not only on its chemical make-up and the number of taste buds a person has, but on past experiences with that or similar foods, how much saliva is mixed into food, and how long the food is chewed. Food that is chewed well has a strong taste. However, food that rests on the tongue for a long time loses its ability to stimulate. This phenomenon is called *sensory adaptation*, or

FIGURE 3.21
Taste Buds Are Found on the Surface of the Tongue

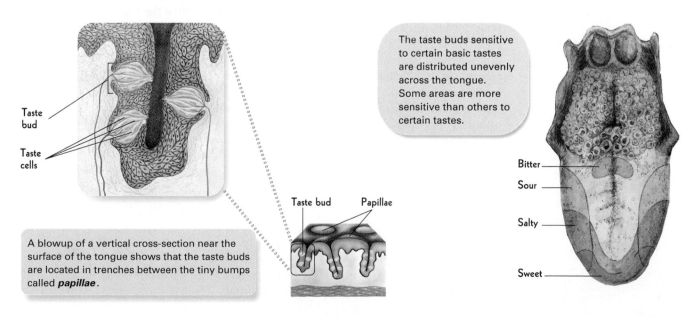

Taste bud
Taste cells

A blowup of a vertical cross-section near the surface of the tongue shows that the taste buds are located in trenches between the tiny bumps called **papillae**.

Taste bud   Papillae

The taste buds sensitive to certain basic tastes are distributed unevenly across the tongue. Some areas are more sensitive than others to certain tastes.

Bitter
Sour
Salty
Sweet

the temporary change in responsiveness of a receptor, often due to repeated high levels of stimulation. A food that loses its texture by being mashed up, blended, or mixed with other foods has less taste and is less appealing to most adults. Thus, a taste experience, much like other perceptual experiences, depends not only on a sensory event but on past experiences and other sensory and perceptual variables.

Smell

Try eating potatoes and onions while holding your nose and you will quickly discover that they taste alike, as do carrots and apples. Smell is such an important sense that those who lose it feel disabled. Like the sense of taste, **olfaction**—the sense of smell—is a chemical sense. That is, the stimulus for smell is a chemical in the air. The olfactory system in human beings is remarkably sensitive: Humans can distinguish approximately 10 000 different scents and can recognize a smell from as few as 40 or 50 molecules of the chemical. For the sensation of smell to occur, chemicals must move towards the receptor cells located on the walls of the nasal passage. This happens when you breathe the chemicals in through your nostrils or take them in through the back of your throat when you chew and swallow food. When a chemical substance in the air moves past the receptor cells, it is partially absorbed in the mucus that covers the cells, thereby initiating the process of smell.

For human beings to perceive smell, information must be sent to the brain. At the top of the nasal cavity is the *olfactory epithelium* (see Figure 3.22), a layer of cells that contains the olfactory receptor cells—the nerve fibres that process odours and transmit information about smell to the olfactory bulbs (the enlargements at the end of the olfactory nerve) and on to higher centres of the brain. There can be as many as 30 million olfactory receptor cells in each nostril, making the olfactory system very sensitive. This fact is dramatically illustrated by perfume manufacturing, which is a complex process. Perfume makers may combine hundreds of scents to make one new perfume; dozens of perfumes have the same basic scent and vary only slightly. The manufacturer's task is to generate a perfume that has a distinctive top note—the first impact of a smell. If the substance that creates a smell is not chemically pure, a middle note and an endnote will follow the top note. The middle note follows after the top note fades away and the endnote remains long after the top and middle notes have disappeared.

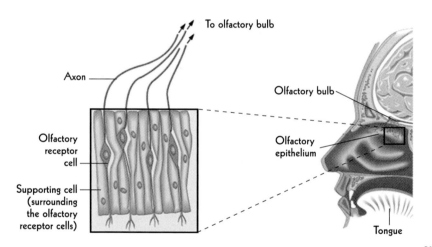

**FIGURE 3.22
The Olfactory System**

Theories of smell involve both the stimulus for smell and the structure of the receptor system. Some theories posit a few basic smells; others suggest many—including fragrant, putrid, fruity, resinous, spicy, and burnt. Psychologists have not agreed on a single classification system for smells, nor do they completely understand how odours affect the receptor cells. Research into the coding of smell is being done, and physiological psychologists make headway each year; for example, we know that memory for odours is long-lasting and that odours can evoke other memories—of past events, childhood, and especially emotional times in our lives (Herz & Engen, 1996). Another area in which important progress has been made is the question of whether and how odours affect human behaviour. We consider this issue next.

Smell and Communication

Animals secrete *pheromones* (pronounced FER-uh-moans)—scented chemical substances that are detected by other animals. Pheromones act as a means of communication. In fact, scents released by one animal even may influence the physiology of another animal.

Pheromones are widely recognized as initiators of sexual activity among animals. For example, female silkworms release a pheromone that can attract male silkworms from miles away. Similarly, when female hamsters are sexually receptive, they emit a highly odorous substance that attracts males (Montgomery-St. Laurent, Fullenkamp, & Fischer, 1988); mice are similarly equipped (Coppola & O'Connell, 1988).

Many animals emit pheromones to elicit specific behavioural reactions; others, notably dogs, use scents in their feces and urine to maintain territories and identify one another. Beavers attempt to keep strangers out of their territory by depositing foul-smelling substances emitted by sacs near the anus. Reindeer have scent glands between their toes that leave a trail for the rest of the herd. Communication through pheromones is found throughout the animal world. But do human beings share this ability?

Although people have always believed that a kind of "chemistry" exists between close friends, few really believed that one person's secretions might alter another person's behaviour. It was generally thought that human beings do not communicate through smell. However, groundbreaking research in the 1970s began to change psychologists' thinking about smell and communication. McClintock (1971) found that the menstrual periods of women living in a college dormitory who were either roommates or close friends became roughly *synchronous*. That is, after the women lived together for several months, their menstrual cycles began and ended at about the same time. McClintock and others began to question whether the synchronization of the menstrual cycles was due to some type of chemical message. In more recent experimental research, McClintock and her colleagues (1998) found that women emit an array of chemical signals that affect synchronicity and behaviour.

The effects of pheromones in animals are profound, but the role of pheromones in human beings remains relatively controversial because of its implications. Nevertheless, perfume makers have been sent into a frenzy of activity trying to make a perfume with pheromone-like capabilities. Is it reasonable for them to assert that perfumes, like pheromones, can attract members of the opposite sex? Probably not. Pheromones probably are not as powerful in human beings as they are in animals, because so many other environmental stimuli affect human behaviour, attitudes, and interpersonal relations.

The Skin Senses

Your skin, an organ of your body, contains a wide range of receptors for relaying information about the *skin senses*—pain, touch, and temperature (warmth and cold). In each case a stimulus is converted into neural energy, and then the brain interprets that neural energy as a psychological experience. Skin receptors ultimately send information to the somatosensory cortex of the brain.

Touch

The skin is more than just a binding that holds your body together. It acts as the housing for your *sense of touch*—your tactile system. The skin of an adult human being measures roughly two square metres and comprises three layers: the epidermis, the dermis, and the hypodermis. The top layer, the *epidermis* (*epi* means "outer," among other things), consists primarily of dead cells and varies in thickness. On the face it is thin; on the elbows and the heels of the feet it is quite thick. The epidermis is constantly regenerating; in fact, every 28 days or so, all of its cells are replaced. The layer underneath the epidermis—the *dermis* (from *derma*, or "skin")—contains live cells as well as a supply of nerve endings, blood, hair cells, and oil-producing (sebaceous) glands. The dermis and epidermis are resilient, flexible, and quite thick. They protect the body against quick changes in temperature and pressure, and the epidermis in particular guards against pain from small scratches, cuts, and bumps. The deepest layer—the *hypodermis* (*hypo* means "under")—is a thick, insulating cushion.

The specialized receptors for each of the skin senses—pain, touch, and temperature—vary in shape, size, number, and distribution. For example, the body has many more cold receptors than heat receptors; it has more pain receptors behind the knee than on the top of the nose. In the most sensitive areas of the hand, there are as many as 1300 receptors per square inch.

The skin sense receptors appear to interact with one another; sometimes one sensation seems to combine with or change to another. Thus, increasing pressure can become pain. Similarly, an itch seems to result from a low-level irritation of nerve endings in the skin; however, a tickle can be caused by the same stimulus and produce a reflex-like response (see *Experiencing Psychology*). Further, people are far more sensitive to pressure in some parts of their bodies than in other parts (compare your fingers to your thigh); the more sensitive areas, such as the neck and the back of the knees, have more receptors than do the less sensitive areas. Complicating matters further, women have greater sensitivity to some pain stimuli than do men and are better able to discriminate painful stimuli (Berkley, 1997).

Many of your determinations of how something feels are relative. When you say a stimulus is cold, you mean it is cold compared to normal skin temperature. When you say an object is warm, you mean it feels warmer than normal skin temperature. When you feel a child's head with the back of your hand and say the child has a fever, you are comparing normal skin temperature to a sick child's elevated skin temperature (and you wouldn't make such a determination immediately after being outside in -10-degree Celsius weather).

Pain

Everyone has experienced an acute painful episode at one time or another: headache, childbirth, dental pain, arthritic pain, or perhaps a kidney stone or stomach flare-up. For most people pain comes and goes, and they are thankful or relieved when it is over. Pain is a perceptual experience with particular negative qualities (Fernandez & Turk, 1992). Pain is the most common symptom found in medical settings; nevertheless, it is adaptive and necessary. In rare cases, children have been born without the ability to feel pain, which places them in constant danger. Their encounters with caustic substances, violent collisions, and deep cuts elicit no painful cautions to avoid such experiences. Further, they do not recognize serious conditions that would send most of us to the doctor for attention—for example, broken bones, deep burns, or the sharp pains that signal appendicitis.

Studying pain is difficult, because pain can be elicited in so many ways. For example, stomach pains can be due to hunger or the flu, toothaches due to a cavity or an abscess, and headaches due to stress or eyestrain. Myriad kinds of pain exist, including sunburn, pain from terminal cancer, labour pains, low back pain, frostbite, and even pain in a "phantom limb" lost as a result of trauma or surgery. Psychologists use several kinds of stimuli to study pain, including chemicals, extreme heat and cold, and electrical stimulation.

Most researchers believe the receptors for pain are small, free nerve endings located throughout the body that are sensitive to intense potentially harmful stimulation—and there are various types, each more sensitive to certain types of stimulation than another. Some areas of the body are more sensitive to pain than others. For example, the sole of the foot and the ball of the thumb are less sensitive than the back of the knee and the neck. Also, though an individual's pain threshold remains fairly constant, different individuals possess different sensitivities to pain. Some people have a low threshold for pain; they will report a comparatively low-level stimulus as being painful. Others have fairly high pain thresholds. When you experience pain,

experiencing psychology

A Ticklish Subject

All of us have been tickled at some point in our lives. Some of us are especially ticklish. We smile, laugh, squirm, and, sometimes, howl when tickled. But why?

Nineteenth-century speculations suggested that people laugh and are ticklish because of a "pleasant state of mind." But today researchers are showing that tickling and its results are in part physical and in large part psychological. People respond to a light touch on the sole of the foot or on the spine, but if they anticipate the touch, if they are with a friend or relative, or if there is an element of surprise, the response is much stronger. That's why people can't tickle themselves—there is no element of surprise, and tickling requires a social interaction and a tension that can occur only between two or more people (Claxton, 1975).

Think back to your childhood. When your mom or dad said, "I'm going . . . to . . . *tickle* you!" and started to wiggle their fingers, you were likely to squirm and giggle even before they touched you. Upon the actual tickle, you may have convulsed in laughter. Those who laugh easily at humour are more likely to respond to tickling (Harris & Christenfeld, 1997). Also, a physiological response to tickling is more likely when with others, particularly friends (Christenfeld et al., 1997), and if one feels comfortable with one's body and is disposed to perceive pleasurable stimuli (Ruggieri et al., 1983).

When researchers used "tickle machines" to lightly stimulate the soles of the feet, the effects of tickling were far more likely to occur when preceded by something else that was funny or when in the presence of another person. Although a tickle response may be a reflexive one, it is highly enhanced by social interactions (Christenfeld et al., 1997). Think of it as top-down *and* bottom-up processing; we laugh because it's a reflex (bottom up) and because of the situation in which we find ourselves (top down). You might laugh at a joke when a friend tells it, but you're more likely to roar at the same joke if a comedian (such as Howie Mandel or Mike Bullard) tells it. And, if the joke is embedded within a long string of other funny jokes, your response would be even greater.

Our response to humour and our ability to be tickled seem to be somewhat related. Both tickling and humour are universal traits found in human beings and in some chimpanzees. They are traits that occur at an early age, and specific pathways can be identified—elements of an evolved response. Indeed, the responses to both humour and tickling serve an evolutionary purpose—those of us with a humorous outlook on life may live longer (Weisfeld, 1993). ■

you know where it hurts, how much it hurts, and the quality of the pain (sharp, burning, localized); your body responds with autonomic nervous system activity—increased heart rate, blood pressure, sweating, and so forth. You then, in turn, respond: you also know whether you are frightened, anxious, or annoyed.

The perception of pain is physical and psychological; much depends on a person's attitudes, previous experiences, and culture. For example, athletes often report not feeling the pain of an injury until after competition has ended. Some cultures are more stoical about pain and teach individuals to endure individual suffering; in Western cultures, there is a widespread illusion that pain and suffering are ennobling (Berkowitz, 1993). Also, boys and girls within Western cultures often are taught to respond differently to pain.

What allows pain suppression? How does the body process, interpret, and stop pain? Gate control theory may offer an answer.

Gate Control Theory. One explanation of how the body processes pain was put forward by Ronald Melzack of McGill University in Montreal and is called the Melzack–Wall gate control theory (Melzack & Wall, 1970). The theory is complex, taking into account the sizes of nerve fibres, their level of development, and the interplay of excitatory and inhibitory cells that can diminish painful sensations. The theory contends that when a signal that normally might indicate a painful stimulus is sent to the brain, it goes through a series of "gates." These gates can be opened either fully or partially or be closed. How far they open determines how much of the original pain signal gets through. A chemical called substance P (standing for pain), released by the sensory nerve fibres, transmits pain impulses across the gates. Research support for gate control theory is sparse, although a variety of drugs, as well as electrical stimulation and acupuncture needles, are thought to close the gates, making the original painful stimulus less potent. Melzack (1993) acknowledges the shortcomings of his idea and its inability to deal with problems such as chronic pain. His most recent formulations suggest that initial, or "early," pain can be blocked at "gates," but continuous, or "late," pain can be sustained by the brain and might only be relieved through non-sensory mechanisms—for example, endorphins.

Endorphins. There have been some exciting breakthroughs in research on pain receptors and the nature of pain. Consider, for example, the study of endorphins. **Endorphins** (from *endogenous*, meaning "naturally occurring," and *morphine*, an opiate painkiller usually derived from opium) are painkillers that are produced naturally in the brain and the pituitary gland. There are many kinds of endorphins, and they help regulate several bodily functions, including the control of blood pressure and body temperature (Bloom, 1981). Endorphins also can produce euphoria and a sense of well-being in the way that morphine does, but to an even greater extent. Stress, anticipated pain, and engaging in athletic activities bring about an increased endorphin level. During and after running, runners often report experiencing a "runner's high," a sensation many believe is related to their increased endorphin level.

Endorphins bind themselves to receptor sites in the brain and spinal cord, thereby preventing pain signals from going to higher levels of the nervous system. Naturally produced endorphins include some that increase tolerance to pain and others that actually reduce pain. *Enkephalin*, for example, is an innate brain endorphin that blocks pain signals (Snyder, 1980). Another naturally produced painkiller, nocistatin, is being tested on a variety of painful conditions and may be able to be synthetically produced (Ito, 1998). Physicians prescribe synthetic endorphins or endorphin-like substances, such as morphine, to block pain when traditional medications are ineffective.

Acupuncture. Many people who suffer chronic, unrelieved pain have sought help from acupuncture. Initially developed in China thousands of years ago, *acupuncture* is a technique in which long, slender needles are inserted into the body at specific locations in order to relieve particular kinds of pain. Controlled studies of acupuncture have yielded varying results. Acupuncture seems to help when needles are placed near the site of pain; this is in contrast to the traditional Chinese view that the key sites are located along life-force meridians found on acupuncture charts! It is possible that the needles stimulate endorphins that may help block the pain (Murray, 1995) or alter serotonin levels (Nash, 1996). For some people, acupuncture may be a reasonable option and an effective treatment (Baischer, 1995). The National Institutes of Health in the United States concluded that acupuncture may be effective for some kinds of pain—migraines, arthritis, and postoperative pain from dental surgery—but that more research is needed because controlled research studies on the results of acupuncture are still inconclusive.

Pain Management. Usually the pain resulting from a headache, toothache, or small cut is temporary and can be alleviated with a simple pain medication such as aspirin. For millions of people, however, aspirin is not enough. For those who suffer from constant pain caused by back injury, arthritis, or cancer, drug treatment either is not effective or is dangerous because of the high dosages required; in addition, each type of pain may require a different treatment. Sometimes painkillers are not prescribed because of fear of addiction—a fear that is often exaggerated by caring, well-meaning family and friends (Melzack, 1990).

New technologies are emerging to help people manage pain. Leaders in pain research reason that something must happen at the site of an injury to trigger endorphin production. What if a drug could stop the whole pain perception process at the actual place where an injury occurs? Researchers are studying the receptor sites in skin tissue and observing how chemicals bind to them. They hope to find compounds that will stop the entire pain perception process, even before endorphin production starts. The compounds they discover may not be total pain relievers; but in combination with other pain medications, such as aspirin, they may be effective.

Practitioners who deal with pain recognize that it can have both physical and psychological sources. Although pain initially may arise from physical complaints, it sometimes continues even after the physical cause abates because it provides other benefits to the sufferer (Fernandez & Turk, 1992). As well, the work of Michael Sullivan at Dalhousie University clearly indicates that psychological factors play a central role in the nature and level of pain that individuals experience (1995). People who score high on his Pain Catastrophizing Scale report experiencing more pain and more negative thoughts during ice-water immersion than do low scorers. Treatment focuses on helping people cope with pain regardless of its origins and increasing a patient's knowledge and skills to control pain (Hardy, 1995).

Hypnosis has been used to treat pain. Patients may be instructed to focus on other aspects of their lives and may be told that after the hypnotic session their pain will be more bearable. Although some suggest that two-thirds of patients who are considered highly susceptible to suggestion can experience some relief of pain through hypnosis, the American National Institutes of Health concluded that a more accurate estimate was 15 to 20 percent.

Anxiety and worry can make pain worse. People who suffer from migraine headaches, for example, often make their condition worse by becoming fearful when they feel a headache coming on. Researchers find that biofeedback training, which teaches people how to relax and cope more effectively, can help those who suffer from chronic pain and migraine headaches—again, results are mixed. Other treatments, closely related to biofeedback, are cognitive coping. A poor or hopeless attitude can make pain worse. Cognitive coping strategies teach patients to have a better attitude about their pain. Patients learn to talk to themselves in positive ways, to divert attention to pleasant images, and to take an active role in managing their pain and transcending the experience.

Kinesthesis and the Vestibular Sense

I f you are a dancer or an athlete, you rely mightily on your body to provide you with information about hand, arm, and leg movements. You try to keep your balance, be graceful, and move about with coordinated skill. Two sensory systems allow for skilled, accurate, and smooth movement—the often ignored, but vitally important, kinesthetic and vestibular systems.

Kinesthesis is the awareness aroused by movements of the muscles, tendons, and joints. It is what allows you to touch your finger to your nose with your eyes closed, leap over hurdles during a track-and-field event, and dance without stepping on your partner's feet. The study of kinesthesis provides information about bodily movements. The movements of muscles around your eye, for example, help you know how far away objects are. Kinesthesia and your other internal sensations (such as an upset stomach) are *proprioceptive cues* (kinesthesia is sometimes called *proprioception*)—sensory cues coming from within your body and providing information about bodily movements and internal sensations.

The **vestibular sense** is the sense of bodily orientation and postural adjustment. It helps you keep your balance and sense of equilibrium. The structures essential to these functions are in the ear. Vestibular sacs and semicircular canals, which are linked indirectly with the body wall of the cochlea, provide information about the orientations of the head and body (Parker, 1980). The vestibular sense allows you to walk on a balance beam without falling off, to know which way is up after diving

Kinesthesis [kin-iss-THEE-sis]: The awareness aroused by movements of the muscles, tendons, and joints.

Vestibular sense [ves-TIB-you-ler]: The sense of bodily orientation and postural adjustment.

into the water, and to sense that you are turning a corner when riding in a car, even when your eyes are closed.

Rapid movements of the head bring about changes in the semicircular canals. These changes induce eye movements to help compensate for head changes and changes in bodily orientation. They also may be accompanied by physical sensations ranging from pleasant dizziness to unbearable motion sickness. Studies of the vestibular sense help scientists understand what happens to people during space travel and under conditions of weightlessness.

Extrasensory Perception

Vision, hearing, taste, smell, touch, and even pain are all part of the normal sensory experience of human beings. Some people, however, claim there are other perceptual experiences that many human beings do not recognize as such. People have been fascinated by *extrasensory perception (ESP)* for hundreds of years. The British Society for the Study of Psychic Phenomena has investigated reports of ESP since the nineteenth century. ESP includes telepathy, clairvoyance, precognition, and psychokinesis. *Telepathy* is the transfer of thought from one person to another. *Clairvoyance* is the ability to recognize objects or events, such as the contents of a message in a sealed envelope, that are not present to normal sensory receptors. *Precognition* is unexplained knowledge about future events, such as knowing when the phone is about to ring. *Psychokinesis* is the ability to move objects by using only one's mental powers.

Experimental support for the existence of ESP is generally weak, and results have not been repeated very often. Moreover, ESP phenomena such as "reading people's minds" or bending spoons through mental power cannot be verified by experimental manipulations in the way that other perceptual events can be. None of these criticisms means that ESP does not exist. However, psychologists see so much trickery and falsification of data and so many design errors in experiments on this subject that they remain sceptical.

Focus

Review
- Why are taste and smell called chemical senses? pp. 103–104
- What is the evidence that animal behaviour is directly affected by pheromones? p. 105
- What are the most and least sensitive parts of the body? p. 106
- Why is the study of pain so complicated? pp. 106–107

Think Critically
- Some individuals are born without a sense of smell. What effect would this have on their sense of taste, and why?
- Why do you think the study of endorphins might have relevance to your life?

Summary and Review

The Perceptual Experience

How does the psychological study of perception help explain individuals' attending to and attaching meaning to stimuli?

■ *Perception* is the process through which people attach meaning to sensory stimuli by means of complex processing mechanisms. Each perceptual system operates in a similar way; although all are different, they share common processes. pp. 76–77

■ *Psychophysics* is the study of the relationship between physical stimuli and people's conscious experience of them. Psychophysical techniques allow researchers to study and approximate the *absolute threshold*—the statistically determined minimum level of stimulation necessary to excite a perceptual system. pp. 77–78

■ If a visual or auditory stimulus is presented so quickly or at such a low volume that a person cannot consciously perceive it, psychologists say that it is presented subliminally. Research on *subliminal perception* is controversial, and many researchers maintain that it can be explained in terms of non-perceptual variables such as motivation, previous experience, and unconscious or critical censoring processes. pp. 78–79

■ The cocktail party phenomenon, whereby a person can hear his or her name spoken across a crowded and noisy room, is a basic finding of selective attention studies, which show that people have limited-capacity attentional abilities. p. 79–80

■ Studies of sensory deprivation have shown that an organism's early experience is important in the development and proper functioning of its perceptual systems. Profound relaxation can occur in an extreme sensory-restricted environment. pp. 80–81

KEY TERMS
sensation, p. 76; perception, p. 76; psychophysics, p. 77; absolute threshold, p. 77; signal detection theory, p. 78; subliminal perception, p. 78

The Visual System

Describe the structures of the visual system.

■ The main structures of the eye are the cornea, pupil, iris, lens, and retina. The retina is made up of 10 layers of cells, of which the most important are the *photoreceptors*, the bipolar cells, and the ganglion cells. The axons of the ganglion cells make up the optic nerve. pp. 82–83

What is the duplicity theory of vision?

■ The duplicity theory of vision states that rods and cones are structurally unique and are used to accomplish different tasks. That is, the two types of receptors have special functions and operate differently: Cones are specialized for colour vision, day vision, and fine acuity, and rods are specialized for low light levels but lack colour abilities and fine acuity abilities. pp. 83–84

What do receptive fields tell researchers about the perceptual process?

■ *Receptive fields* are areas on the retina that, when stimulated, produce changes in the firing of cells in the visual system. Cells at the lateral geniculate nucleus and the *visual cortex* are called feature detectors, and some of them are highly specialized—for example, for motion or colour. p. 84, 86

What are the trichromatic and opponent-process theories of colour vision?

■ The three psychological characteristics of colour are *hue, brightness,* and *saturation.* They correspond to the three physical characteristics of light: wavelength, intensity, and purity. Young and Helmholtz's *trichromatic theory* of colour vision states that all colours can be made by mixing three basic colours and that the retina has three types of cones. Herring's *opponent-process theory* states that colour is coded by a series of receptors that respond either positively or negatively to different wavelengths of light. pp. 87–89

Visual Perception

What is size constancy?

■ *Size constancy* is the ability of the perceptual system to recognize that an object remains constant in size regardless of its distance from the viewer or the size of the retinal image. pp. 90–91

Explain how monocular and binocular depth cues help people see depth.

■ The *monocular depth cues* include motion parallax, the kinetic depth effect, linear perspective, interposition, highlighting and shadowing, atmospheric perspective, and *accommodation.* The two primary *binocular depth cues* are retinal disparity and *convergence.* pp. 92–94

How do perceptual psychologists account for illusions?

■ An *illusion* is a perception of a physical stimulus that differs from measurable reality and the commonly expected appearance; many consider an illusion to be a misperception of stimulation. pp. 94–95

What did the Gestalt psychologists contribute to the understanding of perception?

■ According to a Gestalt idea called the *law of Prägnanz*, stimuli that *can* be grouped together and seen as a whole, or a form, *will* be seen that way. Using the law of Prägnanz as an organizing idea, Gestalt psychologists developed principles of organization for the perception of figures, especially figure–ground relationships. pp. 95–97

KEY TERMS

size constancy, p. 90; shape constancy, p. 91; monocular depth cues, p. 92; accommodation, p. 93; binocular depth cues, p. 93; retinal disparity, p. 93; convergence, p. 94; illusion, p. 94; law of Prägnanz, p. 95

Hearing

What are the key characteristics of sound?

■ *Sound* refers to changes in pressure passing through a gaseous, liquid, or solid medium—usually air. The *frequency* and *amplitude* of a sound wave determine in large part how a listener will experience a sound. pp. 98–99

Describe the anatomy of the ear and how sound is processed.

■ The ear has three main parts: the outer ear, the middle ear, and the inner ear. The eardrum (tympanic membrane) is the boundary between the outer ear and the middle ear. Tiny bones (ossicles) in the middle ear stimulate the basilar membrane in the cochlea, a tube in the inner ear. Place theories of hearing claim that the analysis of sound occurs in the inner ear; frequency theories claim that the analysis of pitch and intensity takes place at higher centres of processing. pp. 99–100

■ Because you have two ears, you can locate the source of sound. A sound made to the left of the head will arrive at the left ear before the right. This creates an interaural time difference. In addition, a sound made to the left will be slightly more intense to the left ear than to the right ear; thus, there is an interaural intensity difference. p. 101

Distinguish between conduction deafness and sensorineural deafness.

■ *Conduction deafness* results from interference in the delivery of sound to the neural mechanism of the inner ear. *Sensorineural deafness* results from damage to the cochlea, the auditory nerve, or higher auditory processing centres. pp. 101–102

KEY TERMS

sound, p. 98; frequency, p. 98; pitch, p. 98; amplitude, p. 98; conduction deafness, p. 101; sensorineural deafness, p. 102

Taste and Smell

Describe the anatomy of the tongue and how it allows for taste differences.

■ The tongue contains thousands of bumps, or papillae, each of which is separated from the next by a "moat." The taste buds are located on the walls of these moats. Each taste bud consists of many taste cells. All taste cells are sensitive to all taste stimuli, but certain cells are more sensitive to some stimuli than to others. p. 103

Why are taste and smell called chemical senses?

■ For taste or smell to occur, chemicals must come into contact with the receptor cells. For the sense of smell, the receptors are located on the walls of the nasal passage. When a chemical substance in the air moves past these receptor cells, it is partially absorbed into the mucus that covers the cells, thereby initiating the process of smell. The olfactory epithelium contains the olfactory receptor cells—the nerve fibres that process odours and enable the individual to perceive smell. pp. 104–105

KEY TERM

olfaction, p. 104

The Skin Senses

Describe the anatomy of the skin.

■ The skin is made up of three layers. The top layer is called the epidermis. The layer underneath the epidermis is called the dermis. The deepest layer, called the hypodermis, is a thick insulating cushion. The skin sense receptors appear to interact with one another; sometimes one sensation seems to combine with or change to another. pp. 105–106

What is the most prominent theory of pain?

■ A widely accepted explanation of how the body processes pain is the Melzack–Wall gate control theory. It suggests that a signal that normally might indicate a painful stimulus passes through a series of gates on its way to the brain. These gates can be opened or closed, and how far they open determines how many pain signals get through. This theory helps account for the fact that certain areas of the body are more sensitive to pain than others. pp. 107–108

What are the body's naturally produced painkillers?

■ *Endorphins* are painkillers that are naturally produced in the brain and pituitary gland. They help regulate several bodily functions, including blood pressure and body temperature. Stress, anticipated pain, and athletic activities bring about an increased endorphin level. p. 108

KEY TERMS

endorphins, p. 108

Kinesthesis and the Vestibular Sense

What sense involves the orientation of the entire body?

■ *Kinesthesis* is the awareness that is aroused by movements of the muscles, tendons, and joints. One kinesthetic sense is the *vestibular sense*—the sense of bodily orientation and postural adjustment. This sense helps you keep your balance and sense of equilibrium. pp. 109–110

KEY TERMS

kinesthesis, p. 109; vestibular sense, p. 109

Extrasensory Perception

Is there a "sixth sense"—ESP?

■ ESP includes telepathy, clairvoyance, precognition, and psychokinesis. Experimental support for the existence of ESP is generally weak. Psychologists remain sceptical about ESP because they see so much trickery and falsification of data, as well as experimental design errors. p. 110

Weblinks

The Joy of Visual Perception: A Web Book
www.yorku.ca/eye
This easy-to-use site is filled with information and graphics on the eye and its functions. If you cannot find an answer to a specific question, you can e-mail the professor who runs the site.

Vision Science
www.visionscience.com
A great tool for finding organizations, individual researchers, bibliographies, and career information about research in human and animal vision.

Auditory Perception Lab
www.ear.berkeley.edu/auditory_lab
This site provides information on projects and research done at the auditory lab at the University of California, Berkeley, and links to information about the ear and its functions, and to the Hearing Sciences Homepage.

Basic Acoustics and Psychoacoustics
www.music.mcgill.ca/auditory/physics.html
Sound is examined in terms of how we hear music. The concepts of pitch, timbre, and loudness are explored. A glossary of related terms and definitions is also included as a link.

Olfaction
www.leffingwell.com/olfaction.html
A research paper on the sense of smell; this Web site includes bibliographical information on related research.

Optical Illusions
www.illusionworks.com
This site offers an introduction to optical illusions and perception. Includes interactive puzzles, demonstrations, and illusions in art as learning devices, as well as a comprehensive bibliography and links to related sites.

Department of Otolaryngology-Head and Neck Surgery
weber.u.washington.edu/~otoweb/ear_anatomy.html
Visit this site organized by the University of Washington School of Medicine to find detailed illustrations and descriptions of the external, middle, and inner ears.

Anomalous Links
www.sonic.net/~comix/anomalies/links/index.htm#e0002
This Web site provides an opportunity to examine parapsychology. A vast collection of links to topics in ESP and a large number of destination links are provided.

Doctor's Guide to Pain Management and Information Resources
www.plsgroup.com/PAINMGT.HTM
News and alerts, pain management information, discussion groups, and links to other sites are all accessible through this site.

Chapter 4
Consciousness

Li has always slept well. His head hits the pillow and he's out. He wakes in the morning refreshed and ready to go. But one particular night, he lay in bed for an hour and a half, unable to drift off. He wasn't stressed or anxious; in fact, he was in a fine mood after a productive and restful day at home. But something was off. As he lay there listening to his wife's quiet, regular breathing and wondering why he was unable to sleep, he grew restless. And then it hit him. The previous night had been the last Saturday in October—the end of daylight savings time. Saturday night he had slept an extra hour. This had thrown off his normal rhythm and was affecting his sleep.

He should have recognized right away that altering his sleep pattern for one night would affect other bodily rhythms as well—and his next night's sleep. Drink alcohol, and you don't sleep normally. Allow yourself to become especially stressed, and the same thing happens. Your hormones, moods, and overall physical health affect your sleep patterns—and vice versa. In some ways, sleep can be considered a barometer of mental and physical health; if you tinker with your normal routine, the change can be reflected in your sleep. Lose too much sleep or sleep badly, and the effects spill over to the next day.

Some lucky people need only five hours of sleep per night—but they are in the minority. Others are able to take an occasional "power nap" to revive themselves—but opportunities for napping are rare, and, again, this solution works for only a small minority. Most people need a solid seven to nine hours of sleep every night.

For many North Americans, however, sleep deprivation has become a way of life. They start their mornings before dawn, and the day is filled with commuting, work, a night class at the community college, an aerobics class, shopping, and household chores. Child-rearing moms and dads also must get the kids off to school, drive them to after-school activities, oversee their homework, and spend "quality time" with them and with each other. High-school students have homework, "obligatory" television, and phone contacts with friends. And then there is the enticing entertainment that is available at all hours—cable TV, computer games, and the Web. Sometimes, people crawl into bed after midnight, exhausted.

So it's no wonder that when they finally do get to bed, many people have trouble sleeping. Part of the problem is that they are constantly on the go, having irregular meals and too few hours in which to relax. Feeling tired each morning, they take stimulants such as coffee for a quick jolt of energy. Then they stumble through the day, doing what has to be done. Unfortunately, there are serious consequences to sleep deprivation. Many auto accidents happen because drivers fall asleep briefly at the wheel. And lack of sleep often causes people to make small mistakes as well—from missed appointments to typing errors. ■

To a great extent, when people are deprived of sleep their normal awareness and responsiveness are altered. For these and other reasons, psychologists are interested in sleep, dreams, and other alterations in consciousness. By studying sleep and other ways that people move from one conscious state to another, researchers learn more about the human brain and its relationship to behaviour.

Consciousness

The human-like robot, Data, in *Star Trek, The Next Generation*, was seeking to be more human, to experience feelings and emotions the way human beings do. He was trying to be sentient, to have subjective feelings and awareness of them. To a great extent Data was trying to develop a human consciousness.

Part of Data's problem, besides not being programmed to be aware of feelings, is that consciousness is difficult to describe, let alone program. Psychologists are acutely aware of this issue. The study of consciousness has waxed and waned as a valid pursuit in psychology. Early psychologists, such as Wilhelm Wundt, studied little else but the content of consciousness; later psychologists, such as William James, studied how consciousness operates. But in the 1920s behaviourists such as John B. Watson argued that consciousness should be eliminated as a subject of psychological study—because it is not a physical structure that can be examined, probed, or diagrammed. As the behavioural approach came to dominate North American psychology, the study of consciousness and thought was all but forgotten. In the 1960s and 1970s when the information processing model and computers were being developed, however, cognitive psychology emerged as a subdiscipline in its own right, investigating thought, perception, memory, and how all of these are interwoven. Consciousness again became a viable topic. The tide had clearly turned; today, consciousness—like other areas of cognitive psychology—is a topic of strong scientific and popular interest.

Defining Consciousness

Almost all psychologists agree that a person who is conscious is aware of the environment; for example, you are conscious when you listen to a lecture (at least some of the time!). However, consciousness also refers to inner awareness—knowledge of your own thoughts, feelings, and memories (sentience); of your own mental shopping list for the afternoon, your anger at a rude driver, and the scent of a lilac that reminds you of your fourth-grade teacher.

When early psychologists studied the mind and its contents, they were studying consciousness. Wundt and his students in the late 1880s had research participants report the contents of their consciousness while sitting still, while working, and while falling asleep. At the turn of the century, Sigmund Freud moved to change the study of consciousness quite dramatically. According to Freud, people have different levels of consciousness—conscious thoughts of which they are aware and unconscious thoughts in the form of needs, wishes, and desires of which they are unaware. He further argued that much of what shapes our actions exists at a level of consciousness to which we do not have access.

The early psychologists came out of a dualistic model, one that saw the mind and body as separate—various dualistic conceptions saw different levels of interaction between the two. *Dualism* has a long and rich tradition that dates back to Descartes, who asserted that the mind and body were completely separate things. Dualism has crept into our language; we say, "These athletes are prepared in both mind and body," suggesting that the mind and body are separate entities having no relationship to one another. But, today, almost all psychologists reject dualistic ideas. The mind does not exist independent of the body; researchers today acknowledge that our mental life has a physiological basis rooted in the brain—this approach is referred to as *materialism*. Not only is materialism the dominant approach, but today's psychologists also take a less black-and-white view of the distinction between "conscious" and "unconscious." They assert that people are more aware of certain mental processes and less aware of others. For example, when you drive along a very familiar route, you suddenly may realize that you drove five kilometres of highway seemingly unaware of what you passed. You know the route so well that you drove automatically, or with less awareness. Cognitive psychologists generally do not speak about the unconscious but instead refer to controlled (deliberate or aware) versus automatic (less aware) processes.

Most psychologists—including the early structuralists, Freud, and today's cognitive researchers—have acknowledged that people experience different *levels* of consciousness. They agree that consciousness can be seen as a process or a continuum—ranging from the sort of alert attention required to read this textbook to dreaming, hypnosis, or drug-induced states. Following this view of consciousness, a person who does not pay attention or who is not alert is not as "conscious" as one who is vigilant and alert. The idea of a continuum of awareness guides many researchers who believe that consciousness is made up of several *levels* of awareness, from alertness to total unresponsiveness. Researchers who favour this view suggest, for example, that a person who is drinking heavily enters, temporarily, a lower (deeper) *level* in the range of conscious levels—that of intoxication. A person who is in a state of consciousness that is dramatically different from ordinary levels of awareness and responsiveness is in an *altered state of consciousness*. A person who is asleep has pretty much "turned off" consciousness (Hobson, 1994).

Not only do researchers acknowledge levels of consciousness, but they also know that some people are better able to think about their own thinking—a process called *metacognition*. Researchers examine metacognition by asking individuals to think about their problem-solving abilities or their perceptual strategies. They ask them to make assessments about their own level of consciousness and their use of information (Flavell & Wellman, 1977; Gleitman, 1985). Researchers ask individuals to monitor their level of alertness and their mood, through the day and over a longer period. You probably know what time of day you are most alert and when you are likely to be sleepy, and you may have noticed that while some of your friends share this pattern with you others do not. Understanding the rhythm to your consciousness is one of many metacognitive skills.

What is the function of consciousness? Clearly, our consciousness allows us to monitor our bodily and mental states. It also allows us, to a certain extent, to control our bodily and mental states. When we feel too anxious, we breathe more deeply. When we are falling asleep we sit up, yawn (to gather some extra oxygen), and perhaps blink. Our consciousness allows us to monitor and control our daily lives; the extent to which we can do this depends on how aware we are, whether we are at a low level of consciousness—such as asleep—or whether in some special situation such as hypnotized, meditating, or drugged. Before we go too far with these ideas, though, let's agree to define **consciousness** as the general state of being aware of and responsive to events within ourselves and in the environment.

Theories of Consciousness

As in other areas of psychology, theory guides research. Several researchers have proposed biologically based theories of consciousness in which understanding the evolution of the human brain is key to understanding consciousness. Jaynes (1976) believes that consciousness originates in differences in the function and physiology of the two hemispheres of the brain (and that in the ancient past, some people who heard God speaking to them actually were listening to the other side of their brain). In a similar way, Robert Ornstein (1977), using physiology and brain structure, suggests that

Consciousness: The general state of being aware of and responsive to events in the environment, including one's own mental processes.

there are two modes of consciousness, each controlled by its own side of the brain. These are the active-verbal-rational mode (called the active mode) and the receptive-spatial-intuitive-holistic mode (called the receptive mode). Ornstein believes evolution has made the active mode automatic; this is the "default," or normal, mode of operation for human beings. Human beings limit their awareness automatically in order to shut out experiences, events, and stimuli that do not relate directly to their ability to survive. When people need to gain perspective and judgment about what they are doing, however, they can expand their normal awareness by using the receptive mode. According to Ornstein, techniques such as meditation, biofeedback, hypnosis, and even the use of certain drugs can help people learn to use the receptive mode, as their primitive ancestors did, to balance the active mode.

Ornstein and his collaborator, David Galin, support many of their ideas with laboratory data showing that the brain is divided and specialized in significant ways. They point out that the left-dominated and right-dominated modes of consciousness operate in a complementary and alternating fashion, one working while the other is inhibited (Galin, 1974; Ornstein, 1976). In Ornstein's (1977) model, intellectual activities take place in the active, or left-dominated, mode; intuitive activities take place in the receptive, or right-dominated, mode. The integration of these two modes underlies the highest human accomplishments. However, since the structure of the brain does not necessarily explain its function, support for this idea is still weak.

Among the newest explanations of consciousness are those from Daniel Dennett (1991, 1996) and Richard Restak (1994). In his book *Consciousness Explained*, Dennett asserts that human beings possess many sources of information, which together create a conscious experience. He argues that the brain creates multiple drafts (copies) of experiences, which are constantly being reanalyzed. According to Dennett, the brain develops a sense of consciousness as well as a sense of self (which is made up of multiple copies of past experiences) through this constant updating and reanalysis of experience. The theory is as yet untested, is not widely accepted, and has been criticized (Mangan, 1993); however, it takes a new path in bringing together perceptual, physiological, and historical information in one individual to explain consciousness. Such ideas are supported by the arguments of neurologist Restak, who asserts in his book *The Modular Brain* that it is the brain's various modules, sections, or parts that control behaviour. Consciousness is not centrally organized but rather resides in these modules; if you lose a module through a car crash or a sporting accident, you will lose certain, but not all, key abilities. Damasio (1995) also follows this line of reasoning and suggests that the modules are hierarchically organized; Calvin (1996) asserts that these modules are at work generating, synthesizing, and creating throughout our lives, when we are awake, asleep, at work, and at play. Calvin argues that it is this activity—which does not always work well—that creates interesting thought patterns and in many cases creative, ingenious thoughts.

Stephen Pinker (1997) maintains that even the best theorists tend to confuse terms when talking about consciousness. A materialist of the first order, Pinker asserts that the mind is what the brain does—nothing more—and that it has evolved as an evolutionary response to the world. Pinker asserts that the mind is a system of organs of computation, designed by natural selection to solve the kinds of problems our ancestors faced in their foraging way of life. Pinker somewhat arrogantly dismisses many psychological issues—guilt, remorse, and fear, for example—as nonsense, arguing that researchers must look only at the machine called the brain. He argues that the "problem" of consciousness can be broken into three issues—sentience, access, and self-knowledge. *Sentience* refers to subjective experience and awareness—feelings. *Access* refers to the ability to report on the content and product of rational thought—we can make deliberate reasoned actions based on memory, rational ideas, and past experiences. Self-knowledge refers to the ability of individuals to recognize that their experiences are uniquely their own and to be aware that they are experiencing as they are doing it. Sentience is difficult to assess, but access and self-knowledge are cognitive issues that can be addressed from a variety of vantage points, including the physiological, such as through fMRI scans and even biofeedback. From Pinker's view, such analysis is crucial because it is the only way to understand the true nature of consciousness. Remember, Pinker argues that the mind is little more than a neural computer, fitted by natural selection with systems for reasoning.

Materialists such as Pinker (1997) who focus on physiology come in sharp contrast to philosophers such as Chalmers (1997) who focus on the role of subjective experience. Consciousness theorists abound and there are no lack of alternative explanations—for example, Damasio (1997) attempts to explain and understand conscious as an interaction between neurology and the environment. Much of the analysis is bio-behavioural—trying to understand the nature of consciousness through an understanding of the brain and its structure and functions. The issues are difficult to frame, the answers are far from complete. To work towards a more complete overall understanding of consciousness, researchers often focus on particular states of consciousness. So, in the remainder of this chapter, we will focus on a wide array of states of consciousness. Some of these states are desirable and normal; others alter human behaviour in less desirable ways. We begin with a very familiar state of consciousness—sleep.

Focus

Review

◆ What are the key characteristics of a definition of consciousness? pp. 116–117
◆ What are the key functions of consciousness? p. 117
◆ Explain the theory that two modes of consciousness exist, each controlled by one side of the brain. pp. 117–118

Think Critically

◆ The differences between levels and states of consciousness may seem slight to you. To help differentiate them, pick one and make a case for it.
◆ Take a few minutes to jot down the contents of your consciousness right now. What would happen if loud music had been playing while you did this compared to soft background music?

Sleep

In January 1964, at age 17, Randy Gardner made history. He set a world's record by staying awake for more than 260 hours—just short of 11 days. A science fair near his San Diego home was the location of his experiment. He enlisted two friends to help keep him awake, and he took no stimulants, not even coffee. After six days, a local physician came to supervise Gardner's progress, much to the relief of his parents. Although he did not suffer any serious physical

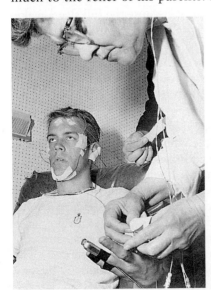

symptoms, there were marked psychological effects. On day two, he had trouble focusing his eyes. On day three, there were mood changes. On day four, he was irritable and uncooperative; he also began to see things. By day six, Gardner had speech difficulties and memory lapses. By day nine, his thoughts and speech were incoherent. On day 10, blurred vision became more of a problem and he was regularly forgetting things. Mornings were his most difficult time, but at no time did he behave in a socially deviant manner.

One of the most interesting aspects of Gardner's adventure is what happened to his sleep after his deprivation. Sleep researcher William Dement followed Gardner's sleep, mental health, physical recovery, and electroencephalogram results for days afterwards. He wanted to see how Gardner recovered, what happened to his sleep patterns, and whether he made up for the sleep he had lost. Dement found that for the three nights following his deprivation, Gardner slept an extra 6.5 hours; and to further aid his recovery, on the fourth night he slept an extra 2.5 hours (Gulevich, Dement, & Johnson, 1966; Johnson, Slye, & Dement, 1965).

These studies of Gardner's sleep loss and his subsequent recovery are part of the history of the study of sleep. Early researchers such as Dement began to realize that sleep and wakefulness follow specific patterns, which can be tracked and predicted. They noted that as you move through the day, your general awareness—responsiveness, thought processes, and physiological responses—changes. On first waking, you may not be fully aware and responsive. You move sluggishly and are slow to realize that the coffee is perking and your toast is burning. Later, at a job or in class, you are probably very alert. But as the day wears on, you find your awareness decreasing; in the evening you may fall asleep in front of the television. Research on sleep is just one part of the larger puzzle of human awareness, human consciousness, and altered states of being. It is a very important part, however, given our increasing tendency to live in a constantly sleep-deprived state (Coren, 1996).

The Sleep–Wakefulness Cycle: Circadian Rhythms

In the far north in summer it is impossible to tell night from day. There is no darkness, activity can continue outdoors 24 hours a day, and you can even get a tee time at midnight. People never seem to sleep; it is as if there *is* no day or night. But people do sleep; unlike Randy Gardner, they give in to their bodily urge to rejuvenate themselves. Their bodies tell them they are tired even if there is no clock on the wall to give them a reminder. Humans are not at the mercy of light and darkness to control their activities, but seem instead to have an internal biological clock ticking to control the sleep–wakefulness cycle. This clock seems to run in about a 24-hour cycle; thus, the term *circadian* was born—from the Latin *circa diem* ("around a day"). **Circadian rhythms** are internally generated patterns of body functions, including hormonal signals, sleep, blood pressure, and temperature regulation, which have an approximate 24-hour cycle and occur even in the absence of normal cues about whether it is day or night.

Human beings are sensitive to light, which helps keep their biological clocks in sync (Boivin et al., 1996). However, when time cues (clocks, windows, temperature changes as the sun goes down) are removed from the environment for a long time, an interesting thing happens—circadian rhythms run a bit slowly. When human beings are placed in artificially lit environments and are allowed to sleep, eat, and read whenever they want to, they sleep a constant amount of time, but on each "day" they go to sleep a bit later (Foster, 1993). This is because the full sleep–wakefulness cycle runs about 24.5 to 25.5 hours. Body temperature and other bodily functions tend to follow a similar circadian rhythm.

Because there are daylight, clocks, and arbitrary schedules, however, circadian rhythms alone do not control sleep and wakefulness. You can see the impact of circadian rhythms when your routine is thrown off by having to work through the night, then sleep, then rise, and so forth—your body's clock may not match your work clock. This disruption becomes especially apparent if you are an airline pilot, a surgeon, or a firefighter—one of the many people who work at night (Czeisler et al., 1990). When you put in long hours that stretch through the night and into the dawn, and when these hours are not regular, you become less attentive, think less clearly, and may even fall asleep from time to time. As well, you may have difficulty allowing your body to adjust to your work schedule because on your days off you naturally want to socialize with your friends and family and they are awake when you normally would be asleep (Coren, 1996). Thus, employers, workers, and consumers need to be aware of the potential decreased efficiency of night workers who vary their schedules, especially airline pilots, police officers, and medical interns. Research shows that circadian rhythms can be reset by shining lights on people's

Circadian rhythms [sir-KAY-dee-an]: Internally generated patterns of body functions, including hormonal signals, sleep, blood pressure, and temperature regulation, that have an approximate 24-hour cycle and occur even when normal day and night cues are removed.

bodies, even while they are asleep (Campbell & Murphy, 1998)—this is an important finding for those who are perpetually readjusting their internal clock, such as frequent air travellers.

Consider the air traveller's common problem—jet lag. If you travel from, say, Toronto to London, England, the trip will take about seven hours. If you leave at 9 p.m., you will arrive in London seven hours later, at 4 a.m.—at least as far as your body is concerned. It seems very late at night. But local London time is 9 a.m. You are exhausted. You finally go to bed and sleep, but your body still has to adjust. You experience exhaustion and disorientation, a set of feelings referred to as *jet lag*. You may want to sleep during the day and stay up at night. If you are experiencing jetlag or if you work long, irregular shifts, your work performance may not be at its peak. Psychologists have learned this through studying sleep, the sleep–wakefulness cycle, and sleep deprivation.

The Sleep of Long-haul Truckers: Research Tells an Interesting Story

Have you ever driven a car for more than six hours? If you have, you probably can remember feeling tired and perhaps even sleepy. Fatigue is a major cause of automobile collisions and many people are killed each year in collisions involving truckers. One possibility is that too many people and some truckers are driving when they are not properly rested.

Driver fatigue, due to sleep deprivation and shifts in circadian rhythms, is often judged to be the number one problem in commercial transportation—the field of professionals who move goods, such as long-haul truckers. Are there data to back up such a claim? A team of researchers (Mitler, Miller, Lipsitz, & Walsh, 1997) from the Scripps Clinic and Research Institute undertook a study of long-haul truck drivers to assess the issue. What's particularly significant about this study is that despite the fact that Western culture in general has been described as sleep deprived, studies of sleep rarely study real, everyday work performance such as truck driving. The researchers reasoned that long-haul truckers would sleep less than they needed to and that their sleep patterns, if measured physiologically, would be altered. Such alteration might lead to situations that could cause accidents on the highway.

Mitler and his colleagues monitored the round-the-clock physiological performance of 80 truck drivers who drove long distances in workdays lasting at least 10 hours. They measured their sleeping behaviour, including how long they slept, how long it took them to fall asleep, brain wave activity, and eye movements; respiration was continuously monitored during sleep and waking activity. Video monitors measured facial expressions during driving. Drivers were given little advice about when or how to sleep, and no financial incentives were offered to sleep or not to sleep. The participants were driving 10 to 13 hours per day, and performance on the various measures was repeatedly tested over a five-day period on more than 200 trips representing 325 000 kilometres.

Younger drivers slept more than older drivers did; their average time in bed (at night plus naps) was 5.18 hours. Overall, drivers actually slept only 4.78 hours per day, about two hours less than their average ideal sleep (as reported in a questionnaire). Drivers who drove during the day slept longer than those who drove at night. For 7 percent of the time they were actually driving, drivers exhibited signs of being in the first stage of sleep, the lightest sleep stage—that is, they were drowsy, showed slow-wave EEGs, and had slow, rolling eye movements. In addition, 56 percent of the participants had at least one six-minute period of drowsiness. The most likely time for such drowsy episodes was in the late night and early morning, between 11 p.m. and 5 a.m.

Professional drivers who spend most of every day on the road put themselves (and other drivers) at risk due to altered sleep cycles and sleep deprivation. Those who drive at night sleep less and have altered sleep cycles. In this study, all long-haul drivers slept less than an optimal amount. Research like this demonstrates that sleep-deprived drivers lapse dangerously into sleep from time to time. Although these truckers did not get into any accidents during this experiment, their lapses into sleep provided evidence that impaired performance can result from sleep deprivation. The implications of this study for airline pilots, emergency room physicians, and those who monitor nuclear weapons seem clear: People who affect the lives of others need to get a proper night's sleep every night.

Sleep: A Restorative Process

Sleep is a natural state of consciousness experienced by everyone. **Sleep** is a non-waking state of consciousness characterized by general unresponsiveness to the environment and general physical immobility. Some psychologists think sleep allows the body to recover from the day's expenditure of energy; they see it as a restorative process. Others perceive sleep as a holdover from a type of hibernation. They believe an organism conserves energy during sleep, when its expenditure would be inefficient (night is not a good time for some animals to catch or produce food). Still others see sleep as a time when the brain itself recovers from exhaustion and overload; they believe sleep has little effect on basic physiological processes in the rest of the body. Horne (1988) asserts that sleep can be divided into two major types: core and optional. *Core sleep* repairs the effects of waking wear and tear on cerebral functions; it is thus restorative. *Optional sleep* fills the time from the end of core sleep until waking. These views of sleep—as physical restoration, hibernation, brain restoration, and core repairs—guide researchers' investigations into sleep patterns.

How much sleep do people really need? Most people require about eight hours a day, but some can function with only four or five hours, while others need as many as nine or ten. Young teenagers tend to need more sleep than college students, and elderly people tend to sleep less than young people do. Most young adults (65 percent) sleep between 6.5 and 8.5 hours a night, and about 95 percent sleep between 5.5 and 9.5 hours (Horne, 1988). Do you think people who are active and energetic require more sleep than those who are less active? Surprisingly, this is not always the case. Bedridden hospital patients, for example, sleep about the same amount of time as people who are on their feet all day. Although the amount of sleep a person needs is determined genetically, heavy exercise, on any particular day, seems to increase a person's need for sleep (Youngstedt, O'Connor, & Dishman, 1997).

Sleep Cycles and Stages: REM and NREM Sleep

The sleep–wakefulness cycle is repetitive, determined in part by circadian rhythms and in part by work schedules and a host of other events. When early sleep researchers such as Nathaniel Kleitman and William Dement studied the sleep–wakefulness cycle, they found stages within sleep that could be characterized through **electroencephalograms** (EEGs)—records of electrical brain patterns—and by eye movements that occur during sleep. Researchers working in sleep laboratories study the EEG patterns that occur in the brain during sleep by attaching electrodes to a participant's scalp and forehead and monitoring the person's brain waves throughout the night. Portable devices now allow the recording of brain waves throughout the day as well (Broughton, 1991).

Recordings of the brain waves of sleeping participants have revealed that during an eight-hour period, people typically progress through five full cycles of sleep (see Figure 4.1). A full sleep cycle lasts approximately 90 minutes. We characterize the first four stages within a cycle as **non-rapid eye movement (NREM) sleep**. The other, very different stage is **rapid eye movement (REM) sleep**—a stage of sleep characterized by high-frequency, low-voltage brain-wave activity, rapid and systematic eye movements, and many vivid dreams. When people first fall asleep, they are in stage one; their sleep is light, and they can be awakened easily. Within the next 30 to 40 minutes, they pass through stages two, three, and four. Stage four is very deep sleep; when partici-

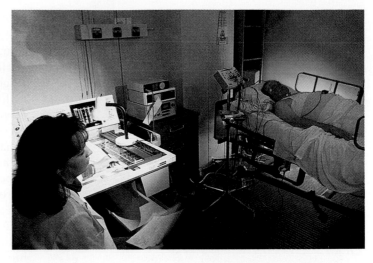

pants leave that stage, they pass again through stage three and then two (both are described in the following paragraph) on their way to REM sleep.

The descent into stage four sleep may take 40 minutes or longer; then a curious event occurs. People move back through stages three, two, and sometimes stage one and then nearly awaken when they go into REM sleep for about 10 minutes. Breathing and heart rate increase, eye movements become rapid, imagery becomes vivid, and other physiological excitement occurs. Also, the longer people sleep (and the more sleep cycles they go through), the more REM sleep they experience (Agnew & Webb, 1973; Barbato et al., 1994). Figure 4.1 shows the distinctive brain-wave patterns of wakefulness, the four stages of NREM sleep, and REM sleep in a normal adult. The waking pattern exhibits a fast, regular rhythm. In stage one, sleep is light; the brain waves are of low amplitude (height) but are relatively fast, with mixed frequencies. Sleepers in stage one can be awakened easily. Stage two sleep shows low amplitude, non-rhythmic activity combined with special patterns called sleep spindles and K complexes. A *sleep spindle* is a rhythmic burst of brain waves that wax and wane for one or two seconds. A *K complex* is a higher-amplitude burst of activity seen in the last third of stage two. Sleep spindles and K complexes appear only during NREM sleep. Sleepers in stage two are in deeper sleep than those

Non-rapid eye movement (NREM) sleep: Four distinct stages of sleep during which no rapid eye movements occur.

Rapid eye movement (REM) sleep: Stage of sleep characterized by high-frequency, low-voltage brain-wave activity, rapid and systematic eye movements, and dreams.

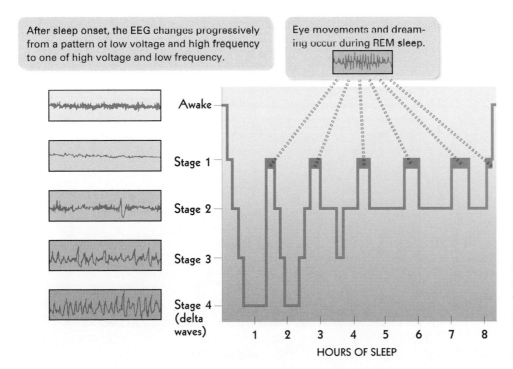

After sleep onset, the EEG changes progressively from a pattern of low voltage and high frequency to one of high voltage and low frequency.

Eye movements and dreaming occur during REM sleep.

Awake

Stage 1

Stage 2

Stage 3

Stage 4 (delta waves)

HOURS OF SLEEP

FIGURE 4.1
EEG Activity during Sleep
EEGs show distinctive and characteristic patterns during the wakeful state, REM sleep, and each of the four NREM sleep stages. Most people complete about five sleep cycles per night.

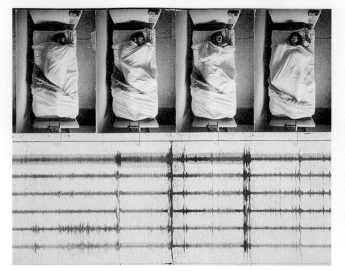

in stage one but still can be easily awakened. Stage three sleep is a transitional stage between stages two and four, with slower but higher-amplitude activity than during stage two. Stage four sleep, the deepest sleep stage, has even higher-amplitude brain-wave traces, called *delta waves*. During this stage, people breathe deeply and have a slowed heart rate and lowered blood pressure. Stage four sleep has two well-documented behavioural characteristics. First, people are difficult to awaken. People awakened from stage four sleep often appear confused and disturbed and take several seconds to rouse themselves fully. Second, people in this stage of sleep generally do not dream as much as they do in REM sleep. Early research on sleep and dreaming suggested that dreams were a sole function of REM sleep, but we now know that dreams during NREM sleep occur and have many of the same characteristics of REM sleep dreams (Foulkes, 1996).

Research participants who are awakened, especially during REM sleep, can report in great detail the imagery and mental activity they have been experiencing. Because REM sleep is considered necessary for normal physiological functioning and behaviour, it might be expected to be a deep sleep; however, it is an active sleep, during which the brain-wave activity resembles that of an aware person. For this reason, REM sleep is often called *paradoxical sleep*. In REM sleep, participants seem agitated; their eyes move and their heart rate and breathing are variable. And yet, participants are difficult to awaken during REM sleep.

In an EEG recorded during a transition from NREM stage two sleep to REM sleep, the first part of the tracing would show a clear K complex, indicating stage two sleep; the last part would show waves characteristic of REM sleep. Researchers can identify the stage in which an individual is sleeping by watching an EEG recording. If delta waves are present, the participant is in stage four sleep. To confirm this, an experimenter may awaken the participant and ask whether he or she was dreaming.

Sleep cycles develop before birth, and they continue to change into adulthood. Initially, sleeping fetuses show no eye movements. Later, they show eye, facial, and bodily movements. Newborns spend a little less than half their sleep time in REM sleep. From age one to age ten, the ratio of REM sleep to stage four sleep decreases dramatically; in later adulthood, there is increased fragmentation of sleep patterns (see Figure 4.2).

FIGURE 4.2
Changes in Sleep Patterns over a Lifetime

Children spend more time in REM sleep than adults do; the proportion of time spent in REM sleep decreases every year. NREM sleep accounts for nearly half of a newborn's sleep time. In adulthood, 80–85% of sleep is NREM.

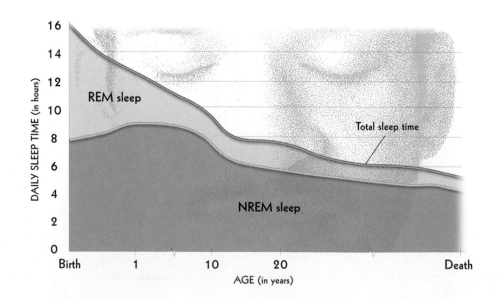

Although REM sleep is an active sleep at all ages, PET scan research shows that not all areas of the brain are equally active. Braun and his colleagues (1998) found that the primary visual cortex is nearly shut down during REM sleep, but that other key visual areas are highly active. This lack of integration of key visual areas may account for some of the confused nature of dreams and their bizarre content. Without interpretation from important visual areas it is like looking at a map without key exits, roads, and directional arrows marked on it. We'll have more to say about this finding in a bit.

Focus

Review

◆ Describe three different theories of the functions of sleep. p. 122
◆ What functions are served by the stages of sleep? pp. 123–125

Think Critically

◆ Describe your own sleep–wakefulness cycle for a day, keeping in mind that sleep specialists have a name for "morning people" (*larks*) and "night people" (*owls*). Are you a lark or an owl?

Sleep Deprivation: Doing without REM

The need for sleep is painfully obvious to anyone who has been deprived of it. Just ask Randy Gardner, who went without sleep for close to 11 days. When people who normally sleep eight hours miss a few hours on a particular night, they may be tired the following day but can function quite well. In truth, much of modern society is sleep deprived—not in the extreme, but enough to give people periods of drowsiness each day. How many times have you seen another student nod off in class despite an interesting lecture or discussion? Why are coffee shops so popular? And why does Tom Petty sing, "I'm so tired of being tired."

What happens to people who are regularly deprived of REM sleep? Research shows that they become anxious and irritable, have difficulty concentrating, and do worse than normal on tests that involve attention and original responses (e.g., Kecklund, Akerstedt, & Lowden, 1997; Plihal & Born, 1997). Long-haul truckers become drowsy when they are deprived of sleep—a usual circumstance—and their performance as drivers suffers (Mitler et al., 1997). As soon as experimental participants deprived of sleep are allowed to have REM sleep again, these psychological ill effects disappear (e.g., Roehrs et al., 1989).

One study deprived participants of all sleep for 205 hours (8.5 days). Researchers found that on the nights immediately after the experiment, participants spent a greater-than-normal amount of time in REM and stage four sleep and the least amount of time in stages one and two—the lightest stages of sleep (Kales et al., 1970; Webb & Agnew, 1975). Similar results were obtained in a study in which participants were partially deprived of REM sleep by being awakened when they showed rapid eye movements. They reported feeling sleepy and spent more time in REM sleep on a subsequent night (Dement, Greenberg, & Klein, 1966). According to Horne (1988), only about 30 percent of lost sleep needs to be recovered, mostly stage four sleep and REM sleep. Think of it as a chequebook where the total amount of REM sleep has to be in balance at the end of a week. After sleep deprivation, on the next night, sleep patterns are altered to bring an individual into balance—the more sleep is lost, the more recovery there is on the next night (Lucidi et al., 1997). *Experiencing Psychology* on page 126 suggests some ways to sleep well.

Some researchers used to believe that serious disruptions of personality might occur from prolonged REM sleep deprivation. But today it is known that serious maladjustments do not occur with sleep deprivation (Bonnet, 1980). With the exception of brain function effects, especially in the cortex, mild sleep deprivation has surprisingly few effects on the rest of the body (Harrison & Horne, 1996). Even more importantly, any changes in cerebral functions that do take place with sleep deprivation are quickly reversed after later sleep (Horne, 1988; Lucidi, 1997). We saw this in the case of Randy Gardner, who exhibited normal sleep patterns after his deprivation.

Is There a Sleep Switch?

If you find yourself in a theatre that's a little too hot, watching a film that's a bit boring, after a night in which you didn't have quite enough sleep, you might start to doze off. Is there a physiological structure that regulates and initiates sleep? Researchers are now suggesting that there may be certain cells deep within the brain that are "turned on" in such situations, while other brain cells are "shut off." Like cells in the visual system, which are activated when exposed to certain stimuli, these specialized brain cells may be selectively active.

Sherin and colleagues (1996) found that when rats were in various stages of sleep, cells in their brains seemed to turn on or off depending on the stage. The specific area of the brain in which these cells are located is the front region of the hypothalamus, called the *ventrolateral preoptic area* (VLPO). When rats were deprived of sleep for 9 to 12 hours, researchers found a certain protein present throughout most of the brain but not in the VLPO; in contrast, when rats were not deprived of sleep, the protein was found in the VLPO but not in the rest of the brain. According to these researchers, this very small area of the brain may constitute a subpopulation of sleep-controlling cells, whose actions determine the organism's state of consciousness.

In humans, there are about 30 000 cells in the VLPO, which produce neurotransmitters that inhibit the firing of other brain cells. In addition, these VLPO cells have connections with other nearby groups of specialized cells. They are thus strategically placed in the chain of neurological events to initiate or inhibit sleep. The VLPO may modulate all of the neurotransmitters involved in wakefulness, arousal, and consciousness—and thus may indeed be the locus of a "sleep switch."

Of course, rats are not human beings, but the physiological processes of rats and humans have shown many parallels. Whether the VLPO, alone or along with some other centre near it, is in fact some kind of master switching mechanism has yet to be determined. Researchers are investigating this hypothesis, looking for alternative explanations, and sorting through the implications for people suffering from sleep disorders as well as those experiencing problems related to jet lag and irregular work schedules.

Sleep Disorders

Do you snore so loudly that you keep others awake; fall asleep at inappropriate times, such as while driving a car; have trouble falling asleep; or sleepwalk? You may have a sleep disorder. People who fall asleep suddenly and unexpectedly have a disorder known as *narcolepsy*. Narcolepsy is probably a symptom of an autonomic nervous system disturbance resulting in lowered arousal, but it also may reflect neurochemical problems (Mamelak, 1991). It is relatively rare, affecting only about 1 in 1000 people.

Another sleep disorder, *sleep apnea*, causes airflow to stop for at least 15 seconds, so the person ceases breathing and wakens briefly. People with this disorder often have as many as 100 apnea episodes in a night; during the day, they are exceedingly sleepy and sometimes have memory losses. Because of their interrupted sleep people with severe apnea may have work-related accidents and severe headaches, and they may fall asleep during the day. Drug therapy and some minor surgical techniques to create better airflow have been used to treat those with sleep apnea—and also may relieve the loud snoring that accompanies the disorder. Monitoring equipment for prolonged breathing pauses also has been used to wake the sleeper (Sheridan, 1985). Sleep apnea affects about 40 in 1000 individuals, but males are more likely than females to suffer from it (Ingbar & Gee, 1985). Sleep apnea also has been proposed as a possible explanation for sudden infant death syndrome (SIDS), in which infants die suddenly during sleep for no obvious reason. Alcohol and other central nervous system depressant drugs often contribute to sleep apnea in adults.

Insomnia, a prolonged inability to sleep, is a very common sleep disorder, often caused by anxiety or depression; 1 in 10 people report suffering from it at some time in their lives. Sleep disturbances and insomnia are especially common among older adults (Prinz et al., 1990). Insomniacs tend to be listless and tired during the day and may use sleeping pills or other drugs to induce sleep at night. Ironically, researchers have found that these drugs do not induce natural sleep; instead, they reduce the proportion of REM sleep (Webb & Agnew, 1975). (Recall that the body's normal response to sleep deprivation is to *increase* REM sleep.) Researchers such as Dement have found that lack of REM sleep may alter normal behaviour; accordingly, people with chronic insomnia should not regularly use drugs that force sleep. Various researchers have proposed behavioural methods that do not rely on drugs to help solve the problem; among these are relaxation training, thought restructuring, and self-hypnosis (e.g., Morin et al., 1994). Vitiello (1989) asserts that diet affects sleep by affecting sympathetic nervous system activity, which may stimulate people in the middle of the night. Research on diet and insomnia is still in its early stages. But since diet affects mood and sleepiness, this idea does have experimental support. Another promising option for insomniacs is discussed in *Brain and Behaviour* on page 128.

Night terrors, another sleep disorder, consist of panic attacks that occur within an hour after a person falls asleep. Sitting up abruptly in a state of sheer panic, a person with a night terror may scream, breathe quickly, and be in a total state of fright. Night terrors are especially common in young children between the ages of three and eight. They usually disappear as a child grows older and do not seem to be a symptom of any psychological disorder. The cause of night terrors is not fully established, but they may be due to electrochemical processes overloading during NREM sleep.

Insomnia: A prolonged inability to sleep.

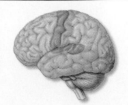

brain and behaviour

Melatonin—A Drug That Induces Sweet Dreams?

I f you were a drug researcher seeking a new drug that could make you a billionaire, you might be looking for a drug that has the effect of melatonin. Melatonin induces a sweet and easy sleep without side effects, even among people with insomnia.

Melatonin is a natural nightcap; it is a hormone normally released by the pea-sized, pineal gland at the base of the brain. Melatonin is involved in keeping the biological clock in sync, among other things (Middleton, Arendt, & Stone, 1997). Melatonin levels in a person's bloodstream vary when the amount of light in the person's environment changes (Mishima et al., 1994) and when circadian rhythms are disturbed (Dollins et al., 1993; Härmä et al., 1993). But research shows that melatonin given in small doses to human beings induces sleep and eases jet lag—quickly, easily, even in midday. Richard Wurtman of the Massachusetts Institute of Technology has reported that, given in very small doses, the hormone is a sleep inducer without sleeping pill side effects such as feeling hung over and losing REM sleep (Dollins et al., 1993). Melatonin has proved especially effective in the treatment of sleep disorders (Jan, Espezel, & Appleton, 1994) and is widely used for jet lag (Brown, 1994). Melatonin has been claimed to positively affect sex drive, life span, heart disease, and even cancer outcomes—these claims have been exaggerated, however, and little evidence exists to support these beneficial effects.

Researchers are not sure how melatonin works. It may fool the body into thinking that it is night. It may act on other brain centres. It may affect other natural sleep-inducing hormones. What researchers do know is that people who take melatonin in small doses have less trouble sleeping. Currently it is available as a nutritional supplement, not yet as a prescription drug.

Should you take melatonin? Lots of people do. But, as a critical thinker, you have to be wary of unproven drugs. Clinical trials with double-blind procedures have yet to be conducted. Dosage levels are untested and people use dosages ranging from as little as one-tenth of a milligram to 200 milligrams. Some people, about 10 percent, report negative side effects including nightmares, headaches, and lowered sex drives. Researchers do not know how the hormone affects old people compared with younger ones. Do men and women respond differently? (There is reason to believe that they do.) Does the drug have any long-term side effects? The potential of melatonin is enormous: It may help people who suffer from sleep disorders; it may aid those who work irregular shifts, including physicians, nurses, and airline pilots. Melatonin may revolutionize how and when people sleep—but the operative word is *may*. The outcome must await carefully controlled, scientific double-blind research on human beings. ■

In *sleepwalking*, a disorder that tends to run in families, an individual appears both asleep and awake at the same time. Sleepwalking is common among children. A sleepwalking child may reach out to a parent for a hug, navigate a darkened room, avoid a piece of furniture, walk into the street, or seem to be trying to accomplish a task—yet still be asleep. More boys sleepwalk than girls, and children who sleepwalk tend to outgrow it as they mature. Brain activity of sleepwalkers, when recorded with an EEG, shows stage four sleep. Research shows that different parts of a sleepwalker's brain display different levels of activity: more primitive motor portions of the brain are active; higher-level cognitive portions are deeply asleep. Contrary to popular belief, there is no danger in waking a sleepwalker. More likely, you may not be able to wake the sleepwalking individual because he or she is so deeply asleep (Hobson, 1994).

Sleep disorders probably have several origins and will require the development of a research methodology, a theory, and a set of treatment plans that reflect the complexity of the problem. To date, no single approach has been found to be universally successful.

Dreams

W hy do some people rarely remember their dreams while others can recall theirs in vivid detail? Do dreams contain hidden meanings and mysterious symbols to be deciphered? Sometimes lifelike, sometimes surreal, and sometimes incoherent, dreams may replay a person's life history or venture into the unknown. Dreams have long occupied an important place in psychology, but only since the 1950s have they come under close scientific scrutiny. Dream research is difficult to conduct; in addition, because the data from dream research are always memories of past events, they are sometimes difficult to quantify and verify (Koulack, 1991) and this is especially true with youngsters who have difficulty reporting dreams from their own perspective (Foulkes & Kerr, 1994).

What Is a Dream?

A **dream** is a state of consciousness that occurs during sleep and is usually accompanied by vivid visual imagery, although the imagery also may be tactile or auditory. During a dream there is an increase in heart rate, the appearance of rapid eye movements, a characteristic brain-wave pattern, and a lack of bodily movements. Although dreams occur more often in REM sleep, they also occur during NREM sleep; during NREM sleep, they tend to be less visual and less bizarre (Casagrande et al., 1996). Dreams during REM sleep are intensely visual, may be action-oriented, and are more likely to be emotional than are NREM dreams. NREM dreams, such as those that occur at the beginning of sleep (Vogel, 1991), are more "thoughtlike" (Foulkes, 1985).

Most people dream four or five times per night, and their dreams last from a few seconds to several minutes. The first dream in a typical night occurs 90 minutes after a person has fallen asleep and lasts for 10 minutes. You dream more in the second part of the night than at the beginning (Casagrande et al., 1996). With about four dreams per night and 365 days per year, a person dreams more than 100 000 dreams in a lifetime. However, people remember only a few of their dreams. Usually, they recall a dream because they woke in the middle of it or because it had powerful emotional content or imagery.

Content of Dreams

Sometimes the content of a dream is related to day-to-day events, to a desire a person wishes to fulfil, or to reliving an unpleasant experience. Sometimes the same dream or a sequence of related dreams is experienced over and over again. Dreams are mostly visual, and they occur mostly in colour. Most dreams are commonplace, focusing on events related to people with whom the person comes into contact frequently—family, friends, or co-workers. Common dream themes include sex, aggressive incidents, and misfortunes. Sounds and other sensations from the environment that do not awaken a sleeper are often incorporated into a dream. For example, when a researcher sprayed water on the hands of sleepers, 42 percent (of those who did not awaken) later reported dreaming about swimming pools, baths, or rain (Dement & Wolpert, 1958).

Dream: A state of consciousness that occurs during sleep and is usually accompanied by vivid visual, tactile, or auditory imagery.

A six-year-old described a dream in which she was being chased by a monster. In the dream she realized that she was dreaming, and turned and made friends with the monster. Like this child, people sometimes report that they are aware of dreaming while the dream is going on; this type of dream is a lucid dream. Most people have had a **lucid dream** at one time or another, particularly as children. When people have experienced a lucid dream, they often report that they were inside and outside of the dream at the same time. For some people this is upsetting, and they may wake themselves from the dream. *Diversity* explores sleeping and dreaming in other cultures (see pages 132 and 133).

Dream Theories

Some psychologists assume that dreams express desires and thoughts that may be unacceptable to the conscious mind. Many therapists who interpret and analyze dreams assume that dreams represent some element of a person that is seeking expression; this view—widely held—suggests that dreams put emotions into a context and that dreaming allows the expression of emotions in a safe place (Hartman, 1995, 1996). Some psychologists see much symbolism in dreams and assert that the content of a dream hides the dream's true meaning. Other psychologists find dreams meaningless. The suggested meaning of a dream depends on the psychologist's orientation. Two theorists who made much of the meaning of dreams are Freud and Jung; both wrote extensively on the meaning of dreams, yet there is little or no scientific support for their theories and much evidence to the contrary (Blagrove, 1996) (see Table 4.1). Others see dreams as a biological phenomenon with little meaning, and cite the fact that dreams are often disconnected and incoherent as evidence of this fact.

Psychodynamic Views. Sigmund Freud described dreams as "the royal road to the unconscious." For Freud, a dream expressed desires, wishes, and unfulfilled needs that exist in the unconscious. In his book *The Interpretation of Dreams* (1900/1953), Freud spoke about the manifest and latent content of dreams. The **manifest content** of a dream consists of its overt story line, characters, and setting—the obvious, clearly discernible events of the dream. The **latent content** of a dream is its deeper meaning, usually involving symbolism, hidden content, and repressed or obscured ideas and wishes—often uncomfortable ones. At the latent level, Freud would say that a dream about a cigar is definitely *not* about a cigar. We will see in Chapters 12 and 16 that Freud used dreams extensively in his theory of personality and in his treatment approach. Freudian psychoanalysts use dream analysis as a therapeutic tool in the treatment of emotional disturbance. Many contemporary therapists use patients' dreams to understand current problems and may see the dreams themselves only as a starting point.

Table 4.1 Theories of Dreaming

Theory	Explanation
Psychodynamic theory	Psychodynamic theorists such as Freud view dreams as expressions of desires, wishes, and unfulfilled needs that exist in the unconscious.
Jungian theory	Jungian theorists see dreams not only as expressions of needs and desires, but as reflections of people's collective unconscious.
Physiological model	Physiological models of dreaming view dreams as combinations of neural signals that are randomly generated and see analysis of dreams as a futile effort to make sense out of random events.

Carl G. Jung (1875–1961) studied Freudian approaches to therapy and personality analysis, and he, too, considered the dream a crucial way to understand human nature. However, Jung, more than Freud, took for granted the idea that a dream was nature's way of communicating with the unconscious and focused on the meaning of dreams. Jung believed that each thing a person dreams has a meaning; dreams are the language through which an individual expresses in an uncensored form the deepest feelings of his or her own mythology. Dreams, for Jung, are very self-oriented

and attempt to make sense of life's tasks, compensate for unconscious urges, and predict the future (McLynn, 1996). Jung asserted that dreams give visual expression to instincts and that each person shares in the **collective unconscious**, a storehouse of primitive ideas and images that they inherit from their ancestors. These inherited ideas and images, whose representations in the individual are termed *archetypes*, are emotionally charged and rich in meaning and symbolism. The archetypes of the collective unconscious emerge in dreams. One especially important archetype is the *mandala*, a mystical symbol, generally circular in form, that in Jung's view represents the striving for unity within a person's self. Jungian therapy focuses on dream analysis as an approach to understanding the human condition. We will consider how Jung focuses on dreams and the collective unconscious of humankind in more detail in our study of personality in Chapter 12.

Today psychoanalytic dream theories still see dreams as keys to the unconscious, but they also suggest that dreams integrate past experiences with current ones to produce a structure of ideas and feelings that are organized and help restore psychological balance. Thus theorists like Fosshage (1997) assert that a dream speaks to us by telling stories of our ongoing psychological transformation. As appealing as these ideas are to some psychologists, there are scant data to suggest that such notions are correct.

Cognitive Views. Many contemporary researchers believe that dreams are connected to reality, have meaning, and even have a "grammar" of their own, without having a hidden, deep, latent content. These cognitive researchers, for example Foulkes (1985, 1996), suggest that dreams express current wishes, desires, and issues with which a person is dealing. Dieters dream of food, those quitting smoking do dream of cigars, and individuals who are depressed dream of bleak futures (e.g., Hajek & Belcher, 1991). Similarly, young lovers dream about the future, and the elderly dream about the past. Not only do we dream about current situations, but our culture and language affect dream content; for example, bilinguals' dream content is related to the language that dominated their waking hours before sleep (Foulkes et al., 1993). Thus, Foulkes (1990) argues that the creation of a dream depends on active, integrative intelligence and that by studying the content of dreams we can study not only development, intelligence, and language, but how cognitive processes develop.

Biological Views. We know that dreaming is neither solely a right- nor left-hemisphere function—both hemispheres are required (McCormick et al., 1997). But both sides of the brain may not be operative simultaneously or even work in congruence. Is it possible that this lack of coordination means that dreams have no underlying meaning and are just random, fleeting images? Two researchers from Harvard Medical School, Allan Hobson and Robert McCarley (1977), believe that dreams (and for that matter all consciousness) have a physiological basis but that they represent little more than incoherent, haphazard, transient images. They argue that during periods of REM sleep, the parts of the brain responsible for long-term memory, vision, audition, and perhaps even emotion are spontaneously *activated* (stimulated) from cells in the hindbrain, especially the pons. The cortex tries to *synthesize*, or make sense out of, the messages it receives from these parts of the brain. Because this activity is not organized by any external stimuli, the resulting dream is often fragmented and incoherent (Hobson, 1989, 1994). Activation-

Does Culture Influence Dream Content?

Freud wrote that dreams were "the royal road to the unconscious" believing, as did many other psychoanalysts of his time and ours, that dreams express the desires and wishes of deeply buried values and experiences. But cognitive researchers, and even some biological scientists, assert that dreams are more a reflection of culture, values, and current experiences. Do our dreams reflect our past or our daily lives?

Two researchers from the University of Helsinki, Punamäki and Joustie (1998), compared the dreams in two cultures that differ in how dream content is viewed—the Finns and the Palestinians. Finnish society does not value or explore dreams as part of the development process; religion, schools, and families focus on consciousness and real work—practical applications. By contrast, Palestinian culture values

and explores multiple levels of reality and consciousness, and prepares children to participate in and interpret dream experiences. Punamäki and Joustie argued that more Palestinian dreams than Finnish ones would be likely to incorporate bizarre images and multiple states of reality. They argued that family background, living circumstances, and religious upbringing focus on issues that might be referred to as individualistic versus collectivist (see p. 16 in Chapter 1 for a review) and that this would show up dreams, with the Finns being individualistic and the Palestinians being more collectivist. Furthermore, they argued that Western dreams likely would be considered private messages from a person's inner core, but Middle Eastern dreams would be more likely to be seen as an external message from sacred forces.

The researchers asked over 200 children from Finnish and Palestinian homes, ages 7 through 12, to keep sleep diaries over a period of one week. Each diary sheet began "Last night I dreamt that . . ." Dreams were analyzed to assess themes such as anxiety and aggression, bizarreness, vividness, atmosphere, and quality of human relationships. Among the Palestinian children, some lived in violent neighbourhoods (Gaza) and some lived in peaceful towns (Galilea).

The results showed that the Palestinians living in violent towns reported dreams of persecution and aggression far more than those living in nonviolent towns and far more than the Finnish children. This was no surprise: Violence in daily life was reflected in dream content. Interestingly, gender, when analyzed, was also an important variable—boys were more likely than

Focus

Review

◆ What suggests that sleep disorders have serious implications for day-to-day behaviour? pp. 127–129
◆ How do researchers know when people dream? p. 129

Think Critically

◆ What, if anything, would probably happen to you if you cut short your normal sleep time by two hours a night for a period of several months?
◆ Keep a notepad at your bedside, and record several nights' dreams immediately on awakening. (You otherwise may forget them by the time you have breakfast.) Which theory of dreaming seems to explain your dreams best?

synthesis theory is supported by researchers who assert that the brain (especially the cortex) basically does its daily "housecleaning" during sleep, scanning previous memories, refreshing old storage mechanisms, and maintaining active memory. Other researchers, however, point out that dreamlike activity occurs even when cells in the pons are not active. In this view, the dream is a random collection of images and means little or nothing of importance. Braun's research (1998) lends support to the idea of disconnects in brain activity; not all parts of the brain are activated during sleep. This lack of integration of brain activity thus may account for the random nature of images and dream content.

girls to experience bizarre imagery, death, terror, and unhappy endings. In both of the nonviolent areas, Palestinian and Finnish, girls were more likely to dream of guilt and shame. Age, which the researchers had hypothesized to have a large effect, was not a potent variable—young children and older ones varied little in dream content because of their age

But contrary to the researchers' assumptions, the results failed to show that Middle Eastern culture would incorporate more multiple levels of reality than Finnish society. In general, the study failed to show that culture and its values dominated dream content at all. What it did show was daily life experiences, such as violence, intruding vividly on dreams. One 10-year-old girl wrote:

I went to school, and on my way I saw a masked man carrying a knife and axe, and I felt afraid of him and I ran away until I reached my mother in the house. I told her why I was shaking: "Mother, mother, on the way to school I saw a masked man." She told me not to be afraid of them, because they do not do anything. So in the dream I felt calm. (p. 338)

In a real-world setting, not in a laboratory, Punamäki and Joustie (1998) showed that the environment in which we live, and our gender, affect dream content. Daily experi-

ences far surpassed cultural themes in the dreams' content. Since culture affects people so greatly in religion, values, and even daily habits, this surprised the researchers. Perhaps the difficulty lies in defining "culture," because the decisive cultural difference may be in the ways society encourages or allows the expression of fear, anger, or aggression. The children in Gaza, one of the violent Palestinian towns, are engaged in a national struggle for independence and may have developed different cultural expectations concerning violence than their peers in Galilea and Finland. The impact of their daily struggle may dominate their dreams, and cultural subtleties may be masked; among the children from Galilea and Finland, cultural differences could not be observed.

Is it possible that dreams do not reflect culture? Perhaps this study did not adequately measure culture in dreaming. Dream content, as assessed through diaries, may not fully explore repressed desires or even culture; it further may be only a single measure of dreaming; and, in this study, it may be inaccurate, because children were doing the recording. Whether culture has an impact is yet to be proved; what was proved, and proved quite decisively, was that daily experiences intrude and dominate the dreams of children. ■

Controlling Consciousness: Biofeedback, Hypnosis, and Meditation

C an you learn to control your own consciousness? Can you manipulate your mental states to achieve certain bodily reactions? Research and anecdotal data suggest that you can. People have long been taught to relax and breathe in special ways so as not to experience pain—for example, during childbirth. Marathons have been won through intense mental concentration that allowed contestants to endure particularly difficult physical circumstances. Laboratory research also shows that people can bring some otherwise autonomic bodily states (see Chapter 2), such as blood pressure, under conscious control through a technique called biofeedback.

Biofeedback

Imagine a special clinic where people could be taught to treat themselves for headaches, high blood pressure, and stress-related illnesses, even for nearsightedness. By learning to influence consciously what are normally involuntary physiological reactions, patients might be able to help themselves. Such a psychological–medical clinic may exist in the future if biofeedback proves to be the healing tool some researchers predict it will be.

Physicians and psychologists once assumed that most biological functions, especially those involving the autonomic nervous system, could not be controlled voluntarily except through drugs or surgery. Since the 1960s, however, studies have explored the extent to which participants can learn to control these functions through biofeedback. **Biofeedback** is a general technique by which individuals can monitor and learn to control the involuntary activity of some of the body's organs and functions. A well-known psychologist, Neal E. Miller, was one of the first researchers to train rats to control certain glandular responses. Miller (1969) suggested that the same techniques could be used to help human beings manage their bodies and behaviour. Since then, studies have shown that people can indeed manipulate their bodies. We do not normally control processes such as blood flow, and in truth, we may not have any conscious awareness of where blood actually flows.

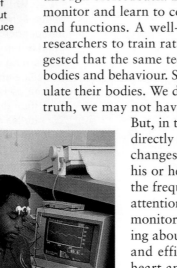

But, in theory, biofeedback gives us that awareness and allows us to directly modify brain systems that control it. The appropriate brain changes are reinforced by the feedback. A relaxed person viewing his or her own brain waves on a monitor, for example, can increase the frequency of those waves by becoming more alert and by paying attention. Similarly, a participant whose heart rate is displayed on a monitor can see the rate decrease as he or she relaxes, thereby learning about the physiological states that allow the body to work easily and efficiently. The person can learn which behaviours relax the heart and lower blood pressure and, in time, can learn to control heart rate and blood pressure by reproducing behaviours associated with reduced heart rate, sometimes without actually being sure how they are doing it.

Some researchers contend that biofeedback training is not effective (Drennen & Holden, 1984); others point out that the same effects can be obtained without real feedback (Plotkin, 1980). Some are sceptical about the long-term effectiveness of biofeedback. Still others claim to have used biofeedback successfully to treat people with stress-related symptoms, hyperactivity, stuttering, depression, nearsightedness, and learning disabilities. For example, Dietvorst (1978) successfully used biofeedback to help heart attack patients reduce their anxiety and fear of future attacks. He trained participants to decrease their level of arousal, and thus their level of anxiety, by monitoring one measure of their autonomic activity—hand temperature.

Many laboratory studies have demonstrated biofeedback's effectiveness in helping people manage a wide range of physiological problems; however, only carefully controlled research will answer persistent questions about its usefulness. For example, under what conditions, with what kinds of problems, and with what types of individuals is biofeedback effective (Middaugh, 1990)? Methodological issues such as those described in Chapter 1 (expectancy effects or attempts to please a researcher, for example) make this a challenging research area.

Hypnosis

"You are falling asleep. Your eyelids are becoming heavy. The weight on your eyes is becoming greater and greater. Your muscles are relaxing. You are feeling sleepier and sleepier. You are feeling very relaxed." These instructions are typical of those used in *hypnotic induction*—the process used to hypnotize people. **Hypnosis** is an altered state of consciousness brought about by procedures that may induce a trance. The generally accepted view of hypnosis is that hypnotized individuals are in a semi-mystical state of consciousness and give up control over much of their behaviour. They are aware of their surroundings and are conscious, but their level of awareness and responses to others are altered. A person's ability to be hypnotized or willingness to follow unconventional instructions given by the hypnotist, such as to make funny noises, is called *hypnotic susceptibility*, or *suggestibility*. Most people can be hypnotized to some extent (Hilgard, 1965). Children between 7 and 14 are the most susceptible; those who daydream also are particularly susceptible (Hoyt et al., 1989). Crawford (1994) argues that highly hypnotizable people have stronger attention-focusing abilities than those who are not suggestible; children certainly fit that characterization.

Effects of Hypnosis. People who have been hypnotized report that they know they have been hypnotized and are aware of their surroundings. Some report being in a special, almost mystical state; most report a sense of time distortion (Bowers, 1979). One reported time distortion effect of hypnosis is *age regression*—the ability to recount details about an experience that took place many years earlier or to feel and act like a child. Because few studies that report age regression during hypnosis have been controlled for accuracy of recall, the authenticity of age regression has been questioned (Nash, 1987). The age at which such recall is said to occur is important, because the ability to remember events before age three is difficult (Perner & Ruffman, 1995). It is possible that individuals report what they believe would have happened at an earlier age.

Heightened memory is another purported effect of hypnosis. Evidence indicates that hypnosis helps participants recall information (e.g., McConkey & Kinoshita, 1988). However, techniques that do not involve hypnosis may work just as well for this purpose. In fact, in a contradictory study by Putnam (1979), hypnotized and non-hypnotized participants were asked to recall events they had seen earlier on videotape. Hypnotized participants made more errors when answering leading questions than did non-hypnotized participants. Putnam suggests that hypnotized participants not only make more errors (misrecollection) but mistakenly believe that their memories are accurate (Sheehan & Tilden, 1983). These results have led researchers to question the use of hypnosis in courtroom settings; in fact, some states do not allow the testimony of hypnotized persons as evidence (Sanders & Simmons, 1983; Smith, 1983).

Hypnosis is also used for pain reduction. In a case reported by E. F. Siegel (1979), hypnosis successfully reduced lower-leg pain in a woman who had undergone an above-the-knee amputation. (The phenomenon of pain in a part of the body that no longer exists is called *phantom pain*; it occurs in some amputees.) Hypnosis also has been used to reduce pain from heat, pressure, and childbirth (Chaves & Dworkin, 1997; Miller & Bowers, 1993). Few studies of pain management, however, are conducted with adequate experimental rigour. Critics of hypnosis note that most patients show signs of pain even when hypnotized. Also, in many cases analgesic drugs (pain relievers) are used along with the hypnotism. Some researchers challenge the ability of hypnosis to reduce pain, reasoning that relaxation and a patient's positive attitude and lowered anxiety account for reported reductions in pain.

Hypnosis continues to be widely used as an aid in psychotherapy. Most clients report that, if nothing else, it is a pleasant experience. Therapists assert that in some cases it can (1) help focus a client's energy on a specific topic, (2) aid memory, or (3) help a child cope with the after-effects of child abuse. Many therapists use hypnosis to help patients relax, enhance their memory, reduce stress and anxiety, lose weight, or stop smoking (Ballen, 1997; Kinnunen & Zamansky, 1997; Kirsch et al., 1995). Some psychologists assert that hypnosis can help athletes concentrate (Morgan, 1992) and help obese patients lose weight (Johnson, 1997). Research into the process and effects of hypnosis continues, with an emphasis on defining critical variables in hypnosis itself and in the participants who are the most and the least easily hypnotized (e.g., Nilsson, 1990) and on ascertaining potential negative effects (e.g., Lynn et al., 1997; Sapp, 1996).

Challenges to Hypnosis. The traditional view of hypnosis is sometimes referred to as a "state" view because it argues that hypnotized individuals are in a state qualitatively different from normal waking consciousness. The traditional state view suggests that various dissociations occur in hypnosis and that there are significant alterations in consciousness aided by special mechanisms of consciousness (Kihlstrom, 1998). This view is sometimes distinguished from more social-cognitive views, sometimes referred to as "non-state" views. But as you will see, such dichotomies are blurred by the data; hypnosis is neither a distinct state nor merely a social phenomenon (Kirsch & Lynn, 1995, 1998); hypnosis does not necessarily rely on special conscious mechanisms (Woody & Sadler, 1998) nor is it an illegitimate conscious state.

The traditional state view is that responses in hypnosis are due to a division of consciousness into two or more simultaneous streams that are separate, distinct, and inaccessible to one another. Hilgard (1986) presents this idea, and Bowers (1992) offers a related theory, but there are little supportive data, physiological or otherwise (Kirsch & Lynn, 1998; Spanos, 1983). Far more evidence supports the long-held view of T. X. Barber, one of the major sceptics of the traditional "state" theory of hypnotism. Barber (1991) and Nicolas Spanos (1991), a researcher at Carlton University until his death several years ago, contend that the concepts of hypnosis and the hypnotic trance are meaningless and misleading. According to them, behaviours of hypnotized participants are no different than behaviours of participants willing to think about and imagine themes suggested to them. If participants' attitudes towards a situation lead them to expect certain effects, those effects will be more likely to occur. Their approach is a social-cognitive view and is sometimes called a *cognitive–behavioural view*; it stresses the role of social processes in changing people's thoughts and behaviour during hypnosis (Lynn, 1992; Barber, Spanos, & Chaves, 1974).

Barber's studies show that participants given task-motivating instructions (such as to concentrate deeply, fix their attention, or breathe deeply) perform similarly to participants who undergo hypnotic induction. Typically, more than half of the participants in experimental groups showed responsiveness to task suggestions, in contrast to 16 percent in control groups that were given no special instructions. From the results, Barber concluded that task-motivating instructions are almost as effective as hypnotic induction procedures in increasing participants' responsiveness to task suggestions.

Barber's studies have received support from other research. Salzberg and DePiano (1980), for example, found that hypnosis did not facilitate performance any more than task-motivating instructions did. In fact, they argued that for cognitive tasks, task-motivating instructions are more effective than hypnosis. But the evidence showing that effects similar to those from hypnosis can be achieved in various ways (e.g., Bryant & McConkey, 1989) does not mean that psychologists must discard the concept or use of hypnosis. It simply means they should reconsider traditional assumptions and stop thinking about hypnosis as either existing or not existing. Rather, they should see it as a topic for continuing research and debate. The ultimate view of hypnosis is unlikely to be strictly state or social-cognitive, but instead will consider motivation, intention, expectancy, memory, and automated responses (Kirsch & Lynn, 1998b).

Meditation

 Meditation has become an important daily routine for one of our colleagues. Previously, searing migraines, stomach pains, and high blood pressure had afflicted her during stressful periods. Despite prescription drugs and frequent visits to the doctor, she had found little relief. Then, at a stress management clinic, she discovered how to ease her tensions through meditation. Now, instead of taking a pill when she feels a migraine coming on, she meditates.

Meditation is a state of consciousness induced by a variety of techniques and characterized by concentration, restriction of incoming stimuli, and deep relaxation to produce a sense of detachment. For centuries meditation has been used to alter consciousness and help relieve health problems. Those who practise it use a variety of positions—sitting, lying, or reclining—and report that it can reduce anxiety, tension headaches, backaches, asthma, and the need for sleep. It also can increase self-awareness and feelings of inner peace (West, 1980, 1982). Meditation is not relaxation, but relaxation is a by-product of meditation.

Practitioners distinguish between two major types of meditation: *mindful* and *concentrative*. Each type uses different techniques to induce an altered state of awareness. Both direct the focus of attention away from the outside world through intense concentration. One begins *mindful meditation* by trying to empty the mind and just be still. As random and intrusive thoughts arise, one notices them (becomes mindful of their content) without reacting to them, judging them good or bad, or dwelling on them. They eventually become mere wisps of thought that pass through consciousness while the person meditating remains serene. Eventually, one becomes aware that the reaction to thought is the problem (suffering) and that reaction is not necessary in order to have thoughts. In *concentrative meditation*, on the other hand, one concentrates on a visual image or a mantra (repetition of a phrase), and when the mind wanders to a random thought, one brings the mind back to the image or mantra without noticing the content of the thought. In this case, the image or mantra is the important thing. This form of meditation is closely tied with religions such as Tibetan Buddhism and Hinduism, but it also has been commercially exploited and because of this has acquired a bad reputation in some circles.

One concentrative approach, *Zen*, is especially popular among those interested in healing and nutritional approaches to health. People using Zen techniques highlight the experience of enlightenment and the possibility of attaining it in this life. Zen techniques urge people to concentrate on their breathing and count their breaths. The immediate aim is to focus attention on a specific visual stimulus; the ultimate aim is to achieve a spiritual state of being.

Supporters of meditation claim that it is a unique state, capable of causing profound physiological and psychological changes. They argue that mindful meditation produces a different mode of cognitive processing by training people to maintain awareness of ongoing events and increasing attention. But a study comparing the physiological responses of meditating participants with those of hypnotized participants found their responses to be nearly identical (Holmes, 1984). Experimental studies also show that individuals trained simply to relax and concentrate have been able to achieve bodily states similar to those who meditate (Fenwick et al., 1977).

Meditation: A state of consciousness induced by a variety of techniques and characterized by concentration, restriction of incoming stimuli, and deep relaxation to produce a sense of detachment.

Focus

Review

◆ What underlying assumption do biofeedback practitioners make when they treat various disorders? p. 134

◆ What is the fundamental difference between the "state" view of hypnosis and the cognitive–behavioural view of hypnosis? p. 136

Think Critically

◆ If daydreamers and those who fantasize easily are ideal participants for hypnosis, does this imply that hypnotized individuals are "faking it" somehow?

◆ Do you think it is reasonable or unreasonable to use hypnosis as an aid in courtroom testimony? Why?

◆ Can you think of a physiological explanation for the effects of rhythmic breathing in meditation?

Drug: Any chemical substance that alters normal biological processes.

Psychoactive drug [SYE-koh-AK-tiv]: A drug that alters behaviour, thoughts, or emotions by altering biochemical reactions in the nervous system, thereby affecting consciousness.

Addictive drug: A drug that causes a compulsive physiological need and that, when withheld, produces withdrawal symptoms.

Substance abuser: A person who overuses and relies on drugs to deal with stress and anxiety.

Psychological dependence: A compelling desire to use a drug, along with an inability to inhibit that desire.

Although most theories that explain the nature and effects of meditation rely on concepts that are not scientifically measurable or observable, some controlled studies have been done. The data from these studies have shown that those who meditate can alter their physiological responses, including oxygen consumption, brain-wave activity, and sleep patterns (Pagano et al., 1976). Such evidence encourages some scientists to continue to investigate meditation for relieving tension, anxiety, and arousal.

Altering Consciousness with Drugs

In each of the past few years, Canadian physicians have written millions of prescriptions for drugs. At least 4 percent of the Canadian population is currently taking tranquillizers. At least 20 percent of adult Canadians use some kind of consciousness-altering drug that changes both brain activity and daily behaviour. We use drugs to help us wake up in the morning, to get us through daily stresses, and to help us sleep. Drugs may be legal or illegal; they may be used responsibly or abused with tragic consequences. A **drug** is any chemical substance that alters normal biological processes. Many widely used drugs are both psychoactive and addictive. A **psychoactive drug** is one that alters behaviour, thoughts, or emotions by altering biochemical reactions in the nervous system, thereby affecting consciousness. An **addictive drug** is one that causes a compulsive physiological need and that, when withheld, produces withdrawal symptoms. Addictive drugs also usually produce tolerance.

In studying drug (or substance) use and abuse, we have to consider the drug itself, its properties, and the context of its use. For example, not all people respond in the same way to the same drug, and one person may respond differently on different occasions. Two important questions we need to ask are the following: Does the drug produce dependence? Are there adverse reactions to the drug for the user or adverse consequences for other people or society (Newcomb & Bentler, 1989)? There is no single explanation for substance use and abuse. Societal factors, individual family situations, medical problems, and genetic heritage are all potentially part of a person's reasons for using or abusing drugs. The use versus abuse issue is an especially problematic one for children, who have to sort out the conflicting messages that society delivers. Newcomb and Bentler (1989) argue, "Adolescents are quite adept at spotting hypocrisy and may have difficulty understanding a policy of 'saying no to drugs' when suggested by a society that clearly says 'yes' to the smorgasbord of drugs that are legal as well as the range of illicit drugs that are widely available and used" (p. 242).

What Is Substance Abuse?

A **substance abuser** is a person who overuses and relies on drugs to deal with stress and anxiety. Most substance abusers turn to alcohol, tobacco, and other readily available drugs such as cocaine and marijuana, but substance abuse is not confined to these drugs. A growing number of people are abusing legal drugs such as tranquillizers and diet pills, as well as illegal drugs such as amphetamines and heroin. A person is a substance abuser if all three of the following statements apply:

- The person has used the abusive substance for at least a month.
- The use has caused legal difficulties or social or vocational problems.
- There is recurrent use in hazardous situations such as driving a car.

Substance abuse can lead to psychological dependence, pathological use, or both. **Psychological dependence** is a compelling desire to use a drug, along with an inability to inhibit that desire. *Pathological use* involves out-of-control episodes of use, such as alcohol binges. Most drugs produce a physiological reaction when they are no longer administered; in general, this reaction is evidence of physical dependence. Without the drug, a dependent person suffers from withdrawal symptoms. **Withdrawal symptoms** are the physiological reactions that occur when an addictive drug is no longer administered to an addict. These reactions may include headaches, nausea, and an intense craving for the absent drug. In addition, addictive drugs usually produce **tolerance**—progressive insensitivity to repeated use of a specific drug in the same dosage and at the same frequency of use. Tolerance forces an addict to use increasing amounts of the drug or to use the drug at an increased frequency to achieve the same effect. For example, alcoholics must consume larger and larger amounts of alcohol to become drunk. Most addictive drugs produce both dependence and tolerance. Shepard Siegel of McMaster University (1984, 1990) has demonstrated that tolerance is only partly due to physiological factors and that addicts become conditioned to the effects of their drugs when taken in familiar settings, requiring more drugs for a comparable high.

Psychoactive drugs change behaviour by altering a person's physiology and normal state of consciousness. Some drugs increase alertness and performance; others promote relaxation and relieve high levels of arousal and tension. Some produce physical and psychological dependence. All psychoactive drugs alter a person's thoughts and moods; they are all considered consciousness-altering drugs.

Why Do People Abuse Drugs?

Some people are likely to develop a substance abuse problem for physiological and genetic reasons; others may have emotional problems caused by stress, poverty, boredom, loneliness, or anxiety. People may turn to drugs to relax, be sociable, forget their worries, feel confident, or lose weight. Parental drug use, peer drug use, poor self-esteem, stressful life changes, divorce, and social isolation have all been implicated.

In any culture, determining the causes of drug abuse is complicated by the definition of addiction. Addictive drugs are generally defined by saying that they are habit forming (reinforcing) or that they produce a physiological dependence—for example, dependence on alcohol or barbiturates. These two processes are not independent, however; physiological processes may lead to addictive reinforcement patterns. Many drugs that affect the brain differently all share the property of being addictive—alcohol and cocaine are two examples. To help develop drug policies, researchers today are attempting to develop models that account for psychological variables such as cravings, physiological variables such as changes in brain structures and firing patterns, and social variables such as family support and therapy.

Substance abusers rarely have identical abuse patterns. Some people use only one drug—for example, alcohol. Others are *polydrug abusers*, taking several drugs; a heroin addict, for example, might also take amphetamines. When amphetamines are difficult to obtain, the person might switch to barbiturates. Some researchers assert that many people are addiction-prone (Sutker & Allain, 1988). Others note that addicts are often ambivalent about whether they want to give up their drug (Bradley, 1990). Still other researchers note that later addictive behaviours can be predicted from antisocial childhood behaviour (Nathan, 1988; Shedler & Block, 1990).

Let's take a closer look at some of the most commonly used drugs and their consciousness-altering properties. We begin with alcohol, the source of one of the most complicated and widespread drug problems in our society.

Alcohol

Alcohol consumption in Canada has been declining over the past decade. According to the Canadian Centre on Substance Abuse (McKenzie, 1997), about 72 percent of

Withdrawal symptoms: Physiological reactions that occur when an addictive drug is no longer administered to an addict.

Tolerance: Progressive insensitivity to repeated use of a specific drug in the same dosage and at the same frequency of use.

urban Canadian adults report having used alcohol at some time; just over 9 percent of those who drink report having problems related to alcohol and just under half a million Canadians are classified as alcoholics. The highest proportions of people reporting problems with alcohol are in the 15- to 24-year-old range.

Alcohol is the most widely used sedative–hypnotic. A **sedative–hypnotic** is any of a class of drugs that relax and calm people and, in higher doses, induce sleep. Because alcohol is readily available, relatively inexpensive, and socially accepted, addiction to this drug is easy to establish and maintain. In fact, most Canadians consider some alcohol consumption appropriate in a variety of situations; they often consume alcoholic beverages before, during, and after dinner, at weddings and funerals, at religious ceremonies, and during sporting events.

Effects of Alcohol. Alcohol is a depressant that decreases inhibitions and thus increases some behaviours that are normally under tight control. For example, it may diminish people's social inhibitions and make them less likely to restrain their aggressive impulses (Steele & Josephs, 1990). The physiological effects of alcohol vary, depending on the amount of alcohol in the bloodstream and the gender and weight of the user (see Figure 4.3). After equal amounts of alcohol consumption, women have higher blood alcohol levels than men do, even allowing for differences in body weight; this occurs because men's bodies typically have a higher percentage of fluid than do women's. With less blood and other fluids in which to dilute the alcohol, women may end up with higher blood alcohol concentrations with fewer drinks than men (Frezza et al., 1990; York & Welte, 1994).

Sedative–hypnotic: A drug that relaxes and calms people and, in higher doses, induces sleep.

FIGURE 4.3
Relationship between Alcohol Consumption and Blood Alcohol Level, by Gender and Weight
Note that 1.0 ounce of alcohol is equivalent to 2 glasses of wine, 2 cans of beer, or 1 mixed drink.

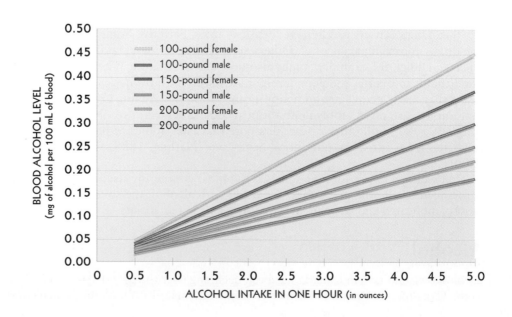

Table 4.2 Behavioural Effects Associated with Various Blood Alcohol Levels

Blood Alcohol Level*	Behavioural Effects
0.05	Lowered alertness, impaired judgment, release of inhibitions, feelings of well-being or sociability
0.10	Slowed reaction time and impaired motor function, less caution
0.15	Large, consistent increases in reaction time
0.20	Marked depression in sensory and motor capability, decidedly intoxicated behaviour
0.25	Severe motor disturbance and impairment of sensory perceptions
0.30	In a stupor but still conscious—no comprehension of events in the environment
0.35	Surgical anesthesia; lethal dose for about 1% of adults
0.40	Lethal dose for about 50% of adults

In milligrams of alcohol per 100 millilitres of blood

With increasing amounts of alcohol in the bloodstream, people typically exhibit progressively slowed behaviour; often they exhibit severe motor disturbances, such as staggering. A blood alcohol level greater than 0.08 percent (0.08 milligrams of alcohol per 100 millilitres of blood) usually indicates that the person has consumed too much alcohol to function responsibly. In all provinces, legal intoxication is a 0.08 percent (or higher) blood alcohol level; police officers may arrest drivers who are found to have at least this level of blood alcohol. Table 4.2 shows the behaviours associated with various blood alcohol levels.

The nervous system becomes less sensitive to, or accommodates to, alcohol with increased usage. After months or years of drinking, drug tolerance develops, and a person has to consume ever-increasing amounts of alcohol to achieve the same effect. Thus, when not in an alcoholic state, a heavy drinker develops anxiety, cravings, and other withdrawal symptoms (Levin, 1990).

Problem Drinkers versus Alcoholics. *Alcohol-related problems* are medical, social, or psychological problems associated with alcohol use. A person who shows an alcohol-related problem such as missing work occasionally because of hangovers, spending a paycheque to buy drinks for friends, or losing a driver's licence because of drunk driving is abusing alcohol. Alcohol-related problems caused by chronic (repeated) alcohol abuse may include liver deterioration, memory loss, and significant mood swings (Nace, 1987). A person with alcohol-related problems, a problem drinker, who also has a physiological and psychological need to consume alcohol and to experience its effects is an **alcoholic**. All alcoholics are problem drinkers, but not all problem drinkers are alcoholics. Without alcohol, alcoholics develop physiological withdrawal symptoms. In addition, they often develop tolerance; a single drink or even a few will not affect them.

Are some people more likely than others to become alcoholics? The answer is yes, according to researchers who study the biological aspects of alcoholism. Researchers assert that genetics, blood and brain chemistry, and specific brain structures predispose some people to alcoholism. Children of alcoholics are more likely to become alcoholics, even if they are raised by non-alcoholic adoptive parents. The correlations suggest that certain individuals' physiology predisposes them to alcoholism.

Alcoholic: A problem drinker who also has both a physiological and a psychological need to consume alcohol and to experience its effects.

An important study of the inheritance factor and the vulnerability of women to alcoholism shows similar results. According to Kenneth Kendler and his colleagues (1994), the transmission of vulnerability to alcoholism from parents to their daughters is due to genetic factors. This study showed that genetic vulnerability was transmitted equally from fathers and mothers to their daughters. It may be that a parent's alcohol use affects a woman's ova or a man's sperm (Cicero, 1994). That inheritance is involved in alcoholism for both men and women is clear; how inheritance interacts with the environment, parental influence (Chassin et al., 1993), and especially thought processes (Goldman et al., 1991) is the question researchers must answer next (Hawkins, Catalano, & Miller, 1992).

Social and Medical Problems. Although alcoholism is seen as a social disease because of its devastating social consequences, it is also a medical problem. Biomedical researchers study the effects of alcohol on the brain, as well as anything about the brains and basic genetics of alcoholics that may predispose them to alcoholism (Tarter & Vanyukov, 1994). Researchers know that chronic excessive drinking is associated with loss of brain tissue, liver malfunctions, and impaired cognitive and motor abilities (e.g., Ellis & Oscar-Berman, 1989).

Treatment Programs. For some alcoholics, psychological and medical treatment is successful. The most widely known program is Alcoholics Anonymous, which helps individuals abstain from alcohol by providing a therapeutic and emotionally nurturing environment. Treatment programs make abstinence their goal. The fundamental assumptions, based on the difficulty alcoholics have controlling their drinking, are that an alcoholic is an alcoholic forever and that alcoholism should be considered an incurable disease (McCrady, 1994).

Some practitioners, on the other hand, believe that limited, non-problem drinking should be the goal of treatment programs (Vaillant & Milofsky, 1982). This view assumes that alcohol abuse is a learned behaviour that therefore can be unlearned. Those who prefer controlled use with the goal of minimizing the harmful effects of alcohol consumption (Fromme et al., 1994; Marlatt et al., 1993) claim that alcohol abuse is merely a symptom of a larger underlying problem, such as poor self-esteem or family instability (Sobell & Sobell, 1982). Researchers such as Marlatt claim that a controlled drinking model is preferable to abstinence-only or "zero tolerance" approaches because it supports any behaviour change that reduces the harm of problems due to alcohol. However, most researchers believe that controlled drinking is not a reliable answer for most alcoholics, although it may be a reasonable alternative for young heavy drinkers who are not yet alcoholics (Nathan & Skinstad, 1987; Rosenberg, 1993).

Family therapy is generally considered an important part of treatment for alcoholism, because the alcohol problem of one family member becomes a problem for the entire family. A multimodal treatment approach (one involving many modes of treatment) is often the best plan; the objective is to combine individual or group therapy with participation in Alcoholics Anonymous or some other self-help group (Levin, 1990). Few systematic, carefully controlled studies of alcoholism and procedures for its treatment exist. Some researchers are investigating the use of behavioural therapies and drugs to control alcohol intake—including drugs such as naltrexone, which has been used to treat heroin addiction but shows positive effects for alcoholism (Kranzler & Anton, 1994). Others are studying the effectiveness of treatment in detoxification centres and halfway houses. Still others are trying to determine who is at risk (who is likely to become an alcoholic), in the hope that early intervention can prevent alcoholism (e.g., Hawkins, Catalano, & Miller, 1992). Table 4.3 presents some of the warning signs that alcoholism is developing.

Other Sedative–Hypnotics

Like alcohol, most barbiturates and tranquillizers are considered to be in the sedative–hypnotic class of drugs (sometimes they are referred to as depressants).

Table 4.3 Warning Signs of Alcoholism

You drink more than you used to and tend to gulp your drinks.	You promise to drink less but do not.
You try to have a few extra drinks before or after drinking with others.	You often regret what you have said or done while drinking.
You have begun to drink alone.	You are beginning to feel guilty about your drinking.
You are noticeably drunk on important occasions.	You are sensitive when others mention your drinking.
You drink the "morning after" to overcome the effects of previous drinking.	You have begun to deny your drinking or lie about it.
You drink to relieve feelings of boredom, depression, anxiety, or inadequacy.	You have memory blackouts or pass out while drinking.
You have begun to drink at certain times, to get through difficult situations, or when you have problems.	Your drinking is affecting your relationships with friends and relatives.
You have weekend drinking bouts and Monday hangovers.	You have lost time at work or school because of drinking.
You are beginning to lose control of your drinking; you drink more than you planned and get drunk when you do not want to.	You are beginning to stay away from people who do not drink.

They relax or calm people, and when taken in higher doses, they often induce sleep. *Barbiturates* decrease the excitability of neurons throughout the nervous system. They calm the individual by depressing the central nervous system. The use of barbiturates as sedatives, however, has diminished; they largely have been replaced by another class of drugs—tranquillizers.

Tranquillizers are a group of drugs (technically benzodiazepines) that sedate and calm people. With a somewhat lower potential for abuse, they are sometimes called *minor tranquillizers*. Valium and Xanax are two of the most widely used tranquillizers prescribed by physicians for relief of mild stress. Such drugs have been widely abused by all segments of society because of their availability.

Opiates: Heroin

Perhaps among the oldest drugs known to human beings are derivatives of the drug morphine, which is a component of the opium produced naturally by some poppy plants. In general, drugs that have such a derivation are referred to as opiates. **Opiates** are a class of drugs with pain-relieving and sedative properties that are addictive and produce tolerance. Heroin is an opiate that dulls the senses, relieves pain, tranquillizes, and induces euphoria. Like many other addictive drugs, heroin is considered biologically reinforcing.

Opiates have been used for everything from relieving children's crying to reducing pain from headaches, surgery, childbirth, and menstruation. Today, most opiates are illegal, but heroin and other opiates (such as morphine, which is illegal when not prescribed by a physician) are readily available from drug dealers. The high cost of these illegal drugs leads many addicts to engage in crime to support their habits.

Heroin can be smoked, swallowed or, more typically, injected into a vein, sometimes as often as four times a day. A recent and especially dangerous trend, because of the likelihood of overdose, is for the user to snort heroin through the nose.

Opiate: A drug with pain-relieving and sedative properties that is addictive and produces tolerance.

Heroin addicts tend to be young, poor, and undereducated. Most become addicts as a result of peer pressure. Estimates of the number of heroin addicts range dramatically, but the most reliable is about 1 percent of the Canadian population. Heroin addicts often use other drugs in combination with heroin; among these are alcohol, barbiturates, amphetamines, and cocaine (the last two drugs will be described in a later section). This polydrug use makes it difficult to classify heroin users as addicts of one drug or another. Moreover, even when classification is possible, treatment is complicated by the medical, psychological, and social problems associated with using many drugs at once.

The major physiological effect of heroin is impaired functioning of the respiratory system. Other effects are some detrimental changes in the heart, arteries, and veins, as well as constipation and loss of appetite. Contrary to popular beliefs, few heroin addicts actually die of overdoses from injections. A lethal dose of the drug would be much larger than that injected even by heavy users. More often than not, heroin addicts die from snorting lethal doses of pure heroin, from taking a mixture of drugs (such as heroin and alcohol), or from disease—especially AIDS, contracted from non-sterile needles and other paraphernalia used to inject the substance into the bloodstream. Some lawmakers advocate community programs to distribute sterile needles to drug users to prevent the spread of AIDS. But, as you might expect, such programs are extremely controversial.

The only major successful treatment program for heroin addiction is methadone maintenance. Like heroin, methadone is an addictive drug and must be consumed daily to avoid withdrawal symptoms. Unlike heroin, however, methadone does not produce euphoria or tolerance in the user, and daily dosages do not need to be increased. Because methadone blocks the effects of heroin, a normal injection of heroin has no effect on individuals who are on methadone maintenance. Moreover, because methadone is legal, many users are able to hold jobs to support themselves and stay out of jail. Research suggests that methadone treatment combined with psychotherapy and behaviour modification techniques to reduce illicit drug use may be far more effective than methadone treatment by itself (Stitzer, 1988). Unfortunately, most methadone treatment programs simply prescribe methadone. Thus, they have been criticized as being unethical because they make money by perpetuating addictive behaviour.

Psychostimulants: Amphetamines and Cocaine

Amphetamines and cocaine are considered psychostimulants and are highly addictive. A **psychostimulant** is any drug that increases alertness, reduces fatigue, and elevates mood when taken in low to moderate doses. *Amphetamines* are a group of chemical compounds that act on the central nervous system to increase excitability, depress appetite, and increase alertness and talkativeness. They also increase blood pressure and heart rate. After long-term use of an amphetamine, a person has cravings for the drug and experiences exhaustion, lethargy, and depression without it.

Cocaine is a central nervous system stimulant and an anesthetic. It acts on neurotransmitters such as norepinephrine (noradrenalin) and especially dopamine (it interferes with the reabsorption of dopamine). It also stimulates sympathetic activity in the peripheral nervous system, causing dilation of the pupils; increases in heart rate, blood pressure, and blood sugar; and decreased appetite. The drug produces euphoria—a light-headed feeling, a sense of alertness, increased energy, sexual arousal, and sometimes a sense of infallibility—but this euphoria is short-lived.

Cocaine can be snorted, smoked, or injected. Snorting is the most popular method. Once inhaled, the drug is absorbed into the tiny blood vessels that line the nose. Within five minutes, the user starts to feel its effects; the peak effect occurs in 15 minutes and may last for 20 to 30 minutes. The processed, smokeable form of cocaine, *crack* (so called because of the crackling sound that often occurs when the mixture is heated), delivers an unusually large dose and induces euphoria in a matter of seconds. While this method of use seems to bring about the fastest effect, it

Psychostimulant: A drug that in low to moderate doses increases alertness, reduces fatigue, and elevates mood.

turns out to be the most addictive. Cocaine also can be injected, since it is soluble in water. However, because of concerns about contracting AIDS through infected needles, intravenous injections are less common than they used to be.

Cocaine is not as widely used in Canada as it is in the Unites States. About 7 percent of American high-school students have used cocaine at least once, while only 1.3 percent of Canadian high-school students report having tried the drug. (Table 4.4 summarizes the effects of cocaine and other commonly abused drugs.) What is the appeal of cocaine? First, cocaine acts as a powerful reward and is highly addictive. In laboratory studies, for example, animals will work incessantly, even to the point of exhaustion, to obtain it. Further, cocaine produces both tolerance and potent urges and cravings. A cocaine high is pleasurable but also brief; users wish to repeat the sensation almost immediately. When the cocaine wears off, its effects give way to unpleasant feelings (known as crashing). These feelings can be alleviated only through more cocaine use (Washton, 1989).

What are some of the problems of cocaine use? At a minimum, the drug is extremely addictive and produces irritability and eating and sleeping disturbances. It also seems to precipitate other disturbances, such as panic attacks. Further, cocaine can produce serious mental disorders, including paranoia, agitation, and suicidal behaviour. Overdosing causes physical problems such as heart attacks, hemorrhages, and heat stroke. Complications associated with cocaine administration include nose sores, lung damage, infection at injection sites, and AIDS. Even those who stop using cocaine often experience medical problems later as a result of damage done to their bodies during the time they were abusing the drug. Using cocaine during pregnancy may result in premature birth, malformations of the fetus, and spontaneous abortions. Lastly, the effects of cocaine are enhanced by its combination with alcohol, but the consequences of this mixture are severe; when people mix cocaine with alcohol they significantly increase the risk of sudden death.

Table 4.4   Commonly Abused Drugs

Type of Drug	Examples of Drug	Effects of Drug	Tolerance?	Physiological Dependence?
Sedative-hypnotics	Alcohol	Reduces tension	yes	yes
	Barbiturates (e.g., Seconal)	Reduce tension; induce sleep	yes	yes
	Tranquillizers (e.g., Valium)	Alleviate tension; induce relaxation	yes	yes
Opiates	Opium Morphine Heroin	Alleviate pain and tension; induce a high	yes	yes
Psychostimulants	Amphetamines	Increase excitability, alertness, and talkativeness; decrease appetite	yes	yes
	Cocaine	Increases alertness, decreases fatigue, stimulates sexual arousal	yes	yes
Psychedelics	Marijuana	Changes mood and perception	no	no

Note: Even though a drug may not produce physiological dependence, it may produce a psychosocial need that compels repeated use.

Because a drug treatment for cocaine addiction has not been developed, psychological therapy is the sole option. Treatment usually includes education, family involvement, group and individual therapy, a focus on abstinence, and long-term follow-up; it is time-intensive and expensive (Hall, Havassy, & Wasserman, 1991).

Psychedelic Drugs

A consciousness-altering drug that affect moods, thoughts, memory, judgment, and perception and that is usually self-administered for the purpose of producing these results is called a **psychedelic**. Psychedelic drugs are sometimes called *hallucinogens*; regardless of their names they have as their principal action creating mind-altering and vivid imagery. The term psychedelic means mind-expanding. The impact of psychedelics varies widely with each individual, and a range of drugs from LSD to Ecstasy fall within this category. Lysergic acid diethylamide (LSD), commonly referred to as "acid," is sold as tablets, capsules, and occasionally in liquid form. With increases in respiration, sweating, and a dry mouth also come rapid mood swings and visual imagery; perception of time and distance changes, and perceptual imagery changes and sometimes frightens users. Although not considered an addictive drug, many LSD users have reported flashbacks—recurring experiences of being high without having taken the drug.

Marijuana

Perhaps the most widely used psychedelic drug is marijuana, the dried leaves and flowering tops of the *cannabis sativa* plant, whose active ingredient is *tetrahydrocannabinol* (THC).

Marijuana can be ingested (eaten), but in Canada it is most commonly smoked, a process in which 20 to 80 percent of the THC is lost. Smoked as a cigarette (called a joint or a nail), in a pipe, or as a cigar (blunts), marijuana alters consciousness, alleviates depression, or merely acts as a distraction. Most users report a sense of elation and well-being; others assert that the drug induces wild flights of fancy. Some users report other, adverse reactions, such as sleeplessness, bad dreams, paranoia, and nausea. There is likely a genetic basis for a person's reaction to the drug; people react differently to it and some individuals are far more susceptible. Marijuana's effects are felt about one minute after smoking, begin to diminish within an hour, and disappear almost completely after three to five hours—although traces of THC can be detected in the body for weeks. Individuals under the influence of marijuana demonstrate impaired performance on simple intellectual and psychomotor tasks. They become less task-oriented and have slower reaction times. Marijuana also interferes with attention and memory. Little is known about how marijuana affects fetal development and reproductive abilities, and about its long-term effects on those who use it from early adolescence until middle age. Marijuana has been widely used only since the late 1960s; it will take a couple of generations before researchers know all of its long-term effects. However, recent research suggests that long-term use can produce lasting brain changes—including problems with attention, memory, and learning—similar to those caused by other major drugs that are abused (Solowij, 1998).

Although researchers agree that marijuana is not physiologically addictive, many argue that it produces psychological dependence. People use and become dependent on marijuana for a variety of reasons. One reason is that it is more easily available than substances such as barbiturates and cocaine. Another reason is the relief of tension that marijuana users experience. Further, most people wrongly believe the drug has few, if any, long-lasting side effects.

Despite considerable social acceptance of marijuana use in Canada, its sale and possession are still against the law. About 25 percent of high-school students report having tried it. For the most part, laws against the sale and possession of marijuana have been ineffective, and the drug is widely available across the country in both urban and rural areas. Some experts consider legalization of marijuana to be a good idea, although few legislators take the idea seriously.

Summary and Review

Consciousness

What are the key characteristics of a definition of consciousness?

- *Consciousness* is a general state of being aware of and responsive to events in the environment, including one's own mental processes. It can range from alert attention to dreaming, hypnosis, or drug-induced states. An *altered state of consciousness* is a pattern of functioning that is dramatically different from that of ordinary awareness and responsiveness. pp. 116–117

KEY TERM
consciousness, p. 117

Sleep

Describe the cycles of sleep and wakefulness.

- A biological clock that ticks within each person controls the sleep–wakefulness cycle; *circadian rhythms* are the internally generated bodily rhythms. When time cues such as daylight and the clock on the wall are removed from the environment, circadian rhythms run a bit slowly. pp. 120–121
- Recordings of the brain waves of sleeping participants have revealed distinct cycles of sleep. Each cycle has four stages of *non-rapid eye movement (NREM) sleep* and one stage of *rapid eye movement (REM) sleep*. During REM sleep, rapid and systematic eye movements occur. A full sleep cycle lasts about 90 minutes, so five complete sleep cycles occur in an average night's sleep.

People deprived of REM sleep tend to catch up on REM sleep on subsequent nights. pp. 123–125

What happens when someone suffers from a sleep disorder?

- Snoring loudly, sleepwalking, and falling asleep at inappropriate times may be signs of a sleep disorder. People who fall asleep suddenly and unexpectedly have a sleep disorder known as narcolepsy. Narcolepsy is probably a symptom of an autonomic nervous system disturbance and lowered arousal but also may reflect neurochemical problems. Another sleep disorder, *insomnia*, is a prolonged inability to sleep, which is often caused by anxiety or depression. pp. 127–128

KEY TERMS
circadian rhythms, p. 120; sleep, p. 122; electroencephalogram (EEG), p. 122; non-rapid eye movement (NREM) sleep, p. 123; rapid eye movement (REM) sleep, p. 123; insomnia, p. 127

Dreams

What evidence supports the assertion that people dream in the middle of the night rather than solely at the end of the evening?

- A *dream* is a state of consciousness that occurs largely during REM sleep and is usually accompanied by vivid visual imagery, although the imagery also may be tactile or auditory. REM sleep occurs four or five times a night, so most people dream four or five times a night. The first dream of a typical night occurs 90

minutes after a person has fallen asleep and lasts for approximately 10 minutes. p. 129

How have key theorists explained dreaming?

- For Freud, a dream expressed desires, wishes, and unfulfilled needs that exist in the unconscious—dreams were "the royal road to the unconscious." Freud referred to the *manifest content* of a dream (its overt story line, characters, and settings) and the *latent content* of a dream (its deeper meaning, usually involving symbolism, hidden content, and repressed or obscured ideas and wishes). p. 130
- Jung took for granted the idea that a dream was nature's way of communicating with the unconscious and saw dreams as the language through which an individual expresses the deepest feelings of his or her own mythology in an uncensored form. He asserted that each person shares in the *collective unconscious*, a storehouse of primitive ideas and images in people's unconscious that are inherited from their ancestors. pp. 130–131
- Hobson and McCarley believe that dreams have a physiological basis and that, during periods of REM sleep, the parts of the brain responsible for long-term memory, vision, audition, and perhaps even emotion are spontaneously activated (stimulated) from cells in the hindbrain, especially the pons. The cortex attempts to synthesize, or make sense out of, the messages. pp. 131–132

KEY TERMS
dream, p. 129; lucid dream, p. 130;
manifest content, p. 130; latent content,
p. 130; collective unconscious, p. 131

Controlling Consciousness: Biofeedback, Hypnosis, and Meditation

Differentiate three keys means of controlling consciousness.

■ *Biofeedback* is the general technique by which individuals can monitor and learn to control the involuntary activity of some bodily organs and functions. Laboratory studies have demonstrated biofeedback's effectiveness in helping people manage a wide range of physiological problems such as headaches and high blood pressure, but only carefully controlled research will answer persistent questions about its usefulness. pp. 133–134

■ *Hypnosis* is an altered state of consciousness brought about by procedures that may induce a trance. Hypnosis can produce special effects such as age regression, heightened memory, and pain reduction. pp. 134–136

■ Physical states produced by *meditation* resemble those achieved by individuals trained to relax and concentrate. The two major types of meditation are mindful and concentrative; both induce an altered state of awareness. People using mindful meditation focus on trying to empty the mind and be still. Concentrative meditation focuses on a visual image or a mantra; when the mind wanders to random thoughts, the person meditating brings attention back to the image or mantra without noticing the content of the thoughts. pp. 136–138

KEY TERMS
biofeedback, p. 134; hypnosis, p. 134; meditation, p. 137

Altering Consciousness with Drugs

What are the different broad categories of drugs?

■ A *drug* is any chemical substance that alters normal biological processes. A *psychoactive drug* is a drug that alters behaviour, thoughts, or emotions by altering biochemical reactions in the nervous system, thereby affecting consciousness. An *addictive drug* is a drug that causes a compulsive physiological need and that, when withheld, produces withdrawal symptoms. p. 138

What are the defining characteristics of a substance abuser?

■ *Substance abusers* have used drugs for at least one month, have experienced legal, personal, social, or vocational problems due to drug use, and have used a drug in hazardous situations. Most researchers agree that no single explanation can account for drug use and abuse. pp. 138–139

How does alcohol affect behaviour, and who is an alcoholic?

■ Alcohol affects behaviour in proportion to its level in the bloodstream and the gender and weight of the user. A person with a blood alcohol level of 0.08 percent or more is generally considered intoxicated; if driving, the person can be arrested. pp. 140–141

■ An *alcoholic* is a person who has alcohol-related problems and who also has a physiological and psychological need to consume alcoholic products and experience their effects. Without alcohol, alcoholics develop physiological *withdrawal symptoms*. In addition, they often develop *tolerance*, whereby a single drink or even a few drinks will not affect them. All alcoholics are problem drinkers, but not all problem drinkers are alcoholics. p. 141

Describe the risks and effects of different classes of drugs.

■ Barbiturates and tranquillizers are in the class of drugs called *sedative–hypnotics*. They relax and calm individuals and, when taken in higher doses, can induce sleep. Barbiturates are considered to produce a deeper relaxation than tranquillizers. Tranquillizers are widely overused because of their availability. pp. 142–143

■ Heroin is one of the class of drugs called *opiates*. It has become a social problem in part because it is illegal; thus, addicts commit crimes to get money to obtain the drug. Heroin addiction has been treated successfully with methadone, which blocks heroin's effects. Methadone programs are criticized, however, because of their lack of treatment to help addicts become totally drug-free. pp. 143–144

■ In general, a *psychostimulant* is any drug that increases alertness, reduces fatigue, and elevates mood when taken in low to moderate doses. Amphetamines and cocaine are psychostimulants. Cocaine is more widely abused in the United States than in Canada; cocaine addiction is difficult to treat and has numerous medical complications. pp. 144–146

■ *Psychedelics* such as marijuana are consciousness-altering drugs that affect moods, thoughts, memory, judgment, and perception and that are usually self-administered for the purposes of producing these results. pp. 146–147

KEY TERMS
drug, p. 138; psychoactive drug, p. 138; addictive drug, p. 138; substance abuser, p. 138; psychological dependence, p. 138; withdrawal symptoms, p. 139; tolerance, p. 139; sedative–hypnotic, p. 140; alcoholic, p. 141; opiate, p. 143; psychostimulant, p. 144; psychedelic, p. 146

Weblinks

Sleep Home Pages
bisleep.medsch.ucla.edu/defaultelse.html
A comprehensive compilation of resources, publications, discussion groups, and organizations relating to the study of sleep and sleep disorders.

Inner TranceFormations Hypnosis Site
www.cet.com/~alanb
This site examines the use of trance and hypnosis as tools for healing and self-discovery and includes information on the history of hypnosis, myths relating to the use of hypnosis, and legal issues.

The Association for the Study of Dreams
www.asdreams.org
This association's home page provides information on journals, discussion groups, and conferences dealing with dreaming.

Psyche: An Interdisciplinary Journal of Research on Consciousness
psyche.cs.monash.edu.au
This is an electronic journal dedicated to exploring the nature of consciousness and its relation to the brain. Articles, book reviews, discussion lists, and links to related sites are included.

The Melatonin and Seasonal Affective Disorder Network
hometown.aol.com/mindbend2/index.htm
Visit this site to find links to newspaper and magazine articles, university research labs, and other Web pages.

SleepNet
www.sleepnet.com
Billed as the site that provides the answers to questions you are too tired to ask, SleepNet's goal is to link all of the sleep information available on the Internet. Sleep labs and forums are found here.

Understanding the Mind-Altering Drugs
nths.newtrier.k12.il.us/academics/science/~goralb/ drugs/main_menu.html
Not only does this site provide a biochemical background for morphine, heroin, and other drugs, it also explains how drugs affect neuroreceptors in the brain.

Tustin Police Department
www.tustinpd.org/drugs.html
The effects, paraphernalia, and dangers of stimulants, depressants, hallucinogens, and designer drugs are detailed at this Web site.

Chapter 5
Learning

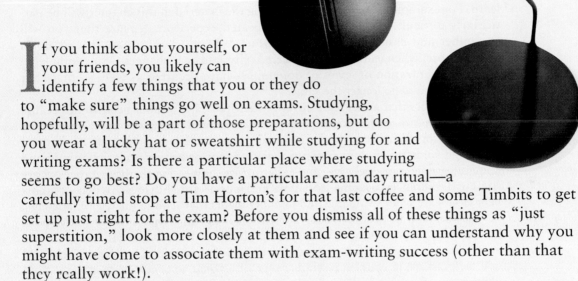

If you think about yourself, or your friends, you likely can identify a few things that you or they do to "make sure" things go well on exams. Studying, hopefully, will be a part of those preparations, but do you wear a lucky hat or sweatshirt while studying for and writing exams? Is there a particular place where studying seems to go best? Do you have a particular exam day ritual—a carefully timed stop at Tim Horton's for that last coffee and some Timbits to get set up just right for the exam? Before you dismiss all of these things as "just superstition," look more closely at them and see if you can understand why you might have come to associate them with exam-writing success (other than that they really work!).

Psychologists have learned that we develop associations between events such as study locations or study clothing, concentration, and success; dentists and pain; and good-looking members of the opposite sex and excitement. Some associations, learned responses, are a long time in coming; others develop quickly, at a young age, and are long-lasting. Psychologists believe that people can be taught new behaviours, new associations, and, if you like, new ways of living. In fact, unteachable, totally reflexive behaviours are few; most human behaviours can be learned, unlearned, and modified. Unlike the proverbial old dog, we can be taught new tricks; we learn from experience with diligence and study.

Learning is at the core of psychology. It affects our personality, our social behaviour, and our development. By the time we reach adulthood, experience has taught us a large number of simple, predictable, learned associations. We know, for example, that a long day at the beach may result in a painful sunburn and that we should approach a strange dog with caution. We also have learned sophisticated, complicated processes, such as how to drive a car and how to appreciate music ranging from Bach to Blue Rodeo. Some people also learn socially deviant behaviours, such as stealing and drug abuse. Whatever the associations are, our ability to learn about the past and to think about and modify our future behaviour is part of what distinguishes human beings from other organisms: We learn and can think about and reflect on that learning.

Learning: A relatively permanent change in an organism that occurs as a result of experiences in the environment.

Conditioning: A systematic procedure through which associations and responses to specific stimuli are learned.

In general, learning is the process by which people acquire new knowledge. Psychologists define **learning** as a relatively permanent change in an organism that occurs as a result of experiences in the environment and that is often *observed in overt behaviour*. This last point means that, because the internal processes of learning cannot be *seen*, psychologists study the *results* of learning. To do so, they may examine such overt behaviour as solving an algebra problem or throwing a ball. They also may measure physiological changes, such as brain-wave activity, heart rate, and temperature. Psychologists' definition of learning has three other important parts: (1) experience in the environment (you find you do better on your exam if you study in your favourite location), (2) change in the organism (you make the pre-exam Tim Horton's stop—over and over again), and (3) permanence (you take very good care of your lucky exam hat so that it lasts through your university or college years).

Behaviour is always being modified; new experiences affect learning, and what is learned may be forgotten. And, along with the external environment, an organism's internal motivation, abilities, and physiological state influence its ability to learn. For example, if you are tired, learning the material in this chapter will be particularly difficult. Also, practice and repeated experiences ensure that you will remember and easily exhibit newly acquired learning, information, and skills. Furthermore, when learning has occurred, physiological changes—for example, in synapse organization or levels of dopamine—have occurred as well, so that after you learn, you're no longer the same.

The factors that affect learning are often studied in animal behaviour, because the genetic heritage of animals is easy to control and manipulate and because all details of an animal's history and environmental experiences can be known. Although some psychologists claim that different processes underlie animal and human learning, most believe—and experiments show—that the basic processes are similar. Differences become apparent and important, however, when complex behaviours are being evaluated and in experiments that require the use of language.

As you read this chapter, ask yourself whether you favour specific study spots, have special fears associated with specific places, or have learned to associate and anticipate exciting, fearful, or special events in your world. Chances are that you will begin to see in yourself a whole range of learned associations that shape your daily interactions. You will see how your conditioning and the resulting associations illustrate the three basic learning processes that are the subject of this chapter: classical conditioning, operant conditioning, and cognitive learning.

Pavlovian, or Classical, Conditioning Theory

You may have noticed that you have developed an association between your favourite study location and success in exams. It involves a small self-deception on your part, but one that gives you some stress relief in preparation for examinations. To a real extent, you have become conditioned.

In a general sense, psychologists use the term *conditioning* to mean learning. But **conditioning** is actually a systematic procedure through which associations and responses to specific stimuli are learned. It is one of the simplest forms of learning. For example, consider what generally happens when you hear the theme from *The X-Files*. You expect that something supernatural or otherworldly will soon appear on your TV screen, because the theme music introduces a show that usually includes alien visitations or weird events—and if you're a fan of the show, you probably feel a pleasant sense of anticipation. You have been *conditioned* to feel that way. In the terminology used by psychologists, the theme music is the *stimulus*, and anticipation is the *response*.

Conditioned behaviours and reflexive behaviours are different. When psychologists first studied conditioning, they found automatic (reflexive) relationships between specific stimuli and responses. Each time a certain stimulus occurs, the same reflexive response, or behaviour, follows. For example, the presence of food in the mouth leads to salivation; a tap on the knee leads to a knee jerk; a bright light in the eye leads to contraction of the pupil and an eye blink. A **reflex** is an involuntary, automatic behaviour in response to a stimulus; it occurs without prior learning and usually shows little variability from instance to instance. Conditioned behaviours, in contrast, are learned. Many people have learned the response of fear to the stimulus of sitting in a dentist's chair, since they associate the chair with drilling and pain. A chair by itself (a neutral stimulus) does not elicit fear, but a chair associated with pain becomes a stimulus that can elicit fear. This is an example of *conditioning*.

Conditioned behaviours may occur so automatically that they appear to be reflexive. Like reflexes, conditioned behaviours are involuntary; unlike reflexes, they are learned. In classical conditioning (to be defined shortly), previously neutral stimuli such as chairs, lights, and buzzers become associated with specific events and lead to responses such as fear, eye blinks, and nervousness. This type of learning, then, involves stimuli of biological significance.

In 1927, Ivan Pavlov (1849–1936), a Russian physiologist, summarized a now famous series of experiments in which he uncovered a basic principle of learning—conditioning. His research began quite accidentally while studying saliva and gastric secretions in the digestive processes of dogs. He knew that it is normal for dogs to salivate when they eat—salivation is a reflexive behaviour that aids digestion—but he noticed that the dogs were salivating *before* they tasted their food. Pavlov reasoned that this might be happening because the dogs had learned to associate the trainers, who brought them food, with the food itself. Anxious to know more about this basic form of learning, Pavlov abandoned his research on gastric processes and redirected his efforts into teaching dogs to salivate to a new stimulus, such as a bell.

Terms and Procedures

The terminology and procedures associated with Pavlov's experiments are precise and can be confusing; but, the basic ideas are actually quite straightforward. Let's explore them systematically. What Pavlov described was **classical conditioning**, or *Pavlovian conditioning*, in which a neutral stimulus is paired with a stimulus that elicits a reflexive response. For example, the process might occur as follows: A researcher first would identify a stimulus that elicits a reflexive response; for instance, an electric shock elicits a flinching or withdrawal response in an animal (or human). The researcher then would pair this reflexive stimulus and response (shock–flinching) with a neutral stimulus (a light). The researcher might turn on the light as the animal is shocked—this would represent one pairing. This would be repeated a number of times, after which turning the light on without shocking the animal produces a flinching response. The animal has learned something about the light and the shock; that is, it has made an association between the light and the shock.

Pavlov called the stimulus that normally produces a response (for example, food) an **unconditioned stimulus**; as its name implies, it elicits relevant activities from the outset, that is, unconditionally. He called the response to this stimulus (for example, salivating) an **unconditioned response**. The unconditioned response occurs involuntarily, without learning, in response to the unconditioned stimulus.

Reflex: An involuntary, automatic behaviour that occurs in response to a stimulus without prior learning and usually shows little variability from instance to instance.

Classical conditioning: A conditioning process in which an originally neutral stimulus, by repeated pairing with a stimulus that normally elicits a response, comes to elicit a similar or identical response. Also known as *Pavlovian conditioning*.

Unconditioned stimulus: A stimulus that normally produces a measurable involuntary response.

Unconditioned response: An unlearned or involuntary response to an unconditioned stimulus.

Conditioned stimulus: A neutral stimulus that, through repeated association with an unconditioned stimulus, begins to elicit a conditioned response.

Conditioned response: A response elicited by a conditioned stimulus.

In a series of experiments, Pavlov taught dogs to salivate in response to a bell. First, he surgically altered the location of each dog's salivary gland to make the secretions of saliva accessible. He then attached tubes to the relocated salivary glands to measure precisely the amount of saliva produced by the food—the unconditioned stimulus. Then he introduced a bell—the new stimulus (see Figure 5.1). He called the bell a neutral stimulus, because the sound of a bell is not necessarily related to salivation and generally elicits only a response of orientation or attention. To demonstrate this prior to training, Pavlov measured the amount of saliva the dogs produced when a bell was rung by itself; the amount was negligible. He then began the conditioning process by ringing the bell and immediately placing food in the dogs' mouths. After he did this several times, the dogs salivated in response to the sound of the bell alone. Pavlov reasoned that the dogs had associated the sound of the bell with the presentation of food. He called the bell, which elicited salivation as a result of learning, a conditioned stimulus. A **conditioned stimulus** is a neutral stimulus that, through repeated association with an unconditioned stimulus, becomes capable of eliciting a conditioned response. As its name implies, a conditioned stimulus becomes capable of eliciting a response because of (conditional upon) its pairing with the unconditioned stimulus. He called the salivation—the learned response to the sound of the bell—a **conditioned response** (the response elicited by a conditioned stimulus). From his experiments Pavlov discovered that the conditioned stimulus (the bell) brought about a similar but somewhat weaker response than the unconditioned stimulus (the food). Pavlov originally called the conditioned response a "conditional" response because it was conditional upon events in the environment—it was dependent on them. Errors in the translation of his writings brought about the term used most often today: conditioned response. The process of Pavlovian conditioning is outlined in Figure 5.2.

**FIGURE 5.1
Pavlov's Experimental
Setup**

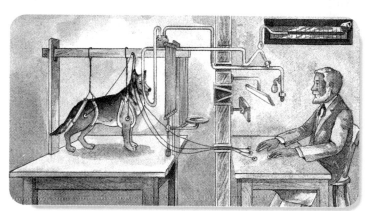

**FIGURE 5.2
The Three Stages of
Classical Conditioning**

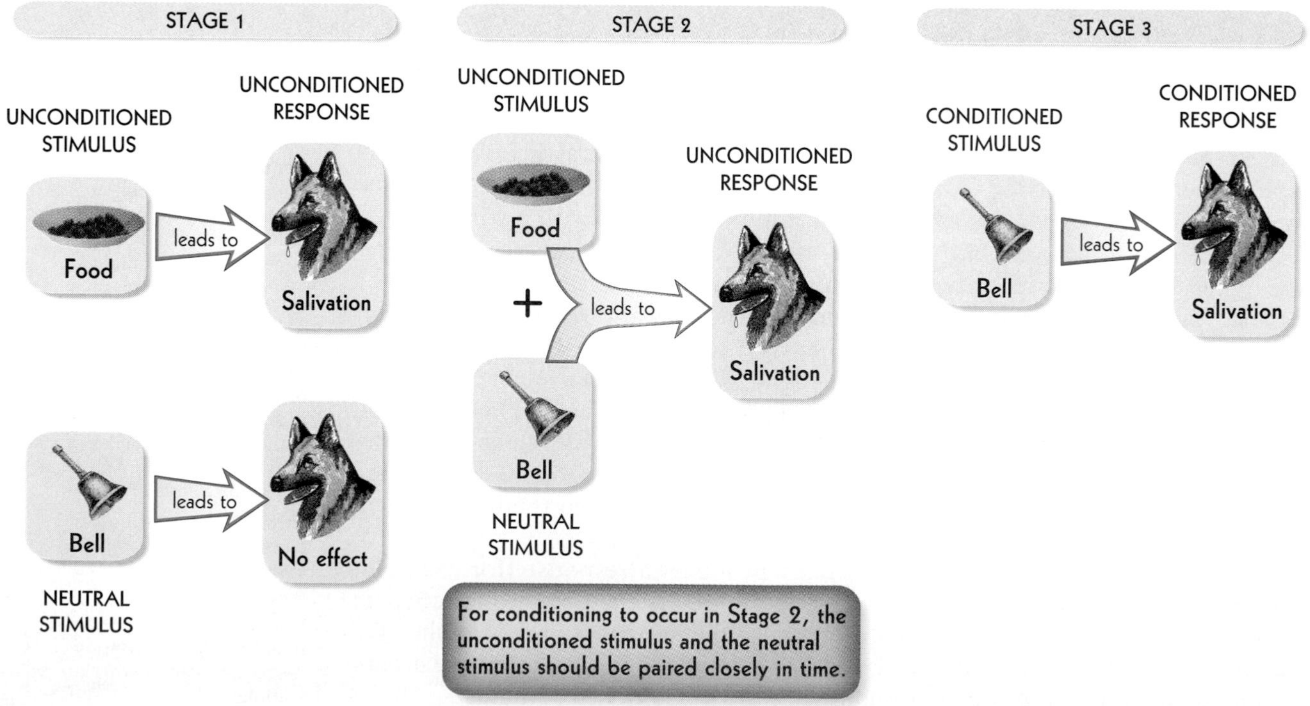

STAGE 1	STAGE 2	STAGE 3

STAGE 1

UNCONDITIONED STIMULUS → UNCONDITIONED RESPONSE

Food — leads to → Salivation

NEUTRAL STIMULUS

Bell — leads to → No effect

STAGE 2

UNCONDITIONED STIMULUS

Food

+

Bell

NEUTRAL STIMULUS

leads to → UNCONDITIONED RESPONSE — Salivation

STAGE 3

CONDITIONED STIMULUS → CONDITIONED RESPONSE

Bell — leads to → Salivation

For conditioning to occur in Stage 2, the unconditioned stimulus and the neutral stimulus should be paired closely in time.

The key characteristic of classical conditioning is the use of an originally neutral stimulus (here, a bell) to elicit a response (here, salivation) through repeated pairing of the neutral stimulus and an unconditioned stimulus that elicits the response naturally (here, food). The conditioned response is acquired gradually. On the first few trials of such pairings, conditioning is unlikely to occur. With additional trials, there is a greater likelihood that the neutral stimulus will yield a conditioned response. Psychologists generally refer to this process as an *acquisition process* and say that an organism has acquired a response. Figure 5.3 shows a typical acquisition curve.

Classical conditioning occurs regularly in the everyday world. When you enter a dentist's office, your heart rate may increase and you may begin to exhibit nervous behaviours because of learned associations you have developed. When classical conditioning occurs, behaviour changes.

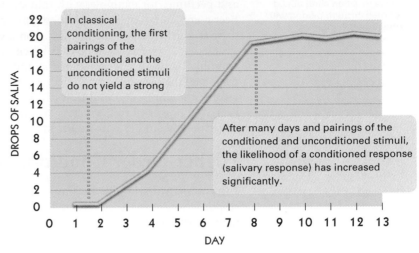

In classical conditioning, the first pairings of the conditioned and the unconditioned stimuli do not yield a strong

After many days and pairings of the conditioned and unconditioned stimuli, the likelihood of a conditioned response (salivary response) has increased significantly.

FIGURE 5.3
A Typical Acquisition Curve

Classical Conditioning in Humans

After Pavlov's success with conditioning in dogs, psychologists were interested in determining whether conditioning also occurs in human beings. In 1931, for example, D. P. Marquis showed classical conditioning in infants. Marquis knew that when an object touches an infant's lips, the infant immediately starts sucking, because the object is usually the nipple of a breast or bottle, from which the infant gets milk. The nipple, an unconditioned stimulus, elicits sucking, an unconditioned response. After repeated pairings of a sound or light with a nipple, infants were conditioned to suck when only the sound or light was presented.

Sucking is one of many reflexive behaviours in human beings; thus it is only one of many responses that can be conditioned. A puff of air delivered to the eye, for example, produces the unconditioned response of an eye blink. When a light or buzzer is paired with puffs of air to the eye, it eventually will elicit the eye blink by itself. This effect can be produced in many animals, as well as in human adults and infants.

The complex equation that allows for learning is not automatic, and depends on a whole array of events, including an organism's past experiences with the conditioned and unconditioned stimulus. This is especially true with complex conditioned responses. Both pleasant and unpleasant emotional responses can be classically conditioned. Consider the following: If a child who is playing with a favourite toy is repeatedly frightened by a sudden loud noise, the child may be conditioned to be afraid each time he or she sees the toy. John B. Watson and Rosalie Raynor explored this type of relationship in 1920 in a now famous experiment with an 11-month-old infant named Albert. The infant was given a series of toys to play with, including a live white rat. One day, as Albert reached for the rat, the experimenters made a sudden ear-splitting noise that frightened the child. After repeated pairing of the noise and the rat, Albert learned the relationship. The rat served as a conditioned stimulus and the loud noise as the unconditioned stimulus; on each subsequent presentation, the rat evoked a conditioned response of fear in Albert. It is important to note that this experiment is considered unethical under the current Canadian Psychological Association guidelines because of the distress caused to Albert and the possibility that the fear, once created, might not be removed effectively.

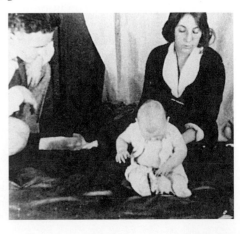

Higher-order conditioning: A
process by which a neutral
stimulus takes on conditioned
properties through pairing with
a conditioned stimulus.

Classical conditioning can be observed simply by watching television, because it is widely used in advertising. Many ads attempt to lead us to associate food, coffee, and perfume, for example, with salivatory responses, relaxation, and sexual appeal. Beer commercials apply conditioning principles by featuring beautiful people enjoying their favourite beer while frolicking on a warm, sunny beach or socializing in a cozy ski chalet. Advertisers hope that when viewers associate the can of beer (a neutral stimulus) with an unconditioned stimulus that naturally elicits a positive emotional response (the pleasant scene), the beer will similarly elicit a positive response. In other words, they hope to condition people to feel good whenever they think about this beer. The powerful role of classical conditioning in advertising has been supported by experimental studies with adults in the laboratory (Stuart, Shimp, & Engle, 1987).

Higher-Order Conditioning

After a neutral stimulus becomes a conditioned stimulus, it elicits the conditioned response whenever it is presented. Moreover, another phenomenon that may occur is **higher-order conditioning**—the process by which a neutral stimulus takes on conditioned properties through pairing with another conditioned stimulus. Suppose a light is paired with mild electric shocks to a dog. On seeing the light, the dog exhibits fear; the light has thus become a conditioned stimulus that elicits a set of fear responses. If a bell is now paired with or presented just before the light, the new stimulus (the bell) can also take on properties of the conditioned stimulus (the light). After repeated pairings, the dog will learn to associate the two events (the light and the bell), and either event by itself will elicit a fear response. When a third stimulus—say, an experimenter in a white lab coat—is introduced, the dog may learn to associate the experimenter with the bell or light. After enough trials, the dog may have conditioned fear responses to each of the three stimuli: the light, the bell, and the experimenter (Pavlov, 1927; Rescorla, 1977). Thus, higher-order conditioning permits increasingly remote associations, which can result in a complex network of conditioned stimuli and responses. At least two factors determine the extent of higher-order conditioning: (1) the similarity between the higher-order stimulus and the original conditioned stimulus, and (2) the frequency and consistency with which the two conditioned stimuli are paired (Rescorla, 1978).

In daily life and in every culture we see evidence of conditioning. The oil light in your car blinks on, your pulse quickens, and you pull over to the side of the road. If you became violently ill with the flu after eating a particular food you may find that you have developed a conditioned taste aversion; you cannot even look at that food again without feeling a bit ill. You may find that even the sound of a dentist's drill is enough to cause feelings of fear. There is universality to these responses—they occur in Japan, Uganda, and Venezuela as well as in Canada. In fact, conditioned taste aversions are among the most powerful conditioned phenomena ever demonstrated. You can see that successful pairing of conditioned and unconditioned stimuli—that is, successful classical conditioning—involves many key variables.

Focus

Review

◆ Identify the fundamental difference between a reflex and a conditioned behaviour. p. 153
◆ Distinguish between a conditioned and an unconditioned response. pp. 153–155

Think Critically

◆ Provide an example of how classical conditioning and higher-order conditioning occur in your life.
◆ Can you think of a situation in which you might want to facilitate higher-order conditioning? How might you increase the likelihood of this kind of learning taking place?

Key Variables in Classical Conditioning

 lassical conditioning is not as simple a process as Pavlov might have thought. As we suggested earlier, such learning is not automatic and depends on a matrix of events, including an organism's past experiences with the conditioned and unconditioned stimulus as well as some key stimulus variables. For example, how bright must the oil light signal in your car be? How loud does the buzzer have to be? How long does the bell have to ring? How sinister must a movie's scary music be? How many times must someone experience pain in a dentist's chair, and how strong does that pain have to be? As with other psychological phenomena, situational variables affect when, if, and under what conditions classical conditioning will occur. Cultural variables are also important; while the principles of conditioning are the same in every culture, what constitutes a fear-producing stimulus will vary from culture to culture.

Some of the most important variables in classical conditioning are the strength, timing, and frequency of the unconditioned stimulus. When these variables are optimal, conditioning occurs easily.

Strength, Timing, and Frequency

Strength of the Unconditioned Stimulus. A puff of air delivered to the eye will easily elicit an unconditioned response, but only if the puff of air (the unconditioned stimulus) is sufficiently strong. Research shows that when the unconditioned stimulus is strong and elicits a quick and regular reflexive (unconditioned) response, conditioning of the neutral stimulus is likely to occur. On the other hand, when the unconditioned stimulus is weak, it is unlikely to elicit an unconditioned response, and conditioning of the neutral stimulus is unlikely to occur. Thus, pairing a neutral stimulus with a weak unconditioned stimulus will not lead reliably to conditioning.

Timing of the Unconditioned Stimulus. For conditioning to occur an unconditioned stimulus usually must be paired with a conditioned stimulus close enough in time for the two to become associated; that is, they must be temporally contiguous. For optimal conditioning, the conditioned stimulus should occur at least half a second (and in many cases substantially longer) before the unconditioned stimulus and overlap with it, particularly for reflexes such as the eye blink. (In Pavlov's experiment, conditioning would not have occurred if the bell and the food had been presented an hour apart.) The two stimuli may be presented together or may be separated by a brief interval. Some types of conditioning can occur with fairly long delays, but the optimal time between the onset of the two stimuli (often cited as half a second) varies from one study to another and depends on many things, including the type of conditioned response sought (e.g., Schwarz-Stevens & Cunningham, 1993).

Frequency of Pairings. Occasional or rare pairings of a neutral stimulus with an unconditioned stimulus at close intervals usually do not result in conditioning (with the exception of food–illness pairings); generally speaking, frequent pairings and pairings that establish a relationship between the unconditioned and the conditioned stimulus are necessary. If, for example, food and the sound of a bell are paired on every trial, a dog is conditioned more quickly than if the stimuli are paired on every other trial. The frequency of the natural occurrence of the unconditioned stimulus is also important. If the unconditioned stimulus does not occur frequently but is always associated with the conditioned stimulus, more rapid conditioning is likely, because one stimulus predicts the other (Rescorla, 1988). Once the conditioned response has reached its maximum strength, additional pairings of the stimuli do not increase the likelihood of a conditioned response. There are exceptions to this general rule, though, and specific one-time pairings can produce learning.

Predictability

A key factor determining whether conditioning will occur is the predictability of the association of the unconditioned and conditioned stimuli. Closeness in time and regular frequency of pairings promote conditioning, but these are not enough. Predictability—being able to anticipate future events—facilitates, and turns out to be a central factor in, conditioning (Rescorla, 1988).

Pavlov thought that classical conditioning was based on contiguity (a close connection between the unconditioned stimulus and the conditioned stimulus). Research now shows, however, that if the unconditioned stimulus (such as the food) can be predicted by the conditioned stimulus (such as the bell), then conditioning is rapidly achieved. Conditioning is achieved not because of the number of times the two events have occurred but rather because of the reliability with which the conditioned stimulus predicts the unconditioned stimulus. Pavlov's dogs learned that bells were good predictors of food; the conditioned stimulus (bells) reliably predicted the unconditioned stimulus (food), so conditioning was quickly achieved.

In Rescorla's (1988) view, what is learned in conditioning is the predictability of events—bells predicting food, light predicting puffs of air to the eye, dentist chairs predicting pain. That there is some sort of relationship between the conditioned and unconditioned stimulus is important. Predictability is one of the key elements in classical conditioning, but without other contextual cues it usually is not enough (Papini & Bitterman, 1990). Many researchers consider predictability to be a cognitive concept; animals and human beings make predictions about the future based on past events in a whole array of circumstances (Siegel & Allan, 1996). As we will see in the next two chapters (on memory and cognition), such thought is based on simple learning but becomes even more complex. You'll also see how the predictability and relationship of events becomes consequential in phenomena such as extinction and spontaneous recovery, considered next.

Extinction and Spontaneous Recovery

Some conditioned responses last for a long time, some for less time. Much depends on whether the conditioned response still predicts the unconditioned one. Consider the following: What would have happened to Pavlov's dogs if he had rung the bell each day but never followed the bell with food? What would happen if you went to the dentist every day for two months, but the dentist only brushed your teeth with pleasant-tasting toothpaste and never drilled, or the drilling that occurred was never accompanied by any discomfort?

If a researcher continues Pavlov's experiment by presenting the conditioned stimulus (bell) but no unconditioned stimulus (food), the likelihood of a conditioned response decreases with every trial; it undergoes extinction. In classical conditioning, **extinction** is the process through which *not* presenting the unconditioned stimulus gradually reduces the probability (and often the strength) of a conditioned response. Imagine a study in which a puff of air is associated with a buzzer that consistently elicits the conditioned eye-blink response. If the unconditioned stimulus (the puff of air) is no longer delivered in association with the buzzer, the likelihood that the buzzer will continue to elicit the eye-blink response decreases over time (see Figure 5.4). When presentation of the buzzer alone no longer elicits the conditioned response, psychologists say that the response has been *extinguished*.

But an extinguished conditioned response may not be gone forever. It can recur, especially after a rest period, in a phenomenon called **spontaneous recovery**. If the dog whose salivation response has been extinguished is placed in the experimental situation again after a rest period of 20 minutes, its salivary response to the bell will recur briefly (although less strongly than before). This behaviour shows that the effects of extinction are not permanent and that the learned association is not totally forgotten (see Figure 5.5).

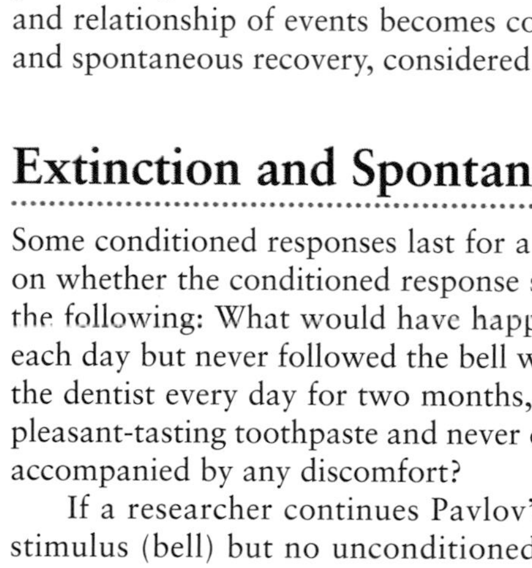

FIGURE 5.4

A Typical Extinction Curve
Numerous experiments have demonstrated that the percentage of times an organism displays a conditioned response decreases over a number of trials in which the unconditioned stimulus is not presented. When presentation of the conditioned stimulus alone no longer elicits the conditioned response, the response has been extinguished.

PERCENTAGE OF CONDITIONED RESPONSES (per minute)

80
70
60
50
40
30
20
10
0

0   10   20   30

NUMBER OF TRIALS IN WHICH THE UNCONDITIONED STIMULUS IS NOT PRESENTED

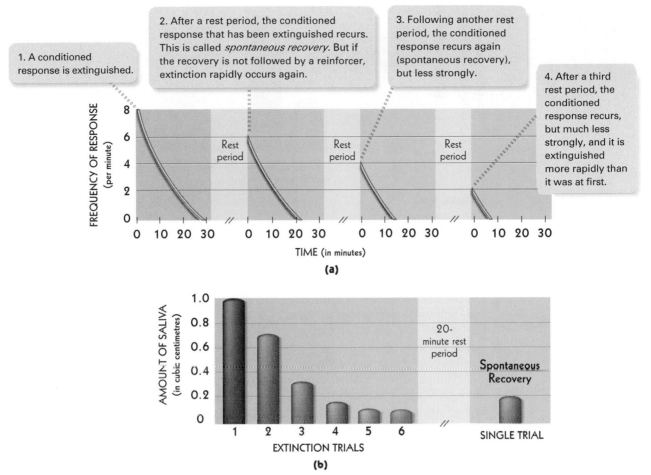

1. A conditioned response is extinguished.

2. After a rest period, the conditioned response that has been extinguished recurs. This is called *spontaneous recovery*. But if the recovery is not followed by a reinforcer, extinction rapidly occurs again.

3. Following another rest period, the conditioned response recurs again (spontaneous recovery), but less strongly.

4. After a third rest period, the conditioned response recurs, but much less strongly, and it is extinguished more rapidly than it was at first.

(a)

(b)

FIGURE 5.5
The Process of Spontaneous Recovery
The graph in part (b) shows some of Pavlov's actual data from an experiment published in 1927. Pavlov brought about extinction in a series of six trials by omitting the presentation of the unconditioned stimulus; but after a 20-minute rest period, spontaneous recovery occurred.

Stimulus Generalization and Stimulus Discrimination

Imagine that a three-year-old child pulls a cat's tail and receives a painful scratch in return. It will not be surprising if the child develops a fear of that cat; but the child actually may develop a fear of all cats, and even of dogs and other four-legged animals. Adults may respond in the same way to similar stimuli—a phenomenon that psychologists call stimulus generalization.

Stimulus generalization occurs when an organism develops a conditioned response to a stimulus that is similar but not identical to the original conditioned stimulus. The extent to which an organism responds to a stimulus similar to the original one depends on how alike the two stimuli are. If, for example, a loud tone is the conditioned stimulus for an eye-blink response, then tones that are somewhat lower but similar also may produce the response. A totally dissimilar tone will produce little or no response. See Figure 5.6 for another example of stimulus generalization.

Stimulus discrimination is the process by which an organism learns to respond only to a specific reinforced stimulus and not to other irrelevant stimuli. Pavlov showed that animals that have learned to differentiate between pairs of stimuli display frustration or even aggression when discrimination is made difficult or impossible. He trained a dog to discriminate between a circle and an ellipse and then changed the shape of the ellipse on successive trials to look more and more like the

Stimulus generalization:
Occurrence of a conditioned response with a stimulus that is similar but not identical to the original conditioned stimulus.

Stimulus discrimination:
Process by which an organism learns to respond only to a specific reinforced stimulus and not to other irrelevant stimuli.

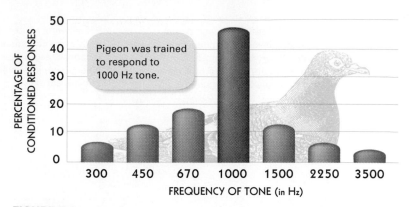

FIGURE 5.6
Stimulus Generalization
Stimulus generalization occurs when an organism (an animal or a human being) exhibits a conditioned response to a stimulus that is similar but not identical to the original conditioned stimulus. In this experiment, a pigeon was trained to respond to a tone of 1000 Hz by pecking a key. Later, the pigeon was presented with tones of different frequencies so that the experimenter could determine whether it would respond to those dissimilar frequencies. Results showed that the percentage of responses decreased as the tone's frequency became increasingly different from the training frequency. *(Based on Jenkins & Harrison, 1960.)*

circle. Eventually, the dog was unable to discriminate between the shapes; it randomly chose one or the other and also became aggressive.

Human beings exhibit similar disorganization in behaviour when placed in work or home situations in which they feel compelled to make a response but don't know how to respond correctly. In such occasions, where one must make a response choice but where choosing a response becomes difficult or impossible, behaviour can become repetitive or limited in scope; people may choose either not to respond to the stimulus or to respond always in the same way (Lundin, 1961; Maier & Klee, 1941). For example, an assembly line employee asked to remove flawed products from a rapidly moving conveyer belt may simply let all products pass or may elect to pull every fiftieth product off the belt, if the flaws are not obvious. Often, therapists must teach maladjusted people to learn to be more flexible in their responses to difficult situations and perhaps to acknowledge when a task is beyond their abilities.

Table 5.1 summarizes four important concepts in classical conditioning: extinction, spontaneous recovery, stimulus generalization, and stimulus discrimination.

Classical Conditioning in Daily Life

You have to admit it. Whether you have noticed it or not, it is very likely that you respond to various types of music with conditioned responses over and over again. Hear a particular kind of music while watching a suspense or horror film and you practically look over your own shoulder. Hear the theme song from *Titanic* and you may get teary-eyed. During your lifetime, you've been conditioned not only to music, but to the sight of good-looking cars and to the thought of walking along a beach with someone you love (especially when it's snowing in Canada during the winter). All of us become conditioned to respond in one way or another, and much of that conditioning is Pavlovian classical conditioning. Let us examine some important examples that have helped us understand ourselves as well as conditioning.

The Garcia Effect. Imagine the following scenario: A six-year-old sits down with her parents after her friends have left her birthday party and eats a ham sandwich with lettuce. She decides that since she is now almost "grown up" she will have mustard on her sandwich, just like her parents. Two hours later, she becomes ill—fever, vomiting, chills, and swollen glands. It was the flu that actually made her ill, but as far as she is concerned, the mustard made her sick. Even now, 16 years later, she still refuses to eat mustard.

Table 5.1 Four Important Concepts in Classical Conditioning

Property	Definition	Example
Extinction	The process of reducing the probability of a conditioned response by presenting the conditioned stimulus alone.	A dog is conditioned by the presentation of food to salivate in response to a tone. When the tone is presented without the food, the dog ceases to salivate to the tone.
Spontaneous recovery	The recurrence of an extinguished conditioned response following presentation of the conditioned stimulus.	A dog's conditioned salivary response to a tone has been extinguished. After a rest period, the dog again salivates in response to the tone, though less than before.
Stimulus generalization	The occurrence of a conditioned response to stimuli that are similar but not identical to the original conditioned stimulus.	A dog conditioned to salivate in response to a high-pitched tone also salivates in response to a somewhat lower-pitched tone.
Stimulus discrimination	The process by which an organism learns to respond only to a specific reinforced stimulus.	A dog is conditioned to salivate only in response to high-pitched tones, not to low-pitched tones.

This association of mustard and nausea is an example of a conditioned taste aversion. In a famous experiment, John Garcia gave animals specific foods or liquids to eat or drink and then induced nausea (usually by injecting them with a drug or by exposing the animals to radiation). He found that after only one pairing of a food or drink (the conditioned stimulus) with the drug or radiation (the unconditioned stimulus), the animals avoided the food or drink that preceded the nausea (see, e.g., Garcia & Koelling, 1971; Linberg et al., 1982).

Two aspects of Garcia's work startled the research community. First, he showed that a conditioned taste aversion could be obtained even if the nausea was induced several hours after the food or drink had been consumed. This contradicted the previously held assumption that the time interval between the unconditioned stimulus and the conditioned stimulus always had to be short, especially if conditioning was to occur quickly. Recent research confirms Garcia's finding (Schafe, Sollars, & Bernstein, 1995). Garcia also showed that not all stimuli could become associated. He tried to pair bells and lights with nausea to produce a taste aversion in rats, but he was unable to do so—learning depended on the relevance, or appropriateness, of the stimuli to one another. This led him to conclude that "strong aversions to the smell or taste of food can develop even when illness is delayed for hours after consumption [but] avoidance reactions do not develop for visual, auditory, or tactile stimuli associated with food" (Garcia & Koelling, 1971, p. 461). Such appropriateness of stimuli may be due to whether they "belong" together in nature; bells and nausea have little to do with one another, but smells and nausea are far more likely to be related in the world and so a smell might quickly become a conditioned stimulus (Hollis, 1997). In the end, Garcia disproved two accepted principles of learning.

Conditioned taste aversion, sometimes called the *Garcia effect*, has adaptive value. In one trial or instance, animals learn to avoid foods that make them sick by associating the smells of poisonous foods with the foods themselves. This clearly has survival value; that is, animals that do not develop rapid aversions to foods that make them sick likely do not survive. Animals that do have this ability survive to reproduce and thus produce offspring that also likely have the rapid aversion ability. Conditioned taste aversion is unaffected by intervening events during the delay between the taste and the illness (Holder et al., 1989). Anyone who has suffered from food poisoning or who has had the misfortune to develop a nasty flu after eating a (formerly!) favourite food can attest to the lasting memory of the food or meal that caused it.

Conditioned taste aversion also has practical uses. Coyotes and wolves often attack sheep and lambs. Garcia laced lamb meat with a substance that causes a short-term illness and put the food on the outskirts of sheep ranchers' fenced-in areas. Coyotes who ate the lamb meat became sick and developed an aversion to lamb. After this experience, they approached the sheep as if ready to attack, but nearly always backed off (see, e.g., Garcia et al., 1976). By using conditioned taste aversion, Garcia deterred coyotes from eating sheep.

Learning and Chemotherapy. Cancer patients often undergo chemotherapy; an unfortunate side effect of the therapy is vomiting and nausea. The patients often lose their appetite and lose weight during treatment. Is it possible that they lose weight because of a conditioned taste aversion? According to researcher Ilene Bernstein (1991), some cancer patients become conditioned to avoid food. They check into a hospital, have a meal, are given chemotherapy, become sick, and thereafter avoid the food that preceded the therapy. Bernstein conducted research with children and adults who were going to receive chemotherapy. Her research showed that patients given foods before therapy, especially foods rich in protein such as eggs and cheese, developed specific aversions to those foods; control groups who were not given those foods before their therapy did not develop aversions to them. Challis and Stam (1992), working at the University of Calgary, identified several factors that seem to predict who will be most influenced by this effect. Basically, depression and anxiety appear unrelated to the effect while self-absorption and focus on one's physical functioning predict a stronger reaction.

Patients develop food aversions even when they know it is the chemotherapy that induces the nausea. Bernstein suggested an intervention based on learning theory: Patients could be given a "scapegoat" food, such as coconut or root beer Lifesavers, just before chemotherapy, so that any conditioned aversion that developed would be to a nutritionally unimportant food rather than to a nutritious food. When Bernstein (1988, 1991) tried this procedure, results were successful with children and adults—they were far less likely to develop food aversions to nutritious foods.

Conditioning of the Immune System. Think of a person's fear of the dentist's chair; chairs, dentists, hygienists, and even the smells associated with the office can lead to fear responses. Classical conditioning explains a wide range of human behaviours, including some physical responses to the world, such as heart rate acceleration and changes in blood pressure.

Substances such as pollen, dust, animal dander, and mold initiate an allergic reaction in many people. Cat fur, for example, may elicit an allergic reaction, such as an inability to breathe, in persons with asthma. Asthma attacks, like other behaviours, can be conditioned to occur. For example, if Lindsay's asthmatic friend has *always* found cat fur in Lindsay's house (a regular pairing), classical conditioning theory predicts that even if all of the cat hair is removed, the friend still may have an allergic reaction upon entering Lindsay's house. (A conditioned stimulus, the house, predicts an unconditioned response, the allergic reaction.) Researchers have shown that people with severe allergies can have an allergic reaction from merely seeing a cat (or entering Lindsay's house, even long after the cat's demise), even if there is no cat fur present.

Even the body's immune system can be conditioned (Ader & Cohen, 1993). Normally, the body releases antibodies to fight disease when toxic substances appear in the blood. In a striking series of studies, animals were classically conditioned in a way that altered their immune responses (Ader & Cohen, 1985, 1993). The experimenters paired a sweet-tasting solution with a drug that produced illness and, as a side effect, also suppressed the immune response. The animals quickly learned to avoid the sweet-tasting substance that seemed to predict illness. When later presented with the sweet-tasting substance alone, the animals showed a reduction in immune system antibodies. The experimenters had classically conditioned an immune system response that was previously thought not to be under nervous system control. This is an intriguing finding.

Conditioning in Addicts. Research also shows that drug users become well conditioned. When heroin addicts inject heroin, their bodies produce compensatory responses to protect them from an overdose; this is a natural response. Shepard Siegel (1984; Seigel & MacCrae, 1984) of McMaster University argues that some of these responses become classically conditioned; that is, they become associated as conditioned responses to the environmental setting in which the addict is injecting the drug. If the addict always injects the drug in the same room, the room itself may serve to initiate compensatory responses, without the heroin ever actually being administered. When a user injects the drug in a new and different location, such compensatory responses are not created—as a result, too much of the drug may be administered, leading to an overdose. A comprehensive theory of drug use, abuse, tolerance, and withdrawal will need to incorporate environmental cues and bodily reactions that are Pavlovian in origin—addicts' bodies react not only to effects of the drug but also in an anticipatory way to the sight of needles, drugs, and locations (Siegel & Allen, 1996).

Pavlov's Understanding Reinterpreted

When Pavlov was busy measuring salivation, he had no reason to consider the complex matrix of variables that we now think about when we evaluate classical conditioning. Pavlov thought about "simple" associations between stimuli. Today, we think about the relevance of a stimulus, its appropriateness, predictability, and ability to create higher-order associations. Pavlov laid the foundation for studying emotions, thoughts, and artificial intelligence because he showed us that organisms learn associations about events in the environment. But these associations are more complex than Pavlov ever thought.

Pavlov focused on specific stimuli and responses; today, researchers are considering how imagined stimuli—thoughts that we have about events—can evoke a response (Dadds et al., 1997). Do thoughts about airplane disasters cause us to avoid air travel? Do images such as hurtling through the air after an airplane collision evoke fears not only of planes but also of heights? Such considerations help us understand, from a conditioning point of view, how behaviour disorders can be established and maintained by thoughts, images, and anticipation of events, all of which can lead to conditioned and sometimes maladaptive behaviours.

Building Table 5.1 summarizes some of the key elements of classical conditioning. Although classical conditioning explains a wide range of phenomena, not all behaviours are the result of such associations. Many complex behaviours result from another form of learning—operant conditioning—which focuses on behaviour and its consequences. Operant conditioning is discussed next.

Focus

Review

◆ How do the variables of strength, timing, and frequency affect learning? p. 157
◆ What happens to the conditioned response if a researcher presents the conditioned stimulus but no unconditioned stimulus? p. 158

Think Critically

◆ What led Garcia to conclude that taste aversion can occur in one trial or one instance? What other examples of learning could occur in one trial or one instance?
◆ What are some of the things that might lead to drug overdoses in addicts who are well conditioned?

Building Table 5.1

Types of Learning: Classical Conditioning

Type of Learning	Procedure	Result	Example
Classical Conditioning	A neutral stimulus (such as a bell) is paired with an unconditioned stimulus (such as food).	The neutral stimulus becomes a conditioned stimulus—it elicits the conditioned response.	A bell elicits a response in a dog.

Operant Conditioning

B ells, whistles, lights, and salivation may occur in the world, and associations may be formed, but in all of these situations the organism, the learner, has little control over the events. A light is presented before food is delivered, and an association is formed. But what happens when a child accidentally breaks a valued clock or a teacher pats a child on the head after class? Do consequences result from such events? Is anything learned? Many psychologists believe that the consequences of behaviour have powerful effects that change the course of subsequent behaviour. Unlike classical conditioning, this view sees the organism as operating on and within the environment, and as a result, the organism receives and observes rewards or punishments. Let's explore this distinction further because it helps explain the how and why of what we do.

Pioneers: B. F. Skinner and E. L. Thorndike

In the 1930s B. F. Skinner (1904–1990) challenged and began to change the way psychologists think about conditioning and learning. In fact, Skinner questioned whether the passive Pavlovian (classical) conditioning that focused on reflexive, automatic responses should be studied at all. Skinner maintained that organisms operate on the environment, with every action followed by a specific event, or consequence. He focused only on an organism's observable behaviour—thought processes, consciousness, brain–behaviour relationships, and the mind were not considered the proper subject matter of psychology. Skinner's early work was in the tradition of such strict behaviourists as Watson, although Skinner ultimately modified some of his own most extreme positions. His 1938 book, *The Behavior of Organisms*, continues to have an impact on studies of conditioning.

According to Skinner, many behaviours are acquired and maintained through operant conditioning, not through Pavlov's classical conditioning. Skinner used the term *operant conditioning* because the organism *operates* on the environment, with every action followed by a specific event, or consequence. **Operant conditioning**, or *instrumental conditioning*, is conditioning in which an increase or decrease in the likelihood that a behaviour will recur (will be repeated) is affected by the delivery of a rewarding or punishing event as a consequence of the behaviour. The conditioned behaviour is usually voluntary, not reflex-like as in classical conditioning. Another key difference between classical conditioning and operant conditioning is that the reward or punishment *follows*, rather than coexists with, the behaviour.

Consider what happens when a boss rewards and encourages her overworked employees by giving them unexpected cash bonuses. If the bonuses improve morale and induce the employees to work harder, the employer's conditioning efforts have

Operant conditioning [OP-er-ant]: Conditioning in which the probability that an organism will emit a response is increased or decreased by the subsequent delivery of a reinforcer or punisher. Also known as *instrumental conditioning*.

been successful. In turn, the employees could condition the boss's behaviour by rewarding her generosity with further increases in productivity, thereby encouraging her to continue giving bonuses. In the laboratory, researchers have studied similar sequences of behaviours followed by rewards. One of the most famous of these experiments was conducted by the American psychologist E. L. Thorndike (1874–1949), who pioneered the study of operant conditioning during the 1890s and first reported his work in 1898. Thorndike placed hungry cats in boxes and put food outside the boxes. The cats could escape from the boxes and get food by hitting a lever that opened a door in each box. The cats quickly performed the behaviour Thorndike was trying to condition (hitting the lever), because doing so (at first by accident and then deliberately) gave them access to food. Because the response (hitting the lever) was important (instrumental) in obtaining the reward, Thorndike used the term *instrumental conditioning* to describe the process and called the behaviours *instrumental behaviours*.

Although Skinner spoke of operant conditioning and Thorndike spoke of instrumental conditioning, the two terms are often used interchangeably. What is important is that both Skinner and Thorndike acknowledged that first the behaviour is *emitted* (displayed), and then a consequence (for example, a reward) follows. This is unlike classical (Pavlovian) conditioning, in which first there is a change in the environment (for example, bells and food are paired) and then the conditioned behaviour (usually a reflexive response) is *elicited* (see Figure 5.7).

In operant conditioning, such as in Thorndike's experiment with cats, an organism emits a behaviour and then a consequence follows. The type of consequence that follows the behaviour is a crucial component of the conditioning, because it determines whether the behaviour is likely to be repeated. Principally, the consequence can be a reinforcer or a punisher. As in classical conditioning, a reward acts as a *reinforcer*, increasing the likelihood that the behaviour targeted for conditioning will recur; in Thorndike's experiment, food was the reinforcer for hitting the lever. A *punisher*, on the other hand, decreases the likelihood that the targeted behaviour will recur. If an electric shock is delivered to a cat's paws each time the cat touches a lever, the cat quickly learns not to touch the lever. Parents use reinforcers and punishers when they link the behaviour of their teenagers to the use of the family car. A teenager on a date is more likely to return home at an appropriate hour if doing so will ensure use of the car again. (We will discuss punishment and its consequences in more detail later in this chapter.)

The Skinner Box and Shaping

Much of the research on operant conditioning has used the apparatus that most psychologists call a Skinner box—even though Skinner never approved of the idea of naming it after him. A **Skinner box** is a box that contains a mechanism for delivering a consequence whenever the animal in the box makes a readily identifiable response that the experimenter has decided to reinforce or punish. In experiments that involve rewards, the delivery mechanism is often a small lever or bar in the side of the box; whenever the animal presses it, the pressing behaviour may be rewarded. Punishment often takes the form of electric shocks delivered through a grid on the floor of the box. Early in Skinner's career, he believed so strongly in creating controlled environments that he devised a controlled living space for his daughter—it became known as the "baby box." The baby box held temperature, light,

FIGURE 5.7
The Process of Operant Conditioning
Operant conditioning is different from classical conditioning in that the behaviour to be conditioned (such as hitting a lever) is reinforced *after* it occurs.

STIMULUS OR CUE — Lever

BEHAVIOUR — Hitting Lever

CONSEQUENCE — Food

Skinner box: Named by others for its developer, B. F. Skinner, a box that contains a responding mechanism (usually a lever) capable of delivering a consequence, often a reinforcer, to an organism.

and humidity at comfortable levels. It also allowed Skinner to "control" the environment and help shape his daughter's behaviour. This personal decision on Skinner's part was quite controversial; although his daughter grew up to be quite normal, ethical questions were raised about manipulating children in this way. However, most of Skinner's work was done with animals—pigeons and rats.

In a traditional operant conditioning experiment, a rat that has been deprived of food for a short time is placed in a Skinner box. The rat moves around the box, often seeking to escape; eventually it stumbles on the lever and presses it. Immediately following that action, the experimenter delivers a pellet of food into a cup. The rat moves about some more and happens to press the lever again; another pellet of food is delivered. After a few trials, the rat learns that pressing the lever brings food. A hungry rat will learn to press the lever many times in rapid succession to obtain food. Today, psychologists use computerized devices to quantify behaviour such as bar pressing and to track the progress an organism makes in learning a response.

Teaching an organism a complex response takes many trials because most organisms need to be taught in small steps, through *shaping*. **Shaping** is the process of reinforcing behaviour that approximates (comes close to) a desired behaviour. To

teach a hungry rat to press a bar in a Skinner box, for example, a researcher begins by giving the rat a pellet of food each time it enters the side of the box on which the bar is located. Once this behaviour is established, the rat receives food only when it touches the wall where the bar is located. It then receives food only when it approaches the bar—and so on, until it receives food only when it actually presses the bar. At each stage the reinforced behaviour (entering the half of the box nearest the bar, touching the wall that houses the bar, and so on) more closely approximates the desired behaviour (pressing the bar). The sequence of stages used to elicit increasingly closer approximations of a desired behaviour is sometimes called the *method of successive approximations*, which means approximately the same thing as *shaping*.

Shaping is effective for teaching animals new behaviours; for example, shaping is used to train a dog to sit on command. The trainer generally does this by pairing a dog treat with a push on the dog's rear while verbally commanding "Sit!" With a treat as a reinforcer following the sitting, the dog begins to sit with less and less pressure applied to its rear; eventually, it sits on command. Shaping was used to train the lions that appear in the film *Ghost in the Darkness*. Shaping is also helpful in teaching people new behaviours. For example, were you taught how to play baseball? If so, first you probably were taught how to hold the bat correctly, then how to swing it, then how to make contact with the ball, and finally how to get a base hit.

Teaching new behaviours by means of operant conditioning is time-consuming and often must be done in several stages, especially if the behaviours are complex. For example, a father who wants his son to make his bed neatly will at first reinforce *all* of the child's attempts at bed-making, even if the results are sloppy. Over successive weeks, the father will reinforce only the better attempts, until finally he reinforces only neat bed-making. Patience is important, because it is essential to reinforce all steps towards the desired behaviour, no matter how small (Fischer & Gochros, 1975). Shaping embodies a central tenet of behaviourism—reinforced behaviours recur. Skinner is the individual most responsible for advancing that notion; psychologists attribute to him the idea that various consequences can redirect the natural flow of behaviour. Among the most important of these consequences is reinforcement.

Reinforcement: A Consequence
That Strengthens a Response

To really understand operant conditioning, you need to study the basic principles of reinforcement. To psychologists, a **reinforcer** is any event that increases the probability of a recurrence of the response that preceded it. Thus, a behaviour followed by a desirable event is likely to recur. Examples of reinforcement abound in daily life: A person works hard in a factory and is rewarded with high pay; a student studies long hours for an examination and is rewarded with a top grade; sales agents call on hundreds of clients and sell lots of their products; young children behave appropriately and receive affection and praise from their parents. The specific behaviours of working hard, studying a great deal, calling on clients, and behaving well for parents are established because of reinforcement. Such behaviours can be taught by means of either or both of two kinds of reinforcers: positive and negative.

Positive Reinforcement. Most people have used positive reinforcement at one time or another. **Positive reinforcement** is the presentation of a rewarding or pleasant stimulus after a particular response, to increase the likelihood that the response will recur. When you teach your dog tricks, you reward it with a biscuit or a pat on the head. When parents are toilet training a two-year-old, they may applaud when the child successfully deposits a bowel movement in the potty; the applause is a reinforcer. The dog and the child continue the behaviours because they have been rewarded with something that is important or desired; their behaviours have been positively reinforced.

Some reinforcers are more powerful than others, and a reinforcer that rewards one person may not have reinforcing value for another. A smile from an approving parent may be a powerful reinforcer for a two-year-old; high grades may be the most effective reinforcer for a student; money may be effective for one adult, while position or status is effective for another. At many corporations, bonuses for effective performance may include colour televisions, stereo systems, or trips to Hawaii.

Negative Reinforcement. Whereas positive reinforcement increases the probability of a response through delivery of a reward, **negative reinforcement** increases the probability of a response through removal of an *aversive* (unpleasant or noxious) stimulus. Negative reinforcement is still reinforcement, because it strengthens or increases the likelihood of a response; its reinforcing properties are associated with its removal. For example, suppose a rat is placed in a maze with an electrified grid that delivers a shock every 50 seconds, and the rat can escape the shock by turning to the left in the maze. The behaviour to be conditioned is turning to the left in the maze; the reinforcement is termination of the painful stimulus. In this case, negative reinforcement—termination of the painful stimulus—increases the probability of the response (going left) because that is the way to turn off the unpleasant stimulus. As another example, consider the last time you took something for a headache. The headache's disappearance (if the drug worked) will negatively reinforce your remedy-taking behaviour.

Noxious or unpleasant stimuli often are used in animal studies of escape and avoidance. In *escape conditioning*, an animal receives a shock just strong enough to cause it to thrash around until it bumps against a bar, thereby stopping the shock. In just a few trials, the animal learns to press the bar to escape being shocked, to bring an unpleasant situation to an end. In *avoidance conditioning*, the same apparatus is used, but a buzzer or some other cue precedes the shock by a few seconds. In this case, the animal learns that when it is presented with a stimulus or cue such as a buzzer, it should press the bar to prevent the shock from occurring—to avoid it. Avoidance conditioning generally involves escape conditioning as well. First the animal learns how to escape the shock by pressing the bar. Then it learns how to avoid the shock by pressing the bar when it hears the buzzer that signals the oncoming shock or it learns to push the bar or to leave the area (if possible) as soon as it is put in the apparatus.

Reinforcer: Any event that increases the probability of a recurrence of the response that preceded it.

Positive reinforcement: Presentation of a rewarding or pleasant stimulus after a particular response, to increase the likelihood that the response will recur.

Negative reinforcement: Removal of an aversive stimulus after a particular response to increase the likelihood that the response will recur.

In avoidance conditioning, the organism learns to respond in such a way that the noxious stimulus is never delivered. For example, to avoid receiving a bad grade on an English quiz, a student may study before an examination or not take an English course at all. And when an adult develops an irrational fear of airplanes, the person may avoid airplane travel. If the person can get to where he or she needs to go by some other means, the person may never unlearn the fear of planes. Thus, avoidance conditioning can explain adaptive behaviours such as studying before an exam, and it can also explain why some people maintain irrational fears.

Most children master both escape and avoidance conditioning at an early age; appropriate signals from a disapproving parent often result in an emitted avoidance response so punishment will not follow. Similarly, just knowing the possible effects of an automobile accident will make most cautious adults wear seatbelts. Both positive and negative reinforcements *increase* the likelihood that an organism will repeat a behaviour. If the reinforcement is strong enough, is delivered often enough, and is important enough to the organism, it can help maintain behaviours for long periods.

The Nature of Reinforcers. The precise nature of reinforcers is a murky issue. Early researchers recognized that events that satisfy biological needs are powerful reinforcers. Later researchers added events that decrease a person's various needs—for example, conversation that relieves boredom, sounds that relieve sensory deprivation, and money that relieves housing congestion. Then, in the 1960s, researchers acknowledged that an array of events can be reinforcers. *Probable behaviours*—behaviours likely to happen, including biological behaviours such as

brain and behaviour
The Biology Behind Learning

Whenever there is learning, there is a relatively permanent change in behaviour, and this change is reflected in our nervous system. Donald O. Hebb (1904–1985), a Canadian psychologist who worked at McGill University, was one of the first to suggest that, with each learning situation, the structure of the brain changes. He argued that cells, synaptic transmission, and neural activity in general become involved in a group that, taken together, fire over and over—he referred to it as a reverberating circuit. The more the circuit that represents a concept or experience is stimulated, the more that learning experience is remembered and the structure of the brain is altered.

Remember that learning is a process made up of unique interactions among hundreds and thousands of neurons in the brain. Using this fact, Hebb (1949) suggested that, when groups of neurons are stimulated, they form specific patterns of neural activity. The evolution of a temporary neural circuit into a more permanent circuit is known as *consolidation*. According to Hebb, consolidation serves as the basis of learning and memory and permits the coding (also known as encoding) of information into long-term memory. If Hebb was correct, when people first sense a new stimulus, only temporary changes in neurons take place; but with repetition, consolidation occurs and the temporary circuit becomes a permanent one.

Many psychologists today believe that the consolidation process provides the key to understanding learning—that individual differences in ability to learn (or remember) may be due to differing abilities to consolidate neural circuits properly. Confirmation of this notion comes from studies using electroconvulsive shock therapy (discussed in Chapter 16) to disrupt consolidation, which results in impaired memory both in human beings and in animals. Further support comes from studies showing that recent (less-consolidated) memories are more susceptible to amnesia loss than are older (more-consolidated) memories (Milner, 1989).

The consolidation process even may play a role in the brain's physiological development. Researchers have compared the brains of animals raised in enriched environments, where toys and other objects are available for the animals to play with and to learn from, with the brains of animals raised in deprived environments. The brains of animals raised in enriched environments have more elaborate networks of nerve cells, with more dendrites

eating and social behaviours such as playing tennis, writing letters, or talking—can reinforce less probable or unlikely behaviours such as cleaning closets, studying calculus, or pressing levers. Researchers call this idea the *Premack principle*, after David Premack, whose influential writings and research fostered it (Premack, 1962, 1965). Parents employ the Premack principle when they tell their children that they can go outside to play *after* they clean up their room.

The Premack principle and its refinements focus on the problem of determining what is a good reinforcer. Therapists and learning theorists know, for example, that something that acts as a reinforcer for one person may not do so for another, and something that acts as a reinforcer on one day may not do so for the same person on the next day. Therefore, psychologists are very careful about determining what events in a client's life—or a rodent's environment—act as reinforcers. If someone were to offer you a reinforcer for some extraordinary activity on your part, what would be the most effective reinforcer? Do reinforcers change with a person's age and experiences, or do they depend on how often the person has been reinforced? Today, researchers are trying to find out ahead of time what reinforcers will work in practical settings such as the home and the workplace (Timberlake & Farmer-Dougan, 1991).

A reinforcer that is known to be successful may work only in specific situations. The delivery of food pellets to a hungry rat that has just pressed a lever increases the likelihood that the rat will press the lever again. But this reinforcer works only if the rat is hungry; for a rat that has just eaten, food pellets are not reinforcing. Psychologists studying learning and conditioning create the conditions for reinforcement by depriving animals of food or water before an experiment. In doing so, they

and more synapses with other neurons (Chang, Isaacs, & Greenough, 1991). This means that when a neuron is stimulated over and over again, it is enriched; it then may branch out and become more easily accessible to further synaptic connections. Such elaboration is greater when organisms are placed in complex, super-enriched visual or auditory environments. These findings may indicate that when key neurons and neurotransmitters are stimulated by reinforcing events, those events may be better remembered and more easily accessed—this may be part of the reason reinforced or practised events are so easily recalled (Kandel & Abel, 1995). Although less research has been done with human beings, Jacobs et al. (1993) found that people with more education have more dendritic elaboration, and Scheibel et al. (1990) found that parts of the body that have more complex usage (fingers versus the wall of the chest) have more elaborate dendritic organization.

If a neuron is stimulated, the biochemical processes involved make it more likely to respond again later; further, its number of dendrites increases because of previous stimulation (Beaulieu & Colonnier, 1988; Lynch & Baudry, 1984). Associations are learned because of synaptic plasticity (the flexibility of neural connections) (Moser et al., 1998; Tracy et al., 1998). Repetition, as in repeated pairings of a conditioned and unconditioned stimulus in classical conditioning, may make learning and remembering easier (Kandel & Abel, 1995)—a concept that fits perfectly with Hebb's original suggestions.

Consolidation theory has been refined and extended by research and shows that a single neuron has many synaptic sites on its dendrites. Not only do cells have many synaptic sites, they can be active in more than one matrix or network of functions. Some neurons may be involved in multiple activities and may exert a stronger influence than others—for example, those cells involved in behaviours where visual and motor activities interact may become especially elaborate. Alkon (1989) showed that there is extensive interaction among those neurons' synaptic sites and with the sites of other neurons. He argued that the spread of electrical and chemical activity from one site to another is critical for initiating learning and memory. He asserted that, on a given neuron, a huge number of different incoming signals can be received and stored. More recently, Alkon has been developing mathematical and computer models to simulate neuronal encoding for memory and to study animal memory. This exciting work also extends Hebb's theories.

Also in its infancy, but very promising, is the finding that specific genes are necessary for the formation of learning and memory. A research team headed by Alcino Silva has isolated a gene, dubbed the *CREB gene*, which is crucial in the consolidation process. Without the presence of this gene, certain proteins are not activated, and memories are fleeting (Bourtchuladze et al., 1994). The impact of the genetic causes of memory and memory loss is yet to be fully understood; the presence of the CREB gene is one link among many in the chain of events from experience to recall, but it seems to be an essential one. ■

Primary reinforcer: A reinforcer (such as food, water, or the termination of pain) that has survival value for an organism; thus, its value does not have to be learned.

Secondary reinforcer: A neutral stimulus that has no intrinsic value for an organism initially but that can become rewarding when linked with a primary reinforcer.

Superstitious behaviour: Behaviour learned through coincidental association with reinforcement.

motivate the animals and allow the delivery of food to take on reinforcing properties. In most experiments, the organism is motivated in some way. Chapter 9 discusses the role of an organism's needs, desires, and physiological state in determining what can be used as a reinforcer.

A **primary reinforcer** is a reinforcer that has survival value for the organism (for example, food, water, or the termination of pain); its value does not have to be learned. Food can be a primary reinforcer for a hungry rat, water for a thirsty one. A **secondary reinforcer** is a neutral stimulus (such as money or grades) that initially has no intrinsic value for the organism but that when linked with a primary reinforcer can become rewarding. Many human pleasures are secondary reinforcers that have acquired value—for example, leather coats that keep people no warmer than cloth ones and sports cars that take people around town no faster than four-door sedans. The secondary reinforcer acquires value because it predicts the primary reinforcer (that is, an association has been made between the secondary and primary reinforcers).

Secondary reinforcers generally are used to modify human behaviour. Approving nods, unlimited use of the family car, and job promotions are secondary reinforcers that act to establish and maintain a wide spectrum of behaviour. Salespeople may work 72-hour weeks to reach their sales objectives. This may happen when their manager, using basic psychology, offers them bonuses for increasing their sales by a specific percentage during a slow month. The manager may reason that increasing the amount of the secondary reinforcer (money) may promote better performance (higher sales). Research shows that increasing or decreasing the amount of a reinforcer can significantly alter an organism's behaviour. Of course, what is reinforcing for one person or one culture, for that matter, may not have the same reinforcing properties for another person or another culture. Money may reinforce some behaviours for some individuals; however, a smile from an approving parent, a salute from a superior officer, or a kiss on the cheek from a loved one may be far more powerful for others.

Superstitious Behaviours. Because reinforcement plays a key role in our learning of new behaviours, parents and educators intentionally try to reinforce children and students on a regular basis. But what happens when a person or animal is *accidentally* rewarded for a behaviour—when a reward has nothing to do with the behaviour that immediately preceded it? Under this condition, people and animals may develop **superstitious behaviour**—behaviour learned through coincidental association with reinforcement. For example, a hockey player may try to extend his scoring streak by always wearing the same "lucky" socks. A student may study at the same place in the library because she earned an A after studying there for the last exam. Many superstitious behaviours—including fear responses to the number 13, black cats, and walking under ladders—are centuries old and have strong cultural associations. Individual superstitious behaviours generally arise from a purely random event that occurred immediately after the behaviour. Thus, a person who happens to wear the same pair of shoes in three bicycle races and wins those races may come to believe there is a causal relationship between wearing that pair of shoes and winning bicycle races.

Animals can learn superstitious behaviours even in a Skinner box. For example, on trials in which a pigeon learns the bar-pressing response, the bird may turn its head to the right before pressing the bar and receiving reinforcement. Although the reinforcement is actually contingent only on pressing the bar, to the pigeon it may seem that both the head turning and the bar pressing are necessary (Skinner, 1948). Therefore, the pigeon will continue to turn its head before pressing the bar.

Punishment: A Consequence That Weakens a Response

You already know that the consequences of an action—whether reward or punishment—affect behaviour. Clearly, rewards can establish new behaviours and maintain them for long periods. How effective is punishment in manipulating behaviour? **Punishment** is the process of presenting an undesirable or noxious stimulus, or removing a desirable stimulus, to decrease the probability that a particular preceding response will recur. Punishment, unlike reinforcement, aims to *decrease* the probability of a particular response. There are two forms of punishment, generally described as positive and negative punishment. In this instance the word *positive* refers to the nature of the contingency. A positive punishment produces a consequence. For example, when a dog growls at visitors, its owner chastises it. When children write on the walls with crayons, their parents scold them or make them scrub the walls clean. In both cases, people indicate displeasure by the delivery of an action in an effort to suppress (decrease) an undesirable behaviour.

Researchers use the same approach—a form of punishment, **positive punishment**—to decrease the probability that a behaviour will recur. They deliver a noxious or unpleasant stimulus, such as a mild electric shock, when an organism displays an undesirable behaviour. If an animal is punished for a specific behaviour, the probability that it will continue to perform that behaviour decreases.

Another form of punishment, **negative punishment**, involves removal of a pleasant stimulus. For example, if teenagers stay out past their curfew, they may lose privileges (be grounded) for a week. If children misbehave, they may be forbidden to watch television. One effective negative punishment is the time-out, in which a person is removed from an environment containing positive events or reinforcers. For example, a child who hits and kicks may be put in a corner where there are no toys, television, or people.

Thus, punishment can involve either adding a noxious event, such as a scolding (positive punishment), or subtracting a positive event, such as TV watching (negative punishment). In both cases, the aim is to decrease the likelihood of a behaviour. (See Figure 5.8 for a summary of the effects of adding or subtracting a reinforcer or punisher.)

Punishment: The process of presenting an undesirable or noxious stimulus, or removing a desirable stimulus, to decrease the probability that a particular preceding response will recur.

Positive punishment: A form of punishment in which an unpleasant stimulus is added in an effort to decrease an undesirable behaviour.

Negative punishment: A form of punishment in which a pleasant stimulus is taken away in an effort to decrease an undesirable behaviour.

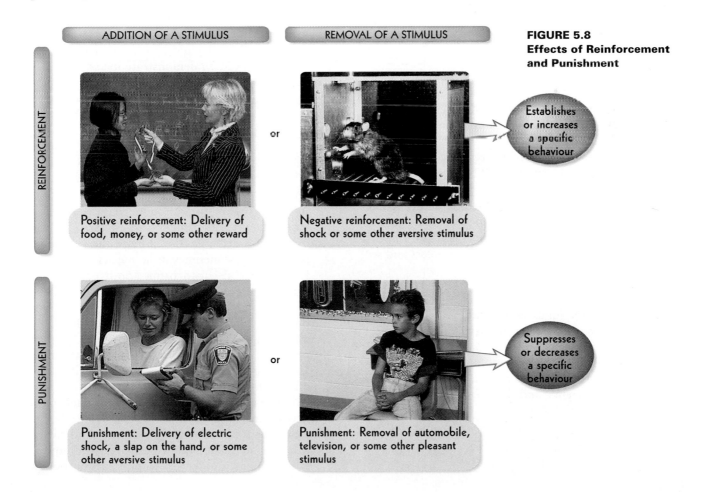

FIGURE 5.8
Effects of Reinforcement and Punishment

ADDITION OF A STIMULUS	REMOVAL OF A STIMULUS	
Positive reinforcement: Delivery of food, money, or some other reward	Negative reinforcement: Removal of shock or some other aversive stimulus	Establishes or increases a specific behaviour
Punishment: Delivery of electric shock, a slap on the hand, or some other aversive stimulus	Punishment: Removal of automobile, television, or some other pleasant stimulus	Suppresses or decreases a specific behaviour

Primary punisher: Any stimulus or event that is naturally painful or aversive to an organism.

Secondary punisher: A neutral stimulus with no intrinsic negative effect on an organism that acquires punishment value through repeated pairing with a primary punisher.

The Nature of Punishers. Just as reinforcers are used for reinforcement, *punishers* are used for punishment. They can be primary or secondary. A **primary punisher** is a stimulus that is naturally painful to an organism; two examples are an electric shock to an animal and a visible look of disapproval by a parent to a small child. A **secondary punisher** is a neutral stimulus that takes on punishing qualities; examples are a verbal no, a shake of the head, or indifference. Secondary punishers can be effective means of controlling behaviour, especially when used in combination with reinforcers for desired behaviours. But, as with reinforcement, what is punishing for one person or in one culture may not have the same properties for another person or in another culture. Indifference may punish some behaviours for some people, but withholding of approval from a stern authority figure may be far more powerful.

Punishment Plus Reinforcement. We have long known that punishment by itself is not an effective way to control or eliminate behaviour. Punishment can suppress simple behaviour patterns, but once the punishment ceases, animals and human beings often return to their previous behaviour. Generally, punishment is most effective if it is severe, if positive alternative behaviours are available, if it quickly follows the behaviour it is intended to reduce, and if it is accompanied by feedback that specifies the relationship between the bad behaviour and the punishment (Schwartz & Robbins, 1995). Therefore, those who study children in classrooms urge the combination of punishment for antisocial behaviour and reinforcement for prosocial behaviour. A combination of private reprimands for disruptive behaviours and public praise for good behaviours is often the most effective method for controlling classroom behaviour.

Limitations of Punishment. A serious limitation of punishment as a behaviour-shaping device is that it suppresses only existing behaviours. It cannot be used to establish new, desired behaviours. Punishment also has serious social consequences (Azrin & Holtz, 1966). If parents use excessive punishment to control a child's behaviour, for example, the child may try to escape from the home so that punishment cannot be delivered. Further, children who receive physical punishments often demonstrate increased levels of aggression when they are away from the punisher. Punishment may control a child's behaviour while the parents are nearby, but it also may alienate the child from the parents.

Research also shows that children imitate aggression. Thus, parents who punish children physically are likely to have children who are physically aggressive (Mischel & Grusec, 1966). A child (or an institutionalized person) may strike out at the person who administers punishment in an attempt to eliminate the source of punishment, sometimes inflicting serious injury. Punishment also can bring about generalized aggression. For example, if two rats in a Skinner box both receive painful shocks, they will strike out at each other. Similarly, punished individuals are often hostile and aggressive towards other members of their group. This is especially true for prison inmates, whose hostility is well recognized, and for class bullies, who are often the children most strictly disciplined by their parents or teachers. Skinner (1988) believed that punishment in schools is unnecessary and harmful; he advocated non-punitive techniques, which might involve developing strong bonds

Focus

Review
- How could a child's undesirable behaviour (hitting the family cat, for example) be shaped to a desired behaviour? p. 166
- What types of reinforcers are most likely to ensure that a behaviour will be repeated? pp. 167–170
- What are some examples showing that probable behaviours can reinforce less probable or unlikely behaviours (the Premack principle)? pp. 168–169
- Distinguish between primary reinforcers and secondary reinforcers. p. 169

Think Critically
- What are the fundamental differences between positive reinforcement, negative reinforcement, and punishment? Give an example of each.
- Your neighbour tells you, "Punishment just doesn't work with my kids any more. I keep escalating the punishments, and they keep acting worse and worse! I don't know what to do!" What do you think is going on here, and what would you advise your neighbour to do?

between students and teachers and reinforcing school activities at home (Comer, 1988). In general, procedures that lead to a perception of control on the part of an individual are much more likely to extinguish undesired behaviour, even when the disciplining agent (often Mom or Dad) is not around.

Further, if punishment is ineffectively or inconsistently delivered, it may lead to **learned helplessness**, in which a person or animal feels powerless to control the punishment and stops making any response at all. Martin Seligman and his colleagues (1975) showed, for example, that dogs first exposed to a series of inescapable shocks and then given a chance to escape further punishment failed to learn the escape response.

Key Variables in Operant Conditioning

s with classical conditioning, many variables affect operant conditioning. Most important are the strength, timing, and frequency of consequences (either reinforcement or punishment).

Strength, Timing, and Frequency of Consequences

Strength of Consequences. Studies comparing productivity with varying amounts of reinforcement show that the greater the reward, the harder, longer, and faster a person will work to complete a task (see Figure 5.9). For example, if you were a gardener, the more money you received for mowing lawns, the more lawns you would want to mow. Similarly, the stronger the punishment, the more quickly and longer the behaviour can be suppressed. If you knew you would be imprisoned for speeding instead of just paying a fine, you probably would start to obey the speed limit.

The strength of a consequence can be measured in terms of either time or degree. For example, the length of time a child stays in a time-out room without positive reinforcements can affect how soon and for how long an unacceptable behaviour will be suppressed. Thus, a two-minute stay might not be as effective as a ten-minute stay. Likewise, a half-hearted "Please don't do that, sweetie" is not as effective as a firm "Don't do that again."

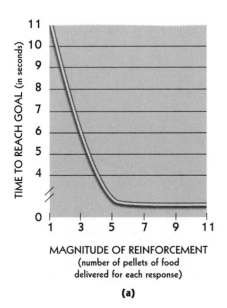

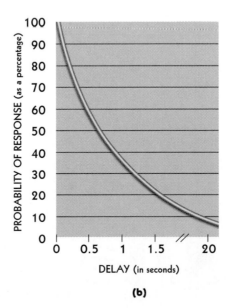

FIGURE 5.9
The Magnitude and Delay of Reinforcement
(a) As the amount of a reinforcer (its strength or magnitude) increases, the time it takes an organism to reach a goal usually decreases. (b) As a delay is placed between a response and reinforcement, the probability that a behaviour will recur decreases. Short delays (or no delays) between a response and reinforcement increase the chances that a behaviour will recur.

Punishment, whatever its form, is best delivered in moderation; too much may be as ineffective as too little. If too much punishment is delivered, it may cause panic, decrease the likelihood of an appropriate response, or even elicit behaviour that is contrary to the goals of the punishment.

Timing of Consequences. Just as the interval between presenting the conditioned stimulus and the unconditioned stimulus is important in classical conditioning, the interval between a desired behaviour and the delivery of the consequence (reward or punishment) is important in operant conditioning. Generally, the shorter the interval, the greater the likelihood that the behaviour will be learned (see Figure 5.9).

Frequency of Consequences. How often do people need to be reinforced? Is a paycheque once a month sufficient? Will people work better if they receive reinforcement regularly or if they receive it at unpredictable times? Up to this point, our discussion has generally assumed that a consequence follows each response. What if people are reinforced only some of the time, not continually? When a researcher varies the frequency with which an organism is to be reinforced, the researcher is said to manipulate the *schedule of reinforcement*—the pattern of presentation of the reinforcer over time. The simplest and easiest reinforcement pattern is *continuous reinforcement*—reinforcement for every occurrence of the targeted behaviour. However, most researchers, or parents for that matter, do not reinforce a behaviour every time it occurs; rather, they reinforce occasionally or intermittently. What determines the timetable for reinforcement? Schedules of reinforcement generally are based either on intervals of time or on frequency of response. Some schedules establish behaviours quickly; however, quickly established behaviours are more quickly extinguished than are behaviours that are slower to be established. (We'll discuss extinction in operant conditioning further in a few paragraphs.) Researchers have devised four basic schedules of reinforcement; two are *interval schedules* (which deal with time periods between reinforced responses), and two are *ratio schedules* (which deal with work output).

Interval schedules can be either fixed or variable. Imagine that a rat in a Skinner box is being trained to press a bar in order to obtain food. If the experiment is on a **fixed-interval schedule**, the reward will follow the first required response that occurs after a specified interval of time since the previous reinforced response. That is, the rat will be given a reinforcer if it presses the bar at least once after a specified time interval, regardless of whether the rat works a great deal or just a little. As Figure 5.10 shows, a fixed-interval schedule produces a scalloped pattern. Just after reinforcement (shown by the tick marks in the figure), both animals and human beings typically respond slowly; just before the reinforcer is due, there is an increase in performance.

FIGURE 5.10
The Four Basic Types of Reinforcement Schedules
Each tick mark indicates presentation of a reinforcer. Steep slopes represent high work rates. In general, the rate of response is higher under ratio schedules than under interval schedules.

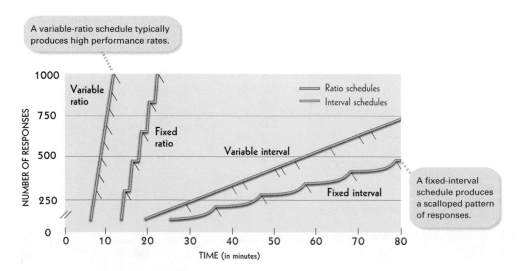

Under a **variable-interval schedule**, the reinforcer is delivered after predetermined but varying amounts of time, as long as an appropriate response is made at least once after each interval following the previous reinforced response. The organism may be reinforced if it makes a response after 40 seconds, after 60 seconds, and then after 25 seconds. For example, if grades are posted at unpredictable intervals during a semester, you probably will check the bulletin board at a fairly regular rate. Rats reinforced on a variable-interval schedule work at a slow, regular rate, without showing the scalloped effect of those on a fixed-interval schedule. The work rate is relatively slow, because the delivery of the reinforcer is tied to time intervals rather than to output. Nevertheless, rats on a variable-interval schedule have a better overall rate of response than those on a fixed-interval schedule.

Ratio schedules, which also can be either fixed or variable, deal with output instead of time. In a **fixed-ratio schedule**, the subject is reinforced for a specified number of responses (amount of work). For example, a rat in a Skinner box might be reinforced after every tenth bar press. In this case, the rat will work at a fast, regular rate until it is reinforced, pause, then begin to work at a fast, regular rate again. It has learned that hard work brings regular delivery of a reinforcer, but that reinforcers do not occur one after the next, so it has learned that it can pause following reinforcement. Figure 5.10 shows that the work rate of a rat on a fixed-ratio schedule is much higher than that of a rat on an interval schedule. In the same way, a teenager who is paid for each lawn mowed (i.e., for the amount of work completed) probably will mow more lawns than a teenager who is paid by the hour.

Variable-ratio schedules can achieve very high rates of response. In contrast to a fixed-ratio schedule, a **variable-ratio schedule** reinforces the subject for a predetermined but variable number of responses (amount of work). Thus, a rat learns that hard work produces a reinforcer, but it cannot predict when the reinforcer will be delivered. Therefore, the rat's best bet is to work at a regular, high rate, thereby generating the highest available rate of response. Sales agents for insurance companies know that the more prospects they approach, the more insurance they will sell. They may not know who will buy, but they do know that a greater number of selling opportunities ultimately will result in more sales. Similarly, gamblers pour quarters into slot machines because although they do not know when they will be reinforced with a jackpot they do know that the slot machine is programmed to pay off at some point. Table 5.2 summarizes the four schedules of reinforcement.

An efficient way to teach a response is to have an organism learn the response on a fixed-ratio schedule, then introduce a variable-ratio schedule. For example, a rat initially can be reinforced on every trial so that it will learn the proper response quickly. It then can be reinforced after every other trial, then after every fifth trial, and then after a variable number of trials. Once the rat has learned the desired response, very high response rates can be obtained even with infrequent reinforcement. When an experimenter implements a *variable*-ratio or a *variable*-interval schedule, the frequency for each ratio or the length of each interval is predetermined,

Table 5.2   Types of Reinforcement Schedules

Schedule	Description	Effect
Fixed-interval	Reinforcement is given for the first response after a fixed time.	Response rate drops right after reinforcement but then increases near the end of the interval.
Variable-interval	Reinforcement is given for the first response after a predetermined but variable interval.	Response rate is slow and regular.
Fixed-ratio	Reinforcement is given after a fixed number of responses.	Response rate is fast and regular.
Variable-ratio	Reinforcement is given after a predetermined and variable number of responses.	Response rate is regular and high.

though it will not appear so to the subject. These schedules can be combined easily for maximum effect, depending on the targeted behaviour (e.g., Zarcone et al., 1997).

Using Schedules of Consequences. The study of reinforcement has many practical implications. Psychologists use the principles of reinforcement to study such frequently asked questions as these: How can I change my little brother's rotten attitude? How can I get more work out of my employees? How do I learn to say no? How do I get my dog to stop biting my ankles? To get your brother to shape up, you can shape his behaviour. Each time he acts in a way you like, however slight, reward him with praise or affection. When he acts poorly, withhold attention or rewards and ignore him. Continue this pattern for a few weeks; as he becomes more pleasant, show him more attention. Remember, reinforced behaviours tend to recur.

Most workers get paid a fixed amount each week. They are on a fixed-interval schedule—regardless of their output, they get their paycheque. One way to increase productivity is to place workers on a fixed-ratio schedule. A worker who is paid by the piece, by the report, by the page, or by the widget is going to produce more pieces, reports, pages, or widgets than one who is paid by the hour and whose productivity therefore does not make a difference. Automobile salespeople, who are known for their persistence, work on a commission basis; their pay is linked to their ability to close a sale. Research in both the laboratory and the business world shows that when pay is linked to output, people generally work harder.

Stimulus Generalization and Stimulus Discrimination

Stimulus generalization and *stimulus discrimination* occur in operant conditioning much as they do in classical conditioning. The difference is that in operant conditioning the reinforcement is delivered only after the organism correctly discriminates between the stimuli. For example, suppose an animal in a laboratory is shown either a vertical or a horizontal line and is given two keys to press—one if the line is vertical, the other if the line is horizontal. The animal gets rewards for correct responses. The animal usually will make errors at first, but after repeated presentations of the vertical and horizontal lines, with reinforcements given only for correct responses, discrimination will occur. Stimulus discrimination also can be established with colours, tones, and more complex stimuli.

The processes of stimulus generalization and discrimination are evident daily. Children often make mistakes by overgeneralizing. For example, a child who knows that cats have four legs and a tail may call all four-legged animals with a tail "cat." With experience and with help, guidance, and reinforcement from his or her parents, the child will learn to discriminate between dogs and cats, using body size, shape, fur, and sounds as criteria. **Stimulus control** may be said to occur when a particular stimulus comes to indicate that a contingency is in place in one situation but not in another. A dog, for example, can learn that it will be punished for entering the kitchen, but only when its owner is in or near the kitchen. The dog's behaviour is under the stimulus control of its owner's presence.

Extinction and Spontaneous Recovery

In operant conditioning, if a reinforcer or punisher is no longer delivered—that is, if a consequence does not follow an instrumentally conditioned behaviour—the behaviour either will not be well established or, if it is already established, will undergo extinction (see Figure 5.11). **Extinction**, in operant conditioning, is the process by which the probability of an organism's emitting a conditioned response is reduced when reinforcement no longer follows the response. Suppose, for example, that a pigeon is trained to peck a key whenever it hears a high-pitched tone.

Stimulus control: Occurs when a particular stimulus comes to indicate that a contingency is in place in one situation but not in another.

Extinction: In operant conditioning, the process by which the probability of an organism's emitting a conditioned response is reduced when reinforcement no longer follows the response.

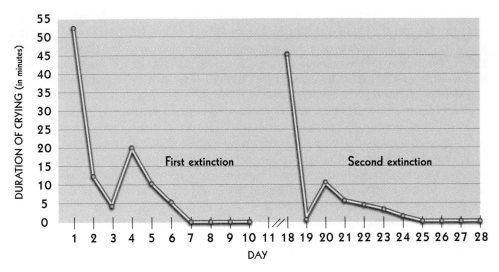

FIGURE 5.11
The Process of Extinction
When an organism's behaviour is no longer reinforced, the likelihood that the organism will continue to respond decreases; psychologists say that the behaviour has undergone *extinction*. Extinction is seen with both animals and human beings. In one study, C. D. Williams found that a child was throwing tantrums at bedtime to get attention. Williams instructed the parents to pay no attention to the tantrums. After several days, the number of minutes the child cried decreased to zero. A week later, an aunt put the child to bed; when the child made a fuss (spontaneous recovery), the aunt reinforced the child with attention. The parents then had to initiate a second extinction process. *(Based on data from Williams, 1959, p. 269.)*

Pecking in response to a high-pitched tone brings reinforcement, but pecking in response to a low-pitched tone does not. If the reinforcement process ceases entirely, the pigeon eventually will stop working. If the pigeon has been on a variable-ratio schedule and thus expects to work for long periods before reinforcement occurs, it probably will work for a very long time before stopping. If it is on a fixed-interval schedule and thus expects reinforcement within a short time, it will stop pecking after just a few trials in which it is not reinforced.

One way to measure the extent of conditioning is to measure how resistant a response is to extinction. *Resistance to extinction* is a measure of how long it takes, or how many trials are necessary, to achieve extinction. Consider a pigeon that is trained to peck when it hears a high-pitched tone and that is rewarded each time it pecks correctly. The pigeon is tested for 30 minutes a day for 60 days. On the sixty-first day it is not reinforced for its correct behaviour. For the first few minutes, the pigeon continues to work normally. But soon its work rate decreases, and by the end of the 30-minute session, it is not pecking at all. When the pigeon is presented with a tone the next day, it again responds with pecking but receives no reinforcement. Within a short time, the pecking behaviour is extinguished. People also show extinction; when researchers removed reinforcers from children who were exhibiting self-injurious behaviour, the self-injuries decreased (Iwata et al., 1994). Certainly parents know that when they stop reinforcing a child's misbehaviour with a lot of attention (even if that attention is negative), the misbehaviours often decrease.

Note that the decrease in response is not always immediately apparent, however. When a reinforcer is withheld, organisms sometimes work harder—showing an initial increase in performance. In such cases, the curve depicting the extinction process shows a small initial increase in performance, followed by a decrease (Allen, Turner, & Everett, 1970).

As in classical conditioning, *spontaneous recovery* also occurs in operant conditioning. If an organism's conditioned work behaviour has undergone extinction and the organism is given a rest period and then retested, the organism will show spontaneous recovery of the behaviour. If the organism is put through this sequence several times, its overall work rate in each session will decrease. After one rest period, the organism's work rate will almost equal what it was when the conditioned response was reinforced. However, after a dozen or so rest periods (with no reinforcements), the organism may make only one or two responses; the level of spontaneous recovery will have decreased markedly. Eventually, the behaviour will disappear completely.

People also show spontaneous recovery. When you answer a question in class, reinforcement or punishment usually follows: The instructor praises you for your intelligence or berates you for your ignorance. However, if the instructor stops reinforcing correct answers or does not call on you when you raise your hand, you will probably stop responding (your behaviour will be extinguished). After a vacation, you may start raising your hand again (spontaneous recovery), but you will quickly stop if your behaviour again is not reinforced. Instructors learn early in their careers that if they want to have lively classes, they need to reinforce not just correct answers but also attempts at correct answers. In doing so, they help shape, or manage, their students' behaviour.

Table 5.3 summarizes four important concepts in operant conditioning: extinction, spontaneous recovery, stimulus generalization, and stimulus discrimination.

Operant Conditioning in Daily Life

 Our world is full of reinforcers and punishers. We can work for rewards such as money. We can volunteer our time for such worthy causes as the Red Cross, shelters for battered women, and AIDS research. Of course, sometimes people feel that there are more punishers in the world than need be. Government taxes our income; the cost of living keeps rising; drunk drivers penalize all of us. But by and large, most of us feel in control of our reinforcers and punishers. As change agents, we know that many of our rewards and punishments are indeed contingent on our behaviours. Each of us, to various extents, experiences operant conditioning in daily life.

Intrinsically Motivated Behaviour. Psychologists have shown that reinforcement is effective in establishing and maintaining behaviour. But some behaviours are intrinsically rewarding—they are pleasurable in themselves. People are likely to repeat intrinsically motivated behaviours for their own sake; for example, they may work on craft projects for the feeling of satisfaction they bring. People are likely to perform extrinsically motivated behaviour, such as working for a paycheque, only for the sake of the external reinforcement. Interestingly, if reinforcement is offered for intrinsically motivated behaviour, performance actually may decrease. Imagine, for example, that a man does charity work because it makes him feel good. Paying the man could cause him to lose interest in the work, because it no longer would offer the intrinsic reward of selfless behaviour. A student pianist may

Table 5.3   Four Important Concepts in Operant Conditioning

Property	Definition	Example
Extinction	The process of reducing the probability of a conditioned response by withholding the reinforcer after the response.	A rat trained to press a bar stops pressing when it is no longer reinforced.
Spontaneous recovery	The recurrence of an extinguished conditioned response following a rest period.	A rat's continued bar-pressing behaviour has undergone extinction; after a rest period, the rat again presses the bar.
Stimulus generalization	The process by which an organism learns to respond to stimuli that are similar but not identical to the original conditioned stimulus.	A cat presses a bar when presented with either an ellipse or a circle.
Stimulus discrimination	The process by which an organism learns to respond only to a specific reinforced stimulus.	A pigeon presses a key only in response to red lights, not to blue or green ones.

lose her desire to practise when her teacher enters her in a competition; practice sessions become ordeals, and the student may wish to stop playing altogether. For every person and for every culture, rewards are individualistic and determined by a host of learning experiences. Chapter 9 considers this issue at greater length, especially the topic of potential hidden costs of rewards.

Electrical Brain Stimulation. Until the 1950s, researchers assumed that reinforcers were effective because they satisfied some need or drive in an organism, such as hunger. Then James Olds (1955, 1969) found an apparent exception to this assumption. He discovered that rats find electrical stimulation of specific areas of the brain to be rewarding in itself.

Olds implanted electrodes in the hypothalamus of rats and attached the electrodes to a stimulator that provided a small voltage. The stimulator was activated only when the rats pressed a lever in a Skinner box. Olds found that the rats pressed the lever thousands of times in order to continue the self-stimulation. In one study, they pressed it at a rate of 1920 times per hour (Olds & Milner, 1954). Rats even crossed an electrified grid to obtain this reward. Animals who were rewarded with brain stimulation performed better in a maze, running faster with fewer errors. And hungry rats often chose self-stimulation over food.

Stimulation of specific areas of the brain initiates different drives and activities. In some cases, it reinforces behaviours such as bar pressing; in others, it increases eating, drinking, or sexual behaviour. Psychologists are still not sure how electrical stimulation reinforces a behaviour such as lever pressing, but they do know that certain neurotransmitters play an important role. For example, when levels of specific neurotransmitters, such as dopamine, are increased after bar pressing, a rat is far more likely to continue bar pressing (P. M. Milner, 1991; White & Milner, 1992). The area of the brain stimulated (initially thought to be the medial forebrain bundle but now recognized to include large parts of the limbic system), the state of the organism, its particular physiological needs, and the levels of various brain neurotransmitters are all important. A hungry rat, for example, will self-stimulate faster than a rat that is not hungry. In addition, a hungry rat generally will choose electrical brain stimulation over food, but will not starve to death by always making this choice.

Behavioural Self-regulation. *Behavioural regulation theorists* assume that people and animals make choices and that they will choose, if possible, activities that seem optimal to them. Rats, for example, spend their time eating, drinking, and running on a wheel—activities they find pleasurable. An experiment by Bernstein and Ebbesen (1978) showed that human beings readjust their activities in a systematic manner. The researchers paid participants to live in an isolated room 24 hours a day, 7 days a week, for several weeks. The room had all the usual amenities of a home—bed, tables, shower, books, cooking utensils, and so forth. The experimenters observed the participants through a one-way mirror and recorded their baseline activity—the frequency of participants' specific behaviours when no restrictions were placed on them. The researchers found, for example, that one participant spent nearly twice as much time knitting as studying. The experimenters used the participant's baseline to determine the reinforcing activity—in this case, knitting.

The experimenters then imposed a contingency. In the case of the participant who liked to knit, for example, they insisted that she study for a specific amount of time before she could knit. If she studied only as much as she did before, she would be able to knit for much less

Focus

Review

◆ Why are variable reinforcement schedules more effective than other reward schedules? pp. 175–176
◆ What happens in extinction? How can researchers measure extinction? pp. 176–178

Think Critically

◆ Would you agree or disagree with the view that all intrinsically motivated behaviours must at some point have been reinforced? Why?
◆ When doing human and animal research on learning, researchers often record baseline activity. Why is such evidence important?

time. As a consequence, the subject altered her behaviour so that she could knit more. She began to study for longer periods of time—eventually more than doubling the time she spent studying. In other words, she regulated her own behaviour through application of the Premack principle (see pp. 164–65).

Other techniques of self-regulation are also based on basic psychological learning principles. Here is an illustration. People with type I diabetes require insulin shots each day. People with type II diabetes (90 percent of the diabetic population) do not require shots each day but are often obese, must take medication daily, and must follow a strict diet. Both groups show poor adherence to their self-care regime: 80 percent use unhygienic techniques, 58 percent administer incorrect doses of insulin, 75 percent do not adhere to the prescribed diet, and 77 percent test their urine incorrectly (Wing et al., 1986). According to Wing and colleagues, if diabetic individuals are to regulate themselves carefully, they must self-observe, self-evaluate, and then self-reinforce. The researchers assert that when people *self-observe* the target behaviour, they are better able to *self-evaluate* their progress. After evaluating their progress, it is crucial that they receive *reinforcement* for adhering to their medical regimen—perhaps by going out for a concert with a friend or by purchasing a long-coveted audiotape or CD. When these procedures are followed, adherence to the medical regimen improves. Self-management turns out to be crucial not only with regards to treating disease processes but within classrooms and other social situations where it can modulate disruptive behaviour (Cavalier, Ferretti, & Hodges, 1997).

Behavioural regulation has other practical applications. It is effective within classrooms and in other social situations where it can modulate disruptive behaviour (Cavalier, Ferretti, & Hodges, 1997). For example, members of Weight Watchers may be told to keep track of when and what they eat, when they have the urge to eat, and what feelings or events precede those urges. The organizers seek to help people identify the events that lead to their eating so that they can control it. Similar procedures also seem to help people in smoking cessation programs. The aim is to help people think clearly, regulate themselves, and thus manage their lives better. This decision process and the focus on thinking are clearly seen in studies of cognitive learning, considered next.

Building Table 5.2 summarizes key points of comparison between classical and operant conditioning.

Building Table 5.2

Types of Learning: Classical Conditioning and Operant Conditioning

Type of Learning	Procedure	Result	Example
Classical Conditioning	A neutral stimulus (such as a bell) is paired with an unconditioned stimulus (such as food).	The neutral stimulus becomes a conditioned stimulus—it elicits the conditioned response.	A bell elicits a response in a dog.
Operant Conditioning	A behaviour is followed by a consequence—either reinforcement or punishment.	The behaviour increases or decreases in frequency.	A rat will press a bar 120 times per hour to achieve a reward or to avoid punishment.

Cognitive Learning

"Enough!" shouted Patrick after four gruelling hours of trying to write a program on his personal computer. Bugs were rampant in his program, all resulting from the same basic problem; but he didn't know what the problem was. After dozens of trial-and-error manipulations, Patrick turned off the computer and went off to study for his history exam. Then, while staring at a page in the text, he saw a difficult phrase that was set off by commas; he thought about it and suddenly realized his programming mistake. He mistakenly had put commas in his program's if–then statements. It was correct English, but incorrect computer syntax.

Patrick solved his problem by thinking. His learning was not a matter of simple conditioning of a simple response with a simple reinforcer, or trial and error. Learning researchers have actively focused on learning that involves reinforcement. Conditioning processes in studies by Pavlov, Thorndike, and Skinner require a reinforcer for behaviour to be maintained. Much of the research on learning has focused on stimuli and responses and their relationship, timing, and frequency. But is a reinforcer always necessary for learning? Can a person learn new behaviours just by thinking or using imagination? These questions are problematic for traditional learning researchers—but not for cognitive psychologists or learning researchers with a cognitive emphasis.

Thinking about a problem allows you to solve the problem and makes other behaviours possible; thus, thinking and imagination become crucial to learning and problem solving (Skinner, 1989). The importance of thinking—the emphasis of cognitive research—is evident even in early learning studies and will be shown over and over again as we examine areas of psychology such as motivation, maladjustment, and therapy. Some of the most famous psychologists of the early part of this century examined learning when reinforcement was not evident and behaviour was not shown. Their early studies focused on insight and latent learning. Some of the studies gave birth to modern studies of cognitive mapping. Recent research has focused on generative learning and observational learning. Still other cognitive research has focused on problem solving, creativity, and concept formation (which will be discussed in Chapter 7). All of this work indicates that there are many different aspects to what is learned and how learning takes place, as the discussion in *Diversity* clearly shows.

Insight

When you discover relationships between a series of events, you may say that you have had an *insight*. Insights usually are not taught to people but rather are discovered after a series of events has occurred. Like Patrick's discovery of the extra commas in his computer program, many types of learning involve both sustained thought and insight.

Discovering the sources of insight was the goal of researchers working with animals during the First World War. Wolfgang Köhler, a Gestalt researcher, showed that chimps developed insights into methods of retrieving food that was beyond their reach. The chimps discovered they could pile boxes on top of one another to reach food or could attach poles together, making a long stick, to grab bananas. They were never reinforced for the specific behaviours that led to their recovering the food; rather, they learned how to get the food through insight, by putting their behaviours together in novel ways. Once a chimp learns how to pile boxes, or once Patrick realizes his programming error, the insight is not forgotten. The insight occurs through thought, without direct reinforcement, but does depend on appropriate prior experience. Once it occurs, no further instruction, investigation, or training is necessary. The role of insight is often overlooked in studies of learning; however, it is an essential element in problem solving, a topic discussed in Chapter 7.

Latent learning: Learning that occurs in the absence of any direct reinforcement and that is not necessarily demonstrated in any observable behaviour, though it has the potential to be exhibited.

Latent Learning

After a person has an insight, learns a task, or solves a problem, the new learning is not necessarily evident. Researchers in the 1920s placed hungry rats in mazes and recorded how many trials it took the rats to reach a "goal"—the spot where food was hidden. It took many days and many trials, but the hungry rats learned the mazes well. Other hungry rats were put into the mazes but were not reinforced with food on reaching the same goal; instead, they merely were removed from the maze. A third group of hungry rats, like the second group, was not reinforced; but after 10 days, these rats were given food on reaching the goal. Surprisingly, in one day, the rats in the third group were reaching the goal with few errors. During the first 10 days of maze running, they must have been learning something but not showing it. After being given a reward, they had a reason to reach the goal quickly.

 Researchers such as E. C. Tolman (1886–1959) argued that this was an example of **latent learning**—learning that is not demonstrated when it occurs. Tolman showed that when a rat is given a reason (such as food) to show learning, the behaviour will become evident. In other words, a rat—or a person—without motivation may not show learning, even if it exists. Tolman's work with rats led him to propose the idea that animals and human beings develop (or generate) a kind of mental map of their world, which allows them to navigate a maze, or even a city street. His early

---

diversity

Do Men and Women Learn Differently?

On many university and college campuses, women are taking women's studies classes as well as traditional literature and math classes in which the students are all women. Educators are recognizing that women students work better in groups, in cooperative efforts that stimulate connections among their ideas and emphasize critical thinking (Gillies & Ashman, 1996). Critical thinking, which focuses on integrating ideas rather than memorizing information, is at the core of such efforts. It builds on the idea that women take advantage of cooperative learning and focus on developing their own voice (point of view) in evaluating research findings (Kohn, 1992). Where possible and appropriate, universities and colleges are taking advantage of unique opportunities to educate women. All around the world, curricula in various disciplines are being designed to take into account the fact that gender differences in learning exist.

Psychologists have been assessing the cognitive learning styles of human beings for decades. In doing so, they have found that males and females do seem to learn differently. As boys and girls, children are taught different behaviours on the playground and in the home, and these behaviours affect the way they learn—at least according to some experts. In general, psychologists argue that boys are more independent and aggressive than girls, and that girls are more cooperative than boys. In general, boys are taught to win, whereas girls are encouraged to enjoy the game and the process of playing and to maintain their relationships with their playmates. Cultural styles affect learning in the classroom as well. As

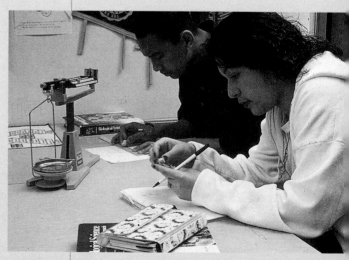

children, both in the classroom and on the playground, boys traditionally have been taught to prevail, whereas girls have been taught to get along,

work laid the foundation for later studies of latent learning (e.g., Chamizo & Mackintosh, 1989) and of generative learning, learning to learn, and cognitive maps. We consider each in turn.

Generative Learning

Modern cognitive psychology is changing the way in which educational psychologists think about learning that occurs in school. According to most cognitive psychologists, in addition to organizing new information in neural structures resembling maps, each individual gives a unique meaning to information being learned. The individual uses his or her existing cognitive maps to interpret the new information. Cognitive psychologists view learning as a *generative process*—that is, the learner generates (constructs) meaning by building relationships between familiar and unfamiliar events (Wittrock, 1987). According to this model, when people are exposed to new information or experiences, they perceive them according to their previous experiences. They then interpret (generate meaning about) the new experiences in ways that are consistent with their prior learning experiences and their memories of those experiences. In other words, they access existing ideas and link new ideas and experiences to them. As a result, they alter their brain structures.

communicate, and cooperate (Kohn, 1992). As a consequence, females tend to learn better in cooperative learning situations, whereas males tend to learn better independently.

Research on the role of learning styles does confirm some differences between men and women—although there are still more differences among women and among men than between men and women. In a study of the test preparation strategies of college students, Speth and Brown (1990) found that men and women differ in how they prepare for multiple-choice versus essay examinations. The women described multiple-choice tests as being more problematic and challenging than did the men. This probably reflects the different approaches to acquiring knowledge, according to Meece and Jones (1996) and Magolda (1990). Magolda found that men viewed learning more as an active, task-oriented process than did women. Magolda also found that men enjoyed the challenge of learning more than the process of learning. Furthermore, according to Crawford and MacLeod (1990), men take a more active participatory role in classrooms than do women, and this role facilitates learning. Yet gender differences in learning styles

tend to be small, to be focused on a narrow range of abilities, and to emerge primarily when a special type of processing is encouraged by test developers, teachers, or employers (Dweck, 1986; Meyers-Levy & Maheswaran, 1991).

Women also may see learning, workplace issues, and relationships differently. These differences show up on the job, where men are more likely than women to focus on winning at all costs. Differences also appear in relationships. Family responsibilities are viewed from sharply different vantage points, as is the raising of children. Parents' well-practised learning styles encourage children's learning and morality from a sometimes distinctly male or female point of view.

Critics sometimes assert that an approach that teaches women differently from men reinforces differences between men and women and encourages sexism. Psychologists know that men and women have different approaches in many areas of life—child care and the workplace are two obvious examples. However, no evidence exists that males and females are born with these differences. Evidence does exist that North Americans are raised in cultures that exhibit, laud, and reinforce

gender differences. It is not surprising that men and women learn about the world differently, that they develop distinctly different world-views, and that these world-views affect their learning styles and their abilities and desires to determine their own destiny (Severiens & Tendam, 1997). Some researchers assert that we need a radical transformation of classroom dynamics (Meece & Jones, 1996); however, as society becomes sensitized to the influences of culture, individuals often seek to gain more freedom from limiting cultural influences. This allows individuals to choose a destiny based on choices made by them, not for them.

Certainly a person's learning style is not linked to and universally predetermined by his or her gender (Severiens & Ten-Dam, 1997). In some cultures, male views of the world tend to predominate; in other cultures, female views of the world are most likely to predominate. In Canadian culture, the extent to which any of us takes a masculine or a feminine approach to learning, cooperation, morality, or any other part of development is highly diverse, varying from family to family, region to region. ■

These modified structures are then encoded in memory and can be accessed later to interpret more new information. The *generative learning model* asserts that learning with comprehension occurs when a person actively links previously learned ideas to new information. Generative learning is thus seen as a constructive process—a process of constantly remodelling and building on existing knowledge.

According to the generative learning model, classroom learning is not so much a matter of engaging in activities and receiving external reinforcement from the teacher or even of receiving knowledge that is transferred from the teacher to the learner. Rather, it is the result of an active process in which the learner plays a critical role in generating meaning and learning. No one other than the learner can build relationships between what the learner already knows and what he or she is currently learning. As a result, what a person actually learns is unique to that person.

Learning to Learn and Cooperative Learning Are Key Facilitators

Most students in their final year of university or college believe they are much better students than they were when they began their post-secondary education. What makes the difference? How do students learn to learn better? Today, educators and cognitive researchers are focusing on *how* information is learned, as opposed to *what* is learned.

Human beings learn how to learn; they learn special strategies for special topics, and they devise general rules that depend on their goals (McKeachie, 1988). When you go fishing, you not only catch fish, but you learn something about the sport of fishing. The techniques for learning how to fish are different from those for learning foreign languages and from those needed to learn mathematics. McKeachie, Pintrich, and Lin (1985) have argued that lack of effective learning strategies is a major cause of low achievement by university and college students. They suggest that there are general cognitive techniques that span topics, which students can use to learn better. Among them are:

- *Elaboration*—translating concepts into one's own language and actively trying to relate new ideas to old ones.
- *Attention*—focusing one's concentrative abilities and staying on task.
- *Organization*—developing skills that allow one to perform the tasks of learning and concept formation in an orderly manner.
- *Scheduling*—developing routine times for studying (which turns out to be a key element of both organization and managing anxiety).
- *Managing anxiety*—learning to focus anxiety on getting a task done, rather than becoming paralyzed with fear.
- *Expecting success*—developing an expectation of success rather than failure.
- *Note taking*—acquiring the skills necessary to take notes that will be a worthwhile learning tool.
- *Learning in groups*—developing good cooperative learning styles that make the most of interactions with other students.

Making students aware of the processes used in learning and remembering is key. This awareness (thinking about thinking and learning about learning) is called *metacognition*. When students think about their own learning they do better; when they act strategically to modify their strategies they learn more (Wynn-Dancy & Gillam, 1997) and are able to do better across a curriculum (Perkins & Grotzer, 1997). Students can better grasp history, chemistry, or economics if they understand *how* to go about studying these topics. Law, psychology, and medicine each require different learning strategies. After people learn *how* to learn, the differences become obvious; indeed, some researchers think of creativity as a metacognitive process involving thinking about one's own thoughts (Pesut, 1990). Individuals can learn to reason, learn, and make better choices across a variety of domains (Larrick, Morgan, & Nisbett, 1990).

Teachers and other students often set expectations, both high and low, for individuals. These expectations can be enhanced through techniques that involve cooperative learning. Cooperation helps students think about how they learn. Students are no longer taken to task for helping one another with their work, because they are now expected to become part of the learning process in a collaborative way—breaking down barriers between learner and teacher. One way to create a better learning environment is to have students cooperate with each other, rather than compete against one another. Research shows that cooperative interactions among students—not just between students and teachers or between students and books—play a significant role in real learning. Teachers who overlook student-to-student teaching may be failing their own courses (Kohn, 1992).

In fact, studies show that forming teams of students in which no one gets credit until everyone understands the material is far more effective than competitive or individualized learning. Whether the students are preschoolers or college age, whether they are studying English or physics, they have more fun, enjoy the subject matter more, and learn more when they work together (Karabenick & Collins, 1997). Students' achievements and attitudes are both improved through cooperative learning (Leikin & Zaslavsky, 1997; Whicker, Bol, & Nunnery, 1997). Another approach to improving learning skills is described in *Experiencing Psychology* on page 186.

Cognitive Maps

Some people are easily disoriented when visiting a new city, while others seem to possess an internal map. These internal maps are sometimes called *cognitive maps*—cognitive representations that enable people to navigate from a starting point to an unseen destination. Cognitive maps must be fairly basic, as they are routinely found in animals. Researchers at the University of Alberta studying cognitive mapping used by animals have shown that pigeons navigate through the effective use of landmarks in the environment (Cheng & Spetch, 1998). How are these cognitive routes perceived and learned? Travel routes can be learned through simple associations: This street leads to that street, that street leads to the pizza parlour, and then you go left. But researcher Gary Allen (1987) asserted that learning routes also involves perceptual and cognitive influences, not just memorization of turns and signs, and he devised a series of studies to demonstrate this. Slides depicting an actual walk through an urban neighbourhood were shown in sequential order to a group of research participants; the same slides were shown in random order to a second group. All participants were then asked to make judgments about the distance from the beginning of the walk to a variety of specific locations. Amazingly, the participants who viewed the random presentation made judgments that were almost as good as those of the participants who viewed the sequential presentation. How did they do it?

Allen contended that the participants formed a cognitive map by using visual information from some slides that overlapped with information in other slides. From these overlaps they pieced together a map of the neighbourhood. (Without the overlap, the pictures would have appeared to show a random walk through different neighbourhoods.) The participants tried to place the randomly ordered slides in sequence mentally by paying attention to particular parts of the visual world they had seen in previous slides. In Allen's words, they attempted to impose "order on a collage of perceptual information" (p. 277).

experiencing psychology

Creating Fluid, Flexible Thinking

I f you drive to school, to the supermarket, or to a friend's house the same way, every day, and have been doing it for years, you've probably passed by short cuts that could get you there more quickly. People develop short cuts in a whole array of behaviours, and some researchers (as we will see in Chapter 13) believe that mental short cuts help account for a limited view not only of road maps but of people. We can learn new routes to work, and new ways to view the world, if we take novel approaches to learning.

Researchers and practitioners, especially psychologists, argue that we need to be more flexible in our approach to learning and not be mindless or passive. So, *how* we watch television, for instance, is as important as *how much* we watch it.

Ellen Langer has argued that the basics of our educational system may be reading, writing, and arithmetic, but that these topics also need to be taught "mindfully." Langer (1989, 1993, 1997) argues that essential information must be placed in a context and used in novel and important ways in order to make the most of the information. Mathematics, for example, can be shown to be important in music, logic, and writing. She has challenged the educational community by arguing that we must take an active role in learning to create aware adults. She suggests that

there are at least seven myths that stunt people's intellectual and learning growth and keep them trapped in tight categorical thinking:

- *The basics should become second nature.* Langer argues that people "overlearn" skills so much that they no longer think about key ideas.

- *Paying attention means staying focused.* Langer maintains that noticing new, diverting ideas and events is important to help us place information in multiple contexts.

- *Delaying gratification is important.* Educators often take the fun out of learning by saying students should learn now and have fun later. Rather, according to Langer, learning is fun, and it should be encouraged as fun.

- *Rote memorization is necessary.* Memorized material often is not retained. When information is critically analyzed and thought about—rather than merely memorized—students learn it better and remember it.

- *Forgetting is a problem.* Sometimes forgetting information can free you to learn new, more important, or more relevant information. Drive the same route every day, so to speak, and you won't consider other alternatives.

- *Intelligence is knowing skills and information.* For Langer, intelligence is thinking flexibly and looking at the world from many perspectives.

- *There are right and wrong answers.* From Langer's point of view, what is correct is context-dependent. Is there a correct way to drive to school? It depends on what your goals are—speed to get to work on time or a leisurely drive? Is capitalism the correct way to run an economic system? Again, if you are a Westerner you will view capitalism differently than if you live in a more socialist country.

The truth is that we need to learn the basics and memorize some key pieces of information, but Langer is worried about how we get there and what we do with the basics. We need to be mindful learners, not passive ones. For example, we all need to know how to read, but we also need to think about what we are reading. Teachers and parents can help children develop thinking skills by asking them questions such as "Was that a good ending?" and "Do you think that if Hamlet had been a princess, rather than an a prince, the story would have unfolded differently? Why?" ■

Allen's research showed that in determining routes human beings pay attention to important landmarks, and that not all landmarks are equally useful. People learn the value of various types of landmarks during childhood. In one study, Edward Cornell of the University of Alberta and colleagues (1992) discovered that young children do not value landmarks the same way that adults do. As they gain experience, children are more likely to pick landmarks that lead to useful choices. Cornell has been able to use the results of his work to develop a set of guidelines to assist police and others to find children who have wandered off and become lost. His guidelines can be used to narrow the search pattern to those areas where the child most likely will be found.

The Theory of Observational Learning

A truly comprehensive learning theory of behaviour must be able to explain how people learn behaviours that are not taught through reinforcement. For example, everyone knows that smoking cigarettes is unhealthy. Smokers regularly try to stop smoking, and most people find their first smoking experience unpleasant. Nonetheless, 12-year-olds light up anyway. They inhale the smoke, cough for several minutes, and feel nauseated. It is a punishing experience for them, but they try it again. Over time, they master the technique of inhaling and, in their view, look "cool" with a cigarette dangling from their fingers. That's the key to the whole situation: The 12-year-olds observe other people with cigarettes, think they look cool, want to look cool themselves, and therefore imitate the smoking behaviour.

Such situations present a problem for traditional learning theorists, whose theories give a central role to the concept of reinforcement. There is little reinforcement in establishing smoking behaviour; instead, there is punishment (coughing and nausea). Nonetheless, the behaviour recurs. To explain this type of learning, Alberta-born, Stanford University psychologist Albert Bandura has contended that the principles of classical and operant conditioning are just two of the ways in which people learn.

During the past 30 years, Bandura's ideas, expressed through observational learning theory, or *social learning theory*, have expanded the range of behaviours that can be explained by learning theory (Woodward, 1982). **Observational learning theory** suggests that organisms learn new responses by observing the behaviour of a model and then imitating it. Observational learning theory focuses on the role of thought in establishing and maintaining behaviour. Bandura and his colleagues conducted important research to confirm their idea that people can learn by observing and then imitating the behaviour of others (Bandura, 1969, 1977b; Bandura, Ross, & Ross, 1963). In their early studies, conducted at the University of Waterloo in Ontario, they showed a group of children some films with aggressive content, in which an adult punched an inflated doll; they showed another group of children some films that had neither aggressive nor passive content. They then compared the play behaviour of both groups and found that the children who had viewed aggressive films tended to play aggressively afterwards, whereas the other children showed no change in behaviour (Bandura, Ross, & Ross, 1963; Bandura & Walters, 1963). Bandura's research and many subsequent studies have shown that observing aggression creates aggression in children, although children do not imitate aggressive behaviour when they also see the aggressive model being punished for the actions.

Building Table 5.3 compares observational learning with the other two major types of learning discussed in this chapter: classical conditioning and operant conditioning.

Everyday experience also shows that people imitate the behaviour of others, especially those whom they hold in high esteem. Parents regularly say to children, "Now watch me . . ." or "Yes, that's the right way to do it." They provide a seemingly endless string of situations in which children can watch and copy their behaviour and then be reinforced for imitation (Masia & Chase, 1997). Children emulate their parents by putting their seatbelts on while riding in a car. You may buy a particular brand of shampoo because your favourite TV star claims to use it. Countless young girls become interested in gymnastics or skating after watching Olympic competitions. Unfortunately, not all observational learning is positive. Alcohol and other drug use often begins when children and teenagers imitate people they admire.

Observational learning theory: A theory that suggests that organisms learn new responses by observing the behaviour of a model and then imitating it. Also known as *social learning theory*.

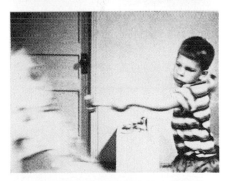

Building Table 5.3

Types of Learning: Classical Conditioning, Operant Conditioning, and Observational Learning

Type of Learning	Procedure	Result	Example
Classical Conditioning	A neutral stimulus (such as a bell) is paired with an unconditioned stimulus (such as food).	The neutral stimulus becomes a conditioned stimulus—it elicits the conditioned response.	A bell elicits a response in a dog.
Operant Conditioning	A behaviour is followed by a consequence—either reinforcement or punishment.	The behaviour increases or decreases in frequency.	A rat will press a bar 120 times per hour to achieve a reward or to avoid punishment.
Observational Learning	An observer attends to a model to learn a behaviour.	The observer learns a sequence of behaviours and becomes able to perform them at will.	After watching TV violence, children are more likely to show aggressive behaviours.

Laboratory studies of observational learning show that people can learn new behaviours merely by observing them, without being reinforced. For example, in a study by Bernal and Berger (1976), subjects watched a film of other participants being conditioned to produce an eye-blink response. The filmed subjects received a puff of air to their eyelids; this stimulus was paired with a tone. After a number of trials, the filmed subjects showed an eye-blink response to the tone alone. The subjects who watched the film also developed an eye blink in response to a tone. Other studies show that people who stutter can decrease their stuttering by watching others do the same (Martin & Haroldson, 1977). Even children who fear animals can learn to be less fearful by watching other children interact with animals (Bandura & Menlove, 1968). Cats, too, learn by observing. John and colleagues (1968) found that cats can learn to avoid receiving a shock through a grid floor by watching other cats successfully avoid the shocks by performing a task.

A key point to remember is that if a person observes an action that is not reinforced, but rather is punished, the person will not imitate that action—at least not right away. Children who observe aggression that is punished do not behave aggressively immediately; nevertheless, they may learn aggressive responses that will become evident in the future. Learning may take place through observation, but performance of specific learning may depend on a specific setting and a person's expectations about the effect of exhibiting the learned behaviours.

Key Variables in Observational Learning

Whether a person learns about an event or a behaviour depends on the extent to which he or she is involved in it. A child who has a direct experience with smoking, for example, is far more likely to remember and copy the behaviour than a child who merely hears about smoking or one who watches a film depicting it. Direct experience will always be a far more potent way for a person to remember and learn (Murachver et al., 1996). In real-world learning situations—classrooms, playgrounds, and homes—children and adults learn best when they are engaged in learning and observing. They are reinforced in some cases, observe and imitate in other cases, and sometimes change the way they are learning in midstream. Greeno (1998) maintains that all learning is active, takes place within a context, constantly changes, and depends on the active participation, consciously or unconsciously, of the learner.

Given that people can learn through many sources, we know that the effectiveness and likelihood of learning is affected by some key elements. One is the *type and power of the model* employed. Nurturing, warm, and caring models, for example, are more likely to be imitated than indifferent, angry ones; authoritative parents are more likely to be imitated than passive ones. In a classroom, children are more likely to participate with and imitate peers whom they see as powerful and dominant.

Another element is the *learner's personality and degree of independence*. Dependent children are more likely to learn from and imitate models than are independent children. Generally, the less self-confidence a person has, the more likely the person is to imitate a model.

A third factor is the *situation*. People are more likely to imitate others when there is uncertainty about correct behaviour. A teenager going on a first date, for example, takes cues about appropriate dress from peers and imitates their behaviour. A person who has never before been exposed to death but who loses someone close may not know what to say or how to express his or her feelings. Watching other people express their grief provides a model for behaviour. But not everyone learns well, and there are sharp differences in how people learn.

Focus

Review

◆ What evidence is there that students who are taught how to learn make gains in many areas, including grades and motivation? pp. 184–186
◆ What fundamental assumptions do observational learning theorists make about reinforcement in the learning process? pp. 187–189

Think Critically

◆ Who are the best types of models for a behaviour that is to be learned through observational learning?

Summary and Review

Pavlovian, or Classical, Conditioning Theory

Identify the fundamental difference between learning and reflexes.

■ *Learning* is a relatively permanent and stable change in an organism that occurs as a result of experiences in the environment. In contrast, *reflexes* occur involuntarily, quickly, and without prior learning. pp. 152–153

Describe how classical conditioning works.

■ *Classical conditioning* involves the pairing of a neutral stimulus (for example, a bell) with an *unconditioned stimulus* (for example, food) so that the *unconditioned response* (for example, salivation) becomes a *conditioned response*. In *higher-order conditioning*, a second neutral

stimulus takes on reinforcing properties by being associated with the *conditioned stimulus*. For classical conditioning to occur, the unconditioned stimulus and the conditioned stimulus usually must be presented in rapid sequence, and the conditioned stimulus must predict the occurrence of the unconditioned stimulus. pp. 153–156

KEY TERMS
learning, p. 152; conditioning, p. 152; reflex, p. 153; classical conditioning, p. 153; unconditioned stimulus, p. 153; unconditioned response, p. 153; conditioned stimulus, p. 154; conditioned response, p. 154; higher-order conditioning, p. 156

Key Variables in Classical Conditioning

What are the most important variables in classical conditioning?

■ The most important variables in classical conditioning are the strength, timing, and frequency of the unconditioned stimulus. p. 157

How may conditioned responses vary depending on the situation?

■ *Extinction* is the process of reducing the likelihood of a conditioned response by withholding (not pairing) the unconditioned and conditioned stimulus. *Spontaneous recovery* is the recurrence of an extinguished conditioned response following a rest period, showing that previously learned associations are not totally forgotten. pp. 158–159

- *Stimulus generalization* is the occurrence of a conditioned response to stimuli similar to, but not the same as, the training stimulus. In contrast, *stimulus discrimination* is the process by which an organism learns to respond only to a specific reinforced stimulus and not to other irrelevant stimuli. pp. 159–160

What are the key findings in studies of conditioned taste aversion?

- In conditioned taste aversion, or the Garcia effect, it takes only one pairing of a food or drink (the conditioned stimulus) with a nausea-inducing substance (the unconditioned stimulus) to make organisms avoid the food or drink that preceded the nausea. Taste aversion can be learned even if the nausea is induced several hours after the food or drink has been consumed; this is important because learning theorists previously had assumed that closeness in time between the two events was essential. pp. 160–161

KEY TERMS
extinction, p. 158; spontaneous recovery, p. 158; stimulus generalization, p. 159; stimulus discrimination, p. 159

Operant Conditioning

What takes place in operant conditioning?

- *Operant conditioning* is conditioning in which an increase or decrease in the likelihood that a behaviour will recur is determined by whether the behaviour is followed by a consequence of reward or punishment. The process often occurs through shaping; *shaping* is reinforcing behaviour that approximates a desired behaviour. A key component of operant conditioning is reinforcement. pp. 164–170

How do reinforcement and punishment work?

- A *reinforcer* is any event that increases the probability that the response that preceded it will recur. *Positive reinforcement* increases the probability that a desired response will occur by introducing a rewarding or pleasant stimulus. *Negative reinforcement* increases the probability that a desired behaviour will occur by removing an aversive stimulus. p. 167

- *Primary reinforcers* have survival value for the organism; their value does not have to be learned. *Secondary reinforcers* are neutral stimuli that have no intrinsic value for the organism initially but that become rewards when they are paired with a primary reinforcer. p. 170

- Punishment, unlike reinforcement, decreases the probability of a particular response. *Punishment* is the process of presenting an undesirable or noxious stimulus, or removing a positive, desirable stimulus, to decrease the probability that a particular preceding response will recur. p. 171

KEY TERMS
operant conditioning, p. 164; Skinner box, p. 165; shaping, p. 166; reinforcer, p. 167; positive reinforcement, p. 167; negative reinforcement, p. 167; primary reinforcer, p. 170; secondary reinforcer, p. 170; superstitious behaviour, p. 170; punishment, p. 171; positive punishment, p. 171; negative punishment, p. 171; primary punisher, p. 172; secondary punisher, p. 172; learned helplessness, p. 173

Key Variables in Operant Conditioning

What are the most important variables affecting operant conditioning?

- The most important variables affecting operant conditioning are the strength, timing, and frequency of consequences. Strong consequences delivered quickly yield high work rates. But consequences do not have to be continuous. Studies of schedules of consequences, especially of reinforcement, have shown that consequences can be intermittent. *Fixed-interval* and *variable-interval* schedules provide reinforcement after fixed or variable time periods. *Fixed-ratio* and *variable-ratio* schedules provide reinforcement after fixed or variable amounts of work. Variable-ratio schedules produce the highest work rates, while fixed-interval schedules induce the lowest work rates. pp. 173–175

Distinguish between extrinsic and intrinsic motivation.

- Psychologists have shown that reinforcement (extrinsic motivation) is effective in establishing and main-

taining behaviour. But some behaviours are intrinsically motivated; they are performed because they are pleasurable in themselves. Behavioural regulation theorists assume that organisms make choices and that, if possible, they will engage in the activities that seem optimal to them. If they are prevented from performing a desired activity, they will readjust their activities. pp. 178–179

KEY TERMS
fixed-interval schedule, p. 174; variable-interval schedule, p. 175; fixed-ratio schedule, p. 175; variable-ratio schedule, p. 175; stimulus control, 176; extinction, p. 176

Cognitive Learning

What is the focus of cognitive learning psychologists?

- Cognitive learning psychologists focus on thinking processes and on thought that helps process, establish, and maintain learning. Some of the early studies focused on insight and latent learning. When you discover relationships between a series of events, psychologists say that you have had an insight. *Latent learning* is learning that occurs in the absence of any direct reinforcement and that is not necessarily demonstrated in any observable behaviour, though it has occurred and has the potential of being exhibited. pp. 181–183

What fundamental assumptions do observational learning theorists make about the learning process?

- *Observational learning theory* (also called social learning theory) suggests that organisms learn new responses by observing the behaviour of a model and then imitating it. Observational learning theory has expanded the range of behaviours that can be explained by learning theorists and focuses on the role of thought in establishing and maintaining behaviour. pp. 187–188

- Some key variables in observational learning are the type and power of the model, the learner's personality and degree of independence, and the situations in which people find themselves. p. 189

KEY TERMS
latent learning, p. 182; observational learning theory, p. 187

Weblinks

Basic Concepts in Classical Conditioning
www.biozentrum.uni-wuerzburg.de/~brembs/classical
This site contains information from various psychology lectures dealing with the principles of classical conditioning.

Operant Conditioning—B. F. Skinner
www.lincoln.ac.nz/educ/tip/43.htm
This site contains an overview of Skinner's theory, along with a bibliography of other references on B. F. Skinner.

The B. F. Skinner Foundation
www.lafayette.edu/allanr/skinner.html
The site contains information about B. F. Skinner and his work, and links to books by and about Skinner.

Examples of Classical Conditioning
www.sfu.ca/~tbauslau/302/cc.html
This site contains 26 questions and answers relating to classical conditioning; you can use them to test your knowledge.

Pavlovian Conditioning
www.users.csbsju.edu/~tcreed/pb/pavcon3.html
This site provides a participatory demonstration of classical conditioning, created by Professor Tom Creed of the College of Saint Benedict/Saint John's University, Psychology Department.

Super Dog—Clicker Training
www.superdog.com/clicker.htm
Examine the application of operant conditioning to dog training at this "superdog" site.

Chapter 6

Memory

With the exception of those times when you are struggling to recall an important study or theory to answer an exam question, you may not think much about the central role that memory plays in how you experience, organize, and live your life. However, your memory gets you through the day by keeping track of your appointments, your belongings, and even your identity. If you have any doubts about the importance of memory, consider a few case studies of people with memory problems.

Is it possible to have too much memory? What if you remembered absolutely everything you saw or heard? Perhaps writing exams might be easier, but there could be a real downside, too. "S," a patient studied by Luria and written about in his book *The Mind of the Mnemonist* (1968), was unable to forget. Even days, months, or years after hearing them, S could remember very long lists of words, letters, or numbers, and could state correctly what he had been wearing and where he had been sitting when he first heard the lists. Everything he heard or read created vivid images in his mind that helped him recall simple information but, for example, made reading books virtually impossible. The first part of a sentence would create one image but the end of the same sentence would suggest another image; this would cause him to start reading the sentence again or risk missing the meaning of the sentence entirely. It could be said that he had too much memory.

What about the opposite case, when memory falls short of what it should be? Imagine what life would be like if you were similar to "H. M." In an attempt to control severe seizures associated with extreme epilepsy, surgeons removed the hippo-campus and several related structures from each side of H. M.'s brain. As a result, H. M. suffers from severe memory problems (Milner, Corkin, & Teuber, 1968; Corkin, 1984). He cannot add new information to his long-term memory. That is, he remembers clearly all that he knew before the surgery but he is unable to store any new memories. This leaves him with a sense that the world is moving on without him. He describes his condition as being "dead but alive." He can experience new events but cannot remember them. As a

consequence his identity, his life, and his world effectively have stopped in time, and yet even that fact is only vaguely available to him.

The central role of memory to identity and functioning also is abundantly clear in the case of people suffering from Alzheimer's. Alzheimer's disease attacks the brain mechanisms that store memories; as the disease progresses patients gradually lose more and more of their memories, and consequently more and more of their identities. The particular tragedy of this disorder is that its onset is usually so gradual that the patients can clearly notice and track its early progress and effects.

Memory is the means by which we store not only our experiences but our reactions to those experiences. We keep track of who we are through our storehouse of memories. So, with the importance of memory clearly in mind, let us look at how memory has been studied by psychologists. ■

Psychologists have long recognized that recalling well-learned facts sometimes can be difficult. Even though something has been *learned*, it may not always be *remembered*. You might easily remember the words to "O Canada," for example, but forget the name of someone you were introduced to last weekend at a friend's house. From Chapter 5, recall that learning is a *relatively* permanent change in the organism that occurs as a result of experience; this change is often, but not always, seen in overt behaviour. **Memory** is the ability to remember past events, images, ideas, or previously learned information or skills; it is also the storage system that allows a person to retain and retrieve previously learned information. Memory allows you to store information and to retrieve it. You may learn something, but this knowledge does you little good without the aid of memory and your ability to reconstruct the past.

Memory: The Brain as Information Processor

Some people tell you that they have a good memory; others tell you that their memory is failing them; still others—often politicians who are being questioned—tell you that they just can't remember. Memory is not a thing that you can weigh; it is not found in one small corner of the brain, with some people having more and others having less of it. Rather, memory is an ability and a process, and it is studied from many different perspectives. Traditionally, psychologists have examined memory solely from a psychological/behavioural perspective, focusing on issues such as what is remembered and what affects memory. Early memory studies at the turn of the century focused on how quickly people learned lists of nonsense words and how long they remembered them or how quickly they forgot them. Early physiological psychologists likened the brain to a huge map with certain areas that code vision, others that code auditory events, and still others that code, analyze, and store memory. Their goal was to discover the spatial layout of the brain and to see how the brain operated. Studies in the post–Second World War era became more practical, focusing on variables such as how the organization of material might affect retention and forgetting. Today, research is focusing on how people code information and use memory aids, imagery, and other learning cues to retrieve information from memory. Researchers also are examining the neuroscience of memory and studying the variables and conditions that determine what is remembered and what is forgotten.

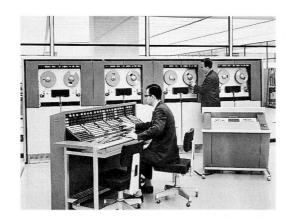

In this age of computers and information technology it is not surprising that researchers have likened the brain to a computer—an information processor—and this has guided their thinking about memory. In the 1960s and 1970s, when the Information Age was still young, researchers began to recognize the brain's complex interconnections and processing abilities. Today, researchers know that the brain is far more complex than ever before thought. The truth is that human brains, of course, are not computers; nor do they work exactly as computers do. They make mistakes, and they are influenced by biological, environmental, and interpersonal events. Nevertheless, enough similarities exist between human brains and computers for psychologists to discuss learning and memory in terms of information processing.

Psychologists use the term *information processing* to refer to organizing, interpreting, and responding to incoming information in the environment in a meaningful way. The information-processing approach typically describes and analyzes a sequence of steps or stages for key memory processes. This approach assumes that the stages and processes are separate, though related, and that each can be analyzed by scientific methods. Although psychologists once considered memory a step-by-step, linear process, today they recognize that many of these steps take place simultaneously, *in parallel*.

In virtually every approach to understanding memory that has been offered, rejected, or modified, researchers seem to agree that three key processes exist. The names of these processes derive from information technologies and will sound familiar to you if you know how computers work. The first process is *encoding*; in the second, data or information is placed in some type of *storage*, either temporarily or permanently; in the third, information is made available through a *retrieval* process. We will use this three-process approach to guide our discussion of memory. You will see that memory involves all three of these processes and that multiple activities take place in multiple memory stores—so that you may be retrieving some information while encoding other information. Memory does not always function linearly, with one step preceding another and not being used again.

Encoding

I f you travel to a foreign country you may find that you are able to manage reasonably well speaking only your own language. With help, you probably will be able to order food and make travel arrangements. However, your experience will be much better if you learn to speak the foreign language. To do this you have to be able to understand the language, and to respond in a meaningful way; this requires encoding.

In Chapter 3, we defined *coding* as the process whereby the perceptual system analyzes stimuli and converts them into electrical impulses. In the same way, the term *encoding* means getting information into the system to be processed, converting it into a usable form. The conversion of an experience into electrochemical energy, coding, is the first step of encoding and establishing a memory. In the language of memory, **encoding** is the organizing of information so that the nervous system can process it, much as a computer programmer writes code that the computer can understand. The means of organization can be visual or auditory and can include taste, touch, temperature, or other sensory information.

Sometimes the entire process of encoding is automatic; at other times it is effortful and requires concentration. Early in their development, people usually have to concentrate to encode information; with practice, such efforts become more automatic. Memory researchers speak of these processes as either controlled or automatic. *Controlled processes* require a great deal of effort and attention, whereas *automatic processes* require little effort and happen without conscious awareness—although certain physiological changes accompany both kinds of processes (Strayer & Kramer, 1990). Most complex memory and cognitive tasks begin as controlled processes; after hundreds of repetitions, they become automatic and easy, requiring little or no attention. (Think about reading. For young children, reading requires effortful encoding; for older children and adults, reading is nearly automatic.) Contemporary memory researchers want to find out how once-difficult tasks become automatic. Closely associated with controlled and automatic processes is the role of *attention*. In general, attention refers to the process of directing mental effort to some features of the environment and not to others. People can either focus their attention on one idea, one event, one person, or one memory task or divide their attention among several tasks or events. Once something is attended to and stored in a person's memory, researchers want to know how that person recalls information so as to make inferences. Even the monitoring of one's own awareness and memory, a process called *metacognition*, has become a focus for researchers.

We encode various kinds of information in a range of ways and to different extents. You will see that what we encode and how well we encode it determine what we remember.

Encoding: The organizing of information so that the nervous system can process it.

Levels of Processing

Does the human brain encode and process some information at a deeper, more complex level than it does other information? Do thinking processes depend on the depth of analysis? Research conducted at the University of Toronto by Fergus Craik and Robert Lockhart (1972) suggested that people encode and process stimuli in different ways, to different extents, and at different levels. Craik and Lockhart called their theory a **levels-of-processing approach**. For example, a person presented with a computer screen displaying, "Cast your vote for Smith, the candidate of distinction," will analyze the message on several levels and in several ways. The lines and angles of the message will be encoded at one level; the words will be encoded for basic meaning and categorized at another level; and the meaning will be encoded, analyzed, and stored at still another, deeper level. According to this view, how information is processed determines how it will be stored for later retrieval.

Cognitive psychologists began to equate the level of processing with the degree or depth of analysis involved. When the level of processing becomes more complex, they theorized, the code goes deeper into memory. Thus, the memory for the lines and angles of the computer message may be fleeting and short-lived, the memory for the words themselves may last longer, and the memory for the meaning of the words may last longest.

Encoding is not a discrete step that happens all at once, before memory stores information. Rather, some levels of encoding happen quickly and easily, whereas other levels take longer and continue for some time. You may continue to encode information while other data are being stored. According to Craik and Lockhart, encoding in various memory levels involves different operations, and memory features are stored in different ways and for different durations.

The levels-of-processing approach generated an enormous amount of research. It explained why some information, such as your family history, is retained for long periods, and other information, such as the dry cleaner's phone number, is quickly forgotten. It also showed that when people are asked to encode information in only one way, they do not encode it in other ways. Thus, when people are not asked to encode words for meaning, but simply to memorize or quickly repeat them (for example, to remember a list of items to buy at the supermarket), they can recall very few of them later.

However, many researchers did not accept the levels-of-processing approach, which dealt primarily with establishing memory. These researchers suggested refinements based on their work on how memories are elaborated on or made distinctive and how recall takes place. For example, the link between encoding and the later process of retrieval is explained by the **encoding specificity principle**, which asserts that the effectiveness of a specific retrieval cue depends on how well it matches up with the originally encoded information. The more sharply your memory cues are defined and paired, the better your recall will be and the less likely you will be to experience retrieval failures. For example, if you learn word processing on a Macintosh, writing a term paper on an IBM or Unix system may be more difficult. To facilitate your access to information stored in memory, you should match the retrieval situation to the original learning situation as much as possible.

Deriving from the encoding specificity principle is the idea of **transfer-appropriate processing**, which occurs when the initial processing of information is similar to the process of retrieval. When there is a close relationship between encoding and retrieval in terms of the modality of information (whether it is visual, auditory, or in some other form) and the processing required, retrieval is enhanced. Researchers have given participants instructions to encode words either for sound or for meaning; if a participant codes for sound but is then asked to recall meaning, recall is far less extensive than if retrieval task and coding task are equivalent (McDermott & Roediger, 1996; Morris, Bransford, & Franks, 1977; Mulligan, 1996; Srinivas,

1996). Such studies suggest that when you study for a test you should study the same way you will be tested: If a test will be in essay format, study by writing essays; if a test will consist of geometry problem sets, study by doing problem sets.

The landmark levels-of-processing research and its subsequent refinements and extensions shape the way cognitive researchers think about memory and thought. These researchers argue that that the way information is encoded may determine how it is stored, processed, and later recalled. They are aware that encoding processes are flexible and are affected by both the cues provided and the retrieval tasks at hand. Encoding processes also are affected by preconceived biases people have; humans tend to notice and encode information that confirms beliefs that they already hold—a tendency called *confirmation bias* (Silverman, 1992).

Neuroscience and Parallel Distributed Processing

Memories are retained in electrochemical form in the brain. Researchers are exploring the neurobiological bases of memory: How does the brain store memories? Where are memories stored? Are memory traces localized or distributed? Researchers using positron emission tomography (PET) techniques (described in Chapter 2) are studying the location, extent, and timing of processing in the brain as it occurs. We will explore the neuroscience approach to memory in more detail later in this chapter.

It should come as no surprise that many researchers believe that the connections within the brain are so sophisticated and interconnected that any simple, multistep model of memory is inadequate. The concept of **parallel distributed processing (PDP)** is an alternative to the levels-of-processing approach that developed from the notion that the brain is organized in neural networks (Rummelhart, Hinton, & McClelland, 1986). The PDP theory suggests that many operations take place simultaneously and at many locations within the brain. This idea is appealing because it is analogous to the way in which information processing occurs in the modern world. At telephone companies, for example, thousands of calls arrive at switching stations simultaneously. Mainframe computers deal simultaneously with jobs from hundreds of users. The PDP model asserts that humans, too, can process and store many events simultaneously.

PDP models apply not only to memory but to perception and learning. Focusing on the biological bases of memory, the PDP model is difficult to characterize in traditional terms, is hard to test experimentally, and has not achieved as wide an acceptance as the information-processing approach. Nevertheless, the PDP model has influenced the way psychologists think about memory.

As we continue to examine the process and structures of memory, try to think of information stored in the brain as books stored in a library. Many kinds of books can be housed in a library—hard covers, paperbacks, books on tape, books on CDs, and online books. Books can be checked out and new ones can be added in parallel—many at a time. Similarly, books can deteriorate with age, be misplaced, or be difficult to locate. Books that you use frequently are the easiest to find—you know exactly where to look for them. Sometimes librarians reorganize the books, storing them differently. We'll return to the library analogy later in this chapter.

Focus

Review
- What are the key assumptions of the information-processing approach to memory? pp. 194–195
- What is the underlying assumption of the levels-of-processing approach to memory? pp. 196–197

Think Critically
- What do you think researchers who focus on parallel distributed processing (PDP) see as the weakest aspect of the information-processing approach?

Storage: The process of maintaining or keeping information available; it also refers to the locations of memory, which researchers call "memory stores."

Sensory memory: The mechanism that performs initial encoding and brief storage of stimuli. Also known as the *sensory register*.

Storage

Suppose a friend of yours goes off to study abroad for a year and stores all of his possessions in your spare closet. He stacks box upon box in your closet and labels each one. He numbers the boxes and develops a master list that he posts on the closet door. You are informed that if he needs anything he will have a copy of the master list, and you will be able to access his books, tapes, and clothes very easily. Your friend has developed an elaborate storage system.

In many important ways, memory uses a similar storage system. **Storage** is the process of maintaining or keeping information readily available; it also refers to the locations of memory, which researchers call "memory stores." Storage may occur for a few seconds or for many years. When people think about memory, they often think solely of storage; they may not consider encoding data into memory, which we've just discussed, or retrieving data from storage, which we will consider soon.

Researchers have conceptualized a three-stage storage system: sensory memory, short-term working memory, and long-term memory. *Sensory memory*, sometimes called the *sensory register*, is the mechanism by which information is initially stored in the brain. When you hear a rock song or touch a piece of silk, you start the sensory memory process by entering, coding, and storing the information temporarily. After the information is stored for a very short time, it is acted upon for a longer period in *short-term working memory*, just as a computer keeps your work in temporary random-access memory. If the electricity goes off before you store information, you lose it. In a similar way, if you read a definition of a word but do not process it adequately, you quickly lose its meaning. The storage mechanism of short-term working memory is fragile; repetition, further encoding, and transfer of information to a final storage place are required. In a computer, information is stored for longer periods of time on a floppy disk or hard disk. In the brain, information is stored in *long-term memory*, from which a person can recall, retrieve, and reconstruct previous experiences.

Sensory Memory

As George Sperling demonstrated in the early 1960s, **sensory memory**, or the *sensory register*, performs initial encoding and provides brief storage of stimuli from which human beings can retrieve information. The brief image of a stimulus appears the way lightning does on a dark evening: The lightning flashes and you retain a brief visual image of it. In his experiments, Sperling (1960) briefly presented research participants with a visual display consisting of three rows of letters. He asked the participants to recite from memory the letters in one of the three rows and cued them as to which row to recite by following the visual display with a tone that varied in pitch. Sperling found that participants were able to recall more than 3 items out of 12 from just a 50-millisecond presentation; as he delayed the cue further, recall decreased (see Figure 6.1). From Sperling's studies and others that followed, researchers concluded that a brief (250-millisecond, or 0.25-second), rapidly decaying sensory memory exists. (*Decay* refers to loss of information from memory as a result of disuse and the passage of time.) Although some researchers have challenged the existence and physiological basis of sensory memory (Sakitt & Long, 1979), most researchers still believe it is the first stage of encoding.

Sensory memory captures a visual, auditory, or chemical stimulus (such as an odour) into a form the brain can interpret. Consider the visual system. Initial coding usually contains information

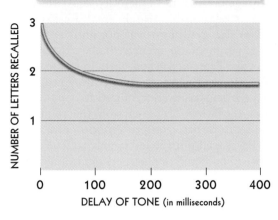

A display like this was presented briefly. Then a tone of varying pitch told the participant which row of four letters to report.

X B D F
M P Z G
L C N H

FIGURE 6.1
Sperling's Discovery of a Visual Sensory Memory
The graph plots participants' accuracy in reporting a specified row of letters. At best, participants recalled about three out of the four letters in a row. As the tone was delayed, the accuracy of recall decreased. But note that there were no further decreases in accuracy when the tone was delayed more than 200 milliseconds. *(Based on data from Sperling, 1960, p. 11.)*

in the form of a picture. Sensory memory establishes the visual stimulus in an electrical or neural form and stores it for 0.25 second with little interpretation, in an almost photographic manner. This visual sensory memory is sometimes called an *icon*, and the storage mechanism is called *iconic storage*. For the auditory system, the storage mechanism is called *echoic storage*; it stores an auditory representation for about three seconds.

Sensory memory is temporary and extremely fragile. Once information is established there, it must be transferred elsewhere for additional encoding and storage or it will be lost. For example, when you locate a phone number you need in a rapidly scrolling computer display, it is established in visual sensory memory (iconic storage). However, unless you quickly transfer the phone number to short-term working memory by writing it down, repeating it over and over to yourself, or elaborating on it by associating it with something else in your memory, you will forget it. Building Table 6.1 summarizes the key processes in sensory memory.

Short-term Working Memory

After reaching sensory memory, stimuli either decay and are lost or are transferred to a second stage—short-term working memory. Initially, researchers spoke of

Building Table 6.1

Key Processes in Sensory Memory

Stage	Encoding	Storage	Retrieval	Duration	Forgetting
Sensory Memory	Visual or auditory (iconic or echoic storage).	Brief, fragile, and temporary.	Information is extracted from stimulus presentation and transferred to short-term memory.	Visual: 250 milliseconds; auditory: about 3 seconds.	Rapid decay of information; interference is possible if a new stimulus is presented.

"short-term memory," to emphasize its brief duration. After extensive research, however, the nature of short-term memory became clearer, and researchers began to recognize its active nature. The name was expanded to acknowledge this quality.

Early Research on Short-term Memory. Thousands of studies were done on the components and characteristics of storage in short-term memory. Early research focused on its duration, its capacity, and its relationship to rehearsal. Researchers had been studying memory and retrieval for decades, but it was not until 1959 that Lloyd and Margaret Peterson presented experimental evidence for the existence of short-term memory. In a laboratory study, the Petersons asked participants to recall a three-consonant sequence, such as *xbd*, after varying intervals. During the intervals, which ranged from 1 to 18 seconds, participants were required to count backwards by threes to prevent them from repeating or rehearsing the sequence. Figure 6.2 presents their results. As the interval between presentation and recall increased, accuracy of recall decreased until it fell nearly to levels that could have been due to chance. The Petersons' experiment, like many others that followed, showed that information contained in short-term memory is available for less than 20 and no more than 30 seconds. After that, it must be transferred to and stored in long-term memory or it will be lost.

In 1956, George Miller argued that human beings can retain about seven (plus or minus two) items in short-term memory. The limited number of items that can be reproduced easily after presentation to short-term working memory is the **memory span**. It usually contains one or two **chunks**—manageable and meaningful units of information. A chunk can be a letter, a group of numbers and words, or even sentences organized in a familiar way for easy encoding, storage, and retrieval. Many people remember their Social Insurance Number in three chunks and their telephone number in two chunks. Chunks can be organized on the basis of meaning, past events, associations, perception, rhythm, or some arbitrary strategy devised by a learner to help encode large amounts of data (Schweickert & Boruff, 1986). Research has confirmed the widespread occurrence of chunking and the use of seven plus or minus two units of information per chunk (Baddeley, 1994). Determining what constitutes a chunk is sometimes difficult, though, because what is perceptually or cognitively grouped together by one individual may be grouped differently by other individuals.

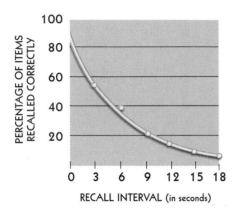

FIGURE 6.2
Results of Peterson and Peterson's Classic Experiment
Peterson and Peterson (1959) found that when they delayed the report of three-letter syllables by having subjects count backwards, accuracy of recall decreased over the first 18 seconds.

Researchers agree that a key operation—rehearsal—is especially important in memory. Rehearsal usually involves more than simply repeating information to prevent it from fading. **Rehearsal** is the process of verbalizing, thinking about, or otherwise acting on or transforming information in order to keep it active in memory. Psychologists distinguish two important types of rehearsal: maintenance and elaborative. **Maintenance rehearsal** is the repetition of information with little or no interpretation. This shallow form of rehearsal involves the physical stimulus, not its underlying meaning.

It principally occurs just after initial encoding has taken place—for example, when you repeat a phone number you need to recall over and over. **Elaborative rehearsal** involves repetition plus analysis, in which the stimulus may be associated with other events and further processed; elaboration links a stimulus to other information. When shoppers attempt to remember the items to be purchased to make that night's dinner, they may organize them in a meaningful pattern, such as the order of the

Memory span: The limited number of items that can be reproduced easily after presentation to short-term memory, usually confined to one or two chunks of information.

Chunks: Manageable and meaningful units of information that can be easily encoded, stored, and retrieved.

Rehearsal: The process of verbalizing, thinking about, or otherwise acting on or transforming information in order to keep it active in memory.

Maintenance rehearsal: The repetition of information with little or no interpretation.

Elaborative rehearsal: Involves repetition and analysis, in which the stimulus may be associated with other events and further processed; elaboration links a stimulus to other information.

aisles in the supermarket. Elaborative rehearsal, when information is made personally meaningful, is especially important in the encoding processes. This type of rehearsal allows information to be transferred into longer-term memory. Maintenance rehearsal alone usually is not sufficient for information to be permanently stored. Actively rehearsed items can be maintained in short-term memory almost indefinitely. In general, however, information held in short-term memory is either transferred to long-term memory or lost.

The Emergence of Working Memory. In the 1970s and 1980s researchers first began formally to think about short-term memory as working memory. Alan Baddeley and Graham Hitch (1974, 1994) view short-term memory as a more complex *working memory*, in which several substructures operate simultaneously to maintain information while it is being processed. Earlier, psychologists often concentrated on single memory tasks, trying to understand each of the components in encoding, storage, and retrieval. But the concept of working memory goes beyond individual stages to describe the active integration of both conscious processes (such as repetition) and unconscious processes (those of which a person is unaware). The emphasis of this model of memory is on how the memory system meets the demands of real-life conscious mental activities such as listening to the radio, reading, or mentally calculating the sum of 74 plus 782.

Short-term working memory is the storage mechanism that temporarily holds current or recently attended-to information for immediate or short-term use. In short-term working memory, information is not simply stored; it is further encoded, then stored or maintained for about 20 to 30 seconds while active processing takes place. A person may decide that a specific piece of information is important; if the information is complicated or lengthy, it will need to be actively repeated or rehearsed. As we saw earlier, *rehearsal* is the process of repeatedly verbalizing, thinking about, or otherwise acting on or transforming information in order to keep it in memory. Researchers generally agree that the more rehearsal, the greater a person's memory for the item to be recalled; even more important, though, is the *type* of rehearsal. Elaborative rehearsal is far more effective than maintenance rehearsal.

To understand how encoding occurs in short-term working memory, imagine a waiter who is given a lengthy and complex order. Once the order is in short-term working memory, it is unlikely that the waiter will remember much of it (except perhaps the first item) after about 30 seconds. Accordingly, he may repeat the order over and over, perhaps associating certain elements of the order with the individuals responsible for them, and continue to rehearse and elaborate on it until he is able to write it down or give it to the chef. Because of the limitations of short-term working memory, rehearsal of information (especially elaborative rehearsal) is crucial for encoding and keeping the information active.

The addition of new information also may *interfere* with the recall of other information in short-term memory. Baddeley and Hitch (1974) demonstrated the limited capabilities of several components, or subsystems, of working memory by having participants recall digits while doing some other type of reasoning task. If one subsystem is given a demanding task, the performance of the others will suffer. One subsystem in working memory encodes, rehearses, and holds auditory information such as a person's name or phone number. Another subsystem is a visual–spatial scratch pad or blackboard, which stores visual and spatial information, such as the appearance and location of objects, for a brief time and then is erased to allow new information to be stored. A third subsystem is a central processing mechanism, like an executive, that balances the information flow and allows people to solve problems and make decisions. This executive controls the processing flow

Short-term working memory: The storage mechanism that temporarily holds current or recently attended-to information for immediate or short-term use and that is composed of several subsystems: a component to encode and rehearse auditory information, a visual–spatial "scratch pad," and a central processing mechanism, or executive, that balances and controls information flow.

FIGURE 6.3
Short-term Working Memory
In short-term working memory, active processing occurs. Information is assumed to be held in a visual–spatial scratch pad and transferred back to an executive, or central processing mechanism. Meanwhile, auditory information is in a rehearsal loop.

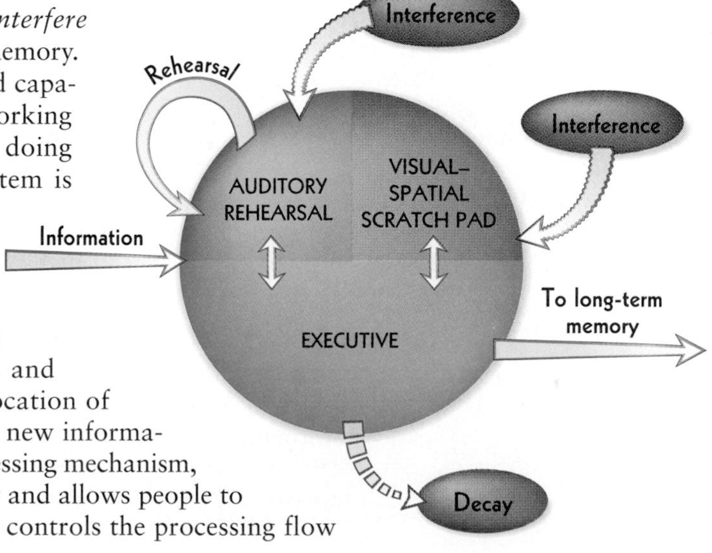

brain and behaviour
The Cellular Basis of Working Memory

A visual–spatial "scratch pad" in working memory is more than an interesting idea or concept; it has a representation in the brain. If you watch a computer display of a brain scan in progress, you can watch short-term working memory functioning. Using both PET and fMRI, researchers can now identify the neural machinery that underlies brain functions, and some of the most exciting research involves studies of the neural activity and brain locations associated with working memory. Working memory requires that some brain structure serve as an "executive" to coordinate, process, and balance the flow of information. Think of working memory as a complex multimodal processor that has to gather data from visual, auditory, and memory processing stores; it has to keep track of, coordinate, supervise, and redeploy cognitive resources to satisfy the storage, reasoning, and recall processes. The prefrontal cortex may be the place where this coordinating, or executive, function is carried out.

The frontal lobes constitute about one-third of the brain; the prefrontal lobes, with their overlying cortex, are the large areas at the very front of the brain, under the forehead. The drive to understand the roles of specific brain areas began years ago, but only recently have Endel Tulving and his colleagues at the Rotman Research Institute of Toronto identified specific memory functions of the prefrontal cortex. They

showed that the left prefrontal cortex is used more in *encoding* new information into episodic memory, whereas the right prefrontal cortex is involved more in episodic memory *retrieval* (Nyberg, Cabeza, & Tulving, 1996; Tulving et al., 1994). Research using PET and fMRI scans shows that when participants engage in various tasks, left and right brain scans are quite different—that is, there is different blood flow in different portions of the prefrontal cortex (Courtney et al., 1998).

When Smith and colleagues (1995) had participants engage in a spatial memory task or an object memory task, the spatial task activated only right-hemisphere regions, whereas the object task activated primarily left-hemisphere prefrontal regions. In later research, Smith (1997) identified different working memory systems for spatial, object, and verbal information. Further, Smith (1997), Joindes (1997), and Gabrieli et al. (1997) showed that as a working-memory task grew more difficult, participants' brain scans became more active, especially in the prefrontal cortex. The prefrontal cortex seems to be selective in what it processes but may take a supervisory role in allowing people to recall past events (Nyberg, 1996; Rugg, 1996; Wheeler, Stuss, & Tulving, 1997).

As the ongoing research unfolds, it is beginning to reveal a complex brain organization with lateral divisions (left versus right) as well as further subdivisions

based on the type of mental task. Owens, Evans, and Petrides (1996) found that two distinct subdivisions of the prefrontal cortex serve different aspects of spatial working memory. The first handles recognition, and the other handles more complex tasks such as mental rotation or naming an example of a category. Alivisatos and Petrides (1997) extended the finding, showing other brain areas involved in complex transformations of spatial mental representations. Still other researchers have shown that output from the prefrontal cortex may be a source of information to other brain areas (Miller, Erickson, & Desimone, 1996).

If the prefrontal cortex is as integral to working memory as researchers think it is, its complexity and involvement in so many verbal, spatial, and language abilities suggests that it may hold a key to understanding problem solving and reasoning. Reasoning requires a person to consider many ideas at once, evaluate them simultaneously, and rule some possibilities as unacceptable and retain others (Carpeneter, Just, & Shell, 1990). Working memory, with its visual–spatial scratch pad and executive function, may be just the mechanism required for reasoning (Kimberg, Esposito, & Farah, 1998). As researchers monitor regional blood flow in the prefrontal cortex, they may be watching actual thought processes (Wheeler, Stuss, & Tulving, 1997). ■

and adjusts it when necessary. Research shows that the type of information being processed by short-term memory—for example, textual information versus textual information with pictures—affects the accuracy of the processing (Kruley, Sciama, & Glenberg, 1994). *Brain and Behaviour* summarizes some current research that supports the existence of short-term working memory.

Building Table 6.2

Key Processes in the First Two Stages of Memory

Stage	Encoding	Storage	Retrieval	Duration	Forgetting
Sensory Memory	Visual or auditory (iconic or echoic storage).	Brief, fragile, and temporary.	Information is extracted from stimulus presentation and transferred to short-term memory.	Visual: 250 milliseconds; auditory: about 3 seconds.	Rapid decay of information; interference is possible if a new stimulus is presented.
Short-term Working Memory	Visual and auditory.	Repetitive rehearsal maintains information in storage, perhaps on a visual–auditory "scratch pad" where further encoding can take place.	Maintenance and elaborative rehearsal can keep information available for retrieval; retrieval is enhanced through elaboration and further encoding.	No more than 30 seconds, probably less than 20 seconds; depends on specific task and stimuli.	Interference and decay affect memory; new stimulation causes rapid loss of information unless it is especially important.

Figure 6.3 on page 201 illustrates the now widely accepted view of short-term memory as working memory. Building Table 6.2 summarizes the key processes in the first two stages of memory.

Long-term Memory

Information such as names, faces, dates, places, smells, and events—both important and trivial—can be found in a relatively permanent form in **long-term memory**. The duration of information in long-term memory is indefinite; much of it lasts a lifetime. The capacity for long-term memory is seemingly infinite; the more information a person acquires, the easier it is to acquire further information. Using the library analogy again, we can say that long-term memory includes all of the books in the library's collection. However, as in a library, information can be lost ("misshelved") or unavailable for some other reason.

Information that is typically encoded and stored in long-term memory either is important (a parent's or friend's birthday, for example) or is used frequently (your telephone number). Getting information into long-term memory often involves rehearsal, but a vivid event or experience can be immediately etched into long-term memory (Schmidt, 1991).

Several types of information are stored in long-term memory. For example, a person may remember the words to "O Canada," the meaning of the word *sanguine*, and how to operate a CD player. Each of these types of information seems to be stored and retrieved in a different way. The information is available to the individual and he or she knows that it is available. For this reason, psychologists refer to such consciously accessible memory as *explicit memory*. Psychologists divide explicit memory into two types: procedural and declarative.

Long-term memory: The storage mechanism that keeps a relatively permanent record of information.

Procedural memory: Memory for the perceptual, motor, and cognitive skills required to complete complex tasks.

Declarative memory: Memory for specific facts.

Consolidation [kon-SOL-ih-DAY-shun]: The evolution of a temporary neural circuit into a more permanent circuit.

Procedural memory is memory for the perceptual, motor, and cognitive skills required to complete complex tasks (see Figure 6.4). Learning how to drive an automobile, in-line skate, wash dishes, or swim involves a series of steps that include perceptual, motor, and cognitive skills—and thus procedural memory. Acquiring these skills is usually time-consuming and difficult at first; but once the skills are learned, they are relatively permanent and automatic. **Declarative memory** is memory for specific facts, such as who won the Grey Cup in 1998 (the Calgary Stampeders!) or when Elvis Stojko last won an Olympic medal. The memory is established quickly, and the information is more likely to be forgotten over time than is information in procedural memory.

The Neuroscience of Coding

Remember, memories are not physical things; rather, they are made up of unique interactions among hundreds and thousands of neurons in the brain. Researchers have sought to understand how these processes take place and where in the brain such coding occurs.

Consolidation. As discussed in detail in the previous chapter (see *Brain and Behaviour*, page 168), Canadian psychologist Donald Hebb (1904–1985) suggested that when groups of neurons are stimulated, they form patterns of neural activity. If a specific group of neurons fires frequently, a reverberating and regular neural circuit is established. This evolution of a temporary neural circuit into a more permanent circuit is known as **consolidation**. According to Hebb, consolidation serves as the basis of short-term memory and permits the coding (also known as encoding) of information into long-term memory. If Hebb is correct, when people first sense a new stimulus, only temporary changes in neurons take place; but with repetition, consolidation occurs and the temporary circuit becomes a permanent one.

The Locations of Memory. Where exactly is memory located? The search for memory—that is, for the memory trace—is long-standing. Early researchers looked for a single place in the brain; later researchers discovered that memory resides in many areas. Some areas may involve every type of memory; others may be used for only one type of memory, such as visual or auditory memory. In addition, because of the many steps and the many sensorimotor features involved, procedural (perceptual, motor, and cognitive) information is probably stored in many more locations than is declarative (factual) information. For example, when you load a videocassette into your VCR, you must coordinate your eye and hand to insert the cassette, and you probably listen and feel (kinesthesis) to sense when the cassette has been inserted far enough. Remembering this relatively simple procedure thus requires a great number of neural connections.

In the 1950s, during brain surgery on patients suffering from epilepsy, Wilder Penfield, a surgeon and researcher at McGill University, and his colleagues explored the cortex with electrodes that were used to stimulate specific neurons. The patients received only local anesthetic, because the brain contains no pain receptors; therefore, they were conscious during surgery. When Penfield stimulated the temporal

FIGURE 6.4
Procedural and Declarative Long-term Memory

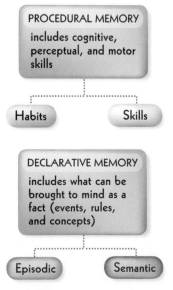

PROCEDURAL MEMORY
includes cognitive, perceptual, and motor skills

Habits   Skills

DECLARATIVE MEMORY
includes what can be brought to mind as a fact (events, rules, and concepts)

Episodic   Semantic

lobe cortex (on either the left or the right side), patients reported seeing images—coherent perceptions of experiences. They also reported auditory perceptions that included speech and music. Familiar and unfamiliar experiences were often intermixed with unrealistic and even strange circumstances (Penfield, 1958; Penfield & Jasper, 1954; Penfield & Mathieson, 1974; Penfield & Milner, 1958; Penfield & Perot, 1963).

Penfield interpreted these reports as true perceptions of past events: His patients were reporting memories elicited by the electrical stimulation (Squire, 1987). Penfield concluded that the temporal lobe stimulation triggered the memory retrievals. The idea that specific brain locations stored specific memories that could be accessed through stimulation was revolutionary.

The initial excitement soon dissipated, however. Stimulation of different brain sites often brought about the same perceptions. In addition, removal of specific sites (because of surgery) failed to destroy the perceptions (Squire, 1987). Other research using similar techniques has shown that when the same site is stimulated repeatedly, different mental images are reported! No consistent mental image has been associated with specific anatomical locations (see Halgren et al., 1978).

Penfield's conclusion that the temporal lobe holds the memory trace has been contested for several reasons. Subsequent work shows that the limbic system and many other brain areas besides the cortex are involved in memory. No single area holds the memory trace. As is often the case with scientific research, although Penfield's work was significant, his conclusions were wrong.

As discussed in the chapter opening, Brenda Milner (1966) reported the case of H. M., a brain-damaged adult whose short-term memory was intact but who was unable to form new long-term memories. As long as he was able to rehearse information and keep it in short-term memory, his recall performance was normal. However, as soon as he could no longer rehearse and had to use long-term memory, his recall became poor. Milner's data provide neurological support for a distinction between short-term and long-term memory. They also focus researchers' attention on the action of specific brain centres and cells and on how cells may change through time and experience.

Until recently, psychologists concentrated on how cells and synapses changed in response to environmental changes, such as deprivation of sound or light. Now, however, researchers use a variety of techniques to investigate the physiological bases of memory (Zola-Morgan, Squire, & Mishkin, 1982). For example, McGaugh (1990) argued that hormones may affect the way in which memories are stored. He pointed out that newly established memories are particularly sensitive to chemical and electrical stimulation of the brain.

Researchers have also sought to determine whether memory traces are localized or distributed throughout the brain. For example, Schacter et al. (1996) and Thompson (1991) assert that the hippocampus plays a key role for certain kinds of memory. But other structures, including the cerebellum, are also important (Thompson & Krupa, 1994). Further, Thompson asserts that procedural memories may be relatively localized but that declarative memories are more widely distributed. Such issues are a long way from being resolved, but research with human beings does show that certain types of memories are stored in certain areas of the brain (Shallice et al., 1994). The coordination of these memory traces may in fact be a hippocampal function. Various studies support the idea that

Focus

Review

◆ How do we know that sensory memory is temporary and fragile? pp. 198–199
◆ How did the Petersons' experiment show that short-term memory exists? p. 200
◆ In what ways is working memory a broader concept than short-term memory? p. 201
◆ What was Penfield's conclusion about the location of memory? Was he correct? pp. 204–205

Think Critically

◆ Explain how consolidation plays a role in the development of the brains of animals, and discuss the implications of this process for human beings.
◆ If you were designing a physiological basis for memory, do you think it would make sense to have memory representations throughout the brain, or do you think memory should be located in a specific place? Why?

the hippocampus takes input stored in many areas and "plays it back" and integrates the data. Researchers assert that such integration may take place during sleep and may be equivalent to consolidation (Gothard et al., 1996; McClelland, McNaughton, & O'Reilly, 1995; Shen & McNaughton, 1996; Wilson & McNaughton, 1994). The role of the hippocampus in memory is still being evaluated (Vargha-Khadem et al., 1997) but research increasingly suggests that the hippocampus, like the prefrontal cortex, may play a central role (Eichenbaum, 1997).

Other researchers are attempting to arrange computer models of the neural networks of the brain (often parallel distributed processing models). Their attempts are fascinating, but are often limited in scope to related groups of brain cells (Sejnowski, Koch, & Churchland, 1988) or to specific types of memories—for example, fearful memories (LeDoux, Romanski, & Xagoraris, 1989) or memory for faces (Damasio, Tranel, & Damasio, 1990). Also, such work doesn't explain many kinds of learning and memory phenomena, such as state-dependent learning, memory for long-forgotten events, or extraordinary memory. A key task for researchers from a neuroscience perspective is to show the relationship between learning and memory and how newly learned information is then stored (Bouton, 1994). The theories that follow from such research help explain a limited range of psychological information about memory (Watkins, 1990), such as learning about smells (Wilson & Sullivan, 1994), but they set the stage for a broader understanding of a more comprehensive, yet-to-be-established theory of learning and memory.

Retrieval

I f your roommate calls you and asks you to go to her desk and find a phone number that she has written inside the front cover of her psychology test, you will likely succeed in finding the number, assuming that you are given clear instructions. Similarly, most memory retrieval is fairly easy; we consciously and explicitly try to remember something and it effortlessly becomes available. But a few things can get in the way, as when you take a test and cannot remember a fact or concept. What are the processes (other than lost books or messy desks) that make retrieval possible or difficult?

Retrieval is the process by which stored information is recovered from memory. Recalling your Social Insurance Number, remembering the details of a phone call, and listing the names of the Seven Dwarfs are retrieval tasks. A person may encode information quickly, develop a well-defined working memory, and enter the information into long-term memory. But once information is coded and stored, the person must be able to retrieve the information and use it in a meaningful way. It turns out that the ability to retrieve information depends on how the information is encoded and stored and what type of information it is. Based on the information content and on the storage and retrieval tasks, psychologists have classified types of memory—episodic and semantic memory and explicit and implicit memory.

Episodic and Semantic Memory. **Episodic memory** is memory for specific events, objects, and situations that are usually personally relevant. It might include what you had for breakfast this morning, the movie you saw last night, or what you did on vacation two summers ago. Studies of memory for events show that people remember them well, especially those events involving themselves. Episodic memory is often specific; a person can describe not only when something happened but also where it happened and the circumstances surrounding it.

When researchers have examined people's ability to remember real-world events (rather than artificially created laboratory events), the results have shown that people have amazingly good memories. These studies are often referred to as *autobiographical memory studies*, because they examine people's memories for

Retrieval: The process by which stored information is recovered from memory.

Episodic memory [ep-ih-SAH-dick]: Memory for specific events, objects, and situations that are usually personally relevant.

their own past (Conway, 1991). People can accurately recognize a person, situation, or event years later (Nelson, 1993). Studies of autobiographical memory suggest that long-term memory is especially durable and fairly easy to access if a helpful retrieval cue is available. The more clearly and sharply defined memory cues are and the more often the memories have been recalled or reconstructed, the more vivid the memories are and the less likely it is that a person will experience retrieval failures (Friedman, 1993).

Semantic memory is memory of ideas, rules, and general concepts about the world. It is based on a set of generalizations about previous events, experiences, and learned knowledge. It is not time-specific; it refers to knowledge that may have been gathered over days or weeks, and it continues to be modified and expanded over a lifetime. Semantic memory develops earlier in childhood than does episodic memory (Tulving, 1993).

Semantic memory seems to be stored at different levels of memory, like sections or floors of a library; therefore, retrieval involves different levels of processing. At superficial levels of processing, the immediate sensory cues are interpreted. At deeper levels, the cues are encoded and categorized according to the kind of information they give and their meanings. At still deeper levels, the meanings are analyzed and synthesized. For example, is the following sentence true or false? "Princess Diana passed away as a result of injuries suffered in an automobile collision in August 1997." To assess the accuracy of this statement, you would need to access several classes of information, including interrelations among times, dates, people, and historic events—which may be complex. The time and effort needed to respond will depend in part on the number of levels of processing required (Tilley & Warren, 1983) and the complexity of the information.

Explicit and Implicit Memory.

Explicit memory is conscious memory that a person is aware of, such as a memory of a word in a list or an event that occurred in the past; generally speaking, most of the tasks we have discussed require participants to recall explicit information. Explicit memory is a conscious, voluntary, active memory store that is accessed relatively easily. When we tap declarative and semantic memory we are tapping explicit memory. In contrast, implicit memory is memory for information or events of which a person is not aware. Considered an almost unconscious process, implicit memory occurs almost automatically and unintentionally.

Researchers examine explicit and implicit memory by using different tasks. Explicit memory usually is examined by tasks such as recall or recognition. Participants are asked to recall a date, fact, or process. Implicit memory tasks *indirectly* test whether a person has knowledge of a previously experienced event that the individual did not consciously try to remember. You may remember things that you are supposed to (explicit memory), but you are also likely to recall things you did not deliberately attempt to learn—for example, the publisher of a book you are studying, the height of a piece of cake you ate, or the brand of a computer in your professor's office. Without any specific awareness, you learn how people stand and how they gesture; you also learn how to run better, play golf, or improve your tennis backhand—often without explicit instructions. Implicit memory demonstrates that people do learn without intentional effort (Boronat & Logan, 1997) and that what they learn explicitly and how they are asked to recall it may affect their implicit recollections (Nelson et al., 1998).

Tulving, Schacter, and Stark (1982) asked research participants to recall long lists of words. In later testing, participants could recall some words and not others; this is no surprise. But the researchers showed that participants could remember superficial characteristics of the previously learned stimuli—even aspects of words that they were unable to recall. This meant that explicit memory (recalling the specific words) was clearly different from implicit memory (having knowledge of the word or event, even without remembering the word or event). Explicit memory is sensitive to the attention paid to a task, the depth of processing, and the retention interval before recall; implicit memory is far more sensitive to the structural and

Semantic memory: Memory for ideas, rules, and general concepts about the world.

Explicit memory: Conscious memory that a person is aware of, such as a memory of a word in a list or an event that occurred in the past.

Implicit memory: Memory for information or events a person is not aware of; considered an almost unconscious process, implicit memory occurs almost automatically.

perceptual elements of a stimulus (Parkin, Reid, & Russo, 1990). Lending physiological support to the explicit/implicit distinction is the finding that these memory stores seem to be found in different locations in the brain (Fleischman, 1997).

The distinction between explicit and implicit memory adds another dimension to researchers' understanding of long-term memory, refining their understanding of the differences between declarative and procedural memory. This distinction suggests that processes of attention and learning of which people are not aware may affect memory. To a certain extent, implicit memory can be considered to be unconscious memory.

Retrieval Success and Failure: Encoding Specificity

Some contemporary researchers assert that every memory is retained and available but that some memories are less accessible than others. Think once again of the library analogy: All of the books in the library are there, but some cannot be found (perhaps because they are misshelved), making retrieval difficult or impossible. When retrieval of information is blocked, that information is effectively forgotten.

Research on retrieval focuses on how people encode information and on the cues that help them recall it. If you are given a cue for retrieval that relates to some aspect of the originally stored information, retrieval is easier, faster, and more accurate. For example, if you were asked to recall the definition of the word *commander*, it would be easy to recall, because the definition refers to the delivery of a command. But if you were asked to recall the meaning of *succor*, the definition ("That which provides relief or care . . .") has no specific cue to help you recall the definition. When a retrieval cue is present, retrieval is easier; this evidence supports the encoding specificity principle.

Recall that the *encoding specificity principle* asserts that the value or effectiveness of a specific retrieval cue depends on how well it matches up with information in the original encoded memory (see p. 198). The more clearly and sharply your memory cues are defined and paired, the better your recall will be and the less likely you will be to experience retrieval failures. To increase your access to information stored in memory, you should match the retrieval situation to the original learning situation as much as possible. The encoding specificity principle is apparent in studies of state-dependent learning.

State-Dependent Learning. Psychologist Gordon Bower (1981) used the following story to describe a phenomenon known as state-dependent learning:

When I was a kid I saw the movie *City Lights* in which Charlie Chaplin plays the little tramp. In one very funny sequence, Charlie saves a drunk from leaping to his death. The drunk turns out to be a millionaire who befriends Charlie, and the two spend the evening together drinking and carousing. The next day, when sober, the millionaire does not recognize Charlie and even snubs him. Later the millionaire gets drunk again, and when he spots Charlie treats him as his long-lost companion. So the two of them spend another evening together carousing and drinking and then stagger back to the millionaire's mansion to sleep. In the morning, of course, the sober millionaire again does not recognize Charlie, treats him as an intruder, and has the butler kick him out by the seat of his pants. The scene ends with the little tramp telling the camera his opinion of high society and the evils of drunkenness. (p. 129)

The millionaire remembers Charlie only when he is intoxicated, the same state in which he originally met him. Psychologists find that information learned while a person is in a particular physiological state is recalled most accurately when the person is again in that physiological state. This phenomenon, known as **state-dependent learning**, is associated with physiological moods and states as well as states involving drugs, time of day (Holloway, 1977), mental illness (Weingartner, 1977), and electro-convulsive shock therapy (discussed in Chapter 16) (Robbins & Meyer, 1970).

State-dependent learning: The tendency to recall information learned in a particular physio-logical state most accurately when one is again in that physi-ological state.

In a typical study of state-dependent learning, Weingartner and colleagues (1976) had four groups of participants learn lists of high- and low-imagery words. To induce intoxication, all participants except those in the control group drank vodka and fruit juice. The control group learned and recalled while sober, a second group learned and recalled while intoxicated, a third group learned while sober and recalled while intoxicated, and a fourth group learned while intoxicated and recalled while sober. The results showed that participants recalled the lists best when they were in the same state in which they had learned the lists. (This is not to say that memory is better under intoxicated conditions. All else being equal, recall is better in sober individuals.)

Several theories attempt to explain state-dependent learning. A widely accepted explanation focuses on how altered or drugged states affect the storage process. According to this view, part of learning involves the encoding of stimuli in specific ways at the time of learning (encoding specificity principle); to access the stored information, a person must evoke the same context in which the encoding occurred (Schramke & Bauer, 1997). When you study for an examination with music in the background but are tested in quiet conditions, your recall may not be as good. The reasons for retrieval failures are not completely clear, but studies of mood and its impact on memory and of state dependent learning may hold the key (Izquierdo & Medina, 1997; Eich, 1995). Studying after exercise, when in a good mood, or when well rested is likely to lead to better recall.

Special Memory: Flashbulb Memory and Extraordinary Memory

In 1973, one of the authors of this text and a group of his friends left school over the lunch hour one day and clustered around a TV watching the final game of the Canada–Russia hockey series. When, in the dying seconds of the third period, Paul Henderson scored his biggest goal ever by slipping the puck past the Russian goaltender, all Canadian spectators went wild. That moment is still vivid in the minds of many Canadians (and is now depicted on a Canadian stamp).

For Canadians too young to remember Henderson's famous goal, the death of Princess Diana may have stuck in their memory. Many people often can recall where they were and what they were doing when they heard the news of the car collision and the later news of Diana's death. Events such as these can mark a point in history for a whole generation. Are they a special kind of memory?

Flashbulb Memory. How did you learn about Princess Diana's death? What were you doing at that moment? What were your first thoughts? Compare the vividness of those memories with your recollection of eating lunch a few days ago.

People vividly remember the circumstances in which they learned of major personal and public events. This phenomenon is often referred to as *flashbulb memory*. Brown and Kulik (1977) argued that there is a special type of memory for events that possess a critical level of emotional impact and what they called *consequentiality*. Most people believe they have flashbulb memories, and Brown and Kulik's work generated an avalanche of debate and research.

Two basic theories explain flashbulb memory. The first focuses on emotion, the second on rehearsal. The emotion approach, sometimes called the *now-print theory*, suggests that recall is facilitated when extraordinary cognitive information overactivates the limbic system (the brain's emotion centre). In addition, information associated with strong emotions may be talked about more, and this rehearsal of information facilitates its recall. The second theory concerns rehearsal and reconstruction. This *reconstructive-script theory* focuses on people telling and retelling the story and gradually filling in, or reconstructing, the story to match a standard story format.

Bohannon (1988) studied people's memories of the *Challenger* space shuttle disaster. Participants were tested at two weeks and then at eight months following the explosion. They were asked both to evaluate their emotions on hearing the news (to test the now-print theory) and to estimate the number of times they had retold the story (to test the reconstructive-script theory). The study's results showed that free recall at eight months was just as good as at two weeks after the explosion, but accurate responses to questions about specific details declined over time. With short delays, either factor (emotion or rehearsal) is sufficient to generate flashbulb memories. But after a delay of eight months, *both* factors are required.

Our level of involvement with a past event is a good predictor of memory. According to Bohannon (1988), simple emotional responses without rehearsal produce good short-term recall only. In the same manner, rehearsal of information that does not have a strong emotional component results in superior short-term memory. Bohannon claims that flashbulb memory is maintained over time *only* "if the flashbulb event was important enough to get the person to repeatedly rehearse the information by telling others" (p. 195). Every person experiences emotional events, and some of these are then rehearsed. When an emotional event is especially significant, and when it is repeatedly rehearsed, both the circumstances and the event have a high probability of being remembered in detail. Multinational research showed that international events do indeed produce flashbulb memories for people in some countries, but not in others—again, the significance of the event, its emotional impact, and a person's involvement in the events and its retelling are key (Conway et al., 1994).

Is flashbulb memory a special kind of memory? McCloskey, Wible, and Cohen (1988) argue, "There is no qualitative distinction . . . between memories for learning about shocking, important events, and memories for learning about expected, trivial events" (p. 181). They assert that flashbulb memory is ordinary memory with no special characteristics. Bohannon's findings on flashbulb memories and the role of emotion and rehearsal in maintaining them are consistent with McCloskey, Wible, and Cohen's argument. Such memories may be vivid, but they must be about emotional events and they must be rehearsed. According to Weaver (1993), what chiefly distinguishes flashbulb memories is the undue confidence people place in their accuracy. The research suggests that there is no special location or encoding mechanism responsible for them.

 Extraordinary Memory. Nearly perfect recall is rare. But is it possible for an average person to develop a remarkable memory? We saw that the memory span for most adults is limited to around seven items, plus or minus two items. Research shows, however, that with practice and the use of special chunking strategies, memory span can be increased greatly. In two different studies, participants' memory spans were increased to 79 digits (Ericsson, Chase, & Faloon, 1980) and 106 digits (Staszewski, 1987). The participants in these experiments developed strategies for effective encoding and efficient retrieval of meaningful chunks of information; the process was effortful and deliberate.

Attempting to increase digit span is a time-consuming process. In the two studies just discussed, 20 months were needed in the first case and 5 years were needed in the second—and the results did not carry over to other study materials. But exceptional memory skills can be seen in other research domains. For example, Staszewski (1988) presented research on "lightning mental calculators"—individuals who can solve complex arithmetic problems (such as 54 917 x 63) with remarkable speed and accuracy. The key to such achievement is steady practice, efficient use of memory, and extensive knowledge of numerical relationships. A person can't train to be a lightning mental calculator without extensive daily and weekly practice. Nor can a person learn to calculate calendar date problems (for example, the day of the week on which July 27, 1946, fell) without extensive practice and considerable knowledge of day, date, and calendar rules (Howe & Smith, 1988). Individuals can learn to overcome working memory limitations, but it requires supervised, prolonged practice that is maintained at high daily levels (Ericsson, Krampe, & Tesch-Römer, 1993). As well, extraordinary musical or athletic skills that take years to perfect provide evidence that procedural memory also benefits from intensive supervised practice (Ericsson & Charness, 1994).

What Facilitates Recall?

Long-term memory studies have brought forth some interesting findings about retrieval and have generated hundreds of other studies focusing on factors that can facilitate or inhibit accurate recall. Two of these factors are primacy and recency effects and imagery. You use both every day.

Primacy and Recency Effects. In a typical memory experiment, a participant may be asked to study 30 or 40 words, with a word presented every 2 seconds. A few seconds or minutes later, the person is asked to recall the words so the researcher can determine whether the information was transferred from short-term to long-term memory. Such experiments typically show an overall recall rate of 20 percent. However, recall is higher for words at the beginning of a list than for those in the middle, a phenomenon termed the **primacy effect**. This effect occurs because no information related to the task at hand is already stored in short-term memory; at the moment a new task is assigned, a person's attention to new stimuli is at its peak. In addition, words at the beginning of a series get to be rehearsed more often, allowing them to be transferred to long-term memory. Thus, the primacy effect is associated with long-term memory processes. However, recall is *even higher* for words at the end of a list—a phenomenon termed the **recency effect**. This effect occurs because these more recently presented items are still being held in short-term memory, where they can still be actively rehearsed, and are not being subjected to any interference from newer information prior to being encoded into long-term memory. The recency effect is thus thought to be related to short-term memory. Figure 6.5 shows the recall rate for words in various positions in a list. It is called a *serial position curve* and presents the accuracy or speed of recall as a function of item position in a list or series of presented items.

In politics, campaign managers attempt to capitalize on the primacy and recency effects through their candidates' speeches. For example, they urge their candidates to speak both very early in the campaign and very late, just before people vote. If several candidates are to speak back-to-back, campaign managers will try to schedule their candidates either first or last. Primacy effects suggest that attention is at its peak at the beginning of the speeches; recency effects suggest that speaking last will be effective because other speakers won't interfere with the transfer of information from short-term to long-term memory. Of course, if days and weeks pass, new information will interfere, and primacy effects will be greater than recency effects.

Imagery. People use perceptual imagery every day as a long-term memory retrieval aid. In **imagery**, people create, recreate, or conjure up a mental picture of a sensory or perceptual experience to be remembered. People constantly invoke images to recall things they did, said, read, or saw. People's imagery systems can be activated by visual, auditory, or olfactory stimuli or by other images (Tracy &

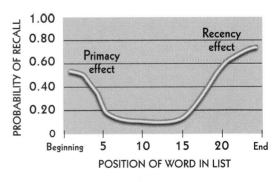

FIGURE 6.5
A Serial Position Curve
The probability of recalling an item is plotted as a function of its serial position on a list of items. Generally, the first several items are fairly likely to be recalled (the primacy effect), and the last several are recalled very well (the recency effect).

Kosslyn had subjects imagine elephants, flies, and rabbits. An imagined rabbit appeared small in size next to an elephant.

Next to a fly, however, an imagined rabbit appeared large in size.

FIGURE 6.7
The Speed of Thought
The speed of thought can be assessed through studies of mental rotation. Shepard and Metzler (1988) asked participants to see as quickly as possible whether visual stimuli were in fact the same stimuli, but rotated, or were different stimuli.

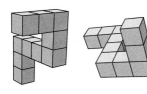

Barker, 1994). Even a lack of sensory stimulation can produce vivid imagery. Imagery helps you answer questions such as these: Which is darker green, a pea or a Christmas tree? Which is bigger, a tennis ball or a baseball? Does the person you met last night have brown eyes or blue eyes?

One technique researchers use to measure imagery is to ask participants to imagine objects of various sizes—for example, an animal such as a rabbit next to either an elephant or a fly. In a 1975 study by Stephen Kosslyn of Harvard University, participants reported that when they imagined a fly, plenty of room remained in their mental image for a rabbit. However, when they imagined an elephant, it took up most of the available space. One particularly interesting result was that the participants required more time and found it harder to see a rabbit's nose when the rabbit was next to an elephant than when it was next to a fly, because the nose appeared to be extremely small in the first instance (see Figure 6.6).

Although they are mental, not physical, phenomena, images have "edges" like those on a photograph—points beyond which visual information ceases to be represented (Kosslyn, 1987). These and other properties of mental images have been useful in a wide variety of studies designed to measure the nature and speed of thought (see, for example, Figure 6.7).

Imagery is an important perceptual memory aid. In fact, a growing body of evidence suggests that it is a means of preserving perceptual information that might otherwise decay. According to Paivio (1971), a person told to remember two words may form an image combining those words. Someone told to remember the words *house* and *hamburger*, for example, might have an easier time remembering those words by forming an image of a house made of hamburgers or of a hamburger on top of a house. When the person is later presented with the word *house*, the word *hamburger* will come to mind. Paivio suggests that words paired in this way become conceptually linked, with the crucial factor being the image.

Focus

Review

◆ What evidence supports the existence of episodic memory? Of semantic memory? pp. 206–207

◆ Differentiate implicit and explicit memory. pp. 207, 208

◆ Why do some researchers conclude that flashbulb memories are not unique memories? p. 210

Think Critically

◆ Is procedural memory more explicit or implicit? What about flashbulb memory? Explain.

◆ Provide three examples of information that you have chunked to facilitate recall.

How images facilitate recall and recognition is not yet fully understood, but one possibility is that an image could add another code to semantic memory. Thus, with two codes, semantic and imaginal, a person has two ways to access previously learned information. Some researchers argue that imagery, verbal encoding mechanisms, and semantic memory operate together to encode and to aid in retrieval (Marschark et al., 1987).

Experiencing Psychology on pages 214 and 215 suggests how you can use the information presented in this chapter to help improve your own memory. Figure 6.8 presents an overall view of the processes of encoding, storage, and retrieval at various stages of memory.

FIGURE 6.8
Encoding, Storage, and Retrieval in Memory
When information enters the memory's information-processing system, it proceeds from sensory memory to short-term working memory and then to long-term memory.

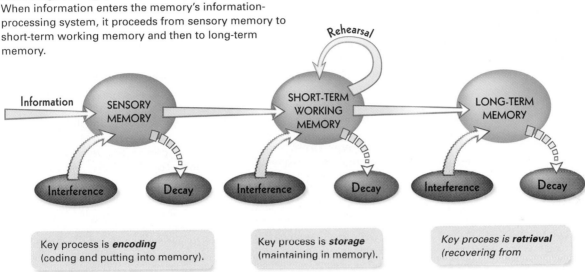

Key process is **encoding** (coding and putting into memory).

Key process is **storage** (maintaining in memory).

Key process is **retrieval** (recovering from

Forgetting: When Memory Fails

Quick! Name your first-grade teacher. Your best friend's middle name. Where you went on your last vacation. In general, your memory serves you amazingly well. Nevertheless, at times you may have trouble recalling the name of someone you know well, where you read an interesting article, or the phone number of a close friend. And have you ever started an exam only to have your mind suddenly go blank? In some ways, forgetting is the opposite, or flip side, of memory—it's the inability to recall, reconstruct or, in general, remember.

There are many causes of forgetting, including not rehearsing information well enough, not making good elaborative associations (links), or not using learned information for a long time. Forgetting also occurs because of interference from other learned information, because information is unpleasant, or because of physiological problems. Moreover, forgetting occurs with both short-term and long-term memory.

Starting with the pioneering work of Hermann Ebbinghaus and others in the latter part of the nineteenth century, many psychologists have studied forgetting. Such research has revealed a great deal about memory processes—in particular, those processes that affect learning and the ability to recall what has been learned.

Early Studies

Some of the first experimenters in psychology studied forgetting, and their work is not forgotten. Sometimes the tasks they created involved paper and pencil, but more

Practice Makes Perfect, or at Least Helps

In studying learning we saw that reinforced behaviour tends to recur; it is learned and remembered. What creates learning? Practice is a key variable but there are several other techniques that can improve memory. Here are some of the most powerful ones; they move from simple strategies to more complex overall approaches. Try using them to learn this chapter's concepts.

Rehearse, Rehearse, Rehearse. If you want to remember something, there is no substitute for rehearsal (see pages 200–202). Maintenance rehearsal, in which you simply reiterate items without attaching any meaning to them, will facilitate recognition or rote recall if you do not have to remember the items for very long. However, if you want to remember ideas for a long time, you need to understand them. This requires the use of elaborative rehearsal. With elaborative rehearsal, you generate meaning as you repeat and think about the information you are learning.

Be an Active Learner. Becoming an active learner means active participation on your part. When you interact with new information, it becomes alive and interesting. By thinking about the new information, asking and answering your own questions, and organizing information in ways that make sense to you, you become an active learner. When you are an active learner, the facts become more than facts—they become meaningful and stay with you.

Generate Personal Meaning. To generate personal meaning out of new material (so that it becomes relevant to your life and needs), you must find ways to connect yourself, your knowledge, and your life experiences to the material you are studying. People have a natural tendency to do this. But if you keep in mind that learning and memory are enhanced when you create personal meaning, you will be more likely to do this intentionally. When you can relate new information to your own life by connecting it to your past or present, to problems you need to solve, or to events in the world, you make it important. And you are much more likely to understand it, remember it, and use it.

Practice over Time. You will benefit from practice if you review your notes soon after class or write a summary of an article soon after reading it. When you plan to study, however, distributing practice and rehearsal over time becomes important. This means studying a particular subject for a relatively short time every day or every other day, instead of trying to cram all of your studying into one long session. If you stick with a schedule for doing schoolwork so that you can avoid cramming, you can make use of the distributed practice principle. In doing so, you will increase the amount of material you learn and remember within the same total amount of study time.

Plan on Relearning. Memory studies show that most forgetting occurs right after something has been learned. They also show that if you go back and relearn (rehearse again) the same material, you learn it more quickly and forget less of it (see page 215). Whenever you study, review what you have already learned before you move forward to new information. In this way, you will be making use of the relearning principle.

Take Advantage of the Primacy and Recency Effects. Research concerning the primacy and recency effects (see page 211) shows that you are most likely to remember information received at the beginning and at the end of a study session or lecture. Therefore, instead of forcing yourself to have long, drawn-out study sessions, take a short (5- to 10-minute) break after you have studied for 20 to 30 minutes. Taking breaks will enhance your learning and memory because it will increase the number of times that the primacy and recency effects can work to your advantage

Focus to Prevent Interference. You can facilitate memory storage by doing whatever you can to avoid unnecessary interference (see pages 218–219). For example, when you are studying, focus on one course or one learning task at a time. If you are studying for a big test on Shakespeare, study Shakespeare until you feel confident you have learned the material.

Make Use of Chunking. Chunking allows us to increase the capacity of our working memory (see page 200). For instance, consider the word *psychoneuroendocrinology*, which refers to the subfield of psychology ("psycho . . . ology") that investigates the influence on the nervous system ("neuro") of hormones ("endocrin"). What if you had to learn this word so that you could spell it on an essay exam? How would you do it with the limited capacity of short-term memory? You would use chunking. To remember the long word, you would break it into small chunks: *psycho-neuro-endocrin-ology*.

Another way to use chunking is to group ideas together in organized ways. For example, you might list some factors that increase recall as one chunk of things to remember and some factors that contribute to forgetting as another chunk.

Use Mnemonics. If you transform information that is abstract, difficult, or still unlearned into information that is personally meaningful, it will be easier to remember. Using mnemonics, or memory aids, allows you to combine seemingly unrelated items into an organized format, rhyme, or jingle so you can easily remember all of the items. For example, as a child you may have learned the notes of the treble-clef musical scale, EGBDF, by using the mnemonic jingle "Every Good Boy Does Fine." The more you can relate unfamiliar information that you want to recall to familiar information that you already know, the easier it will be for you to learn and remember it.

Use Mediation. Mediation is a bridging technique that allows you to link two items to be remembered with a third item (or image) that ties them together and serves as a cue for retrieval. Cermak (1975) uses the names *John* and *Tillie* as an example. John reminds someone of a bathroom, which can be associated with the image of tiles, which sounds and is spelled somewhat like Tillie. Therefore, remembering a tiled bathroom helps the person remember the names John and Tillie.

Make Use of the von Restorff Effect. If one item in a group of things stands out because it differs from the other items, like the cow among the egrets in the photo, it will be easier to learn and remember. This is known as the *von Restorff effect*. You can make use of this effect by deliberately making an idea you want to remember stand out. Do this by using a coloured highlighter on your notes, by exaggerating the meaning of the idea you want to remember, by making the idea seem funny or bizarre in your mind, or by emphasizing the distinctiveness of the idea in your mind as you think about it.

Review in Different Contexts and Modalities. The place where you learned something can be an important retrieval cue.

For example, when you see a familiar receptionist in a gymnasium, you may not be able to remember how you know that person. Try to review and rehearse information in different settings. Also, try learning and studying through more than one sensory modality. For example, if you hear a lecture (auditory modality), write down what you hear (tactile–kinesthetic and visual modality). If you have been developing mnemonics on paper, try saying them out loud. If you have been outlining a chapter aloud, write down or draw a map of the key ideas.

Prepare the Environment. Because there is so much to learn and remember, you can facilitate the task if you prepare your environment (Brown, 1989). Limit the number of opportunities for people to distract you from your task. Study in a quiet place where there are few people. Avoid visual clutter in your study area; it is a distraction from the task at hand. Limit the number of tasks you are working on so as to focus your attention and thus stay tuned into one task. Finish the tasks that you start so they will not take further attention. Keep a notebook handy to jot down ideas, insights, and potential mnemonics. ■

often they merely involved the experimenter, a participant, and some information to be learned. Computers were unheard of, and techniques that psychologists use today would not have made sense.

Relearning. Using the technique of *relearning*, Hermann Ebbinghaus (1850–1909) studied how well people retain stored information. Ebbinghaus earnestly believed that the contents of consciousness could be studied by scientific principles. He tried to quantify how quickly participants could learn, relearn, and forget information. Ebbinghaus was the first person to investigate memory scientifically and systematically, which made his technique as important as his findings.

In his early studies, in which he was both researcher and subject, Ebbinghaus assigned himself the task of learning lists of letters in order of presentation. First he strung together groups of three letters to make nonsense syllables such as *nak, dib, mip,* and *daf.* He then recorded how many times he had to present lists of these nonsense syllables to himself before he could remember them perfectly. Ebbinghaus found that when the lists were short, learning was nearly perfect in one or

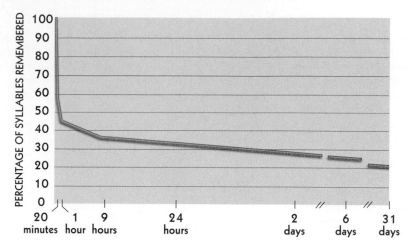

FIGURE 6.9
Ebbinghaus's Forgetting Curve
Ebbinghaus found that most forgetting occurs during the first 9 hours after learning.

ELAPSED TIME BETWEEN LEARNING OF SYLLABLES AND MEMORY TEST

two trials. When they contained more than seven items, however, he had to present them over and over for accurate recall.

Later, Ebbinghaus performed learning experiments with other participants. He had them learn lists of words and then, after varying amounts of time, measured how quickly the participants relearned the original list. If participants relearned the list quickly, Ebbinghaus concluded that they still had some memory of it. He called this learning technique the *saving method*, because what was initially learned was not totally forgotten. (See Figure 6.9 for Ebbinghaus's "forgetting curve.")

Practice. Following Ebbinghaus's lead, from the 1930s through the 1960s, many researchers investigated the best ways for people to learn new material and relearn forgotten skills. In one 1966 study, Baddeley and Longman wanted to learn which of two types of practice resulted in more optimal learning and retention: intensive practice at one time (*massed practice*) or the same amount of practice over several intervals (*distributed practice*). To answer this question, they taught postal workers to touch-type.

The participants were divided into four groups, each member of which practised for the same number of hours using either distributed practice or massed practice. One group practised typing for one hour a day, the second practised for two hours a day, the third practised for one hour twice a day, and the fourth practised for two hours twice a day. The dependent variable was how well they learned to type—that is, the number of accurate keystrokes per minute. A typing test showed that distributed practice (typing one hour a day for several days) was more effective. From this experiment and others, researchers have learned that the effectiveness of distributed practice depends on many variables, including the method, order, and speed of presentation. Distributed practice is especially effective for perceptual motor skills, where eye–hand coordination is important.

In the 1970s, researchers began to study the best way to present information to be learned. (This interest paralleled the innovations being carried out at that time in public schools, including open classrooms, the "new math," and cooperative learning.) They found, for example, that if one item in a list differs from the others (say, one plant name in a list with nine animal names), the different item is learned more easily. This is the phenomenon called the *von Restorff effect*.

Measures of Retention

As teachers, we hope our students will be able to recall key ideas, recognize important concepts, reconstruct elements of our lectures, and be able to visualize key graphs and other images. We hope students will associate the facts in meaningful, personally relevant ways. But first, they have to be able to learn and access the information. Recall, recognition, reconstruction, and pictorial memory are all measures of *retention*. The most widely investigated measures of retention have been recall and recognition. *Recall* is remembering the details of a situation or idea and placing them together in a meaningful framework (usually without any cues or aids). Asking someone to name the make of the vehicle Princess Diana was riding in at the time of the fatal collision is a test of recall. *Recognition* is remembering whether one has seen a stimulus before—whether the stimulus is familiar. Asking someone whether the same vehicle was a Mercedes is a test of recognition. *Reconstruction* is the procedure of restoring a disrupted sequence of events (for example, a series of events in a person's history) to its original order. This is often aided by *pictorial memory*.

Recall. In recall tasks, participants are asked to remember previously presented information. (Essay exams require you to recall information.) In experiments, the information usually comprises strings (or lists) of digits or letters. A typical study might ask participants to remember 10 nonsense syllables, which are presented one at a time on a screen every half-second. The participants then would have to repeat the list at the end of the five-second presentation period.

Three widely used recall tasks are free recall, serial recall, and paired associate tasks. In *free recall tasks*, participants can recall items in any order, much as you might recall the items on a grocery list. *Serial recall tasks* are more difficult; the items must be recalled in the order in which they were presented, as you would recall a telephone number. In *paired associate tasks*, participants are given a cue to help them recall the second half of a pair of items. In the learning phase of a study, the experimenter might pair the words *tree* and *shoe*. In the testing phase, participants would be presented with the word *tree* and would have to respond with the correct answer, *shoe*. People are amazingly good at such tasks; we recall groups of words, events, animals, and so forth together, which, of course, lends credence to the idea that information is contained in semantic networks.

Recognition. In a multiple-choice test, you are asked to recognize relevant information. Psychologists have found that recognition tasks can help them measure subtle differences in memory ability better than recall tasks can. That's because, although a person may be unable to recall the associated details contained in a previously studied fact, he or she may recognize the fact. Asked to name the capital of Prince Edward Island, you would probably have a better chance of answering correctly if you were given four options: Halifax, Charlottetown, Sherbrooke, or Regina.

Reconstruction. Here's a test of your memory: What did Neil Armstrong say when he first set foot on the moon? Few people can recall Armstrong's words exactly, but most can probably recognize them or reconstruct them approximately. Researchers have shown that people often "construct" memories of past events; these constructions are close approximations but not exact memories. For example, you might reconstruct Armstrong's speech as being something about man's first steps on the moon being important for all mankind. Or you might update his words to be more gender-neutral, having to do with one person's steps moving all people forward. (Armstrong's exact words were "That's one small step for man, one giant leap for mankind.")

In 1932, English psychologist Sir Frederick Bartlett reported that when college students tried to recall stories they had just read, they changed them in interesting ways. They shortened and simplified details, a process called *levelling*; they focused on or emphasized certain details, a process called

Schema [SKEEM-uh]: A conceptual framework that organizes information and makes sense of the world by laying out a structure in which events can be encoded.

Decay: Loss of information from memory as a result of disuse and the passage of time.

Interference: The suppression of one bit of information by another received either earlier or later or the confusion of the two pieces of information.

sharpening; and they altered facts to make the stories fit their own views of the world, a process called *assimilation*. In other words, the students constructed memories that to some degree distorted the events.

Contemporary explanations of this *reconstructive memory* have centred on the constructive nature of the memory process and on how people develop a **schema**—a conceptual framework that organizes information and makes sense of the world. Because people cannot remember *all* of the details of an event or situation, they retain key facts and lose minor details. Schemas group together key pieces of information. In general, people try to fit an entire memory into some framework that will be available for later recall. For example, the hockey-watching author's schema for life in Canada during 1973, the year that Canada won the Canada–Russia hockey series, might include memories such as listening to an Eric Clapton song about sheriff homicide, graduating from high school, and losing sleep as a result of watching a new film called *The Exorcist*.

Pictorial Memory. Related to reconstruction is the study of *pictorial memory*, in which researchers test how well people can remember visual images. The results of these studies show that people are amazingly good at recognizing images they have seen before. In fact, Haber (1979) found that participants could recognize thousands of pictures with almost 100 percent accuracy. In 1970, Standing, Conezio, and Haber showed participants thousands of slides, each for a few seconds. They then presented pairs of slides, only one of which the participants had seen before, and asked the participants to identify which of the pair they had seen. The participants recognized the previously seen slides with greater than 95 percent accuracy. More recent studies have repeated the results of Standing and his colleagues, and researchers have developed other approaches as well. The research suggests that pictorial information may be encoded, stored, and retrieved differently from other information; pictorial memory may work so well because of activation of complex memory representations (Intraub, 1980; Intraub, Gottesman, & Bills, 1998; Standing, 1973).

Key Causes of Forgetting

We forget for a myriad of reasons, and information can be lost from both short-term and long-term memory. Two concepts, decay and interference, help explain losses from memory in powerful ways (see Figure 6.10).

Decay of Information. Decay is the loss of information from memory as a result of disuse and the passage of time. In decay theory, unimportant events fade from memory, and details become lost, confused, or fuzzy if not recalled every once in a while. Another way to look at decay theory is this: Memory exists in the brain in a physiological form known as a *memory trace*. With the passage of time and a lack of active use, the trace disintegrates, fades, and is lost. *Diversity* explores the decline of memory functions with age.

Decay theory was popular for many years but is not widely accepted today. Many early studies did not consider several important variables that affect memory processes, such as the rate and mode of stimulus presentation. Although decay is a small part of the final explanation of forgetting, it is probably less important than other factors, such as interference.

Interference in Memory. Interference is the suppression of one bit of information by another received either earlier or later or the confusion of the two pieces of information. In interference theory, the limited capacity of short-term memory

FIGURE 6.10
Decay and Interference in Short-term Working Memory and Long-term Memory
The transfer of information from short-term working memory to long-term memory is crucial for accurate recall at a later time. Note that decay and interference affect both stages of memory.

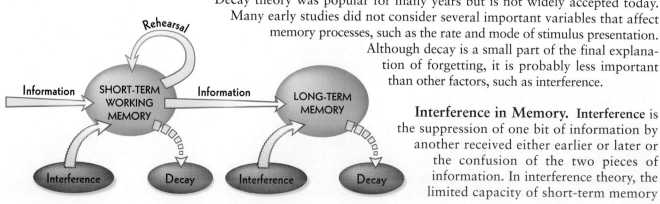

Does Memory Have to Decline with Age? A Bit.

A high-school student very likely will be able to remember the name of every teacher he has ever had while a 40-year-old may not be able to remember no more than a few names without effort. The 40-year-old's memory has not started to deteriorate; in fact, she likely has far more facts at her disposal that the high-school student. However, she may need to wade through some more recently acquired facts or names to find the ones she wants, and some memories may actively interfere with the recall of the teachers' names. Such recall can be complicated, and as time passes, perhaps impossible. Daniel Schacter (1996) points out the complexity of recalling people's names and especially of piecing together a story from the past or recalling a college or university experience: Who was there? When did it happen? Was it when I was a sophomore? What happened first? Was I living in the dorm that semester?

Is it inevitable that memories fade away as you get older? Does memory become fuzzy? Disjointed? Here today, gone tomorrow? Like many things psychological, the answer isn't simple. After age 30 there are slight declines in some types of memory, such as free recall of lists of syllables. Recall and some other memory abilities show deterioration after age 50, and still more deterioration after age 75. The frontal lobe has been implicated in this deterioration in older adults, at least in some tasks (West, 1998).

But like many things, all memory tasks are not created equal. Some are far more difficult. Knowing how to launch a 12-metre sailboat is quite different from knowing the first name of the Kramer character from *Seinfeld*. Further, many memory tasks depend on a speedy response.

How do you respond while driving in the left-hand lane when the turn signal is yellow? When someone says, "Quick, who briefly interrupted Pierre Trudeau's many years as prime minister?" you may know the answer (Joe Clark)—but not right away. Speeded responses cloud the issue of memory research because although the answer or response may be there, older individuals often respond more slowly, sometimes due to other age-related problems

such as atherosclerosis. Another complicating factor is that memory research is often done with different participants at different ages—500 people at age 30, another 500 at age 50, and still a third group of people at age 75. But such research, which does not follow young people as they get older, makes interpretations difficult, because there are many differences among those three groups of people and differing environmental situations affect participants.

When Lars-Goran Nilsson undertook a study that examined the

same individuals over a 10-year period, he and his colleagues found that deterioration depends on the question the researcher asks. Older individuals forget the source of information more than the facts that were learned (Erngrund, Mantayla, & Nilsson, 1996). Educational level also was important. Although there are age-related deficits in semantic memory (ideas, concepts, rules), higher levels of education forestalled the effects of age on problem solving (Backman & Nilsson, 1996; Diehl, Willis, & Schaie, 1995).

In general, researchers conclude that memories of older adults (especially of the oldest adults) do not play back like those of younger ones. Still, there are things you can do to minimize age-related declines in memory skills. People who make a conscious effort to learn new things as they continue to get older lose less—it is a matter of "use it or lose it!" Research shows that if you think you are forgetful, you will be (Ereber et al., 1997)—so think positively. Research also shows that active involvement in learning and memory—for example, through elaborative rehearsal—facilitates recall; so stay involved, be creative, and don't become passive. Older adults do not monitor their day-to-day activities and abilities as well as younger people do, and often, even when given more study time, do not use it as effectively as younger adults; decline in recall can be offset by better time management techniques (Dunlosky & Connor, 1997). Talking about learning, doing, and recalling—planning to act—facilitates recall; so plan for the future. Since it is predicted that there may be as many as 2.5 million North Americans over age 100 in the twenty-first century, research into ways to improve people's memories will continue to be important. ∎

Proactive interference [pro-AK-tiv]: Decrease in accurate recall of information as a result of the effects of previously learned or presented information. Also known as *proactive inhibition*.

Retroactive interference [RET-ro-AK-tiv]: Decrease in accurate recall of information as a result of the subsequent presentation of different information. Also known as *retroactive inhibition*.

makes it susceptible to interference from, or confusion among, other learned items. That is, when competing information is stored in short-term memory, the crowding that results affects a person's memory for particular items. For example, if someone looks up a telephone number and is then given another number to remember, the second number probably will interfere with the ability to remember the first one. Moreover, interference in memory is more likely to occur when a person is presented with a great deal of new information. (In this text, you are being provided with a great deal of new information. Organizing your studying into coherent chunks will help you avoid confusing the information you are trying to enter into long-term memory.)

Research on interference theory shows that the extent and nature of a person's experiences both before and after learning are important. For example, someone given a list of nonsense syllables may recall 75 percent of the items correctly. However, if that person had earlier been given 20 similar lists to learn, the number of items correctly recalled would be lower; the previous lists would interfere with recall

of the current list. If the person subsequently were given additional lists to learn, recall would be even lower. Psychologists call these interference effects proactive and retroactive interference (or inhibition). **Proactive interference**, or *proactive inhibition*, is a decrease in accurate recall of information as a result of the effects of previously learned or presented information. **Retroactive interference**, or *retroactive inhibition*, is a decrease in accurate recall as a result of the subsequent presentation of different information. (See Figure 6.11 for an illustration of both types of interference.) Proactive and retroactive interference help explain recall failures in long-term memory.

Here is an illustration of proactive and retroactive interference: Suppose that you attend a series of speeches, each of which is five minutes long. According to psychological research on proactive and retroactive interference, you will be most likely to remember the first and last speeches. There will be no proactive interference with the first speech and no

FIGURE 6.11
Proactive and Retroactive Interference
In memory, proactive and retroactive interference occur when information interferes with (inhibits recall of) other information.

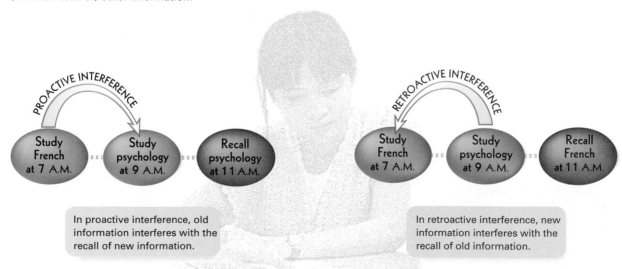

RED	BLUE
GREEN	ORANGE
BLACK	BLACK
BLUE	BLUE
ORANGE	GREEN
GREEN	BLUE
ORANGE	RED
BLUE	BLUE
BLACK	ORANGE
RED	GREEN
BLUE	RED

FIGURE 6.12
"The Stroop Test"

*Source: Baron/Earhard/Ozier,
Psychology, Second Canadian Edition
(Scarborough: Prentice Hall Canada,
1998), p. 116.*

The Stroop effect. Two lists are presented in five colours; red, green, blue, black, and orange. In order to experience the Stroop effect you must say the colour of the ink of each word. Try to ignore the words themselves. First name aloud the colour of each word in the list on the left as quickly as you can. Next say the colour of the words from the list on the right. You will discover that it is much easier to say the colours of the words on the left in which the colours and words correspond. To say the colours of the words on the right you have to suppress your automatic desire to read the word. That is, your knowledge of the word's contents *interferes* with your ability to name the colour of the ink that the word is printed in. This effect is named for the psychologist who discovered it (Stroop, 1935).

retroactive interference with the last speech. Your memory of the middle speeches, however, will suffer from both proactive and retroactive interference.

Interference in Attention. Interference has long been a potent explanatory factor in memory and perception studies. For many years it was used to explain what is called the *Stroop effect* (Stroop, 1935). (See Figure 6.12 for an example of this phenomenon.)

The Stroop test is a procedure in which people are presented with the names of colours, printed in ink that is not the colour named; for example, the word *red* may be printed in blue ink. Participants are asked to name the colour of the ink. Most people find it difficult to attend to the colour of the ink alone (the Stroop effect), because of an apparently automatic tendency to read the word, which produces interference. This explanation has been popular, but attention, rather than interference, is now considered more important in explaining the Stroop effect (MacLeod, 1991).

Special Types of Forgetfulness

Psychologists have learned that there are special kinds of forgetting that are not so easily explained by mere decay or simple interference. You have probably heard about these kinds of forgetting in the popular press, but psychologists have given them special attention in studies of eyewitness testimony and of motivated forgetting.

Eyewitness Testimony. You've seen it on television dozens of times. A witness is asked to look through a book of mug shots in the hopes that he can identify a perpetrator. A mug shot is identified; the witness identifies the perpetrator. If the witness is then shown a lineup of six individuals, he is now more likely to identify the perpetrator than if he wasn't shown the mug shots. When a witness looks through a book of mug shots it actually biases him to choose the perpetrator from the lineup. The witness is more confident that he is identifying the correct perpetrator during the lineup, although the mug shot is actually what is being remembered.

If someone witnesses an accident or a crime, can that person accurately report the facts of the situation to the police or the courts? The answer is yes and no. The police and the courts generally have accepted *eyewitness testimony* as some of the best evidence that can be presented. Eyewitnesses are people who saw the crime, have no bias or grudge, and swear to tell (and recall) the truth. But do they?

If memory is a reconstructive process, as many psychologists contend, it is not a literal reproduction of the past (Schacter, 1996). In fact, research shows that eyewitnesses often forget; they recall events incorrectly, make mistakes, and sometimes identify the wrong people as being involved in the events (Bekerian & Bowers, 1983; E. F. Loftus, 1979). When people make such incorrect identifications, they are often confident in their judgments (Wells, Luus, & Windschitl, 1994). Nevertheless, eyewitnesses of the same event often report seeing different things. Langman and Cockburn (1975) recorded the 1968 eyewitness testimony of people who reported seeing Sirhan Sirhan shoot American Senator Robert F. Kennedy (brother of President John F. Kennedy). Even though many of the eyewitnesses were standing next to one another, they reported seeing different things. In addition, identification of a criminal, even in a lineup, is prone to significant mistakes (Navon, 1990), although techniques have been developed to improve the accuracy of lineup identifications (Sporer, 1993; Wells, 1993).

To complicate the matter, eyewitnesses often enhance their memories over time (recall Bartlett's theory of assimilation). Harvard law professor Alan Dershowitz (1986) asserts that the memories of witnesses—particularly those with a stake in the eventual outcome—tend to get better with the passing of time. Dershowitz calls this process *memory enhancement* and argues that it occurs when people fit their hazy memories into a coherent theory and pattern of other results. Ironically, the more detailed a witness is (even about irrelevant details), the more credible that witness is assumed to be, even if he or she is recalling things inaccurately (Bell & Loftus, 1989).

Much of this also applies to "ear witnesses," people who are asked to identify a voice they have heard before. Daniel Yarmey (1994) of the University of Guelph has studied this issue extensively. Generally he finds that witnesses do a poorer job of identifying people from voice alone, but that the identification rate improves as the length of the voice sample increases.

Whether the witness's memory is weakened, clouded, or confused or whether retrieval processes are impaired is still not clear; but repeated interrogation of a witness can modify the witness's memory—enhancing the recall of some details and even inducing forgetting of other details—even when no misinformation is contained in the questioning (Shaw, Bjork, & Handal, 1995). When a person feels that another eyewitness has corroborated an identification, his or her confidence increases. However, a witness's confidence is not necessarily related to the accuracy of his or her identification (Sporer et al., 1995); when another witness identifies someone else, that confidence quickly decreases (Luus & Wells, 1994).

Motivated Forgetting—Memory and Childhood Abuse. Freud (1933) was the first to formally suggest the idea of motivated forgetting—that unwanted or unpleasant events might be lost in memory simply because people want to forget them. He stated that such loss occurs through repression—the burying of unpleasant

ideas in the unconscious, where they remain inaccessible. Most researchers agree that *motivated forgetting* probably exists in some form. But they have found it hard to measure and difficult to demonstrate experimentally, even though anecdotal clinical evidence abounds.

For nearly two decades Elizabeth Loftus (1991, 1993, 1997), shown in the photo, has been asking whether recall of previously forgotten, traumatic events—for example, being sexually abused as a child—is due to memory enhancement, overinflation of facts, or the planting of such memories. She has extrapolated her laboratory findings to real-life situations involving old memories—and has caused a furor by viewing with scepticism professionals who treat victims of sexual abuse. These professionals assert that their clients' memories, often from many years before, are vivid, accurate, and truthful. The research is inconclusive: Children and adults can be led to enhance their memories (Lindsay, 1993); false memories can be implanted (Loftus, 1997; Pezdek, Finger, & Hodge, 1997; Seamon, Luo, & Gallo, 1998); such memories can remain well preserved over time (Brainerd, Reyna, & Brandse, 1995) and are reported with confidence (Zaragoza & Mitchell, 1996). Ceci and Bruck (1993) hold that adults and even very young children are capable of accurately recalling events that occurred early in their lives; however, the age at which people can recall events is debated, because most people have few recollections before age six and even fewer before age three (Eacott & Crawley, 1998).

The debate among professionals has grown intense, dividing the experts and pitting clinical psychologists against researchers. Some memory researchers have asserted that sexually abused victims could not forget such childhood events for long durations (Pendergrast, 1997; Garry & Loftus, 1994) and that there is nothing special about a traumatic memory (Shobe & Kihlstrom, 1997). Researchers assert that some misguided therapists are helping some people "recover" events that never occurred (Ofshe & Singer, 1994; Poole et al., 1995). Others argue that this is not the case, and argue that scientific findings do not all support the explanation that disclosures of childhood abuse are inevitably the result of therapist suggestion (Olio, 1994, Williams, 1994).

Many researchers have pointed out that there are three key questions: First, can someone forget horrible experiences and remember them years later? Second, is there a potential physiological basis for such recall? And third, is memory fallible? Clinical psychologists speak to the first issue; physiologists speak to the second; and memory researchers speak to the third. Research shows that memory is indeed fallible; people do forget, and people make mistakes, can be led on, and can attribute information to the wrong people. There may be perceptual and physiological explanations for some of these findings (Payne et al., 1997; Schacter, 1997). However, many men and women have been abused as children; such events can be corroborated, and people can repress horrific experiences and have their memories recur when they are adults and can better cope with them.

To be the critical thinkers that they were trained to be, researchers and clinicians alike need to listen to the evidence closely, and examine this contentious issue (Pope, 1996). Does repressed memory exist? Yes. Is memory fallible? Yes. Are some people's memories unreliable and subject to suggestion? Yes. Are some people's memories recollections of real events? Yes. Regardless of the source of the memories, the pain of individuals who recover unpleasant repressed memories of their childhood is real; psychologists are trying to help them.

Neuroscience of Forgetting: Studies of Amnesia

Much of the early work on the neuroscience of memory began with the study of patients in hospitals who for one reason or another had developed amnesia, often as the result of an accident. Television soap operas frequently portray people with amnesia, but in fact the condition is relatively rare. **Amnesia** is the inability to remember information, usually because of physiological trauma (such as a blow to the head). Typically, amnesia involves loss of memory for all events within a specific period.

There are two basic kinds of amnesia: retrograde and anterograde. **Retrograde amnesia** is the inability to remember events and experiences that preceded a traumatizing event. The loss of memory can cover the period just before the event, as in the minutes leading up to an accident, or a period of several years before it. Recovery

Amnesia [am-NEE-zhuh]: Inability to remember information (typically all events within a specific period) usually due to physiological trauma.

Retrograde amnesia [RET-ro-grade]: Loss of memory for events and experiences that occurred in a period preceding the amnesia-causing event.

tends to be gradual, with earlier events remembered before more recent ones. **Anterograde amnesia** is the inability to remember events and experiences that occur *after* an injury or brain damage. People suffering from anterograde amnesia are stuck in the lives they lived before being injured; new events are often completely forgotten. For example, if the onset of the amnesia occurred in 1996, the person may be able to remember clearly the events of 1995, or earlier, but have a difficult time recalling what he or she did only half an hour ago. The person may meet someone for the hundredth time, yet think he or she is being introduced to a perfect stranger. The person is able to learn some new information, but this is highly dependent on how the information is presented (Hamann & Squire, 1995). Amnesia most typically affects the transfer of information from working memory to long-term memory. Ultimately, most amnesic patients have difficulty forming new long-term memories.

Most people who develop amnesia do so because of head injury; others develop symptoms because of Korsakoff's syndrome, an affliction resulting from drinking

Building Table 6.3

Key Processes in the Stages of Memory

Stage	Encoding	Storage	Retrieval	Duration	Forgetting
Sensory Memory	Visual or auditory (iconic or echoic storage).	Brief, fragile, and temporary.	Information is extracted from stimulus presentation and transferred to short-term memory.	Visual: 250 milliseconds; auditory: about 3 seconds.	Rapid decay of information; interference is possible if a new stimulus is presented.
Short-term Working Memory	Visual and auditory.	Repetitive rehearsal maintains information in storage, perhaps on a visual–auditory "scratch pad" where further encoding can take place.	Maintenance and elaborative rehearsal can keep information available for retrieval; retrieval is enhanced through elaboration and further encoding.	No more than 30 seconds, probably less than 20 seconds; depends on specific task and stimuli.	Interference and decay affect memory; new stimulation causes rapid loss of information unless it is especially important.
Long-term Memory	Salient or important information processed by short-term working memory is transferred into long-term memory through elaborative rehearsal.	Storage is organized on logical and semantic lines for rapid recall; organization of information by categories, events, and other structures aids retrieval.	Retrieval is aided by cues and careful organization; errors in retrieval can be introduced; long-term memory is fallible.	Indefinite; many events will be recalled in great detail for a lifetime.	Both decay and interference contribute to retrieval failure.

too much, eating too little, vitamin deficiencies, and brain damage. Diseases, especially viral ones, can cause amnesia as well. These types of causes for amnesia may seem completely unrelated, but research shows that head injury, Korsakoff's syndrome, and viral disease affect a group of loosely related neural circuits that link the temporal lobes, hippocampus, and frontal lobes. In studying patients with brain damage or those who have undergone surgery for major epileptic attacks, researchers have found that the hippocampus (see pp. 55–56) may play a critical role in the transfer of new information to long-term memory. Milner showed that if certain regions of the brain are damaged or removed, people can remember old information but not new information (Milner, 1966; Milner, Corkin, & Teuber, 1968). The ability to remember remote events seems to depend on brain mechanisms that are separate and distinct from those required for new learning of recent events (Shimamura & Squire, 1986). These studies do not conclusively confirm the existence of separate places or processes in the brain for different types of memory, but they are suggestive. Moreover, research on learning and memory of emotional responses by Kim and Fanselow (1992) supports the idea that memory is not a single process or one encoded in a single place (Shen & McNaughton, 1996; Shallice et al., 1994). MRI studies indicate that men and women who have undergone traumas show changes in the size of various areas of the brain, especially the hippocampus. All of this research supports an important point: Memories may be coded in one or many places, and they may be affected by a range of physical events, past experiences, and current ones—thus, memory is as much a process as it is an event or a thing.

Building Table 6.3 summarizes key processes in the three stages of memory and forgetting.

Focus

Review

◆ What view of memory reflects the fact that recall and recognition tap different processes? p. 217
◆ Distinguish retrograde from anterograde amnesia. pp. 223–224

Think Critically

◆ Why do you think distributed practice is more effective than massed practice for learning?
◆ How do interference explanations of forgetting explain errors in retrieval?

Summary and Review

Memory: The Brain as Information Processor

Describe memory.

■ *Memory* is the ability to remember past events or previously learned information or skills; it is also the storage system that allows retention and retrieval of information. p. 194

KEY TERM
memory, p. 194

Encoding

What is the information-processing approach to memory, and what is encoding?

■ The information-processing approach assumes that each stage of learning and memory is separate, though related, and is analyzable by scientific methods. pp. 194–195

■ *Encoding* is the organizing of information so that the nervous system can process it; it involves the process of getting things into the system. p. 195

■ The *encoding specificity principle* asserts that the value or effectiveness of a specific retrieval cue depends on how well it compares with and contains information from when the original memory was encoded. The more clearly and sharply memory cues are defined, the better recall will be. p. 196

What are the underlying assumptions of the levels-of-processing approach? Of parallel distributed processing?

■ The *levels-of-processing approach* holds that a person can process a stimulus in different ways, to different extents, and at different levels. When the level of processing becomes more complex, the code goes deeper into memory. pp. 196–197

■ The concept of *parallel distributed processing (PDP)* developed from the notion of the brain being organized in neural networks; it suggests that many operations take place simultaneously and at many locations within the brain. p. 197

encoding, p. 195; levels-of-processing approach, p. 196; encoding specificity principle, p. 196; transfer-appropriate processing, p. 196; parallel distributed processing (PDP), p. 197

Storage

Describe the role of sensory memory.

■ *Sensory memory* is the mechanism that performs initial encoding and brief storage of sensory information. The visual sensory memory is sometimes called an icon, and the storage mechanism is iconic storage. The storage mechanism for the auditory system is echoic storage. Once information is established in sensory memory, it must be transferred elsewhere for additional encoding or it will be lost. pp. 198–199

Describe short-term working memory.

■ *Short-term working memory* is the memory storage system that temporarily holds current or recently acquired information for immediate or short-term use. Information is maintained in short-term memory for about 30 seconds. In short-term working memory, active processing takes place, including rehearsal and the transfer to long-term memory. Short-term working memory is seen as being made up of three subsystems: a subsystem to encode and rehearse auditory information; a "scratch pad," or holding place for information; and a central processing mechanism, or executive, that balances the information flow. pp. 199–200

■ The brief and limited number of items that can be reproduced easily after presentation is called the *memory span*. The immediate memory span usually contains one or two *chunks*—manageable and meaningful units of information. p. 200

What is rehearsal?

■ *Rehearsal* is the process of repeatedly verbalizing, thinking about, or otherwise acting on or transforming information to be remembered. *Maintenance rehearsal* is the repetitive review of information with little or no interpretation; this shallow form of rehearsal involves the physical stimulus, not the underlying meaning. *Elaborative rehearsal* involves repetition in which the stimulus may be associated with other events and be further processed; this type of rehearsal is usually necessary to transfer information to long-term memory. pp. 200–201

How does long-term memory operate?

■ *Long-term memory* is the memory storage system that keeps a relatively permanent record of information. It is divided into procedural memory and declarative memory. *Procedural memory* is memory for the perceptual, motor, and cognitive skills necessary to complete a task; *declarative memory* is memory for specific facts. Declarative memory is further subdivided into *episodic memory*, or memory for specific events, objects, and situations that are usually personally relevant, and *semantic memory*, or memory for ideas, rules, and general concepts about the world. pp. 203–204

How does consolidation affect remembering?

■ *Consolidation* is the evolution of a temporary neural circuit into a more permanent circuit. If a neuron is stimulated, the biochemical processes involved make it more likely than non-stimulated neurons to respond later; further, the number of dendrites in the neuron increases because of previous stimulation. p. 204

Can stimulation of specific cortical areas prompt recall from memory?

■ When Penfield stimulated the temporal lobe cortex, patients reported seeing images—coherent perceptions of experiences. More recent research shows, however, that no consistent mental images are associated with specific anatomical locations. Further research has proved that no single area holds memory traces. pp. 204–205

storage, p. 198; sensory memory, p. 198; memory span, p. 200; chunks, p. 200; rehearsal, p. 200; maintenance rehearsal, p. 200; elaborative rehearsal, p. 200; short-term working memory, p. 201; long-term memory, p. 203; procedural memory, p. 204; declarative memory, p. 204; consolidation, p 204

Retrieval

Distinguish between episodic and semantic memory.

■ *Episodic memory* is chronologically dated memory for specific events, objects, and situations. Episodic memories often are very specific and usually are personally relevant; a person can describe when and where something happened, and the circumstances surrounding the event. By contrast, *semantic memory* is memory of ideas, rules, and general concepts about the world. It is based on a set of generalizations about previous events, experiences, and learned knowledge. pp. 206–207

Differentiate between implicit and explicit memory.

■ *Explicit memory* is conscious memory that a person is aware of, such as the presentation of a word in a list or an event that occurred in the past; generally speaking, most recall tasks require participants to explicitly recall information. Explicit memory is a conscious, voluntary, active memory store. In contrast, *implicit memory* is memory for information or events that a person is not aware of. Considered an almost unconscious process, implicit memory occurs unintentionally and almost automatically. Researchers study the two types of memory by using different tasks. pp. 207, 208

■ *State-dependent learning* is the tendency to recall information learned in a particular physiological state, such as being inebriated, most accurately when one is again in that physiological state. pp. 208–209

What distinguishes the primacy effect from the recency effect?

■ The *primacy effect* results in the more accurate recall of items presented first; the *recency effect* results in the more accurate recall of items presented last. p. 211

What is imagery?

■ *Imagery* is a cognitive process in which a mental picture is created of a sensory event. People's imagery systems can be activated by visual, auditory, or olfactory stimuli. Even a lack of sensory stimulation can produce vivid imagery. pp. 211–213

Forgetting: When Memory Fails

How are recall, recognition, and reconstruction different aspects of memory?

■ Recall is remembering the details of a situation or idea and placing them together in a meaningful framework (usually without any cues or aids). Recognition is remembering whether one has seen a stimulus before—whether the stimulus is familiar. Research on reconstructive memory focuses on the constructive nature of the memory process and how people develop a *schema*—a conceptual framework that organizes information and makes sense of the world. pp. 217–218

How and why is information lost from memory?

■ *Decay* is the loss of information from memory as a result of disuse and the passage of time. According to interference theory, the limited capacity of short-term memory makes it susceptible to *interference* or confusion. *Proactive interference* is a decrease in accurate recall as a result of the effects of previously learned or presented information. *Retroactive interference* is a decrease in accurate recall as a result of the subsequent presentation of different information. pp. 218, 220

Distinguish retrograde from anterograde amnesia.

■ *Amnesia* is the inability to remember information, usually because of some physiological trauma (such as a blow to the head). *Retrograde amnesia* is the inability to remember events that preceded a traumatizing event; *anterograde amnesia* is the inability to remember events that occur after an injury or brain damage. pp. 223–225

Weblinks

Investigating Short-Term Memory
www.ucs.mun.ca/~mathed/Stats/memory14.htm
This site, from Memorial University (Newfoundland), includes a quiz to test the way in which words are recalled.

Recovered Memory Project
www.brown.ed/Departments/Taubman_Center/Recovmem/Archive.html
An in-depth look at the operation of recovered memory in legal proceedings and case studies. Includes links to other studies and criticisms of theories of recovered memory, including ideas about "false memory syndrome."

Short-Term Memory
www.as.ua.edu/psychology/cognitive/stm.htm
A description of how short-term memory works, with a graphic demonstration.

The Memory Page
www.premiumhealth.com/memory
Mnemonic techniques to help you improve your memory, along with suggestions on how to use your memory when studying, a list of books, and links to related Web sites.

Educational Psychology Interactive: The Information Processing Approach
www.valdosta.peachnet/edu/~whuitt/psy702/cogsys/infoproc.html
Diagrams, charts, and definitions help to define the Stage Model of Information Processing at this comprehensive Web site.

Selected Traumatic Amnesia Publications
dynamic.uoregon.edu/%7Ejjf/trauma.html
This site contains a number of abstracts of articles written about amnesia.

Skeptic's Dictionary
wheel.ucdavis.edu/~btcarrol/skeptic/memory.html
Amnesia, cryptomnesia, and repressed memories are a few of the controversial types of memories discussed at this Web site.

Chapter 7

Cognition: Thought and Language

Larry Barnett was more or less typical of men his age. At age 52, his kids were finishing college, he was at his peak earning potential, he didn't smoke, he drank only occasionally, and he didn't exercise very much. In fact, his wife called him a "weekend warrior," suggesting that he expended energy only on the weekends. That day seemed like any other day—driving in congested traffic to get to a stressful office. But, unlike any other day, an event was taking place within Larry's body, one that would change the course of his life forever. Larry suffered a stroke behind the wheel of his well-padded Volvo. He lost consciousness, slammed into the car in front of him, spun around, and wound up on the side of the highway. Other cars were damaged, but no lives were lost. Larry lay in the hospital for three weeks in a semi-coma. Six weeks after the incident Larry awoke and began to do better.

But, some pieces of Larry's intellectual life had been disconnected. Larry seemed aware of the world around him and was able to process what people were saying. Yet he had trouble speaking. He seemed to know things but was unable to articulate what he knew. If shown a picture of a cat and asked to identify it, he would indicate that he knew what it was. In fact, if asked questions about cats—for example, if they had four legs, if they purred, if they had long tails—he knew the correct answers. However, if asked to name the animal, he couldn't. Larry Barnett was suffering brain damage due to his stroke.

Parts of his brain that connected the sections involved in speech, language, and thought were damaged. After a stroke, if a patient is lucky, some parts of the brain may recover, some may have to be retrained, and some take over for other portions. A long road lay ahead for Larry. Neuroscientists understand what happens when a stroke occurs and that the common, day-to-day behaviours that we all take for granted are intricately interwoven and easily damaged. Speech, language, and thinking are separate yet interconnected processes, all of which rely on the brain. ■

Many biologists and neuroscientists assert that most psychologically complex phenomena, such as speech and language, can be explained by the laws of evolution, molecular biology, and physics (E. G. Wilson, 1998). Many social scientists, however, argue that social phenomena, human interactions, and especially the thought and language of human beings are sufficiently complex, original, and spontaneous that they are far more than the sum of their parts: molecules, genes, and DNA. Human behaviour is sufficiently rich in its subtleties that no single variable explanation, which fails to recognize differences among individuals, can explain it.

Researchers have recognized that thought and language are separate, but closely related, concepts. Language provides human beings with a unique vehicle for expressing thoughts, planning for the future, and analyzing the past. Thought allows human beings to reflect on the past, assess it carefully, and develop new, unique ideas and technology. This chapter therefore discusses both cognition (thought)—especially as it relates to perceiving, learning, remembering, and using information, some of the topics of the previous three chapters—and language, the symbolic system people use to communicate their thoughts to others. Perhaps for some biologists this analysis would be too global and elaborate—but for many social scientists, it is the accepted one.

Cognitive Psychology: An Overview

How are a tiger and a domestic cat similar? Who is the governor general of Canada? How is an omelette made? Answering each of these questions requires a different mental procedure. To answer the first question, you likely drew mental images of both felines and then compared the images. In answering the second question, you simply may have known the right name because of news stories. To answer the third question, you likely mentally walked through the procedure of preparing an omelette and described each step. The thinking you used to answer all of these questions required knowledge, language, and images.

Cognitive psychology is the study of the overlapping fields of perception, learning, memory, and thought; it is the study of how people attend to, acquire, transform, store, and retrieve knowledge (and increasingly, as cognitive neuroscience, it is also the study of how these processes are accomplished within the brain). In a real sense, cognitive psychology is the overall study of thought; we have been discussing it for the past three chapters, and it will help us understand other fields such as intelligence (Chapter 8). In this chapter, however, we will focus on two core topics of cognitive psychology: thought and language. The word *cognition* derives from the Latin *cognoscere*, "to know." Cognitive psychologists are interested primarily in mental processes that influence the acquisition and use of knowledge as well as the ability to *reason*, the process by which people generate logical and coherent ideas, evaluate situations, and reach conclusions. Cognitive researchers assume that mental processes exist, that people are active processors, and that cognitive processes can be studied primarily using techniques that measure time to respond and the accuracy of responses (Ashcraft, 1989).

The history of cognitive psychology began in the late nineteenth century. As we saw in Chapter 1, the main areas of study at the start of psychology were mental processes, thought, and the internal workings of the mind, discerned through introspection. In the 1920s, behaviourism—with its focus on directly observable behaviour—became the mainstream psychology, and there was little reference to internal cognitive processes. Discussion and research of such "mentalistic" phenomena as imagery were avoided, because these phenomena were deemed fleeting and incapable of being observed and measured.

In the 1940s, psychology changed in profound ways. During the Second World War rudimentary computers that could store instructions in their memory were

Cognitive psychology: The study of the overlapping fields of learning, perception, memory, and thought, with a special emphasis on how people attend to, acquire, transform, store, and retrieve knowledge.

being built—they were massive, expensive, and relatively slow. After the war, there was an influx of returning veterans in colleges and universities, which necessitated a massive infusion of new faculty members. Many of these new students and faculty members studied computers, computer science, and a new field called artificial intelligence. The post-war years were marked by prosperity and optimism about the future and about our ability to understand ourselves and our place in the world. In the late 1950s and early 1960s, the flow charts and concepts such as encoding, storage, and retrieval used to construct, program, and run computers were used to begin to construct models of how human "computers" or minds processed information. Research into the nature of human thinking had begun in earnest.

The intellectual world wasn't concerned solely with computers, though. Jean Piaget (whom we will discuss in a later chapter) argued that children think *differently* than adults. George Miller (1956) speculated on exactly how humans code information. Noam Chomsky (1957) suggested that language acquisition is a "wired-in" process. Donald Broadbent (1958) wrote on the nature of attention and thought. Ulric Neisser (1967) published an important book called *Cognitive Psychology*. Also in 1967, Posner and Mitchell published one of the first true experimental studies of cognitive processes. In 1972, Fergus Criak of the University of Toronto (Craik & Lockhart, 1972) proposed a new model for understanding memory processes, and Endel Tulving (1972) of the Rottman Institute advanced memory research on another front. Also in 1972, an influential book by Allen Newell and Herbert Simon, *Human Problem Solving*, altered the way psychologists thought about this topic by discussing the information-processing capacities of the mind and how attention is shared and divided in the various stages of decision making. Researchers like Newell and Simon, and the next wave of theorists in cognitive studies, came from psychology, biology, linguistics, computer science, and philosophy (especially logic). Research began to examine such questions as these: How does thought develop in children? How many pieces of information can a person code at one time? How much can someone pay attention to? How do the eyes scan text during reading? How do people make inferences—determining, for example, that if a blue jay is a bird and all birds have wings, a blue jay has wings? Is a penguin, then, a bird, too?

It is sometimes hard to pinpoint exactly what cognitive psychology is. But understanding thought, reasoning, and the interplay between human beings and their environment continues to be a central concern for cognitive researchers. This means understanding not only how thought takes place, but how it takes place within a context—the environment— and how people extract information from the environment (E. Gibson, 1992; Neisser, 1992). This chapter demonstrates the breadth of cognitive psychology and its growth since its origins in the 1950s. We begin with the study of concept formation, which is crucial for all cognition.

Concept Formation: The Process of Forming Mental Groups

E ach day, people solve problems, make decisions, and behave logically, often following steps that are complicated, but orderly. Many researchers conceive of reasoning itself as an orderly process that takes place in discrete steps, one set of ideas leading to another (Rips, 1990). To perform this

Sexist Language Affects Thinking

In churches, synagogues, and mosques around the country people are trying out, and getting used to, gender-neutral language. In some liturgies God is not being referred to as "Father" and our "forefathers" are being referred to as our *ancestors*. We now speak of Abraham, Isaac, and Jacob *and* Rebecca, Rachel, and Leah. Research shows that these changes affect listeners' responses to liturgy and sermons (Greene & Rubin, 1991). Gender-neutral language is becoming accepted and commonplace—while Captain James T. Kirk, of the original *Star Trek* series, said: "To boldly go where no *man* has gone before," Captain Jean-Luc Picard, of the more recent version of the series, spoke of "boldly go[ing] where no *one* has gone before."

Over the last three decades, psychologists have become particularly aware of the role of language in shaping people's conceptual structures. If you have a concept that all nurses are women, then when a man wearing a white lab coat enters your hospital room, you assume he is a doctor. In general, the English language has evolved in such a way that words define many roles as male, except for those roles that traditionally have been assumed by women (e.g., nurses, teachers) (Bem, 1993). Walk down any street where construction is being done and you are likely to see the warning sign "Men Working." Today, even though you are likely to see women as part of the work crew, the sign probably still reads the same.

Concepts of the world first form in childhood, as children hear stories from parents and teachers. They tell of pioneers who travelled to the West with their wives, children, and farm animals. Fairy tales say that the king rules the castle. Children and adults learn that the law was written to be acceptable to a "reasonable man" (lawyers even call it the *reasonable man standard*). Language with a sexist bias expresses stereotypes and expectations about men and women. Thus, many positive descriptive words are thought of as masculine (for example, *successful, strong, independent*, and *courageous*). Women traditionally have been described as *gentle, loving*, and *patient*. When language indicative of strength or courage is applied to a woman, it is often in the context of incongruity—for example, "She thinks like a man."

That women are thought of as loving and patient and men are thought of as successful and strong is important to psychologists who study concept formation, problem solving, and language. Such concepts set an attitude and an approach on the part of men and women to a whole range of behaviours. Bem (1993) asserts that people view the world through a male point of view and that this is assumed to be the preferred value system. In business, men have been assumed to be task-oriented problem solvers. Women, by contrast, have been assumed to be people-oriented rather than problem-oriented and, as a consequence,

process, people need to employ rather complex forms of thought—every decision involves the ability to form, manipulate, transform, and interrelate concepts. **Concepts** are the mental categories people use to classify events and objects according to common properties. Many objects with four wheels, a driver's seat, and a steering wheel are automobiles; "automobiles" is a concept. More abstract is the concept of "justice," which has to do with fairness, ethics, and equity. "Animal," "computer," and "lecturer" are all examples of concepts that have various *exemplars* (specific members of the category). The study of *concept formation* is the examination of the way people organize and classify events and objects, usually in order to solve problems.

Concepts make events in the world more meaningful by helping people organize their thinking. People develop progressively more complex concepts throughout life. Early on, infants learn the difference between "parent" and "stranger." Within a year, they can discriminate among objects, colours, and people and comprehend such simple concepts as "animal" and "flower." By age two they can verbalize these differences.

Much of what young children are taught involves *classification*—the process of organizing things into categories—because this is a key to organizing and under-

Concept: A mental category used to classify an event or object according to a common property.

have been wrongly stereotyped as less effective in business. And, in fact, many men and women do fit such stereotypes; perhaps because they were raised in environments in which the stereotypes were accepted, they reflect the stereotypes in their day-to-day behaviour.

Research supports the idea that men and women are perceived and treated differently and that they speak differently. Frable (1989) concluded that if people believe in gender-specific abilities, they are likely to apply that belief when making decisions. Frable found that people with strong gender-typed ideas were especially likely to pay attention to the gender of a job applicant and then to devalue the interview performance of women. McDonaugh (1992) found that interviewers not only devalue the résumés of women in general but devalue even more the résumés of women who are members of a minority or who are less attractive. Thus, racial and physical stereotyping complicates gender stereotyping. Gender differences in language use are usually context-dependent; researchers know that men's and women's language is different (Ariel & Giora, 1992), but they also know that it must be considered within a larger social context of ethnicity, class, age, and gender—not to mention social norms (Wodak & Benke, 1997).

While the stereotypes continue to exist, some women and men are becoming more androgynous (*androgyny* is the state of consciously possessing both male and female characteristics). Today, people are more accepting of individuals who express androgynous characteristics—for example, men who cook and women who are engineers. Even more importantly, people are becoming more sensitive to how language shapes their concept of the world and their problem-solving abilities. McMinn and colleagues (1990) found that those who used gender-neutral language in writing were also likely to use gender-neutral language in conversation. However, they also found that it is difficult to change the use of sexist language, perhaps because certain ways of speaking have become acceptable within communities and not just by individuals (McMinn et al., 1991). Further, avoiding sexist language is just a beginning; sexism and the behaviour that follows from it are deeply embedded in people's thoughts and actions.

There have been some changes within Western culture, however. No longer do only men fix telephones wires and only women work as telephone operators; today people are encouraged to be everything they might be, regardless of gender. Even Canadian astronauts are both male and female. Despite some lingering sexism, boys *and* girls currently in primary school are more likely to be encouraged to solve problems creatively, to approach science and math problems with excitement, and to be caring, warm human beings. ■

standing this complex world (see Figure 7.1). Think back to your early school years and to TV shows such as *Sesame Street*. You were taught to classify colours; different animals (and their sounds); shapes such as triangles, circles, and squares; and the letters in the alphabet. You learned to recognize that the people in your house—mother, father, sister, and brother—are a group called a "family." The process of developing concepts through the process of classification is lifelong and constantly changing. It involves separating dissimilar events and finding commonalties (Medin, 1989). But what is the best way to study the processes by which children and adults classify and organize information? Does the way they organize information affect their thinking, and does that effect vary depending on whether they are thinking about a male or a female? *Diversity* examines how words can affect behaviour.

Concept formation is relatively easy to study in controlled laboratory situations. Psychologists design laboratory studies in which the participants form concepts through a range of tasks. For example, suppose you were asked to make judgments in response to questions such as this: Is a bicycle a toy or a vehicle? The experimenter would time your response and also ask you to express your thought processes out loud.

FIGURE 7.1
Classification Tasks Require Choosing among Alternatives That Share Properties
In a typical classification task for children, the objective is to circle the picture that is most like the sample.

SAMPLE

Prototype: An abstraction of a pattern, object, or idea stored in memory, against which similar patterns are evaluated to see how closely they resemble each other; it is the best example of a class of items.

A key requirement in laboratory situations studying concept formation is that participants understand and be able to form rules—statements of how features are related. For example, if all objects that have four sides and are red are exemplars of a target concept, participants can learn that any time they see a red rectangle or square, they should press a button. Here is a common task used in laboratory investigations of concept formation: An experimenter presents you with a stimulus and tells you that something about the objects makes them similar. You are asked to identify this characteristic, this rule. Each time the researcher presents a stimulus, you ask whether it has the property (characteristic) being targeted; and the experimenter answers yes or no. Suppose the first stimulus is a picture of a large bird. The experimenter tells you that it is a *positive instance* (a stimulus that is an example of the concept under study). You now know that the concept may be largeness or being a bird. The second stimulus is a small red bird; the experimenter says that this, too, is a positive instance. You now know that size is not important. The third stimulus is a large blue bird; it, too, is a positive instance. Although the property could be "things that fly" or "animals," you surmise that the relevant property is being a bird. When, on the fourth trial, the stimulus is a small blue toy car and the experimenter says it is a *negative instance* (a stimulus that is not an example of the concept), you might say with conviction that being a bird is the concept.

Laboratory studies allow for examination of how concepts are formed and organized. But concepts in the real world are not always so clear-cut. For example, you know that professors and high-school instructors are teachers, but do priests and ministers qualify as teachers? Do scout troup leaders qualify? Is the prime minister of Canada a teacher? Each of these individuals acts as a teacher—at least, from time to time. The same problem exists with concepts such as "family." One concept of a family consists of two parents and 2.4 kids. But what of single-parent families, blended families, adoptive families, communal families, extended families? Many researchers define a family as any group of people who care about each other in significant ways. You can see that concepts are often fuzzy.

Eleanor Rosch has asserted that when people are presented with *fuzzy concepts*, they tend to define them in terms of *prototypes*, or best examples, of a class of items (Rosch, 1973, 1978). A **prototype** is an abstraction of a pattern, object, or idea stored in memory, against which similar patterns are evaluated to see how closely they resemble each other; it is the best example of a class of items. A high-school English teacher may be a prototype of a teacher; ministers, hiking instructors, and psychologists are also examples, but not "best" examples. Some concepts make for easily defined prototypes; others are hard to define. When you think about the concept of "furniture," you recognize that chairs, sofas, and tables are good examples—but telephones, pianos, and mirrors are all furniture as well; this is a fuzzy concept. The concept of "computer modem" is much less fuzzy: There may be a few shapes and sizes, but nearly all computer modems do the same thing, in pretty much the same way—they allow for digital computer signals to be reconfigured and sent along analog telephone communication lines. Of course, many variables affect how easily concepts are defined, including properties of the concept as well as an individual's unique experiences with that concept. It is these experiences that help people build strategies and solve problems.

Focus

Review

◆ What is the fundamental difference between a positive and a negative instance in concept formation? p. 234
◆ How do we use prototypes in forming concepts? p. 234

Think Critically

◆ What are the implications for psychologists of the fact that cognitive psychology is so broad and covers so many aspects of psychology?
◆ Where do you think people store information that is fuzzy in its conceptual nature?

Problem Solving: Confronting Situations That Require Solutions

You are generally unaware of your cognitive processes; you don't usually think about thinking. And yet you are thinking all the time—sorting through choices, deciding where to go, what to do, and when to do it. When you think, you engage in a wide variety of activities, from daydreaming to planning your next few steps on a mountain path.

How do you manage to study for your psychology exam when you have an English paper due tomorrow? How can you arrange your minuscule closet so all of your clothes and other belongings will fit in it? Your car gets a flat tire on the Trans-Canada Highway; what should you do? These are all problems to be solved. In important ways, your approaches to these dilemmas represent some of the highest levels of cognitive functioning. Human beings are wonderful at **problem solving**, at confronting situations that require going beyond the available information (insight) or that require information gaps to be filled in. Because you can form concepts and group things together in logical ways, you are able to organize your thoughts and attack a problem to be solved. Psychologists believe that the process of problem solving has four stages, summarized in Figure 7.2.

Huge differences exist in people's problem-solving abilities; but psychologists can help people become more effective problem solvers. Recall from Chapters 1 and 3 that Gestalt psychologists analyzed the world in terms of perceptual frameworks and argued that the mind organizes the elements of experience to form something unique. As we saw in Chapter 5, Wolfgang Köhler (1927/1973), a Gestalt researcher, showed that chimps could solve problems by developing *insights* into methods of retrieving food beyond their reach. They discovered they could pile up boxes to reach the food or attach poles together to make a long stick with which to grab the food. Once the insight occurred, no further instruction, investigation, or training was necessary. Insight is not essential to problem solving, but hints, cues, and prior experience all support the process of developing insight and finding essential elements—an advantage in problem solving (Kaplan & Simon, 1990).

When people, and machines for that matter, solve problems they tend to use two basic approaches: algorithms and heuristics. An **algorithm** is a procedure for solving a problem by using a set of rules to implement particular steps over and over again until the problem is solved. Many mathematics problems (for example, finding a square root) make use of algorithms. Algorithms are precise and usually are implemented exhaustively until the solution is reached.

Algorithms also are used in a wide variety of real-life problems, from increasing the yield of a recipe (say, by doubling each ingredient) to writing a computer program (even a relatively simple program requires several algorithms). To implement an algorithm, you follow the rules regarding which task to implement at which point in the procedure. For example, an algorithm for doubling a recipe might be: "Find the list of ingredients. For each ingredient, find the measured amount of the ingredient, multiply that amount by two, and use the product as the new amount for the ingredient. Repeat this procedure until there are no more ingredients listed in the recipe." It's monotonous, but it works. However, because algorithms are sets of rules and procedures that *must* be followed, the necessary time and effort may make them impractical for some uses. Chess-playing computer programs like "Deep Blue" use algorithms to calculate which of all possible chess moves is best at a given moment. Human problem solvers, such as chess master Gary Kasparov, use rules-

FIGURE 7.2
Stages in Problem Solving
Problem solving can be conceived of as a four-stage process.

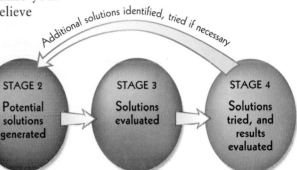

Additional solutions identified, tried if necessary

| STAGE 1 | STAGE 2 | STAGE 3 | STAGE 4 |
| Problem identified, and complexity assessed | Potential solutions generated | Solutions evaluated | Solutions tried, and results evaluated |

Problem solving: The behaviour of individuals when confronted with a situation or task that requires insight or determination of some unknown elements.

Algorithm [AL-go-rith-um]: A simple, precise, and exhaustive problem-solving procedure that follows a set of rules to implement a step-by-step analysis, as in working out a math problem.

of-thumb so that they do not have to follow rigid sets of rules to solve problems. These rules-of-thumb are an integral part of heuristic strategies.

Heuristics are sets of strategies that act as flexible guidelines—not strict rules and procedures—for discovery-oriented problem solving. Heuristic procedures reflect the processes used by the human brain, and involve making rough estimates, guesses, and subjective evaluations that might be called hunches, or intuitions (Bowers et al., 1990). For example, the coach of a hockey team might evaluate the team's first-period performance and intuit that different plays might better its chances against that opponent. To contrast heuristics with algorithms, we can use an example from the game of chess. When deciding on a move, a person (or computer) using an algorithm strategy would repeatedly consider every possible move in terms of its probability for long-term success, then choose the one with the highest likelihood of success. A person using a heuristic strategy would consider only the moves he or she believed most likely to lead in the general direction of a successful outcome. These moves would not be given statistical probabilities of outcomes; instead, the heuristic strategist would ask, "Which move has enhanced my strategic position in the game in the past?" Another example occurs when we work out a complex division problem or a percentage calculation without the benefit of a calculator. The steps we follow in working out the problem represent algorithms but the confidence we have in our answer is more likely based on a heuristic (that is, a rough estimate of what the correct answer should be).

Several different heuristic approaches exist, most of which centre on the goal that is to be achieved. For example, in **subgoal analysis**, a problem is taken apart or broken down into several smaller steps, each of which has a subgoal. In calculating a complex formula, for example, you first might break the task down into a series of simpler questions. In **means–ends analysis**, the current situation or position is compared with the desired end (the goal) in order to determine the most efficient means of getting from one (the current position) to the other (the goal). For example, would a calculator be of assistance in calculating the formula, or would it be worth taking the time to enter the problem into your computer? The objective is to reduce the number of steps needed to reach the goal. A **backwards search** involves working backwards from the goal or endpoint to the current position, both to analyze the problem and to reduce the steps needed to get from the current position to the goal. For example, determining whether some of the component parts of the larger problem be solved at a glance by drawing on previous experiences or memory. People often use all three of these heuristic approaches, but they may be limited, by a psychological set or expectation, to using only one problem-solving approach.

Table 7.1 summarizes the major advantages and disadvantages of algorithms and heuristics.

Barriers to Good Problem Solving

Although people's problem-solving abilities are usually quite good, they may be subject to certain limitations. Among these limitations are functional fixedness and mental set; researchers study these hindrances to gain a better understanding of the processes of problem solving.

Functional Fixedness: Cognition with Constraints. When a four-year-old refuses to wear a raincoat because it is not raining outside he may insist that it is obvious to any fool that raincoats are only for rain. Explaining that the coat also

Heuristics [hyoo-RISS-ticks]: Sets of strategies that act as guidelines, not strict rules and procedures, for discovery-oriented problem solving.

Subgoal analysis: A heuristic procedure in which a task is broken down into smaller, more manageable steps, each of which has a subgoal.

Means–ends analysis: A heuristic procedure in which the problem solver tries to move closer to a solution by comparing the current situation with the desired goal and determining the most efficient way to get from one to the other.

Backwards search: A heuristic procedure in which a problem solver works backwards from the goal or endpoint to the current position, both to analyze the problem and to reduce the steps needed to get from the current position to the goal.

Table 7.1 Algorithms and Heuristics: Two Approaches to Problem Solving

Approach	Procedure	Advantages	Disadvantages	Example
Algorithm	Exhaustive, systematic consideration of all possible solutions; a set of rules.	Solution is guaranteed.	Can be very inefficient, effortful, time-consuming.	Computer chess programs are typically based on a set of pre-defined rules and moves.
Heuristics	Strategies; rules-of-thumb that have worked in the past.	Efficient; saves effort and time.	Solution is not guaranteed.	Person attempting to repair a car uses past experience to rule out a whole range of potential problems.

could be used to keep him warm on cool spring days may be effective in getting him to put on the coat. In this exchange, the four-year-old is exhibiting a basic characteristic of most people: functional fixedness. **Functional fixedness** is the inability to see that an object can have a function other than its stated or usual one. When people are functionally fixed, they have limited their choices and conceptual framework; they see too few meanings or responses to an object or idea. In many ways this constitutes a breakdown in problem solving.

Studies of functional fixedness show that often the name or the meaning given to an object or tool limits its function (Arnon & Kreitler, 1984). In a typical study, a participant is presented with a task and provided with tools that can be used in various ways. One laboratory problem used to show functional fixedness is the two-string problem (see Figure 7.3). In this task, a person is put in a room in which there are two strings hanging from the ceiling and some objects lying on a table. The task is to tie the two strings together, but it is impossible to reach one string while holding the other. The only solution is to tie a weight (such as a magnet or a pair of pliers) to one string, set it swinging back and forth, take hold of the second string, and wait until the first string swings within reach. This task is difficult because people's previous experiences with objects such as pliers may prevent them from considering using them in such novel ways.

Functional fixedness: The inability to see that an object can have a function other than its stated or usual one.

FIGURE 7.3
The Two-String Problem
In the two-string problem, the person must set one string in motion in order to tie the strings together. This solution illustrates that sometimes in order to solve problems people need to overcome functional fixedness and use tools in new ways.

Mental Set. Psychologists have found that most individuals are flexible in their approaches to solving problems. In other words, they do not use preconceived, or "set," solutions but often think about objects, people, and situations in new ways. However, sometimes people develop a rigid strategy, or approach, to certain types of problems. Avoiding a rigid approach would allow an astronaut to make a device for filtering air out of duct tape and other spare parts (remember the scene from the film *Apollo 13?*). These solutions require limber thought processes.

According to the principle underlying this problem-solving limitation, prior experience predisposes a person to make a particular response. Most of the time, this predisposition, or readiness, is useful and adaptive; for the most part, what worked in the past will work in the future. Sometimes, however, the biasing effect of a set is not productive. Creative thinking requires that people break out of their *mental set*—their limited ways of thinking about possibilities. Having a mental set is the opposite of being creative. It limits innovation and prevents a person from solving new and complex problems (McKelvie, 1984; Holland, 1975). In an increasingly complex and changing world, such limitations can be problematic. Here's a problem that is difficult because of a mental set. In Figure 7.4, draw no more than four lines that will run through all nine dots—without lifting your pen from the paper. The answer is provided in Figure 7.5 on page 240.

Experiencing Psychology offers suggestions for overcoming barriers to problem solving and improving your critical thinking skills.

Creative Problem Solving

A number of Canadian cities have had problems in the past with young people hanging around subways or other transit stations and creating disturbances or intimidating transit users. In Calgary, the problem was creatively addressed relatively inexpensively, without installing expensive video surveillance systems or hiring more security. Instead, classical music was played through the existing address system; most of the young people moved on and the problems ceased.

Creativity is the ability to develop original, novel, and appropriate responses to a problem, to break out of functional fixedness. An *original response* is a response not copied from or imitative of another response; that is, the respondent originated the idea. In this discussion, it means a response that is not usually given. A *novel response* is a response that is new or that has no precedent. Unless an original and novel solution is also appropriate, however, psychologists do not call it creative. An *appropriate response* is a response that is reasonable in terms of the situation. Building your home out of soap bubbles may be an original and novel idea, but it is clearly not appropriate. A key issue in creativity is how people break mental sets and become more creative in their thinking (Greeno, 1989). You don't have to be an Einstein or a Picasso to be creative, as the Calgary transit solution demonstrated. To ensure that a creative solution is appropriate, effective problem solvers form a hypothesis and then test it to evaluate potential solutions. Creativity is simply a different way of thinking.

Being exceptionally bright or a good conversationalist, having novel responses, or even appropriate ones, does not make someone "creative." According to well-known creativity researcher Mihalay Csikszentmihalyi (1996) (pronounced CHICK-sent-me-high-ee), creative individuals are those who have changed the culture in some way that involves original thinking. He cites people like Wayne Gretzky, who by everyone's definition is a talented, gifted athlete—but who is not creative, according to Csikszentmihalyi. Csikszentmihalyi asserts that creativity is the process of redefining or transforming your domain (either in your professional field or in an area of interest such as gardening, music, or painting) or creating a new domain.

FIGURE 7.4
The Nine-Dot Problem
Because people tend to group things in familiar ways, it is hard for them to overcome their psychological set to connect the nine dots as instructed.

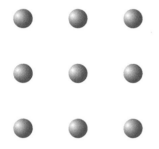

Try to connect all nine dots with no more than four lines, without lifting your pen from the paper.

Creativity: The ability to develop original, novel, and appropriate responses to a problem, to break out of functional fixedness.

experiencing psychology

Be a Critical Thinker

Every day, people have to make judgments, classify ideas, follow logic, and solve complex problems—that is, engage in reasoning. Yet reasoning abilities vary from person to person, and some people are better than others at forming concepts, making decisions, and solving problems. As we saw in Chapter 1, being a critical thinker means that you have to:

- Avoid biases.
- Evaluative alternatives and outcomes.
- Avoid oversimplifications.
- Determine the relevance of facts.
- Question facts.
- Consider all arguments.
- Be open-minded.
- Be tolerant of ambiguity.

There are several other key ideas to make you especially good at critical thinking.

Don't fixate on availability. Things that come to mind quickly are not necessarily the best solutions to problems. Don't necessarily choose the first answer that comes to mind.

Don't generalize too quickly. That most elements in a grouping follow a pattern does not mean that all elements in the grouping will follow the pattern. For example, the fact that you have seen dozens of red roses does not mean that all roses are red.

Don't stick with an easy decision. People often stick with solutions that work, even though other solutions may work even better. Consider all of the alternatives.

Don't stick with a decision that fits pre-existing ideas. People often too quickly accept ideas that conform to their previously held views. This is a serious mistake for researchers who want to be open to new ideas.

Don't test only some of the available ideas or premises. If you do not evaluate all of the available ideas, premises, alternatives, or conclusions, you are likely to miss the correct, or most logical, answer.

Don't be emotional. Sometimes people become emotionally tied to a specific idea, premise, or conviction. When this happens, the likelihood that they can critically evaluate the evidence drops sharply. Critical thinkers are cool and evaluative, not headstrong and emotional.

Don't be constrained by old ideas. Opening yourself up to new ideas may require conscious effort. For example, committees formed to evaluate problems and recommend solutions often define the problem, write down all possible solutions, and then evaluate the possibilities—an effective problem-solving technique called brainstorming. In **brainstorming**, people try to generate as many possible solutions as they can without making any initial judgments about the validity of those solutions. This procedure can be used to illuminate alternative solutions to problems as diverse as how a city can dispose of its waste and how a topic for a group project can be selected. The rationale behind brainstorming is that people will produce more high-quality ideas if they do not have to evaluate the suggestions immediately. Brainstorming attempts to release the potential of the participants: to free them from potential functional fixedness, increase the diversity of ideas, and promote creativity. ■

A Three-Stage Process. Morris Stein (1974) defined the creative process as involving three stages: hypothesis formation, hypothesis testing, and communication of results. In hypothesis formation, a person tries to formulate a new response to a problem, which is not an easy task. A person must confront the situation and think of it in non-stereotyped ways, exploring paths not previously explored.

When people sort through alternatives to try to solve a problem, they attempt to focus their thinking, discarding inappropriate solutions until a single appropriate option remains. To do so, they *converge* on an answer (or use convergent thinking skills). **Convergent thinking** is narrowing down choices and alternatives to arrive at a suitable answer. **Divergent thinking**, in contrast, is widening the range of possibilities and expanding the options for solutions; this lessens the likelihood of functional fixedness or mental set. Guilford (1967) defined creative thinking as divergent thinking. According to other psychologists, any solution to a problem that can be worked out only with time and practice is not a creative solution. To

Brainstorming: A problem-solving technique that involves considering all possible solutions without making initial evaluative judgments.

Convergent thinking: In problem solving, the process of narrowing down choices and alternatives to arrive at a suitable answer.

Divergent thinking: In problem solving, widening the range of possibilities and expanding the options for solutions.

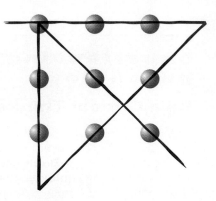

FIGURE 7.5
The Nine-Dot Solution
Here is a creative solution to the nine-dot problem presented in Figure 7.4. Note that you have to think beyond your psychological set and not see the nine dots as forming a square.

foster creativity, people need to rethink their whole approach to a task (Greeno, 1989). Successful entrepreneurs know this to be the case (McClelland, 1987), and those who develop new technologies, products, and services are often well rewarded for their creativity. Business schools are paying closer attention to developing creativity in marketing courses, and researchers are examining the roles of creativity and insight in solving problems (Kaplan & Simon, 1990). Csikszentmihalyi (1996) asserts that we must break new boundaries, transforming business, the arts, or science, to be really creative.

Investing in Creativity. Robert Sternberg has developed a novel approach to studying creativity. He argues that we bring six interactive resources to a problem: intelligence, thinking styles, knowledge, personality, motivation, and environment. When people get involved with a solution that others have ignored or dismissed, they can be creative and productive and later "sell" their idea. This notion of working on undervalued problem solutions and marketing them later is why Sternberg calls his approach an *investment theory of creativity* (Sternberg & Lubart, 1993, 1996). Sternberg argues that if people emphasize their interactive resources like thinking style and motivation, they can be more creative; he contrasts this approach with traditional ideas of creativity that often define truly creative people as those with exceptionally high levels of certain personality attributes. From Sternberg's point of view, anyone who brings all six interactive resources to bear on a problem can be creative.

Focus

Review

◆ What are the fundamental differences between heuristics and algorithms? pp. 235–236
◆ Identify and describe three things research has shown to be effective for improving problem-solving abilities. p. 239

Think Critically

◆ What do you think creates functional fixedness? How do you think you could help yourself break through it to solve a problem?
◆ In school settings, people solve verbal problems and answer questions that might be considered silly in many other settings. What does this say about school experiences?

Reasoning and Decision Making: Generating Ideas and Reaching Conclusions

D eciding whether to take a run at lunchtime, have a sandwich and soft drink, or study for an upcoming quiz may be a regular decision for you. Each option has benefits and costs; because you make this decision day in and day out, the process usually occurs quickly. But how do you make such decisions? When cognitive psychologists study *thinking* they generally attempt to study the systematic day-to-day processes of reasoning and decision making (Galotti, 1989). **Reasoning** is the purposeful process by which people generate logical and coherent ideas, evaluate situations, and reach conclusions. The system or principles of reasoning used to reach valid conclusions or inferences is called **logic**. You can think about reasoning and logic as proceeding in an ordered way or as comprising a process in which ideas and beliefs are continuously updated in a loose, unstructured way (Rips, 1990)—both approaches are valid, and both types of reasoning occur.

Decision making means assessing and choosing among alternatives. You make decisions that involve the probability of some event (how likely is it that my friends will want to go on this trip with me?) and others that involve expected value (how important is *this* trip, rather than some other one?). Your decisions vary from the trivial to the complex: what to eat for breakfast, which courses to take, what career to pursue. The trivial decisions are usually made quickly, without much effort, and unconsciously. The complex ones require conscious, deliberate thought and effort. Sometimes your decision making is logical. At other times you are not sure how things will work out or whether your decision-making process is valid.

Psychologists have devised numerous approaches for looking at the thought processes of individuals. We will examine three of these: (1) formal reasoning, or syllogisms—situations for which there is a single correct answer; (2) logical decision making; and (3) situations in which the answer or decision is less certain and which therefore involve estimating probabilities.

Syllogisms: Formal Reasoning

One of the traditional ways to study thinking, reasoning, and decision-making processes is to provide research participants with deduction tasks such as syllogisms. A **syllogism** is a sequence of statements, or *premises* (usually two), followed by a conclusion. The task is to decide whether the conclusion is warranted based on the assumption that the premises are true.

A psychologist can analyze each decision in the process and thus follow participants' thoughts. People are not particularly good at solving abstract syllogisms; more concrete ones are easier to follow. Consider the following syllogism.

> Premise 1: All professional hockey players can skate well.
> Premise 2: Theoren Fleury is a professional hockey player.
> Conclusion: Theoren Fleury can skate well.

Is the conclusion logical? Do the two premises allow you to conclude that Theoren Fleury skates well? In the preceding example, it is easy to see that the conclusion is accurate. Because logic assumes that the premises are true, however, you can devise a syllogism in which the conclusion validly follows from the premises but is really false—because one or more of the premises are false. For example, if you changed premise 1 to "All professional hockey players are American," you could logically come to the valid (but false) conclusion that "Theoren Fleury is American."

Of course, it's not always easy to accept what may be the perfectly logical results of this sort of reasoning. Research by Val Thompson (1996) at the University of Manitoba indicates that the believability of the premises strongly affects the acceptability of the conclusion. That is, even if the conclusion follows logically from the premises, we may not accept it if the premises are hard to believe. Being able to reach logical conclusions when the premises are odd or hard to believe (assuming they are true) is one of the strengths of logic.

Learning how to use logic, and especially how to check the truth of premises, can help you to become a better critical thinker and decision maker. By being sceptical about the premises on which conclusions are based and by systematically evaluating the truth of premises you can think the way a detective does, using logical decision-making skills to eliminate possibilities one by one.

Reasoning: The purposeful process by which people generate logical and coherent ideas, evaluate situations, and reach conclusions.

Logic: The system or principles of reasoning used to reach valid conclusions or inferences.

Decision making: Assessing and choosing among alternatives.

Syllogism [SILL-oh-jiz-um]: A sequence of statements, or premises (usually two), followed by a conclusion; the task is to decide whether the conclusion is warranted.

Uncertainty: Estimating Probabilities

How do people decide what to wear, where to go, or how to answer a question on a test? How do they decide when something is bigger, longer, or more difficult? Many decisions are based on formal logic, some are based on carefully tested hypotheses, and some are based on educated guesses. Making an educated guess implies knowing something from past experience. When you see rain clouds, for example, you guess—but cannot be 100 percent certain—that it will rain. The likelihood of rain is expressed as a percentage—that is, as a probability.

Psychological factors, especially previous events, affect how people estimate probabilities of events. Consider a study conducted by Daniel Kahneman, who worked at the University of British Columbia, and his colleague Amos Tversky (Tversky & Kahneman, 1973) in which participants were asked to judge whether a list of names contained more men than women. Participants were given the names of 40 famous people—20 men and 20 women, with a probability of 50 percent of each gender. In one case, the participants read a list in which the men were more famous than the women; in another, the participants read a list in which the women were more famous than the men. After reading their respective lists, the participants were asked if their list contained more men or women. The participants who read the list with more famous men said there were more men on the list; those who read the list with more famous women said there were more women on the list. The critical variable affecting the results was the participants' familiarity with the names of the famous people. In other words, the fact that the people of one gender were more famous affected the participants' perceptions and their estimates of probability.

People make probability estimates of all types of behaviours and events. In election years, they estimate the likelihood of a Liberal victory. On the basis of past experience, they estimate the probability of staying on a study schedule, an exercise regime, or a diet. They can judge whether a particular event increases or decreases the probability of another event. When several factors are involved, their compounding and mitigating effects alter the probability of the outcome. For example, the probability that there will be rain when there are thunderclouds, high winds, and low barometric pressure is much higher than the probability of rain when there are only a few thunderclouds.

Study participants asked to make probability judgments about the real world, particularly about fairly rare events such as airplane crashes, are less likely to make accurate judgments than people given laboratory problems (Swets, 1992). The farther in the future the event to be predicted is, the more ambiguity exists for the predictor; also, people are likely to be affected by past behaviour and therefore make mistakes about the future (Payne, Bettman, & Johnson, 1992). Also, according to Norman Brown (1997) at the University of Alberta, people judge the frequency of target events by trying to recall as many similar events as possible and then counting their recollections. This strategy, of course, is significantly influenced by how the questions are asked and the contexts in which they are posed. People make mistakes and errors in judgment and may act irrationally. They may ignore key pieces of data and thus make bad (or irrational) decisions that are not based on probability. Sometimes, people's world-views colour their probability decision making. If an individual's moral system, religious belief, or political view points in one direction (for example, Christianity versus Buddhism or capitalism versus communism), that individual's strategies and decision estimates will be influenced in that direction.

Finally, people are not machines or computers; their creativity, past experiences, and humanness affect results, sometimes in unpredictable ways. However, cognitive psychologists have suggested ways for individuals to become the most efficient learners and thinkers they can be, and researchers have found that people can be taught to weigh costs and benefits more accurately and to be less influenced by their frames of reference (Larrick, Morgan, & Nisbett, 1990; Payne, Bettman, & Johnson, 1992). Research by Kevin Dunbar (1994) at McGill University, for example, indicates that the stated goals of a sample research project (finding evidence that supports a hypothesis) strongly affect whether the researcher can look past expectations and react appropriately to negative research findings. One way to break out of traditional frames of reference is to use analogies. When researchers examined how students could best learn scientific concepts, they found that analogies and metaphors were especially useful. Details are reported back well through traditional learning of text, but analogies—especially creative ones—provide conceptual bridges that facilitate learning, memory, and concept development (Donnelly & McDaniel, 1993). For example, a lawyer arguing a case before a jury may use the metaphor of a chain to describe the case he or she is trying to build. The opposing lawyer, however, may be able to do damage to the chain metaphor, as chains are only as strong as their weakest link—refute one fact and the chain breaks.

Barriers to Good Decision Making

In the same way that people's problem solving can be hampered by mental sets, their decision making can be hindered by a range of stumbling blocks.

Gambler's Fallacy. If you know about probability, you know that people have misconceptions about the probabilities of events. A common fallacy is the *gambler's fallacy*—the belief that the chances of an event occurring increase if the event has not occurred recently or that things can be done to increase the odds of winning. This fallacy has resulted in millions of people leaving thousands of dollars in the casinos of Las Vegas. Every time you flip a coin, the chance of it turning up "heads" is still 50 percent—regardless of what happened on the last flip, or on the last 10 flips. And every pull of a slot machine has the same likelihood of making you a winner, regardless of what happened on the last pull, even if you think you are "due for a win."

Belief in Small Numbers. Limiting the number of observations we make also contributes to poor decision making. When we choose to draw conclusions from a small sample of individuals or observations—a *belief in small numbers*—results are likely to be far more variable and not representative of a larger sample. Even a single compelling story example can influence us. The truth is that people are willing to infer conclusions from a small sample—say 10 neighbours—and assume that such a sample is representative of an entire town, state, or country.

Availability Heuristic. Although it is generally known that air travel is quite safe—safer than walking through the parking lot of a nearby shopping mall—many people are still afraid to fly. People with such fears overestimate the probability of events in their lives and are likely to make poor decisions when they follow those beliefs. Such exaggeration is probably due to the wide media attention given to infrequent catastrophic events; accordingly, such information is more "available" than other information and therefore it is easy to think of examples of these events. Psychologists refer to this phenomenon as the *availability heuristic*—the tendency to judge the probability of an event by how easy it is to think of examples of it. The number of fatalities due to plane crashes, tornadoes, and icebergs is overestimated by most people.

Overconfidence. When people develop ideas about the world they often become overconfident and overestimate the accuracy of their judgments and knowledge. Such *overconfidence* is a major stumbling block to good decision making. Imagine the surprise of a student who is rejected from the only law school she applied to because she was sure—absolutely convinced—that she would be accepted. Individuals become so committed to their ideas and beliefs that they are more often confident than correct; when challenged they often become more rigid and fixed in their beliefs. Individuals should gather as much information as possible before becoming so confident.

Focus

Review

◆ What is the advantage for psychologists using syllogisms in research? p. 241
◆ Identify and describe several barriers to making good decisions. pp. 243–244

Think Critically

◆ Do you agree or disagree with the idea that people are often not good at estimating the probability of events in the world? Why?
◆ Can you think of a political situation or crisis where overconfidence or confirmation bias contributed to bad decisions?

Confirmation Bias. Perhaps the greatest challenge to making good decisions is that people tend to cling to beliefs despite contradictory evidence; psychologists call this phenomenon the *confirmation bias*. People tend to discount information that does not fit with their pre-existing views. Salespeople who were once star performers often cling to the belief that they are "Number One" long after their ascendancy has faded—and despite objective sales data. People continue to believe in ESP or other psychic phenomena even as negative evidence accumulates. People rarely look back on missed opportunities to invest; rather, they seek to confirm their good judgment by showing how they have made money (or not lost it) through the investments they did make. Such a narrow, single-minded focus certainly can lead to poor reasoning and decision making. As you will see when we study social psychology in Chapter 13, the confirmation bias leads to stereotypes and prejudices that are often ill-informed and wrong.

Artificial Intelligence

 s the 1990s have unfolded and people have given thought to the millennium, much has been written about the role of computers in society. There is no question that computers have transformed what we do and how we do it. Today's computers are small, fast, and powerful; in some ways, they reflect the values of our society—power, speed, and disposability after four years or so. By simulating specific models of the human brain, computers help psychologists understand human thought processes. Specifically, computers help shape theoretical development (as in hypotheses about information processing and perception), assist researchers in investigating how people solve problems, and enable psychologists to test models of certain aspects of behaviour, such as memory. They also assist human beings in performing many real-life chores. When computer programs implement or produce some type of human activities, they are said to involve *artificial intelligence* (*AI*).

The Computer as Information Processor

In Chapters 3 and 6, you learned how researchers break down many perception and memory problems into small steps, using the information-processing approach. The information-processing approach to perception, memory, and problem solving is a direct outgrowth of computer simulations. Flow charts showing how information from sensory memory reaches short-term working memory and long-term memory rely implicitly on a computer analogy. Those who study memory extend the computer analogy further by referring to hypothetical storage areas in the brain as "buffers" and biological information-processing mechanisms as "central processors." Basically, both computers and human brains are viewed as symbol-manipulating devices. The information-processing approach is widely used, although it has come under attack as reducing everything to its smallest element (Bruner, 1990).

The most widely investigated aspect of computer simulation and artificial intelligence is problem solving. Playing chess was one of the first human activities that researchers tried to duplicate with computers, and ever since then human beings like Gary Kasparov have been challenging the computers for dominance—with some modest successes and some notable failures! Jonathan Schaeffer of the computer science department at the University of Alberta has taken game modelling to new heights by designing a program called Chinook that plays checkers so well that it is now, in fact, the world champion, having beaten several top-ranked players in tournament play. If you think your checkers skills are pretty good, try them out against Chinook at www.cs.ualberta.ca/~chinook/. Good luck!

Computers can solve complicated problems involving large amounts of memory. The most sophisticated programs incorporate aspects of human memory and decision making and have been used to solve a wide array of problems, including issues of computer chip design and human resource management (Lawler & Elliot, 1996).

Human beings are hampered by their limited attention span and their limited ability to work on more than one task at a time. In contrast, computers can operate hundreds or even thousands of processors (decision switches) at once. Supercomputers, in turn, are made up of many of these powerful computers operating simultaneously (in parallel) to solve problems.

Although computers can be programmed to process information in similar ways to human beings and can process certain complex information infinitely more quickly, they lack human ingenuity and imagination. In addition, computers do not have a referential context in which to interpret situations. When you ask a grocer, "Halibut?" and the grocer responds, "Wednesday, after 4, downtown only," you understand the meaning of this answer: Halibut will be available on Wednesday, after 4 p.m., when the shipment has arrived at the downtown branch of the grocery chain. Human beings understand the context—that fish are shipped only occasionally, to some stores, at certain times during the week. They understand the concepts of branch stores, fresh fish, and selective shipments. Computers do not have such contexts. Further, they cannot evaluate their own ideas or improve their own problem-solving abilities by developing heuristics.

Neural Networks

As we have seen, the comparison of the brain to a computer is a compelling one. Interesting research has focused on the brain's ability to represent information in a number of locations simultaneously. Take a moment to imagine a computer. You may conjure up an image of an IBM or a Macintosh, a laptop or a mainframe terminal. You also may start thinking about programming code, computer screens, even Nintendo. Your images of specific computers or representations of what the computers can do are stored and coded at different places in the brain. No one suggests that you have a "computer corner" where all information about computers is stored. Since various pieces of information are stored in different portions of the brain, their electrical energy must be combined at some point, in some way, for you to use the word *computer*, understand it, and visualize it what it stands for.

The brain has specific processing areas. However, these areas are located throughout the brain, and thus a "convergence" zone, or centre, is necessary to mediate and organize the information, according to University of Iowa researchers Damasio and Damasio (1992). Thus, signals from physically distant clusters of neuronal activity come together in convergence zones to evoke words, develop sentences, and fully process ideas and images about the subject at hand—such as pianos. That convergence zones are located away from specific pieces of information helps explain why some stroke victims and patients with various brain lesions (injuries) can tell you some things about pianos but not everything they once knew. For example, a stroke victim may be able to look at a picture of a piano and tell you that it has keys and a pedal but be unable to name it. According to Damasio and Damasio's view, a key convergence zone has been damaged.

The idea of convergence zones has led to the development of models of where and how the brain operates to represent the world, develop concepts, solve problems, and process day-to-day tasks like reading and listening (Posner & Pavese, 1998). It also helps explain why people who have had damage to the visual cortex can sometimes have knowledge of things that they do not acknowledge seeing. This residual vision—sometimes referred to as *blindsight*—is attributed to secondary, less important visual pathways. Wessinger, Fenrich, & Gazzaniga (1997) reported cases of individuals who could not see various objects, but yet had visual abilities—blindsight. Such multistage models of knowledge of the world—with multiple sources of input—suggest convergence zones and multiple levels and layers of processing.

In recent years, mathematicians, physiologists, and psychologists have joined forces to develop specific models of how neural structures represent complicated information (e.g., Hinton, 1992). Their work is often based on the concept of *parallel distributed processing (PDP),* which suggests that many operations take place simultaneously and at many locations within the brain (an idea introduced in Chapter 6). Most computers can perform only one operation at a time—admittedly very quickly, but still only one at a time. In contrast, the largest of modern computers can operate hundreds or even thousands of processors at once. Today's supercomputers are made up of many powerful computers that operate simultaneously (in parallel) to solve problems. PDP models assert that the brain can process many events, store them simultaneously, and compare them to past events (Grossberg, 1995). PDP models also incorporate perception and learning; they combine data from studies of eye movements, hearing, the tactile senses, and pattern recognition to present a coherent view of how the brain integrates information to make it meaningful. PDP models can even account for nodes, units, or (in the Damasios' terminology) convergence zones that store different types of information in different ways (McClelland, 1994).

To study parallel distributed processing, researchers have devised artificial neural networks. These networks typically are composed of interconnected "units" that serve as model neurons. Each unit, or artificial neuron, receives signals of varying and modifiable weight, to represent signals that would be received by a real dendrite. Activity generated by the unit is transmitted as a single outgoing signal to other neural units. Both input and output to units can be varied electronically, as can interconnections among units. Layers of units can be connected to other layers, and the output of one layer may be the input to another.

A neural network is, of course, believed to be a physical entity in the brain, but researchers usually prefer to use computers to create complex, fast, electronic neural networks that simulate specific activities. For example, computer-simulated neural networks have sophisticated pattern recognition abilities and can be taught to recognize handwritten letters and other simple patterns. A network can be presented with a stimulus, say the letter A. If the network (the computer program) responds that the stimulus was an H, the signal strength of some of the synaptic junctions can be altered to make the network respond appropriately. In addition, a network can learn to recognize a range of forms that look like the letter A. In this case, the network is said to have learned a *prototype.* Prototypes may constitute the network's basis of form and letter perception. While potentially useful in their own right, these networks also provide rich explanations of how human neural networks actually might be functioning.

 Processing within neural networks can proceed from the top down or from the bottom up. We saw in Chapter 3 (p. 76) that when researchers examine sensation and perception they usually adopt a bottom-up processing or analysis approach that starts at the most fundamental level of sensation—where the stimulus meets the receptors—and works up to more complex perceptual tasks involving interpretation. Neural network analysis also can proceed from the top down. This type of analysis zeros in on processes such as selective attention.

An interesting aspect of networks is what happens when one portion of a network is partially destroyed. The network does not crash, but it makes mistakes, much as the brain would. When portions of the brain are ablated (surgically destroyed or removed) or injured in an accident, the person is still able to complete some tasks. For example, one patient lost the ability to perceive motion, seeing the world instead as a series of still photos. This made crossing the road very hazardous, as she would glance up and see a stationary image of a car and assume it was safe to cross when in fact the car was bearing down on her and would hit her if she proceeded across the street.

Neural networks, like the brain, learn and remember. A neural network learns when the weights or values associated with various connections change over time. Sophisticated networks learn quickly and easily, and modify themselves based on experience. The connections between various units within the network are changed because of experience in a way that reflects Hebb's theory: Those units that are frequently activated will become more pronounced, will have a lower threshold of activation, and will be more easily accessed in the future (Posner, DiGirolamo, & Frenandez-Duque, 1997). This access is part of the retrieval process; easy access means easy retrieval, and both are dependent on clear, unambiguous learning.

That neural networks operate efficiently is clear; but they're fallible. Although they can learn speech and handwriting, chess and checkers strategies, and spatial layouts, they are subject to error (see Nass et al., 1995). Furthermore, they do not have the creativity and personality that human beings possess. They lack a sense of humour and the ingenuity that perseverance, motivation, and intelligence brings to a task. Neural networks help us understand human cognition, but they will not take its place.

Focus

Review

- How can the human brain be compared to a computer? pp. 244–245
- Describe the fundamental idea of a convergence zone. p. 245
- What is a neural network? pp. 246–247

Think Critically

- What do you think has made the human brain develop in such a way that it exhibits creativity and humour, which a computer cannot do?
- What are the implications of the Damasios' idea that information is stored all over the brain and brought together in convergence zones for neuroscientific studies of memory and thought? For locating the memory store?

Language

The doorbell rings. You open the door and see someone wearing sunglasses, a T-shirt, and pink-and-green swim trunks. The person says, "Tell your roommate to get her stick. It's six-foot and glassy." Some people might interpret this to mean that the roommate owns some kind of long Plexiglas pogo stick. A surfer, however, would grab a surfboard (stick) and head to the beach, where six-foot-high waves are breaking on a beautiful, windless day (making the ocean's surface "glassy"). Although the words sound the same to surfer and non-surfer, their interpretation will be radically different, because surfers use particular terms and expressions when talking about their sport. Linguists have a name for the study of how the social context of a sentence affects its meaning: *pragmatics*. A **language** is a system of symbols, usually words, that convey meaning; in addition to the symbols, a language also has rules for combining symbols to generate an infinite number of messages (usually sentences). Therefore, language is symbolic, it is a structured system, it is used to represent meaning, and it is generative, allowing an infinite number of sentences to be created. We will examine these key elements in a moment. But for now, think about how amazing it is that we have such complex language structure, and that we are able to process it so effortlessly, despite its complexity. Some

Language: A system of symbols, usually words, that convey meaning; in addition, it also has rules for combining symbols to generate an infinite number of messages.

researchers have questioned whether two people who speak the same language but use different expressions to describe conditions think about the world in different ways. Does language determine thought, or do all people think alike, regardless of their language? Ultimately, what is the influence of culture on language?

Thought, Culture, and Language

In the 1950s researchers discovered that Inuit languages had many more nouns to refer to snow than English does. From this finding, anthropologist and linguist Benjamin Whorf reasoned that the Inuit languages shaped Inuits' thinking about snow—that is, verbal and language abilities must affect thought directly. In Whorf's view, the structure of the language that people speak directly determines their thoughts and perceptions (Whorf, 1956). To investigate Whorf's claim, cognitive psychologist Eleanor Heider Rosch studied the language structure and colour-naming properties of two cultures with different languages (Heider, 1971, 1972; Heider & Olivier, 1972; Rosch, 1973). Every language has ways of classifying colours, although no language includes names for more than 11 basic colours (Berlin & Kay, 1969). Rosch's research participants were English-speaking Americans and native speakers of Dani, the language of a primitive Stone Age tribe (the Dani) in Papua New Guinea. In Dani there are only two basic colour names: *mola* for bright colours and *mili* for dark colours. In English there are many ways of classifying colours, usually based on hues; for example, red, blue, yellow, green, turquoise, pink, and brown. If language determines thought, as Whorf claimed, then the English speakers and the Dani would show different ways of thinking about colour.

Rosch showed both groups of participants single-colour chips for five seconds each. After a delay of 30 seconds, she asked the participants to pick the same colour from a group of 40 colour chips. Whorf's hypothesis predicted that since the Dani have only two basic color-naming words, they would confuse colours within a group. Two different hues from the *mola* category would be considered the same basic colour. However, neither the Dani nor the English-speaking participants confused colours within categories. The Dani's two-colour language structure did not limit their ability to discriminate or remember colours; that is, it did not, as Whorf claimed, determine their perception.

In the same manner, even though human beings are sensitive to odours, they have an impoverished language structure to describe them. Research shows that although odours are easily detected, naming such odours can be difficult. Such names are often based on personal experiences and sometimes are coded in terms of a personal biographical event (for example, Granddad's pipe tobacco, Mother's perfume, Aunt Maria's attic) (Richardson & Zucco, 1989). Linguistic processes play a limited role in the processing of smell; the language of odours is determined by factors other than simply perceptions of odours. The work of Rosch and many other researchers has put to rest Whorf's idea that language determines thought (Lillo-Martin, 1997).

Culture, however, has a great influence on both language and thought. Fairly rigid linguistic customs reflect hundreds of years of history; for example, in the French language, there are formal and informal means of address. The word "you" for friends is *tu*; in more formal settings, one uses *vous*. Japan has even greater culturally determined distinctions in formality of language; who a person is in the workplace—boss, manager, supervisor, worker—affects how he or she is addressed and whether he or she will be shown deference. (In Chapter 17, we will consider workplace psychology in more detail.) Language is thus an expression of racial, geographic, cultural, and religious tendencies (Williamson, 1991).

Many people are bilingual, speaking at least two languages. Although bilingualism promotes cognitive flexibility, research shows that when bilingual people are asked to respond to a question, take a personality test, or otherwise interact in the world, they do so in a culturally bound way—depending on the language in which they respond. When responding to a personality inventory written in Chinese, native speakers of Chinese are likely to reflect Chinese values; when they respond to an English version of the same personality test, their responses are more likely to reflect Western values (Dinges & Hull, 1993). As Hunt and Agnoli (1991, p. 377) assert, "The language people speak is a guide to the language in which they think." The even deeper question of whether the human brain is innately structured so as to facilitate various cognitive and linguistic functions is explored in *Brain and Behaviour* on page 250.

As Matsumoto (1994) asserts, language and culture are intertwined; culture affects language, *and* it affects a person's attitudes and world-view. Along with studies of culture, Rosch's studies suggest that language does not determine thought, but rather subtly influences it. Recall from *Diversity* (pages 232–233) that a person's language can shape his or her world-view and expectations—for example, influencing expectations for women or men. Although various languages have developed specific grammars and thought processes, they have probably done so in response to specific environments, events, and cultures. It may be adaptive to discriminate among many kinds of snow or supervisors, but language does not directly determine thoughts. Rather, thoughts about snow and supervisors help shape language and the specific words in it.

Linguistics

Throughout the ages and in every culture, human beings have shaped their thoughts into language and have employed words to order their thoughts. Tens of thousands of years ago, our cave-dwelling ancestors put their thoughts into words to organize hunting parties. Several millennia later, Egyptian scribes used hieroglyphics (pictorial characters) to represent the spoken word. Today, world leaders employ oratory to rouse their constituencies to moral behaviour and social progress, professors verbally instruct students in the various fields of human knowledge, and people from all walks of life use language to exchange ideas with others or to solve problems mentally. Without this ability, human civilization could never exist. In many ways, language and thinking define humanity.

Linguistics is the study of language structure and language change, including speech sounds, meaning, and grammar. **Psycholinguistics** is the psychological study of language, of how language is acquired, perceived, understood, and produced. Among other things, psycholinguists seek to discover how children learn the complicated rules necessary to speak correctly. Children are astonishingly adept at understanding and using the basic rules of language. Even 18-month-olds, who have vocabularies of perhaps only 50 words, comprehend a great deal of what is said to them; we say that their *receptive vocabulary* is greater than their *productive vocabulary*. However, productive vocabularies increase very rapidly in the number of words that are used and in their forms. By age six, most children have vocabularies of about 10 000 words and by the time most people have reached adulthood they recognize about 40 000 words!

The miracle of language acquisition in children has long fascinated linguists and psycholinguists. Studies show that children first acquire the simple aspects of language, then learn progressively more complex elements and capabilities. Studies also have revealed *linguistic structures*—the rules and regularities that exist in, and make it possible to learn, a language. The following section examines three major areas of psycholinguistic study: *phonology*, the study of the sounds of language; *semantics*, the study of the meanings of words and sentences; and *syntax*, the study of the relationships among words and how they combine to form sentences. In each of these areas, researchers have tried to identify the universal characteristics that exist in all languages.

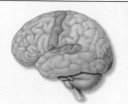

brain and behaviour
Is Anything About Thought Hard-wired?

Are some people just naturally better problem solvers? Are the brains of geniuses organized in some special way? Researchers have conducted EEG studies to see if there are observable differences in the brain waves, brain structure, and neuroanatomical details of gifted and talented people. But this early research yielded few important or consistent findings (e.g., Beisteiner et al., 1994; Martindale et al., 1984). Among other research problems, individual differences in brain-wave patterns are sufficiently great that any differences that are found in the gifted are not necessarily significant.

Research from PET scans and language studies are beginning to suggest where some types of thought or information processing may be located in the brain. PET scans, which trace the distribution and timing of activity in the brain while a person is involved in a cognitive task, show that key brain areas do seem to be involved in certain key functions (Abdullaev & Posner, 1998). The occipital lobe becomes more involved in visual activities, the temporal lobe in more cognitive functions, and the

left superior temporal gyrus in auditory language comprehension (Cabeza & Nyberg, 1997). PET scan studies thus lend credence to the traditional view that there is a considerable correspondence between brain structure and function.

New research is constantly challenging traditional findings. Language functions traditionally have been thought to be based solely in the left hemisphere for right-handed people (90 percent of the population). An area on the left side of the brain, called the sylvian fissure, has been thought responsible for the expression and comprehension of spoken and written language—closely associated activities. But Christiana Leonard and her colleagues (1996) found that, as children grew older and developed more sophisticated language ability, left-right asymmetries disappeared. Furthermore, Baynes and colleagues (1998) found that writing abilities may be located on the right side of the brain. Baynes found that in a patient who had undergone a surgical split-brain procedure (see Chapter 2, p. 63), in which the left and right sides of the brain are disconnected, the ability to read

and speak were left-brain activities but writing was a right-brain activity. This finding—that spoken and written language can be controlled by independent hemispheres—needs to be substantiated, but it raises new thoughts about the modularization of brain function. Some researchers think that the brain may consist of many more modules or parts than previously thought, and that these parts may operate both independently and together to create language. Other researchers using different techniques are reaching similar conclusions (Stone et al., 1996).

So, is the brain hard-wired for some activities? Perhaps. We saw in Chapter 2 that the brain is plastic, malleable, and sensitive to experience; that is, it changes over time. The brain may have specific structures and functions that are hard-wired, but their proper operation requires sophisticated control and coordination that may be dependent on experience and even on the context in which people find themselves. Perhaps it is this coordination that allows all of us to develop a thinking style that is different from that of others (Sternberg, 1997). ■

Language Structure

 The key components of language are its sounds, how its sounds acquire meaning, and its overall organization. Let's consider these elements, known more formally as phonology, semantics, and syntax.

Phonology. The crying, spitting, and burping noises that infants first make are caused by air passing through the vocal apparatus. By about six weeks, infants begin to make speechlike cooing sounds. During their first 12 months, babies' vocalizations become more varied and frequent. Eventually a baby can combine sounds into pronounceable units. As psychologists have studied people's speech patterns, they have helped define a field—phonology. **Phonology** is the study of the patterns and distribution of speech sounds in a language and the tacit rules for their pronunciation.

Phonology: The study of the patterns and distribution of speech sounds in a language and the tacit rules for their pronunciation.

The basic units of sound that compose the words in a language are called **phonemes**. In English, phonemes are the sounds of single letters, such as *b, p, f,* and *v,* and of combinations of letters, such as *th* in "these." All of the sounds in the English language are expressed in 45 phonemes; of those, just 9 make up nearly half of all words. **Categorical speech perception** refers to the ability to discriminate sounds that belong to the same phonemic class. Janet Werker and Richard Tees at the University of British Columbia (Werker & Tees, 1984; Werker & Pegg, 1992) have clearly demonstrated that infants can make more distinctions among phenomes than adults can. Unlike mature speakers of their native language, infants are able to distinguish the differences between speech sounds that do not actually exist in their native language. However, in the second half of their first year, as infants focus on the phonemic distinctions that are important in their native language, they begin to lose the ability to respond to sounds outside of their usual language environment. That is, they tune in the sounds contained in the language they will learn to speak and tune out the sounds that are not relevant.

At about one year of age, children make the first sounds that can be classified as real speech. Initially they utter only one word, but soon are saying as many as four or five words. Once they have mastered approximately 100 words there is a rapid increase in the size of their vocabulary; interestingly, the timing of this "vocabulary spurt" varies from one child to another (Dromi, 1997). Words consist of **morphemes,** the basic units of meaning in a language. A morpheme consists of one or more phonemes combined into a meaningful unit. The morpheme *do,* for example, consists of two phonemes, *d* and *o.* Adding prefixes and suffixes to morphemes can form other words. Adding *un-* or *-ing* to the morpheme *do,* for example, results in *undo* or *doing. Morphology* is the study of word meaning.

No matter what language people speak, one of their first meaningful utterances is the morpheme *ma.* It is coincidental that *ma* is a word in English. Other frequently heard early words of English-speakers are *bye-bye, dada,* and *baby.* In any language, the first words often refer to a specific object or person, especially food, toys, and animals. In the second year, a child's vocabulary may increase to more than 200 words, and by the end of the third year, to nearly 900 words. (Figure 7.6 illustrates vocabulary growth through age seven.)

Phoneme [FOE-neem]: A basic unit of sound in a language.

Categorical speech perception: The ability to discriminate sounds that belong to the same phonemic class.

Morpheme [MORE-feem]: A basic unit of meaning in a language.

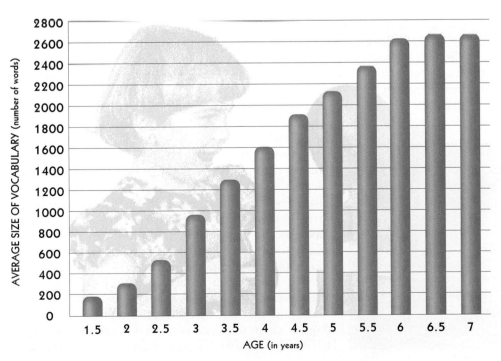

FIGURE 7.6
Vocabulary Changes in Childhood
The average size of children's vocabulary increases rapidly from age 1½ until age 6, when children are fully functional—with a vocabulary of more than 2500 words.

(Adapted from Moskowitz, 1978 on work done by Smith.)

Semantics [se-MAN-ticks]: The analysis of the meaning of language, especially of individual words.

Syntax [SIN-tacks]: The way that words and groups of words combine to form phrases, clauses, and sentences.

Semantics. At first, babies do not fully understand what their parents' utterances mean. But as more words take on meaning, the growing child develops semantic capability. **Semantics** is the analysis of the meaning of language, but especially of individual words, the relationships among words, and the significance of words within particular contexts.

Consider how a four-year-old child might misconstrue what her father says to her mother: "I've had a terrible day. First, the morning traffic made me a nervous wreck. Then, I got into an argument with my boss, who became so furious he almost fired me." The child might think her father got into a car accident and was nearly set on fire. In trying to understand what is being said, a child is faced with understanding not only the meanings of single words but also the relationships of those words to other words. As everyone who has attempted to learn a new language knows, the meaning of a sentence is not always the same as the meanings of the individual words added together. Although children acquire words daily, the words they acquire mean different things, depending on their context. Of course, even adults use only a small set of words over and over again; most other words are used rarely. People who learn a new language usually concentrate on the most widely used words. Teachers of French or Spanish rarely attempt to have students learn the words for *aura* or *modality*. The focus tends to be on basic, utilitarian vocabulary and syntax.

Syntax. Young children use single words to represent whole sentences or ideas; they say, "Milk" or "Blankie." We understand that they mean that they want more milk, or that they want their blanket. Linguists call such one-word utterances *holophrases*. Eventually, they begin to combine words into short sentences, such as "Mama, look" or "Bye-bye, Daddy." This slightly expanded, but still reduced, speech in which unimportant words are left out is referred to as *telegraphic speech* or *telegraphese*. This type of speech is only observed in children who are learning languages in which word order conveys meaning, such as French or English. Over a period of time children must learn to convey meaning using appropriate grammatical structures. **Syntax** is the way that words and groups of words combine to form phrases, clauses, and sentences. Syntactic capability enables children to convey more meaning. For example, children acquire a powerful new way of making their demands known when they learn to combine the words *I want* or *give me* with appropriate nouns. Suddenly, they can ask for cookies, toys, or Mommy without any of them being within pointing range. The rewards that such linguistic behaviour brings children are powerful incentives for them to learn more language. Children begin to use sentences at different ages; but once they begin, they tend to develop at similar rates (R. Brown, 1970).

The rate at which language skill develops largely depends on the nature of the language being learned. For example, English grammar relies heavily on word order and less on adding suffixes to words (morphology). Inuktitut, spoken by Inuit in Canada's North, relies more heavily on morphology than on word order to convey meaning. As a result, telegraphic speech is not seen among Inuit toddlers. As well,

the Turkish language relies on inflections to communicate meaning, whereas Serbo-Croatian uses word order (similar to English and French) as well as inflection. Because word order systems are more complex, those languages are acquired more slowly than systems based partly or completely on inflection.

Early studies of children's short sentences suggested that descriptions of the positions and types of words used could characterize early speech, but later analyses showed these descriptions to be inadequate. Later investigations suggested that young children possess an innate grammar and that they use grammatical relationships in much the same ways that adults do (McNeill, 1970). That is, they have an understanding of the rules

Table 7.2 Early Linguistic Milestones

Age	Language Activity
12 weeks	Smiles when talked to; makes cooing sounds spontaneously
16 weeks	Turns head in response to human voices
20 weeks	Makes vowel and consonant sounds while cooing
6 months	Changes from cooing to babbling
12 months	Imitates sounds; understands some words
18 months	Uses 3–50 words (some babies use very few words at this age—as few as 3—while others use as many as 100); understands basic speech
24 months	Uses between 50 and as much as 250 words; uses two-word phrases
30 months	Uses new words daily; has good comprehension of speech; vocabulary of about 500 words
36 months	Has vocabulary of more than 850 words; makes grammatical mistakes, but their number decreases significantly with each passing week

for word order that goes beyond the small sentences they can produce. **Grammar** is the linguistic description of how a language functions, especially in terms of the rules and patterns used for generating appropriate and comprehensible sentences.

Table 7.2 summarizes some of the linguistic milestones in a child's life.

Transformational Grammar

In 1957 linguist Noam Chomsky, a brilliant theoretician, described a radical approach to grammar that changed many psychologists' views of language development. When it was first introduced, Chomsky's theory was seen as extreme, even reactionary, and, from a behaviourist perspective (then a dominant theory), "mentalistic." Chomsky (1959) argued that the behaviourists' views failed to adequately describe many important facets of language development, particularly the concept of linguistic structures. Rather than learning language through reinforcement, Chomsky claimed that each person is born with the ability to transform a finite set of rules into an infinite number of meaningful sentences. For example, English speakers can create an infinite number of word combinations even when confined to a fixed word order such as subject-verb-object (Mary kissed Juan, Marc washed the dishes, dogs chase cats, etc.). Furthermore, Chomsky argued that the meaningful message of a sentence is stored differently from the words used to compose it (Chomsky, 1986, 1990). One of his best known example sentences is *Colourless green ideas sleep furiously*. This sentence is grammatical but meaningless. We know that it is meaningless despite having no previous experience with this sentence. The behaviourist perspective could not account for this phenomenon.

Surface and Deep Structures. The fundamental idea of Chomsky's **transformational grammar** is that each sentence has both a surface structure and a deep structure. (See Figure 7.7 for an example of how transformational rules work.) The **surface structure** is the organization of a sentence that is closest to its written or spoken form. It is usually the actual sentence, such as *Alex gave Mary a dog*. It shows the words and phrases that can be analyzed into their grammatical categories. The **deep structure** is the underlying meaning of the sentence. Thus, the sentences *Alex gave Mary a dog* and *Mary was given a dog by Alex* have different surface structures but the same deep structure.

Grammar: The linguistic description of how a language functions, especially the rules and patterns used for generating appropriate and comprehensible sentences.

Transformational grammar: An approach to the study of language that assumes that each sentence has both a surface structure and a deep structure.

Surface structure: The organization of a sentence that is closest to its written or spoken form.

Deep structure: The underlying meaning of a sentence.

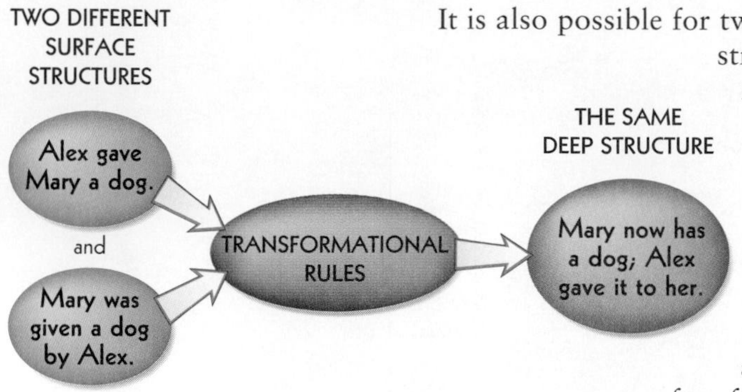

Alex gave
Mary a dog.

and

Mary was
given a dog
by Alex.

TRANSFORMATIONAL
RULES

THE SAME
DEEP STRUCTURE

Mary now has
a dog; Alex
gave it to her.

It is also possible for two deep structures to be derived from a single surface structure. To understand transformational grammar more clearly, consider this sentence: *Visiting relatives can be a pain.* Although the sentence is simple, it has two distinct meanings: that relatives who visit can be annoying guests or that going to visit relatives can be an annoying chore. Transformational grammar accounts for these two meanings by showing that for the same surface structure, there are two possible deep structures. To a great extent, the meaning of a word or a sentence is far more important than its surface form, or structure.

FIGURE 7.7
Chomsky's Concepts of Surface Structure and Deep Structure
Two different surface structures lead to the same meaning through transformational rules.

Abstraction in Language. Imagine that a friend phones you to tell you about a severe-storm warning he just heard over the radio. Most likely, he won't recite the radio announcement verbatim but instead will relay in his own words the storm's estimated arrival time, wind velocities, and probable amount of precipitation. That is, your friend will tell you what he remembers best from the announcement—its concepts, not its exact wording. This suggests that memory for verbal exchanges is not literal-minded and passive but rather an active compilation of concepts.

Researchers made this same argument more than 60 years ago. In 1932, English psychologist F. C. Bartlett published results from studies that are consistent with more recent studies (Mandler & Johnson, 1977; Stein & Glenn, 1979).

Bartlett asked people to read a short story heavy with plot information. After a few minutes, the participants had to recall the story. They retold the story to another person, who retold it to another, and so forth. Bartlett examined the retelling of the story from person to person to see what happened to the details as time passed. Bartlett found that the stories grew shorter, less detailed, and more informal. Some events were altered, and others were introduced to fit the altered story line. Bartlett argued that his participants built a *schema* (an organized structure in memory) of the events of the story, and the schema was what they remembered (see Chapter 6, page 218). Bartlett thus asserted that the participants abstracted the key elements of the story for memory organization and recall; for Bartlett, memory was an active reconstruction.

Focus

Review

◆ What evidence did researchers use to determine whether the structure of spoken language determines people's thoughts and perception? pp. 248–249

◆ Identify the fundamental difference between surface structure and deep structure. pp. 253–254

◆ Summarize Bartlett's evidence for the existence of schemas with regard to verbal exchanges. p. 254

Think Critically

◆ If a person is going to learn a second language, where is the best place to do it, and when? Why?

Language Acquisition

T hat human beings acquire language is one of our uniquely defining characteristics. It is a major achievement in the life of a child, continues to define us as adults, and separates us from other species (Bickerton, 1995). All of our historic and cultural achievements, let alone advances in science and technology, depend on the use of language. Language development is an individual achievement that occurs within a sociocultural context (Clark, 1996). Since language is a unique human gift, a special ability, was there an evolutionary turn of events that set humans apart in this respect (MacWhinney, 1998)? If language is based on the evolutionary development of biological structures, two things should be true: (1) Many aspects of language ability should be evident early in life. (2) All children, regardless of their culture or language, should develop syntax and grammar (an understanding of language patterns) in a similar way. If environmental factors account for language acquisition, the role of learning should predominate. Consider, for example, what happens when people take their first course in Spanish, French, or English. They recognize that they will learn to communicate in a new language that includes a new grammar, new written forms, and new pronunciation. They may buy study aids: books, dictionaries, and tapes. They may read about the country in which the language is spoken, talk to someone who speaks the language, and rely on foreign language teachers. In general, they *prepare* to acquire the new language. But what about infants learning their very first language, how are they prepared to learn it? Are they prepared at all? In trying to resolve the nature–nurture debate over language acquisition, researchers investigate the development of language through a number of approaches, including observational studies of infants and children, case histories of sensory-deprived infants, studies of reading-disabled or brain-damaged individuals, and experiments with chimpanzees.

Learning Theories

The learning approach to language acquisition is quite simple. As discussed earlier, behaviourists like Skinner argued that children are reinforced for specific language behaviours. We speak and understand language because specific language structures (i.e., grammatical categories) are reinforced and repeated. For example, a child might say, "Want cookie" every time she sees a favourite grandparent who regularly supplies cookies. Skinner argued that vocalizations that were not reinforced decreased in frequency. Skinner would explain that a child reared in Quebec might learn French because that's what they heard and were reinforced for speaking. Thus, behaviourists would argue that babies, as they learn language, observe models produce language, imitate their models, and then are reinforced for their own language behaviour (Bates & Elman, 1996). Babies attend in a focused way, listen intently, and repeat sounds that they hear, especially those that they have heard before (Saffran, Aslin, & Newport, 1996). Infants are attentive listeners and parents modify their speech so that it is short, direct, repetitive, and intentionally exaggerated. (Kuhl et al., 1997).

A behaviourist might describe the following scenario. As a baby produces sounds, parents often repeat the baby's words in proper English so that the baby can hear its words spoken correctly. Parents also reinforce the baby by responding in some way to the baby's utterance. The baby might say, "Daddy, baby, wasue." In response, the parent may say, "You want Daddy to give you water?" The baby smiles, is given a drink, and the process continues until eventually, over days and weeks, the baby learns the "proper" words and word order. Thus, learning approaches use traditional learning (operant conditioning) theories and more modern (social/observational learning) theories to explain the acquisition of language.

Biological Theories

Learning theories emphasize the role of environmental influences, or nurture, in language acquisition. But learning theories cannot account for the fact that people have the ability to generate an almost infinite number of correctly formed sentences in their native language. This means that people can comprehend sentences they have never heard and generate sentences they have never before produced. Because this ability cannot be acquired solely through imitation or instruction, many researchers, like Noam Chomsky (1957) and George Miller (1965), assert that human beings are biologically equipped with an innate, unique capacity to acquire and develop language. Such nativist positions assume that a hypothetical structure, a language acquisition device or LAD (Chomsky, 1957), exists to process and facilitate the learning of language.

Although Miller and Chomsky (1957) do not exclude experience as a factor in shaping children's language, they claim that human nature itself, through a LAD, allows children to pay attention to language in their environment and ultimately to use it. Nonetheless, even the strongest proponents of the nature (biological) argument do not contend that a specific language is inborn. Rather, they agree that a predisposition towards language exists and that human beings are born with a "preprinted" blueprint for language. A child who is not exposed to language cannot acquire language; both nature and nurture exert an influence. As a child matures, the blueprint provides the framework through which the child learns a language and its rules (e.g., Kuhl et al., 1992). Three major sources of evidence support the biological side of the nature–nurture debate: (1) studies of brain structure, lateralization, and convergence zones, (2) studies of learning readiness, and (3) studies of language acquisition in children and chimpanzees.

Brain Structure, Lateralization, and Convergence Zones. As early as 1800, researchers knew that the brain of a human being was specialized for different functions. At that time, researchers began mapping the brain and discovered that if certain areas were damaged (usually through accidents), the injured person suffered from severe disorders in language abilities. Later work, some of it conducted by Norman Geschwind (1972), led to the idea of *lateralization*—the localization of a particular brain function primarily in one hemisphere. As Chapter 2 showed, considerable evidence suggests that the left and right hemispheres of the brain (normally connected by the corpus callosum) have some distinctly different functions.

Some researchers argue that the brain has unique processing abilities in each hemisphere. For example, for most people, important language functions are predominantly, but not exclusively, left-hemisphere functions (Corina, Vaid, & Bellugi, 1992). However, the available evidence for hemispheric specialization is not clear-cut. Although each hemisphere seems to play a dominant role in some functions, it interacts with the other hemisphere in the performance of other functions (Baynes et al., 1998).

Antonio Damasio asserts that the brain has many specific language-processing areas, some of which are lateralized (Damasio & Damasio, 1992). Information about a single thing or event may be stored in multiple locations throughout the brain. However, data connect through a convergence zone, or centre, that mediates and organizes all of the relevant information. Thus, signals from physically distant clusters of neuronal activity come together in convergence zones to elicit words, generate sentences, and fully process language.

Learning Readiness. Researcher Eric Lenneberg (1921–1975) claimed that human beings are born with a grammatical capacity and a readiness to produce language (Lenneberg, 1967). He theorized that language simply develops as people interact with their environment. One important aspect of this theory is that a child's capacity to learn language depends on the maturation of specific neurological structures. Lack of maturity of certain brain structures limits infants' ability to speak in the first months of life. But the structural maturation that has occurred by about 18 to 24 months permits children to acquire grammar. Lenneberg's view derives in part from observations that most children learn the rules of grammar at a very early age.

Lenneberg believed that the brain continues to develop from birth until about age 13, with the greatest developmental leap taking place around age 2. During this period, children develop grammar and learn the rules of language. After age 13, there is little room for improvement or change in their neurological structure. Lenneberg supported this argument with the observation that brain-damaged children can relearn some speech and language, whereas brain-damaged adolescents or adults who lose language and speech are unable to completely regain the lost ability. Lenneberg's view is persuasive, but some of his original claims have been seriously criticized (e.g., Kinsbourne, 1975).

Language Studies with Chimpanzees

We have long known that animals communicate with one another. Whales use clicks and squeals, and monkeys make various sounds to signal one another, especially when predators appear. But do animals communicate with one another through language? If they do, is that language the same as, similar to, or totally different from the language of human beings? Most importantly, what can human beings learn from animals about the inborn aspects of language?

Some researchers claim that not only human beings but also other organisms—perhaps suprisingly, parrots—may have some rather sophisticated language acquisition skills. Irene Pepperberg (Pepperberg, 1994; Pepperberg, Brese, & Harris, 1991), for example, has conducted an extensive series of studies on a number of parrots, including Alex, who she bought in 1977. Alex can name 50 objects, name colours, and count to 8. He can classify objects by both number and colour and shows evidence of understanding the concepts of *same* and *different*. As well, there is evidence that he may practise speech in private in ways similar to that of young human language learners. Pepperberg's work with Alex challenges us to consider that parrots may not be simply mimicking words and phrases but actually may be using words and language is a way that reflects a richer internal ability than they have been credited with in the past (at least by non-parrot owners!).

The suggestion that parrots may have complex language ability is controversial, but even more hotly debated is the question of whether chimpanzees are born with a grammatical capacity and readiness for language.

Chimp Language? The biological approach to language suggests that human beings are "prewired"—born with a capacity for language. Experience is the key that unlocks this existing capacity and allows its development. The arguments for and against the biological approach to language acquisition use studies showing that chimpanzees naturally develop some language abilities. Playful and curious, chimps share many physical and mental abilities with human beings. Their brains have a similar organization, and some language-like functions may even be lateralized in chimpanzees (Gannon et al., 1998). This is an especially important and interesting finding because psychologists generally have believed that only human beings exhibited brain asymmetries related to lateralization of language functions. Researchers are not sure what this lateralization means, but hope that it will provide some insight into chimp language abilities. What it does *not* mean is that chimps have human language structure does not necessarily imply its function.

Chimps are especially useful to study because researchers can control and shape the environment in which chimps learn language, something they cannot do in studies involving human beings. For these reasons, chimpanzees have been the species of choice for psychologists studying language in animals.

However, all attempts to teach animals to talk have failed. Until recently, this failure led most psycholinguists to conclude that only human beings have the capacity to acquire language.

Herbert Terrace's work at Columbia University challenged the findings of previous investigators by suggesting that chimps do not have language abilities and that the data reported so far had shown only that the chimps were mimicking their teachers' signs (Terrace, 1979, 1980). Other researchers at the Yerkes Primate Center have presented additional challenges to primate language acquisition (Savage-Rumbaugh et al., 1983). They claim not only that chimp language is different from that of human beings but also that the *purpose* of chimp language is different. Unlike young children, who spontaneously learn to name and point to objects (often called *referential naming*), chimps do not develop such communication skills spontaneously. Terrace (1985) agrees that the ability to name objects is a basic part of human consciousness. He argues that, as part of socialization, children learn to refer to various inner states: feelings, thoughts, and emotions. Chimps can be taught some naming skills, but the procedure is long and tedious. Children, on the other hand, develop these skills easily and spontaneously at a young age. Accordingly, researchers such as R. J. Sanders (1985) assert that chimps do not interpret the symbols they use in the same way that children do. These researchers question the comparability of human and chimp languages.

Although few psychologists are completely convinced about the role of language in chimp communication, their criticisms do not diminish the chimps' language abilities or their accomplishments in other areas, such as mathematics (Rumbaugh, Savage-Rumbaugh, & Hegel, 1987; Boysen & Berntson, 1989) and comprehension (Sevcik & Savage-Rumbaugh, 1994). Researchers also do not rule out language and speech processing in some chimps. Chimp language remains an emerging part of psychology; researchers such as Savage-Rumbaugh assert that basic ideas about the nature of language must be reevaluated—the linguistic feats of the chimps are just too impressive. The answers are far from complete, but the quest is exciting and being extended to other species, including dolphins (Herman, Kuczaj, & Holder, 1993; Schussterman & Gisner, 1988).

Social Interaction Theories: A Little Bit of Each

The development of language is a wonderful example of how debates in psychology emerge, grow, and help us understand human behaviour. Early learning theorists took an unbending view of the role of reinforcement in language development. Later, biological researchers assumed that the physical underpinning of language was just too strong to deny the role of physiology in language. But neither view by itself is correct. Children are born with a predisposition to language—there is no doubt about that. And nearly everybody will agree that children are reinforced for their language behaviour. But all language takes place within a social setting that changes daily with different caretakers and with the moods and needs of both child and caregivers. So while language may be in part innate and in part reinforced, the rigid, unbending views of innate grammars, reinforced behaviours, and polarized approaches are probably too limited in their conception of language acquisition (Seidenberg, 1997).

As we do with so many other behaviours, we must consider the context in which language occurs. At feeding time, babies are far more likely to express their needs vocally because they are hungry. During play times, babies are far more likely to be self-centred, making utterances that do not necessarily have communicative functions. Parents often articulate words, sentences, and emotional expressions in a teaching mode when talking to babies. For example, we know that infants acquire phonetic properties of their native language in the early months of life by listening to adults speak.

A key to understanding language acquisition is to consider not only the structure of language, but also its function and the context in which it is learned, expressed, and practised. For human beings, who are very much social organisms, that expression takes place within groups of people where communication serves a vital function as a way for children to get attention and make their needs known. So, while a child may be "prewired" for language and reinforced for using language correctly, language nearly always takes place in an interactive social setting.

Focus

Review

◆ What is the crucial assumption of biological approaches to language acquisition? pp. 255–256
◆ Terrace claimed there are important differences between chimp language and the language of human children. What are those differences? p. 257

Think Critically

◆ The two learning approaches to language acquisition—conditioning and imitation—differ with respect to what key underlying principle? (Think back to Chapter 5.)

Summary and Review

Cognitive Psychology: An Overview

How do cognitive psychologists approach the field of psychology?

■ *Cognitive psychology* is the study of the overlapping fields of perception, learning, memory, and thought. Cognitive psychology focuses on how people attend to, acquire, transform, store, and retrieve knowledge. Cognitive psychologists study thinking; they assume that mental processes exist, are systematic, and can be studied scientifically. Cognitive psychologists believe that individuals are active participants in analyzing their world. pp. 230–231

KEY TERM
cognitive psychology, p. 230

Concept Formation: The Process of Forming Mental Groups

What is involved in the process of concept formation?

■ *Concepts* are the mental categories used to classify events and objects according to common properties. Concept formation involves classifying and organizing objects by grouping them with or isolating them from others on the basis of a common feature. In laboratory studies of concept formation, participants are presented with stimuli that are either positive or negative instances of a concept. They are asked to identify the concept. pp. 232–234

■ A *prototype* is an abstraction of a pattern, object, or idea stored in memory, against which similar patterns are evaluated to see how closely they resemble each other; it is the best example of a class of items, for example, a teacher, president, or bluebird. p. 234

KEY TERMS
concept, p. 232; prototype, p. 234

Problem Solving: Confronting Situations That Require Solutions

What are the fundamental differences between algorithms and heuristics?

■ When computer programs implement some types of human activities, they are said to involve artificial intelligence (AI). *Algorithms* are problem-solving procedures that use a set of rules to implement a particular series of steps. *Heuristics* are sets of strategies that act as guidelines, not strict rules, for problem solving. pp. 235–236

■ In *subgoal analysis*, a problem is taken apart, or broken down, into several smaller steps, each of which has a subgoal. In *means–ends analysis*, the current situation or position is compared with the desired end to determine the most efficient means for getting from one to the other. p. 236

What are some barriers to good problem solving?

■ *Problem solving* consists of realizing that a problem exists and assessing its complexity, devising solutions, evaluating those solutions, and assessing results. The ability to develop insight into situations gives a person an advantage in problem solving. p. 235

■ *Functional fixedness* is the inability to recognize that an object can have a function other than its stated or usual one. Functional fixedness has been shown to be detrimental to problem solving. To help eliminate functional fixedness, some people use the technique of *brainstorming*. pp. 236–237, 239

■ *Creativity* is the ability to develop responses that are original, novel, and appropriate. According to Guilford, creative thinking is divergent thinking. *Divergent thinking* is the production of new information from known information, or the generation of logical possibilities. In contrast, *convergent thinking* is the process by which possible options are selectively narrowed until they converge on one answer. pp. 238–239

KEY TERMS
problem solving, p. 235; algorithm, p. 235; heuristics, p. 236; subgoal analysis, p. 236; means–ends analysis, p. 236; backwards search, p. 236; functional fixedness, p. 237; creativity, p. 238; brainstorming, p. 239; convergent thinking, p. 239; divergent thinking, p. 239

Reasoning and Decision Making: Generating Ideas and Reaching Conclusions

Differentiate between reasoning and decision making.

■ *Reasoning* is the purposeful process by which people generate logical and coherent ideas, evaluate situations, and reach conclusions. The system or principles of reasoning used to reach valid conclusions or inferences is called *logic*. *Decision making* is the assessment of alternatives; people make decisions that sometimes involve the probability of occurrence of an event or the expected value of the outcome. p. 241

What are some key elements of the decision-making process?

■ A *syllogism* is a sequence of statements, or premises (often two, and assumed to be true), followed by a conclusion; the task is to decide (deduce) whether the conclusion is valid. Psychologists analyze the decision-making process by having participants describe the steps of their thinking process. p. 241

■ Psychological factors, especially previous events, affect how people estimate probabilities of behaviours and events. Sometimes people ignore key pieces of data, however, and thus make bad (or irrational) decisions not based on probability; at other times, people's world-views influence their decision making. pp. 242–244

KEY TERMS
reasoning, p. 241; logic, p. 241; decision making, p. 241; syllogism, p. 241

Artificial Intelligence

What is artificial intelligence?

■ When computer programs implement or produce some type of human activities, they are said to involve artificial intelligence (AI). A computer analogy of perception and reasoning has been the model for most studies of AI; this work is often based on the concept of *parallel distributed processing (PDP)*, which suggests that many simultaneous operations take place at many brain locations. pp. 244–246

Describe how neural networks work.

■ Electronic neural networks simulate specific cognitive activities, including pattern recognition, recognition of handwriting, planning computer moves, and recognizing spatial layouts. Neural networks, like the brain, learn and remember by noting changes in the weights or values associated with various connections. Such networks use top down and bottom up processing to solve problems. Those units that are frequently activated will become more pronounced, may have a lower threshold of activation, and are more easily accessed. pp. 245–247

Language

How are language, thought, and culture interrelated, and what are the key elements of language?

■ Whorf assumed that language structure determined thought. However, research shows that language structure alone is unlikely to account for the way people think, because language is also an expression of culture. pp. 248–249

■ *Linguistics* is the study of language, including speech sounds, meaning, and grammar. *Psycholinguistics* is the study of how people acquire, perceive, understand, and produce language. *Phonemes* are the basic units of sound in a language; *morphemes* are the basic units of meaning. *Semantics* is the study of the meaning of language components. *Syntax* is how words and groups of words are related and how words are arranged into phrases and sentences. *Grammar* is the linguistic description of a language, in terms of its rules and patterns for generating comprehensible sentences. pp. 249–253

■ *Transformational grammar*, developed by Chomsky, is an approach to studying the structure of a language. It assumes that each sentence has both a *surface structure* and a *deep structure*. In general, researchers conclude that the meaning of a sentence (deep structure) and the level of its analysis are more important than the specific words (surface structure). pp. 253–254

KEY TERMS
language, p. 247; linguistics, p. 249; psycholinguistics, p. 249; phonology, p. 250; phoneme, p. 251; categorical speech perception, p. 251; morpheme, p. 251; semantics, p. 252; syntax, p. 252; grammar, p. 253; transformational grammar, p. 253; surface structure, p. 253; deep structure, p. 253

Language Acquisition

How do theorists explain language acquisition?

■ Learning plays an important part in language acquisition. However, people have the ability to generate an unlimited number of correctly formed sentences in their language. This ability cannot be acquired solely through imitation or instruction, which suggests the existence of an innate grammar or language ability. pp. 255–256

■ Damasio asserts that the brain has specific language-processing areas, some of which are lateralized. Information about a thing or event may be stored in multiple locations throughout the brain. However, data are connected through a convergence zone, or centre, that mediates and organizes the information. p. 256

■ A key to understanding language acquisition is to consider not only the structure of language but also its function and the context in which it is learned, expressed, and practised. Communication serves a vital function and nearly always takes place in an interactive, social setting. p. 258

Weblinks

Center for Research in Language
crl.ucsd.edu
Links to research in psychology and linguistics from students, professors, and researchers, along with posts on opportunities to study further in this field.

Exploration of Language
www.mc.maricopa.edu/academic/cult_sci/antrho/Language/
A wide range of audio clips in different languages helps demonstrate the fundamentals of historical linguistics and other language principles.

Foreign Languages for Travellers
www.travlang.com/languages/index.html
Pick any language you do not know, then click on a phrase or sentence to hear how it is spoken.

International Society for General Semantics
www.crl.com/~isgs/isgshome.html
This site describes the activities of this California-based organization, and provides general information on semantics and links to references.

Neural Network Technology
wardsystems.com/cando.htm
The world of artificial intelligence is the focus of this Web site. Free downloads, links, and information about neural networks are all available.

Philosophy and Chiropractic
www.national.chiropractic.edu/humanities/phillips.html
A chiropractor employs techniques of logical analysis and formal reasoning to present his philosophy and basic theoretical views about health and well-being.

Language May Influence Cognition
www.apa.org/monitor/oct98/cog.html
This essay briefly examines how the language you speak determines how you think.

Chapter 8

Intelligence

Ivetka and Mikael's daughter, Tatiana, was doing so well in school that her teacher contacted them to suggest that they consider placing Tatiana in a Gifted and Talented Education (GATE) program. Ivetka and Mikael were thrilled, and Tatiana was excited about the prospect of a new challenge. As they gathered the application materials together, they began to discover quite a bit about our society's current methods of measuring intelligence. They found, for example, that Tatiana would have to take the Weschler Intelligence Scale for Children (WISC). Her score on this test would be reported as a percentile and would represent the percentage of children of the same age in North America who scored at or below Tatiana's score.

The WISC includes a number of different kinds of vocabulary tests and tests of logic, arithmetic, and spatial reasoning. It is believed to measure a child's intellectual ability and to predict her school achievements. Ivetka and Mikael learned that, generally, Tatiana must obtain an overall score (an intelligence quotient, or IQ) of 130 or higher (100 is the average score, and only about 2 percent of the population obtain scores at or above 130) if she is to be considered for a GATE program. As parents, they would have to decide whether they wanted Tatiana to take the WISC (there was a long waiting list for a school psychologist who could administer the test, and private psychologists charge several hundred dollars for this service). As well, they had to decide what to tell Tatiana about the test. They worried about how she would feel if the results were not what they all hoped (Ivetka and Mikael would, of course, continue to love and value her regardless of the results!). In the end, though they knew that some difficult decisions lay ahead of them, they felt the benefits outweighed the downside and decided to go ahead with the application.

Parents such as Ivetka and Mikael often ask, "What do IQ tests measure?" They might also ask, "Can we boost our child's score through special training? How well does a person's score predict school success? Are intelligence and achievement the same thing or can we increase achievement in a person of limited intelligence?" You might also ask social policy questions: Is it fair to train some students for such tests? Should economically comfortable students be allowed an advantage because they can seek out specialized training? Most importantly, you might ask, "What is intelligence?" ■

Evaluating intellectual capabilities is a complex task, for there is more to intelligence than test scores. Intelligence tests do not measure other mental characteristics that are important to success, such as motivation, creativity, and leadership skills. People demonstrate effective and intelligent behaviour in many ways, but not necessarily in all areas. Some people, for example, can write a complicated computer program but not a short story. Moreover, intelligence must be defined in terms of the situations in which people find themselves. Intelligent behaviour for a dancer is very different from intelligent behaviour for a scientist, and both types of behaviour are different from intelligent behaviour for a child with a learning disability.

No single test—such as a test of verbal ability, or knowledge of English literature, or math skills—is a clear measure of intelligence. Psychologists therefore use a variety of tests as well as other data—among them interviews, teacher evaluations, and writing and drawing samples—to evaluate an individual's current standing, to make predictions about future performance or behaviour, and to offer suggestions for remedial work or therapy. In spite of their drawbacks, tests do have strong predictive value; for example, intelligence tests generally can predict academic achievement, and achievement tests generally can predict whether someone will profit from further training in a specific area.

In this chapter, we will consider individual differences in intelligence by way of theories, tests, and controversies. We also will examine two special populations with respect to intelligence: the gifted and the mentally retarded. But first, let's begin with the very basic, but difficult, question: What is intelligence?

What Is Intelligence?

Human beings are capable of artistic greatness, such as Michelangelo's frescos in the Vatican or Yo Yo Ma's virtuoso cello performances. Humans can achieve enormously difficult tasks such as building the pyramids with relatively primitive tools; we exhibit great compassion for others, as did Gandhi and Mother Teresa; and we are capable of communicating effectively with each other to bring about peace. We are an intelligent species that can think about our past, predict our future, and use our abilities for good as well as for evil; our capabilities and achievements are immense. But how can we quantify these achievements? Should we? From a historical perspective, it is not clear how one can even begin to compare Michelangelo's frescos to the achievements of Mother Teresa. But how do we compare individual achievement at a given point in time? How do we predict future outcomes?

From a scientist's point of view, the important task becomes quantifying intelligence so as to make accurate measurements and predictions about human behaviour. And so the intelligence test was designed, or as most of us know it, the IQ test. Everyone has heard of IQ tests, but do they actually measure intelligence? Can any test measure it? Further, what causes us to be so intellectually different from one another?

What is intelligence? For some psychologists, intelligence is all mental abilities; for others, it is the basic general factor necessary for all mental activity; for still others, it is a group of specific abilities. However, all agree that intelligence is a concept, a hypothetical structure, not an identifiable thing.

Early psychologists sought to separate normal children from mentally retarded children, and developed tests to do so. Later researchers developed elaborate theories of the "factors" that make up intelligence. Along the way, they developed complicated testing procedures. From the beginning, researchers have sought to know the source of intelligence. Is it inherited from our parents through genetics or from our learning and environment? The history of psychology has been punctuated with thousands of research papers on intelligence and its nature. Part of the problem is defining what intelligence is and is not. Part is determining whether intelligence has one or many components. And again, part is determining what causes intelligent behaviour—nature or nurture.

Recognizing these complexities, we can still formulate a working definition of intelligence: **Intelligence** is the overall capacity of the individual to act purposefully, to think rationally, and to deal effectively with the environment. By this definition, intelligence is expressed behaviourally. It is shown in the ways people act and in their abilities to learn new things and to use previously learned knowledge. Most importantly, intelligence has to do with people's ability to adapt to the cultural environment in which they learned about the world. Intelligence is thus not a thing but a process, a product, and a capacity, which is affected by a person's day-to-day experiences in the environment. One's intelligence is *not* his or her IQ, a score derived from a test; we'll have much more to say about IQ tests later in this chapter.

Theories of Intelligence: One Ability or Many?

All people are not equally intelligent all of the time; nor are the conditions under which people will exhibit their intelligence clear. This fact of individual differences, or variation among people, in behaviour has been of enduring interest to psychologists. Psychologists do study individual behaviour and how it varies over time and circumstances, but at times they seem more interested in making generalizations about people. E. B. Titchener, an early psychologist, studied the speed of a single person's mental processes but paid little or no attention to variations among the people he was studying. John Watson, known as the father of behaviourism, denied the relevance of individual differences in intelligence. Researchers who examine intelligence today, however, *do* focus on individual differences. In the early 1900s, a large body of data describing the characteristics considered to be involved in intelligence emerged. The data included information on age, ethnicity, gender, socioeconomic status, and environmental factors. From these data, researchers developed theories about the nature of intelligence and ways to test it.

A key issue has been, and continues to be, whether there is a single intelligence or many. Today, the most influential approaches to this question are factor theories, Gardner's theory of multiple intelligences, Robert Sternberg's "triarchic" theory, and the theory proposed by Vygotsky.

Factor Theories. Factor theories of intelligence use a correlation technique known as *factor analysis* to discover what makes up intelligence. **Factor analysis** is a statistical procedure designed to discover the independent elements (factors) in any set of data. In testing, it attempts to find a cluster of items that measure a common ability. Results of tests of verbal comprehension, spelling, and reading speed, for example, usually correlate highly, suggesting that some underlying attribute of verbal abilities (a factor) determines a person's score on those three tests.

In the early 1900s, Charles E. Spearman (1863–1945) used factor analysis to show that intelligence consists of two parts: a general factor affecting all tasks, which he termed the *g factor*, and several specific factors necessary to perform particular tasks. According to Spearman, some amounts of both the general and the specific factors were necessary for the successful performance of any task. Thus, to read a map, you need a certain amount of the *g factor* and a certain amount of specific spatial abilities. This basic approach to intelligence is known as the *two-factor theory of intelligence*. Debate exists about whether a *g-factor* approach is well-grounded or whether it results more from the tests used and the factor-analysis procedures chosen; nonetheless, there is still support for the idea that a single general factor underlies otherwise diverse cognitive abilities (Brody, 1997).

Louis L. Thurstone (1887–1955) further developed Spearman's work by postulating a general factor analogous to Spearman's, as well as seven other factors, each representing a unique mental ability. Known as the *factor theory approach to intelligence*, Thurstone's theory included the seven factors that he considered to be the basic abilities of human beings: verbal comprehension, word fluency, number facility, spatial visualization, associative memory, perceptual speed, and reasoning. The factor theory approach is not universally accepted. Some researchers continue to assert that there is a general factor of intelligence and that it cannot be separated into distinct parts that account for specific processes (Jensen & Weng, 1994); rather, the same overall factor accounts for success in both academic and work pursuits (Kranzler & Jensen, 1991; Ree & Earles, 1992). In contrast to this perspective, contemporary thinkers such as Gardner, considered next, assert that human beings have multiple intelligences.

Gardner's "Multiple Intelligences." Many researchers have proposed that there are multiple types of intelligence, and they readily acknowledge that traditional intelligence tests do not measure them. Howard Gardner has been at the leading edge of this theoretic view (1983/1993, 1995; Gardner & Hatch, 1989). Gardner argues that human competencies, of which there are many, do not all lend themselves to measurement on a single standard test of verbal ability. He criticizes IQ tests because they rely so heavily on a blend of logical and linguistic abilities; he further asserts that to understand intelligence we must examine not only "normal" people but also the artistically and intellectually gifted as well as other less gifted special populations. He maintains that we have multiple intelligences, where "an intelligence" is an ability to solve a problem or create a product within a specific cultural setting. He defines eight criteria for establishing an intelligence (see Table 8.1).

Gardner's view has been both widely praised and criticized. It has been praised for its recognition of the cultural context of intelligence, its recognition of multiple competencies, its more culture-free view of intelligence, and its ability to develop a framework in which to analyze intelligence in school and other applied settings. The criticisms of Gardner's view focus on terminology—for example, are *talents* intelligence? Critics assert that Gardner's separate "intelligences" are all highly correlated with one another, and all measure the same thing. Further, critics argue that

Table 8.1 Gardner's Multiple Intelligences

Type of Intelligence	Exemplar	Core Components
Linguistic	Poet Journalist	Sensitivity to the sounds, rhythms, and meanings of words; sensitivity to the different functions of language
Logical–mathematical	Scientist Mathematician	Sensitivity to and capacity to discern logical or numerical patterns; ability to handle long chains of reasoning
Musical	Composer Violinist	Ability to produce and appreciate rhythm, pitch, and timbre; appreciation of the forms of musical expressiveness
Spatial	Navigator Sculptor	Capacity to perceive the visual–spatial world accurately and to perform transformations on initial perceptions
Bodily–kinesthetic	Dancer Athlete	Ability to control bodily movements and to handle objects skilfully
Naturalist	Botanist Chef	Ability to make fine discriminations among the flora and fauna of the natural world or the patterns and designs of human artifacts
Interpersonal	Therapist Salesperson	Capacity to discern and respond appropriately to the moods, temperaments, motivations, and desires of other people
Intrapersonal	Person with detailed, accurate, self-knowledge	Access to one's own feelings and the ability to discriminate among them and draw on them to guide behaviour; knowledge of one's own strengths, weaknesses, desires, and intelligence

Source: H. Gardner & T. Hatch, Multiple intelligences go to school: Educational implications of the theory of multiple intelligences, Educational Researcher, 18(8) (1989), 6; with adaptation based on personal communication from H. Gardner (1996).

they seem to resemble lists of learned things and personality styles, rather than competencies or intelligence. Still other critics assert that Gardner's eight intelligences are merely descriptions of competencies that provide no more insight into the overall nature of intelligence that a single IQ score.

Ultimately, Gardner's work will have to stand the test of scientific scrutiny. Can it be tested? Does it help us understand human behaviour? Does it lead to good predictions about behaviour? The scientific jury is still out, but it certainly has influenced another multiple intelligence view, that of Robert Sternberg.

Sternberg's "Triarchic" Theory. Robert J. Sternberg of Yale University takes an information-processing view of intelligence. He argues (1986a) that " the essence of intelligence is that it provides a means to govern ourselves so that our thoughts and actions are organized, coherent, and responsive to both our internally driven needs and to the needs of the environment." Sternberg has criticized not only today's widely used tests of intellectual ability, which attempt to gauge intelligence on the basis of traditional theories, but also many elements of the theories themselves. He maintains that traditional tests used to make decisions about admissions to university programs—including the LSAT, GRE, and even the IQ test—measure only limited aspects of behaviour and do not predict future success very well (Sternberg & Williams, 1997).

Sternberg (1986a, 1997) finds intelligence tests too narrow and contends that they don't adequately account for intelligence in the everyday world. He argues that researchers have focused for too long on how to measure intelligence, rather than on more important questions such as: What is intelligence? How does it change? What can individuals do to enhance it? Sternberg reasons that some tests measure individual mental abilities, while others measure the way in which the individual operates in the environment. He asserts that a solid theory of intelligence must account for both individual mental abilities and the ability of people to use their capabilities in the environment. Sternberg focuses not on how much intelligence people have but on how they use it, which makes his theory far more applicable across cultures. Sternberg's ideas have evolved over the last decade, and he now uses terminology and ideas that are easy to understand. He focuses on *successful intelligence*, an ability to adapt to, shape, and select environments to accomplish one's goals and the goals of society. Sternberg (1985, 1997) has described a "triarchic" theory of intelligence presenting three dimensions, each of which covers a different aspect of intelligence: analytic, practical, and creative (see Figure 8.1).

The *analytic* dimension deals with an individual's ability to use intelligence for problem solving in specific situations where there is one right answer. This part of the triarchic theory focuses on how people shape their environments so that their competencies can be best used. Analytical intelligence is valued on tests and in the classroom. For example, an individual might organize problems in a meaningful way, perhaps by grouping similar items together. The analytic dimension does not refer to any mental operations that are required to solve problems, and thus it is likely to be culture-free. It may apply to an African herdsman using leaves to build walls for a dwelling, a machinist cleaning a well-used lathe, or a student solving a math problem.

The *practical* dimension addresses a person's application of experience with the external world and everyday tasks. According to this part of Sternberg's theory, a

FIGURE 8.1
Sternberg's Triarchic Theory of Intelligence

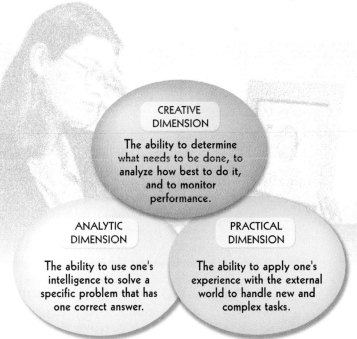

CREATIVE DIMENSION
The ability to determine what needs to be done, to analyze how best to do it, and to monitor performance.

ANALYTIC DIMENSION
The ability to use one's intelligence to solve a specific problem that has one correct answer.

PRACTICAL DIMENSION
The ability to apply one's experience with the external world to handle new and complex tasks.

test measures this facet of intelligence if it assesses both a person's ability to handle novel tasks and the person's mastery of tasks in an automatic manner. Examples of such mastery through experience are memorizing verb forms in a foreign language or troubleshooting malfunctioning electronic equipment. Initially, such tasks are difficult and tedious, but practice makes them nearly automatic.

The *creative* dimension is the glue that holds the other two subtheories together. It describes the mental mechanisms underlying what are commonly considered intelligent behaviours. Creative intelligence includes a person's ability to determine the tasks that need to be done, to determine the order in which the tasks should be undertaken, to analyze their parts, to decide which information should be processed, and to monitor performance. This is the aspect of intelligence necessary to write a love poem, a novel, or a computer program. Tasks that can be used to measure the elements of creative intelligence are analogies, vocabulary, and syllogisms.

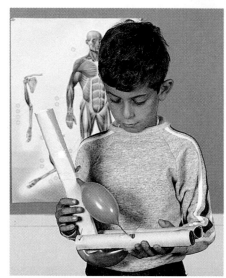

Few behaviours engage all three dimensions of intelligence, so Sternberg asserts that various tasks measure intelligence to a different extent. Eating is a behaviour that is adaptive but does not show novelty, or the use of non-trivial abilities. Similarly, turning on a light switch is adaptive and automatic, but does not demonstrate the other dimensions of intelligence. Thus, from Sternberg's point of view, new tests are needed to analyze fully the three basic dimensions of intelligent behaviour. To be good predictors of a person's academic achievement, tests must look at the person's knowledge of the world—practical intelligence or common sense—in addition to the person's verbal comprehension and mathematical reasoning (Sternberg et al., 1995). Too often, children do poorly in school and in society despite having obvious intellectual skills. They often do not know how to allocate their time or how to work effectively with other people. These skills need to be taught, because some students do not develop them on their own (Sternberg, 1997b). As Ceci (1991) asserts, schools foster the learning of specific skills, not necessarily general problem-solving abilities. In addition, schools often foster specific ways of thinking about problems, but researchers and tests need to value alternative modes of thought and creativity.

Sternberg and Gardner have teamed up on a research project to develop a curriculum to help students develop practical intelligence by learning to think without boundaries (brainstorm), break down mindsets (free themselves from functional fixedness), and see novel solutions in the world (exercise creativity).

Vygotsky's View. Lev Vygotsky (1896–1934) was a Russian psychologist who saw intellectual development as part of a social world that includes communication, with the self and with others. Intelligence is not one task but many tasks that are interwoven. Children, for example, engage in private speech to plan their own actions and behaviour; when they use such speech, they do better in various intellectual tasks. Vygotsky suggests that private speech helps a child understand his or her world. For Vygotsky (1934/1962) even the earliest speech is essentially social and useful and a key part of intelligence; this social speech comes first, followed by egocentric (self-directive) speech, then inner speech. In 1930 Vygotsky wrote, "the most significant moment in the course of intellectual development . . . occurs . . . when speech and practical activity, two previously completely independent lines of development, converge" (Vygotsky, 1930/1978, p. 24). According to Vygotsky, to properly understand intellectual development we must examine the dynamics and interactions of these two activities.

Vygotsky argued that when children are presented with tasks that are outside of their current abilities, they need the help of society to accomplish them. The child eventually incorporates new skills and ideas in his or her repertoire of behaviour and thus shows intelligence. Since children solve practical tasks with the help of their own inner speech, psychologists need to examine how and when that speech develops. Vygotsky ultimately argued that psychologists must examine not only the result of intellectual growth but the process of getting there as well.

One aspect of intellectual functioning that is lacking in all of the theories discussed thus far is our understanding of social-emotional events and experiences. Being able to predict and respond appropriately to our own and others' emotional states is the central factor in successful diplomacy and is essential to getting along well in the world.

Emotions—A Different Kind of Intelligence?

Being highly intelligent is no guarantee of success in life. It is true that doing well in school is important in getting ahead. But there is more to success in business, and in life, than superior cognitive ability. You probably know individuals who are quite bright intellectually, but who have little common sense, few leadership skills, or very little motivation. In 1995, Daniel Goleman, a psychologist who writes a regular science column for the *New York Times*, published a book entitled *Emotional Intelligence*, in which he claims that one's emotional life can matter much more than one's intellectual life.

Goleman argues that traditionally defined intelligence stands alongside and separate from emotional intelligence. According to Goleman, emotional intelligence seems to be the key to getting ahead in life. Emotional intelligence includes self-awareness, impulse control, persistence, self-motivation, the ability to recognize emotions in others, and social agility. Goleman gives credit to psychologists such as Gardner and Sternberg who stress the multiplicity of intelligence, but he feels that they don't go far enough.

Cognitive ability and emotional intelligence are not mutually exclusive. Highly intelligent people can be bright and productive, but they also can be cold, unresponsive, and detached (low emotional intelligence). Alternatively, a bright, productive person can be outgoing, cheerful, poised, sympathetic, and caring (high emotional intelligence). Goleman's assertion is that, all other things being equal, those with high emotional intelligence will nearly always do better than those with low emotional intelligence. Of course, people who are bright do not have only low or high emotional intelligence. Like other types of intelligence, emotional intelligence is displayed in a wide range of degrees.

Goleman proposes that people who develop a high emotional intelligence can better manage the difficulties of life, such as inappropriate aggression, eating disorders, depression, or alcoholism. He argues that people can be taught to recognize emotions and understand relationships, to develop better frustration tolerance and anger management, to focus better on the task at hand and pay attention (thus becoming less impulsive), and to take another person's perspective. Goleman's point has been emphasized by researchers who assert that only when people can accurately perceive, appraise, and express their emotions, can they better harness their intellectual lives. Mayer and Salovey (1997) argue that when people use their emotions to facilitate thought they can help regulate emotions and thus facilitate growth. Mayer and Salovey try to separate the effects of emotion and intelligence, and assert that each affects the other; they contend that a definition like Goleman's focuses too much on the motivational properties of emotional states and too little on the feelings of emotions.

Psychologists have to ask some critical questions: To what extent are cognitive ability and emotions independent? Are they affected by the

Focus

Review

- Identify the key features of a definition of intelligence. p. 265
- On what fundamental grounds do Gardner and Sternberg criticize intelligence tests? pp. 266, 267

Think Critically

- What evidence might Gardner or Sternberg use to argue that existing IQ tests measure some people's behaviour only some of the time?
- What are the implications for researchers of Vygotsky's claim that we must examine the process of intelligence, not just its product?
- Is love a smart, intellectually efficient idea or feeling? How might we separate a person's feelings and thoughts from his or her intelligence? Or can we?

same environmental variables? Can emotional intelligence be fostered, boosted, or enhanced? (We will see in Chapter 10 that programs such as Better Beginnings, Better Futures have successfully enhanced academic skills. Might the same be done for emotional intelligence?) How do we measure Goleman's criteria for emotional intelligence? Psychologists know a great deal about both intelligence and emotion, but there is little research evidence to support this new concept of emotional intelligence, despite its intuitive appeal. Until solid, systematic research is done, it remains an interesting working hypothesis, an imaginative idea that deserves investigation. It very likely will be tested in longitudinal studies over the next decade or two.

The Process of Test Development

You may have been administered one or more intelligence tests during your school years. If they were administered, these tests may have determined your educational track from elementary school onwards. But psychologists are among the first to admit that intelligence tests have shortcomings, and researchers continue to revise these tests to correct their inadequacies and ensure that they have practical benefits and applications in educational, occupational, and clinical settings (Daniel, 1997).

Intelligence tests have had a long history. In the late nineteenth and early twentieth centuries, Alfred Binet (1857–1911), a Frenchman, became interested in psychology and began to study behaviour. He later employed Theodore Simon (1873–1961), a 26-year-old physician; their friendship and collaboration became famous. In 1904, Binet was commissioned to identify procedures for educating children in Paris who suffered from mental retardation. Binet was chosen for the task because he had been lobbying for action to help the schools. (Only recently had schools been made public, and retarded children were doing poorly and dropping out.) In 1905, Binet and Simon set a goal to separate normal children from children with mental retardation. As Stagner (1988) suggests, this may have been the first government-sponsored psychological research.

Binet coined the phrase *mental age*, meaning the age level at which a child is functioning cognitively, regardless of chronological age. Binet and Simon developed everyday tasks, such as counting, naming, and using objects, to determine mental age. The scale they developed is often considered the first useful and practical test of intelligence. Ninety years later, psychologists are still following some of their recommendations about how tests should be constructed and administered. In fact, one of the most influential intelligence tests in use today—the Stanford–Binet test—is a direct descendant of Binet's and Simon's early tests.

Developing a Test

Imagine that you are a seven-year-old child taking an intelligence test, and you come to the following question: "Which one of the following tells you the temperature?" Below the question are pictures of the sun, a radio, a thermometer, and a pair of mittens. Is the thermometer the only correct answer? Suppose there are no thermometers in your home, but you often hear the temperature being given on radio weather reports. Or imagine that you "test" the temperature each morning by standing outside to feel the sun's strength, or that you know it's cold outside when your parents tell you to wear mittens. According to your experiences, any one of the answers to the question might be an appropriate, intelligent response.

What Does a Test Measure? Your predisposition to respond to this hypothetical test question based on your experience—your cultural biases—illustrates the complexity of intelligence test development. In general, a *test* is a standardized device for examining a person's responses to specific stimuli, usually questions or problems. Because there are many potential pitfalls in creating a test, psychologists follow an elaborate set of guidelines and procedures to make certain that their questions are properly constructed. First, a psychologist must decide what the test will measure. For example, will it measure musical ability or knowledge of geography, mathematics, or psychology? Second, the psychologist needs to construct and evaluate items for the test that will give examiners a reasonable expectation that success on the test means something. Third, the test must be standardized.

Standardization. **Standardization** is the process of developing uniform procedures for administering and scoring a test and for establishing norms. **Norms** are the scores and corresponding percentile ranks of a large and representative sample of individuals from the population for which the test was designed. A **representative sample** is a sample of individuals who match the population with whom they are to be compared on key variables such as socioeconomic status and age. Thus, a test designed for all Canadian university students might be given to 2000 students, including an equal number of males and females, 16 to 20 years old, who graduated from large and small high schools, from different areas of Canada, and who represent different ethnic groups and socioeconomic levels.

Standardization ensures that there is a basis for comparing future test results with those of a standard reference group. After a test is designed and administered to a representative sample, the test developers examine the results to establish norm scores for different segments of the test population. Knowing how people in the representative sample have done allows psychologists and educators to interpret future individual test results properly. The scores of those in the representative sample serve as a reference point for comparing individual scores.

Normal Curve. Test developers generally plot the scores of the representative sample on a graph that shows how frequently each score occurs. On most tests some people score very well, some score very poorly, and most score somewhere in the middle. When test scores are distributed in that way, psychologists say they are *normally distributed*, or fall on a normal curve. A **normal curve** is a bell-shaped graphic representation of data arranged to show what percentage of the population falls under each part of the curve. As Figure 8.2 illustrates, most people fall in the middle range, with a few at each extreme. An individual's test score can then be used to estimate his or her rank in the general population by noting where it falls on the normal distribution. (The Appendix discusses the normal distribution in detail.)

Scores. The simplest score on a test is the **raw score**—the number of correct answers unconverted or transformed in any way. The raw score, however, is seldom a true indicator of a person's ability. For many tests, particularly intelligence tests, raw scores need to be adjusted to take into account a person's age, gender, and grade level; that is, to ensure they are being compared to an appropriate comparison group. Such scores commonly are expressed in terms of a **standard score**—a score that expresses an individual's position relative to those of others based on the mean score and how scores are distributed around it. If, for example, a 100-item intelligence test is administered to students in grades 3 and 11, test developers expect those in grade 11 to answer more items correctly than those in grade 3. To adjust for these differences in age, scoring procedures provide for each student's score to be compared to the score typically achieved by other students at the same grade level. Thus, if those in grade 11 typically answer 70 questions correctly, a student in grade 11 who answers 90 questions correctly will have done better than most other students at

Standardization: The process of developing uniform procedures for administering and scoring a test and for establishing norms.

Norms: The scores and corresponding percentile ranks of a large and representative sample of individuals from the population for which a test was designed.

Representative sample: A sample of individuals who match the population with whom they are to be compared on key variables such as socioeconomic status and age.

Normal curve: A bell-shaped graphic representation of data arranged to show what percentage of the population falls under each part of the curve.

Raw score: A test score that has not been transformed or converted in any way.

Standard score: A score that expresses an individual's position relative to those of others based on the mean score and how scores are distributed around it.

FIGURE 8.2
A Normal Distribution
The bell-shaped curve shows a standard normal distribution. As in normal distributions of height, weight, and even intelligence, very few people are represented at the extremes.

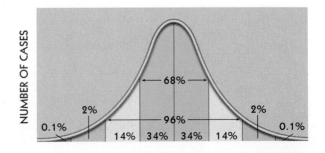

NUMBER OF CASES

68%
2%
96%
2%
0.1%
14% 34% 34% 14%
0.1%

that grade level. Similarly, if those in grade 3 usually answer 25 questions correctly, a student in grade 3 who answers 15 questions correctly will not have performed as well as other students at that grade level. A standard score is generally a **percentile score**—a score indicating what percentage of the test population obtained a lower score. If, for example, someone's percentile score is 84, then 84 percent of the people taking the test obtained a lower score than that person did.

Intelligence Quotients. Perhaps the oldest and most widely recognized test is the intelligence test. Binet's test clearly qualifies as an intelligence test—even though it was a relatively crude one. In the early 1900s, intelligence was measured by a simple formula. To obtain an intelligence quotient (IQ), a psychologist divided a person's mental abilities, or mental age, by the person's chronological age and multiplied the result by 100. (See Table 8.2 for examples.) Mental ages of children were estimated from the number of correct answers on a series of test items; the higher the number, the higher the mental age.

A problem with the traditional formula—mental age divided by chronological age, then multiplied by 100—is that young children are far more variable in their answers than are older children or adults; it is as if their intelligence is less stable, less repeatable, and more subject to change. This variability makes predictions and comparisons difficult. To simplify measures of IQ, psychologists and testers began using **deviation IQ**—a standard IQ test score for which the mean and variability remain constant at all ages. According to deviation IQs, a child of 9 and an adolescent of 16, each with an IQ of 116, have the same position relative to others who have taken the same IQ test. Both are above the eighty-fourth percentile; that is, both scored better than 84 percent of all others their age who took the same IQ test.

Of all the achievements by psychologists in making tests useful, perhaps the most important is ensuring that tests are both reliable and valid. If a student obtains different scores on two versions of the same test, which score is correct? Furthermore, does the test measure what it is supposed to measure and only that?

Reliability

Reliability refers to the consistency of test scores. **Reliability** is a test's ability to yield the same or similar scores for the same individual through repeated testing. (When a researcher says that test scores have consistency, the researcher is assuming that the person taking the test is in the same emotional and physiological state each time the test is administered.) If a test's results are not consistent over several testing sessions or for two comparable groups of people, useful comparisons are impossible; in effect, the test cannot be trusted. Of course, a single person's score is likely to vary from administration to administration of a test; this is unavoidable, as human beings are not machines. So a test rarely will be perfectly reliable, but the real question is, "Is it generally consistent and does it yield similar results on other testings?"

Table 8.2   Traditional Calculation of Intelligence Quotient for Three People

	Person 1	Person 2	Person 3
Mental Age (MA)	6 years	15 years	15 years
Chronological Age (CA)	6 years	18 years	12 years
MA ÷ CA	6 ÷ 6 = 1	15 ÷ 18 = 0.83	15 ÷ 12 = 1.25
(MA ÷ CA) x 100	1 x 100 = 100	0.83 x 100 = 83	1.25 x 100 = 125
IQ	100	83	125

There are several ways to determine whether a test is reliable. The simplest method, termed *test–retest*, is to administer the same test to the same person on two or more occasions. If, for example, the person achieves a score of 87 one day and 110 another, the test is probably not reliable (see Table 8.3). Of course, the person might have remembered some of the test items from one occasion to the next. To avoid that problem, testers use the *alternative-form method*, which involves giving two different versions of the same test. If the two versions test the same characteristic, differing only in the test items used, both should yield the same result. Another way to test reliability is to use the *split-half method*, which involves dividing a test into two parts; on a reliable test, the scores from the two halves should yield similar, if not identical, results.

Even the most reliable test will not yield identical results each time it is taken; however, a good test will have a relatively small standard error of measurement. The *standard error of measurement* is the number of points by which a score varies because of imperfect reliability. Consider an IQ test that has a standard error of measurement of 3, for example. If someone scores 115 on that test, the test developer can state with a high degree of confidence that the individual's real score is between 112 and 118—3 points above or below the obtained score.

Validity

If a psychology exam included questions such as "What is the square root of 647?" and "Who wrote *The Grapes of Wrath*?" it would not be a valid measure of your knowledge of psychology. That is, it would not be measuring what it is supposed to measure. To be useful, a test must have not only reliability, but also **validity**—the ability to measure only what it is supposed to measure and to predict only what it is supposed to predict.

Types of Validity. *Content validity* is a test's ability to measure the knowledge or behaviour it is intended to measure. A test designed to measure musical aptitude should not include items that assess mechanical aptitude or personality characteristics. Similarly, an intelligence test should measure only intelligence, not musical training, cultural experiences, or socioeconomic status.

In addition to content validity, a test should have *predictive validity*—the ability to predict a person's future achievements with at least some degree of accuracy. Critics of intelligence tests like to point out, however, that test scores are not always accurate predictors of people's performance, that the correlation between IQ test scores and school grades is only about 0.6 at best (1.0 represents perfect correlation). Tests cannot take into account high levels of motivation or creative abilities. Nevertheless, many law schools use the Law School Admission Test (LSAT) scores of applicants to decide who should be accepted for admission—thus assuming that the scores accurately predict ability to succeed in law school.

Table 8.3 Test–Retest Reliability

Test–retest reliability indicates whether people who are given the same or a similar test on repeated occasions achieve similar scores each time.

	Test with High Reliability		Test with Low Reliability	
	First Testing	**Second Testing**	**First Testing**	**Second Testing**
Person 1	92	90	92	74
Person 2	87	89	87	96
Person 3	78	77	78	51

Halo effect: The tendency for one particular or outstanding characteristic of an individual (or a group) to influence the evaluation of other characteristics.

Two additional types of validity are *face validity*, the extent to which a person can judge a test's appropriateness by reading or examining the test items, and *construct validity*, the extent to which a test actually captures or measures the hypothetical quality or particular trait it is supposed to measure, such as intelligence, anxiety, or musical ability.

A Critique of Intelligence Test Validity. There are six basic criticisms of the validity of intelligence tests and testing. The first is that there is no way to measure intelligence because no clear, agreed-upon definition of intelligence exists. The defence to this argument is that, although different IQ tests seem to measure different abilities, the major tests have face validity. Face validity is the appropriateness of test items "on their face"—that is, their appropriateness to someone examining the items. Intelligence tests generally contain items requiring problem solving and rational thinking, which in middle-class society are accepted as tests of intelligence.

The second criticism is that because IQ test items usually consist of *learned information*, they reflect the quality of a child's schooling rather than the child's actual intelligence. The response to this challenge is that most vocabulary items on IQ tests are learned in the general environment, not in school; moreover, the ability to learn vocabulary terms and facts seems to depend on the general ability to reason verbally. Further, other measures of ability, including the Ravens' Progressive Matrices (a nonverbal, untimed test that requires inductive reasoning on perceptual patterns), seem independent of schooling and correlate highly with traditional IQ test scores. A problem with this response is that it assumes that children's experiences in the general environment have been fairly similar and it does not take into account variation due to cross-cultural experiences.

The third criticism is that *school settings* may adversely affect IQ and other test scores, not only because tests are often administered inexpertly but also because of the halo effect (e.g., Crowl & MacGinitie, 1974). The **halo effect** is the tendency for one particular or outstanding characteristic of an individual (or a group) to influence the evaluation of other characteristics. A test administrator can develop a positive or negative feeling about a person, a class, or a group of students that may influence the administration of tests or the interpretation of test scores (Nathan & Tippins, 1990). People who defend testing against this charge acknowledge that incorrectly administered tests are likely to result in inaccurate test scores, but they claim that this effect is less powerful than opponents think it is, especially among properly trained test administrators.

Two other criticisms of testing are less directly related to the issue of validity. One criticism is that some people are *test-wise*. These individuals make better use of their time than others, guess the tester's intentions, and find clues in the test. Practice in taking tests improves these people's performance. The usual defences are that the items on IQ tests are unfamiliar even to experienced test takers and that the effects of previous practice are seldom or never evident on IQ tests. Another criticism is that individuals' scores often depend on their *motivation to succeed* rather than on actual intelligence. Claude Steele has argued that whenever members of ethnic or other minorities concentrate explicitly on a scholastic task, they worry about confirming negative stereotypes of their group (Steele, 1997; Steele & Aronson, 1995). This extra burden may drag down their performance, through what Steele calls *stereotype threat*—people fear being reduced to a stereotype and then do worse because of their fear. Defenders of IQ tests agree that examinees' motivation and attitudes towards tests are important; however, they deny that the IQ tests themselves may influence motivation.

Focus

Review

◆ Why is the normal curve an essential part of the process of standardization? p. 271
◆ What fundamental assumption underlies the use of a representative sample? p. 271

Think Critically

◆ Which of the criticisms of intelligence tests and testing is most significant, in your opinion? Why?
◆ Why might a psychologist not want parents to know their child's IQ score?

Lastly, success in Canada—economic, social, and political—is heavily influenced by one's academic achievement and the ensuing opportunities that emerge from completing university or college. In making educational placement decisions on the basis of IQ test scores, it is argued that our society creates the correlation between academic success, schooling, and IQ test scores. The defence, again, is that IQ test scores correlate with other measures of intelligence that seem to be independent of schooling.

Critics of IQ tests are concerned about the interpretation of scores. It is important to remember that intelligence tests generally are made up of different subtests or subscales, each of which yields a score. There also may be a general score for the entire test. All of these scores require knowledgeable interpretation; that is, test scores must be given a context that is meaningful to the person who receives the information. Without such a context, a score is little more than a number. The interpretation of test scores is the key to understanding IQs; without such interpretation, a single IQ score can be biased, inaccurate, or misleading.

Three Important Intelligence Tests

What is the best intelligence test? What does it measure? Can you study for an intelligence test to get a higher score? The three tests we will examine here—the Stanford–Binet Intelligence Scale, the Wechsler scales, and the Kaufman Assessment Battery for Children—are all widely used, were developed using careful research, and predict performance well. Their results correlate well with one another. Research shows that these tests are reliable and valid. It is important to recall that IQ tests initially were developed to predict school success; therefore, items were chosen that would be reflective of a typical school curriculum. We'll begin by examining the first real IQ test, the Stanford–Binet Intelligence Scale.

Stanford–Binet Intelligence Scale

Most people associate the beginning of intelligence testing with Alfred Binet and Theodore Simon. As noted earlier, Binet collaborated with Simon to develop the Binet–Simon Scale in 1905. The original test actually was 30 short tests arranged in order of difficulty and consisting of such tasks as distinguishing food from nonfood and pointing to objects and naming them. The Binet–Simon Scale was heavily biased towards verbal questions and was not well standardized.

From 1912 to 1916, Lewis M. Terman revised the scale and developed an intelligence test now known as the Stanford–Binet Intelligence Scale. (*Stanford* refers to Stanford University, where the test was further developed.) In the Stanford–Binet, a child's mental age (intellectual ability) is divided by that child's chronological age and multiplied by 100 to yield an intelligence quotient (IQ). For decades psychologists have used the original and revised versions of the Stanford–Binet scale. This test traditionally has been a good predictor of academic performance, and many of its subtests correlate highly with one another.

A new version of the Stanford–Binet Intelligence Scale, published in 1986, contains items designed to avoid favouring men or women or stressing ethnic stereotypes. It is composed of four major subscales and tests individuals aged 2 through 23, yielding one overall IQ score. The test administration time varies, because the number of subtests given is determined by age. All examinees first are given a vocabulary test; along with their age, this test determines the level at which all other tests begin. There are 15 possible subtests, which vary greatly in content. Some require verbal reasoning, others require quantitative reasoning, and still others require abstract visual reasoning. In addition, there are tests of short-term memory.

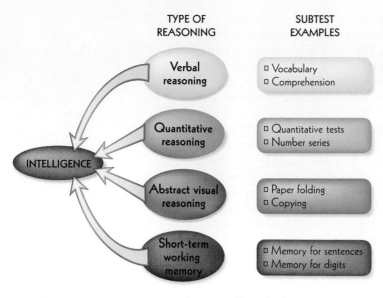

TYPE OF REASONING

- Verbal reasoning
- Quantitative reasoning
- Abstract visual reasoning
- Short-term working memory

INTELLIGENCE

SUBTEST EXAMPLES

- □ Vocabulary
- □ Comprehension

- □ Quantitative tests
- □ Number series

- □ Paper folding
- □ Copying

- □ Memory for sentences
- □ Memory for digits

FIGURE 8.3
The Modern Stanford–Binet Intelligence Scale
The most recent version of the Stanford–Binet Intelligence Scale measures intelligence with a composite score made up of four scores on broad types of mental activity: verbal reasoning, quantitative reasoning, abstract visual reasoning, and short-term working memory. Each of the scores is obtained through a series of subtests that measure specific mental abilities.

Each of the subtests consists of a series of levels, with two items at each level. The tester begins by using entry-level items and continues until a higher level on each subscale is established (until the test taker fails a prescribed number of items). (See Figure 8.3 for a description of the new Stanford–Binet Intelligence Scale.)

Raw scores, determined by the number of items passed, are converted to a standard score for each age group. The new Stanford–Binet scale is a powerful test; one of its great strengths is that it can be used over a wide range of ages and abilities. Nonetheless, like all tests, it has limitations. One of these limitations is that examinees are not given the same battery of subtests at different ages; this makes comparisons across age groups difficult (Sattler, 1992). However, the new Stanford–Binet scale correlates well with the previous version, as well as with the Wechsler scales and the Kaufman Assessment Battery for Children (which are examined next).

Wechsler Scales

David Wechsler (1896–1981), a Romanian immigrant who earned a Ph.D. in psychology from Columbia University, was influenced by Charles Spearman and Karl Pearson, two English statisticians with whom he studied. In 1932, Wechsler was appointed chief psychologist at Bellevue Hospital in New York City; there, he began making history. In the 1930s, Wechsler recognized that the Stanford–Binet Intelligence Scale was inadequate for testing the IQs of adults. He also maintained that some of the Stanford–Binet items lacked validity. In 1939, Wechsler developed the Wechsler– Bellevue Intelligence Scale to test adults. In 1955, the Wechsler Adult Intelligence Scale (WAIS) was published; it eliminated some technical difficulties of the Wechsler–Bellevue scale. The latest revision of the test is the WAIS–III.

Wechsler also developed the Wechsler Intelligence Scale for Children (WISC), which covers children aged 6 through 16. It was revised in 1974, becoming the WISC–R; the 1991 revision is the WISC–III. Table 8.4 shows some of the typical subtests included in the WISC–R. In 1967, the Wechsler Preschool and Primary Scale of Intelligence (WPPSI) was developed for children aged 4 through 6 1/2; it was revised in 1989, becoming the WPPSI–R.

The Wechsler scales group test items by content. For example, all of the information questions are presented together, and all of the arithmetic problems are presented together. The score on each subtest is calculated and converted to a standard (or scaled) score, adjusted for the test taker's age. The scaled scores allow for a comparison of scores across age levels. Thus, an 8-year-old's scaled score of 7 is comparable to an 11-year-old's scaled score of 7. An overall IQ score is reported as well as subscale scores. Thousands of studies have been conducted to assess the reliability and validity of the Wechsler scales.

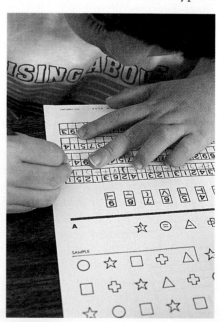

Table 8.4   Typical Subtests of the WISC–R

Verbal Test		Performance Test	
Subtest	**Type of Task**	**Subtest**	**Type of Task**
Information	When questioned, recall a general fact that has been acquired in a formal or informal school setting	Picture completion	Point out the part of an incomplete picture that is missing
Similarities	Use another concept in describing how two ideas are alike	Picture arrangement	Put a series of pictures that tell a story in the right sequence
Arithmetic	Solve a word problem without pencil and paper	Block design	Use real blocks to reproduce a picture of a block design
Digit span	Recall an orally presented string of digits	Object assembly	Put the pieces of a jigsaw-like puzzle together to form a complete object
Vocabulary	Define a vocabulary word	Coding	Given a key that matches numbers to geometric shapes, fill in a form with the shapes that go with the listed numbers
Comprehension	Answer a question requiring practical judgment and common sense		

Kaufman Assessment Battery for Children

Many intelligence tests have been criticized for being biased in that some of their questions are geared towards the white, middle-class, male experience. Psychologists Alan and Nadeen Kaufman contend that their Kaufman Assessment Battery for Children (K–ABC) uses tasks that tap the experience of all people, regardless of background. A memory task in the K–ABC, for example, might ask a child to look at a picture of a face and then pick it out from pictures of other faces a few moments later.

The K–ABC was designed especially for assessment of and intervention in school problems. School psychologists, the primary users of the K–ABC, act as evaluators and consultants to families and schools, helping them to set and achieve appropriate educational goals. The K–ABC consists of four global scales. Three of these measure mental processing abilities (sequential processing, simultaneous processing, and a composite of the two); the fourth scale assesses achievement. The Kaufmans believe that the sequential- and simultaneous-processing scales measure abilities synonymous with intelligence—that is, the ability to process information and the ability to solve problems (Kaufman, 1983). A sequential task requires that stimuli be manipulated in sequential order. For example, a child might be asked to repeat a series of digits in the order in which the examiner presented them. A simultaneous-processing task involves organizing and integrating many stimuli at the same time. Here, a child might be asked to recall the placement of objects on a page that was presented only briefly.

The K–ABC assesses how well and in what way a child solves problems on each task, minimizing the role of language and of acquired facts and skills. A separate part of the test, the achievement scale, involves demonstrating such skills as

Focus

Review

◆ What were some of the drawbacks of the early versions of the Stanford–Binet Scale, and what positive changes were made to the test in the late 1980s? pp. 275–276

◆ What did Wechsler set out to "fix" about the Stanford–Binet Scale when he designed his test? p. 276

◆ What is seen as the main advantage of the K–ABC over other tests? p. 277

Think Critically

◆ Imagine that you were asked to assess a child who was having trouble academically in grade three. Which test would you use and why? Would you answer differently if you were told that the student was a recent immigrant from a non-English-speaking country? After testing, would you know enough to make recommendations?

reading comprehension, letter and word identification, and computation. These tasks resemble those typically found on other IQ tests in that they are heavily influenced by language experience and verbal ability.

Although early research on the K–ABC shows it to be a promising IQ test (German, 1983; Zins & Barnett, 1983), it also has its critics. Sternberg (1984) has been especially critical of the assumptions on which the K–ABC is founded, particularly ideas about how sequential processing proceeds and whether it reflects important elements of thought. Still, many practitioners consider it child-oriented and easy to administer. A final evaluation of the K–ABC is probably still a decade away.

The Environmental and Biological Partnership

 ver the past 20 years, minority groups have joined psychologists and educators in challenging the usefulness of testing in general and of intelligence testing in particular.

Cultural Biases?

A major argument against IQ testing is that the tests are culturally biased and thus effectively discriminate against individuals who do not come from the test makers' environments—usually white, middle-class, and suburban. A test item or subscale is considered culturally biased when, with all other factors held constant, its content is more difficult for members of one group than for those of other groups. To understand how a test can be culturally biased, imagine that the child of an impoverished migrant worker is given the multiple-choice temperature problem posed earlier. If the child is unfamiliar with thermometers and radios, he might choose the sun as the best answer. Because experiments have shown some tests to be culturally biased, some educators and parents have urged a ban on tests in all public schools, especially IQ tests. They argue that groups of individuals who are not exposed to the same education and experiences as the middle-class group for whom the tests were designed are bound to perform less well and, as a consequence, may not be provided appropriate educational opportunities. Table 8.5 lists some questions that might bias an intelligence test. (How many children could answer the questions on Test B? Yet a person who *did* know the answers would clearly have intelligence of a particular type.)

Table 8.5 Tests Can Be Constructed to Have a Bias

Test A	Test B
1. What are the colours in the Canadian flag?	1. Of what is butter made?
2. Who is the prime minister of Canada?	2. Name a vegetable that grows above ground.
3. What is the longest river in Canada?	3. Why does seasoned wood burn more easily than green wood?
4. How can banks afford to pay interest on the money you deposit?	4. About how often do we have a full moon?
5. What is the freezing point of water?	5. Who was the prime minister of Canada during The Second World War?
6. What is a referendum in government?	6. How can you locate the pole star?

Clearly, those who interpret IQ tests must be particularly sensitive to any potential biases. Biases can exist, but well-respected psychologists (Sattler, 1992; Vernon, 1979) support the view that they do not exist in such tests as the WISC–III. It may be more appropriate to say that any bias that exists in relation to IQ tests is determined by how the results are used (a point that will be examined shortly). Someone may score poorly on an IQ test due to a lack of understanding of the language in which it was administered (an issue testers are trained to watch for), or as a result of growing up in poverty or in a different cultural community. All of these factors can contribute to IQ test performance in ways that could lead to misreading a child's intellectual potential. Consequently, the meaning of IQ test score differences must be interpreted very carefully (Helms, 1992).

IQ tests cannot predict or explain all types of intellectual behaviour. They are derived from a small sample of a restricted range of cognitive activities. Intelligence can be demonstrated in many ways; an IQ test provides little information about someone's ability to be flexible in new situations or to function in mature and responsible ways. Intelligence tests do reflect many aspects of people's environments—how much individuals are encouraged to express themselves verbally, how much time they spend reading, and the extent to which parents have urged them to engage in academic pursuits (e.g., Barrett & Depinet, 1991).

Since the early 1970s, the public, educators, and psychologists have scrutinized the weaknesses of IQ tests and have attempted to eliminate cultural bias in testing by creating better tests and establishing better norms for comparison. The tests have attempted to control the influences of different cultural backgrounds (Helms, 1992). However, even the courts acknowledge the complexity of the issues involved in IQ tests and testing (Elliott, 1987). In isolation, IQ scores mean little. Information about an individual's home environment, personality, socioeconomic status, and special abilities is crucial to understanding intellectual functioning. *Diversity* on page 280 further examines cultural differences in testing.

Genetic and Environmental Impact

If you were born into a well-bred, upper-class family and had access to school and appropriate family connections, you likely would be smart. Or so thought Sir Francis Galton in the nineteenth century. Galton was among the first to speculate that genetics is involved with intelligence, arguing that intelligence is passed from generation to generation. But today psychologists recognize that both the genetic heritage established before birth (nature) and people's life experiences (nurture) play an important role in intelligence. Researchers have used child-rearing studies to help unravel the key variables. In a classic environmental study, a researcher administered IQ tests to children reared in different communities in the Blue Ridge Mountains, an isolated area 160 kilometres west of Washington, D.C. (Sherman & Key, 1932). Most of the adults in these communities were illiterate, and communication with the outside world was limited. The investigators concluded that lack of language training and school experience accounted for the children's poor scores on standardized tests, particularly on tests involving calculations and problem solving. Moreover, because the IQ scores of the children were highest in the communities with the highest social development and lowest in the communities with the poorest social development, the researchers concluded that the children's IQs developed only as their environment demanded development. Persistent poverty clearly has detrimental effects on children (McLoyd, 1998). Still, Angoff (1988) has asserted that children from impoverished homes can achieve more on IQ tests, and other standardized tests, if "cognitive training begins early in life and continues for an extended period . . . and is carried out in a continuously supportive and motivating atmosphere" (p. 719).

Few would debate the idea that the environment, and especially schooling, has a potent effect on intellectual tasks (Ceci & Williams, 1997). But efforts to unravel the fixed genetic component from the environmental impact have required some sophisticated research and statistical techniques. The main goal of such studies has

Cross-cultural Differences Are Small and Narrowing

Cross-cultural differences in IQ scores, LSAT scores, and other measures of achievement or ability are narrowing (National Center for Educational Statistics, 1996). This may be due to more equal opportunities under the law, to federal intervention programs for the culturally disadvantaged, or to socioeconomic factors that affect home environments. As more minority-group students enrol in mathematics courses in high school, the better they do on achievement tests. In addition, differences between groups have tended to decrease over the last two decades (Williams & Ceci, 1997). Furthermore, differences within groups are often greater than differences between groups, a fact that minimizes the importance of between-group differences (Zuckerman, 1990).

There are three factors that may create observed differences between groups, but their relative importance has yet to be established. As a case in point, consider blacks, who—as a group—do somewhat less well on average on intelligence tests than do whites. The first factor being debated is the possibility of a genetic component. Philippe Rushton (1988), a controversial psychologist at the University of Western Ontario, has argued in favour of a genetic explanation, but he has been criticized widely. The second factor is that blacks are disproportionately represented among those who live in culturally impoverished areas. The third factor is that IQ tests may contain a built-in vocabulary bias against blacks.

People from different backgrounds and cultures differ on a variety of dimensions—there is no doubt about that. A cross-cultural study of 320 Israeli children whose parents had emigrated from Europe, Iraq, North Africa, or Yemen showed that the four groups tended to exhibit four different patterns of cognitive abilities (Burg & Belmont, 1990). Differing patterns of cognitive ability are not surprising; cultures vary considerably in their world-view and in their conception of time, space, people, and what is important. Thus, historical and cultural background has a significant effect on people's patterns of mental ability and achievement (Geary, 1996). When psychologists test a child from Ontario or British Columbia, his or her culture is clearly different from a child from Papua New Guinea, and so the instrument used to test the child must be culturally relevant (Greenfield, 1997). Flynn (1987) showed that IQ scores are changing around the world, and he concluded that schooling, educational emphasis, and family values in various cultures were affecting the test scores—not that people in certain cultures were getting smarter. Schooling clearly fosters the cognitive processes that contribute to high IQ scores (Ceci & Williams, 1997).

One conclusion is becoming strikingly clear: *Rather than measuring innate intellectual capacity, IQ tests measure the degree to which people adapt to the culture in which they live.* In many cultures, to be intelligent is to be socially adept. In Western society, because social aptitude is linked with schooling, the more schooling you have, the higher your IQ score is likely to be (Ceci & Williams, 1997). All individuals have special capabilities (both intellectual and other), and how these capabilities are regarded depends on the social environment. Being a genius in traditional aboriginal cultures may include being a good storyteller; in other cultures, it may mean being astute and aggressive (Eysenck, 1995). In Western countries, however, the concept of giftedness too often is attached to high academic achievement alone. Concern about the implications of this limited conception of intelligence is one reason why educators in some settings are placing less emphasis on IQ scores.

Critics of standardized testing have been vocal and persuasive, and their arguments cannot be discounted. Researchers today assert that the typical intelligence test may be too limited because it does not take into consideration the many forms of intelligent behaviour that occur outside the testing room, within our diverse society (Frederiksen, 1986; Sternberg & Wagner, 1993). Frederiksen suggests that real-life problem situations might be used to supplement the usual psychological tests. This view is consistent with Sternberg's (1986a) idea that intelligence must be evaluated on many levels, including the environment in which a person lives and works. If this type of evaluation were to take place, IQ scores could become better predictors of both academic and occupational success (Wagner, 1997). Yet, in spite of all of the limitations of IQ scores, research continues to show that they are still the best overall predictor of school performance (Ree & Earles, 1992, 1993).

Table 8.6 summarizes some misconceptions about intelligence tests and testing. ■

Table 8.6 Some Misconceptions about Intelligence Tests and Testing

Misconception	Reality
Intelligence tests measure innate intelligence.	IQ scores measure some of an individual's interactions with the environment; they never measure only innate intelligence.
IQs never change.	People's IQs change throughout life, but especially from birth through age 6. Even after this age, significant changes can occur.
Intelligence tests provide perfectly reliable scores.	Test scores are only estimates. Every test should be reported as a statement of probability, such as "There is a 90% chance that the test taker's IQ falls within a 6-point range of the reported score (from 3 points above to 3 points below)."
Intelligence tests measure all aspects of a person's intelligence.	Most intelligence tests do not measure the entire spectrum of abilities related to intellectual behaviour. Some stress verbal and nonverbal intelligence but do not adequately measure other areas, such as mechanical skills, creativity, or social intelligence.
A battery of tests reveal everything necessary to make judgments about a person's competence.	No battery of tests can give a complete picture of any person. A battery can only illuminate various areas of functioning.

Source: Adapted from Sattler, 1992.

been to determine the **heritability** of traits, the proportion of a trait's variation in a population of individuals that is genetically determined. Heritability of some traits is easily seen. Children who have two tall parents have an excellent likelihood of being tall—the heritability of height is thus high, and we can say that heredity is a key factor in determining height. When we say that a trait is heritable, especially when we attach a percentage to that heritability—say, for example, 50 percent—we mean that *in a group* of people, 50 percent of the variation (differences) among them is attributable to heredity. This does *not* mean, however that we can say that 50 percent of a *specific person's* intelligence, height, or any other variable is determined by heredity. One last caution: Although heritability is biologically based, even highly heritable traits such as height can be modified by the environment. Deprive a child of a nutritious diet and the child will not grow normally, but if you then feed the child well during growth years, you are likely to see growth spurts.

Estimates of the heritability of intelligence have varied widely, as have research techniques that attempt to measure it. To estimate how much of intelligence is heritable, researchers have studied adopted children, who are raised apart from their biological parents (e.g., Scarr & Weinberg, 1994). Researchers examine intelligence test scores and other measures of cognitive ability to compare an adopted person's score with those of the biological parents, adoptive parents, biological siblings, and adoptive siblings. The goal is to determine whether scores later in life more greatly resemble those of biological relatives or adoptive relatives. A French adoption study showed a 14-point increase in IQ scores in children from impoverished homes after they were adopted into families in a higher socioeconomic class (Schiff et al., 1982). This study demonstrated that environment has a strong effect on intellectual abilities. Other data from adoptive homes, however, strongly suggest that the biological mother's IQ has a more important effect than the adoptive home environment. In fact, as time passes there is a decrease in the relationship of the IQs of an adopted child and the adoptive parents and an increase in correlation with the IQs of biological parents (Bouchard et al., 1990; Plomin et al., 1997; Scarr & Weinberg, 1994). Eysenck (1998) provides an explanation, asserting that when an adopted child is young, his environment is determined solely by the adopted parents, which leads to a correlation between their IQs. But as the child grows older and makes choices about his life and interests, his biological predispositions lead him to be selective about the environments in which he participates; the result is a greater correlation

Heritability: The proportion of a trait's variation in a population of individuals that is genetically determined.

with the IQs of his biological parents. There are variations, of course; for example, Scarr and Weinberg (1994) found differences between sons and daughters, with sons being more influenced by family environment. The researchers suggest that parents invest in their sons' futures—regardless of their abilities and achievements—in ways that they do not invest in their daughters' futures.

One type of adoptive study compares the intellectual abilities of identical twins who were separated at birth through adoption; because the twins share the same genetic heritage, any differences in IQ scores *must* be the result of environmental influences. Figure 8.4 summarizes the correlation between IQ scores and child-rearing environments for both related and unrelated children in different studies. If genetics were the sole determinant of IQ scores, the correlation for identical twins should be as close to 1.0 as test reliability will allow, whether they are reared together or apart. Also, the correlation should not decrease when any two siblings (twins or not) are raised apart from each other. However, identical twins raised together and those raised apart do not have identical IQ scores—although their scores are similar (Bouchard et al., 1990). Bouchard and colleagues conclude that about half of the similarities in IQ test scores between identical twins can be accounted for by genetics—not the 70 to 80 percent that

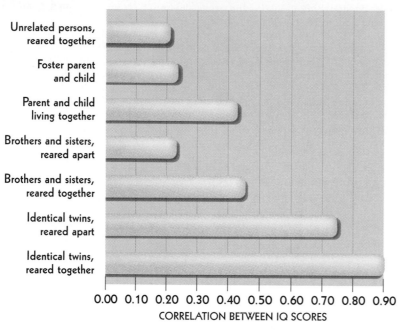

FIGURE 8.4
Correlations between IQ Scores of Persons of Varying Relationships
The closer the biological relationship of two individuals, the more similar their IQ scores—strong support for a genetic component to intelligence.

(Based on data from Bouchard & McGue, 1981, and Erlenmeyer-Kimling & Jarvik, 1963.)

some researchers claim. This finding lends strong support to the idea that the environment must play an equally important role in determining IQ scores (e.g., Johnson, 1991; Plomin et al., 1994). Interestingly, most data about the role of genetics in IQ scores come from studies of identical twins and their performance early in life (Chorney et al., 1998). Only recently have data emerged from studies of older identical twins who have lived full lives and had a wide range of experiences (McClearn et al., 1997; Pedersen et al., 1992). Such data confirm the idea that about half of the similarity in the IQ scores of identical twins—even into old age—can be accounted for by genetics (Petrill et al., 1998). *Brain and Behaviour* explores some ways in which identical twins are and are not alike.

There are volumes of data from child-rearing studies that attempt to demonstrate the genetic and environmental components of intelligence. In general, research shows that, to a great extent, genetics and environment contribute equally to IQ scores (Pedersen et al., 1992; Pedersen, Plomin, & McClearn, 1994). However, to frame nature versus nurture as a debate with a winner and a loser is a mistake, as the two work together in partnership. There is a myth that if a behaviour or characteristic is genetic, it cannot be changed. But genes do not fix behaviour; instead, they establish a range of possible reactions. Environments determine the extent to which the range of genetic potential will be expressed and success will be achieved in a variety of intellectual and social fronts (Ceci & Williams, 1997). Thus, the study of nature, nurture, and social environments together ultimately will answer key questions (Neisser et al., 1996; Plomin, 1994).

brain and behaviour
Identical Twins May Not Be So Identical

I n studying intelligence, researchers often seek samples of identical twins, technically called monozygotics. As we saw in Chapter 2, identical twins share the same genetic heritage. But things are more complicated than that, because identical twins are not always exactly identical. This complicates the study of intelligence.

Some monozygotics exhibit mirror imaging, or asymmetry, in various traits; researchers call them asymmetric twins. For example, one twin may be left handed, while the other is right-handed; such twins also may show different cerebral dominance. It turns out that the asymmetries sometimes are quite pervasive. The same pattern may appear for footedness, facial features, and aspects of internal organs. Body hair patterns are often asymmetrical, and asymmetric twins often throw and draw with opposite sides of the body. When they develop serious illnesses, such as polio, or they have congenital malformations, the disorders strike opposite sides of the body (Gedda, 1961). The causes of the asymmetries are not clear, but several factors have been suspected. The actual process of splitting in the embryo seems to be implicated; for example, is there one placenta or two (about one-third of identical twins have two separate placentas)? When there are two placentas, fetal blood supply often is not equal. Finally, birth order may be important, as the second-born twin suffers a greater risk of oxygen deprivation due to the extended duration of that twin's birth (Phelps, Davis, & Schartz, 1997).

Perhaps most interesting from a psychological point of view—and especially important in studies of intelligence—is that asymmetric twins show different cognitive abilities. When one twin excels at verbal tasks, the other is often superior at spatial tasks. When one is mathematically oriented, the other seems adept at verbal skills. This raises an important methodological issue in studies of brain–behaviour relationships. Researchers have always assumed that identical twins are genetically exactly the same, but studies of asymmetric twins show us that this is not the case. When using identical twins, researchers trying to sort out the nature–nurture issue probably should use only those twins that are as identical as possible—not asymmetric twins. ■

The Bell Curve

Publication of *The Bell Curve*, by Richard J. Herrnstein and Charles Murray (1994), stirred up a whirlpool of debate. While its comments are directed at American society, the questions it raises are worthy of consideration by Canadians. Among its controversial positions are that IQ is largely genetically determined, that minority groups are increasingly trapped in low-IQ environments while individuals with higher IQs use the educational system to leave their original neighbourhoods, and that any attempts to reverse this situation are doomed to failure. Let's take a look at what these authors claimed and see whether critical thinking supports these claims.

Key Arguments. *The Bell Curve* asserts that the United States is ruled by a cognitive elite that is selected by IQ tests, SAT scores (the Scholastic Aptitude Test is a general test of intellectual ability taken by university-bound American high-school students), and admission to prestigious universities. This elite is said to occupy the top of the socioeconomic ladder, while the rest of American society is assigned to inferior and subordinate status—and, Herrnstein and Murray claim, the situation is likely to stay that way. They write: "Mounting evidence indicates that demographic trends are exerting downward pressure on the distribution of cognitive ability in the United States, and that the pressures are strong enough to have social consequences" (p. 342). They also say that "if women with low scores are reproducing more rapidly than women with high scores, the distribution of scores will, other things equal, decline, no matter whether the woman with the low scores came by them through nature or nurture." Herrnstein and Murray suggest that, unless something is done to correct, alter, or somehow modify the present trend, the United States will be permanently split between a ruling cognitive elite and a large, growing, and powerless underclass consisting primarily of low-IQ blacks, whites, Hispanics, and immigrants. Yet Herrnstein and Murray consider it futile to attempt to raise the poor, the disadvantaged, and the cognitively impaired above the limits of their own genetics. They maintain: "The story of attempts to raise intelligence is one of high hopes, flamboyant claims, and disappointing results" (p. 389).

The Bell Curve further asserts that intelligence determines who is rich, middle class, or poor in the United States—that is, that the United States' class structure is mostly determined by genetic causes. Although many researchers believe that intelligence is substantially heritable, as we saw earlier in this chapter, the differences *within* groups of people tend to be greater than the differences *between* groups of people. Any differences between groups may or may not have a genetic reason; in fact, evidence in favour of a genetic cause is far from conclusive (Ceci, Rosenblum, & Kumpf, 1998). Thus, the implications of IQ test score differences between ethnic groups are far less meaningful or important than Herrnstein and Murray assert.

Implications. In *The Bell Curve*, Herrnstein and Murray wrote about the implications for social policy of differences in intelligence, maintaining that there are problems associated with low cognitive ability—crime and social decay—that are not likely to be solved by outside interventions. To put it bluntly, their argument is that the so-called underclass, as a group, is intellectually inferior, which leads them to devalue the potential benefits of affirmative action programs. This is a key point. Ultimately, Herrnstein and Murray conclude that there is no way out for the underclass; no matter how many remedial educational programs are introduced, individuals will be hampered by cognitive disabilities created by their genetics.

A completely opposite point of view is held by others (Neisser et al., 1996). For example, Myerson and his colleagues (1998) argue that tests of academic ability are taken at the point in life when ability differences are most pronounced. Blacks gain more from university or college education than do whites; if IQ test scores were examined as students finished college, the gap in IQ scores would be much smaller. Jonathan Crane (1994) continues the argument by asserting that changes in society are the solution to closing that gap. Crane writes: "There is simply no valid evidence that the race gap in cognitive test scores is caused by genetically determined differences in intellectual capacity. In contrast, there is a good deal of evidence that supports an environmental explanation of the gap" (p. 202).

Critical Analysis. Although any debate about race, ethnicity, IQ, and genetics is inherently controversial, Herrnstein and Murray present data in a way that makes careful critical analysis especially difficult. For example, they omit much historical data, fail to separate the effects of nature and nurture in some early childhood data, present limited new data, and make a series of questionable claims and assumptions. Among their assumptions are that IQ represents a general quality, that IQ largely or solely reflects genetics, that IQ is fixed and immutable, and that a causal relationship exists between IQ and problematic social behaviours. Leading psychologists, however, recognize the multidimensional nature of intelligence, the modifiability of intelligence, and the fact that IQ is not the only predictor of performance on a job or in life (Sternberg, 1995) and that it is often not a very good one (Wagner, 1997).

Conclusions. A key point to note as students of psychology is that Herrnstein and Murray present a vision of a future in which people of high and low IQs would have their respective places in society—commensurate with their IQs. But intelligent behaviour is not a single thing—it is more a process than a collection of single abilities—and even though everyone cannot be a brain surgeon, intelligence is far more complicated than an IQ score can reflect. Despite its weaknesses, perhaps the value of *The Bell Curve* is that it raised for debate once again many useful questions about intelligence.

Stability of Intelligence Test Scores

Many people have taken an intelligence test at some time. Was the test you took in grade 2 a good predictor of your academic ability when you were in grade 10? Or should you have been retested? Does an IQ score remain stable over a long period of time? Early examinations of IQ score stability showed that the IQ scores of infants did not correlate well with their IQ scores when they were school age (Bayley, 1949). Researchers quickly realized that it is not possible to measure the same capabilities in infants that can be measured in older children and adults. Further, correlations of the IQ scores of school-age children and adults show that such scores can change, sometimes substantially. Yet some research indicates that certain predictions can be made from infant IQ scores (DiLalla et al., 1990; Rose & Feldman, 1995). A key idea is that while IQ test scores may remain stable, the information that is tested varies quite substantially over the years. First-graders are asked substantially different items than are sophomores in high school—what remains stable is their score in relation to their peers.

What about the IQ scores of adults? Do IQ scores remain stable throughout adulthood? In general, psychologists have shown that intelligence and achievement test scores at first increase with age, then level off in adulthood, only to decline in late adulthood (Schaie, 1993). The results of a 40-year IQ study showed that, in general, the intellectual functioning of men increased slightly around age 40 and then gradually declined to earlier levels when the men were in their fifties (Schwartzman et al., 1987). Despite the passage of 40 years, cognitive performance remained relatively stable. The effect of aging on IQ scores is a complicated issue, because some aspects of the scores decrease more with age than do others. For example, numerically based portions of IQ tests tend to show a more significant decrease with advancing age than do verbally based portions (Schaie, 1993). In addition, not everyone shows age-related IQ declines; people who continue their education throughout their lives show relatively small decreases.

Ample evidence now exists to confirm that IQ scores remain relatively stable once test subjects reach adulthood. However, the scores of infants and children are so prone to change that they are not reliable predictors of later IQ scores. Of course, a child who achieves a high score on an IQ test at age 9 is likely to do well at age 18—perhaps even better. The data show enough fluctuation, though, especially at younger ages, to make predictions uncertain.

Experiencing Psychology on page 286 discusses changes in IQ scores over the past several decades.

Gender Differences

Many psychologists believe there are gender differences in verbal ability, with girls surpassing boys in most verbal tasks during the early school years. However, most differences have been due to the cultural expectations fostered by parents and teachers. For example, parents and teachers have long encouraged boys to engage in spatial, mechanical tasks. Two interesting events have occurred in Canada in recent decades, though. First, many parents have been encouraging boys *and* girls to acquire math, verbal, and spatial skills; that is, they have endeavoured to avoid gender-role stereotyping. Second, the observed cognitive differences between boys and girls have been diminishing each year.

It turns out that the old consensus about gender differences is at least exaggerated and at most simply wrong (Halpern, 1997). Hyde and Linn (1988) examined 165 research studies on gender differences in verbal ability; these studies had tested a total of 1 418 899 people. Although Hyde and Linn did find a gender difference in favour of females, this difference was so small that they claimed it was not worth mentioning. They further argued that more refined tests and theories of intelligence are needed to examine any gender differences that may exist. The differences found today exist only in certain special populations; for example, among

Why Your IQ Is Up

O ver the last eight decades, the data indicate that IQ test scores have risen by as much as 25 points. Are people smarter now? Or were people less intelligent then? We know that IQ tests are not a measure of innate ability; rather, they measure vocabulary and how well people have learned analytical, critical thinking, and reasoning skills. Consider what is included on today's IQ tests—analogies, antonyms, complex puzzle solutions, spatial logic, and basic geometry and trigonometry. These call for a level of problem-solving skills that would have baffled the average person when IQ tests were first developed at the turn of the twentieth century; similarly, we would all look pretty smart if we

took the IQ tests developed by Binet in the early 1900s. This rise in IQ test scores is called the Flynn effect, after James R. Flynn, who first noted the substantial rise in scores (Flynn, 1987, 1998).

Several factors might be at work. We are healthier and better nourished than previous generations were. We focus more on critical thinking skills than on rote information learning. We are more test-wise, having been tested constantly in school settings. Further, students today are challenged by everything from video games to computers to complex puzzles—all of which require higher levels of reasoning and practice. Therefore, it isn't so amazing that on an IQ test where the types of question have remained

stable—especially on puzzle and spatial abilities—test scores are up. In the end, psychologists conclude that students today may be learning critical thinking skills, which may increase the IQ test scores. ■

Focus

◆ If IQ tests do not examine innate ability, what do they measure? pp. 278–279

Think Critically

◆ What conclusions about nature versus nurture can be drawn when correlations between IQ scores and child-rearing environments for both related and unrelated children are examined?

◆ If you had to design a series of selection procedures for admission to a high school, a college, or a program for gifted students, what procedures would you choose?

the very brightest mathematics students, boys continue to outscore girls, although the boys' scores are quite variable (Hedges & Nowell, 1995). Boys are motivated to achieve more and strive harder at math, in part because more of them have career aspirations that involve mathematical skills. As a consequence of these aspirations, boys tend to take additional and more advanced math courses, which puts them still further ahead on standardized tests. It is important to remember that the small gender differences (and ethnic differences) that do exist are based on group averages and say nothing about individual abilities (Halpern, 1997; Suzuki & Valencia, 1997). In general, it is fair to say that differences between the test scores of males and females are disappearing (Geary, 1998), and that this change is occurring in many cultures (Skaalvik & Raukin, 1994).

Exceptional Individuals

 anadian society is oriented towards looking for, testing, and educating special or exceptional children. As early as during the first few weeks of grade one, most children take some kind of reading readiness test; by the end of grade four, students usually are classified and labelled according to their projected development, again largely on the basis of tests. Educators often use the term *exceptional* to refer to people who are gifted as well as to those who suffer from learning disabilities, physical impairments, and mental retardation.

Giftedness

Gifted individuals represent one end of the continuum of intelligence and talent. Exceptional ability is not limited to cognitive skills, however. Most six-year-olds enrolled in a ballet class probably will show average ability, but ballet teachers report that an occasional child will exhibit a natural ability for dance. In the same way, many children and adults learn to play the piano, but only a few excel at it. And over a wide range of behaviours, some people excel in a particular area but are only average in other areas.

The phenomenon of gifted children has been recognized and discussed for centuries. Some gifted children, like Mozart, display their genius musically. Others display it in science; many great scientists made their most important theoretical discoveries very early in their careers. There is no universally accepted definition of *giftedness* (just as there is no universally agreed-on definition of *intelligence*). Gifted children may have superior cognitive, leadership, or performing arts abilities. Moreover, they require special schooling that goes beyond the ordinary classroom; their instruction needs to be individualized (Detterman & Thompson, 1997). Without it, these children may not realize their potential. In truth, all children need individualized instruction because most students—especially the gifted—are underchallenged (Winner, 1997). There is no federally mandated program for gifted students in Canada. Each school board or district may have a special program for the gifted; however, some school systems have none, and others allocate special instruction only in brief periods or to small groups and still do not challenge the extraordinarily gifted. Some systems provide special schools for children with superior cognitive abilities, performing arts talents, or science aptitude. The special needs of gifted students (and of those with mental retardation—considered next) should not be addressed for only one day a week, only in grades one through six, or with traditional teaching techniques.

Mental Retardation

The term *mental retardation* covers a wide range of behaviours, from slow learning to severe mental and physical impairment. Many people with mental retardation are able to cope well. Most learn to walk and to feed and dress themselves; many learn to read and are able to work. In 1992, the American Association on Mental Retardation adopted a new formal definition of mental retardation:

> **Mental retardation** refers to substantial limitations in present functioning. It is characterized by significantly subaverage intellectual functioning, existing concurrently with related limitations in two or more of the following applicable adaptive skill areas: communication, self-care, home living, social skills, community use, self-direction, health and safety, functional academics, leisure, and work. Mental retardation manifests before age 18.

This definition requires that practitioners consider (1) cultural and linguistic diversity, (2) how adaptive skills interact with a person's community setting, (3) the fact that specific skills

Mental retardation: Below-average intellectual functioning, as measured on an IQ test, accompanied by substantial limitations in functioning that originate before age 18.

often exist with limitations, and (4) the likelihood that life functioning generally will improve with age.

There are a variety of causes for mental retardation—from deprived environments (especially for those with mild retardation) to genetic abnormalities, infectious diseases, and physical trauma (including trauma caused by drugs taken by the mother during pregnancy). There are two broad ways to classify mental retardation. The first focuses on biological versus environmental causes; the second, more prevalent, approach focuses on levels of retardation as reflected in behaviour.

I

Levels of Retardation. A diagnosis of mental retardation involves three criteria: a lower-than-normal (below 70) IQ score as measured on a standardized test, such as the WISC–III or the WAIS–III; difficulty adapting to the environment; and the presence of such problems before age 18. There are four basic levels of mental retardation, each corresponding to a different range of scores on a standardized IQ test (see Table 8.7 and Figure 8.5): mild, moderate, severe, and profound.

FIGURE 8.5
Mental Retardation in the Population

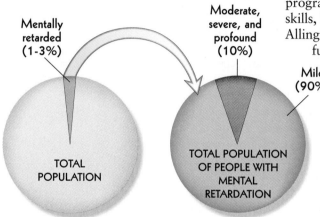

Mild Retardation. Approximately 90 percent of those classified as mentally retarded have mild mental retardation (Wechsler IQ score of 55–69). Through special programs, they are able to acquire academic and occupational skills, but they generally need extra supervision of their work (e.g., Allington, 1981). As adults, people with mild mental retardation function intellectually at about the level of 10-year-olds. Thus, with some help from family and friends, most people with mild mental retardation can cope successfully with their environment.

Moderate Retardation. People with moderate mental retardation (Wechsler IQ of 40–54) account for approximately 6 percent of those classified as mentally retarded. Most live in institutions or as dependants of their families. Those who are not institutionalized need special classes; some can hold simple jobs, although few are employed. People with moderate mental retardation are able to speak, write, and interact with friends, but their motor coordination, posture, and social skills are clumsy. Their intellectual level is equivalent to that of five- to six-year-olds.

Severe Retardation. Only about 3 percent of the people with mental retardation are severely retarded (Wechsler IQ of 25–39). People with severe mental retardation show great motor, speech, and intellectual impairment and are almost totally dependent on others to take care of their basic needs. Severe retardation often results from birth disorders or traumatic injury to the brain.

Table 8.7 Mental Retardation as Measured on the Wechsler Scales

Classification	Wechsler IQ Score	Percentage of the Mentally Retarded
Mild	55–69	90
Moderate	40–54	6
Severe	25–39	3
Profound	Below 25	1

Profound Retardation. Only 1 percent of the people with mental retardation are classified as profoundly retarded (Wechsler IQ below 25). These people are unable to master even simple tasks and require total supervision and constant care. Their motor and intellectual development is minimal, and many are physically underdeveloped. Physical deformities and other congenital defects (such as deafness, blindness, and seizures) often accompany profound mental retardation.

Educating and Employing Those with Mental Retardation. Until recently, thousands of children were given a substandard education after doing poorly on an intelligence test. Labelled as slow learners or perhaps even as mentally retarded, these children received neither special education nor special attention. The situation is somewhat better today. In the United States, federal legislation (Public Law 94–142, the Education for All Handicapped Children Act) ensures individualized testing and educationally relevant programs for all children. In Canada there is no such legislation, but nonetheless our education systems are significantly more inclusive of children with special needs than they used to be.

Mainstreaming—the integration of all children with special needs into regular classroom settings, whenever appropriate, with the support of special education services—has been tried to varying degrees within our educational systems. In mainstreaming, children are assigned to a regular class for at least half of their school day. They spend the rest of the day in special education classrooms or vocational training situations. Although research studies have produced conflicting data on the effectiveness of mainstreaming, psychologists and educators generally support it (Zigler & Hodapp, 1991).

Real progress has been made with mainstreaming, but problems remain in many school settings. Too often children are mainstreamed not into the academic (classroom) aspects of school, but only into its social aspects (athletics, lunch). This is done to avoid stigmatization, but one consequence is a lack of delivery of adequate special academic services to children who require them (Zigler & Hodapp, 1991). Because of such problems, some schools now keep students with special education needs in regular classrooms and bring support to them rather than bringing the children to supportive services—an approach called *inclusion*. Not without its critics, inclusion focuses on the needs of individual children in new ways; research on its success is still a decade away.

Mainstreamed children can become good workers. Companies are realizing that if people with mild mental retardation are placed in the right job, are properly trained, and are effectively motivated, they can be counted on to be good workers. As a result, many companies now hire workers with mental retardation who were once thought to be unemployable.

There are some drawbacks to hiring such workers. One is that training them often requires extra patience. Even a relatively simple task may have to be broken down into 30 or 40 individual steps. As well, workers with mental retardation sometimes need help to remain focused on their job. Nonetheless, there are many great success stories. Those workers who have been through training programs do exceptionally well. Workers with mental retardation are likely to stay in jobs that others tire of. In addition, they may be more dependable, motivated, and industrious than other workers.

Mainstreaming: The integration of all children with special needs into regular classroom settings, whenever appropriate, with the support of special education services.

Focus

Review

◆ What are the implications of mainstreaming children with mental retardation? p. 289

Think Critically

◆ A diagnosis of mental retardation involves a lower-than-normal IQ score. What does this imply about IQ tests as a predictor of behaviour? What might be some characteristics of a different kind of test for diagnosing mental retardation?

Summary and Review

What Is Intelligence?

Identify the key qualities of a definition of intelligence.

- Intelligence is the overall capacity of the individual to act purposefully, to think rationally, and to deal effectively with the environment. p. 265

Describe several different approaches to intelligence.

- A *factor analysis approach* to evaluating intelligence uses correlational techniques to determine which tasks are involved in intellectual ability. In factor analysis, many tasks are given to a person, scores are derived for each task, and correlations are computed. The assumption is that tasks with high correlations test similar aspects of intellectual functioning. p. 265

- Gardner maintains that people have multiple intelligences (at least eight). An intelligence is an ability to solve a problem or create a product within a specific cultural setting. He argues that not all human intelligences, or competencies, lend themselves to measurement by a test, and he ciriticizes IQ tests because they place so much emphasis on linguistic and logical-mathematical skills. p. 266

- Sternberg takes an information-processing view of intelligence. Like Gardner, whose view is that intelligence has many parts, Sternberg's "triarchic" theory divides intelligence into three dimensions: analytic, practical, and creative. Sternberg focuses on adaptation to the world. pp. 267–268

- Vygotsky argued that the most significant moment in the course of intellectual development occurs when speech and practical activity, two previously completely independent lines of development, converge and that researchers need to study the processes of intelligence, in a social context, not just the product of the intelligence. p. 268

KEY TERMS
intelligence, p. 265; factor analysis, p. 265

The Process of Test Development

Why were Binet and Simon significant in the development of intelligence tests?

- Binet coined the phrase *mental age*, meaning the age level at which a child is functioning cognitively. He

and Simon developed everyday tasks, such as counting, naming, and using objects, to determine mental age. The scale they developed is considered the first useful and practical test of intelligence. p. 270

How can intelligence tests be developed fairly and accurately?

- *Standardization* is the process of developing uniform procedures for administering and scoring a test. This includes developing *norms*—the scores and corresponding percentile ranks of a large and representative sample of test takers from the population for which the test was designed. A *representative sample* is a sample of individuals who match the population with whom they are to be compared, with regard to key variables such as socioeconomic status and age. p. 271

- A *normal curve* is a bell-shaped graphic representation of data arranged to show what percentage of the population falls under each part of the curve. The simplest score on a test is the *raw score*—the number of correct answers unconverted or transformed in any way. Scores are commonly expressed in terms of a *standard score*—a score that expresses an individual's position relative to those of others and based on the mean score and how scores are distributed around it. A standard score is generally a *percentile score*—indicating what percentage of the test population would obtain a lower score. A *deviation IQ* is a standard IQ test score for which the mean and variability remain constant at all ages. pp. 271–272

- A test is considered *reliable* if it yields the same or similar score for the same individual on repeated testing. There are several types of reliability. All tests have some degree of unreliability. The standard error of measurement is the number of points by which a score varies because of the imperfect reliability of a test. A test's *validity* is its ability to measure what it is supposed to measure; without validity, proper inferences from test results cannot be made. pp. 272–273

- There are several basic criticisms of—and defences for—the validity of intelligence tests and testing. The first focuses on the definition of intelligence. The second focuses on learned information. The third is

that school settings may adversely affect IQ scores. Another criticism of testing is that some people may be test-wise, which improves performance. A fifth criticism is that IQ test scores may depend on people's motivation to succeed. Lastly, our society helps create the correlation between academic success, schooling, and IQ test scores. pp. 274–275

- Critics of IQ tests are concerned about the interpretation of scores. It is important to remember that intelligence tests generally are made up of different subtests or subscales, each yielding a score. There also may be one general score for the entire test. All of these scores require knowledgeable interpretation; that is, test scores must be given a context that is meaningful to the person who receives the information. Without such a context, a score is little more than a number. p. 275

KEY TERMS
standardization, p. 271; norms, p. 271; representative sample, p. 271; normal curve, p. 271; raw score, p. 271; standard score, p. 271; percentile score, p. 272; deviation IQ, p. 272; reliability, p. 272; validity, p. 273; halo effect, p. 274

Three Important Intelligence Tests

What are the chief differences between the Kaufman Assessment Battery for Children (K–ABC) and the Stanford–Binet and Wechsler scales?

- The Stanford–Binet Intelligence Scale consists of four major subscales and one overall IQ test score. It has been a good predictor of academic performance, and many of its tests correlate highly with one another; its newer items minimize gender and racial characteristics. pp. 275–276

- The Wechsler scales group test items by content. The score on each subtest is converted to a standard (or scaled) score, adjusted for the subject's age. The test yields verbal, performance, and overall IQ scores. p. 276

- The K–ABC consists of four global scales. Three of the scales measure mental processing abilities—sequential processing, simultaneous processing, and a composite of the two; the fourth scale assesses achievement. p. 277

The Environmental and Biological Partnership

What is the evidence to show that cultural variables and gender affect intelligence test scores?

■ Although researchers find differences among the IQ test scores of various racial and cultural groups, they find little or no consistent and conclusive evidence of bias in these tests. The evidence of many studies conducted with a variety of intelligence tests and ethnic minority groups indicates that intelligence tests are not culturally biased. But IQ test scores alone mean little and must be interpreted in the context of a person's life (including schooling). Intelligence can be demonstrated in many ways, including maturity and responsibility. pp. 278–279

■ Cross-cultural differences exist and express themselves in IQ test scores; for this reason many psychologists (1) de-emphasize overall test scores, (2) focus on interpretation of tests, (3) remember that IQ test scores do not measure innate ability, and (4) focus on intellectual functioning in the context of real-life situations. p. 279

■ Proponents of the environmental (nurture) view of intelligence believe that intelligence tests do not adequately measure a person's adaptation to a constantly changing environment. Many researchers claim that current theorizing will never resolve the issue of nature versus nurture, because factors such as family structure, family size, and other environmental variables are important and impossible to measure accurately. Some traits have a high degree of hereitability. *Heritability* is the proportion of a trait's variation in a population of individuals that is genetically determined. Genetics (nature) does not fix a person's intelligence; it sets a framework for the environment to shape it. pp. 279–282

■ The old consensus about gender differences in verbal and mathematical abilities is at least exaggerated, and at most simply wrong; gender differences in verbal ability are so small that they can be ignored. pp. 285–286

KEY TERM
heritability, p. 281

Exceptional Individuals

Describe the ends of the continuum of intelligence—giftedness and mental retardation—and their implications for educational settings.

■ Giftedness is having superior cognitive, leadership, or performing arts abilities. Gifted children represent one end of a continuum of intelligence abilities. Such individuals need special schooling to meet their special needs. p. 287

■ *Mental retardation* is below-average intellectual functioning together with substantial limitations in adaptive behaviour, originating before age 18. Retardation can affect communication, self-care, home living, social skills, self-direction, health and safety, leisure activities, and work. There are four basic levels of mental retardation; each corresponds to a specific range of scores on a standardized intelligence test. The behaviours associated with mental retardation vary from slow learning to an inability to care for oneself because of impaired physical, motor, and intellectual development. pp. 287–288

■ *Mainstreaming* is the integration of all children with special needs into regular classroom settings wherever appropriate and with the support of special services. The purpose of mainstreaming is to help normalize the life experiences of children with special needs; unfortunately this is most often done in social settings rather than academic ones. p. 289

KEY TERMS
mental retardation, p. 287; mainstreaming, p. 289

Weblinks

Sternberg's Triarchic Theory
www.gwu.edu/~tip/stem.html
An overview of Sternberg's triarchic theory, with examples, references for further reading, and links to Web pages on other theories of learning and intelligence.

Howard Gardner
www.ed.psu.edu/insys/esd/gardner/menu.html
Howard Gardner comments on various topics dealing with intelligence and schooling. Includes audio and video links.

Is Intelligence Inherited?
www.yorku.ca/bethune/bc1850/intellig.htm
This site from York University examines the study of intelligence and explores intelligence testing, genetics and intelligence, and other factors that might influence intelligence levels. It includes links to related sites.

Intelligence
Pavlov.psyc.queensu.ca/~kang/psyc100/intelligence/ppframe.htm
This site, from the psychology department at Queen's University, outlines theories of intelligence, the use and reliability of intelligence testing, and genetic influences on intelligence.

Body, Mind & Spirit—What's Your EQ?
www.utne.com/cgi-bin/eq
Visit this site and take an Emotional Intelligence test. A series of situations are presented, and you can choose from four possible responses to each situation.

Intelligence Test
www.execpc.com/~rtodd/int-test.html
Attempt these questions to challenge your mental flexibility and creativity.

Chapter 9

Motivation and Emotion

Yusif is a 50-something businessman. He works out at the gym three times a week and rides 100 kilometres a week on his mountain bike. His goals are to push his body to do things it hasn't done before, and to burn enough calories to keep his weight down. He is motivated by the fact that his father had heart problems. With that family history, along with a tendency to put on weight too easily, he has some real reasons to work out. He wants to live to a ripe old age and do it in good health. He also wants to feel stronger and thus more self-confident, and to be part of the group who work out regularly at the gym; the atmosphere there is very positive and supportive. His workouts make him feel like a 16-year old, if he ignores the crackling of his joints. And his regular exercise regimen also means that he can eat just about anything he wants without gaining weight.

If you work out at the gym, run or walk, or do other things for exercise on a regular basis, think for a moment about why you do that, about what drives you to keep your exercise routine going.

Perhaps you are motivated by the fact that there are heart or blood pressure problems in your family, or maybe you have realized that you must raise your metabolic rate to avoid putting on extra weight. Maybe you have found that fitness and regular exercise reduce the symptoms of stress, especially around exam times, and that exercise makes you feel alert and self-confident. On the other hand, perhaps you run or work out with a friend or two and they tend to hound you into going along to the gym, even if you don't feel like it much. Of course, you simply could enjoy hanging out at the gym with other fit people. You can see that motivation is personal and powerful.

A person's exercise routine, or lack thereof, illustrates several key concepts in psychology. Why do some people continue to strive for success while others give up with a single failure or are content to enjoy life at a more relaxed pace? Why will one person spend a free afternoon watching soap operas and munching potato chips while another will use the time for an eight-kilometre run and a quick study session before dinner? Why do some people crave the excitement of competition while others seem to shy away from it? What drives people to take action? And what makes them so emotional about it? ■

Motivation: Any condition, although usually an internal one, that can be inferred to initiate, activate, or maintain an organism's goal-directed behaviour.

Theories of Motivation

R esearchers have always sought to discover what drives people to take various actions—from simple, seemingly instinctual actions such as eating to complex actions such as learning to juggle. Many theories of motivation have been developed to explain human behaviour, but no single theory can explain all behaviour. An understanding of the interacting forces that impel us must begin with a definition of *motivation*. The word derives from the Latin *movere*, meaning "to move," and refers to the forces that energize. **Motivation** is any condition, although usually an internal one, that can be inferred to initiate, activate, or maintain an organism's goal-directed behaviour.

Let's examine the four basic parts of this definition of motivation. First, motivation reflects an *internal condition* that cannot be directly observed—one reason why its effect has to be inferred. The condition may develop from simple physiological needs or from complex psychological desires, such as the desire to help others, to obtain approval, or to earn a higher income. Second, motivation is an *inferred concept* that links a person's internal conditions to external behaviour. It cannot be observed directly, but an observer can infer its presence from its behavioural effects. Third, motivation *initiates, activates, or maintains behaviour*. Because you are motivated to control your weight and keep fit, you may initiate an exercise regimen, which you then hope to maintain. Fourth, motivation generates *goal-directed behaviour*. Goals vary widely across individuals and situations. Some goals are concrete and immediate—for example, to eat, to remove a painful stimulus, or to win a diving match. Other goals are more abstract and long-term; the behaviour of someone who studies hard, for example, may be motivated by desires to maximize learning, to obtain good grades, and to get a good job.

In the end, motivation can be considered the study of what we choose to do, why we choose to do it, and how much energy we spend doing it (Edwards, 1999). Motivation theories fall into six broad categories—evolutionary theories, drive theory, arousal theory, expectancy theories, cognitive theory, and humanistic theory—each of which has generated research activity. We will examine each of these categories in turn and then look at some basic types of motivation, before discussing how emotions and motivation are intertwined.

Evolutionary Theories

In the early days of psychology, theorists like Konrad Lorenz spoke of *instincts*, referring to fixed behavioural patterns that animals produce without learning. What these researchers studied were often elaborate stereotyped behaviour patterns associated with hunting and mating. Researchers quickly realized that the study of such rigid behaviour patterns—whether of geese or wolves—had limited relevance to human beings. But their early theorizing did give way to a more contemporary, *evolutionary perspective* that asserts that natural selection, the process of selective reproduction of the fittest organisms, would explain certain basic human behaviours. Animals, and human beings for that matter, who are motivated to engage in behaviours that make it more likely they will succeed, stay alive, and reproduce are more likely to be represented in the population. Ultimately, only the fittest organisms contribute to the gene pool.

Evolutionary theorists have examined basic motivations that help an organism survive, for example, eating, drinking, and sleeping. They have studied reproductive behaviour, pain avoidance, and temperature regulation and have examined emotions such as fear, as we'll see later in this chapter. In each case, they conclude that organisms that develop and flourish are those that have evolved physically and mentally through natural selection; further, and most importantly, these changes are grounded in brain structure and function. Evolutionary theorists do not discount learning; rather, they assert that organisms that have learned well have done so due to adaptive brain structures. They contend that through successive generations, over millions of years, evolutionary selection results in more advanced, evolved organisms that are better suited to their environments and that are motivated to succeed, reproduce, and pass on their genetic heritage.

Drive Theory

Some of the most influential and best-researched motivation theories are forms of drive theory. **Drive theory** is an explanation of behaviour that assumes that an organism is motivated to act because of a need to attain, reestablish, balance, or maintain some goal that helps with the survival of the organism or the species. Stimuli such as hunger and pain create, energize, and initiate such behaviour. A person who is hungry, perhaps a homeless person, may spend most of his or her time looking for food; the individual will be driven to seek food.

A **drive** is an internal aroused condition that directs an organism to satisfy some physiological need. Drive theory focuses on **need**—a state of physiological imbalance usually accompanied by arousal. (We will explore arousal in greater depth in the next section.) Physiological needs are said to be mechanistic, because the organism has no choice but to be pushed, pulled, and energized by them, almost like a machine. An organism motivated by a need is said to be in a *drive state*. Both animals and human beings in a drive state show goal-directed behaviour. Their goal is often to attain **homeostasis**—a tendency to attempt to maintain a constant state of inner stability or balance. The processes by which organisms seek to reestablish homeostasis are a key part of drive theory. For example, a thirsty animal—one depleted of its normal level of body fluids—will seek out water to reestablish its body fluid level (psychologists refer to this normally maintained level as a steady state). In motivation theory we often refer to the goal that satisfies a need as an *incentive*. Incentives can be positive and lure us, like food or a sexually attractive person, or they can repel us and cause us to avoid a painful situation or someone we dislike. Behaviours such as eating and drinking, which reduce a biological need (and reestablish homeostasis), are reinforced when its incentive is attained; such behaviours are therefore especially likely to recur. Behaviours such as juggling, which does not reduce a biological need, are less likely to recur—if they even happen in the first place. (See Figure 9.1 for an overview and examples of drive theory.)

In examining motivation from a drive reduction point of view, psychologists seek to understand such simple behaviours as eating and drinking. As Abraham Maslow (1962, 1969) suggested, a person's physiological need for food and water generally must be satisfied before any other needs. However, drive theory clearly does not explain all, or even most, motivated behaviour; besides, difficult-to-define concepts such as "need" and "hunger" vary from person to person. The history of motivation theory is marked by distinct shifts from one theory to another. For example, though many early researchers focused on the internal conditions—needs—that impel organisms to action, contemporary researchers such as Joseph LeDoux (whose work will be discussed later in the chapter) recognize that some human motives are biological, others are learned through conditioning, and still others result from people thinking about and evaluating their needs and their behaviours.

Arousal Theory

A characteristic of all motivational systems is that they involve arousal. **Arousal** is generally thought of as activation of the central nervous system, the autonomic nervous system, and the muscles and glands. Some motivational theorists suggest that organisms

Drive theory: An explanation of behaviour that assumes that an organism is motivated to act because of a need to attain, reestablish, balance, or maintain some goal that helps with the survival of the organism or the species.

Drive: An internal aroused condition that directs an organism to satisfy physiological needs.

Need: A state of physiological imbalance usually accompanied by arousal.

Homeostasis: A tendency to attempt to maintain a constant state of inner stability or balance

Arousal: Activation of the central nervous system, the autonomic nervous system, and the muscles and glands; according to some motivational theorists, organisms seek to maintain optimal levels of arousal by actively varying their exposure to arousing stimuli.

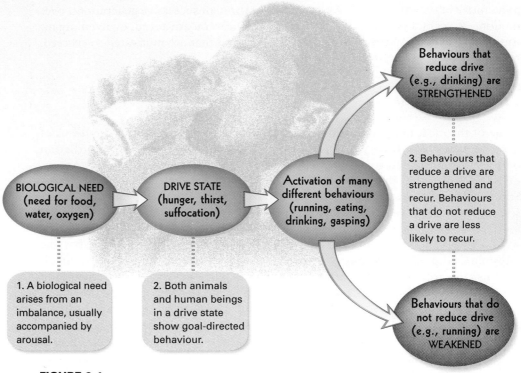

FIGURE 9.1
An Overview of Drive Theory

I seek to maintain optimal levels of arousal by actively varying their exposure to arousing stimuli.

Unlike hunger and thirst, lack of sensory experience does not result in a physiological imbalance; yet both human beings and animals seek sensory stimulation. When deprived of a normal amount of visual, auditory, or tactile stimulation, some adults become irritable and consider their situation or environment intolerable. Kittens like to explore their environment, young monkeys will investigate mechanical devices and play with puzzles, and people seem motivated or impelled to seek sensory stimulation. (However, in some situations people and animals seek to avoid stimulation—for example, when they are sick or in need of rest.)

But a lack of sensory stimulation or a need to reduce some drive fails to explain many basic behaviours. *Arousal theory* attempts to bridge the gap by explaining the link between a behaviour and a state of arousal. R. M. Yerkes and J. D. Dodson first scientifically explored the link between performance and arousal in 1908. They described a relationship involving arousal and performance that ultimately was called the *Yerkes–Dodson law*. This law suggests that arousal and level of task difficulty are related: On easy tasks, moderate to high levels of arousal produce maximum performance; but, on difficult tasks, low levels of arousal yield better performance. Think of athletics: In a 100-metre sprint, a fairly high level of arousal may facilitate performance, but in a more complex triathlon, where strategy is necessary, too much arousal may yield poor decision making, for example, by going all-out too soon in a multihour event. Contemporary researchers have refined the Yerkes–Dodson law by suggesting that when a person's level of arousal and anxiety is either too high or too low, performance will be poor, especially on complex tasks. The inverted U-shaped curve in Figure 9.2 illustrates this relationship between level of arousal and level of performance.

Thus, people who do not care about what they are doing have little anxiety but also have little arousal, and therefore usually perform poorly in both work and play. If arousal increases to the point of high anxiety, performance also suffers. Think of an activity that you practise often, and in which you occasionally either compete or perform publicly. For example, you may be a diver, an actor, or a member of a debating team. Chances are you performed most poorly when you were not interested in practising or when you were exceedingly nervous about your performance, such as during an important competition. Conversely, you probably did your best when you were eager to practise or when you were moderately excited by the competition. This phenomenon explains why some baseball players perform exceptionally well at the beginning of the season, when pressure is only moderately high, and then commit numerous errors when pressure mounts—for instance, in the final games of the World Series. It also explains why the same tasks at different points in our lives seem to bring far more interest, pressure, and concern. High-school juniors are far more concerned about final exams than are fifth-graders or college graduates. And even among high-school students, events are interpreted differently; pressure surrounding final exams varies depending on how important they are to a student and how prepared that student is for them.

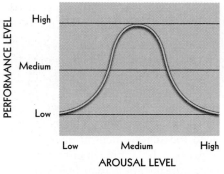

FIGURE 9.2
Performance and Arousal
Performance is at its peak when arousal is at moderate levels; too much or too little arousal results in low performance levels.

Canadian researcher Donald Hebb (1904–1985) suggested that behaviours vary from disorganized to effective, depending on a person's level of arousal. He demonstrated that human functioning is most efficient when people are at an optimal level of arousal (Hebb, 1955). It is important to realize that the stimulus itself—for example, final exams, the World Series, or a date on Saturday night—does not produce arousal; it is a person's internal response to these events that determines how he or she behaves. Hebb's theory shifted researchers' focus from stimuli, drives, and needs to the idea that arousal energizes behaviour but does not direct it. The development of optimal-arousal theories helped psychologists explain the variation in people's responses to situations in terms of a state of internal arousal rather than solely in terms of responses to stimuli. This shift in emphasis marked a subtle but important transition from a strictly mechanistic drive reduction theory towards learning, expectancy, and more cognitive theories. (See Building Table 9.1 for a comparison of drive and arousal theories.)

Building Table 9.1

Drive and Arousal Theories of Motivation

Theory	Theorist	Principally Explains	Key Idea	View of Behaviour
Drive	Hull	Learning through stimulus–response associations and drive reduction	*Homeostasis*—the organism seeks physiological balance.	Largely mechanistic
	Nisbett	Obesity		
Arousal	Hebb	Optimal arousal	Performance depends on level of arousal.	The efficiency of behaviour is determined by the level of physiological arousal.

Expectancy Theories

If you expend enormous energy in the gym, you expect to see results. You feel that you have a right to see your muscles tone, endurance increase, and weight remain stable. You expect this because of past experiences and what you have read or been told about physical fitness. Your motivation is, in part, based on expectancies. **Expectancy theories** connect thought and motivation and are explanations of behaviour that focus on people's expectations of success in reaching a goal and their need for achievement as energizing factors. A key element of these theories, often expressed by achievement researcher David McClelland (1958), is that people's expectations guide their behaviours. The motives and needs that people develop are not initiated by some physiological imbalance. Rather, people learn through their interactions in the environment to have needs for mastery, affiliation, and competition. These needs are based on their expectations about the future and about how their efforts will lead to various rewarding outcomes.

To understand some important concepts related to expectancy theory, we can consider someone's desire to be better at golf. That desire means hours of practice, which require them to deprive themselves of other pleasures (not that golfing is onerous!). Psychologists argue that such motives for striving at golf originate partly in social needs. A **motive** is a specific (usually internal) condition, typically involving some form of arousal that directs an organism's behaviour towards a goal. Unlike a drive, which always has a physiological origin, a motive does not necessarily need to have a physiological explanation. Thus, although you may be motivated to be thin and fit, there is no *urgent* physiological need for you to be so. A **social need** is an aroused condition that directs people towards establishing feelings about themselves and others and towards establishing and maintaining relationships. Your social needs, for example, probably have included winning approval from family, friends, and other people with whom you interact or work. The needs for achievement and affiliation are affected by many factors, including socioeconomic status and race and experiences from birth onwards. The need to feel good about oneself often leads to specific behaviours through which a person strives to be evaluated positively (Geen, 1991). This topic will be explored in more detail later in this chapter when we discuss achievement, as well as when we consider social psychology in Chapter 13. (See Building Table 9.2 for a comparison of expectancy theories and drive and arousal theories.)

Cognitive Theory

In the study of motivation, **cognitive theory** is an explanation of behaviour that asserts that people are actively and regularly involved in determining their own goals and the means of achieving them. Like expectancy theory, cognitive theory focuses on thought as an initiator and determinant of behaviour. However, more than expectancy theory does, cognitive theory emphasizes the role of conscious decision making in all areas of life. For example, you are actively involved in deciding how much time you will spend studying for a psychology exam, how hard you will work to become an accomplished pianist, or how much commitment you will give to a new diet or exercise routine.

As early as 1949, Donald Hebb anticipated how cognitive theory would influence psychology to move away from mechanistic views of motivation and behaviour by suggesting that it is unsatisfactory to equate motivation with biological need. Other factors, such as arousal and attention, are also important determinants of motivation. Contemporary researchers consider, and many emphasize, the role of active decision making and the human capacity for abstract thought. These cognitive theorists assume that individuals set goals and decide how to achieve them.

Cognitive Controls. Cognitive theory holds that if you are aware of—and think about—your behaviour, motivation, and emotions and you attempt to alter

Building Table 9.2

Drive, Arousal, and Expectancy Theories of Motivation

Theory	Theorist	Principally Explains	Key Idea	View of Behaviour
Drive	Hull	Learning through stimulus–response associations and drive reduction	*Homeostasis*—the organism seeks physiological balance.	Largely mechanistic
	Nisbett	Obesity		
Arousal	Hebb	Optimal arousal	Performance depends on level of arousal.	The efficiency of behaviour is determined by the level of physiological arousal.
Expectancy	McClelland	Achievement motivation	Humans learn the need to achieve.	Partly cognitive, partly mechanistic—achievement is a learned behaviour.

your thoughts, you can control your behaviour. Cognitive psychologists maintain that if human beings are aware of their thought patterns, they can control their reasoning and ultimately their overt behaviour. We will see in Chapter 16 that this idea is used extensively by therapists to help people with various maladjustments. In explaining motivation, cognitive psychologists show that arousal can be under voluntary cognitive control. Through instruction and self-help techniques, people can alter their behaviour by changing their thoughts and thus their expectancies (e.g., Norris, 1989). That thoughts can alter behaviour also becomes evident when we consider intrinsic and extrinsic motivation.

Intrinsic and Extrinsic Motivation. A child may love playing checkers, doing puzzles, or colouring in colouring books. Why do some activities seem like fun and others seem like work? Are there things psychologists can do to make activities fun? What are the critical variables?

In general, psychologists find that some activities are intrinsically fun—people like to do them for their own reward. Others, however, are not nearly as much fun; people need to be motivated to perform them, either with reinforcers or with threats of punishment. Psychologists talk about *intrinsic* and *extrinsic* motivation—whether things are done for fun or for rewards. **Extrinsic motivation** is supplied in the form of rewards that come from the external environment. Praise, a high grade, and money given for a particular behaviour are extrinsic rewards. Such rewards can strengthen existing behaviours, provide people with information about their performance, and increase feelings of self-worth and competence. In contrast, behaviours engaged in for no apparent reward except the pleasure and satisfaction of the activity itself arise from **intrinsic motivation**. Edward Deci (1975) suggests that people engage in such behaviours for two reasons: to

Extrinsic motivation [ecks-TRINZ-ick]: Motivation supplied by rewards that come from the external environment.

Intrinsic motivation [in-TRINZ-ick]: Motivation that leads to behaviours engaged in for no apparent reward except the pleasure and satisfaction of the activity itself.

obtain cognitive stimulation and to gain a sense of accomplishment, competence, and mastery over the environment. Individuals vary widely with respect to the need for cognitive stimulation; each person's experiences and genetic make-up affect the strength of this need (Cacioppo et al., 1995).

In studies focusing on intrinsic motivation, Deci compared two groups of university-age participants engaged in puzzle solving. One group received no external rewards, while the other group did receive rewards. Deci found that participants who initially were given rewards generally spent less time solving puzzles when rewards were no longer given. Those who were never rewarded, on the other hand, spent the same amount of time solving puzzles on all trials (Deci, 1972). Lepper and Greene (1978) referred to this phenomenon as the *hidden cost of rewards*; today, we refer to it as the overjustification effect. The **overjustification effect** is the decrease in likelihood that an intrinsically motivated task, after having been extrinsically rewarded, will be performed when the reward is no longer given.

Research on the overjustification effect has been extensive and controversial. The earliest research focused on the basic finding that extrinsic rewards can have detrimental effects; however, newer research suggests that these detrimental effects occur only under restricted and avoidable situations (Eisenberger & Cameron, 1996; Pittenger, 1997; Snelders & Lea, 1996). In fact, Eisenberger and Cameron assert that when goals are attainable, extrinsic rewards have negligible effects on intrinsic motivation, but that some people report liking the task better after verbal extrinsic rewards. Cialdini and colleagues (1998) have developed techniques to undermine or overcome the overjustification effect with children by giving them controlled rewards and attributing the rewards to the child's internal abilities. In the same way, Cordova and Lepper (1996) found that a child's depth of engagement in learning could be enhanced by giving the child feedback and by personalizing the task.

Psychologists continue to explore the effects of providing extrinsic rewards for intrinsically motivated behaviours. Baumeister and Tice (1985) showed that when people with high self-esteem are rewarded for intrinsically motivated behaviours, they aspire to excel and seek opportunities to do so. But when people with low self-esteem are rewarded for intrinsically motivated behaviours, they aspire to be only adequate or satisfactory. It is not surprising, then, that intrinsic motivation is, at least in part, related to a person's past experiences and current level of self-esteem. Other variables, such as the type of task undertaken and the type of reward received, can influence the level of intrinsic motivation. The combination of intrinsic motivation, external rewards, self-esteem, and perhaps new and competing needs affects day-to-day behaviour. (In Chapter 13 we will consider what happens when goals and needs conflict and how animals and human beings behave in situations that have both positive and negative aspects.)

Focus

Review

◆ How does drive theory explain motivation? p. 295

◆ Under what conditions is intrinsic motivation lessened when rewards are offered? What is the overjustification effect? p. 300

Think Critically

◆ In what way did humanistic theory grow from cognitive theory? Did expectancy theories grow from drive theory?

◆ Why is humanistic theory difficult to test experimentally?

Humanistic Theory

Your physiological readiness, expectations, and learned behaviour work together to determine your success in any sport or fitness activity you attempt. One of the appealing aspects of humanistic theory is that it recognizes the interplay of behavioural theories and incorporates some of the best elements of the drive, arousal, expectancy, and cognitive approaches for explaining motivation and behaviour.

Humanistic theory is an explanation of behaviour that emphasizes the entirety of life rather than individual components of behaviour. It focuses on human dignity, individual choice, and self-worth. Humanistic psychologists believe that individuals' behaviour must be viewed within the framework of the individuals' environment and values. As we saw in Chapter 1, one of the founders and leaders of the humanistic approach was Abraham Maslow (1908–1970), who assumed that people are essentially good—that they possess an innate inclination to develop their potential and to seek beauty, truth, and harmony.

Maslow believed that people are born open and trusting and can experience the world in healthy ways. In his words, people are naturally motivated towards self-actualization. **Self-actualization** is the final level of psychological development in which individuals strive to realize their uniquely human potential—to achieve everything they are capable of achieving. This includes attempts to minimize ill health, to attain a superior perception of reality, and to feel a strong sense of self-acceptance. (Of course, such *self*-preoccupation is a very Western characteristic; many elements of Maslow's theory would not hold up in some Eastern cultures.)

Maslow's influential theory conceives of motives as forming a hierarchy, which can be represented as a pyramid, with fundamental physiological needs at the base and the needs for love, achievement, understanding, and self-actualization near the top (see Figure 9.3). According to Maslow, as lower-level needs are satisfied, people strive for the next higher level; the pyramid culminates in self-actualization.

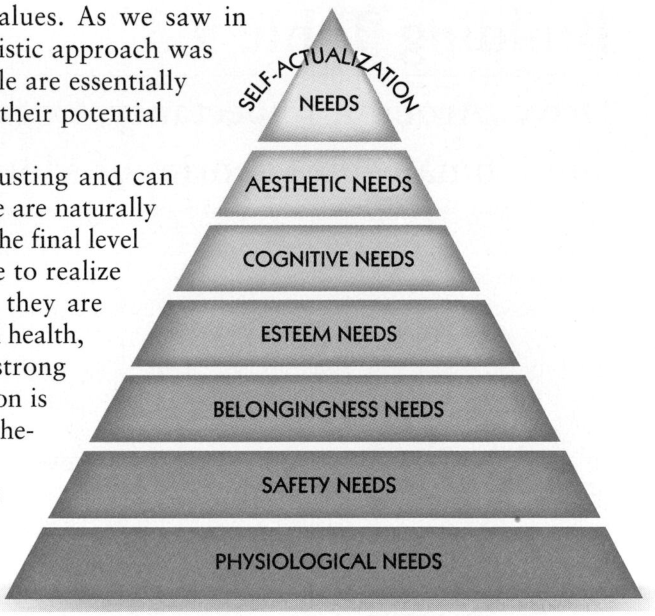

Building Table 9.3 adds Deci's cognitive theory and Maslow's humanistic theory to the comparative summary of motivation theories.

Although Maslow's theory provides an interesting way to organize aspects of motivation and behaviour and their relative importance, its global nature makes experimental verification difficult. Moreover, his levels of motivation seem closely tied to middle-class Western cultural experiences; Western cultures are highly individualistic compared to Eastern cultures, which are more collectivist. So Maslow's theory may not be valid for all cultures or socioeconomic strata. His theory, like many other motivation theories, does not explain how other components of people's lives interact with behaviour. For example, how does a person maintain a need for privacy and independence and still have a need to be with other people? Also, humanistic theory does not deal with how people develop the need to seek beauty, truth, and harmony. Again, this reveals its culture-bound Western approach—Eastern cultures and religions incorporate ways to develop and meet this need, including meditation and exercise.

FIGURE 9.3
Maslow's Hierarchy of Needs
Physiological needs are at the base of the pyramid. Successively higher levels represent needs that are increasingly learned social ones.

Hunger: A Physiologically Based Need

N ow that you understand the theoretical work that has been done on motivation, let's look at a few very basic *types* of motivation. All of us have been hungry, felt sexually aroused, and experienced such learned motives as those for achievement. These three motivators—food, sex, and achievement—illustrate how motivation leads to both basic biological behaviours and some complex and culturally determined ones. It is to those types of motivation that we turn next, beginning with perhaps the most basic, drive-based motivation—hunger. You will see that in motivation, as in other areas of psychology, there is a complex interplay of biology and learning with one or the other predominating at different times.

Physiological Determinants of Hunger

We don't eat only to gain nutrition the way animals do; we also eat to taste. We know the power of tastes, sights, and smells—they evoke hunger, or at least desire. When

Self-actualization: In humanistic theory, the final level of psychological development in which individuals strive to realize their uniquely human potential—to achieve everything they are capable of achieving, including minimizing ill health, attaining a superior perception of reality, and feeling a strong sense of self-acceptance.

Building Table 9.3

Drive, Arousal, Expectancy, Cognitive, and Humanistic Theories of Motivation

Theory	Theorist	Principally Explains	Key Idea	View of Behaviour
Drive	Hull	Learning through stimulus–response associations and drive reduction	*Homeostasis*—the organism seeks physiological balance.	Largely mechanistic
	Nisbett	Obesity		
Arousal	Hebb	Optimal arousal	Performance depends on level of arousal.	The efficiency of behaviour is determined by the level of physiological arousal.
Expectancy	McClelland	Achievement motivation	Humans learn the need to achieve.	Partly cognitive, partly mechanistic—achievement is a learned behaviour.
Cognitive	Deci	Intrinsic motivation	Intrinsic motivation is self-rewarding because it makes people feel competent.	Cognitive—motivation is inborn, but extrinsic rewards often decrease it.
Humanistic	Maslow	Learned needs for fulfilment and feelings of self-actualization	Self-actualization	Cognitive—humans seek to attain self-actualization after they have fulfilled basic needs for food and security.

you are hungry, you may feel stomach pain or become weak or dizzy—sensations that impel you to seek food. What causes these sensations? Physiological explanations of hunger focus on the concept of homeostasis and hormones. A delicate balance—a *homeostasis*—of food and fluid intake is necessary for proper physiological functioning; any imbalance results in a drive to restore the balance. For example, when a person experiences fluid deprivation and the resulting cellular dehydration, homeostatic mechanisms come into play. The person is put into a drive state in which the mouth and throat become dry, cueing the person to drink. Thirst is not a result of dryness in the mouth or throat, and simply placing water in the mouth will not reduce thirst. The body seeks to maintain homeostasis, and when the internal regulator drops below a key point—almost like a thermostat—certain actions are put into play.

Similarly, the *glucostatic approach* to explaining hunger argues that the principal physiological cause of hunger is a low blood sugar level, which accompanies food deprivation and creates a chemical imbalance. In the body, sugar is quickly broken down into glucose, which is crucial to cellular activity. When the blood sugar (glucose) level is low, the body sends warning signals to the brain; the brain immediately responds by generating hunger pain in the stomach. Hunger depends directly on levels of blood sugar (and other metabolites), which trigger the central nervous system circuits that control eating. Experiments with animals in which the nerves between stomach and brain were severed show that the animals continued to eat at appropriate times—when their blood sugar levels were low. These experiments provide evidence for the glucostatic approach.

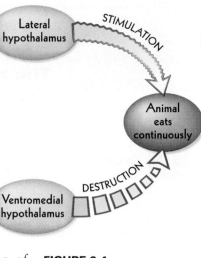

FIGURE 9.4
The Effects of the Hypothalamus on Eating Behaviour
The stimulation or destruction (ablation) of a rat's hypothalamus alters the rat's eating behaviour; in addition, the location of the hypothalamic stimulation—ventromedial or lateral—affects the results.

The amount of food people eat does not necessarily affect the feeling of hunger—at least not right away. A hungry adult who eats steadily for five minutes may still feel hungry on stopping. But 30 minutes later, after the food has been converted into sugar, the person may no longer feel hungry. The type of food eaten determines how soon the feeling of hunger disappears. A candy bar loaded with easily converted sugar will take away hunger pain faster than foods high in protein. High-protein foods such as meat, cheese, and milk take more time to digest and to elevate blood glucose.

Much of current knowledge about hunger and eating behaviour comes from studies of the hypothalamus, a region of the forebrain (see Chapter 2, page 55). Researchers have argued that two areas of the hypothalamus are partly responsible for eating behaviour: the ventromedial hypothalamus and the lateral hypothalamus. (See *Brain and Behaviour*.) The *ventromedial hypothalamus* (the "stop eating" centre) is activated to stop an organism from eating when the blood sugar level is high, or when this part of the hypothalamus is electrically stimulated. The *lateral hypothalamus* (the "start eating" centre) is activated to drive the organism to start eating when the blood sugar level is low, or when this part of the hypothalamus is stimulated. The lateral hypothalamus has been shown to play a direct role in eating behaviour (both hunger and satiety), while the ventromedial hypothalamus has a more indirect role. For example, the ventromedial hypothalamus may influence eating by stimulating the hormonal and metabolic systems (Powley, 1977). As

Figure 9.4 shows, researchers have used lesioning (surgical) techniques to destroy the ventromedial and lateral areas of the hypothalamus in rats. This destruction caused the opposite effects of stimulation.

What happens when the motivation to eat, the hormonal system, or perhaps genetics leads a person to overeat and eventually to become obese?

Hunger and Obesity: What Causes Overeating?

Despite the signs of health consciousness—low-fat foods, health clubs, sports gear—it seems that there is an ever-growing tendency in Canada to be ever growing; a recent national survey suggested that 51 percent of Canadians are overweight (Health Canada, 1994). This proportion has been rising steadily in recent decades. Certain laws of nature cannot be broken, and unfortunately, one of these laws is that calories not expended will be stored as fat. Why are Canadians eating too much, too often? Are Canadians overweight because of junk food, time spent watching television, or not enough exercise? How do psychologists explain obesity? Two types of explanations are physiological and psychological.

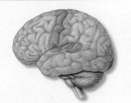

brain and behaviour
The Hunt for the Neurobiology of Eating

From diet pills to liposuction, North Americans are searching for an easy way out of obesity and their bad eating habits. On radio shows and in coffee shops, people talk about their desire for a quick weight control fix. Is such a possibility real? What if we could identify a brain centre that could be controlled by medication? What if obesity and its consequences could be avoided?

From a psychobiologist's point of view, obesity isn't just a case of bad eating habits. There has to be a brain mechanism involved, and the search for it has been exciting. Early brain researchers suggested the existence of specific feeding and satiety centres—of "switches" that signalled when to start and stop eating. Although a satiety centre may be located in the hypothalamus, researchers later discovered that many levels of the brain are involved, from subcortical structures such as the hypothalamus and amygdala to the highly evolved cortex (Roland, Li, & Morien, 1996).

Today, researchers are attempting to look at the neural foundations of eating through three principal techniques: surgery, neurochemistry, and direct measurement. Their aim is to discover all of the structures involved in eating behaviour so as to learn why we eat and overeat. The task is daunting.

The earliest research examined eating and brain mechanisms through surgical and lesioning techniques. Behaviour was evaluated after damage to selected sites of the brain was induced. The early research on satiety centres used surgical techniques; researchers damaged the hypothalamus, and eating behaviour was altered. These were exciting research findings because they linked brain structures to specific functions. What the early researchers did not realize, however, was that invasive surgical techniques disrupt not just a specific site, but connected ones as well. The idea of surgical "isolation" of a site was flawed.

To enhance site-specific precision, neurochemistry techniques were then developed. Neurotransmitters, agonists or antagonists (which enhance or oppose neural transmission, see Chapter 2, p. 47), are introduced to different brain locations—without surgical trauma or invasive cutting, to knock out specific sites and thereby establish and confirm links between structure and function. Although more accurate, like lesioning, too many other structures were affected regardless of how specific the damage was. As a technique neurochemistry offered little more than invasive surgery.

Over the last decade, the hunt for a technique to link structure to function was significantly enhanced as various direct measurements of brain tissue were made. Small probes are inserted into specific brain tissue of animals to allow for "online" monitoring of living cells (Roland, Li, & Morien, 1996). Even more encouraging, because it can be done with humans, is functional magnetic resonance imaging (fMRI; see Chapter 2, p. 60). Using fMRI, researchers can trace changes in

Physiological Explanations of Obesity. If you have an overweight parent, the likelihood of being overweight increases dramatically, even if you were thin as a youngster. Some researchers insist that the reason is genetic and that fixed behavioural and biological patterns are inherited (Bar-Or, 1998; Comuzzie & Allison, 1998). Researchers offer a number of biobehavioural explanations (Spiegelman et al., 1998), including homeostatic mechanisms (Woods et al., 1998), specific proteins (Hotamislgil et al., 1996), and lower metabolic rates (Laessle, Wurmser, & Pirke, 1997). In the 1990s, the scientific journals were awash with findings of an "obesity" gene, which was said to hold the key to overeating and obesity. Researchers suggested that the gene directs the production of a hormone that tells the brain how much fat is stored in the body; this information ultimately governs eating behaviour and energy expenditures (Puigserver et al., 1998). Researchers reported that if the protein product of the obesity gene was injected into animals, it caused the animals to lose weight and maintain weight loss. The research on obesity genes ultimately may lead to a pill that may help some individuals lose and maintain weight (Campfield, Smith, & Burn, 1998). However, for years researchers have found other physiological reasons for obesity—genetics may be just one explanation.

brain function while a person eats. The sections of the brain responsible for eating will show an increase in metabolism (blood flow), which ultimately will lead to a signal change in the fMRI image. As people grow hungry and eat, we can locate the corresponding brain activation. Such studies can de done with human beings and allow for alternating experimental conditions—for example, changes in hunger levels or changes in concentration of sugar levels in food in the same individual.

Through a combination of these three techniques researchers have been able to isolate brain mechanisms, structures, and substances involved in feeding behaviour. We now know

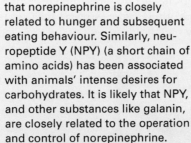

that norepinephrine is closely related to hunger and subsequent eating behaviour. Similarly, neuropeptide Y (NPY) (a short chain of amino acids) has been associated with animals' intense desires for carbohydrates. It is likely that NPY, and other substances like galanin, are closely related to the operation and control of norepinephrine.

Isolating a brain structure or neurotransmitter is just the beginning. Nearly any food affects eating behaviour, but so do other hormones. Insulin, for example, which helps the body to metabolize sugars, directly affects eating behaviour. As we saw in Chapter 2, insulin is a hormone secreted by the pancreas; it is released into the bloodstream when blood sugar (glucose) is present, to allow the blood sugar to be taken into the body's cells. Eating food that quickly increases blood sugar levels, such as candy, also triggers the pancreas to release insulin quickly. The body cells then quickly take in the blood sugar, and the blood sugar level once

again falls. Thus, a hungry person who consumes a candy bar generally finds that, after an initial feeling of relief from hunger, even greater hunger will rapidly recur. The blood sugar level is now low again, often even lower than before the person ate. Manipulation of insulin turns out to be a powerful mechanism of control. And neurotransmitters like serotonin, which can be stimulated through eating certain types of food (like chocolate), affect eating, mood, and depression. Depression, in turn, affects eating behaviours; some people eat when they are depressed, while others shy away from food.

What makes this complicated system even more perplexing is the knowledge that eating behaviours are affected by the hypothalamus, the amygdala, and various cortical locations. Each of the brain substances and hormones that researchers identify affects each one of these brain structures somewhat differently. What all of this means, to psychologists and to dieters, is that why we eat and when we eat is not simply a matter of "I see it, I want it," or "Just exercise a little willpower." People eat for a variety of complex psychological and biological reasons. The techniques of neurobiology are just beginning to help us understand its intricacy. ∎

One of the first psychologists to offer a physiological explanation was Richard Nisbett (1972), who proposed an explanation based on *fat cells*. He asserted that people are born with different numbers of fat cells and that the number of fat cells a person has determines the person's eating behaviour and propensity towards obesity. Body fat is stored in fat cells, so people born with many fat cells are more likely to be obese than those born with few fat cells. Although the number of fat cells a person has is genetically determined, the size of each cell is affected both by genetics and by nutritional experience early in life. Dieting, in this explanation, decreases only the *size*, not the *number*, of fat cells. Moreover, the body "wants" to maintain the size of fat cells at a constant level, so people who have shrunk the size of their fat cells by dieting will experience a constant sense of food deprivation. Thus, permanent weight loss becomes extremely difficult. This accounts for the finding that about two-thirds of people who lose weight gain it back within a year.

Closely associated with the fat cell explanation of obesity is some researchers' view that each person has a *set point*—a level of body weight that is maintained by the body. The central idea of the set point explanation is that the body seeks to maintain and will always reestablish a homeostatic weight. The set point, which differs from person to person, is determined by many factors, including genetics, early nutrition, current environment, and learned habits.

Further, some studies suggest that people can inherit both a tendency to overeat and a slow metabolism. A slow (or low) metabolism uses available energy (calories) from food efficiently; unused calories tend to be stored as fat. For example, the Pima Indians of Arizona are prone to obesity; 80 to 90 percent of the tribe's young adults are dangerously overweight. According to Ravussin and colleagues (Norman et al., 1998; Ravussin et al., 1988; Tataranni et al., 1997), who spent years researching their habits, the Pima have unusually low metabolisms. During any 24-hour period, the typical Pima (who is as active as the average American) burns about 80 calories less than is considered normal for his or her body size. Ravussin's view is that the Pima, whose ancestors spent generations in the desert, where they went through periods of famine, developed a metabolism that coped with on-again, off-again eating patterns. However, in the twentieth century the Pima abandoned their traditional diet (which was low in fat) and ate like other Americans. The Pima's genes, which had developed a disposition to being "thrifty" and storing fat, became a liability as the proportion of fat in their diet increased.

People don't have the luxury of choosing their genetic heritage, but that does not mean that those who inherit a predisposition towards obesity are condemned to become fat or to lead an otherwise unhealthy lifestyle. The body's natural predisposition and its molecular operation (Woods et al., 1998) work to keep weight the same—maintaining homeostasis. Therefore, attempts to lose weight through intake regulation alone (such as dieting) are prone to failure and tend to lead to what is called *yo-yo dieting*, or recurring cycles of dieting and weight gains. However, weight control—even small changes in one's set point—can be achieved through significant increases in physical activity.

Psychological Explanations of Obesity. Physiological make-up isn't the only important factor in eating behaviour. The social environment is rampant with food-oriented messages that have little to do with nutritional needs. Advertisements proclaim that merriment can be found at a restaurant or a supermarket. Parents coax good behaviour from their children by promising them desserts or snacks. Thus, eating acquires a significance that far exceeds its role in satisfying physiological needs: It serves as a rationale for social interaction, a means to reward good behaviour, and a way to fend off unhappy thoughts and reduce stress (Greeno & Wing, 1994).

Consider a man's attempts to maintain his weight after losing 75 pounds through diet and exercise. Suddenly, he notices food even more than before. Every time he sees food advertised on billboards or on television, he wants to eat. All of the social events he attends seemed to feature a delectable spread of appetizers, which he is tempted to sample in order to be "sociable." And whenever he becomes anxious, his first impulse is to seek the comfort of food. However, by separating eating behaviours linked to hunger from those that were learned emotional responses, he manages to control his eating behaviour and avoid gaining weight even five years later. Researchers continue to explore the causes of overeating. Their efforts have led to some interesting findings, especially when dieters are compared to non-dieters.

We know that the body seeks to maintain weight, to maintain a homeostatic position (Wood et al., 1998). We also know that we live in an environment that promotes excessive food intake and, although it encourages it, creates multiple opportunities to avoid physical activity. The problem is that the body has developed great mechanisms for maintaining weight gain, and weak mechanisms for shedding weight gain when it is not needed (Hill & Peters, 1998). Through the last five decades researchers have identified four key factors that contribute to overeating. First, food is readily and easily available—from drive-through windows to frozen meals. Second, portion sizes are growing ever bigger—fast food restaurants have super-size meals. Third, our diets are higher in fat than ever before—fat contains nearly twice the caloric intake per gram as proteins or carbohydrates. Fourth, most children and adults do not engage in regular, sustained physical activity. Put all of this together—low physical activity, eating too much, too often, of the wrong things—and the result is an overweight population that has trouble losing weight.

When researchers such as Stanley Schachter and colleagues (Schachter, Goldman, & Gordon, 1968) investigated eating patterns, they found evidence that led them to infer that the mere sight of food motivates overweight people to eat more than normal-weight people. They contended that the availability of food, its prominence, and other external cues tell individuals when to eat (too much, too fast, and too often), and obese people respond more readily to such cues than normal-weight individuals do. Schachter's work set off wide-ranging research into the psychological variables that cause overeating in the obese.

Differences between the eating habits of obese and normal-weight individuals exist; however, research shows that the differences are small and inconsistent (Rodin, 1981). The obese tend to be oversensitive to food cues, when compared to normal-weight individuals; furthermore, obese individuals underestimate their food intake (Laessle, Wurmser, & Pirke, 1997). Anyone who is on a diet will tell you that external cues trigger food cravings. But many obese individuals are nearly always on a diet, so it is not surprising that they constantly have food cravings. It may not be that the obese are more sensitive to external cues than normal-weight individuals, but rather that *those who are dieting* (which the obese often are) are more sensitive to such cues.

In the end, the unfortunate truth is that people who have lost weight often must take in fewer calories to maintain their weight than those who have never been obese. This means that formerly obese people have a particularly difficult time keeping their weight down. A cycle of dieting and regaining weight makes permanent weight loss difficult because the body adjusts itself to burn fewer calories after a weight loss (in order to make better use of the diminished resources, as in a famine). To make matters worse, even small disorders of the autonomic nervous system might play a role in keeping obese people fat (Klesges, Isbell, & Klesges, 1992) and genetics may play a stronger role than the environment in weight maintenance.

The latest research and assertions are forcing a critical evaluation of all previously collected data. They imply that physiological mechanisms may play a much larger role than psychological ones in eating behaviour. Today, there is no simple answer to the nature-versus-nurture question about obesity, and attempts to treat obesity must incorporate a "reasonable weight" that is based on aesthetic and health standards for the wide range of individuals with obesity problems. Such plans must incorporate biological and environmental factors as well as cognitive states—the thoughts that the obese have when they are overeating (Grilo & Shiffman, 1994).

Eating Disorders

Singer Anne Murray's daughter Dawn Langstroth has struggled with anorexia. In 1997, when she was 17 years old and 5 feet 9 inches tall, she weighed 120 pounds. In trying to lose weight to advance in her modelling career she had all but stopped eating, sometimes only drinking juice for days. Her skin was grey and her hair was falling out. After treatment in a Florida clinic she is now healthy but must monitor her condition carefully. Canadian ballet dancer Evelyn Hart also has spoken publicly about her eating disorder. Many dancers, models, and gymnasts must monitor their weight carefully—in some cases, this can lead to eating disorders.

Eating disorders are psychological disorders characterized by gross disturbances in eating behaviour and in the way individuals respond to food. Two important eating disorders are anorexia nervosa and bulimia nervosa. These disorders are very much culture-bound and Western diseases; other cultures have their own culture-bound disorders, but eating disorders such as anorexia nervosa and bulimia nervosa are found in wealthy, Western, industrialized societies. Eating disorders affect about 3 percent of women at some time during their lives.

Anorexia Nervosa. Anorexia nervosa, a starvation disease that affects as many as 40 out of every 10 000 young women in North America, is an eating disorder characterized by an obstinate and wilful refusal to eat. Individuals with the disorder, usually adolescent girls from middle-class families, have a distorted body

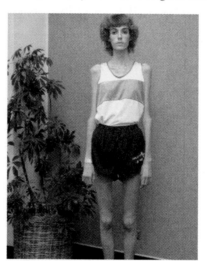

image. They perceive themselves as fat if they have any flesh on their bones or if they deviate from their idealized body image. They intensely fear being fat and relentlessly pursue thinness. The anorexic's refusal to eat eventually brings about emaciation and malnutrition (which may bring about a further distortion of body image). Victims can sustain permanent damage to their heart muscle tissue, sometimes resulting in death.

Many therapists believe that anorexia nervosa has strictly psychological origins. They cite poor mother–daughter relationships, excessively protective parents, other negative family interactions, and escapes from self-awareness as the main causes (Walters & Kendler, 1995). Others are exploring possible physiological contributions to the disorder (Walsh & Devlin, 1998), including the many changes taking place at puberty that might influence its emergence (Attie & Brooks-Gunn, 1989), as well as prejudice against the obese (Crandall, 1994). Some psychologists believe that people with eating disorders may lack a hormone that is thought to induce a feeling of fullness after a meal.

People with anorexia nervosa need a structured setting, and therapists often hospitalize them to help them regain weight. To ensure that the setting is reinforcing, hospital staff members are always present at meals. Individual and family therapy is provided. Clients are encouraged to eat and are rewarded for consuming specified quantities of food. Generally, psychotherapy is also necessary to help these people attain a healthy self-image and body weight. Even after treatment at well-known centres like Sheena's Place in Toronto, however, as many as 50 percent suffer relapses within a year.

Bulimia Nervosa. Bulimia nervosa is an eating disorder characterized by binge eating followed by purging. It tends to occur in normal-weight women with no history of anorexia nervosa. The bingeing (recognized by the person as being abnormal) is accompanied by a fear of not being able to stop eating. Individuals who engage in binge eating become fearful of gaining weight, and become preoccupied with how others see them (Striegel-Moore, Silberstein, & Rodin, 1993). Therefore, they often purge themselves of unwanted calories, mostly through vomiting and the use of laxatives and diuretics. Other methods include compulsive exercising and weight-reduction drugs. Bulimics often suffer from depression (Specker et al., 1994). The medical complications of bulimia are serious and include cardiovascular and gastrointestinal problems, menstrual irregularities, blood and hormone dysfunctions, muscular and skeletal problems, and sharp swings in mood and personality.

Men and women are affected by eating disorders in similar ways (Olivardia et al., 1995), but the ratio of female to male bulimics is 10 to 1. Researchers theorize that more women believe that fat is bad and thin is beautiful. Women of higher socioeconomic class are at greater risk of becoming bulimic, as are professionals whose weight is directly related to achievement, such as dancers, athletes, and models. Disharmonious family life and maladjusted parents who inflict psychological and physical abuse on a child are correlated with the incidence of bulimia—although there is by no means a causal relationship (Rorty, Yager, & Rossotto, 1994). Women with bulimia also have lower self-esteem than women who eat normally, and they may have experienced some kind of clinical depression in the past (Klingenspor, 1994). Reports of alcohol dependency and a family history of bulimia are sometimes reported (Garfinkel et al., 1997; Kozyk, Touyz, & Beumont, 1998).

Some bulimics eat as a means of lightening their mood, regulating tension, and escaping from self-awareness (Heatherton & Baumeister, 1991). After bingeing, however, they feel guilty. To lessen their guilt and the potential consequence of gaining weight, they purge themselves. Researchers believe that the purges reduce feelings of guilt. Some bulimics become so involved in food-related behaviours that they avoid contact with other people. The exact role of dieting in bulimia is unclear because many bulimics don't regularly engage in dieting (Lowe, Gleaves, & Murphy-Eberenz, 1998). The problems don't disappear completely when treated; one study found that after not being diagnosed as bulimic for an entire decade, women who had once been so diagnosed were much thinner than others in their communities (Sullivan et al., 1998).

Focus

Review

◆ What is the evidence that individuals are motivated to eat or drink because of a lack of food or fluid in the body? pp. 302–303
◆ What suggests that obesity may be gentically based, at least in part? pp. 304-306

Think Critically

◆ Individuals respond to food in different ways depending on the time of day. How might this factor have affected Schachter's research participants, causing obese and normal-weight participants to behave differently?
◆ If, as some researchers claim, there is a physiological basis to anorexia nervosa, why is it less prevalent in other cultures?

Sexual Behaviour: Physiology Plus Thought

When it was first reported that Prince Charles had had a long-standing affair with friend and confidant Camilla Parker-Bowles, the London tabloids had a field day. American President Bill Clinton's affairs have had a similar effect in the United States. People's preoccupation with the sex lives of national figures indicates that they are fascinated with and often define themselves in terms of their sexuality—a type of motivation that, unlike physiologically based hunger, is not necessary to sustain life. So we immediately see an important difference between sexual behaviour and activities like food seeking. The sexual behaviour of lower organisms is controlled largely by their physiological and hormonal systems. In contrast, in human beings the sex drive is to a great extent under psychological control.

This means that not only physiology, especially sex hormones, but ideas, past behaviours, emotions, expectations, and goals all influence the sexual behaviour of human beings. The relative contributions of these factors vary. For some people, sights, sounds, and smells are sexual initiators, triggers for sexually motivated behaviour. For others, thoughts, feelings, and fantasy either initiate or in many cases satisfy sexual impulses. Men and women respond differently, the old respond differently than the young, the religious background of individuals affects their sexual behaviour, and the culture in which a person is raised has profound influences. Western ideas about sexuality differ significantly from Eastern approaches, and even within Western cultures there exists great diversity. For example, Europeans are more open and expressive sexually than are Canadians. And the British find sexual indiscretions among politicians more outrageous and titillating than do Canadians, who find ethical scandals less entertaining. Keeping in mind this cultural diversity, let us first look at some of the initiators of sexual behaviour, at the physiology of sexual behaviour, and then at the sexual behaviours in which human beings engage.

What Initiates the Sex Drive?

Hardly a day goes by that you are not bombarded with sexually suggestive advertisements. Perfume ads abound in magazines; attractive, and often half-clad, models sell cars. Youthful, sexually desirable men and women sell sports equipment; even toothpaste is sold by alluring women and men. Advertisers use learning principles to pair attractive people and situations with their products in the hope that their products will assume an arousing glamour—and to hint that if you use their product, you may become as alluring as their models. The advertisers are seeking to initiate activity—buying activity—by activating the sexual drive. They know, of course, that people's thoughts, rather than their hormones, direct buying behaviour. But hormones do play a vital role in sexual behaviour.

Sex Hormones. Sexual behaviour in human beings is in part under hormonal control, and the sex hormones differ for men and women. In males, the testes are the principal producer of androgens, the male sex hormones. In females, the ovaries are the principal producer of estrogens, the female sex hormones. (In reality there are many different male and female sex hormones, but we can refer to them generically as androgens and estrogens.) The release of androgens (especially testosterone) and estrogens (especially estradiol) signals and accelerates the onset of the secondary sex characteristics in developing teenagers. Once they are postpubescent, their bodies produce sufficient levels of androgens and estrogens to create a desire and willingness to engage in sexual behaviours—if they choose to. In men, androgens (especially testosterone) stay at pretty much the same level on a day-to-day basis; in women, estrogen levels vary throughout the menstrual cycle, and when the menstrual cycle ceases at menopause, estrogen levels fall. Both men and women can be sexually receptive and active regardless of their hormone level.

People share with animals a hormonally based sexual urge that is determined, in part, by brain structures such as the hypothalamus (Swaab & Hofman, 1995). But in animals, hormones exert profound effects on behaviour, activating an organized set of sexual responses. Most of these responses in animals are under direct hormonal control and are not exhibited without hormonal activation. For example, if the hormone-generating testes of male rats are removed, the animals show a marked decrease in sexual activity. Similarly, most female animals are sexually responsive *only* when hormones are released into the bloodstream (when they are "in heat"). Human beings, on the other hand, can choose whether to respond sexually to encounters at any given time. In fact, in human beings the removal of hormone-generating organs may not affect sexual behaviour at all (depending on the person's age), because sexual motivation is influenced by social and psychological factors as much as by physiological ones—if not more so.

Sights, Sounds, Smells, and Fantasy. In animals, a female may show her sexual receptivity by releasing pheromones; this acts as a trigger for sexual activity (see Chapter 3, page 105). Other times, a suggestive movement or circling around a nest may signal receptivity and will trigger sexual behaviour in another animal. However, because they are not so directly under hormonal control, human beings can be aroused, become interested, and seek out or be responsive to sexual stimulation because of the sight of something sexual, an erotic sound, or the smell of a familiar and arousing scent. Thought plays an enormous role in the sexual behaviour of human beings; people's thoughts, fantasies, emotions, and images initiate and activate sexual desire and activity.

Sexual Response Cycle

Excitement phase: The first phase of the sexual response cycle, during which there are initial increases in heart rate, blood pressure, and respiration.

Vasocongestion: In the sexual response cycle, engorgement of the blood vessels, particularly in the genital area, due to increased blood flow.

Plateau phase: The second phase of the sexual response cycle, during which the sexual partners are preparing for orgasm, autonomic nervous system activity increases, and there is further vasocongestion.

Orgasm phase: The third phase of the sexual response cycle, during which autonomic nervous system activity reaches its peak and muscle contractions occur throughout the body, but especially in the genital area, in spasms.

Resolution phase: The fourth phase of the sexual response cycle, during which the body naturally returns after orgasm to its resting, or normal, state.

When human beings become sexually aroused, they go through a series of four phases (stages). The phases, which together are known as the *sexual response cycle*, are the excitement phase, the plateau phase, the orgasm phase, and the resolution phase.

The **excitement phase** is the first phase of the cycle, during which there are initial increases in heart rate, blood pressure, and respiration. A key characteristic of this phase is **vasocongestion**—engorgement of the blood vessels, particularly in the genital area, due to increased blood flow. In women, the breasts and clitoris swell, the vaginal lips expand, and vaginal lubrication increases; in men, the penis becomes erect. The excitement phase is anticipatory and may last from a few minutes to a few hours. Physical contact, fantasy, or even smells may initiate it.

The **plateau phase** is the second phase of the sexual response cycle, during which the sexual partners are preparing for orgasm. Autonomic nervous system activity, such as the heart rate, increases. In women, the clitoris withdraws and the vagina becomes engorged and fully extended; in men, the penis becomes fully erect, turns a darker colour, and may secrete a bit of fluid, which may contain sperm.

The **orgasm phase** is the third phase of the sexual response cycle, during which autonomic nervous system activity reaches its peak and muscle contractions occur throughout the body, but especially in the genital area, in spasms. An *orgasm* is the peak of sexual activity. In men, muscles throughout the reproductive system contract to help expel semen; in women, muscles surrounding the outer vagina contract. Although men experience only one orgasm during each sexual response cycle, women are capable of multiple orgasms. An orgasm lasts only a few seconds and is an all-or-none activity; once a threshold for orgasm is reached, the orgasm occurs.

The **resolution phase** is the fourth phase of the sexual response cycle, during which the body naturally returns to its resting, or normal, state. This return takes from one to several minutes, varying considerably from person to person. During this phase, men usually are unable to achieve an erection for some amount of time, called the *refractory period*.

Like many other physiological events, the sexual response cycle is subject to considerable variation. Some people go through a lengthy plateau phase; others may have a longer resolution phase.

Human Sexual Behaviour

While our culture is saturated with sexually suggestive advertisements and sexually explicit movies and television, it shows considerable reluctance to scientifically examine and talk about sexual behaviour. Efforts to examine sexuality in a systematic way often are viewed with scepticism, supported by the general belief that the government (or the researchers it funds) have no place in the bedrooms of the nation.

Sex Surveys: What's Normal? Despite this reluctance to look at data, over the years various sexual surveys, attitude questionnaires, and in-depth interviews have been conducted. The most famous study was conducted by biologist Alfred Kinsey and his colleagues (1948, 1953) in the United States. The Kinsey study used to be the main source of information about human sexual attitudes and behaviour. This was unfortunate, because while quite comprehensive, the study was not representative of the population; data were collected in face-to-face interviews with a sample of largely white, middle-class people from the U.S. east coast and the Midwest. In addition, the interviewers often coaxed answers from participants in a belligerent way; this was hardly dispassionate, careful science. But contemporary researchers such as Morton Hunt (1974), Masters, Johnson, and Kolodny (1994), and Laumann and colleagues (1994, 1998) have now extended Kinsey's work.

When the Kinsey studies were first published, the public was shocked. The data regarding homosexuality seemed incredible. Kinsey and his colleagues received considerable criticism—initially for the data they produced, more recently for their methods. Now, after more than four decades, it is clear that Kinsey's statistics were often accurate but in some cases may have overrepresented or underrepresented contemporary sexual behaviour. For example, the Kinsey study may have overrepresented the number of men who were homosexual (10 percent). The most striking example of underrepresentation may be the figures representing the premarital sexual behaviour of women. While Kinsey reported some premarital sexual behaviour in women, it was, in fact, far more frequent. Since the Kinsey days, major changes in sexual behaviour have taken place and continue to occur. The fear of AIDS during the last decade has caused young men and women to alter their sexual behaviour; among individuals in their twenties, for example, the number of sexual partners people are willing to have has decreased. Despite historic reports of differences on many measures, men and women are becoming more alike in sexual attitudes and behaviours (Oliver & Hyde, 1993). Let's examine some of the patterns.

In general, reports about sexual practices show that individuals engage in sexual behaviours more frequently when they are younger than when they are older. For example, the frequency of intercourse decreases from the early twenties to the fifties or sixties (Call, Sprecher, & Schwartz, 1997). Similarly, the duration spent in any specific sexual activity decreases with increasing age. Within couples in Western culture, patterns of sexual practices are predictable; elements of sexual activity, particularly foreplay, rarely occur in isolation. One behaviour, such as petting, often or at least usually precedes another, such as intercourse. Compared with other industrialized countries, Canada has a lower median age of onset of sexual activity (Durex, 1998). While our sex lives are predictable, and not as active as many assume, they are reported by most people as being satisfactory (Laumann et al., 1994).

Laumann's study of sexual practices in the United States is the most recent and most comprehensive North American study of the last four decades. In it, 3432 men and women aged 18 to 59 in randomly selected households throughout the country were administered questionnaires and face-to-face interviews. The results showed that men and women are more likely today than in the 1940s to have intercourse before marriage and that there has been a slow and steady decrease in the age of first intercourse (see also Feldman et al., 1997; Wadsworth et al., 1996). Men think about sex more often than women; about 54 percent of men think about sex daily, compared to only 19 percent of women. Interestingly, married men and women have more sex than do non-married young people—shattering a myth that the young and footloose are the most sexually active. Only one-third of people aged 18 to 59 have sex with a partner as often as twice a week. Many behavioural scientists found the results of Laumann's study predictable—but there were some surprises. Most women (90 percent) and most men (75 percent) reported that they had not had any extramarital sexual affairs (Laumann et al., 1994, p. 214). This may reflect in part a fear of sexually transmitted diseases; in any event, our society is not as sexually promiscuous as daytime soap operas would have you believe. Another finding that surprised some researchers was that only 5.3 percent of men and 3.5 percent of women had had homosexual intercourse with someone since puberty. More importantly, only 2.8 percent of men and 1.4 percent of women identified themselves as exclusively homosexual. The Laumann percentages are substantially less than the

10 percent that was reported by Kinsey in the 1950s, and they have been substantiated with similar estimates from other researchers (Cameron & Cameron, 1998; Sell, Wells, & Wypij, 1995). There is some uncertainty, though, about the reliability of the methods used to collect this information. A recent study done at the University of Calgary, for example (Bagely & Tremblay, 1998), suggests that when given the opportunity to respond via computer in a manner that guarantees anonymity, the percentage of males indicating a homosexual orientation moves up towards the 10 percent originally reported by Kinsey.

A key approach that the Laumann study used was to define sexuality and sexual behaviour within the context of how people live. The researchers found that individuals have sex with people they know and live with (most often spouses) and that when people are sexually active, they think about and desire sex more than do individuals who are not sexually active. Further, when people do engage in an extramarital affair, it is usually not a one-night stand with a stranger met on a train but a relationship with a person they know (Wadsworth et al., 1996). The Laumann study shows that contemporary sexual behaviour has changed. Today, people express their sexuality more often and more openly—and seek to understand their own feelings and behaviour. Laumann's team (Michael et al., 1998) reports a wide variety in sexual behaviours, especially compared with other cultures. People today also are paying attention to sexually transmitted diseases, especially to the spread of AIDS, a topic discussed in Chapter 13; nevertheless, risk-taking sexual behaviours, such as not using condoms, continues at disconcertingly high rates (Downey & Landry, 1997). Further, people today are confronting the issue of sexual orientation more forthrightly, at least more than in previous decades.

Sexual Orientation. Sexual orientation is the direction of one's sexual interests. A person with a *heterosexual orientation* has an erotic attraction to and preference for members of the opposite sex; an individual with a *homosexual orientation* has an erotic attraction to and preference for members of his or her same sex. A *bisexual orientation* is an erotic attraction to members of both sexes. Before the Kinsey studies, people were considered either heterosexual or homosexual; but Kinsey introduced the idea of a continuum of sexual behaviours: from exclusively homosexual behaviours through some homosexual behaviours, to mostly heterosexual behaviours, to exclusively heterosexual behaviours. Kinsey recognized, and opened the door for other researchers to recognize, that a homosexual encounter does not make a person homosexual. Also, a person may have a homosexual or bisexual orientation without ever having had a homosexual sexual experience. It is thus an overgeneralization and a mistake to label a person as to sexual orientation based solely on a single, or even multiple, sexual behaviours (Haslam, 1997).

The Kinsey report startled psychologists when it announced a high frequency of homosexual behaviour among men (37 percent) and suggested that 1 in 10 men was primarily homosexual in orientation. Some studies since have suggested that the numbers may be lower, placing them at about 2.5 to 3 percent (Laumann et al., 1994). There is still a stigma attached to gays living openly, and as such research reports must be interpreted carefully. As a study done at the University of Calgary (Bagely & Tremblay, 1998) indicates, these estimates can be significantly affected by how the questions about sexual orientation are asked, and the true figure for urban populations actually may be close to 10 percent.

The causes of homosexuality have been debated for decades, and the argument has developed into a classic nature-versus-nurture debate. The nurture side asserts that homosexual behaviour is under voluntary control to a great extent, that it is learned, and that it can be changed by means of effective, consistent, and long-term therapy. Bem (1996) developed a theory that suggested that childhood temperament leads to atypical gender activities and preferences. This is followed by feelings of difference from same-sex peers; these feelings then lead to arousal and heightened

Focus

Focus

Review

◆ What evidence exists to suggest that thought plays an especially important role in human sexual behaviour? pp. 310–311

◆ Briefly summarize the nature and nurture sides of the debate about the development of a homosexual orientation. pp. 313–314

Think Critically

◆ Should the federal government engage in or fund studies of sexual behaviour? Why or why not?

◆ Many scientific discoveries concerning genetics raise ethical questions: For example, should parents be allowed to pre-screen their unborn child for a genetic marker for homosexuality? Can you think of other examples?

autonomic activity. Bem suggests that such arousal by people you are not like—the exotic—leads to sexual arousal, and so, the exotic becomes erotic. Bem's ideas have not yet been put to experimental tests. Bem and others who support a nurture view see a basic flaw in conclusions from genetic studies, family studies, and research on brain chemistry—they assert that researchers have mixed up the causes of sexual orientation with the effects (Byne, 1994).

On the nature side are those who assert that homosexuality is indeed inborn, fixed, and genetically determined. They cite data showing that homosexual men and women knew when they were young children that they were "different" and point out that attempts to change gay men and women through therapy, prayer, and drugs are mostly ineffective. Further, recent studies isolating brain structures, genes, and familial patterns of homosexuality (even among twins separated at birth) increasingly lend support to a nature argument (LeVay & Hamer, 1994). The weight of the evidence leans towards the physiological—or nature—side of the debate, though it is important to remember that this evidence is correlational in nature and therefore causal inferences should be made very cautiously. Twin studies show a high concordance rate for homosexuality among fraternal and identical twins. In extended families, gay men tend to come from families where there are many other gay men; further, Hamer found genetic evidence associated with gay men (Hamer et al., 1993). High levels of specific hormones have been found at birth among babies who later became male homosexuals. Lastly, both Simon LeVay (1991) and Swaab and Hoffman (1995) found that portions of the hypothalamus of gay men differ from those of heterosexual men. The impact of this evidence has been profound. Gay men and lesbians are leaving mental health counselling, seeking civil rights protection, and feeling better about themselves and their sexuality.

Achievement: A Social Need

P ersonality psychologists such as Henry Murray assert that key events and situations in people's environment determine behaviour. Murray used the word *press* for the way these environmental situations may motivate a person (Murray, 1938). The environment may *press* an individual to excel at sports, be a loving caretaker to a grandparent, or achieve great wealth. The *press* of poverty may produce a social need for financial security; it therefore may cause a person to work hard, train, and become educated to achieve wealth.

The most notable theories for measuring the results of press are expectancy theories that focus specifically on the **need for achievement**—a social need that directs people to strive constantly for excellence and success. According to such achievement theories, people engage in behaviours that satisfy their desires for success, mastery, and fulfilment. Tasks not oriented towards these goals are not motivating and either are not undertaken or are performed without energy or commitment. There may be even more negative effects when people feel that making an effort is useless.

One of the leaders in early studies of achievement motivation was David C. McClelland, whose early research focused on the idea that people have strong social motives for achievement (McClelland, 1958). McClelland showed that achievement

Need for achievement: A social need that directs people to strive constantly for excellence and success.

motivation is learned in an individual's home environment during childhood. Adults with a high need for achievement had parents who stressed excellence and who provided physical affection and emotional rewards for high achievement. These individuals also generally walked early, talked early, and had a high need for achievement even in elementary school (e.g., Teevan & McGhee, 1972). A high need for achievement is most pronounced in first-born children, perhaps because parents typically have more time to give them direction and praise. It is also especially evident in cultures, for example in many Asian cultures, that stress achievement-related activities and foster a fear of academic failure in children (Eaton & Dembo, 1997).

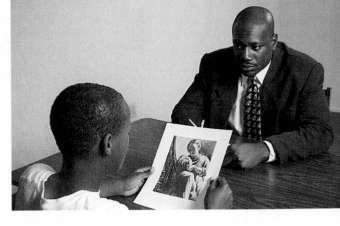

Achievement motives often are measured in terms of scores derived from an analysis of the thought content of imaginative stories. Early studies of people's need for achievement used the *Thematic Apperception Test (TAT)*. In this test, people are shown scenes with no captions and vague themes, which are thus open to interpretation. The test takers are instructed not to think in terms of right or wrong answers but to answer four basic questions for each scene:

1. What is happening?
2. What has led up to this situation?
3. What is being thought?
4. What will happen next?

Using a complex scoring system, researchers analyze participants' descriptions of each scene. They have found that persons with a high need for achievement tell stories that stress success, getting ahead, and competition (Spangler, 1992).

With tests such as the TAT, a researcher can quickly discern which individuals have a high need for achievement and which have a low need. For example, Lowell (1952) found that when he asked participants to rearrange scrambled letters (such as *wtse*) to construct a meaningful word (*west*), subjects with a low need for achievement improved only slightly at the task over successive testing periods. In contrast, participants who scored high in the need for achievement showed greater ongoing improvement over several periods of testing (see Figure 9.5). The researchers reasoned that, when presented with a complex task, persons with a high need for achievement find new and better ways of performing the task as they practise it, whereas those with a low need for achievement try no new methods. People with a high need for achievement constantly strive towards excellence and better performance; they have developed a belief in their self-efficacy and in the importance of effort in determining performance (Carr, Borkowski, & Maxwell, 1991; McClelland, 1961).

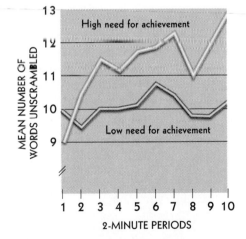

FIGURE 9.5
Performance on a Scrambled-Letter Task
The graph shows performance on a scrambled-letter task for successive two-minute periods. Performance is affected by a person's overall approach to achievement-related tasks. Participants with a low need for achievement improved overall; however, those with a high need for achievement improved even more.

(Based on data from Lowell, 1952.)

The need for achievement seems to be closely related to the amount of risk people are willing to take. Some researchers claim that children exposed to praise are likely to be more achievement-oriented and thus willing to take on higher levels of risk. To test this idea, Canavan-Gumpert (1977) presented first-grade and sixth-grade girls in a New York suburban school with math problems, then praised them for correct answers and criticized them for incorrect answers. After a practice task in which they were praised or criticized, the girls chose problems at one of eight levels of difficulty. The praised students had more optimistic expectations, higher standards, and

Focus

Review

◆ Define *need for achievement*, and explain how psychologists measure it. pp. 314–315
◆ What is a self-fulfilling prophecy? p. 316

Think Critically

◆ Do you think that second- and third-born children have needs that are different from or greater than those of first-born children? What might those needs be?

greater confidence about their future performance. They chose problems at the highest level of difficulty, accepting the risk of failure. The criticized students were dissatisfied with their performance and chose problems at the lowest difficulty level. The most important finding of this study is that praise and criticism directly affected girls' risk-taking behaviour and, ultimately, their need for achievement.

The goals people set and the amount of risk they are willing to take also are affected by the kind of needs that motivate them, their experiences, and even their moods (Hom & Arbuckle, 1988). The expression *self-fulfilling prophecy* suggests that those who expect to succeed will do so and those who don't expect to succeed won't. Expectations for success and failure can influence the outcome of an effort if those expectations help shape the person's behaviour (Elliott & Dweck, 1988). A teacher who expects a student to fail, for example, may treat the student in ways that increase the likelihood of the student's failure; things tend to turn out just the way the teacher expected (or prophesied) they would. Expectancy thus becomes a key component in explaining behaviour, especially in people with a high need for achievement. For example, a person pushed towards success by parents, drama instructors, or sports coaches may develop a high need for achievement; after positive experiences, such an individual typically will set challenging but attainable performance goals (Dweck & Leggett, 1988).

Emotion

Wildly popular, strikingly beautiful, and highly controversial, Princess Diana led a life of fairy tales, but was tragically killed in an automobile accident in 1997. People's responses to her sudden death were intense; worldwide, flowers overflowed in the streets outside British embassies; hundreds of thousands lined the streets of London to solemnly honour Diana and her family. People were motivated by an internal need to express their grief and show support to Diana's family; letters were written, flowers continued to pour in, and tears were shed.

People were saddened, and yet their grief energized many to donate time and money to charities that Diana had sponsored.

That motivation and emotion are interconnected should come as no surprise. Grief causes people to engage in acts of kindness. Anger can cause you to hurl an object across a room or to lash out at a friend. Happiness can make you smile all day long or stop to help a motorist with a flat tire. Fear can electrify you and make your legs pump faster as you sprint down a dark, shadowy alley. Although emotions, including love, joy, and fear, can motivate behaviour, these emotional states and categories remain fuzzy (Rosch, 1978). As *Experiencing Psychology* shows, even such a seemingly universal state as happiness has yet to be fully understood.

experiencing psychology

Happy Days

So much of our lives are fraught with tension; as children we are on a schedule—get to the bus on time, go to soccer lessons, do homework, go to church. We then want to get into university, land the right job, find the perfect partner. We seek the right house, neighbourhood, and church affiliation. And the list goes on. In therapy, psychologists find that people just want to be happy, to have some joy in their lives. Nevertheless, as a topic of study, happiness has received relatively little attention—at least compared with fear, anger, depression, and schizophrenia.

What is happiness? Is it tranquillity, satisfaction, joy, or contentment? Psychologists tend to refer to happiness as a state of subjective well-being, a person's evaluation of his or her life. Such evaluations are both cognitive, realistic judgments of facts (wealth or health, for example) and affective or feeling-based (pleasant or unpleasant reaction to reality). Most people report fairly positive subjective well-being—they are happy (Veenhoven, 1993)—despite the fact that objective measures of their situation often show them to be disadvantaged economically (Diener & Diener, 1996). People worldwide report overall happiness in work, leisure, and marriage, with the exception of the very poorest societies. Happy people tend to be optimistic, have high self-esteem, feel good, and sleep well; happiness seems unrelated to some variables that many people think are important—age, gender, ethnicity, educational level, financial status, and physical attractiveness.

Like all things human, there is variation; some people are happier than others. The happiest individuals have close personal relations with other people, are involved in their work, are well rested, and are goal-oriented (Aron & Aron, 1997; Meyers

& Diener, 1995). When people are happy, fluctuations in their lives, financial or otherwise, tend to make little difference. Happy people, whether rich or poor, seem to have a stable set of feelings about their situations, so that an infusion of money or financial setbacks, for example, does not tend to change their level of happiness. Research shows that as people's financial and other circumstances improve, their happiness levels—their subjective well-being—remains stable (Diener, 1998). People adapt to new levels of wealth; they eat better, wear better clothes, and live in bigger houses—but they come to accept those things, so their relative level of subjective well-being stays the same. Furthermore, as people adapt to new levels of health or wealth, they remember the past and recognize that others are less well off, and this too makes people feel happier.

Perhaps subjective well-being is randomly distributed or perhaps it is distributed among people, as is height, such that very few people are extremely short or tall and very few people are extremely miserable or ecstatic about life. Lykken & Tellegen (1996) make such a biologically based argument; they speculate (p. 189): "It may be that trying to be happier is as futile as trying to be taller and therefore is counterproductive." Although most people are happy, they argue that this is genetically determined and that individual differences in happiness are a matter of chance.

Still, people *want* to be happy; in fact, above all other things—money, fame,

even health—people seek happiness. According to psychologist Mihaly Csikszentmihalyi (1997) (pronounced CHICK-sent-me-high-ee), with so many emotional responses available, happiness can be achieved only if people find *flow*. Flow occurs when a person's skills are engaged in overcoming a challenge that is reasonable. When people are engaged in activities, often with friends or family, they feel less self-conscious, they feel strong, and hours pass by in minutes. From Csikszentmihalyi's view, happiness follows from flow, from engagement. Whether a physician or a clerk in a department store, an individual can engage with other people, show interest, understand the impact of his or her job, or life for that matter, on others. Csikszentmihalyi argues that each of us can transform our lives, find flow, and then achieve happiness by complete engagement with what we do and with whom we do it.

Although it is true that happiness stays pretty stable over life and that most people report being happy, most psychologists, like Csikszentmihalyi, remain optimistic that happiness can be increased through personal striving, maintenance of close relationships, and a positive attitude (e.g., DeNeve & Cooper, 1998). They argue that if you can be positive you can brighten your life, other people's lives, and the human condition. In a way, psychology is an optimistic profession; psychologists unabashedly admit to this bias. We don't assume that our lives are fixed and that trying to do or be better is counterproductive. ■

What Is Emotion?

The word *emotion* is an umbrella term referring to a wide range of subjective states, such as love, fear, sadness, and excitement. We all have emotions, talk about them, and agree on what represents them; but this agreement is not scientific. The psychological investigation of emotion has led to a more precise definition. Most psychologists acknowledge that emotion consists of three elements: feelings, physiological responses, and behaviours. An **emotion** is a subjective response (feeling), usually accompanied by a physiological change, which is often interpreted by an individual and then readies the individual for some action that is associated with a change in behaviour. People cry when they are sad, have increased energy when they are excited, and breathe faster, sweat, feel nauseated, and salivate less (causing a dry mouth) when they are afraid. Some physiological changes precede an emotional response. For example, just before an automobile crashes, the people involved show physiological arousal, muscle tension, and avoidance responses—that is, they brace themselves in anticipation. Other changes are evident only after an emotion-causing event. It is only after the auto accident that people shake with fear, disbelief, or rage.

Emotions are often sharp and automatic and evident early in life. A loud noise scares people and a warm touch is likely to soothe. Such events create physiological changes and people often respond to these changes by altering other aspects of their behaviour. When they are startled, they may scream. If they are injured, they may become angry and seek revenge or retribution. When they are in love, they may act tenderly towards others. In some situations, people respond automatically; in others, they think about acting out their feelings but may not express them in directly observable ways. Emotional expressions sometimes seem contradictory; consider Juliet's claim that "parting is such sweet sorrow." Although emotions may seem to be written all over people's faces, appearances can be deceiving and difficult to interpret.

Psychologists focus on different aspects of emotional behaviour. The earliest researchers catalogued and described basic emotions (Bridges, 1932; Wundt, 1896). Others tried to discover the physiological bases of emotion (Bard, 1934). Still others focused on how people perceive bodily movements and on how they convey emotions to others through nonverbal mechanisms such as gestures or eye contact (Ekman, 1992). We have learned that people experience the same *kinds* of emotions, but their intensity and quality vary. One person's sense of joy is different from another's. Thus, emotions have a private, personal, and unique component. This subjective element is called *feelings*. Subjective feelings are difficult to measure, so most researchers focus on the physiological and behavioural aspects of emotion. This focus tends to shift research from the internal process to action or readiness for action. Researchers are studying a range of observable and measurable aspects of emotions, such as whether one hemisphere of the brain dominates emotion (R. J. Davidson, 1992); the biochemical components of emotions, including blood glucose levels and hormone changes (Baum, Grunberg, & Singer, 1992); physiological responses such as heart rate and blood pressure; and behavioural responses such as smiling and crying.

Feelings, Physiology, and Behaviour. Psychologists' definition of emotion has three central elements: feelings, physiology, and behavioural responses. Each of these has been examined extensively.

When we hear a loud noise and are startled, we often freeze up. When surprised by friends with a birthday cake, we may be delighted. When kissed by a loved one, we feel soothed. Over the years researchers have tried to identify the "basic" emotional expressions of feeling. But such cataloguing is difficult because strong cultural expectations are placed on emotional responses; fear can be praised or punished in various cultures and as a child we may learn to hide our "basic" emotions. One noted researcher (Izard, 1977) isolated 10 such basic emotions (joy, interest, surprise, sadness, anger, disgust, contempt, fear, shame, and guilt). Different accounts of emotion emerge every few years, adding or subtracting, for one reason or another, one or two emotional states (e.g., Kelner & Buswell, 1997). Among psychologists the most widely studied emotion has been fear, largely because fear has a strong physiological basis and is evident among all primates.

In many of the early studies of emotion, fear was studied both behaviourally and physiologically. Behaviourally, fear is evident in children and adults; in fact, it is the principal symptom of maladjusted people. People who are depressed and anxious report feeling afraid. They are afraid of life, work, taking action, and even inaction. The maladjusted fear punishment, and often success. Fear leads to worry and anxiety and a cycle of inaction.

Recent research has revealed that physiologically, the amygdala, within the limbic system, is crucial to fear. That is, when the amygdala is damaged, removed, or chemically altered with drugs, fear responses are altered. Fear can be initiated by stimulating the amygdala, and associated symptoms can be initiated or suppressed with its alteration. The amygdala sits close within the brain and has loose connections to the hippocampus; in human beings, when the amygdala or the hippocampus is altered, people may show fear but not know why, or they may recognize the fear but not show emotional reactions. LeDoux (1996) shows that subcortical amygdala responses seem automatic, but are, in fact, tied to the more complex memory systems that tell people about the past, the present, and how to interpret physiological arousal.

Behaviourally, psychologists have recognized that facial expressions provide reliable clues to people's feelings—with or without studying physiology. Facial expressions are easily observed and interpreted by others and are thought of as an accurate index of a person's emotional states. People are extremely good at detecting changes in facial expressions (Edwards, 1998). There are asymmetries in facial expressions in both infants and adults, and adults can easily discern those differences. Best and Queen (1989) found that the left side of the face (controlled by the right side of the brain in most people) may be more expressive than the right side of the face, especially in adults (Rothbart, Taylor, & Tucker, 1989), and research shows that upper portions of the face may be more expressive than lower portions (Asthana & Mandal, 1997). Because the right side of the face may be more readily under the control of the left side of the brain, people may be able to inhibit right-face expression more easily than left-face expression. Nevertheless, although facial expressions (on either side) are good indicators of emotion, they are only indicators; a happy expression or a turned-down mouth can mask real emotions. For a demonstration that emotions are both easy and difficult to read, see Figure 9.6.

People also display emotion through gestures, body language, and voice tone and volume (Izard & Saxton, 1988). Examples include a lowered head, shaking fists, and laughter, as well as clenched teeth, limpness, and loss of energy. The autonomic nervous system responds differently to differences among emotions (Levenson, 1992). Researchers have studied the smiling responses of infants, children, and adults by examining when and under what conditions smiling is evoked and then lost (Carlson, Gantz, & Masters, 1983). Researchers also have conducted cross-cultural studies of smiling (Levenson et al., 1992) and have found commonalties in what brings about emotional responses such as smiling, although not all researchers find responses that are the same (Ekman, 1992) or that occur to the same extent (Pittam et al., 1995). Most emotional responses are expressed cross-culturally, but they vary in degree; while anthropologist Ruth Benedict characterized Japanese culture as a shame culture and Canada and the United States as guilt cultures, it is crucial to note that she overstated the case. The Japanese know guilt, and we know shame; the guilt/shame distinction is not an either/or distinction, but rather a gradation of emotional response (Heider, 1994).

The expression of emotion is affected by context and by subtle variables. Facial characteristics are important; people prefer more feminine faces in both men and women—the Leonardo DiCaprio look—and this is a powerful determinant of attractiveness (Perrett et al., 1998). But looks are only part of the story. For example, we have all stood in lines at a grocery store and observed the behaviour of the clerks to different customers. Psychologists have, in fact, studied the emotional

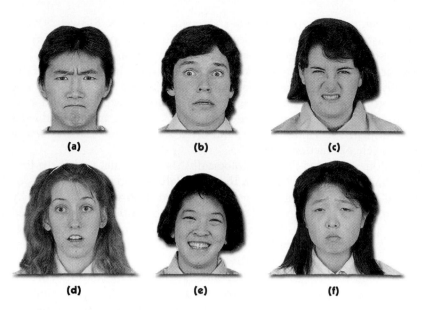

FIGURE 9.6
Recognizing and Naming Emotions
Look carefully at the six photographs. Which of the following six emotions is portrayed in each photo?

1. Happiness   3. Fear   5. Surprise
2. Sadness   4. Anger   6. Disgust

Answers: (a) 4; (b) 3; (c) 6; (d) 5; (e) 1; (f) 2

expressions of store clerks and their responses to customers. In one study (Rafaeli, 1989), a range of variables was considered: the clerk's gender, the wearing of a smock with a nametag on it, the presence of other clerks, and the customer's gender. Although the results were complicated, the emotional expressions of clerks were affected by nearly all of the variables. Female clerks displayed positive emotions more often than male clerks, male customers received positive emotional responses more often than female customers, and clerks who were made especially aware of their role (because they were wearing smocks) were more expressive than other clerks. Complex emotional behaviour cannot be explained by one simple variable such as gender or dress.

Can We Control Emotions? Psychologists know that physiological arousal from one event can lead to enhanced emotional arousal at another—they call this excitation transfer. Does this happen without awareness? People are not passive—that is, they do not respond automatically to environmental or internal stimuli—and they can learn to control emotional expression or hold in their rage or excitement. This view asserts that people manage or determine their emotional states in purposeful ways by constantly evaluating their environment and feelings. Through this appraisal, they alter their level of arousal.

Arousal is an essential component in emotion, as we've seen, and researchers show that people can use cognitive means to control their arousal level and therefore their emotions. Even young infants show some forms of emotional restraint and control, and an infant's control of emotion continues to develop, especially at the end of the first year (Kopp, 1989).

Central to the idea of arousal affecting emotion is the concept that people can "read" or evaluate biological signals in their own body. People learn to evaluate their arousal, understand what it means, and use that information to modulate their response. Understanding the flush of sexual excitement can lead to a variety of behaviours; understanding the adrenalin rush of a challenge to a fight can lead to other behaviour. The first step is to discern what the excitement is about. For psychologists studying the behaviour of disturbed individuals, the interaction of arousal, emotion, and thought has become increasingly important. Even in normal individuals, too high a level of arousal can produce extreme emotional responses and lead to disorganized, less effective behaviour. Many maladjusted individuals, such as those suffering from the manic stages of bipolar disorders, have so high a level of arousal that they cannot organize their thinking or behaviour (see Chapter 15, pages 541–542).

Some studies show that people can control their body's biochemistry. In a study by Lazarus and Alfert (1964), participants were able to manipulate their electrodermal response when told in advance about a painful procedure shown in a film. Thus, emotion and its expression reflect both a person's motivations and basic biochemistry (Carver & Scheier, 1990). People also control their emotions because of strong cultural expectations. In Canada and the United States, for example, children and women have greater permission to cry and express emotions than men do. But in Latin America, men are expected to be emotional.

Expectations and cognitive appraisals of situations seem to be key elements in physiological and subsequent behavioural expressions of emotion (C. A. Smith, 1989). Expectations that are biased in one direction or another can lead to some unusual consequences; for example, if a person suffers from hypochondriasis (see Chapter 15, pages 536–537), any ache, pain, or quickness of breath may lead the person to experience dire feelings about his or her health.

Varieties of Emotional Experience. Robert Plutchik (1980) suggests that emotions can be mixed (just as colours are) to yield new varieties of emotional experience. He has devised a conceptual circle to characterize emotional responses (see Figure 9.7). Neighbouring primary emotions (shown inside the circle) are mixed to yield more complex emotions (shown outside the circle). So, for instance, a person experiencing joy and anticipation may feel a sense of optimism; similarly, surprise and sadness when mixed may be experienced as disappointment. Such models are interesting ways to think about the range of human emotional responses; however, there is as yet little data to support them.

Not all researchers consider all elements of a definition of emotion in their studies. One study may focus on emotional expression; another will focus on physiological reactions. There are basic emotions that appear to be innate, such as fear, anger, sadness, joy, disgust, and surprise; these are often considered survival emotions. More complex emotions, such as pride, love, and envy, are more likely to be learned, thought about, and evaluated; we consider them to be more cognitively based emotions. In considering emotions researchers have developed theories to help explain them; not surprisingly, they tend to have physiologically based theories that tend to explain only some emotions very well and more complex, cognitive theories that tend to explain well feelings that are learned.

Diversity on page 322 explores the extent of emotional differences between men and women.

FIGURE 9.7
An Alternative Conception of Emotional Range: Plutchik's Circle
Plutchik (1980) suggests that human emotions can be mixed (just as colours are) to yield new varieties of emotional experience.

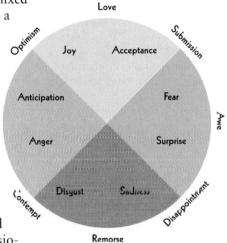

Physiological Theories of Emotion

Many researchers feel that our happiness, rage, and even sexual pleasure are physiologically based. They argue that the wide range of emotions that human beings experience and express is controlled in large part by a series of neurons located in an area deep within the brain—the limbic system. The *limbic system* is composed of cells in the hypothalamus, the amygdala, and other cortical and subcortical areas. Studies of these crucial areas began in the 1920s, when Bard (1934) found that the removal of portions of the cortex of cats produced sharp emotional reactions to simple stimuli such as a touch or a puff of air. The cats would hiss, claw, bite, arch their backs, and growl—and their reactions did not seem directed at any specific person or target. Bard referred to this behaviour as *sham rage*. Later researchers

Stereotypical Beliefs About Emotion and Gender

In our society, it is widely believed that women are more emotionally expressive than men, and that they more readily express warmth and affection as well as fear, vulnerability, and sadness. And men are believed to express less warmth and affection and to be more angry. These beliefs about the way men and women operate in our society are widely accepted. However, research shows that these stereotypes may reflect reality in part because the stereotypes themselves help shape it! People who do not conform to generally held beliefs might be punished through social rejection; similarly, people who do conform are rewarded for such behaviours.

Most people do not recognize that gender differences are more socially constructed than biologically constructed. Consider, for example, the gender stereotype that males express more anger than females. This stereotype is largely inaccurate. It is inaccurate because it focuses on the behavioural expression of anger through aggression but ignores the expression of anger through other modalities. For example, women often verbalize more intense anger and for longer periods of time than do men—especially in close heterosexual relationships. Men more frequently "stonewall" their wives by inhibiting facial actions and minimizing their listening as well as eye contact. Although some stereotypical behaviours are supported by research data, research by Leslie Brody (1997) suggests that gender differences can be either minimized or maximized depending on the social and cultural context. She asserts that the reason we continue to stereotype women as less expressive of anger is that we do not consider multiple modes of expression. She also points out that the context in which anger is expressed affects how we perceive it; for example, Hall (1984) suggests that people moderate their behaviour with the opposite sex so that it approaches the other sex's norms. So, both males and females are often equally expressive to female friends even though females indicate that they are more expressive towards intimate others than are males.

Expression of anger also depends on where the individual is in the life cycle and whether he or she is rearing children. People's expression of aggression diminishes during child-rearing years, and men who are principal caregivers of children tend to be similar in their emotional expressiveness towards children and less aggressive than males who are not engaged in child-rearing. We also know that women in Western cultures, more than men, still tend to be in positions of low power and status. In such positions, women may be more likely to interpret situations as being less controllable and risky for expressing anger (Lips, 1994). In cross-cultural studies in Africa, LeVine (1966) showed that because of labour migration and changes in workloads, power and status levels between the two sexes began to shift—as a consequence, both sexes begin to express the emotions stereotypically associated with the other.

In the end, stereotypes about gender and emotion tend to be imprecise and are exaggerated. They tend to ignore the modality in which an emotion is expressed. They ignore the content of the situation and the culture of the emotional expression. ■

stimulated portions of the brain with electrical current and found that the visual system was also important in emotions. They deduced that the cortex was integrating visual information and hypothalamic information to produce emotional behaviour. Two major physiological (biological) approaches to the study of emotion dominated psychology for decades: the James–Lange theory and the Cannon–Bard theory. Both are concerned with the physiology of emotions and with whether physiological change or emotional feelings occur first. More recent theories, like that of LeDoux (1996), focus on specific brain structures.

The James–Lange Theory. According to a theory proposed by both William James (1842–1910) and Carl Lange (1834–1900) (who are given joint credit since their approaches were so similar), people experience physiological changes and then interpret them as emotional states (see Figure 9.8). People do not cry because they feel sad; they feel sad because they cry. People do not perspire because they are afraid; they feel afraid after they perspire. In other words, the James–Lange theory says that people do not experience an emotion until after their bodies become aroused and begin to respond with physiological changes; that is, feedback from the body produces feelings or emotions (James, 1884; Lange, 1922). For this approach, in its most simplified form, *feeling* is the essence of emotion. Thus, James (1890, p. 1006) wrote, "Every one of the bodily changes whatsoever it be is felt, acutely or obscurely, the moment it occurs."

A modern physiological approach suggests that facial movements, by their action, can create emotions. Called the *facial feedback hypothesis*, this idea expresses the view that sensations from the face, or facial feedback, provide cues or signals to the brain that help us determine our emotional response. In some ways this approach derives from the James–Lange theory. For example, when specific facial movements create a change in blood flow to and temperature of the brain, pleasant feelings occur. According to Zajonc, Murphy, and Inglehart (1989), a facial movement such as a smile or an eye movement may release the appropriate emotion-linked neurotransmitters (Izard, 1990; Ekman, 1993). Some neurotransmitters may bring about pleasant emotions and others unpleasant ones. Crying, for example, is associated with a mixture of sympathetic, parasympathetic, and somatic activation (Gross, Fredrickson, & Levenson, 1994). Zajonc and his colleagues argue that facial movements alone are capable of inducing emotions; anecdotally, children (and adults) often do feel a bit happier when their parents and friends coax them to smile. This theory is still relatively new and has not yet been tested extensively by other researchers. However, you can test it yourself by holding a pencil in your teeth for a few minutes (which makes you smile) and see if this makes you feel better than when you hold a pencil in your lips for a few minutes (which makes you frown).

The Cannon–Bard Theory. Physiologists, notably Walter Cannon (1871–1945), were critical of the James–Lange theory. Cannon and P. Bard, a colleague, argued that the physiological changes in many emotional states were identical. They reasoned as follows: If increases in blood pressure and heart rate accompany feelings of both anger and joy, how can people determine their emotional state simply from their physiological state? Cannon spoke of undifferentiated arousal—the same physiological reaction for fight and flight.

Cannon argued that when a person is emotional, two areas of the brain—the thalamus and the cerebral cortex—are stimulated simultaneously (he did not realize the full nature of the limbic system). Stimulation of the cortex produces the emotional component of the experience; stimulation of the thalamus produces physiological changes in the sympathetic nervous system.

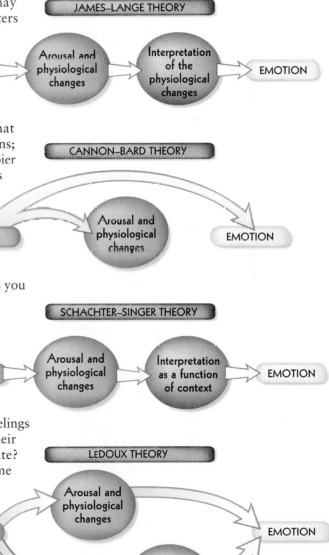

FIGURE 9.8
Theories of Emotion
In the *James–Lange theory*, arousal precedes interpretation. In the *Cannon–Bard theory*, arousal and emotion occur simultaneously. According to the *Schachter–Singer theory*, the interpretation of arousal depends on the context. According to LeDoux, the physiological basis of an emotion occurs first, and the subjective interpretation follows a separate but related pathway in the brain.

JAMES–LANGE THEORY

EVENT → Arousal and physiological changes → Interpretation of the physiological changes → EMOTION

CANNON–BARD THEORY

EVENT → Arousal and physiological changes → EMOTION

SCHACHTER–SINGER THEORY

EVENT → Arousal and physiological changes → Interpretation as a function of context → EMOTION

LEDOUX THEORY

EVENT → Arousal and physiological changes → EMOTION
EVENT → Memories and interpretation → EMOTION

According to Cannon (1927), emotional feelings *accompany* physiological changes (see Figure 9.8); they do not *produce* such changes.

The truth is that when Cannon and Bard were putting together their theory they knew relatively little about how the brain operated. For example, physiological changes in the brain do not happen exactly simultaneously. Further, people report that they often have an experience and then have physiological and emotional reactions to it. Neither the James–Lange nor the Cannon–Bard approach considered how thoughts about a situation might alter their physiological reactions and emotional responses. But the James–Lange and Cannon–Bard approaches provided a conceptual bridge to newer, more modern approaches.

LeDoux's Emotional Brain. Joseph LeDoux (1993, 1995, 1996) has been investigating the physiological bases of emotion—especially fear—and discovering the central role of the amygdala and the structures with which it is connected. LeDoux asserts that a person's feelings and subjective experiences are initiated by primitive subcortical brain mechanisms. He asserts in his popular book, *The Emotional Brain*, that through the process of natural selection and evolution our brain has evolved to detect fearful situations and respond rapidly to them, with heart rate increase and muscle tension for example. His view is that responses like the fear response are hard-wired into the brain's circuit, and that subjective responses follow through closely associated but different routes. LeDoux reasons that fear responses—like freezing up at the sight of a natural predator—are nature's evolutionary responses. You respond automatically without thought. In referring to a prairie dog who sees its natural predator, the bobcat, LeDoux (1996, p. 176) argues, "The sight or sound of the bobcat goes straight to your amygdala and out comes the freezing response." But such automatic responses are quick fixes, and in human beings, control and thought are initiated and they determine subsequent actions. LeDoux asserts that we use our memory system, especially working memory, to make decisions about current situations and what to do next.

For LeDoux, emotional experiences are determined first by stimulation of the amygdala with its automatic responses. Second, the amygdala creates arousal in various other brain structures. Next, the arousal and automatic responses created by the amygdala create changes in the body—release of hormones, sweating, facial changes—and these bodily changes create information, feedback to the brain. The higher centres in the brain sense basic bodily reactions and interpret them (Kleinke, Peterson, & Rutledge, 1998). Remember what William James said, "We don't cry because we are sad, but rather, we are sad because we cry." LeDoux also argues that we don't have to be aware of a stimulus to be fearful; he cites data from experiments on subliminal perception to argue that you can have a feeling without a conscious stimulation (Zajonc, 1984). In the end, LeDoux (1996) asserts that there may be two routes for emotions, one subcortical and one cortical. His view is very much an evolutionary one; evolution has prepared us for certain events in our world that should yield a basic emotional response. Fear of heights, snakes, or insects has an evolutionary basis as these situations can cause danger. Our thoughts, past experiences, and memories then affect how we respond. Of course, our modern world has changed very quickly from that of our ancestors, and such fears today may lead to unnecessary phobias—snakes and tarantulas are not part of the world of most people.

For many biological psychologists the underpinnings of our emotional lives are biochemical and based in evolution. But even the staunchest supporters of this approach recognize that our complex and evolved brain has developed a wide range of emotional states. Our emotional repertoire is far too complex to be solely based on automatic evolutionary responses.

Cognitive Theories of Emotion

Fear, sadness, rage, and excitement all have readily recognizable emotional and physiological manifestations. But what about more complex emotions? Consider, for example, pride, embarrassment, or self-esteem. Consciousness of self requires a far more subtle and complex analysis—one that focuses on thought (Lewis, 1995). Cognitive theories of emotion focus on mental interpretation as well as physiology. These theories follow logically in the history of psychology, because thought processes have become extremely influential. Cognitive theorists argue that emotion theories must incorporate interpretation, anticipation, and even problem solving (Parrott & Schulkin, 1993).

The Schachter–Singer Approach. The Schachter–Singer view of emotion is a cognitive approach that focuses on emotional activation and incorporates elements of both the James–Lange and the Cannon–Bard theories. Schachter and Singer observed that people do indeed interpret their emotions, but not solely from bodily changes. They argued that people interpret physical sensations within a specific context (see Figure 9.8). They knew that bodily states, including chemically induced states brought on by alcohol or other drugs, can change moods. But observers cannot interpret what a person's emotional behaviour means unless they know the situation in which it occurs. If a man cries at a funeral, observers suspect he is sad; if he cries at his daughter's wedding, they suspect he is joyful. Thus, according to the Schachter–Singer view, an emotion is created by cognitive factors as a person tries to account for a state of perceived activation (Lang, 1994).

To demonstrate their contention, Schachter and Singer (1962) injected volunteers with epinephrine (adrenalin), a powerful stimulant that increases physiological signs of arousal such as heart rate, energy level, and even sensations of butterflies in the stomach. The participants were not aware of the usual effects of the epinephrine, however. They compared these participants to a control group who weren't injected with epinephrine. To see if they could affect how participants interpreted their aroused state, Schachter and Singer manipulated the settings in which the volunteers experienced their arousal. The researchers hired undergraduates and paid them to act either happy and relaxed or sad, depressed, and angry. The hired students—called "stooges"—pretended that they too were volunteers in the drug study. However, they were given injections of salt water, not epinephrine. Their emotional behaviour was strictly an act. The "happy" stooges shot wads of paper into a wastebasket and flew paper airplanes around the room. The "angry" ones complained about the questionnaire they had to fill out and voiced their dissatisfaction with the experiment.

All of the experimental participants showed increased physiological arousal when compared to control particpants. Those who interacted with the happy stooges reported that the drug made them feel good; those who interacted with the angry ones reported feeling anger. Schachter and Singer reasoned that when people see no immediate external cause for their physiological arousal (especially when arousal levels are low), they will label their feelings in terms of the thoughts available to them—in this case, thoughts stimulated by their interactions with the stooges.

Schachter and Singer had the kernel of an important idea; arousal intensifies emotions, but it is not as diffuse as they thought. People don't live in a vacuum of experiences. For example, when people first smoke marijuana or take other psychoactive drugs, they tend to approach the experience with definite expectations. If told the drug will produce feelings of hunger, new users will report feeling hunger; if told the drug is a downer, new users often interpret their bodily sensations as depressive. In Schachter and Singer's view, people experience internal arousal, become aware of the arousal, seek an explanation for it, identify an external cue, and then label the arousal. In an important way, arousal provides the fuel, the energy, of emotion, but the labelling determines the emotion that is felt.

Valins (1966) argued that actual physiological arousal is not a prerequisite for labelling of emotion; cognitive processes alone will suffice (see Harris & Katkin, 1975). Reisenzein (1983) argues that Schachter and Singer's theory overestimates the role of arousal and that arousal, at best, merely intensifies an emotional experience. Today, we recognize that Schachter and Singer's view probably overstated the role of cognitive processes as the determiner of emotion, but it stimulated researchers like Damasio (1994) to think about this important component and make it part of their theories.

Multicultural Emotions. Phillip Shaver and his colleagues have sought to identify the basic emotions that all people experience and the ways in which they are experienced. Shaver suggested that there are basic emotions that almost all people will describe when asked to identify emotions, but these basic categories can overlap, and many other emotional states can be grouped under them. Schwartz and Shaver (1987) contend that people's emotional knowledge is organized around these emotional categories and that people exhibit characteristic behaviours with each emotion. Along with others (Ekman, 1994; Izard, 1994), Schwartz and Shaver also assert that these emotions appear cross-culturally and that researchers have to understand this overall structure before they can define an overall theory of emotion. Each culture may put its own value on an emotion and have different traits that trigger it. For example, love is an extremely powerful emotion in the United States; but in Sumatra, one of the chief islands of Indonesia, nostalgia is the most powerful emotion (Heider, 1991). Shaver believes that we have to better understand the overall structure and concept of emotion. Paul Ekman (1993) concurs and asserts that some aspects of emotion may be culture-specific, while others may be universal. Researchers have just begun to use the proper techniques to ask the right questions about the extent to which emotional expression is indeed universal; the debate continues (Izard, 1994; Russell, 1994).

Lie Detection?

Many physiological changes are due to an increase in activity in the sympathetic branch of the autonomic nervous system. When the sympathetic nervous system is activated, a range of responses takes place almost simultaneously. Fear, for example, may slow or halt digestion, increase blood pressure and heart rate, deepen breathing, dilate the pupils, decrease salivation (causing a dry mouth), and tense the muscles. Researchers recognized that the autonomic nervous system provides direct, observable, measurable responses that can be quantified in a systematic manner. This realization led to the development of what is commonly called the lie detector, or polygraph device.

 The polygraph test, or lie detector test, is perhaps the most widely recognized recorder of emotion. A polygraph device records changes in the activity of the sympathetic branch of a person's autonomic nervous system. Most autonomic nervous system activity is involuntary, and lying is usually associated with an increase in autonomic activity.

A trained polygraph operator compares a person's autonomic responses to a series of relatively neutral questions to the person's responses to questions about the issue being explored. During non-controversial questions (such as a request for the person's name or address), autonomic activity remains at what is considered the baseline level. During critical questions (such as whether the person used a knife as a weapon), however, a person with something to hide usually shows a dramatic increase in autonomic nervous system activity.

Not all people, however, show distinct or marked autonomic nervous system changes when they are emotionally aroused (Bashore & Rapp, 1993). Habitual liars show little or no change in autonomic activity when they lie; they seem to be able to lie without becoming emotionally aroused (Honts, 1994). Equally important is the finding that some people who tell the truth may register changes in autonomic nervous system activity because of anxiety. This means that a truthful individual who takes a lie detector test may appear to be lying when the individual is in fact telling the truth. In a study of lie detectors, researchers examined innocent and guilty individuals accused of theft (Kleinmuntz & Szucko, 1984). Although guilty people often were declared guilty by the lie detector and innocent people often were declared innocent, 37 percent of innocent people were declared guilty! In summary, lie detectors are subject to significant errors in both directions—there is no evidence of a unique physiological response to deceit (Kleinmuntz & Szucko, 1984; Patrick & Iacono, 1989; Saxe, 1994).

Today, most jurisdictions do not accept the results of lie detector tests as valid evidence in court, especially in criminal cases. The Canadian Psychological Association also has expressed strong reservations about polygraph tests, asserting that their use may afflict psychological damage on innocent persons. The association's concerns stem in part from the knowledge that some people can control their emotions and do not respond automatically to external stimuli, whereas other people are less able to control their emotions and may overreact to external stimuli.

Focus

Review

◆ Identify the fundamental ideas that distinguish the James–Lange, Cannon–Bard, LeDoux, and Schachter–Singer theories of emotion. pp. 323–335

◆ Why are lie detectors unscientific? pp. 326–327

Think Critically

◆ Do you think lie detectors should be used in the public or private sector? Why?

◆ Do you think that there are universal emotions? Why?

Summary and Review

Theories of Motivation

Distinguish between a motivation and a need.

■ *Motivation* is an internal condition that appears by inference to initiate, activate, or maintain an organism's goal-directed behaviour. Motivation is inferred from behaviour and is caused by needs, drives, or desires. A *need* is a state of physiological imbalance that is usually accompanied by arousal. pp. 294–295

Differentiate the various theories of motivation.

■ The *evolutionary perspective* asserts that natural selection, the process of selective reproduction of the fittest animals, explains certain basic human behaviours. Those who are motivated to succeed, stay alive, and reproduce are more likely to be represented in the population with the ultimate gene pool coming from the fittest organisms. Evolutionary theorists conclude that through natural selection changes are evident in brain structure and function and that evolution creates more advanced, evolved organisms that are motivated to succeed, live, and pass on their genetic heritage. pp. 294–295

■ *Drive theory* is an explanation of behaviour that assumes that an organism is motivated to act because of a need to attain, reestablish, balance, or maintain some goal that helps with the survival of the organism or the species. A mechanistic drive explanation of behaviour views the organism as being pushed, pulled, and energized, almost like a machine. Drive theories often focus on *homeostasis*, a tendency to attempt to maintain a constant state of inner stability or balance. p. 295

■ According to *optimal arousal theories*, individuals seek an optimal level of stimulation. The Yerkes–Dodson law asserts that behaviour varies from disorganized to effective to optimal, depending on the person's level of *arousal*. Contemporary researchers have extended the idea by suggesting that when a person's level of arousal and anxiety is too high or too low, performance will be poor, especially on complex tasks. An inverted U-shaped curve describes the relationship between arousal and effectiveness of behaviour. pp. 295–297

■ *Expectancy theories* are explanations of behaviour that focus on people's expectations of success in reaching a goal and their need for achievement. p. 298

■ *Cognitive theory* emphasizes the role of active decision making in all areas of life. It emphasizes the role of thoughts and individual choices regarding life goals and the means of achieving them. Cognitive theory moves away from mechanistic descriptions of behaviour and emphasizes the role of human choice and expression. Cognitive theory focuses on (1) thought as an initiator and determinant of behaviour, and (2) the role of active decision making in all areas of life. pp. 298–299

■ *Intrinsic motivation* gives rise to behaviours that a person performs in order to feel competent and self-determining. *Extrinsic motivation* is supplied by rewards that come from the external environment; they tend to decrease the recurrence of intrinsically motivated behaviour. pp. 299–300

■ *Humanistic theory* explains behaviour by emphasizing the entirety of life rather than the individual components of behaviour. Humanistic psychologists believe that individuals' behaviour must be viewed within the framework of the individuals' environment and values; humanistic theory focuses on human dignity, individual choice, and self-worth. pp. 300–301

KEY TERMS

motivation, p. 294; drive theory, p. 295; drive, p. 295; need, p. 295; homeostasis,

p. 295; arousal, p. 295; expectancy theories, p. 298; motive, p. 298; social need, p. 298; cognitive theory, p. 298; extrinsic motivation, p. 299; intrinsic motivation, p. 299; overjustification effect, p. 300; humanistic theory, p. 300; self-actualization, p. 301

Hunger: A Physiologically Based Need

What causes hunger?

■ The glucostatic approach argues that the principal physiological cause of hunger is a low blood sugar level, which accompanies food deprivation. A delicate balance of food and fluid intake—a homeostatic state—is necessary for proper functioning. Genetics and disorders of the autonomic nervous system also may play a role in eating behaviour. Physiological make-up isn't the only important factor in eating behaviour; people's experiences also teach them how to interact with food. pp. 301–303

■ There is no clear, convincing, simple answer to the question of nature versus nurture regarding obesity. Genetics plays a role, but a person's history with food, level of obesity, and current weight all contribute to the likelihood of recurrence or development of obesity. pp. 303–307

■ *Anorexia nervosa*, a starvation disease, is an eating disorder characterized by the obstinate and wilful refusal to eat. *Bulimia nervosa* involves binge eating accompanied by a fear of not being able to stop eating. Bulimics often purge themselves of unwanted calories by vomiting and by using laxatives and diuretics. pp. 308–309

KEY TERMS
eating disorders, p. 308; anorexia nervosa, p. 308; bulimia nervosa, p. 308

Sexual Behaviour: Physiology Plus Thought

What are the rules of thought and of hormonal influences in human sexual behaviour?

■ Sexual behaviour in human beings is in part under hormonal control, and the hormones are different for men and women. In men, the testes are the principal producers of androgens, or male sex hormones; in women, the ovaries are the principal producers of estrogens, or female hormones. p. 310

■ Thought plays an enormous role in the sexual behaviour of human beings; our own thoughts, fantasies, and images initiate and activate sexual desire and activity. p. 311

How many phases does the sexual response cycle have?

■ When human beings become sexually aroused, they go through a series of four phases (stages). The phases, which together are known as the sexual response cycle, are the *excitement phase*, the *plateau phase*, the *orgasm phase*, and the *resolution phase*. p. 311

How have North Americans' sex lives changed over the last 40 years?

■ The Laumann study, the most recent and comprehensive study of the last four decades, has shown that the sex lives of Americans are predictable and not as active as many assume, although most are happy with their sex lives. The Laumann study showed that men and women are more likely today than they were 40 years ago to have had intercourse before marriage and that there has been a slow and steady decrease in the age of first intercourse. Men think about sex more than women, and married men and women have more sex than single young people. pp. 312–313

■ A person with a heterosexual orientation has an erotic attraction and preference for members of the opposite sex; an individual with a homosexual orientation has an erotic attraction and preference for members of the same sex. According to the Laumann study, only 2.8 percent of men and 1.4 percent of women identify themselves as exclusively homosexual in orientation. This is substantially less than the 10 percent reported by Kinsey in the 1950s. p. 313

KEY TERMS
excitement phase, p. 311; vasocongestion, p. 311; plateau phase, p. 311; orgasm phase, p. 311; resolution phase, p. 311

Achievement: A Social Need

How does expectancy theory explain the need for achievement?

■ *Need for achievement* is a social need that directs a person to strive constantly for excellence and success. According to expectancy theory, people engage in behaviours that satisfy their desires for success, mastery, and fulfilment. Tasks not oriented towards these goals are not motivating and either are not undertaken or are done without energy and commitment. Need for achievement can be measured by tests such as the TAT. pp. 314–315

KEY TERM
need for achievement, p. 314

Emotion

Identify the fundamental ideas that distinguish various theories of emotion?

■ An *emotion* is a subjective response (feeling), usually accompanied by a physiological change, which is often interpreted by the individual and then readies the individual for some action that is associated with a change in behaviour. Emotions are aroused internal states; they may occur in response to either internal or external stimuli. p. 318

■ The James–Lange theory of emotion states that people experience physiological changes and then interpret those changes as emotions. The Cannon–Bard theory states that when people experience emotions, two areas of the brain are stimulated simultaneously, one creating an emotional response and the other creating physiological change. pp. 323–324

■ LeDoux asserts that there are two routes for emotions, one subcortical and one cortical. His view is very much an evolutionary one; evolution has prepared us for certain events in our world that should yield a basic emotional response. p. 324

■ According to the cognitive view of emotion, for example Schachter–Singer's approach, people interpret physiological changes within specific contexts and infer emotions from these cues. p. 325

■ Shaver showed that there are basic emotions that most people display regardless of their culture. These categories can overlap, and many other emotional states can be grouped under them. p. 326

KEY TERM
emotion, p. 318

Weblinks

Theories of Emotion
www.people.memphis.edu/~clong/emotiont.htm
Early theories of emotion and related research are detailed on this site. Important questions about theories of emotion are put forward, and links are provided to some answers.

Anorexia Nervosa and Bulimia Association
www.ams.queensu.ca/anab
This non-profit organization, based in Kingston, Ontario, provides information on eating disorders and supports people suffering from them.

Sexual Orientation Resources on the WWW
www.ualberta.ca/~cbidwell/hsms/hsresgay.htm
The University of Alberta has set out links to general information resources, organizations and networks, and educational and research sites dealing with issues relating to sexual orientation.

The Couch Potato's Lament
www.health-line.com/articles/hl941202.htm
This article from *Healthline* magazine cites popular excuses for not exercising, as well as explanations of exercise patterns and why people get off track with regards to their workout plan.

Depression
www.psych.helsinki.fi/~janne/asdfaq/2.html
Visit this site for a more detailed answer to the question, "What is depression?" For more information about depression, go to the "see also" items at the end of the Web page.

The Entrepreneur Test
www.liraz.com/webquiz.htm
This interactive test will help you assess if you have what it takes to be an entrepreneur.

The American Polygraph Association
www.polygraph.org
This site offers descriptions, applications, discussions about validity and reliability, and other facts about the polygraph test.

Chapter 10

Child Development

Raj and Maya watched as their 12-year-old daughter, Tina, walked up to the baseline, tennis racquet in hand. She prepared to serve, concentration written all over her face. As he watched Tina standing there, looking so determined and confident, Raj could hardly believe how grown-up she looked. It seemed like only yesterday that Tina was taking her first unsteady steps, and before he knew it, she'd be choosing a career! As he thought about it realistically, though, he realized that the process of growing up really had taken a long time. Tina, like all human infants, was utterly helpless for a long time, and relied completely on Raj and Maya for all of her needs. It took a year for her to be able to walk, another year before she could talk, and, of course, she was still not yet quite grown. She would likely not leave home until her late teens or early twenties.

Children accomplish an amazing amount in their first 12 years, and much of the dramatic developmental acquisitions (walking, language, social interaction) emerge in the first four to six years. Especially when things go wrong (for example, trouble with friends or in school), but when they go right as well (for example, a good report card or a flawless piano recital), parents wonder and worry about the causes of development. Why do children turn out the way they do? Who or what is ultimately responsible for their developmental outcomes? Are good, or troubled, children born that way or are these outcomes consequences of how they have been treated during their "formative" years? The answers to these questions matter not only to parents and child psychologists but also to society at large as it struggles to decide what to do about things like the Young Offenders Act (legislation addressing young people who have come to the attention of the law). Parents, teachers, and even judges speculate about the causes that underlie child development outcomes—about who or what is responsible for child development.

Most people today acknowledge that home interactions are crucial in developing a child's personality. They aren't the only influence—certainly biological factors weigh in heavily—but they are nevertheless crucial. Psychologists know that crucial developmental processes take place in the early years of life. They know that both nature and nurture play key roles in development, and that children develop differently. Some are cognitively advanced; others are average or slow. But how much, or how well, any child achieves milestones of development is affected by a complex interaction of nature and nurture. ■

Part of the goal of this chapter will be to focus on normal developmental processes in children—physical, cognitive, moral, emotional, and social development. We will also see how people's genetic make-up interacts with their environments to produce unique individuals. Our examination will help explain how parents can affect their children's development so profoundly. The next chapter will look at adolescence, adulthood, and aging—showing that development is a process that lasts a lifetime.

Key Issues, Theories, and Research Designs

D evelopmental psychology is the study of the lifelong, age-related processes of change in the physical, cognitive, emotional, and social domains of functioning; such changes are rooted in biological mechanisms that are genetically controlled (for example, maturational processes involved in the growth of the nervous system) as well as in social interactions. Psychologists study all of these changes—biological, maturational, and social—to find out how people grow, develop, and transform from young children to mature, functioning adults and to learn what causes those changes. Developmental psychologists recognize that development involves gains and losses over time as people respond in positive and negative ways to life's experiences. They also recognize that development must be viewed from multiple perspectives and within a historical context. Today's developmental researchers acknowledge that the interaction of genetics and the environment is a complex issue (Smith and Thelan, 1993) and that there is considerable diversity in developmental growth (Baltes, 1987). In their study of development, psychologists have focused on a few key issues, theories, and research methods to unravel the causes of behaviour. The goal is always the same: to describe, explain, predict, and potentially help manage human development.

Key Issues

There are a number of key issues in the study of development that help researchers form their questions and construct their theories. Three of the most important are nature versus nurture, stability versus change, and continuity versus discontinuity.

Nature versus Nurture. One way to look at individual development is to consider to what extent the developing person's abilities, interests, and personality are determined by evolutionary or biological influences, by *nature*, or by environmental influences, by *nurture*. The nature-versus-nurture issue has been raised before, in Chapters 2 and 8. Attempting to separate biological from environmental causes of behaviour is a complex matter and one of the classic theoretical issues in this area of psychology; the answer to any specific question about human behaviour usually involves the interaction of both nature and nurture.

To separate the roles played by genetics and the environment, researchers have studied identical twins (who share the same genetic make-up) who have been reared apart (in different environments). In doing so, they have found extraordinary similarities between such siblings beyond the obvious genetic traits such as height, hair colour, or allergies (Lykken, McGue, Tellegen, & Bouchard, 1992). In one study, Lykken and his colleagues found an identical twin who was an accomplished story-teller with a collection of amusing anecdotes. Later, his twin brother was asked if he knew any funny stories. "Why, sure," he responded, and leaning back with a practised air, he continued, "I'll tell you a story." Other twins shared interests in dogs, smoked the same cigarettes, or were both politically conservative. One pair of twins shared a phobia for water at the beach; both would enter the water backwards, and then only up to their knees. In the Lykken study there were two firefighters, two gunsmiths, and two people who obsessively counted things; all of these pairs were identical twins. Lykken and his colleagues (1992) argued that genetics plays an especially important role in human development. But many psychologists believe that although genetics plays a crucial role in development, a child's environment has an equal, if not more important, impact. They argue that children's experiences in and outside of the home can expand or hinder the developmental possibilities provided by genetics. Similarly, many parents think they can enhance their children's environment and optimize the likelihood of their living stimulating, well-reasoned, satisfying lives.

Stability versus Change. Do individuals stay pretty much the same throughout their lives—cognitively, emotionally, and socially—or do they change, adapt, emerge from, and be affected profoundly by events in their environment? The issue of stability versus change is a recurring theme in developmental psychology. It is closely associated with nature and nurture, because when researchers assume stability they often assume that stable traits—for example, shyness— are inherited and genetically determined. Those who favour an environmental view are more likely to believe that people change over the course of a lifetime because of unique life events—for example, the loss of a sibling in a car accident or exposure to chicken pox, which later may be implicated in the development of multiple sclerosis.

Continuity versus Discontinuity. A third debate focuses on development as continuous or discontinuous. A *continuous view* sees development as a process of gradual growth and change with skills and knowledge added one bit at a time, with one skill building on another. Development also can be viewed as *discontinuous*, with growth, maturation, and understanding of the world occurring at various stages with changes appearing abruptly—almost suddenly. For example, a 12-month-old does not seem to recognize herself in a mirror, but in a few short months she will show that she does recognize herself by touching her nose in curiosity if a blob of red rouge has secretly been placed on it.

Key Theories

Most developmental psychologists also have a point of view about development—a theoretical orientation. They develop orderly, coherent ideas that describe, explain, and hopefully predict behaviour from a particular theoretic perspective. Developmental theories give shape and order to sets of data about physical, cognitive, and social development. Some developmental theories today reach back to early psychological leaders for ideas; other developmental theories have modernized earlier ideas; still others are breaking new ground, looking at development and maturation from unique vantage points. These theories reflect the history of psychology and the diversity of the discipline.

Psychoanalytic. One of the earliest modern theories of development was Freud's. As you will see when we study personality in Chapter 12, Freud believed that early childhood experiences, especially those before the age of six, shape a person's biologically determined urges—leading, for example, to the development of a conscience. Interestingly, Freud never studied children; his theories developed out of studies of disordered adults. We'll have much more to say about Freud later. Erik Erikson, who we will discuss in detail in the next chapter, took Freud's view and modified it making it more focused on normal personality development, more focused on development across the life span, and more sensitive to social and cultural influences on development, rather than focusing on sexual and aggressive impulses.

Behaviourism. In sharp contrast to the psychoanalytic tradition, which emphasizes the unconscious and the role of early childhood experiences, behaviourists focused on observable, quantifiable behaviours. Clark Hull focused on drive reduction theories, which consider how people are motivated by biological needs. B. F. Skinner focused on the antecedents of behaviour and the reinforcers following behaviour. Behaviourists have claimed that a child's development can proceed in any number of directions depending entirely on his or her particular reinforcement history. Today many behaviourists also consider cognitive aspects of behaviour and how thought influences behaviour.

Cognitive Theory. The development of thought has been studied closely by a number of researchers. The key theorist in this area, Jean Piaget, argued that development occurs in an orderly, biologically determined manner, but also emphasized that development involves a process of adaptation to the world in which a child adjusts to its ever-changing demands. Piaget developed an exceedingly influential theory of cognitive development (Flavell, 1996). A second cognitive theory, *the information-processing perspective,* views human beings as problem solvers who attempt to make sense of the world. These theorists attempt to look more closely at basic processes such as attention, memory, and problem solving and offer an alternative way of describing and explaining why young children think differently than older children. Most information-processing approaches see people as active decision makers responding to environmental demands; these approaches attempt to explain how hard-wired brain systems work by enabling people to learn from and build on their experiences.

Ecological Systems Theory. A distinctly different approach that has had a wide impact is *ecological systems theory.* Developed by a number of researchers, with Urie Bronfenbrenner at its forefront, this approach argues that children develop within a system of complex human relationships and that those relationships exist in a series of overlapping and non-overlapping immediate environments such as families and neighbourhoods and larger environments such as communities, provinces, and countries. Children grow within families, within larger family relationships, within neighbourhoods and workplaces, and within a country and culture that stresses certain values. This approach emphasizes the role of culture and social relationships in the small world of individuals and in larger society. You will see that Bronfenbrenner shares this theoretic perspective with others. For example, Lev Vygotsky, who stressed that dialogue between children and members of society fuels child development, promoted a sociocultural perspective over 70 years ago. His work, along with Bronfenbrenner's, reminds us that we have to look at behaviour in the social context in which it occurs because we do not live in a social vacuum.

Key Research Designs

Good researchers know that the method they use to study a problem often influences the results. To interpret what the results might mean, a researcher must, at a minimum, take into account the particular research design used. In developmental research, two widely used designs for describing developmental changes are the cross-sectional and the longitudinal designs. In the *cross-sectional research design,* a psychologist will compare many different individuals of different ages at the same time to determine how they differ on some important dimension. In the *longitudinal research design,* a psychologist studies the same group of people repeatedly over time to examine changes that have occurred over a long period of time.

Each design has its advantages and disadvantages. For example, the cross-sectional design suffers from the fact that the participants' backgrounds (parents, family income, and nutrition) differ. Moreover, if differences between age groups are observed, it is difficult to determine if such differences are due to development or to pre-existing differences. The various age groups being examined may have had different life experiences—for example, one generation may have received substantially less education than the next and that factor will affect results when measuring IQ.

Lastly, with this design, individual differences are impossible to assess because participants generally are tested only once.

But the longitudinal design also has problems. It requires repeated access over time to the same people, but some participants may move, withdraw from the study, or even die. Also, after repeated testing on the same task (even though the tests may be months or years apart), participants may improve because of practice (that is, experience with taking the test may improve performance). If testing occurs over a long period of time, the tests themselves may become obsolete. Longitudinal research sometimes takes years to complete; this can cost a lot of money. Also, if the welfare of children could be affected (for example, by a study that examines which approach to teaching children how to read works best), it may be desirable to implement the study's results as quickly as possible rather than waiting for 5-, 10-, or 20-year outcome data. Another disadvantage to this design is that important changes may occur in the environment and/or in the social worlds of the participants, making it difficult to discern whether observed changes should be attributed to development or to environmental change. For example, if a group of children in Bosnia was tested for stability of personality, it would be difficult to conclude that their particular traits were due to development and not influenced by the extreme circumstances of their lives. See Figure 10.1 for a comparison of the cross-sectional and longitudinal research designs.

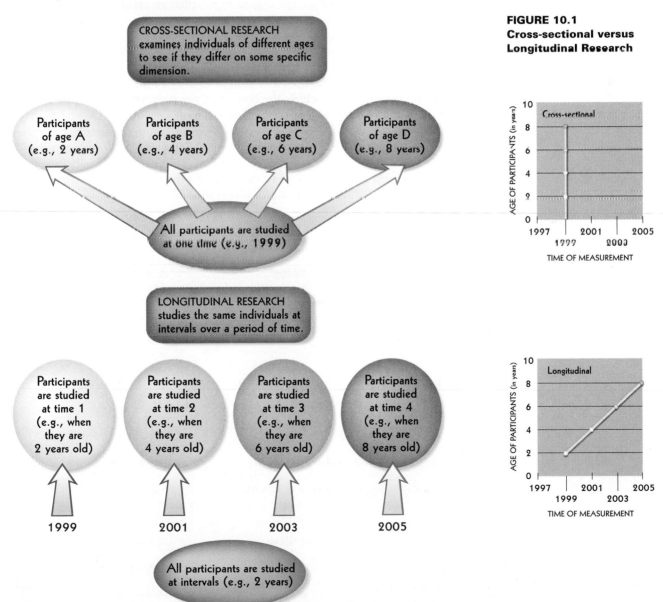

FIGURE 10.1
Cross-sectional versus Longitudinal Research

Zygote [ZEYE-goat]: A fertilized egg.
Embryo [EM-bree-o]: The prenatal organism from implantation to the eighth week following conception.
Fetus [FEET-us]: The prenatal organism from the eighth week following conception until birth.

The First 10 Months

U nderstanding how and why adolescents turn out the way they do can't be done by examining a mere slice of their lives and saying that "this caused that"; the truth is that human behaviour is sufficiently complex and affected by so many subtle influences that developmental change has multiple sources. Those sources began with our basic constitution, our biology—our bodies. Our development begins long before birth. Developmental events before birth are referred to as *prenatal* development; in the month after birth, they are *neonatal* development.

Prenatal Development

The lifelong journey of human development begins with conception. Conception occurs when an ovum and a sperm join in a woman's fallopian tube to form a **zygote**—a fertilized egg. During the next seven to nine days, the zygote floats down the fallopian tube to implant itself in the blood-lined wall of the uterus. From the time implantation is complete (about the second week following conception) until the eighth week after conception, the organism is called an **embryo**. Then, from the eighth week until birth, the organism is called a **fetus**. On average, maturation and development of the fetus takes 266 days, or about 38 weeks. Table 10.1 summarizes the prenatal (before birth) and postnatal (after birth) periods of development.

Although the prenatal environment—especially the mother's diet (Sigman, 1995)—can have an influence, the basic characteristics of an individual are established at conception; these include the colour of the hair, skin, and eyes; the sex (gender); the likelihood that the person will be tall or short, fat or lean; and perhaps basic intellectual abilities and personality traits. Within 10 hours, the zygote divides into four cells, forming a *blastocyst*. During the first week, a cluster of about a dozen cells drifts from the fallopian tube to the uterus. There, the cells begin the process of *differentiation*: Organs and other parts of the body begin to form. Some cells form the *umbilical cord*—a group of blood vessels and tissues that connect the

Table 10.1 Life Stages and Approximate Ages in Human Development

Period	Life Stage	Approximate Age
Prenatal period	Zygote	Conception to day 7 to 9
	Embryo	To week 8
	Fetus	Week 8 to birth
Postnatal period	Neonate	Birth to 1 month
	Infancy	1 to 18 months
	Toddlerhood	18 months to 3 years
	Early childhood	3 to 6 years
	Middle childhood	6 to 13 years
	Adolescence	13 to 20 years
	Young adulthood	20 to 40 years
	Middle adulthood	40 to 65 years
	Late adulthood	65 plus

zygote to the placenta. The **placenta** is a mass of tissue in the uterus that acts as the life-support system for the fetus by supplying oxygen, food, and antibodies and by eliminating wastes—all by way of the mother's bloodstream.

Table 10.2 summarizes the major physical developments during the prenatal period.

Harmful Environmental Effects

People have long assumed that the behaviour of a pregnant woman affects prenatal development. Medieval European doctors advised pregnant women that uplifting thoughts would help their babies develop into good, happy people, while fright, despondency, and negative emotions might disrupt the pregnancies and possibly influence the infants to become sad or mean-spirited. Research with animals shows that stress during pregnancy has effects on the emotional development of offspring, as indicated when the offspring are later tested as adults (Pfister & Muir, 1992).

Table 10.2   Major Developments during the Prenatal Period

	Age	Size	Characteristics
First trimester **1–12 weeks**	7–9 days	150 cells	Zygote attaches to uterine lining.
	2 weeks	Several thousand cells	Placental circulation established.
	3 weeks	1/10 inch	Heart and blood vessels begin to develop. Basics of brain and central nervous system form.
	4 weeks	1/4 inch	Kidneys and digestive tract begin to form. Rudiments of ears, nose, and eyes are present.
	6 weeks	1/2 inch	Arms and legs develop. Jaws form around mouth.
	8 weeks	1 inch, 1/30 ounce	Bones begin to develop in limbs. Sex organs begin to form.
	12 weeks	3 inches, 1 ounce	Gender can be distinguished. Kidneys are functioning, and liver is manufacturing red blood cells. Fetal movements can be detected by a physician.
Second trimester **13–24 weeks**	16 weeks	6½ inches, 4 ounces	Heartbeat can be detected by a physician. Bones begin to calcify.
	20 weeks	10 inches, 8 ounces	Mother feels fetal movements.
	24 weeks	12 inches, 1½ pounds	Vernix (white waxy substance) protects the body. Eyes open; eyebrows and eyelashes form; skin is wrinkled. Respiratory system is barely mature enough to support life.
Third trimester **25–38 weeks**	28 weeks	15 inches, 2½ pounds	Fetus is fully developed but needs to gain in size, strength, and maturity of systems.
	32 weeks	17 inches, 4 pounds	A layer of fat forms beneath the skin to regulate body temperature.
	36 weeks	19 inches, 6 pounds	Fetus settles into position for birth.
	38 weeks	21 inches, 8 pounds	Fetus arrives at full term—266 days from conception.

11 weeks

4 weeks

20 weeks

Teratogen [ter-AT-oh-jen]: A substance that can produce developmental malformations (birth defects) during the prenatal period.

While a fetus is not affected by the mother's condition to the extent suggested by medieval doctors, the environment and life-support systems provided by the mother do influence the embryo and fetus from conception until birth. Environmental factors such as diet, infection, radiation, and drugs affect both the mother *and* the baby. The child is especially affected during *critical periods*, during which there is rapid development and special sensitivity to environmental stimuli. During the first two years of life, the brain is especially sensitive; neuronal connections are undergoing many changes. Although the basic architecture of the brain is in place before birth, how individual connections of neurons are made is subject to considerable influence or damage.

Substances that can produce developmental malformations (birth defects) during the prenatal period are known as **teratogens.** Birth defects are the leading cause of death of infants in their first year of life in North America. Probably the most widely known teratogen is alcohol. If the mother drinks alcoholic beverages in early and middle pregnancy, the baby is more likely to be born prematurely, to have a lower birth weight, and to suffer from mental retardation or attention-deficit disorder (Streissguth, Barr, & Martin, 1983). Extreme effects are associated with a syndrome called *fetal alcohol syndrome (FAS)*. These children often have smaller brains, heart defects, and distinctive facial abnormalities and are mentally retarded. In many cases other defects are also present. Although these affects are typically observed in the offspring of alcoholic mothers, the mother does not have to be an alcoholic, or even a heavy drinker, in order to cause these effects. One study showed that drinking more than three ounces of 100-proof liquor per day during pregnancy was significantly related to a deficit in four-year-olds' intelligence test scores and poor attention span (Streissguth et al., 1989). Any deficits that occur usually are related to both the amount of alcohol consumed and when it was consumed during the pregnancy. It is estimated that about 350 children are born each year in Canada with FAS (Statistics Canada, 1992).

Studies also show that many drugs can affect prenatal development. High doses of aspirin, for example, may cause fetal bleeding, although the evidence is controversial (Werler, Mitchell, & Shapiro, 1989). Cigarette smoking constricts the oxygen

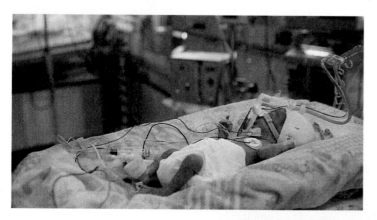

supply. Babies born to mothers who smoke cigarettes tend to be of lower birth weight, may be at increased risk for cleft palate and childhood cancers, and are more likely to die in infancy. Certain drugs, including tranquillizers, can be teratogenic, producing potentially irreversible malformations of the head, face, and limbs as well as neurological disorders (Kopp & Kaler, 1989; Lester & Dreher, 1989). Tragically, in recent years, hundreds of thousands of infants, such as the one in the photo, have been born addicted to various illegal drugs. Infants born to mothers who smoked crack during pregnancy suffer from low birth weight and central nervous system damage (Kaye, Elkind, Goldberg, & Tytun, 1989). Users of cocaine during pregnancy give birth to babies at increased risk for sudden infant death as well as a number of behavioural and physical problems (Fox, 1994; Kandall, Gaines, Habel, Davidson, & Jessop, 1993). The influence of drugs can be especially severe during the embryonic stage of development—a critical period—when the mother may not realize she is pregnant.

Newborns Come Well-equipped

Newborns grow rapidly—seemingly almost overnight—and they are not nearly as helpless as many people believe. At birth infants can hear, see, smell, and respond to the environment in adaptive ways; in other words, they have good sensory systems. They also are directly affected by experience. To help infants develop in optimal ways, psychologists try to find out how experience affects their perceptual development. In doing so, psychologists need to discover how infants think, what they perceive, and how they react to the world. Researchers therefore have devised ingenious ways of "asking" newborns questions about their perceptual world, such as: What are a child's inborn abilities and reflexes? When do inborn abilities become evident? How does the environment affect inborn abilities?

Growth. An infant who weighs 7.5 pounds at birth may weigh as much as 20 or 25 pounds by 12 months. At 18 months, the infant is usually walking and beginning to talk. For psychologists, infancy continues until the time when the child begins to represent the world abstractly (eg. through language). Thus, *infancy* is the period from 1 to 18 months (the infant is referred to as a neonate in the first month); *childhood* is the period from 18 months to about age 13—when *adolescence* begins.

The rapid growth that occurs in the early weeks and months after birth is quite extraordinary and mirrors embryonic development in important ways. A newborn's head is about one-fourth of its body length; a two-year-old's head is only one-fifth of its body length. This pattern of growth is called the *cephalocaudal trend* (from the Greek word *kephalé*, "head," and the Latin word *cauda*, "tail"). Another growth pattern—the *proximodistal trend*—has growth moving from the centre (proximal part) of the body outward (to the more "distant" extremities). That is, the head and torso grow before the arms, legs, hands, and feet do. Thus, a newborn's head is about the same circumference as the torso, and an infant's arms and legs are quite short, relatively speaking—but this changes very quickly (see Figure 10.2).

During the period of infancy and childhood, the child grows physically from a being that requires constant care, attention, and assistance to a nearly full-size, independent person. This process of growth and maturation begins at birth. At the end of the first year and the beginning of the second year of life, children can walk, climb, and manipulate their environment—skills that often lead parents to use safety devices that block stairways, lock cabinets, and prevent medicine bottles from being opened. There is significant variability in the age at which a child begins to walk or climb. Some babies develop early; others are slow to develop these physical abilities. However, the age at which these specific behaviours occur seems unrelated to any other major developmental abilities, except in cases of severe delay.

Figure 10.3 shows the major achievements in motor development in the first two years.

Newborns' Reflexes. Touch the palm of a newborn baby and you'll probably find one of your fingers held in the surprisingly firm grip of a tiny fist. The baby is exhibiting a reflexive reaction. Babies are born with innate *primary reflexes*—unlearned responses to stimuli. Some, such as the *grasping reflex*, no doubt helped

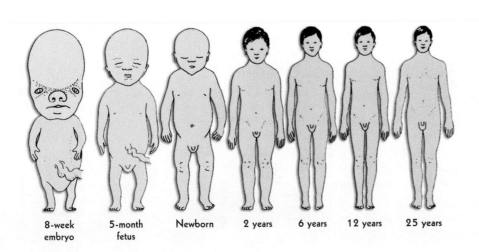

8-week embryo   5-month fetus   Newborn   2 years   6 years   12 years   25 years

FIGURE 10.2
The Cephalocaudal Trend of Growth
Body proportions change dramatically from fetal stages of development until adulthood.

(From Berk, 1994.)

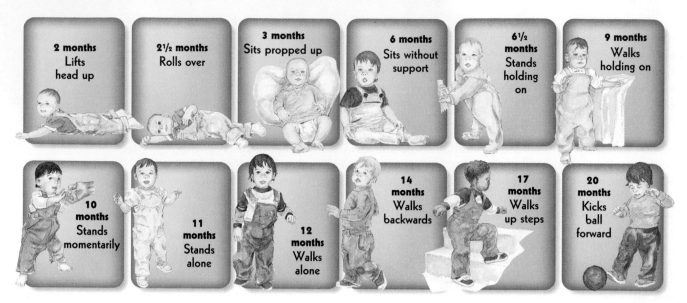

FIGURE 10.3
Development of Motor Skills in the First Two Years
Infants typically develop motor skills in the sequence shown here. Normal, healthy infants may reach any of these milestones earlier or later than these average ages.

Babinski reflex: A reflex in which a newborn projects its toes outward and up when the soles of its feet are touched.

ensure survival in humanity's primate ancestors. Most of these reflexes disappear over the course of the first year of life. Physicians use the presence or absence of primary reflexes to assess neurological damage at birth and to evaluate an infant's rate of development. Table 10.3 summarizes the primary reflexes and their duration. One primary reflex exhibited by infants is the **Babinski reflex**—a projection of the toes

Table 10.3 Newborns' Reflexes

Reflex	Initiated By	Response	Duration
Eye blink	Flashing a light in the infant's eyes	Closing both eyes	Continues throughout life
Babinski	Gently stroking the sole of the infant's foot	Flexing the big toe; fanning out the other toes	Usually disappears near the end of the first year
Withdrawal	Pricking the sole of the infant's foot	Flexing of the leg	Present during the first 10 days; present but less intense later
Plantar	Pressing a finger against the ball of the infant's foot	Curling all the toes under	Disappears between 8 and 12 months
Moro	Making a sudden loud sound	Extending the arms and legs; then bringing arms towards each other in convulsive manner; crying	Begins to decline in 3rd month; gone by 5th month
Rooting	Stroking the infant's cheek lightly with a finger or a nipple	Turning the head towards the finger, opening the mouth, and trying to suck	Disappears at approximately 3 to 4 months
Sucking	Placing a finger in the infant's mouth	Sucking rhythmically	Often less intense and less regular during the first 3 to 4 days of life but continues for several months

outward and up in response to a touch to the sole of the foot. Another is the **Moro reflex**—an outstretching of the arms and legs and crying in response to a loud noise or a sudden, unexpected change in the environment. Newborns also exhibit the **rooting reflex**—the turning of the head towards a mild stimulus (such as a breast or hand) that touches their lips or cheek. They show the **sucking reflex** in response to a finger placed in their mouth and the **grasping reflex** in response to an object touching the palms of their hands—infants vigorously grasp objects touching their palm or fingers.

Moro reflex: A reflex in which a newborn stretches out its arms and legs and cries in response to a loud noise or a sudden, unexpected change in the environment.

Rooting reflex: A reflex in which a newborn turns its head towards a mild stimulus that touches its lips or cheek.

Sucking reflex: A reflex in which a newborn makes sucking motions when presented with a stimulus to the lips, such as a nipple.

Grasping reflex: A reflex in which a newborn vigorously grasps any object touching its palm or fingers or placed in its hand.

At first, an infant's abilities and reflexes are innate (biologically determined by the human genetic code). Gradually, learned responses, such as reaching for desired objects or grasping a cup, replace reflex reactions. The baby's experiences in the environment become more important in determining development. These complex interactions between nature and nurture follow a developmental time course that continues throughout life.

Infant Perception: Fantz's Viewing Box. An avalanche of research on infant perception shows that newborns have surprisingly well-developed perceptual systems. Robert Fantz (1961) did some of the earliest work on infant perception. He designed a viewing box in which he placed an infant; he then had a hidden observer or camera record the infant's responses to stimuli (see Figure 10.4).

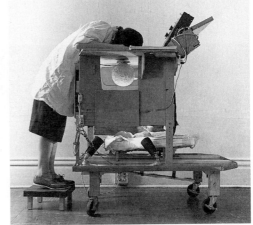

The exciting part of Fantz's work was not that he asked interesting questions but that he was able to get "answers" from the infants. By showing infants various pictures of faces and patterns and recording their eye movements, he discovered the infants' visual preferences. He recorded how long and how often the infants looked at each picture and calculated the total time they spent viewing each type of picture. Because they spent more time looking at pictures of faces than at pictures of random squiggles, Fantz concluded not only that they could see different patterns but that they preferred faces.

Other researchers confirm that human and non-human infants prefer complex visual fields over simple ones, curved patterns over straight or angular ones, and human faces over random patterns or faces with mixed-up features (Walton & Bower, 1993; Wilson & Goldman-Rakie, 1994). Even in the first few months of life, babies can discriminate among facial features and prefer attractive faces to less attractive ones (Langlois et al., 1990, 1991). Newborns look at pictures of their parents more than at pictures of strangers (de Haan & Nelson, 1997). Babies as young as three months can discern a caregiver's shift of attention by observing their eyes and then shift their own attention to the same object or event (Hood, Willen, & Driver, 1998). Also, as the photos show, babies sometimes respond to caregivers by imitating their facial expressions (pursed lips, stuck-out tongues). Research in this area with very young infants is controversial, and not all researchers are able to find consistent imitation in young infants (Abravanel & deYong, 1997; Meltzoff, 1996).

By seven months, infants know happy faces and sounds and can discriminate among them. According to Arlene Walker-Andrews (1997), they recognize emotional

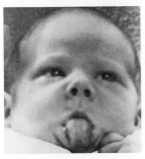

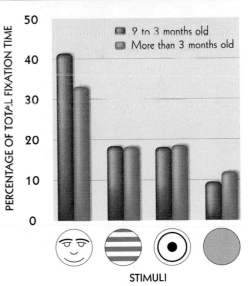

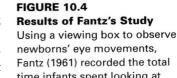

STIMULI

FIGURE 10.4
Results of Fantz's Study
Using a viewing box to observe newborns' eye movements, Fantz (1961) recorded the total time infants spent looking at various patterns. He found that they looked at faces or patterned material much more often than they looked at plain fields.

expressions. Using a procedure similar to Fantz's, Walker-Andrews (1986) observed five- and seven-month-old infants who saw films of people with angry or happy facial expressions making angry or happy sounds. (The lower third of each face was covered so that the infants could not match the sounds to the lips.) Walker-Andrews showed that seven-month-old infants could tell when the sound and facial expression did not match, but five-month-olds could not. This research suggests a timetable by which infants develop the ability to discriminate among facial expressions.

Infant perception is quite good; it follows a maturational timetable, but there are discontinuities in perceptual development. At first, babies attend to the most prominent features in the world; as time passes, they attend to, recognize, and respond to the world based on their recognition of people and situations—they begin to make more cognitive-based perceptual decisions (Bhatt, 1997; Bronson, 1997).

The Visual Cliff. Gibson and Walk conducted a classic developmental research study in 1961. They devised the *visual cliff method* to determine the extent of infants' depth perception. In this method the researcher places an infant who can crawl on a glass surface, half of which is covered with a checkerboard pattern. The

same pattern is placed several feet below the transparent half of the glass surface. Infants can crawl easily from the patterned area onto the transparent area. Infants who lack depth perception should be willing to crawl onto the transparent side as often as onto the patterned side. Conversely, infants who have depth perception should refuse to crawl onto the transparent side, even when encouraged to do so by their mothers. Walk and Gibson found that nine-month-olds avoided the transparent surface, thus proving that they have depth perception.

In sum, newborns enter the world with the ability to experience, respond to, and learn from the environment. In general, therefore, psychologists say that the sensory systems of newborns are well formed but still developing; their development is very much shaped by experience, which ultimately alters brain connections permanently (M. Leon, 1992). Newborns are thus genetically equipped and ready to learn, perceive, and experience the world; their brains develop, neurons interconnect, and the complexity of neuronal development continues. Recall from Chapter 3 that, although most of the connections of a newborn's visual system are present at the birth, the proper functioning of the system is sensitive to and depends on experience (Wong et al., 1995) and the tasks given to the individual (Jacobs & Kosslyn, 1995). Without proper and varied perceptual experiences, less than optimal brain development occurs. Babies' development proceeds in a certain order and according to a rough timetable of developmental events during infancy and early childhood. These events are the topics considered next.

Focus

Review

◆ What are the fundamental differences between the psychoanalytic and the cognitive views of development? p. 333–334

◆ What is the evidence that the embryonic stage is crucial for fetal development? p. 338

Think Critically

◆ What ancient survival value might each of the primary reflexes have had?

◆ What survival function might infants' preferences for human faces have?

Cognitive Development

W hy do some automobiles have childproof locks and windows? Why do parents use gates to guard stairs and gadgets to keep kitchen cabinets closed? Why are young children's toys made so that small parts cannot come off? The answer: Children are inquisitive and much more intelligent than many people give them credit for. Even three-month-olds can learn the order of a list of items, and when given age-appropriate prompts can remember that information a day later (Gulya et al., 1998).

The physical development of infants is visible and dramatic; parents of infants will tell you that their babies seem to grow and change every day. The cognitive changes that occur in young children are less visible but no less dramatic. Children are continually developing, both physically and cognitively; they focus their attention on coping with an ever-expanding world and, as they mature, can determine causes of events. Much of this developing ability is cognitively based (Miller & Aloise, 1989). Figure 10.5 on page 344 shows some of the many cognitive activities of the first 12 months. Without question, the leading figure of the twentieth century in studying and theorizing about children's and adults' cognitive development was Jean Piaget; his work laid the foundation for our current understanding of the development of thought.

Jean Piaget's Insights

Swiss psychologist Jean Piaget (1896–1980) came to believe that the fundamental development of all cognitive abilities takes place during the first two years of life; many psychologists and educators agree. Piaget devised ingenious procedures for examining the mysteries of cognitive development of young children; he looked at what children did well, what mistakes they made, and when and how they gained insights into the world. Piaget's theory focuses on *how* people think instead of on *what* they think, making it applicable to people in all societies and cultures. Perhaps Piaget's greatest strength, however, was his description of how a person's inherited capacities interact with their actions in the environment to produce a cognitively functioning child and adult. Although psychologists initially were sceptical of Piaget's ideas, and some criticisms persist, many researchers have shown that his assumptions are generally correct and can be applied cross-culturally. There are also dissenters (notably Russian psychologist Lev Vygotsky, whose theories we will consider later), who stress culture's role in shaping thought processes (Rogoff & Morelli, 1989). Piaget had a stronger child emphasis, asserting that cognitive development grows out of the interaction between biological changes that take place within a child and a child's experience in using the mind to try to understand the world. What Piaget did best was focus on the details of a child's cognitive life; he observed them in minute detail and noticed discontinuities in children's limitations and abilities at various ages. It was from these observations that he developed his approach. Piaget's explanations of cognitive development follow the child's movement from a self-centred infant to an independent, thinking adolescent. He believed that this development is due to fundamental changes in how the child's thinking is organized.

Key Concepts. Piaget believed that developmental changes in cognition occur as children try to make sense of their experiences. He called organized ways of interacting with the environment and experiencing the world **schemes**; schemes are mental structures or basic ways of knowing or making sense out of experience, but also include actions (such as looking, reaching, and grasping). Initially, infants and toddlers develop schemes for motor behaviours, like realizing that reaching out and touching an object will move it. Schemes develop because a child realizes that a particular action is associated with a particular outcome. Those results then, in turn,

Scheme: In Piaget's view, a specific mental structure; an organized way of interacting with the environment and experiencing it.

1 week
- See patterns, light, and dark
- Are sensitive to the location of a sound
- Distinguish volume and pitch
- Prefer high voices
- Will grasp an object if they touch it accidentally
- Stop sucking to look at a person momentarily

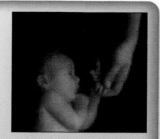

1 month
- Become excited at the sight of a person or a toy
- Look at objects only if in their line of vision
- Prefer patterns to plain fields
- Coordinate eyes sideways, up, and down
- Follow a toy from the side to the centre of the body

2 months
- Prefer people to objects
- Stare at human faces; become quiet at the sound of a human voice
- Are startled at sounds and make a facial response
- Perceive depth
- Coordinate eye movements
- Reach out voluntarily instead of grasping reflexively
- Discriminate among voices, people, tastes, and objects

3 months
- Follow moving objects
- Glance from one object to another
- Distinguish near objects from distant objects
- Search with eyes for the source of a sound
- Become aware of self through exploration
- Show basic signs of memory

4 to 7 months
- See the world in colour and with near-adult vision
- Pull dangling objects towards them
- Follow dangling or moving objects
- Turn to follow sound and vanishing objects
- Visually search out fast-moving or fallen objects
- Begin to anticipate a whole object when shown only part of it
- Deliberately imitate sounds and movements
- Recall a short series of actions
- Look briefly for a toy that disappears

8 to 12 months
- Put small objects into containers and pull them out of containers
- Search behind a screen for an object after they see it hidden there
- Hold and manipulate one object while looking at another object
- Recognize dimensions of objects

FIGURE 10.5
Infants' Perceptual and Cognitive Milestones

(After Clarke-Stewart, Friedman, & Koch, 1985, p. 191.)

may affect the child's future behaviour and development; for example, the child learns that the amount of force they use will determine how far the object will move. This entire process of constructing schemes through actions on and in the environment is called *adaptation*. As adaptation continues, a child organizes his or her schemes into more complex mental representations, linking one scheme with another. Ultimately, schemes develop about play, make-believe, and the permanence of objects, for example. For a child to develop schemes, and for mental structures to grow more complex, two key processes must occur: assimilation and accommodation.

Both children and adults use the processes of assimilation and accommodation to deal with new information and experiences. **Assimilation** is the process by which a person absorbs new ideas and experiences and incorporates them into existing schemes. **Accommodation** is the process of modifying previously developed schemes to adapt them to new experiences. A child who learns to grasp a ball demonstrates assimilation by later grasping other round objects in a manner similar to the one used to grasp the ball. This assimilated behaviour then serves as a foundation for accommodation. The child can learn new and more complex behaviours for grasping forks, crayons, and sticks by modifying the earlier response—for example, by widening or narrowing the grasp. The two processes alternate in a never-ending cycle of cognitive growth throughout the four stages of development that Piaget described. The stages and processes involved are part of an active construction of reality and the world—babies and young children piece together their own constructions of the world, rather than directly absorb what adults teach them. Importantly, Piaget asserts that children are active in their own cognitive development and therefore are not simply passive recipients of knowledge and information.

Four *stages* of cognitive development are central to Piaget's theory. Piaget believed that just as standing must precede walking, each stage of cognitive development must precede the next. For example, a preschooler does not understand the logical relationship between height and width. Therefore, even if a parent carefully measures a soft drink equally into two different-sized glasses, the preschooler feels cheated if the level of the soft drink in his shorter, wider glass is lower than that in his older brother's taller, narrower glass. The older brother understands that differences in height can compensate for differences in width and is therefore unsympathetic to the preschooler's "illogical" demand for more soda pop. Piaget's stages are associated with approximate ages. The exact age for each stage varies with the individual, but children in all cultures go through the same stages in the same order. Piaget acknowledged the complex interaction of environmental influences and genetic inheritances; nevertheless, he felt strongly that the order of stages was invariant. The four developmental stages he proposed are the sensorimotor stage, the preoperational stage, the concrete operational stage, and the formal operational stage.

The Sensorimotor Stage. Piaget considered the **sensorimotor stage**, which extends from birth to about age two, to be of critical importance, because the foundation for all cognitive development is established during this period. Consider the enormous changes that take place during the first two years of life. At birth an infant is a totally dependent, reflexive organism. Within weeks, infants learn some simple behaviours. They ingenuously smile at their caregivers; they attend to objects in their visual range, such as mobiles hanging overhead; they appear captured by human voices; they anticipate events in the environment, for example, by arching their backs in anticipation of being picked up. At two to three months, infants develop some motor coordination skills (Clifton et al., 1993; Thelen, 1994), a memory for past events, and an ability to predict future visual events (Gulya et al., 1998; Haith & McCarty, 1990). According to Piaget, this early acquisition of memory is a crucial foundation for further cognitive development.

By the age of six to eight months, infants seek new and more interesting kinds of stimulation. They can sit up and crawl. No longer willing just to watch what goes on around them, they begin to actively manipulate their environment, attempting what Piaget called "making interesting sights last." They may throw a toy or their food onto the floor from their high chair over and over again so that they can watch the adults around them run about and react. Infants at this stage exhibit some fairly sophisticated cognitive abilities. For example, Karen Wynn (1992) suggests that infants at this age have some very basic numerical reasoning abilities that lay the foundation for further arithmetic reasoning development (Starkey, 1992). At about eight months, infants can form simple intentions, and they attempt to overcome obstacles in order to reach goals. They can now crawl to the other side of a room to where the cat is lying or follow a parent into the next room.

Assimilation: According to Piaget, the process by which a person absorbs new ideas and experiences and incorporates them into existing schemes.

Accommodation: According to Piaget, the process of modifying previously developed schemes to adapt them to new experiences.

Sensorimotor stage: The first of Piaget's four stages of cognitive development (covering roughly the first two years of life), during which the child begins to interact with the environment and the rudiments of memory are established.

From about eight months on, babies develop *object permanence*—the ability to realize that objects continue to exist even when they are out of sight. Prior to the development of object permanence, when an object moves out of a baby's range of sight, the baby "forgets" about it. After object permanence develops, the baby realizes that the object is just out of view. This creates a fundamental change in how the baby interacts with the environment. For example, infants can now begin to search in simple ways for objects that are no longer in sight. Although the exact age at which object permanence becomes evident has not yet been established, Renée Baillargeon (1994, 1996) has shown the existence of object permanence for some tasks in four-month-olds—earlier than Piaget believed possible. In general, Baillargeon (1998) asserts that infants have knowledge of the physical world and that they have a specialized learning ability that guides their acquisition of such knowledge with various aspects of object permanence evolving gradually throughout the sensorimotor stage. She believes that Piaget's tasks for establishing the presence of object permanence were overly dependent on motor (reaching) responses and feels that Piaget missed the presence of object permanence in young children because they had not yet developed this motor skill.

In the second half of the sensorimotor stage (from about 12 to 24 months), children begin to walk, talk, and to deliberately act on their environment. Object permanence is more fully developed; the child can now follow a ball that rolls away and can search for his or her mother after she has left the room. Children also begin to use language to represent the world, an ability that allows them to create a symbol (word/idea) for an object.

The Preoperational Stage. In the **preoperational stage**, which lasts from about age two to age six or seven, children begin to use their newfound ability to represent the world symbolically. By age two, a child can talk about Grandma, Daddy, doggy, cookies, Big Bird, going bye-bye, and other objects and events. They can now engage in games of pretend (using a broom for a horse), they can defer imitation (sitting in a toy box imitating a bus driver from a trip with Grandpa two week ago), and they can use language. They are not restricted to the immediate present. No longer an uncoordinated, reflex-oriented organism, the child has become a thinking, walking, talking human being. The abilities to represent and to use symbols mark the beginning of the preoperational stage. Nonetheless, children continue to think about specifics and cannot deal with thoughts that are not easily represented visually.

A key element of the preoperational stage—which affects a child's cognitive and emotional behaviour—is egocentrism. **Egocentrism** is the inability to understand the role that perspective can play in a situation. If a child has seen a toy hidden or a present wrapped, he will not be able to separate this "privileged" information (which he now knows) from what others know, and will expect others to know where to look for the hidden toy or what is in the wrapped package. Because of cognitive immaturity, a young child talking on the phone will answer questions by nodding her head in silence. The child still cannot put herself in the caller's (or anyone else's) position. Egocentrism also leads them to interpret the world entirely from their own perspective. For example, they respond to questions such as "Why does it snow?" with answers such as "So I can play in it."

At the end of Piaget's preoperational stage, children are just beginning to understand the difference between their ideas, feelings, and interests and those of others. This process of **decentration**—understanding the concept of perspective or point of view and thus being able to recognize other people's feelings, ideas, and viewpoints—continues for several years. It allows the child to become less preoccupied with their own perspective and to see other points of view or more than one aspect of a situation.

Piaget further held that children's understanding of space and their construction of alternative visual perspectives is limited during the preoperational stage. Recent evidence, however, suggests that Piaget may have underestimated the visual perspective abilities of children by using tasks that were too complex. For example, Piaget asked children about what a doll would see when it was placed on the other side of a

Preoperational stage: Piaget's second stage of cognitive development (lasting from about age two to age six or seven), during which initial symbolic thought is developed.

Egocentrism [ee-go-SENT-rism]: The inability to understand the role that perspective can play in a situation; self-centredness.

Decentration: Understanding the concept of perspective or point of view and thus being able to recognize other people's

detailed model of three mountains. He claimed that children either were confused about what the doll would see or attributed their own view to the doll. When much simpler displays are used (for example, three Disney character dolls arranged in a simple circle) children as young as three years of age show a rudimentary grasp of what someone seated opposite them would see and how it would differ from what they themselves see. Research now shows that even three-year-olds can solve certain visual and space perspective problems previously thought to be solely in the domain of 7- to 10-year-olds (Newcombe & Huttenlocher, 1992).

The Concrete Operational Stage.

The **concrete operational stage** is Piaget's third stage of cognitive development, lasting from approximately age 6 or 7 to age 11 or 12; during this stage children develop the ability to understand constant factors in the environment, rules, and higher-order symbolic systems such as arithmetic and geography. They can look at a situation from more than one point of view and can evaluate different aspects of it. They have gained sufficient mental maturity to be able to distinguish between appearance and reality and to think ahead one or two moves in checkers or other games. During this stage, children discover what remains logically constant in the world; they learn rules and understand the reasons for them. For example, a child learns to wear a raincoat on a cloudy morning, anticipating rain later in the day.

The hallmark of this stage is an understanding of **conservation**—the ability to recognize that the appearances of objects may be transformed by changing their shape, for example, yet still be the same at an underlying level such as their number, weight, substance, or volume. This concept has been the subject of considerable research. In a typical conservation task, a child is shown three beakers. Two beakers are short, squat, and half full of water; a third is tall, thin, and empty (see Figure 10.6). The experimenter pours the water from one short, squat beaker into the tall, narrow one and asks the child which beaker has more water. A child who does not understand the principle of conservation (such as the younger brother from our earlier example) will claim that the taller beaker contains more water. A child who is able to conserve liquid quantity will recognize that the same amount of water is contained in both the tall and the short beaker. A child who has mastered one type of conservation (for example, conservation of liquid quantity) often cannot immediately transfer that knowledge to other conservation tasks (for example, the idea that two stacked weights weigh the same as the two weights placed side by side).

Concrete operational stage: Piaget's third stage of cognitive development (lasting from approximately age 6 or 7 to age 11 or 12), during which the child develops the ability to understand constant factors in the environment, rules, and higher-order symbolism.

Conservation: The ability to recognize that perceptual changes (such as the "shape" of a liquid put in a different container) may not indicate that an underlying quality has changed (for example, the liquid still has the same weight, substance, or volume).

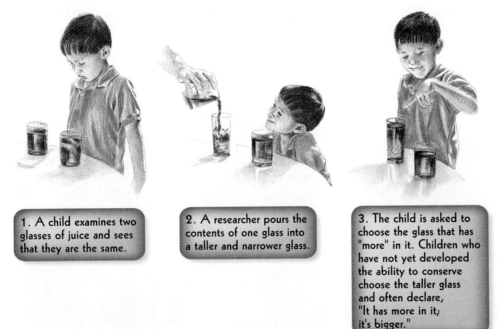

1. A child examines two glasses of juice and sees that they are the same.

2. A researcher pours the contents of one glass into a taller and narrower glass.

3. The child is asked to choose the glass that has "more" in it. Children who have not yet developed the ability to conserve choose the taller glass and often declare, "It has more in it; it's bigger."

FIGURE 10.6
Development of Conservation
Conservation is the ability to recognize that an object that has been transformed is still the same object, regardless of any changes it has undergone.

Formal operational stage:
Piaget's fourth and final stage
of cognitive development
(beginning at about age 12),
during which the individual can
think hypothetically, can consider all future possibilities, and
is capable of deductive logic.

A child who masters the concept of conservation realizes that specific facts are true because they follow logically, not simply because they are observed. Thus, the child infers that the tall glass *must* have the same amount of water because no water was added or subtracted when the water was poured into it. Cognitive and percep-tual cognitive abilities continue to develop as children mature and, slowly and in different ways, begin to grasp new and ever more difficult concepts (Flavell, Green, & Flavell, 1989).

The Formal Operational Stage. The **formal operational stage** is Piaget's fourth and final stage of cognitive development (beginning at about age 12), during which the individual can think hypothetically, can consider all future possibilities, and is capable of deductive logic. Unlike children in the concrete operational stage, whose thoughts are still tied to the data of concrete situations, adolescents can engage in abstract thought. They do this by forming hypotheses that allow them to think of different ways to represent situations, organizing them into all possible relationships and outcomes. The cognitive world of adolescents is full of informal theories of logic and ideas about themselves and life; they now can undertake scien-tific experiments where they form and test hypotheses.

By age 12, the egocentrism of the sensorimotor and preoperational stages has for the most part disappeared, but a new egocentrism has developed (Elkind, 1967). According to Inhelder and Piaget (1958, pp. 345–346): "The adolescent goes through a phase in which he attributes an unlimited power to his own thoughts so that the dream of a glorious future or of transforming the world through ideas (even if this idealism takes a materialistic form) seems to be not only fantasy, but also an effective action which in itself modifies the empirical world." This phase is thought to be a result of the adolescents' first experiences with their new, formal operational way of viewing the world and their place in it. With time and experience, the ego-centrism and naïve hopes of adolescents eventually decrease as they face and deal with the challenges of life that we will explore further in the next chapter.

Piaget's stages of cognitive development are summarized in Figure 10.7.

Putting Piaget in Perspective. Parents, educators, and psychologists can enhance children's cognitive development by understanding how cognitive abilities develop. For example, Piaget recognized that parental love and parent–child inter-actions are always important to a child's development, but he asserted that they are *essential* in the first two years of life. For a child to develop object permanence, to learn how to make interesting sights last, and to develop the rudiments of numerical reasoning, it is necessary for caregivers to provide abundant physical and cognitive stimuli, especially stimuli that move and change colour, shape, and form. Research confirms that children and animals given sensory stimulation from birth through the early months develop more quickly both cognitively and socially than those who

**FIGURE 10.7
Piaget's Stages of
Cognitive Development**

SENSORIMOTOR STAGE	PREOPERATIONAL STAGE	CONCRETE OPERATIONAL STAGE	FORMAL OPERATIONAL STAGE
(Age 0–2) The child begins to interact with the environment.	(Age 2–6 or 7) The child begins to represent the world symbolically.	(Age 7–11 or 12) The child learns rules such as conservation.	(Age 12–adulthood) The adolescent can transcend concrete situations and think about the future.

are not given such stimulation. Parents and educators who agree with Piaget have devoted their efforts to ensuring that the first years of life are ones in which stimulation is great, curiosity is encouraged, and exploration is maximized. A key to an enriched environment is that children be given the freedom to manipulate objects and see them from multiple vantage points; expensive toys are not necessary—variety is the key. Psychologists advising governments about early intervention programs such as Better Beginnings, Better Futures in Ontario agree that an enriched preschool environment could help children from disadvantaged backgrounds.

Although Piaget's ideas have had an enormous influence on the ways psychologists think about children's development, some researchers have problems with his approach. Psychologist Rochel Gelman argues that researchers like Piaget tend to underestimate younger children's abilities. For example, Shatz and Gelman (1973) found that two-year-olds change the length of their sentences on the basis of whom they are talking to, using shorter sentences when speaking to younger children. The researchers argue that this ability may reflect a level of cognitive maturity beyond that of an "egocentric" preoperational child. Like Gelman, many other researchers claim that Piaget may have overestimated the degree of egocentrism in young children. Baillargeon asserts that Piaget also underestimated the visual perspective abilities of infants. She holds that abilities such as understanding what actually happens to objects when they are hidden, which Piaget saw as developing at 18 months, can be found at 6 months of age and earlier (Miller & Baillargeon, 1990). Most recently, Baillargeon (Baillargeon, 1998; Needham, Baillargeon, & Kaufman, 1998) has argued that infants are born with specialized learning mechanisms that allow for their acquisition of knowledge about the physical world—an interesting assertion that needs further research.

Vygotsky's Sociocultural Theory: An Alternative to Piaget

Piaget saw the child as an organism that is self-motivated to abstract reality from the world. The child, he held, is a busy constructor of reality, making interesting sights last, inventing games, and learning abstract rules. But Lev Vygotsky (1896–1934) saw the child not as alone in this task but as part of a social w filled with communication with the self and others. For Vygotsky, children constantly trying to extract meaning from the social world and master higher-order concepts and are aided in this by the ways in which their exp ences are structured by parents, teachers, siblings, peers, and others (Bru 1997). At first, children's mental life expresses itself in interaction with o people. Later, children engage in *private speech* (speech out loud, but to the selves) to plan and guide their own actions and behaviour; when they u such speech, they do better in various tasks (Bivens & Berk, 1990). It important to note that Piaget believed that private speech was egocentric, d not involve perspective taking, and therefore had no communicative inter or more general purpose. Vygotsky suggests just the opposite; private speech is essential in that it is self-directive and thus helps a child understand his or her world and that of other people. Think of the last time you engaged in a complex task—for example, putting something together or playing a video game—and admit that you may have been talking to yourself a bit at the time. For Vygotsky (1934/1962) even the earliest speech is essentially social and useful; in fact, he asserts that social speech comes first, followed by private speech, then inner speech (fully

Focus

Review

◆ What is the difference between assimilation and accommodation? p. 345
◆ From Piaget's point of view, why are the first two years a critical time for cognitive development? pp. 348–349
◆ How is Vygotsky's approach different from Piaget's? pp. 349–350

Think Critically

◆ Assuming that Piaget did in fact overestimate the extent of egocentrism in young children, what might be another explanation for apparently egocentric behaviour in a child?
◆ What are the implications of Vygotsky's view that the most significant moment in intellectual development occurs when speech and practical activity converge?
◆ Describe how you might use scaffolding to teach a child a game.

internalized speech). Vygotsky wrote that "the most significant moment in the course of intellectual development . . . occurs . . . when speech and practical activity, two previously completely independent lines of development, converge" (Vygotsky, 1930/1978, p. 24).

To a great extent, Vygotsky focused much of his writing on trying to understand what he called *culturally patterned dialogue*. Vygotsky emphasized extracting meaning from the world, especially through verbal (social) interchanges, and he particularly tried to examine the culture, situation, and context through which meaning is extracted. Vygotsky's approach can be considered *sociocultural* (Bruner, 1997), as it focuses on the social and cultural roots of human knowledge and development.

Vygotsky was especially concerned with how other people provide information about culture to children. From a Vygotskian perspective, skills and knowledge are culture bound (Meadows, 1998). In Chapter 5, we considered the role of cooperative learning in education and saw that when students cooperate in teams they do better. Vygotsky's theory would predict such a result.

Vygotsky held that when children are presented with tasks that are just outside of their current abilities, they need the help of culture and society—usually parents—to accomplish them. Vygotsky referred to the *zone of proximal development* as the difference between what children can do on their own and what they can accomplish with the aid of a parent, teacher, sibling, or peer (or a large purple dinosaur, for that matter). When more skilled individuals help a child, the child can try out new skills and eventually incorporates those new skills and ideas into his or her repertoire of behaviour. The child can engage in an interactive process that can also be referred to as *scaffolding*, where one person sets a structure for another that enables that person to succeed at a task that they could not accomplish alone. As a child learns, the adult gradually removes the scaffolding and makes the task slightly harder or more complicated so that the child learns the next rules of engagement. This interactive, collaborative process leads to developmental advancement for the child (Meadows, 1998; Stringer, 1998).

Moral Reasoning

F ew children make it to adolescence without squabbling with their siblings. The adult in charge usually tells them to stop fighting with their sister or brother and announces that such behaviour is "unacceptable." As children grow, they develop the capacity to assess for themselves what is right and wrong. They decide what actions, such as helping the homeless or turning in a cheater, are right, wrong, acceptable, or unacceptable. Most people at one time or another are faced with decisions that challenge their conscience. The classic example, often presented to children, is whether they should turn in a wallet to the police that has no identification but contains $100. From childhood on, individuals develop **morality**—a system of learned attitudes about social practices, institutions, and individual behaviour that allows a person to evaluate situations and behaviour as being right or wrong, good or bad.

Morality: A system of learned attitudes about social practices, institutions, and individual behaviour that allows a person to evaluate situations and behaviour as being right or wrong, good or bad.

Attitudes about specific outcomes, such as who gets the window seat, as well as decisions about important moral issues develop and change throughout life. Beginning in their preschool years, children learn from their parents the behaviours, attitudes, and values considered appropriate and correct in their culture. Morality also is communicated by teachers, religious and community leaders, and friends. As children mature, they acquire attitudes that accommodate an increasingly complex view of reality. Your views of morality when you were 10 years old probably differ from your views today. But do they? Or is the reasoning and judgment of a child, a preteen, or an adolescent as sound as that of an adult?

Piaget and Kohlberg

Piaget examined children's ability to analyze questions of morality and found the results to be consistent with his ideas about cognitive development. Young children's ideas about morality are based on what others (their parents) tell them is right or wrong (called *heteronomous*, meaning directed by someone else); young children expect that immediate consequences will follow any transgression. When playing a game, a young child pays only passing attention to the rules, and, in marble games, for example, seems to assume that everyone will go home with their own marbles at the end of the day. Older children, on the other hand, recognize that rules are established to regulate social interaction, for example, in peer groups. Older children have developed a sense of *moral autonomy* (meaning self-directed morality), which allows them to recognize that situational factors affect perceptions and that if they play by the rules all involved should recognize that the game proceeded "fairly" despite who wins (Piaget, 1932).

According to Piaget, as children develop cognitively, their moral judgments move away from inflexibility and towards relativity (to context). When young children are questioned about lying, for example, they respond that it is always bad under any circumstances—a person should never lie. Between the ages of 5 and 12, however, children recognize that lying may be permissible in special circumstances—for example, when you lie to a bully so that he will not hurt your friend or when you lie to avoid hurting someone else's feelings.

Piaget's theory of moral development was based on descriptions of how children responded to specific kinds of questions about moral situations and the ages at which they gave different answers. The research of Harvard psychologist Lawrence Kohlberg (1927–1987) grew out of Piaget's work both on moral development and on general cognitive development. Kohlberg believed that moral development in general proceeds through three levels, each of which is divided into two stages (though he eventually dropped the sixth stage, as he could not find a significant number of people who used it consistently). The central concept in Kohlberg's theory is *justice*, the idea that morality ultimately comes down to a sophisticated or principled balance of individual rights and responsibilities. In his studies of moral reasoning, Kohlberg presented moral dilemmas to people of various ages and asked them to describe what the stories meant to them and how they felt about them (Kohlberg, 1969). Table 10.4 shows how Kohlberg's theory of moral development and Piaget's theories of moral and cognitive development compare.

Three Levels of Morality. In one of Kohlberg's stories, Heinz, a poor man, considers stealing a drug for his wife, who will die without it. Presented with the story of Heinz, people at level 1, *preconventional morality*, either condemn Heinz's behaviour or justify it based on what he gets out of it (for example, prison time or a wife that lives). People at level 2, *conventional morality*, have internalized society's rules and say that Heinz broke the law by stealing and should go to jail or that the marital contract obliges him to do all he can to save his wife. Only people who have reached level 3, *postconventional morality*, can see that although Heinz's action was illegal, it may be justified on the principled grounds that the right to life takes precedence over rights to property (see Figure 10.8).

Table 10.4 A Comparison of Piaget's Cognitive and Moral Theories and Kohlberg's Theory on Moral Development

Piaget Cognitive	Piaget Moral	Kohlberg Moral
Sensorimotor and preoperational (birth to 6 or 7 years)	Heteronomous morality	Level 1—Preconventional morality Stage 1: Obedience and punishment orientation Stage 2: Naively egoistic orientation
Concrete operational (7 to 11 or 12 years)	Autonomous morality	Level 2—Conventional morality Stage 3: Good-child orientation Stage 4: Authority-and-social order maintaining orientation
Formal operations (12 years and beyond)		Level 3—Postconventional morality Stage 5: Contractual–legalistic orientation Stage 6: Conscience or principle orientation

Young children at level 1, *preconventional morality*, base their decisions about right and wrong on the likelihood of avoiding punishment and obtaining rewards. A child in this stage would say it is "bad" to pull the cat's tail "because Mom will send me to my room." Level 2, *conventional morality*, is first adopted by school-aged children; they conform to avoid the disapproval of other people. At this stage, a 10-year-old might choose not to try cigarettes because he values being viewed as a good boy and knows his parents and friends disapprove of smoking. A process that considers the implications of a person's behaviour also governs level 2 judgments: What would the general social consequences be if everyone behaved in that manner? The social order is understood to function so long as people generally attend to the rules that make it work.

As individuals move towards level 3, *postconventional morality*, they become more able to move beyond fixed rules and laws and focus on principles. The principles at issue here are the sort found in documents such as the Canadian Charter of Rights and Freedoms or the U.S. Constitution. In level 3 morality, people make

FIGURE 10.8
Development of Morality over Time
In Kohlberg's theory of morality, a distinct progression of moral development emerges over a child's life. Children do not often achieve the highest, or postconventional, levels of moral reasoning.

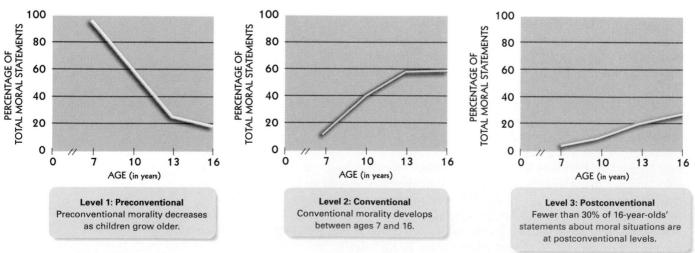

Level 1: Preconventional
Preconventional morality decreases as children grow older.

Level 2: Conventional
Conventional morality develops between ages 7 and 16.

Level 3: Postconventional
Fewer than 30% of 16-year-olds' statements about moral situations are at postconventional levels.

judgments on the basis of their perception of the needs of society, with the goal of maintaining community welfare and order. Only a minority reaches level 3. In advanced stages of level 3, people make judgments on the basis of personally constructed moral principles, rather than societal teachings. Conscientious objection (breaking laws or refusing to engage in behaviour viewed as morally wrong) is associated with this stage. For example, a person may recognize that laws such as segregation laws are unjust because they violate a basic principle of respecting the rights of all people.

Being capable of the highest level of moral reasoning does not guarantee that people will always operate at that level. Research conducted at the University of British Columbia by Brian de Vries and Lawrence Walker (1986) indicates that when thinking about issues such as capital punishment, about one-quarter of participants used reasoning that was a full stage lower than their highest possible stage. Much research is being done to determine what influences people's moral reasoning.

Gender Differences: Gilligan's Work

Criticisms of Kohlberg's pioneering research came from Carol Gilligan (1982, 1994, 1997), who found that people look at more than justice when they analyze moral conflicts. She discovered that people also are concerned with caring, relationships, and connections with other people.

Though Kohlberg and his colleagues generally had not reported any gender differences, Gilligan did. *Gender differences* are, of course, differences between males and females in behaviour or mental processes. Gilligan noted differences between males and females in their inclinations towards caring and justice. She found that females are more concerned with care, relationships, and connections with other people—she hypothesized a feminine orientation to moral issues. As younger children, girls are socialized towards a morality of caring, whereas boys are socialized towards a morality of justice. Drawing on work by Nancy Chodorow (1978), Gilligan asserts that the difference between boys and girls is established by gender socialization and by the child's relationship with the mother. Where children spend more time with their mothers or other female caregivers during their preschool years, Gilligan argues that boys, who have identified with their fathers as being male, work at being essentially different from the female adults who are caring for them. This establishes autonomy, assertiveness, and self interest as central developmental goals. By identifying with their female caregivers, girls do not have to sever the close social ties that developed between them during the dependency of infancy and develop a sense of self based on those and other connections and relationships. These, of course, are socialization stereotypes and are intended to indicate the general directions in which males and females are socialized in Western society. Males can and do think in terms of connectedness and caring just as females can and do think in terms of autonomy and justice.

Gilligan asserts that the transition to adolescence is a crucial time, during which girls may develop their own voice—a voice based on caring and connection that too often is muted and suppressed (Gilligan, 1997). Gilligan shows that boys respond to Kohlberg's Heinz dilemma by indicating that sometimes people must act on their own to do the right thing. Girls, in contrast, are more likely to look for ways to discuss differences and seek compromise. Like Kohlberg, Gilligan argues that the development of caring follows a time line, with caring initially felt only towards oneself, later felt towards others, and ultimately (in some people) a more mature stage of caring for truth. Gilligan's work has been influential with respect to psychologists' evaluations of morality. Yet there is concern that her approach perpetuates gender stereotyping—women as nurturing, men as logical. Despite widespread acceptance of her view that Kohlberg's work is biased against women, there exists surprisingly little research examining just how these two models might function in normal development (Lapsley, 1996; Lollis, Ross, & Leroux, 1996).

Focus

Review

◆ Distinguish the key differences between pre-conventional, conventional, and postconventional morality. pp. 351–352
◆ What was Gilligan's main criticism of Kohlberg's work? p. 353

Think Critically

◆ What is a potential problem with using Kohlberg's stories (such as the one about Heinz) to study moral development?

Does women's inclination towards caring show itself in other cultures? Stimpson, Jensen, and Neff (1992) examined questionnaire responses of women in Korea, China, Thailand, and the United States. Their results show that Gilligan's work on socialized differences in moral orientation holds up in the three non-Western cultures, and they speculate that differences in caring between men and women initially may have a biological origin.

The study of morality, justice, and caring has gone beyond Kohlberg's original view. For example, Kitwood (1990) argues that only after people have developed a sense of themselves can they fully care about others; he thus combines personality theory (discussed in Chapter 12) with studies of morality. Moral reasoning and behaviour, and especially moral socialization, have to be studied within the context of the total person and that consideration means examining gender, cultural, ethnic, and age differences.

Emotional and Social Development

Anne Frank, the Jewish girl who hid in an attic from the Nazis (and who ultimately was killed) during the Second World War, eloquently thanked the people who helped hide her and her family in her diary. She wrote extensively of her dedication and gratitude to the people who were making sacrifices and putting their own lives at risk to help her family; she affirmed the morality of their actions. For an adolescent, Anne showed extraordinary emotional maturity. Making moral decisions is not independent of a person's emotional life. In fact, morality without the "heat" of emotional response would not seem particularly moral. Emotions are an aspect of human behaviour that begin to develop shortly after birth with the attachments that infants form with caregivers.

Attachment: The Earliest Emotions

Attachment is the formal term psychologists use to describe the strong emotional tie that a person feels towards significant others. Attachment theory plays an important role in the emotional development of children. People's ability to express emotion and form attachments develops from birth through adulthood. Attachment behaviours develop in the early weeks and months of life and are evident during adolescence and adulthood, when people form close loving bonds with others. Most researchers consider these behaviours to be innate, even though they unfold slowly over the first year of life and are reinforced by caregivers. Emotional expressions—including attachment behaviours—not only appear in all cultures (see Chapter 9) but are found in deaf and blind people and in people without limbs, who have limited touch experiences (Izard & Saxton, 1988). Attachment, emotional expressions, and the bonds that form among people have been studied in depth. Heavily influenced by classic early work with rhesus monkeys done by Harry Harlow, this research was extended in the 1970s by work on bonding.

Classic Work: Attachment in Rhesus Monkeys. To find out how people develop attachment behaviours, Harry Harlow (1905–1981), a psychologist at the

Attachment: The strong emotional tie that a person develops towards significant others.

University of Wisconsin, focused on the development of attachment in rhesus monkeys. Harlow's initial studies were on the nature of early interactions among monkeys. But he found that monkeys raised from birth in isolated bare-wire cages away from their mothers did not survive, even though they were well fed. Other monkeys, raised in the same conditions but with scraps of terry cloth in their cages, survived. Terry cloth is hardly a critical variable in the growth and development of monkeys, yet its introduction into an otherwise bare cage made the difference between life and death for these infant rhesus monkeys. Harlow inferred that the terry cloth provided some measure of security. That conclusion led him to attempt to discover whether infant monkeys had an inborn need for love or warmth.

In a classic experiment, Harlow placed infant monkeys in cages along with two wire-covered shapes resembling adult monkeys. One figure was covered with terry cloth; the other was left bare. Both figures could be fitted with bottles to provide milk. In some cases, the wire figure had the bottle of milk; in other cases, the terry-cloth figure had the bottle. Harlow found that the infant monkeys clung to the terry-cloth figures whether or not they provided milk. As well, they rushed to the terry-cloth figure whenever they were frightened or anxious, a clear sign of attachment. He concluded that the wire figure, even with a bottle of milk, could not provide the comfort that the terry-cloth figure could provide (Harlow & Zimmerman, 1958).

Another of Harlow's findings was that regardless of which figure had the bottle, none of the monkeys grew up to be totally normal. They were more aggressive and fearful than monkeys raised normally. They also were unable to engage in normal sexual relations. And some of the infants raised with wire figures exhibited self-destructive behaviours (Harlow, 1962). These findings indicate that there is clearly more to attachment than just clinging to terry cloth.

Bonding. In the 1970s and 1980s, it was widely, though incorrectly, believed that parents bond to their infants soon after delivery. **Bonding** is a special process of emotional attachment that may occur between parents and babies in the minutes and hours immediately after birth. It is neither a reflex nor a learned behaviour. Pediatricians Marshall Klaus and John Kennell (1983) argued that a mother is in a state of heightened sensitivity to her child immediately after delivery and that she begins to form unique, specific attachment to the child at that time. But research has not supported claims for bonding. Eyer (1992) asserts that there is no evidence to support the existence of bonding and that, for humans at least, it is a fictional concept. Despite this, keeping parents and infants together in the hospital shortly after birth as advocated by Klaus has been welcomed by many parents (Kennell, Voos, & Klaus, 1979). There is no doubt, however, that the parent–infant attachment deepens in the first months of life.

Attachment in Infants. John Bowlby (1907–1990) studied the close attachment between mothers and their newborns. Bowlby (1977) argued that an infant's emotional tie with its caregiver is innate and evolves as a set of behavioural responses that promote survival. Bowlby asserted that an infant's very early interactions with its parents are crucial to normal development. In support of this view, research now shows that mothers recognize their newborns by smell, touch, and sound (Kaitz et al., 1992), and that newborn infants similarly recognize their mothers (Leon, 1992). Many psychologists consider the establishment of a close and warm parent–child relationship to be one of the major developmental milestones of the first year of life. This attachment is considered to be a key developmental event that helps an infant develop basic feelings about trust and security.

By the age of seven or eight months, after achieving object permanence, attachment to the mother may become so strong that her departure from the room causes a fear response, especially to strangers; this response is known as *separation anxiety* and reflects insecurity on the part of the infant. When infants fear that the principal caregiver, usually the mother, may not be consistently available, they become clingy

Bonding: A special process of emotional attachment that may occur between parents and babies in the minutes and hours immediately after birth.

and object to her disappearing (Ainsworth, 1979; Bowlby, 1988; Cassidy & Berlin, 1994). Infants also may demonstrate a heightened fear of strangers at this time. In attempting to analyze attachment to parents, influential research conducted in Canada by Mary Ainsworth used a procedure called the *strange situation technique*, in which babies from 12 to 24 months of age are observed with parents, removed briefly from them, and then reunited. Research with this technique shows that most babies (about 60 percent) are secure; they are distressed by a parent leaving but are easily comforted. Other babies (about 20 percent) are neither distressed by separations nor comforted by reunions—these babies are categorized as *avoidant* and are considered to have an insecure attachment. Still other babies (about 15 percent) are *resistant*; these babies seek closeness to the parent but when separated are angry and then show mixed feelings of both anger and proximity seeking when they are reunited (Ainsworth, Blehar, Waters, & Wall, 1978). Lastly, some babies (about 5 percent) are characterized as *disoriented*; they show confused, contradictory attachment behaviours and may act angry, sad, or ambivalent at any time (Main & Soloman, 1990). Although attachment theory has been criticized for being largely based on behaviours observed during stressful situations that are somewhat artificial (Field, 1996), it is nevertheless a good predictor of later developmental outcomes (Ainsworth, 1989; Brennan & Shaver, 1996).

Researchers find that secure babies have mothers who are affectionate and appropriately responsive (Isabella, Belsky, & von Eye, 1989). According to some researchers, this mother–child relationship facilitates both current behaviours and later cognitive and emotional development (Cassidy & Berlin, 1994; Hewlett et al., 1998). Not all researchers agree, and cross-cultural work shows significant variations (e.g., Tronick, Morelli, & Ivey, 1992), but studies indicate that the quality and nature of the mutual closeness formed between the young child and the mother can make a difference (Hewlett et al., 1998). Children who have not formed warm, close attachments early in life lack a sense of security and become anxious and overly dependent. As six-year-olds, they are perceived as more aggressive and less competent than their more secure counterparts (Cohn, 1990). Those who have close attachments require less discipline and are less easily distracted (Lewis & Feiring, 1989). There is evidence that early attachment relationships are predictive of other relationships as the child gets older. Ratings of older children's relationships with their mothers, for example, are positively correlated with ratings of infant attachment. Similarly, ratings of attachments with early teachers tend to predict the perceptions of later teachers. Such data led Howes, Hamilton, and Philipsen (1998) to conclude that early attachments exist in a wide variety of domains and affect later development.

Once established, early attachment is fairly stable. Babies are fairly resilient (Kier & Lewis, 1997) and brief separations from parents, as in child-care centres, do not adversely affect attachment. Influential psychologist Mary Ainsworth (1979) asserts that early attachment affects the child's later friendships, relations with relatives, and enduring adult relationships; other research confirms that people's relationships as adults are related to the attachment styles they had as children (Brennan & Shaver, 1995). Adoptive parents can form the same type of secure, close attachment to the child as biological parents. A caretaking atmosphere that is warm, consistent, and governed by the infant's needs is the key to forming a secure attachment. Both adoptive and biological parents can provide such an atmosphere, and both adoptive and biological children can form strong secure attachments to their parents (Singer et al., 1985). In recent years large numbers of children have been adopted from orphanages in countries such as Romania. Their early experiences were far less than optimal, but following adoption by Canadian parents their circumstances improved greatly. The studies featured in *Experiencing Psychology* (see pages 358 and 359) provide some insight into the effects of early experiences and changes in parenting on attachment behaviour.

Can we go so far as to say that early childhood experiences such as attachment *determine* who and what we later become? There is little doubt that attachment is important, but it doesn't necessarily determine who we become. That is, human beings have an amazing ability to adapt, survive, and negotiate the future. Michael Lewis (1997, 1998) cautions that researchers often overestimate the effects of attachment and how it determines our future, and that separation anxiety at age 1 has little to with adjustment at age 18, let alone at age 35. Lewis studied infants' attachment at age 1 and again at age 18 in terms of attachment to family and friends; he found that secure attachment did not protect children from later maladjustment, nor did insecure attachment predict later trouble. Is attachment important? The answer is surely yes. Does it affect our adjustment as an adult? Probably. Does it *determine* our adjustment as an adult? The answer is probably no, because too many of life's events, chance circumstances, and good and bad decision making affect our life course.

Emotional Exchanges. Verbal exchanges and other emotional interactions between infants and their caregivers increase significantly as infants mature. Dialogues in the form of gestures, smiles, and vocalizations become more common. Mothers and fathers initiate these interactions as often as infants do. This early play is good for babies, as long as the babies are not overstimulated and annoyed by too much excitement (Singer & Singer, 1990).

Verbal exchanges help establish ties, teach language, inform infants about the world, and socialize them. These exchanges seem to occur universally, between all infants and parents. In a cross-cultural study, parents in four countries—Argentina, France, Japan, and the United States—all used similar types of speech when speaking to their infants (Bornstein et al., 1992). There were some differences, of course. For example, Japanese mothers were more willing than mothers from the other countries to speak ungrammatically to their infants, using nonsense words, songs, and rhyme. But the similarities among cultures outweighed the differences. The researchers concluded: "[The] universal aspects of infancy . . . appear . . . to exert control over the content of maternal speech" (p. 601).

Interactions between parents and babies are especially important for ensuring optimal development. In an experiment in which mothers remained still and expressionless, their infants appeared sad and turned away from them (Cohn & Tronick, 1983). The key implication of this research is that the mere presence of a parent is not enough; the parent must interact both physically and verbally with the infant (Sorce & Emde, 1981) and must pay attention to the infant (Jones & Raag, 1989). There are some cultural differences in the ways parents respond to infants (Camras et al., 1992). In a study of mother–infant interactions with participants from Kenya, Mexico, and the United States, researchers found that women in Kenya were more likely to be soothing and protective to young infants, while women in the United States were more verbally active and played a great deal. The cultural differences that appeared were evident at four months and were even more pronounced at nine months. How such verbal and emotional responsiveness on the part of mothers affects later development is a matter of speculation and a promising area for future research. These same researchers found that across cultures a mother's level of schooling affected her responsiveness. In comparing women from Mexico and the United States, the researchers found that women who had more schooling were more verbally responsive than women with less schooling (Richman, Miller, & LeVine, 1992).

Several other important variables influence the type and amount of interaction between parents and infants. One is the baby's physical attractiveness (Hildebrandt, 1983). People judge especially beautiful babies as more competent, more likable, and healthier than average-looking or unattractive babies (Stephan & Langlois, 1984). Adults are more likely to play with, speak to, tweak, jiggle, or smile at attractive babies (Langlois et al., 1995). This is not surprising; psychologists know that

F ollowing the fall of the Berlin Wall and the beginning of massive social restructuring in Eastern Europe, Canadians became dramatically aware of the plight of the youngest citizens of these changing countries. Perhaps most poignant were the conditions of infants and young children living in orphanages in Romania. With birth control unavailable and abortion illegal, many parents had children they could not care for and who were thus turned over to the state (Marcovitch et al., 1994). These children were living in developmentally hazardous conditions, often with infant to caregiver ratios of between 10 and 20 to 1. They had no toys or consistent stimulation, and feedings largely were conducted by propping up a bottle or having the infants hold their own bottles. Children would spend 20 to 24 hours a day in their cribs. As Elinor Ames of Simon Fraser University observed (Ames, 1990), their living conditions amounted to severe deprivation; possibly, this represented the most extreme form of systematic deprivation ever documented.

The public response to descriptions and pictures of these infants was significant and rapidly led to a large number of Canadians trying to adopt Romanian children and remove them from the conditions that were threatening their short-term welfare and long-term development. Between January 1990 and April 1991, 1013 Romanian children were issued visas to come to Canada for adoption (Ames & Carter, 1992). Past research had clearly indicated that children who spent their early years in similar conditions were at increased risk for less-than-optimal developmental outcomes, even if they were eventually placed in stable family environments. What would the Canadian experience of the Romanian orphans be like? How would they fare developmentally relative to Canadian children? Would the amount of time they spent in the orphanages be related to a level of developmental delay? Would early problems diminish with time spent with Canadian adoptive families?

Follow-up studies of these children and their experiences with their Canadian adoptive families have been conducted independently by Elinor Ames and her colleges and by Sharon Marcovitch of the Child Development Clinic at Toronto's Hospital for Sick Children. The results obtained so far have been very instructive about the effects of the early orphanage experiences, but also reasonably

people are biased by the attractiveness of others, whether children or adults (Ritter & Langlois, 1988). As well, mothers talk more to babies than do fathers (Leaper, Anderson, & Sanders, 1998). The baby's own behaviour is also important. Clarke-Stewart (1973) found that the more often the child looked, smiled, or vocalized to the mother, the more affectionate and attached to the child she became and, further, the more responsive she was to her child's distress. Tronick and Cohn (1989) concur. They have found that infants and mothers both change their behaviour in reaction to each other, and they argue that neither the baby nor the mother is a passive recipient of the other's emotions. Both are active participants in forming the attachment.

Temperament: Enduring Emotions

During the earliest months of life, some infants smile or reach out to a new face and readily accept being held or cuddled. Others are more inhibited. Still others exhibit extreme reticence, even distress, in the presence of strangers. As adults, *xenophobic* infants (those who fear strangers) are likely to be inhibited, meek, and wavering (Caspi, Elder, & Bem, 1988). Researchers know, however, that for most people there is only modest stability of such infant behaviours over time. In very extreme cases—such as xenophobia, where traits such as intense shyness or diffidence are in evidence—stronger stability of these traits over time is observed. This does not deny a genetic component to temperament but rather suggests that what is observed in

positive about the longer-term developmental outcomes for these children.

A key variable seemed to be the amount of time the children spent in an orphanage before adoption. Generally, those adopted before six months of age (Marcovitch et al., 1994) and those who spent little or no time in an orphanage prior to adoption had few developmental delays upon arrival in Canada, and their adoptive parents reported fewer problems related to their care (Fischer, Ames, Chisholm, & Savoie, 1997). Children who spent more time in orphanages arrived in Canada with more medical problems and eating problems (often eating all they were offered until their parents decided they had had enough). As well, they were more likely to have sleeping problems, the most common being a tendency to lie in bed in the morning without signalling that they had awakened. They were more likely to engage in rocking behaviour, most commonly when they were tired or alone. They were more likely to have problems with siblings and peers, the most common being a tendency to withdraw from or not engage in social interac-tion. Overall, children who spent more time in an orphanage exhib-ited a range of developmental delays when compared to non-orphaned preschool children (Fischer, Ames, Chisholm, & Savoie, 1997; Marcovitch et al., 1994).

As bleak as this may sound, the final results of these investigations are actually positive. First, it is worth noting that the vast majority of these problems were present when the children first arrived in Canada. Except with regards to medical prob-lems, the adoptive parents coped with the children effectively on their own, and with few exceptions all reported significant improvement in all problem areas through the preschool years. While researchers will have to wait until the children enter school to get a clear picture of where they stand developmentally relative to their Canadian peers, it appears that things are headed in the right direction.

As a final note, some of the researchers in this area (Fischer, Ames, Chisholm, & Savoie, 1997) have speculated as to whether it is appropriate to characterize the pat-tern of problems presented by these children as reflecting developmental abnormality. They point out that a similar pattern of problem behaviour in a non-orphanage-reared child very likely would raise serious con-cerns about the developmental course that child was following. But consideration of the conditions within Romanian orphanages may suggest an alternative hypothesis. Could it be that the "problem" behaviours of these children actually reflect adaptations, on their part, to a very unusual environment? For example, there would be no point in indicating they were awake if no one was going to interact with them, no reason to learn to attend to satiety cues (which indicate a person is full) when they were constantly under-fed, and no reason to expect them to be able to interact with siblings and peers if they have had no experience with the sort of energetic interac-tions we routinely see in children. The hope is that, with the new opportunities they now have as a result of being adopted into Canadian families, these children will learn to adapt to their new, more positive environments and get back on track developmentally. There is encouraging evidence that they are doing just that. ■

---

infancy is not necessarily what is seen later on. Further, what parents observe (social wariness with unfamiliar people) is different than the shyness that teachers observe (concern about social evaluation of peers), and so shyness—social inhibition and anxiety—varies in different situations and exhibits itself in changeable ways (Eisenberg et al., 1998).

Temperament refers to early-emerging and long-lasting individual differences in the intensity and especially the quality of a person's emotional reactions. Some psy-chologists believe that each person is born with a specific type of temperament: easygoing, wilful, outgoing, or shy, to name a few. Newborns, infants, and children, like the adults they will eventually grow to be, are all different from one another. Generalizations from one child to all children are impossible, and even generaliza-tions from a sample of children to all children must be made cautiously. So many variables can affect a child's growth and development that researchers have painstakingly tried to determine which variables are critical and which are less important. Thomas and Chess (1977), in their pioneering work in the New York Longitudinal Study, in which a sample of children were studied from birth into adulthood, point out that temperament is not fixed and unchangeable.

Data from the New York Longitudinal Study show that children tend to fall into four broad categories: easy (40 percent), difficult (10 percent), slow to warm up (15 percent), and unique (35 percent). *Easy* children are happy-go-lucky and adapt easily to new situations. This type of child would react to the first day of kindergarten with interest and excitement. *Difficult* children resist environmental change and often react poorly. This type of child would react to the first day of

Temperament: Early-emerging and long-lasting individual differences in the intensity and especially the quality of a person's emotional reactions.

kindergarten with fear and intense anxiety, perhaps throwing a tantrum and refusing to enter the room. *Slow-to-warm-up* children respond slowly, have low-intensity responses, and often are negative. This type of child would react to the first day of kindergarten with anxiety, clinging to the parent. Many children are *unique* and show a variety of emotional reactions.

Many researchers contend that some specific initial temperamental characteristics may be long-lasting and biologically based. For example, Jerome Kagan and his colleagues found that two- and three-year-olds who were *extremely* inhibited—that is, cautious and shy—tended to remain that way for four or more years. They also found physiological evidence (an increase in autonomic nervous system activity, as well as overarousal of the amygdala and hypothalamus, for example) that these children may be more sensitive to change and unfamiliarity (Kagan & Snidman, 1991a; Kagan, 1997). That is, minor changes in the environment are sufficient to arouse the autonomic nervous system in these children. Daniels and Plomin (1985) found an important relationship between the shyness of two-year-old adopted infants and the shyness of their biological mothers. Their findings suggest that genetic factors play a role in shyness. Studies of identical twins on a range of emotional dimensions, especially temperament, also show strong concordance (similarity between twin pairs), supporting a strong genetic component (Emde et al., 1992). Even maternal actions, such as time spent in daylight during pregnancy, may have an effect; Gortmaker and colleagues (1997) found that short exposure to daylight during pregnancy was associated with a higher likelihood of shy behavior in offspring. Further evidence for a biological predisposition comes from studies of basic physiological responses; infants' heart rates in response to a distracting stimulus are known to predict temperament (Huffman et al., 1998).

However, shyness and other aspects of temperament can be changed; human behaviour is the product of deliberate thought processes as well as biological forces. A child's temperament affects his or her interaction with parents in important ways and may determine in part how the parents treat the child; in other words, there is a reciprocal and mutually reinforcing influence. Parents recognize that they affect their child's temperament and personality; they assume that their child-rearing practices will have important influences on development. Moreover, shyness is somewhat culturally determined; in one cross-cultural study, researchers found that in China shyness among students helps them gain acceptance from teachers; the opposite tends to be true for students in Western countries (Chen, Rubin, & Li, 1995).

Brain and Behaviour further explores the role of parental nurturing.

Early Social Development and Child-rearing

In any bookstore, you'll find shelves lined with how-to books on child-rearing written by physicians, parents, psychologists, and others. The variety of approaches and experts shows that ideas about child-rearing are complicated and constantly changing. As society changes, so do beliefs and practices related to children's social development and ideas about how children form a sense of identity and self. As children move cognitively from egocentrism to a point where they can view themselves in relation to the rest of the world, they also develop the ability to think about social relationships. As we will see, children have not one but many environments in which they develop socially.

Regardless of culture, parents respond positively to good behaviours in children and negatively to bad ones. Although cultural differences exist (scheduling children's time and behaviours in France and non-interference and acceptance by Swedish parents, for example), parents worldwide respond to their children in similar ways (Honig & Chung, 1989). Although parents exert a powerful influence on children, it is not the sole influence. Despite vast differences in the ways that individual parents treat children, most children turn out all right. Some researchers, such as Harris (1998), assert that this is because a child's many environments, especially his or her play groups, exert profound effects on social development.

brain and behaviour
The Nurture Assumption

Perhaps the most important issue in developmental psychology is the nature *versus* nurture issue. For decades researchers have explored this dichotomy trying to prove that one is more important than the other. Today, it is pretty much a given that such a dichotomy is misleading at best and wrong at worst. Most behaviours are a combination of genetics and environment—of biological factors interacting with environmental ones. In the case of development, the issue is especially important. Parents have a belief—and it has been the conventional wisdom for five decades—that what they do with their children matters a great deal and that their role in shaping a child's behaviour is paramount. This belief is so ingrained that social critics and researchers alike, for example, Sylvia Hewlett and Cornel West (1998), have called for a national recommitment to parenting with support by business, government, and society at large.

But in the last decade, researchers have presented strong evidence suggesting that biology counts more than previously thought in the nature-nurture debate. Typical of such research is the evidence collected by Robert Plomin in collaboration with many other researchers. Plomin has studied twins who have been reared apart and together, babies and very old people, and adopted children and their biological and adoptive parents. Plomin's research concludes that genetics plays an important role in creating differences in cognitive abilities; children are cognitively most like their biological parents, especially as they become older (Chorney et al., 1998; Plomin et al., 1997; Petrill et al., 1998; Plomin, Petrill, & Cutting, 1997).

So, the role of genetics in cognitive development seems strong. Genes seem to play a key role in other aspects of development as well. For example, temperament has a genetic basis (Kagan, 1997). The list goes on: alcoholism, aggression, shyness, and creativity also are genetically linked. Theorists like Edward O. Wilson (1998) contend that it all comes down to the laws of physics and DNA's genetic code (Hamer & Copeland, 1998). So, are parents working with a flawed assumption—that they make a difference (other than through their genetic contribution)? Over the years, most psychologists have argued that genetics only play a part and do not account for the whole of a child's development. Parents, and the individuals themselves, can affect the expression of the genetic code, work thorough developmental problems, and with hard work and dedication, change some of the effects of genetics and biology. Psychologists argue that there is plasticity in the brain and that experience continues to shape us throughout our lives.

The truth is that psychology is an optimistic profession; psychologists assume that our lives are not fixed by genetic inheritance and that every person strives for positive change. Their view has been substantiated by thousands of research studies that show the important role of environment.

But one theorist, Judith Rich Harris (1995, 1998), suggested in a controversial book that most psychologists have got it wrong—in fact, she suggested that they have it backwards. She acknowledged the role of genetics and was quick to admit that some things cannot be denied, such as a biological and genetic predisposition to music or verbal ability. But Harris, a science writer with a master's degree in psychology, also contended in *The Nurture Assumption* that *peers*—not parents—are the key players in shaping children's behaviour. In the nature-versus-nurture controversy, playmates, schoolmates, and society provide the influence that counts. Harris based her idea on observations of how children tend to do what peers do, rather than what parents want. She pointed out that parents may treat two children identically, but the children will wind up behaving very differently because of their different experiences in the schoolyard. She argues that researchers have been unable to identify how parenting styles affect a child's personality. Furthermore, she notes that adopted children's personalities are not like the personalities of their adoptive parents. Harris concluded that genetics plays a big role—perhaps as much as 50 percent—but the rest of the variation between children is due to environmental influences that are not parental.

Children seek to be different from their parents, according to Harris. Children seek to differentiate themselves from parents and be like friends, schoolmates, and even teachers. How do we explain, then, that children of warm, accepting parents tend to grow up to be well adjusted? As for negative outcomes, Harris claims that genetics, not parents, make the difference. She concludes, "As for what may be wrong with you: Don't blame it on your parents" (p. 362).

Harris's writings were featured prominently in the popular press because, on the one hand, her ideas challenged one of our society's most firmly held beliefs—that

continued on next page

parents matter. On the other hand, critics argue that the book received attention because it panders to parents' concerns about the effectiveness of their child-rearing practices—in some ways, it lets them off the hook. Harris's ideas caused a furor in the ranks of child development professionals, who argued that her ideas are flawed. For example, psychologists point out that peers do not begin to exert their effects until age six to eight. Psychological studies argue that most adult personality traits are laid down long before this age. Further, a child's verbal abilities are well predicted by the amount of time parents spend talking with children—again, before peers have their impact. In addition, for better or worse, children identify with their parents and imitate them. Lastly, much of Harris's data comes from questionnaires with adults about their past behaviour, and little comes from actual observation of children—a far more accurate assessment of children's behaviour or tendencies.

Do parents matter? Sure they do—they matter a great deal (Resnick et al., 1997). Do they matter as much as we have thought in the past? Harris contends that they do not matter as much as we thought, arguing that peers and other non-parental influences matter more. In the heredity versus environment issue (nature versus nurture) Harris focuses on the influence of the non-parental environment. Though research has not validated it, she argues that parents have overestimated their impact on their children. Harris's work has yet to be tested, and many mainstream psychologists find it a flawed theory, even outrageous. Many dismiss it and argue that parental influences are genuine, subtle, elaborate, and difficult to measure scientifically. Some worry that parents may begin to ignore children or neglect them as a result of Harris's book.

Harris's notion challenges one of the fundamental ideas associated with brain and behaviour—that genetics counts in a child's development, but that parental environment is largely responsible. Instead, Harris suggests that genetics counts and parents count somewhat, but that peers have the most significant influence on children's developing personalities. Research aimed at testing her theory in the future hopefully will clarify both the nature and the truth of her claims. ■

Social development begins soon after birth, with the development of an attachment between parents and their newborn. The nature of a child's early interactions with parents is a crucial part of personality development. Infants have a great need to be hugged, cuddled, and nurtured. However, although love is a critical variable for positive development, as psychoanalyst Bruno Bettelheim (1987) said, "Love is not enough." Ultimately, the most important job for parents is to teach their children both how to become independent and how to interact with others.

The First Months. In the first year of life, social interactions among children are limited; infants need constant attention and are self-centred. Basically they are unable to recognize any needs other than their own. In the second half of the first year of life, children exhibit strong attachments to parents and other caregivers, along with fear of strangers.

As early as nine months, infants show they like to play games by indicating their unhappiness when an adult stops playing with them (Ross & Lollis, 1987). They play by themselves, but as they grow older, especially beyond two years of age, they engage in more social play with other children (Howes, Unger, & Seidner, 1989).

By the beginning of their second year, children have begun to understand that they are separate from their parents—they are developing a conscious sense of self. They learn to differentiate themselves from others, to manipulate the world, and to interact with other people. As they enter the preoperational stage, egocentrism gradually gives way to increased social interaction. At age 2, children are better at controlling their emotional responses than they were at 18 months. They generally play alone or alongside other children, but they prefer to play with an adult than with other two-year-olds (Jennings, Curry, & Connors, 1986). Gradually, however, they begin to socialize with their peers.

Sharing. The noted pediatrician Benjamin Spock once said that the only two things children will share willingly are communicable diseases and their mother's age. Actually, from age two until they begin school, children vacillate between quiet conformity and happy sharing, on the one hand, and making stubborn negative demands and exhibiting egocentric behaviour, on the other. Because sharing is a socially desirable behaviour, learning to share becomes a top priority when they enter a child-care centre, nursery school, or kindergarten. (*Experiencing Psychology* on pages 364 and 365 discusses some developmental issues associated with day care.)

Very young children do not understand the concept of sharing—particularly the idea that if you share with another child, the other child is more likely to share with you. In a laboratory study of sharing, researchers observed a series of two children separated by a gate. Initially one child was given toys and the other wasn't; then the situation was reversed. The researchers found that none of the children shared spontaneously; however, 65 percent shared a toy when asked to do so by their mother. Moreover, a child who was deprived of a toy after having shared one often approached the child who now had the toy. One child even said, "I gave you a toy. Why don't you give me one?" Children do not initiate sharing at a young age; but once they share, they seem to exhibit knowledge about reciprocal arrangements (Levitt et al., 1985). Of course, sharing is more likely among children who are friends because they have more intense social activity and make more frequent attempts at conflict resolution (Newcomb & Bagwell, 1995).

Entry into kindergarten helps break down egocentrism; however, many other factors can either promote or retard this aspect of development. One variable is the type of toys children play with. Quilitch and Risley (1973) provided young children with two kinds of toys—those generally played with by one child at a time (isolate toys) and those designed for use by two or more children at the same time (social toys). All of the children played with both kinds of toys, but some were first given social toys and others were first given isolate toys. After the initial play period, more of the children who had been given social toys first chose to play with other children. The researchers concluded that the kinds of toys given to children altered the degree of egocentrism exhibited in their play.

Hildy Ross of Waterloo University has extensively studied the impact of parental intervention on the sharing and fighting behaviours of siblings. When parents step in to mediate a sibling argument, the result is most often positive and in line with the parents' view of the situation (Ross, 1996; Perlman & Ross, 1997a) and sometimes, but not always, leads to more sophisticated, less violent solution strategies (Perlman & Ross, 1997b).

Does Gender Make a Difference?

A generation ago, many parents tended to strongly encourage "masculine" traits such as athletic prowess in their sons and "feminine" traits such as empathy in their daughters. Parents often accepted and promoted a gender-based social environment. Today, many parents de-emphasize gender-based interests in their children, seeking to reduce or eliminate society's tendency to stereotype people, their interests, and their occupations on the basis of gender. This trend is also reflected in children's literature through carefully crafted gender-neutral photographs and story lines (Kortenhaus & Demarest, 1993). This de-emphasis of gender-associated behaviours has led to a more even distribution of scores on various measures of cognitive ability (Feingold, 1993).

Obviously, there are both similarities and differences between the genders. When young people are given equal schooling, measures of academic performance for boys and girls tend to be equal. Socially, both men and women value intelligence and a sense of humour in the opposite sex. Men and women differ in their biological make-up, and their experiences, biologically and environmentally, are not the same; for example, small but fairly consistent gender differences exist in domains closely related to sex and mating (Buss, 1995). For example, Buss indicates that males have a slightly stronger preference for younger women, while women show a

Child Care

Psychologist Sanda Scarr (1998) puts it truthfully, if bluntly: Child care exists so parental employment can continue. But child care can help in children's development, and has been used throughout the twentieth century to intervene with disadvantaged children. For families in which both parents have jobs, as well as for single-parent families, child care is a necessity. Child care is becoming increasingly diverse as parents seek alternative arrangements for their children. While their parents work, most preschool children are cared for in their own homes or other people's homes, often by babysitters, relatives, friends, or grandparents. Child-care centres provide care for about 23 percent of preschool children who have working mothers and fathers.

Because of numerous variables, it isn't easy to determine the effects of child care. These variables include, among other things, the child's age at entry into a child-care program, the child's family background, the security of the child's attachment to parents, and the stability of the child-care arrangement (Belsky, 1990). In addition, as Nina Howe of Concordia University points out, the quality of the care received must be closely considered if viable conclusions about the effects of child care are to be reached (Howe & Jacobs, 1995). Infant care is stressful for parents; it is thus very important that child-care environments be supportive not only for infants but for the parents as well. If parents are overly anxious about child-care arrangements, this stress will affect their children (Harms, 1994). A child's home environment and socialization can, of course, moderate or eliminate any potential negative consequences of child care (Broberg et al., 1997). In addition, when there is parental harmony, parent–child relationships are enhanced, regardless of child-care arrangements (Erel & Burman, 1995; Willoughby & Glidden, 1995).

Some research has questioned current child-care practices and asserts that there is a basis for concern about the impact of child care on development (Bates et al., 1994; Kim, 1997). This research suggests that infants who receive more than 20 hours of child care per week display more avoidance of their mothers when they are reunited than do infants who spend only a couple of hours a week in child care (Belsky & Rovine, 1988). But more recent research (Caruso & Corsini, 1994) suggests that even when children enter day care at a young age, the impact of 33 hours of child care a week is minimal.

Psychologists are especially interested in the relationship between child care and attachment, because they believe that a child's emotional security depends on a strong, loving bond with a primary caretaker, usually the mother (Kagan, Kearsley, & Zelazo, 1980). Contrary to popular belief, studies of attachment behaviours find that non-parental care does not reduce a child's emotional attachment to the mother (Etaugh, 1980). Moreover, there is no evidence that routine temporary separations, such

slight preference for older men. Buss claims that these ratings reflect evolutionary differences in preference for fertile women (by men) and for stable relationships (by women). The theory is that these distinct preferences support strategies that increase the likelihood that one's genes will survive through mating.

Researchers are aware that their pre-existing ideas and, sometimes, their politically correct desires to minimize differences may contaminate or obfuscate the truth. Thus, Alice Eagly (1995) argues that researchers must deal responsibly with issues of gender differences. Research in this area is controversial. Men and women talk differently with their sons and daughters—women talk more than men, although the gender of the child matters little (Leaper, Anderson, & Sanders, 1998). Some psychologists assert that the way we talk to and treat boys and girls is creating special problems. For example, Pollack (1998) argues that society has such strong expectations about how boys should behave—independent, strong, and tough—that the pressure puts them at risk for various psychological problems. The truth is that society puts similar, but different, pressure on girls—to be independent, strong, and feminine—and some see these pressures as conflicting. Children today sometimes get mixed messages, and they certainly have higher expectations placed on them than was true a generation ago (Maccoby, 1998).

as those experienced with child care for preschool children, create psychological trauma later in life (Bates et al., 1994).

Considerable evidence suggests that a stimulating, varied environment is necessary for optimal cognitive development and that high-quality child-care centres provide a stimulating environment. High-quality child care means an experienced, qualified, and well-paid staff, a low staff-to-child ratio, and a low staff turnover (Scarr, Eisenberg, & Deater-Deckard, 1994). In a study of middle-class children, Bates and his colleagues (1994) found no differences in intellectual functioning between children enrolled in high-quality child-care centres and children reared at home. In fact, high-quality child-care centres may increase children's positive social interactions with peers (Egeland & Niester, 1995), may make

children happier (Vandell, Henderson, & Wilson, 1988), and may help prevent the declines in cognitive functioning that sometimes occur in children who are not exposed to varied environments (e.g., Burchinal, Lee, & Ramey, 1989). Further, in child-care centres there is often considerable sharing among children; this is an activity not normally done at home, and it can produce positive effects (Davis & Thornburg, 1994; Moorehouse, 1991). Therefore, there is evidence that first-class child-care centres can yield positive effects (Davis & Thornburg, 1994). When parents are involved, even a little, in the day-care situation, parental and child satisfaction are even higher (Cronan, Walen, & Cruz, 1994; Fagan, 1994a, 1994b).

Typical of recent research is a longitudinal study conducted in Sweden by Anders Broberg and colleagues (1997). The researchers studied 146 children from 16 months of age to age 8. They measured an array of abilities, especially cognitive ability. Results showed that children who spent more time interacting with caregivers, at home or in day care, scored better on tests of verbal ability. Involvement in small groups was important in predicting mathematical ability. The researchers concluded that day care did not place their subjects at any

disadvantage. Other research found virtually no difference between home-care and day-care children in personality or attachment (NICHD Early Child Care Research Network, 1997; Schoelmerich et al., 1995).

Researchers generally assert that good-quality child care "is neither a benefit nor a detriment to the development of children from stable low-risk families" (Scarr & Eisenberg, 1993, p. 638). The long-term impact of child care on children seems negligible (Morrison, Ispa, & Thornburg, 1994). Scarr (1998, p. 95) concludes, "Widely varying qualities of child care have been shown to have only small effects on children's current development and no demonstrated long-term impact, except on disadvantaged children, whose *homes* put them at developmental risk." Further, and perhaps most importantly, young children's development must be studied within a context of multiple factors—home, parent harmony, school, playground relationships and activities, grandparents, nutrition. From an ecological perspective, a child's development usually is not going to be determined by a single factor such as non-parental care (Brontenbrenner, 1979) and psychologists must look at the joint influences of family care, child care, school, and even culture. ■

One reality is that from the moment of birth, parents may begin treating their children differently on the basis of gender; from the beginning, girls and boys have different life experiences (Carli, 1997). For example, few people have gender neutral names such as Pat, Terry, Chris, or Lee (van Fleet & Atwater, 1997). Parents try to determine just the right name, one that will send just the right message, generally a name that will be gender appropriate. Psychologists are especially aware of *gender stereotyping*. In general, a stereotype is a fixed, overly simple, often wrong, and often negative idea about traits, attitudes, and behaviours attributed to others. A **gender stereotype** is an expectation of specific patterns of behaviour—overly simple, often wrong, and often negative ideas about traits and attitudes—based on gender. Young boys are given footballs; young girls are given Barbie dolls. Boys wear blue; girls wear pink. And these distinctions have an impact at an early age (Leinbach, Hort, & Fagot, 1997). Is this a problem?

Despite the sense you may have that there are significant differences in how parents raise their sons and daughters, in fact, most of the differences in the way boys and girls are raised are small (Lytton & Romney, 1991). The gender differences that do exist tend to result from many factors—many of which are subtle. For example, boys tend to be assigned chores that take them away from people (such as

Gender stereotype: An expectation of specific patterns of behaviour—overly simple, often wrong, and often negative ideas about traits and attitudes—based on gender.

yard work and walking the dog), whereas girls tend to be assigned chores that keep them close to people, such as food preparation or dishwashing. As a consequence, some researchers assert, girls interact more with people and therefore may become more nurturing. In the same manner, boys may excel at manipulating objects and tools, while girls have fewer opportunities for inventive play. And both girls and boys may receive approval and praise for their "gender-appropriate" behaviours, and these ideas are then reflected in their behaviour (Karniol & Ada, 1997). Not only are reinforced behaviours important, but (according to social learning theory) children learn gender-based ideas merely by watching the behaviour of adults of their own gender (Luecke-Aleska et al., 1995). Television is another source of gender-based ideas—ideas that have fluctuated between extremes over the years and are often exaggerated (Olson & Douglas, 1997), especially in children's cartoons (Thompson & Zerbinos, 1997).

Some psychologists argue that the differences in self-concept discussed earlier in the context of Gilligan's critique of Kohlberg's theory of moral development suggest that there are masculine and feminine orientations towards knowledge. The masculine approach views knowledge and expertise as things to be won or acquired, while the feminine approach views them as the outcomes of relational or collaborative activity (Belenkey, Clinchy, Goldberger, & Tarule, 1988; Goldberger, 1997).

Evidence exists that there may be biological, especially hormonal, influences underlying some observed gender differences; that is, children may have pre-existing preferences for gender-based behaviours (Berenbaum & Snyder, 1995). Researchers know that 18-month-old boys and girls show greater involvement with toys conventionally associated with their own gender—boys like trucks and girls like dolls—even if parents have not promoted play with gender-stereotyped toys (Caldera, Huston, & O'Brien, 1989). This suggests a biological influence (Berenbaum & Snyder, 1995). Further, starting at age three and continuing into early adolescence, children prefer same-sex playmates (Maccoby, 1998). According to Eleanor Maccoby (1998) this characteristic is reliable, cuts across a variety of situations, and is difficult to change. Gender segregation does not happen solely because children have been given "boy" toys or "girl" toys; nor does it result solely from inborn temperamental differences that lead to rough-and-tumble play for boys and more sedate play for girls (Berenbaum & Snyder, 1995). Children know they are members of one gender or the other. This knowledge binds members of each gender together and differentiates them from members of the other gender. Children with widely different personalities are drawn together solely on the basis of their shared gender. Maccoby (1998) asserts that gender differences are minimal when children are observed individually but become more evident in social groups.

It is apparent that both biological and environmental influences are important factors in determining gender differences. However, gender differences in behaviour are small and are obvious only in certain situations, such as on the playground (Oliver & Hyde, 1993). Furthermore, gender differences are decreasing as people become more **androgynous**—adopting behaviours shared by both genders—and endorsing nontraditional roles for both men and women (Twenge, 1997). As parents consider the implications of research on gender differences, they must use critical thinking skills. They should foster, among other things, children's achievement, moral values, and self-esteem. None of these values is gender-based; both boys and girls can and should be taught to play, learn, reason, and solve problems. All children should be taught basic human values, which are not gender-specific.

The Research Process (see pages 368 and 369) discusses differences in the ways fathers and mothers approach their roles.

Androgynous: Exhibiting behavioural traits associated with both sexes.

Friendships: The Company We Keep

When you like someone who likes you, there is good chance that you call yourselves friends. Although some people have many and others have few, most people, at one time or another, find someone with whom they share values, ideas, and thoughts. At its simplest, a *friendship* is a close emotional tie between two peers (Kerns, 1998). Children develop their first friendships around age three. They develop more friends in elementary school, and most high-school students report having three to five good friends. Among adolescents, as much as 29 percent of waking hours are spent with friends; among adults, for a variety of reasons, the time spent interacting with friends drops to 7 percent. If you had a number of friends as a child, you are more likely to have a number as an adult, even if you don't spend a great deal of time with each one of them.

According to Hartup and Stevens (1997) there are some important developmental consequences to having friends. Those children and adolescents who have friends tend to be more socially competent than those who do not. Having friends provides someone to confide in, to be afraid with, to grow with. Having friends sets the stage for intimacy with adults. Elementary school children tend to form same-gender friendships; cross-gender friendships are rare. Likewise, children choose friends of the same ethnicity and age (Aboud & Mendelson, 1998). With youngsters, friendships lead to cooperation rather than competition, at least more so than with non-friends (Hartup, 1989). Furthermore, when children have friends in their classroom, they do better in school (Ladd, 1990). Adolescent friendships generally provide a place for sharing and intimacy (although occasionally they can be filled with conflict over social or political issues, drugs, gangs, and sexual behaviour) (Berndt, 1992). When friendships fall apart, self-confidence is undermined (Keefe & Berndt, 1996).

Among adults, friendships between two women differ from those between two men, and both differ from friendships between a man and a woman. Western cultural expectations for specific gender-based behaviours often control male-female interactions in friendship. Women talk more about family, personal matters, and doubts and fears than men do; men talk more about sports and work than women do. Women in general find friendships more satisfying than men do (Elkins & Peterson, 1993); nevertheless, many men also experience and seek intimacy and support in friendships (Botschner, 1998).

Research supports the notion that closeness is the key variable that defines a friendship. Ideally, close friends participate as equals, enjoy each other's company, have mutual trust, provide mutual assistance, accept each other as they are, respect each other's judgment, feel free to be themselves with each other, understand each other in fundamental ways, and are intimate and share confidences (Davis & Todd, 1984).

From a developmental point of view, friends are an important resource cognitively and emotionally from childhood through old age (Hartup & Stevens, 1997). Friends contribute to the socialization process on age-related tasks. Friends provide supportive and intimate relationships that set the stage for later intimacies between them and other people. But not all friendships are alike, and the meaning of a friendship is buried below the surface conversation of shopping, school, or jobs. The intimacy of a friendship comes from shared interests, values, and a sense of closeness.

Erik Erikson and the Search for Self

Developing an awareness of the self as different from others is a key to early childhood social development. Self-perception begins when the child recognizes that he or she is a separate person, different from other people; the self becomes more differentiated as a child develops an appreciation of his or her own inner mental world. As children develop a concept of themselves, they develop self-esteem and

Is Dad's Time Quality Time?

Both of the male authors of this book are good dads. Each often took charge of child care, changed diapers, and was attentive to his daughters' needs. But the research literature suggests that they probably didn't spend as much time with their children as their partners did. They may have not been as communicative with their daughters as their partners were (Fagan, 1997). The North American family is undergoing dramatic changes. During the past two decades, women have entered the workforce in unprecedented numbers and, in so doing, have changed the shape, structure, and fabric of family life. In some homes, men stay home while their partners work. Regardless of who is the principal breadwinner, many mothers are spending less time with their young children. Are fathers picking up the slack? Do fathers spend enough time with their children? Do fathers engage in basic caregiving, play, or both? Is Dad's time "quality" time? And down the road, how much do fathers contribute to adolescent maladjustment when compared to mothers?

The Concept of Quality Time. Today's fathers are more interested in their newborns and may be involved in their upbringing from the first moments of life, as evidenced by the fact that many more fathers are now present in the delivery room than was formerly true. Fathers are loving and responsive caregivers; they are concerned with their children's welfare (Fagan, 1997). Still, some men view parenting as a voluntary activity in which they help or assist their partners, who are the primary caregivers. Two words often used in describing fathers' interactions with children are *quality* and *quantity*. Fathers sometimes assert that they spend limited time with their children but that this time is "quality" time. Two Syracuse University researchers, Hoosain and Roopnarine (1994), studied the *quality* and *quantity* of interactions between fathers and their children to determine whether this is true.

Methods. Among other groups, the researchers studied 23 two-parent African-American families in which the father worked full-time and the mother worked part-time. Each family was middle-income and had a child younger than two; all of the families lived in Syracuse, New York. Both mothers and fathers were professionals, such as nurses, doctors, teachers, and social workers.

Both parents were asked to fill out a parental involvement questionnaire to assess their involvement in child-care activities. Mothers and fathers rated their degree of involvement with their children in six areas: bedtime routines, physical care (such as diaper changing and bathing), feeding, singing, playing, and soothing the child.

Results. Some fathers spent large amounts of time with their children, others spent very little. Some spent quality time (time devoted to active involvement with a child, as opposed to mere presence); others did not. For example, compared with the mothers, the fathers rated themselves as being less involved in singing to infants, in bedtime routines, in the physical care of infants, in offering comfort when infants cried, in feeding, and in playing with the infants. In fact, the fathers spent about 42 percent as much time as the mothers in caregiving activities. The estimates for these African-American fathers and children are quite similar to those of white American fathers and their children, as we will see.

Play turned out to be a prominent feature of the time fathers spent with their infants; in fact, the fathers were twice as likely to be involved in play

significant attachments to others. Such cognitive, and then social, changes do not take place in isolation. They are influenced by the nature of a child's early attachments, by the cultural world in which the child grows, by child-rearing practices, and by how children are taught and learn to think about the causes of events in the world. The construction of an identity—a self—occurs slowly and gradually and is affected by many variables.

Perhaps no one is more closely associated with the challenges of social development and self-understanding than the psychoanalyst Erik H. Erikson (1902–1994). With sharp insight, a linguistic flair, and a logical, coherent approach to studying human behaviour, Erikson, who studied with Sigmund Freud in Austria, developed a theory of *psychosocial* stages of development. Each of his stages leads to the development of a unique aspect of self, and the stages help define how a person

as in basic caregiving activities (see also Hossain & Roopnarine, 1995). The gender of the infant did not seem to be important in determining the extent of play or basic caregiving for either mothers or fathers.

Conclusions. This study suggests that child care is a priority among middle-class African-American fathers, but that fathers play with their infants more than they engage in basic caregiving. It also suggests that they play with their sons and daughters equally. These data are consistent with other research. For example, Grossman, Pollack, and Golding (1988) studied the quality and quantity of interactions between fathers and their first-born five-year-old children. To measure quantity, the researchers had the fathers estimate the average amount of time they spent with their children on weekdays and weekends, with respect to both playtime and caretaking. To measure quality, the researchers had the subjects perform a play task in the home. The researchers recorded the quality of the interactions during play in terms of warmth (was the parent critical or reinforcing?), attention, and responsiveness.

Grossman, Pollack, and Golding (1988) found that fathers were attentive; but they also found that the amount of time men spend with their children is directly affected by their partners. In general, men married to autonomous, self-sufficient, competent women spend less time with their children. The quality of the time a father spends with his children seems to be enhanced a great deal if the father has high feelings of self-worth; it is also enhanced by the mother's attitudes (Beitel & Parke, 1998). For example, if the mother is highly supportive of a father's involvement, father involvement may be high or low depending on the father, his work schedule, and his predisposition. But if a mother opposes or is not supportive of father involvement, the father will not be involved regardless of his individual disposition.

In the end, Fagan (1996) concluded, as did Hoosain and Roopnarine, that African-American men were good and attentive fathers. It is important to note that research on fathers and their children is limited; in a review of the impact of fathers on later adolescent maladjustment, only 1 percent of studies focused solely on fathers, while 48 percent focused exclusively on mothers (Phares & Compas, 1993). Further, the quality and quantity of time men spend with their children cannot be analyzed in isolation, because both aspects are affected by personal psychological variables as well as by marital factors and even the gender of the child (Beitel & Parke, 1998; Parke, 1995). For example, when a marriage is satisfying, fathers spend more time with their children (Willoughby & Glidden, 1995). Moreover, men are more likely to engage in affectionate touch with younger sons than older ones, and some studies find that daughters receive less attention from fathers than do sons (Harris & Morgan, 1991; Salt, 1991). Although we know that fathering is good for children, we also know that it is good for men—it enhances their self-esteem and feelings of competence.

In general, fathers are seen as less affectionate than mothers and more likely to engage in play than in caregiving (Sun & Roopnarine, 1996; Hoosain & Roopnarine, 1994). Although most children understand that their fathers love and care for them, they often, not surprisingly, feel closer to their mothers. But there are still many unanswered questions. Do some types of men marry autonomous women because they want little to do with their children? Do children seek out the more playful parent? Do children seek out the more autonomous parent? In what kinds of play do fathers engage? The research continues. ■

develops a role, attitudes, and skills as a member of society. According to Erikson, a series of basic psychological conflicts determines the course of development. His theory is noted for its integration of a person's disposition and environment with historical forces in the shaping of the self. Erikson's theory describes a continuum of stages (including dilemmas and crises) through which all individuals must pass. Each stage can have either a positive or a negative outcome. New dilemmas emerge as a person grows older and faces new responsibilities, tasks, and social relationships. A person may experience a dilemma as an opportunity and face it positively or may view the dilemma as a catastrophe and fail to cope with it effectively.

Table 10.5 lists the first four psychosocial stages in Erikson's theory, with their age ranges and the important events associated with them. (We will look at Erikson's later stages, covering adolescence and adulthood, in Chapter 11.) Stages 1

Table 10.5 Erikson's First Four Stages of Psychosocial Development

Stage	Approximate Age	Important Event	Description
1. Basic trust versus basic mistrust	Birth to 12–18 months	Feeding	The infant must form a loving, trusting relationship with the caregiver or develop a sense of mistrust.
2. Autonomy versus shame/doubt	18 months to 3 years	Toilet training	The child's energies are directed towards the development of physical skills, including walking and controlling the sphincter. The child learns control but may develop shame and doubt if not handled well.
3. Initiative versus guilt	3 to 6 years	Independence	The child continues to become more assertive and to take more initiative but may be chastised for being too forceful, which can lead to guilt feelings.
4. Industry versus inferiority	6 to 12 years	School	The child must deal with demands to learn new skills or risk a sense of inferiority, failure, and incompetence.

through 4 of Erikson's theory cover birth through age 12. We now take a closer look at each of these stages.

Stage 1 (birth to 12 to18 months) involves the development of *basic trust versus basic mistrust*. During their first months, according to Erikson, infants make distinctions about the world and decide whether it is a comfortable, loving place in which they can feel basic trust. At this stage, they develop beliefs about the essential reliability of people. If their needs are adequately met, they learn that their world is a predictable and safe place. Infants whose needs are not met learn to distrust the world.

During stage 2 (18 months to 3 years), toddlers must resolve the crisis of *autonomy versus shame and doubt*. That is, they must begin to take effective control of aspects of their behaviour in socially acceptable ways. Success in toilet training and other tasks involving control leads to a sense of autonomy and more mature behaviour. Difficulties dealing with control during this stage result in fears and a sense of shame and doubt.

In Erikson's theory, stage 3 (3 to 6 years) is that of *initiative versus guilt*, when children develop the ability to use their own inventiveness, drive, and enthusiasm. During this stage they either gain a sense of independence and good feelings about themselves or develop a sense of guilt, lack of acceptance, and negative feelings about themselves. If children learn to dress themselves, clean their rooms, and develop friendships with other children, they can feel a sense of mastery; alternatively, they can be dependent or regretful.

During stage 4 (6 to 12 years), children must resolve the issue of *industry versus inferiority*. That is, as they enter formal schooling, they must develop a sense of their own competence, and this sense forms the basis of their self-esteem. Children either develop feelings of competence and confidence in their abilities or experience inferiority, failure, and feelings of incompetence.

Focus

Review

◆ How do we know that attachment exists? pp. 354–357
◆ Cite evidence to suggest that some traits, such as shyness, are inborn. pp. 359–360
◆ Identify two key variables that affect the quality of child care. pp. 364–365

Think Critically

◆ In what ways do you think physical and emotional development might interact?
◆ What are the implications for later emotional development of cross-cultural differences in responsiveness towards infants?
◆ What do you think happens in a modern Canadian family when a child does not successfully master a stage of Erikson's development, such as autonomy versus shame and doubt? How might the response be different in a Japanese or Russian family?
◆ Should employers provide day care for their employees' children? What might be the implications for workers and employers of doing so?

A key point of Erikson's theory is that children must go through each stage, resolving its crises as best they can. Many factors have a bearing on the successful navigation of these stages. Of course, children grow older whether they are ready for the next stage. A person still may have unresolved conflicts, opportunities, and dilemmas from previous stages. This can cause anxiety and discomfort and make resolution of advanced stages more difficult. Because adolescence is such a crucial stage for the formation of a firm identity, the environment surrounding an adolescent becomes especially important. We will turn to this topic in the next chapter.

Summary and Review

Key Issues, Theories, and Research Designs

What are the different views on, theories about, and methods of studying development?

- A key issue in development is to consider to what extent a person's abilities, interests, and personality are determined primarily by biological, genetic influences (*nature*) or primarily by environmental influences (*nurture*). The issue of *stability* versus *change* is a recurring theme and is closely associated with nature and nurture, because when a researcher assumes stability the researcher often assumes that stable traits are inherited and genetically determined. Those favouring an environmental view are more likely to believe that people change with life's events. A *continuous view* sees development as a process of gradual growth and change; but development can also be viewed as discontinuous, with growth, maturation, and understanding of the world occurring at various key periods and change appearing abruptly. pp. 332–333

- In the cross-sectional research design, researchers compare people of different ages to determine if they differ on some important dimension. In the longitudinal design, researchers study a group of people, usually over a period of time, to determine whether changes have occurred. pp. 334–335

KEY TERMS
developmental psychology, p. 332

The First 10 Months

Distinguish between an embryo and a fetus.

- From implantation until the eighth week following conception, the prenatal organism is called an *embryo*; from the eighth week until birth, it is called a *fetus*. p. 336

- In the first months of life, an embryo is especially sensitive to teratogens. A *teratogen* is a substance that can produce developmental malformations in a fetus; common teratogens include alcohol and other drugs. p. 338

How is a newborn equipped to deal with the world?

- When a child is born, it comes prepared with a set of primary reflexes; among them are the *Babinski reflex*, the *Moro reflex*, the *rooting reflex*, the *sucking reflex*, and the *grasping reflex*. Newborns also have surprisingly well-developed perceptual systems. pp. 339–342

KEY TERMS
zygote, p. 336; embryo, p. 336; fetus, p. 336; placenta, p. 337; teratogen, p. 338; Babinski reflex, p. 340; Moro reflex, p. 341; rooting reflex, p. 341; sucking reflex, p. 341; grasping reflex, p. 341

Cognitive Development

What is the difference between assimilation and accommodation?

- Piaget's theory focuses on how people think, instead of on what they think. Piaget identified two processes that enable the individual to gain new knowledge: assimilation and accommodation. *Assimilation* is the process of dealing with new information in terms of existing schemes. *Accommodation* is the process of modifying one's existing thought processes and knowledge schemes in response to new information. p. 345

Describe Piaget's stages of cognitive development.

- Piaget believed that cognitive development occurs in four stages, each of which must be completed before the next stage begins. In the *sensorimotor stage*, covering roughly the first two years of life, the child begins to interact with the environment, and the rudiments of intelligence are established. pp. 345–346

- The *preoperational stage* lasts from about age two to seven, when initial symbolic thought is developed. *Egocentrism*, the inability to perceive a situation or event except in relation to oneself, flourishes in this stage. At the end of the preoperational stage, children begin the process of *decentration*, gradually moving away from self-centredness. pp. 346–347

- The *concrete operational stage* lasts from approximately age 7 to 12; the child develops the ability to understand constant factors in the environment, rules, and higher-order symbolism. pp. 347–348

- The *formal operational stage* begins at about age 12, when the individual can think hypothetically, consider all future possibilities, and use deductive logic. p. 348

How does Vygotsky's approach differ from Piaget's?

- For Vygotsky, a child is part of an active social world in which communication with others and self-speech (private or self-directive speech) helps the child understand his or her world and that of other people. Vygotsky held that when children are presented with tasks that are outside of their current abilities, they need the help of scaffolded social situations to accomplish them. pp. 349–350

KEY TERMS
scheme, p. 343; assimilation, p. 345; accommodation, p. 345; sensorimotor stage, p. 345; preoperational stage, p. 346; egocentrism, p. 346; decentration, p. 346; concrete operational stage, p. 347; conservation, p. 347; formal operational stage, p. 348

Moral Reasoning

How has morality been studied?

■ *Morality* is a system of learned attitudes about social practices, institutions, and individual behaviour that people use to evaluate situations and behaviour as being right or wrong, good or bad. Piaget and Kohlberg studied moral reasoning, focusing on how people make moral judgments about hypothetical situations. Their theories differ in that Piaget's stages cover development up to the beginning of the concrete operational stage while Kohlberg's model covers it up through formal operational reasoning. pp. 350–353

What was Gilligan's main criticism of Kohlberg's work?

■ Whereas Kohlberg showed that young children base their decisions about right and wrong on the likelihood of avoiding punishment and obtaining rewards, Gilligan found that children also were concerned with caring, relationships, and connections with other people. Most important, Gilligan found important differences between males and females. As younger children, girls are socialized towards a morality of caring, while boys are socialized towards a morality of justice. pp. 353–354

KEY TERM
morality, p. 350

Emotional and Social Development

What evidence is there that attachment exists?

■ *Attachment* is the strong emotional tie that a person feels towards a special person in his or her life. Harlow found that infant monkeys clung to terry-cloth figures whether or not they provided milk. He concluded that a wire figure could not provide the comfort that a terry-cloth one could provide. pp. 354–355

■ *Bonding* is a special process of emotional attachment theorized to occur between parent and child in the minutes and hours immediately after birth. However, it is a controversial idea that has little research support. p. 355

■ Bowlby was one of the first to study the close attachment between mothers and their babies. Ainsworth and Main showed that when removed from the mother, a baby develops characteristic responses of being secure, avoidant, resistant, or disoriented. Once established, early attachment is fairly permanent. Verbal exchanges between child and caregiver help establish ties, teach language, inform infants about the world, and socialize them. pp. 355–357

How permanent is temperament?

■ *Temperament* refers to early-emerging long-lasting individual differences in the intensity and especially the quality of emotional reactions. Temperament is not fixed and unchangeable; still, many researchers contend that some specific initial temperamental characteristics may be long-lasting and biologically based. pp. 358–360

How do children begin to develop a sense of self?

■ By the beginning of their second year, children have begun to understand that they are separate from their parents—they are developing a sense of self. Very young children do not understand the concept of sharing—particularly the idea that sharing with another child makes the other child more likely to share with them. pp. 362–363

How do children learn gender roles?

■ Gender stereotyping means having expectations for specific behaviour patterns based on a person's gender. While parents do reinforce children selectively based on their gender, especially at young ages, gender differences in behaviour are small and apparent only in certain situations, such as on the playground and in groups. pp. 365–366

What is friendship?

■ Friendship is a close emotional tie between peers. Close friends ideally interact as equals, enjoy each other's company, have mutual trust, provide mutual assistance, accept each other as they are, respect each other's judgment, feel free to be themselves with each other, understand each other, and share confidences. Children develop their first friendships around age three. High-school students typically report having three to five good friends. Adolescents spend as much as 29 percent of their waking hours with friends. Among adults in Western cultures, expectations for specific gender-based behaviours often control male–female interactions in friendship. p. 367

Describe Erikson's stage theory of psychosocial development.

■ Erikson describes psychosocial development throughout life as a series of stages during which people resolve various psychosocial issues. His theory suggests that at each stage a successful or unsuccessful resolution of a dilemma determines personality and social interactions. pp. 368–371

KEY TERMS
attachment, p. 354; bonding, p. 355; temperament, p. 359; gender stereotype, p 365; androgynous, p. 366

Weblinks

Jean Piaget Society
www.piaget.org/index.html
This home page of the Society for the Study of Knowledge and Development focuses on the life and work of Piaget. The organization's collection of publications and symposia are accessible from this site.

Jean Piaget Archives
www.unige.ch/piaget/biog.html
Visit this site to read Piaget's biography.

Kohlberg Tutorial
**snycorva.cortland.edu/~ANDERSMD/KOHL/content.
HTML**
This site contains information on Kohlberg's theory of moral development, and a link to information on Piaget's theory.

Classic Theories of Child Development
idealist.com/children/cdw.html
An overview of the work of Margaret Mahler, Sigmund Freud, and Erik Erikson, with a month-to-month look at development from 1 to 36 months.

The Institute of Child Study
www.oise.utoronto.ca/ICS
This site contains information on the research and researchers at this centre, which is part of the University of Toronto's Ontario Institute for Studies in Education.

Fetal Alcohol Syndrome
www.uchsc.edu/ahec/fas/
Access this site to learn more about FAS, how it can be prevented, and what can be done for infants suffering from it.

Developmental Milestones
www.uky.edu/Medicine/Departments/itec/mileston.htm
The University of Kentucky developed this site, which contains a detailed listing of developmental milestones. This list contains all of the developmental events of childhood and is thus very useful as a study aid.

Attachment Home Page
www.attach-bond.com/
This site is dedicated to helping parents and children develop strong attachments and bonds. It provides links to other attachment, parenting, and therapy sites.

Temperament and Social Behavior
www.mentalhealth.com/mag1/p5h-ch02.html
Read a brief article by Jerome Kagan, a leading researcher in temperament, about shyness and timidity in children.

Chapter 11

Adolescence and Adulthood

At the time, Sarah was fairly sure that all of the problems that arose during her teenage years were someone else's fault entirely (her parents, her teachers, the world in general). She had a rough fourteenth year: Her hormones were raging and her emotions were running wild; she was the oldest child in the family, and her parents didn't really know how to deal with her frequent and massive mood swings. She was lucky; the big issues were staying out late, allowance, and cleaning her room. She felt her parents weren't giving her enough freedom, her allowance wasn't enough, and that it was her business if her bedroom looked like a tornado had hit it.

It all seems so simple now, a few years later. A curfew, a couple of dollars, and some junk on the floor seem like small issues. But during the time that doors were slamming and blood pressure was going up, she and her parents feared they'd end up hating each other.

Her parents had thought the terrible twos were bad—with emotional outbursts from a cranky and obstinate small child. But as parents of an adolescent, they were dealing with someone who could express her anger easily, wilfully, and with a flair for the dramatic.

The truth is that every age—infancy, childhood, adolescence, adulthood, and late adulthood—brings its own joys and difficulties. Psychologists see human development as a process of growth and change that is influenced by a person's biological inheritance, life experiences, thoughts—and a certain amount of chance. For example, moving from one province to another changes people's lives; a divorce is unsettling; a death in the family can be devastating; winning the lottery can jolt a person from poverty to luxury and from anonymity to fame. So, in addition to normal, predictable developmental changes, once-in-a-lifetime happenings can permanently alter physical, social, and personality development. Normative life events are typical for most men and women in a culture; we can think of them as commonly experienced major events, like having children or retiring from work. Other life events are idiosyncratic; they are low-probability events like the death of a sibling or a major health problem. It is easy to pay attention to idiosyncratic events because they are often so compelling, but because normative life events affect most people, psychological theories have focused on them. ■

This chapter discusses some of the developmental changes that occur during adolescence and adulthood and traces the psychological processes underlying these changes. You'll see that a person's *chronological age* (actual age in years) is sometimes different from his or her *functional age* (the way the person actually performs in life). For example, some adolescents act "beyond their years," older and wiser than is expected of their peers. Among older adults—especially those over 65—some function in ways that seem more like what one would expect of people in their forties and fifties (Neugarten, 1968).

Adolescence: Bridging the Gap

A t age 14, despite what they might think, young people are not yet mature; they haven't yet grown up and aren't yet ready to face the world—or their parents—as an adult. Quite frankly, that's the way it should be. They continue to show childlike behaviours, but are changing and becoming more adult-like.

Adulthood is the period in life when people are relatively free of parental influence, especially financially, and accept responsibility for themselves. In Western culture, the transition from childhood to adulthood brings dramatic physical, cognitive, social, and emotional changes. Generally, this transition occurs between the ages of 12 and 20, a period known as *adolescence*, which bridges childhood and adulthood but is like neither of those states. **Adolescence** is the period extending from the onset of puberty to early adulthood. **Puberty** is the period when the reproductive system matures; it begins with an increase in production of sex hormones, occurring at and signalling the end of childhood. Although adolescents are like adults in many ways—they are nearly mature physically and mentally, and their moral development is fairly advanced—their emotional development may be far from complete and they have not yet become economically self-sufficient or taken on adult roles such as regular work and taking care of themselves (including paying bills and making day-to-day decisions independently).

Adolescence in Multiple Contexts

Adolescence is often referred to incorrectly as an inevitable time of storm and stress—of raging hormones—and for some adolescents this is indeed the case. It is a popular stereotype that adolescents are in a state of conflict resulting in part from a lack of congruity in their physical, cognitive, social, and emotional development. But like most stereotypes, a sweeping generalization that adolescence is especially tough is not accurate. Furthermore, there are multiple influences that initiate and maintain change in an adolescent's physical, cognitive, social, and emotional development. However, there is evidence that some adolescents certainly do experience conflict during this period. Consider alcohol abuse. Most adolescents know that drinking is illegal, harmful, and potentially deadly when combined with driving. Yet some are not mature enough to withstand peer pressure and make a conscious decision not to drink and drive and they may experience terrible consequences from poor decision making.

But storm and stress is not the whole picture of adolescence. *Most* adolescents go through this period of multiple changes without significant psychological difficulty (Larson & Ham, 1993). Although spurts of hormones effect adolescents' reactions, non-biological factors in turn moderate the effects of adolescents' moods (Buchanan, Eccles, & Becker, 1992; Eccles et al., 1993). Adolescence may be a challenging life period, just as adulthood is, but fewer than 30 percent of adolescents have serious difficulties (Eccles et al., 1993). Most adolescents have normal conflicts with parents or peers, and some have atypical problems, such as poverty; in

Adolescence [add-oh-LESS-sense]: The period extending from the onset of puberty to early adulthood.

Puberty [PEW-burr-tee]: The period during which the reproductive system matures; it begins with an increase in production of sex hormones and occurs at (and signals) the end of childhood.

addition, adolescents' coping mechanisms, or ways of dealing with these stressors, may not yet be fully mature.

Thus, the current consensus among psychologists is that adolescence is not ordinarily a time of great psychological turmoil (Powers, Hauser, & Kilner, 1989) and that adolescents have no more psychological disturbances than the rest of the population (Hauser & Bowlds, 1990). This does not mean that adolescence is conflict-free or that parent–child relationships do not change during this period (Larson & Ham, 1993); what it does mean is that adolescence does not *have* to be a stressful time (Galambos, 1992; Paikoff & Brooks-Gunn, 1991). Conflict frequency and intensity increases in early adolescence, is stable in middle adolescence, and decreases as adolescents reach 17 to 20 years of age (Laursen, Coy, & Collins, 1998). In the end, most adolescents have positive, healthy emotional and social development during these years.

It is almost a cliché for a teenager in Canada to feel that "no one understands me," but it is difficult to imagine a teenager growing up in the jungles of Papua New Guinea expressing the same sentiment. His focus during the teen years is not self-expression but learning specific skills. Thus, the problems of adolescence must be considered in a cultural context. Even when adolescents grow up in the same country, they experience life's joys and disappointments in different ways. Some teenagers come from disadvantaged economic groups. Some grow up in luxury. Others are exposed to racial prejudice, alcohol and other drug abuse, non-supportive families, or other stressful situations that lead them to feel a lack of control over their lives.

Unfortunately, most research on adolescence has been conducted on white, middle-class teenagers. But researchers now understand that the life experiences of whites, blacks, First Nations people, Asians, and other groups are not all alike. More recently, studies have compared the experiences of different groups and examined the cultural differences among groups as well as the diversity that exists within cultural groups. The reality is that there is often more diversity within a group than between groups. Researchers are also increasingly recognizing the similarities between groups.

Physical Development in Adolescence

The words *adolescence* and *puberty* are often used interchangeably, but in fact they mean different things. As noted earlier, puberty is the period during which the reproductive system matures. The age when puberty begins varies widely; some girls begin to mature physically as early as age eight, some boys at nine or ten (Marshall & Tanner, 1969). The average age of achieving sexual maturity—the first menstruation for a girl, the first ejaculation for a boy—is 13, plus or minus a year or two (on average, girls enter puberty a year or two before boys). Just before the onset of sexual maturity triggered by an increase in growth hormones, boys and girls experience significant *growth spurts*, gaining as much as 12 centimetres in a single year.

By the end of the first or second year of the growth spurt, changes have occurred in body proportions, fat distribution, bones and muscles, and physical strength and agility. In addition, the hormonal system has begun to trigger the development of secondary sex characteristics. **Secondary sex characteristics** are the genetically determined physical features that differentiate the sexes; they are not directly involved with reproduction, but they help distinguish men from women, for example, beards and chest hair in males and breasts in females. (*Primary sex characteristics* are those associated principally with the reproductive organs such as the vagina, uterus, and ovaries in females and the testes in males; they are present at birth.) Boys experience an increase in body mass and a deepening of the voice, as well as the growth of pubic, underarm, and facial hair. Girls experience an increase in the size of the breasts, a widening of the hips, and the growth of underarm and pubic hair. Puberty ends with the maturation of the reproductive organs, at which time boys produce sperm and girls begin to menstruate. The first ejaculation for boys and the first menstrual cycle for girls (called menarche) are usually memorable events. The order and sequence of these pubertal changes is predictable, but as noted earlier, the age at which puberty begins and the secondary sex characteristics emerge is quite variable from person to person.

Puberty has received a good deal of research attention. For example, researchers have found that as boys pass through puberty, they feel more positive about their bodies, whereas girls are more likely to have negative feelings. These effects are not simply related to gender. Rather, research suggests that the positive or negative feelings about their bodies are affected by the adolescents' perception of the "normality" of their maturational timing. Moreover, these timing effects are opposite for males and females, with early maturation being perceived as positive for males but negative for females (Peterson, 1987).

Researchers find that in junior high school, early-maturing boys enjoy several advantages, including increased confidence, superior athletic prowess, greater sexual appeal, and higher expectations from teachers and parents (Apter et al., 1981; Livson & Peskin, 1967, 1980). Early-maturing girls, on the other hand, seem to be at a disadvantage, experiencing negative body images, greater difficulty at home and at school, and less popularity with their female peers (Ge, Conger, & Elder, 1996; Graber et al., 1997). But these differences in adolescence often do not hold up in adulthood; the stresses of being an early or late maturer may help teenagers become adept at coping (Macfarlane, 1971). Many who were at a disadvantage in the adolescent years become self-assured, independent, and flexible as adults. The truth is that so many factors go into the making of a self-assured adult that we are not sure how significant the impact of early or late maturation is.

Puberty itself does not create psychological maladjustment; but becoming an adolescent means emerging as an adult, socially and sexually, and this takes some significant adjustment. New forces affect the self-image of adolescents; and although these forces create new stresses, most adolescents perceive their new status as desirable. Maturation has implications for social development, because young people often gravitate to and choose environments and activities that complement their genetic tendencies.

Cognitive Development in Adolescence

As children mature physically, they also develop cognitively in rather complex ways. Piaget and Vygotsky showed (see Chapter 10) that children's cognitive development has both biological and social components. But cognitive development does not stop in adolescence. Because most adolescents are now in the formal operational stage, can think about the world abstractly, and can develop hypotheses, they learn new cognitive strategies. Teenagers gain an expanding vocabulary, seek out creative solutions, and can fully use higher mental functions. Problem solving often becomes a focus for adolescent thought. For a brief time, many adolescents become egocentric, idealistic, and critical of others—which may make decisions about everyday issues difficult for them.

Developing new cognitive abilities—moving into Piaget's formal operations—is quite liberating for adolescents. Teenagers begin to understand the world and its subtleties and can think about the world abstractly. This newfound ability is not always easy, as adolescents sometimes become argumentative and difficult. According to Inhelder and Piaget (1958, pp. 345–346): "The adolescent goes through a phase in which he attributes an unlimited power to his own thoughts so that the dream of a glorious future or of transforming the world through ideas (even if this idealism takes a materialistic form) seems to be not only fantasy, but also an effective action which in itself modifies the empirical world." Part of the problem is that teenagers become wrapped up in themselves and their own thoughts—in short, they become quite egocentric. This transitional period, and its attendant *adolescent egocentrism*, leads to two cognitive distortions that were first documented by David Elkind (1967). The first is called the **imaginary audience**—the feeling adolescents have that they are "on stage," that there is an imaginary audience always watching them and the belief that this audience is as concerned about the adolescent's thoughts and behaviours as he or she is. "Everyone will notice," thinks a teenager, referring to his or her first pimple, or whatever else. The adolescent egocentrically believes the world is watching and therefore will do whatever is necessary to avoid embarrassment—usually by behaving like all of his or her friends or by seeking solitude.

Not only do adolescents believe that they are on stage, but they also develop an inflated sense of their own importance. This cognitive distortion is called the **personal fable**—the belief that their own ideas are special and unique, that other people cannot understand them, and that they are invulnerable so that risky behaviours, such as unsafe sex, that might harm other people will not harm them (Elkind & Bowen, 1979). The personal fable can lead to tragedy such as with the individual who thinks that he or she would never crash the car and can drive after drinking.

The imaginary audience and the personal fable may not be as much a return to childhood egocentrism as a side effect of cognitive growth and the ability to think about thinking. Adolescent egocentrism may be a bridging mechanism that allows adolescents to take on new roles, break away from parents, and integrate new views of the self (Lapsley, 1993). Whatever its origins, it starts to disappear by late adolescence (Vartanian & Powlishta, 1996).

Cognitive differences between boys and girls and between male and female adolescents are minimal. As we saw in Chapter 8, gender differences in verbal and mathematical abilities are exceedingly small (Hyde, Fennema, & Lamon, 1990). The cognitive differences found in recent research studies exist only in certain special populations—for example, among the very brightest mathematics students, where boys continue to outscore girls at least at the high-school level. However, boys' scores are especially variable (Hedges & Nowell, 1995). This does not mean that no differences are apparent; on certain tests (such as the SAT), males as a group outperform females in mathematics (Park, Bauer, & Sullivan, 1998). What it does mean is that when certain socioeconomic and cultural variables are controlled, gender differences are small and unimportant and refer only to overall group differences, not to the individual's likelihood of accomplishment.

Researchers are still trying to determine whether basic differences in intelligence exist between males and females and, if so, under what conditions. Biologically based mechanisms may account for some gender-based cognitive differences, but learning and social forces are far more potent in establishing and maintaining gender role stereotypes and gender-specific attitudes (see Chapter 5, pp. 182–183).

Imaginary audience: A cognitive distortion experienced by adolescents, in which they see themselves as "on stage," with an imaginary audience always watching them.

Personal fable: A cognitive distortion experienced by adolescents, in which they believe they are so special and unique that other people cannot understand them and risky behaviours will not harm them.

Emotional and Social Development in Adolescence

Early childhood social interactions as well as advances in cognitive development profoundly affect adolescent social adjustment. When children make poor adjustments early on, the likelihood of making good adolescent adjustments, social and otherwise, decreases. When Cairns and Cairns (1994) tracked 695 young people growing up over a 14-year period, they noticed that the youngsters' early patterns of social adjustment became predominant as the years went by. These researchers argue that the trajectories of social development do not change much; troubled boys and girls stay troubled, and happy and well-adjusted children are more likely to stay well adjusted. But regardless of their previous adjustment, the egocentrism of the *imaginary audience* that they think exists and the *personal fable* that they invent complicates their emotional and social adjustment.

Adolescents develop a self-image based on beliefs about themselves that are both cognitively and emotionally based; but significant others (parents and peers) also generate expectations and beliefs about adolescents, and these beliefs also have an impact (Cairns & Cairns, 1994). So an adolescent's personality and sense of self-esteem is affected by his or her stage of cognitive development and by childhood experiences, events such as the timing of puberty and how peers and parents react to that timing. Some of these effects can be modified. For example, parents and teachers can help both early- and late-maturing adolescents with their feelings about body image. Research shows that involvement with athletics can be a buffer against the initially negative feelings that sometimes arise during this period. For both girls and boys, increased time spent in sports is associated with increased satisfaction with body image and higher self-ratings of strength and attractiveness. Physical activity is associated with higher levels of achievement, weight reduction, improved muscle tone, and stress reduction, all of which contribute towards a positive self-image (Kirshnit, Richards, & Ham, 1988).

There are sharp individual differences in the development of adolescent self-esteem. Early adolescence, compared with middle or late adolescence, is associated with lower self-esteem and with feelings of insecurity, inadequacy, and shyness. Self-esteem is affected by a number of factors, including the number and types of relationships with others, ethnicity, socioeconomic level, and gender. Adolescents in a minority culture must form an ethnic or racial identity within the majority culture. This adds an element to identity formation and self-esteem that is absent in adolescents who are members of the majority culture. Socioeconomic factors also influence self-esteem. Although the effects of poverty on self-esteem are most marked in middle childhood, low income continues to exert an effect in adolescence, causing adolescents to be hostile, depressed, and unmotivated (Garbarino, Dubrow, Kostelny, & Pardo, 1992).

An additional important factor in the development of self-esteem is gender. In spite of the rapidly changing role of women in Western culture, young women often develop low self-esteem by the time they reach high school, despite the fact that their early childhood ambitions and dreams may have been similar to those of males. Television and the print media as well as school systems that still favour males in many domains contribute to the lower self-esteem of young women. Despite enormous historical gains, there is still a need to change many attitudes and behaviours (Rhode, 1997). This idea will be explored in further detail below.

Two additional important influences on self-esteem and personality are parents and peers. Theories disagree about the relative influence of peers versus parents (Harris, 1998), but most indicate that adolescents' attitudes fall somewhere between those of their parents and those of their peers (Paikoff & Brooks-Gunn, 1991). As was argued in Chapter 10, some assert that the influence of peer groups is especially formidable—especially in the early years of adolescence when the belief in an *imaginary audience* is still great. *Peer groups* are people who identify with and compare themselves to one another. They often consist of people of the same age, gender, and race, although adolescents may change their peer group memberships and may belong to more than one group. As adolescents spend more time away from parents and home, they experience increasing pressure to conform to their peer groups' values in relation to society, government, religion, music, and even fast-food restaurants; the desire for conformity especially affects same-sex peer relations (Bukowski et al., 1993). Peers sometimes praise, sometimes cajole, and constantly pressure one another to conform to behavioural standards, including standards for dress, social interaction, and forms of rebellion, such as shoplifting or taking drugs (Farrell & Danish, 1993). Most importantly, peers influence the adolescent's developing self-concept. *Diversity* (see pages 382 and 383) discusses a particular type of peer interaction—youth groups and youth gangs.

However, there is no question that adolescents also are responsive to parental influence (Resnick et al., 1997). While adolescents are working to pull away from their parents and establish a sense of autonomy, they also need to maintain a sense of connection and attachment to their parents. An adolescent's self-esteem and self-confidence are affected by parents and their style of raising a child (Resnick et al., 1997)—for example, are they authoritative, nurturing, and firm, or are they rigid and controlling? In the end, both parents and peers set standards by which the adolescent judges his or her own behaviour and contribute to self-esteem, confidence, and social and emotional adjustment. Some of that social adjustment is gender-based, as we will see in the next section.

Who Am I? The Search for Gender Identity

Gender matters. In fact, gender matters a great deal in both childhood and adulthood (Maccoby, 1998). Being a man or a woman in the Western world carries with it certain burdens. Men and women have different expectations for themselves and for members of the opposite sex and those expectations create gender inequality. It is widely held that "once upon a time" women suffered bad feelings about themselves and serious discrimination, but that those days are over. The truth is that that the attitudes and values of white males still dominate our society (Rhode, 1997). Serious disparities in employment, pay, status, and leadership roles continue to exist. This is a societal problem, but it stems from how people develop and nurture their gender identity and that of the opposite sex.

We saw in Chapter 10 that gender differences are differences between males and females in behaviour or mental processes. Extensive research has revealed few significant biologically determined behavioural differences between the genders. Although girls often reach developmental milestones earlier than boys, this difference usually disappears by late adolescence (L. Cohn, 1991). Rather, it appears that experience and learning—the way a person is raised and taught—have a profound impact on observed differences in gender-based behaviours.

Gender Identity. As noted earlier, a key feature of adolescence is that it is a period of transition and change. Adolescents must develop their own identity, a sense of themselves as independent, mature individuals. One important aspect of identity is **gender identity**—a person's sense of being male or female. Children develop gender identity by age three. By age four or five, children realize that their gender identity is permanent; that is, they know that changing their hair, clothing, or behaviour does not alter their gender. By this age they have segregated themselves in play groups according to gender (Maccoby, 1998). This means that adolescents have a clear sense of gender identity well before puberty.

But consider the experience that adolescents have when their bodies change in appearance very rapidly, sometimes in unpredictable ways. During the transition to adulthood, adolescents often try out various behaviours, including those relating to male–female relationships and dating. Some adolescents become extreme in their orientation towards maleness or femaleness. Boys, especially in groups, may become aggressive; girls may act submissively, be especially concerned with their looks, and focus on bonding with other girls. This exaggeration of traditional male

Gender identity: A person's sense of being male or female.

If There Are Young People Are There Gangs?

I n his song "Northern Frontier" on his latest CD *xray sierra*, Tom Cochrane sings about the deaths of Joseph Beeper Spence and Jeff Giles in Winnipeg, both of whom were innocent bystanders killed by members of the "deuce" and "i.p." (Indian Posse) gangs basically for being in the wrong place at the wrong time. Do we have a problem with youth gangs in Canada? Are gangs an inevitable part of life? Are all adolescent gangs organized in the same ways and to the same extent? Before you jump to what may seem like obvious conclusions, think for a minute about how your answers may be influenced by the portrayals of youth gang activity in the American media (e.g., movies like *Dangerous Minds* and especially television). Think about whether the assumption that full-blown gang activity is an inevitable part of adolescents' lives is a valid one, or whether it is just that—an assumption.

There is youth gang activity in Canada but gangs do not exist in every high school. This is emphasized by students like Janice Crave

from Courtney, British Columbia, who wrote of her concern about the assumption she noticed in an American questionnaire on gangs that there are gangs wherever there are young people (Crave, 1998). Gangs are mainly an urban phenomenon. While specific acts of violence are difficult to connect to gang activity (because police charge individuals, not groups), the amount and level of violent offences by young people in Canada is on the increase (Mathews, 1993). A number of police forces across the country, including in Vancouver and Toronto, operate gang crime units. There is an increasing problem with gangs of middle-class youth in Toronto, native gangs in Winnipeg, and Asian gangs in Vancouver and Toronto. What are Canadian youth gangs like and what sorts of forces draw young people into (or steer them away from) involvement in gang activities?

First, it is important to realize that the nature and extent of gang activity in Canada is in no way as serious as that found in the United States (Bala et al., 1994). Though the nature and extent of the violent images regularly presented to us via American

media may be contributing to the increase in violence among Canadian youth, it is also contributing to an overestimation of the extent and seriousness of youth gang activities in Canada (Federation of Canadian Municipalities, 1994).

Second, despite the tendency of some older citizens to view groups of three or more young people as a gang, there is uncertainty as to just how to define a gang. They definitely should be distinguished from peer groups, which are a central part of normal adolescent development. Researchers identify a continuum of youth crime organization ranging from a group to a gang. A group is a collection of friends that is loosely organized, has no clear leadership structure, has only spontaneous involvement in violence (if at all), and has little or no involvement in crime for profit (Mathews, 1993). Groups are likely to spend their time hanging out in malls and around convenience stores and street corners, and would describe themselves as friends. In the middle of this continuum are groups that gather mainly to engage in crime (for example, house break-ins), then go their

---

or female behaviours, called *gender intensification*, is often short-lived but may be related to the increased feelings of self-esteem that boys feel during adolescence and the decreased self-esteem that girls experience (Block & Robins, 1993).

Many psychologists believe that once gender identity is firmly established, children and adolescents attempt to bring their behaviour and thoughts into conformity with generally accepted gender-specific roles. **Gender schema theory** asserts that children and adolescents use gender as an organizing theme to classify and interpret their perceptions about the world (S. L. Bem, 1985; Maccoby, 1988). (Recall from Chapter 6 that a schema is a conceptual framework that organizes information and makes sense of the world. See Figure 11.1 on page 384 for a description of gender schema theory.) Young children decide on appropriate and inappropriate gender behaviours by processing a wide array of social information. They develop quick shorthand concepts of what boys and girls are like; then they try to behave consistently with those concepts. Thus, they show preferences for gender-related toys, activities, and vocations. In fact, children's and, later, adolescents' self-esteem and feelings of worth often are tied to their gender-based perceptions about themselves, many of which are determined by identification with the same-gender parent

Gender schema theory: The theory that children and adolescents use gender as an organizing theme to classify and interpret their perceptions about the world.

separate ways when the crimes are completed. At the other end of this continuum are criminal youth gangs, which are highly organized, have a clear leadership hierarchy, are systematically violent, and are involved in crime for profit as a major activity (Mathews, 1993). These gangs have initiation rituals, recognizable clothing, and "turf" (or territory) that they protect. They are more likely to use violence systematically and to have a noticeable effect on their communities. They also may be linked to adult gangs. To quote a young gang member, "A group is a group of friends. A gang is a group of trouble" (Mathews, 1993).

To understand Canadian groups/gangs and the young people involved in them requires that you consider the developmental stage of adolescence and the diverse context in which Canadian young people are growing and living. Adolescence is a time when young people begin to stand on their own both cognitively and socially, and their peer groups provide them with support for their emerging identities. A standard theory holds that gangs provide a level of support and access to social power, status, and resources such as money for young people growing up in severely economically challenged areas

(Haskell, 1961). The actual role that the social context plays in the formation of youth groups in Canada partially fits this model but varies significantly by region.

In Winnipeg, for example, youth groups fall closer to the gang end of the continuum and a large proportion of their members is aboriginal. Both poverty and a lack of strong social organization and future prospects contribute to the formation of these gangs (Smith, 1996). In southern Ontario, a lot of gang-related activity involves middle-class youth who are involved for thrills rather than monetary payoff. In Toronto, the groups/gangs are quite diverse; some are ethnically based and others have mixed membership

(Mathews, 1990). In British Columbia (and to a lesser extent in Toronto), the focus is on Asian gangs consisting of members drawn together either by their immigrant status (and thus their common language and lack of easy access to money and status) or by the drug trade (Nyhuus, 1998).

The question of what to do about youth gangs is a difficult one, and not easy to answer from a psychological point of view. Certainly work can be done to help communities become better informed about the actual extent of the problem. In the case of youth groups, interventions at the community level that find or create other, more positive activities and facilities for young people can help. Specific social problems can be addressed in other areas; for example, committing necessary resources to English as a second language (ESL) training to speed assimilation may be of value. Finally, recognizing the difficult social problems faced by aboriginal youth is a necessary step in addressing the problem in areas such as Winnipeg. Most of these approaches focus on providing support for more positive adolescent development—something that must occur if this problem is to diminish. ■

(Heilbrun, Wydra, & Friedberg, 1989). For example, young people may relate their self-worth to how much their behaviour matches that of adult males or females or to how well they fulfil society's view of gender roles (see Hudak, 1993). There are some sharp differences between teenage boys and girls in self-esteem (Block & Robins, 1993) and in rates of depression, with girls being twice as likely to be depressed as boys (Nolen-Hoeksema & Girgus, 1994).

Gender Roles. **Gender roles** are the full range of behaviours generally associated with one's gender; these roles help people establish who they are. However, in the course of establishing gender roles, people sometimes adopt **gender role stereotypes**—beliefs about gender-based behaviours that are strongly expected, regulated, and reinforced by society. Men, for example, may learn to hide their emotions; Western culture frowns on men who cry in public and reinforces men who appear strong and stoic when faced with sorrow or stress (Fisher & Good, 1998). Women are expected to behave in a passive and nurturing manner, suppressing anger. In the workplace, gender role stereotypes still exist and heavily influence wages and promotions (Hoffman & Hurst, 1990; Pomerleau et al., 1990). According to Statistics

Gender roles: The full range of behaviours generally associated with one's gender, which help one establish who one is. Also known as *sex roles*.

Gender role stereotypes: Beliefs about gender-based behaviours that are strongly expected, regulated, and reinforced by society.

Canada (1996), on average, women in Canada earn about 73 cents for each dollar that men earn—this discrepancy is referred to as the wage gap. The *wage gap* exists largely because women still predominate in many lower-paid jobs.

Influences processing of social information

Society's beliefs about the traits of females and males

GENDER SCHEMA

Influences self-esteem (only behaviours or attitudes consistent with gender schema are acceptable)

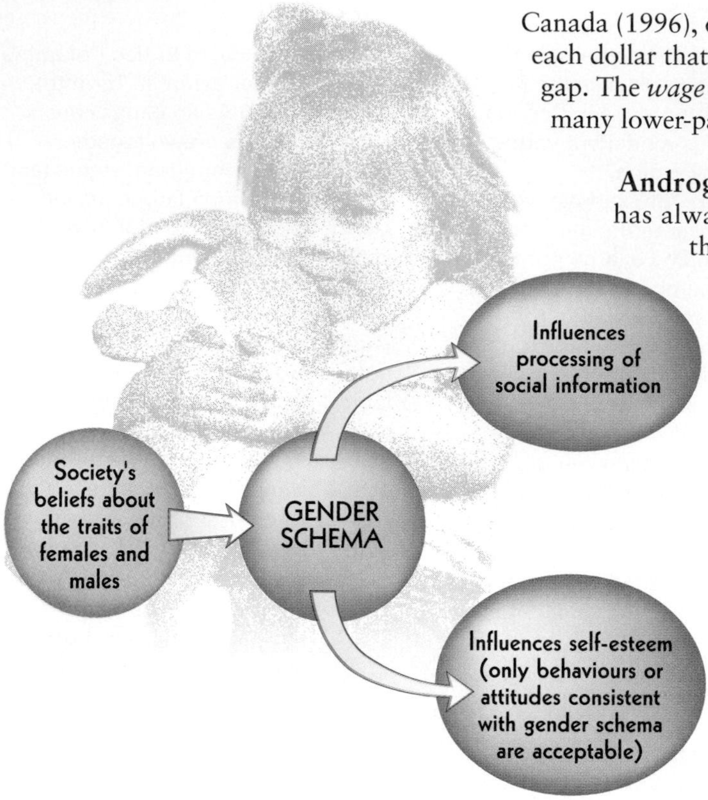

FIGURE 11.1
Gender Schema Theory
According to gender schema theory, children and adolescents use gender as an organizing theme for classifying and interpreting their perceptions about the world.

Androgyny. Developing a gender identity in adolescence has always been part of the transition to adulthood. Today, this task is more complicated, especially for women. In earlier decades of this century, most educated Canadian women were expected to pursue marriage and homemaking, which were considered full-time careers. Today, women's plans often include a career outside the home as well as child-rearing. In recent years, many women and men have developed new attitudes about gender roles—attitudes that encourage *both* traditionally masculine traits and traditionally feminine traits. They have adopted behaviours that are **androgynous**— that represent a blend of valued masculine-stereotyped and feminine-stereotyped traits. Androgynous men and women may fix cars, have careers, do housework, and help care for children; they can be both assertive and emotionally sensitive. More than ever before, men today disparage violent toughness as part of the masculine role (Fisher & Good, 1998). Several studies have found that people who rate high in androgynous characteristics tend to feel more fulfilled and more competent when dealing with social and personal issues (S. L. Bem, 1993; Stake, 1997). Other studies have indicated that an androgynous or masculine self-view is associated with higher self-esteem in both males and females (Rose & Montemayor, 1994). As people become more androgynous in Canada, it will be interesting to see if this trend affects adolescents' friendships, which are discussed in *The Research Process* (see pages 386 and 387).

Sexual Behaviour During Adolescence

Times have changed a great deal. In the 1950s, maintaining one's status as chaste until marriage was considered a virtue; if sexual intimacy was engaged in, it was between young adults who had committed themselves to one another. Today, sexual intimacy is seen as a rite of passage and a way of gaining adult status; about 50 percent of Canadian girls and boys age 15 to 19 have engaged in sexual intercourse at least once. This is an important finding, as sexually active teenagers are at greater risk for alcohol abuse, sexually transmitted diseases, and academic failure, among other negative outcomes (Maticka-Tyndale, 1997). What has initiated these changes?

In human beings, learned attitudes have a greater influence than biological factors in determining sexual behaviour; and people first learn about such behaviour at home. Parents' attitudes and behaviour affect children—whether, for instance, parents hug and kiss openly, seem embarrassed by their bodies, or talk freely about sexual issues. The influence of parents in sexual matters was shown in a study that examined how parents' discipline and control influence teenagers' sexual attitudes and behaviour. Miller and colleagues (1986) surveyed more than 2000 teenagers and their parents about parental discipline and teenage sexual behaviour. The results showed that sexual permissiveness and intercourse were more frequent among adolescents who viewed their parents as not having rules or not being strict. Sexual behaviours, especially intercourse, were less frequent among teenagers who reported that their parents were strict. In addition, close relationships with parents and feelings of family support have been associated with later age at first intercourse (Brooks-Gunn & Furstenberg, 1989).

Androgynous: Having both stereotypically male and stereotypically female characteristics.

Canadian adolescents view sexual intimacy as an important and normal part of growing up; premarital heterosexual activity has become increasingly common among adolescents, especially 13- to 17-year-olds. About 60 percent of male teenagers and 50 percent of female teenagers have intercourse by age 18 (Maticka-Tyndale, 1997). There are great individual differences in age at first intercourse and in the subsequent frequency of intercourse. It is not uncommon for first intercourse to occur at age 14 or 15 and then for the teenager not to have intercourse again for a year or two (Furstenberg, Brooks-Gunn, & Chase-Lansdale, 1989). Dreyer (1982) suggests four reasons for the early expression of sexual behaviour. First, adolescents are reaching sexual maturity at younger ages than in previous decades. Second, knowledge and use of contraception are becoming more widespread, thus eliminating the fear of pregnancy. Third, adults' sexual attitudes and behaviours are changing. And finally, adolescents consider sexual behaviour to be normal in an intimate relationship.

More relaxed attitudes about adolescent sexual behaviour have brought about increased awareness of contraception and of the problems of teenage pregnancy. Nevertheless, about 24 000 teenagers between age 15 and 19 give birth each year (Statistics Canada, 1996). This rate is less that half of that found in the United States (Unicef, 1998). The more engaged students are with schooling, the less likely they are to become pregnant (Manlove, 1998). The consequences of childbearing for teenage mothers are serious. Teenage mothers are more likely to smoke and to have low-birth-weight infants; they are also less likely to receive timely prenatal care. Furthermore, a young woman's chances for education and employment become more limited, and many young women are forced to rely on public assistance. Most studies indicate that women who bear children early in their lives will not achieve economic equality with women who postpone parenthood until they are adults (Furstenberg & Hughes, 1995); adolescent pregnancy is also associated with abuse of alcohol and other drugs and depression (Martin, Hill, & Welsh, 1998).

Current studies show that, despite the threat of AIDS, teenagers and college students still engage in regular sexual activity, often without appropriate protection. Comprehensive school-based health-care programs that emphasize the complete picture of sexuality (attitudes, contraception, motivation, and behaviour) reduce the risk of pregnancy in teenagers. But for many parents and teenagers alike, such programs are controversial.

Focus

Review

- What evidence exists to show that gender-based behaviours are strongly expected, regulated, and reinforced by society? pp. 383–384
- Identify several androgynous traits. p. 384

Think Critically

- As people become more androgynous, how do you think it will affect adolescent friendships? How might it change the nature of courting? Of marriage?

Adulthood: Years of Stability and Change

C anadian adults today often have vastly different life experiences than did adults of the 1950s, whose lives tended to follow more predictable and prescribed timetables. In the 1950s, many people married when they were in their late teens or early twenties and had children soon after. Wives frequently stayed at home to raise the children, while husbands went to work to support the family. Today's adults tend to marry later, and some don't marry at all. Many people are postponing or rejecting parenting. While some women choose to stay at home

After the closing night of the high-school play, a father drops his daughter off for a celebratory overnight cast party. He is surprised—perhaps a bit shocked—to find out that the overnight party is a coed sleepover! Such events were unheard of when he was in high school. But today, high-school students commonly have cross-gender friendships, some of which are intellectually and emotionally—but not sexually—intimate. High-school students seek intimate relationships with friends—male and female—for a range of reasons, not the least of which is to find someone who will bolster their self-esteem. We know that adolescents are especially vulnerable emotionally, feel that the whole world is watching them, and often have poor body images. It's no surprise, then, that having friends and expressing intimacy are high on their list of priorities.

Adolescents with friends do better in school and are less likely to experience psychological problems. But whom do adolescents seek out? Do boys seek out girls, and vice versa? With whom are adolescents likely to be more intimate? With whom are boys and girls more comfortable? A team of researchers at the University Miami School of Medicine (Lundy, Field, McBride, Field, & Largie, 1998) seeking to answer these questions videotaped eleventh- and twelfth-grade adolescents during interactions with friends and had observers rate the interactions.

The Question. The researchers knew that adolescents seek out "best friends" and wanted to know which of three pairs—male-male, female-female, or male-female—produced the highest levels of comfort and playfulness in their interactions. They also sought to know if this changed from grade 11 to grade 12. With whom do high-school students develop the most comfortable feelings?

Method. Eighteen high-school students (11 females and 7 males) were studied over a two-year period during grades 11 and 12. They were asked to name their best same-sex friends and best opposite-sex friends. These friends were then also asked to participate.

The best-friend pairs, same-sex and opposite-sex, were seated face to face across a small table and asked to have conversations about anything they wanted. The 10-minute conversations were videotaped. Students then completed a questionnaire. Saliva samples were collected before videotaping and after the questionnaire to assess arousal levels (cortisol levels in saliva can yield a measure of arousal).

to raise children, many are concentrating on careers; some of these women's husbands raise the children. Many grown children are returning home after college, and divorce has broken up numerous families. The 1950s stereotype of a well-ordered, simple family structure has changed sharply in a relatively short period of time.

The Canadian adult life experience today is also different from that of other cultures. Canadians share some commonalties with people in other Western cultures, but very few with people in Third World countries. These cultural differences have not been widely studied. In addition, until the 1970s developmental psychologists in Western cultures concentrated largely on white, middle-class infants and children.

Psychologists are now focusing on development across cultures and throughout the life span. They are recognizing that a person encounters new challenges in every stage of life. Researchers study adult development by looking at the factors that contribute to stability or change, to a sense of accomplishment or feelings of despair, and to physical well-being or diminished functioning. To illustrate this, think about the decades after retirement, which can be a time of stability and feelings of completion and well-being, or a difficult, unhappy time full of physical and emotional troubles. Researchers today also are examining the differences between men and women, with emphasis on the unique experiences of women. Minorities are being studied, and theories are recognizing and focusing on cultural diversity.

The questionnaire asked how the participants felt during the taping, how they rated their friend, and what level of intimacy they had with that friend. Participants also self-assessed their self-esteem, anxiety, and levels of depression. Each of the videotaped interactions was coded by the researchers for positive to negative states of attentiveness and feeling on three dimensions: *interested* (looking at, leaning towards the other person); *animated* (looking intensively, fast talking, exaggerated facial expression); and *playfulness* (funny faces, laughing, mimicry). The raters did not know that the pairs of participants in each videotape were best friends—they were thus blind to friendship status.

Results. The analysis of the data showed that the males in grade 12 reported being slightly happier than when they were in grade 11 and happier than either group of females. All of the participants—males and females—were more comfortable when they were in same-sex pairs than in cross-sex pairs. The grade 12 boys had the lowest peer intimacy scores. Compared to males, females engaged in more interactions and animated behaviour; furthermore, this gender difference increased in grade 12. Both males and females showed decreases in playfulness as they grew older. The saliva tests showed that the most stressed interactions were among grade 11 boys in cross-gender interactions.

Conclusions. The changes that occurred from grades 11 to 12 were small and often subtle—grade 11 and 12 adolescents are very similar. Far more important, and perhaps the key finding of the study, was that while both males and females preferred same-sex friends, they developed more comfortable feelings in cross-sex relationships as they grew older. The female-female interactions were the most involved and intimate. Like previous research (Sharabany, Gershoni, & Hoffman, 1981), this study found that males de-emphasize feelings and emotional support as components of relationships and stress their instrumental, helping components. The females, more than the males, focused on feelings. There was more synchrony, matching of behaviour, as both males and females grew older.

Intimacy grows as people develop, and the nature of their relationships changes. Males and females are more likely to interact well as they enter adulthood, but cultural expectations for support and help or feelings and intimacy have strong effects among adolescents. Males and females prefer same-sex friends during the adolescent years; they feel more intimate, comfortable, and less anxious with people of the same sex. ∎

Psychologists also are recognizing that a person's career, not just the person's family or life stage, is a defining characteristic of adulthood. Adults spend an enormous amount of time and energy on their careers, which until recently have been examined relatively little by psychologists. Building Table 11.1 summarizes the major changes in functioning in young, early, and middle adulthood.

The Search for Identity: Adult Stage Theories

Some theorists—perhaps the more poetic—think of life as a journey along a road from birth to death. This metaphor is encapsulated in Erik Erikson's stage theory, in which people move through a series of stages and must resolve a different dilemma in each stage in order to develop a healthy identity.

Erik Erikson—Revisited. An important aspect of Erikson's stage theory is that it encompasses the entire life span. At each stage, people attempt to solve a particular dilemma and they move towards greater maturity as they pass from stage to stage. In Chapter 10 we addressed stages 1 to 4, which focused on childhood. Let's now consider the stages that begin with adolescence.

Erikson's stage 5, *identity versus role confusion*, marks the end of childhood and the beginning of adolescence. According to Erikson, the growth and turmoil of

Building Table 11.1

Major Changes in Important Domains of Adult Functioning

Age	Physical Change	Cognitive Change	Work Roles	Personal Development	Major Tasks
Young Adulthood, 18–25	Peak functioning in most physical skills; optimal time for child bearing	Cognitive skills high on most measures	Choice of career, which may involve several job changes	Conformity; task of establishing intimacy	Separate from family; form partnership; begin family; find job; create individual life pattern
Early Adulthood, 25–40	Good physical functioning in most areas; health habits during this time establish later risks	Peak period of cognitive skill on most measures	Rising work satisfaction; major emphasis on career or work success; most career progress steps made	Task of passing on skills, knowledge, love (generativity)	Rear family; establish personal work pattern and strive for success
Middle Adulthood, 40–65	Beginning signs of physical decline in some areas (strength, elasticity of tissues, height, cardiovascular function)	Some signs of loss of cognitive skill on timed, unexercised skills	Career reaches plateau, but higher work satisfaction	Increase in self-confidence, openness	Launch family; redefine life goals; redefine self outside of family and work roles; care for aging parents

adolescence creates an "identity crisis." The major task for adolescents is to resolve that crisis successfully by forming an *identity*: a sense of who they are, where they are going, and their place in the world. Adolescents have to form an identity that is multifaceted and includes vocational choices, religious beliefs, gender roles, sexual beliefs, and ethnic customs. The task is daunting, and this is one reason why adolescence is such a key stage of development. From Erikson's view, the failure to form an identity leaves the adolescent confused about adult roles and unable to cope with the demands of adulthood, including the development of mature relationships with members of the opposite sex (Erikson, 1963, 1968). The special problems of adolescence—which occasionally include rebellion, suicidal feelings, and drug problems—also must be dealt with at this stage.

Stage 6 (young adulthood) involves *intimacy versus isolation*. Young adults begin to select other people with whom they can form intimate, caring relationships. They learn to relate on an emotionally deep basis with members of the opposite sex and commit to a lasting relationship. Failure to resolve the dilemma of intimacy results in feelings of isolation.

In stage 7 (middle adulthood), *generativity versus stagnation*, people become more aware of their mortality and develop a concern for future generations. They now hope to convey to the next generation, particularly to their children, information, love, and warmth. They do so through acts of caring (Bradley & Marcia, 1998). As adults, they hope to guide the following generations; otherwise they will stagnate (remain self-absorbed), feeling that they have done nothing for the next generation.

In stage 8 (late adulthood), *ego integrity versus despair*, people decide whether their existence is meaningful, happy, and cohesive or wasteful and unproductive. Many individuals never fully complete stage 8, and some do so with regrets and a feeling that life is too short. Those who do master and complete this stage feel fulfilled, with a sense that they understand, at least partly, what life is about.

Table 11.1 summarizes stages 5 to 8 of Erikson's theory.

Levinson's Life Structures. Another noted theorist, Daniel Levinson, has devised a different stage theory of adult development. He agrees that people go through stages and that they share similar experiences at key points in their lives. He also agrees that studying those shared experiences allows psychologists to help people better manage their lives. Unlike Erikson, however, Levinson does not see life as a journey towards some specific goal or objective leading to maturity. Rather, he believes that a theory of development should lay out the eras during which individuals master various developmental tasks. In his words (Levinson, 1980, p. 289): "We change in different ways, according to different timetables. Yet, I believe that everyone lives through the same developmental periods in adulthood . . . though people go through them in their own ways."

Levinson (1978) suggests that, as people grow older, they adapt to the demands and tasks of life. He describes four basic eras in the adult life cycle—adolescence, early adulthood, middle adulthood, and late adulthood—each with distinctive qualities and different life problems, tasks, and situations. Each era also brings with it different *life structures*—unique patterns of behaviour and ways of interacting with the world. These are the "themes" of one's life at a given time, as reflected in two or three major areas of chosen commitment. Levinson's theory highlights periods of questioning and doubt alternating with periods of stability. The so-called midlife crisis is one of those major questioning periods.

During *adolescence* (ages 11 to 17), young people enter the adult world but are still immature and vulnerable. During *early adulthood* (18 to 45), they make their first major life choices regarding family, occupation, and style of living. Throughout this period, adults move towards greater independence and senior positions in the community. They raise their children, strive to advance their careers, and launch

Table 11.1 Erikson's Last Four Stages of Psychosocial Development

Stage	Approximate Age	Important Event	Description
5. Identity versus role confusion	Adolescence	Peer relationships	The teenager must achieve a sense of identity that encompasses occupation, gender roles, sexual behaviour, and religion.
6. Intimacy versus isolation	Young adulthood	Love relationships	The young adult must develop intimate relationships or suffer feelings of isolation.
7. Generativity versus stagnation	Middle adulthood	Parenting and work	Each adult must find some way to contribute to and support the next generation.
8. Ego integrity versus despair	Late adulthood	Reflection on and acceptance of one's life	Ideally, the person arrives at a sense of acceptance of oneself as one is and a sense of fulfilment.

their offspring into the adult world. Early adulthood is an era of striving for, gaining, and accepting responsibility. By the end of this era, at about age 45, most people are no longer caring for young children but increasingly may be involved in assisting aging parents.

The much-discussed midlife crisis occurs at the end of early adulthood. In fact, Levinson calls particular attention to it, asserting that most adults experience a crisis in their early forties. During this era, people often realize that their lives are half over—that if they are to change their lives, they must do so now. Of those who are dissatisfied with the life they have made, some resign themselves to their original course; others decide to change, grow, and strive to achieve new goals. (This era is similar to Erikson's stage 7, generativity versus stagnation.)

Middle adulthood spans the years from 46 to 65. Adults who have gone through a midlife crisis now learn to live with the decisions they made during early adulthood. Career and family usually are established. People experience either a sense of satisfaction, self-worth, and accomplishment or a sense that much of their life has been wasted. It is often during this period that people reach their peak in creativity and achievement (Simonton, 1988). In the middle of this era, some people go through a crisis similar to that of early adulthood. Sometimes it is a continuation of the earlier crisis; at other times it is a new one (see *Experiencing Psychology*).

The years after age 50 are ones of mellowing. People approaching their sixties begin to prepare for late adulthood, making whatever major career and family decisions are necessary before retirement. People in their early sixties generally learn to assess their lives not in terms of money or day-to-day successes but according to whether life has been meaningful, happy, and cohesive. At this time, people stop blaming others for their problems. They are less concerned about disputes with other people. They try to optimize their life, because they know that at least two-thirds of it has passed and they wish to make the most of their remaining years. Depending on how well people come to accept themselves at this stage, the next decade may be one of great fulfilment or great despair.

Levinson's fourth and final era, *late adulthood*, covers the years from age 65 on. During retirement, many people relax and enjoy the fruits of their labours. Children, grandchildren, and even great-grandchildren can become the focus of an older person's life.

Levinson's stage theory is a bit more rigid about its timetable than is Erikson's, and it focuses on developmental tasks, or themes. Levinson's theory is an alternative to Erikson's, but both suffer from being hard to evaluate experimentally.

Gender Differences in Adult Stages. Levinson developed his theory by studying 40 men in detail over several years. His subjects were interviewed weekly for several months and again after two years. Spouses were interviewed, and extensive biographical data were collected. Levinson's theory has achieved wide acclaim, but it has also been challenged. A major shortcoming is that it was based on information gathered from a small sample of middle-class men between the ages of 35 and 45. It did not consider gender differences.

Women apparently follow life stages similar to those for men. As children, women are taught different values, goals, and approaches towards life, which often are reflected later in their choice of vocations, hobbies, and intellectual pursuits. Historically, women have pursued different career paths than men. More recently, women are increasingly entering areas previously dominated by men. For example, women now comprise nearly half of all law school students. However, this does not mean that all female attorneys choose to follow the traditional path from associate to partner that is generally chosen by males. In *The Seasons of a Woman's Life* (1996), Levinson points out the complexities of women's lives based on his interviews with a small sample of women. According to Levinson, women must deal with contradictory roles and responsibilities, which makes tracking of their life stages and transitions a complex task.

The developmental course of women, and especially of women's transitions, is similar to that of men; but some women tend to experience transitions and life

experiencing psychology

Are Crises Unavoidable?

Clearly, people go through transitions in life. At certain junctures, new decisions must be made and people must reassess who they are, where they are going, and how they want to get there. But does everyone go through a midlife crisis? A distinction should be drawn between a transition and a crisis. A *transition* suggests that a person has reached a time in life when old ways of coping are giving way to new ones, old tasks have been accomplished, and new ways of living are emerging. A person in transition must face new dilemmas, challenges, and responsibilities, which often require reassessment, reappraisal, and the development of new skills. A *crisis*, in contrast, occurs when old ways of coping become ineffective and a person is helpless—not knowing what to do and needing new, radically different coping strategies. Crises often are perceived as painful turning points in people's lives.

Not everyone experiences the infamous midlife *crisis*, but most people pass through a midlife *transition*; and some pass through two, three, or even more transitions. At around age 30, a transition may occur; during this transition, careers and relationships begun in a

person's twenties are reevaluated and sometimes rejected. In the transitions of early and middle adulthood—including the midlife "crisis" at about age 40—people reorient their career and family choices. Sometimes parents experience another transition, called the *empty nest syndrome*, when their children leave home. The empty nest syndrome usually is not too stressful and is less likely to be a problem for people who are engaged in paid employment outside the home than for those whose lives centre on their children (Adelmann et al., 1989). Transitions also occur at retirement, not only for the retiree but also for the spouse.

People who experience midlife transitions normally show no evidence of increased maladjustment or increased rates of suicide or alcoholism. For some people, however, midlife changes can be difficult. Like adolescents, some adults grapple with the transitions in their lives, while others sail through them, not perceiving them as difficult or painful. Their attitudes depend on their unique personalities and their ways of coping with the world. Thus the term *midlife crisis* may be a misnomer. As Levinson

(1980) suggests, it should more properly be called a *midlife transition*—a transition that may be more difficult for some individuals than others. In fact, it is best to think of such transitions as normative; most people experience midlife transitions, and some people experience several of them. The idea of a universally experienced midlife *crisis* has little scientific support. ■

events at later ages and in more irregular sequences (Smart & Peterson, 1994). In addition, women experience events such as midlife transitions differently than men. While some men approach a midlife crisis at age 40 as a last chance to hold on to their youth, many women see it as a time to reassess, refocus, and revitalize their creative energies (Apter, 1995; Levinson, 1996). At 50, many women become suddenly aware of their aging due to physical changes in their body—especially declining fertility—and this creates a different type of transition (Jarrett & Lethbridge, 1994; Pearlmann, 1993).

In a major study of women's transitions, Mercer, Nichols, and Doyle (1989) identified a developmental progression for women. They considered especially the role of motherhood and how it influences the life courses of women. In the *launch into adulthood era* (ages 16 to 25), women break away from families to go to school, marry, and work. In the *levelling era* (ages 26 to 30), many women readjust their life course; this is often a time for marriage, separation, or divorce. In the *liberation era* (ages 36 to 40), women focus their aspirations, grow personally, and may initiate or change careers. Mercer and colleagues did not find major transitions for women in the years from 40 to 60; they found greater flux and crises in earlier and later years. In the *regeneration/redirection era* (ages 61 to 65), women, like men, adjust to their life choices and prepare for retirement and a more leisurely lifestyle. These two latter stages (liberation and regeneration) are times of great empowerment for women, when growth, regrowth, and purpose are often redefined and reinforced, resulting in a sense of true contentment. In the last stage of life, the *creativity/destructiveness era* (age 65 and on), women are challenged to adapt to health changes and the loss of spouses and friends; this time also may be characterized by a surge of creativity or, sometimes, depression.

Women still face discrimination in the workplace, and society continues to be ambivalent in its expectations for women. Women still have the primary burden of family responsibilities, especially child care; in the aftermath of a divorce, the woman usually gets physical custody of the children. Women often must juggle multiple roles, which place enormous burdens on them (K. J. Williams et al., 1991). The assumption of solo child-care responsibility after divorce has sharp economic consequences that alter the lifestyle, mental health, and course of life stages for women (McBride, 1990). Further, the issues in women's transitions are often different from those in men's; women tend to focus more on intimacy and relationships than do men (Caffarella & Olson, 1993). Thus, obvious life-stage differences exist for men and women—whether they are upper, middle, or lower class—but even greater differences exist *within* groups of demographically similar men or women. Even popular accounts of life span development such as Gail Sheehy's *New Passages* (1995) and *Men's Passages* (1998) recognize the enormous individual differences that exist in people's ability to alter, customize, and create their life courses.

Physical Development in Adulthood

One hundred years ago only about half of all Canadians who reached age 20 lived beyond age 65. Today most people live well into their seventies, but despite this longevity we know little about the middle to late adult years. The reality is that psychologists study childhood physical development extensively, but in comparison pay little attention to adult physical development. Although physical development in adulthood is slower, less dramatic, and sometimes less visible than in childhood and adolescence, it does occur.

Fitness Changes. Most of the adult years are years of health and fitness; the leading cause of death, for example, for people aged 25 to 44 is an unintentional injury—for example, from a motor vehicle crash. Psychologists often speak of fitness as involving both a psychological and a physical sense of well-being. Physically, human beings are at their peak of agility, speed, and strength between ages 18 and 30. From 30 to 40 there is some loss of agility and speed. And between 40 and 60, much greater losses occur. In general, strength, muscle tone, and overall fitness deteriorate gradually from age 30 on. People become more susceptible to disease. Respiratory, circulatory, and blood pressure problems are more apparent; lung capacity and physical strength are significantly reduced. Decrease in bone mass and strength occur, especially in women after menopause; the resulting condition is called *osteoporosis*. Immune system responsivity and the ability to fight disease diminish significantly among older adults.

Sensory Changes. In early adulthood, most sensory abilities remain fairly stable. But between ages 40 and 50 adults must contend with almost inevitable sensory losses that become more pronounced as they age. Vision, hearing, taste, and smell require increasingly higher levels of stimulation to respond at the same levels as younger people's senses do. Older people, for example, usually are unable to make fine visual discriminations without the aid of glasses, have limited capacity for dark adaptation, and often have some degree of hearing loss, especially in the high-frequency ranges. Reaction time slows and visual acuity decreases; the risks of glaucoma, cataracts, and retinal detachment increase. By age 65, many people can no longer hear very high-frequency sounds, and some are unable to hear ordinary speech. Hearing loss is greater for men than for women.

Sexual Changes. In adults of both sexes, advancing years bring changes in sexual behaviour and desire as well as physical changes related to sexuality. For example, in the child-rearing years, women's and men's sexual desires are sometimes moderated by the stresses of raising a family and juggling a work schedule. But sexual activity remains a vital part of the lives of middle-aged adults. Although many people continue to experience sexual enjoyment to a similar or greater extent than in their younger years, there may be differences in their physical reactions. Men may need more time to achieve erection and women experience a thinning of the vaginal walls that may make intercourse painful. For women, midlife hormonal changes lead to the cessation of ovulation and menstruation at about 50 years, a process known as *menopause*. Menopause generally is not seen as a crisis for most but as a transition after which women no longer have to deal with pregnancy issues; for some, however, it is perceived as a crisis signalling the beginning of old age and a lack of youthful femininity. At about the same age, men's testosterone levels decrease, their ejaculations are weaker and briefer, and their desire for sexual intercourse typically decreases from previous levels (Rowland et al., 1993). Nevertheless, older people continue to engage in sexual activities and find them enjoyable, and a significant percentage continue to find their sexual activities more satisfying than when they were younger (National Council on Aging, 1998).

Theories of Aging. The quest for eternal youth has inspired extravagant attempts to slow, stop, or reverse the physical process of aging. Alchemists in the Middle Ages tried in vain to concoct an elixir of life. Ponce de Leon organized an expedition to the New World in 1512 to find the fabled fountain of youth. And in the past century, some people attempted to revive youthful vigour with everything from strong laxative therapy (to clean the colon) to injections of cells from lamb fetuses. In recent years, scientists seem to have dramatically increased the life span of some laboratory animals by feeding them calorie-restricted diets.

Despite the centuries-long search for the secret of eternal youth, psychologists and physicians have been examining the behavioural and physiological changes that accompany aging only since the early 1970s. Three basic types of theories—based on heredity, external factors, and physiology—have been developed to explain aging. Although each emphasizes a different cause for aging, it is most likely that aging results from a combination of all three.

Genes determine much of a person's physical make-up; thus, it is probable that *heredity*, to some extent, determines how a person ages and how long he or she will live. Much supporting evidence exists for this genetic argument. For example, long-lived parents tend to have long-lived offspring. However, researchers still do not know *how* heredity exerts its influence over the aging process, simply that there are multiple mechanisms of aging, some of which are hereditary (Jazwinski, 1996).

External, or *lifestyle*, *factors* also affect how long a person will live (Kimmel, 1980). For example, people who reside on farms live longer than those who reside in cities; normal-weight people live longer than overweight people; and people who do not smoke cigarettes, who are not constantly tense or hostile, who wear seatbelts, and who are not exposed to disease or radiation live longer than others. Because data on external factors are often obtained from correlational studies, cause-and-effect statements cannot be based on them; it is reasonable to assume, however, that external factors such as disease, smoking, and obesity affect a person's life span.

Several theories use *physiological explanations* to account for aging. Because a person's physiological processes depend on both hereditary and environmental factors, these theories rely on both concepts. The *wear-and-tear theory* of aging claims that the human organism simply wears out from overuse, like a machine (Hayflick, 1994); this idea has intuitive appeal but little research support. What little research does support this information focuses on how the body uses its energy stores and indicates that the more active a life a person lives, the less efficient may be the body's use of energy and the faster the aging process (Levine & Stadtman, 1992). A related theory, the *homeostatic theory*, suggests that the body's ability to adjust to stress and other variations in internal conditions decreases with age. For example, as the ability to maintain a constant body temperature decreases, cellular and tissue damage occur and aging results. Similarly, when the body can no longer control the use of sugar through the output of insulin, signs of aging appear. It is important to note, however, that aging may be the *cause* of deviations from homeostasis, rather than the result.

It is also important to distinguish between primary and secondary aging. *Primary aging* is the normal, inevitable change that occurs among human beings and is irreversible, progressive, and universal. Such aging happens despite good health; a consequence of such aging is that a person is more vulnerable to society's fast-paced and sometimes stressful lifestyles. *Secondary aging* is aging due to extrinsic factors such as disease, environmental pollution, or smoking. Lack of good nutrition is a secondary aging factor that is a principal cause of poor health and aging among lower-income elderly Canadians.

Cognitive Changes in Adulthood

Perhaps the most distressing change that may occur with aging is a decline in cognitive ability. Although many people believe that declines in intellectual functioning are steep and universal, they are not. It is difficult to predict exactly what and how much change will occur in intellectual functioning. A major problem is defining intellectual functioning. Older people are likely to do poorly on standardized intelligence tests, not because their intelligence is low but because the tests require the manipulation of objects during a timed interval—and older people often have a slower reaction time or decreased manual dexterity (often because of arthritis). To overcome these disadvantages, researchers have devised new methodologies for studying intelligence in older people.

Although most research indicates that cognitive and intellectual abilities typically decrease with advancing age, many of the changes are of little importance for day-to-day functioning (Schaie, 1994). For example, overall vocabulary decreases only slightly. Moreover, some of the changes observed in laboratory tasks are small and can be forestalled or reversed through cognitive interventions. In addition, many older persons do not do well on intelligence tests because they are not as motivated as younger persons to score highly. Yet there is no doubt that the brain encodes information differently in the young than in the old. Memory changes, for example, probably result from changes in cortical activation during encoding (Grady et al., 1995).

For more than 35 years, K. Warner Schaie has been following thousands of men and women and testing them at regular intervals on various cognitive tasks. He argues that there is extreme variability in both the types and causes of cognitive deficits. He suggests that changes in health and family situation may produce severe biological and psychological consequences that in turn affect intellectual functioning (Schaie, 1994). See Table 11.2 for a summary of age-related changes in intellectual skills through adulthood.

Whatever the causes, changes in intellectual functioning that occur with age and that influence behaviour are seldom devastating. Many researchers suggest a "use it and you are less likely to lose it" approach. Up to the ages of 60 through 65, there is little decline in learning or memory; motivation, interest, and recent educational

Table 11.2 Summary of Age-Related Changes in Intellectual Skills

Ages 20–40	Ages 40–65	Age 65 and Older
Peak intellectual ability between about 20 and 35	Maintenance of skill on measures of verbal intelligence; some decline of skill on measures of performance intelligence; decline usually not functionally significant till age 60 or older	Some loss of verbal intelligence; most noticeable in adults with poorer health, lower levels of activity, and less education
Optimal performance on memory tasks	Little change in performance on memory tasks, except perhaps some slowing later in this period	Slowing of retrieval processes and other memory processes; less skilful use of coding strategies for new memories
Peak performance on laboratory tests of problem solving	Peak performance on real-life problem-solving tasks and many verbal abilities	Decline in problem-solving performance on both laboratory and real-life tests

Source: Adapted from Bee (1987).

experience (or lack of it) are probably more important in a person's ability to master complex knowledge than is age.

Researchers generally acknowledge that some age-related decrements do occur (e.g., Craik, 1994; Salthouse, 1995; Verhaeghen & Salthouse, 1997); however, such effects are often less apparent in cognitively active individuals (Shimamura et al., 1995). When deficits do occur, older individuals can compensate to optimize their performance. The truth is that most Canadians are aging well (Johnson, 1995) and that with appropriate support systems—health and social support systems—older individuals can do just fine, especially in pragmatic, everyday situations (Baltes, 1993).

It is important to remember that despite evidence that old age takes a toll, there are many remarkable examples of intellectual achievement by people 70 years of age or older. Golda Meir, for example, became prime minister of Israel at age 70. Chief Dan George's prominent film career began in his 70s. Arthur Rubinstein, the Polish-born concert pianist, gave one of his greatest recitals at age 81. Older individuals have a certain wisdom that comes with the experience of having lived a long life.

Personality Development in Adulthood

A basic tenet of most personality theories is that, regardless of day-to-day variations, an individual's personality remains stable over time. That is, despite frequently observed deviations from people's normal patterns of development, the way a person copes with life tends to remain fairly consistent throughout that individual's lifetime. But research shows that personality also may be sensitive to the unique experiences of the individual, especially during the adult years. According to Haan, Millsap, and Hartka (1986), children's and adolescents' personalities tend to remain stable. The researchers collected data from a longitudinal sample of participants, who were asked to describe themselves on variables such as self-confidence, assertiveness, dependability, and warmth. Important shifts, some related to cognitive maturity, occurred in many variables once the participants reached adulthood. For example, adults are likely to be more assertive and self-confident than when they were younger. However, once established such shifts remain stable. Further, major life events—for example, a child's tragic death, a highly stressful job situation, or a divorce—not surprisingly, can alter a person's overall outlook on life.

The data from this study are not easy to generalize from, because the researchers did not take into account changing societal values and expectations. Nevertheless, the data suggest that the adult years are filled with great personal challenges and opportunities and therefore are years in which people need to be innovative, flexible, and adaptive. Positive changes during adulthood—the development of a sense of generativity, the fulfilment of yearnings for love and respect—usually depend on some degree of success at earlier life stages. Adults who continue to have a narrow outlook are less likely to experience personality growth in later life.

As we have seen, researchers now recognize that the male-dominated psychology profession of the 1950s generated a host of personality theories based on studies of men that failed to highlight women's unique personality and development issues adequately. Personality researchers now acknowledge that contemporary women face challenges in the workforce and the home that were not conceived of three decades ago. These challenges have given rise to the "supermom" phenomenon of women who are expected to do it all—home, family, career, personal satisfaction—within the same span of years. Serious research into the psychological life of women is just beginning to emerge.

Aspects of personality development are discussed in further detail in Chapter 12.

Focus

Review

◆ In each of Erikson's eight stages, people face dilemmas. What are the overall consequences of a poor outcome at any one stage? pp. 387–389

◆ What evidence suggests that there is a distinction between a transition and a crisis in an adult's life? p. 391

◆ What is the evidence that intelligence test scores decrease among aging people because of non-cognitive factors? p. 394

Think Critically

◆ What do you think are the implications of the finding that women follow a different developmental progression than do men?

Late Adulthood: Limitations and Possibilities

No human being has lived past 122 years of age. Most of us will not achieve such longevity, but as we grow older, we age experientially as well as physically; that is, we gather experiences and expand our worlds. Nevertheless, in Western society, growing older is not always easy, especially because of the negative stereotypes associated with the aging process. Today, however, people are healthier than ever before, are approaching later years with vigour, and look forward to second and sometimes third careers. In general, being over age 65 brings with it new developmental tasks—retirement, coping with health issues, and maintaining a long-term standard of living.

How older people view themselves depends in part on how society treats them. Many Asian and African cultures greatly respect the elderly for their wisdom and maturity; in such societies, grey hair is a mark of distinction, not an embarrassment. In contrast, Western cultures tend to be youth-oriented and people spend a fortune on everything from hair dyes to facelifts to make themselves look younger. However, because the average age of North Americans is climbing, how the elderly are perceived by others and how they perceive themselves may be changing.

Approximately 12 percent of the Canadian population—or more than 3.6 million Canadians—are 65 years of age or older. According to Statistics Canada (1998), the proportion of elderly people is expected to increase to 16 percent of the total population by the year 2016, when the number of Canadians over 65 will exceed 5.8 million. Figure 11.2 illustrates how Canada's population has been growing older over the past few decades. At present, the average life expectancy at birth

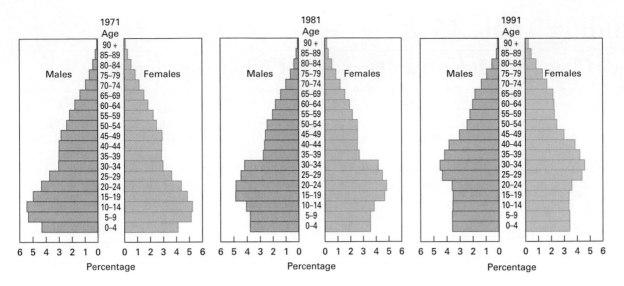

FIGURE 11.2

A Nation Growing Older

Note that, in 1971, the baby boom shows up in the 5 to 19 years age category; by 1991, the baby boom is in the 25 to 39 years age category.

Source: Statistics Canada, Figure 14.1 "Age Pyramids of Canada for Selected Years Since 1951," adapted from "Report on the Demographic Situation in Canada, 1992," Catalogue No. 91–209.

in Canada is about 78 years, and the oldest of the old— those over 85—are the most rapidly growing elderly age group. Life expectancy is different for men and women, however. Women live about six years longer than men, on average.

For many people, the years after age 60 are filled with new activities and excitement. Both men and women enjoy doing things that they may not have been able to do before because of family commitments. Canadian seniors receive 60 percent of their income from private pensions, investments, and earnings and 40 percent from government pensions and benefits. The median income of Canadian families headed by a senior was about $33 000 (Health Canada, 1998). Most seniors maintain close friendships and stay in touch with family members. Some, however, experience loneliness and isolation because many of their friends and relatives have died or they have lost touch with their families. In Canada, there are now as many people over the age of 65 as there are under the age of 8; yet funding for programs to support the health and psychological well-being of older people is relatively limited.

Myths, Realities, and Stereotypes

There is a widely held myth that older people are less intelligent than younger people, less able to care for themselves, inflexible, and sickly. The reality is that many elderly people are as competent and capable as they were in earlier adulthood. They work, play golf, run marathons, socialize, and stay politically aware and active. Most older adults maintain a good sex life (Bretschneider & McCoy, 1988) and positive mental health. Of course, as was pointed out at the beginning of this chapter, some people will conduct life's activities in a frail, disorganized manner, even when young; others, although chronologically old, are youthful and vigorous. Building Table 11.2 summarizes important changes in adult functioning through late adulthood.

Building Table 11.2

Major Changes in Important Domains of Adult Functioning

Age	Physical Change	Cognitive Change	Work Roles	Personal Development	Major Tasks
Young Adulthood, 18–25	Peak functioning in most physical skills; optimal time for child bearing	Cognitive skills high on most measures	Choice of career, which may involve several job changes	Conformity; task of establishing intimacy	Separate from family; form partnership; begin family; find job; create individual life pattern
Early Adulthood, 25–40	Good physical functioning in most areas; health habits during this time establish later risks	Peak period of cognitive skill on most measures	Rising work satisfaction; major emphasis on career or work success; most career progress steps made	Task of passing on skills, knowledge, love (generativity)	Rear family; establish personal work pattern and strive for success
Middle Adulthood, 40–65	Beginning signs of physical decline in some areas (strength, elasticity of tissues, height, cardiovascular function)	Some signs of loss of cognitive skill on timed, unexercised skills	Career reaches plateau, but higher work satisfaction	Increase in self-confidence, openness	Launch family; redefine life goals; redefine self outside of family and work roles; care for aging parents
Late Adulthood, 65–75+	Significant physical decline on most measures	Small declines for virtually all adults on some skills	Retirement	Integration of ideas and experiences, perhaps self-actualization; task of ego integrity	Cope with retirement; cope with declining health; redefine life goals and sense of self

Ageism. Stereotypes about the elderly have given rise to **ageism**—prejudice against the elderly and the discrimination that follows from it. Ageism is prevalent in the job market, in which older people are not given the same opportunities as their younger co-workers, and in housing and health care. Ageism is exceptionally prevalent in the media—on television and in newspapers, cartoons, and magazines—and in everyday language (Schaie, 1993). Schmidt and Boland (1986) examined everyday language to learn how people perceive older adults. They found interesting differences. For example, *elder statesman* implies that a person is experienced, wise, or perhaps conservative. However, *old statesman* might suggest that a person is past his prime, tired, or useless. The term *old people* may allude to positive elements in older adults—for example, being the perfect grandparent—or to negative qualities such as grouchiness or mental deficiencies. What does *old* mean?

Ageism: Prejudice against the elderly and the discrimination that follows from it.

Older people who are perceived to represent negative stereotypes are more likely to suffer discrimination than those who appear to represent more positive stereotypes. This means that an older person who appears healthy, bright, and alert is more likely to be treated with the same respect shown to younger people. By contrast, an older adult who appears less capable may not be given the same respect or treatment. In Chapter 16, we'll see that first impressions have a potent effect on people's behaviour. This seems to be particularly true for older people. An older person's physical appearance may evoke ageism on sight, whereas a younger person may not be judged until more data is obtained. In any case, ageism can be reduced if people recognize the diversity that exists among aging populations.

Brain Disorders. You might assume that aging is inevitably accompanied by *senility*, a term once used to describe cognitive changes that occur in older people. Today, psychologists know that cognitive deficits are caused by brain disorders, sometimes termed *dementias*, that occur only in *some* older people. **Dementias** are long-standing impairments of mental functioning and global cognitive abilities in otherwise alert individuals, causing a memory loss and related symptoms. The leading cause of degenerative dementia in Canada is Alzheimer's disease. Only a small proportion of people aged 60 to 65 suffer from dementias. The percentage begins to increase after 65 years of age to 2.4 percent of people between 65 and 74 years of age, 11.1 percent of people aged 75 to 84, and 34.5 percent of those aged 85 and older (Canadian Study of Health and Aging Working Group, 1994).

More than 70 conditions cause dementias. Among them are arteriosclerosis (hardening of the arteries), Parkinson's disease, Huntington's disease, syphilis, and multiple sclerosis. Moreover, the failing immune systems of AIDS patients can cause brain infections, which in turn can lead to dementia. Memory loss often first occurs for recent events and later occurs for past events. Additional symptoms include loss of language skills, reduced capacity for abstract thinking, personality changes, and loss of a sense of time and place. Severe and disabling dementias affect about 316 500 Canadians. With the increasing number of elderly citizens, these statistics are on the rise.

Some conditions that cause dementia can be treated, and that treatment often halts (but does not necessarily reverse) the dementia. Such *reversible dementias*, which can be caused by malnutrition, alcoholism, or toxins (poisons), usually affect younger people. *Irreversible dementias* are most commonly of two types: multiple infarct dementia and Alzheimer's disease. *Multiple infarct dementia* usually is caused by two or more small strokes (ruptures of small blood vessels in the brain); it results in a slow degeneration of the brain. A well-known cause of dementia—Alzheimer's disease—is discussed in *Brain and Behaviour* (see pages 400 and 401).

> **Dementia:** A long-standing impairment of mental functioning and global cognitive abilities in otherwise alert individuals, causing memory loss and related symptoms.

Death: The End of the Life Span

People's overall health deteriorates as they age. For men, the probability of dying doubles in each decade after midlife. In some people, blood pressure rises, cardiac output decreases, and the likelihood of stroke increases, often as a result of cardiovascular disease, which also affects intellectual functioning by decreasing blood flow to the brain. Some individuals experience *terminal drop*—a rapid decline in intellectual functioning in the year before death. Some researchers attribute this change to cardiovascular disease, claiming that decreased blood flow (and resulting decrease in oxygen) to the brain causes declining mental ability and, ultimately, failing health. However, although there is evidence for the terminal drop, no satisfactory method exists for predicting death on the basis of poor performance on intelligence or neuropsychological tests (Botwinick, 1984).

If you are young, perhaps an adolescent, you are more likely than older people to die from automobile accidents or AIDS. But the majority of the population die at an older age and so the leading causes of death in Canada are heart disease, cancer, strokes, and accidents; in fact, 7 out of 10 older Canadians die from heart disease,

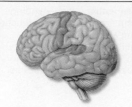

brain and behaviour
Alzheimer's Disease

Alzheimer's disease is a chronic and progressive disorder of the brain and the most common cause of degenerative dementia. Memory loss, language deterioration, poor visual/spatial skills, and an indifferent attitude characterize Alzheimer's disease. Named after Dr. Alois Alzheimer, a German physician who first studied its symptoms, it could well be the most widespread neurological disorder of all time. As the Canadian population grows older, the number of cases of Alzheimer's disease increases. Currently, there are about 202 500 diagnosed Alzheimer's patients in Canada and nearly 20 million worldwide; in addition, there are a large number of undiagnosed cases (Anonymous, 1994). One recent estimate suggests that the numbers may be greater than those usually cited: 1 in 20 people over 65 may have the disease, and almost half of those over 85 may have it (Evans et al., 1989). Alzheimer's disease affects women more than men, even after adjusting for the higher number of women who survive to old age. Because Alzheimer's is a degenerative disease, its progression can-

not be stopped; it is irreversible and ultimately ends in death. To date, there is no fully effective method of prevention, treatment, or cure. What causes this disease? What is its psychological impact on the Canadian population? How does it affect families?

Psychological Effects. The impact of Alzheimer's disease on the patient is enormous; the disease severely damages the quality of life. At the beginning patients are not necessarily stripped of their vigour or strength, but they slowly become confused and helpless. Initially, they may forget to do small things. Later, they may forget appointments, anniversaries, and the like. The forgetfulness is often overlooked at first. Jokes and other coping strategies cover up for memory losses and lapses. The memory losses are not always apparent, and some days are better than others. Ultimately, however, the disorder grows worse. Alzheimer's patients start to have trouble finding their way home and remembering the names of their spouses and children. At least initially, episodic more than semantic memory retrieval is affected and short-term

rather than long-term memory is more likely to be impaired (Bäckman & Lipinska, 1993). Patients' personalities also change. They may become abrupt, abusive, and hostile to family members. Within months, or sometimes years, they lose their speech and language functions. Eventually, they lose all control of memory and even of basic bodily functions.

What Causes Alzheimer's Disease? A definitive diagnosis of Alzheimer's disease can be made only by an examination of brain tissue after death; a tangled bundle of neurons is the typical finding. Brain scans usually confirm that the patient's neurons seem to be twisted, gnarled, and coated with *plaque* (fibrous tissue that impedes neural transmission). We call these tangled bundles of fibres *neurofibrillary tangles*. Levels of neurotransmitter substances—specifically acetylcholine—are usually low, and there is usually a loss of functioning neurons.

Pertinent scientific findings about the causes of the disease come from a wide variety of sources. In a major report to the

cancer, or stroke. The number of Americans who succumb to heart disease has decreased because of improved health, reduced smoking, and positive lifestyle changes among Americans. Strokes take their toll every year by cutting off the blood supply to the brain; strokes are significantly less common among men and women who do not smoke, who manage their high blood pressure, and who exercise regularly. But cancer continues to increase; despite good cure rates, half of all cancers are found in men and women over the age of 65. A healthy lifestyle decreases the likelihood of disease, and research shows that older adults can achieve the fitness levels of younger adults (Danner & Edwards, 1992). Reducing risk factors can reduce needless early deaths, and this is best accomplished through health promotion and education (Becker, 1993).

Everyone recognizes that death is inevitable, but in the twentieth century few people actually witnessed death (Aiken, 1985). Before the twentieth century, most people died in bed at home, where other people were likely to be with them. Today,

Alzheimer's disease [ALTZ-hy-merz]: A chronic and progressive disorder of the brain that is the most common cause of degenerative dementia.

U.S. Congress, the Advisory Panel on Alzheimer's Disease (1995) argued that there are multiple routes to the disease. Correlational research shows that Alzheimer's disease tends to run in families, which suggests a genetic basis or at least a predisposition to the disorder. Some researchers posit a depletion of enzymes; others suggest an accumulation of toxins; still others focus on neurotransmitters, insensitivity of receptors, and metabolic patterns (Joseph, 1992). Genetic mutations have been implicated. Blood supply problems, immune system factors, head injuries, nutrition, and viruses—both latent viruses and newly introduced ones—also have been proposed as contributors to the disease.

In studying cell biology, researchers have found a highly orchestrated form of cell death—referred to as *apoptosis*, or programmed cell death—that seems to be implicated in Alzheimer's. Some proteins found in the brain and body seem to drive cells to apoptosis when conditions are right (Barinaga, 1998). Proteins that accumulate in the brain of Alzheimer's patients seem to kill cells involved in memory unless another specific protein (called a *nerve growth factor*, or NGF) is bound to that protein (Rabizadeh et al., 1993). Researchers speculate that memory loss might be averted or stopped by treating cells with NGF or other drugs that mimic the actions of NGF.

No one yet knows the causes of Alzheimer's disease or has developed an effective treatment. Researchers are beginning to think that there are many types of Alzheimer's disease, some of which may be hereditary and some of which may be generated by early life events, such as head

injuries. Research is showing that there may be specific genes on specific chromosomes that cause nearly all of the cases of early-onset familial Alzheimer's; such research may lead to an understanding of the biochemical causes of the disease (Sherrington et al., 1995). Discovery of these genes also may lead to diagnostic tests for at-risk members of a family that harbours the genes.

Implications for Families.
The expected increase in the elderly population means that we will see more and more Alzheimer's patients. The financial and emotional cost to patients and their families is astounding because patients can live in a dependent, non-functional state for more than a decade. Caring for the patient imposes immense physical, emotional, and financial hardships. The patient's loved ones "walk a tightrope between meeting the patient's needs and preserving their own well-being" (Heckler, 1985, p. 1241). Alzheimer's disease changes family life in irreversible ways; most patients are placed in nursing homes or hospitals after extensive and exhausting care at home. Brody, Lawton, and Liebowitz (1984, p. 1331) assert: "In the overwhelming majority of cases, nursing home placement occurs only after responsible family caregivers have endured prolonged, unrelenting caring (often for years) and no longer have the capacity to continue their caregiving efforts." The total cost of care for Alzheimer's patients in Canada is currently estimated at more than $3.9 billion per year (Ostbye & Cross, 1995). ∎

---

nearly 80 percent of Canadians die in hospitals and nursing homes. **Thanatology,** the study of the psychological and medical aspects of death and dying, has become an interdisciplinary specialty. Researchers and theorists in several areas—including theology, law, history, psychology, sociology, and medicine—have come together to better understand death and dying. For psychologists, dealing with the process of dying is especially complicated because people do not like to talk or think about death. Nevertheless, considerable progress has been made towards understanding the psychology of dying.

Kübler-Ross's Stage Theory. Elisabeth Kübler-Ross has become famous for her studies of the way people respond psychologically to their impending death (see, e.g., Kübler-Ross, 1969, 1975). She believes that people in Western society fear death because it is unfamiliar, often hidden away in hospitals. She suggests that a way to reduce this fear is to involve members of a dying person's family more

Thanatology: The study of the psychological and medical aspects of death and dying.

closely in what is, in fact, a very natural process. She contends that it is better for people to die at home than in an unfamiliar hospital room. In addition to imposing emotional stress on the terminally ill patient, impending death also causes stress for the patient's family. Kübler-Ross has drawn attention to the additional stress on family members created by interactions with doctors, especially in traditional, impersonal hospital settings. Like many other physicians and psychologists, she believes that a more home-like setting can help patients and their families deal better with death. One answer to the problem of death in institutional settings is the hospice, discussed below.

Kübler-Ross was one of the first researchers to use a stage theory to discuss people's fear of their own death and the death of loved ones. According to Kübler-Ross, people who learn that they are terminally ill typically go through five stages: *denial*, which serves as a buffer against the shocking news; *anger* directed against family, friends, or medical staff; *bargaining*, in which people try to gain more time by "making a deal" with God, themselves, or their doctors; *depression*, often caused by the pain of their illness and guilt over inconveniencing their family; and finally, *acceptance*, in which people stop fighting and accept death.

Criticisms of Kübler-Ross's Theory. Kübler-Ross's theory has been subject to considerable criticism. Not all researchers find the same sequence of events in the dying process (Stephenson, 1985). They argue that the sequence outlined by Kübler-Ross does not apply to all people and that the stages are not necessarily experienced in the order she suggests. However, Kübler-Ross contends that her theory was intended to be an overall outline, not a strict set of stages or steps.

Kübler-Ross also has been criticized for her research techniques. Her interviews were not very systematic; she offers few statistics, and some of her ideas rely more on intuition than on facts established through scientific methods. Specifically, her data-gathering techniques have been highly subjective. Schaie and Willis (1986) have suggested that the ideas put forth by Kübler-Ross should not be considered a theory but "an insightful discussion of some of the attitudes that are often displayed by people who are dying" (p. 483). Although Kübler-Ross's ideas about death and dying may not be valid in every case, many practitioners find them useful in guiding new medical staff through the difficult task of helping the dying, especially those who are facing premature death because of illnesses such as cancer.

Whether one accepts Kübler-Ross's stages as typical, it is clear that, as in all areas of life, different people approach death with different attitudes and behaviours. In general, people fear the process of dying and the accompanying pain, disability, and dependency that often precede death—although they are more fearful of death in middle age than at any other time in the life cycle. Religious people fear death less than others, and financially stable people have less negative attitudes towards death than do poor people. Moreover, most psychologists believe that the ways in which people have dealt with previous times of stress in their lives largely predict how they will deal with death.

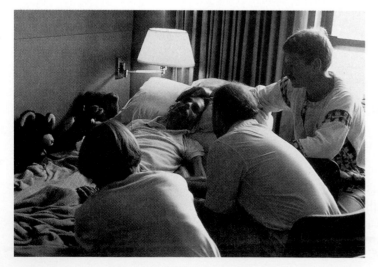

Hospice Care

Hospices initially were conceived of as special facilities established to provide efficient and humane care to terminally ill patients and their families. They were to address emotional, social, and spiritual needs in addition to physical ones, and to combine humane treatment with sensitivity to the financial costs of patient care (Butterfield-Picard & Magno, 1982; Smyser, 1982). A hospice is thus an alternative source of care that helps provide a variety of resources to terminally ill patients and their families. Hospice care takes psychological principles used in therapy and puts them to work in the day-to-day care of the terminally ill. Hospice care focuses on the psychological needs of the patient, while acknowledging that death is inevitable and imminent.

The hospice approach is not appropriate for every dying person. It requires specific kinds of commitment from the patient and family members. Therefore, before providing care, hospices evaluate both the patient and the family. Hospices and their staff operate under a different set of guidelines from those used by hospitals and nursing homes that care for the terminally ill (Butterfield-Picard & Magno, 1982):

- Control of decisions concerning the patient's care rests with the patient and the family.
- Many aspects of traditional care, such as life-support procedures, are discontinued when the patient desires.
- Pain is kept to a minimum so that the patient can experience life as fully as possible until death.
- A team of professionals is available around the clock.
- Surroundings are home-like rather than clinical; often the patient is actually at home.
- When possible, family members and the hospice team are the caregivers.
- Family members receive counselling before and after the patient dies.

Family members who use hospices, as well as friends and practitioners, have to deal with ethical and practical questions about care and costs, life-support systems, and medications. To help these concerned individuals, researchers and applied psychologists are exploring issues such as how to determine exactly when death occurs, how the dying should be treated, and how families and friends can cope better with the dying process, with grief over their loss, and with guilt about their feelings of relief.

Focus

Review

◆ What are the effects of Alzheimer's disease? pp. 400–401
◆ What are the key ideas that Kübler-Ross has posited, and what criticisms have been put forth about those ideas? pp. 401–402
◆ What are the goals of hospices? pp. 402–403

Think Critically

◆ How might the cognitive changes associated with aging influence the health and well being of older adults?
◆ What special emotional problems might need to be addressed when a terminally ill person enters a hospice program?

Summary and Review

Adolescence: Bridging the Gap

Distinguish between puberty and adolescence.

- *Puberty* is the period during which the reproductive system matures; it signals the end of childhood. There is considerable variation among individuals as to its time of onset. *Adolescence* is the period extending from the end of childhood (often defined as the onset of puberty) to early adulthood. p. 376

What are the major changes experienced by adolescents?

- Changes in intellectual abilities, body proportions, and sexual urges (together with changing relationships with parents and peers) create enormous challenges for adolescents. For some, this period is problematic emotionally. Adolescents also develop cognitive distortions like the *imaginary audience* and the *personal fable* in which they see themselves as "on stage" all the time and so special and unique that other people cannot understand them. The challenges of adolescence, however, must be considered in a cultural context, because most of the research on adolescence has been conducted with white, middle-class American teenagers—who are clearly not representative of all adolescents. pp. 376–379

- *Secondary sex characteristics* are the genetically determined physical features that differentiate the sexes;

they are not directly involved with reproduction, but help distinguish men from women—for example, bodily hair patterns, pitch of voice, and muscle development. p. 378

Characterize cognitive and social development in adolescence, especially with respect to gender similarities and differences.

■ Cognitive differences between male and female adolescents are minimal, but social differences are important and real. Adolescents develop a self-image based on a set of beliefs about themselves; other people also generate expectations and beliefs about adolescents, and these beliefs affect them. The influence of peer groups, people who identify with and compare themselves, is formidable. pp. 378–381

■ *Gender identity* is a person's sense of being male or female. Parents are the first and most important forces shaping gender identity; they influence a child from birth. Peers and schools are important sources of information as well. *Gender schema theory* asserts that children and adolescents use gender as an organizing theme to classify and understand their perceptions about the world. pp. 381–383

■ Most people adopt *gender role stereotypes*—beliefs about gender-based behaviours that are strongly expected, regulated, and reinforced by society. But today, *androgyny*, the condition in which some stereotypically male and some stereotypically female characteristics are apparent in one individual, is more common than in the past. pp. 383–384

How have adolescent sexual behaviour and attitudes changed in recent years?

■ Adolescents view sexual intimacy as a normal part of growing up, and premarital heterosexual activity has become more common among adolescents, especially 13- to 17-year-olds. More relaxed attitudes concerning adolescent sexual behaviour have brought about increased awareness among adolescents about contraception and pregnancy. Yet teen pregnancy is still widely prevalent; thus, increased awareness does not imply that the problem is being solved. pp. 384–385

Adulthood: Years of Stability and Change

Describe Erikson's last four stages of psychosocial development.

■ Erikson's stage 5, identity versus role confusion, marks the end of childhood and the beginning of adolescence; adolescents must decide who they are and what they want to do in life. Stage 6 (young adulthood) involves intimacy versus isolation; young adults begin to select other people with whom they can form intimate, caring relationships. In stage 7 (middle adulthood), generativity versus stagnation, people become more aware of their mortality and develop a particular concern for future generations. Finally, in stage 8 (late adulthood), ego integrity versus despair, Erikson asserts that people decide whether their existence is meaningful, happy, and cohesive or wasteful and unproductive. pp. 387–389

Describe Levinson's theory of adult development.

■ According to Levinson's stage theory of adulthood, all adults live through the same developmental periods, though people go through them in their own ways. His theory of adult development (which was generated from data on males) describes four basic eras: adolescence, early adulthood, middle adulthood, and late adulthood. Each has distinctive qualities and different life problems, tasks, and situations. pp. 389–390

Differentiate life transitions and crises.

■ Nearly everyone has transitions in life, but not everyone experiences them as crises. A transition suggests that a person has reached a time in life when old ways of coping are giving way to new ones. A crisis occurs when old ways of coping become ineffective and a person feels helpless, not knowing what to do. p. 391

Do women's life stages parallel men's?

■ Women do not necessarily follow the same life stages as men. Women tend to experience transitions and life events at later ages and in more irregular sequences than those reported by Levinson; consequently, Mercer, Nichols, and Doyle suggested a developmental progression for women that features five transitional eras: launch into adulthood, levelling, liberation, regeneration/redirection, and creativity/destructiveness. pp. 390–392

Describe the effects of aging.

■ Physical development and aging continue throughout adulthood. In general, strength, muscle tone, and overall fitness deteriorate from age 30 on. There are also sensory changes, including increased reaction time after age 65. Sexual behaviour and desire typically change and physical changes related to sexuality occur in adults of both sexes. pp. 392–393

■ Primary aging is the normal, inevitable change that occurs with age and is irreversible, progressive, and universal. Secondary aging is aging due to extrinsic factors such as disease, environmental pollution, and smoking. p. 394

■ Most research indicates that cognitive abilities decrease with advancing age, but many of the changes that occur later in life are of little importance for day-to-day functioning and affect only some people. p. 394

■ Personality development is sensitive to the unique experiences of the individual, especially during the adult years. Major life events (deaths, divorce, etc.) can alter a person's overall outlook on life. pp. 395–396

Late Adulthood: Limitations and Possibilities

Who are the aged, and how is life different in late adulthood?

■ In general, being over age 65 classifies a person as being aged. Approximately 12 percent of the Canadian population—more than 3.6 million Canadians—are 65 or older. p. 396

■ *Ageism* is discrimination on the basis of age, often resulting in the denial of rights and services to the elderly. p. 398–399

- Brain disorders called *dementias* involve losses of cognitive or mental functioning. Reversible dementias, which may be caused by malnutrition, alcoholism, or toxins (poisons), usually affect younger people. Irreversible dementias are of two types: multiple infarct dementia and Alzheimer's disease. p. 399

- Currently, there are about 202 500 diagnosed Alzheimer's patients in Canada. *Alzheimer's disease* is a degenerative disorder whose progression cannot be stopped; it is irreversible and ultimately ends in death. Individuals who suffer from

Alzheimer's disease slowly lose their memory. Within months, or sometimes years, they lose speech and language functions. Eventually, they lose all bodily and mental control. pp. 400–401

What are the essential elements of Kübler-Ross's theory of dying?

- Kübler-Ross has described dying as a process involving five stages: denial, anger, bargaining, depression, and finally, acceptance. Although controversial and not widely accepted by the scientific community, Kübler-Ross's ideas have generated much interest. p. 402

How can hospices aid the dying and their families?

- Hospice care is a special approach that helps provide humane care to terminally ill patients and their families. Hospice care is not appropriate for every dying person. It requires specific kinds of commitment from the patient and family members. pp. 402–403

KEY TERMS
ageism, p. 398; dementia, p. 399; Alzheimer's disease, p. 400; thanatology, p. 401

Weblinks

Adult Development and Aging
www.iog.wayne.edu/apadiv20
This site is the home page of the division of the American Psychological Association dedicated to adult development and aging, and offers information on research and links to related study and research programs and employment opportunities.

Aging and Mental Alertness
www.wellweb.com/seniors/mental.HTM
This site is devoted to discussion and information about aging and mental alertness. Tips for exercising perceptive abilities are listed.

The Gerontological Society of America
www.geron.org/
The aim of this organization is to promote research in aging and to disseminate knowledge to researchers, practitioners, and decision makers. The society has created a student organization to provide students with an opportunity to be participants in the field of gerontology.

Bereavement Information
www.bereavement.demon.co.uk/lbn/reading.html
This British site lists the different emotions you may feel during the grieving process, as well as helpful books on the topic.

Closer Look at Teen Pregnancy
www.intac.com/~jdeck/tahra/Tp1.html
This documentary was photographed in Ohio and Kentucky during February 1995. It is intended to give a personal look at how two girls' lives changed once they had children.

Erikson Tutorial Home Page
snycorva.cortland.edu/~ANDERSMD/ERIK/welcome.HTML
From Cortland College comes this listing and discussion of Erikson's eight stages of psychosocial development. Erikson's biography and links to related sites also are provided.

Demographics of Divorce
www.hec.ohio-state.edu/famlife/divorce/demo.htm
Explore the effects of divorce on family life. Statistics, causes, trends, and living arrangements are discussed at this Web site.

Chapter 12

Personality and Its Assessment

Choose the best answer:

What has had the greatest impact on who you are as a person?

A. Your parents—you turned out pretty much the way they wanted you to.

B. Your parents—but you turned out not at all like they intended; in fact, just the opposite.

C. You—you decided the person that you wanted to be and you've become that person.

D. You—but you really can't remember ever deciding to be this way; you've always been who you are.

If you asked a personality psychologist why you turned out the way you did, the answer clearly would depend on his or her orientation to personality. A behaviourist would answer A—your parents shaped your behaviour, especially during the early years. A psychoanalytically oriented psychologist (a follower of Freud) would choose B—your parents shaped you especially during the early years, and in reaction to those events you choose opposite behaviours to hide, disguise, or repress your anger. A humanist would choose answer C, arguing that you decided who you would become because you are a free agent always trying to be your best. Finally, a biologically oriented psychologist most likely would choose D and assert that you have little choice in personality and that much of your personality is laid down at conception by your genetic make-up.

The correct answer is probably *none of the above*, because personality is a mixture of our biological predisposition, learning, shaping, and choosing. Personalities are a blend of traits, our current environment, and recent learning. The fact is that characterizing people is a complicated process, especially when we try to do this using only a very small sample of the range of behaviours in which they engage. The reality is that few phenomena are as resistant to easy definition and assessment as the human personality. ■

For psychologists, **personality** is a set of relatively enduring behavioural characteristics (including thoughts) and internal predispositions that describe how a person reacts to the environment. What gives people consistency in their behavioural characteristics? To answer this question, some personality theorists focus on day-to-day behaviours that characterize people; others focus on inner conflicts that could shape personality. Some see a human being as an individual who reacts to the environment. Others emphasize the internal, even genetic, influences that impel a person to action. Personality theorists must consider social psychological concepts such as attitudes, motivational concepts such as expectancies, and even biological theories such as those suggesting inherited predispositions towards such personality characteristics as shyness. The earliest personality theorists (for example, Freud) tended to think of personality as something stable within the individual. Later theorists began to recognize that personality depends on a host of environmental situations. Contemporary theorists, especially the behavioural and cognitive ones, often focus more on environmental determinants of personality than on internal predispositions.

Personality theories are a set of interrelated ideas and facts put forward to coherently explain and predict behaviour and mental processes. Being able to predict and explain behaviour enables psychologists to help people anticipate situations and express their feelings in manageable and reasonable ways. Personality theories focus on a few key questions, and the answers they offer vary with each theoretic perspective:

- Does nature or nurture play a greater role in day-to-day behaviour?
- Do unconscious processes direct behaviour?
- Are human behaviour patterns fixed or changeable?
- Does a person's behaviour depend on the situation?
- What makes people behave consistently across situations?

We will begin by examining psychoanalytic theory—an approach to personality that focuses on the unconscious and how thoughts and ideas contained therein direct day-to-day behaviour. This approach is the well-known and widely disputed theory of Sigmund Freud.

Psychoanalytic Theory

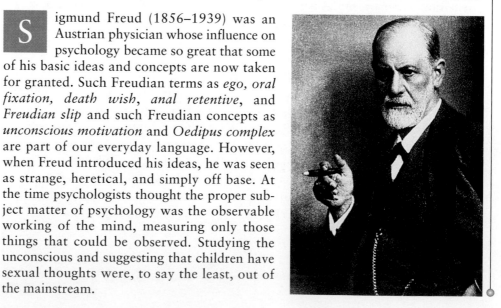

Sigmund Freud (1856–1939) was an Austrian physician whose influence on psychology became so great that some of his basic ideas and concepts are now taken for granted. Such Freudian terms as *ego, oral fixation, death wish, anal retentive,* and *Freudian slip* and such Freudian concepts as *unconscious motivation* and *Oedipus complex* are part of our everyday language. However, when Freud introduced his ideas, he was seen as strange, heretical, and simply off base. At the time psychologists thought the proper subject matter of psychology was the observable working of the mind, measuring only those things that could be observed. Studying the unconscious and suggesting that children have sexual thoughts were, to say the least, out of the mainstream.

At first Freud used hypnosis and later a process known as "free association" to treat people with physical and emotional problems. (We will discuss free association later.) Most of his patients were from the middle and upper classes of Austrian society. Many were society matrons—women of wealth and position—who, because they lived in a repressive society, had limited opportunities for the release of anxiety and tension. Freud noticed that many of them needed to discuss their problems and often felt better after having done so. From his studies of hypnosis and his work with these patients, he began to conceptualize a theory of behaviour; many of his early conclusions focused on the role of sexual frustrations in producing physical symptoms. Over time, Freud developed an elaborate theory of personality and an accompanying approach to therapy. His approach to personality came to be called *psychoanalytic theory*, his method of therapy *psychoanalysis*.

Three Key Concepts

Many psychological theories have key concepts around which they grow. Freud's theory has three key concepts: psychic determinism, unconscious motivation, and conflict. **Psychic determinism** is a psychoanalytic assumption that all feelings, thoughts, actions, gestures, and speech have a purpose and are determined by some action or event that happened to an individual in the past. Adults, for example, do not have accidental slips of the tongue; nor do they frown or change mood by accident. Instead, past events affect all of today's actions. **Unconscious motivation** is a psychoanalytic assumption that behaviour is determined by desires, goals, and internal states buried deep within the unconscious, of which an individual is unaware. By definition, people are unaware of the contents of the unconscious and even of its very existence.

Freud also theorized that people are constantly in *conflict*. They are energized and act the way they do because of two basic instinctual drives—*life*, which prominently features sex and sexual energy, and *death*, which features aggression. These instincts are buried deep within the unconscious and are not always socially acceptable. Freud wrote little about aggression until late in his life; he focused mainly on sexual instincts, which he termed the **libido**—the instinctual (and sexual) life force that, working on the pleasure principle and seeking immediate gratification, energizes the id. (The id will be discussed further in the next section.) In his later writings, Freud referred to the libido as "life energy." His critics assert that he was inordinately preoccupied with sexual matters.

When people exhibit socially unacceptable behaviours or have feelings they consider socially unacceptable, especially sexual feelings, they often experience self-punishment, guilt, and anxiety—conflict. Freud's theory thus describes a conflict between a person's instinctual (often unconscious) need for gratification and the demands of society for socialization. In other words, it paints a picture of human beings caught in a conflict between basic sexual and aggressive desires and society's demands. A gentleman from Vienna, Austria, of the Victorian era might have wished to hit an offensive drunk, but the social rules of that time did not allow such behaviour. For Freud, a person's basic desire is to maximize instinctual gratification while minimizing punishment and guilt.

Structure of Consciousness and the Mind

In his theory, Freud considered the sources and consequences of conflict and how people deal with it. For Freud, a person's source of energy to deal with conflict is biologically determined and lies in the structure of consciousness.

Structure of Consciousness. According to Freud, consciousness consists of three levels of awareness. The first level, the **conscious**, consists of the thoughts, feelings, and actions of which people are aware. The second level, the **preconscious**,

Psychic determinism [SYE-kick]: A psychoanalytic assumption that all feelings, thoughts, actions, and gestures have a purpose and are determined by past actions or events.

Unconscious motivation: A psychoanalytic assumption that behaviour is determined by desires, goals, and internal states buried deep within the unconscious, of which an individual is unaware.

Libido [lih-BEE-doe]: In Freud's theory, the instinctual (and sexual) life force that, working on the pleasure principle and seeking immediate gratification, energizes the id.

Conscious: Freud's first level of awareness, consisting of the thoughts, feelings, and actions of which people are aware.

Preconscious: Freud's second level of awareness, consisting of mental activities of which people can become aware if they closely attend to them.

Unconscious: Freud's third level of awareness, consisting of mental activities beneath people's normal awareness.

Id: In Freud's theory, the source of a person's instinctual energy, which works mainly through the pleasure principle.

Ego: In Freud's theory, the part of personality that seeks to satisfy the individual's instinctual needs in accordance with reality.

Superego [super-EE-go]: In Freud's theory, the moral aspect of mental functioning, comprising the ego ideal (what a person would ideally like to be) and the conscience, and taught by parents and society.

consists of mental activities of which people can become aware if they closely attend to them. The third level, the **unconscious**, consists of the mental activities beneath people's normal awareness. They become aware of these activities only through specific therapeutic techniques, such as dream analysis. Suppose that a woman decides to become a psychotherapist for a *conscious* reason. She tells her family and friends that she wants to help people. Later, during an introspective moment, she realizes that her *preconscious* motivation for becoming a psychotherapist stems from a desire to resolve her own unhappiness. Finally, through psychoanalysis, she discovers that she hungers for love and intimacy, which her parents denied her. *Unconsciously*, she has been hoping that her future patients will satisfy that hunger by making her feel needed.

Id, Ego, and Superego. According to Freud's theory, the primary structural elements of the mind and personality are three mental forces (not physical structures of the brain) that reside, fully or partially, in the unconscious—the id, the ego, and the superego. Each force accounts for a different aspect of functioning (see Table 12.1).

The **id** is the source of a person's instinctual energy, which, according to Freud, is either sexual or aggressive. The id works through the *pleasure principle*; that is, it tries to maximize immediate gratification through the satisfaction of raw impulses. Deep within the unconscious, the demanding, irrational, and selfish id seeks pleasure. It does not care about morals, society, or other people.

While the id seeks to maximize pleasure and obtain immediate gratification, the **ego** (which grows out of the id) is the part of the personality that seeks to satisfy the individual's instinctual needs in accordance with reality; that is, it works by the *reality principle*. The ego acts as a manager, adjusting cognitive and perceptual processes to balance the person's functioning, control the id, and keep the person in touch with reality. For example, a four- or five-year-old boy at the checkout line in a grocery store sees candy—his id says take the candy. The ego may recognize that he could steal the candy but it acknowledges that he is likely to be caught and punished. Working on the reality principle, the boy realizes that gratifying his id by stealing the candy is dangerous.

As a child grows, the superego develops. In Freud's theory, the **superego** is the moral aspect of mental functioning, comprising the ego ideal (what a person would ideally like to be) and the conscience, and is taught by parents and society. The superego tells the id and the ego whether gratification in a particular instance is ethical. It attempts to control the id by internalizing parental authority (whether rational or irrational) through the process of socialization and by punishing transgressions with feelings of guilt and anxiety. When the boy mentioned earlier is older and is sent to the store with two dollars to buy a loaf of bread, upon seeing the candy at the checkout line the id says, "Steal it." The ego sees that is it is possible that he may not get caught because the store is so hectic—the ego may be giving into the id a bit. Then the superego is heard from—taking the candy would be morally wrong, it

Table 12.1   Comparison of Freud's Three Systems of Personality

Id	Ego	Superego
Represents biological aspect	Represents psychological aspect	Represents societal aspect
Unconscious	Conscious and preconscious	Conscious, preconscious, and unconscious
Pleasure	Reality	Morality
Seek pleasure and avoid pain	Adapt to reality; know true and false	Represent right and wrong
Immediate gratification	Safety and compromise	Perfection

would be stealing. Shame would accrue if Mom found out. The ego and superego thus attempt to modulate the id and direct it towards appropriate behaviour. (See Figure 12.1 for a description of Freud's levels of consciousness and mental forces.)

Development of Personality

Freud strongly believed that if people examined their past they could gain insight into their current behaviour. This belief led him to create an elaborate psychosexual stage theory of personality development. Freud believed that the core aspects of personality are established early, remain stable throughout life, and are changed only with great difficulty. He argued that all people pass through five critical stages of personality development: oral, anal, phallic, latency, and genital (see Table 12.2). At each of the key stages, Freud asserted, people experience conflicts and issues associated with *erogenous zones*—areas of the body that when stimulated give rise to erotic or sexual sensations.

Oral Stage. The concept of the **oral stage** is based on the fact that the instincts of infants (from birth to about age two) are focused on the mouth as the primary pleasure-seeking centre. Infants receive oral gratification through feeding, thumb sucking, and cooing during the early months of life, when their basic feelings about the world are being established. Relying heavily on symbolism, Freud contended that adults who consider the world a bitter place (referring to the mouth and taste senses) probably had difficulty during the oral stage of development and may have traits associated with passivity and hostility. Their problems would tend to focus on nurturing, warmth, and love.

Anal Stage. The **anal stage** is Freud's second stage of personality development, from age two to about age three, during which children learn to control the immediate gratification they obtain through defecation and become responsive to the demands of society. At about age two or three, children learn to respond to some of their parents' and society's demands. One parental demand—potty training—is that

Oral stage: Freud's first stage of personality development, from birth to about age two, during which infants obtain gratification primarily through the mouth.

Anal stage: Freud's second stage of personality development, about age two to age three, during which children learn to control the immediate gratification they obtain through defecation and become responsive to the demands of society

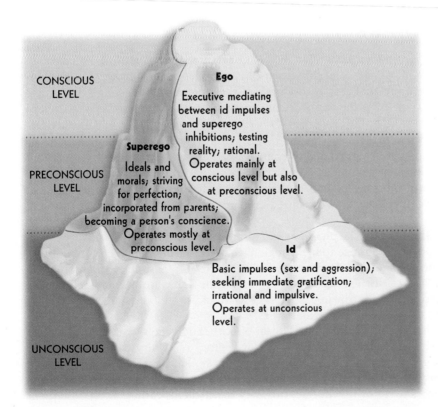

FIGURE 12.1
Freud's View of Mental Forces
Freud viewed consciousness as having three levels: the conscious, the preconscious, and the unconscious. Freud theorized that just as the greater part of an iceberg is hidden beneath the surface of the sea, most of the contents of the mind are below the level of conscious awareness. The ego is mainly a conscious and preconscious mental force. The superego operates mostly as a preconscious mental force. The id operates solely at an unconscious level.

Table 12.2 Freud's Five Psychosexual Stages of Personality Development

Stage		Erogenous Zone	Conflicts/ Experiences	Adult Traits (Especially Fixations) Associated with Problems at a Stage
Oral (birth to 2 years)		Mouth	Infant achieves gratification through oral activities such as feeding, thumb sucking, and cooing.	Optimism, gullibility, passivity, hostility, substance abuse
Anal (2 to 3 years)		Anus	The child learns to respond to some parental demands (such as for bladder and bowel control).	Excessive cleanliness, orderliness, messiness, rebelliousness
Phallic (4 to 7 years)		Genitals	The child learns to realize the differences between males and females and becomes aware of sexuality.	Flirtatiousness, vanity, promiscuity, chastity, disorder in gender identity
Latency (7 to puberty)		None	The child continues developing but sexual urges are relatively quiet.	Not specified
Genital (puberty on)		Genitals	The growing adolescent shakes off old dependencies and learns to deal maturely with the opposite sex.	Not specified

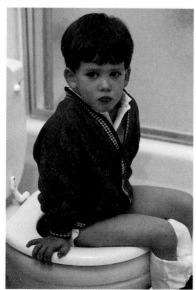

children control their bodily functions of urination and defecation. Freud maintained that most two- and three-year-olds experience pleasure in moving their bowels, and the anal area is the focus of their pleasurable feelings. This stage therefore establishes the basis for conflict between the id and the ego—between the desire for infantile pleasure and the demand for adult, controlled behaviour. Freud claimed that during the anal stage, children develop certain lasting personality characteristics related to control, such as neatness and orderliness, that reflect their toilet training. Thus, adults who had difficulty in the anal stage would tend to have problems that focus on orderliness (or lack of it) and also might be compulsive or disorganized in many behaviours.

Phallic Stage. The **phallic stage** is Freud's third stage of personality development, from about age four through age seven, during which children obtain gratification primarily from the genitals. At about age four or five, children become aware of their sexuality. Freud claimed that numerous feelings are repressed so deeply during this stage that children (and later adults) are unaware of many of their sexual urges.

During the phallic stage, children pass through the Oedipus (or Electra) complex. The **Oedipus complex** includes feelings of rivalry with the parent of the same sex and love of the parent of the opposite sex, ultimately resolved through identification with the parent of the same sex. The Oedipus complex for males thus refers to a boy's love for his mother, hostility towards his father, and consequent fear of castration and punishment by the father. In resolving the Oedipus complex, the boy eventually accepts his father's close relationship with his mother. Rather than feel excluded by it, he chooses to gratify his need for his mother's attention by identifying with his father. In this way, a young boy begins to model his behaviour after that of his father. For females, Freud argued that the Oedipus complex, sometimes termed the *Electra complex*, follows a slightly different course. Freud held that when a young girl realizes that she has no penis, she develops what Freud called *penis envy*. He suggested that she could symbolically acquire a penis by attaching her love to her father. A young girl then might ask her father to marry her so they can raise a family together. When she realizes that this is unlikely, she may identify with her mother and copy her mother's behaviour as a means of obtaining (or sharing in) her father's affection. Like the young boy, the young girl identifies with the parent of the same sex in the hope of obtaining affection from the parent of the opposite sex. For both boys and girls, the critical component in resolving the Oedipus complex is the development of identification with the parent of the same sex. Adult traits associated with problems at this stage usually involve sexuality and may be seen in vanity, promiscuity, or excessive worry about chastity.

Whether the Oedipus complex explains behaviour is controversial and widely debated, especially because many people find the idea sexist and degrading to women. There is no doubt about Freud's view of women; he saw them as weaker and less rational than men and believed they should be subservient to men. Today, most researchers believe that Freud's notion of penis envy was imaginative but unconvincing, overdrawn, and lacking credibility (Stagner, 1988; Webster, 1995). Is the Oedipus complex a good explanation of the dynamics of four- and five-year-olds with their parents? Today most researchers think not.

Latency Stage. The **latency stage** lasts from about age seven until puberty. During this period, children develop physically, but sexual urges are inactive (latent). Sexual urges, fears, and frustrations are suppressed; much of children's energy is channelled into social or achievement-related activities. Some psychoanalysts believe that this stage has disappeared from Canadian society because of rapid maturation into adolescence.

Genital Stage. When people reach the last stage of development, the **genital stage**, the sexuality, fears, and repressed feelings of earlier stages are once again exhibited. Over the course of the genital stage, the adolescent shakes off dependence on parents and learns to deal with members of the opposite sex in socially and sexually mature ways. Some members of the opposite sex, who were ignored during the latency stage, are now seen as attractive and desirable. Many unresolved conflicts and repressed urges affect behaviour during this stage. Ideally, if people have passed through previous stages of development without major incident, they will develop conventional relations with members of the opposite sex. If not, they may continue to struggle with unresolved conflicts within their unconscious throughout their adult life.

Unresolved Conflicts

As children proceed from one developmental stage to the next, they adjust their views of the world. Successfully passing through one stage to the next requires the resolution of that stage's principal conflict. Freud likened it to military troops moving from battle to battle—failure to successfully resolve one battle or conflict weakens an army at its next battle. According to Freud, if children do not successfully pass through a stage and resolve its principal conflicts they acquire a fixation and an unrelenting use of defence mechanisms.

Fixations. A **fixation** is an excessive attachment to some person or object that was appropriate only at an earlier stage of development. A person who becomes

Phallic stage [FAL-ick]: Freud's third stage of personality development, about age three to age seven, during which children obtain gratification primarily from the genitals.

Oedipus complex [ED-i-pus]: Occurring during the phallic stage, feelings of rivalry with the parent of the same sex and love of the parent of the opposite sex, ultimately resolved through identification with the parent of the same sex; in girls this process is called the *Electra complex*.

Latency stage [LAY-ten-see]: Freud's fourth stage of personality development, from about age seven until puberty, during which sexual urges are inactive.

Genital stage [JEN-it-ul]: Freud's last stage of personality development, from the onset of puberty through adulthood, during which the sexual conflicts of childhood resurface (at puberty) and are often resolved (during adolescence).

Fixation: An excessive attachment to some person or object that was appropriate only at an earlier stage of development.

fixated is said to be arrested at a particular stage of development. Fixation at one developmental stage does not prevent all further development, but unless people master each stage successfully, they cannot fully master the later stages. For example, a child who does not successfully pass through the phallic stage probably has not resolved the Oedipus complex and may feel hostility towards the parent of the same sex. The child may suffer the consequences of this unresolved conflict, often sexual in nature, throughout life.

Fixations or partial fixations usually occur because of frustration or overindulgence that hinders the expression of sexual or aggressive energy at a particular psychological stage. According to Freud, good personality adjustment generally involves a balance among competing forces. The child, and later the adult, should be neither too self-centred nor too moralistic. Parents who are restrictive, punitive, and overbearing or those who are indifferent, smothering, or overindulgent produce emotionally disturbed children who have a difficult time coping with life because of the resulting fixations. What happens when a person becomes fixated? According to Freud, the person develops defence mechanisms and sometimes maladjustment.

Defence Mechanisms. A **defence mechanism** is an unconscious way of reducing anxiety by distorting perceptions of reality. Everyone defends against anxiety from time to time. Defence mechanisms allow the ego to deal with the uncomfortable feelings that anxiety produces. In fact, people are typically unaware that they are using defence mechanisms. Nonetheless, people who use them to such an extent that reality is sharply distorted can become maladjusted.

Freud described many kinds of defence mechanisms but identified repression as the most important. In **repression**, anxiety-provoking thoughts and feelings are totally relegated to the unconscious. When people repress a feeling or desire, they become unaware of it. Thus, a young boy who was abused by a football coach later in life becomes a father who, without being able to say why, refuses to allow his athletic son to try out for the team.

In addition to repression, Freud observed five other key defence mechanisms:

- **Projection**—the mechanism by which people attribute their own undesirable traits to others as a way of avoiding the anxiety they might experience if they acknowledged their strong feelings. Has anyone ever come up to you and said "Are you mad at me?" and you had no idea what they were talking about? They may, in fact, have been mad at you. In the same way, a woman with deep aggressive tendencies may see other people as acting in an excessively aggressive way and deny that she has such tendencies herself. Similarly, a man who is anxious about his own anger may see others as being overly hostile.

- **Denial**—the mechanism by which people directly refuse to accept reality or to recognize the true source of their anxiety. Someone with strong sexual urges may dispute any interest in sex rather than deal with those urges. A student who is failing a mathematics course may seem unconcerned and tell friends that all is well academically. You remind a friend of something embarrassing they did and they reply, "I never did that!" Or a friend becomes somewhat aggravated in a conversation, so you say, "Don't get angry." They reply, "I'M NOT ANGRY!"

- **Reaction formation**—the mechanism by which people defend against anxiety by adopting behaviours opposite to their true feelings. A classic example of the use of reaction formation as a defence mechanism is the behaviour of a person who has strong sexual urges but becomes extremely chaste. Similarly, a student athlete who is extraordinarily competitive may choose to sit out a meet rather than risk a potentially disheartening failure.

- **Sublimation**—the mechanism by which socially unacceptable impulses are redirected into acceptable ones. Thus, a man who has sexual desires for

Defence mechanism: An unconscious way of reducing anxiety by distorting perceptions of reality.

Repression: A defence mechanism by which people block anxiety-provoking thoughts and feelings from conscious awareness and push them into the unconscious.

Projection: A defence mechanism by which people attribute their own undesirable traits to others.

Denial: A defence mechanism by which people directly refuse to accept reality or to recognize the true source of their anxiety.

Reaction formation: A defence mechanism by which people adopt behaviours opposite to their true feelings.

Sublimation [sub-li-MAY-shun]: A defence mechanism by which socially unacceptable impulses are redirected into acceptable ones.

someone he knows is off limits (perhaps a cousin) may channel that desire into working 14-hour days for his church. Similarly, a student who is anxious about academic work may channel his energy into artistic endeavours, athletics, or community activities.

■ **Rationalization**—the mechanism by which people reinterpret undesirable feelings or behaviour to make them appear acceptable. For example, a shoplifter may rationalize that no one will miss the things she steals or that she needs the things more than other people do. A student may cheat, asserting to himself that his failure would hurt his parents far too much for them to bear. Finally, upon breaking up, your partner tells you that it's nothing you've done—they just need "more space."

When a person's defence mechanisms cause reality to become seriously distorted, it is a cause for concern. Overreliance on defence mechanisms leads to maladjustment.

Rationalization: A defence mechanism by which people reinterpret undesirable feelings or behaviour to make them appear acceptable.

Freud Today

When Freud's psychosexual theory of development was first proposed around 1900, it received considerable unfavourable attention. It was considered absurd to suggest that young children had sexual feelings towards their parents. Yet if you watch young children and the ways in which they respond to and identify with their parents, you will see that there are elements of truth to Freud's conception of personality development. Little girls do tend to idolize their fathers, and little boys often become strongly attached to their mothers. And there is clear research evidence that individuals use projection as a defence mechanism (Newman, Duff, & Baumeister, 1997).

Despite these observations, Freud's theories have been sharply criticized for numerous reasons. Some psychologists object to Freud's basic conception of human nature, his emphasis on sexual urges towards parents, and his idea that human behaviour is so biologically determined. Others reject his predictions about psychosexual stages and fixations. Still others assert that his theory does not account for changing situations and the differing cultures in which people live. Many people find Freud's ideas about women contentious and problematic. Freud's case histories are today seen by many as intellectually contrived (Webster, 1995). At a minimum, his ideas are controversial; many psychologists do not regard them as valid, and view them as almost completely untestable; some assert that Freud did not even remember his own work correctly (Schatzman, 1992). In addition, Freud used poorly defined terms, he occasionally failed to distinguish between observation and inferences he made from them, and he confused correlation with causation. Almost all agree that his theory is fuzzy and because it can be stretched to account for any outcome, it makes predictions about an individual's behaviour almost impossible to test. Freud's theory also has to be considered in a cultural context. In the Victorian era, Austrian society, with its rigid standards of behaviour, and Freud's wealthy patients biased him in directions that few theorists would adopt today.

Regardless of whether Freud has had the final say about human behaviour, his influence on psychology and on Western culture exceeds that of any other personality theorist, past or present. His theory weaves together his clinical experiences with patients, his speculations about human nature, and his own complex and dark personality. In many ways, Freud's theory paved the way for other developmental stage theories, such as those of Piaget, Erikson, and Levinson, who made more specific predictions about behaviour.

Cultural Determinants of Personality

As already noted, Freud's practice was with Austrian society matrons. This seems simple enough, but consider the implications. Freud developed a theory from dealing with a particular group of patients whose day-to-day behaviour, personalities, and problems were shaped by the culture in which they lived. *Culture*, as we have seen, refers to the norms, ideals, values, rules, patterns of communication, and beliefs adopted by a group of people. Within a culture, there may be different social classes, but all of the people have the same basic set of norms.

Cultural diversity is apparent as one travels from country to country. For example, if travelling from England to Spain, through France, and then to Germany and Turkey, one sees distinctly different value systems, lifestyles, and personalities. Modes of dress and attitudes about work, family, and religion differ. Culture is significant, because it shapes how people raise their children, the values they teach, and family life.

Cultural values shape personality. Therefore, personality theories must be considered in a cultural context. Western society values competitiveness, autonomy, and self-reliance; in addition, Western conceptions of personality focus on the individual. By contrast, non-Western cultures value interdependence and cooperation; they focus more on groups in constructing conceptions of personality. For developing adolescents, one culture may stress conformity to rules, strict adherence to religious values, and obedience to parental authority. In contrast, another culture may stress independence, free thought, experimentation, and resistance to parental authority.

Within Canadian culture, there are significant variations based on heritage. Aboriginal peoples, for example, add diverse experiences to the Canadian cultural mix (for example, a profound realization of the importance of environmental or family context in understanding individuals), as do people from French and English backgrounds and immigrants from broadly diverse cultural backgrounds.

The large number of variables makes the study of culture and personality a complicated task. Adjustments and refinements must be made to take account of ethnicity, gender, age, and class, as well as culture. Accordingly, every personality theory, concept, and approach must be considered and evaluated from a multicultural perspective. For example, a person from Japan is likely to view embarrassment and saving face as far more potent social values than does a person raised in Canada. We will come back to this multicultural theme later in this chapter, when we examine the theory of Walter Mischel. He argues that the context in which behaviour occurs must be a focus of personality psychologists.

Neo-Freudians—Dissent and Revision

There is no question that Freud has had an enormous impact on psychological thought. But modern theorists, including some of Freud's students, have found what they consider to be serious omissions, errors, and biases in Freudian theory. Many of these theorists have developed new ideas loosely based on Freud's original conception, but usually attributing greater influence to cultural and interpersonal factors; they have become known as **neo-Freudians**.

Some neo-Freudians (Alfred Adler, for instance) have argued that people are not driven solely by sexual instincts. Others (Erich Fromm, for example) have argued that the ego has more of a role than Freud thought in controlling behaviour. Still others (Karen Horney, for instance) have focused on the central role of anxiety in shaping personality and maladjustment. Many theorists (Harry Stack Sullivan, for example) have attributed a greater influence to cultural and interpersonal factors. A number of the neo-Freudian theories (Carl Jung's, for instance) have been more optimistic and future-oriented. While traditional psychoanalysts begin by focusing

Neo-Freudians: Personality theorists who have proposed variations on the basic ideas of Freud, usually attributing a greater influence to cultural and interpersonal factors than Freud did.

on unconscious material in the id and only later try to increase the patient's ego control, many practising neo-Freudians focus on helping people to develop stronger control of their ego and to feel better about their "selves." Carl Jung is one of the best known of the neo-Freudians; we'll explore his influential theory next.

Jung's Analytical Psychology

Carl Gustav Jung (1875–1961) was a psychiatrist who became a close friend and follower of Freud. However, Jung, a brilliant thinker, ultimately broke with Freud over several key issues. Compared to Freud, Jung placed relatively little emphasis on sex. He focused instead on people's desire to blend their basic drives (including sex) with real-world demands. Thus, Jung saw people's behaviour as less rigidly fixed and determined. He also emphasized the search for meaning in life and focused on religiosity. By 1911, Jung and Freud were exchanging angry letters. In 1917, when Jung declared his disagreements with Freud, he and Freud severed their relationship—Freud was intolerant of followers who deviated too much from his positions (and you might think about what Freud himself would have to say about such behaviour).

Jung chose to differentiate his approach from Freud's by calling it an *analytic approach* rather than a *psychoanalytic approach*. Like Freud, Jung emphasized unconscious processes as determinants of behaviour, and he believed that each person houses past events in the unconscious. Jung's version of the unconscious was slightly different, however. Unlike Freud, Jung held that the unconscious anticipates the future and redirects a person's behaviour when the person is leaning too much in one psychological direction. Thus, for example, if a person is using too many defence mechanisms, the unconscious can anticipate problems and help the person deal with anxiety rather than distort it.

In addition, Jung developed a new concept central to his ideas—that of the collective unconscious. The **collective unconscious** is a shared storehouse of primitive ideas and images in the unconscious that are inherited from one's ancestors. These inherited ideas and images are emotionally charged, rich in meaning and symbolism, and contained in the form of **archetypes** within a person's unconscious. The archetypes of the collective unconscious emerge in art, in religion, and especially in dreams. One especially important archetype is the *mandala*, a mystical symbol, generally circular in form, that in Jung's view represents the striving for unity within a person's self. Jung pointed out that many religions have mandala-like symbols; indeed, Hinduism and Buddhism use such symbols as aids in meditation. Another archetype is the concept of mother; each person is born with a predisposition to react to certain types of people or institutions as mother figures. Such figures are considered warm, accepting, and nurturing; some examples are the Virgin Mary, one's godmothers, and the Earth. There are archetypes for

wise older men and wizards and for mothers good and bad. Jung found rich symbolism in dreams and used archetypes such as the mandala and the mother to help people understand themselves.

Jung's ideas are widely read but not widely accepted by mainstream psychologists. Although his impact on psychoanalytic theory is important, Jung himself never achieved prominence in leading psychological thought. Some theorists even view his theories as mere poetic speculation.

Another psychologist who broke with Freud—but who made a more lasting impact on psychological thought—was Alfred Adler, whom we consider next.

Collective unconscious: In Jung's theory, a storehouse of primitive ideas and images in the unconscious that are inherited from one's ancestors.

Archetypes [AR-ki-types]: In Jung's theory, emotionally charged ideas and images that have rich meaning and symbolism and are contained within a person's unconscious.

Adler's Fulfilment Approach

Freud heavily influenced Alfred Adler (1870–1937) and some psychologists consider his theory to be simply an extension of Freud's. Adler was a Viennese physician who had an unhappy childhood. He recalled being compared to his older brother, who seemed to be better liked because of his physical prowess and attractiveness. Perhaps his unhappy childhood and feelings of inferiority led Adler to believe that people strive to become the best they can be. When Adler broke with Freudian traditions, he focused much more on human values and social interactions.

Adler differed with Freud concerning two key points. First, Adler viewed human beings as striving to overcome obstacles in order to fulfil themselves, rather than for pleasure. Second, Adler viewed the social nature of human beings as much more important than did Freud. Adler met with Freud weekly; however, in 1911, Freud denounced him because of sharp, irreconcilable differences in their views of personality. The break between the two theorists was hostile, and Freud sought and was successful in expelling Adler from mainstream psychoanalytic groups (Webster, 1995).

Structure of Personality. According to Adler, people are motivated, or energized, by natural feelings of inferiority, which lead them to strive for completion, mastery, and ultimately perfection. Thus, feelings of inferiority are not always detrimental. A sense of inferiority can compel people to strive for mastery and thereby express their core tendencies, both as individuals and as members of society.

Adler recognized that people seek to express their need for mastery in different areas of life. Some seek to be superior artists; others seek to be superior social advocates, parents, or corporate executives. Thus, each person develops a unique lifestyle, in which attitudes and behaviours express a specific life goal or an ideal approach to achieving mastery. Adler eventually sought to develop an "individual" psychology, arguing that people have to be analyzed as unique human beings.

Adler stressed fulfilment through individual striving towards specific goals. He recognized that people often develop unrealistic expectations for themselves, sometimes to the extent that the goals they set can be considered fictional. Adler termed the effort to accomplish life goals that are unrealistic and unlikely to be achieved by most people *fictional finalism*. Examples are winning the Pulitzer Prize for literature or becoming a millionaire (Adler, 1969). However, it is these fictional goals, which are often unconscious, that motivate people and set up unique patterns of striving.

Development of Personality. Adler believed that children's social interactions are particularly important in determining eventual personality characteristics. Adler and his followers relied heavily on the idea that early relationships with siblings, parents, and other family members determine the lifestyle an individual eventually chooses. It therefore follows, Adler asserted,

Focus

Review

◆ What are the fundamental assumptions about human behaviour on which Freud's theory is based? p. 409

◆ Why did Freud believe the unconscious to be so important in personality? p. 410

◆ What is the fundamental function of all of Freud's defence mechanisms? p. 414

◆ To which of Freud's fundamental assumptions did the neo-Freudians react? p. 416

Think Critically

◆ What is it about a society that can shape a personality theorist's point of view?

◆ Adler's view of personality development was radically different from Freud's. What implications did this difference have for Adler's theory of personality development?

Table 12.3   Some of Adler's Hypotheses about Birth Order

Birth Order	Hypothesis
Only child	The centre of attention, dominant; often spoiled because of parental timidity and anxiety; extremely feminine or masculine in orientation
First born	Dethroned from a central position with the birth of a sibling; thus has negative attitudes and feelings towards the second child and a passion for domination; protective and helpful towards others
Second born	Actively struggling to surpass others
Last born	The most pampered (the smallest and weakest); not unhappy; able to excel by being different

that birth order is important. A first-born child, for example, is likely to have a different relationship with people and is thus likely to develop a lifestyle different from that of a third-born child. First borns are pushed by parents towards success, leadership, and independence and so tend to have a high need for achievement. Their early experiences make it likely that they will choose careers reflecting that need for achievement, such as corporate executive or politician. Third-born children, on the other hand, usually are more relaxed about achievement. A young child who feels competitive with an older sibling, however, may develop a strong need for achievement that will drive the child towards public success. Sulloway (1996) concurs, arguing that children strive to maximize parental investment in them, adapting a strategy to their own family, and that this is bound to bring about sibling rivalry. (See Table 12.3.)

Humanistic Approaches

Dehumanizing was the term that many psychologists used to describe psychoanalytic theory; Freud characterized people as too primitive, and his theory was viewed by many as too deterministic. Humanistic approaches developed in the 1950s in part as a backlash against Freud's theory and attempted to humanize the study of personality by focusing on the unique qualities of human beings.

Unlike Freudians and neo-Freudians, who want to understand relationships between children and parents, humanistic theorists are more interested in people's conceptions of themselves and what they would like to become. In general, *humanistic theories* assume that people are motivated by internal forces to achieve personal goals. Humanistic psychology focuses not on maladjustment or abnormal behaviour but on healthy people.

Humanistic theories emphasize fulfilment and, as already suggested, were developed partly in response to Freud's theory, which stresses the conflict of inner forces. Whereas Freud saw people in conflict warding off evil thoughts and desires with defences, humanistic psychologists see people as basically decent (although some of their specific behaviours may not be). Moreover, humanistic fulfilment theories enable theoreticians and practitioners to make predictions about specific behaviours.

Sometimes humanistic theories are called *phenomenological approaches*, because they focus on the individual's unique experiences with and ways of interpreting the things and people in the world (phenomena). These approaches are more likely to examine immediate experiences than past ones and are more likely to deal with an individual's perception of the world than with a therapist's perception of the individual. Finally, they focus on self-determination; people carve their own destinies from their own vantage points and in their own ways. Two well-known psychologists, Abraham Maslow and Carl Rogers, whose theories are examined next, represent the humanistic approaches.

Abraham Maslow

No single individual is more closely associated with humanistic phenomenological psychology than Abraham Maslow (1908–1970). In Chapter 9 we examined Maslow's theory of motivation, which states that human needs are arranged in a pyramidal hierarchy in terms of their importance and potency. Lower needs—food and water, for example—are powerful and drive people towards fulfilling them. In the middle of the pyramid of needs are safety, then belongingness, then self-esteem. At the top of the pyramid is self-actualization. The higher a need is on the hierarchy, the more distinctly human the need is.

As a humanist, Maslow believed that human beings are born healthy and undamaged, and he had a strong bias towards studying well-adjusted people. Maslow spoke about personality in terms of human uniqueness and the human need for self-actualization—the process of growth and the realization of individual potential. He focused not on what was missing from personality or life but on what one might achieve in realizing one's full potential. The process of realizing potential and of growing is the process of self-actualizing. Critics of Maslow find his notions too fuzzy (as they do Freud's) and view his approach to psychology as romantic and never fully developed. Also, his theory is virtually untestable because he provided little discussion or explanation of the nature of self-actualizing tendencies. Carl Rogers presented a more complete and scientific humanistic approach.

Rogers and Self Theory

Carl Rogers (1902–1987) began to formulate his personality theory during the first years of his practice as a clinician in Rochester, New York. He listened to thousands of patients and was among the first psychologists to tape-record and transcribe his interactions with patients. What Rogers's patients said about their experiences, their thoughts, and themselves led him to make three basic assumptions about behaviour: (1) Behaviour is goal-directed and worthwhile. (2) People are innately good, so they will almost always choose adaptive, enhancing, and self-actualizing behaviours. (3) How people see their world determines how they will behave.

Key Concepts. Rogers believed that personal experiences provide an individual with a unique and subjective internal frame of reference and world-view. He believed that **fulfilment**—an inborn tendency directing people towards actualizing their essential nature and thus attaining their potential—is the motivating force of personality development. Thus, people strive naturally to express their capabilities, potential, and talents. Rogers's personality approach is *unidirectional*, because it always moves in the direction of fulfilment. This does not mean that an individual's personality undergoes uninterrupted growth. During some periods, no growth is evident. However, for Rogers, a person's core tendency is to actualize and enhance life. Rogers liked the analogy of a seed, which if watered grows into a strong, healthy plant—a representative member of its species.

Structure of Personality. Rogers's theory of personality is structured around the concept of self. By **self** he means the perceptions individuals have of themselves and of their relationships to other people and to various aspects of life. The self-concept is how people see their own behaviour and internal characteristics. As mentioned before, Rogers's theory assumes that individuals are constantly engaged in the process of fulfilling their potential—of actualizing their true self.

Rogers suggested that each person has a concept not only of self but also of an ideal self. The **ideal self** is the self that a person ideally would like to be (such as a

Fulfilment: In Rogers's personality theory, an inborn tendency directing people towards actualizing their essential nature and thus attaining their potential.

Self: In Rogers's theory of personality, the perceptions individuals have of themselves and of their relationships to other people and to various aspects of life.

Ideal self: The self that a person ideally would like to be.

competent professional, a devoted mate, or a loving parent). According to Rogers's theory, each person's happiness lies within that person's conception of self. A person is generally happy when agreement exists between the real (Rogers used the term *phenomenal*) self and the ideal self. Great discrepancies between the real and the ideal selves create unhappiness, dissatisfaction, and, in extreme cases, maladjustment.

Rogers's focus on the self led him to his basic principle—that people tend to maximize their self-concept through **self-actualization**. In the self-actualization process, the self grows, expands, and becomes social. People are self-actualized when they have expanded their self-concept and developed their potential to approximate their ideal selves by attempting to minimize ill health, be fully functioning, have a clear perception of reality, and feel a strong sense of self-acceptance. When people's self-concepts are not what they would like them to be, anxiety develops. Rogers saw anxiety as useful because it motivates people to try to actualize their best selves, to become all they are capable of being.

Development of Personality. Unlike Freud, Rogers suggested that personality development occurs continuously, not in stages. He contended that development involves regular self-assessment in order to master the process of self-actualization—which takes a lifetime.

Rogers was particularly aware that children develop basic feelings about themselves early in life. The self-assessments of children who are told that they are beautiful, intelligent, and good are radically different from those of children who are told that they are bad, dirty, stupid, and a general nuisance. Rogers did not claim that negative feelings towards children's behaviour should not be expressed; rather, children should have a sense that they themselves are worthwhile and good, although a specific behaviour that they exhibit might be unacceptable. Rogers suggested that children must grow up in an atmosphere in which they can experience life fully. This involves their recognizing both the good and the bad sides of their behaviour.

The Importance of Self-Concepts. People with rigid self-concepts guard themselves against potentially threatening feelings and experiences. Rogers suggested that these people become unhappy when they are unable to fit new types of behaviour into their existing self-concepts. They then distort their perceptions of their behaviour in order to make the perceptions compatible with the self-concepts. A man whose self-concept includes high moral principles, rigid religious observance, and strict self-control, for example, probably becomes anxious when he feels envy. Such a feeling is inconsistent with his self-concept. To avoid anxiety, he denies or distorts what he is truly experiencing. He may deny that he feels envy, or he may insist that he is entitled to the object he covets.

A changing world may threaten a person's self-concept. The person then may screen out difficult ideas or thoughts; this tends to create a narrow outlook, a limited conception of the world, and a restriction on personal growth. But individuals can reduce or eliminate their fear by broadening their frame of reference and by considering alternative behaviours. People with healthy self-concepts can allow new experiences into their lives and can accept or reject them. Such people move in a positive direction. With each new experience, their self-concepts become stronger and more defined, and the goal of self-actualization is brought closer.

Individual Development. Rogers's concept of personality shows a serious concern for individual development. Rogers stressed that each person must evaluate her or his own situation from a personal (internal) frame of reference, not from the external framework of others.

Freud's and Rogers's theories of personality make fundamentally different assumptions about human nature and about how personality is expressed. Freud saw biologically driven human beings in conflict; Rogers saw human beings as inherently good and trying to be everything they could be. Freud was strongly deterministic, whereas humanists are strongly oriented towards free will. Humanists believe people can rise above biologically inherited traits and can use decision-making

Self-actualization: The fundamental human need to strive to fulfil one's potential; from a humanistic view, a final level of psychological development in which a person attempts to minimize ill health, be fully functioning, have a superior perception of reality, and feel a strong sense of self-acceptance.

Building Table 12.1

Psychoanalytic and Humanistic Approaches to Personality

Approach	Major Proponent	Core of Personality	Structure of Personality	Development	Cause of Problems
Psychoanalytic	Sigmund Freud	Maximizes gratification while minimizing punishment or guilt; instinctual unconscious urges direct behaviour	Id, ego, superego	Five stages: oral, anal, phallic, latency, genital	Imbalances between the id, ego, and superego, resulting in fixations
Humanistic	Carl Rogers	Actualizes, maintains, and enhances the experiences of life through the process of self-actualization	Self	Process of cumulative self-actualization and development of sense of self-worth	Incongruence between self and concept of ideal self

processes to guide behaviour. The treatment procedures that developed out of the theories of Freud and Rogers—psychoanalysis and client-centred therapy (the latter will be discussed in Chapter 16)—are fundamentally different. (See Building Table 12.1 for a summary of the psychoanalytic and humanistic approaches.)

Next, we examine an approach to personality that focuses on traits and on the specific behavioural responses that individuals make throughout their lives.

Trait and Type Theories: Dispositions

B oth ancient philosophers and medieval physicians believed that the proportions of body fluids (called humours) determined a person's temperament and personality. Cheerful, healthy people, for example, were said to have a *sanguine* (cheerful, hopeful, and self-confident) personality because blood was their primary humour; those who had a preponderance of yellow bile were considered hot-tempered. Like their medieval counterparts, some early psychologists based their personality theories on the traits that people openly exhibit, such as shyness, impulsiveness, and aggressiveness. Research shows that many of these easily observed characteristics do predict other behaviours. For example, extremely shy people are more likely than others to be anxious and lonely and to have low self-esteem (DePaulo et al., 1989), and adolescents with behaviour problems often have low self-esteem (Harper & Marshall, 1991). Theories based on these observations—trait and type theories of personality—make intuitive sense and thus have been very popular. They focus on broad, stable behavioural dispositions.

Trait theorists study specific traits. A **trait** is any readily identifiable stable quality that characterizes the way in which an individual differs from other individuals. Someone might characterize one leader as energetic and forward-looking and another as tough and patriotic. Such characterizations present specific ideas about

Trait: Any readily identifiable stable quality that characterizes the way in which an individual differs from other individuals.

these people's traits and dispositions. Traits can be evaluated on a continuum, so a person can be extremely shy, very shy, shy, or mildly shy. (The trait of shyness is investigated in more detail in *Brain and Behaviour* on page 424.) For some personality theorists, traits are the elements that make up our personality.

Type theorists group together traits common to specific personalities. **Types**, therefore, are categories in which broad collections of traits are loosely tied together and interrelated. Although the distinction between traits and types sometimes blurs, as Gordon Allport (1937, p. 295) explained, "A man can be said to *have* a trait; but he cannot be said to *have* a type. Rather he fits a type."

Types: Categories of personality in which broad collections of traits are loosely tied together and interrelated.

Allport's Trait Theory and Cattell's Factor Theory

The distinguished psychologist Gordon Allport (1897–1967) was a leading trait theorist who suggested that each individual has a unique set of personality traits. According to Allport (1937/1998), if a person's traits are known, it is possible to predict how the person will respond to various events in the environment. Allport quickly discovered that while thousands of traits characterize people's behaviour, some are more dominant than others.

Allport decided that traits could be grouped into three kinds: cardinal, central, and secondary. *Cardinal traits* are ideas and enduring characteristics that determine the direction of a person's life. A clergyman's cardinal trait may be belief in and devotion to God; a civil rights leader's may be the desire to rectify social and political injustices. Allport noted that many people have no cardinal traits. The more common *central traits* are reasonably easy to identify; they are the qualities that characterize a person's daily interactions, the basic units of personality. Allport believed that central traits—including self-control, apprehension, tension, self-assuredness, forthrightness, and practicality—adequately describe many

personalities. For example, tennis legend John McEnroe could be characterized as self-assured and hot tempered, lacking emotional control; Woody Allen's typical film persona could be described as tense and apprehensive. *Secondary traits* occur in response to specific situations. For example, a person may have a secondary trait of xenophobia—a fear and intolerance of strangers or foreigners. Secondary traits are more easily modified than central traits and are not necessarily exhibited on a daily basis.

Everyone has different combinations of traits, which is why Allport claimed that each person is unique. To identify a person's traits, Allport recommended an in-depth study of that individual. If Allport's theory were followed to its logical conclusion, knowing a person's traits would allow a psychologist to predict how that person would respond to the environment—that is, what the person's behaviour would be. This has not yet come about. Psychologists such as Allport and Raymond B. Cattell have argued, however, that it is possible to tell a great deal about a person just by knowing a few of the person's traits. Cattell (1965) used the technique of *factor analysis*—a statistical procedure in which psychologists analyze groups of variables to detect which are related—to show that groups of traits tend to cluster together or form *factors*. Thus, researchers find that people who describe themselves as warm and accepting also tend to rate themselves as high on nurturance and tenderness and low on aggression, suspiciousness, and apprehensiveness. Researchers also see patterns within professions; for example, artists may see themselves as creative, sensitive, and open, while accountants may describe themselves as careful, serious, conservative, and thorough-minded.

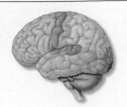

brain and behaviour
Overcoming Shyness

A bout 40 percent of adults report being shy, and for many of them **shyness** is a serious behaviour problem that inhibits personal, social, and professional growth. Shy people show extreme anxiety in social situations; they are extremely reticent and often overly concerned with how others view them. They fear acting foolishly; as a consequence, they may develop clammy hands, dry mouth, excessive perspiration, trembling, nausea, blushing, and a need to go to the bathroom frequently. Shyness makes people avoid social situations and makes them speak softly, when they speak at all (Schmidt et al., 1997). Shy people also avoid approaching other people (Asendorpf, 1989). In contrast to bold children, shy children are more likely to have higher heart rates (Arcus, 1994). Most shy people report that they have always been shy, and half of all shy people feel they are shyer than other people in similar situations (Carducci & Stein, 1988). The causes of extreme shyness have been thought to be biological in origin (Kagan, Reznick, & Snidman, 1998), although the exact mechanism that might underlie it is still unknown. Genetic predispositions are suggested, and research shows that even a mother's exposure to daylight during pregnancy affects hormonal and other biological mechanisms that affect her newborn's shyness (Gortmaker et al., 1997). Personality researchers contend that certain personality traits, including shyness, are long-

lasting. Jerome Kagan found that two- and three-year-olds who were extremely cautious and shy tended to remain that way for years (Kagan, 1997a; Schmidt et al., 1997). Daniels and Plomin (1985) also found an important relationship between adopted infants' shyness at two years of age and the shyness of their biological mothers. This finding also suggests that genetic factors play an important role in shyness (Hamer & Copeland, 1998; Lykken et al., 1992).

Although Kagan also suggests that extreme shyness may have a biological basis, he believes that shyness emerges because people develop distorted self-concepts—negative views about their competencies and a lack of self-esteem (Kagan, 1997b). Such individuals view themselves in a poor light, as having few social graces. These thoughts, combined with actions such as withdrawal and nervousness, set a person up for social failure. When negative events occur, the person then says, "See,

I was right." A person's thoughts about her or his shyness, bodily reactions, and social behaviours thus perpetuate the shyness (Bruch, Berko, & Haase, 1998). A parent's shyness and sociability can affect these thoughts; the more sociable are parents, the less shy are children (Chung & Doh, 1997). The consequences of being shy can be profound; shy children marry later and have children later in life (Kerr, Lambert, & Bem, 1996); such life-course decisions affect career decisions as well.

Treatment programs exist to help people overcome extreme shyness (Carducci & Stein, 1988). If you are shy, here are some things you can do:

■ Rehearse what you want to say before speaking.

■ Build your self-esteem by focusing on your good points.

■ Accept who you are.

■ Practise smiling and making eye contact.

■ Observe the behaviour of others whom you admire, and copy it.

■ Think about how others feel; remember that about 40 percent of all people feel the way you do (i.e., are shy).

■ Begin some relaxation training, perhaps involving self-hypnosis, yoga, or even biofeedback.

■ Think positively; having a positive attitude about yourself and other people can go a long way towards helping to overcome shyness. ■

Shyness: Extreme anxiety in individuals who are socially reticent and often overly concerned with how they appear to others, often leading to avoidance of social situations.

Eysenck's Type Theory

Whereas Allport and Cattell focused on traits, Hans Eysenck (1916–1997) focused on higher levels of trait organization, or what he called *types*. Each type incorporates elements at a lower level (traits), and each trait incorporates lower-order qualities (habits). Eysenck (1970) argued that all personality traits could be grouped along three basic dimensions: emotional stability, introversion or extroversion, and psychoticism.

Emotional stability is the extent to which people control their feelings. At one extreme of this dimension, people can be spontaneous, genuine, and warm; at the other, they can be controlled, calm, flat, unresponsive, and stilted. The dimension of *introversion or extroversion* has to do with the extent to which people are withdrawn or open. Introverts are socially withdrawn and shy; extroverts are socially outgoing and open and like to meet new people. Eysenck's third dimension, *psychoticism*, is sometimes called tough- or tender-mindedness. At one extreme, people are troublesome, opposed to authority, sensation-seeking, insensitive, and risk-taking; at the other, they are warm, gregarious, and tender.

Eysenck argued that personality has a biological basis but emphasized that learning and experience also shape an individual's behaviour. For example, he said that introverts and extroverts possess different levels of arousal in the cortex of the brain. Accordingly, persons of each type seek the amount of stimulation necessary to achieve their preferred level of arousal. For example, a person who prefers a low level of arousal, in which stimulation is less intense, may become a security guard or a librarian; a person who prefers a high level of arousal, which is reflected in outward behaviour, may become a race car driver or a politician. There are many people who may be characterized as sensation seekers; they climb mountains, ride dirt bikes, gamble at the track, or take drugs. *Diversity* on page 426 explores the question of whether people who are religious share a personality type.

The idea of a biological component to traits is widely debated (Bullock & Gilliland, 1993; Heath & Martin, 1990) and not yet resolved. Most psychologists assert that some traits may be passed on genetically—at least to some extent (e.g., Hamer & Copeland, 1998; Plomin, 1994a). Behavioural geneticists consider the environment to be a minimal influence, but most psychologists maintain that environmental influences are so strong that much of a person's personality is shaped by day-to-day interactions.

The Big Five

Because of trait theory's popular appeal and common-sense approach, researchers today still find it attractive. However, rather than speaking of hundreds of traits or of a few types, many theorists now agree that there are five broad trait categories. These categories have become known as the *Big Five* (McCrae & Costa, 1987):

- *Extroversion–introversion*, or the extent to which people are social or unsocial, talkative or quiet, affectionate or reserved.
- *Agreeableness–antagonism*, or the extent to which people are good-natured or irritable, courteous or rude, flexible or stubborn, lenient or critical.
- *Conscientiousness–undirectedness*, or the extent to which people are reliable or undependable, careful or careless, punctual or late, well-organized or disorganized.
- *Neuroticism–stability*, or the extent to which people are worriers or calm, nervous or at ease, insecure or secure.
- *Openness to experience*, or the extent to which people are open to experience or closed, independent or conforming, creative or uncreative, daring or timid.

Although dozens of traits can describe people, researchers think of the Big Five categories as "supertraits," the important dimensions that characterize or organize personality (McCrea & Costa, 1990, 1994). Research has been supportive, showing stability of the Big Five (Borkeneau & Ostendorf, 1998); the Big Five hold up cross-

Is There a Religious Personality Type?

When you picture a "religious" person, who comes to mind? Do you think of Mother Teresa? The Dalai Lama? Your rabbi or priest? Does your image involve acts of kindness performed by a spiritual person, or do you envision someone who is repressed, rigid, and inflexible? It turns out that there are so many different forms of religious expression that whatever your image, you probably are partly right. But is religiousness a personality trait? Does one's personality determine whether one will be religious? Religious expression exists in enormous diversity, including worship services, community outreach, and individual acts of kindness. Individuals of all ages pray (Levin & Taylor, 1997). From a psychologist's point of view, religion can play a key role in many people's lives, but it is expressed in many forms, with seemingly endless variation (Melton, 1993).

Some people have strong, stereotyped views of those who are religious. But researchers have found, usually through questionnaires and surveys, a more complicated and subtle picture of individual religious development. People who are religious—regardless of their tradition, ethnicity, or culture—don't tend to be one personality type. Some religious individuals are indeed authoritarian individuals who adopt strict guidelines and make use of rigid punishments to raise their children.

But a similar number of religious people are non-authoritarian. When all of the data are taken together, it turns out that authoritarianism is not correlated in any direct way with being religious (Stark, 1971). Similarly, the religious, across all groups, tend not to be any more or less suggestible to ideas than are other individuals, although within some religious denominations greater suggestibility is seen.

Religious individuals who are deeply committed to a life of faith report a sense of well-being. Researchers have tried to separate whether this sense of well-being comes from being religious or emerges due to other reasons (Paloutzian & Ellison, 1991). Paloutzian (1996) concludes that spiritual well-being is an overriding sense of the quality of daily life, but that religion is just one part of a person's life that creates that sense of peace. For example, it turns out that spiritual well-being is positively related to people's feelings about their own health (Chamberlain & Zika, 1992).

In the end, those who are religious aren't of one personality type. They aren't more upbeat, nor are they more reserved. They aren't any more or less authoritarian, dogmatic, or balanced than the non-religious. Religious people feel better than the non-religious— their sense of well-being is greater. But remember that correlation is not equivalent to causation—being religious does not necessarily *cause* one to feel better or to be a more effective person.

The role of religion in our lives has just begun to be explored in psychology, and research on it has yet to be integrated into mainstream psychology (Kirkpatrick, 1997)—this is quite astonishing, given the large role that it plays in so many lives. Researchers have just begun to explore how, and whether, religion shapes personality or how personality shapes religious experience. Some of the latest research efforts have looked at differences in religiousness from feminist (Neitz, 1995), developmental (Tamminen, 1994), and cross-cultural perspectives (Chia & Jih, 1995). ■

culturally (Costa & McCrea, 1998; McCrea et al., 1998; Trull & Geary, 1997), and there may be genetic influences (Bouchard & Hur, 1998). The Big Five may help us understand children's personalities (Shiner, 1998), although little research has been conducted on children and personality development.

The Big Five is easily understood (Sneed, McCrae, & Funder, 1998), can be used to make predictions about happiness (DeNeve & Cooper, 1998), and can be used in practical situations like mate selection (Botwin, Buss, & Shackelford, 1997), job performance (Mount, Barrick, & Stewart, 1998), and therapy (Matthews et al., 1998). However, as good as the Big Five is, it is still only a model that psychologists use to help them understand personality; it is not necessarily a final or complete description of personality (Bouchard, 1997). And not all researchers agree with the categories (Deniston & Ramanaiah, 1993; Wiggins & Trapnell, 1992). For example, researchers recently found evidence for two additional dimensions (excellent–ordinary and evil–decent); therefore, the Big Five soon may be considered the Big Seven (Almagor, Tellegen, & Waller, 1995; Benet-Martinez & Waller, 1997). Moreover, some elements of personality are not typed well by the Big Five (Schinka, Dye, & Curtiss, 1997), especially in the area of health-related concerns (Marshall et al., 1994); more research is needed into the meaning of the factors.

Criticisms of Trait and Type Theories

Trait and type theories are appealing because they characterize people along important dimensions, providing simple explanations for how individuals behave. The idea of traits as accurate predictors of behaviour has been supported by some research (Funder, 1995), but more often psychologists have criticized these theories on six basic fronts. First, they argue that trait theories are not actually personality theories. That is, they do not make good predictions about behaviours or explain why the behaviours occur. Some psychologists claim that trait theories are merely lists of behaviours arranged into a hierarchy without solid evidence that the hierarchy relates to human behaviour. Second, most trait theories do not tell which personality characteristics last a lifetime and which are transient. Major events can alter traits and types. Third, since an individual's behaviour depends on the situation or context, traits cannot predict behaviour (Schmit & Ryan, 1993). Some researchers contend that the failure of trait theories to account for situational differences is a crucial weakness. Fourth, trait theories do not account for changing cultural elements. If you test the same person at 10-year intervals, the person's traits likely will be different. But society also will be different, as will people's values and ideas. Trait and type theories do not account for these changing cultural norms. Fifth, not only does each culture change, but the differences between cultures (for example, between Western and Eastern cultures) are great, and trait theories do not account for them (Matsumoto, 1996). Finally, trait and type theories do not explain how people develop traits. Nor do they explain why traits change.

Trait and type theories continue to evolve, and debate continues as to the number of stable traits (Zuckerman et al., 1993). However, psychologists want personality theories that (1) explain the development of personality, (2) predict maladjustment, and especially (3) explain why a person's behaviour can be dramatically different in different situations. Theories that attempt to describe, explain, and predict behaviours with more precision tend to be behavioural ones, the next major group of theories that we will examine.

Focus

Review

- What does self-actualization mean in the context of Maslow's and Rogers's personality theories? pp. 420–421
- Distinguish between a trait and a type. pp. 422–423
- What is a fundamental criticism of trait and type theories? p. 427

Think Critically

- What do you think is the most important way humanistic theory differs from Freudian theory?
- Many psychologists accept the Big Five, but perhaps they should consider a Big Six, Big Seven, or Big Four. What do you think of the inclusiveness of the Big Five? Are five dimensions too many or not enough to characterize individual differences in personality?

Behavioural Approaches: Learning Is Key

 eople often try to figure out what goes on inside the worlds of their heroes, movie stars, athletes, and political figures; they try to glimpse what their personal and professional lives might be like and infer things about their personality. But B. F. Skinner, a leader of American behaviourism, would have argued that such an exercise is a waste of time—you cannot see inside people's minds. He and behavioural colleagues would argue that speculating about private, unobservable behaviour is fruitless. He would further assert that inner drives, psychic urges, and the need for self-actualization are impossible-to-define concepts.

Behaviourists assert that concepts like psychic urges are not the proper subject matter of personality study. Behavioural theorists are practical. They believe that people often need to change aspects of their lives quickly and efficiently and that many people do not have the time, money, or energy for lengthy therapy or personality analysis. Consider the behavioural self-treatment that Redford Williams proposes for Type A people—those hard-driving, ambitious, highly competitive people who, according to cardiologists, are at high risk of heart attacks (R. L. Williams, 1989). Williams says that the lethal elements in Type A individuals are hostility and cynical mistrust, and he outlines steps that such individuals can take to reduce hostility and develop a more trusting attitude and a healthier heart. One step is hostility monitoring—recording angry feelings in a "hostility" journal. Another is thought stopping—mentally yelling "Stop!" whenever hostile thoughts start forming. If behaviourists are correct in saying that personality is equivalent to the sum of a series of responses, then Williams's self-treatment program should help Type A individuals change their health-endangering personalities.

Key Behavioural Concepts

Behaviourists look at personality very differently than do any of the theorists described so far. They generally do not look inward, and instead look only at overt behaviour. Behavioural approaches are often viewed as a reaction to the conceptual vagueness of traditional personality theories. Behavioural personality theorists assert that personality develops as people learn from their environments. The key word here is *learn*. According to behaviourists, personality characteristics are not long-lasting and fixed; instead, they are subject to change. Thus, for behaviourists such as Skinner, personality is the sum of a person's learned tendencies.

Does personality change? *The Research Process* (see pages 430 and 431) discusses how two researchers studied the constancy of personality by examining the behavioural characteristics of a group of women over a period of 20 years.

Precisely Defined Elements. Behavioural theories tend to centre on precisely defined elements, such as the relationship between stimuli and responses, the strength of stimuli, and the strength, duration, and timing of reinforcers. All of these can be tested in a laboratory or clinical setting. By focusing on stimuli and responses, behaviourists avoid conceptualizing human nature and concentrate instead on predicting behaviour in specific circumstances. As a result, their assertions are more easily tested than are those of other theorists. Behaviourists see the development of personality simply as a change in response characteristics—a person learns new behaviours in response to new environments and stimuli.

Responses to Stimuli. For most behaviourists, the structural unit of personality is the response to stimuli. Any behaviour, regardless of the situation, is seen as a response to a stimulus or a response in anticipation of reinforcement (or punishment). When an identifiable stimulus leads to an identifiable response, researchers predict that every time that stimulus occurs, so will the response. This *stimulus–response relationship* helps explain the constancy of personality. For example, whenever a teacher has something unpleasant to discuss with one of his students, he may say, "Would you stay and see me after school?" The student's response is often to tense up and become defensive. The student has learned through repetition over the years that such initial responses are predictable: The stimulus of a request for an after-school meeting leads to an initial response of defensiveness.

Behaviour Patterns. Using behavioural analysis, psychologists can discover how people develop behaviour patterns (such as eating their vegetables or being hostile) and why behaviour is in constant flux. The behavioural approach suggests that learning is the process that shapes personality and that learning takes place through experience. Because new experiences happen all the time, a person is constantly learning about the world and changing response patterns accordingly. Just as there are several learning principles involving the use of stimuli, responses, and reinforcement, there are several behavioural personality theories. These theories are based on classical conditioning, operant conditioning, and observational learning.

Classical Conditioning

Most people are fearful or anxious at times. Some are fearful more often than not. How do people become fearful? What causes constant anxiety?

Many behavioural psychologists maintain that people develop fearfulness, anxiety, and a timid personality through classical conditioning, in which a neutral stimulus is paired with another stimulus that elicits some response. Eventually, the neutral stimulus can elicit the response on its own. For example, many people fear rats. Because rats are often encountered in dark cellars, a person may learn to fear dark cellars; that is, dark cellars become a feared stimulus. Later, the person may develop a generalized fear of dark places. If the person sees a train for the first time in a darkened station that looks like a cellar, the person may learn to fear trains. Classical conditioning thus allows researchers to explain the predictability of a person's day-to-day responses to specific stimuli. It describes the relationship between one stimulus and a person's expectation of another, as well as the predictable response the person makes (Rescorla, 1988).

Operant Conditioning

In operant conditioning, behaviour is followed with a consequence, such as reinforcement or punishment. According to behaviourists, personality can be explained as spontaneous behaviour that is reinforced. For example, when a person is affectionate and that behaviour is reinforced with smiles and hugs, the person is likely to continue to be affectionate.

Behavioural psychologists often use the operant learning principles of reinforcement and punishment to help children control themselves and shape their own personalities. Consider a problem of school discipline in which a 10-year-old boy frequently used obscenities in school (Lahey, McNees, & McNees, 1973). In an hour's time, the child would utter as many as 150 obscene words and phrases. To deal with the problem, whenever the child uttered an obscene word, psychologists would take him out of the classroom for a minimum of five minutes and place him in a well-lit, empty room. They told him he would be placed in this room every time he made an obscene utterance. In a few days, the average number of obscenities decreased dramatically, from more than two a minute to fewer than five an hour. Using operant conditioning, the researchers were able to modify an element of this boy's personality.

The time-out procedure is often used in learning situations in both classrooms and laboratories. As with any reinforcement or punishment procedure, the subject learns that the procedure is contingent on behaviour. In the example given, the time-out was punishment. The child found it rewarding to be in the classroom and punishing to be in the time-out room. Thus, to remain in the classroom and avoid being put in the time-out room, he learned not to utter obscenities.

Observational Learning

Observational learning theories assume that people learn new behaviours by watching the behaviours of others. The theory contends that an observer will imitate the

Plaster or Plasticity: Does Personality Change?

Is a person's personality fixed in time like a plaster cast, or does it mold itself through experience enough to be considered plastic? Does personality change over time, or does it stay the same from adolescence through old age? Are personality changes the same for men and women? Trait theorists assume that personality remains much the same over the life span. Shy people remain shy; high-school pranksters become retirement-home pranksters. Stage theorists such as Erik Erikson and Daniel Levinson (discussed in Chapter 11), on the other hand, contend that people change during their life span. These psychologists believe in an adult developmental life cycle. But are there gender differences in the course of personality development? Many researchers think there are, particularly before and during adolescence (L. D. Cohn, 1991).

Hypotheses. Unfortunately, most personality and adult life cycle studies have been conducted with men—who represent less than half of the population. Do women's personalities change in a similar way to men's? Do the personalities of career-oriented women change and those of family-oriented women stay the same? Helson and Moane (1987), of the University of California at Berkeley, studied the personalities of a group of women, starting when the women were of college age and continuing to midlife. In a second study, husbands and wives were studied (Wink & Helson, 1993). A third study compared three samples of women who were adults in the 1950s, early 1960s, and late 1960s (Helson, Stewart, & Ostrove, 1995). The primary objective of all of these studies was to discover whether personality changes are obvious across different life paths and whether those changes support theories of adult development and personality. A second objective was to compare the life cycles of men and women, since previous long-term studies had failed to address that vital issue. The researchers wondered whether life cycles for adulthood need to be rethought. Do women have midlife transitions, as men do?

Method. Helson and Moane began their work in 1958 at Mills College, a private women's college located in Oakland, California. They gathered information from the same 81 women at ages 21, 27, and 43. In using this longitudinal method, they studied a single group of people at different times to determine whether changes had occurred over time. (For a review of this method, see Chapter 10, page 334.) The researchers used several measures of personality, including the California Psychological Inventory (CPI). The CPI, which is commonly used to study people from mid-adolescence to old age, is a test of normal personality. Designed to assess effectiveness in interpersonal functioning, it examines confidence, independence, responsibility, socialization, self-control, tolerance, and flexibility, among other dimensions.

Correlational Results. The results, reported as correlations among the different measures of personality, showed interesting stabilities and changes. For example, when the women were between the

behaviours of a model and thus develop a specific set of behavioural tendencies. Personality is thus seen as developing through the process of observation and imitation.

Observational learning theories stress the importance of the relationship between the observer and the model in eliciting imitative behaviour. When children view the behaviour of a parent or other important figure, their imitative behaviour is significantly more extensive than when they observe the actions of someone less important to them. For example, a boy is more likely to adopt his father's hurried behaviour than his neighbour's relaxed attitude, even if he spends roughly equal amounts of time with each.

People can learn abnormal, as well as acceptable, behaviour and personality characteristics through imitation. In fact, the most notable behaviour that people observe and then imitate may be violence. As we will see in Chapter 13, children who observe a violent TV program are more willing to hurt others after watching the program. If children observe people who are reinforced for violent, aggressive behaviour, they are more likely to imitate that behaviour than more socially desirable behaviours.

ages of 21 and 27, they took control of their lives, acknowledged differences between the way the world ought to be and the way it was, and scored higher on tolerance, social maturity, and femininity than they did later in life. At ages 27 and 43, they scored higher in the areas of dominance, independence, and confidence, but lower in flexibility and femininity. The changes from 27 to 43 were greater than the changes from 21 to 27. As the women grew older, they became more organized, committed, and work-oriented, but less open to change.

The results of this study are consistent with adult life cycle theories of development that have focused on men. From ages 21 to 43, there were increases in self-discipline and commitment to duties; this typically occurs with men, too. The women became more confident, independent, and work-oriented. Until age 27, the changes were small, but after age 27, the women focused less on gender-specific tasks such as child care and more on gaining independence and confidence and on developing a career. Later in life, women became happier than their husbands, but both men and women were happier in late adulthood than in their child-rearing years (Wink & Helson, 1993).

Conclusions. Like Daniel Levinson (1996), both Helson and Moane (1987) and Wink and Helson (1993) maintain that women's and men's personalities change in consistent and predictable ways between the ages of 21 (young adulthood) and 43 (middle age). They believe, for example, that a career requires a person to develop skills, confidence, and insight into others—things that were not necessary at earlier life stages for some women. From the researchers' view, personality is not static; rather, it is a constantly evolving set of skills and abilities acquired to cope with the demands and dilemmas that face maturing individuals. This view is consistent with that of stage theorists like Levinson, but it presents problems for trait theorists (e.g., McCrae & Costa, 1994), who assert that personality is stable during the life span.

Implications. The researchers conducted their studies during a time of rapid change in women's roles in society, from 1960 through 1985. Were the changes that occurred then similar to the changes that are taking place now or to the changes that will occur in the next 20 years? Women aged 21 to 27 today may not show the same patterns. Research is addressing various possibilities. For example, Helson and Picano (1990)

have shown that women who filled more traditional roles early in life but later joined the labour force are able to adapt their personalities to new sets of demands. This is especially true if they are well educated and seek independence—traits more typically found in women of the most recent generations than in older, more traditionally raised participants (Helson, Stewart, & Ostrove, 1995).

The 1960 to 1985 research did not specifically address the implications for personality of certain lifestyle variations; many women, for example, opt for a career first and children later. Socioeconomic status and societal changes determine so many lifestyle, educational, and work issues that they need to be examined, too. Further, new research must consider results in a historical context, taking into account changing political, social, and moral values. Finally, a 20-year longitudinal study of college women of the 1990s will be needed to determine whether Helson and Moane's findings are still valid for today's generation. ■

Observational learning theories assume that learning a new response through imitation can occur without reinforcement, but that later reinforcement acts to maintain such learned behaviour and thus to maintain personality characteristics. Most people, for example, have observed aggressive, hostile behaviour in others but still choose different ways to express emotions. Together, the imitative aspects of observational learning theories and the reinforcement properties of conditioned learning can account for most behaviours. For example, a daughter may become logical and forthright by watching her lawyer mother prepare arguments for court cases and seeing her win.

Researchers who focus on observational learning recognize that people choose to show some behaviours and to omit others. Accordingly, some researchers focus on observational learning in combination with another element—thought (cognition). The cognitive approaches to personality, which we will examine next, focus on the interaction of thoughts and behaviour.

Cognitive Approaches: Dynamics of Personality

Behaviourists, especially the early behaviourists, were single-minded in their belief that psychologists should study only observable, measurable behaviour. But, of course, human beings have an inner psychic life; they think about things and react emotionally, and those thoughts and reactions are not always evident in observable behaviour. In important ways, cognitive approaches to personality appeared as a reaction to strict behavioural models, adding a new dimension. The cognitive emphasis is on the interaction of thoughts and behaviour. Cognitive approaches consider the uniqueness of human beings, especially of their thought processes, and assume that human beings are decision makers, planners, and evaluators of behaviour. Rather than viewing people as having stable traits, cognitive approaches assume that people are more fluid and dynamic in their behaviour and responses to the world.

Cognitive views have been influenced by the humanistic idea that people are essentially good and strive to be better. George Kelly (1955) was one of the first psychologists to assert that people make rational choices in trying to predict and manage events in the world. Many contemporary researchers claim that people can change their behaviour, their conceptions of themselves, and their personalities in a short time if they are willing to change their thoughts.

Key Cognitive Concepts

From a cognitive point of view, the mere association of stimuli and responses is not enough for conditioning and learning to occur in human beings; thought processes also have to be involved. Thought and behaviour affect one another. According to cognitive theory, a person exhibits learned behaviour that is based on the situation and personal needs at a particular time. If thought and behaviour are closely intertwined, then when something affects a person's thoughts, it should also affect his or her behaviour. If a man who adopts "thought stopping" as a therapy technique mentally yells, "Stop!" whenever his thoughts become hostile, he should be successful in quelling his disagreeable language.

One of the key concepts of the cognitive approach to personality is the idea that people develop self-schemata. As we saw in Chapters 6 and 11, a *schema* is a conceptual framework by which people make sense of the world. Self-schemata (*schemata* is the plural of *schema*) are series of ideas and self-knowledge that organize how people think about themselves. They are often global themes that help individuals define themselves. A man's self-schemata may comprise a self-schema that involves exercise, another that concerns his wife, and still others that are about schoolwork, family, and religious feelings. Cognitive researchers assert that people's self-schemata help shape their day-to-day behaviour. They may affect people's adjustment, maladjustment, and ability to regulate their own behaviour. Thus, someone who holds a self-schema for being in control of her emotions may find the death of a loved one a unique challenge to normal day-to-day coping mechanisms.

Over the years, a number of cognitive constructs and theories have been developed, dealing with how people perceive themselves and their relationship with the world. Many classic theories that attempt to explain all aspects of personality and behaviour have been criticized because they are difficult to study scientifically. The ego in Freud's theory, for example, is not a physiological structure or state that can be manipulated or studied. Similarly, the concepts of self and of maximizing potential in Rogers's theory are difficult to measure and assess. As a reaction to imprecise grand theories, psychologists have developed smaller, better-researched theories. These theories, many of which follow a cognitive approach, account for specific behaviours in specific situations. Because their concepts are well defined, they are easier to test. We will consider three such concepts and theories next: Julian Rotter's concept of locus of control, Albert Bandura's concept of self-efficacy, and Walter Mischel's concept of cognitive social learning. Each helps clarify different aspects of personality.

Locus of Control

When patients seek the help of a therapist they often do so because they feel "a lack of control" in their life. And often the task of therapy is to help clients realize what forces are shaping events and what they can do to gain a sense of control. One widely studied cognitive–behavioural theory that is often used to help researchers and therapists is locus of control, introduced in the 1950s and systematically developed by Julian Rotter and Herbert Lefcourt. *Locus of control* involves the extent to which individuals believe that a reinforcer or an outcome is contingent on their own behaviour or personal characteristics rather than being a function of external events not under their control or simply unpredictable (Lefcourt, 1992; Rotter, 1990). Rotter focused on whether people place their locus of control inside themselves (internal) or in their environments (external). Locus of control influences how people view the world and how they identify the causes of success or failure in their lives. In an important way, it reflects people's personalities—their views of the world and their reactions to it.

To examine locus of control, Rotter developed a test consisting of a series of statements about oneself and other people. To determine whether your locus of control is internal or external, ask yourself to what extent you agree with the statements in Table 12.4. People with an internal locus of control feel a need to control their environment. They are more likely to engage in preventive health measures and dieting than are external people. University students characterized as having an internal locus of control are more likely than others to profit from psychotherapy and to show high academic achievement (Lefcourt & Davidson-Katz, 1991). Similarly, hospital nurses characterized as having a strong internal locus of control are more likely to attempt to reform unjust situations (Parker, 1993). In contrast, people with an external locus of control believe they have little control over their lives. A university student characterized as having an external locus of control may attribute a poor grade to a lousy teacher, feeling there was nothing he or she could have done to get a good grade. Individuals who develop an internal locus of control, on the other hand, feel they can master any course they take because they believe that through hard work they can do well in any subject—in general they report less stress in their lives (Carton & Nowicki, 1994; Carton, Nowicki, & Balser, 1996).

Table 12.4   Statements Reflecting Internal versus External Locus of Control

Internal Locus of Control		External Locus of Control
People's misfortunes result from the mistakes they make.	*versus*	Many of the unhappy things in people's lives are partly due to bad luck.
With enough effort, we can wipe out political corruption.	*versus*	It is difficult to have much control over the things politicians do in office.
There is a direct connection between how hard I study and the grade I get.	*versus*	Sometimes I can't understand how teachers arrive at the grades they give.
What happens to me is my own doing.	*versus*	Sometimes I feel that I don't have enough control over the direction my life is taking.

INTERNAL LOCUS OF CONTROL

SPECIFIC EXPECTANCY: Hard work leads to wealth. ⟷ SPECIFIC BEHAVIOUR: Long hours at new job ⟷ GENERAL EXPECTANCY: I control my reinforcements.

EXTERNAL LOCUS OF CONTROL

SPECIFIC EXPECTANCY: Luck is the most important tactic in becoming wealthy. ⟷ SPECIFIC BEHAVIOUR: Punching a clock and doing only what is required at a new job ⟷ GENERAL EXPECTANCY: I have no control over my reinforcements.

FIGURE 12.2
Locus of Control
A person's general expectations about life are determined in a three-part process: Specific expectancies result in specific behaviours, which are reinforced. This cycle eventually leads to a general expectancy about life, which underlies either an internal or an external locus of control.

Self-efficacy: A person's belief about whether he or she can successfully engage in and execute a specific behaviour.

People develop expectations based on their beliefs about the sources of reinforcement in their environments. These expectations lead to specific behaviours. Reinforcement of these behaviours in turn strengthens expectancy and leads to increased belief in internal or external control (see Figure 12.2). Not surprisingly, in therapeutic situations where self-esteem is an issue, psychologists often seek to bolster a client's self-esteem by helping them recognize the things they can control effectively (Betz, 1992).

Locus of control integrates personality theory, expectancy theories, and reinforcement theory. It describes several specific behaviours but is not comprehensive enough to explain all, or even most, of an individual's behaviour. For example, people often develop disproportionately negative thoughts about themselves and acquire a poor sense of self-esteem. Sometimes this is shown in the behaviour pattern known as *shyness* (which was discussed in *Brain and Behaviour* on p. 424). Bandura's theory, which we examine next, specifically addresses people's thoughts about their own effectiveness.

Self-Efficacy

Albert Bandura developed one of the most influential cognitive theories of personality. His conception of personality began with observational learning theory and the idea that human beings observe, think about, and imitate behaviour (Bandura, 1977a). Bandura played a major role in reintroducing thought processes into learning and personality theory.

Bandura argued that people's expectations of mastery and achievement and their convictions about their own effectiveness determine the types of behaviour they will engage in and the amount of risk they will undertake (Bandura, 1977a, 1977b). He used the term **self-efficacy** to describe a person's belief about whether he or she can successfully engage in and execute a specific behaviour. Judgments about self-efficacy determine how much effort people will expend and how long they will persist in the face of obstacles (Bandura, 1997).

A strong sense of self-efficacy allows people to feel free to select, influence, and even construct the circumstances of their own lives. Also, people's perceived self-efficacy in managing a situation heightens their sense that they can control it (Conyers, Enright, & Strauser, 1998). Thus, people who have strong beliefs in their self-efficacy are more likely than others to attribute success to variables within themselves rather than to chance factors, and are more likely to pursue their own goals (Bandura, 1988; McAuley, Duncan, & McElroy, 1989). Because people can think about their motivation, and even their own thoughts, they can effect changes in themselves and persevere during tough times (Sterrett, 1998).

Bad luck or non-reinforcing experiences can damage a developing sense of self-efficacy. Observation of positive, prosocial models during the formative years, on the other hand, can help people to develop a strong sense of self-efficacy that will encourage and reinforce them in directing their own lives. Bandura's theory allows individual flexibility in behaviour. People are not locked into specific responses to specific stimuli, as some strict behaviourists might assert. According to Bandura, people choose the behaviours they will imitate, and they are free to adapt their behaviour to any situation. Self-efficacy both determines and flows from feelings of self-worth. Accordingly, people's sense of self-efficacy determines how they may present themselves to other people. For example, a man whom others view as successful may not share that view, and a man who has achieved little of note to society may consider himself a capable and worthy person. Each of these men will present himself as he sees himself (as a failure or a worthy person), not as others see him.

Bandura's theory is optimistic. It is a long way from Freud's view, which argues that conflicting biologically based forces determine human behaviour. It is also a long way from a strict behavioural theory, which suggests that environmental contingencies shape behaviour. Bandura believes that human beings have choices, that they direct the course of their lives. He also believes in a process called *reciprocal determinism* in which people both determine and are determined by the interactions they have with others and their environments.

Gender and Self-Efficacy. Men and women develop differently, both physiologically and socially, and this difference affects their self-efficacy. As children, boys are more likely than girls to play in large groups where opportunities for discussion are minimized; girls, in contrast, more frequently play in small groups in which interpersonal awareness is more likely to be heightened. In addition, boys may be encouraged more than girls to become involved in competitive, achievement-related activities (L. D. Cohn, 1991). In general, adult males have higher self-esteem than females, and this gender difference stays fairly constant across ages, educational levels, and cultures (Feingold, 1994).

Self-efficacy is affected by the cultural variables that define men's and women's roles. Research that has manipulated participants' view of performance on various tasks shows that a person's sense of self-efficacy is related to that person's fulfilment of culturally mandated, gender-appropriate norms (Josephs, Markus, & Tafarodi, 1992). Men more than women focus on independence and distinctiveness; women more than men focus on interdependence and good relations. From these different focuses, both men and women derive a sense of self-efficacy.

Cognitive Social Learning

Like Bandura, Walter Mischel claims that thought is crucial in determining human behaviour; like Bandura, Mischel believes that both past experiences and current reinforcement are important. But Mischel is an *interactionist*—he focuses on the interaction of people and their environment (Mischel, 1983). Mischel and other cognitive theorists argue that people respond flexibly to various situations. They change their responses based on their past experiences and their assessment of the present situation (Brown & Moskowitz, 1998). This process of adjustment is called *self-regulation*. People make subtle adjustments in their tone of voice and overt behaviour (their personality), depending on the context in which they find themselves. Those who tend to be warm, caring, and attentive, for example, can in certain situations become hostile and aggressive.

People's personalities, and particularly their responses to any given stimulus, are determined by several variables (Mischel, 1979): *competencies* (what people know and can do), *encoding strategies* (the way they process, attend to, and select information), *expectancies* (their anticipation of outcomes), *personal values* (the importance they attach to various aspects of life), and *self-regulatory systems* (the systems of rules they have established for themselves to guide their behaviour).

Mischel has had a great impact on psychological thought because he has challenged researchers to consider the idea that traits alone cannot predict behaviour, that the context of the situation must be considered. The context means not only the immediate situation but also the culture in which a person lives and was raised, as well as other variables such as the gender and age of the person whose behaviour is being predicted. Day-to-day variations in behaviour should not be seen as aberrations, but rather as meaningful, predictable responses (Brown & Moskowitz, 1998).

Cognitive Theories Evolve

From the view of cognitive personality theorists, human uniqueness can best be explained by the idea that reinforcement, past experiences, current feelings, future expectations, and subjective values all influence people's responses to their environments. Human beings have characteristic ways of responding, but those ways—

Focus

Review

◆ Identify three key behavioural concepts used to explain personality development. pp. 428–429
◆ What is locus of control? p. 433
◆ Why is Mischel called an interactionist? p. 435

Think Critically

◆ What are some possible explanations a cognitive psychologist might offer for the constancy of personality?
◆ If a person has an internal locus of control, under what conditions do you think he or she would be likely to develop maladjustment or extreme anxiety?

their personalities—change, depending on specific circumstances.

Cognitive theories of personality are well researched but not yet complete; they do not, for example, clearly explain the development of personality from childhood to adulthood. They also are not yet well integrated. Bandura, for example, has shifted his focus from observational learning to self-regulation to self-efficacy without tying the threads of those research areas together. Bandura never claimed to develop a complete theory of personality and this incompleteness signifies that personality research and theory are exceedingly complex and subtle—further research and new ideas are still needed to generate more complete, sophisticated theories.

Personality theories are diverse, and their explanations and accounts of specific behaviours vary sharply. Each one views the development of personality and maladjustment from a different vantage point. See Building Table 12.2 for an overall summary of the personality theories presented in this chapter.

When a practitioner, regardless of orientation, meets a client, there are several ways the client can be evaluated. These techniques are the focus of personality assessment, the topic we will consider next.

Personality Assessment

When you think to yourself that your neighbour is a fun-loving guy, that your mom is an affectionate person, or that your brother is politically skilful you are making assessments of their personality. We all do it from time to time, and psychologists do it systematically.

Assessment is the process of evaluating individual differences among human beings by techniques such as tests, interviews, observations, and recordings of physiological processes. Psychologists who conduct assessments are constantly seeking ways to evaluate personality in order to explain behaviour, to diagnose and classify maladjusted people, and to develop treatment plans when necessary. Many individuals and organizations give tests—school systems may give IQ tests, for example—but these are not full-blown assessments. Businesses conduct assessments for personnel selection; assessments are also used to supplement psychological research on personality types.

Therapists sometimes conduct assessments of clients who may be in distress. In this forum, an assessment is done by a psychologist who has a relationship with a client, and the type of examination used is determined by the client's needs (Matarazzo, 1990). Often, more than one assessment procedure is needed to provide all of the necessary information, and many psychologists administer a group, or *battery*, of tests. The goal of the examiner is to use a variety of available tests so that when the information is taken together, an intelligent, informed conclusion can be drawn. As Kaufman (1990, p. 29) asserts, "Psychologists need to be shrewd detectives to uncover test interpretations that are truly 'individual' . . . and will ultimately help the person referred for evaluation."

A psychologist may assess personality with the Minnesota Multiphasic Personality Inventory–2nd Edition (MMPI–2) (discussed later in this section), intelligence with the WAIS–III (an intelligence test), and a specific skill (such as coordination) with some

Assessment: The process of evaluating individual differences among human beings by techniques such as tests, interviews, observations, and recordings of physiological processes.

Building Table 12.2

Psychoanalytic, Humanistic, Trait and Type, Behavioural, and Cognitive Approaches to Personality

Approach	Major Proponent	Core of Personality	Structure of Personality	Development	Cause of Problems
Psychoanalytic	Sigmund Freud	Maximizes gratification while minimizing punishment or guilt; instinctual unconscious urges direct behaviour	Id, ego, superego	Five stages: oral, anal, phallic, latency, genital	Imbalances between the id, ego, and superego, resulting in fixations
Humanistic	Carl Rogers	Actualizes, maintains, and enhances the experiences of life through the process of self-actualization	Self	Process of cumulative self-actualization and development of sense of self-worth	Incongruence between self and concept of ideal self
Trait and Type	Gordon Allport	Organizes responses in characteristic modes	Traits	Process of learning new traits	Having learned faulty or inappropriate traits
Behavioural	B. F. Skinner	Reduction of social and biological needs that energize behaviour through learned responses	Responses	Process of learning new responses	Having learned faulty or inappropriate behaviours
Cognitive	Several, including Rotter, Bandura, and Mischel	Responses depend on a changing environment, and the person responds after thinking about the environmental context	Responses determined by thoughts	Process of thinking about new responses	Inappropriate thoughts or faulty reasoning

other specific test. More confidence can be placed in data gathered from several tests than in the data from a single test; as *Experiencing Psychology* on page 438 shows, no single test can characterize a personality completely. Hundreds of psychological tests exist; there are more than 100 tests just for measuring the various elements of anxiety. The purpose of the testing determines the type of tests administered.

experiencing psychology

Can Personality Be Assessed Accurately with a Single Test?

W hether you are trying to select a career path or develop smoother working relationships with your co-workers, you might find that personality tests can help you. Personality tests, along with interest and ability tests, for example, can be useful in predicting vocational preferences. One of the tests frequently used for this purpose was developed in the 1960s by Peter Myers and Isabel Briggs.

The Myers–Briggs Type Indicator, often called the MBTI, is a test based on Jung's theory of personality. Jung proposed that each individual favours specific modalities, or ways of dealing with and learning about the world; the modalities that you prefer define your personality type. The MBTI asks you to choose between pairs of statements that deal with your preferences or inclinations. For instance: "Do you think that having a daily routine is (a) an easy way to get things done, or (b) difficult even when necessary?"

The MBTI is scored so that an individual is characterized as predominantly at one pole or another on four distinct dimensions:

Extroversion–Introversion (E or I), Sensing–Intuition (S or N), Thinking–Feeling (T or F), and Judging–Perceptive (J or P). An individual can score high in each of these bipolar dimensions. The various possible combinations yield 16 personality types. For example, an ENFP type is an individual whose principal modes are extroversion, intuition, feeling, and perception. This person feels a greater relatedness to the outer world of people than to the inner world of ideas (E), tends to look for possibilities rather than work with what is known (N), makes decisions based on personal values rather than logic (F), and shows a preference for a spontaneous way of life rather than an orderly existence (P).

Unfortunately, the MBTI has many problems. It can be scored in sophisticated ways, but often it is simply interpreted by unskilled examiners for purposes of vocational counselling. The MBTI was normed for students in grades 4 through 12, so it is best used for individuals of those ages. Cultural vantage points are not considered, and individual differ-

ences are not taken into account. Further, the likelihood of maladjustment is not considered, nor is the development of personality. Further, the ability of the MBTI to reliably predict work or other behaviour has not been solidly demonstrated.

In fairness, the MBTI is a quick and easy way to gather basic data about personality; when combined with other personality instruments such as the MMPI–2, the California Psychological Inventory, and the 16PF questionnaire, it can be useful in helping a skilled clinician evaluate important elements about an individual—for example, stress level (Ware, Rytting, & Jenkins, 1994). Research also shows that the MBTI can be used to assess the quality of therapeutic relationships and the extent to which people are able to perceive consumer messages, and that it can be helpful in designing techniques for classroom management (Carland et al., 1994; Claxton & McIntyre, 1994; Nelson & Stake, 1994). But, as we saw in Chapter 8, no single test score can reveal everything about an individual, despite what some might claim. ■

Objective Personality Tests

 Next to intelligence tests, the most widely given tests are *objective personality tests*. These tests, sometimes called *personality inventories*, generally consist of true/false or multiple-choice questions. The aims of objective personality tests vary. Raymond Cattell developed a test called the 16PF (the name refers to 16 personality factors) to screen job applicants and to examine individuals who fall within a normal range of personality functioning. The California Psychological Inventory (CPI) is used primarily to identify and assess normal aspects of personality. Using a large sample of normal subjects as a reference group, it examines personality traits such as sociability, self-control, and responsibility. Well-constructed personality tests turn out to be valid predictors of performance in a wide array of jobs; this is true for people of various ethnicities and minority status groups (Hogan, Hogan, & Roberts, 1996).

One of the most widely used and best-researched personality tests is the Minnesota Multiphasic Personality Inventory–2nd Edition (MMPI–2). The original MMPI was widely used, and the second edition, published in 1989, is considered to be a major revision. The MMPI–2 consists of 567 true/false statements that focus on attitudes, feelings, motor disturbances, and bodily complaints. A series of sub-scales examine different aspects of functioning and measure the truthfulness of the examinee's responses; these subscales, called the clinical and validity scales, are shown in Table 12.5. In 1992 a special version of the MMPI, called the MMPI–A, was developed for adolescents. Items on this test cover adolescent issues such as eating disorders, substance abuse, and family and school problems. Typical statements on the MMPI–2 include:

I tire easily.
I become very anxious before examinations.
I worry about sex matters.
I become bored easily.

The MMPI–2 can be administered individually or to a group. The test takes 90 minutes to complete and can be scored in less than half an hour. It provides a profile

Table 12.5 The Clinical and Validity Scales of the MMPI–2

Scale Name	Interpretation
Clinical Scales	
1. Hypochondriasis (Hs)	High scorers reflect an exaggerated concern about their physical health.
2. Depression (D)	High scorers are usually depressed, despondent, and distressed.
3. Hysteria (Hy)	High scorers complain often about physical symptoms, which have no apparent organic cause.
4. Psychopathic deviate (Pd)	High scorers show a disregard for social and moral standards.
5. Masculinity/femininity (Mf)	Extreme scorers show "traditional" masculine or feminine attitudes and values.
6. Paranoia (Pa)	High scorers demonstrate extreme suspiciousness and feelings of persecution.
7. Psychasthenia (Pt)	High scorers tend to be highly anxious, rigid, tense, and worried.
8. Schizophrenia (Sc)	High scorers tend to be socially withdrawn and to engage in bizarre and unusual thinking.
9. Hypomania (Ma)	High scorers are emotionally excitable, energetic, and impulsive.
10. Social introversion (S)	High scorers tend to be modest, self-effacing, and shy.
Validity Scales	
1. Cannot say (?)	High scorers may be evasive in filling out the questionnaire.
2. Lie (L)	High scorers attempt to present themselves in a very favourable light and possibly tell lies to do so.
3. Infrequency (F)	High scorers are presenting themselves in a particularly bad way and may well be "faking bad."
4. Defensiveness (K)	High scorers may be very defensive in filling out the questionnaire.

Projective tests: Personality-assessing devices or instruments in which examinees are shown a standard set of ambiguous stimuli and asked to respond in an unrestricted manner.

that lets psychologists assess an individual's current level of functioning and characteristic way of dealing with the world, and it provides a description of some specific personality characteristics. The MMPI–2 also enables psychologists to make reasonable predictions about a person's ability to function in specific situations, such as working in a mental hospital or as a security guard. Many businesses today require job applicants to take the MMPI–2 as part of the screening process for certain jobs.

Generally, the MMPI–2 is used as a screening device for maladjustment. Its norms are based on the profiles of thousands of normal people and a smaller group of psychiatric patients. These norms show the range of scores that "normal" individuals obtain on each scale. In general, a score significantly above normal may be considered evidence of maladjustment. The test has built-in safeguards to prevent test takers from controlling the test's outcome. Interpretation of the MMPI–2 generally involves looking at patterns of scores, rather than at a single scale.

Nearly 5000 published studies have examined the validity and reliability of the original MMPI. For the most part, these studies have supported the MMPI as a valid and useful predictive tool. The MMPI–2 was standardized using a much larger sample (2600 people) of subjects, who were more representative of the overall population than were the initial group of subjects. It includes questions that focus on eating disorders and drug abuse; older questions that had a gender bias have been revised. Because many of the test's traditional features remain unchanged, the refinements and modifications should only improve its predictive validity (Butcher et al., 1990). Yet the MMPI–2 is by no means a perfect instrument for valid predictions about future behaviour; it should be considered as only one in a battery of tests (Helmes & Reddon, 1993).

Projective Tests

The fundamental idea underlying the use of projective techniques is that a person's unconscious motives direct daily thoughts and behaviour. To uncover a person's unconscious motives, psychologists have developed **projective tests**—devices or instruments used to assess personality in which an examinee is shown a standard set of ambiguous stimuli and asked to respond in an unrestricted manner. The examinees are assumed to project their unconscious feelings, drives, and motives onto the ambiguous stimuli. Clinicians assess the deeper levels of an examinee's personality structure and uncover motives of which the individual may not be aware. They tend to be used by psychoanalytically oriented psychologists, they do not have the standard psychometric properties associated with tests like an IQ test, and they are less reliable than objective personality tests, but they help complete a picture of psychological functioning.

Rorschach Inkblot Test. One classic projective test is the *Rorschach Inkblot Test* (see Figure 12.3). Ten inkblots are shown to the person, one at a time. Five are black and white, two have some red ink, and three have various pastel colours. The inkblots are symmetrical, with a specific shape or form. Examinees tell the clinician what they see in the design, and a detailed report of the response is made for later interpretation. Aiken (1988, p. 390) reports a typical response:

FIGURE 12.3
The Rorschach Inkblot Test
In a Rorschach Inkblot Test, the psychologist asks a person to describe what he or she sees in an inkblot such as this one. From the person's descriptions, the psychologist makes inferences about his or her drives, motivations, and unconscious conflicts.

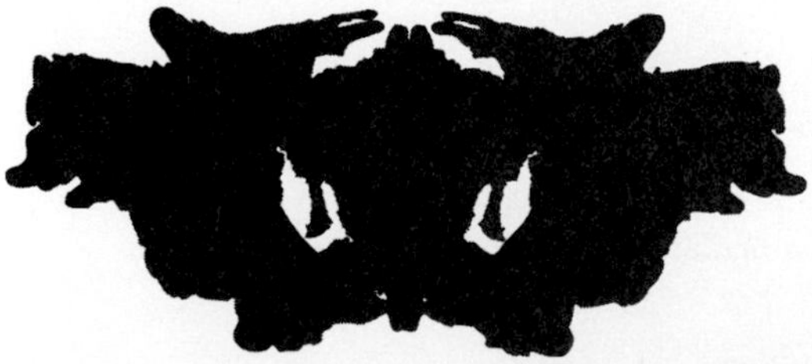

> My first impression was a big bug, a fly maybe. I see in the background two facelike figures pointing toward each other as if they're talking. It also has a resemblance to a skeleton—the pelvis area. I see a cute little bat right in the middle. The upper half looks like a mouse.

After the inkblots have been shown, the examiner asks specific questions, such as "Describe the face-like figures" and "What were the figures talking about?" Although norms are available for responses, skilled interpretation and good clinical judgment are necessary for placing an individual's responses in a meaningful context. Long-term predictions can be formulated only with great caution (Exner, Thomas, & Mason, 1985) because of a lack of substantive supporting research (Wood, Nezworski, & Stejskal, 1996).

Thematic Apperception Test. The *Thematic Apperception Test* (TAT) is much more structured than the Rorschach. (The TAT was discussed in Chapter 9 as one way to assess a person's need for achievement.) It consists of black-and-white pictures, each depicting one or more people in an ambiguous situation; examinees are asked to tell a story describing the situation. Specifically, they are asked what led up to the situation, what will happen in the future, and what the people are thinking and feeling. The TAT is primarily useful as part of a battery of tests to assess a person's characteristic way of dealing with others and of interacting with the world.

To some extent, projective tests have a bad reputation among non-psychoanalytically oriented psychologists. Most argue that the interpretation of pictures is too subjective and prone to error. Even when they use projective tests, practising clinicians often rely heavily on behavioural assessment approaches, discussed next.

Behavioural Assessment

Traditionally, *behavioural assessment* focused on overt behaviours that could be examined directly. Today, practitioners and researchers examine cognitive activity as well. Their aim is to gather information to both diagnose maladjustment and prescribe treatment. Four popular and widely used behavioural assessment techniques are behavioural assessment interviews, naturalistic observation, and self-monitoring.

Behavioural Assessment Interviews. Any psychological assessment is likely to begin with an interview. Interviews are personal, giving the client (and the client's family) an opportunity to express feelings, facts, and experiences that might not be expressed through other assessment procedures. Interviews yield important information about the client's family situation, occupational stresses, and other events that affect the behaviour being examined. They also allow psychologists to evaluate the client's motivations as well as to inform the client about the assessment process.

Behavioural assessment interviews tend to be systematic and structured, focusing on overt and current behaviours and paying attention to the situations in which these behaviours occur. The interviewer will ask the examinee about the events that led up to a specific response, how the examinee felt while making the response, and whether the same response might occur in other situations. Through this type of interview, the clinician has the opportunity to select the problems to be dealt with in therapy and to set treatment goals. Many clinicians consider their first interview with a client to be a key component in the assessment process. Interviews reveal only what the interviewee wishes to disclose, however, and are subject to bias on the part of the interviewer. Nonetheless, when followed up with other behavioural measures, interviews are a good starting point.

Naturalistic Observation. In behavioural assessment, naturalistic observation involves an observer entering a client's natural environment and recording the occurrence of specified behaviours at predetermined intervals. Ideally there should be two observers to check for accuracy and reliability, but most often there is only one observer. In a personality assessment, for example, psychologists might observe how often a child jumps out of his seat while in a school classroom or how often a hospitalized patient refers to her depressed state. The purpose of naturalistic observation as a behavioural assessment technique is to observe people without interfering with their behaviour. The strength of the approach is in providing information that might

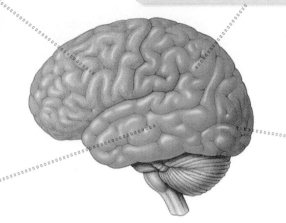

FRONTAL LOBES: These lobes are integrally involved in ordering information and sorting out stimuli. Damage to this area may affect concentration and attention, abstract thinking ability, concept formation ability, foresight, problem-solving ability, speech, and fine motor ability.

PARIETAL LOBES: These lobes contain reception areas for the sense of touch and for the sense of body position. Damage to this area may result in disorganization, distorted self-perception, and deficits in the sense of touch.

OCCIPITAL LOBES: These lobes contain visual reception areas. Damage to this area could result in blindness in all or part of the visual field or deficits in object recognition, visual scanning, visual integration of symbols into wholes, or recall of visual imagery.

TEMPORAL LOBES: These lobes contain auditory reception areas as well as certain areas for the processing of visual information. Damage to this area may affect sound discrimination, recognition, and comprehension; music appreciation; voice recognition; and auditory or visual memory storage.

FIGURE 12.4
Some Brain–Behaviour Characteristics for Selected Sites in the Brain

(Adapted from Cohen et al., 1988.)

Self-monitoring: An assessment procedure in which a person systematically counts and records the frequency and duration of his or her own specific behaviours.

otherwise be unavailable or difficult to piece together. For example, observation can help psychologists learn the sequences of events that can lead up to an outburst of antisocial behaviours.

Naturalistic observation is not without its problems, however. How does a researcher record behaviour in a home setting without influencing that behaviour by simply being present? Do naturalistic samples of behaviour in one setting represent interactions in other settings? Does the observer have any biases, make inaccurate judgments, or collect inadequate data? Although naturalistic observation is not perfect, it is a powerful technique.

Self-Monitoring. Self-monitoring is an assessment procedure in which a person systematically counts and records the frequency and duration of his or her own specific behaviours. One person might record the number and duration of symptoms such as migraine headaches, backaches, or feelings of panic. Another person might self-monitor his or her eating or sleeping patterns, sexual behaviour, or smoking. Self-monitoring is inexpensive, easy to do, and applicable to a variety of problems. While there is concern about the reliability of the data, self-monitoring reveals information that otherwise might be inaccessible, and it enables practitioners to probe the events that preceded the monitored activity to see if some readily identifiable pattern exists. In addition, self-monitoring helps clients become more aware of their own behaviours and the situations in which they occur.

Neuropsychological Assessment

Personality changes and some forms of maladjustment sometimes result from a brain disorder or a malfunction in the nervous system (see Figure 12.4 for examples). One way to detect such disorders is neuropsychological assessment. (Neurologists are physicians who study the

Focus

Review

◆ What is the goal of a projective test? pp. 440–441
◆ Identify the techniques of behavioural assessment. pp. 441–442

Think Critically

◆ Do you think the TAT and the Rorschach Inkblot Test achieve their goals?
◆ What aspects of personality do you think a personality test might be unable to characterize?

physiology of the brain and its disorders; neuropsychologists are psychologists who study the brain and its disorders as they relate to behaviour.) Neuropsychology is a traditional area in experimental psychology and employment of its techniques enables practitioners to watch for signs of neuropsychological disorders.

The signs of neuropsychological disorders may become evident through the use of traditional assessment devices such as histories (a history of headaches, for example), intelligence tests (showing slow reaction times), or observation of the client during a session (the occurrence of head motions or muscle spasms). Thus, if a child who makes obscene gestures or remarks frequently and inappropriately accompanies them with facial tics, the practitioner may suspect the existence of the neurological disorder known as Tourette's syndrome, in which such behaviours are often evident. Psychologists who see evidence of neuropsychological deficits often refer the client with the problem to a neuropsychologist or neurologist for further evaluation.

Summary and Review

Psychoanalytic Theory

What are the fundamental assumptions about human behaviour and the mind that underlie Freud's theory?

■ *Psychic determinism* suggests that actions or events that happened to an individual in the past determine all current thoughts, feelings, actions, gestures, and speech. *Unconscious motivation* suggests that behaviour is determined by desires, goals, and internal states of which an individual is unaware. Freud also theorized that people are constantly in conflict because of two basic instinctual drives buried deep within the unconscious—life, which prominently features sex and sexual energy, and death, which features aggression. p. 409

■ Freud's structure of *personality* includes three levels: *conscious, preconscious,* and *unconscious.* The primary structural elements of the mind and personality—the id, the ego, and the superego—are three forces that reside, fully or partially, in the unconscious. The *id,* which works through the pleasure principle, is the source of human instinctual energy. The *ego* tries to satisfy the instinctual needs in accordance with reality. The *superego* is the moral branch or aspect of mental functioning. pp. 409–411

■ Freud described the development of personality in terms of five consecutive stages: oral, anal, phallic, latency, and genital. In the *oral stage* newborns' instincts are focused on the mouth—their primary pleasure-

seeking centre. In the *anal stage* children learn to control the immediate gratification obtained through defecation and become responsive to the demands of society. In the *phallic stage* children obtain gratification primarily from the genitals. During this stage, children pass through the *Oedipus complex* (or Electra complex). In the *latency stage,* sexual urges are inactive. The *genital stage* is Freud's last stage of personality development, during which the sexual conflicts of childhood resurface at puberty and are resolved in adolescence. pp. 411–414

What is the fundamental function of all of Freud's defence mechanisms?

■ *Defence mechanisms* such as *projection, denial, reaction formation, sublimation,* and *rationalization* reduce anxiety by distorting one's perceptions of reality. Defence mechanisms allow the ego to deal with anxiety. For Freud, the most important defence mechanism is *repression*—in which people block anxiety-provoking feelings from conscious awareness and push them into the unconscious. pp. 414–415

To what fundamental assumptions of Freud did the neo-Freudians react?

■ A *neo-Freudian* (such as Jung or Adler) is a psychologist who modified or varied some of the basic ideas of Freud; these theorists usually attributed a greater influence to cultural and interpersonal factors than did Freud. Some neo-Freudians argued that Freud overemphasized sex and ignored many other key

issues. Other neo-Freudians asserted that the ego has more of a role than Freud thought in controlling behaviour and shaping personality. pp. 416–417

■ Jung emphasized unconscious processes as determinants of behaviour and believed that each person houses past events in the unconscious. The *collective unconscious* is a collection of emotionally charged ideas and images that have rich meaning and symbolism. In Adler's theory, people strive for mastery or perfection. This tendency is often prompted by feelings of inferiority. According to Adler, individuals develop a lifestyle that allows them to express their goals in the context of human society. pp. 417–419

KEY TERMS
personality, p. 408; psychic determinism, p. 409; unconscious motivation, p. 409; libido, p. 409; conscious, p. 409; preconscious, p. 409; unconscious, p. 410; id, p. 410; ego, p. 410; superego, p. 410; oral stage, p. 411; anal stage, p. 411; phallic stage, p. 413; Oedipus complex, p. 413; latency stage, p. 413; genital stage, p. 413; fixation, p. 413; defence mechanism, p. 414; repression, p. 414; projection, p. 414; denial, p. 414; reaction formation, p. 414; sublimation, p. 414; rationalization, p. 415; neo-Freudians, p. 416; collective unconscious, p. 417; archetypes, p. 417

Humanistic Approaches

What does self-actualization mean in the context of Maslow's and Rogers's personality theories?

■ In Maslow's theory, *self-actualization* is the process of realizing one's innate human potential to become the best one can be. The process of realizing potential, and of growing, is the process of becoming self-actualized. p. 420

■ The humanistic approach of Rogers states that *fulfilment* is the motivating force of personality development. Rogers focuses on the concept of *self*; the *ideal self* is the self that a person ideally would like to be. Persons with rigid self-concepts guard themselves against threatening feelings; they become unhappy when they are unable to fit new types of behaviour into their current self-concepts. pp. 420–422

KEY TERMS
fulfilment, p. 420; self, p. 420; ideal self, p. 420; self-actualization, p. 421

Trait and Type Theories: Dispositions

Distinguish between a trait and a type.

■ A *trait* is any readily identifiable stable quality that characterizes the ways in which an individual differs from other people; a *type* is a category in which broad collections of traits are loosely tied together and interrelated. A person can be said to have a trait, but a person fits a type. pp. 422–423

Describe the ideas of Allport, Cattell, and Eysenck regarding traits.

■ Allport argued that if you know a person's traits, it is possible to predict how he or she will respond to stimuli. Cardinal traits are ideas and behaviours that determine the direction of a person's life. Central traits are the qualities that characterize a person's daily interactions. Secondary traits are specific behaviours that occur in response to specific situations. Cattell used the technique of factor analysis to show that groups of traits tend to cluster together. Eysenck focused on types, which are higher levels of trait organization. Eysenck argued that all personality traits can be grouped along three basic dimensions: emotional stability, introversion–extroversion, and psychoticism. pp. 423–426

What are the Big Five?

■ Although dozens of traits exist, researchers think of the Big Five as "supertraits," the important dimensions that characterize personality. These are extroversion–introversion, or the extent to which people are social or calm; agreeableness–antagonism, or the extent to which people are good-natured or irritable; conscientiousness–undirectedness, or the extent to which people are reliable or undependable; neuroticism–stability, or the extent to which people are nervous or at ease; and openness to experience, or the extent to which people are independent or conforming. pp. 425–426

KEY TERMS
trait, p. 422; types, p. 423; shyness, p. 424

Behavioural Approaches: Learning Is Key

What are the key aspects of behavioural approaches to personality?

■ Behavioural theories of personality centre on precisely defined elements, such as the relationship between stimuli and responses, the strength of stimuli, and the strength, duration, and timing of reinforcers. For behaviourists, the structural unit of personality is the response. All behaviours are seen as responses to stimuli or as responses waiting for reinforcement. Behavioural psychologists try to discover behaviour patterns and use learning principles to help clients control their behaviour and shape their personalities. pp. 428–429

Identify three key behavioural concepts used to explain personality development.

■ Behavioural psychologists who focus on classical conditioning maintain that people develop fearfulness and anxiety through the process in which a neutral stimulus is paired with another stimulus that elicits some response. According to behaviourists who focus on operant conditioning, personality can be explained as spontaneous behaviour that is reinforced. Observational learning theorists see personality as developing through the process of observation and imitation and point out that learning can occur independent of reinforcement. pp. 429–431

Cognitive Approaches: Dynamics of Personality

What are the key ideas of the cognitive approach to personality?

■ The cognitive approach emphasizes the interaction of a person's thoughts and behaviour. It considers the uniqueness of human beings and assumes that human beings are decision makers, planners, and evaluators of behaviour. Cognitive views assert that people make rational choices in trying to predict and manage events in the world. One of the key concepts of the cognitive approach is the idea that people develop self-schemata—series of ideas and self-knowledge that organize how a person thinks about himself or herself. p. 432

■ Locus of control, according to Rotter, is the extent to which individuals believe that a reinforcement or an outcome is contingent on their own behaviour or personal characteristics, rather than not being under their control or being unpredictable. People classified as having an internal locus of control feel in control of their environment and future; people with an external locus of control believe that they have little control over their lives. pp. 433–434

■ *Self-efficacy*, in Bandura's theory, is a person's belief about whether he or she can successfully engage in and execute a specific behaviour. Judgments about self-efficacy determine how much effort people will expend and how long they will persist in the face of obstacles. A strong sense of self-efficacy allows people to feel free to select, influence, and even construct the circumstances of their lives. pp. 434–435

■ Cognitive theories of personality have reintroduced thought into the equation of personality and situational variables. They have focused on how people interpret the situations in which they find themselves and then alter their behaviour. Mischel argues that people change their responses based on their past experiences and their current assessment of the situation to suit the present situation. This process of adjustment is called *self-regulation*. pp. 435–436

KEY TERM
self-efficacy, p. 434

Personality Assessment

Describe assessment.

■ *Assessment* is the process of evaluating individual differences among human beings by techniques such as tests, interviews, observations, and recordings of physiological processes. Many psychologists administer a group, or battery, of tests. The goal is to use the variety of tests available so that when information is taken together, intelligent and informed conclusions can be drawn. p. 436

What is the MMPI–2?

■ The MMPI–2 consists of 567 true/false statements that focus on attitudes, feelings, motor disturbances, and bodily complaints. Clinical and validity subscales examine different aspects of functioning and measure the truthfulness of the examinee's responses. The MMPI–2 is used as a screening device for maladjustment. pp. 438– 440

What is the goal of a projective test?

■ *Projective tests* such as the Rorschach Inkblot Test and the TAT use ambiguous stimuli and ask examinees to respond in an unrestricted manner. Examinees are thought to project unconscious feelings, drives, and motives onto the ambiguous stimuli. p. 440

Identify the techniques of behavioural assessment.

■ Four popular and widely used behavioural assessment techniques are behavioural assessment interviews, naturalistic observation, self-monitoring, and neuropsychological assessment. Behavioural assessment interviews tend to be systematic and structured, focusing on overt and current behaviours and paying attention to the situations in which these behaviours occur. Naturalistic observation involves observing a client in the natural environment and recording the occurrence of specified behaviours at predetermined intervals. In *self-monitoring*, a person systematically records the frequency and duration of his or her own specific behaviours. Neuropsychological assessment is the study of the brain and its disorders as they relate to behaviour. pp. 441–443

KEY TERMS
assessment, p. 436; projective tests, p. 440; self-monitoring, p. 442

Weblinks

The Official Abraham Maslow Publications Site
www.maslow.com/index.html
This site features information on books, articles, and audiovisual materials by or about Abraham Maslow.

Personality and Consciousness
www.wynja.com/personality/theorists.html
You can search for books or information by a theorist's name. This Web site also provides links to more information on each theorist.

Freud Museum London
www.freud.org.uk
The home page for a museum dedicated to Sigmund Freud and his work. Learn about Freud's life and research, or link to other publications about his theories.

Concepts of Person, Self, Personal Identity: Bibliography and Texts
www.canisius.edu/~gallaghr/pi.html
A great reference to online texts and bibliographies, journals, associations, and institutions dealing with personal identity.

Keirsey Temperament and Character Web Site
www.keirsey.com
Take the online personality questionnaire to discover to which of the 16 character types you belong. This test is based on the Myers–Briggs Type Indicator test.

Carl Jung Homepage
www.cgjung.com/
Visit this Web site to access links to Jungian educational centres, related organizations and multilingual sites, and articles and article discussion forums.

The Alfred Adler Institute of San Francisco
ourworld.compuserve.com/homepages/hstein/
Philosophy and theology, parenting and teaching, questions and answers, theory and practice, and how they all relate to Adler's theories are discussed at this comprehensive Web site.

Minnesota Multiphasic Personality Inventory-2 (MMPI-2)
assessments.ncs.com/assessments/tests/mmpia.htm
This site provides detailed information about the MMPI-2 scale.

Personality and Consciousness
www.wynja.com/personality/top.html
This site provides descriptions of a number of personality theorists, such as Freud, Maslow, Jung, and Adler. A list of books about each theory is also available to order through Amazon.com.

Chapter 13

Social Psychology

Littleton, Colorado. April 20, 1999. At Columbine High School, in a quiet, middle-class suburb, the lives of 12 students and 1 teacher were ended in a massacre that shook the nation and gained worldwide attention. Stunned and grieving, parents, teachers, and schoolmates asked themselves "Why?" and "What went wrong?" Soon, media analysts and editorial writers were probing the causes as well. No one will ever know for sure what went so terribly wrong in the lives of Eric Harris and Dylan Klebold, the two high-school students who planned and executed the devastating massacre.

Eight days later, just as many Canadians were comfortably referring to the Littleton tragedy as an "American problem," a troubled 14-year-old walked into W. R. Myers High School in Taber, Alberta. With a sawed off .22 calibre rifle, he shot and killed 17-year-old Jason Lang and seriously wounded another student.

While trying to help the traumatized families and friends of the victims of both incidents, psychologists became aware, yet again, of how little we really know about one another, and about how our actions and words influence others. If the boys who gunned down their peers had been treated differently, would these tragedies have been averted? Were there key events or interactions that shaped the boys' attitudes and behaviours? Many questions like these will be asked again and again as the families and friends of the victims try to recover from their shock and grief. ■

Psychologists recognize that people's behaviour is shaped by early experiences, by others in their lives, and by daily influences such as advertising, new friends, and school experiences. People are not programmed machines that stay the same forever; they examine other people's nonverbal messages, looking beyond their smiles, and they resist (or give in to) attempts to change their attitudes or gain their compliance. No person is an island, unaffected by other people's attitudes and behaviour. You may be beginning to recognize that what people wear, whom they vote for, and what they value are affected by an array of social variables.

In this chapter, we examine the social world of interactions among individuals and within groups. We will see that other people affect each individual's attitudes and self-perceptions and exert powerful influences on individual behaviour. **Social psychology** is the study of how individuals influence and are influenced by the thoughts, feelings, and behaviours of others—it is the scientific study of how we think about and interact with other people.

This chapter looks at some of the traditional concepts in social psychology: attitudes, social cognition, and social interactions. These concepts help psychologists understand of behaviour that occurs when more than one person is involved—that is, of social behaviour. Our focus at first will be on how individual attitudes are affected by other people.

Attitudes: Our Dispositions and Inclinations

Attitudes are long-lasting patterns of feelings and beliefs about other people, ideas, or objects that are based in a person's past experiences and shape his or her future behaviour. They are usually evaluative and serve certain functions, such as guiding new behaviours and helping the individual interpret the world efficiently (Eagly & Chaiken, 1993). Attitudes are shaped by how a person perceives other people, how others perceive him or her, and how the person *thinks* others see him or her. Try to recall a time when you were discussing an uncertain or new issue with friends (for example, what to make of a movie you had all just seen or what to think about a recent news event). You may recall offering your view somewhat tentatively and even adjusting it as you were speaking in response to the comments, facial expressions, and body postures of those to whom you were speaking. In other situations you may be more sure of your position and less likely to change it in response to the reactions of others. Most of the time social influences on our attitudes are less obvious but they are there nonetheless.

Dimensions of Attitudes

Football fans are often fanatical in their attitudes; their enthusiasm is earnest and they often back up their feelings with visible support for the team. Yet not everybody appreciates football, and even people who like it may find the hoopla that surrounds a big game to be a bit much. People's feelings and beliefs about football, or any other subject, are a crucial part of their attitudes. Attitudes have three dimensions—cognitive, emotional, and behavioural—each of which serves a specific purpose.

The *cognitive dimension* of an attitude consists of thoughts and beliefs. When someone forms attitudes about a group of people, a series of events, or a political philosophy, the cognitive dimension of those attitudes serves a function by helping the person categorize, process, and remember the people, events, and philosophy. The *emotional dimension* of an attitude involves evaluative feelings, such as like or dislike.

For example, some people feel excited when in a large crowd while others may feel apprehensive or afraid. The *behavioural dimension* of an attitude determines how people actually show their beliefs and evaluative feelings (Eagly, 1992), such as by voting in accordance with their political beliefs or attending rap concerts. Behaviourally, attitudes function to shape specific actions. Individuals do not always publicly display their attitudes, of course, especially when the attitudes are not yet firmly established or when attitudes and behaviours are inconsistent. For example, many more people cognitively and emotionally support a nuclear arms freeze than give their time, energy, or money to organizations supporting this cause (Gilbert, 1988).

When people have very strongly held attitudes about a specific topic, they are said to have a *conviction*. Once people form a conviction, they think about it and become involved with it (which makes convictions long-lasting and resistant to change). This is especially true of religious and political convictions (Abelson, 1988). For example, despite strong evidence to the contrary, many people still believe that American President John F. Kennedy was assassinated by agents of the CIA in a plot to overthrow the government. Once people have adopted a belief, it functions to justify a wide range of behaviours and to interpret new information about events.

What variables determine how attitudes are formed, displayed, or changed? Why are some attitudes hard to modify and others relatively easy? We will take up each of these questions in the following sections, beginning at the beginning—with attitude formation.

Forming Attitudes

Though it some day may be discovered that there is a genetic predisposition to develop one type of attitude over another, the most common current position is that attitudes are formed through learning that begins early in life. Thus, psychologists rely on learning theories to explain how children form attitudes. Three learning theory concepts that help explain attitude formation are classical conditioning, operant conditioning, and observational learning (see Chapter 5 for a review and detailed explanation of these concepts).

The association of people, events, and ideologies with certain attitudes often goes unnoticed because it happens so effortlessly. However, such associations can shape children's views of and emotional responses to the world, thereby forming the basis of their future attitudes as adults. (See Figure 13.1 for an application of this process to attitude formation in adults.) For example, suppose a parent never has a good word to say about the Reform party ("red-necked right-wingers" and so on). *Classical conditioning* pairs the formerly neutral stimulus (the Reform party) with an unconditioned stimulus (derogatory comments). Because derogatory comments naturally elicit negative feelings, the resulting negative feelings can be considered an unconditioned response. If a child overhears such remarks repeatedly, the Reform party eventually will evoke a response of negative feelings (now a conditioned response) in the child.

A key principle of *operant conditioning* is that reinforced behaviours are likely to recur; this principle helps explain how attitudes are maintained over time. In socializing their children, parents express approval for and reinforce ideas and behaviours consistent with their own "correct" view of the world. Such approval and reinforcement help children adopt their parents' "correct" attitudes.

FIGURE 13.1
Classical Conditioning in Attitude Formation
In attempting to create positive attitudes towards a product or idea, advertisers use classical conditioning techniques. They pair the product or idea with an attractive, desirable individual or situation to evoke a positive response.

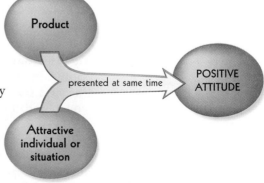

According to the concept of *observational learning*, people establish attitudes by watching the behaviour of those they consider significant and then imitating that behaviour. The new attitudes people learn eventually become their own. Suppose that a young girl sees her father react angrily to a TV news story that contradicts a tenet of the family's religious faith. The next time the child hears a similar argument, she will be likely to mimic her father's attitude, which may affect her own attitude.

Predicting Behaviour from Attitudes

Social psychologists can assess people's attitudes, but whether those attitudes predict behaviour depends on numerous variables. Among these, four key variables are attitude strength, vested interest, specificity of attitudes, and accessibility of attitudes.

Attitudes are better predictors of behaviour when the *attitude strength* is strong and there are few competing outside influences, such as conflicting advertising appeals or advice from friends. A person who believes strongly in the health hazards of cigarette smoke, even after being bombarded with cigarette company advertisements, would most likely continue to work actively for a nonsmoking environment. Furthermore, attitudes people consider to be personally important (in which they have a *vested interest*) are more likely to be shown in behaviour and to stay intact, regardless of how situations change over time (Krosnick, 1988). If a parent believes strongly in improving their child's educational opportunities, they will be far more likely to attend PTA meetings. The extent to which a belief is part of a person's self-concept is also a good predictor of both the strength of the belief and the likelihood that the person will act on it (Pomerantz, Chaiken, & Tordesillas, 1995).

Attitudes also are more likely to foretell behaviour when they are *specific* and the situation requiring a decision closely matches the situation to which the attitude applies. Global attitudes, and even stereotypes about people, do not predict specific behaviours very well (Haddock, Zanna, & Esses, 1994). For example, a person may have a broadly liberal political attitude, but only a specific attitude about health care, welfare reform, or government waste will predict whether the person will vote for a specific political candidate. Lastly, attitudes predict behaviour best when they are *accessible*, that is, well formed and easily remembered (Fazio 1990). When people have sharply delineated ideas about a political position, they can easily decide how favourably they rate a new candidate. When they cannot easily remember or articulate their views, making such judgments is more time-consuming and the outcomes are less predictable.

Persuasion: Changing Attitudes

Television is one of the prime ways that politicians and marketing executives try to change our attitudes. Both know that since people learn attitudes, they can change them or learn new ones. Changed attitudes may impel a person to do almost anything—from voting Reform, to trying a new brand of soap, to undergoing a religious conversion, to becoming a fan of jazz. In the 1950s, Carl Hovland was one of the first social psychologists to identify key components of attitude change: the communicator, the communication, the medium, and the audience.

The Communicator. To be persuasive, a communicator—the person trying to effect attitude change—must project integrity, credibility, and trustworthiness. If people don't respect, believe, or trust the communicator, they are unlikely to change their attitudes. People with "mature" faces have more control and influence in personal interactions (Berry & Landry, 1997). Researchers also have found that the perceived power, prestige, celebrity, prominence, modesty, and attractiveness of the communicator are extremely important (Chaiken & Eagly, 1993; Cialdini, 1994; Dabul et al., 1998). Credibility is also an important characteristic. A credible communicator is perceived as a trustworthy expert. For example, a spokesperson from Health Canada has a greater ability to change your views about cigarette smoking in the workplace than does a local school board member.

Information received from friends is considered more influential than information from the communications media. For example, Costanzo and colleagues (1986, p. 528) suggest: "Media sources are effective in creating awareness of a new technology, but interpersonal sources exert a far greater influence on the decision to adopt a new technology." Communicators who share characteristics with their audience are more persuasive than communicators who are seen as different from their audience. Leonard-Barton (1981) showed that the best predictor of whether a person will purchase solar energy equipment is the number of the person's acquaintances who currently own such devices. Similarly, a teenager is more likely to follow a close friend's advice on the use of condoms than that of an unknown public health official (Jaccard et al., 1990).

The Communication. A clear, convincing, and logical argument is the most effective tool for changing attitudes—especially attitudes with emotional content, such as those concerning capital punishment or legalized abortion (Millar & Millar, 1990). This is especially true in Western culture, where appeals to logic and reason, rather than to authority and tradition, are more prevalent than in Japan, for example. The more highly involved the audience is, the more important the logic of the argument becomes. Audiences that have a low level of involvement are more likely to be swayed by superficial variables. If you have strong attitudes about capital punishment you are not going to change your mind simply because an attractive celebrity speaks against your position. You will focus on the content of the message rather than on the characteristics of the communicator.

Communications that arouse fear are effective in motivating attitude change, especially when health issues are concerned and the communicator does not overdo the fear appeal (Robberson & Rogers, 1988). For example, think of some of the anti-smoking messages you've seen on television. What techniques do they use to induce fear? Fear works; college students who come to fear AIDS are more likely to use condoms (Boyd & Wandersman, 1991), and fear of cancer can be motivating in some situations (Wandersman & Hallman, 1993). In fact, research is now beginning to show that negative information tends to influence people more strongly than comparably extreme positive information (Ito, Larsen, Smith, & Cacioppo, 1998). This is particularly true if the report of dire consequences also includes something that people can do to avoid the danger (Gleicher & Petty, 1992; Rogers, 1983).

Researchers have also found that if people hear a persuasive message often enough, they begin to believe it, regardless of its validity. Repeated exposure to certain people or situations can also change attitudes (R. F. Bornstein, 1989). For example, after seeing numerous TV commercials that show a particular brand of battery outperforming the competition, a viewer may change his or her attitude towards the product from neutral to positive. Similarly, someone who is seen frequently is more likely to be viewed positively than is someone who is seen less frequently; this is called the *mere exposure effect* (Jacoby et al., 1989).

The Medium. The way in which communication is presented—its medium—influences people's receptiveness to attitude change. Today, one of the most common avenues for attempts to change attitudes is the mass media, particularly television. After all, the goal of TV commercials is either to change or to strengthen people's behaviour. Commercials exhort viewers to drink Pepsi instead of Coke, to say no to drugs, or to vote Liberal instead of Reform or Conservative. Research shows that TV advertising is one of the most influential media of attitude change in the Western world; this is no surprise, given that in the average household the television is on for more than four hours every day.

Nevertheless, face-to-face communication often has more impact than communication through television or in writing. Thus, even though candidates for public office rely heavily on TV, radio, and printed ads, they also try to meet people face to face, sometimes taking to the road to bring their message directly to the people. This is important because research shows that in politics the impact of bursts of advertising in the mass media is often overrated. Television may serve only to strengthen pre-existing ideas, and then only if advertising campaigns are massive (and expensive) and pre-existing ideas are weak (Sears & Kosterman, 1994).

The Audience. Attitude changes can occur. However, openness to attitude change is in part age- and education-related. People are most susceptible to attitude change in their early adult years; susceptibility to change drops off in later years (Krosnick & Alwin, 1989). People of high intelligence are less likely to have their opinions changed, and people with high self-esteem tend to be similarly unyielding (Rhodes & Wood, 1992). However, when a friend tries to change a person's attitudes, attitude change is far more likely (Cialdini, 1994).

Attitude change is complicated, and researchers have shown that a number of other variables are also important. For example, attitude change is more likely when the targeted attitude is not too different from an existing one (McCaul, Jacobson, & Martinson, 1998); it is also more likely when the audience is not highly involved with a particular point of view (Johnson & Eagly, 1989). For example, changing the attitudes of politically involved citizens is more difficult than altering those of uninvolved citizens (Johnson & Eagly, 1989; Ottati, Fishbein, & Middlestadt, 1988). Research also shows that people who positively anticipate a new idea or who feel that others around them are inclined to change their views are likely to exhibit attitude change (Boninger et al., 1990; Cialdini, 1994). The extent of attitude change can also be affected by prevalent attitudes in a particular region of the country, as was seen in the most recent referendum on separation in Quebec.

Changing attitudes, and ultimately behaviour, can be difficult if people have well-established habits or are highly motivated in the opposite direction. Consider attitudes towards smoking. Although most people generally believe in the serious health consequences of smoking, 30 percent of Canadians still smoke. Getting people to stop smoking—or to not start—takes more than fostering positive attitudes about health; it also requires instilling a new habit in people and removing an old one. Education can be helpful, as can devices to help people remember not to smoke (such as warning buzzers or strings on fingers); nevertheless, smoking behaviour, once established, is hard to stop due to physical addiction and psychological dependence.

Experiencing Psychology shows some tried-and-true techniques that have been used for decades to influence attitudes, change behaviours, and obtain favours.

Cognitive Approaches: The Elaboration Likelihood Model. Decades of research have identified the components of attitude change. But researchers only recently have begun to focus on what happens cognitively to individuals whose attitudes are being changed. Various theories attempt to understand individuals' thought processes so as to be able to predict actual attitude change. One such theory, proposed by Richard Petty and John Cacioppo (1981, 1985), suggests that people generally want to have valid attitudes and beliefs that will prove helpful in the face of day-to-day challenges and problems (Petty et al., 1994). This model is called the **elaboration likelihood model**—a view of attitude change suggesting that it can be accomplished via two routes: central and peripheral. (See Figure 13.2 for an overview of this model.) These two routes explain why people can be logical in some situations and illogical in others.

The *central route* emphasizes the content of the message; conscious, thoughtful consideration; and elaboration of arguments. Attitude change via this route depends

Elaboration likelihood model: A theory suggesting that there are two routes to attitude change: central, which focuses on thoughtful, elaborative considerations, and peripheral, which focuses on less careful, more emotional, and even superficial considerations.

experiencing psychology

Techniques to Induce Attitude Change

How do people influence one another? What techniques promote attitude change? Managers, salespeople, parents, and politicians all apply principles of social psychology in their work. They influence people regularly by using social psychology techniques such as the foot in the door, the door in the face, the ask-and-you-shall-be-given approach, lowballing, modelling, and incentives.

Foot-in-the-Door Technique. To get someone to change an attitude or grant a favour, begin by asking for a small attitude change or a small favour. In other words, get your foot in the door. Ask to borrow a quarter today, a dollar next week, and money for your tuition within a month.

The essence of the foot-in-the-door technique is that a person who grants a small request is likely to comply with a larger request later. However, it works only if the person first grants the small favour, and it works best if there is some time between the first, small request and the later, large one. A person who says no to the first favour may find it even easier to say no to subsequent ones (Kilbourne, 1989).

Door-in-the-Face Technique. To use the door-in-the-face technique, first ask for something outrageous; then later ask for something much smaller and more reasonable. Ask a friend to lend you $100; after being turned down, ask to borrow $5. Your friend may be relieved to grant the smaller favour.

The the door-in-the-face technique appears to work because people do not want to be seen as turning someone down twice, and it works best if there is little time between requests. To look good and maintain a positive self-image, people agree to the lesser of two requests.

Ask-and-You-Shall-Be-Given Technique. When people ask for money for a good cause, whether the request is large or small, they usually will get a positive response. Ask someone who has given before and the request is even more likely to be granted (Doob & McLaughlin, 1989), especially if the person is in a good mood (Forgas, 1998). Fundraisers for universities, churches, and museums know that asking usually will get a positive response. Research indicates that asking in an unusual way can pique a person's interest, turn the potential donor aside from his or her well-rehearsed script of saying no, and increase the likelihood of giving (Santos, Leve, & Pratkinis, 1994).

Lowballing Technique. Lowballing is a technique by which a person is influenced to make a decision or commitment because of the low stakes associated with it. Once the decision is made, the stakes may increase; but the person will likely stick with the original decision. For example, if a person agrees to buy a car for $9000, they may still buy it even if several options are added on, increasing the price to $10 000. Lowballing works because people tend to stick to their commitments, even if the stakes are raised. Changing one's mind may suggest a lack of good judgment, may cause stress, and may make the person feel as if he or she is violating an (often imaginary) obligation.

Modelling. Showing good behaviour, such as conserving energy or saying no to drugs, to someone else increases the likelihood that the person will behave similarly. The person being observed is a model for the desired behaviour. Modelling, which is examined in Chapter 5, is a powerful technique for influencing behaviours and attitudes by demonstrating those behaviours and expressing those attitudes. When well-known athletes exhibit generosity of spirit and act like good sports, they serve as models for youngsters who aspire to careers such as theirs.

Incentives Technique. Nothing succeeds better in eliciting a particular behaviour than a desired incentive. Offering a 16-year-old use of the family car for setting the dinner table every night usually results in a neatly set dinner table. Offering a large monetary bonus to a sales agent for achieving higher than usual year-end sales performance usually boosts sales efforts. Behaviour changes occur—the person is doing it for an incentive—but attitude changes may not follow—the 16-year-old sets the table, but still hates doing so. ■

on how effective, authoritative, and logical a communication is. Confronted with scientific evidence on the effects of second-hand smoke on people's health (especially the prevalence of respiratory diseases), most people conclude through the central route that second-hand smoke is in fact detrimental to health. That is, unless they are highly motivated to believe otherwise, they conclude that the scientific arguments against smoking are too strong to refute.

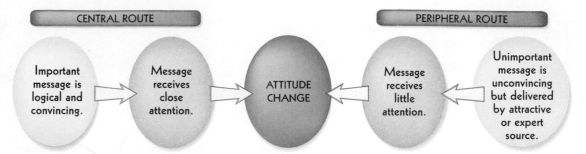

| CENTRAL ROUTE | | | | PERIPHERAL ROUTE | |

| Important message is logical and convincing. | Message receives close attention. | ATTITUDE CHANGE | Message receives little attention. | Unimportant message is unconvincing but delivered by attractive or expert source. |

FIGURE 13.2
Elaboration Likelihood Model
According to the elaboration likelihood model, attitude change can occur through the central route or the peripheral route.

The *peripheral route* emphasizes a more superficial, less careful, and more emotional evaluation of the message. This route has an indirect but nevertheless powerful effect, especially when there are no convincing or strong arguments that can motivate the use of the central route. This is what happens frequently with political messages (DeBono, 1992; Petty et al., 1993). Toronto Mayor Mel Lastman, shown in the photo, uses emotion-laden language to get his message across. Whether a person accepts a message through this route depends on how the person perceives its pleasantness, its delivery, and its similarity to well-established personal attitudes, and on the characteristics of the communicator. Think of an infomercial that you may have seen on television that attempts to sell exercise equipment. Such commercials often make their pitch while featuring attractive models and an upbeat, eager (and trim) audience. You may believe the evidence presented only because a convincing, seemingly honest, and fit person has expressed confidence in the product. The attitude change you may show—a desire to buy the product—often stems largely from emotional or personal rather than logical arguments and therefore may not be long-lasting (Petty et al., 1993).

The key idea of the elaboration likelihood model is that sometimes people form or change attitudes because of thoughtful, conscious decisions (central route) or because of more superficial, emotional, and quick ideas or feelings (peripheral route). The central route is used when people have the ability, time, and energy to think through arguments carefully; the peripheral route is more likely to be used when decisions are less important, motivation is low, time is short, or the ability to think through arguments is impaired (Petty et al., 1994).

When Does Behaviour Determine Attitudes?

Is it possible that your attitudes don't determine your behaviour, but that just the opposite occurs—your behaviour shapes your attitudes? There is mounting evidence that to a certain extent this is the case. In weight control programs and alcohol abstinence programs, group facilitators first try to change behaviours (abstain from alcohol, for example). In such situations, the theory is that positive attitudes about a new life will *follow* changes in behaviour.

A dramatic example of attitudes following a set of behaviours occurred in the 1970s. In a study that came to be known as the Stanford Prison Experiment (Haney, Banks, & Zimbardo, 1973; Haney & Zimbardo, 1998) normal, well-adjusted, male college students volunteered to play a role as prisoners or guards in a simulated prison in the basement of the psychology building at Stanford University. Guards were dressed in uniforms and given billy clubs, reflective sunglasses, whistles, and the power to enforce rules. Prisoners were locked in cells and dressed in hospital gowns with numbers on them, rubber sandals, and caps made from nylon stockings. The researchers originally had planned to observe the students over a two-week period to see how completely they adopted the roles of prisoner and guard. However, within a few days "guards" were verbally abusing and degrading "prisoners." Prisoners became passive, obedient, and withdrawn, and many were suffering intense psychological pain, anxiety, and depression. The experiment was aborted after only six days. Remember that at all times each person was aware that he was participating in an experiment, that the "prison" was a simulation. Yet personal identities seemed to become submerged within these new roles. The study showed that students could play a role—guard or prisoner—and quickly

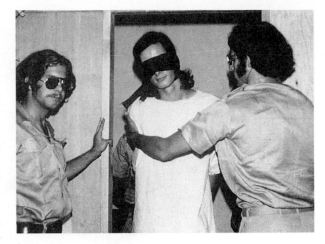

adapt to that role, enacting attitudes that were consistent with it. Imagine how powerful roles become in shaping behaviour in real institutions (e.g., prisons, hospitals) where roles are well-defined. This research study would not be allowed to be conducted today due to ethical considerations.

If people are so heavily influenced by the situations in which they find themselves, can psychologists ever say that people are the same from one situation to another? The answer to such a question may come from studies of cognitive consistency.

Searching for Cognitive Consistency

People often try to maintain consistency among their various attitudes and between their attitudes and their behaviour. *Consistency* refers to a high degree of coherence among elements of behaviour and mental processes; such coherence leads to orderly living and enables people to make decisions about their future behaviour without having to filter out numerous alternatives.

Cognitive Dissonance. Imagine the dilemma faced by a scientist who smokes cigarettes and who finds through her research that cigarettes do indeed cause cancer. As a scientist, she must find the physical evidence compelling; as a smoker, she recognizes that she has smoked for years, feels fine, and has a 92-year-old grandmother who still smokes. How does she reconcile these opposing facts? Moreover, what further confusion would she suffer if she learned that a chest X-ray found that her grandmother's lungs are totally clear?

When people's various attitudes conflict with one another or when their attitudes conflict with their behaviour, they feel uncomfortable. Leon Festinger (1919–1989) called this feeling of tension **cognitive dissonance**—the state of discomfort that results when a discrepancy exists between two or more of a person's beliefs or between a person's beliefs and overt behaviour. Based on the premise that people seek to reduce such dissonance, Festinger (1957) proposed a *cognitive dissonance theory*. According to the theory, when people experience conflict among their attitudes (see Figure 13.3) or between their attitudes and their behaviour, they are motivated to change either their attitudes or their behaviour. Cognitive dissonance theory also may be considered to be a type of motivation theory, because it suggests that people become energized to do something (Elliot & Devine, 1995). Consider an example of behavior–attitude conflict. Suppose you are a strong proponent of animal rights. You support your local animal rights organization and Greenpeace, refrain from eating meat, and are repulsed by fur coats. Then you win a raffle and are awarded a stylish black leather coat. Wearing the coat goes against your beliefs, but it feels good, you know it looks great on you, and all of your friends admire it. According to cognitive dissonance theory, you are experiencing conflict between your attitudes (animal rights) and your behaviour (wearing the coat). To relieve the conflict, you either will stop wearing the coat or will modify your attitude (leather becomes a more acceptable choice). People choose the most direct method (the one

Cognitive dissonance [COG-nuh-tiv DIS-uh-nins]: The state of discomfort that results when a discrepancy exists between two or more of a person's beliefs or between a person's beliefs and overt behaviour.

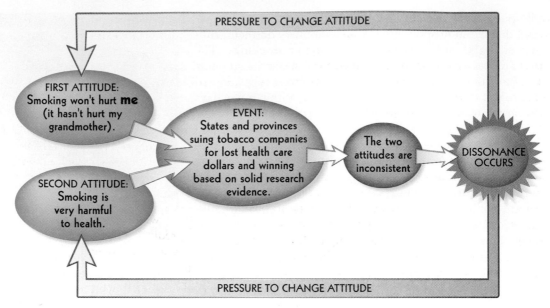

FIGURE 13.3
Cognitive Dissonance
A person often holds conflicting attitudes or behaves in ways that are inconsistent with his or her attitudes. When an event challenges one of those attitudes or the behaviour, the person is motivated to change the attitude or behaviour because of cognitive dissonance.

that is the easiest) to reduce dissonance (Stone et al., 1997). Psychologists have devised measures for a person's preference for consistency (Cialdini, Trost, & Newsom, 1995), but not all people are consistent, nor do all psychologists suggest that consistency is important.

An Alternative to Cognitive Dissonance Theory. Social psychologist Daryl Bem (1972) claims that people do not change their attitudes because of internal states such as dissonance. He has proposed **self-perception theory**—an approach to attitude formation in which people are assumed not to know what their attitudes are until they examine their behaviour. Bem argues that people infer their attitudes and emotional states from their behaviour. First they search for an external explanation; if no such explanation is available, they then turn to an internal one. That is, people simply look at their behaviour and say, "I must have liked this if I behaved this way." For example, if you are angry when a salesperson calls you at home but respond to the call in a warm and polite manner, you may infer that you liked the product or the salesperson (or at least that you didn't hate it as much as you thought you might). See Figure 13.4 for a comparison of the traditional view of attitude formation and Bem's view.

FIGURE 13.4
Two Views of Attitudes
Does behaviour follow from attitudes (the traditional view), or do attitudes follow from behaviour (Bem's view)?

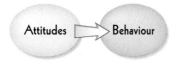

TRADITIONAL VIEW
Attitudes shape behaviour; behaviour follows from attitudes.

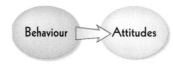

BEM'S VIEW
Behaviour is interpreted; then attitudes are formed.

Bem's research is supported to some extent by the cognitive work of Stanley Schachter (which we reviewed in Chapter 9). Schachter showed that research participants inferred aspects of their emotional states from both their physical states and the situations in which they found themselves. Thus, a person who is physically aroused and surrounded by happy people reports feeling happy. A person who is physically aroused and in a hostile situation reports feeling angry.

Reactance Theory. Leading a consistent and coherent life with a clear set of attitudes may be satisfying, but attitudes are often challenged. Have you ever been ordered to do something and found that you wanted to do exactly the opposite? According to social psychologist Jack Brehm (1966), whenever people feel that their

Self-perception theory: An approach to attitude formation in which people are assumed to infer their attitudes based on observations of their own behaviour.

freedom of choice is being unjustly restricted, they are motivated to reestablish that freedom. Brehm calls this form of negative influence *reactance*. In **reactance**, the inconsistency lies between a person's self-image as being free to choose and the person's realization that someone else is trying to force him or her to choose a particular alternative.

Reactance theory is consistent with the notion of forbidden fruit. Forbidden activities often become more attractive. Choosing the forbidden fruit may provide an individual with a sense of autonomy. An adolescent who is told he cannot befriend members of a minority group may seek out members of that group more often. When coercion is used, resistance follows. According to reactance theory, the extent of reactance is directly related to the extent of the restriction on freedom of choice. If a person does not consider the choice very important and if the restriction is slight, little reactance develops. The wording or delivery of the restriction also affects the extent of reactance. People who are told they *must* respond in a certain way are more likely to react negatively than if they merely receive a suggestion or are given a relatively free choice.

Focus

Review

◆ What is the relationship between attitudes and behaviour? pp. 448–449, 450
◆ What evidence is there that a good communicator can effectively change attitudes? pp. 450–451
◆ What evidence is there that modelling can induce attitude change? p. 453

Think Critically

◆ Under what conditions are attitudes most likely to predict behaviours? Can you think of situations where existing attitudes will not predict future behaviours?

Social Cognition: The Impact of Thought

On meeting someone for the first time, you might say, "I really like him!" or "I can't put my finger on why, but she irritates me." Often, first impressions are based on nothing more than the other person's appearance, body language, and speech pattern. Yet these impressions can have lasting effects. How do people form attitudes about others? In this section, we will move outward from individual attitudes to the broader world of social cognition—one's view of the social environment.

Social cognition is the thought processes involved in making sense of events, other people, oneself, and the world in general by analyzing and interpreting them. It focuses on social information in memory, which affects judgments, choices, evaluations, and, ultimately, behaviour (Fiske, 1992). Social cognition is a useful and pragmatic (results-oriented) process in which people often use mental short cuts to help them organize the world. The process often begins with attempts to understand other people's communications, which can be verbal (words) or nonverbal (looks, gestures, body movements, and other means of expression), and to form impressions of the people. The process by which a person uses the behaviour and appearance of others to infer their internal states and intentions is known as **impression formation**; sometimes the impressions are accurate, but certainly not always. We will look at impression formation in more depth later in this section, when we study attribution.

Organizing the World Using Mental Short Cuts

We saw earlier that people use their attitudes to help them make decisions and organize their lives. In a related way, using mental short cuts helps people process

Reactance: A pattern of feelings and subsequent behaviours aimed at reestablishing a sense of freedom when there is an inconsistency between a person's self-image as being free to choose and the person's realization that someone is trying to force him or her to choose a particular alternative.

Social cognition: The thought processes involved in making sense of events, other people, oneself, and the world in general by analyzing and interpreting them.

Impression formation: The process by which a person uses the behaviour and appearance of others to infer their internal states and intentions.

information and decreases the information overload that they might otherwise experience in their complex lives. People seek to be "cognitive misers," processing information superficially unless they are motivated to do otherwise. As Susan Fiske (1992, p. 879) asserts, "Social cognition operates in the service of practical consequences." To help themselves make decisions people develop pragmatic rules of thumb.

One rule of thumb is *representativeness*; individuals or events that appear to be representative of other members of a group are quickly classified as such, often despite a complete lack of evidence. If you see a six-foot-six 19-year-old, you are likely to think that he plays basketball—without knowing anything else about him, let alone his interests or abilities. Another rule of thumb is *availability*; the easier it is to bring to mind instances of one category, type, or idea, the more likely it is that the category, type, or idea will be used to describe an event. Politicians associate memorable images and ideas—often stark, vivid ones—with themselves or their opponents. Television ads that associate polluted waters with a current premier tie him or her to bad environmental policy. The more vivid the image, the more likely this will be available and remembered by voters. Still another rule of thumb is the *false consensus effect*; people tend to believe that others agree with them. Whatever their view on a politician or a social issue, people believe that most other people believe the way they do. The last rule of thumb is *framing*; the way in which information is organized and the context in which it is presented to people helps determine whether people are likely to accept it easily, ignore it, or reject it. Consider the different impacts of these two public health warnings: "95 percent of the population will not be affected by the disease and only 5 percent will become seriously ill" and "Due to the disease, 5 percent of you will become seriously ill, although the rest of you will be unaffected." Or compare these statements: "This great new car costs under $9999" and "This great new car costs about $10 000"—$9999 sounds a lot better than $10 000.

When other people's behaviour fits neatly into a person's conceptions of the world, the individual can use little effort to make judgments about it. One of the most powerful ways of sending easily interpreted signals is nonverbal communication.

Assessing the World Using Nonverbal Communication

Impression formation often begins with nonverbal communication. Cues or actions that involve movements of the body, especially the face, provide **nonverbal communication**. When a person irritates you, it may be a gesture, a grimace, or an averting of the eyes that generates your bad feelings—not the words that they speak (Ambady & Rosenthal, 1993). Nonverbal communication is difficult to suppress and is easily accessible to observers (DePaulo, 1992). Three major sources of nonverbal communication are facial expressions, body language, and eye contact.

Facial Expressions and Body Language. Many of the conclusions you draw about other people are based on their facial expressions. Most people, across cultures, can distinguish six basic emotions in the facial expressions of other people: happy, sad, angry, fearful, surprised, and disgusted. A simple expression such as a smile, for example, gives others a powerful cue about a person's truthfulness. Research shows that when a person smiles, both the smile and the muscular activity around the eyes help determine if the truth is being told or if the person is smiling to mask another emotion (Ekman & Keltner, 1997). *The Research Process* examines this phenomenon in more detail.

People also convey information about their moods and attitudes through body positions and gestures—**body language**. Movements such as crossing the arms, lowering the head, and standing rigidly can all communicate negative attitudes. On the other hand, when a server in a restaurant moves closer to a table and makes direct

the research process

Hiding the Truth

Can you deceive others by smiling when you're telling a lie? Not very well, according to Paul Ekman (Ekman, Friesen, & O'Sullivan, 1988; Ekman & Keltner, 1997). In the early 1970s, Ekman noted that facial features and gestures provide complex information to an observer, especially when a person tries to be deceitful. He observed that subtle facial cues accompany various types of smiling and that people cannot mask true emotions with a grin. He tested this idea experimentally by having participants view people telling about pleasant experiences and then view people lying about experiences, trying to make unpleasant ones seem pleasant.

Method. Ekman and his colleagues (Ekman, Friesen, & O'Sullivan, 1988) identified several types of smiles: happy smiles, false smiles, listening smiles, and masking smiles (smiles meant to deceive or hide a real emotion). They hypothesized that facial muscles around the eyes and nose signal the real meaning of a smile. Using a concealed camera, the research team videotaped participants who

first truthfully described a film that was mildly enjoyable. Then the participants watched an unpleasant film about skin burns and amputations and were asked to conceal negative feelings when describing the film. Could the participants convince another person that they had watched a pleasant film?

Results. The researchers scored close-ups of the participants' faces with respect to which facial muscles moved. Facial muscle movements such as pulling the brows together, wrinkling the nose, and raising the brows were categorized; the results showed that smiles of true enjoyment involved eye muscle activity more often than did feigned smiles of enjoyment. When a participant tried to conceal negative emotions with a happy but false smile, noticeable changes occurred in the muscles. The results support the researchers' contention that genuinely happy smiles differ from other smiles in that they appear more quickly and fade more slowly.

Conclusions. This study shows that smiles are not a single category of behaviour but are multifaceted. A

person can convey different social signals through a smile. From a social psychologist's view, this is important because it confirms that people are tuned in to fine elements of behaviour; a person can discriminate between types of smiles and can assign different meanings to them. Thus, for example, research shows that deceptive salespersons reveal their falseness through non-verbal cues (DePaulo & DePaulo, 1989). Similarly, your boss may be smiling, but a mere lift of an eyebrow (Frank, Ekman, & Friesen, 1998) or a couple of millimetres' change in the distance between the eyebrows is enough to cause a dramatic change in your thoughts or overt behaviour (Frank & Ekman, 1997; Ekman & Keltner, 1997). ■

eye contact, tips increase (Lynn & Mynier, 1993). Body language may differ according to culture and gender. In Western cultures, the energetic and forceful way that younger people walk makes them appear sexier, more carefree, and happier than older people (Montepare & Zebrowitz-McArthur, 1988); yet this is culture-bound—body language is not viewed in the same way in non-Western cultures. A pensive, reflective posture or a deferential movement or head position might signal composure, confidence, and status in Japan, for example (Matsumoto & Kudoh, 1993). In addition, gestures have different meanings in different societies. For example, the North American A-Okay sign is a rude gesture referring to sexual acts in many cultures. Research also shows that in Western cultures women are often better than men at communicating and interpreting nonverbal messages, especially facial expressions (Sogon & Izard, 1987). Women are more likely to send nonverbal facial messages but are also more cautious in interpreting nonverbal messages sent to them by men.

Eye Contact. Researchers are well aware of another source of nonverbal communication: *eye contact*. The eyes convey a surprising amount of information about feelings. A person who is looking at you may glance briefly at you or may stare. You may glance or stare back. You probably would gaze tenderly at someone you were fond of but avoid eye contact with someone you did not trust or like or did not know well (Teske, 1988). Frequent eye contact between two people may indicate that they like or are sexually attracted to each other.

People tend to judge others based on the eye contact they engage in, making inferences (attributions) about others' internal dispositions from the degree of eye contact. Canadians generally prefer modest amounts of eye contact rather than constant or no eye contact. Job applicants, for example, are rated more favourably when they make moderate amounts of eye contact, speakers who make more rather than less eye contact are preferred, and witnesses testifying in a court trial are perceived as more credible when they make eye contact with the attorney questioning them (DePaulo, 1992). However, all of this is true only in Western cultures, which foster an individualistic stance; in some non-Western cultures—for example, Japan or among First Nations people—making direct eye contact may be a sign of disrespect, arrogance, and even a challenge.

Inferring the Causes of Behaviour: Attribution

If you see people standing in line at a bus stop, you can be fairly certain that they wish to take a bus. Similarly, if you saw a man at the bus stop reading the Muslim holy book, the Koran, you might infer that he is a devout Muslim. In getting to know others, people often infer the causes of their behaviour. When they do, they are making attributions. **Attribution** is the process by which a person infers other people's motives and intentions by observing their behaviour. It also can involve a search for causes for environmental events as well. Through attribution, people decide how they will react towards others or to new situations, in an attempt to evaluate and make sense of their social world. Attribution may seem like a fairly straightforward process based on common sense. However, it must take into account internal as well as external causes of behaviour. Someone making an *internal attribution* thinks the behaviour comes from within the person, from the individual's personality or abilities. Someone making an *external attribution* believes that person's behaviour is caused by outside events, such as the weather or luck.

People can be mistaken when they infer the causes of another person's behaviour. Suppose that the man you saw reading the Koran is actually a Catholic taking a world religions class that uses the book as a text. In that case, your original attribution (that he is a Muslim) was wrong. It is also easy to see that culture shapes attributions; Morris and Peng (1994) found that accounts of certain crimes in English-language newspapers were *dispositional* (based on internal attributions) in tone, but that Chinese newspapers were more *situational* (based on external attributions) in their explanations of the same crimes.

Harold Kelley's (1972, 1973) theory of attribution suggests that people use three criteria to decide whether the causes of a behaviour are internal or external: *consensus*, *consistency*, and *distinctiveness* (see Figure 13.5). According to Kelley, to infer that someone's behaviour is caused by internal characteristics, you must believe (1) that few other people in the same situation would act in the same way (low consensus), (2) that the person has acted in the same way in similar situations in the past (high consistency), and (3) that the person acts in the same way in different situations (low distinctiveness). To infer that a person's behaviour is caused by external factors, you must believe (1) that most people would act that way in that

Attribution: The process by which a person infers other people's motives and intentions by observing their behaviour.

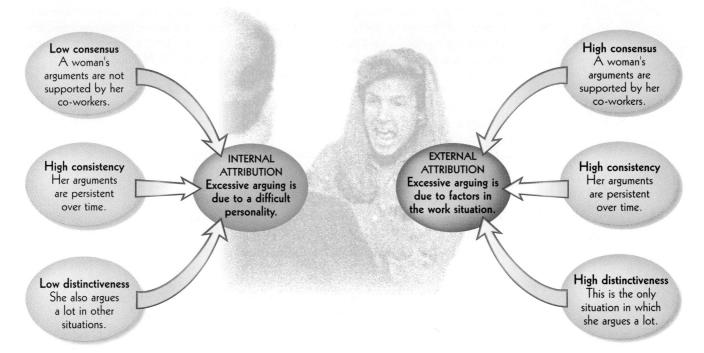

FIGURE 13.5
Attributional Thinking
Kelley's attributional model outlines three criteria for determining the causes of behaviour: consensus, consistency, and distinctiveness. According to the theory, assigning an internal attribution to a person's behaviour is usually the result of low consensus, high consistency, and low distinctiveness. When a person's behaviour shows high consensus, consistency, and distinctiveness, others tend to attribute the causes of the behaviour to external reasons.

sort of situation (high consensus), (2) that the person has acted that way in similar situations in the past (high consistency), and (3) that the person acts differently in other situations (high distinctiveness).

To see how Kelley's theory works, suppose that a man in an office gets into an argument with his supervisor, but other people in the same office do not enter into the discussion (low consensus). Also suppose that the man has argued about the same issue on other occasions (high consistency). Finally, assume that he argues with everybody (low distinctiveness). In such a case, people would no doubt attribute the argument to the individual's personality; the man is simply argumentative. Now suppose (1) that many of the man's co-workers join in and support him in the debate (high consensus), (2) that the man has argued about the same issue in the past (high consistency), but (3) that he does not argue in other situations (high distinctiveness). People would then be more likely to attribute the argument to situational factors, such as the supervisor's incompetence.

Why People Make Attributions. Why do people make attributions? What motivates a person to want to know the causes of other people's behaviour? The accepted explanation is that individuals engage in the process of attribution to maintain a sense of control over their environment. It helps people feel competent and masterful, because they think that knowledge about the causes of behaviour will help them control and predict similar events in the future (Burger & Hemans, 1988). People also make attributions to quickly make sense of their world. If a person's behaviour fits in with a pattern already observed, why analyze it in depth? People are quick to make causal attributions if the behaviour being observed is not unusual.

Errors in Attribution. Residents of Garrison Keillor's Lake Wobegon, Minnesota, are strong women, good-looking men, and children who are all above average. Like Keillor's fictional characters, most of us tend to see ourselves in flattering ways—

we often have unrealistically positive views of our abilities and perceptions of our control of the world. Wobegoners, like the rest of us, tend to see themselves and the rest of their peer group as above average (Klar & Giladi, 1997). These perceptions are often self-enhancing and even egocentric (Farwell & Wohlwend-Lloyd, 1998). Social psychologists have found that people are often especially error-prone or biased in their attributions concerning the behaviours of others. Sometimes they make errors because they use mental short cuts that are not accurate. Two of the common types of errors that have been identified are the fundamental attribution error and the actor–observer effect.

When people commit the **fundamental attribution error**, they assume that other people's behaviour is caused by internal dispositions and underestimate situational influences. For example, a man may have lost his temper, and we assume that he is hot-tempered; however, the truth is that it was only because he was overcharged for an item that he lost his temper. We observe the behaviour of others and tend to discount or not pay attention to the circumstances.

The **actor–observer effect** is the tendency to attribute the behaviour (especially failings) of others to dispositional causes but to attribute one's own behaviour to situational causes. An individual knows himself or herself in many situations and observes much variety in day-to-day behaviour; outside observers, on the other hand, have less information to go on and are more likely to make dispositional attributions. A young child who falls may say, "I slipped on the ice." When a friend falls, however, the same child may say, "You're clumsy." If you fail an exam, you may blame it on your roommate, whose radio prevented you from concentrating on your studies. But when someone else fails an exam, you may wonder about that person's ability.

Errors in attribution are often judgments made in a limited context with limited knowledge. Often they do not help people cope any better—they simply assign blame (Tennen & Affleck, 1990). Errors in attribution cause people to blame rape victims, for example (Bell, Kuriloff, & Lottes, 1995). Some errors in attribution come from the fact that people generally perceive themselves as having more positive traits than others and as being more flexible in their ability to adapt (Sande, Goethals, & Radloff, 1988). This tendency has been seen cross-culturally (Liebrand, Messick, & Wolters, 1986) but often does not exist to the same extent in other cultures (Matsumoto, 1994). This has important implications in business relationships, where goodwill and trust are important; if a business person tends to see others as less (or more) flexible than the people in his or her company, this may alter a negotiation in a fundamental way.

Self-Serving Bias. The **self-serving bias** is people's tendency to evaluate their own positive behaviours as being due to their own internal traits and characteristics but to blame their failures and shortcomings on external, situational factors. People may develop a self-serving bias because it helps meet their *need for self-esteem*. This bias can be seen as an adaptive response that helps people deal with their limitations and gives them the courage to venture into areas they normally might not explore. People also make such attributions about themselves to help maintain a sense of balance by resolving inconsistencies between old and new information about themselves (Snyder & Higgins, 1988). Often, a person who makes an excuse about some negative personal behaviour has shifted the cause of the behaviour to a less central element of personality or to situational factors. This behaviour results in enhanced image building and a sense of control. Furthermore, a self-serving bias allows people to present themselves to others in a positive light (Celuch & Slama, 1995). The self-serving bias is more common in men than women and in Western than non-Western cultures (Cross & Madson, 1997).

Errors in attribution contribute to the self-serving bias. People tend to take credit for their successes but to blame others for their failures; that is, people assume that good things happen to them because they deserve it and that bad things happen to other people because those individuals deserve that. When something bad happens to you, you may blame it on bad luck or circumstances; when something bad happens to others, you may blame it on their careless or reckless behaviour.

Fundamental attribution error: The tendency to attribute other people's behaviour to dispositional (internal) causes rather than situational (external) causes.

Actor–observer effect: The tendency to attribute the behaviour of others to dispositional causes but to attribute one's own behaviour to situational causes.

Self-serving bias: People's tendency to evaluate their own positive behaviours as being due to their own internal traits and characteristics, but to blame their failures and shortcomings on external, situational factors.

Self-perceptions Depend on Your Cultural Context

P sychologists know that men and women perceive themselves differently. So do teenagers and people over age 65, people from the West and those from the East, and Canadians and Americans. In this box we will look at a sampling of the ways in which self-perceptions vary among different groups of people in Canada.

In studies conducted in Western cultures it is routinely found that people adopt a self-serving bias, rating their own actions more positively than the actions of others, even when the behaviours are indistinguishable. But this self-serving bias is not found among Asian study samples. It usually is argued that this is due to a Western orientation towards individualism and an Asian orientation towards collectivism (where the individual is only regarded as part of a group). Steven Heine and Darrin Lehman at the University of British Columbia (Heine & Lehman, 1997a) wondered whether this difference would be noted if participants were asked to rate a family member or their university rather than themselves. Perhaps people from collectivist cultures would show a self-serving bias in reference to the groups they belonged to, if not towards themselves. In fact, the researchers found a lack of self-serving bias among Asian participants generalized to both rating family members and rating their universities. This suggests that Asian participants do not think in self-biased terms even at the level of the groups they belong to, whereas Western participants extend their self-serving bias to include all levels of groups to which they belong.

In a related study, Heine and Lehman (1997b) asked Canadian and Japanese participants to rate, rank, and re-rate 10 compact discs. Occasionally this task led to participants ranking CDs they previously had liked low on their list or CDs they previously had not liked high on their lists. This potentially led to feelings of tension or cognitive dissonance (due to the discrepancy between their stated beliefs and their past listening behaviours). When given an opportunity to discuss or rationalize their ratings virtually all of the Canadian participants did so, whereas virtually none of the Japanese participants seemed to feel a need to rationalize their choices. Again, this likely reflects different cultural approaches to self-concept. The Canadian participants' independent approach to self-conceptualization caused a need to justify or rationalize their choices, as in Western cultures responsibility for past actions ultimately is assumed by the individual. In Japanese culture, on the other hand, the self is viewed in interdependent terms and, as such, the individual is not viewed as being solely responsible for his or her actions.

There is enormous diversity among individuals, families, and cultural values within any community. Parenting, education, and ethnicity affect each person's self-perception. When social psychologists develop theories of self-perception, ethnicity must be taken into account. People are diverse, and the research data show that culture affects how they perceive themselves. ■

The impact of errors in attribution and the self-serving bias can be seen in society at large. For example, Claude Steele has asserted that whenever members of minority groups concentrate on scholastic tasks, they worry too much about the risk of confirming their group's negative stereotype (Steele, 1997; Osborne, 1997; Aronson, Quinn, & Spencer, 1998). This burden may drag down their performance through what Steele calls *stereotype threat*. Stereotype threat probably occurs in part because a situational, academic pressure threatens global self-esteem; people fear being reduced to a stereotype and then stop trying and ultimately do worse because of the fear. This behaviour—no longer trying—is referred to as *disidentification*; it suggests that there was once a relationship between academic success and self-esteem, but it

Prejudice: Negative evaluation of an entire group of people, typically based on unfavourable (often incorrect) ideas or stereotypes about the group.

Stereotypes: Fixed, overly simple, often incorrect, and often negative ideas about traits, attitudes, and behaviours attributed to groups of people.

Discrimination: Behaviour targeted at individuals or groups with the aim of holding them apart and treating them differently.

no longer exists. Unless minorities (older adults, gang members) are resilient to such threats, their performance is likely to suffer (Steele, 1997). Such an attitude may inhibit people from having realistic goals, thus setting them up for disappointment.

People constantly seek the reasons for other people's behaviour in order to make judgments about them. Most people also regularly reflect on their own behaviour and in doing so form self-perceptions. *Diversity* further examines the influence of ethnicity on self-perception.

Prejudice: The Darker Side of Attitudes

People's ideas, about themselves and others, help define who they are, how they view the world, and ultimately how they behave. But what happens when the ideas, values, or activities of another person or another group of people are different from yours? What happens when you do not know the other group of people well, or at all? Why do some people form negative evaluations of certain groups, such as aboriginal people, Asians, Jews, or lesbians and gay men? In this section, we will explore the darker side of attitudes and attributions about others—prejudice—and how it can be prevented.

Prejudice is a negative evaluation (an attitude) of an entire group of people that is typically based on unfavourable (and often incorrect) ideas or stereotypes about the group. It is usually based on a small sample of experience with an individual from the group being evaluated, or even on no direct experience. **Stereotypes** are fixed, overly simple, often incorrect, and often negative ideas about traits, attitudes, and behaviours attributed to groups of people. Among others, people hold stereotyped ideas about First Nations people, lawyers, blonde women, and hockey players; the stereotypes, often shared by many people, can lead to prejudice.

Prejudice, as an attitude, is composed of a cognitive belief (all Xs are stupid), an emotional element (I hate those Xs), and often a behaviour (I am doing everything I can to keep those Xs out of my neighbourhood). When prejudice is translated into behaviour, it is called **discrimination**—behaviour targeted at individuals or groups with the aim of holding them apart and treating them differently. You can think of discrimination as prejudice in action. One common type of discrimination is *sexism* (prejudice based on gender), which involves accepting the strong and widely held beliefs of rigid gender role stereotyping (examined in Chapter 11). Overt discrimination based on gender is illegal, but it still exists, and many people's expectations for women are still based on old stereotypes about gender. For example, many people expect all women to be nurturing towards children (Glick & Fiske, 1997; Swim et al., 1995; Allen, 1995).

Sometimes people are prejudiced but do not show that attitude in their behaviour; that is, they do not discriminate. Merton (1949) referred to such individuals as *cautious bigots* (unlike true bigots, who are prejudiced and who also discriminate). People sometimes show *reverse discrimination*, bending over backwards to treat an individual more positively than they should, solely to counter their own pre-existing biases or stereotypes (Chidester, 1986). That is, someone prejudiced towards First Nations people may be overly solicitous towards a First Nations person and may evaluate the person favourably on the basis of standards different from those used for others. This, too, is discrimination. (Table 13.1 illustrates the interaction between prejudice and discrimination.)

A related concept is *tokenism*, in which prejudiced people engage in positive but trivial actions towards members of a group they dislike. A male executive may make a token gesture towards the women on his staff, or a manager may hire a token Asian. By engaging in tokenism, a person often attempts to put off more important actions, such as changing overall hiring practices. In this person's mind, the trivial behaviour justifies the idea that he or she has done something for the disliked group. Tokenism has negative consequences for the self-esteem of the person to whom it is applied, and it perpetuates discrimination by suggesting that only one member of the disliked group was good enough to be given a job. In the end, social psychologists generally conclude that stereotyping promotes prejudice, and that prejudice promotes discrimination.

Table 13.1 Prejudice and Discrimination

Prejudice and discrimination interact in such a way that one can be evident without the other.

	Presence of Prejudice	Absence of Prejudice
Presence of Discrimination	An employer believes that non-whites cannot do quality work and does not promote them, regardless of their performance.	An employer believes that all people can do quality work but does not promote minorities because of long-held company policies.
Absence of Discrimination	An employer believes that non-whites cannot do quality work but promotes them on the basis of their performance rather than following preconceived ideas.	An employer believes that all people can do quality work and promotes people on the basis of their performance on the job.

What Causes Prejudice? The causes of prejudice cannot be tied to a single theory or explanation. Like so many other psychological phenomena, prejudice is a cross-cultural phenomenon (Pettigrew et al., 1998); it has multiple causes and can be examined within an individual, between individuals, within a group, or within society (Duckitt, 1992). We will consider four theories to explain prejudice: social learning theory, motivational theory, cognitive theory, and personality theory.

According to *social learning theory*, children *learn* to be prejudiced; they watch parents, other relatives, teachers, peers, and neighbours engage in acts of discrimination, which often include stereotyped judgments and racial slurs; they then incorporate those ideas into their own behavioural repertoire. After children have observed such behaviours, they are then reinforced (operant conditioning) for exhibiting similar behaviours. Thus, through imitation and reinforcement, a prejudiced view is transmitted from one generation to the next.

We saw in Chapter 9 that people are motivated to succeed, to get ahead, and to provide for basic as well as high-level emotional needs. If people are raised to compete against others for scarce resources, this competition can foster negative views of competitors. *Motivational theory* thus asserts that individuals learn to dislike specific individuals (competitors) and then generalize that dislike to whole classes of similar individuals (races, religions, or cultures). Gordon Allport asserted that the arousal of competition followed by erroneous generalizations creates specific prejudice towards minority groups (Allport, 1954/1979; Gaines & Reed, 1995). This helps make minorities that are seen as economic competitors into scapegoats—for example, Jews in Nazi Germany and Japanese Canadians during the Second World War. Research conducted with children, adolescents, and adults shows that people who are initially seen as friends or as neutral others are sometimes treated badly when turned into competitors. Competition for jobs among immigrants also can create prejudice, particularly in times of economic hardship.

Cognitive theorists assert that people think about individuals and their groups of origin as a way of organizing the world. Cialdini (1993) argues that there are so many events, circumstances, and changing variables in their lives that people cannot analyze all of the relevant data about any one thing easily. People thus devise mental short cuts to help them make decisions. One of those short cuts is to stereotype individuals and the groups they belong to—for example, all French Canadians, all homeless people, all men, all lawyers. Research shows that people use such short cuts to socially categorize individuals on traits such as athleticism, intelligence, gender, and ethnicity, and that they develop illusory correlations about social groups and their behaviours (Schaller, 1991; Spears & Haslam, 1997; Stone, Perry, & Darley, 1997). An *illusory correlation* is an unsubstantiated and incorrect correlation between two events or situations that appear, by inference, to be related. By devising such short cuts in thinking, people develop ideas about who is in an *in group*—that is, who is a member of a group to which those people belong or want to belong. The division of the world into groups labelled "in" versus "out" or "us" versus "them" is known

Social categorization: The process of dividing the world into "in" and "out" groups.

as **social categorization.** Not only do people divide the world into in groups and out groups, but they tend to see themselves and other members of an in group in a favourable light; doing so bolsters their self-esteem and occurs almost automatically (Devine, 1989; Fiske, 1998).

As we saw earlier in this chapter, when judging other people, individuals make fundamental attribution errors. They assume that other people's behaviour is caused by internal dispositions—which may not be true—and that other people are all alike, at least most of the time (Lambert, 1995). They underestimate situational influences and overestimate dispositional influences on other people's behaviour, and then they use those behaviours as evidence for their attitudes (prejudices). Thus, hostilities between Arabs and Israelis in the Middle East, Catholics and Protestants in Ireland, and blacks and whites in South Africa are perpetuated.

Researchers such as Susan Fiske (1998) assert that when people develop stereotypes about groups—who's in and who's out—the stereotype and the prejudice that follows is a more complex affair than previously thought. For example, there are groups that some people like but do not respect, or vice versa. In some circles, the traditional housewife is liked but not respected; similarly, militant feminists may be respected but not liked. This duality of liking/respecting may translate into complex social behaviours such as sexism and racism in which individual members of a given group are treated benevolently while the group as a whole is treated with hostility (Glick & Fiske, 1997; Glick et al., 1997; Monteith, Zuwerink, & Devine, 1994).

Personality psychologists assert that a person who develops prejudices has a "prejudice-prone personality." In fact, some personality tests examine the extent to which people are likely to be prejudiced. For example, one common personality type is the *authoritarian personality*. Authoritarian people may have been fearful and anxious as children and may have been raised by cold parents who withheld love and regularly used physical punishment. Bob Altemeyer of the University of Manitoba has studied authoritarianism extensively and has shown that, in addition to having its roots in experiences of fear and aggression, it is related to early experiences with parents and religious activities that promote a strong reverence for authority (Altemeyer, 1988). To gain control and mastery as adults, such individuals become aggressive and controlling over others. They see the world in absolutes—good versus bad, black versus white. They also tend to blame others for their problems and to become prejudiced towards those people (Adorno et al., 1950). The relationship between personality and prejudice has its roots in psychoanalytic theory and is hotly debated.

Can similar forms of resentment be expressed in nonracial terms? The answer is clearly yes. As *Brain and Behaviour* shows, someone may be prejudiced against fat people because he or she holds people responsible for their behaviour—a Western value. The result is resentment and subtle prejudice.

How to Reduce and Eliminate Prejudice.
To reduce and eliminate prejudice, people can teach rational thinking, try to judge others based on their behaviour, promote equality, and avoid labels that perpetuate stereotypes (Jussim et al., 1995). Changing a behaviour, and then letting attitudes follow in due course, can reduce prejudice. For example, once people have worked on a community project with a member of a different culture, lived with a person of another

Focus

Review

- Identify the key characteristics of nonverbal communication. pp. 458–460
- Describe the fundamental difference between dispositional and situational interpretations of the causes of behaviour. pp. 460–461
- How do psychological theories explain the development of prejudice? pp. 464–466

Think Critically

- Can you describe any useful functions that errors in attribution have served for you or a friend in the last few months? Have such errors helped someone feel more intelligent, more worthwhile, or less at fault?
- In Canada prejudice has been instrumental in the poor treatment of First Nations people, women, the aged, gays and lesbians, and many minority groups. What are some effective techniques (not necessarily governmental policies) that can be used to help eliminate prejudice, correct previous injustices, and make for a more tolerant society?

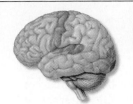

brain and behaviour

Double Whammy Against Fat People

Fat people have a lot going against them—biology probably is not on their side, nor are the prejudicial attitudes that they may experience. On the biological side, the brain and the regulation of hormones are central reasons why, once people get fat, they stay fat. As discussed in Chapter 9, nearly any food affects eating behaviour, but so do hormones. Insulin, for example, affects eating behaviour. Neurotransmitters like serotonin, which can be stimulated through eating certain foods, like chocolate, affect eating, mood, and depression. Eating behaviours also are affected at the hypothalamic level, the amygdala, and at various cortical locations. Researchers' understanding of neurobiology is just beginning to help them understand the intricacies of eating.

But there are not only biological shackles on the obese—there are social consequences as well. People see fat individuals as unattractive, aesthetically displeasing, and even emotionally impaired. They are described as "weak-willed" by some; their peers rate them as unlikable. Employers don't want to hire them, health care workers ignore them, and fat people are less likely to attend college than thin people.

According to Christian Crandall (Crandall, 1994; Crandall & Martinez, 1996), who studied anti-fat biases, anti-fat attitudes are at an all-time high; they are overt and widely held. Why do people hold this view so strongly? Crandall maintains that two factors are key. First, Canadians and Americans believe that thinness is good; over the last 40 years they have developed a cultural preference for thinness—indeed, the popular media extol thinness as virtuous and obesity as disagreeable at best. Second, the conservative Protestant ethic of willpower, self-determination, and the idea that "a person can be anything that he or she wants to be" is at the core of Canadian and American values. So, a fat person comes to be seen as personally responsible for his or her "deviant" behaviour. Stereotypes of fat people (gluttonous, lacking in willpower) lead to prejudice against them and then to discrimination in employment and other areas of life. Fat people often try to compensate, perhaps by being overly friendly or helpful (Miller & Myers, 1998).

Following this reasoning, it is no surprise that Canadians and Americans are anti-fat. We view obesity as a personal imperfection. But other cultures don't have such polarized views. In Mexico, Central American countries, and Africa the obese are not stigmatized—and the emotional consequences of being overweight are not so evident (Rothblum, 1990, 1992; Cogan et al., 1996).

Anti-fat prejudice offers an opportunity for researchers to study stereotyping, prejudice, and discrimination. It will be interesting to see if researchers compare prejudice against fat people with other prejudices such as racism and sexism. Whereas biology may be a key determinant of obesity, social attitudes about it affect millions of people in equally detrimental ways. ■

race, or prayed with members of a different religious faith, their emotional views of them as individuals change (Pettigrew, 1997).

A society can pass laws that mandate equal treatment for all people—for example, those that forbid discrimination in the workplace or in the housing market. Such laws generally reflect changing beliefs (Bobo & Kluegel, 1997). Voters can elect officials on the basis of their competence, throw them out of office on the basis of their incompetence, and make gender-neutral judgments of performance. Former prime minister Kim Campbell and former governor general Jean Sauvé were judged by their performance, not by their gender. Svend Robinson, widely perceived as a highly principled politician due to his integrity and character, has the ability to transform people's views of the role of homosexuals in our society (Sigelman, 1997).

Psychologists—and students of psychology—must be especially sensitive to the need to think about *individuals* rather than about groups. Through examination of individuals, psychologists become sensitive to the wide diversity of human behaviour. Although it is tempting to derive broad generalizations about behaviour and the causes of behaviour, researchers must focus on individuals. When they focus on individuals, they see that human beings are engaged in and are affected by an array of behaviours.

Social Interactions: The Power of People and Situations

How you initiate a conversation with someone you haven't met before is a task all of us have had to deal with. When people interact with one another, complex new realms of possibility open up. For this reason, social psychologists pay close attention to the interactions among individuals. From obeying authority to watching television to helping a person in distress, day-to-day social interactions can be exceedingly complex, involving intricate variables. This is what makes the study of social behaviours so exciting.

Social Influence

Parents try to instil specific values in their children. An adolescent may admire the hairstyle or mannerisms of an attractive peer and decide to adopt them. Professors urge students to shed preconceived ideas. The behaviour or appearance of a celebrity may be emulated by adoring fans. Religious leaders exhort their followers to live in certain ways. Social interactions affect individual behaviour in profound ways; when people are members of a group, their social interactions are often even more striking than their individual behaviour.

One kind of social interaction is **social influence**, or the way in which one or more people alter the attitudes or behaviour of others, either directly or indirectly. People exert powerful influences on others, and psychologists have attempted to understand how this influence operates. Studies of social influence have focused on two topics: conformity and obedience.

Conformity. When someone changes attitudes or behaviours to be consistent with other people or with social norms, the person is exhibiting **conformity**; he or she is trying to fit in. The behaviours the person may adopt include positive, prosocial behaviours such as wearing seatbelts, volunteering time and money for a charity, or buying only products that are safe for the environment. Sometimes, however, people conform to counterproductive, antisocial behaviours, such as drug abuse or mob violence.

People conform to the behaviours and attitudes of their peer or family groups. A successful young executive may wear conservative dark suits and drive a BMW to fit in with office colleagues. Similarly, the desire to conform can induce people to do things they might not do otherwise. An infamous example is the My Lai massacre, in which American soldiers slaughtered Vietnamese civilians during the Vietnam War. While several factors account for the soldiers' behaviour (including combat stress, hostility towards the Vietnamese, and obedience to authority), the soldiers also yielded to extreme group pressure. The few soldiers who refused to kill the civilians hid that fact from their comrades. One soldier even shot himself in the foot to avoid becoming part of the slaughter.

Groups strongly influence conformity. Solomon Asch (1907–1996) found that people in a group adopt the values and standards set by the group. Examples of conformity to group standards range from an individual refraining from speaking during a public address to a whole nation discriminating against a particular ethnic group. Studies also show that individuals conform to group norms even when they are not pressured to do so. Consider what happens when an instructor asks a class of 250 students to answer a relatively simple question, but no one volunteers. When asked, most students will report that they did not raise their hand because no one else did. Asch (1955, p. 6) stated:

> The tendency to conformity in our society [is] so strong that reasonably intelligent and well-meaning young people [being] willing to call white black is a matter of concern. It raises questions about our ways of education and about the values that guide our conduct.

Social influence: The way in which one or more people alter the attitudes or behaviour of others.

Conformity: People's tendency to change attitudes or behaviours to be consistent with other people or with social norms.

Suppose you have agreed to participate in an experiment. You are seated at the end of a table next to four other students. The experimenter holds up a card and asks each of you to pick which of two lines is longer, A or B. You quickly discover that the task is simple. The experimenter holds up successive pairs of lines and each participant correctly identifies the longest. But, after several rounds, you notice that the first person has chosen line A instead of line B, though B is obviously longer. You are surprised when the second person also chooses line A, then the third, then the fourth. Your turn is next. You are sure that line B is longer but the four people before you have all chosen line A. What do you do?

In 1951 Asch performed a similar experiment to explore conformity. Seven to nine individuals were brought into a room and asked to judge which of three lines matched a standard (see Figure 13.6). However, only one group member—the naïve participant—was unaware of the purpose of the study. The others were collaborators of the researcher, and they deliberately gave false answers to try to influence the naïve participant. Asch found that one-third of naïve participants went along with the group, even though the majority answer was obviously wrong and even though the group exerted no explicit, or directly observable, pressure on that person.

It turns out that the relative number of individuals purposely giving wrong answers is a critical variable. When one or two individuals pick the wrong line, the tendency to conform is considerably less than when ten do. Another important variable is whether there are any dissenting votes. If even 1 of 15 people disagrees with the other participants, the naïve participant is more likely to choose the correct line.

How do groups influence individual behaviour? One conformity variable is the *amount of information* provided when a decision is to be made. When people are uncertain of how to behave in ambiguous situations, they seek the opinions of others. For example, people who are unsure of how they should vote in an election often will ask trusted friends for advice. People tend to accept the advice of those they like and those who are similar to them.

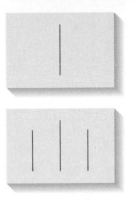

FIGURE 13.6
Asch's Classic Study of Conformity
Participants were shown cards like these and asked to choose the line on the lower card that was the same length as the line on the upper card. The confederates deliberately chose incorrect answers to see if the unsuspecting participant would go along with the majority.

Another important variable that affects the degree of conformity is the *relative competence* of the group. People are more likely to conform to the decision of a group if they perceive its members as being more competent than they themselves are. This pressure becomes stronger as group size increases. A first-year student in a large class of first-, second-, and third-year students may not answer even a simple question if no one else speaks up because they assume that their classmates are more competent than they are.

Position within a group also affects individual behaviour. A person who confidently believes that a group holds them in high esteem will respond independently. If they are insecure about their status they may respond as the group does because they fear losing status.

The *public nature of behaviour* also determines people's responses. Individuals are more willing to make decisions that are inconsistent with those of their group when the behaviour is private. In a democracy, for example, voting is done privately so as to minimize group pressure on how individuals vote.

Why do people tend to conform? Several theories have attempted to explain this phenomenon. The *social conformity approach* states that people conform to avoid the stigma of being wrong, deviant, out of line, or different from others. According to this view, people want to do the right thing, and people define as right whatever is generally accepted (Festinger, 1954). Another explanation for why individuals in a group conform—or don't conform—is *attribution*. When a person can identify causes for other people's behaviour and strongly disagrees with those causes, conformity disappears (Ross, Bierbrauer, & Hoffman, 1976). The issue of *independence* also helps explain conformity (or the lack of it). Although most people would like to be independent, independence is risky. People in a group may have to face the consequences of their independence, such as serious disapproval, peer pressure to conform, being seen as deviant, becoming less powerful, or simply being left out. Finally, conformity is partly a matter of *expediency*; conforming conserves mental energy. Recall Cialdini's (1993) argument that people face too many events, circumstances, and changing variables to be able to analyze all the relevant data. People therefore need short cuts to help them make decisions. It is efficient and easy for people to go along with others whom they trust and respect, especially if key elements of a situation fit in with their views.

It is important to recognize that not everyone conforms to group pressures all the time—especially when other people disagree with the group. Both everyday experience and research show that *dissenting opinions* help counteract group influence and conformity. Even one or two people in a large group can seriously influence decision making. Moreover, when group decision making occurs, a consistent opposing voice (think of South African leader Nelson Mandela) can exert substantial influence and foster a sense of liberation, even when the opposition is devoid of power or status (Kitayama & Burnstein, 1994). Not surprisingly, analysis of cross-cultural studies shows that countries with collectivist cultures exhibit more conformity than do countries with individualistic cultures (Bond & Smith, 1996).

Obedience and Milgram's Study. **Obedience** is compliance with the orders of another person or a group of people. The studies on obedience by Stanley Milgram (1933–1984) are classic, and his results and interpretations still generate debate today. Milgram's work focused on the extent to which an individual will obey a person in authority. His studies showed that ordinary people were remarkably willing to comply with those they saw as legitimate authority figures.

Imagine that you are one of the participants in Milgram's 1963 study at Yale University. You and a man you do not know are brought into a laboratory and are told that you will be participating in an experiment on paired-associate learning. You draw lots to determine who will be the teacher and who will be the learner. The drawing is actually rigged so that you will be the teacher and the man (who is collaborating with the experimenter) will be the learner.

The learner/collaborator is taken to an adjoining room, where you cannot see him. You are shown a shock-generating box containing 30 switches, with labels that

range from "15 Volts: Slight Shock" to "420 Volts: Danger: Severe Shock" to "450 Volts: XXX." You are told to shock the learner by hitting one of the switches every time he makes an error on a test he will be given.

As the test continues, the experimenter and an assistant, both wearing white lab coats, encourage you to increase the shock voltage by one level each time the learner makes a mistake.

As the shock level rises, the learner/collaborator screams as if he is suffering increasing pain. When the intensity reaches the point of intense shock (255–300 volts), the learner stops responding vocally to the test stimulus and pounds on the walls of the booth. The experimenter tells you to treat the learner's lack of vocal response as an error and to continue increasing the levels of shock. What would you do?

This was the basic scenario of the Milgram study. As Figure 13.7 shows, 65 percent of the participants in the study continued to shock the learner until they had delivered shocks at all levels. (As you may have guessed by now, the learner/collaborators were not actually receiving shocks but only pretending to be in pain.)

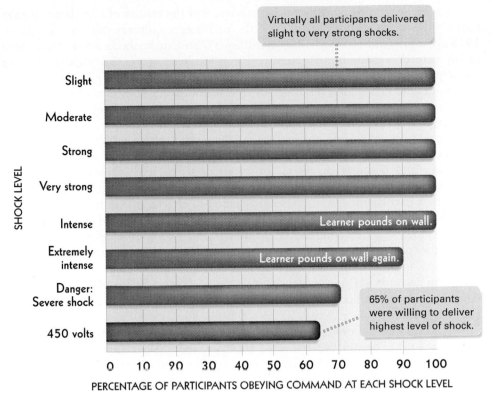

FIGURE 13.7
Milgram's Obedience Study

(Based on data from Milgram, 1963.)

Virtually all participants delivered slight to very strong shocks.

Learner pounds on wall.

Learner pounds on wall again.

65% of participants were willing to deliver highest level of shock.

SHOCK LEVEL

Slight

Moderate

Strong

Very strong

Intense

Extremely intense

Danger: Severe shock

450 volts

0   10   90   30   40   50   60   70   80   90   100

PERCENTAGE OF PARTICIPANTS OBEYING COMMAND AT EACH SHOCK LEVEL

However, not all of Milgram's participants were obedient. Moreover, the presence of others who refused to continue shocking the learner reduced the probability of obedience to as little as 10 percent (Milgram, 1965; Powers & Geen, 1972). These data suggest that obedience is sensitive to both authority and peer behaviour. The fact that an individual's ability to resist coercion improves in the presence of an ally who also resists indicates the importance of other social influences on behaviour.

Did conducting the study at the prestigious Yale University influence the participants? Milgram (1965) suggested that his experiment might have involved a particular type of experimental bias—*background authority*. To investigate the issue, Milgram conducted a second study in an office building in Bridgeport, Connecticut. Participants were contacted by mail and had no knowledge that Milgram or his associates were from Yale. In this second study, 48 percent of the participants, as compared with 65 percent at Yale, delivered the maximum level of shock. Although this was not a big difference, Milgram inferred that the perceived function of an institution could induce obedience in participants. Moreover, an institution's qualitative position within a category (for example, a prestigious versus a little-known university) may be less important than the type of institution it is (for example, a university rather than a company office).

Explaining Milgram's Results. Why did so many participants in Milgram's experiments obey the wishes of the authority figure? One reason is that they were volunteers. Volunteers often bring undetected biases to an experimental situation, and one such bias is a willingness to go along with authority. When instructed to shock, Milgram's participants did what they were told and, once they started, could not find a solid reason to stop. Another explanation derives from learning theories. Children learn that authority figures, such as teachers and parents, know more than they do and that taking their advice generally proves beneficial. As adults, they maintain those beliefs and apply them to authority figures such as employers, judges, government leaders, and so on. Cialdini (1993) also notes that obedience has practical advantages, such as helping people make decisions quickly: "It is easy to allow ourselves the convenience of automatic obedience. . . . We don't have to think, therefore we don't" (p. 178).

Researchers repeated Milgram's methods, and the results of one study suggest that obedience to authority is not specific to Western cultures (Shanab & Yahya, 1978). People tend to obey those in authority, and such obedience is even more highly valued in many non-Western cultures. Students at the University of Jordan participated in a similar study; as in the original Milgram study, about 65 percent were willing to give high levels of shock to other students. Milgram's findings apply to men and women, old and young; they show that the social world and people's interactions within it are strongly affected by others.

In any study of social influence, researchers worry about ethics, and Milgram's experimental methods certainly raised ethical issues. The primary issue was one of deception and potential harm to those who participated. Obtaining unbiased responses in psychological research often requires deceiving naïve participants. To ensure that participants do not have any lasting ill effects, researchers debrief them after the experiment. **Debriefing** is informing participants about the true nature of the experiment after its completion, including an explanation of hypotheses, methods, and expected or potential results. Researchers debrief participants *after* the experiment to preserve the validity of the responses while taking ethical considerations into account. Of course, debriefing must be done clearly and with sensitivity, especially in studies like Milgram's, which could affect a participant's self-concept and self-esteem.

Milgram's participants were fully debriefed and shown that they had not harmed the other person. Nevertheless, critics argued, the participants came to realize that they were capable of inflicting severe pain on other people. Milgram therefore had a psychiatrist interview a sample of his obedient participants a year after the study. No evidence of psychological trauma or injury was found. Moreover, one study reported that participants viewed participation in the obedience experiment as a positive experience. They did not regret having participated; nor did they report any short-term negative psychological effects (Ring, Wallston, & Corey, 1970). Today, due to ethical constraints that are now in place, Milgram's research and its variations would not be allowed in research laboratories.

Studies of social influence, especially conformity and obedience studies, show us that people exert powerful influences on individuals and that those influences are even greater when a group exerts them. One person may influence us, but when a group of people attempt to influence us, the effect is extremely powerful. Let's look at the effects of groups on individual behaviour and how individuals behave within groups.

Groups: Sharing Common Goals

"Membership has its privileges," according to American Express. In appealing to people's desire to be part of a group, the credit card company is employing psychological principles to sell its product and engender loyalty. To make the American Express group as attractive as possible, the company has run magazine ads featuring famous athletes, actors, politicians, and business people who are cardholders. Who wouldn't want to identify with such an elite group?

Membership does confer certain advantages, which is why people belong to all kinds of groups. There are formal groups, such as the Canadian Psychological Association, and informal ones, such as a lunch group of co-workers. A **group** can be either a large number of people working towards a common purpose or a small number of people (even two) who are loosely connected by some common goals or interests. By joining a group, people indicate that they agree with or have a serious interest in its purpose. If a major function of the Canadian Cancer Society is to raise money for cancer research, a person's membership indicates an interest in finding a cure for cancer. It generally has been thought that groups function well and enhance performance; research shows, however, that such effects of groups are modest and that the larger effect that emanates from a group is a sense of cohesion, solidarity, and commitment to a task (Mullen & Copper, 1994).

Social Facilitation. Individual behaviour is affected not only by membership in a group but also by the mere presence of a group. **Social facilitation** is a change in performance that occurs when people believe they are in the presence of other people. For example, there is anecdotal evidence that a person practising a sport at which he or she is accomplished may do even better when other people are watching. A person who is less accomplished, however, may do worse when other people are around. Research studies that examine people's performance at various tasks—for example, keyboard data entry—show this effect (Aiello & Kolb, 1995).

How the presence of others changes a person's behaviour, and whether it changes the behaviour for better or worse, is illustrated in Figure 13.8. This figure is based on Robert Zajonc's (1965) *drive theory of social facilitation*. According to Zajonc, the presence of others produces heightened arousal, which leads to a greater likelihood that an individual will exhibit a particular response (Jackson & Latané, 1981; Zajonc, 1965).

But the exact nature of this heightened arousal is a source of some debate. One theory of social facilitation suggests that fear of evaluation—not the mere presence of people—brings about changes in performance (see Innes & Young, 1975). If an auto mechanic knows that a customer is watching him repair an engine, he is likely to increase his work speed to convince the observer of his efficiency and professionalism. Bond and Titus (1983) suggest that the effects of social facilitation are often overestimated. They caution that a model of social facilitation must take into account the actual and believed presence of observers, as well as the perceived importance of the evaluation by the perceived observers. Thus, being evaluated by a friend has a different effect than being evaluated by a superior or even a stranger (Buck et al., 1992).

A decrease in an individual's effort and productivity as a result of working in a group is known as **social loafing**. Suppose you and several fellow students are working on a group project for one your classes. Would you expend as much effort as a member of the group as you would have expended if you had had to complete a project on your own? Research confirms the social loafing effect—you probably would not work as hard in the group. In an experiment in which individuals were instructed to clap their hands and cheer, they clapped and cheered less loudly when they were part of a group (Latané, Williams, & Harkins, 1979).

Most psychologists claim that social loafing occurs when individual performance within a group cannot be evaluated; that is, poor performance may go undetected, and exceptional performance may go unrecognized. Consequently, people feel less pressure to work hard or efficiently. One study showed that as group size

Social facilitation: Change in performance that occurs when people believe they are in the presence of other people.

Social loafing: A decrease in productivity that occurs when an individual works in a group instead of alone.

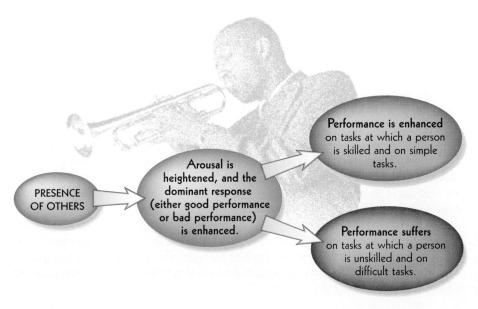

PRESENCE OF OTHERS

Arousal is heightened, and the dominant response (either good performance or bad performance) is enhanced.

Performance is enhanced on tasks at which a person is skilled and on simple tasks.

Performance suffers on tasks at which a person is unskilled and on difficult tasks.

FIGURE 13.8
Social Facilitation
The presence of others may either help or hinder a person's performance. The presence of others heightens arousal, and heightened arousal leads to better performance on tasks a person is good at and worse performance on difficult tasks.

increased, individual members believed their own efforts were more dispensable—the group could function without their help. "Let George do it" became the prevailing attitude (Kerr & Bruun, 1983). Such findings are evident cross-culturally; even Jordanian students, who come from a society that stresses cohesion and group cooperation, worked less hard when they were working together than when working alone (Atoum & Farah, 1993).

Social loafing is minimized when the task is attractive and rewarding and the group is cohesive and committed to high task performance (Karau & Williams, 1997). It is also less apparent when a group is small, when the members know one another well, and when a group leader calls on individuals by name or lets it be known that individual performance may be evaluated (Williams, Harkins, & Latané, 1981). Some researchers have noted decreased social loafing when individuals have the opportunity to assess their own performance relative to an objective standard or relative to other people's performance, even though no one else is evaluating them (Harkins & Szymanski, 1988; Szymanski & Harkins, 1993). As with so many other social phenomena, a wide array of variables can alter the extent of social loafing; yet researchers conclude that social loafing is a robust phenomenon that occurs across a wide variety of tasks and situations (Karau & Williams, 1997; Prattarelli & McIntyre, 1994).

Group Polarization. In groups, people may be willing to adopt behaviours slightly more extreme than their individual behavioural preferences. They may be willing to make decisions that are risky or even daring. A person who is unwilling to invest money in a venture may change his or her mind on hearing that other members of the group are investing. Some early research on group decision making focused on the willingness of individuals to accept more risky alternatives when other members of the group did so; this research described such individuals as making a *risky shift* in their decisions.

In a group, individuals initially perceive themselves as being more extreme than the other members of the group. They also believe they are more fair, more right-minded, more liberal, and so on. When they discover that their positions are not very different from those of others in the group, they shift, or become *polarized*, to show that they are even more right-minded, fairer, or more liberal. They also may become more assertive in expressing their views. Shifts or exaggerations that take place among group members after group discussions are referred to as **group polarization**; in individuals, such a shift is known as a *choice shift* (Zuber, Crott, & Werner, 1992).

A *persuasive argument* explanation of the polarization phenomenon asserts that people tend to become more extreme after hearing views similar to their own. A person who is mildly liberal on an issue becomes even more liberal, more polarized. The explanation therefore suggests that people in a group often become more wedded to their initial views instead of becoming more moderate. If other people in the group hold similar views, that may polarize them even more. The effects of group polarization are particularly evident among juries. After group discussion, jury members are likely to decide on their initial views and argue for them more strongly. Thus, individual jury members with an initially doubting view towards a witness will have even deeper doubts after group discussions; their initial view becomes a verdict.

Another explanation for group polarization is *diffusion of responsibility*—the feeling of individual members of a group that they cannot be held responsible for the group's actions. If a church youth group makes a decision to invest money, for example, no single individual is responsible. Diffusion of responsibility may allow the teenagers to make far more extreme investment decisions as a group than they would individually.

Social comparison also may play a role in group polarization. People compare their views with the ideas of others whom they respect and who may hold more extreme attitudes than they do. Feeling as right-minded as their colleagues, they become at least as liberal or as conservative as their peer group—they polarize their views.

Group polarization:
Exaggeration of individuals' pre-existing attitudes as a result of group discussion.

After a group becomes polarized, many people in the group may share the same opinion. When such an event occurs (as it often does with government officials), people sometimes fall into a trap called *groupthink*.

Groupthink: The tendency of people in a group to seek agreement with one another when reaching a decision, usually prematurely.

Groupthink. Studies of decision making in government have often focused on the concept of **groupthink**—the tendency of people in a group to seek agreement with one another when reaching a decision, usually prematurely. Groupthink occurs when group members reinforce shared beliefs in the interest of getting along rather than effectively evaluating alternative solutions to the problem. The group does not allow its members to disagree, accept dissenting opinions, or evaluate options realistically (Janis, 1983). Groupthink discredits or ignores information not held in common, and thus cohesive groups are more likely to exhibit it (Mullen et al., 1994). See Figure 13.9 for a summary of the factors leading to groupthink.

Studies of history and government offer several examples of groupthink resulting in defective decision making, including the ill-fated decision to launch the space shuttle "Challenger" against the advice of engineers on the launch team (Moorhead, Ference, & Neck, 1991). Another example of groupthink may have been the calling of the budget vote in the House of Commons that brought down the Joe Clark government. In hindsight, it is clear that the Progressive Conservatives did not have enough support to pass the budget, but at the time they seemed certain that all would go well with the vote. This groupthink proved to be costly, as Joe Clark was forced to resign after having served only nine months as prime minister and Pierre Trudeau and the Liberals regained power in the election that followed.

Social psychologist Ivan Steiner (1982) suggests that groupthink occurs when members' overriding concern is to maintain group cohesiveness and harmony. Maintaining cohesiveness helps individuals believe that the group cannot make mistakes. In addition, strong leaders often insulate a group from information or from other people to keep the group thinking in one direction (McCauley, 1989).

Despite the intuitive appeal of the groupthink concept, however, research support for it is minimal. Nevertheless, Aldag and Fuller (1993) assert that despite its lack of empirical support, groupthink is a defective process that people should guard against. They argue that groupthink can happen and that research into leaders, committees, and technology needs to focus on the variables that may create it or help defend against it (Miranda, 1994).

Unrestrained Group Behaviour. The presence of other people can arouse people (social facilitation), can make them less active (social loafing), can cause them to make extreme decisions (group polarization), or can lead to consensus-making poor decisions (groupthink). So, when placed in a group, normally thoughtful people have been known to take part in bad decision making and even very irrational behaviours. Consider mob violence. When people engage in a riot, looting, or a beating, individuals explain their behaviour not in terms of individual responsibility but as a group decision.

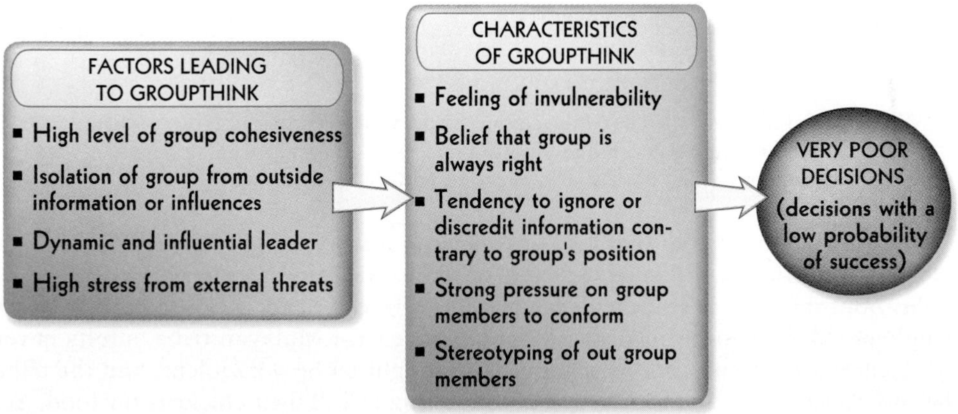

FIGURE 13.9
Groupthink: Development and Results

FACTORS LEADING TO GROUPTHINK	CHARACTERISTICS OF GROUPTHINK	VERY POOR DECISIONS (decisions with a low probability of success)
■ High level of group cohesiveness ■ Isolation of group from outside information or influences ■ Dynamic and influential leader ■ High stress from external threats	■ Feeling of invulnerability ■ Belief that group is always right ■ Tendency to ignore or discredit information contrary to group's position ■ Strong pressure on group members to conform ■ Stereotyping of out group members	

A key component of unrestrained behaviour such as mob violence is *anonymity*. Anonymity produces a lack of self-awareness and self-perception that leads to decreased concern with social evaluation. When people have fewer concerns about being evaluated, they are more willing to engage in inappropriate or irrational behaviours. When there is violence or illegal drug use among a crowd at a rock concert, people feel less responsible. The view that no single individual can be held responsible for the behaviour of a group arises out of **deindividuation**—the process by which individuals lose their self-awareness and distinctive personalities in the context of a group and may engage in anti-normative behaviour (Diener et al., 1980). Deindividuation (and its accompanying arousal) can lead to shifts in people's

perceptions of how their behaviour will be viewed—and thus to less controlled, less self-conscious, or less careful decisions about behaviour. With deindividuation, people alter their thoughts about decisions.

Groups such as the military, prisons, and cults use deindividuation to encourage their members to conform. In boot camp, military recruits are made to feel that they are there to serve the group, not their conscience. In prisons, inmates are made to wear uniforms and cut their hair short and are assigned numbers. With their unique personality stripped away, they are no longer treated as individuals and are made to behave as members of one large prison group. A cult persuades members to go along with group beliefs and acquire a sense of obligation to the group by asking individual members to perform increasingly taxing services on the group's behalf. In the end, an individual's behaviour in a group often becomes distorted, more extreme, and less rational; the group leads members to feel less accountable for their own actions. Research on deindividuation suggests it may not be this clear-cut (e.g., Prentice-Dunn, 1991; Postmes & Spears, 1998)—so, this popular and appealing idea is in a state of flux. Like many theories in psychology it is being evaluated and reevaluated to ensure its durability.

Aggression and Violence: The Dark Side of Human Behaviour

Our social interactions with people are sometimes quite inconsequential; we say hello to others as we pass them on the street, for example. Other times our interactions affect family or work relationships, such as when we recognize kindness or good work in our family or co-workers. But social interactions also include the dark side of people's behaviours, including their aggressive and violent acts—children and adults kill cats, set fires, and engage in acts of terror. People strike out at others, behave aggressively and violently, and the cause often is not apparent or justified. As we will see in this section, social interactions are shaped by a wide array of events in people's lives.

> We killed, killed, killed. The Malays would stop and go through people's pockets and take their watches and money. We did not think of watches or money. We thought only of killing. . . . [W]e were drunk with blood.

A Semai soldier told that tale to American anthropologist Robert K. Dentan (1968), who lived with the man's tribe for more than a year. What is most remarkable about the story is that the Semai are among the gentlest people on earth. Not a single murder has been recorded among this central Malayan tribe, adults never physically attack one another, children are taught to be nonviolent, and the tribe has no police force. The Semai regret even having to kill their chickens for food. Yet

Deindividuation: The process by which individuals in a group lose their self-awareness and concern with evaluation and may engage in anti-normative behaviour.

despite their pacifist heritage, Semai tribesmen were recruited and trained by the British to fight Communist guerrillas in the early 1950s. When their comrades fell in battle, the Semai avenged themselves on the enemy with terrible ferocity. One veteran reported drinking the blood of a man he killed. On their return home, however, the Semai soldiers returned to their pacifist ways.

In contrast, the Yanomamo of Brazil and Venezuela are among the most violent people on earth. Their murder rate is extraordinarily high, and an estimated 44 percent of the men aged 25 or older have participated in at least one killing. Yet other South American tribes are as peaceful as the Yanomamo are violent. If people can be either loving or violent, what compels them to act one way or the other?

When people feel unable to control situations that affect their lives, they may become frustrated, angry, and aggressive. Social psychologists define **aggression** as any behaviour designed to harm another person or thing. An aggressive person may attempt to harm others physically through force, to harm them verbally through gossip, rumours, or irritating comments, or to harm them emotionally by withholding love. On a larger scale, whole countries attempt to harm others through economic sanctions or by acts of war. Three major theoretical explanations for aggressive behaviour are instincts, acquired drives, and a cognitive model.

Instincts. Some psychologists believe that many aspects of behaviour, including aggression, are inborn (see DiLalla & Gottesman, 1991); but most psychologists, the Canadian Psychological Association, and the American Psychological Association (1990) do not agree. Those who believe that people are genetically predisposed towards aggression are termed *nativists*. An early nativist was Freud, who suggested that people have a destructive desire to release aggression against themselves, a death instinct he called *thanatos*. However, Freud never fully developed this concept, and today his conceptualization of the death instinct is not widely accepted.

Another nativist was the ethologist and Nobel laureate Konrad Lorenz (1903–1989), who investigated aggressive behaviour through naturalistic observation. He noted that although animals of the same species fight with one another, they often use signals that tell them to avoid fighting or to stop fighting well before serious injury or death occur. According to Lorenz (1964), aggression is instinctive and spontaneous; the aggressive instinct serves to maximize the use of food, space, and resources. Lorenz stressed the social implications of people's aggressive instincts, focusing on their adaptive values.

Both animals and human beings can be aggressive; whether that aggression is inhibited or expressed depends on the organism's previous experiences and current social context, such as whether the organism is being provoked or whether it has been raised in a hostile environment (Lore & Schultz, 1993).

Acquired Drives. Another explanation for aggressive behaviour is that the frustration of goal-directed behaviour leads to aggression—this is the *frustration–aggression hypothesis*, initially proposed by Dollard and colleagues (1939). This theory relies on observations demonstrating that people involved in everyday goal-oriented tasks often become aggressive or angry when frustrated. For example, ordinarily you may be unlikely to become upset if another car pulls out into traffic in front of you. However, if you are in a hurry to get to work, you might honk or mutter angrily at the other driver. On a larger scale, the violence between Catholics and Protestants in Northern Ireland is fuelled in part by intense competition for decent jobs in a depressed economy.

Berkowitz (1964) examined the evidence for the frustration–aggression hypothesis and proposed a modified version of it. He suggested that frustration creates a

Aggression: Any behaviour designed to harm another person or thing.

readiness for aggressive acts rather than producing actual aggression. He showed that, even when frustration is present, certain events or situations must exist before aggression occurs—for example, a weapon lying on a table. In a later reformulation, Berkowitz (1989) suggested that frustrations generate aggressive inclinations to the extent that they arouse negative feelings in the frustrated individual (Berkowitz, 1990). Berkowitz's conception accounts for the instances when people don't become aggressive when frustrated. Although many psychologists find the frustration–aggression hypothesis too simplistic, it is beneficial—in part because it has led to other research that helps describe behaviour, for example, cognitive theory.

Cognitive Psychology. Theories are perishable; they eventually become outdated and are replaced. This has been especially true in the study of aggression. Old ideas about aggression being inborn and people having inherited tendencies to violence have come to be considered wrong; see Table 13.2. Early research (described in Chapter 5) was based on learning theory explanations of how children learn aggressive behaviour, popular in the 1950s and 1960s. Later, with the increasing influence of Skinner's behaviourism, researchers focused on more refined, operant interpretations of aggression. They studied the effects of punishing children for aggressive behaviour and rewarding them for non-aggressive behaviour. (A shift towards observational (social) learning theory occurred in the 1970s, and the effects of television viewing were a prime focus—see *Experiencing Psychology* on pages 480–481). In the 1980s, cognitive explanations of aggression became prevalent, and researchers began to speak in terms of thought, interpretations, and expectations.

Leonard Eron's work is typical of much contemporary social psychological research. He shifted his explanations of aggression from simple motivational drive reduction ideas (described in Chapter 9) to social learning ideas, and finally to a cognitive–behavioural analysis. Eron (1987) conducted a longitudinal study of aggression over 22 years. He examined and tracked the entire third-grade population (870 students) of Columbia county, a semi-rural area in New York state. Eron's early work in the 1960s examined external psychological conditions that might cause aggression, especially parental attitudes towards children (Lefkowitz et al., 1977). In the late 1970s Eron and other aggression researchers began to probe the influences in children's lives that cause them to *interpret* the world in a way that makes them aggressive. These researchers started looking at the data within a cognitive frame of reference: An aggressive child responds to the world with combativeness because the child has internalized aggressive ideas. Eron (1987, p. 441) argued: "It was what the subjects were saying to themselves about what they wanted . . . what might be an effective or appropriate response . . . that helped determine how

Table 13.2 A Tendency to Violence Is Not Inherited

Many scientific groups have adopted a statement called the Seville Statement on Violence, which asserts that the use of scientific data to support war is wrong and is based on erroneous assumptions.

The following statements are scientifically incorrect:

We have inherited a tendency to make war from our animal ancestors.

War or any other violent behaviour is programmed into our human nature.

Through the course of human evolution, aggression more than any other characteristic has been programmed into human behaviour.

Humans have a violent brain.

War is caused by instinct or any other specific inborn motivation.

Source: Adapted from the Seville Statement on Violence (APA, 1994).

aggressive they are today." So, like Eron, researchers today are examining how stimuli in an individual's environment may elicit thoughts and emotional responses that give way to aggressive behaviour (Bushman & Geen, 1990). These stimuli include a difficult personal situation and frustrating social conditions (Staub, 1996). They also are considering the possibility of a hormonal, brain disorder, or genetic link or defect that may predispose individuals towards aggression (Berhardt, 1997; Cadoret et al., 1995).

A key variable that may predispose people to aggression is self-esteem. The conventional wisdom traditionally has been that people with low self-esteem—unfavourable global impressions of themselves—are more likely to be violent and aggressive. But a review of research shows that crime, violence, and aggression are not *caused* by low self-esteem. According to Roy Baumeister (Baumeister, Smart, & Boden, 1996; Bushman & Baumeister, 1998) aggression is caused by threats to a person's level of esteem. When favourable views about one's self are threatened, contradicted, mocked, or challenged, people become aggressive. This view suggests that those who fail to adjust their self-appraisal—despite evidence to the correctness of the new view—become aggressive. There are some strong direct implications of such an idea. Western society places a strong emphasis on helping develop individuals' self-esteem. But development of self-esteem doesn't protect individuals from threats to it. Baumeister suggests that societal pursuit of high self-esteem for everyone may end up doing considerable harm given the fact that it is impossible to insulate everyone from threats to it. Research on how threats to self-esteem affect aggression has yet to be done, but the idea holds considerable promise.

Gender Differences in Aggression. Many people believe that men are naturally more aggressive than women. They refer to aggressive contact sports such as football and boxing, the aggressive role of men in business, the overwhelming number of violent crimes committed by men, and the traditional view that men are more likely than women to be ruthless and unsympathetic. It is also generally accepted that more masculine people are more aggressive (Kogut, Langley, & O'Neal, 1992) and this idea is reflected in children's toys (Dietz, 1998) and on television (Browne, 1998). But are men really more aggressive than women?

To learn more about gender differences in aggression, two psychologists at Purdue University, Alice Eagly and Valerie Steffen (1986), searched the psychological literature from a 15-year period for studies of adults exposed to standardized situations designed to induce aggressive behaviour. They found 63 experiments that compared gender differences in aggressive behaviours. Most of the studies were conducted in laboratories, although some were conducted in field settings. The laboratory experiments were often teacher–learner situations, in which a teacher had to deliver shocks to a learner (similar to the Milgram studies). The field experiments typically involved the experimenter cutting in line in front of an unsuspecting person, causing mild frustration that could turn into anger and aggression.

Eagly and Steffen confirmed what people had already observed—men are more *physically* aggressive than women—a finding supported by others (Harris & Knight-Bohnhoff, 1996). But they also found that both men and women use *psychological* aggression such as verbal abuse and angry gestures. They suggest that the differences in aggression that appear between men and women are directly related to the perceived consequences of the aggression. Women in many cultures have been raised to feel especially guilty if they cause physical pain; men have not been raised with those values, at least not to the same extent. However, gender roles in Canadian society are changing, so it may be that gender differences in willingness to cause pain—and act aggressively—will diminish in the future. Research supports the idea that the context and situation in which people find themselves alters the nature and extent of aggression in men and women towards individuals of their own and the opposite gender (Harris, 1994, 1996; Olson, 1994). The research picture is complicated and some important and subtle effects occur. For example, research shows that the age at which aggression occurs varies in men and women; girls develop antisocial behaviours in adolescence, rather than earlier as do boys.

experiencing psychology

Exposure to Violence

E xposure to violence in its many forms has been likened to a public health epidemic; violence is seen on city streets, in rural communities, and on the worldwide stage. Violence is almost commonplace, and its impact on childhood development grows daily (Osofsky, 1995). Nowhere is violence and aggression, especially sexual aggression, more prevalent than on television (MacKay & Covell, 1997). And most children aged 2 to 11 spend more hours watching television (an average of almost 22 hours a week) than they spend in any other activity except sleep; in addition, they are often indiscriminate viewers (Huston et al., 1992; Kubey & Csikszentmihalyi, 1990). Television thus serves as a major source of children's imitative behaviour. For example, watching television has

been shown to affect children's career aspirations. Furthermore, it may alter their overall aggressive thoughts and their views of life and may decrease their creativity (Bushman & Geen, 1990; Valkenberg & van der Voort, 1994).

The fact that television portrays so much aggressive behaviour concerns parents and educators, as well as social psychologists. Half of all prime-time TV characters are involved in violent activity of some kind; about one-tenth kill or are killed; the perpetrators of these crimes go unpunished in nearly three-quarters of violent scenes. Sixty-one percent of television programs contain violence—and that violence is often glamorized (Smith et al., 1998). Moreover, about 20 percent of males appearing on TV shows are engaged in law enforcement, whereas less than 1 percent

are in law enforcement in the real world. Although the overall amount of violence on television is staggering, some programs account for a disproportionate number of violent acts overall (Gunter & Harrison, 1998).

Research generally supports the contention that viewers who frequently watch violent programs on television are more likely to be aggressive than are viewers who see less TV violence (Hogben, 1998; Wood, Wong, & Chachere, 1991). Further, one study found that children exposed to large doses of TV violence are less likely to help a real-life victim of violence; another found that viewers of violence were less sympathetic to real-life victims than were non-viewers (Huston et al., 1992). Viewers of violence also are more fearful of becoming victims of violent acts. One study

Furthermore, early maturing girls are at higher risk for psychological problems and aggressive behaviours (Loeber & Strouthamer-Loeber, 1998). Some social behaviours may be genetically programmed and may have an evolutionary basis, but the weight of the evidence leans towards socialization (Archer, 1996). We are just beginning to assess some of these important issues such as gender and the developmental course of aggression.

Domestic Assault. Will today's children create a gentler society? Will they deal with marital conflict through reason and caring? Or will the couples of tomorrow be

even more violent than today's are? A national survey of Canadian police departments in 1996 revealed 21 901 cases of spousal assault (the victim was female in 89 percent of the cases). Nearly 30 percent of all married couples report at least one violent episode (Bunge & Levett, 1998). Assaults are more common among younger couples and thus many women have experienced assault in various forms long before marriage. According to research by Don Dutton at the University of British Columbia, abusers are threatened, jealous, and fearful and they mask these emotions with anger (Dutton, 1998). High levels of conflict, low socioeconomic status, low levels of academic achievement, alcohol abuse, young children at home, and exposure to violence as a child are correlated with

found that the viewing of violence at age 8 predicted aggressive behaviour at age 19 (Eron & Huesmann, 1980). Children who play violent video games also seem to act more aggressively at later ages (Schutte et al., 1988), and even infants can become fearful by watching television (Meltzoff, 1988). According to Stacy Smith and her colleagues in the National Television Violence Study (1998) violence on television hasn't changed appreciably—neither its overall prevalence or how it is treated have changed much. How does watching violence on television affect viewers? Smith and her colleagues describe some of the key effects of viewing violence on television:

- It weakens viewers' inhibitions.
- It may suggest new ideas and techniques to the uninitiated.
- It may activate or stimulate existing aggressive ideas and behaviours.
- It reduces a person's overall emotional sensitivity to violence—it desensitizes people.
- It introduces a fear of being victimized by violence

Of course, television also can have positive effects on children. In one study, children exposed to shows such as *Sesame Street* and *Mister Rogers' Neighborhood*, which focus on topics such as sharing and caring, were more likely to engage in prosocial behaviour with other children than children in a control group who did not watch those shows (Coates, Pusser, & Goodman, 1976). But watching a lot of any kind of television has a deleterious impact on children's reading comprehension skills (Koolstra, van der Voot, & van der Kamp, 1997).

Research on the effects of television and other media is tricky. Often the effects are subtle because potential influences—violence, sex, and education—are sometimes combined in one program. For example, some assert that children are "protected" from the effects of violence by the knowledge that what they see is not real (Davies, 1997); but young children are not able to make this distinction. In the end, the data are fairly clear: Programming, for better or worse, can affect children. So, how, when, and how often information is conveyed to children ultimately has important social implications (Calvert, 1998; Sell, Ray, & Lovelace, 1995). Social psychologists interested in public policy are suggesting requirements for at least a certain amount of educational programming for children on every station and for controls to protect children from advertising that exploits their special vulnerability (Huston et al., 1992; Smith et al., 1998). ■

domestic violence (Dearwater et al., 1998; Magdol et al., 1998). Further, younger adults (under age 30) are more likely to engage in domestic violence than are older adults (O'Leary et al., 1989), and such behaviours (pushing, shoving, slapping) are fairly stable—a person who is aggressive early in a relationship stays that way. While domestic violence against men exists, the vast majority of cases involve men abusing women. There continue to be many myths about physical abuse in close relationships; Table 13.3 describes some of them.

Is there some event, action, or predisposition that makes a man abuse his partner? Early explanations of domestic violence focused on mental disorders, and many research studies show that men who assault women suffer from personality disorders such as those we will examine in Chapter 15. Other explanations of domestic violence, indeed violence in general, focus on evolutionary and biological predispositions (e.g., Cadoret et al., 1995; Stoff & Cairns, 1996). Evolutionary theory and its closely related sociobiological theory, for example, explain aggressive behaviours as attempts to

Table 13.3 Myths about Physical Abuse in Close Relationships

Violence in close relationships never happens to people like me.

People never tell anyone about violence in their relationships.

Only males inflict violence on their partners.

Women stay in abusive relationships only because they are passive.

In couples, there is a cycle of violence.

Battered women are masochistic; their batterers are mentally ill.

Violence nearly always involves the use of alcohol.

Source: Adapted from Marshall & Vitanza, 1994, p. 263.

Prosocial behaviour: Behaviour that benefits someone else or society but that generally offers no obvious benefit to the person performing it and that may even involve some personal risk or sacrifice.

maximize the likelihood that the aggressors and their offspring will survive (Keller, 1997).

Differing from these psychiatric and biological theorists, many sociologists and psychologists believe that assaults on women by their partners are generated by social rules supporting male dominance and culturally determined gender roles (Richie, 1994). Although society is changing, the traditional image of couples places the male in the dominant role and the woman, especially women of colour, in a vulnerable role. According to this view, men are merely living up to cultural expectations (Sommers-Flanagan, Sommers-Flanagan, & Davis, 1993), and the court system often supports such biases (Richie, 1994).

The overall picture is complex. Dutton (1998) proposes that people grow and develop within a social context and suggests that a valid explanation of domestic violence must examine at least four factors that are an outgrowth of the social context and lead to a specific personality configuration:

- The cultural values of the individuals (Do they see men and women as equal?)
- The social situation of those involved (Are they employed?)
- The cohesiveness of the family unit (Do they communicate?)
- The level of individual development (Do they express feelings well? Do they excuse violence? Have they witnessed family violence?)

Dutton asserts that a comprehensive theory of domestic violence must evaluate a potentially assaultive male with respect to each factor. Although some interpretations view violence against women as the misuse of power by men (L. Walker, 1989), Dutton's approach considers a complex mix of variables as the determinants of such behaviour. Unlike most domestic assault models, which focus on one level of analysis (communication, personal values, or, perhaps, job stress), Dutton's approach suggests multiple levels, with the importance of each level differing for each assault case. Although it is often tempting to rely on simple models of domestic assault, the reality is that human beings are complex, and the causes of assault must be understood in a broader context.

Another specific type of aggressive behaviour—rape—is discussed in *Experiencing Psychology*.

Focus

Review

- Identify the key findings and the ethical issues raised by Milgram's study. pp. 470–472
- Distinguish between social facilitation and social loafing. pp. 473–474
- Identify the social variables that are important in explaining unrestrained group behaviour. pp. 475–476

Think Critically

- Consider some famous dissenters in history. How did their refusal to conform to group pressure affect their lives? How did their dissent influence society?
- How might it be possible to shape a society to make it less aggressive?

Prosocial Behaviour

Are small-town people more helpful than city people? It turns out that they are, and that this is true all over the world (Yousif & Korte, 1995); but what factors are at work, and under what conditions are people helpful? For example, if you are walking down the street with a bag of groceries and you drop them, what is the likelihood that someone will help you pick them up? Will a bystander who observes a serious accident or a crime help the victim? What attributions will the bystander make about the causes of an incident? What attitudes about helping behaviour or about people being victims will the bystander bring to the incident? Psychologists want to find out when, and under what conditions, someone will help a stranger. They are examining the likelihood of **prosocial behaviour**—behaviour that benefits someone else or society

experiencing psychology

Developing a Theory of Rape

Rape is forcible sexual assault on an unwilling partner, usually a woman. The legal definition of rape generally is broadened to include any sexual assault (usually intercourse) that occurs without freely given consent.

Most rapes are planned, often in a meticulous manner; rape is seldomly an impulsive act prompted by a spontaneous sexual or aggressive feeling. Rape should be considered a violent crime rather than a sexual crime. Labelling rape as a sexual assault obscures the violent, brutal nature of the crime and often places the victim on the defensive in a courtroom. Research shows that people often blame the victim, particularly if she knew the rapist (Kanekar et al., 1991).

More than 27 000 sexual assaults are reported each year in Canada (Statistics Canada, 1997); many experts assert, however, that this is only one-quarter of the actual number. Rape is underreported to the criminal justice system (Koss, 1993). For example, one research study found that 27 percent of college women had experienced situations in which rape was attempted, and 7.5 percent of college men reported initiating acts that meet the definition of rape (Koss, Gidycz, & Wisniewski, 1987). Although these results cannot necessarily be generalized to the entire population, rape and attempted rape seem to be far more common than was previously believed. Many rape victims know their assailants. On college campuses today, rape or attempted rape by an acquaintance—sometimes known as *date rape*—is receiving increased attention from law enforcement officials, who acknowledge its high prevalence (Ellis, 1994). As well, there is concern in the United States (and to a lesser extent here in Canada) about "date rape drugs" such as Rohypnol (a sedative 10 times stronger than Valium) that can be slipped into a woman's drink and render her totally helpless.

The Rapist. Because rape is a violent crime, researchers have sought to understand the characteristics and motivations of the rapist. Several facts about rapists are coming into focus. They tend to be young, often between 15 and 25. Many have willing sexual partners; half of all convicted rapists are married, although their high level of aggressiveness probably precludes happy and stable marriages or other satisfactory relationships.

Rapists may have some history of sexual dysfunction and they often have committed another sex-related offence, although these findings are not consistent across all studies (Furby, Weinrott, & Blackshaw, 1989). Rapists tend to be more responsive to violence than are other men and are less able to understand cues and messages from women who say no. Rapists' levels of maladjustment vary from slight to extreme when measured on psychological tests (Kalichman et al., 1989). Men who assault and rape women often view their attacks not as rape but as "mere" assault (Bourque, 1989). Various classifications of rapists have emerged—from those who rape on a whim to angry rapists to violent and sadistic rapists. No firm classification system is yet in place.

Most research shows that between 15 and 25 percent of male college students engage in some level of sexual aggression, usually towards women (Malamuth & Sockloskie, 1991). Most rapists think the likelihood of being punished is small, and this is considered to be one of the contributory factors in rape (Ellis, 1991). A comprehensive theory of rape will have to account for both its aggressive and its sexual nature (Barbaree & Marshall, 1991). Research in this area is ongoing. ■

---

but that generally offers no obvious benefit to the person performing it and that may even involve some personal risk or sacrifice.

Altruism: Helping without Rewards. Why does Peter Beneson, the founder of Amnesty International, devote so much time and effort to helping "prisoners of conscience" around the world? What compelled Mother Teresa to wander Calcutta's streets and attend to the wounds and diseases of people no one else will touch? Why did Oskar Schindler risk his life to save 1100 Jews from the Nazi death camps during the Second World War?

Altruism consists of behaviours that benefit other people and for which there is no discernible extrinsic reward, recognition, or appreciation (Quigley, Gaes, & Tedeschi, 1989). However, does an altruistic person truly expect no reward for good acts? Isn't the feeling of well-being after performing an altruistic act a type of reward? Does the altruist expect a reward in an afterlife?

Rape: Forcible sexual assault on an unwilling partner, usually a woman.

Altruism [AL-true-ism]: Behaviours that benefit other people and for which there is no discernible extrinsic reward, recognition, or appreciation.

Sociobiology: A theory based on the premise that even day-to-day behaviours are determined by the process of natural selection—that social behaviours that contribute to the survival of a species are passed on genetically from one generation to the next and account for the mechanisms producing behaviours such as altruism.

Bystander apathy: The unwillingness of witnesses to an event to help, an effect that increases when there are more observers.

Many behaviourists contend that an element of personality directs people to seek social approval by helping. According to this view, people with a high need for achievement are more likely than others to be helpful, and people may continue to be helpful because the positive consequences of their actions are self-reinforcing (Batson et al., 1991; Puffer, 1987). From a behavioural view, intrinsically rewarding activities become powerful behaviour initiators; thus, when you have a relationship with a person, the person's affection and approval make you more likely to be caring and helpful (Batson, 1990). Further, once kindness and helpfulness become well established and even routine, individuals are more likely to help others, such as the homeless, disadvantaged senior citizens, and orphans.

Other theorists argue that biological drives underlie altruistic behaviour. Consider the following scenario. An infant crawls into a busy street. A truck is approaching. The infant's mother darts in front of the oncoming vehicle and carries her child to safety. Most people would say that love impelled the mother to risk her life to save the child. Sociobiologists would argue that the mother committed her brave deed so her genes would be passed on to another generation.

The idea that people are genetically predisposed towards certain behaviours was described by Edward Wilson, a Harvard University zoologist, in his 1975 book *Sociobiology: A New Synthesis*. Wilson argued that biological, genetic factors underlie all behaviour. But he went one step further. He founded a new field, **sociobiology**, based on the premise that even day-to-day behaviours are determined by the process of natural selection—that social behaviours that contribute to the survival of a species are passed on via the genes from one generation to the next. Natural selection accounts for the mechanisms that have evolved to produce altruistic behaviours (Crawford & Anderson, 1989). For the sociobiologist, genetics is the key to daily behaviour.

Psychologists hotly debate sociobiological theory, because it places genetics in a position of primary importance and minimizes the role of learning. Most psychologists feel strongly that learning plays a key role in the day-to-day activities of human beings. People *learn* to love, to become angry, to help or hurt others, and to develop relationships with those around them. But although sociobiology is too fixed and rigid for most psychologists, it does raise interesting questions about the role of biology and genetics in social behaviour.

Behavioural theories and sociobiology are two ways of explaining why people help others. People don't always help, however. One important area of research seeks to explain why.

Bystander Apathy: Failing to Help. The study of helping behaviour has taken some interesting twists and turns. For example, psychologists have found that in large cities, where potentially lethal emergencies (accidents, thefts, stabbings, rapes, and murders) occur frequently, people often exhibit bystander apathy—they watch, but seldom help. **Bystander apathy** is the unwillingness of witnesses to an event to help; this unwillingness increases with the number of observers, a fact that has been termed the *bystander effect*. In a well-known incident in New York City in 1964, Kitty Genovese was walking home when a man approached her with a knife. A chase ensued, during which she screamed for help. He stabbed her, and she continued screaming. When lights came on in nearby buildings, the attacker fled. But when he saw that no one was coming to his victim's aid, he returned and stabbed her again. The assault lasted more than 30 minutes and was heard by dozens of neighbours; yet no one came to the victim's aid. This is a classic case of bystander apathy.

Bibb Latané and John Darley (1970) investigated bystander apathy in a long series of studies. They found that in situations requiring uncomfortable responses, people must choose between helping and standing by apathetically. They must decide whether to introduce themselves into a situation, especially when there are other bystanders. But they first have to decide what is going on (is this an emergency or not?) and often are misled by the *apparent* lack of concern among other bystanders to conclude that nothing bad is really going on after all—so they don't help. Latané and Darley reasoned that when people are aware of other bystanders in an emergency situation, they also may be less likely to help because they experience *diffusion of responsibility* (the feeling that they cannot be held responsible). To test their hypothesis, the researchers brought college students to a laboratory and told them they were going to be involved in a study of people who were interested in discussing college life in New York City. They explained that, in the interest of preserving people's anonymity, a group discussion would be held over an intercom system rather than face-to-face, and that each person in the group would talk in turn. In fact, in each experimental session there was only one true participant. Assistants who worked for the researchers prerecorded all of the other conversations.

The independent variable was the number of people the naïve participant thought were in the discussion group. The dependent variable was whether and how fast the naïve participant reported as an emergency an apparently serious seizure affecting one of the "other participants." The future "seizure victim" spoke first; he talked about his difficulties in adjusting to college and mentioned that he was prone to seizures, particularly when studying hard. Next, the naïve participant spoke. Then came the prerecorded discussions by assistants. Then the "seizure victim" talked again. After a few relatively calm remarks, his speech became increasingly loud and incoherent; he stuttered and indicated that he needed help because he was having "a-a-a real problem—er—right now and I—er—if somebody could help me out it would—it would—er—er sh-sure be good." At this point, the experimenters began timing the speed of the naïve participant's response.

Each naïve participant was led to believe that his or her discussion group contained two (participant and victim), three (participant, victim, and one other person), or six (participant, victim, and four other people) people. That is, in the two-person group, participants believed they were the only bystanders; in the three-person group, they thought there was one other bystander. When participants thought they were the only bystander, 85 percent of them responded before the end of the seizure. If they thought there was only one other bystander, 62 percent of the participants responded by the end of the seizure. When participants thought there were four additional bystanders, only 31 percent responded by the end of the seizure (see Figure 13.10).

In general, research has shown that bystanders will help under some conditions. For one thing, people's self-concepts and previous experiences affect their willingness to intercede. Bystanders who see themselves as being especially competent in emergencies (such as doctors and nurses) are likely to help a victim regardless of the number of people present (Pantin & Carver, 1982). If the person who needs help has a relationship with the person who can offer help, help is more likely to be given (Batson, 1990). Research in cities of various sizes shows that people who live in small communities are more likely to help (Levine et al., 1994). Also, personality characteristics of the individual involved in a bystander situation are important. Men respond more often than women (Salminen & Glad, 1992). Tice and Baumeister (1985), however, found that participants with a high degree of masculinity were less likely to respond. They contended that highly masculine subjects might be especially fearful of embarrassment. In Western cultures, the personality characteristics of men, in general, emphasize strength and aggression rather than sensitivity and nurturing. This finding is supported by work showing that women are more likely than men to help friends, and that when women do so, they do it in a nurturing rather than a problem-solving way (Belansky & Boggiano, 1994).

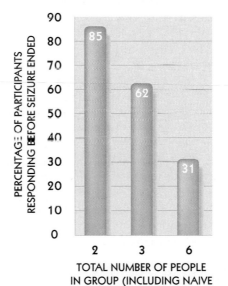

FIGURE 13.10
The Bystander Effect
In a classic bystander apathy study, as the number of people in the group increased, the willingness of the naïve participant to inform the experimenter that the victim had suffered a seizure decreased.

(From Latané & Darley, 1970.)

Relationships and Attraction

Some people feel that they are living a life that is predetermined and that relationships with others—especially love relationships—are a part of their personal destiny. It turns out that people who believe in romantic destiny—that people are meant for each other—tend to have long relationships, if they let a relationship begin in the first place (Knee, 1998). But relationships with friends, lovers, and spouses are intricate. What is it about your friends that attracts you and makes you want to maintain a relationship with them in the first place? We saw in Chapter 9 that people develop relationships to fulfil their needs for warmth, understanding, and emotional security. Psychologists also know that people are attracted to those who live or work near them, whom they consider good-looking, who share their attitudes, and with whom they spend time. Social psychologists in particular study **interpersonal attraction**, the tendency of one person to evaluate another person (or a symbol or image of another person) in a positive way.

Proximity. People are more likely to develop a relationship with a neighbour than with someone who lives several blocks or kilometres away. Three decades of research show that the closer people are geographically—whether this means where they work or where they live—the more attracted they will be. A simple explanation is that they are likely to see each other more often, and repeated exposure leads to familiarity, which leads to attraction. Another reason is that attraction is facilitated by the anticipation of a relationship with someone encountered frequently. In addition, if people are members of a group, such as a computer club, a volunteer organization, or an aerobics class, they perceive themselves as sharing the same feelings, attitudes, and values as others in the group. That perception leads to attraction.

Physical Attractiveness. Within seconds of seeing a person, you are able to decide if they are attractive to you (Locher et al., 1993). Research shows that people feel more personal regard and ascribe more power, status, and competence to individuals they find physically attractive than to those they don't; we saw this earlier when we discussed who could best change people's attitudes (Dion, Pak, & Dion, 1990; Feingold, 1992a, 1992b).

Attractiveness is affected by subtle but powerful variables. For example, in a recent study both men and women were shown facial images of Caucasian and Japanese females and males that had been "feminized" or "masculinized" by a computer (Perrett et al., 1998). Both Caucasian and Japanese participants preferred and rated as most attractive the faces that were feminized. Interestingly, both men and women tend to find more appealing men who are more feminine looking than rugged. The researchers suggested that computer alteration of men's faces to make them slightly feminine makes them appear less menacing and softens other features that are associated with negative traits. The researchers assert that more feminine faces appear younger and that people's preferences for young faces are correlated

with their preference for feminized faces. Such results are probably no surprise to Leonardo DiCaprio's agent.

Volumes of research show that people are attracted romantically, at least at first, to those whom they find attractive (Cunningham, Barbee, & Pike, 1990). In general, people will judge an attractive individual to have more positive traits and characteristics than an unattractive one, especially when appearance is the first information provided (DeSantis & Kayson, 1997). Attractive people are granted more freedom and are perceived as being more fair, competent, and healthy than unattractive people (Cherulnik, Turns, & Wilderman, 1990; Kalick et al., 1998). For example, attractive college professors are seen as better teachers and are less likely to be blamed if a student receives a failing grade in a course (Romano & Bordieri, 1989). But such findings about attractiveness are a distinctly Western phenomenon; values about attractiveness differ cross-culturally, and different cultures appraise various elements of life in different ways (Matsumoto & Kudoh, 1993).

How important is attractiveness when it comes to dating? Do people always select the most attractive person for a date? Research shows that people prefer attractive dates, and some studies show that people seek out those of their own level of attractiveness. But other variables also seem to play an important role; educational level, intelligence, socioeconomic status, and similarity of previous experiences all weigh heavily in the choice of whom to date and eventually marry (Feingold, 1988a). Although physical attractiveness and youthfulness are initially important in the selection of dates and mates (especially among men), appearance is just one variable among many (Sprecher, Sullivan, & Hatfield, 1994).

In a typical physical attractiveness experiment, participants are given two identical job résumés, each of which has a different picture attached to it. Results show that people will evaluate the résumé of the person they find physically attractive more positively than that of the other person, even though the qualifications of the "applicants" are the same (e.g., Frieze, Olson, & Russell, 1991). Attractive people are preferred in the workplace, as dates, and as friends; they are also thought to be less menacing (Eagly et al., 1991). In one research study, for example, participants were given information about a hypothetical sex offender, including a facial photograph and a conviction record (Esses & Webster, 1988). The subjects judged physically unattractive sex offenders as less likely to restrain their behaviour in the future than better-looking but equally dangerous sex offenders.

Liking Those Who Share the Feeling and Who Hold Similar Attitudes.
Learning theorists contend that people are attracted to and form relationships with those who give them positive reinforcement and that people dislike those who punish them. The basic idea is simple: You like the people who like you. Moreover, if you like someone, you tend to assume (sometimes incorrectly) that the other person likes you in return and that the two of you share similar qualities. This tendency is especially prevalent in people who need social approval (Jacobs, Berscheid, & Walster, 1971).

Another attribute that affects the development of relationships is real or perceived similarity in attitudes and opinions. If you perceive someone's attitudes as similar to your own, there is an increased probability that you will like that person. Having similar values, interests, and background is a good predictor of a friendship (e.g., Miller, 1990). Similarly, voters who agree with the views of a particular political candidate tend to rate that person as more honest, friendly, and persuasive than the politicians with whom they disagree.

Researchers also have found that, conversely, if you already like someone, you will perceive that person's attitudes as being similar to your own. For example, voters who like a particular political candidate, perhaps because the candidate is warmhearted or physically attractive, will tend to minimize their attitudinal differences.

That you like those who like you is explained by cognitive consistency theory, which suggests that sharing similar attitudes reduces cognitive dissonance (the phenomenon we examined earlier). In your natural inclination to avoid dissonance, you are attracted to those you believe share similar attitudes; shared attitudes in turn lead to attraction and liking. Learning theories also suggest that you like people with similar attitudes because similar attitudes are reinforcing to you. As long as you think the other person's attitudes are genuine, such liking will continue.

Friendships and the Role of Equity.
Jerry and Elaine, Joey and Chandler, and Pooh and Piglet—liking each other and sharing ideas and values have been the bases of many friendships. *Friendship* is a special two-way relationship between people. According to one influential group of researchers, if two people's behaviours, emotions, and thoughts are related, and the people are dependent on one

another, a close relationship exists (Kelley et al., 1983). Closeness is reported by many researchers as the key variable that defines a friendship, although *close* must be defined so that all researchers mean the same thing when they use the word (Berscheid, Snyder, & Omoto, 1989).

Ideally, friends participate as equals, enjoy each other's company, have mutual trust, provide mutual assistance, accept each other as they are, respect each other's judgment, feel free to be themselves with each other, understand each other in fundamental ways, and are intimate and share confidences (Davis & Todd, 1984). Reciprocity and commitment between people who see themselves as equals are essentials of friendship (Hartup, 1989). Compared with casual friends, close friends interact more frequently across a wider range of settings, are more exclusive, and offer each other more benefits (Hays, 1989).

As we saw in Chapter 10, elementary school children tend to form same-gender friendships; cross-gender friendships are rare. With youngsters, friendships lead to cooperation rather than competition, at least more than with non-friends (Hartup, 1989). Furthermore, when children have friends in the classroom, they do better in school (Ladd, 1990). Adolescent friendships sometimes provide a place for sharing and intimacy, although they also can be filled with conflict over social or political issues, drugs, gangs, and sexual behaviour (Berndt, 1992). Among adults, friendships between two women differ from those between two men; and both differ from friendships between a man and a woman. Western cultural expectations for specific gender-based behaviours, such as who helps with child care or who initiates sexual activity, often control male-female interactions in friendship. Women talk more about family, personal matters, and doubts and fears than men do; men talk more about sports and work than do women. Women in general find friendships more satisfying than men do (Elkins & Peterson, 1993).

Equity plays an important role in close relationships. **Equity theory** states that people attempt to maintain stable and consistent interpersonal relationships in which the ratio of members' contributions is balanced. This ensures that all members are treated fairly. People in close relationships usually have a sense of balance in the relationships and believe they will stay together for a long time (Clark & Reis, 1988).

According to equity theory, one way in which people maintain a balanced relationship is to make restitution when it is demanded. Apologies help restore a sense of autonomy and fairness to a wronged individual. Similarly, people who do favours expect favours in return, often using the principle of equity unconsciously in day-to-day life. If a friend helps you move into your new apartment, you may be expected to lend her a hand when she has to take an old refrigerator to the dump. Research shows that when a person senses inequity in a situation, her or his feeling about the other person is affected—especially when the other person is being treated better (Griffeth, Vecchio, & Logan, 1989).

 Intimate Relationships and Love. People involved in a close relationship also may be intimate with one another. In **intimacy** each person is willing to self-disclose and to express important feelings and information to the other person; in response, the other person usually acknowledges the first person's feelings, making each person feel valued and cared for (Reis & Shaver, 1988). Research shows that self-disclosure tends to be reciprocal; people who disclose themselves to others are usually recipients of intimate information (Collins & Miller, 1994). When people self-disclose they validate each other; that is, they accept each other's positive and negative attributes. Although such self-disclosure is important, revealing secrets and intimate information is not always beneficial to individuals (Kelly & McKillop, 1996).

Unfortunately, there is little research on intimate relationships outside of marriage. Psychologists know much more about intimate relationships between pairs of people, especially men and women, when sex, love, and marriage become involved (Miller, 1990). Communication, affection, consideration, and self-disclosure between friends have been studied relatively little. However, important individual

Equity theory: In social psychology, the theory that people attempt to maintain stable and consistent interpersonal relationships in which the ratio of members' contributions is balanced.

Intimacy: A state of being or feeling in which each person is willing to self-disclose and to express important feelings and information to the other person; such behaviours are usually reciprocated.

and gender differences do exist in friendships. For example, women more than men incorporate close relationships into their view of themselves and let those views affect their thoughts and behaviours (Cross & Madson, 1997). Women more than men evaluated same-sex friendships very positively (Veniegas & Peplau, 1997). Furthermore, in relationships, men are more self-disclosing with a woman than they are with another man; in general, men are less likely to be self-disclosing and intimate than are women (Dindia & Allen, 1992).

Love, emotional commitment, and sex are the parts of intimate relationships that most people think of when they hear the word *intimacy*. People in love relationships often express feelings in unique ways—they give flowers, take moonlit walks, write lengthy letters, and have romantic dinners. According to psychologists, love has psychological, emotional, biochemical, and social factors. Consider this array of definitions of *love*:

- Fromm (1956) focused on the idea that mature love is possible only if a person achieves a secure sense of self-identity. He said that when people are in love, they become one and yet remain two individuals.
- Heinlein (1961) wrote that love "is a condition in which the happiness of the other person is essential to your own."
- Branden (1980) suggested that love is "a passionate spiritual, emotional, sexual attachment . . . that reflects a high regard for the value of each other's person."
- Tennov (1981) believed that the ultimate state of romantic love is one called "limerance": a head-over-heels involvement and preoccupation with thoughts of the loved one.

All of these definitions are right, and none are. Many classifications of love have been suggested, and all have some overlapping components. One influential classification is Sternberg's (1986b) view, which sees love as having three components: intimacy, commitment, and passion. *Intimacy* is a sense of emotional closeness. *Commitment* is the extent to which a relationship is permanent and long-lasting. *Passion* is arousal, some of it sexual, some intellectual, and some inspirational. When all three components are present, the highest type of love—*consummate love*—results. Another view (Hendrick & Hendrick, 1986) includes six distinct varieties of love: passionate, game-playing, friendship, logical, possessive, and selfless (see Table 13.4).

Different as these classifications may be, researchers have nonetheless identified some common elements in love relationships. Love usually involves the idealization of another person; people see their loved ones in a positive light. It also involves caring for another person and being fascinated with that person. Love includes trust, respect, liking, honesty, companionship, and sexual attraction. A central element is commitment; however, Bev Fehr and Jim Russell (1991), in work at the University of British Columbia, suggested that love and commitment may not be separable, because one usually follows from, or is part of, the other.

What happens when love disappears? People in a close emotional relationship who break up, whether married or not, experience emotional distress. Sadness, anger, loss, and despair are among the emotions experienced by people at the end of a close relationship. However, research shows that the extent of those feelings is determined by an individual's level of security. If you lose a lover or spouse, your reaction will be determined not only by the loss of your relationship but also by your own basic feelings of security, attachment, and anxiety (Simpson, 1990).

Love is a state, but it is also an act and a series of behaviours. Thus, although a person may be in love, most psychologists think of love in terms of the behaviours that demonstrate it, including remaining faithful sexually and showing caring behaviours (D. Buss, 1988). Yet researchers also wish to know whether love has a biological basis. According to David McClelland (1986), two sources exist for understanding love: analytical self-reports ("I think I have fallen in love") governed by the left side of the brain, and emotional reports governed by the right side of the brain (an idea we examined in Chapters 2 and 4). In McClelland's view, the right brain can tell the

Table 13.4   Six Varieties of Love

Variety of Love	Sample Items
Passionate love	My lover and I were attracted to each other immediately after we first met.
	My lover and I became emotionally involved rather quickly.
Game-playing love	I have sometimes had to keep two of my lovers from finding out about each other.
	I can get over love affairs pretty easily and quickly.
Friendship love	The best kind of love grows out of a long friendship.
	Love is really a deep friendship, not a mysterious, mystical emotion.
Logical love	It is best to love someone with a similar background.
	An important factor in choosing a partner is whether or not he (she) will be a good parent.
Possessive love	When my lover doesn't pay attention to me, I feel sick all over.
	I cannot relax if I suspect that my lover is with someone else.
Selfless love	I would rather suffer myself than let my lover suffer.
	Whatever I own is my lover's to use as he (she) chooses.

Source: From Hendrick and Hendrick (1986).

individual about emotional experiences that are not consciously processed. McClelland argues that these emotional processes influence physiological processes and behaviours (the sweaty palms, the racing heart) that are not directly under our conscious control. In some ways, McClelland writes, there are two psychologies of love: an analytic left-brain understanding and an emotional right-brain understanding. McClelland's view, particularly his physiologically based explanation of love, has yet to achieve wide acceptance, because most researchers assert that love derives from environmental rather than biological variables (Waller & Shaver, 1994).

Love is expressed differently in every culture, and even within a culture there are enormous variations in its expression. Two researchers from the University of Keele in England, Robin Goodwin and Daniel Tang (1991), used questionnaires to examine whether British and Chinese university students in Hong Kong valued the same traits in friends and romantic partners. Results showed that, overall, romantic partners were expected to be more honest and caring than friends were expected to be. In addition, the British students stressed sensitivity and humour in romantic partners and friends, but the Chinese students stressed creativity and astuteness about money. Other results support

Focus

Review

◆ What is the key psychological explanation for bystander apathy? pp. 484–485

◆ Identify the fundamental characteristics of a close relationship. pp. 486–488

Think Critically

◆ Provide a psychological explanation of why you probably will like someone whose attitudes you perceive as similar to your own. Why might that person be able to influence you to do things that you otherwise might not do?

◆ Psychologists know that people like those who are similar to themselves. What psychological principles could you call on to increase the likelihood that you will get a job or be promoted in the job you are in?

these conclusions. When Susan Sprecher and her colleagues (1992) compared love attitudes and experiences among Japanese, Americans, and Russians, they found distinct cultural differences. For example, the Japanese were less romantic than the other groups; the Americans were more likely to associate love with marriage than were the other groups; and the Russians were the most excitable and had the most trouble staying calm when in love.

Cultural differences in love relationships vary in part because of the nature of marriages themselves. In cultures where marriages are arranged by parents, love comes about slowly over time. In cultures where passionate love is equated with happiness, such as in Canada, love is often seen to wane over time; but in cultures where romantic, passionate love is valued less, the depth of relationships and the waning of passion are viewed differently and have a different time course. Psychologists know far too little about love relationships in this and other cultures; yet love is a basic human emotion that is nurtured from birth to death and is easily seen in every culture. As psychologists discern the key elements of friendships, they will be more likely to tackle the even more complicated topic of love and how it should be nurtured.

Summary and Review

Attitudes: Our Dispositions and Inclinations

What is social psychology?

- *Social psychology* is the study of how individuals influence and are influenced by the thoughts, feelings, and behaviours of others. p. 448

What is the relationship between attitudes and behaviour?

- *Attitudes* are long-lasting patterns of feelings and beliefs about other people, ideas, or objects that are based in people's experiences and shape their future behaviour. Attitudes are usually evaluative and have cognitive, emotional, and behavioural dimensions, each of which serves a function. Attitudes are formed early in life through learning processes. Social psychologists can assess people's attitudes, but whether those attitudes predict behaviour depends on a number of variables, including attitude strength, vested interest, specificity of attitudes, and accessibility of attitudes. pp. 448–460

What are the key components of attitude change?

- There are four key components of attitude change, each of which affects the extent of change that may take place: the communicator, the

communication, the medium, and the audience. The *elaboration likelihood model*, proposed by Petty and Cacioppo, asserts that there are two routes to attitude change: central and peripheral. The central route emphasizes rational decision making; the peripheral route, which is more indirect and superficial, emphasizes emotional and motivational influences. pp. 450–454

- Cognitive explanations of attitudes and attitude change include cognitive dissonance and reactance theory. *Cognitive dissonance* is the discomfort that results when an individual maintains two or more beliefs, attitudes, or behaviours that are inconsistent with one another. *Reactance* is the pattern of feelings and subsequent behaviours aimed at reestablishing a person's sense of freedom when there is an inconsistency between the person's self-image of being free to choose and the person's realization that someone is trying to force him or her to choose a particular alternative. pp. 455–457

KEY TERMS
social psychology, p. 448; attitudes, p. 448; elaboration likelihood model, p. 452; cognitive dissonance, p. 455; self-perception theory, p. 456; reactance, p. 457

Social Cognition: The Impact of Thought

What is social cognition?

- *Social cognition* is the thought process of making sense of events, people, oneself, and the world in general through analyzing and interpreting them. Often, to save time, people use mental short cuts to make sense of the world, developing rules of thumb. p. 457

How are nonverbal communication and attribution theory used in the study of social cognition?

- *Nonverbal communication* is information provided by cues or actions that involve movements of the body, especially the face. These sources of information help people make judgments about other people and about events in the world. pp. 458–460

- *Attribution* is the process by which someone infers other people's motives and intentions from observing their behaviour and deciding whether the causes of the behaviour are dispositional (internal) or situational (external). Attribution helps people make sense of the world, organize their thoughts quickly, and maintain a sense of control over the environment. It helps people feel competent and masterful and maintain a sense of balance, because it helps them predict similar events in the future. pp. 460–461

Describe the most common attribution errors.

■ Two of the most common errors in attribution are the fundamental attribution error and the actor–observer effect. The *fundamental attribution error* is the tendency to attribute other people's behaviour to dispositional rather than situational causes. The *actor–observer effect* is the tendency for people to attribute the failings of others to dispositional causes but to attribute their own failings to situational causes. Sometimes these errors occur because of a *self-serving bias*; that is, people's tendency to evaluate their own behaviour as worthwhile, regardless of the situation. pp. 461–464

Define prejudice and identify the theories that explain it.

■ *Prejudice* is a negative evaluation of an entire group of people. Prejudice is typically based on *stereotypes*—fixed, overly simple, often incorrect, and often negative ideas, usually about traits, attitudes, and behaviours attributed to groups of people. Prejudice often leads to *discrimination*, behaviours targeted at individuals or groups with the aim of holding them apart and treating them differently. Prejudice has multiple causes and can be accounted for, at least to some extent, by social learning theory, motivational theory, cognitive theory, and personality theory. pp. 464–466

KEY TERMS
social cognition, p. 457; impression formation, p. 457; nonverbal communication, p. 458; body language, p. 458; attribution, p. 460; fundamental attribution error, p. 462; actor–observer effect, p. 462; self-serving bias, p. 462; prejudice, p. 464; stereotypes, p. 464; discrimination, p. 464; social categorization, p.466

Social Interactions: The Power of People and Situations

Explain social influence and conformity.

■ *Social influence* is the way in which one or more people alter the attitudes or behaviour of others, either directly or indirectly. Social influence is easily seen in studies of conformity. *Conformity* occurs when a person changes attitudes or behaviours to be consistent with other people or with social norms. pp. 468–470

What is obedience, and what did Milgram's studies of obedience demonstrate?

■ *Obedience* is the process by which a person complies with the orders of another person or group of people. Milgram's studies demonstrated that an individual's ability to resist coercion is limited (65 percent of participants in one study delivered what they thought were the highest possible levels of shock to another person), although the presence of an ally who refuses to participate reduces obedience and underscores the importance of social influences on behaviour. pp. 470–472

What are social facilitation and social loafing?

■ *Social facilitation* in groups is a change in performance that occurs when people believe they are in the presence of other people. The change can be either positive or negative. *Social loafing* is a decrease in an individual's effort and productivity as a result of working in a group. pp. 473–474

Identify three processes that may occur in group decision making and that may or may not be helpful.

■ Extremes of group behaviour include *group polarization*, the exaggeration of pre-existing attitudes as a result of group discussion; *groupthink*, the tendency of people in a group to seek concurrence with one another; and *deindividuation*, the process by which the individuals in a group lose their self-awareness, self-perception, and concern with evaluation and ultimately may engage in antisocial, anti-normative behaviour. pp. 474–476

Describe aggression, prosocial behaviour, and bystander apathy.

■ *Aggression* is viewed by social psychologists as any behaviour designed to harm another person or thing. *Prosocial behaviour* exhibits itself in *altruism*, behaviours that benefit someone else or society but that generally offer no obvious benefit to the person performing them. In contrast, *bystander apathy* is the unwillingness of witnesses to an event to help, especially when they are among numerous observers. pp. 476–477, 482–485

Define interpersonal attraction and indicate some key findings in studies of it.

■ *Interpersonal attraction* is the tendency of one person to evaluate another person (or a symbol or image of another person) in a positive way. The process of attraction involves the characteristics of both the people involved and the situation. People give more personal regard and ascribe more power, status, and competence to people they find attractive than to those they don't. pp. 486–487

Define friendship and love and distinguish between them.

■ Reciprocity, closeness, and commitment between people who see themselves as equals are essentials of friendship. *Equity theory* holds that people attempt to maintain stable, consistent relationships in which the ratio of members' contributions is balanced. Love usually involves the idealization of another person. People see their loved ones in a positive light, care for them, and are fascinated with them; love also involves trust and commitment. According to Sternberg, love has three components: intimacy (a sense of emotional closeness), commitment (the extent to which a relationship is permanent), and passion (arousal, some of it sexual, some intellectual, and some inspirational). pp. 487–489

KEY TERMS
social influence, p. 468; conformity, p. 468; obedience, p. 470; debriefing, p. 472; group, p. 472; social facilitation, p. 473; social loafing, p. 473; group polarization, p. 474; groupthink, p. 475; deindividuation, p. 476; aggression, p. 477; prosocial behaviour, p. 482; rape, p. 483; altruism, p. 483; sociobiology, p. 484; bystander apathy, p. 484; interpersonal attraction, p. 486; equity theory, p. 488; intimacy, p. 488

Weblinks

Social Psychology Network
www.wesleyan.edu/spn
A huge database on all aspects of social psychology. Includes information on textbooks, journals, courses, and research groups, as well as links to other psychology information.

Society for Personality and Social Psychology
www.spsp.org
Information on the society's activities and publications, and on careers in psychology.

Psychology Page
www.iit.edu/~azamoma/psych.html#social
Social categorization and the origins of prejudice are addressed here through a discussion of stereotypes in an essay entitled "Impressions and Levels of Prejudice" by Omar Azam.

Social Influence and Social Cognition
www.nimh.nih.gov/publicat/baschap5.htm#socinf
To learn more about persuasion and persuasive techniques, visit this site devoted to social influence that is sponsored by the National Institute of Mental Health.

Car Buyer's Tactics
www.pyramidwest.com/tactics.html
This is one of the most useful and informative sites regarding application of psychological knowledge to everyday life situations. Read about specific compliance tactics used by car salespeople.

The Altruistic Personality and Prosocial Behavior Institute
www.humboldt.edu/~spo1/altru.htm
Visit this site to learn more about prosocial behaviour. Publications and links to other Web sites are listed.

Types of Love
topchoice.com/~psyche/love/fehrtyp.html
This site goes into great depth about theories of love, in particular, the theories of both Sternberg and Hatfield.

Chapter 14

Stress and Health Psychology

Going out for a drive on Sunday afternoon is part of our popular culture—dad and mom ensconced in the front seat; son and daughter squabbling in the back seat. Although this semi-idyllic scene can still be found on the road, the reality for most people on the streets of Canada is traffic, congestion, and frustration. There are too many cars, people, and lights; in our fast-paced society there never seems to be enough time to get where we want to go.

For most commuters, and even on Sunday outings, life on the road means tailgating, congestion, fumes, and occasionally an out-of-control driver. Weaving in and out of lanes has become common, but old and young drivers alike are beginning to fear those who get out of control when they drive. Psychologists call this phenomenon "road rage"—people losing control of their emotions and responding violently to others on the roadway in reaction to a traffic disturbance. In most cases, the traffic situations these people encounter are typical of today's normal driving conditions and higher traffic volumes. But such drivers' reactions are far from typical. Some of them have slammed into other cars, run over bicyclists, drawn guns, and shot drivers who were in their way to express frustration or anger at their driving. The wheel, the car, and the highway have become weapons for expressing frustration, anger, and stress.

Experts say that aggressive driving behaviours are triggered by a variety of stimuli. Some are provoked by the actions of another driver; others are set off by roadway congestion. People who exhibit aggressive behaviours cross all age, ethnic, socioeconomic, and gender lines. Even usually "mild-mannered" people behave aggressively when behind the wheel, perhaps only when they're on the road. Those who are characteristically cynical, rude, angry, or aggressive are prone to get angry more often. These people "rage" at home, at work, *and* on the road. Canadian figures are not available, but in testimony given before the U.S. House of Representatives (1997) it was reported that aggressive driving—tailgating, speeding, running red lights, giving other drivers dirty looks or obscene gestures—has increased 51 percent over the last five years. For example, between 1990 and 1996, there were at least 10 037 incidents of

road rage that resulted in 218 deaths and 12 000 injuries.

Of course, everybody experiences bad moods, anger, and stress from time to time. As a student, you face a variety of stressors: studying for more than one exam in the same week; juggling studies with a part-time job, children, or both; getting along with a roommate or partner in cramped quarters. Stressors are a reality for everyone. Some suffer from stress-related health problems, such as high blood pressure and insomnia. Others try to escape from stress by turning to alcohol and other drugs. People can deal with stressors in either positive or negative ways; unfortunately, many don't cope effectively, and some even may take their frustrations out on the road. ■

In this chapter, we will examine the nature of stress, learn how to cope with it, and look at the interrelationship of health and stress. We also will look into how motivation, learning, and personality work together to influence the ability to cope with stress in day-to-day life.

Stress

P opping antacid tablets like candy, launching into tirades at co-workers or friends, pounding their fists on tables, and downing cocktails each night are a way of life for many people who succumb to stress caused by their jobs, families, and financial burdens. One person may have a high-pressure job that affects her social life and causes daily migraines. A co-worker may manage the same amount of stress in more positive ways, without suffering negative health consequences. Herein lies an important point: Different people evaluate and handle stress different ways.

What Is Stress?

A **stressor** is an environmental stimulus that affects an organism in physically or psychologically injurious ways, usually producing anxiety, tension, and physiological arousal. **Anxiety** is a generalized feeling of fear and apprehension that may be related to a particular event or object and is often accompanied by increased physiological arousal. Physiological arousal, often the first change that appears when a person responds to a stressor, includes changes in the autonomic nervous system that bring about increased heart rate, faster breathing, higher blood pressure, sweating palms, and dilation of the pupils.

Whenever something negatively affects someone, physically or psychologically, the person may experience the effect as stress. **Stress** is a nonspecific, often global response to real or imagined challenges or threats; it is an emotional response, a result. The key is that not all people view a stimulus, situation, challenge, or threat in the same way; *a person must view a situation as stressful for it to be stressful.* This broad definition recognizes that everyone experiences stress at some time, but that stress is also an interpreted state; stress is a response on the part of an individual. Richard Lazarus (1993), a leader in the study of emotion and stress, asserts that people *actively negotiate* between the demands of the environment (stressors) and personal beliefs and behaviours. This active negotiation is what cognitive researchers refer to as *cognitive appraisal.* Sometimes the arousal that stressors bring about initiates positive actions; sometimes the arousal's effects are detrimental. Thinking "I can't possibly handle this!" is likely to lead to a less positive response than is thinking "This is a big challenge for me!" (Lyubomirsky & Tucker, 1998). Figure 14.1 provides an overview of the responses to stressors that occur after a cognitive appraisal.

What determines whether a particular event will be stressful? Beyond cognitive appraisal, the answer lies in the extent to which people are familiar with the event, how much they have anticipated the event, and how much control they have

FIGURE 14.1
The Effect of Cognitive Appraisal on Responses to Stressors
Depending on how a potential stressor (for example, entering a tied game in overtime) is evaluated, its impact can vary emotionally, physiologically, and behaviourally.

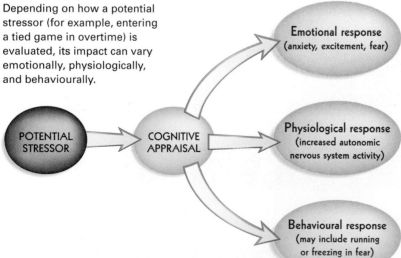

over the event and their response to it. The first exam written in a class generally produces particular anxiety because even well-prepared students do not know about the instructor's testing style. Subsequent exams are less anxiety producing for well-prepared students because they know what sort of exam questions to expect. When people can predict events and are familiar with them, they feel that they are more in control and can have some impact on their future.

Sources of Stress

You may never do this, but imagine that you have left a term paper until the last minute. As you scramble through the library trying to find appropriate references, you begin to realize that most of the sources for your project are signed out and that several other students also are looking for the few remaining relevant books and journals. How would you feel? There are three broad types of situations that cause stress: frustration, conflict, and pressure.

Frustration. When people are hindered from meeting their goals, they often feel frustrated. **Frustration** is the emotional state or condition that results when a goal—work, family, or personal—is thwarted or blocked. When people believe they cannot achieve a goal (often because of situations beyond their control), they may experience frustration. When you are unable to obtain a summer job because of a lack of experience, it can cause feelings of frustration. When a grandparent becomes ill, you may feel helpless; this can cause frustration. When there is an environmental threat over which people have no control, frustration is often the result (Hallman & Wandersman, 1992).

Some frustrations are externally caused. Examples are time lost in rush hour traffic or your grandparent's illness. Specific people cause other frustrations; your boss may be unfair in his appraisal of you, or your child or roommate may watch television while you are trying to study. You can sometimes alleviate the frustration of dealing with other people by taking some action; this action, however, may place you in conflict, another type of stress.

Conflict. When people must make difficult decisions, they may be in a state of conflict. **Conflict** is the emotional state or condition in which people have to make difficult decisions about two or more competing motives, behaviours, or impulses. Consider the difficult decisions of American draftees who did not want to fight in the Vietnam War but also did not want to flee to Canada or face imprisonment. Or what happens if a person's goals and needs conflict—if a student must choose between two equally desirable academic courses, both of which will advance the student's career plans but which meet at the same hour?

One of the first psychologists to describe and quantify such conflict situations was Neal Miller (1944, 1959). Miller developed hypotheses about how animals and human beings behave in situations that have both positive and negative aspects. In general, he described three types of conflicts that result when situations involve competing demands: approach–approach conflicts, avoidance–avoidance conflicts, and approach–avoidance conflicts.

Approach–approach conflict is the conflict that results when a person must choose between two equally attractive alternatives or goals (for example, two wonderful job offers). Approach–approach conflict generates discomfort and a stress response; however, people usually can tolerate it because either alternative is pleasant. **Avoidance–avoidance conflict** is the conflict that results from having to choose between two equally distasteful alternatives or goals (for example, paying your taxes or facing prosecution). **Approach–avoidance conflict** is the conflict that

Frustration: The emotional state or condition that results when a goal—work, family, or personal—is thwarted or blocked.

Conflict: The emotional state or condition in which a person has to make difficult decisions about two or more competing motives, behaviours, or impulses.

Approach–approach conflict: Conflict that results from having to choose between two equally attractive alternatives or goals.

Avoidance–avoidance conflict: Conflict that results from having to choose between two equally distasteful alternatives or goals.

Approach–avoidance conflict: Conflict that results from having to choose an alternative or goal that has both attractive and repellent aspects.

APPROACH–APPROACH CONFLICT

Movies (+) → ← Theatre (+)

AVOIDANCE–AVOIDANCE CONFLICT

Studying (−) → ← Cleaning (−)

APPROACH–AVOIDANCE CONFLICT

Delicious (+)

Hot fudge sundae

High in calories (−)

FIGURE 14.2
Three Types of Conflict
In approach–approach conflict, people have to choose between equally appealing alternatives. In avoidance–avoidance conflict, people have to choose between equally distasteful alternatives. In approach–avoidance conflict, people are faced with a single alternative that is both appealing and distasteful.

results from having to choose an alternative or goal that has both attractive and repellent aspects. Studying for an exam, which can lead to good grades but is boring and difficult, is an approach–avoidance situation. As Figure 14.2 shows, any of the three types of conflict situations will lead to a different degree of stress. Miller developed principles to predict behaviour in conflict situations, particularly in approach–avoidance situations: (1) the closer a person is to a goal, the stronger the tendency is to approach the goal. (2) When two incompatible responses are available, the stronger one will be expressed. (3) The strength of the tendency to approach or avoid is correlated with the strength of the motivating drive. (Thus, someone on a diet who is considering a hot fudge sundae may yield to temptation if desire for the sundae is stronger than the desire to lose weight.) People regularly face conflict situations that may cause them to become anxious. Moreover, if conflicts affect day-to-day behaviour, people may exhibit symptoms of maladjustment.

Pressure from Work, Time, and Life Events. Arousal and stress may occur when people feel **pressure**—the emotional state or condition resulting from the real or imagined expectations of others for certain behaviours or results. Although individual situations differ, pressure is common to almost everyone. Most of the time, it is associated with work, a lack of time, and life changes.

Work that is either overstimulating or understimulating can cause stress. Work-related stress also can come from fear of being let go or retired, of being passed over for promotion, or of organizational changes. In addition, the physical work setting may be too noisy, crowded, or isolated. Work-related pressure from deadlines, competition, and professional relationships (to name just a few possibilities) can cause a variety of physical problems. People suffering from work stress may experience migraines, sleeplessness, hunger for sweets, overeating, and intestinal distress. Stress at work often leads to an impaired immune system, which in turn leads to illness, resulting in lost efficiency and absenteeism (Levi, 1990). Stress at work also often "spills over" to non-work hours and leads to other problems like alcoholism—at least some of the time (Grunberg, Moore, & Greenberg, 1998).

Individuals with high-stress jobs, particularly where the stress is constant and the stressors are beyond the individual's control, show the effects most dramatically. Air traffic controllers and surgeons, for example, are responsible for the lives of other people every day and must be alert and organized at all times. If they work too many hours without relief, they may make a fatal mistake. Other examples of high-stress jobs are social workers, customer service agents, waiters and waitresses, and emergency workers.

Lack of time is another common source of stress. Everyone faces deadlines: Students must complete papers and tests on time, auto workers must keep pace with the assembly line, and taxpayers must file their returns by April 30. People have only a limited number of hours each day in which to accomplish tasks; therefore, many people carefully allocate their time to reduce time pressure. They may establish routines, make lists, set schedules, leave optional meetings early, and set aside leisure time in which to rid themselves of stressful feelings. If they do not handle time pressures successfully, they may begin to feel overloaded and stressed.

A third common source of stress is life events. Even positive situations may cause stress. Consider marriage. Marriage unites people as partners, companions, lovers, and friends. Nonetheless, adjusting to married life means becoming familiar with new experiences, responding to unanticipated events, and having less control over many aspects of day-to-day experiences—all of which can be stressful. Also, at times, interpersonal discord arises. One partner may not be fulfilling marital or role obligations or may be causing the spouse to feel left out; both possibilities may bring

Pressure: The emotional state or condition resulting from the real or imagined expectations of others for certain behaviours or results.

about stress and even health problems (Tesser & Beach, 1998).

We will examine stressful life events in more detail later in this chapter. In addition to major life events, however, it is also clear that a great deal of stress may be attributed to the simpler trials of day-to-day life. Table 14.1 presents the 10 daily hassles most frequently cited as sources of stress. It turns out that these daily hassles increase stress and predict symptoms like headaches (Fernandez & Sheffield, 1997).

Our Response to Stress

During rehearsal for a choral concert, a number of elementary school children developed nausea, shortness of breath, and abdominal pains. At the choir performance that evening, several of the children collapsed on stage. At another school, sixth-graders became dizzy and fainted during their graduation program. In both cases, the children were diagnosed as suffering from stress-related disorders. Feeling stress and trapped in situations that didn't allow them to escape from it, the children responded with symptoms of physical illness. People experience stress in a wide variety of ways. Some individuals experience modest increases in physiological arousal, while others may exhibit significant physical symptoms. In extreme cases, people become so aroused, anxious, and disorganized that their behaviour becomes maladaptive or maladjusted. The basic idea underlying the work of many researchers is that stress activates a biological predisposition towards maladjustment (Monroe & Simons, 1991).

Emotion, Physiology, and Behaviour. Psychologists who study stress typically divide the stress reaction into emotional, physiological, and behavioural components. *Emotionally*, people's reactions often depend on their frustration, their work-related pressures, and their day-to-day conflicts. When frustrated, people become angry or annoyed; when pressured, they become aroused and anxious; when placed in situations of conflict, they may vacillate or become irritable and hostile. *Physiologically*, the stress response is characterized by arousal. Recall that

Table 14.1 Life's Little Hassles— The Top 10

1. Concerns about weight

2. Health of a family member

3. Rising prices of common goods

4. Home maintenance

5. Too many things to do

6. Misplacing or losing things

7. Yard work or outside home maintenance

8. Property, investments, or taxes

9. Crime

10. Physical appearance

Source: Kanner et al., 1981.

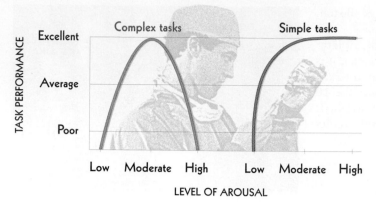

Excellent

Average

Poor

TASK PERFORMANCE

Complex tasks   Simple tasks

Low   Moderate   High   Low   Moderate   High

LEVEL OF AROUSAL

FIGURE 14.3
Effects of Arousal on Task Performance
When arousal is low, task performance is poor or non-existent. Performance is usually best at moderate levels of arousal. High levels of arousal usually improve performance on simple tasks but impair performance on complex tasks (such as surgery).

when psychologists refer to arousal, they usually mean changes in the autonomic nervous system that cause increased heart rate, faster breathing, higher blood pressure, sweating palms, and dilation of the pupils. Arousal is often the first change that occurs when a person feels stressed. *Behaviourally*, stress and its arousal response are connected. As we saw in Chapter 9, psychologist Donald Hebb (1972) has argued that effective behaviour depends on a person's state of arousal. When people are moderately aroused, they behave with optimal effectiveness. When they are underaroused, they lack the stimulation to behave effectively. Overarousal tends to produce disorganized and ineffective behaviour, particularly if the tasks people undertake are complex. (Figure 14.3 shows the effects of arousal on task performance.)

Nevertheless, a moderate amount of arousal and the stress that accompanies it may be unavoidable. Stress and the concomitant arousal keep people active and involved. They impel students to study, drive athletes to excel during competition, and help business people to strive for further success. In short, stress and arousal can help people achieve their potential.

Burnout. **Burnout** is a state of emotional and physical exhaustion, lowered productivity, and feelings of isolation, often caused by work-related pressures (Kalimo & Mejman, 1987). People who face high-pressure conditions on a daily basis often feel debilitated, hopeless, and emotionally drained and eventually may stop trying. Although burnout is most often work-related, pressures caused by family, financial, or social situations can create the same feelings. Burnout victims develop negative self-concepts because they are unable to maintain the high standards they have set for themselves. They often cease to be concerned about others and have physical as well as social problems.

Health Consequences. A research study found that stress contributes to a person's susceptibility to the common cold (Cohen, Tyrrell, & Smith, 1993). Mothers have long told people to reduce their levels of stress to keep from getting sick, and research now supports their advice. Stress does not directly cause disease. However, it contributes to many diseases, including the six major causes of death in Canada: heart disease, cancer, lung ailments, accidental injuries, cirrhosis of the liver, and suicide. In general, stress affects the immune system, making people more vulnerable to disease (Cohen, Tyrrell, & Smith, 1991; Cohen & Williamson, 1991; Herbert et al., 1994). More specifically, when stress responses go unexpressed, people show increased levels of autonomic nervous system activity such as increased heart rate and blood pressure (Hughes, Uhlmann, & Pennebaker, 1994). This, in turn, can lead to higher blood pressure, which has been linked to heart disease and other ailments. Stress also may lead to headaches, backaches, decreased productivity, and family arguments. Stress is often correlated with flare-ups of peptic ulcers (Levenstein et al., 1996). At a minimum, stress-related illnesses are causing an increase in medical costs for both individuals and employers. Extreme stress has been implicated in sudden heart attacks (Bosma et al., 1998; Kamarck & Jennings, 1991).

Stress afflicts children as well as adults, and some children are more vulnerable to it than others. Children are particularly unable to change or control the circumstances in which they find themselves (Band & Weisz, 1988). They may experience stress in school, stress caused by an abusive parent, stress from their parents' divorce, or stress from peer pressure. Like adults, they often show their stress response in physical symptoms. Also like adults, children have to appraise a situation as stressful in order for it to be experienced as stressful.

Burnout: A state of emotional and physical exhaustion, lowered productivity, and feelings of isolation, often caused by work-related pressures.

Studying Stress: Focus on Physiology

Psychologists want to know how today's increasingly complex lifestyles affect the physical and psychological well-being of individuals. For example, does intense competition make business people more susceptible to heart attacks? How can psychologists help people cope with life stressors, such as having a baby? How can therapists help veterans who are traumatized by war? These questions have helped researchers develop theories of stressors. One of the best-known theories is Hans Selye's general adaptation syndrome.

Selye's General Adaptation Syndrome. Working first at McGill University and then at the University of Montreal, Hans Selye (1907–1982) conducted a systematic study of stressors and stress. He investigated the physiological changes in people and animals that were experiencing various amounts of stress. Selye conceptualized people's responses to stress in terms of a *general adaptation syndrome* (1956, 1976). (A *syndrome* is a set of responses; in the case of stress, it is a set of behaviourally defined physical symptoms.) Selye's work initiated thousands of studies on stress and stress reactions, and Selye himself published more than 1600 articles on the topic.

According to Selye, people's response to a stressor occurs in three stages: (1) an initial short-term stage of alarm, (2) a longer period of resistance, and (3) a final stage of exhaustion (see Figure 14.4). During the *alarm stage*, people experience increased physiological arousal. They become excited, anxious, or frightened. Bodily resources are mobilized. Metabolism speeds up dramatically, and blood is diverted from the skin to the brain, resulting in a pale appearance. (The response is much like the fight-or-flight syndrome, in which the sympathetic nervous system is activated; see Chapter 2.) Later on in the stress response, people also may experience loss of appetite, sleeplessness, headaches, ulcers, or hormone imbalances; their normal level of ability to cope with stressors decreases.

Because people cannot stay highly aroused for very long, the initial alarm response usually leads to *resistance*. During this stage, physiological and behavioural responses become more moderate and sustained. People in the resistance stage often are irritable, impatient, and angry, and they may be constantly tired. This stage can persist for a few hours, several days, or even years, although eventually resistance begins to decline. For example, couples who suffer traumatic divorces sometimes exhibit anger and emotional fatigue for years after the conflict has been resolved in court.

The final stage is *exhaustion*. If people don't reduce their level of stress, they can become too exhausted to adapt. The air traffic controller who takes no vacations, works long shifts, and is expected to do more with less help may show symptoms of maladjustment or withdrawal. In extreme cases of constant stress, as in war, serious illness and death may occur. Of course, not everyone shows the same behaviours.

Holmes–Rahe Scale. Among the many researchers Selye inspired to study stressors and refine his theory are Holmes

FIGURE 14.4
Selye's General Adaptation Syndrome
According to Hans Selye, a person's response to a stressor can be divided into three stages: alarm, resistance, and exhaustion.

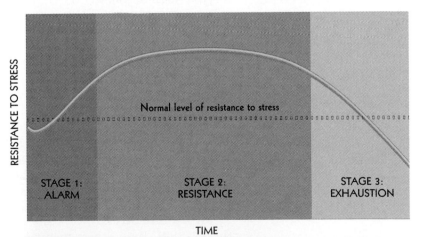

RESISTANCE TO STRESS

Normal level of resistance to stress

STAGE 1: ALARM

STAGE 2: RESISTANCE

STAGE 3: EXHAUSTION

TIME

During the first stage, the body mobilizes its resources.

In the second stage, the body establishes resistance; if the stress continues, resistance eventually begins to decline.

In the third stage, resistance is depleted, leading to exhaustion.

and Rahe. Their basic assumption is that stressful life events, especially when occurring in combination, will damage health (Holmes & Rahe, 1967; Rahe, 1989). *Stressful life events* are prominent events in a person's day-to-day circumstances that necessitate change.

To test their assumption, the researchers devised the Social Readjustment Rating Scale—a scale on which individuals identify significant life events (changes) that they've experienced over the past two years (Table 14.2 shows part of this scale). Each event is rated for its influence on a person. The death of a spouse, divorce, and illness are rated as high stressors; changes in eating habits, vacations, and holidays are rated lower. A person's total score is an index of stress and the likelihood of illness in the next two years. According to Holmes and Rahe, a person who scores above 300 points will be likely to suffer a stress-induced physical illness.

Although widely used, the Holmes–Rahe scale has been sharply criticized on a number of dimensions. First, for many people who score high on the scale, a direct relationship between health and life events has not been found (Krantz, Grunberg, & Baum, 1985). People have support systems, friends, and activities that influence how, when, and under what conditions stressors will affect them. Some psychologists therefore question the validity of the scale in predicting illness (Theorell et al., 1986). Another criticism stems from the fact that the scale was based on a study of young, male navy personnel, whose characteristics do not necessarily match those of the general Canadian and U.S. population, especially older people and women (Dohrenwend & Shrout, 1985). In addition, the scale includes only major life events. As well, the scale does not allow for an assessment of the role of interpretation in a person's perception of stress. For some people a separation or divorce might be devastating while for others it may provide a sense of relief. The stressors faced by most people are seldom big life crises; they are day-to-day irritations, but they do cause stress over the years (Whisman & Kwon, 1993).

The results of a study of the effects of both major life events and daily hassles on the reported health of elderly subjects showed that hassles are more closely related to psychological and physical ill health than are major life events (Chamberlain & Zika, 1990). Other studies found that flu, headaches, sore throats, and backaches also were related to daily hassles and stressors (DeLongis, Folkman, & Lazarus, 1988); that stressful life events are related to the quality of intimate, close relationships (Tesser & Beach, 1998); and that there may be a genetic predisposition to high levels of autonomic system activity in response to stressful life events (Kendler et al., 1993). It is not surprising that people with an external locus of control (see Chapter 12, pages 433–434), little social support (to be discussed in a later section), and high levels of stress see life as much more difficult than others do (Jorgensen & Johnson, 1990). *Diversity* (see page 504) examines the influence of culture on the ways people perceive and handle stressors.

Heart Disease and Stress

Heart disease and high blood pressure account for more than half of deaths each year in Canada. Physicians and psychologists view these silent killers as a disorder of lifestyle. Three components of day-to-day life are being studied in connection with high blood pressure and heart disease: work-site stress, Type A behaviour, and physiological reactivity. Intense research into each of these biobehavioural factors has altered heart patient treatment, because it is becoming clear that all three are related and interact in complex ways (Jorgenson et al., 1996).

Work-Site Stress. Work-site stress increases the prevalence of heart attacks (Levi, 1990). Researchers theorize that this may happen because physiological components of the stress response (such as increased heart rate and elevated blood pressure) place extra burdens on the heart over many years. The likelihood that you will have a heart attack increases significantly if you are an air traffic controller or a surgeon, for example, because these jobs are fraught with potential stressors. Other

Table 14.2 A Portion of the Holmes–Rahe Social Readjustment Rating Scale

Rank	Life Event	Value
1	Death of spouse	100
2	Divorce	73
3	Marital separation	65
4	Jail term	63
5	Death of close family member	63
6	Personal injury or illness	53
7	Marriage	50
8	Fired at work	47
9	Marital reconciliation	45
10	Retirement	45
11	Change in health of family member	44
12	Pregnancy	40
13	Sex difficulties	39
14	Gain of new family member	39
15	Business readjustment	39
16	Change in financial state	38
17	Death of a close friend	37
18	Change to different line of work	36
19	Change in number of arguments with spouse	35
20	Mortgage or loan for major purchase	31
21	Foreclosure of mortgage or loan	30
22	Change in responsibilities at work	29
23	Son or daughter leaving home	29
24	Trouble with in-laws	29
25	Outstanding personal achievement	28
26	Wife [or husband] begins or stops work	26
27	Begin or end school	26
28	Change in living conditions	25
29	Revision of personal habits	24
30	Trouble with boss	23
31	Change in work hours or conditions	20
32	Change in residence	20
33	Change in schools	20
34	Change in recreation	19
35	Change in church activities	19
36	Change in social activities	18
37	Loan for lesser purchase (under $10 000)	17
38	Change in sleeping habits	16
39	Change in number of family get-togethers	15
40	Change in eating habits	15
41	Vacation	13
42	Christmas	12
43	Minor violations of the law	11

jobs may cause stress by demanding too little or too much of a worker. Stress is also affected by a person's degree of *autonomy*—the extent to which the person controls the speed, flow, and level of work. A position with high demands and low control increases stress. A factory worker, for example, usually has little control over the work and therefore may experience stress.

Men are more likely than women to develop heart disease related to work-site stress. However, in recent years more women have entered the workforce. When their situations are similar, men and women seem to have similar rates of heart disease (Hamilton & Fagot, 1988).

Fitting in and Getting By: The Stress of Immigration and Stress on the Farm

We all have a pretty good idea about what sorts of things cause stress in our own lives, but what do we know about people whose lives are different than our own? Consider the experiences of immigrants to Canada. And then think about a group that is supposed to be living right—farming families who work the land and make an honest living.

Moving from your country of origin and starting a new life in another country involves a lot of change. You may not know the language spoken there, you may not have a job, and you may not have any friends or any members of your cultural group to talk to and lean on for support while you adjust to the new country. It certainly would be a stressful experience. Research into ethnicity and behaviour often shows striking differences because the world-view and life experiences of different groups are unique. Everyone, regardless of ethnicity, is similarly and adversely affected by the difficult times in life. Nevertheless, how individuals respond is in part dependent on their culture and the values that it espouses, reinforces, and expects (Crystal et al., 1994).

A study conducted in Toronto by Ken and Karen Dion (Dion, Dion, & Pak, 1992) explored the factors involved in predicting the level of stress experienced by new members of the local Chinese community. The study focused on psychological factors, and revealed that an individual's general level of psychological hardiness was directly related to the level of stress he or she experienced. Specifically, people with a higher sense of personal control over their circumstances and with a higher level of self-esteem were likely to report fewer psychological stress symptoms and also reported having experienced less discrimination.

Participants' level of adaptation to life in Toronto also was related to their level of education, the socio-economic level of their job, and their proficiency with English. In other words, the more successful and the more adapted they were to Canadian life, the less stress they experienced.

In addition, Cynthia Baker (1993) found that the level of stress experienced during the period of adjustment that immigrants go through when they first arrive in Canada is significantly lessened if they settle in an area that already has a large community of people from their cultural background. Clearly, social support that one can relate to and draw upon is a significant factor in positive adjustment to a new country.

In light of the above results you might think that people who have been established, sometimes for generations, on Canadian farms would be far less likely to experience significant levels of stress. In fact, if you were to assess stress levels among Canadian farmers using common stress scales you might find this to be true, but you would have failed to capture a clear picture of what farming life is like. It is worth noting that most measures of life stress tend to focus on stressors most often experienced by city dwellers and do not do a particularly good job of tracking the stresses experienced by members of farming communities.

While far more connected with the rest of the world than they were even 40 years ago, Canadian farming families today are in business for themselves in a very uncertain segment of the economy. Farm families experience high levels of stress due to the financial realities of farming and are further stressed by their lack of control over the most influential variables in their lives, including government policies, weather, and market conditions. All of these factors contribute to sleep and health disruptions, a greater number of arguments, and trouble concentrating (Walker & Walker, 1987; Walker, Walker, & MacLennan, 1986). Farm families in which the members support each other do better than ones that do not deal well with the stresses of farm living (Keating, 1987). Financial assistance for farm products is fairly readily available, but assistance in developing resources to cope with stress is offered to farming families only rarely.

In summary, most people experience their share of stress. In understanding the nature of this stress and how people cope with it, psychologists must not assume that all life situations and cultural contexts are the same. Only when researchers look past this assumption can they begin to study the stress in people's lives, let alone assist them to cope with it effectively. ■

Type A Behaviour. In the late 1950s, physicians Friedman and Rosenman identified a pattern of behaviour that they believe contributes to heart disease: Type A behaviour (Friedman & Rosenman, 1974). **Type A behaviour** occurs in individuals who are competitive, impatient, hostile, and always striving to do more in less time. (**Type B behaviour** occurs in people who are calmer, more patient, and less hurried.)

Early studies of Type A behaviour showed a strong association with heart disease; that is, Type A individuals were more likely than Type B individuals to have heart attacks. More recent research, however, suggests that no such relationship exists (Johnson, Espenes, & Gillard, 1998; Lilla et al., 1998). Some elements of Type A behaviour do seem to be related to heart disease (Hart, 1997), but the overall Type A behaviour pattern is not. For example, hostility and anger have been related to heart disease (Morren, 1998; Madigan, Dale, & Cross, 1998), as have suspiciousness and mistrust (Weidner et al., 1989). Culture plays a role; some consider Type A behaviour and its relationship to heart disease to be a Western phenomenon, mainly involving middle-aged, North American businessmen (Helman, 1992). One important research finding is that expressing the emotions associated with stress verbally or in writing decreases the risk of health problems (Berry & Pennebaker, 1993; Friedman, 1996). Another important finding is that although women experience more periods of distress than do men, they are less likely to stay distressed (Almeida & Kessler, 1998). People who are extremely anxious, depressed, angry, and unhappy have a higher rate of heart disease than do other people (T. Q. Miller et al., 1991), although the physiological mechanism underlying this is unclear (Suls & Wan, 1993). In sum, Type A behaviour patterns exist; however, a direct relationship between overall Type A behaviour and heart disease, or other disorders for that matter, is minimal or nonexistent (Koehler, Kuhnt, & Richter, 1998; Matthews, 1988).

Physiological Reactivity. A possible third factor relating stress to heart disease is how the body reacts to stressors. This is called *reactivity*, or *physiological reactivity*. A situation interpreted as stressful may cause a rapid physiological response, triggering processes that lead to heart disease. Research shows that Type A behaviour patterns are associated with increased physiological reactivity (Contrada, 1989), long-lasting emotional distress (Suls & Wan, 1989a, 1989b), and increased feelings of anger and hostility (Suarez & Williams, 1989). People who are physically fit react better physiologically to stressful situations than those who are not fit. But it is still not clear whether increased reactivity predisposes people to high blood pressure and heart disease or whether those predisposed to high blood pressure and heart disease show reactivity.

Work-site stress, aspects of Type A behaviour, and physiological reactivity are individually correlated to heart disease, but research suggests that these factors are also interactive; that is, they affect one another (Krantz et al., 1988). From a psychologist's viewpoint, this is an important finding requiring further investigation. First, much more research is needed to better understand these factors. Laboratory studies of stress are not the same as real-world situations (Lassner, Matthews, & Stoney, 1994). Second, although behavioural factors contribute to heart disease, researchers need to determine the relative importance of these factors. Third, psychologists need to find interventions that help individuals learn to control negative emotions arising from excessive stress and so decrease the likelihood of heart disease (Frasure-Smith, Lespérance, & Talajic, 1993). Fourth, and most important, more research is needed on how an individual's culture and world-view affect work-site stress, Type A behaviour, and physiological reactivity. For example, research shows that Japanese Americans who were the most traditional in Japanese cultural views (collectivistic, for example) had the lowest incidence of heart disease when compared with Japanese Americans who were the least traditional in terms of Japanese values (Matsumoto, 1996). Another factor affecting stress levels is one's approach to getting tasks done in a timely manner, as discussed in *The Research Process* (see pages 506 and 507).

Type A behaviour: Behaviour characterized by competitiveness, impatience, hostility, and constant efforts to do more in less time.

Type B behaviour: Behaviour characterized by more calmness, more patience, and less hurrying than that of Type A individuals.

Post-traumatic Stress Disorder

The effects of wars on the people who fight on the front lines have long been the subject of research and speculation. The term *shell-shock* was used to describe the severe stress reactions of many young men to the trench warfare of the First World War, but no systematic cure, other than removal from the front lines and rest, was developed. In fact, it was not until the Vietnam War that significant research was undertaken into this aspect of stress. This severe stress-related disorder is now termed **post-traumatic stress disorder (PTSD)**—a mental disorder that may become evident after a person has undergone severe stress caused by some type of disaster.

Origins and Symptoms. Victims of rape, natural disasters (tornadoes, earthquakes, hurricanes, floods), and disasters caused by human beings (wars, train wrecks, toxic chemical spills) often suffer from PTSD. Many survivors of the 1989 San Francisco earthquake still fear the double-decker freeways of California, which took several lives when they collapsed in the quake. PTSD is also still evident long after the 1980 volcanic eruption of Mount St. Helens (Shore, Vollmer, & Tatum, 1989). In Canada, a PCB fire in 1988 required evacuation of over 1500 families and led to a significant increase in PTSD symptoms (Breton, Valla, & Lambert, 1993). Divers trying to recover the wreckage and victims of the terrible September 1998 crash of Swissair flight 111 suffered symptoms of PTSD after a prolonged period of the gruesome work. The likelihood that a person will experience PTSD at some time during his or her life is about 8 percent (Kessler et al., 1995).

Post-traumatic stress disorder (PTSD): A mental disorder that may become evident after a person has undergone severe stress caused by some type of disaster; common symptoms include vivid, intrusive recollections or re-experiences of the traumatic event and occasional lapses of normal consciousness.

the research process

Procrastination and Stress

Why do now what you can put off until tomorrow? The answer is that if you habitually put things off, your work will suffer and so may your health.

Doing your work in a timely fashion is considered to be appropriate, rational adult behaviour, especially in Western culture. But an awful lot of us procrastinate from time to time; and some people procrastinate—put off, delay, make excuses for lateness—very often. Critics of procrastinators call them lazy or self-indulgent and argue that their work performance suffers due to high stress levels. Defenders—many of them procrastinators themselves—assert that the work performance is the same, sometimes better, because of heightened stress to get the job

done. They'll argue, "I do my best work under pressure." But do they?

Diana Tice and Roy Baumeister (1997) investigated the effects of procrastination on the quality of work performance, stress, and illness. Students were given an assignment with a deadline. Procrastinators were identified using a standard scale that identifies them compared with non-procrastinators. The students' well-being was assessed with self-reports of stress and illness. Finally, task performance was checked by ascertaining whether students turned in assignments early, on time, or late.

The researchers hypothesized that procrastination might show poorer performance and health and higher stress levels. Alternatively,

they acknowledged that there might indeed be benefits due to intense, last-minute efforts.

Participants and Method.
The participants were volunteer students taking a health psychology course. They were assigned a term paper and were told that if they could not make the due date they automatically would be given an extension. Dates on which the papers were turned in were recorded, and questionnaires about health and stress were filled out when the students turned in their papers. Papers were graded by an instructor who did not know who turned in which paper and when. This type of research design is referred to as a blind study.

Common symptoms of post-traumatic stress disorder are vivid, intrusive recollections or re-experiences of the traumatic event and occasional lapses of normal consciousness (Wood et al., 1992; Morgan et al., 1997). People may develop anxiety, depression, or exceptionally aggressive behaviour; they may avoid situations that resemble the traumatizing events. Such behaviours eventually may interfere with daily functioning, family interactions, and health. Research on PTSD is attempting to identify a possible genetic predisposition (True et al., 1993), a physiological explanation (Tryon, 1998), and psychological causes such as motivated forgetting of difficult circumstances (Foa & Riggs, 1995; Karon & Widener, 1998). An increasing number of studies are focusing on the psychological aftermath of natural disasters such as earthquakes, tornadoes, and floods (Wood et al., 1992), as well as the impact on survivors of traumatic events like the Holocaust of the Second World War (Yehuda et al., 1998) and the displacement of refugee children (Ajdukovic & Ajdukovic, 1998). Many more studies have focused on military personnel and especially Vietnam veterans and on those who have experienced life-threatening situations (e.g., Keane, 1998; Rosebush, 1998; Ursano et al., 1995).

Results. As expected, procrastinators turned in their papers late. Procrastinators received lower grades than the non-procrastinators. Interestingly, procrastinators' scores were negatively correlated with stress and reporting of symptoms—that is, the more a student was a procrastinator the fewer stress and wellness problems he or she had. The procrastinators thus reported feeling better, but had poorer grades.

Discussion. It appears that procrastination brings short-term benefits to health. Procrastinators benefit from the carefree, casual situation they create for themselves—stress is lowered and illness is reduced. But when Tice and Baumeister conducted another study to assess whether these effects were the same at all points in the semester, they found that the procrastinators experienced much more stress late in the semester than the non-procrastinators did. In fact, when the impact of procrastination is considered in light

of time (early or late in the semester), the effects are negative—total stress and illness are higher for procrastinators. As the researchers put it, the early benefits of tardiness are outweighed by the later costs of stress and ill health. Especially important is the finding that procrastinators produced inferior work—postponing work seemed to lead to compromises and sacrifices in quality.

There were some design flaws and limitations in this research. First, participants were not randomly assigned. Second, some people wind up doing their work late for reasons other than procrastination, such as family emergencies or illness. Third, although stress, illness, and procrastination are related, correlation does not prove a causal effect. And, of course, university students are not representative of all people and so these results cannot be generalized to the entire population.

Implications. The study suggests that procrastination should be considered a self-defeating behaviour because it is associated with stress, illness, and inferior performance. Of course, some procrastinators mistakenly believe that they can improve performance by postponing it, but evidence to support this view is scant. In the end, procrastination is not adaptive—procrastinators end up suffering more and performing worse than non-procrastinators. Procrastinators of the world, get organized! ■

The Vietnam Veteran. Much of what we know about PTSD we have learned from studies of Vietnam veterans. Although most veterans of the Vietnam War do not suffer from the disorder, thousands of them do. While most Canadians tend to identify the Vietnam War with the United States, between 10 000 and 40 000 Canadians served in Vietnam with American units. If anything, their experiences with PTSD are more serious than those of American veterans, mainly due to the lack of recognition of their involvement in Canada as well as their isolation from other veterans who could share their experiences (Stretch, 1990, 1991).

Decades later, these Vietnam veterans still endure sleeping problems, difficulty in concentrating, and feelings of alienation, and relive painful experiences. Many Vietnam veterans did not experience symptoms until months or even years after their return home. Those who suffer from PTSD seem more likely than others to have other stressful events in their lives and other adjustment problems, which in turn make the disorder worse—a vicious circle (McFall, Mackay, & Donovan, 1991).

The Vietnam War created unique psychological problems. Survival—not heroism—was the primary concern of many military personnel. Some turned to drugs or alcohol to alleviate fear. Moreover, the combatants, most of whom were drafted, knew that many people at home vehemently opposed the conflict. Finally, many of the soldiers were whisked home without ceremony or a chance to reacclimate gradually (Hobfoll et al., 1991).

For many complicated psychological, political, and social reasons, mental health practitioners have not always been as responsive as they might have been to those suffering from PTSD. This has occurred in part because, as we will see in the next section, other variables (such as a high degree of resilience) can lessen the impact of the trauma of war on many individuals (Sutker et al., 1995). Still, too often, veterans have been held responsible for how they experience traumatic stress. Now that psychologists recognize PTSD, special help in the form of workshops and therapy is becoming available, and drug therapies are being assessed (Vinar, 1998).

Focus

Review

◆ What is the link between stress and ill health? pp. 500–505
◆ Why is appraisal a key component of stress? p. 496
◆ What are the symptoms of post-traumatic stress disorder? pp. 506–507

Think Critically

◆ What do you think defines a catastrophe?
◆ Do you see yourself as a Type A person or a Type B person? Do you know any Type A people? Does their health seem to be affected?

Coping

M ost people have ways to cope with anxiety and with the physical ailments produced by stress. Some people seek medical and psychological help; others turn to alcohol and other drugs. Others seem to lack resources and do not cope well when they find themselves in stressful circumstances.

What Is Coping?

Coping: The process by which a person takes some action to manage, master, tolerate, reduce, or minimize environmental or internal demands that cause or might cause stress and that will tax the individual's inner resources.

In general, *coping* means dealing with a situation. However, for a psychologist, **coping** is the process by which a person takes some action to manage, master, tolerate, reduce, or minimize environmental and internal demands that cause or might cause stress and that will tax the individual's inner resources. This definition of coping involves five important components. First, the coping is constantly changing and being evaluated and is therefore a process or a strategy. Second, coping involves managing situations, not necessarily bringing them under complete control. Third, coping is effortful; it does not happen automatically. Fourth, coping aims to manage cognitive as well as behavioural events. Finally, coping is a learned process.

Many types of coping strategies exist; a person may use a few or many of them. Coping begins at the biological level. People's bodies respond to stress with specific reactions, including changes in hormone levels, in autonomic nervous system activity, and in the amount of neurotransmitters in the brain. Effective coping strategies occur at the psychological level when people learn new ways of dealing with their vulnerabilities.

Resilience, Coping Skills, and Social Support

A crucial factor that determines how well people cope with their problems is resilience. **Resilience** is the extent to which people are flexible, are less easily impaired by events, and respond adaptively to external or internal demands. A person who is resilient is said to be less vulnerable to stressors. Resilience depends on **coping skills**—the techniques people use to deal with changing situations and stress. People who have effective coping skills to guide them are prepared to deal with stress-related situations and are thus less vulnerable (Wiebe, 1991). People with poor or less well-developed coping skills may be extremely vulnerable and incapable of dealing with stress. This is especially true in children, who, because they are young, are less likely to have well-developed coping skills (Hilsman & Garber, 1995). In some cases, children even may develop a sense of *learned helplessness*; they may have found that rewards and punishments are not contingent on their behaviour, so they learn not to try to cope, thereby remaining helpless (Job & Barnes, 1995). Faced with poor coping skills and a loss of control, some adults, too, stop responding. (We examined learned helplessness in Chapter 5.)

The level of social support available to them affects people's resilience and vulnerability. **Social support** consists of the comfort, recognition, approval, and encouragement available from other people, including friends, family, members of organizations, and co-workers. Even animals can provide social support (Siegel, 1990). When people feel supported by others' emotional concern and displays of caring, they can cope better with extraordinary pressure. Support is especially valuable when it is offered by someone who is important to the vulnerable person (Dakof & Taylor, 1990; Kessler et al., 1992). In addition to (and sometimes in place of) friends and family, group therapy (examined in Chapter 16) can be especially effective in alleviating anxiety. In group therapy, other people in similar situations can offer concern and emotional support.

Defence-oriented and Task-oriented Coping Strategies

According to psychologist Richard S. Lazarus (1982), people faced with constant stress use either defence-oriented or task-oriented coping strategies. *Defence-oriented coping strategies* do not reduce stressors; however, they help people protect themselves from their effects. These strategies ease stress, thereby enabling people to tolerate and deal with disturbances. As we saw in Chapter 12, people may use defence mechanisms to distort reality in order to defend themselves against life's difficulties. One such mechanism is *rationalization*, in which people reinterpret reality to make it more palatable. If your boyfriend or girlfriend dumps you, you may cope by telling your friends that you "never really liked him/her that much anyway." Similarly, a person who is turned down for a job may rationalize that he didn't want to work for the company after all. Another defence mechanism is *reaction formation*. A

Resilience: The extent to which people are flexible, are less easily impaired by events, and respond adaptively to external or internal demands.

Coping skills: The techniques people use to deal with changing situations and stress.

Social support: The comfort, recognition, approval, and encouragement available from other people, including friends, family, members of organizations, and co-workers.

FIGURE 14.5
**Developing a Stress
Reduction Program**
Developing a stress reduction
program is a task-oriented
coping strategy.

1.
What is
distressing
me?

- Biases
- Background
- Assumptions
- Environment
- Value system
- Inferences
- Attitudes

4.
What
results can
I see?

2.
How am I
handling it now,
and what can
I do about it?

3.
How have I
put my plan
into action?

woman who dreads her tedious work but is excessively cheerful at the office has developed a reaction formation. She is expressing a feeling that is the opposite of her true one.

Stress management is becoming increasingly important to highly stressed individuals. Counsellors commonly treat stress by first identifying the stressor and then helping the client modify behaviour to cope with it. Through therapy, a person troubled by stressful situations can learn to cope by untangling personal feelings, understanding the sources of the stress, and then modifying behaviour to alleviate it. Students about to enter college or university, for example, often show signs of stress. They're worried about academic pressures, social life, and overall adjustment. At some schools, incoming students can receive counselling to learn how to deal with their stress. Similarly, stress management seminars, in which psychologists help business executives deal with stress in the corporate world, are becoming popular. The aim of both the counselling and the seminars is the same: to modify people's responses to stressors by replacing maladaptive responses with more useful ones.

Most psychologists, and especially behavioural psychologists, recommend *task-oriented coping strategies* for managing stress. The strategies usually involve several tasks, or steps (see Figure 14.5). Essentially, these steps are (1) identifying the stressor, (2) choosing an appropriate course of action for stress reduction, (3) implementing the plan, and (4) evaluating its success. A person's biases, attitudes, value systems, and previous environmental stressors affect each of these steps (which are not always undertaken in order).

Identifying the Stressor. Since stress-producing situations exist in many areas, identifying the stressor is often difficult. A person may be experiencing problems with their workload, their finances, their social life, and their roommate. They must decide what is causing them the most stress and whether their problems with their social life, for example, are in some way tied to their work situation. The difficulty of identifying specifically what is causing feelings of stress is not limited to students or young people. Older people seem to have as much difficulty as younger people in identifying and controlling sources of stress (Lazarus & DeLongis, 1983).

Choosing the Action. Once the stressor is identified, people need to choose among several coping strategies. For example, they can withdraw from a stress-inducing situation by quitting work, leaving a spouse, or declaring bankruptcy. More often, they turn to other people or other methods of coping.

Because arousal and excitement usually accompany stress, people may cope by using *relaxation techniques*. These techniques include biofeedback, hypnosis, and meditation, all of which help people refocus their energies. Exercise such as aerobics, jogging, or racquetball is another effective way for a person to relax, relieve stress, and improve mood states (Aganoff & Boyle, 1994; Steptoe, Kimbell, & Basford, 1998).

Many people manage stress and anxiety with *cognitive coping strategies*; that is, they prepare themselves to handle pressure through gradual exposure to increasingly intense stressors (Janis, 1985). Chapter 9 discussed a study in which people viewing a film with painful scenes were able to control their emotional responses (Lazarus & Alfert, 1964). This study suggests that people can learn to manage their stress by using their thought processes. Building on this finding, a major goal of current research on stress is to prepare people to react in constructive ways to early warning signs of stress.

Research shows that people can help with stress by talking to themselves and using imagery (Ilacqua, 1994). The self-talk procedure, which is used widely, is effective in helping people confront stressors and cope with pain and the feeling of being overwhelmed (Turk, Meichenbaum, & Genest, 1983). By talking to themselves, people gain control over their emotions, arousal, and stress reactions; this technique is especially useful before noxious or painful medical procedures such as chemotherapy (Ludwick-Rosenthal & Neufeld, 1988).

Implementing the Plan. Stress management counsellors help people prepare for stressful situations by providing them with new ideas—a process called stress inoculation. **Stress inoculation** is the procedure of giving people realistic warnings, recommendations, and reassurances to help them prepare for and cope with impending dangers or losses. Sometimes stress inoculation involves a single technique, such as breathing deeply and regularly. At other times it is more elaborate, involving graded exposure to various levels of threats or detailed information about a forthcoming procedure (Janis, 1985). Janis likens stress inoculation to an antibiotic given to ward off disease. It helps people to defend themselves and to cope with stressors when they occur. Essentially, stress inoculation does the following:

- Increases the predictability of stressful events.
- Fosters coping skills.
- Generates self-talking.
- Encourages confidence about successful outcomes.
- Builds a commitment to personal action and responsibility for an adaptive course of action.

Evaluating the Success of the Plan. A well-designed coping plan includes evaluation of the plan's success. Have the techniques been effective? Is there still more to do? Are new or further actions needed? All of these questions need to be answered as part of the task-oriented coping strategy.

To cope well both at home and at work, people should be task-oriented, self-monitoring, realistic, open to supportive relationships, and patient (Sarason & Sarason, 1987). They also need to eat sensibly, get enough sleep, stand up for themselves from time to time, find a hobby, take refuge in family—and sometimes, when things get too extreme, escape. Most importantly, people have to believe in themselves and in their ability to cope well with stress (Bandura et al., 1988). It can sometimes be very helpful to anticipate events that may cause stress—that is, to engage in **proactive coping**, or taking action in advance of a potentially stressful situation to prevent it, modify it, or prepare for it before it occurs. Proactive coping precedes the stressful situation and requires different skills than does coping with an immediate stressor (Aspinwall & Taylor, 1997). *Experiencing Psychology* (see page 512) examines this strategy in more detail.

Coping, Health, and a Positive Attitude

Applied psychologists claim that simply maintaining a positive attitude can help a person cope with stress and can even reduce its physical symptoms. People who believe they have control over their lives, health, and well-being are more relaxed and happier than those who do not (Rodin, 1986; Thompson et al., 1993). An upbeat mood, a positive sense of personal control, and even a self-serving bias (a way of looking at things that makes you look or feel better) can facilitate such worthwhile behaviours as helping others and evaluating people favourably (Meyers & Diener, 1995). Applied psychologists suggest that people who have positive attitudes even may live longer.

Sometimes, reframing or rethinking a situation serves as a rationalization to make it less anxiety producing, as we saw in Chapter 12. One study, however,

Stress inoculation [in-OK-you-LAY-shun]: The procedure of giving people realistic warnings, recommendations, and reassurances to help them prepare for and cope with impending dangers or losses.

Proactive coping: Taking action in advance of a potentially stressful situation to prevent it, modify it, or prepare for it before it occurs.

experiencing psychology

A Stitch in Time— Proactive Coping

If you recognize that you are going to have a challenging semester next fall, you might arrange a full-time job over the summer to ensure only light part-time work when school starts. By doing so (whether you think of it that way or not), you are already coping with your tough fall semester.

Psychologists have spent decades examining how people cope when stressors occur, how they marshal friends, social support, and emotional strength and take specific actions. But little research has been conducted on the activities that people also may engage in—preparing in advance. Anticipating a lonely holiday season, a student in a foreign country, far from home, may plan a skiing expedition. Recognizing that job opportunities and advancement seem to be shrinking in one's chosen profession, a person might choose to take courses, train, and put a new spin on what she does.

Lisa Aspinwall and Shelley Taylor (1997) have asserted that proactive coping is really a five-stage process. First, we *accumulate resources,* mustering time, money, and social support and managing current situations. Next, we *recognize* that a stressful event is coming. Then we *appraise* the event for its difficulty and its potential impact. Fourth, we *engage in preliminary coping,* to see what we can do now to prevent or minimize a threat. And finally, we *elicit and use feedback* to assess whether we have averted a future stressor.

The truth is that many stressors in life can be avoided or minimized. If we understand what we can do, in advance, to help avoid them, our lives will be better. This is proactive coping—an active process that requires people to be practical and take action, not just seek emotional support or avoidance. In the view of Aspinwall and Taylor, we can lead happier lives if we take care, think ahead, and take action. ■

showed that people who engage in such small self-deceptions may be healthier than people who focus on their anxiety. In an unpublished study that ran from 1946 through 1988, Peterson and Seligman (reported in DeAngelis, 1988) found that those who made excuses for negative events in 1946 had better health in 1988. Such results indicate that people who emphasize the negative aspects of life's events may develop learned helplessness. They may then choose inaction because they believe themselves to be powerless in controlling events. Taking a positive approach and believing in your own abilities will help ward off stress and avoid the fear and arousal that come from feelings of despair and low self-esteem (Bandura et al., 1988). Seligman (1988) argues that optimism helps people achieve goals and cope more effectively; for example, optimistic salespeople substantially outsell their pessimistic colleagues. Maintaining an optimistic attitude is likely to help people engage in self-protective behaviours that will foster change for the better (Ewart, 1991; Scheier & Carver, 1993).

The Conservation of Resources. People can develop a positive attitude by conserving resources. A person's home, personal relationships, and status as a valued worker, good student, or community leader are important resources to those who have them. Hobfoll (1989) suggests that people strive to retain, protect, and build their resources; the potential or actual loss of these valued resources is threatening. In Hobfoll's view, when these resources are under attack, people try to defend themselves. They attempt to ward off the attack or replace the lost resources by, say, seeking a new marriage or leadership position or by gaining some new competence or financial strength. When a person is experiencing stress because of a threat to personal resources, treatment might mean shifting the person's focus of attention, reinterpreting the threat, helping the person see how the lost resource might be replaced (for example, by finding a new job), and reevaluating the threat.

Effective Coping Strategies. Taking responsibility for preventive behaviours can be an important step towards better physical and mental health (Ewart, 1991). There are a number of steps you can take to cope, manage stress, and stay healthy:

- *Increase exercise.* People are able to cope better when they improve their physical fitness, usually by exercising. In addition, increased exercise will lower blood pressure and reduce the risk of heart disease.
- *Eat well.* People feel better and cope better when they eat well and have a balanced diet. This also means not being overweight.
- *Sleep well.* People react better to life when they have had a good night's sleep; reaction time improves, as does judgment.
- *Be flexible.* Life is unpredictable; accept that fact and day-to-day changes and surprises will be easier to handle.
- *Keep stress at school or the office.* Work-related stressors should be kept in the work environment. Bringing stressors home will only make stress worse. People are more likely to be involved in substance abuse and domestic violence when they bring stressors home with them.
- *Communicate.* Share your ideas, feelings, and thoughts with the significant people in your life. This will decrease misunderstanding, mistrust, and stress.
- *Learn to relax.* In our fast-paced society, people seldom take the time to relax and let uncomfortable ideas and feelings leave them. Learn meditation, yoga, or deep breathing. Schedule some time each day for yourself.
- *Seek support.* Social support from family, friends, and self-help groups will help you appraise situations differently. Remember, you have to appraise a situation as stressful for it to be stressful. Social support helps you keep stressful situations in perspective.

Brain and Behaviour (see page 514) discusses **psychoneuroimmunology (PNI)**, the study of how psychological processes and the nervous system affect and, in turn, are affected by the body's natural defence system—the immune system.

Psychoneuroimmunology (PNI) [SYE-ko-NEW-ro-IM-you-NOLL-oh-gee]: The study of how psychological processes and the nervous system affect, and in turn are affected by, the body's natural defence system—the immune system.

Health psychology: Subfield concerned with the use of psychological ideas and principles in health enhancement, illness prevention, diagnosis and treatment of disease, and rehabilitation processes.

Focus

Review

- What does it mean to be resilient? p. 509
- Identify several coping strategies that can be used to deal with daily hassles. p. 513
- What is the connection between the immune system, attitudes, and health? p. 514

Think Critically

- From your own experience, what coping techniques are more effective than others?
- Do you think that undergoing stress inoculation might allow people to build an immunity to stress?

Health Psychology

I n the past, most people died from causes beyond their control—influenza, tuberculosis, and pneumonia, for example. Today, the leading causes of death in Canada—heart disease, cancer, stroke, and accidents—can be controlled to some extent by environmental and behavioural variables. Psychologists believe there is a direct relationship between people's health and their behaviour. **Health psychology** is the psychological subfield concerned with the use of psychological ideas and principles in health enhancement, illness prevention, diagnosis and treatment of disease, and rehabilitation processes. It is an action-oriented discipline that assumes that people's ideas and behaviours contribute to the onset and prevention of illness. A closely related field, *behavioural medicine*, integrates behavioural

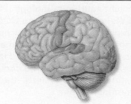

brain and behaviour
Rose-coloured Glasses for Your Immune System

Before you go to the gym for a workout or out for a bike ride—especially if it's very early in the morning—you may have to give yourself a pep talk. It's a psychological technique that we all use. And when you become stressed in the middle of an exam, you may (or you should!) talk to yourself, saying things like "take a deep breath." Again, this is a little common-sense psychology. But does it go further than that? Can we harness our body's own defence mechanisms? Can we directly or indirectly affect our brain and behaviour? Today some psychologists think we can, and the evidence is mounting.

Research in psychoneuro-immunology (PNI) shows that the immune system (which fights disease) responds to a person's moods, stress level, and basic attitudes about life (Herbert et al., 1994; Keicolt-Glaser et al., 1998). According to PNI researchers, the brain provides information to the immune system about how and when to respond (Altman, 1998; Miller, 1998). The nervous and immune systems seem to be linked, each producing substances that alter the functions of the other (Greer & Brady, 1998; Maier & Watkins, 1997). The brain—especially after activation of the sympathetic nervous system—

sends to the immune system signals that trigger its disease-fighting ability, including the production of white blood cells and other types of disease-fighting cells (Biondi & Zannino, 1997; Overmier & Gahtan, 1998). The immune system sends signals to the brain that alter its functioning (Maier, Watkins, & Fleshner, 1994). Thus, the immune system of a person with a positive, upbeat attitude responds better and faster than does that of a person who is depressed and lethargic (Ader & Cohen, 1993; O'Leary, 1990). Consider people whose loved ones have recently died; they consistently show higher rates of illness and depression (Connor & Leonard, 1997). Today, many AIDS patients are provided with counselling designed to bolster their immune systems by improving their attitudes; this may help them live longer.

Not all researchers agree about the role of positive illusions and thoughts (e.g., Colvin & Block, 1994), but most psychologists agree that thoughts and ideas play an important role both in preventing illness and in determining how people respond to becoming sick (Biondi & Zannino, 1997; Leonard, 1998). Some psychologists still find it difficult to accept the idea

that the immune system responds to mental attitudes. Researchers, however, are beginning to realize the power of positive thinking on certain bodily processes (Herbert & Cohen, 1993; O'Leary, 1990). Of course, even though positive attitudes and thoughts can be beneficial, they can go only so far in helping to alleviate illness, and only with some people (Manuck et al., 1991). Sometimes having a positive attitude and practising meditation, exercise, and other traditional coping techniques fail to reduce stress. Wearing rose-coloured glasses from time to time can be beneficial; however, continuous self-deception can lead to maladjustment, lies, and a badly distorted view of reality. ■

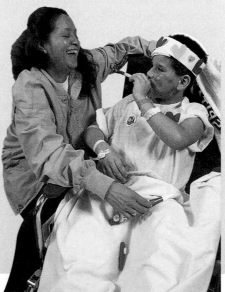

science with biomedical knowledge and techniques; it is narrower in focus than health psychology (Agras, 1992).

Traditionally, physicians have looked at health as the absence of disease. A person who was not experiencing adverse effects from infection, an injury, or an abnormal condition of some kind was considered healthy. Now, however, physicians and psychologists acknowledge that health refers not just to the absence of disease but to the total welfare of a person in terms of social, physical, and mental well-being. This concentration on social, physical, and mental well-being places health and psychology in the same corner, with a focus on the positive side—health promotion.

Health and wellness are now seen as conditions people can actively pursue by eating well, exercising regularly, and managing stress effectively (Cowen, 1991). Unlike medicine, which focuses on specific diseases, health psychology looks at the broad principles of thought and behaviour that clarify fundamental psychosocial mechanisms and affect all areas of a person's life. Today, researchers are focusing on the positive effects of health-promoting behaviours (Millar & Millar, 1995).

Educating people about prevention and wellness and discovering the variables that affect health are central goals of health psychologists. And many health psychologists focus on disease prevention—for example, preventing the spread of AIDS, considered in *Experiencing Psychology*, (see pages 516 and 517) is of great concern.

Variables That Affect Health and Illness

You can set a positive tone to your life, enhance feelings of belonging, and see the positive side of things. You can laugh more than other people and wear "rose-coloured glasses"; this helps ward off the impact of negative or difficult life events (Kuiper & Martin, 1998). The reality is that our attitudes, behaviour, and outlook affect health and illness—but they are affected by complex interrelationships among many events (Lefcourt & Thomas, 1998). Accordingly, health researchers have explored five variables that correlate strongly with health and illness: personality, cognitions, social environment, gender, and sociocultural variables (Rodin & Salovey, 1989).

Personality. Do certain personality variables predispose people to illness? Or does illness predispose a person to a specific personality? Some evidence suggests that angry, hostile people are more prone to illness than are optimists. But which comes first? Perhaps the lack of illness causes optimism, or at least a positive lifestyle. The role of personality variables in illness and health is still unclear, and much more research is needed (as we saw when we examined the role of Type A behaviour in heart disease, page 505).

Cognitions. People's thoughts and beliefs about themselves, other people, and situations affect health-related behaviours. For example, one important variable is the extent to which people believe they control their lives, including health and illness. People with an internal locus of control (examined in Chapter 12) are more likely to take charge of their illnesses and attempt to get better than are people with an external locus of control. When people sense that they can control their own health, they are more likely to engage in health-conscious behaviours, such as eating complex carbohydrates, decreasing their consumption of saturated fat, and exercising more. But when people fear events like tornadoes or floods—often because they have recently lived through one—they tend to be at higher risk for stress-related symptoms, including high blood pressure. Researchers have long known that stress lowers resistance—although they do not know how or why—to colds and other diseases (Cohen et al., 1998).

Social Environment. Family, close friends, and work can be sources of social support—a key element in helping a person maintain health and recover from illness. Greater self-esteem, positive feelings about the future, and a sense of control are characteristic of people with strong social support. Adults in stable, long-term relationships such as marriage are less likely to be ill than are people devoid of strong social support networks (Cohen et al., 1997a, 1997b; Lorenz et al., 1997); in addition, the children of stable relationships are likely to be healthier than the children of non-stable relationships (Gottman & Katz, 1989). Support from co-workers and supervisors in the work environment also may facilitate health (Repetti, Matthews, & Waldron, 1989). Individuals with social support are more likely to engage in preventive dental health, proper eating habits, and the use of safety practices that extend life, such as wearing seatbelts.

experiencing psychology

AIDS—Education and Prevention

People who are infected with the human immuno-deficiency virus (HIV—the virus that causes AIDS) can harbour it for many years without developing a full-blown case of AIDS. However, once people develop AIDS, they generally die within two years of diagnosis because their immune systems can no longer fight off diseases and infections. A great deal is known about AIDS, but at present there are no preventive vaccines or cures, although complicated "cocktails" of drug treatments significantly slow the virus's destructive course in many people. Some people, fearing contamination, still shun AIDS patients. Because most people with AIDS are infected through sexual contact or intravenous drug use, some attach a moral stigma to the disease. For all of these reasons, AIDS is accompanied by devastating psychological consequences.

Fifty-four thousand people in Canada are infected with HIV. Most people who have AIDS are between 20 and 49 years of age. HIV infection/AIDS is one of the leading causes of death among those aged 25 to 40. Reports from Health Canada (1998) and the United Nations show that more than 1000 deaths per year from AIDS occur in Canada. Worldwide, 30 million people are infected. Although at present some jurisdictions have a greater percentage of cases than others, most experts believe that this disparity will disappear in time (Rosenberg, 1995).

There is some good news. Due to better treatments that slow the HIV infection's natural course, the incidence of new cases has dropped significantly; furthermore, death among people with AIDS has declined as much as 25 percent. But as HIV infection continues and deaths are slowed, the number of

people living with HIV and AIDS continues to rise.

Few other diseases are accompanied by so many losses. AIDS patients face the loss of physical strength, mental acuity, ability to work and care for their families, self-sufficiency, social roles, income and savings, housing, the emotional support of friends and loved ones, and ultimately life itself. Some schools have prohibited any children who have AIDS, or even those who have family members with AIDS, from attending classes. People with AIDS have been fired, and co-workers have quit their jobs to avoid them; judges have held legal hearings on closed-circuit television to avoid contact with people who have AIDS. For many people with AIDS, self-esteem fades rapidly as they blame themselves for having contracted the disease. This self-blame leads to depression, anxiety, self-anger, and a negative outlook

Gender. Some health concerns apply only to women (menopause, for example), and others affect women disproportionately (for example, eating disorders). Therefore, the health concerns of women differ from those of men. Seventy percent of all psychoactive medications prescribed are for women, and two-thirds of all surgical procedures are performed on women (Ogur, 1986; Travis, 1988). While women generally have enjoyed an advantage in longevity, the gap in average life span between men and women has been decreasing. Women's changing lifestyles and work patterns are highly correlated with increased medical problems and decreased average life span. Further, as Rodin and Ickovics (1990) assert, the redefinition of gender roles and the changing social support structure for women affect health, medical treatment, and psychological functioning.

Sociocultural Variables. Cultural background, age, ethnic group, and socioeconomic class also are important variables that affect health. Although women tend to visit physicians more often than men, in some cultures the quality of their treatment is not equal to that given to men. As well, with advancing age, people are more likely to become ill or depressed (although there is much individual variation) (Dura, Stukenberg, & Kiecolt-Glaser, 1990). Often, illness among the elderly is affected by other variables, such as loneliness and isolation from family. Health is strongly related with healthy behaviours like eating well and exercising; when age, education, and income are taken into account there are no strong ethnic differences

on life. Families and friends become similarly affected as they cope with a dying loved one and face their own inability to understand the disease. Those who have lived with AIDS and AIDS-related diseases for a decade or more have expected to die; many, if not all, of their friends have died and they may have been economically devastated. But through the use of improved therapies many now feel healthy again (although not cured). Now these people have to figure out how to live again as a relatively healthy person; like their ill counterparts, some feel guilty, others feel depressed, but some take hold of and make the best of their newfound lease on life.

In their AIDS prevention efforts, psychologists pay particular attention to high-risk behaviours so as to help individuals avoid risky situations. High-risk behaviours are those that directly expose people to the blood or semen of others who are likely to have been exposed to the virus—in other words, to others who are also likely to have engaged in high-risk behaviours. Often, individuals who have engaged in high-risk behaviours are sexually promiscuous men and women, homosexual or bisexual men, or present or past intravenous drug abusers. Heterosexuals who have had sexual contact with carriers of AIDS are at significant risk. In Canada, about 10 percent of known AIDS cases occur from heterosexual sex. But, according to the American Center for Disease Control and Prevention, heterosexual sex accounts for 71 percent of reported AIDS cases in other parts of the world. (See Figure 14.6.) Everywhere, adolescents are at especially high risk because they, more than adults, are likely to engage in unprotected sexual activity and they have some of the highest rates of sexually transmitted diseases, including HIV.

AIDS education aimed at young people is critically important, because education can be effective in changing behaviour. Nevertheless, in the case of AIDS, the relationship often does not hold up—people who know about AIDS, its transmission routes, and prevention still engage in risky behaviours (Helweg-Larsen & Collins, 1997). For example, among sexually active high-school students, only 54 percent reported using a condom the last time they had intercourse (Centers for Disease Control and Prevention, 1996). AIDS education, and research in general, has ignored gender as a crucial variable; but recent analyses show that women often respond better than men do to education about high-risk behaviours (Amaro, 1995). Further, when men and women communicate better, they are more likely to minimize the risks of transmission (Dolcini et al., 1995). ■

(Kim et al., 1998). It also may be that an individual's tendency to seek medical assistance will vary depending on the examples set by their parents or by whether they grew up in Canada with a national health plan or in the United States where, without private insurance, visits to the doctor can be very expensive.

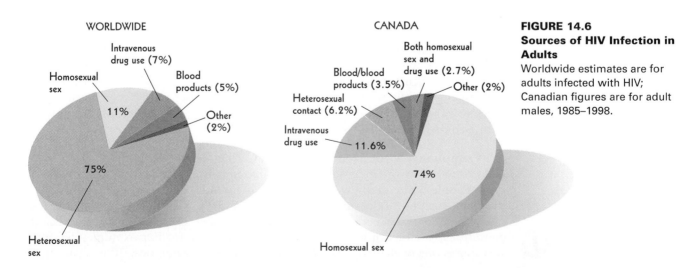

WORLDWIDE

Intravenous drug use (7%)

Homosexual sex

Blood products (5%)

11%

Other (2%)

75%

Heterosexual sex

CANADA

Both homosexual sex and drug use (2.7%)

Blood/blood products (3.5%)

Other (2%)

Heterosexual contact (6.2%)

Intravenous drug use

11.6%

74%

Homosexual sex

FIGURE 14.6
Sources of HIV Infection in Adults
Worldwide estimates are for adults infected with HIV; Canadian figures are for adult males, 1985–1998.

The Psychology of Being Sick

When a person is sick with an illness that impairs day-to-day functioning, the effects can be devastating. The impact on the individual can be profound, both psychologically and economically. Illness seriously affects both the sick person and family members. Health psychologists are concerned not only with the links between stress and illness but with how people cope with illness when it occurs.

Seeking Medical Care. When do people seek medical care? What are the variables that prompt a person to try to get help to become well and healthy? Most people avoid medical care and advice except when it becomes absolutely necessary. Usually, when people have a visible symptom (rashes, cuts, swellings, and fever) and the symptom appears threatening, painful, and persistent, they seek professional help. They are more likely to seek such help when they are sure the problem is physical rather than psychological and when they think that medical attention will provide a cure. If they think medical attention will be a waste of time, or if they dread a diagnosis, they often delay seeking help.

There are gender differences in people's willingness to seek medical attention. Women seek medical help more than men do, have more medical visits, and take more prescription medication (Rosenstock & Kirscht, 1979). However, men have a shorter life span than do women and have higher rates of ulcers, heart disease, and stroke. Men may be less willing to seek medical attention because they perceive it as a weakness in character. On the other hand, women often seek a doctor's care for normal, non-pathological conditions (situations not caused by disease) such as pregnancy, childbirth, and menopause and therefore may be more willing to seek medical attention for other types of conditions.

Major cultural differences also exist in health-care seeking; a country's technological, economic, and political system shape health-care delivery, as does its general level of economic development. These factors, in turn, affect individuals' willingness to seek health care and to trust health-care providers. Power relationships and trust (two culturally determined variables) greatly affect health-care seeking. For example, Matsumoto (1996) describes research showing that Japanese women trust their physicians less than American women do, yet are more likely to comply with a physician's advice for an invasive medical procedure.

The Sick Role. When people do what they think will help them get well, they are adopting a *sick role*. For most people, this means taking specific steps to get well, relieving themselves of normal responsibilities, and realizing that they are not at fault for their illness. Of course, a person can also adopt behaviours associated with illness when in fact there is no illness or pathology.

Unfortunately, many people blame the ailing person for being sick, even though the illness may be unrelated to any preventive measures a person might have taken. Sick people usually are relieved of normal responsibilities, such as working or taking care of the family. When they are in the hospital, they give over to physicians and nurses the responsibility for their care. Although Western culture fosters an attitude that people should be cheerful when sick, it is normal for sick people to be slightly depressed or even angry, especially when hospitalized (R. S. Lazarus, 1984). Because sickness is generally seen as a temporary state, we expect people to get well and to work towards that end—taking medication, sleeping, and, especially, complying with medical advice.

Compliance with Medical Advice. Getting people to adhere to health regimens or to follow their physicians' advice has long been a focus of health psychologists. People will comply with specific recommendations for a particular health problem, such as "Take three tablets a day for 10 days." However, they are less likely to adhere to general recommendations for diet, exercise, and overall health conditions, such as quitting smoking or relaxing more. For example, cigarette smoking is one of the largest health concerns today, causing over 20 percent (more than 40 000 people) of deaths annually in Canada. Yet about 6 million Canadian adults, 30 percent of the population, continue to smoke (Health Canada, 1996).

Compliance with medical advice depends on the severity of the problem. If an illness causes pain or discomfort, people are more likely to comply with a regimen of treatment to alleviate the discomfort. People are more receptive to medical treatment when it is specific, simple, and easy to do, has minimal side effects, and brings about immediate relief (Klonoff, Annechild, & Landrine, 1994). Also, people seeking a cure or relief of specific symptoms are more likely to be cooperative than are people merely seeking wellness or prevention. When long-term exercise is the prescribed treatment, most people drop out of a program within six months. Even when the impact of not taking a preventive medication is serious, people are not especially compliant; this is especially true for lengthy or difficult treatments, such as four-times-daily insulin injections (Hanson et al., 1989).

Compliance with a health-care regimen is increased when the regimen is tailored to the person's lifestyle and habits. Even written agreements between practitioners and clients can be helpful. Health psychologists have found that clients are more likely to adhere to treatments when a physician's influence and the family support systems are substantial. Social support from family and friends turns out to be particularly valuable in getting even very sick people to comply with guidelines for treatment (DiMatteo & DiNicola, 1982). Helping people to build resourcefulness, manage stress, and understand the implications of their medical regimen is key to improved compliance (Aikens et al., 1992).

Health Psychology and Adaptive Behaviour

Health psychologists focus on adaptive behaviours that will improve people's day-to-day lives. They encourage preventive programs at work and educate people about ways to manage stress and about other positive approaches towards health that will enhance and prolong life. They frequently conduct stress management workshops to help managers and workers cope with increasing pressures and workloads; they also help people quit smoking, control their alcohol intake, follow exercise programs, and practise good nutrition.

Today, health psychologists attempt to change people's behaviour before it gets out of hand. Health psychology is an action-oriented discipline, and as men and women seek more healthful lifestyles, psychologists are playing an instrumental role in their quest. Sometimes, health psychologists focus on preventive behaviours— use of condoms to prevent the spread of AIDS, regular exercise, and so on. At other times, they help people deal with existing problems such as obesity, diabetes, and high stress levels. Let's examine three of the ways that health psychologists assist in dealing with health problems: behavioural interventions, pain management, and stress management.

Behavioural Interventions. To manage existing health disorders and help prevent disease, behavioural interventions are necessary and important. Health psychologists know that many lifestyle behaviour problems can be modified; these include smoking, excessive drinking, drug abuse, overeating, and a lack of exercise. Excess caloric intake leads to obesity—and obesity in turn often leads to hypertension (high blood pressure), which causes heart disease.

Some interventions are community-based. Consider drug abuse. Most people first encounter drugs in schools, in both city and suburban settings. As a result, strong efforts are made to achieve drug-free schools. To a great extent, these sorts of plans have been moderately successful; they are action-oriented and attempt to educate students and involve the community in dealing with drug use and abuse and, especially, prevention. Other interventions are made on an individual level. For example, the likelihood that a person will stick to an exercise regime is increased when friends, relatives, and coaches make prompts and phone calls (Lombard, Lombard, & Winett, 1995).

Pain Management. Severe and disabling pain is symptomatic of some illnesses. Such pain can take three forms: (1) *chronic pain*, which is long-lasting and ever-present; (2) *periodic pain*, which comes and goes; and (3) *progressive pain*, which is ever-present and increases in severity as the illness progresses. Many people suffer from chronic pain, such as headaches, lower back pain, and arthritis. Some types of chronic pain can be treated with drugs, surgery, or other medical interventions; other types may call for nontraditional psychological techniques.

Two nontraditional techniques for pain management are hypnosis and biofeedback (discussed in Chapter 4). Other techniques include behaviour modification and cognitive therapy. Behaviour modification uses learning principles (see Chapter 5) to teach people new effective behaviours and to help them unlearn old maladaptive behaviours. People undergoing this type of therapy learn to relax after a twinge of pain rather than focus on the pain, thus making it worse. Chapter 16 discusses how cognitive therapy uses behaviour modification techniques to help people acquire new thoughts, beliefs, and values that can help in pain management.

Stress Management. Because stressors exist in everyone's life—whether school exams, parent or peer demands, natural disasters, illness, death, divorce, inflation, or financial difficulties—many health psychologists focus on stress and its management. With the help of health psychologists, employers are sponsoring programs for managing stress in the workplace (Glasgow & Terborg, 1988). These programs usually involve education, exercise, nutrition, and counselling. The results are fewer workdays lost to illness and lower health-care costs.

Stress management also results in fewer lost lives (Gebhardt & Crump, 1990). When patients who were hospitalized for heart attacks were treated for stress symptoms after their release from the hospital, they had fewer subsequent heart attacks than did a control group who did not receive specific stress treatments (Frasure-Smith & Prince, 1989).

Focus

Review

◆ Under what conditions do people comply with medical advice? pp. 518–519

Think Critically

◆ What are the implications of the finding that women seem to respond better than men to education about high-risk behaviours that may lead to AIDS?

Summary and Review

Stress

Why is appraisal such a key component of stress?

■ *Stress* is a nonspecific, often global response to real or imagined challenges or threats; it is an emotional response, a result of something. It is a normal part of living and depends on a person's appraisal of a situation. Stress is caused by *stressors*—environmental stimuli that affect an organism in either physically or psychologically injurious ways. p. 496

What kinds of conflicts result in stress?

■ *Approach–approach conflicts* arise when a person must choose between two equally pleasant alternatives, such as two wonderful jobs. *Avoidance–avoidance conflicts* occur when a choice involves two equally distasteful alternatives, such as paying your taxes or facing prosecution.

Approach–avoidance conflicts result when a choice or goal has both attractive and repellent aspects, such as eating a delicious but fattening dessert. pp. 497–498

■ Emotionally, people's reactions often depend on their *frustration*, their work-related *pressures*, and their day-to-day *conflicts*. Physiologically, the stress response is characterized by arousal. Behaviourally, stress and its arousal response are related. When people are moderately aroused, they behave with optimal effectiveness; when they are under-aroused, they lack the stimulation to behave effectively. pp. 497–500

Describe three stages of Selye's general adaptation syndrome.

■ Selye characterized stress responses as a general adaptation syndrome with three stages: alarm, resistance,

and exhaustion. During the alarm stage, people experience increased physiological arousal and mobilize bodily resources. During resistance, physiological and behavioural responses become more moderate and sustained. During exhaustion, if people don't relieve their stress, they can become too exhausted to adapt; at that point, they again become extremely alarmed, and they finally give up. p. 501

Characterize Type A behaviour.

■ *Type A behaviour* occurs in individuals who are competitive, impatient, hostile, and always striving to do more in less time. Some elements of Type A behaviour, such as anger and hostility, seem to be related to heart disease, but the overall Type A behaviour pattern does not seem to be related. p. 505

What is the link between stress and ill health?

- People exposed to high levels of stress for long periods of time may develop stress-related disorders, including physical illness. *Post-traumatic stress disorder (PTSD)* may become evident after a person has undergone extreme stress caused by some type of disaster. pp. 506–507

KEY TERMS
stressor, p. 496; anxiety, p. 496; stress, p. 496; frustration, p. 497; conflict, p. 497; approach–approach conflict, p. 497; avoidance–avoidance conflict, p. 497; approach–avoidance conflict, p. 497; pressure, p. 498; burnout, p. 500; Type A behaviour, p. 505; Type B behaviour, p. 505; post-traumatic stress disorder (PTSD), p. 506

Coping

Distinguish various forms of coping.

- *Coping* is the process by which a person takes some action to manage, master, tolerate, reduce, or minimize environmental and internal demands that cause or might cause stress and that will tax the individual's inner resources. *Coping skills* are the techniques people use to deal with changing situations and stress. *Proactive coping* is taking action in advance of a potentially stressful situation to prevent it or modify it before it occurs. pp. 508–509, 511

- Defence-oriented coping strategies do not reduce stressors but instead help people protect themselves from their effects. Most psychologists recommend task-oriented coping strategies. These strategies usually involve several tasks or steps: (1) identifying the stressor, (2) choosing an appropriate course of action for stress reduction, (3) implementing the plan, and (4) evaluating its success. pp. 509–511

- *Stress inoculation* increases the predictability of stressful events, fosters coping skills, generates self-talking, encourages confidence about successful outcomes, builds a commitment to personal action and responsibility for an adaptive course of action, and gives people realistic warnings, recommendations, and reassurances to help them prepare for and cope with impending dangers or losses. p. 511

- *Psychoneuroimmunology (PNI)* is the study of how psychological processes and the nervous system affect the body's immune system and how, in turn, the immune system influences psychological processes. pp. 513–514

KEY TERMS
coping, p. 508; resilience, p. 509; coping skills, p. 509; social support, p. 509; stress inoculation, p. 511; proactive coping, p 511; psychoneuroimmunology (PNI), p. 513

Health Psychology

What is the role of health psychology?

- *Health psychology* is the use of psychological ideas and principles to help enhance health, prevent illness, diagnose and treat disease, and rehabilitate people. Health psychology is an action-oriented discipline that focuses on preventive health measures as well as intervention in existing conditions. pp. 513–515

- Health psychologists can highlight the distinction between high-risk and low-risk behaviour in AIDS prevention. They can be involved in educating youth, the uneducated, and other high-risk populations; they also can counsel AIDS patients and their families. pp. 516–517

Under what conditions do people comply with medical advice?

- When people do what they think will help them get well, they are adopting a sick role. Research shows that people are more receptive to medical treatments when the treatments are specific, simple, easy to do, and have minimal side effects. pp. 518–519

KEY TERM
health psychology, p. 513

Weblinks

Stress at the Workplace
www.frt.com/stress.htm
Improving tolerance for stress, acute treatment, and a definition of stress are all discussed in this current article.

Dr. Orman's Special Report for the Holiday Season
www.stresscure.com/health/holidays.html
Visit this site to discover the top 10 causes of stress during Christmas, and discover how to deal with financial stress during the holidays.

Hassles
www.stresscure.com/health/expcting.html
Public speaking, raising children, relationship conflicts, and emotional distress are all part of life's everyday stresses. This site discusses each of these hassles and how you can cope with them.

Emotions and Health
www.pins.co.uk/upages/probertm/pa.htm
Are you worrying yourself sick? This concern is examined at this site, where the link between stress and the immune system is explored.

OncoLink: Coping with Cancer
www.oncolink.upenn.edu/psychosocial/coping/
The University of Pennsylvania provides information on coping with cancer. Links to articles such as "Amusing Ways to Handle Stress," "Decision Support for Patients with Breast Cancer," and "Guided Imagery and Music" are all accessible from the home page.

Health Psychology
freud.apa.org/divisions/div38/home.html
The American Psychological Association sponsors this site dedicated to understanding health and illness.

The HIV and AIDS Project
www.cpa.ca/hiv/home.html
Visit this site for information on AIDS prevention and on living with HIV and AIDS. The contacts, links, discussion forums, and information on this site are organized by the Canadian Psychological Association and Health Canada.

Chapter 15

Psychological Disorders

It was 11 a.m. on a cold, dark Sunday morning when he felt his life starting to change—for the worse. He'd slept badly the night before; in fact, he'd awakened in the middle of the night, drenched in a cold sweat. But that was just the beginning. Rob Terman was slowly slipping into a depressed state. At first he became moody, unable to concentrate at work; later, he became withdrawn from his family. He chalked it up to an early midlife crisis and decided that he needed a new girlfriend. But the truth was that things got worse—over a period of two months, he lost weight, had great difficulty sleeping, developed an array of physical complaints, and lost interest in his usual activities and friends. This once active, sports-oriented guy was taken over by sadness. Angry about most things and despondent most of the time, Rob found that all areas of his life were being affected. Exasperated about the smallest things and anxious about nearly everything, losing sleep, losing weight, and abusing alcohol on the weekends, Rob finally realized he needed help. (We will tell you about Rob's search for help at the start of the next chapter but don't worry, things worked out for him.)

We live in a crazy world—at least it seems so if you watch the local daily news. Television reports of crime sprees and mass shootings seem ubiquitous. There is no doubt in our minds—and, we're sure, in yours—that people who engage in such senseless acts of violence are, at best, in deep trouble psychologically. We call them deranged and mentally ill—or we assume that they must be. Such individuals have more going on than a tough experience in first-grade reading. But what about people who engage in behaviours that some people see as abnormal, but not crazy or bizarre?

In 1999 there was considerable discussion about Calista Flockhart, star of Fox television's *Ally McBeal*, and her extreme thinness. Flockhart claimed she was just thin, but many critics and psychologists asserted that she had an eating disorder. This issue grabbed the public's attention because nearly 1 in 150 girls suffer from the eating disorder anorexia nervosa, a topic we discussed in Chapter 9 (p. 308). Flockhart's weight and her eating behaviours are between her and her doctors, but they raise questions about mental illness: When has someone gone over the line? How different must a person's behaviour be to qualify as abnormal? Is Flockhart's eating behaviour any stranger than that of an old man who leaves a multimillion-dollar fortune to his cats? Is becoming extremely thin and avoiding food any stranger than taking a midwinter dip in an ice-covered lake, as members of the Polar Bear Club do, or than undergoing extensive cosmetic surgery to obtain a "perfect" face? In this chapter we will consider the very broad range of issues and disorders that together make up human abnormal psychology. ∎

What Is Abnormal Behaviour?

B ankview is an older neighbourhood in Calgary made up of a mix of houses and apartment buildings. Until he lost parts of his feet to frostbite several years ago a man known as the Bankview Bottle Picker lived beside a park under the overhang of an apartment garage. He slept on an old mattress and kept warm in the winter months with a large collection of blankets and old sleeping bags he had found in various dumpsters in the area. When interviewed from time to time by the local media he refused to discuss his past but was open about the fact that he drank excessively and that he spent his days collecting bottles and cans in neighbourhood garbage cans and bins that could be cashed in to buy booze. Many local residents made a point of putting any bottles or cans they were throwing out beside their garbage cans in order to make it easier for the Picker to find them. He refused offers of more substantial assistance and he and the neighbourhood basically got used to each other.

Is this behaviour abnormal? To some extent, it depends on where you live, because every society has its own definition of abnormal behaviour. In Russia, for example, people were once regularly placed in mental institutions for homelessness or political dissent. Generally, however, behaviour classified as abnormal is more than odd. In any single month, about 15 percent of adults in our population meet the criteria for having a mental disorder; that is, they exhibit symptoms of abnormality (Reiger et al., 1988).

A Definition

Abnormal behaviour is behaviour characterized as (1) atypical, (2) socially unacceptable, (3) distressing, (4) maladaptive, and/or (5) the result of distorted cognitions. Let's consider these five distinguishing characteristics in turn.

First, abnormal behaviour is *atypical*. Many behaviours are unusual; however, abnormal behaviours tend to be so unusual as to be statistically rare. For example, you would not consider ear or body piercing among teenagers to be abnormal, because the practice is fairly common today. However, washing one's hands every few minutes during the day until they are raw is atypical. Of course, not all atypical behaviour is necessarily abnormal. The athleticism and grace of Wayne Gretzky is statistically uncommon but not abnormal and Einstein's rare genius was considered atypical. On the other hand, most people would not hesitate to label drug abuse as abnormal behaviour, even though it is not as atypical as it once was.

Second, in addition to being atypical, abnormal behaviour is also often *socially unacceptable*. To some degree, ideas about what is normal and abnormal vary according to cultural values, which are in a constant state of flux. What is acceptable in one culture may be labelled unacceptable in another. Similarly, behaviour that was considered unacceptable 25 years ago, such as males wearing earrings or piercing other body parts, may be considered acceptable today. A behaviour that is judged abnormal, however, is one that is unacceptable to society in general.

Third, a person's abnormal behaviour often causes *distress* to that person or to those around the person. While feelings of anxiety or distress are normal in many situations, prolonged anxiety (distress) may result from abnormal behaviour. You may feel anxious while you are preparing to speak in front of a group; however, constant, unrelenting anxiety, the avoidance of any situation that might require simply interacting with other people, and fear of people in general suggest a problem.

Fourth, abnormal behaviour is usually *maladaptive*, or self-defeating to the person exhibiting it. Maladaptive behaviour, such as drug abuse, is harmful and nonproductive. It often leads to more misery and prevents people from making positive changes in their lives.

Abnormal behaviour: Behaviour characterized as atypical, socially unacceptable, distressing, maladaptive, and/or the result of distorted cognitions.

Last, abnormal behaviour is often the result of *distorted cognitions* (thoughts). For example, a young man with distorted cognitions may falsely believe that people are out to get him. A woman suffering from distorted cognitions associated with major depression may believe that she is worthless, stupid, and unlovable.

In recent years, psychologists have begun to describe behaviour in terms of *maladjustment* rather than *abnormality*. The distinction is important because it implies that maladaptive behaviour can, with treatment, be adjusted and become adaptive and productive. The term *maladjustment* also emphasizes specific behaviours rather than labelling the entire person.

Because of the phenomenon of the self-fulfilling prophecy, it is important for therapists and other professionals to label people as little as possible. The idea that an abnormal response pattern might make some kind of sense given certain life circumstances cannot be ignored. For example, an adolescent may be presented to a psychologist as "the problem in the family" when in reality the problem actually has to do with how the mother and father (and other siblings) react and interact around the adolescent—in effect making *them* the problem. By focusing on specific behaviours, psychologists try to avoid the negative consequences of "labelling" their clients.

To summarize, abnormal behaviour is characterized as atypical, socially unacceptable, distressing, maladaptive, and/or the result of distorted cognitions. There are, of course, exceptions to this definition. Nevertheless, this definition provides psychologists with a solid framework from which to explore abnormal behaviour and its treatment.

Perspectives on Abnormality

Before prescribing treatment, mental health practitioners want to know why a person is maladjusted, because establishing the cause of a disorder can sometimes help define a treatment plan. Therefore, practitioners often turn to theories and models that attempt to explain the causes of abnormality. A **model** is a guideline, perspective, or approach that helps scientists discover relationships among data; it uses a structure from one field to help describe data in another. Psychologists use models to make predictions about behaviour. An attempt to explain a school phobia as at least partially due to attachment issues is one example of a model that allows for the design of possible treatments. These models form the basis of **abnormal psychology**, the field of psychology concerned with the assessment, treatment, and prevention of maladaptive behaviour. Several models help explain abnormal behaviour: medical–biological, psychodynamic, humanistic, behavioural, cognitive, sociocultural, legal, and interactionist.

Medical–Biological Model. Thousands of years ago, people believed that abnormal behaviour was caused by demons that invaded an individual's body. The "cure" often involved a surgeon performing *trephination*—drilling a hole into the skull to allow the evil force to escape. Even as recently as a few hundred years ago, people with psychological disorders were caged and treated like animals. Early reformists, such as French physician Philippe Pinel, advocated the medical model and proposed that abnormal behaviour could be treated and cured, like an illness. When scientists showed that syphilis could cause mental disorders, the medical model gained even greater acceptance and led to more humane treatment and better conditions for those with psychological disorders.

The *medical–biological model* of abnormal behaviour focuses on the biological and physiological conditions that cause abnormal behaviours. This model deals with a range of mental ailments, such as those caused by mercury poisoning or viral attacks on brain cells. It focuses on genetic abnormalities, problems in the central nervous system, and hormonal

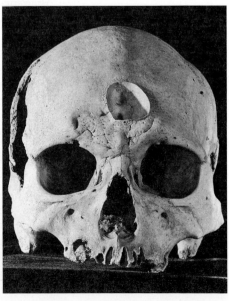

Model: A guideline, perspective, or approach derived from data in one field and used to help describe data in another field.

Abnormal psychology: The field of psychology concerned with the assessment, treatment, and prevention of maladaptive behaviour.

changes. It also helps explain and treat substance abuse problems and schizophrenia, two disorders that may have a strong biological component. Proponents of the medical–biological model might explain the Bankview Bottle Picker's lifestyle as resulting from a chemical or hormonal imbalance that alters judgment.

Many of the terms and concepts used in psychology and psychiatry are borrowed from medicine; they include *treatment*, *case*, *symptom*, and *syndrome*, as well as *mental illness*. The medical model assumes that abnormal behaviour, like other illnesses, can be diagnosed, treated, and often cured. This approach has not gone unchallenged, however. Its critics say that it does not take advantage of other psychological insights, such as those derived from cognitive or behavioural models. A major—but not surprising—disadvantage of the medical model is that it emphasizes drug treatment and often involves hospitalization rather than solving psychological problems by psychological means.

Psychodynamic Model. The *psychodynamic model* of abnormal behaviour is based on Freud's theory of personality (discussed in Chapter 12). This model assumes that psychological disorders result from anxiety produced by unresolved conflicts and forces of which a person may be unaware. It asserts that maladjustment occurs when a person relies on too many defence mechanisms or when defence mechanisms fail. A depressed person's behaviour might be explained as loneliness, despair, or anger turned inward. Although many depressed individuals are bright and capable, their behaviour might be seen as a reaction to fear of competing caused by low self-esteem that was initiated in childhood. Treatment usually involves helping a patient become aware of motivations and conflicts so that the person can have a healthier lifestyle. We will explore psychodynamic approaches to treatment in more detail in Chapter 16.

Humanistic Model. Like the psychodynamic model, the *humanistic model* of abnormal behaviour assumes that inner psychic forces are important in establishing and maintaining a normal lifestyle. Unlike psychodynamic theorists, however, humanists believe that people have a good deal of cognitive control over their lives. The humanistic model focuses on individual uniqueness and decision making. It contends that people become maladjusted when their expectations far exceed their achievements. In the case of a depressed person, a humanist might focus on her dignity, self-respect, and quest for independence. Humanistic treatment usually involves helping maladjusted people to discover and accept their true selves, formulate more realistic self-concepts and expectations, and become more like their ideal selves.

Behavioural Model. The *behavioural model* of abnormal behaviour states that such behaviour is caused by faulty or ineffective learning and conditioning patterns. Two fundamental assumptions of behavioural (learning) theorists are that disordered behaviour can be reshaped and that more appropriate, worthwhile behaviours can be substituted through traditional learning techniques (see Chapter 5). Behavioural theorists assume that events in a person's environment reinforce or punish various behaviours selectively and, in doing so, shape personality and may create maladjustment. Proponents of the behavioural model might explain a depressed man's behaviour by noting that he was being reinforced for behaving in sad and depressed ways.

Cognitive Model. The *cognitive model* of abnormal behaviour asserts that human beings engage in both prosocial and maladjusted behaviours because of their thoughts. As thinking organisms, individuals decide how to behave; abnormal behaviour is based on false assumptions or unrealistic coping strategies. Practitioners of the cognitive perspective treat people with psychological disorders by helping them develop new thought processes that instil new values. Some assert that depressed people might have developed wrong ideas about their *self* (that it is worthless), their *future* (that it holds no prospects), and the *world* (that it is a nasty, dangerous place). Using the cognitive model, a practitioner might assist a depressed client to replace maladjusted thoughts and behaviours with positive, worthwhile ones. The practitioner might treat such a person by helping him to formulate more rational self-concepts and to adopt more effective coping strategies.

Sociocultural Model. According to the *sociocultural model* of abnormal behaviour, people develop abnormalities within and because of a context—the context of the family, the community, and the society. Researchers, especially cross-cultural researchers, have shown that people's personality development and their disorders reflect their culture, the stressors in their society, and the types of disorders prevalent in their society. Relying heavily on the learning and cognitive frameworks, the sociocultural model focuses on cultural variables as key determinants of maladjustment. Thus, a depressed symptom pattern might be viewed as the culturally appropriate response to a particular life event.

As researchers examine the frequency and types of disorders that occur in different societies, they also note some sharp differences within each society. Within a specific society, disorders vary as a function of the decade in which they occur and the age and gender of the clients. In China, for example, depression is relatively uncommon but stress reactions in the form of physical ailments are frequent. Canadians, Americans, and Europeans report guilt and shame when they are depressed; depressed individuals in Africa, on the other hand, are less likely to report these symptoms but are more likely to report somatic (physical) complaints. Specific disorders seem highly culture-specific; for example, *amok* (as in "running amok") is a disorder characterized by sudden rage and homicidal aggression and is seen in some Asian countries, such as Malaysia and Thailand. Brought on by stress, sleep deprivation, and alcohol consumption, the behaviour can be broken down into a series of stages. Similarly, *anorexia nervosa*, discussed in Chapter 9, is a disorder primarily confined to the West. Researchers now recognize, therefore, that some disorders are *culturally indigenous*; that is, specific to a culture (Simons & Hughes, 1993).

Legal Model. The *legal model* of abnormal behaviour defines such behaviour strictly in terms of guilt, innocence, and sanity. Consider Dorothy Joudrie, a Calgary women who was charged with shooting her husband, Earl. Dorothy, who had been an alcoholic for many years, had been beaten by her husband for a number of years, though the beatings had stopped 18 years before the shooting. Claiming she had no memory of the incident, Dorothy shot Earl six times at close range with a small-caliber handgun. She seemed unaware of her actions and even Earl said that she looked and sounded very calm during the shooting. At her trial all of the psychiatrists, even those called by the prosecution, agreed that Dorothy was in a dissociative state at the time of the shooting. Based on this evidence the jury found her not criminally responsible for her actions. She was placed in a mental hospital and released within a year, though she is still undergoing treatment.

The term *insane* is a legal term, not a psychological one. Insanity refers to a condition that excuses people from responsibility and protects them from punishment. From the legal point of view, a person cannot be held responsible for a crime if, at the time of the crime, the person lacked the capacity to recognize right from wrong or to obey the law.

Although perhaps useful for judicial purposes, the legal definition of abnormal behaviour is too focused to be useful in treating clients. It is also a misconception that insanity is widely used as a defence. The legal system tends to mix mental illness, sin, law, theology, and people's need for retribution and forgiveness. Therefore, the insanity defence is a murky concept, even though TV dramas wrongly portray it as a mainstay of the legal system that is applied according to clear-cut, focused, and consistent guidelines.

Interactionist Model. Each of the models we've examined—medical–biological, psychodynamic, humanistic, behavioural, cognitive, sociocultural, and legal—views maladjustment from a different perspective. No single model can explain every kind of abnormal behaviour. Despite their philosophical incompatibilities, however, each model has value. For some disorders (such as phobias), learning theory offers an explanation of the cause and prescribes an effective course of treatment. For other disorders (such as schizophrenia), medical–biological theory explains a significant part of the problem. Consequently, many psychologists use an *interactionist model* (sometimes called an *eclectic model*) of abnormal behaviour, one drawing on all of these perspectives. The practitioners use the best of each of two or more models. For example, a therapist could treat a depressed patient by arranging for antidepressant drugs (medical–biological approach), helping the patient develop new, optimistic thought processes (cognitive approach), and teaching the patient adaptive behaviours to eliminate depression-inducing stress (behavioural approach).

Be a Critical Thinker. People have developed a range of ideas about abnormality, and a veil of misunderstanding still surrounds mental illness in many people's minds. For example, many individuals still think that a mental illness lasts forever and that people are incurable. They sometimes worry that the mentally ill are dangerous, violent, or out of control. Other people may believe (incorrectly!) that the mentally ill have contributed to their disorders by not living properly, by displaying poor character, or by making bad decisions. The truth is that more people get better from mental illness than those who do not; that few people who suffer from mental illness are violent; and that most people with various mental illnesses suffer quietly and bear their pain privately. Thus, few people are incurable, violent, or bizarre. Treatment with therapy, drugs, and love, care, and support from family members and friends are the key ingredients.

As you examine each of the psychological disorders presented in this chapter, think about whether you favour one model of maladjustment over another. Do you have a cognitive bent, or do you favour a more psychodynamic approach? Perhaps you are more behavioural in your beliefs. Regardless of a practitioner's predispositions, it is important that symptoms be carefully evaluated so proper diagnoses can be made. People who are suffering need to be helped, not ignored, especially since a wide variety of treatments are available (Isaac & Armat, 1990).

Next, we will consider a system that has been developed to help practitioners make diagnoses. The system is presented in the *Diagnostic and Statistical Manual of Mental Disorders*.

Diagnosing Maladjustment: The *DSM–IV*

Ask psychologists and psychiatrists to describe or explain some of your more interesting relatives and they are likely to indicate that they are odd but not mentally ill. Trying to sort out odd or idiosyncratic from mentally ill by diagnosing maladjusted behaviour is a complicated process.

Diagnostic and Statistical Manual of Mental Disorders. Most Canadian psychologists and psychiatrists use a system for diagnosing maladjusted behaviour called the *Diagnostic and Statistical Manual of Mental Disorders* (*DSM*), devised by the American Psychiatric Association. The current edition of the manual is the fourth, the *DSM–IV*, published in 1994. Its goals are (1) to improve the reliability of diagnoses by categorizing disorders according to observable behaviours, and (2) to ensure that the diagnoses are consistent with research evidence and practical experience (Widiger et al., 1991). The system designates 16 major categories of maladjustment and more than 200 subcategories. (Table 15.1 lists some of the major classifications.) The *DSM* also cites the **prevalence** of each disorder—the percentage of the population displaying the disorder during any specified period. For most psychological disorders, researchers also know the lifetime prevalence—the statistical likelihood that a person will develop the disorder during his or her lifetime.

An important feature of the *DSM* is that diagnostic information for any individual is laid out on five different dimensions. The *DSM* refers to these dimensions

Prevalence: The percentage of a population displaying a disorder during any specified period.

as axes; the manual thus uses what is called a *multiaxial* system in order to be as informative, precise, reliable, and valid as possible about an individual's condition. Axis I describes the *major disorders* themselves. Axis II describes *personality disorders and mental retardation*. Axis III describes *current medical conditions* that might be pertinent to understanding or managing the individual's mental disorder—such as alcoholics who may have cirrhosis of the liver. Axis IV, *psychosocial or environmental problems*, refers to life stresses or familial support systems that may or may not facilitate a person's treatment or recovery. These include economic, job, or educational problems. Finally, Axis V comprises a *global assessment of functioning*, which reports the clinician's overall assessment of the client's functioning in the psychological, social, and occupational domains of the client's life in the past year. These five axes, when viewed together, help a clinician fully describe the nature of a person's maladjustment. It is important to note that there may not be an assessment on a particular axis. For example, there may be no medical condition to report on Axis III. Table 15.2 describes the axes of the *DSM–IV*.

The *DSM–IV* helps clinicians know how common psychological disorders are and what the *prevalence* of a disorder is. It often cites the *lifetime prevalence*, that is, the likelihood that a person will experience the disorder at some time during their life. A typical *DSM–IV* statement might read, "The lifetime prevalence for this disorder in young adult females is approximately 1% 3%; the rate of occurrence of this disorder in males is approximately one-tenth of that in females" (p. 548). (The disorder being referred to is bulimia nervosa, see pp. 308–309.)

Table 15.1 Major Classifications of the *Diagnostic and Statistical Manual of Mental Disorders*, Fourth Edition

Disorders First Diagnosed in Infancy, Childhood, and Adolescence

Delirium, Dementia, and Other Cognitive Disorders

Substance-Related Disorders

Schizophrenia and Other Psychotic Disorders

Mood Disorders

Anxiety Disorders

Somatoform Disorders

Factitious Disorders

Dissociative Disorders

Sexual and Gender Identity Disorders

Eating Disorders

Sleep Disorders

Impulse Control Disorders

Note: Each classification is further broken down into subtypes.

Table 15.2 The Axes of the *DSM-IV*

Axis	Description
Axis I	Symptoms that cause distress or significantly impair social or occupational functioning
Axis II	Personality disorders—personality patterns that are so pervasive, inflexible, and maladaptive that they impair interpersonal or occupational functioning
Axis III	Medical conditions that may be relevant to the understanding or treatment of a psychological disorder
Axis IV	Psychosocial and environmental problems (such as negative life events and interpersonal stressors) that may affect the diagnosis, treatment, and prognosis of psychological disorders
Axis V	Global assessment of functioning—the individual's overall level of functioning in social, occupational, and leisure activities

Source: Adapted from Diagnostic and Statistical Manual of Mental Disorders, *Fourth Edition,* American Psychiatric Association, 1994.

You might think that a diagnostic manual would be straightforward, like an encyclopedia of mental disorders. However, the *DSM* has met with some resistance and controversy; because committees wrote it, it represents various compromises. Some psychologists applaud its recognition of social and environmental influences on behaviour. Others take issue with the way it places disorders together based on symptoms rather than causes. Still others argue that the *DSM* is too precise and complicated. Some assert that, despite its rigour, it is still not precise enough. Others have concerns about potential gender bias against women (e.g., Hartung & Widiger, 1998). Still others believe the *DSM* should go beyond its descriptive approach and include problem-oriented and problem-solving information rather than just symptoms. Many psychologists are unhappy with the use of psychiatric terms that perpetuate a medical rather than a cognitive-behavioural model. Finally, although small in number, some even assert that the *DSM* pathologizes everyday behaviours and that practitioners then use the legitimated psychiatric terms for political and monetary gain (Kutchins & Kirk, 1997).

The *DSM* is continually being evaluated and revised to reflect the latest scientific knowledge, and thus is an evolving system of classification (Clark, Watson, & Reynolds, 1995). *Experiencing Psychology* illustrates the process by asking, "Is there such a thing as chronic fatigue syndrome? And is it a disorder?"

Diversity and Diagnoses. The *DSM* is by no means the final word in diagnosing maladjustment, and its reliability is not completely known; rather, it is a developing system of classification. In addition, it needs to become more sensitive to issues of diversity. Not all ethnic groups exhibit symptoms of every disorder; nor do all members of one ethnic group have an equal likelihood of exhibiting specific symptoms.

Research shows that the likelihood of a specific diagnosis is indeed related to ethnicity. For example, Asians receive more diagnoses of schizophrenia than do whites (Paradis, Hatch, & Friedman, 1994), despite the fact that Asians in general do not seek mental health services as often as whites do (Uba, 1994). In the United States, Hispanic Americans receive fewer diagnoses of schizophrenia than do whites (Flaskerud & Hu, 1992). Similarly, Koreans are more likely to be diagnosed as depressed than are people in Taiwan, the Philippines, the United States, or Canada (Crittenden et al., 1992). The rates of a specific disorder in a particular country probably reflect racial, religious, and cultural biases; they especially reflect the specific culture-bound symptomatology that a society considers normal. As suggested earlier, various cultures allow for, and perhaps encourage, specific symptomatology. Culture and its effects on clinical diagnosis and treatment plans are underresearched and constitute an important area of concern for practising psychologists. The Canadian Psychological Association and the American Psychological Association (1993) state that practitioners must:

- Recognize cultural diversity.
- Understand the role of culture and ethnicity in development.
- Help clients understand their own sociological identification.
- Understand how culture, race, gender, and sexual orientation interact to affect behaviour.

Focus

Review

- What are the advantages and disadvantages of the medical–biological model of abnormal behaviour? pp. 525–526
- Identify the distinguishing characteristics of the psychodynamic, humanistic, and cognitive models of abnormal behaviour. pp. 526–527
- What are the goals of the *DSM*, and what are its potential advantages and disadvantages? pp. 528–530

Think Critically

- Do you think there are any behaviours that are perceived as abnormal in all cultures? Explain.
- If you had a say in what the next edition of the *DSM* would look like, what would you add to make it more useful?

experiencing psychology

The Emergence of a New Disorder?

I s there such a thing as a "new" disorder? Or do psychologists just relabel a disorder that they have long known existed? There are some politics involved in classifying mental disorders (generally due to financial considerations), and some science. Chronic fatigue syndrome is a case in point.

Chronic fatigue syndrome, often referred to as CFS, has emerged as a diagnostic category in the last decade—although it has not yet been included as a diagnostic category in the *DSM*. The most significant symptom of CFS is debilitating fatigue, but other symptoms also appear, including sore throat, muscle pain, and sleep problems. The entertainer Cher (shown in the photo) is one of the current sufferers from CFS—does she have a medical problem or a mental disorder? Initially, most researchers assumed that CFS was a relatively rare disorder that existed as an offshoot of a host of other psychiatric disorders, such as depression. Many practitioners minimized the seriousness and prevalence of CFS. Many considered it a strictly physical disorder, not psychological at all. However, over the last decade practitioners and researchers alike have rethought their positions.

CFS is a poorly understood, threatening affliction that can severely stress a patient's individual coping mechanisms and thus affect social and occupational relationships. Thus, the practitioner must assess the impact of the illness in the context of the patient's life background, as well as be alert to signs of overpowering distress. Such signs could include heightened interpersonal difficulties, substance abuse, unnecessary avoidance of people and activities, extreme helplessness, difficulty tolerating dependency, panic, misplaced anger, self-blame and guilt, and hopelessness.

CFS seems to have a fairly high prevalence. But the rate depends partly on how the disorder is defined. Some definitions require a definite onset of the disorder and substantial reductions in occupational, social, and personal activities. Other definitions require as many as eight symptoms; others require only four. So, the number of symptoms a

researcher requires to diagnose an individual with CFS determines its relative frequency within specific populations. Furthermore, family doctors are often the ones who make a referral to a psychologist or psychiatrist when they suspect a patient of having CFS. Therefore, a physician's preconceived notion of whether CFS is a medical condition or a psychological one is important. A great deal of controversy and speculation surrounds CFS. Is it a single disorder or a mix of problems? What is its relationship to infections, the immune system, and mood disturbances?

In reviewing the history, politics, and science of CFS, Leonard Jason and his colleagues (Jason et al., 1997) argued that psychologists, through research and careful evaluation, have to determine definitive diagnostic criteria. Only then can true estimates of prevalence be established. After these two elements are determined, researchers will be better able to establish effective treatment plans (Friedberg & Jason, 1998)

Does CFS exist? The answer is probably yes. Is it often mixed up with other disorders? Again, the answer is probably yes. More research is necessary to differentiate CFS from other disorders that share some of its symptoms. A biopsychological model that explains the disorder with reference to both medical and psychological aspects may be the most constructive way to approach the problem (Johnson, 1998). ■

In the remainder of this chapter, we will explore some of the most important disorders described in *DSM–IV* and their consequences. We begin with anxiety disorders.

Anxiety, Somatoform, and Dissociative Disorders

Everyone experiences anxiety, just as everyone experiences stress (as we discussed in Chapter 14). Most people feel anxious in specific situations, such as before taking an examination, competing in a swim meet, or delivering a speech. Although anxiety can be a positive, motivating force, its effects also can be debilitating; left untreated, chronic anxiety eventually may impair a person's health. Those who have had serious enough anxiety problems to have been hospitalized are at increased risk for suicide (Allgulander, 1994). Anxiety disorders are so common in the general population that they warrant special consideration. Research into them, however, is not extensive; and there is a genuine lack of research on special populations or ethnic groups (Last & Perrin, 1993). What has emerged in recent years has been the finding that at least some anxiety-related traits may have a genetic basis, and that symptoms sometimes can be alleviated through various drugs that facilitate serotonin transmission (Lesch et al., 1996). Let's look at the scope of the disorders.

Defining Anxiety

Anxiety is customarily considered a generalized feeling of fear and apprehension that may be related to a particular event or object and is often accompanied by increased physiological arousal. Psychologists recognize that anxiety is a key symptom of maladjustment—not necessarily the cause of maladjustment. Thoughts, environmental stimuli, or perhaps some long-standing and as yet unresolved conflict causes apprehension, fear, and its accompanying autonomic nervous system arousal. Feelings of not being able to control a situation are common in both children's and adults' anxiety; some researchers speculate that childhood anxiety and a perceived sense of lack of control may lead to similar, if not identical adult feelings—and this may lead to adult disorders (Chorpita & Barlow, 1998). This may be the case with generalized anxiety disorders, considered next.

Generalized Anxiety Disorders

Every disorder represents a different pattern of behaviour and maladjustment, and the *DSM–IV* classifies disorders under a variety of diagnostic categories. Those in which anxiety is the prominent feature are designated as generalized anxiety disorders. A **generalized anxiety disorder** is an anxiety disorder characterized by persistent anxiety occurring on more days than not for at least six months, sometimes with autonomic hyperactivity, apprehension, problems with motor tension, and difficulty in concentrating. People with a generalized anxiety disorder feel anxious almost constantly, even though nothing seems to provoke their anxiety. Fears often revolve around health, money, family, or work. Unable to relax, they have trouble falling asleep; they tend to feel tired and have trouble concentrating. They often report excessive sweating, muscle tension, headaches, and insomnia. They are tense and irritable, are unable to concentrate, have difficulty making decisions, and may hyperventilate (Rapee, 1986).

DSM–IV states that a person must show persistent anxiety to receive this diagnosis. When such chronic anxiety has no obvious source, it is called free-floating anxiety. **Free-floating anxiety** is persistent anxiety not clearly related to any specific object or situation, accompanied by a sense of impending doom.

People with a generalized anxiety disorder show impairment in three areas of functioning. One area is *motor tension*—the person is unable to relax and exhibits jumpiness, restlessness, and tension. The second area is *autonomic hyperactivity*—

Anxiety: A generalized feeling of fear and apprehension that may be related to a particular event or object and is often accompanied by increased physiological arousal.

Generalized anxiety disorder: An anxiety disorder characterized by persistent anxiety on more days than not for at least six months, sometimes with autonomic hyperactivity, apprehension, problems with motor tension, and difficulty in concentrating.

Free-floating anxiety: Persistent anxiety not clearly related to any specific object or situation, accompanied by a sense of impending doom.

the person sweats, has a dry mouth, has a high resting pulse rate, urinates frequently, and may complain of a lump in the throat. The third area is *vigilance*—the person has difficulty concentrating and is irritable and impatient.

Phobic Disorders

Do you know someone who is petrified at the thought of an airplane ride, who avoids crowds at all cost, or who shudders at the sight of a harmless garden snake? That person may suffer from a **phobic disorder**—an anxiety disorder involving an excessive, unreasonable, and irrational fear of, and consequent attempt to avoid, specific objects or situations. People with phobic disorders exhibit avoidance and escape behaviours, show increased heart rate and irregular breathing patterns, and report thoughts of disaster and severe embarrassment. Many psychologists agree that, once established, the relief a person derives from escaping or avoiding the feared situation maintains phobias.

One key to diagnosing a phobic disorder is that the fear must be excessive and disproportionate to the situation. Most people who fear heights would not avoid visiting a friend who lived on the top floor of a tall building; a person with a phobia of heights would, however. Fear alone does not distinguish a phobia; both fear and avoidance must be evident.

Mild phobic disorders occur in about 7.5 percent of the population. They are, in fact, relatively common in well-adjusted people. Severe, disabling phobias occur in less than 0.05 percent of the population, typically in patients with other disorders (Seif & Atkins, 1979). Phobias occur most frequently between the ages of 30 and 60 and occur about equally in men and women (Marks, 1977). There are an infinite number of objects and situations towards which people become fearful. Because of the diversity and number of phobias, *DSM* classifies three categories of phobia (though there are many subtypes): agoraphobia, social phobia, and specific phobia.

Agoraphobia. **Agoraphobia** is a marked fear and avoidance of being alone or isolated in open and public places from which escape might be difficult or embarrassing. This phobia is accompanied by avoidance behaviours that eventually may interfere with normal activities. It can become so debilitating that it prevents the individual from going into any open space, travelling in airplanes or through tunnels, or being in crowds. People with a severe case may decide never to leave their home, fearing that they will lose control, panic, or cause a scene in a public place. Agoraphobia is often brought on by stress, particularly interpersonal stress. It is far more common in women than in men, and it is often accompanied by other disorders.

Symptoms of agoraphobia are hyperventilation, extreme tension, and even cognitive disorganization (Zitrin, 1981). Agoraphobics often are seriously depressed; they often feel weak and dizzy when they have an attack and often suffer from severe panic attacks. *Panic attacks* are characterized as acute anxiety, accompanied by sharp increases in autonomic nervous system arousal, that is not triggered by a specific event; persons who experience such attacks often avoid the situations that are associated with them, thus perpetuating the agoraphobia (McNally, 1994). Some cognitive psychologists think of a panic attack as a "fear of fear"; attempting to avoid anxiety because they are so sensitive to it and its symptoms, people may panic while trying to avoid the symptoms of being fearful (McNally et al., 1997).

Agoraphobia is complicated, incapacitating, and extraordinarily difficult to treat. According to Freud and other psychoanalysts, traumatic childhood experiences may cause people to avoid particular objects, events, and situations that produce anxiety. Freudians speculate that as young children, agoraphobics may have feared abandonment by a cold or non-nurturing mother, and the fear has generalized to a fear of

abandonment or helplessness. Most researchers today find Freudian explanations of phobic behaviour unconvincing. As an alternative, modern learning theory suggests that agoraphobia may develop because people avoid situations they have found to be painful or embarrassing. Failed coping strategies and low self-esteem have been implicated (Williams, Kinney, & Falbo, 1989). Despite much research, no simple cause for the disorder has been found.

Social Phobia. Whereas a person with agoraphobia may avoid all situations involving other people, a person with a social phobia tends to avoid situations involving possible exposure to the scrutiny of other people. A **social phobia** is an anxiety disorder characterized by fear of, and a desire to avoid, situations in which one might be exposed to scrutiny by others and might behave in an embarrassing or humiliating way. A person with a social phobia avoids eating in public or speaking before other people. Such a person also avoids evaluation by refusing to deal with people or situations in which evaluation and a lowering of self-esteem might occur (Williams, Kinney, & Falbo, 1995). Social phobia is more than being shy, as shy individuals don't astutely avoid circumstances that make them uncomfortable or self-conscious. Social phobia disrupts normal living and social relationships. The dread of attending a social function can begin weeks in advance and lead to debilitating symptoms.

Specific Phobia. A **specific phobia** is an anxiety disorder characterized by irrational and persistent fear of a specific object or situation, along with a compelling desire to avoid it. Most people are familiar with specific phobias; see Table 15.3 for some examples. Among specific phobias are *claustrophobia* (fear of closed spaces), *hematophobia* (fear of the sight of blood), and *acrophobia* (fear of heights). Many specific phobias develop in childhood, adolescence, or early adulthood. Most people who have fears of heights, small spaces, water, doctors, or flying can calm themselves and deal with their fears, but those who cannot (true phobics) often seek the help of a psychotherapist when the phobia interferes with their health or day-to-day functioning. Treatment using behaviour therapy is typically effective.

Obsessive–Compulsive Disorders

Being orderly and organized is an asset for most people in today's fast-paced, complex society. However, when orderliness becomes a driving concern, a person may be suffering from an obsessive–compulsive disorder. An **obsessive–compulsive disorder** is an anxiety disorder characterized by persistent and uncontrollable thoughts and

Table 15.3   Some Common Specific Phobias

Acrophobia (fear of high places)	Hematophobia (fear of blood)
Ailurophobia (fear of cats)	Mysophobia (fear of contamination)
Algophobia (fear of pain)	Nyctophobia (fear of darkness)
Anthropophobia (fear of men)	Pathophobia (fear of disease)
Aquaphobia (fear of water)	Pyrophobia (fear of fire)
Astraphobia (fear of storms, thunder, and lightning)	Thanatophobia (fear of death)
	Xenophobia (fear of strangers)
Claustrophobia (fear of closed places)	Zoophobia (fear of animals)
Cynophobia (fear of dogs)	

irrational beliefs (obsessions) that cause performance of intrusive and inappropriate compulsive rituals that interfere with daily life. The unwanted thoughts, urges, and actions of people with obsessive–compulsive disorders focus on maintaining order and control. About 2 percent of the population suffer from obsessive–compulsive disorders. Of those with the disorder, about 20 percent have only obsessions or compulsions; about 80 percent have both.

People with obsessive–compulsive disorders combat anxiety by carrying out ritual behaviours that reduce tension; they feel that they have to *do* something. If they do not perform these compulsive acts, they may develop severe anxiety. Their thoughts have extraordinary power to control actions. For example, a person obsessed with avoiding germs may wash his hands a hundred times a day and may wear white gloves to avoid touching contaminated objects. A person obsessed with punctuality may become extremely anxious if she happens to arrive late for a dinner date. Adolescents with obsessive–compulsive disorders tend to wash and rewash, check, count, repeat, touch, and straighten their environment (March, Leonard, & Swedo, 1995). A person may compulsively write notes about every detail of every task before permitting himself to take any action. Here is an account of fairly severe obsessive–compulsive behaviour:

> I used to write notes to remind myself to do a particular job, so in my mind there was a real risk that one of these notes might go out of the window or door. . . . My fear was that if one of these papers blew away, this would cause a fatality to the person carrying out my design project. . . . I found it difficult to walk along the street, as every time I saw paper I wondered if it was some of mine. I had to pick it all up, unless it was brown chocolate paper, or lined paper, which I didn't use. And before I got on my bike, I checked that nothing was sticking out of my pockets and got my wife to recheck. . . . I couldn't smoke a cigarette without taking it to bits and checking there was no document between the paper and tobacco. I couldn't even have sex because I thought a piece of paper might get intertwined into the mattress. (Melville, 1977, pp. 66–67)

Freud and other psychodynamic theorists believed that obsessive–compulsive disorders come largely from difficulties during the anal stage of development, when orderliness and cleanliness are often stressed. Learning theorists argue that bringing order to a person's environment reduces uncertainty and risk and thus is reinforcing. Because reinforced behaviours tend to recur, these behaviours become exaggerated during times of stress. Neuroscience-oriented theorists now believe strongly that factors such as dysfunction in the basal ganglia, chronic levels of elevated arousal, a genetic link, and brain trauma explain obsessive–compulsive disorders (Last et al., 1991). Research on the neuroanatomy that may underlie the disorder has proceeded at a fast pace, although with varying conclusions—it turns out that results are difficult to replicate. It may be that obsessive symptoms and compulsive symptoms have a different anatomical locus; patients who are medicated (who would otherwise qualify as good participants) are often excluded from studies. So although the neuroscience of obsessive–compulsive disorder is making headway, there is still much to understand (Wilson, 1998).

Practitioners report that full-blown and dramatic cases of obsessive–compulsive disorders are relatively rare. Treatment often includes drugs (such as Anafrinil, Prozac, or Zoloft; see Chapter 16) combined with relaxation exercises (March, Leonard, & Swedo, 1995). Such treatment helps change ideas about stress and the consequences of anxiety. Family support and family psychotherapy are also helpful; families are taught that they should neither encourage the behaviours nor participate in the person's rituals. In fact, research shows that when clients are given training to

Somatoform disorders [so-MAT-oh-form]: Disorders characterized by real physical symptoms not under voluntary control and for which no apparent physical cause exists.

Somatization disorder: A somatoform disorder characterized by recurrent and multiple physical complaints of several years' duration for which medical attention has been ineffective.

Conversion disorder: A somatoform disorder characterized by the loss or alteration of physical functioning for no apparent physiological reason.

Hypochondriasis [hy-po-kon-DRY-a-sis]: A somatoform disorder characterized by an inordinate preoccupation with health and illness, coupled with excessive anxiety about disease.

refrain from compulsive behaviours after exposure to anxiety-producing ideas, people, or events, the training decreases compulsive acts and associated anxiety (Marks et al., 1986). Today, self-help groups, greater awareness of the disorders, and drug therapies are leading to successful treatment. Somatoform and dissociative disorders, discussed next, are harder to understand and treat.

Somatoform Disorders

If you were a writer for a TV soap opera, you might have on your desk a copy of *DSM–IV*, with the page turned down at somatoform and dissociative disorders. These disorders are relatively rare and are studied less than other disorders; however, they make for fascinating reading and study.

Somatoform disorders are disorders that involve real physical symptoms that are not under voluntary control and for which no apparent physical cause exists. Evidence suggests that the causes are psychological. Three types of somatoform disorders are somatization disorders, conversion disorders, and hypochondriasis. People suffering from these disorders are also frequently diagnosed as having personality disorders, which we will discuss later in this chapter (Bass & Murphy, 1995).

Somatization Disorders. A **somatization disorder** is a somatoform disorder characterized by recurrent and multiple physical complaints of several years' duration for which medical attention has been ineffective. Despite physicians' inability to help, those with the disorder tend to seek medical attention at least once a year. The disorder typically begins before age 30. It is diagnosed in only about 1 percent of females and is even rarer in males.

Patients with such disorders feel sickly for much of their lives and may report muscle weakness, double vision, memory loss, and hallucinations. Other commonly reported symptoms include gastrointestinal problems, painful menstrual periods with excessive bleeding, sexual indifference, and pains in the back, chest, and genitals. Anxiety and depression often beset patients.

Individuals with somatization disorders generally have a host of emotional problems that cause their physical complaints. However, at times some of the physical conditions are not psychologically caused, and physicians must be especially careful to treat medically those conditions that need treatment and not to dismiss all of the patient's problems as psychological.

Conversion Disorders. A **conversion disorder** is a somatoform disorder characterized by the loss or alteration of physical functioning for no apparent physiological reason. People suffering from conversion disorders often lose the use of their arms, hands, or legs or their vision or other sensory modality. They may develop a combination of ailments. For example, a patient may become not only blind but also deaf, mute, or totally paralyzed. Although patients may be unaware of the relationship, conversion disorders generally are considered a way to escape from or avoid extremely distressing situations. Also, the attention and support that patients sometimes receive because of the symptoms may cause them to maintain the disorder. Conversion disorders often are associated with a history of psychosomatic illness. Men and women are equally likely to develop conversion disorders, which, like somatization disorders, are rare.

Hypochondriasis. When a person spends a lot of time going to physicians with all types of bodily complaints for which the physicians can find no cause, psychologists suspect hypochondriasis. **Hypochondriasis** is a somatoform disorder characterized by an inordinate preoccupation with health and illness, coupled with excessive anxiety about disease. Hypochondriacs believe, erroneously, that they have grave afflictions. They become preoccupied with minor aches and pains and often miss work and create alarm among family members. Every ache and minor symptom is examined, interpreted, and feared.

Psychodynamic views of hypochondriasis believe that focusing on the symptoms of illness keep the person from dealing with some other painful sources of stress. Behavioural psychologists focus on how the illness can be reinforcing: People are given extra attention and care, and the illness diverts attention from tasks at which the individual may not be succeeding. By focusing on illness, a person may avoid dealing with marital problems, financial affairs, and educational goals. Of course, to the hypochondriac the fears and anxiety are real. Only through psychotherapy can the true causes of the excessive attention to symptoms be addressed.

Dissociative Disorders

Dissociative disorders are disorders characterized by a sudden but temporary alteration in consciousness, identity, sensory/motor behaviour, or memory. Although relatively rare, these disorders are quite noticeable and sharply delineated. They include dissociative amnesia and dissociative identity disorder.

Dissociative Amnesia. Dissociative amnesia (formerly called *psychogenic amnesia*), one of several dissociative disorders, used to be grouped with other disorders. Today, however, psychologists recognize it as a separate disorder. **Dissociative amnesia** is a dissociative disorder characterized by the sudden and extensive inability to recall important personal information, usually information of a traumatic or stressful nature. The memory loss is too extensive to be explained by ordinary forgetfulness. Often the amnesia is brought on by a traumatic incident involving physical injury or death. For example, a woman who experiences a brutal sexual assault may be unable to remember anything from the moments immediately preceding the attack until days after the attack. The condition, which is relatively rare, occurs most often during wars or natural disasters.

Dissociative Identity Disorder: Multiple Personality. Another form of dissociative disorder, often associated with dissociative amnesia but presenting a dramatically different kind of behaviour, is dissociative identity disorder, more commonly known as *multiple personality*. **Dissociative identity disorder** is characterized by the existence within an individual of two or more distinct personalities, each of which is dominant at particular times and directs the individual's behaviour at those times. Each personality has unique traits and different memories and behavioural patterns. For example, one personality may be adaptive and efficient at coping with life, while another may exhibit maladaptive behaviour. Some people's alternate personalities are of the opposite sex or of different ages. Each personality is often unaware of any other one, although in some cases they eavesdrop on each other (Putnma et al., 1989; Steinberg, 1995; Schacter et al., 1989). Each personality, when active, acknowledges that time has passed but cannot account for it. The switch from one personality to another usually is brought on by stress.

Despite the impression given by popular movies and books such as *The Three Faces of Eve* and *Sybil*, multiple personality is a rare disorder, with only a few hundred well-documented cases in history. Many people erroneously confuse multiple personality with schizophrenia, a much more common disorder involving only one personality that we'll examine later in this chapter (Steinberg et al., 1994).

Psychologists have little data on the causes of dissociative identity disorder and debate about how best to classify it (Gleaves, 1996). For some, there is doubt as to whether multiple personality actually exists; it is unrecognized by some practitioners (Huapaya, 1994; Lowenstein, 1993).

Dissociative disorders: Disorders characterized by a sudden but temporary alteration in consciousness, identity, sensory/motor behaviour, or memory.

Dissociative amnesia: A dissociative disorder characterized by the sudden and extensive inability to recall important personal information, too extensive to be explained by ordinary forgetfulness.

Dissociative identity disorder: A dissociative disorder characterized by the existence within an individual of two or more distinct personalities, each of which is dominant at particular times and directs the individual's behaviour at those times.

Focus

Review

◆ What is free-floating anxiety? p. 532
◆ Identify the central elements of an obsessive–compulsive disorder. pp. 534–535
◆ What evidence might suggest that a person is suffering from somatization disorder? p. 536

Think Critically

◆ What are the implications of dissociative identity disorder for traditional theories of personality?

Other psychologists assert that it nearly always can be traced back to severe, prolonged child abuse. Some psychologists think people invent multiple personalities to avoid taking responsibility for their own behaviour, especially when they have committed criminal acts. Others think some therapists subtly encourage patients to show symptoms of this disorder so that the therapists can achieve recognition. In any case, dissociative identity disorder is well known; it is vivid and interesting, and much more research is needed before comprehensive theories and effective treatments will become available.

Personality Disorders

P eople who exhibit inflexible and long-standing maladaptive ways of dealing with the environment that typically cause stress and/or social or occupational difficulties may have one of the **personality disorders**. Often, these disorders are identified in childhood or adolescence and persist throughout adulthood. People with personality disorders are easy to spot but difficult to treat. Paul Bernardo (shown in the photo), who was declared a dangerous offender and convicted of the rapes and murders of several young women in southern Ontario, has been classified by many as having a serious personality disorder.

Types of Personality Disorders

People with personality disorders are divided into three broad clusters: those whose behaviour appears (1) odd or eccentric, (2) dramatic, emotional, and erratic, or (3) fearful or anxious. We will now consider six specific personality disorders: paranoid, borderline, histrionic, narcissistic, antisocial, and dependent.

Paranoid Personality Disorder. Fitting into the first cluster, by showing odd or eccentric behaviour, are people suffering from *paranoid personality disorder*, who have unwarranted feelings of persecution and who mistrust almost everyone. They are hypersensitive to criticism and have a restricted range of emotional responses. They have strong fears of being exploited, and of losing control and independence. Sometimes they appear cold, humourless, even scheming. As you might expect, people with paranoid personality disorder are suspicious and seldom able to form close, intimate relationships with others.

Borderline Personality Disorder. Fitting into the second cluster, individuals with *borderline personality disorder* have trouble with relationships; they show a pattern of instability with interpersonal relationships, self-image, and affect. In addition they are often impulsive. They are sometime suicidal; they report feelings of emptiness and are sometimes inappropriately angry. Easily bored and distracted, such individuals fear abandonment. Individuals with borderline personality disorder often sabotage or undermine themselves just before a goal is to be reached—for example, by dropping out of school just before graduation.

Histrionic Personality Disorder. Fitting into the second cluster, because of dramatic, emotional, and erratic behaviours, are those people with *histrionic personality disorder*. Individuals with this disorder seek attention by exaggerating situations in their lives. They have stormy personal relationships, are excessively emotional, and demand constant reassurance and praise.

Narcissistic Personality Disorder. Closely related to histrionic personality disorder, and also classified in the second cluster, is *narcissistic personality disorder*. People with this disorder have an extremely exaggerated sense of self-importance, expect favours, and need constant admiration and attention. They show a lack of caring for others and they react to criticism with rage, shame, or humiliation.

Personality disorders: Disorders characterized by inflexible and long-standing maladaptive ways of dealing with the environment that typically cause stress and/or social or occupational difficulties.

Antisocial Personality Disorder. Still another disorder of the second cluster, and perhaps the most widely recognized personality disorder, is the antisocial personality disorder. An **antisocial personality disorder** is characterized by egocentricity, behaviour that is irresponsible and that violates the rights of other people (lying, theft, delinquency, and other violations of social rules), a lack of guilt feelings, an inability to understand other people, and a lack of fear of punishment. Individuals with this disorder may be superficially charming, but their behaviour is destructive and often reckless. A person often demonstrates symptoms of the condition prior to early adolescence but must be at least 18 years old before a diagnosis may be made. Prior to adulthood the child or adolescent may be diagnosed with conduct disorder. The individual displays a blatant disregard for others and appears to lack a moral conscience.

A person who frequently changes jobs, does not take proper care of his or her children, is arrested often, fails to pay bills, and lies constantly displays behaviours typical of antisocial personality disorder. Such people are relatively unsocialized adults: They are unwilling to conform to and live by society's rules, and their behaviour often brings them into conflict with society. Antisocial people consistently blame others for their behaviour. They seldom feel guilt or learn from experience or punishment. The disorder occurs six times more often in men than in women. Cold-blooded killers, such as Clifford Olson and Paul Bernardo, display extreme forms of this disorder, although most people with the disorder exhibit it through less deadly and sensational behaviours. As many as 3 percent of all individuals may be diagnosed with antisocial personality disorder.

Adopted children separated at birth from antisocial biological parents are likely to show antisocial behaviour later in life; this and other evidence suggests a genetic (nature) contribution to the disorder (Lyons et al., 1995; Nigg & Goldsmith, 1994). Another fact that suggests a genetic factor is that the nervous systems of people diagnosed as having antisocial personality disorder may be different from those of normal people. When normal people do something wrong, their autonomic nervous system reacts with symptoms of anxiety, such as fear, heart palpitations, and sweating. Evidence suggests that *decreased* autonomic arousal is characteristic in people with antisocial personality disorders (Patrick, 1994). These people do not function at sufficiently high levels of autonomic nervous system arousal, do not experience the physiological symptoms of anxiety, and thus do not learn to associate those symptoms with antisocial behaviour.

On the environmental (nurture) side, some psychologists believe that poor child-rearing practices and unstable family situations render individuals with antisocial personality disorder unable to learn fear, guilt, and punishment avoidance. Such people seem to have learned maladaptive functioning from their family situations and consequently to have developed inappropriate behaviours. Also, the symptoms of antisocial personality disorder often are seen first in a person's interactions with family members (Ge et al., 1996). Family relationships become strained, and some people suffering from the disorder may become involved in domestic violence—including child abuse, which we examine below. If the environmental viewpoint is correct, antisocial personality disorder may be a learned behaviour. Or, more likely, both physiological and socialization factors may contribute to it.

Dependent Personality Disorder. Fitting into the third behaviour cluster, by acting fearful or anxious, are individuals whose behaviour is characteristic of *dependent personality disorder*. Such people are submissive and clinging; they let others make all of the important decisions in their lives. They try to appear pleasant and agreeable at all times. They act meek, humble, and affectionate in order to keep their protectors. Overprotective, authoritarian parenting seems to be a major initiating cause of dependency (R. F. Bornstein, 1992).

Psychological Maltreatment of Children

The psychological maltreatment of children often takes the form of child abuse. Child abuse is not classified as a personality disorder, but many child abusers suffer from personality and other disorders. Many practitioners see child abuse as an outcome of previous psychological maltreatment of the abuser. **Child abuse** is the physical, emotional, or sexual mistreatment of children and is implicated in children's development of antisocial personality disorder. The impact on an abused child's self-esteem is profound (Romans et al., 1995; Trickett & Putnam, 1993), although victimized children can recover well with treatment (Kendall-Tackett, Williams, & Finkelhor, 1993).

In 1996 children under 18 years of age made up 24 percent of the Canadian population and accounted for 22 percent of violent victimization. Eighteen percent of physical assaults were directed towards children, as were 60 percent of reported sexual assaults (Bunge & Levett, 1998). Females are victimized more than males (Knutson, 1995). Victimization is easier to detect through overt behaviours in young children than it is in school-age children (Campis, Hebden-Curtis, & DeMaso, 1993). Research shows that not all cases are reported and that even some treated cases go unreported by therapists, though the therapists are bound by law to report them; further, the rate of child abuse has not decreased in recent years (Kalichman & Craig, 1991; Knutson & Selner, 1994).

The Child Abuser. Who are the child abusers? Only about 5 percent of child abusers exhibit symptoms of very disturbed behaviour. Most abusive parents seem quite normal by traditional social standards and sometimes have a prominent place in the community.

Physically abusive parents often have unusually high expectations for their children and distorted perceptions of the children's behaviour. They are generally less satisfied with their children than are non-abusive parents, and they perceive child-rearing as more difficult than do non-abusive parents (Trickett & Susman, 1988). Abusive parents are not necessarily more discipline-oriented, power-oriented, or authoritarian with their children, but they tend to rely on ineffective child management techniques, including aversive control, blaming, scapegoating, threats, verbal degradations, and physical punishment (Emery, 1989a, 1989b; Milner & Chilamkurti, 1991). Most parents who were abused as children do not abuse their own children. Formerly abused children are, however, significantly more likely than others to be abusers themselves, especially if they do not have a stable, emotionally satisfying, supportive relationship with a mate (Egeland, Jacobvitz, & Sroufe, 1988; Worling, 1995). Societal attitudes towards family privacy, poverty, and difficult children also play a role in child abuse. Belsky summarizes it well (1993, p. 427): "There is no one pathway to these disturbances in parenting; rather maltreatment seems to arise when stressors outweigh supports and risks are greater than protective factors."

Prevention. Most psychologists and social workers consider child abuse an interactive process involving parental incompetence, environmental stress, and poor child management techniques. Therefore, both psychologists and social workers attempt to change family systems and patterns of interaction. Parents can be taught different coping skills, impulse control, effective child management techniques, and constructive ways to interact with their children. When these techniques are applied in early intervention programs for parents at risk of child abuse, they produce encouraging results. Children of potentially abusive parents who have undergone such therapy seem to have fewer and less intense behaviour problems. Yet evaluations of such programs are equivocal. Reppucci and Haugaard (1989), for example, conclude: "We cannot be sure whether prevention programs are working" (p. 1274). These researchers argue that it is urgent and essential to conduct extensive investigation of the full range of preventive efforts.

Focus

Review

◆ Identify the distinguishing characteristics of a person diagnosed as having an antisocial personality disorder. p. 539

Think Critically

◆ Describe a preventive program that could be instituted to help decrease child abuse.

Mood Disorders

Everyone experiences sad moods at one time or another. Ending a long-term intimate relationship, feeling overwhelmed during final exams, mourning the death of a close friend or family member, and experiencing serious financial problems all can be sources of depression. We use the term *depression* in a colloquial sense every day. But when people become so depressed or sad that a long-term change occurs in their outlook and overt behaviour, they may be suffering from *clinical depression*. Depression is considered to be a type of mood disorder. Mood disorders can involve the extremes of energy and emotion. Mood disorders, which include *bipolar disorders* and *depressive disorders*, sometimes may be precipitated by a specific event, although for many individuals the symptoms develop gradually.

Bipolar Disorders

Gustav Mahler, a nineteenth-century Austrian composer and conductor, apparently suffered from a bipolar disorder. At age 19, he wrote to a friend:

> Much has happened within me since my last letter; I cannot describe it. Only this: I have become a different person. I don't know whether this new person is better; he certainly is not happier. The fires of a supreme zest for living and the most gnawing desire for death alternate in my heart, sometimes in the course of a single hour.

Bipolar disorders, which originally were known as *manic–depressive disorders*, get their name from the fact that patients' behaviour vacillates between two extremes: mania and depression. The *manic phase* is characterized by rapid speech, inflated self-esteem, impulsiveness, euphoria, and decreased need for sleep. Patients in the manic phase are easily distracted, get angry when things do not go their way, and seem to have boundless energy. A person in the *depressed phase*, which often follows the manic phase, is moody and sad, with feelings of hopelessness.

About 1 percent of the population suffers from bipolar disorders; men and women are equally likely to be affected. Although Mahler's bipolar disorder started when he was still in his teens, people who suffer from bipolar disorders are often in their late twenties before they begin to manifest the symptoms overtly, and these disorders often continue throughout life. Patients can be relatively normal for a few days, weeks, or months between episodes of excitement and depression, or they can rapidly vacillate between excitement and depression. The key component of bipolar disorders is the shift from excited states to depressive states of sadness and hopelessness. The disorder seems to have a biological basis and patients often respond fairly well to drug treatment, especially to lithium and other drugs that are considered second- and third-generation drugs (a topic that will be discussed in Chapter 16) (Barnodes, 1998; Post et al., 1998). The nature of bipolar disorders often can contribute to lack of client compliance with their treatment plan, making outcomes difficult to predict. As many as 50 percent of individuals who suffer from bipolar disorder also exhibit maladaptive personality traits, such as experiencing obsessions or being overly dependent or narcissistic (Peselow, Sanfilipo, & Fieve, 1995). Table 15.4 lists the signs and symptoms of mania and depression in bipolar disorders.

Depressive Disorders

Bonnie Strickland (1988) said, "Depression has been called the common cold of psychological disturbances . . . which underscores its prevalence, but trivializes its impact." At any time, about 1.3 million Canadians are suffering from this disabling disorder (Statistics Canada, 1995). And many of those people are misdiagnosed, not diagnosed, and not receiving treatment, despite its availability (Hirschfeld, 1997). Listen to the words of American novelist William Styron, who describes in his 1990 memoir, *Darkness Visible*, his state of mind during a period of depression:

Bipolar disorder: A mood disorder characterized by vacillation between two extremes, mania and depression; originally known as manic–depressive disorders.

Table 15.4 Bipolar Disorder Involves Cycles of Mania and Depression

	Manic Behaviour	Depressive Behaviour
Emotional characteristics	Elation, euphoria Extreme sociability, expansiveness Impatience Distractibility Inflated self-esteem	Gloominess, hopelessness Social withdrawal Irritability
Cognitive characteristics	Desire for action Impulsiveness Talkativeness Grandiosity	Indecisiveness Slowness of thought Obsessive worrying about death Negative self-image Delusions of guilt Difficulty in concentrating
Motor characteristics	Hyperactivity Decreased need for sleep Sexual indiscretion Increased appetite	Fatigue Difficulty in sleeping Decreased sex drive Decreased appetite Decreased motor activity

Depressive disorders: A general category of mood disorders in which people on a day-to-day basis show extreme and persistent sadness, despair, and loss of interest in life's usual activities.

Major depressive disorder: A depressive disorder characterized by loss of interest in almost all of life's usual activities; a sad, hopeless, or discouraged mood; sleep disturbance; loss of appetite; loss of energy; and feelings of unworthiness and guilt.

He [a psychiatrist] asked me if I was suicidal, and I reluctantly told him yes. I did not particularize—since there seemed no need to—did not tell him that in truth many of the artifacts of my house had become potential devices for my own destruction: the attic rafters (and an outside maple or two) a means to hang myself, the garage a place to inhale carbon monoxide, the bathtub a vessel to receive the flow from my opened arteries. The kitchen knives in their drawers had but one purpose for me. Death by heart attack seemed particularly inviting, absolving me as it would of active responsibility, and I had toyed with the idea of self-induced pneumonia—a long frigid, shirt-sleeved hike through the rainy woods. Nor had I overlooked an ostensible accident, à la Randall Jarrell, by walking in front of a truck on the highway nearby. . . . Such hideous fantasies, which cause well people to shudder, are to the deeply depressed mind what lascivious daydreams are to persons of robust sexuality.

When depressed, people are more than blue, or sad. As Styron shows, depression is debilitating, dangerous, and overwhelming. **Depressive disorders** are a general category of mood disorders in which people on a day-to-day basis show extreme and persistent sadness, despair, and loss of interest in life's usual activities. The main difference between depressive disorders and bipolar disorders is that people with depressive disorders show no vacillation between excitement and depression; they tend to be depressed more often than not. One type of depressive disorder, major depressive disorder, is eight times more common than bipolar disorders.

Major depressive disorder, one of several depressive disorders, is characterized by loss of interest in almost all of life's usual activities; a sad, hopeless, or discouraged mood; sleep disturbance; loss of appetite; loss of energy; and feelings of unworthiness and guilt. Someone experiencing major depressive disorder is not merely experiencing fleeting anxiety or sadness, although this disorder may be triggered by a specific event, such as the loss of a loved one, a job, or a home, or some failure in life. Sufferers show at least some impairment of social and occupational functioning, although their behaviour is not necessarily bizarre.

Symptoms. The symptoms of major depressive disorder include poor appetite, insomnia, weight loss,

loss of energy, feelings of worthlessness and intense guilt, inability to concentrate, and sometimes thoughts of death and suicide (Buchwald & Rudick-Davis, 1993; Irwin, Smith, & Gillin, 1992). Depressed patients have a gloomy outlook on life, an extremely distorted view of current problems, a tendency to blame themselves, and low self-esteem (Maddux & Meier, 1995). They often withdraw from social and physical contact with others. Every task seems to require a great effort, thought is slow and unfocused, and problem-solving abilities are impaired. Individuals who display symptoms have other problems as well; for example, decrease in bone density and heightened risk of osteoporosis occur in those who suffer from depression, and depression is associated with abnormal brain activity in the frontal lobes and with immune system problems (George, Ketter, & Post, 1993; Herbert & Cohen, 1993; Schweiger et al., 1994).

Depressed people also may have **delusions**—false beliefs that are inconsistent with reality, held despite evidence that negates them, and may induce feelings of guilt, shame, and persecution. Seriously disturbed patients show even greater disruptions in thought and motor processes and a total lack of spontaneity and motivation. Such patients typically report that they have no hope for themselves or the world; nothing seems to interest them. They are often extremely self-critical (Blatt, 1995). Some feel responsible for serious world problems such as economic depression, disease, or hunger. They report strange diseases and may insist that their body is disintegrating or that their brain is being eaten from the inside out. Most people who exhibit symptoms of major depressive disorder can describe their reasons for feeling sad and dejected; however, they may be unable to explain why their response is so deep and so prolonged.

Psychologists say that many people suffering from major depressive disorder are poor at reality testing. *Reality testing* is a person's ability to judge the demands of the environment accurately and to deal with those demands. People with poor reality testing are unable to cope with the demands of life in rational ways because their reasoning ability is grossly impaired.

Onset and Duration. A major depressive episode can occur at any age, although people who experience these episodes usually undergo the first one before age 40. Symptoms are rapidly apparent and last for a few days, weeks, or months. Because so many different circumstances can be involved in depressive reaction, the extent of depression varies dramatically from individual to individual. Episodes may occur once or many times. Stressful life events are sometimes predictors of depression (Monroe, Simons, & Thase, 1991). Major depressive disorder is not exclusively an adult disorder; researchers also find evidence of it in children and adolescents (Larson et al., 1990). When children show depression, they often have other symptoms, especially anxiety and loneliness. Treatment plans must be flexible and must take into account the array of family situations in which children find themselves—divorce, foster care, or an environment of alcoholism or child abuse, for example.

Prevalence. According to Statistics Canada (1995), over 1.25 million Canadians suffer from major depressive disorders in a given year. Women are two to three times as likely as men to be diagnosed as depressed and are more likely to express feelings of depression openly (Culbertson, 1997; Sprock & Yoder, 1997). It is unclear why women experience more depression than men; research on gender differences in both causes and treatment is limited (Strickland, 1992).

According to several studies, people born around 1960 suffer up to 10 times as many episodes of major depressive disorder as did their grandparents or great-grandparents (Lewinsohn et al., 1993). This may be due to changes in diagnosis, in reporting frequency, or perhaps in the stressors in society; the answer is not yet clear. In addition, people in developing countries are far less likely to develop the passivity, feelings of hopelessness, diminished self-esteem, and suicidal tendencies that typify Westerners afflicted by major depressive disorder. Martin Seligman (1988) suggests that the increased incidence of depression stems from too much emphasis on the individual, coupled with a loss of faith in supportive institutions such as family, country, and religion.

Delusions: False beliefs that are inconsistent with reality, held despite evidence that negates them, and may induce feelings of guilt, shame, and persecution.

Clinical Evaluation. How does a practitioner know if a person is suffering from major depressive disorder? A complete clinical evaluation comprises three parts: a physical examination, a psychiatric history, and a mental status examination. The *physical examination* rules out thyroid disorders, viral infection, and anemia—all of which cause a slowing down of behaviour. A neurological check of coordination, reflexes, and balance is part of this exam, to rule out brain disorders. The *psychiatric history* attempts to trace the course of the apparent disorder, genetic or family factors, and past treatments. Finally, the *mental status examination* scrutinizes thought, speaking processes, and memory; it includes interviews and may include tests for psychiatric symptoms (among them the MMPI–2) and projective tests such as the TAT (see Chapter 12). All of this is done because, among other things, it is important to distinguish between major depressive disorder and dysthymic disorder. In *dysthymic disorder* people experience a mild but chronic depressed mood for more days than not, for at least two years, along with poor appetite, insomnia, low self-esteem, and feelings of hopelessness. This disorder often goes undiagnosed and untreated; people begin to act, and to be treated, as if this "sad" personality is normal. Yet dysthymic disorder spreads a thin veil of sadness over a person's life; individuals with the disorder are less likely to marry, more likely to divorce, and are often underemployed or unemployed. They report being self-critical, have low interest in life's activities, and show occupational and social impairment. Dysthymic disorder is not

brain and behaviour
Genetic Vulnerability and the Neurochemistry of Depression

Thousands of people in Canada are taking medication daily for depression; Prozac, Zoloft, and Elavil are now household names. Researchers and clinicians have found that when these medications are given to people who exhibit symptoms of depression, within a few weeks the depressed mood lifts and people can get on with their lives. At this point, they often seek psychological therapy. Practitioners who prescribe such medication make a fundamental assumption—depression is caused by a biological imbalance of various brain substances. The causes of the imbalance are in dispute but practitioners know that in many, indeed in the great majority of, cases, medications that alter the levels of certain neurotransmitters affect depression.

If depression is biologically based, are some people born with a predisposition to depression? Indeed, depression may be geneti-

cally based, especially its most severe forms (Lyons et al., 1998). We know that children of depressed parents are more likely than other children to be depressed; further, twin studies indicate that genetic factors play a substantial role in depression (Barnodes, 1998; Kendler et al., 1992, 1993). But most research today is focusing on the idea that, for whatever reason, people's depression is caused by an insufficient amount of a neurotransmitter in the brain. Research shows that if the level of key neurotransmitters at receptor sites in the brain is increased, depression is alleviated. Because traumatic events decrease these neurotransmitter levels, being in a stressful situation could bring about depression.

Part of our awareness of how drugs work to alleviate depression comes from our understanding of how neurotransmitters move from one neuron to the next. Neurotransmitters held within

vesicles in one neuron are released, move across the synaptic space, and attach at a binding site at the next neuron. (See Chapter 2, p. 45.) The receptors have binding sites for particular neurotransmitters. This is an important point because a specific neurotransmitter can and will

as severe as major depressive disorder but it lasts longer and often occurs alongside it; clinicians often diagnose dysthymic disorder in persons who initially were seeking help for a major depressive episode.

Causes of Major Depressive Disorder

Most psychologists believe that major depressive disorder is caused by a combination of biological, learning, and cognitive factors. Biological theories suggest that chemical and genetic processes can account for depression. (*Brain and Behaviour* describes the biological approach to understanding depression.) Learning theories suggest that people develop faulty behaviours. Cognitive theories suggest that irrational ideas guide behaviour. For example, learned helplessness theories suggest that people choose not to respond by giving up. Let's look at each explanation in more detail.

Learning and Cognitive Theories. Learning and cognitive theorists argue that people learn depressive behaviours and thoughts. People with poor social skills who never learn to express prosocial behaviours and who are punished for the behaviours they do exhibit experience the world as aversive and depressing. In support of this idea is the finding that children of depressed patients, having been exposed to so many depressive behaviours, are more likely than other children to be

influence only those cells that have receptors for it. Four of the key neurotransmitters believed to be involved in depression are dopamine, norepinephrine, epinephrine, and serotonin. They are called *mono*amines because they are synthesized from a single amino acid.

When monoamines are released and are meant to bind to the next cell but do not, the neurotransmitter is then either neutralized or taken back up by the neuron that released it in a process called *reuptake*. (Again, see Chapter 2 for a refresher on this process.) If reuptake occurs before the neurotransmitters (in this case, the monoamines) are able to bind at the receptor sites, synaptic transmission is incomplete. This disruption of transmission may be important in the development of symptoms of depression. When people are given drugs that do not allow the neurotransmitters to be neutralized or restored to the releasing cell, the neurotransmitter is more likely to bind and depression is averted.

With each passing month there is new support for what researchers generally call the *monoamine theory of depression*, which suggests that major depression results from a deficiency of available monoamines or inefficient monoamine receptors (Mann et al., 1996; Soares & Mann, 1997). The monoamine theory of depression is based on the finding that three classes of drugs, each in a different way, block reuptake and keep people from being depressed. These drugs—monoamine inhibitors, tricyclics, and serotonin-reuptake inhibitors—all block the reuptake of monoamines (especially serotonin and norepinephrine). The evidence in support of this theory comes from a range of domains, including genetic studies, the effectiveness of selective serotonin-reuptake inhibitors, and reduced levels of serotonin.

Remember that the brain has about 10 billion receptors, so the process is anything but simple. For example, serotonin plays a complicated role, and there are at least seven families of closely chemically related neurotransmitters. Thus, many drug variations can be devised to block reuptake, that is, to limit the process by which neurotransmitters are reabsorbed before they can reach and bind at receptor sites. One of those drugs, Prozac, has received a great deal of media attention because it is prescribed so widely and has helped so many people.

The research continues on monoamines because researchers do not fully understand their actions. For example, after a patient takes serotonin-reuptake inhibitors alleviation of depression takes weeks to occur, even though the changes in blood levels of neurotransmitters happens in days; this inconsistency is difficult to understand. In addition, other drugs that also block monoamine reuptake do not have antidepressant effects. Further, despite the availability of dozens of approved antidepressant drugs, relief for many patients remains elusive. Widely respected researchers like Elliot Valenstein (1998) have questioned brain chemistry explanations and argue that a quick fix via the use of pills is not the whole answer. Others agree and the next decade of research should prove illuminating because, as you will see in Chapter 16, some researchers assert that psychological forms of therapy are as effective or more effective than drug therapy (Antonuccio, Danton, & DeNelsky, 1995). ■

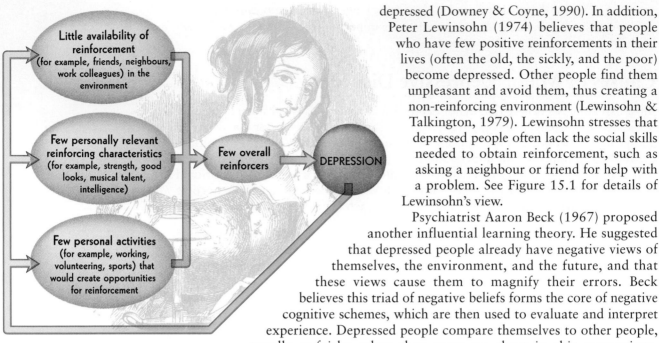

FIGURE 15.1
Lewinsohn's View of Depression
According to Lewinsohn, some people have few reinforcers available in the environment. This lack of reinforcers causes depression, which then leads to even fewer reinforcers.

depressed (Downey & Coyne, 1990). In addition, Peter Lewinsohn (1974) believes that people who have few positive reinforcements in their lives (often the old, the sickly, and the poor) become depressed. Other people find them unpleasant and avoid them, thus creating a non-reinforcing environment (Lewinsohn & Talkington, 1979). Lewinsohn stresses that depressed people often lack the social skills needed to obtain reinforcement, such as asking a neighbour or friend for help with a problem. See Figure 15.1 for details of Lewinsohn's view.

Psychiatrist Aaron Beck (1967) proposed another influential learning theory. He suggested that depressed people already have negative views of themselves, the environment, and the future, and that these views cause them to magnify their errors. Beck believes this triad of negative beliefs forms the core of negative cognitive schemes, which are then used to evaluate and interpret experience. Depressed people compare themselves to other people, usually unfairly; when they come up short in this comparison, depressed people see the difference as disastrous. They see the human condition as universally wretched, become angry, and view the world as a place that defeats positive behaviour. Their poor self-concept and negative expectations about the world produce negative future expectations that lead to depression. All of this is magnified in depressed adolescents, who also are experiencing many bodily changes that may heighten their risk of depression (Allgood-Merton, Lewinsohn, & Hops, 1990).

Beck (1967, 1972, 1976) theorized that depression does not cause negative feelings but that negative feelings and expectations cause depression. Research supports Beck's theory. Depressed people are harsher on themselves than non-depressed people are, and they have particularly low levels of self-expectations and self-esteem (Maddux, 1995). They make judgments based on insufficient data, they overgeneralize, and they exaggerate the negative outcomes in their lives. According to Beck, being depressed causes poor judgments and thus affects people's cognitions. Beck's theory is influential among psychologists for two reasons. First, it is consistent with the notion that depression stems from a lack of appropriate positive reinforcements in people's environments. Second, it acknowledges both cognitive and environmental variables such as family interactions.

Learned Helplessness. What would you do if you failed every exam you took, regardless of your efforts? What happens when a person's hopes and dreams are constantly thwarted, regardless of the person's behaviour? The result may be **learned helplessness**—the behaviour of giving up or not responding, exhibited by people or animals who have learned that rewards and punishments are not contingent on behaviour.

Seligman (1976) has suggested that people's beliefs about the causes of their failures determine whether they will become depressed. When they attribute their failures to unalterable conditions within themselves ("my own weakness, which is unlikely to change"), they acquire low self-esteem (Maddux & Meier, 1995). That is, when people come to believe that eventual outcomes are unrelated to anything under their control, they develop learned helplessness and become pessimistic rather than optimistic. For example, a man who comes to believe that his effort to meet new people by being outgoing and friendly never works may stop trying. Eventually he will choose not to respond to the environment, because he has learned that his behaviour makes no difference (Peterson & Seligman, 1984). According to Seligman, the major cause of learned helplessness is an organism's belief that its response will

Learned helplessness: The behaviour of giving up or not responding, exhibited by people or animals who have learned that rewards and punishments are not contingent on behaviour.

not affect what happens to it in the future. The result of this belief is anxiety, depression, and, eventually, non-responsiveness. The opposite of learned helplessness is *learned optimism*—a sense that the world has positive outcomes, which leads people to see happy things in their lives (Seligman, 1991). Seligman asserts that *learning* is the key to a sense of doom or optimism. Seligman (1988) argues that the environment, not genetics, is the cause of pessimism, depression, and helplessness, especially when people believe that they are responsible for long-standing failures in many areas of their lives. When learned helplessness is operative, people adopt the view that they cannot change highly aversive life events (Abramson, Metalsky, and Alloy, 1989).

The idea that learned helplessness is a key factor in depression has received research support, although the way this factor operates is not yet fully understood (Joiner & Wagner, 1995; Overmeier 1998). The effects of helplessness and depression are poignant and painful. They influence a person's day-to-day life, work environment, and family roles—especially parenting (Downey & Coyne, 1990). People who develop such ideas assume that their depression will last forever and blame themselves most of the time. Such self-blame is strongly associated with the Western ideal that people must assume personal responsibility for their acts, at least as compared to non-Western countries where cooperative efforts are especially valued.

A Vicious Cycle. Many variables determine whether an individual will develop a mood disorder, or any other disorder for that matter. Some people, because of family environment, genetic history, or brain chemistry, are more vulnerable than others. **Vulnerability** is the sum of a person's predispositions towards developing the disorder. The more vulnerable the individual is, the less necessary are environmental stress or other disorders (such as anxiety) to the initiation of a mood disorder. This is the vulnerability–stress hypothesis, sometimes termed the *diathesis–stress model*.

Some people lack good social skills, and this puts them at a disadvantage. They say the wrong things, chose the wrong options, and find few reinforcers in their lives. Needless to say, this leads to negative thinking. To a substantial extent, a person's thoughts affect, even determine, his or her depression. At the same time, a person's depression determines his or her thoughts. Adding one or more stressful life experiences and a sense of learned helplessness to the mix creates a vicious cycle of events that keep a person feeling depressed. And when depressed, people are often irritable and pessimistic, and they tend to annoy the people around them—they're sort of depressing. The consequence is that people avoid them—yet another cause for feeling bad. This "common cold of psychiatric disturbances" affects millions and leaves them feeling as if they are in a dark, lonely place feeling deficient and incapable of moving ahead. Untamed and unmanaged, this vicious cycle leads to self-blame, further isolation, loneliness, and sometimes suicide.

Vulnerability: A person's diminished ability to deal with demanding life events.

Suicide

Depressed individuals are at greater risk for suicide than are non-depressed individuals. Fortunately, most people who think about suicide do not actually commit the act; but when people become depressed and feel hopeless, the likelihood that they will commit suicide increases sharply (Rifai et al., 1994). Each day, about 10 people in Canada commit suicide; over 3700 Canadians commit suicide each year (Health Canada, 1994). These individuals are often lonely, guilt-ridden, and depressed. They believe things cannot and will not get better, and that suicide is their best option. They are unable to see their other options because they are so distressed.

A distinction must be drawn between attempters and completers. *Attempters* try to commit suicide but are unsuccessful. They tend to be young and impulsive, are more often women than men, and are more likely to make nonfatal attempts such as wrist slashing. *Completers* succeed in taking their lives. They tend to be white, male, and older, and they use highly lethal techniques of self-destruction, such as handguns. Although estimates vary with age and gender, there are an estimated 10 to 25 attempted suicides for every completed one.

Who commits suicide? More than four times as many men as women actually complete suicides. Among adolescents, suicide is the second leading cause of death (after accidents) compared to adults where it is the ninth leading cause of death; 1 out of every 1000 adolescents attempts suicide each year (Health Canada, 1994). The elderly, the divorced, and former patients with psychological disorders have a higher likelihood than others of attempting and committing suicide. Alcoholics have a high rate of suicide; First Nations people do, as well, partly because alcoholism is a common problem for them (Murphy et al., 1992; Young & French, 1993). (*Diversity* discusses the higher rate of suicide among Canada's aboriginal population.) People who have been suffering from major depression are more likely to attempt suicide while they are recovering, when their energy level is higher, than at the depths of depression; during the worst part of a depressive episode, a person is usually too weak, divided, and lacking in energy to commit suicide. Although only 15 percent of depressed people are suicidal, most suicide-prone individuals are depressed.

Are there warning signs of suicide? Research shows that predicting suicide is difficult but not impossible (Shneidman, 1994). There are several indicators: changes in personal appearance, a dramatic drop in quality of schoolwork, changes in drug abuse patterns, decreased appetite, the giving away of prized possessions, and, most important, a depressed attitude. Nearly everyone who is suicidal exhibits depression, shown by changes in sleeping patterns (especially insomnia), a diminished ability to concentrate, fatigue, feelings of worthlessness, and decreased problem-solving abilities (Hughes & Neimeyer, 1993). In addition, 86 percent of those who complete suicide have attempted suicide before. Clearly, suicide attempters may become suicide completers if no one intervenes and helps them after a first attempt.

Causes. The causes of suicide are as complex as the people who commit suicide. For some individuals who take their own lives, societal pressures serve as a catalyst. For others, the catalysts may be the responsibility of aging parents, substance abuse that impairs judgment, or traumatic or humiliating events. For still other people, a long-standing series of psychological disorders may predispose them to suicide. The psychological antecedents for suicide are about the same in non-Western and Western cultures (Cheng, 1995). Table 15.5 presents some of the many myths about suicide and counters them with facts.

Psychologists cite an array of factors that may influence a suicide attempt. *Biological psychologists* assert that certain neurotransmitters, especially serotonin, have been linked to disorders that predispose individuals to suicide; for example, research shows that there are alterations in the serotonin system of those who attempt and complete suicide (Arango, Underwood, & Mann, 1992; Rifai, Reynolds, & Mann, 1992; Roy et al., 1991). *Behavioural psychologists* suggest that past experiences with suicide (such as seeing the effects of suicide on friends and relatives of a person who committed suicide) reinforce people's attempts to commit suicide. Other people who have taken their lives also may serve as models for suicidal behaviour, although this is not always the case (Gibson & Range, 1991). *Psychodynamically oriented psychologists* suggest that the suicidal person is turning hostility and anger inward. Freud might argue that the act of suicide is the ultimate release of the aggressive instinct. *Cognitive psychologists* assert that suicide is the failure of a person's problem-solving abilities in response to stress or, alternatively, that the person's cognitive assessment is that the future is hopeless. *Humanistic psychologists* see suicide as a waste of a human being's potential, and they attempt to help suicidal and depressed patients focus on the meaning in their lives so that they can fulfil rather than destroy themselves. Many theorists, regardless of orientation, focus on a person's attempt to avoid self-awareness (Baumeister, 1990).

Suicide in Canada's Aboriginal Communities

I f you're a member of an ethnic or other minority group, research suggests that you are more likely than non-minority individuals to suffer from an anxiety disorder and to be at risk for suicide (Paradis, Hatch, & Friedman, 1994). Canada's aboriginal people have a rate of suicide higher than that of other segments of our population.

The estimated suicide rate among registered Indians may be approximately two and a half times as large as that in the general population, although this rate varies dramatically from community to community (Mao et al., 1992). There are indications that this dramatically higher suicide rate is true of aboriginals who dwell in reserves, and that the rates for aboriginals living outside of reserves are comparable to those for the general population (Cooper et al., 1992). In remote northern communities the suicide rate has been found to be as high as seven times that found in the general population (Ross & Davis, 1986).

What sorts of factors might begin to account for these higher rates of suicide among Canada's aboriginal populations? Alcohol abuse is one factor (Kettl & Bixler, 1993), but so is a general lack of social control in the light of radical economic change, resettlement, isolation, and breakdown of immediate and extended families (Charles, 1991). High levels of anomie (being cut off from normal ways of living) characterize many of these communities (Berlin, 1985). Young aboriginals, who are more likely to have had a chaotic family background, have felt pressure both to belong to their traditional culture and to achieve in North American culture, without receiving adequate support in either direction. Clearly, solutions to this problem will not be solely psychological, but also will require economic and societal intervention. The fact that there are aboriginal communities in which the suicide rate is indistinguishable from the national average ought to suggest that community-based solutions are possible. These types of solutions, in fact, are being examined in more detail. All of these factors are part of the multicultural research problems that psychologists are only now beginning to recognize. ■

Adolescent suicide has received a great deal of attention because it is surprisingly prevalent. The suicide rate among teenage males is six times higher than that among teenage females (O'Donnell, 1995). Adolescents who attempt suicide often see a wide discrepancy between their high personal ambitions and seemingly meagre results. The causes of adolescent suicide are complex and still not fully understood, but the increasing pressures and stress encountered by adolescents in Canada today certainly contribute to the rising number of suicides. Adolescents face an extremely competitive workforce, alternating pressures to conform and to be an individual, and a social situation teeming with violence, crime, and drugs. Often, angry and frustrated adolescents exhibit other self-destructive behaviours, such as drug use, in addition to feelings of hopelessness and low self-esteem (Kashani, Reid, & Rosenberg, 1989). Prevention efforts must focus on counselling, education, and reduction of the risk factors that lead to suicide.

Prevention. Most individuals who attempt suicide really want to live. However, their stress and their sense of helplessness about the future tell them that death is the only way out. This is even more true of adults than of adolescents (Cole, 1989). Some people are helped by crisis intervention and by counsellors they

Table 15.5 Myths and Facts about Suicide

Myth	Fact
1. Suicide happens without warning.	1. Suicidal individuals give many clues; 80% have to some degree discussed with others their intent to commit suicide.
2. Once people become suicidal, they remain so.	2. Suicidal persons remain so for limited periods—thus there is value in restraint.
3. Suicide occurs almost exclusively among affluent or very poor individuals.	3. Suicide tends to occur in the same proportion at all economic levels of society.
4. Virtually all suicidal individuals are mentally ill.	4. This is not so, although most are depressed to some degree.
5. Suicidal tendencies are inherited or run in families.	5. There is no evidence for a direct genetic factor.
6. Suicide does not occur in primitive cultures.	6. Suicide occurs in almost all societies and cultures.
7. In Japan, ritual suicide is common.	7. In modern Japan, ritual suicide is rare; the most common method is barbiturate overdose.
8. Writers and artists have the highest suicide rates because they are "a bit crazy to begin with."	8. Physicians and police officers have the highest suicide rates; they have access to the most lethal means, and their work involves a high level of frustration.
9. Once a person starts to come out of a depression, the risk of suicide dissipates.	9. The risk of suicide is highest in the initial phase of an upswing from the depth of depression.
10. People who attempt suicide fully intend to die.	10. People who attempt suicide have diverse motives.

Source: Meyer & Salmon, 1988.

can talk to. But a primary goal should be to help eliminate conditions that lead to and foster suicide, including availability of guns, alcoholism, drug abuse, and emotional isolation (Maris & Silverman, 1995).

When a person makes a suicide threat, take it seriously. Most people who commit suicide leave clues to their intentions ahead of time. Statements such as "I don't want to go on" or "I'm a burden to everyone, so maybe I should end it all" should be taken as warning signs. When people begin to give their possessions away or write letters with ominous overtones to relatives and friends, these are signs, too. If you know someone you think may be contemplating suicide, here are some steps you can take (Curran, 1987):

- Talk about stressors with the person who is at risk. The more the suicidal individual talks, the better. Don't be afraid to talk about suicide; it will not influence your friend or relative to commit suicide.

- Help the person who is contemplating suicide to seek out a psychologist, psychiatrist, counsellor, or parent. A person thinking of suicide needs counselling.

- Do not keep a contemplated suicide a secret. Resist the person's attempts to force you to

Focus

Review

- Identify the key characteristics of a bipolar disorder. p. 541
- What are the essential characteristics of major depression? pp. 542–543
- Describe how learned helplessness can lead to depression. pp. 546–547

Think Critically

- What are the implications of the finding that many people who experience manic episodes also suffer from personality disorders?
- How might Szasz (who claimed that mental illness is just a label) explain the behaviour of a person showing depressive symptoms?
- If you have known someone who has committed suicide, do the psychological theories discussed in this section make sense with respect to that person? Why or why not?

remain quiet about such confidences. Tell the person's spouse, parent, guardian, or counsellor. Unless you are certain that these people already know, you should tell someone responsible for your friend's or relative's welfare.

Bipolar and depressive disorders leave people unable to cope effectively on a day-to-day basis. An even more disabling disorder is schizophrenia, which we examine next.

Schizophrenia

Schizophrenia is considered to be the most devastating, complex, puzzling, and frustrating of all mental disorders; people with this disorder lose touch with reality and are often unable to function in a world that makes no sense to them. The word *schizophrenia* means "split-mind" and the split refers to a severing of the emotional and intellectual aspects of the person's personality and fragmentation of thought processes. When Eugen Bleuler coined the term *schizophrenia* in 1911, he argued that its main symptom was seriously disorganized thinking, perceptions, emotions, and actions. (A caution: Schizophrenia is not split personality. People sometimes confuse the notion of a "split mind" with dissociative identity disorder, which is characterized by the existence within one person of two or more distinct personalities; that disorder was covered earlier in this chapter, on p. 537.)

A person with schizophrenia is said to have a schizophrenic disorder; this is because schizophrenia really represents a range of disorders. There is no single symptom or group of symptoms that characterizes all people who are suffering with schizophrenia. **Schizophrenic disorders** are a group of disorders characterized by a loss of contact with reality and by deterioration of social and intellectual functioning. Age of onset for men generally occurs between 18 and 25, and for women occurs between 26 and 45. The reason for this sex difference is not known (Gottesman, 1991; Straube & Oades, 1992). People diagnosed as having a schizophrenic disorder often show serious personality disintegration. They may be considered **psychotic**—suffering from a loss of contact with reality that is wide-ranging and interferes with their ability to meet the ordinary demands of life.

Schizophrenia begins slowly, with more symptoms developing as time passes. It affects 1 in 100 people in Canada (Bland et al., 1988) and accounts for almost 25 percent of all mental hospital admissions each year. The diagnosis occurs more frequently among lower socioeconomic groups, non-whites, and younger people (Lindsey & Paul, 1989).

Essential Characteristics of Schizophrenic Disorders

People with schizophrenic disorders display sudden significant changes in thought, perception, mood, and overall behaviour. How they think about themselves, social situations, and other people—social cognition—becomes seriously distorted (Penn et al., 1997). Those changes often are accompanied by distortions of reality and an inability to respond appropriately in thought, perception, or emotion. Some symptoms are *positive symptoms*, exhibited by their presence—for example, delusions or hallucinations. Some symptoms are *negative symptoms*, exhibited by their absence—for example, an inability to experience pleasure. Not all of the symptoms of the disorder are present in any given patient, although most patients display a number of these symptoms.

Thought Disorders. One of the first signs of schizophrenia is difficulty maintaining logical thought and coherent conversation. People with schizophrenia

Schizophrenic disorders [SKIT-soh-FREN-ick]: A group of disorders characterized by a loss of contact with reality and by deterioration of social and intellectual functioning.

Psychotic [sye-KOT-ick]: Suffering from a loss of contact with reality that is wide-ranging and interferes with their ability to meet the ordinary demands of life.

disorders show disordered thinking and impaired memory (Sengel & Lovallo, 1983). They also may suffer from *delusions* (false beliefs). Many have delusions of persecution and believe that the world is a hostile place. These delusions often are accompanied by delusions of grandeur, in which the patient erroneously believes that he or she is a particularly important person. This importance becomes the reason for the persecution. Sometimes patients take on the role of an important character in history—for example, Jesus Christ or the Queen of England—and imagine that people are conspiring to harm them. Delusional thought is often apparent in schizophrenics' speech, in which sentence structure, words, and ideas become fragmented, jumbled, and disordered, creating a "word salad" of thoughts. Thus, a patient might be heard to say, "Your Highness, may I more of some engine to my future food, for His Lowness." Memory is seriously disturbed, especially working memory (Schooler et al., 1997). Remember that working memory holds information for a brief period so that further processing can take place and allow people to respond as a task demands. It is not surprising that when a system that is so important to thought and language fails, both thought and speech patterns become disorganized and often incoherent.

Perceptual Disorders. Another sign of schizophrenic disorders is the presence of **hallucinations**—compelling perceptual (visual, tactile, olfactory, or auditory) experiences without a real physical stimulus. Auditory hallucinations are the most common. The patient reports hearing voices originating outside of his or her head—these voices typically abuse, threaten, make accusations against, or humiliate the patient. The voices may comment on the patient's behaviour or direct the patient to behave in certain ways (Bentall, 1990). For example, convicted serial killer David Berkowitz (known to most people as Son of Sam) claimed that his neighbour's dog told him to kill, though it is not clear whether he was actually schizophrenic or just convincingly portraying the symptoms. Hallucinations have a biological basis and are caused by abnormal brain responses (Asaad & Shapiro, 1986).

Emotional Disorders. One of the most striking characteristics of schizophrenia is the display of inappropriate **affect**—emotional responses. A patient with schizophrenia may become depressed and cry when told her favourite relative is coming to visit, yet laugh hysterically at the death of a close friend or relative. Some patients display no emotion (either appropriate or inappropriate) and seem incapable of experiencing a normal range of feeling. Their affect is constricted, or *flat*; they express no variation in mood. They show blank, expressionless faces, even when presented with a deliberately provocative remark or situation. Other patients exhibit *ambivalent* affect. They go through a wide range of emotional behaviours in a brief period, seeming happy one moment and dejected the next.

Types of Schizophrenia

The term *schizophrenia* is a catchall for patients displaying many symptoms; however, there are actually five types of schizophrenia—disorganized, paranoid, catatonic, residual, and undifferentiated—each with different symptoms, diagnostic criteria, and causes (see Table 15.6). Regardless of the type, a diagnosis of schizophrenia requires the presence of the following features:

- Loss of contact with reality
- Involvement of more than one area of psychological functioning
- Deterioration in social and intellectual functioning
- Onset of illness generally before age 45
- Duration of illness of at least six months

Disorganized Type. The **disorganized type of schizophrenia** is characterized by severely disturbed thought processes, frequent incoherence, delusions, and

Hallucinations [ha-LOOSE-in-AY-shuns]: Compelling perceptual (visual, tactile, olfactory, or auditory) experiences without a real physical stimulus.

Affect: A person's emotional responses.

Disorganized type of schizophrenia: A major type of schizophrenia, characterized by severely disturbed thought processes, frequent incoherence, delusions, and inappropriate affect.

Table 15.6 Types and Symptoms of Schizophrenia

Type	Symptoms
Disorganized	Frequent incoherence; disorganized behaviour; blunted, inappropriate, or silly affect
Paranoid	Delusions and hallucinations of persecution or grandeur (or both) and sometimes irrational jealousy
Catatonic	Stupor in which there is a negative attitude and marked decrease in re-activity to the environment, or an excited phase in which there is agitated motor activity not influenced by external stimuli and which may appear or disappear suddenly
Residual	History of at least one previous episode of schizophrenia with prominent psychotic symptoms but at present a clinical picture without any prominent psychotic symptoms; continuing evidence of the illness, such as inappropriate affect, illogical thinking, social withdrawal, or eccentric behaviour
Undifferentiated	Prominent delusions, hallucinations, incoherence, or grossly disorganized behaviour, which do not meet the criteria for any other types or which meet the criteria for more than one type

inappropriate affect. Patients may exhibit bizarre emotions, with periods of giggling, crying, or irritability for no apparent reason. Their behaviour can be silly, inappropriate, or even obscene. They show a severe disintegration of normal personality, a loss of contact with reality, and often poor personal hygiene. Their chances for recovery are poor. Ted Kaczynski, the American Unabomber, refused to allow prosecution psychiatrists to examine him, although he exhibited a mental deterioration that convinced many that his crimes were the product of schizophrenia.

Paranoid Type. The paranoid type of schizophrenia is one of the most difficult to identify and study, because those suffering from it generally are able to manage their lives reasonably well. The **paranoid type of schizophrenia** is characterized by hallucinations and delusions of persecution or grandeur (or both), and sometimes irrational jealousy. Paranoid schizophrenics may actively seek out other people and not show extreme withdrawal from social interaction. Their degree of disturbance varies over time. (The paranoid type of schizophrenia is different from the paranoid personality disorder.)

Paranoid schizophrenics may be alert, intelligent, and responsive. However, their delusions and hallucinations impair their ability to deal with reality, and their behaviour is often unpredictable and sometimes hostile. They may see bizarre images and are likely to have auditory hallucinations. They may think they are being chased by ghosts or by intruders from another planet. They may believe certain events in the world have a particular significance to them. If, for example, a newscaster wears a blue shirt, a paranoid schizophrenic patient may believe that the newscaster is doing so to signal that the patient is responsible for all of the bad news they report that day. Compared to patients with other types of schizophrenia, patients with the paranoid type of schizophrenia develop symptoms at a later age and have a better chance of recovery (Fenton & McGlashen, 1991).

Paranoid type of schizophrenia [PAIR-uh-noid]: A major type of schizophrenia, characterized by hallucinations and delusions of persecution or grandeur (or both), and sometimes irrational jealousy.

Catatonic Type. The **catatonic type of schizophrenia** is characterized by displays of excited or violent motor activity or by stupor. That is, there are actually two subtypes of the catatonic type of schizophrenia—excited and withdrawn—both of which involve extreme overt behaviour. *Excited* catatonic patients show excessive activity. They may talk and shout continuously and engage in seemingly uninhibited, agitated, and aggressive motor activity. These episodes usually appear and disappear suddenly and without obvious cause. *Withdrawn* catatonic patients tend to appear stuporous—mute, negative, and basically unresponsive. Although they occasionally exhibit some signs of the excited type, they usually show a high degree of muscular rigidity. They are not immobile but have a decreased level of speaking, moving, and responding, although they usually are aware of events around them. Withdrawn catatonic patients may use immobility and unresponsiveness to maintain control over their environment; their behaviour relieves them of the responsibility of responding to external stimuli.

Residual and Undifferentiated Types. People who show symptoms attributable to schizophrenia but who remain in touch with reality are said to have the **residual type of schizophrenia**. Such patients show inappropriate affect, illogical thinking, or eccentric behaviour. They have a history of at least one previous schizophrenic episode. It is fairly common for patients to switch back and forth between types of schizophrenia (Kandler, Gruenberg, & Tsuang, 1985).

Sometimes it is difficult to determine which category a patient most appropriately fits into (Gift et al., 1980). Some patients exhibit all of the primary features of schizophrenia—prominent delusions, hallucinations, incoherence, and grossly disorganized behaviour—but do not fit neatly into the categories of disorganized, catatonic, paranoid, or residual. Individuals with these characteristics are said to have the **undifferentiated type of schizophrenia**.

Causes of Schizophrenia

What causes people to lose their grasp on reality with such devastating results? Are people born with schizophrenia, or do they develop it as a result of painful childhood experiences? Researchers of schizophrenia take markedly different positions about its origins. Biologically oriented psychologists focus on chemicals in the brain and a person's genetic heritage; their basic argument is that schizophrenia is a brain disorder. Learning theorists argue that a person's environment and early experiences cause schizophrenia. The arguments for each approach are compelling, but most theorists adopt a *diathesis–stress model* asserting that people with an underlying genetic predisposition or vulnerability develop the disorder when they are beset with a stressful life situation. Let's look at the data.

Biological Causes. Substantial evidence exists to suggest the presence of some kind of biological determinant of, or predisposition to, schizophrenia. People born with that predisposition have a greater probability of developing schizophrenia than do other people. In early or middle fetal development, brain connections may go awry and result in later cerebral malfunctioning (Waddington, 1993). This may be because key RNA molecules may be missing when the major neurotransmitters, such as GABA (discussed in Chapter 2), are forming (Akbarian et al., 1995). Using this evidence, researchers assert that schizophrenia is caused by brain chemistry and perhaps by an impaired autonomic nervous system response (Hollister et al., 1994).

About 1 percent of the Canadian population is schizophrenic; when one parent has schizophrenia, however, the probability that an offspring also will develop the disorder increases to between 3 and 14 percent. If both parents have schizophrenia, their children have about a 35 percent probability of developing it. (Figure 15.2 shows the likelihood of the relatives of schizophrenics developing the disorder.) It is now generally accepted that schizophrenia runs in families; the children and siblings of schizophrenic patients are more likely to exhibit maladjustment and schizophrenic symptoms than are other people (Kety et al., 1994). Researchers have been looking for a gene that might carry specific traits associated with schizophrenia, although such efforts have had only limited success (Markow, 1992).

Researchers are aware that the family environment of children of schizophrenics is unusual. Therefore, they acknowledge that the genetic evidence is only suggestive and that environment also likely plays a role in the development of the disorder. If schizophrenia were totally genetic, the likelihood that identical (monozygotic) twins, who have identical genes, would both show the disorder if one did would be 100 percent. (This likelihood of shared traits is referred to as the **concordance rate**.) But studies of schizophrenia in identical twins show concordance rates that range from 15 to 86 percent (DiLalla & Gottesman, 1995; Torrey et al., 1994), suggesting that other factors are involved. In one important study, analysis of brain structures showed subtle but important brain abnormalities in a schizophrenic individual whose non-schizophrenic identical twin did not show the brain abnormality. Such studies assert that non-genetic factors must exert an important influence on schizophrenia and are critical in its development (DiLalla & Gottesman, 1995). Nevertheless, most researchers agree that genetics is a fundamental factor in the disorder. The concordance rate for schizophrenia in identical twins is almost five times that in fraternal twins. Moreover, identical twins reared apart from their biological parents and from each other show a higher concordance rate than do fraternal twins or controls (Stone, 1980).

Support for a biological basis for schizophrenia comes from other sources as well, notably studies of biochemical processes and drugs. Like many discoveries in science, the discovery of the first antipsychotic drug—chlorpromazine—happened by accident in the 1950s. First used as an antihistamine, the drug was found to have calming effects on patients, including agitated schizophrenic patients. This drug was followed by others, such as reserpine, leading to further breakthroughs in drug treatment for schizophrenia, all of which contributed to a better understanding of the biochemistry of the disorder.

Researchers today readily acknowledge that neurotransmitters and their actions contribute to the development of schizophrenia; this understanding initially led to the *dopamine theory of schizophrenia*. The dopamine theory of schizophrenia asserts that too much dopamine or too much activity at dopamine receptors causes schizophrenia by overstimulating the brain, and that using antipsychotic drugs, which decreases dopamine levels of activity, can avert schizophrenic symptoms. Dopamine pathways are considered one of the main sites of biochemical disturbances in the brain (Fang, 1996; Masotto & Racagni, 1995). A class of drugs, the *phenothiazines*, appears to block receptor sites in the dopamine pathways. When patients with schizophrenia are given phenothiazines, many of their disturbed thought processes and hallucinations disappear. Conversely, drugs that stimulate the dopamine system and increase brain dopamine levels (such as amphetamines) aggravate existing schizophrenic disorders. It turns out that there are subtypes of dopamine receptors, and that a number of medications collectively called *neuroleptics* inhibit schizophrenic symptoms, especially positive symptoms (O'Connor, 1998). A revision of the dopamine hypothesis to a *dopamine-seratonin interaction hypothesis* has been proposed (Kapur & Remington, 1996; Megens & Kennis, 1996). This newer theory is based on patients' responses to some of the newer drugs—the atypical antipsychotics—that block receptors to both dopamine and seratonin.

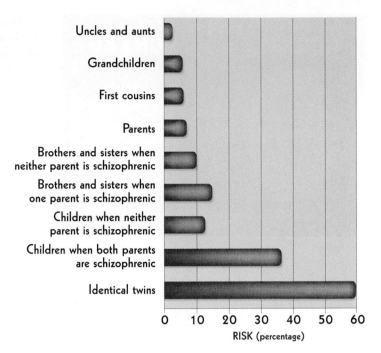

FIGURE 15.2
The Risk That Various Relatives of a Schizophrenic Person Will Develop Schizophrenia
The more closely two individuals are related, the greater the likelihood that if one develops schizophrenia, the other will, too.

Concordance rate: The degree to which a condition or trait is shared by two or more individuals or groups.

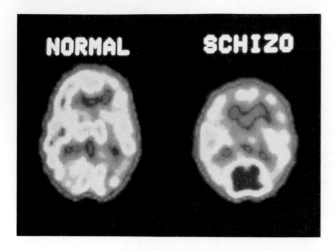

Biochemistry is not the whole story—if it were, we could cure or control symptoms for all patients with schizophrenia. Certain portions of the brains of schizophrenic patients and their relatives exhibit abnormalities, although it is not yet clear whether schizophrenia causes the abnormalities or the abnormalities cause schizophrenia (Cannon & Marco, 1994). For example, the *brain ventricles* (hollow areas normally filled with fluid) are enlarged in some schizophrenic patients, leaving less space for neurons (Raz & Raz, 1990; Suddath et al., 1990). Furthermore, some structures, notably the frontal lobes, show reduced blood flow and functioning in schizophrenics (Resnick, 1992). As well, schizophrenic patients demonstrate altered levels of the number of binding sites for serotonin in the prefrontal cortex (Burnet, Eastwood, & Harrison, 1996; Kahn, Davidson, & Davis, 1996). When Buchsbaum and Hazlett (1997) examined the literature on brain-imaging studies in schizophrenic patients compared with normal individuals, they found that the brains of schizophrenic patients showed anatomical structures that looked like the brains of older normal participants. Therefore, they suggest that in some patients schizophrenia may mimic a rapid aging process that prematurely affects the brain.

In sum, researchers now assert that genetic and biochemical factors and brain abnormalities all predict a specific risk for schizophrenia. While many stress factors (which are the focus of environmental researchers) may contribute to schizophrenia, a genetic component seems to be the most important factor.

Environmental Factors. Some psychologists believe that in addition to critical genetic factors, environmental interactions also may determine the onset and ultimate development of schizophrenia (see Figure 15.3), although there is no evidence that environmental factors alone *cause* schizophrenia.

Other more behavioural explanations of schizophrenia are based on traditional learning principles (explored in Chapter 5). The behavioural approach argues that faulty reinforcement and extinction procedures, as well as social learning processes, can account for schizophrenia. Imagine a child brought up in a family where the parents constantly argue, where the father is an alcoholic, and where neither parent shows much affection for the other or for anyone else. Such a child, receiving no reinforcement for interest in events, people, and objects in the outside world, may become withdrawn and begin to exhibit schizophrenic behaviour. Lidz (1973) argues that children who grow up in such homes adopt the family's faulty view of the world and of relationships and thus are likely to expect reinforcement for abnormal behaviours. Growing up in such an emotionally fragmented environment may predispose individuals to emotional disorder and eventual schizophrenia (Miklowitz, 1994; Walker et al., 1983).

Even in families in which marital conflict is absent, parents sometimes confuse their children or have difficulty communicating effectively. Once a person has developed schizophrenia, researchers

FIGURE 15.3
The Vulnerability–Stress View of Schizophrenia
According to the vulnerability–stress view of schizophrenia, the environment triggers behaviours in people who are predisposed to schizophrenia.

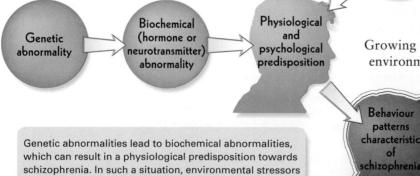

Genetic abnormalities lead to biochemical abnormalities, which can result in a physiological predisposition towards schizophrenia. In such a situation, environmental stressors can trigger the behaviour patterns of schizophrenia.

have found that families often affect the developmental course and severity of the illness experienced by the patient. When a family has an interaction style characterized by hostility, criticism, emotional overinvolvment, and a lack of boundaries (overintrusiveness), psychologists say that that their level of *expressed emotions* is high. When patients return to families with high levels of expressed emotion, their relapse rate is higher than it is in families with low levels of expressed emotion. In addition, parents can, for example, place their children in a situation that offers inconsistent messages, a **double bind**. Initially described by Bateson as an explanation for the causes of schizophrenia (Bateson et al., 1956), double bind situations usually occur between individuals with an intense emotional attachment, such as a child and a parent (Mishler & Waxler, 1968). The parents express the need for strong affectionate relationships, but when the child makes an overture they are rejected. Indeed, research shows that schizophrenic patients are less accurate than control participants in the reception of emotional communication (Fagan & Silverthorn, 1998). Ineffective communication of this kind, if played out consistently, may shape an environment of confusion conducive to the development and maintenance of schizophrenia. What Bateson saw as a cause of schizophrenia may be more a pattern of a lack of communication skills, especially during stressful periods (Docherty, Hall, & Gorinier, 1998).

According to learning theory, a person who receives a great deal of attention for behaviours that other people see as bizarre is likely to continue those behaviours. People who fail to develop effective social skills are more at risk for bizarre behaviours (Mueser et al., 1990). Other reinforcement theories suggest that bizarre behaviour and thoughts are themselves reinforcing, because they allow the person to escape from both acute anxiety and an overactive autonomic nervous system.

Nature and Nurture. Many variables determine whether an individual will develop schizophrenia. Some people, because of family environment, genetic history, or brain chemistry, are more vulnerable than others. As we have already seen when examining mood disorders, *vulnerability* is a person's diminished ability to deal with demanding life events. The more vulnerable the individual is, the less necessary are environmental stress or other disorders (such as anxiety) to the initiation of a schizophrenic episode. *The Research Process* on page 558 examines the question of who is most vulnerable for schizophrenia.

To summarize, although the exact causes of schizophrenia are still unknown, research suggests the following:

- The production and activity of specific types of chemical substances in the brain are associated with schizophrenia.

- A connection exists between genetics and schizophrenia, although genetic factors alone cannot account for its development.

- Environmental factors (such as the presence of marital conflict and double binds) may contribute to the development of schizophrenia. Among these factors, early childhood relationships may be especially important.

- The most likely cause of schizophrenia is a biological predisposition in the individual, which may be aggravated by a climate of emotional immaturity, lack of effective communication, and emotional instability. There is, however, no evidence to suggest that poor family relations cause the illness.

Double bind: A situation in which an individual is given two different and inconsistent messages.

Focus

Review

- Identify the essential characteristics of the five major types of schizophrenia. pp. 551–552
- How are concordance rates used in research on the causes of schizophrenia? p. 555

Think Critically

- How likely would it be for a homeless person to be diagnosed as schizophrenic? Explain.
- Why do researchers place more emphasis on longitudinal research than on cross-sectional research in studying schizophrenia?

Vulnerability, High-risk Studies, and Schizophrenia

C an schizophrenia be prevented? Do some people have a vulnerability to schizophrenia that is triggered by stressful situations? According to the vulnerability–stress hypothesis, a person's susceptibility to schizophrenia depends on genetic factors, birth factors, and stress during infancy, childhood, and adolescence. The Genain quadruplets—three of whom were diagnosed as

schizophrenic—provide a classic example of the genetic link. The vulnerability-stress approach assumes that when stressors appear, schizophrenia and its symptoms may appear; the more stressors there are, the more likely it is that schizophrenia will surface. Some people can tolerate a great deal of stress; others can tolerate very little before schizophrenia materializes.

Psychologists have conducted longitudinal studies of schizophrenia, following children of schizophrenic mothers and fathers from birth to adulthood. These studies, known as *high-risk studies* because the participants are assumed to be at higher risk than the general population, have produced important results. The high-risk approach is effective because:

■ Participants can be studied before the disorder develops.

■ The data are relatively unbiased, because it is not known whether the child will become schizophrenic.

■ Data can be gathered from the individuals and their families (not from doctors or hospital records) and therefore are not influenced by patients' likelihood of seeking particular medical assistance.

Many high-risk studies underway throughout the world, including some that started in the 1960s, are now assessing the likelihood of schizophrenia in mature adults. The Copenhagen High-Risk Project is one such study. Since 1962, Mednick, Parnas, and Schulsinger (1987) and Cannon, Mednick, and Parnas (1990) have followed a sample of people who were at high risk for schizophrenia, as well as a group of control individuals who were not considered at risk for schizophrenia. This study focused on mothers and their children. The mothers of the high-risk children were schizophrenic, while the mothers of the children in the control group were not schizophrenic. The schizophrenic and control mothers were matched for age, social class, education, and urban–rural differences. Psychological tests were given at periodic intervals. The results showed that if a child's mother was schizophrenic, the child was at least eight times more likely than usual to develop schizophrenia. Moreover, if the birth experience was traumatic, there was increased

likelihood of schizophrenia. The results also showed that poor maternal supervision was related to the development of schizophrenia.

Other high-risk projects report similar results. The University of Rochester Child and Family Study, which began in 1972, shows that when parents are maladjusted, their children often need psychological care (Wynne, Cole, & Perkins, 1987). The Stony Brook High-Risk Project has reported that considerable family discord, poor parenting skills, and marital conflict are related to psychological problems in children. The relationship between these variables and psychological problems is magnified when there is a schizophrenic parent (Weintraub, 1987). An Israeli high-risk study that did a 25-year follow-up found similar results (Ingraham et al., 1995).

There is no doubt that children of schizophrenic parents are at greater risk for developing schizophrenia. However, researchers are most interested in the high-risk children who never develop the disorder. What makes them different? Researchers believe that family relationships are an important dimension. If children of schizophrenic parents live in a household filled with discord, fighting, alcoholism, and poor discipline, they are much more likely to develop the disorder. Burman and colleagues (1987, p. 364) conclude: "Stressful environments will tend to produce schizophrenia in genetically predisposed individuals."

The vulnerability–stress hypothesis may prove to be the most accurate predictor of schizophrenia. It appears that in some people who are more vulnerable than others, stressors may spark the psychiatric disorder. ■

Summary and Review

What Is Abnormal Behaviour?

Provide a definition of abnormal behaviour and explain the major perspectives on abnormality.

■ *Abnormal behaviour* is atypical, socially unacceptable, distressing, maladaptive, and/or the result of distorted cognitions. p. 524

■ The medical–biological model focuses on the biological and physiological conditions that initiate abnormal behaviours. The psychodynamic model focuses on unresolved conflicts and forces of which a person may be unaware. The humanistic model assumes that people can control their own lives; it focuses on individual uniqueness and decision making. The behavioural model states that abnormal behaviour is caused by faulty or ineffective learning and conditioning patterns. The cognitive model looks at people's ideas and thoughts. The sociocultural model examines abnormalities within the context of culture, the family, the community, and society. The legal model defines abnormal behaviour strictly in terms of guilt, innocence, and sanity. The interactionist model draws on all of these perspectives. pp. 525–528

What are the goals of the *DSM*, and what are its potential advantages and disadvantages?

■ The *DSM–IV* is the latest edition of the diagnostic manual that mental health practitioners use to diagnose and classify mental disorders. It describes behaviour in terms of its characteristics and its *prevalence*. The manual uses what is called a multiaxial system in order to be as informative, precise, reliable, and valid as possible about an individual's condition. Its goals are to improve the reliability of diagnoses and to make sure that diagnoses are consistent with research evidence and practical experience. Some psychologists applaud the *DSM* for its recognition of social and environmental influences on behaviour; others take issue with the way it places disorders together based on symptoms rather than causes. Still others argue that it is too precise and complicated, and that it has a bias against women. pp. 528–530

What are the essential characteristics of chronic fatigue syndrome (CFS)?

■ The most significant symptom of CFS is debilitating fatigue, but other symptoms also appear, including sore throat, muscle pain, and sleep problems. These symptoms sometimes lead to aggravated interpersonal difficulties, substance abuse, unnecessary avoidance of people and activities, extreme helplessness, and/or difficulty tolerating any dependency, panic, displacement of anger self-blame and guilt, and hopelessness or despair. p. 531

KEY TERMS
abnormal behaviour, p. 524; model, p. 525; abnormal psychology, p. 525; prevalence, p. 528

Anxiety, Somatoform, and Dissociative Disorders

What are the chief characteristics of anxiety, somatoform, and dissociative disorders?

■ *Anxiety* is a generalized feeling of fear and apprehension, often accompanied by increased physiological arousal, and may or may not be related to a specific event or object. p. 532

■ A *generalized anxiety disorder* is characterized by persistent anxiety of at least a month's duration. It can include autonomic hyperactivity, impairments in motor tension, and vigilance. Irrational fear and avoidance of certain objects or situations characterize a *phobic disorder*; people are not truly phobic unless they avoid situations that make them fearful. pp. 532–533

■ Individuals with *obsessive–compulsive disorders* have persistent and uncontrollable thoughts and irrational beliefs, which cause them to perform compulsive rituals that interfere with normal daily functioning. The focus of these behaviours is often on maintaining order and control. pp. 534–535

■ People with *somatoform disorders* have real physical symptoms with no apparent physical cause. *Somatization disorders* are somatoform disorders characterized by recurrent and multiple complaints of several years' duration for which medical attention has not been effective. *Conversion disorders* are somatoform disorders characterized by the loss or alteration of physical functioning for no apparent physiological reason. *Hypochondriasis* is a somatoform disorder characterized by an extreme preoccupation with health and illness, anxiety about disease, and imagined afflictions. pp. 536–537

■ *Dissociative disorders* are disorders characterized by a sudden but temporary alteration in consciousness, identity, sensory/motor behaviour, or memory. These disorders, though quite noticeable, are relatively rare. p. 537

KEY TERMS
anxiety, p. 532; generalized anxiety disorder, p. 532; free-floating anxiety, p. 532; phobic disorders, p. 533; agoraphobia, p. 533; social phobia, p. 534; specific phobia, p. 534; obsessive–compulsive disorder, p. 534; somatoform disorders, p. 536; somatization disorder, p. 536; conversion disorder, p. 536; hypochondriasis, p. 536; dissociative disorders, p. 537; dissociative amnesia, p. 537; dissociative identity disorder, p. 537

Personality Disorders

What are the chief characteristics of five key personality disorders?

■ People who have unwarranted feelings of persecution and who mistrust almost everyone are said to be suffering from the type of *personality disorder* called paranoid personality disorder. Submissive and clinging behaviours are characteristic of people with a dependent personality disorder. Dramatic, emotional, and erratic behaviours are characteristic of the histrionic personality disorder. The narcissistic personality disorder is characterized by an extremely exaggerated sense of self-importance, an expectation of special favours, and a constant need for attention; people with the disorder show a lack of caring for others and react to criticism with rage, shame, or humiliation. The *antisocial personality disorder* is characterized by behaviour that is irresponsible and destructive and violates the rights of others; persons with antisocial personality disorder have no fear of punishment and are egocentric. pp. 538–539

KEY TERMS
personality disorders, p. 538; antisocial personality disorder, p. 539; child abuse, p. 540

Mood Disorders

What are the major mood disorders and their essential characteristics?

■ *Bipolar disorders* get their name from the fact that patients' behaviour vacillates between two extremes: mania and depression. p. 541

■ Patients diagnosed with *major depressive disorder* have a gloomy outlook on life, particularly slow thought processes, loss of appetite, an exaggerated view of current problems, loss of energy, and a tendency to blame themselves. p. 542

■ The monoamine theory of depression suggests that major depression results from deficient monoamines or inefficient monoamine receptors. This theory is based on the finding that three classes of drugs block reuptake of monoamines, each in a different way, and keep people from being depressed. Learning theories argue that reinforcement patterns and social interactions determine the course and nature of depression. pp. 544–546

■ *Vulnerability* is a person's diminished ability to deal with demanding life events. The more vulnerable the individual is, the less necessary are environmental stress or other disorders (such as anxiety) to the initiation of a mood disorder. p. 547

Who attempts suicide?

■ Most people who think about suicide do not actually commit the act. Attempters try to commit suicide but are unsuccessful; completers succeed in taking their lives. More than three times as many men as women actually succeed in ending their lives, although four times as many women as men attempt to do so; each year 1 in 1000 adolescents attempt suicide. pp. 547–549

KEY TERMS
bipolar disorder, p. 541; depressive disorders, p. 542; major depressive disorder, p. 542; delusions, p. 543; learned helplessness, p. 546; vulnerability, p. 547

Schizophrenia

Identify the essential characteristics of the five major types of schizophrenia.

■ Schizophrenia is a group of disorders characterized by a loss of contact with reality and by deterioration of social and intellectual functioning. Individuals with *schizophrenic disorders* often show serious personality disintegration, with significant changes in thought, mood, perception, and behaviour. Some symptoms are *positive symptoms*—they exhibit themselves by their presence; some symptoms are *negative symptoms*—they exhibit themselves by their absence, for example, an inability to experience pleasure. p. 551

■ Severely disturbed thought processes characterize the *disorganized type of schizophrenia*. Patients have *hallucinations* and delusions and are frequently incoherent. The *paranoid type of schizophrenia* is among the most difficult to identify and study, because outward behaviour often seems appropriate to the situation. Patients actively may seek out other people and may not show extreme withdrawal from social interaction. There are actually two subtypes of the *catatonic type of schizophrenia*—excited and withdrawn. People who show symptoms attributable to schizophrenia but

who remain in touch with reality are diagnosed as having the *residual type of schizophrenia*. Some patients exhibit all of the essential features of schizophrenia but do not fall clearly into any one of the other categories—these individuals are classified as suffering from the *undifferentiated type of schizophrenia*. pp. 552–554

How are concordance rates used in research on the causes of schizophrenia?

■ The *concordance rate* is the degree to which a condition or trait is shared by two or more individuals or groups. Concordance rates between siblings are often examined, especially those for twins, who share a genetic heritage. Biological studies suggest that the cause of schizophrenia must be to some extent genetic, as is shown by much higher concordance rates for identical twins than for fraternal twins. p. 555

What is the dominant theory of the neurochemistry of schizophrenia?

■ The *dopamine theory of schizophrenia* asserts that too much dopamine or too much activity at dopamine receptors causes schizophrenia, and that using antipsychotic drugs, which decrease dopamine levels of activity, can avert schizophrenic symptoms. p. 555

■ Several variables determine whether an individual will develop schizophrenia. Some people, because of family environment, genetic history, or brain chemistry, are more vulnerable than others. The more vulnerable the individual is, the less necessary are environmental stress or other disorders to the initiation of a schizophrenic episode. p, 557

KEY TERMS
schizophrenic disorders, p. 551; psychotic, p. 551; hallucinations, p. 552; affect, p. 552; disorganized type of schizophrenia, p. 552; paranoid type of schizophrenia, p. 553; catatonic type of schizophrenia, p. 554; residual type of schizophrenia, p. 554; undifferentiated type of schizophrenia, p. 554; concordance rate, p. 555; double bind, p. 557

Weblinks

What Is Depression?
www.psych.helsinki.fi/~janne/asdfaq/2.html
Visit this site for a more detailed answer to the question "What is depression?" For more about depression, link to the "see also" items listed at the end of the page.

Online Resources for People with Bipolar Disorder
www.moodswing.org/index.shtml
Explore bipolar disorder in more detail at this site. Topics include what to do if you have just been diagnosed, what to do if a family member or friend has just been diagnosed, and available treatments.

Anxiety Disorders Association of America
www.adaa.org/4_info/4d_sp/4d_01.htm
Acrophobia, claustrophobia, agoraphobia, and other anxiety disorders are discussed at this site. You can also take a test to determine which phobias you may have.

Schizophrenia Society of Ontario
www.web.net/~sso/
News archives, contact names, and in-depth explanations about schizophrenia are accessible at this Web site.

Antisocial Personality Disorder
www.mentalhealth.com/dis1/p21-pe04.html
Visit this site for a detailed description and explanation of personality disorders in general.

American Academy of Child and Adolescent Psychiatry
www.aacap.org/factsfam/suicide.htm
Read a discussion of teen suicide at this site. The signs of adolescents that might be considering killing themselves are listed.

Chapter 16

Therapy

When we last left Rob (at the beginning of Chapter 15) he had decided that his sleep loss, weight loss, and serious alcohol use on weekends indicated that he needed help. That help came from his company's in-house nurse, who referred him to a psychologist who was part of a extended care plan set up for his company. Early on, the psychologist had Rob go for a physical check-up; after consultation with the psychologist, the physician felt that Rob should take an antidepressant for a short time to combat his depression. Prozac was prescribed—and it helped a great deal. In fact, within 10 days Rob's mood started to lift, which made his weekly session with his therapist much easier. Problems came into sharper focus. His energy was greater. Rob started to see his issues clearly and even started to mend a strained relationship with his father and brother. The struggle from the depths of despair to recovery was long and tough, though. It involved months of therapy dealing with diverse issues, including self-esteem, distorted ideas about work demands, and his relationship with his dad and brother.

Was it the psychological therapy that helped, or was it the drug? The truth is that it was probably a combination of the drug therapy and the psychotherapy that helped Rob to move ahead. Would one have worked without the other? Perhaps—but the combination turned out to be extremely effective. Many researchers think that this is the key to therapy, but others insist on approaches involving only psychotherapies or only drug therapies, especially for depression. A great deal depends on the disorder. ■

In some important ways therapy is changing; people are relying more and more on drugs for the treatment of anxiety and depression. But many psychologists think that professionals involved in the mental heath area pathologize people's problems and overdiagnose them as psychological disorders (Kutchins & Kirk, 1997) and that they overmedicate patients (Valenstein, 1998). The reality is that the causes of people's disorders—the initiators of unhappiness—are not usually biological. When people have marital problems, let work relationships get to them, or start to view the world too rigidly, help from a therapist—not a drug—is usually more effective. Overall mental health and therapy is complicated by two facts today. First, cuts to the health care system are putting pressure on practitioners to find fast, efficient cures that are helpful, but also less costly. Second, some disorders, especially disorders like depression, often are undiagnosed and therefore remain untreated (Hirschfeld, 1997). Let's look at the available therapies and sort out the issues to determine what works best, and when.

Therapy Comes in Many Forms

M any sources and types of treatment are available for people who are having difficulty coping with their problems (see Figure 16.1). When a person seeks help from a physician, mental health counselling centre, or drug treatment centre, an initial working diagnosis is necessary. Does the person have medical problems? Should the person be hospitalized? Is the person dangerous? If psychotherapy is in order, what type of practitioner is best suited for the person? There are two broad types of therapy: biologically based therapy and psychotherapy.

Biologically Based Therapy and Psychotherapy

Biologically based therapy traditionally has been called *somatic therapy*; this term refers to treatment of psychological disorders by means of treatments for the body, including therapy that affects hormone levels and the brain. For example, severely depressed individuals may need antidepressants; those diagnosed as having schizophrenia may need antipsychotic drugs; those with less severe disorders may be advised to change their diet and exercise more, because exercise has mood-enhancing effects for many disorders (Byrne & Byrne, 1993). We will examine some of these biological therapies later in this chapter. But first, we will explore the broad array of psychological therapies that are available for people suffering from life problems or maladjustment.

Psychotherapy is the treatment of emotional or behavioural problems through psychological techniques. It is a change-oriented process, sometimes fairly emotional, whose goal is to help individuals cope better with their problems and achieve more emotionally satisfying lifestyles. Psychotherapy accomplishes its goal by teaching people how to relieve stress, improve interpersonal communication, understand previous events in their lives, and/or modify their faulty ideas about the world. Psychotherapy helps people improve their self-image and adapt to new and challenging situations.

Of course, different cultures perceive different outcomes as optimal. Thus, in Canada, enhancing self-esteem through accomplishment may be seen as an optimal goal of psychotherapy. In Asia, an outcome that improves family harmony may enhance self-esteem, even though achieving that goal means working for collective rather than personal good. This difference in goals is highlighted in *Diversity*; it is also recognized

FIGURE 16.1
Types of Treatment
A 1993 study of nearly 23 million people with mental health or substance abuse problems showed that such people seek help from a variety of sources.

(Adapted from Narrow et al., 1993.)

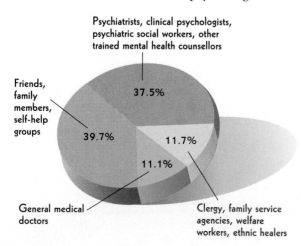

Psychiatrists, clinical psychologists, psychiatric social workers, other trained mental health counsellors

Friends, family members, self-help groups

37.5%

39.7%

11.7%

11.1%

General medical doctors

Clergy, family service agencies, welfare workers, ethnic healers

Asian Canadians and Mental Health

A sian Canadians are as difficult to characterize as a group as French Canadians or Protestants. That is, there are considerable differences within each of these groups, including diversity in language, education, traditions, and socioeconomic levels. However, like any other ethnic experience, the Asian-Canadian experience requires a unique perspective in the study of psychology. This perspective raises psychologists' sensitivity and understanding of the rich Asian-Canadian cultural heritage. This is important because Asian Canadians comprise a rapidly increasing percentage of our population. Although the prevalence of mental disorders among Asian Canadians is quite comparable to other groups (Yamamoto, Rhee, & Chang, 1994) and although they do seek counselling, they are more likely to report bodily ailments as an initial complaint to a therapist (Lippincott & Mierzwa, 1995). According to research conducted by Peter Waxer of York University (1990), Asian Canadians also are more likely to show a preference for a directive approach to therapy (where the therapist tells the client what they need to do or change). To understand the mental health of Asian Canadians, psychologists must understand what healing means, what family means, and the role of spirituality in Asian cultural traditions—and the relationship of these variables to therapy (Gerber, 1994; Tempo & Saito, 1996). As

Tsai and Uemura (1988) assert, one must understand at least three core cultural values that shape the responses of Asian Canadians to stress and to the world: family, harmony, and stoicism.

In traditional Asian cultures, the *family* is the primary source of emotional support. The most important family relationship is not the global husband–wife–children relationship but rather the parent–child relationship. A person is defined by roles in the family, which include parent roles, grandparent roles, and child roles. A deferential and respectful relationship to elders is maintained, with an emphasis on prescribed roles; these family roles and responsibilities provide support.

Harmony results from maintaining dignity and minimizing shame. This is a key goal if an Asian Canadian is to have a good relationship with family and self. Preserving dignity, or "face," maintains a person and the person's family and community. If everyone preserves such dignity, interpersonal harmony is optimized.

Asian Canadians also rely on personal strength and a sense of *stoicism*; that is, restraint is valued and emotional maturity means suffering silently and suppressing emotions. The open expression of emotion is discouraged.

These three values—family, harmony, and stoicism—could tend to keep Asian Canadians from using mental health services provided in the community (Tsai & Uemura, 1988). Asian Canadians may subject themselves to enormous levels of stress before seeking outside help; as a group, they tend to seek such help only in extreme crises. They are far more likely to ask for help from family, thus maintaining harmony and saving face by appearing stoic to those outside the family. For example, Japanese Canadians suffered many emotional problems during the Second World War, when they were relocated away from the west coast to inland areas. Those who were moved lost land and possessions and suffered with great dignity and stoicism; to this day, however, survivors of the relocations still bear emotional burdens.

A challenge for psychologists is to reach out to the Asian-Canadian community by making psychological services available in a way that minimizes shame, improves family unity, and respects cultural differences. The therapeutic alliance must respect the Asian family, its life cycle, its traditions, and the types of problems presented to practitioners (Tempo & Saito, 1996). Often, emphasizing family bonds—perhaps through family therapy—is an effective technique, as is relying on traditional and familiar Asian-Canadian philosophical traditions. Not all Canadians have the same needs. ■

by professional organizations such as the Canadian Psychological Association, the American Psychological Association (1993), and the American Psychiatric Association (1995).

Is Psychotherapy Necessary and Effective?

The mass media and the images it presents to the public often shape the reputation of psychotherapy. Talk show psychologist Frasier Crane on *Frasier* bumbles through his own life; Barbra Streisand, in her role as a psychiatrist in the film *Prince of Tides*, stretched the ethical boundaries by sleeping with her client's brother. These images, as well as talk show pop psychology, make many ask, "Is psychotherapy really necessary or effective?" Some researchers note that many clients could outgrow or otherwise find relief from their symptoms without psychotherapy. Others assert that psychotherapy is more art than science. Still others believe that psychotherapy provides only temporary relief. Let's consider some of these arguments.

Placebo Effects. A **placebo effect** is a therapeutic change that occurs as a result of a person's expectations of change rather than as a result of any specific treatment. Is the benefit of psychotherapy largely a placebo effect? Physicians report that people sometimes experience relief from their symptoms when they are given sugar pills and are told that the pills are medicine. In much the same way, some patients in psychotherapy may show relief from their symptoms simply because they have entered therapy and now are committed to and expect change. For some people, just the attention of a therapist and the chance to express their feelings can be therapeutic. One research study even showed that clients who paid for therapy had a better therapeutic outcome than clients who did not pay; researchers recognize and pay particular attention to such nonspecific effects (Roberts et al., 1993; Yoken & Berman, 1984).

But any placebo effect in psychotherapy is likely to be temporary. Any long-lasting therapeutic benefits generally will come about from the client's and therapist's efforts. Research studies that compare traditional psychotherapies with placebo treatment show that the traditional therapies are consistently more effective (Lipsey & Wilson, 1993).

Psychotherapy Research. In 1952, an important paper by Hans Eysenck challenged the effectiveness of psychotherapy, claiming that it produces no greater change in maladjusted individuals than do naturally occurring life experiences. Thousands of studies attempting to investigate the effectiveness of therapy followed. These studies showed what clients and therapists have known for decades: that Eysenck was wrong (Bachar, 1998; Lipsey & Wilson, 1993; Smith, Glass, & Miller, 1980). Although some psychologists continue to challenge the effectiveness of psychotherapy, most are convinced that it is effective with a wide array of clients (e.g., Kazdin, 1991; Lindfors et al., 1996; Seligman, 1995). The effectiveness of therapy and people's speed of response vary with the type of problem—for example, anxiety and depression respond more rapidly than do personality disorders (Kopta et al., 1994).

Is one type of therapy more effective than another? Many researchers contend that most psychotherapies are equally effective; that is, regardless of the approach a therapist uses, the results are often the same (Wampold et al., 1997). However, some newer and trendier approaches—ones that often appear in popular magazines—tend to be less reliable and reflect a culture eager to try the new, unproved, and fascinating. Critics such as Robyn Dawes (1994) assert that many therapists do not properly take research findings into account and that some therapists—often those with little training—don't do the right thing for their clients by ignoring the facts and looking for the exotic or easy way out. But if most of the legitimate therapies are effective, there must

Placebo effect [pluh-SEE-bo]: A therapeutic change that occurs as a result of a person's expectations of change rather than as a result of any specific treatment.

be some common underlying component that makes them successful. Both the Canadian Psychological Association and many individual researchers are seeking to systematize research strategies to investigate effectiveness; this research will lead to a clearer picture of which approaches are best for certain disorders, for clients of various ages, and for particular types of clients (Chambless & Hollon, 1998; Kazdin & Weiss, 1998). Furthermore, researchers are suggesting ways to validate therapy research in the laboratory and the real world (Goldfreid & Wolfe, 1998). Table 16.1 presents some generally recognized signs of good progress in therapy.

Which Therapy, Which Therapist?

Before 1950, there were about 15 types of psychotherapy; today, there are hundreds. Some focus on individuals, some focus on groups of individuals (group therapy), and others focus on families (family therapy). Some psychologists even deal with whole communities; these *community psychologists* focus on helping individuals, groups, and communities develop a more action-oriented approach to individual and social adjustment. A therapist's training usually will determine the type of treatment approach he or she takes. Rather than using just one type of psychotherapy, many therapists take an *eclectic approach*—that is, they combine several different techniques in their treatment.

A number of systematic psychotherapeutic approaches are in use today. Each can be applied in several formats—with individuals, couples, or groups—and each will be defined and examined in greater detail in later sections of this chapter. Some practitioners use *psychodynamically based approaches*, which loosely or closely follow Freud's basic ideas. These therapists' aim is to help patients understand the motivations underlying their behaviour. They assume that maladjustment and abnormal behaviour occur when people do not understand themselves adequately. Practitioners of *humanistic therapy* assume that people are essentially good—that they have an innate disposition to develop their potential and to seek beauty, truth, and goodness. This type of therapy tries to help people realize their full potential and find meaning in life. In contrast, *behaviour therapy* is based on the assumption that most behaviours, whether normal or abnormal, are learned. Behaviour therapists encourage their clients to learn new adaptive behaviours. Growing out of behaviour therapy and cognitive psychology (see Chapters 1 and 7) is *cognitive therapy*, which focuses on changing a client's behaviour by changing his or her thoughts and perceptions.

Most of the therapy approaches that we will discuss adopt a single theoretic point of view that guides research and practice. Certainly a clear example will be psychoanalysis, which prescribes a clear set of guidelines for therapy and its process. But a new approach called *psychotherapy integration* has developed. Psychotherapy integration is not a single-theory approach, but rather tries to look beyond any one theory of therapy to see what can be learned from other perspectives and is open to integrating diverse theories and techniques.

Psychotherapy integration is more than an eclectic approach (a bit of this and a bit of that) because the goal is to integrate theories to solve problems. Research on psychotherapy integration

Table 16.1 Signs of Good Progress in Therapy

The client is providing personally revealing and significant material.

The client is exploring the meanings of feelings and occurrences.

The client is exploring material avoided earlier in therapy.

The client is expressing significant insight into personal behaviour.

The client's method of communicating is active, alive, and energetic.

There is a valued client–therapist working relationship.

The client feels free to express strong feelings towards the therapist—either positive or negative.

The client is expressing strong feelings outside of therapy.

The client is moving towards a different set of personality characteristics.

The client is showing improved functioning outside of therapy.

The client indicates a general state of well-being, good feelings, and positive attitudes.

Source: Mahrer & Nadler, 1986.

is difficult, however, because hypotheses from these new points of view are difficult to generate. Arkowitz (1997) argues that psychotherapy integration does not try to develop one, overarching view of therapy, but rather suggests that it is a way of thinking about and doing psychotherapy that reflects an openness to points of view other than the one with which a therapist is most familiar. In some important ways, psychotherapy integration is a process, a way of thinking, and it may help psychologists define the future of psychotherapy. Another ongoing development that may prove a better avenue to explore is research on prevention of disorders, discussed in *The Research Process*.

Let's return for a moment to Rob Terman, whose problems were outlined in our chapter opener. What type of therapy would best suit his situation? As mentioned before, the appropriateness and effectiveness of the different kinds of therapy vary with the type of disorder being treated and the goal of the client. Research to discover the best treatment method often is conducted for specific disorders, such as depression (Robinson, Berman, & Neimeyer, 1990). Results from such studies usually limit their conclusions to a specific method for a specific problem. For example, individual psychodynamic therapy has a good success rate for people with anxiety and adjustment disorders, but it is less successful for those with schizophrenia. Long-term group therapy is more effective than short-term individual therapy for people with personality disorders. Behaviour therapy is usually the most effective approach with children, regardless of the disorder.

the research process

Prevention Instead of Treatment?

When psychologists conduct research they often have set a research agenda. They might ask: What is the best therapy for anorexia nervosa? What is the optimal number of sessions for therapy to be effective? Or perhaps they seek to know if combination treatments of drugs and talking therapy work better than either drugs or talking therapy alone. But before a research agenda can be set, scientists must establish what needs to be studied, discovered, or examined. Such was the case with prevention science; psychologists were not sure that mental disorders could be prevented or how to study their prevention. For example, can depression be prevented the way you prevent a child from being exposed to a cold virus?

But innovative and promising work has been done in prevention. Researchers and practitioners have begun to map out a new field for research, have helped set a research agenda, and are suggesting that psychological disorders can be averted before they occur. David Reiss and Richard Price (1996) outlined that research agenda. To help *prevent mental disorders*, they first argue that we need to do research to learn (1) how we reduce the risk of developing a disorder, and (2) what protective factors people can develop to assist them when their level of risk is high. For example, can we reduce the likelihood that a person will be among people who themselves are disordered, alcoholic, or ineffective communicators? Second, they assert that research is necessary on how to *identify preclinical cases* so that full-blown disorders can be prevented. Third, they argue that research is necessary into how one disorder often leads to another and is associated with another. For example, a disorder like social phobia might lead to other symptoms, perhaps panic attacks and then agoraphobia—psychologists need to know what precedes what.

From a research perspective, the key is that prevention research offers the possibility of new insights into the development of disorders, the mechanisms that cause disorders, and the social and community context in which disorders develop. This is a tall order, but the research process first requires agenda setting. Reiss and Price and their colleagues who work in the prevention field are challenging researchers to do this work to help better the human condition. Prevention science requires a unique combination of scientist and practitioner (Goldfried & Wolfe, 1996). It also requires an active collaboration among psychologists, but such work may bridge an important gap in the field's understanding of psychological disorders and their treatment. ■

Therefore, Rob could receive effective treatment from a variety of therapists (Wampold et al., 1997). One therapist might focus on the root causes of his maladjustment. Another might concentrate on eliminating his symptoms: sadness, anxiety, and alcohol abuse. Besides the therapeutic approaches, some characteristics of the therapists themselves affect the treatment; among these characteristics are gender, ethnicity, personality, level of experience, and degree of empathy. Garfield (1998) suggests that research on which variables are the most important in therapeutic change is not being given enough attention, because key combinations may lead to superior outcomes.

Although there are differences among the various psychotherapies and therapists, there are also some commonalties. In all of the therapies, clients usually expect a positive outcome, which helps them strive for change. Figure 16.2 presents an overview of outcomes when psychotherapy is combined with efforts to change. In addition, clients receive attention, which helps them maintain a positive attitude. Moreover, no matter what type of therapy is involved, certain characteristics must be present in both the therapist and the client for therapeutic changes to occur. For example, good therapists communicate interest, understanding, respect, tact, maturity, and ability to help. They respect their clients' ability to cope with their troubles (Fischer, 1991). They use suggestion, encouragement, interpretation, examples, and perhaps rewards to help clients change or rethink their situations. But clients must be willing to make some changes in their lifestyles and ideas. A knowledgeable, accepting, and objective therapist can facilitate behaviour changes, but the client is the one who makes the changes (Lafferty, Beutler, & Crago, 1989).

Variables such as the client's social class, gender, age, education, therapeutic expectations, and level of anxiety are also important. For example, therapists need to understand the unique life stresses experienced by women. Similarly, they must address the special obstacles facing clients of various ethnic and other minority groups (Sue, 1998). In general, the therapist and client must form an alliance to work together purposefully (Luborsky, Barber, & Crits-Cristoph, 1990); such alliances are helped if the therapist and client share some values (Kelly & Strupp, 1992). Because psychoanalysis is based on the development of a unique relationship between the therapist and the patient, compatibility is especially critical. The patient and the therapist usually decide within the first few sessions whether they feel comfortable working with each other.

Table 16.2 presents an overview of the major practitioners of psychotherapy, including their earned degrees and their activities. The table includes some practitioners who do not have as much training in psychotherapy as do psychologists—for example, nurses and social workers. These types of practitioners often work as part of a team, along with a clinical psychologist or psychiatrist, in delivering mental health services to clients.

To better understand the issues involved in psychotherapy, in the next sections we will look

FIGURE 16.2
Goals of Psychotherapy
An important goal of psychotherapy is engaging the client in the process of change. Once initiated, psychotherapy, along with efforts to change, can affect a host of problems, including specific maladaptive behaviours, distorted thoughts, inner conflicts, and interpersonal relationships.

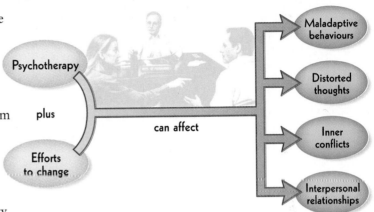

Focus

Review

◆ What is the essential difference between biologically based therapy and psychotherapy? p. 564

Think Critically

◆ Imagine that you are undergoing treatment for anxiety or depression. What would you expect to gain, lose, or change during therapy?

◆ Why do you think some disorders respond more quickly to therapy than others do?

◆ What are the implications of the fact that in Central and South America there are dramatically different mental health services available for the rich and the poor?

Table 16.2 Psychotherapy Practitioners and Their Activities

Type of Practitioner	Degree	Years of Education beyond Undergraduate Degree	Activities
Clinical or counselling psychologist	PhD (Doctor of Philosophy or PsyD (Doctor of Psychology)	5–8	Diagnosis, testing, and treatment using a wide array of techniques, including insight and behaviour therapy. Cannot prescribe medication.
Psychiatrist	MD (Doctor of Medicine)	8	Biomedical therapy, diagnosis, and treatment, often with a psychoanalytic emphasis
Social worker	MSW (Master of Social Work)	2	Family therapy or behaviour therapy, often in community-based settings such as hospitals
Psychiatric nurse	BSN (Bachelor of Science in Nursing) or MA (Master of Arts)	0–2	Inpatient psychiatric care, supportive therapy of various types
Counsellor	MA (Master of Arts, often in counselling)	2	Supportive therapy, family therapy, vocational readjustment, alcoholism and drug abuse counselling

more closely at the four major psychotherapeutic approaches: psychodynamic, humanistic, behaviour, and cognitive therapies. Then we will examine group therapy and the biologically based approaches.

Psychoanalysis and Psychodynamic Therapies

Psychoanalysis is a lengthy insight therapy developed by Freud that aims at uncovering conflicts and unconscious impulses through special techniques, including free association, dream analysis, and transference. Many other psychologists use a therapy loosely connected to or rooted in Freudian theory. These psychologists refer to their therapies as **psychodynamically based therapies—** therapies that use theory, approach, or techniques derived from Freud, but that reject or modify some of the elements of Freud's theory.

Sigmund Freud believed that the exchange of words in psychoanalysis causes therapeutic change. According to Freud (1920/1966, p. 21):

> The patient talks, tells of his past experiences and present impressions, complains, and expresses his wishes and his emotions. The physician listens, attempts to direct the patient's thought-processes, reminds him, forces his attention in certain directions, gives him explanations and observes the reactions of understanding or denial thus evoked.

Freud's therapy is an **insight therapy**—a therapy that attempts to discover relationships between unconscious motivations and current abnormal behaviour. Insight therapy has two basic assumptions: (1) that becoming aware of one's motivations helps one change and become more adaptable, and (2) that the causes of maladjustment are unresolved conflicts that the person was unaware of and therefore unable

Psychoanalysis [SYE-ko-uh-NAL-uh-sis]: A lengthy insight therapy developed by Freud that aims at uncovering conflicts and unconscious impulses through special techniques, including free association, dream analysis, and transference.

Psychodynamically based therapies [SYE-ko-dye-NAM-ick-lee]: Therapies based loosely on Freud's psychoanalytic theory, using a part of that approach but rejecting or modifying some of its elements.

Insight therapy: Therapy that attempts to discover relationships between unconscious motivations and current abnormal behaviour in order to change that behaviour.

to deal with. The goal of insight therapy is to treat the causes of abnormal behaviours rather than the behaviours themselves. In general, insight therapists try to help people see life from a different perspective so they can choose more adaptive lifestyles.

Goals of Psychoanalysis

Many individuals who seek psychotherapy are unhappy with their behaviour but are unable to change it. As we saw in the discussion of Freud's theory of personality (Chapter 12), Freud believed that conflicts among a person's unconscious thoughts and processes produce maladjusted behaviour. The general goal of psychoanalysis is to help patients understand the unconscious motivations that direct their behaviour. Only when they become aware of those motivations can they begin to choose behaviours that lead to more fulfilling lives. In psychoanalysis, patients are encouraged to express healthy impulses, strengthen day-to-day functioning based on reality, and perceive the world as a positive rather than a punishing place.

To illustrate the psychoanalytic approach, suppose that Rob Terman seeks the help of a psychologist who uses a psychodynamically based therapy. The psychologist might attempt to discover the source of Rob's problems by asking him to describe how he relates to his parents—especially to his father. Rob realizes that he has sought his father's love all of his life. Through therapy he realizes that he is torn between love for his father and rage towards him. He discovers that he has been incapable of expressing anger appropriately towards him. In addition, he confronts the fact that he is angry about his father's affection for his brother. Frustrated and hostile, he has lost interest in work, lost his self-esteem, and become depressed.

Techniques of Psychoanalysis

In general, psychoanalytic techniques are geared towards the exploration of early experiences. In traditional psychoanalysis, the patient lies on a couch and the therapist sits in a chair out of the patient's view. Freud believed this arrangement would allow the patient to be more relaxed and feel less threatened than if the therapist was in view. Today, however, many followers of Freud prefer face-to-face interactions with patients.

Two major techniques used in psychoanalysis are free association and dream analysis. In **free association**, the patient is asked to report whatever comes to mind, regardless of how disorganized it might be, how trivial it might seem, or how disagreeable it might feel. A therapist might say, "I can help you best if you say whatever thoughts and feelings come to your mind, even if they seem irrelevant, immaterial, foolish, embarrassing, upsetting, or even if they're about me, even very personally, just as they come, without censoring or editing" (Lewin, 1970, p. 67). The purpose of free association is to help patients learn to recognize connections and patterns among their thoughts and to allow the unconscious to express itself freely.

In **dream analysis**, patients are asked to describe their dreams in detail; the dreams are interpreted and used to provide insight into unconscious motivations. Sometimes lifelike, sometimes chaotic, sometimes incoherent, dreams at times may replay a person's life history and at other times may venture into the person's current problems. Freud believed that dreams represent some element of the unconscious seeking expression. Psychodynamically oriented therapists see much symbolism in dreams; they assert that the content of a dream hides its true meaning.

Free association: A psychoanalytic technique in which a person reports to the therapist his or her thoughts and feelings as they occur, regardless of how trivial, illogical, or objectionable their content may appear.

Dream analysis: A psychoanalytic technique in which a patient's dreams are interpreted and used to provide insight into the individual's unconscious motivations.

Interpretation: In Freud's theory, the technique of providing a context, meaning, or cause of a specific idea, feeling, or set of behaviours; the process of tying a set of behaviours to its unconscious determinant.

Resistance: In psychoanalysis, an unwillingness to cooperate by which a patient signals a reluctance to provide the therapist with information or to

help the therapist understand or interpret a situation.

Transference: A psychoanalytic phenomenon in which a therapist becomes the object of a patient's emotional attitudes about an important person in the patient's life, such as a parent.

Working through: In psychoanalysis, the repetitive cycle of interpretation, resistance to interpretation, and transference.

Many therapists use patients' dreams to gain insight into patients' current problems. The goal of dream analysis is to help therapists reveal patients' unconscious desires and motivations by discovering the meaning of their dreams.

Both free association and dream analysis involve the therapist's interpretation. **Interpretation**, in Freud's theory, is the technique of providing a context, meaning, or cause of a specific idea, feeling, or set of behaviours; it is the process of tying a set of behaviours to its unconscious determinant. With this technique, the therapist tries to find common threads in a patient's behaviour and thoughts. Patients' use of *defence mechanisms* (ways of reducing anxiety by distorting reality, examined in Chapter 12) is often a sign of an area that may need to be explored. For example, if a male patient avoids the subject of women, invariably deflecting the topic with an offhand remark or a joke, the therapist may wonder if some kind of defensive avoidance is going on. The therapist then may encourage the patient to explore his attitudes and feelings about women in general and about his mother in particular.

Two processes are central to psychoanalysis: resistance and transference. **Resistance** is an unwillingness to cooperate by which a patient signals a reluctance to provide the therapist with information or to help the therapist understand or interpret a situation, sometimes to the point of belligerence. For example, a patient disturbed by her analyst's unsettling interpretations might become angry and start resisting treatment by missing appointments or failing to pay for therapy. Analysts usually interpret resistance as meaning either that the patient wishes to avoid discussing a particular subject or that an especially difficult stage in psychotherapy has been reached. To minimize resistance, analysts try to accept patients' behaviour. When a therapist does not judge but merely listens, a patient is more likely to describe feelings thoroughly.

In transference, patients transfer feelings from earlier relationships to the therapist. **Transference** is a psychoanalytic phenomenon in which a therapist becomes the object of a patient's emotional attitudes about an important person in the patient's life, such as a parent. For example, if Rob Terman's therapist is a man and he becomes hostile towards him, a psychoanalyst would say that he is acting as though the therapist were his father; that is, he is directing attitudes and emotional reactions from that earlier relationship towards the therapist (Butler & Strupp, 1991). Most importantly, because the psychotherapist will respond differently than Rob's father might have, Rob can experience the conflict differently, which will lead him to a better understanding of the issue. By permitting transference, the therapist gives patients a new opportunity to understand their feelings and can guide them in the exploration of repressed or difficult material. The examination of thoughts or feelings that previously were considered unacceptable (and therefore often were repressed) helps patients understand and identify the underlying conflicts that direct their behaviour.

Psychoanalysis, with its slowly gained insights into the unconscious, is a gradual and continual process. Through their insights, patients learn new ways of coping with instinctual urges and develop more mature means of dealing with anxiety and guilt. The cycle of interpretation, resistance to interpretation, and transference occurs repeatedly in the process of psychoanalysis and sometimes is referred to as **working through**.

Criticisms of Psychoanalysis

Freud's theory has not been universally accepted; even his followers have disagreed with him. One group of psychoanalysts, referred to as *ego analysts* or *ego psychologists*, has modified some of Freud's basic ideas. *Ego analysts* are psychoanalytic practitioners who assume that the ego has greater control over behaviouur than Freud suggested and who are more concerned with reality checking and control over the environment than with unconscious motivations and processes. Like Freud, ego analysts believe that psychoanalysis is the appropriate method for treating patients with emotional problems. Unlike Freud, however, they assume that people have voluntary control over whether, when, and in what ways their biological urges will be expressed.

A major disagreement between ego analysts and traditional psychoanalysts has to do with the role of the id and the ego. (Recall from Chapter 12 that the id operates on the pleasure principle, while the ego operates on the reality principle and tries to control the id's impulsive behaviour.) A traditional Freudian asserts that the ego grows out of the id and controls it—but an ego analyst asserts that the ego is independent of the id, controls memory and perception, and is conflict-free. Whereas traditional psychoanalysts begin by focusing on unconscious material in the id and only later try to increase the patient's ego control, ego analysts try to help clients develop stronger egos. They may ask a client to assertively take control of a situation—to let reason, rather than feeling, guide a specific behaviour pattern. From an ego analyst's point of view, a weak ego may cause maladjustment by its failure to perceive, understand, and control the id. Thus, by learning to master and develop their egos—including moral reasoning and judgment—people gain greater control over their lives.

Critics of psychoanalysis contend that the approach is unscientific, imprecise, and subjective; they assert that psychoanalytic concepts such as id, ego, and superego are not linked to real things or to day-to-day behaviour. Other critics object to Freud's biologically oriented approach, which suggests that a human being is a mere bundle of energy caught in conflict and driven towards some hedonistic goal. These critics ask: Where in this approach does human free will come in? Also, elements of Freud's theory are untestable, and some are sexist. Freud conceived of men and women in prescribed roles; most practitioners today find this idea objectionable.

Quite aside from these criticisms, the effectiveness of psychoanalysis is open to question. Research shows that psychoanalysis is more effective for some people than for others. It is more effective, for example, for people with anxiety disorders than for those diagnosed as schizophrenic. In addition, younger patients improve more than older ones. In general, studies show that psychoanalysis can be as effective as other therapies, but no more so (Garfield & Bergin, 1986).

Psychoanalysis also has certain disadvantages. The problems addressed in psychoanalysis are difficult, and a patient must be highly motivated and articulate to grasp the complicated and subtle relationships being explored. Further, because traditional psychoanalysis involves meeting with an analyst for an hour at a time, five days a week, for approximately five years, psychoanalysis is typically extremely costly. Many people who seek therapy cannot afford the money or the time for this type of treatment.

Building Table 16.1 (see page 574) presents a summary of the key components of the psychoanalytic view of therapy. Humanistic therapies, which we will examine next, are neither as time-consuming nor as comprehensive in their goals as is psychoanalysis.

Focus

Review

◆ Define resistance and transference. p. 572
◆ What basic criticism of psychoanalysis do ego analysts offer? pp. 572–573
◆ Identify the disadvantages of psychoanalysis. p. 573

Think Critically

◆ Why do you think most practitioners feel that psychoanalysis is not the most appropriate treatment for marital discord?

Humanistic Therapies

 umanistic therapies, unlike psychoanalytic therapies, emphasize the uniqueness of the human experience, the ability to reflect on conscious experience, and the idea that human beings have free will to determine their destinies.

Building Table 16.1

Key Components of Psychoanalytic Therapy

Therapy	Nature of Psycho-pathology	Goal of Therapy	Role of Therapist	Role of Unconscious Material	Role of Patient's Insights	Techniques
Psycho-analytic	Maladjust-ment reflects inadequate conflict reso-lution and fix-ation in early development.	Attainment of maturity, strengthened ego functions, reduced con-trol by uncon-scious or repressed impulses.	An *investiga-tor*, uncover-ing conflicts and resis-tances.	Primary in classical psy-choanalysis; less empha-sized in ego analysis.	Includes not solely intellec-tual under-standing but also emotional experiences.	Analyst takes an active role in inter-preting the dreams and free associa-tions of patients.

Client-centred therapy: An insight therapy, developed by Carl Rogers, that seeks to help people evaluate the world and themselves from their own perspective by providing them with a nondirective environ-ment and unconditional positive regard. Also known as *person-centred therapy*.

Humanistic psychologists tend to focus on the present and future rather than on the past and assert that human beings are conscious, creative, and born with an innate desire to fulfil themselves. To some extent, humanistic approaches, being insight-oriented, are an outgrowth of psychodynamically based insight therapies: They help basically healthy people to understand the causes of their behaviour, both normal and maladjusted—but they focus on helping people take responsibility for their futures by promoting growth and fulfilment. Client-centred therapy and Gestalt therapy are two types of humanistic therapies that focus on such self-determination.

Client-centred Therapy

Client-centred therapy, or *person-centred therapy*, is an insight therapy that seeks to help people evaluate the world and themselves from their own perspective by providing them with a nondirective environment and uncondi-tional positive regard (which we will soon look at in more detail). Carl Rogers (1902–1987) first developed client-centred therapy. Rogers was a quiet, caring man who turned the psycho-analytic world upside-down when he introduced his approach. He focused on the person, listening intently to his clients and encouraging them to define their own "cures." Rogers saw peo-ple as basically good, competent, social beings who move for-ward and grow. He believed that people move towards their ideal selves throughout life, maturing into fulfilled individuals through the process of self-actualization.

Rogerian therapists hold that problem behaviours occur when the environment prevents a person from developing his or her own innate potential. If children are given love and rein-forcement only for their achievements, for example, as adults they may see them-selves and others almost solely in terms of achievement. Rogerian treatment involves helping people evaluate the world from their own perspective and improve their self-regard. A Rogerian therapist might treat Rob Terman by encouraging him to explore his past goals, current desires, and expectations for the future, and then asking whether he can achieve what he wants through a new relationship with a woman or even at work. Table 16.3 presents the basic assumptions underlying Rogers's approach to treatment.

Techniques of Client-Centred Therapy. Because its goal is to help clients discover and actualize their as-yet-undiscovered selves, client-centred therapy is nondirective. **Nondirective therapy** is a form of therapy in which the client determines the direction of therapy while the therapist remains permissive, almost passive, and accepts totally the client's feelings and behaviour. In nondirective therapy the therapist does not dominate the client, but instead encourages the client's search for growth and self-discovery.

The use of the word *client* rather than *patient* is a key aspect of Rogers's approach to therapy (*patient* connotes a medical model). In psychoanalysis, the therapist *directs* patients' "cure" and helps patients understand their behaviour; in client-centred therapy, the therapist *guides* clients and helps them realize what they feel is right for themselves. Clients are viewed as the experts on their own experience. The clients direct the conversation and the therapist helps them organize their thoughts and ideas simply by asking the right questions, by responding with words such as "oh," and by reflecting back the clients' feelings. Even a small movement, such as a nod or gesture, can help clients stay on the right track. Clients learn to evaluate the world from their own vantage point, with little interpretation by the therapist. Thus, in a meeting with a client, therapists often *paraphrase* a client's ideas, ask clients to clarify and *restate* ideas and feelings in other words, and *reflect* back to clients what they have just said so that a client can hear his or her own words again.

A basic tenet of client-centred therapy is that the therapist must be a warm, accepting person who projects positive feelings towards clients. To counteract clients' negative experiences with people who were unaccepting, and who thus have taught them that they are bad or unlikable, client-centred therapists accept clients as they are, with good and bad points; they respect them for their worth as individuals, showing them *unconditional positive regard* and respect. *Empathic understanding*, whereby therapists communicate acceptance and recognition of clients' emotions and encourage clients to discuss whatever feelings they have, is an important part of the therapeutic relationship.

Client-centred therapy can be viewed as a consciousness-raising process that helps people expand their awareness so as to construct new meanings. Initially, clients tend to express the attitudes and ideas they have adopted from other people. Thus, Rob Terman might say, "I should make top sales figures," implying "because my father expects my success." As therapy progresses and he experiences the empathic understanding of the therapist, he will begin to use his own ideas and standards when evaluating himself (Rogers, 1951). As a result, he may begin to talk about himself in more positive ways and try to please himself rather than others and thus construct new meanings. He may say, "I should make top sales figures only if they mean something to me," reflecting a more positive, more accepting attitude about himself. As he begins to feel better about himself, he eventually will suggest to the therapist that he knows how to deal with the world and may be ready to leave therapy.

Criticisms of Client-Centred Therapy. Client-centred therapy is acclaimed for its focus on the therapeutic relationship. No other therapy makes clients feel so warm, accepted, and safe. These are important characteristics of any therapy, but critics argue that they may not be enough to bring about long-lasting change.

Critics of client-centred therapy assert that lengthy discussions about past problems do not necessarily help people with their present difficulties and that an environment of unconditional positive regard may not be enough to bring about desired

Table 16.3 Rogers's Assumptions about Human Beings

1. People are innately good and are effective in dealing with their environments.

2. Behaviour is purposeful and goal-directed.

3. Healthy people are aware of all their behaviour; they choose their behaviour patterns.

4. A client's behaviour can be understood only from the client's point of view. Even if a client has misconstrued events in the world, the therapist must understand how the client sees those events.

5. Effective therapy occurs only when a client modifies his or her behaviour, not when the therapist manipulates it.

Nondirective therapy: A form of therapy in which the client determines the direction of therapy while the therapist remains permissive, almost passive, and accepts totally the client's feelings and behaviour.

behaviour changes. They believe that this therapy may be making therapeutic promises that cannot be fulfilled and that it focuses on concepts that are hard to define, such as self-actualization.

Gestalt Therapy

With the aim of creating an awareness of a person's whole self, Gestalt therapy differs significantly from psychoanalysis. **Gestalt therapy** is an insight therapy that emphasizes the importance of a person's being aware of current feelings and situations. It assumes that human beings are responsible for themselves and their lives and that they need to focus not on the past but on the present, the "here and now." As such, Gestalt therapy is concerned with current feelings and behaviours and their representation in a meaningful, coherent whole.

Frederick S. ("Fritz") Perls (1893–1970), a physician and psychoanalyst trained in Europe, was the founder and principal proponent of Gestalt therapy. He was a dynamic, charismatic therapist, and many psychologists followed him and his ideas closely. Perls assumed that the best way to help clients come to terms with anxiety and other unpleasant feelings was to focus on their current understanding and awareness of the world, not on past situations and experiences.

Gestalt therapy aims at expanding clients' awareness of their current attitudes and feelings so they can respond more fully and appropriately to current situations. Gestalt psychologists help people deal with feelings of what Perls termed *incomplete Gestalts*—that is, unfinished business or unresolved conflicts, such as previously unrecognized feelings of anger towards a spouse or envy of a brother or sister. Only when people become aware of the here and now can they become sensitive to the tension and repression that made their previous behaviour maladaptive. Thus, a major goal of therapy is to get people in touch with their feelings so they can construct an accurate picture of their psychological world.

Gestalt therapy examines current feelings and behaviours of which a client may be unaware. Usually, the therapist asks the client to concentrate on current feelings about a difficult past experience. For example, a Gestalt therapist may ask a client to relive a situation and discuss it as if it were happening in the present.

Another technique is to have clients change the way they talk; a client who thinks she has trouble being assertive might be asked to speak assertively to each member of a group. Still another technique is to ask clients to behave in a manner opposite to the way they feel; a man who feels hostile or aggressive towards his boss, for example, might be asked to behave as though their relationship were warm and affectionate. The underlying assumption is that feelings expressed in the present can be understood and dealt with more easily than can feelings remembered from the past. For these reasons, Gestalt therapy is considered an *experiential therapy*.

Some critics believe Perls was too focused on individuals' happiness and growth, that he encouraged the attainment of these goals at the expense of other goals. Critics assert that Gestalt therapy focuses too much on feelings and not enough on thought and decision making. Finally, critics point out that Gestalt therapy may work well for healthy people who want to grow but that it may not be as successful for severely maladjusted people who cannot make it through the day.

Building Table 16.2 presents a summary of the key components of the psychoanalytic and humanistic views of therapy.

Focus

Review

♦ Why is Rogers's therapy termed *client-centred*? p. 574

♦ What is the fundamental aim of Gestalt therapy? p. 576

♦ Briefly describe the major differences between client-centred therapy and Gestalt therapy. pp. 574–577

Think Critically

♦ What are the implications for a theory of therapy of assuming that people are inherently good, as Rogers did?

♦ How might psychodynamic and humanistic therapists use hypnosis differently?

Building Table 16.2

Key Components of Psychoanalytic and Humanistic Therapies

Therapy	Nature of Psycho-pathology	Goal of Therapy	Role of Therapist	Role of Unconscious Material	Role of Patient's Insights	Techniques
Psycho-analytic	Maladjust-ment reflects inadequate conflict reso-lution and fix-ation in early development.	Attainment of maturity, strengthened ego functions, reduced con-trol by uncon-scious or repressed impulses.	An *investiga-tor*, uncover-ing conflicts and resis-tances.	Primary in classical psy-choanalysis; less empha-sized in ego analysis.	Includes not solely intellec-tual under-standing but also emotional experiences.	Analyst takes an active role in inter-preting the dreams and free associa-tions of patients.
Humanistic	Incongruity between the real self and the potential, desired self; overdepen-dence on oth-ers for gratifi-cation and self-esteem.	To foster self-determina-tion, release human poten-tial, expand awareness.	An *empathic person*, in honest en-counter with client, sharing experience.	Emphasis is primarily on conscious experience.	There is more emphasis on *how* and *what* questions than *why* questions.	Help client to see the world from a different per-spective and to focus on the present and the fu-ture instead of the past.

Behaviour Therapy

B ehaviour therapy has become especially popular in the last three decades for three principal reasons. First, sometimes people have problems that may not warrant an in-depth discussion of early childhood experiences, an exploration of unconscious motivations, a lengthy discussion about current feelings, or a resolution of inner conflicts. Examples of such problems are fear of heights, anxiety about public speaking, marital conflicts, and sexual dysfunction. In these cases, behaviour therapy may be more appropriate than psychodynamically based or humanistic therapies. Second, people seek behaviour therapy because health care systems are seeking quicker, less expensive solutions to everyday problems. Last, behaviour therapy can be very effective. As you will see, behaviour therapy is very focused on current behaviour and on designing solutions to problems.

Goals of Behaviour Therapy

Behaviour therapy is a therapy based on the application of learning principles to human behaviour. Also called *behaviour modification*, it focuses on changing overt behaviours rather than on understanding subjective feelings, unconscious processes, or motivations. It uses learning principles to help people replace maladaptive behav-iours with new, better ones. Behaviour therapists assume that people's behaviour is

Behaviour therapy: A therapy based on the application of learning principles to human behaviour that focuses on changing overt behaviours rather than on understanding subjective feelings, uncon-scious processes, or motiva-tions. Also known as *behaviour modification*.

influenced by changes in their environment, in the way they respond to that environment, and in the way they interact with other people. Unlike psychodynamically based therapies, behaviour therapy does not aim to discover the origins of a behaviour; it works only to alter it. For a person with a nervous twitch, for example, the goal would be to eliminate the twitch. Thus, behaviour therapists treat people by having them first unlearn old, faulty behaviours and then learn new, more acceptable or effective ones.

Behaviour therapists do not always focus on the problems that caused the client to seek therapy. If they see that the client's problem is caused by some other situation, they may focus on changing that situation. For example, a man may seek therapy because of a faltering marriage. However, the therapist may discover that the marriage is suffering because of the client's frequent and acrimonious arguments with his wife, each of which is followed by a period of heavy drinking. The therapist then may discover that both the arguments and the drinking are brought on by stress at work, aggravated by the client's unrealistic expectations regarding his performance. In this situation, the therapist may focus on helping the client develop standards that will ease the original cause of the problem—the tension felt at work—and that will be consistent with the client's capabilities, past performance, and realistic likelihood of future performance.

Unlike psychodynamic and humanistic therapies, behaviour therapy does not encourage clients to interpret past events to find their meaning. Although a behaviour therapist may uncover a chain of events leading to a specific behaviour, that discovery generally will not prompt a close examination of the client's early experiences.

When people enter behaviour therapy, many aspects of their behaviour may change, not just those specifically being treated. Thus, a woman being treated for extreme shyness may find not only that the shyness decreases but also that she can engage more easily in discussions about emotional topics and can perform better on the job. Behaviourists argue that once a person's behaviour has changed, it may be easier for the person to manage attitudes, fears, and conflicts.

Behaviour Therapy versus Psychodynamic and Humanistic Therapies

Behaviourists are dissatisfied with psychodynamic and humanistic therapies for three basic reasons: (1) psychodynamic and humanistic therapies use concepts that are almost impossible to define and measure (such as the id and self-actualization); (2) some studies show that patients who do not receive psychodynamic and humanistic therapies improve anyway; and (3) once a therapist has labelled a person as abnormal, the label itself may lead to maladaptive behaviour. (Although this is true of any type of therapy, psychodynamic therapy tends to use labels more than behaviour therapy does.) Behaviour therapists assume that people display maladaptive behaviour not because they are abnormal but because they are having trouble adjusting to their life situations; if they are taught new ways of coping, the maladjustment will disappear. A great strength of behaviour therapy is that it provides a coherent conceptual framework.

However, behaviour therapy is not without its critics. Most insight therapists, especially those who are psychodynamically based, believe that if only *overt* behaviour is treated, as is often done in behaviour therapy, symptom substitution may occur.

Symptom substitution is the appearance of one overt symptom to replace another that has been eliminated by treatment. Thus, insight therapists argue that if a therapist eliminates a nervous twitch without examining its underlying causes, the client will express the underlying disorder by developing some other symptom, such as a speech impediment. Behaviour therapists, on the other hand, contend that symptom substitution does not occur if the treatment makes proper use of behavioural principles. That is, if an acceptable replacement behaviour is effectively reinforced, negative behaviours should be extinguished. Research shows that behaviour therapy is at least as effective as insight therapy and is more effective in some cases (Jacobson, 1991; McGlynn, 1990; Snyder, Wills, & Grady-Fletcher, 1991).

Symptom substitution: The appearance of one overt symptom to replace another that has been eliminated by treatment.

Techniques of Behaviour Therapy

Behaviour therapists use an array of techniques, often in combination, to help people change their behaviour; chief among these techniques are operant conditioning, counterconditioning, and modelling. In addition to using several behavioural techniques, the therapist may use some insight techniques. A good therapist will use whatever combination of techniques will help a client most efficiently and effectively. The more complicated the disorder being treated, the more likely it is that a practitioner will use a mix of therapeutic approaches—a *multimodal approach* (e.g., Blanchard et al., 1990).

Behaviour therapy usually involves three general procedures: (1) identifying the problem behaviour and its frequency by examining what people actually feel, think, and do; (2) treating the client, perhaps by reeducation, communication training, or some type of counterconditioning (such treatment strategies are individually tailored to a client); and (3) continually assessing whether there is a behaviour change. If the client exhibits the new behaviour for several weeks or months, the therapist concludes that treatment was effective. Let's now explore the three major behaviour therapy techniques: operant conditioning, counterconditioning, and modelling.

Operant Conditioning

Operant conditioning procedures are used with different people in different settings to achieve a wide range of desirable behaviours, including increased reading speed, improved classroom behaviour, and the maintenance of personal hygiene. As we saw in Chapter 5, operant conditioning to establish new behaviours often depends on a *reinforcer*—any event or circumstance that increases the probability that a particular response will recur. Rob Terman could employ operant conditioning to help himself adopt more positive responses towards himself. For example, he could ask his girlfriend to praise him every time he honours his own best judgment or is honest about his feelings.

One of the most effective uses of operant conditioning is with children who are antisocial, slow to learn, or in some way maladjusted. Operant conditioning is also effective with patients in mental hospitals. Ayllon and Haughton (1964), for example, instructed hospital staff members to reinforce patients for psychotic, bizarre, or meaningless verbalizations during one period and for neutral verbalizations (such as comments about the weather) during another. As expected, the relative frequency of each type of verbalization increased when it was reinforced and decreased when it was not reinforced (see Figure 16.3).

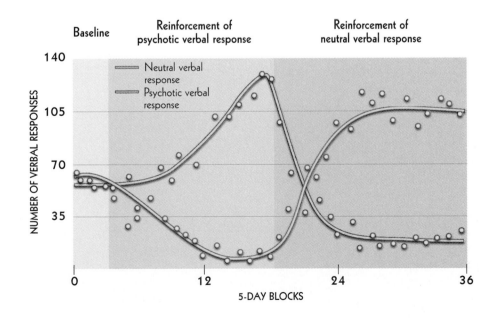

FIGURE 16.3
Reinforcement Increases Desired Behaviours
A study by Ayllon and Haughton (1964) found that reinforcement affected the frequency of psychotic and neutral verbal behaviour in hospitalized patients.

Token Economies. One way of rewarding adaptive behaviour is with a **token economy**—an operant conditioning procedure in which individuals who engage in appropriate behaviour receive tokens that they can exchange for desirable items or activities. In a hospital setting, for example, some rewards might be candy, new clothes, games, or time with important people in the patients' lives. The more tokens people earn, the more items or activities they can obtain.

Token economies are used to modify behaviour in social settings, usually with groups of people. They aim to strengthen behaviours that are compatible with social norms. For example, a patient in a mental hospital might receive tokens for cleaning tables, helping in the hospital laundry, and maintaining certain standards of personal hygiene and appearance. The level of difficulty of the behaviour or task determines the number of tokens earned. Thus, patients might receive 3 tokens for brushing their teeth but 40 tokens for engaging in helping behaviours.

Ayllon and Azrin (1965) monitored the performance of a group of hospitalized patients who were involved in doing simple work tasks for 45 days. They found that when tokens (reinforcement) were contingent on performance, the patients produced about four times as much work per day as when tokens were not delivered. (See Figure 16.4, in which some of the researchers' results are presented.) Token economies become especially effective when combined with other behavioural techniques (Miller, Cosgrove, & Doke, 1990). We will examine two of these techniques next—extinction and punishment first, followed by time-out.

Extinction and Punishment. As we saw in Chapter 5, extinction and punishment can decrease the frequency of a behaviour. For example, if reinforcers are withheld, extinction of an undesired behaviour will occur. Suppose a six-year-old girl refuses to go to bed at the designated time. When she is taken to her bedroom, she cries and screams violently. If the parents give in and allow her to stay up, they are reinforcing the crying behaviour: The child cries; the parents give in. A therapist might suggest that the parents stop reinforcing the crying behaviour by insisting that their daughter go to bed and stay there. Chances are that the child will cry loudly and violently for two or three nights, but the behaviour eventually will be extinguished (C. D. Williams, 1959).

Another way to decrease the frequency of an undesired behaviour is to punish it. Punishment often involves the presentation of an aversive stimulus. In the laboratory,

Token economy: An operant conditioning procedure in which individuals who engage in appropriate behaviour receive tokens that they can exchange for desirable items or activities.

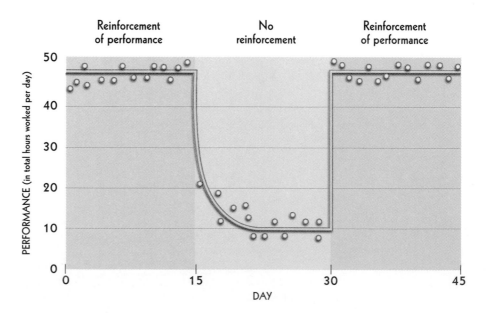

FIGURE 16.4
Token Economies Change Performance Effectively
Ayllon and Azrin (1965) found that tokens increased the total number of hours worked per day by a group of 44 patients.

researchers might provide slight electric shocks to get adult participants to stop performing a specific behaviour. Usually, punishment for undesired behaviours is combined with positive reinforcement for desired behaviours because, as we saw in Chapter 5, a serious limitation of punishment as a behaviour-shaping device is that it suppresses only existing behaviours. It cannot be used to establish new, desired behaviours.

Research also shows that people, especially young people, imitate aggression. Thus, a child (or an institutionalized person) in therapy may strike out at the therapist who administers punishment in an attempt to eliminate the source of punishment, sometimes inflicting serious injury. Punishment also can bring about generalized aggression. This is especially true for prison inmates, whose hostility is well recognized, and for class bullies, who are often the children most strictly disciplined by their parents or teachers. Skinner (1988) believed that punishment is harmful; he advocated non-punitive therapeutic techniques. This might involve the therapist working to reinforce specific prosocial activities. In general, procedures that lead to a perception of control on the part of a client are much more likely to lead to nonoccurrence of undesired behaviour.

Time-out. As we saw in Chapter 5, **time-out**—the physical removal of a person from sources of reinforcement in order to decrease the occurrence of undesired behaviours—is an effective operant conditioning procedure. Suppose a boy regularly throws a temper tantrum each time he wants a piece of candy, an ice-cream cone, or his little brother's toys. With the time-out procedure, whenever the child misbehaved, he would be placed in a restricted area away from the rest of the family, without sweets, toys, television, or other people. He would be required to stay in the restricted area (such as a chair or a time-out room) for a short period, such as 5 or 10 minutes; if he left the area, more time would be added. Not only would the child not be getting what he wanted, he also would be removed from any potential source of reinforcement. Time-out is used principally with children; it is especially effective when it is combined with positive reinforcers for appropriate behaviour and is administered by a knowledgeable parent or child-care specialist (Crespi, 1988).

Counterconditioning

A second major technique of behaviour therapy is **counterconditioning**—a process of reconditioning in which a person is taught a new, more adaptive response to a familiar stimulus. For example, anxiety is one of the first responses people show when they are maladjusted, fearful, or lacking in self-esteem. If a therapist can condition a person to respond with something other than anxiety—that is, *counterconditioning* the person—a real breakthrough will be achieved, and the person's anxiety will be reduced.

Joseph Wolpe (1915–1997) was one of the initial proponents of counterconditioning. His work in classical conditioning, especially in situations in which animals show conditioned anxiety responses, led him to attempt to inhibit or decrease anxiety as a response in human beings. His therapeutic goal was to replace anxiety with some other response, such as relaxation, amusement, or pleasure.

Behaviour therapy using counterconditioning begins with a specific stimulus (S1), which elicits a specific response (R1). After the person undergoes counterconditioning, the same stimulus (S1) should elicit a new response (R2) (Wolpe, 1958). There are two basic approaches to counterconditioning: systematic desensitization and aversive counterconditioning.

Systematic Desensitization. **Systematic desensitization** is a three-stage counterconditioning procedure in which people are taught to relax when presented with stimuli that formerly elicited anxiety. First the client learns how to relax; then the client describes the specific situations that arouse anxiety; finally the client, while deeply relaxed, imagines increasingly vivid scenes of the situations that elicit anxiety. In this way, the client is gradually, step by step, exposed to the source of anxiety, usually by imagining (while relaxed) a series of progressively more fearful or anxiety-provoking situations. With each successive experience, the client learns relaxation rather than fear as a response. Eventually, the client actually approaches the real-life situation.

Flying in an airplane, for example, is a stimulus situation (S1) that can bring about an inappropriate fear response (R1). With systematic desensitization therapy, the idea of flying (S1) eventually can elicit a response of curiosity or even relaxation (R2). The therapist first might ask the relaxed client to imagine sitting in an airplane on the ground, then to imagine the airplane taxiing, and eventually to imagine flying though the billowing clouds. As the client practises relaxation while imagining the scene, he or she becomes able to tolerate more stressful imagery and eventually may perform the imagined behaviour—in this case, flying in an airplane. Eventually, practising and becoming desensitized in real-world situations produces the most lasting effects (Hoffart, 1996). For example, if therapists combine systematic desensitization with changing people's ideas about the world—cognitive therapy, which we examine later in this chapter—they find that people cope better. Through systematic desensitization and cognitive therapy people can lose their fears of flying.

Systematic desensitization is most successful for people who have problems such as impulse control or who exhibit forms of anxiety, such as phobias. It is not especially effective for people who exhibit serious psychotic symptoms; nor is it the best treatment for situations involving interpersonal conflict.

Aversive Counterconditioning. Before therapy, clients often do not avoid a stimulus that prompts inappropriate behaviour. This is where aversive counterconditioning, another form of counterconditioning, can be used. **Aversive counterconditioning** is a counterconditioning technique in which an aversive or noxious stimulus is paired with a stimulus that elicits an undesired behaviour so that the client will adopt a new, more worthwhile behaviour in response to the familiar stimulus and thus cease the undesired behaviour. As with systematic desensitization, the objective is to teach a new response to the original stimulus. A behaviour therapist might use aversive counterconditioning to teach an alcoholic client to avoid alcohol. The first step might be to teach the person to associate alcohol (the original stimulus) with the sensation of nausea (a noxious stimulus). If verbal instruction is not enough, the therapist might administer a drug that causes nausea whenever alcohol is consumed. The goal is to make the drinking of alcohol unpleasant. Eventually, the treatment will make the client experience nausea just at the *thought* of consuming alcohol, thus causing the client to avoid alcohol. This approach is limited, of course, by the ability of the client to realize that it was the drug and not the alcohol that made him or her sick.

Modelling

Both children and adults learn behaviours by watching and imitating other people—in other words, by observing models. Children learn table manners, toilet behaviour, and appropriate responses to animals by observing and imitating their parents and other models. Similarly, the music you listen to, the styles of clothing you wear, and the social or political causes you support are determined, in part, by the people around you.

According to Albert Bandura (1977a), as part of behaviour therapy, modelling is most effective in three areas: (1) teaching new behaviour, (2) helping to eliminate fears, especially phobias, and (3) enhancing already existing behaviour. By watching the behaviour of others, people learn to exhibit more adaptive and appropriate behaviour. Bandura, Blanchard, and Ritter (1969), for example, asked people with snake phobia to watch other people handling snakes. Afterwards, the watchers' fear of snakes was reduced.

One problem with modelling is that people may observe and imitate the behaviour of inappropriate models. We saw in Chapter 3 that people imitate violent behaviours that they have observed on television and in movies. Further, many adolescents become involved in abuse of alcohol and other drugs because they imitate their peers. Such imitation often occurs because of faulty thinking about situations, people, or lifelong goals. When people have developed a faulty set of expectations that guide their behaviour, cognitive therapy may be in order.

Behaviour Therapy in a Contemporary Context

Behaviour therapy along with cognitive therapy (to be considered next), with which it is closely allied, have been influenced heavily by health care changes. A care orga-nization (such as Blue Cross) will specify what services it will cover and usually how much money it will commit to specific types of treat-ments in a given coverage period. While they do not directly stipulate what type of therapy is to be offered (as sometimes occurs with managed care organizations in the United States), there is an incentive (due to limited financial reimburse-ment) to consider briefer forms of therapy. Many psychologists view insurance for care and managed care, such as is found in the United States, as a crisis, a nightmare, and the downfall of psychotherapy (Fishman & Franks, 1997). In contrast, behaviour therapists, more than other therapists, have become allies of care organiza-tions because of the close alignment of their shared goals, especially the goals of efficiency.

Building Table 16.3 on page 584 presents a summary of the key components of the psycho-analytic, humanistic, and behavioural views of therapy.

Focus

Review

- ◆ Identify the fundamental reasons why behaviourists are dissatisfied with psychodynamic and humanistic therapies. p. 578
- ◆ For what disorders is the behaviour therapy technique of operant conditioning especially effective? pp. 579–582

Think Critically

- ◆ How would the therapy process differ if a practitioner used behaviour therapy or Gestalt therapy with a person who was suffering from low self esteem?
- ◆ Why do you think modelling is especially effective in the treatment of phobias?

Cognitive Therapy

G rowing out of behaviour therapy and the developing study of cognitive psychology is *cognitive therapy*, which focuses on changing a client's behaviour by changing his or her thoughts and perceptions. Cognitive psy-chologists have had a profound impact in many areas of psychology, especially in therapy. In the past, behaviour therapists were concerned only with overt behaviour; today, many incorporate thought processes into their treatments. For this reason their work is often called cognitive behaviour therapy. Researchers now suggest that thought processes may hold the key to managing many forms of maladjustment.

Therapists who use *cognitive restructuring* (cognitive therapy) are interested in modifying the faulty thought patterns of disturbed people (Mahoney, 1977). This type of therapy is effective for people who have attached overly narrow or other-wise inappropriate labels to certain situations; for example, such a person may believe that sex is dirty or that assertiveness is unwomanly. Whenever presented

Building Table 16.3

Key Components of Psychoanalytic, Humanistic, and Behaviour Therapies

Therapy	Nature of Psychopathology	Goal of Therapy	Role of Therapist	Role of Unconscious Material	Role of Patient's Insights	Techniques
Psychoanalytic	Maladjustment reflects inadequate conflict resolution and fixation in early development.	Attainment of maturity, strengthened ego functions, reduced control by unconscious or repressed impulses.	An *investigator*, uncovering conflicts and resistances.	Primary in classical psychoanalysis; less emphasized in ego analysis.	Includes not solely intellectual understanding but also emotional experiences.	Analyst takes an active role in interpreting the dreams and free associations of patients.
Humanistic	Incongruity between the real self and the potential, desired self; overdependence on others for gratification and self-esteem.	To foster self-determination, release human potential, expand awareness.	An *empathic person*, in honest encounter with client, sharing experience.	Emphasis is primarily on conscious experience.	There is more emphasis on *how* and *what* questions than *why* questions.	Help client to see the world from a different perspective and to focus on the present and the future instead of the past.
Behaviour	Symptomatic behaviour stems from faulty learning or learning of maladaptive behaviours.	To relieve symptomatic behaviour by suppressing or replacing maladaptive behaviours.	A *helper*, helping client unlearn old behaviours and learn new ones.	Not concerned with unconscious processes.	Irrelevant and unnecessary.	Clients learn new responses, establish new behaviours, and eliminate faulty or undesirable ones.

with a situation that involves sex or assertiveness, the person will respond in a way that is determined by his or her thoughts about the situation rather than by the facts of the situation.

Cognitive therapy is derived from three basic propositions:

- Cognitive activity affects behaviour.
- Cognitive activity can be monitored.
- Behaviour changes can be effected through cognitive changes.

Cognitive therapy typically focuses on current behaviour and current thoughts. It is not especially concerned with uncovering forgotten childhood experiences, although it can be used to alter thoughts about those experiences. As shown by Keith Dobson from the University of Calgary (1989) and other researchers (Jacobson & Hollon, 1996; Simons et al., 1995), it has been used effectively to treat depression. Other reserachers (Lipsey & Wilson, 1993) have shown that cognitive therapy can be used to effectively treat bulimia, weight loss, anger, and adolescent behaviour problems. When cognitive restructuring is combined with other psychological techniques, such as reinforcement, that help the person make behavioural changes, findings are even more supportive (Kirsch, Montgomery, & Sapirstein, 1995). Cognitive therapy has gone through three decades of development and its effectiveness and future look promising (Beck et al., 1994; Brown & Barlow, 1995; Gaffer, Tsaousis, & Kemp-Wheeler, 1995; Mahoney, 1993).

> **Rational–emotive therapy:** A cognitive behaviour therapy that emphasizes the importance of logical, rational thought processes.

Rational–Emotive Therapy

The best-known cognitive therapy is **rational–emotive therapy**—a cognitive behaviour therapy that emphasizes the importance of logical, rational thought processes. Researcher Albert Ellis developed this therapy more than 30 years ago. Most behaviour therapists assume that abnormal behaviour is caused by faulty and irrational *behaviour* patterns. Ellis and his colleagues, however, assume that it is caused by faulty and irrational *thinking* patterns (Ellis, 1970; Ellis & Harper, 1961). They believe that if faulty thought processes can be replaced with rational ones, maladjustment and abnormal behaviour will disappear.

According to Ellis, psychological disturbance is a result of events in a person's life that give rise to irrational beliefs leading to negative emotions and behaviours. Moreover, these beliefs are a breeding ground for further irrational ideas (Dryden & Ellis, 1988). Ellis (1988) argues that people make formal demands on themselves and on other people, and they rigidly hold on to them no matter how unrealistic and illogical they are.

Thus, a major goal of rational–emotive therapy is to help people examine the past events that produced the irrational beliefs. Ellis, for example, tries to focus on a client's basic philosophy of life and how it is self-defeating. He thus tries to uncover the client's thought patterns and help the client recognize that the underlying beliefs are faulty. Table 16.4 lists 10 irrational assumptions that, according to Ellis, cause emotional problems and maladaptive behaviours. They are based on people's needs to be liked, to be competent, to be loved, and to feel secure. When people place irrational or exaggerated value on these needs, the needs become maladaptive and lead to emotional disturbance, anxiety, and abnormal behaviour. If rational–emotive therapy is successful, the client adopts different behaviours based on new, more rational thought processes. Research supports the effectiveness of the approach (Abrams & Ellis, 1994; Haaga & Davison, 1993), and Ellis (1993) asserts that rational–emotive therapy has broad applications in both therapy and classroom settings.

Beck's Approach

Another cognitive therapy that focuses on irrational ideas is that of Aaron Beck (1963). As we saw in Chapter 15, Beck's theory assumes that depression is caused by people's distorted cognitive views of reality, which lead to negative views about the world, themselves, and the future, and often to gross overgeneralizations. For example, people who think they have no future—that all of their options are blocked—and who undervalue their intelligence are likely to be depressed. Such individuals form appraisals of situations that are distorted and based on insufficient (and sometimes wrong) data. The goal of therapy, therefore, is to help them to develop realistic appraisals of the situations they encounter and to solve problems (Beck, 1991). The therapist acts as a trainer and co-investigator, providing data to be examined and guidance in understanding how cognitions influence behaviour (Beck & Weishaar, 1989).

Table 16.4   Ellis's Outline of 10 Irrational Assumptions

1. It is a necessity for an adult to be loved and approved of by almost everyone for virtually everything.

2. A person must be thoroughly competent, adequate, and successful in all respects.

3. Certain people are bad, wicked, or villainous and should be punished for their sins.

4. It is catastrophic when things are not going the way one would like.

5. Human unhappiness is externally caused. People have little or no ability to control their sorrows or to rid themselves of negative feelings.

6. It is right to be terribly preoccupied with and upset about something that may be dangerous or fearsome.

7. It is easier to avoid facing many of life's difficulties and responsibilities than it is to undertake more rewarding forms of self-discipline.

8. The past is all-important. Because something once strongly affected someone's life, it should continue to do so indefinitely.

9. People and things should be different from the way they are. It is catastrophic if perfect solutions to the grim realities of life are not immediately found.

10. Maximal human happiness can be achieved by inertia and inaction or by passively and without commitment "enjoying oneself."

Source: Ellis & Harper, 1961.

According to Beck (1976), a successful client passes through four stages in the course of correcting faulty views and moving towards improved mental health: "First, he has to become aware of what he is thinking. Second, he needs to recognize what thoughts are awry. Then he has to substitute accurate for inaccurate judgments. Finally, he needs feedback to inform him whether his changes are correct" (p. 217).

Meichenbaum's Approach

Some researchers, among them Donald Meichenbaum, believe that what people say to themselves determines what they will do. Therefore, a key goal of therapy is to change the things people say to themselves. According to Meichenbaum, the therapist has to change the client's appraisal of stressful events and the client's use of self-instructions, thus normalizing his or her reactions (Meichenbaum, 1993).

A strength of Meichenbaum's theory is that self-instruction can be used in many settings for many different problems (Dobson & Block, 1988). It can help people who are shy or impulsive, people with speech impediments, and even those who are schizophrenic (Meichenbaum, 1974; Meichenbaum & Cameron, 1973). Rather than attempting to change their irrational beliefs, clients learn a repertoire of activities they can use to adjust their behaviour when it seems problematic. For example, they may learn to conduct a private monologue in which they work out adaptive ways of thinking and coping with situations. They can then discuss with a therapist the quality and usefulness of these self-instructional statements. They may learn to organize their responses to specific situations in an orderly, more easily exercised set of steps.

Building Table 16.4 provides an overall summary of the psychoanalytic, humanistic, behavioural, and cognitive approaches to individual therapy.

Building Table 16.4

Key Components of Psychoanalytic, Humanistic, Behaviour, and Cognitive Therapies

Therapy	Nature of Psychopathology	Goal of Therapy	Role of Therapist	Role of Unconscious Material	Role of Patient's Insights	Techniques
Psychoanalytic	Maladjustment reflects inadequate conflict resolution and fixation in early development.	Attainment of maturity, strengthened ego functions, reduced control by unconscious or repressed impulses.	An *investigator*, uncovering conflicts and resistances.	Primary in classical psychoanalysis; less emphasized in ego analysis.	Includes not solely intellectual understanding but also emotional experiences.	Analyst takes an active role in interpreting the dreams and free associations of patients.
Humanistic	Incongruity between the real self and the potential, desired self; overdependence on others for gratification and self-esteem.	To foster self-determination, release human potential, expand awareness.	An *empathic person*, in honest encounter with client, sharing experience.	Emphasis is primarily on conscious experience.	There is more emphasis on *how* and *what* questions than *why* questions.	Help client to see the world from a different perspective and to focus on the present and the future instead of the past.
Behaviour	Symptomatic behaviour stems from faulty learning or learning of maladaptive behaviours.	To relieve symptomatic behaviour by suppressing or replacing maladaptive behaviours.	A *helper*, helping client unlearn old behaviours and learn new ones.	Not concerned with unconscious processes.	Irrelevant and unnecessary.	Clients learn new responses, establish new behaviours, and eliminate faulty or undesirable ones.
Cognitive	Maladjustment occurs because of faulty, irrational thought patterns.	To change the way clients think about themselves and the world.	A *trainer* and *co-investigator*, helping the client learn new, rational ways to think about the world.	Little or no concern with unconscious processes.	Irrelevant to therapy but may be used if they do occur.	Clients learn to think situations through logically and to reconsider many of their irrational assumptions.

Focus

Review
◆ According to Ellis, what are the consequences of developing irrational beliefs? p. 585
◆ Compare rational–emotive therapy and Beck's approach to cognitive therapy. pp. 585–586

Think Critically
◆ The cognitive approach has been criticized by some as being too mechanistic, ignoring underlying causes of problems such as poverty or exposure to violence. Do you agree or disagree with this concern? Why?

Cognitive therapy in its many forms has been used with adults and children, and with specialized groups such as women and the elderly (Davis & Padesky, 1989; DiGiuseppe, 1989; Glantz, 1989). It can be applied to such problems as anxiety disorders, marital difficulties, chronic pain, and (as is evident from Beck's and Dobson's work) depression. Cognitive therapy continues to make enormous strides. It is influencing an increasing number of theorists and practitioners who conduct both long-term therapy and brief therapy (which is considered in *Experiencing Psychology*).

Group therapy: A psycho-therapeutic process in which several people meet as a group with a therapist.

Group Therapy

W hen several people meet as a group to receive psychological help, the treatment is referred to as **group therapy**. This technique was introduced in the early 1900s and has become increasingly popular since the Second World War. One reason for its popularity is that the same therapist might see 8 to 10 clients in just one hour. Another reason for the popularity is that the therapist's fee is shared among the members of the group, making group therapy less expensive than individual therapy.

Group therapy also can be more effective than individual therapy (McRoberts, Burlingame, & Hoag, 1998), since the social pressures that operate in a group can help shape the members' behaviour. In addition, group members can be useful models of behaviour for one another, and groups provide frequent and varied opportunity for mutual reinforcement and support.

Technique and Formats

The techniques used in group therapy are determined largely by the nature of the group and the orientation of its therapist. The group may follow a psychoanalytic, client-centred, Gestalt, behavioural, or other approach. No two groups are alike, and no two groups deal with individual members in the same way.

In traditional group therapy, 6 to 12 clients meet on a regular basis (usually once a week) with a therapist in a clinic or hospital or in the therapist's office.

Generally, the therapist selects members on the basis of what they can gain from and offer to the group. The goal is to construct a group whose members are compatible (though not necessarily the same) in terms of age, needs, and problems. The duration of group therapy varies; it usually takes longer than 6 months, but there are a growing number of short-term groups (under 12 weeks) (Rose, 1991). The format of traditional group therapy varies, but generally each member describes her or his problems to the other members, who in turn relate their experiences with similar problems and how they coped with them. This gives individuals a chance to express their fears and anxieties to people who are warm and accepting; each member

experiencing psychology

Health Insurance and Brief Therapy

Whether psychologists like it or not, there is a new model for psychotherapy in town—and it is often a short, cognitive one. Professionals and patients have been forced by health care systems and health insurance companies into a model that, for economic reasons, is often short, focused—and sometimes especially effective (Cummings, Budman, & Lawrence, 1998). The model rejects many of the traditional ideas of the various therapies discussed so far in this chapter. Its proponents reject the idea that any one therapeutic approach can help all people with any behavioural or emotional problem. It rejects the belief that a person's unconscious or life history *must* be understood fully before the client can end therapy. Finally, it disavows the idea that the therapist and the client have to resolve past or future psychological problems during psychotherapy sessions.

Sometimes termed *brief therapy*, this therapeutic approach is based on a blend of psychotherapeutic orientations and skills (Cummings, 1986). A basic goal is to give clients what they need; the therapy therefore focuses on treating clients' problems efficiently and getting clients back on their own as quickly as possible. The time frame varies from therapist to therapist and client to client, but 6 weeks is common and 16 to 24 weeks is considered lengthy. One of its objectives is to save clients time and money. Although insurance companies or health care systems may place limits on the number of sessions, clients may remain in therapy longer if they feel the need and are willing and able to continue to pay. They also can return if they need help in the future. The key distinction of this changing approach to therapy is that more and more therapists are thinking in terms of *planned* short-term treatments (Messer & Wachtel, 1997).

The therapist makes sure that treatment begins in the first session of brief therapy. He or she strives to perform an *operational diagnosis* that answers this question: Why is the client here today instead of last week, last month, last year, or next year? The answer indicates to the therapist the specific problem for which the client is seeking help. Also in the first session, "every client makes a therapeutic contract with every therapist" (N. A. Cummings, 1986, p. 430; Goulding, 1990). The goals of therapy are established and agreed on by the client and the therapist, and the therapy is precise, active, and directive, with no unnecessary steps (Clarkin & Hull, 1991; Lazarus & Fay, 1990).

Published research on brief therapy is encouraging, suggesting that the therapy is effective and that its effects are long-lasting (e.g., Barber & Ellman, 1996; Shefler, Dasberg, & Ben-Shakhar, 1995). Research has been limited to relatively few clients with a narrow range of problems. Nonetheless, researchers have found brief therapy to be effective when treatment goals and procedures are tailored to the client's needs and the time available. It can be especially effective with couples (Donovan, 1998) and when combined with cognitive restructuring (Ellis, 1990).

Brief therapy is not a cure-all. As with all therapies, its aim is to help relieve clients' suffering, and it will be effective with some clients and with some problems some of the time (Franko & Erb, 1998). Further research on brief therapy is being conducted now, and its future will depend on the results of that research. ■

eventually realizes that everyone has emotional problems. Group members also have opportunities to role play (try out) new behaviours in a safe but evaluative environment. In a mental health centre, for example, a therapist might help members relive past traumas and cope with their continuing fears. Finally, in group therapy, members can exert pressure on an individual to behave in more appropriate ways. Sometimes the therapist is directive in helping the group cope with a problem. At other times the therapist allows the group to resolve a problem independently.

Nontraditional Group Therapy

Two nontraditional techniques sometimes used in group therapy are psychodrama and encounter groups. **Psychodrama** is a group therapy procedure in which members act out their situations, feelings, and roles. It stems from the work of J. L. Moreno, a Viennese psychiatrist who used this technique in the 1920s and 1930s. Those who participate can practise expressing their feelings and responding to the feelings of others. Even those who do not participate can see how others respond to different emotions and situations. Psychodrama can help open the floodgates of emotion and can be used to refine social skills and define problem areas that need to be worked on further (Naar, 1990).

All kinds of other groups come together to learn more about their feelings, behaviour, and interactions. In the 1960s and 1970s such groups were termed **encounter groups**; today they often taken on specialized names such as "The Special Awareness Group" or the "Mediation as a Way of Life Group." These groups are designed to offer people experiences that will help them self-actualize and develop better interpersonal relationships and a sense of authenticity or genuineness. (Self-actualization, which we examined in Chapters 9 and 12, is the process by which people move towards fulfilling their potential.) These encounter groups also enable their members to work on resolving their own problems and perceiving—and ultimately minimizing—the effects of their problems on others. Each encounter group is unique. Some are like regular therapy groups. In others, the therapist participates minimally, if at all. Some researchers believe that encounter groups made up of specific types of people—such as drug addicts, alcoholics, or singles—have an advantage in therapy.

Family Therapy

A special form of group therapy is family therapy. **Family therapy** is therapy in which two or more people who are committed to each other's well-being are treated at once in an effort to change the ways in which they interact. (Marital, or couple, therapy is thus a subcategory of family therapy.) A *family* is defined as any group of people who are committed to one another's well-being, preferably for life (Bronfenbrenner, 1989). Today it is widely recognized that families are often non-traditional; there are blended families and single-parent families, among others. Different kinds of families are shaping the way people respond to the world and must be considered as part of the cultural context in which psychologists view behaviour. And even for traditional families, life has grown more complicated because of the increasing need to juggle work and family responsibilities and cope with crime and health problems such as AIDS.

With families facing new kinds of problems, family therapy is now widely used by a large number of practitioners, especially social workers. Family therapy aims to change the ways in which family members interact. Currently, brief family therapy is more common and symptom relief (immediate problem resolution) is usually the first goal, but certainly not the only goal. From a family therapist's point of view, the real patient in family therapy is the family's structure and organization. While parents may identify one member of their family—perhaps a delinquent child—as the problem, family therapists believe that, in many cases, that person simply may be a scapegoat. The so-called problem member becomes the focus of the family's attention, which turns away from structural problems that are difficult to confront. Any clinician who works with a person who has some type of adjustment problem also must consider the impact of this problem on the people that individual interacts with.

Sometimes family therapy is termed *relationship therapy*, because relationships are often the focus of the intervention, especially with couples (Jacobson & Addis, 1993). Research on effectiveness indicates that, like other forms of therapy, family therapy and marital (couple) therapy are effective (Pinsof, Wynne, & Hambright,

1996; Shadish et al., 1993). However, because of the myriad of variables found within families, doing such research is complicated to say the least (Lebow & Gurman, 1995).

Family therapists often attempt to change *family systems*. This means that treatment takes place within the ongoing, active social system that is a marriage or a family (Fruzzetti & Jacobson, 1991). Therapists assume that there are multiple sources of psychological influence: Individuals within a family affect family interactions, and family interactions affect individuals; the family is thus an interactive system (Sturges, 1994). For example, when a mother labels a son "lazy" because he is not working, the son may feel shame but may act out his feeling as anger. He may lash out at his father's poor work habits and lack of success. This may be followed by a squabble over who supports the family and so forth. The mother's attitude may lead to a clash among all of the individuals within the closed system, the family. The family systems approach has become especially popular in faculties of social work, in departments of psychology, and even in colleges of medicine, where patients are often seen in a family setting. A useful technique in family therapy is to *restructure* the family's interactions. If a son is responding too submissively to his domineering mother, for example, the therapist may suggest that the son be assigned chores only by his father.

An issue that often emerges in family therapy is how families become enmeshed in one member's problems—for example, depression, alcoholism, drug abuse, child abuse, or anxiety disorders. Such involvement often becomes devastating for the whole family. This problem is termed *codependence*. Codependence is not a disorder in the *DSM–IV*. In fact, the families of people with disorders such as substance abuse often have gone relatively unnoticed. But practitioners who treat whole families, not just the person suffering from maladjustment, view codependence as an additional type of adjustment problem—not for the patient but for the patient's family and friends.

The codependents—the family members or friends—are often plagued by intense feelings of shame, fear, anger, or pain; they cannot express those feelings, however, because of an intense desire to please and care for the person suffering from the disorder or addiction. Codependent children may believe that their job is to take care of their maladjusted parents. Codependent adults may strive to help their maladjusted spouses, relatives, or friends with problems. They often think that if they were perfect, they could help the maladjusted individual. In some cases, people actually *need* the person to stay disordered; for example, families sometimes unwittingly want a member with a problem to remain dependent on them so they can stay in a controlling position. Practitioners often see patients with alcoholism or cocaine addiction whose friends or family members are codependent.

Some researchers believe the family systems approach is as effective as individual therapy—and more effective in some situations (Ford et al., 1998). Not all families profit equally from such interventions, however. Family therapy is difficult with families that are disorganized or in which not all members participate. Younger couples and families seem to have better outcomes; when depression is evident, outcomes are not as good (Lebow & Gurman, 1995). In addition, some family members may drop out of therapy; this almost always has negative consequences (Prinz & Miller, 1994).

In the end, family therapy today is eclectic, borrows from many schools of therapy, and is willing to consider a broad range of families and problems (Guerin & Chabot, 1997). Family therapists join with families in helping them change because they acknowledge and recognize that change of one sort or another is inevitable in a dynamic system. They further assert that

Focus

Review

◆ Identify the advantages of various forms of group therapy over individual therapy. pp. 588–589

Think Critically

◆ Why do you think that having several people in treatment together makes such a difference in group therapy? Isn't getting a great deal of one-on-one attention—individual therapy—likely to produce superior results?

only a small change is necessary to make a big difference. Most family therapists assert that clients have the strength and resources to change and that people don't need to understand the origins of a problem to solve it. Finally, there is no *one* solution to family problems—especially given today's complicated families (Selekman, 1993).

Biologically Based Therapies

hen an individual is referred to a practitioner for help, the usual approach involves some form of psychological treatment. This generally means psychological therapy that may be based on psychodynamic, humanistic, behavioural, or cognitive theories. For some patients, however, psychotherapy is not enough. Some may be too profoundly depressed; others may be exhibiting symptoms of bipolar disorders (manic depression) or schizophrenia; still others may need hospitalization because they are suicidal. This is where the potential role of biologically based therapies emerges. These therapies may include medication, hospitalization, and the involvement of physicians. They generally are used in combination with traditional forms of psychotherapy, in a multimodal approach. Biologically based therapies fall into three broad classes: psychosurgery (rarely used), electroconvulsive therapy (occasionally used), and drug therapy (often used).

Psychosurgery and Electroconvulsive Therapy

Psychosurgery is brain surgery; it was used in the past to alleviate symptoms of serious mental disorders. A particular type of psychosurgery commonly performed in the 1940s and 1950s was *prefrontal lobotomies*, in which a surgeon would sever parts of the brain's frontal lobes from the rest of the brain. The frontal lobes were thought to control emotions; their removal destroyed connections within the brain, making patients docile. Patients lost the symptoms of their mental disorders, but they also became overly calm and completely unemotional. Some became unable to control their impulses, and an estimated 1 to 4 percent died from the operation.

Today, despite advances in technology and in the precision of the operation, psychosurgery is rarely used for three basic reasons. First, drug therapy has proved

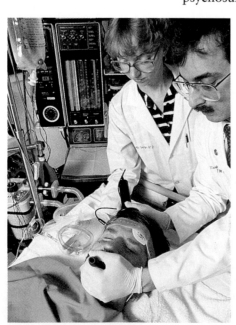

more effective than surgical procedures. Second, the long-term effects of psychosurgery are questionable. Third, and most important, the procedure is irreversible and therefore morally objectionable to most practitioners and to patients and their families. Its widespread use during the 1940s and 1950s is considered by many to have been a serious mistake.

Electroconvulsive therapy (ECT), or *shock treatment*, once widely employed with depressed individuals, is a treatment for severe mental illness in which a brief application of electricity to the head is used to produce a generalized seizure (convulsion). The duration of the shock is less than a second, and patients, who are sedated and on muscle relaxants at the time of treatment, are treated in 3 to 12 sessions over several weeks. In the 1940s and 1950s, ECT was routinely given to severely disturbed patients in mental hospitals. Unfortunately, it often was used on patients who did not need it (mostly women) and by overzealous physicians who wished to control unruly patients. Today, ECT is not a common treatment. According to the National Institutes of Health, fewer than 2.5 percent of all psychiatric hospital patients are treated with ECT.

Is ECT at all effective? Could drug therapy or traditional psychotherapy be used in its place? ECT is effective in the short-term management of severely depressed individuals, those suffering from extreme episodes of mania, and people with psychotic depression (Flint & Rifat, 1998); it is sometimes used when a particular patient is at risk of suicide (Cohen et al., 1997; Mukherjee, Sackeim, & Schnurr, 1994). However, its effects are only temporary if it is not followed by drug therapy and psychotherapy (Parker et al., 1992). Generally speaking, ECT should be used as a last resort, when other forms of treatment have been ineffective and when a patient is not responsive to medications. ECT is not appropriate for treating schizophrenia or for managing unruly behaviours associated with other disorders.

The medical risk of death during the administration of ECT is low (Coffey et al., 1991). However, there is a potential for memory loss and for a decreased ability to learn and retain new information that may endure for several weeks. In addition, ECT may frighten patients and can leave them with feelings of shame and of being stigmatized (Fink, 1997). If practitioners determine that ECT is warranted, the law requires (and medical ethics demand) that the patient has the right to accept or reject the treatment. Much more research is needed to determine the full effects of ECT and the groups for whom the treatment may be beneficial.

Drug Therapy

In this fast paced society, people seem to want quick fixes. During every election campaign, politicians promise a quick fix for the economy, a new plan to eliminate poverty, or a simple solution to concerns over youth violence. In the same manner, people often want to take drugs to alleviate emotional problems. Drug therapy is an important form of treatment, especially for anxiety, depression, and schizophrenia. It is the most widely used biologically based therapy, and it is effective when used correctly and carefully. But several key issues must be stressed. Dosages are especially important and must be monitored; too much or too little of certain drugs is dangerous. Long-term use of many drugs is ill advised. Further, no drug will permanently cure the maladjustment of people who are not coping well. Last, physicians and psychiatrists must be sensitive to the issues of overmedication and long-term dependence on drugs.

Drug therapy can be an effective method for treating a variety of disorders. But often clinicians are reluctant to turn to drug therapy until after traditional forms of psychotherapy have failed—which may cause a delay in the patient's healing. Drug therapy is sometimes used in combination with traditional talking therapy (see *Experiencing Psychology* on page 594).

In the last decade, clinical psychologists in some American jurisdictions have sought the ability to prescribe prescriptions for a limited class of drugs. The argument is that patients would benefit by the better integration of medications and psychological techniques (Hines, 1997; Tuckman, 1997); but this is a controversial proposition even among psychologists (Gutierrez & Silk, 1998; Plante, Boccaccini, & Anderssen, 1998). Those who support the idea recognize that additional training would be necessary and that licensing authority would need to be instituted (Klusman, 1998). Provincial colleges of psychologists in Canada are watching this American debate with interest.

When physicians (often psychiatrists) do administer drugs, people may experience relief from symptoms of anxiety, mania, depression, and schizophrenia. Drugs for the relief of mental problems are sometimes termed *psychotropic drugs*; they are usually grouped into four classes: antianxiety drugs, antidepressant drugs, antimania drugs, and antipsychotic drugs.

Antianxiety Drugs. Antianxiety drugs, or tranquillizers, (technically *anxiolytics*) are mood-altering substances. Widely used in Canada, these drugs reduce stressful feelings, calm patients, and lower excitability. Librium, Xanax, and Valium are trade names of the most widely prescribed antianxiety drugs. When taken occasionally to help a person through a stressful situation, such drugs are useful. They also help manage anxiety in a person who is extremely anxious, particularly when

experiencing psychology

Talking Therapy, Drug Therapy, and Depression

Depression is the most common disorder seen by the medical, psychiatric, and psychological communities. Nearly 20 percent of the population will experience a depressive episode at one time or another. Women are twice as likely as men to be diagnosed as depressed; the aged are more likely than others to be depressed, as are widows and people with lower incomes (Coryell, Endicott, & Keller, 1992; Umberson, Wortman, & Kessler, 1992).

Treatment for depression traditionally has involved insight-oriented therapy, drug therapy, or a combination of the two. Insight therapy has been used to help patients gain an understanding of the causes of their feelings of sadness. Drug therapy has proved especially effective in altering brain activity in ways that alleviate depressive symptoms. Prozac and Zoloft are two popular and effective drugs. Most practitioners and theoreticians believe that the most effective treatment is drugs in combination with psychotherapy.

New research is challenging this idea, however. In the last decade, psychologists have found that (1) psychotherapy is especially effective for depression; (2) the benefits of psychotherapy for depression are long-lasting; and (3) most importantly, combinations of psychotherapy and drug therapy are *not* necessarily more effective than

either of the treatments alone (Persons, Thase, & Crits-Christoph, 1996). In important reviews of the research literature on the treatment of depression, Muñoz and colleagues (1994) argued that psychotherapy is more effective than medicine in depression; Antonuccio, Danton, and DeNelsky (1995) came to the same conclusion. Robinson, Berman, and Neimeyer earlier argued (1990) that drug therapy alone or traditional psychotherapy alone is equally effective for patients suffering from depression. These researchers' findings startled some members of the psychological community because they challenged the long-held idea that combination treatments are the most effective. The three researchers acknowledge that drug therapy plus psychotherapy may be the most effective treatment for some other disorders. Research shows them to be correct—for example, for anxiety disorders in adolescents a combination of drug therapy and behaviour therapy is especially effective (Kearney & Silverman, 1998). However, for the types of drugs examined by Robinson and his colleagues and for patients suffering from clinical depression, the result was clear: The combination treatment provided no additional benefit over drug therapy alone or psychotherapy alone.

The work of these researchers raises a question: How many people

are being given drugs when they don't need them? The answer is unclear; but with each passing month, new research on various disorders and on the role of psychotherapy and drug therapy continues to emerge (Southwick & Yehuda, 1993). For example, Wexler and Cicchetti (1992), like Muñoz and colleagues (1994), argue that psychotherapy alone has the advantage. These studies led Antonuccio to assert that "when treating depression, there is no stronger medicine than psychotherapy" (1995, p. 451). In a review of studies on psychotherapy and depression, Antonuccio, Danton, and DeNelsky (1995, p. 582) wrote: "there is a tendency to underestimate the power and cost-effectiveness of a caring, confidential psychotherapeutic relationship in the treatment of depression . . . for those who do not respond to psychotherapy, the costs and benefits of drug treatments or combined treatments can then be carefully weighed." Today, most therapists are practical and say that an initial treatment with psychotherapy alone perhaps might be followed by combination treatment. There are likely to be further studies showing which types of depressive disorders can best benefit from drug therapy, which from insight therapy, which from cognitive therapy, and which from combinations of drug therapy and traditional talking therapies. ■

the person is also receiving some form of psychotherapy. However, long-term use of antianxiety drugs without some adjunct therapy is usually ill advised because they are highly addictive and potentially fatal if mixed with alcohol. Today, physicians are wary of patients seeking antianxiety drugs for management of daily stress; they worry about substance abuse and an overreliance on drugs to get through the day.

Antidepressant Drugs. As their name suggests, antidepressants (technically *thymoleptics*) are sometimes considered mood elevators. They work by altering the level of neurotransmitters in the brain. With the wide availability of antidepressants, it is surprising that half of those who have been depressed for more than 20 years have never taken an antidepressant (Hirschfeld et al., 1997). Depression often goes undiagnosed and likely is undertreated.

One kind of antidepressant, selective serotonin reuptake inhibitors (SSRIs), or simply serotonin reuptake inhibitors, blocks the reuptake of serotonin. When a neuron sends a key neurotransmitter (usually serotonin or norepinephrine) across a synapse, there is often an excess of the neurotransmitter; this excess is then reabsorbed into the transmitting neuron (a process called *reuptake*). In depressed individuals, often too little of the neurotransmitter is absorbed into the next cell because of the reuptake—antidepressants block this reuptake.

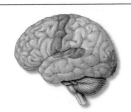

brain and behaviour
A Best-Selling Medication—Prozac

Since its introduction in 1987 about 28 million people have taken the drug Prozac. Along with two other drugs, Zoloft and Paxil, which are close to Prozac in chemical make-up, this "wonder drug" is so popular that pharmacies need whole shelves to stock the supply necessary for one week. Yearly sales of such drugs are upward of $4 billion.

Many people who take Prozac and its sister medications feel better—their symptoms of depression lift, their appetites return, and the gloomy outlook seems less bleak. People who take the drug feel so much better that they do better in their work and their relationships, and life seems to turn around. The drugs decrease the likelihood of new episodes of depression (Montgomery & Kasper, 1998) and work well for older adults (Mittmann et al., 1997; Salzman, 1997) and even for children (Ryan & Varma, 1998).

The number of side effects from drugs like Prozac is small compared to drugs used earlier. Those drugs had potent side effects—increased heart rate, increased blood pressure, nausea, and sleepiness, to name a few. So one reason why Prozac has been so successful is that it is relatively free of serious side effects. But it is not totally without them.

Researchers have long known that drugs that affect the reuptake of monoamines (serotonin, dopamine, norepinephrine, epinephrine) can lighten some depressive symptoms. But the runaway success of Prozac has startled practitioners and researchers alike. They are surprised because not everyone who takes Prozac feels better. Furthermore, there are some side effects to Prozac, including a diminution of sexual appetite. Originally intended for shorter durations—six months or so—Prozac is now being taken for years on end. Are people staying on the drug too long? Researchers are wondering if the drug (among many others) is being over-prescribed (Messer & Wachtel, 1997). How many people who take the drug actually need it? How many were not properly diagnosed?

The effects of this class of drugs are so quickly evident, and the side effects so few, that psychologists worry that the original problems—low self-esteem or depression over a bad relationship, for example—may not get the attention they deserve. SSRIs have an important place in the treatment of people with various disorders—but most psychologists feel they should be part of a full treatment program that also involves—or should involve—short-term or perhaps even long-term psychotherapy.

Some researchers have questioned whether explanations of depression, schizophrenia, and a host of other disorders can rely solely on brain chemistry explanations (Valenstein, 1998). They argue that easy explanations and quick fixes through drugs are rarely the complete answer to psychological problems. Will new drugs evolve that will be better, more refined, and more potent than today's SSRIs? The answer is undoubtedly yes. Will drugs alone solve people's psychological problems? The answer is surely no. Are they part of a solution for some people? The answer is unquestionably yes. ∎

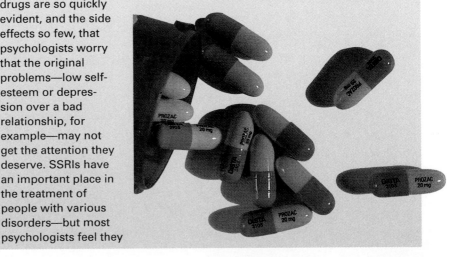

Drugs such as Prozac, Zoloft, and Paxil are SSRI antidepressants. These drugs account for the majority of antidepressant sales in Canada and the United States. *Brain and Behaviour* discusses the success of Prozac (see page 595). Extremely depressed people who take these antidepressants often become more optimistic and less sad and redevelop a sense of purpose in their lives. These medications allow many people to function outside a hospital setting. The drugs can take as long as four weeks to reach their full effectiveness, and daily use is necessary.

Antidepressants also include two other major categories of drugs: tricyclics and monoamine oxidase (MAO) inhibitors. Both types of drugs are potent. The tricyclics (named for their chemical structure) act like SSRIs in blocking reuptake, but MAO inhibitors work by breaking down the enzyme (monoamine oxidase) that destroys the neurotransmitters norepinephrine and serotonin. The tricyclics are prescribed much more often than the MAO inhibitors because they pose less danger of

Table 16.5 Drugs Commonly Used to Treat Psychiatric Disorders

Effect Group	Chemical Group	Generic Name	Trade Name	Function	Common Side Effects
Antianxiety (anxiolytic)	Benzodiazepines	Diazepam Chlordiazepoxide Alprazolam Clonazepam	Valium Librium Xanax Klonapin	Increases neurotransmission of GABA	Addictive, fatal when mixed with alcohol, slurred speech, dry mouth, lightheadedness, diminished motor control. May cause "rebound anxiety" at a *more* intense level than prior to medication
	Nonbenzodiazepine	Buspirone	Buspar	As above	Not addictive, takes longer to be effective
Antidepressant (thymoleptic)	Tricylics	Amitriptyline Imipramine Nortriptyline Desipramine Doxepin Clomipramine	Elavil Tofranil Pamelor Norpramin Sinequan Anafranil	Block reuptake of serotonin *and* norepinephrine	Dry mouth, dizziness, blurred vision, weight gain
	Monoamine oxidase inhibitors	Phenelzine Tranylcypromine	Nardil Parnate	Blocks the breakdown of norepinephrine and serotonin, making more available for transmission	Dangerous rise in blood pressure if patient does not follow dietary restrictions
	Serotonin reuptake inhibitors	Fluoxetine Sertraline Paroxetine Fluvoxamine	Prozac Zoloft Paxil Luvox	Blocks the reuptake or reabsorption of only serotonin	Nausea, insomnia, diarrhea, headache, anxiety, loss of sexual desire or response
Antimanic (thymoleptic)	Lithium carbonate	Lithium	Eskalith Lithonate Lithobid	Uncertain	Weight gain, tremors, dry mouth, thirst, toxic at high levels, excessive urination, fatigue
	GABA agonist	Valproic acid	Depakene	Better for fast cycling disorders	
Antipsychotic (neuroleptic)	Phenothiazines	Chlorpromazine Trifluoperazine Fluphenazine Thioridazine	Thorazine Stelazine Prolixin Mellaril	Block neurotransmission of dopamine, effects positive symptoms	Sedation, constipation, dry mouth, blurred vision, cardiac irregularities, tremors and muscle spasms, restlessness, a shuffling gait. Can produce permanent Parkinson's-like motor disorders involving shaking, loss of voluntary muscle control, and stiff muscles
	Atypical antipsychotic	Clozapine Risperidone	Clozaril Risperdal		

medical complications. (Patients on MAO inhibitors have to adhere to special diets and some other restrictions to prevent adverse physical reactions to the drugs.) To help a patient suffering from a severe bout of depression, a physician might prescribe a commonly used tricyclic such as imipramine (Tofranil) or amitriptyline (Elavil), which will have fewer serious side effects and alleviate symptoms in the majority of people with depressive problems.

Research on the effectiveness of antidepressant drugs is controversial. Some researchers assert that these drugs have major effects, while others report only modest help from the drugs (Greenberg et al., 1992; Schulberg & Rush, 1994). Research using double-blind procedures and carefully controlled conditions continues, especially with drugs that have specific actions on depressive behaviours (Dubovsky & Thomas, 1995; Roose et al., 1994). The impact of new research findings will be profound, because the number of people with depressive disorders is substantial.

Antimania Drugs. Lithium carbonate, the only effective antimania drug (also technically a *thymoleptic*), has come into wide use for patients with bipolar (manic–depressive) disorders because it relieves the manic elements. Psychiatrists find that when a daily maintenance dose is taken, lithium is especially helpful in warding off future episodes of mania. The dosage of any drug is important, but in the case of lithium it is especially important because lithium is toxic at high doses. Too much produces noxious side effects such as weight gain, tremors and dry mouth; too little has no effect. No drug will cure individuals with bipolar disorder of all of their symptoms and will solve all of their problems (for example, lithium is less effective with young patients). In general, however, lithium allows some patients to cope better, to control their symptoms, and to seek other therapies that allow them to manage their lives in the most productive way possible (Moncrieff, 1997). The same is true of other drugs in this class, including valproic acid, or valproate.

Antipsychotic Drugs. Antipsychotic drugs (technically *neuroleptics*) are used mainly for people who suffer from the disabling disorder of schizophrenia. These drugs reduce hostility and aggression in violent patients and make their disorders more manageable. They also reduce delusions and allow some patients to manage life outside a hospital setting.

Most of the antipsychotic drugs prescribed are phenothiazines, the most common of which is chlorpromazine (Thorazine). They seem to work on the positive symptoms of schizophrenia by altering the level and uptake of the neurotransmitter dopamine—but this is uncertain (Lidsky et al., 1997). As with antidepressants, dosages of antipsychotic drugs are crucial. Further, if patients are maintained on antipsychotic drugs for too long, other problems can emerge, such as blurred vision, sedation, cardiac abnormalities, and dry mouth. Another serious side effect is *tardive dyskinesia*—a central nervous system disorder characterized by involuntary, spasmodic movements of the upper body, especially the face and fingers, and including leg jiggling and tongue protrusions, facial tics, and involuntary movements of the mouth and shoulders. See Table 16.5 for a detailed listing of some common drugs used to treat psychiatric disorders and their common side effects. The atypical antipsychotic drugs, which reduce both major positive and negative symptoms, may act by affecting specific groups of dopamine neurons. These drugs are costly and one, Clozaril, causes a potentially fatal blood disorder in a small percentage of patients (Alvir et al., 1993).

Focus

Review
- What are the ethical implications of psychosurgery and of electroconvulsive therapy (ECT)? pp. 592–593
- What are the major classes of psychotropic drugs, and what evidence exists to show their effectiveness in which situations? pp. 593–597

Think Critically
- What is the implication of the lag time that occurs before some drug treatments have an effect?
- If drug therapy is so effective, why aren't more people being treated in this way?
- What is the solution to the problem of the overprescription of medications, especially antidepressants?

Summary and Review

Therapy Comes in Many Forms

What is the essential difference between biologically based therapy and psychotherapy?

■ Two broad types of therapy are biologically based therapy and psychotherapy. *Biologically based therapy* refers to treatment of emotional or behavioural problems by means of treating the body. *Psychotherapy* is treatment through psychological techniques. p. 564

Is therapy necessary and effective in the long run?

■ A *placebo effect* is a nonspecific therapeutic change that occurs as a result of a person's expectations of change rather than as a direct result of a certain treatment. However, any long-term therapeutic effects come from the client's and therapist's efforts. p. 566

KEY TERMS
psychotherapy, p. 564; placebo effect, p. 566

Psychoanalysis and Psychodynamic Therapies

According to psychoanalytic theory, what causes maladjustment and what processes are involved in treatment?

■ *Insight therapies*, which include *psychodynamically based therapies*, assume that maladjustment and abnormal behaviour are caused by people's failure to understand their own motivations and needs. Insight therapists believe that once patients understand the motivations that produce maladjusted behaviour, the behaviour can be changed. p. 570

■ According to Freud, conflicts among a person's unconscious thoughts and processes produce maladjusted behaviour. Classical Freudian *psychoanalysis* often involves a process of *free association, dream analysis, interpretation, resistance,* and *transference*; collectively, this repetitive cycle is referred to as *working through*. pp. 571–572

What are the basic criticisms of psychoanalysis?

■ *Ego analysts* are psychoanalytic practitioners who are often critical of classical Freudian analysis and believe that the ego has greater control over behaviour than Freud suggested. They are more concerned with reality testing and control over the environment than with unconscious motivations and processes. p. 573

■ Critics of psychoanalysis contend that the approach is unscientific, imprecise, and subjective. Other critics object to Freud's biologically oriented approach, which suggests that a human being is a mere bundle of energy caught in conflict and driven towards some hedonistic goal. Further, many elements of Freud's theory are sexist or untestable. p. 573

KEY TERMS
psychoanalysis, p. 570; psychodynamically based therapies, p. 570; insight therapy, p. 570; free association, p. 571; dream analysis, p. 571; interpretation, p. 572; resistance, p. 572; transference, p. 572; working through, p. 572

Humanistic Therapies

Briefly describe the major differences between client-centred therapy and Gestalt therapy.

■ *Client-centred therapy* aims to help clients realize their potential by learning to evaluate the world and themselves from their own point of view. This approach is a *nondirective therapy*, and the therapist conveys unconditional positive regard while letting the client set the agenda for therapy. pp. 574–575

■ *Gestalt therapy* encourages individuals to get in touch with their current feelings and become aware of their current situations. Gestalt techniques are designed to help clients become more alert to their significant feelings and to their surroundings in the "here and now." p. 576

KEY TERMS
client-centred therapy, p. 574; nondirective therapy, p. 575; Gestalt therapy, p. 576

Behaviour Therapy

Identify the basic assumptions and techniques of behaviour therapy.

■ *Behaviour therapy*, or behaviour modification, is a therapy based on the application of learning principles to human behaviour. It focuses on changing overt behaviours rather than on understanding subjective feelings, unconscious processes, or motivations. It attempts to replace old behaviours with new, more adaptive ones. p. 577

■ Techniques of behaviour therapy include *token economies, time-out,* and *counterconditioning. Systematic desensitization* is a three-stage counterconditioning procedure in which a person is taught to relax while imagining increasingly fearful situations. pp. 580–582

■ As part of behaviour therapy, modelling is especially effective in three areas: (1) teaching new behaviour, (2) helping to eliminate fears, especially phobias, and (3) enhancing already existing behaviour. pp. 582–583

KEY TERMS
behavior therapy, p. 577; symptom substitution, p. 578; token economy, p. 580; time-out, p. 581; counterconditioning, p. 581; systematic desensitization, p. 582; aversive counter conditioning, p. 582

Cognitive Therapy

What are the basic propositions of cognitive therapy?

■ The three basic propositions of cognitive therapy are: (1) Cognitive activity affects behaviour; (2) cognitive activity can be monitored; (3) behaviour changes can be effected through cognitive changes. p. 584

■ *Rational–emotive therapy* emphasizes the role of logical, rational thought processes in behaviour. It assumes that faulty, irrational thinking patterns are the cause of abnormal behaviour. p. 585

KEY TERM
rational–emotive therapy, p. 585

Group Therapy

What is group therapy, and what is the function of family therapy?

■ *Group therapy* is therapy used to treat several people simultaneously for emotional and behavioural problems. The techniques used by a therapy group are determined by the nature of the group and the orientation of its therapist. pp. 588–589

■ *Family therapy* attempts to change family systems, because individuals affect family processes and family processes affect individuals. Treatment takes place within an ongoing, active social system such as a marriage or family. pp. 590–592

KEY TERMS
group therapy, p. 588; psychodrama, p. 590; encounter group, p. 590; family therapy, p. 590

Biologically Based Therapies

What are the major types of biologically based therapies and the major classes of psychotropic drugs?

■ The major biologically based therapies are psychosurgery, electroconvulsive therapy, and drug therapy. *Psychosurgery* (brain surgery) is a generally outmoded method of treatment used to alleviate symptoms of serious mental disorders. *Electroconvulsive therapy (ECT)* is a treatment for severe mental illness in which a brief application of electricity to the head is used to produce a generalized seizure. pp. 592–593

■ Drugs for the relief of mental problems usually are grouped into four classes: antianxiety drugs, antidepressant drugs, antimania drugs, and antipsychotic drugs. Such drugs often work by altering the level of neurotransmitters in the brain. For example, when a neuron sends a key neurotransmitter across a synapse, there is often an excess of the neurotransmitter; this excess is then reabsorbed into the transmitting neuron—reuptake. In depressed individuals, too little of the neurotransmitter is often absorbed into the next cell because of the reuptake—but antidepressants block such reuptake. pp. 593–5978

KEY TERMS
psychosurgery, p. 592; electroconvulsive therapy (ECT), p. 592

Weblinks

Internet Mental Health Guide
www.mentalhealth.com
This Web page covers many treatment issues, including the use of drugs.

Association for Humanistic Psychology
ahpweb.org/index.html
The home page of an international organization "dedicated to the exploration and healing of the human mind, body and soul" presents its magazine and journal and provides links.

American Association for Marriage and Family Therapy
www.aamft.org
An in-depth resource site for couples, families, educators, academics, and practitioners.

Association for Advancement of Behavior Therapy
server.psyc.vt.edu/aabt
The home page of a professional, interdisciplinary association concerned with the use and possible benefits of behaviour therapy provides information about journals and conferences.

American Psychoanalytic Association
apsa.org/pubinfo/about.htm
To learn more about psychoanalysis and psychoanalytic therapy, visit this home page. How to find a psychoanalyst, who can benefit from psychoanalysis, and who is a psychoanalyst are all discussed.

Behavior Online
www.behavior.net/gestalt.html
This detailed essay is an introduction to Gestalt therapy.

How to Start a Self-Help/Advocacy Group
www.libertynot.org/mha/chouse/shag.html
The Center for Mental Health Services provides information on topics such as how to begin a group, your first meeting, and the role of professionals in self-help groups.

Rational Emotive Behavior Therapy
www.threeminutetherapy.com/rebt.html
For a complete yet brief description of rational–emotive therapy, visit Dr. Edelstein's "Three Minute Therapy" page.

Antianxiety Medications
pharmacology.tqn.com/library/weekly/bl970717.htm
An introduction to antianxiety medications, such as benzodiazepines, is provided at this Web site.

Chapter 17

Applied Psychology

Lorraine Finn is one of the new breed of coaches. She isn't a mom, she isn't a gym teacher; she's married, young, athletic, feminine, and focused on one thing and one thing only: winning. Lorraine coaches the little league team in the afternoon, the high-school team in the early evening, and the insurance company's senior league on weekends. She has a mantra that she repeats over and over: Keep your eye on the ball. And she means this literally and figuratively. She urges, coerces, and yells at players to focus and watch the ball. "You can't hit what you don't see," she says. Figuratively, she keeps telling her players, young and old, to focus on the task at hand—playing ball, having fun, and winning.

In some ways, Lorraine thinks of herself as the president of a company trying to motivate employees. Her job, she feels, is to keep her players motivated, working hard, focused on the task at hand, enjoying the challenge, and ultimately winning ball games. Lorraine took a minor in psychology in college. In fact, she took 21 credit hours in the discipline because she found it so relevant. Among other things, she studied and focused on learning, motivation, health psychology, and personality. She found psychology relevant to day-to-day living and especially to coaching baseball

Applied psychology is the branch of psychology that uses psychological principles to help solve practical problems of everyday living—whether those problems come up on the job, at school, or on the playing field. Consider Lorraine and baseball, for example. Applied psychologists examine how the basics of behaviour, such as learning and memory, affect day-to-day athletic activities. They also consider how coaches like Lorraine can motivate athletes to demonstrate peak performance by using common psychological mechanisms to help them visualize possibilities, overcome obstacles, and achieve fulfilment. To a great extent, applied psychologists help people better manage their own behaviour. Whether you are the coach of the Montreal Canadiens, the neighbourhood house hockey league director, or a manager making human resource decisions, the resources and psychological principles of applied psychology go a long way. ■

In this chapter we consider an array of fields in which psychology is indeed applied to modern life. We begin with the workplace, because this is the place where psychological principles have been systematically studied and applied for so long—even as far back as John B. Watson, who applied psychology to a Maxwell House coffee advertising campaign in 1915.

Industrial/Organizational Psychology

Work consumes a high proportion of a person's waking hours, and how we work, where we work, and why we work are important questions. Increased global competition, changes in information technology, and industrial reengineering are fast changing the world of work. As productivity has become increasingly important to business, industrial/organizational psychology has grown in importance. **Industrial/organizational (I/O) psychology** is the study of how individual behaviour is affected by the work environment, by co-workers, and by organizational practices. It is the study of people not only in industry but in government, hospitals, universities, and non-profit organizations. I/O psychologists study behaviour in large and small businesses—from small biotech startups to large multinational corporations. In all of these environments, key concerns are how well individuals perform their duties and relate to one another; I/O psychology is increasingly being applied to address those concerns through provision of research-based answers to pressing organizational problems (Cascio, 1995). Large companies have I/O psychologists on site, working in their human resources departments, and small companies hire them as consultants.

I/O psychologists pay close attention to the type of company in which they work, because companies vary in their organizational structures, and worldwide companies vary even more. Given today's increasingly global economy, I/O psychologists must take into account global multicultural differences among organizations. Many companies reflect an organizational structure that in turn reflects their society. Asian companies—in Korea, for example—often reflect a family orientation, where people work hard for the good of the entire family. This affects hiring decisions, firing, promotions, hierarchies, and the general work ethic. Culture especially affects how decisions are made; in Japan, for example, plans for new ideas are often drafted from the bottom up, rather than emanating from higher levels of an organization as they often do in Canada and the United States. The entire corporate mind-set may vary from culture to culture, and from company to company within each culture. Some companies, especially those in Latin American countries, are extremely hierarchical in nature, according high respect to authority figures; some companies in developing countries are more loosely organized in terms of who does what; in North America, there is often some flexibility as to who is allowed to assume various roles.

In general, I/O psychology can be divided into four broad areas: human resources psychology, motivation of job performance, job satisfaction, and leadership. *Human resources psychology* focuses on the personnel functions of placing people in their jobs, training them, promoting, determining benefits, and evaluating performance. Such functions take place both before people begin to work for an organization and as an ongoing process within the organization. *Motivation of job performance* is a key area for I/O psychologists; they study not only rewards and success at work but also workers' influence on management and management's concerns about itself. *Job satisfaction* and other aspects of happiness at work are concerns of workers and employers alike. Finally, the study of *leadership* focuses on the key attributes of leaders—people who influence other people's behaviour towards the attainment of agreed-upon goals.

Applied psychology: The branch of psychology that uses psychological principles to help solve practical problems of everyday living.

Industrial/organizational (I/O) psychology: The study of how individual behaviour is affected by the work environment, by co-workers, and by organizational practices.

Human Resources Psychology

Job analyses: Careful descriptions of the various tasks and activities that are required for employees to do their jobs, along with the necessary knowledge, skills, and abilities; such analyses describe what gets done and how it gets done.

Human resources, or personnel, psychologists are involved in a broad array of activities related to employment—from helping employers choose among prospective job candidates, to determining compensation packages, to facilitating on-the-job training, to arranging termination programs when businesses must downsize. To help organizations succeed, human resources psychologists must consider the internal conditions of an organization (its size, structure, and business strategies) as well as external conditions (legal, social, political, cultural) (Jackson & Schuler, 1995). Among the most important tasks is helping organizations select among well-trained, qualified candidates for specific positions. Today, finding the right people for jobs occurs within the overall context of an organization's *strategic planning*. This high-level planning, which is finalized at the top levels of the organization, includes forecasting the organization's future needs, establishing specific objectives, and implementing programs to ensure that appropriate people will be available when needed (Jackson & Schuler, 1990).

Job Analyses. An important step in the strategic planning process is ensuring that there are well-qualified personnel to fill all of the company's needs. Companies often prepare **job analyses**—careful descriptions of the various tasks and activities that are required for employees to do their jobs, along with the necessary knowledge, skills, and abilities. Thus, there is an analysis of *what* gets done and *how* it gets done. This means specifying performance criteria—behaviours—that are required of employees. For example, a computer programmer might be expected to write code, debug the code of other programmers, and evaluate the efficiency of the code. Job analysis also means enumerating the qualifications for employment. For example, a computer programmer might need a college degree in computer science, two or three years of experience, and top-notch hands-on computing skills.

A *functional job analysis*, sometimes called an FJA, describes each type of work and the level of complexity of each job. An FJA is appealing to I/O psychologists because—like operationally defined behaviour in a research study—it is concrete, observable, and measurable. In an FJA there are three hierarchies of worker functions, and in each hierarchy there is an analysis of what gets done and how. In most jobs, workers have to deal with data (information), people (co-workers, subordinates, or customers), and things (objects). Within each of these types of work there are various levels of complexity. With data, individuals may have to compare, contrast, or copy data; on a more complex level, they also may have to analyze or synthesize data from different sources. With people, individuals may have to take instructions, help others, or serve others; on a more complex level, they may have to supervise, instruct, negotiate with, or mentor other people. With things, individuals may handle, carry, sort, or tend; on a more complex level, they may be altering, preparing, or fixing equipment.

There are other ways to measure what a job is, what gets done on a job, and who is best suited to specific work. For example, the *position analysis questionnaire* is widely used to ask those who know the job best to analyze their own jobs. On this questionnaire, workers fill out up to 194 statements describing a given job (McCormick, Jeanneret, & Mecham, 1972). The position analysis questionnaire has questions in six major areas: information sources (where the worker gets data from), mental processes (what decision making is required), work output (what physical work is required), relationships with others (communication skills), job context (physical working conditions), and other (licensing, criticality of position, special clothes, etc.).

The FJA and the position analysis questionnaire are widely used instruments, but there are many other such tests and analysis instruments, and most of them work equally well (Levine et al., 1983). All have a similar goal: Employers need to ensure that jobs are appropriate and have the correct scope. A job should not be too big or encompass too many tasks; nor should it be too limiting and so focused that it becomes boring and repetitive. Ideally, jobs should allow employees some level of responsibility for and control over how they do their work. Two of the key tasks of an I/O psychologist are balancing the scope and complexity of jobs and helping employers create jobs that will be motivating.

Selection Procedures. Employers want to hire individuals who will enjoy their work, suit the company's needs, and be productive. I/O psychologists develop specific selection procedures, including tests, to produce the best match between employers and employees. The selection procedures for jobs with large firms are often complicated and time-consuming.

Selection procedures have one basic goal—predicting the success of job candidates to help an employer determine which candidates to hire and which to reject. Employers and researchers use application forms, interviews, work samples, and tests to make comparisons between people looking for a job. Subtle factors can be at work in selection procedures, and evaluators have to pay particular attention to these factors—for example, to guard against the influence of their own moods

(Baron, 1993), an applicant's expensive clothes or unattractive looks, and other non–job-related characteristics that have nothing to do with an applicant's true capabilities (Forsythe, 1990).

There exist a wide range of selection methods that involve everything from tests of mental ability to peer rating, examination of experience, interests, and even handwriting. But research shows that that the best measures to help employers decide who to hire are mental ability tests, work sample tests, and integrity tests—and when these are combined, employers are even more likely to choose a candidate that will work out well (Schmidt & Hunter, 1998).

Tests of general mental ability come in many forms and test many abilities; most are paper-and-pencil tests and can be administered in groups or individually. They can focus on measures of general or specific abilities; intelligence tests are widely used measures of general ability in jobs that require high-level cognitive skills. Other standardized cognitive tests, such as those for general ability and specific verbal or mathematical knowledge, are good predictors of both academic success and certain types of job performance (Ree, Earles, & Teachout, 1994; Schmidt, Onex, & Hunter, 1992). However, an important question for I/O psychologists is whether such tests (or any tests for that matter) are the *best* predictors of job performance (or even if they are *valid*, *sufficient* predictors). This question has become especially important because of a large number of lawsuits filed by those who argue the tests discriminate against them. *Diversity* addresses this issue of equal employment opportunity further.

Work samples are hands-on simulations of all or part of a job's tasks. Depending on the job, there may be tests of spatial abilities (for air traffic controllers), perceptual accuracy (stenographers, proofreaders), or motor abilities (firefighters). Each test is used to help the employer determine if a job candidate's abilities match the job's requirements. Tests of managerial ability, which sometimes present the applicant with a simulated in box to sort through, also have been devised and have proved successful at indicating who will be a good manager (Berman & Miner, 1985).

One type of test that has seen significantly increased use across different kinds of jobs is the *test of integrity*. Some such tests focus on attitudes about theft, including rationalizations about "acceptably" small amounts of on-the-job theft. Other tests examine integrity more indirectly, by looking at characteristics such as dependability, conscientiousness, and thrill seeking. Finally, tests such as the MMPI–2, which screens for maladjustment, are also used to reveal people of low integrity. Although

Gender, Ethnicity, and Employee Selection

I magine that you are in charge of hiring several new employees for your company. You think you ought to use several screening tests in addition to one or more interviews in order to decide who are the best candidates for the jobs. But how should you select tests and conduct interviews to avoid any concerns about discrimination in your hiring practices? How can you be certain that your procedures will be fair for all applicants whether they are male, female, members of visible minorities, aboriginal, disabled, or older persons? As Steven Cronshaw of the universities of Guelph and Waterloo indicates in his book *Industrial Psychology in Canada* (1991) you first must ensure that any tests you use can be proven to be valid predictors of skills that are directly relevant to the job in question. This usually requires that a detailed job analysis be conducted and that the test or tests to be used have been demonstrated to accurately predict the skill required for that job. Intelligence tests, for example, may have good validity for some purposes, but unless you can point to data that clearly indicate that IQ test scores predict job success you should not ethically, and you cannot legally, use that test in your selection procedures. A specific example involves a decision by the Canadian Human Rights Commission that required CN Rail to discontinue its use of the Bennett Mechanical Aptitude test in selecting some of its blue-collar employees, as CN could not demonstrate that the test was a valid predictor of performance in those jobs. The ruling indicated that because women scored lower on the test on average and because of the lack of validity data, the practice of using the test as part of the selection procedure was discriminatory. I/O psychologists are trained in these activities and could help you to avoid running into problems with this and other pieces of legislation to be discussed in *Experiencing Psychology* on page 609.

Surprisingly little is known about gender, minority group status, and interview outcomes. Most research has been done with college students, with simulated interviews and involved questionnaires rather than real-life observations of job interviews. Several key variables determine the results of interviews. First, the *interview structure*, or lack thereof, affects results. Second, *job complexity* is a key variable because technical jobs tend to attract a self-selected group of applicants. Women, minorities, and males all do about as well in this domain, probably because they all have the skills necessary to do the job before they walk into the interview. Third, when there is a *low number of women or minority applicants*, some interviewers may hold the view that the best candidates for jobs must be within the majority group.

Interviewers must be trained to ask questions and attend only to information that is directly relevant to the job in question. For example, marital status is not a relevant issue but ability to travel, relocate, or work shifts may be important job-relevant considerations. Culturally based differences in interpersonal style may not be relevant to the job requirements but could influence the interviewer's reaction to the applicant if the interviewer is not anticipating them. For example, aboriginal people believe extensive eye contact to be a sign of disrespect, yet in Western culture consistent eye contact is believed to indicate honesty and liking. As well, another Western custom not consistently shared by aboriginal populations involves nodding and saying "uh-huh" at regular intervals to indicate that you follow and understand the speaker. In both of these cases, an interviewer not making adjustments for job-irrelevant cultural differences may form an unfairly negative impression of an aboriginal applicant. Again, training designed by I/O psychologists can deal with these issues in a straightforward manner.

In the end, to be fair and hire the best possible candidate employers probably want to use structured interviews, because they are a selection alternative with high validity. But what they may want more than anything else is more data from researchers on this issue. ■

such tests are controversial—many feel that individuals may be misdiagnosed or wrongly classified as lacking in integrity—their usage is on the increase, and they are seen as an alternative that is better than not testing at all (Camara & Schneider, 1994; Sackett, 1994).

Although, when taken in combination, mental ability, work samples, and integrity are good predictors, there are other that are important. We live in a fast-changing service-based economy, in which jobs in the service sector account for about 79 percent of all employment. The rise of the Internet and Internet sales over the last five years shows how an economy and job requirements can rapidly change the life of a business. Thus, many employers want their employees to be able to provide high-quality customer service and to be creative, adaptable, resilient, empathic, and understanding with customers—and technologically adept. Since these abilities are now being considered important as job qualifications (Cascio, 1995), it is not surprising that the use of tests to measure elements of personality in the workplace has increased markedly in the last decade. Several million such tests are administered yearly. Personality tests are used more to find specific behaviour patterns that are well suited to a type of job than to screen out people who may be abnormal (Hogan, Hogan, & Roberts, 1996). For example, some people who exhibit Type A behaviour patterns (discussed in Chapter 14) do better at some types of high-pressure work, such as being a commodities trader, than at others, such as meticulously checking a manuscript for typographical errors (Lee, Ashford, & Bobko, 1990). Tests of personality and interests, however, are difficult to correlate with job performance; for example, outgoing individuals may be good salespeople, but quiet, introspective individuals often can be just as persuasive.

Tests are just one way to gather information about applicants. Biographical data can help paint an accurate picture of an individual, as can work samples, letters of recommendation, and exercises in which job candidates take part in general discussions about work. Interviews can be important in determining the fit of an applicant with a position—but research shows that interviewers often make final decisions about applicants within the first minutes of an interview! Also, sometimes interviewers' judgments are based more on negative information provided than on positive information. Structured interviews—in which each applicant is asked the same questions in a certain way, in a certain order, and in the same manner—work better than do unstructured interviews (Arvey & Campion, 1982).

Training. Once a company has made a hiring decision about a new employee, a period of training nearly always follows. *Training* is the process by which organizations systematically teach employees skills to improve their job performance. Most

corporations offer systematic training, which typically begins by teaching employees about the organization and its goals. A new employee may need to learn specific skills, such as how to use a computer program or how to sell in a new industry. Training individuals about specific tasks can be simple or complex. For example, a new sales manager must learn not only about the products she will sell but also about the territory she will manage, the employees she will supervise, and the specific needs of her customers.

A variety of methods are available for training. At the simplest levels are lectures, films, and videotapes. Self-paced instruction, whereby a person works with materials at his or her own pace, is often used. Training programs often also use discussion groups, simulations, and on-the-job procedures; a training program may involve an apprenticeship or a mentoring relationship, with regular guidance and performance appraisals by a more senior person on the job. Letting employees watch others so that they can observe and imitate is particularly effective. However, some people respond better than others to any training methods. And finding mentors for women has sometimes been difficult because of smaller numbers of women in upper management.

In today's fast-paced, highly technological workplace, even seasoned employees need training and retraining. In large organizations, training is an ongoing process as new products and technologies are introduced. I/O psychologists typically break training into a multistep set of learning objectives. Because it provides very specific goals for knowledge and skill acquisition, this method of training is often particularly effective at helping employees identify their strengths and weaknesses. It also helps employees pinpoint specific obstacles to overcome and opportunities for improvement.

Training may be the simple process of reviewing a new tool or procedure, such as introducing an executive to the Internet, teaching a secretary a new word-processing program, or working with custodians to promote recycling efforts. It also may be an elaborate process that involves the employee in active on-the-job participation—perhaps programming a robot or pitching a product to clients. Training may include repetitive practice, particularly with highly technical equipment. It often involves moving from a teaching classroom or sales meeting to the field, store, or actual workplace. Finally, training usually involves feedback, so employees can learn whether the new skill or knowledge has been successfully acquired.

I/O psychologists take training especially seriously, because business or organizational success requires well-trained employees. Accordingly, to ensure good training researchers seek to know what the successful outcomes of training are—that is, what constitutes good work performance. In a way, researchers look at the desired outcome and work backwards to determine how employees should be trained. I/O psychologists look at how employees have reacted to recent training by examining work products, final exams, or results immediately after a training procedure. Results are, after all, what employers want. Effective training produces changes in employees' ability to deliver results, whether in the form of better-quality products, clearer communications, or more effective supervision.

Performance Appraisal. Have you ever been evaluated by an employer? Bosses are sometimes good at appraising work, but they also may overlook your best efforts and remember your mistakes, or they may not accurately convey how they feel about your performance. What makes a boss good at evaluating employees?

The process by which a supervisor periodically evaluates job-relevant strengths and weaknesses of a subordinate is called **performance appraisal**. Performance appraisals are especially important because they often are used to determine salaries, layoffs, firings, transfers, and promotions (Harris, Gilbreath, & Sunday, 1998). Supervisors have always made such appraisals, and researchers have tried in the past 70 years to find ways for them to do it more systematically. Methods to improve the appraisal process typically involve more active thinking on the part of supervisors.

The problem with performance appraisals is that they often are done inaccurately by people with few skills in evaluation and with few diagnostic aids. Supervisors generally report that they dislike conducting appraisals. They don't like to review their subordinates, and many acknowledge that they do not have strong evaluative skills. Further, supervisors have just as many inappropriate biases as anyone else (Swim et al., 1989), including the tendency to make attribution errors (pointed out in Chapter 13). And even when performance appraisals are done well, research shows that people's pay is more often associated with the quantity of their work than with its quality (Jenkins et al., 1998).

What are the criteria, or standards, on which a worker is judged? There is usually no ultimate criterion, no comprehensive measure of performance, by which to judge a worker, because multiple performance criteria enter into evaluation. A worker's quantity of work is often important, but so is its quality. Relationships with other workers also enter into an appraisal of performance. Researchers have devised scales of performance in areas such as sales volume, relationship with customers, and quality of interworker communication; these can be helpful diagnostic tools. But because these skills often overlap, multiple or composite scales have been devised. None has proved totally satisfactory.

Performance appraisal: The process by which a supervisor periodically evaluates the job-relevant strengths and weaknesses of subordinates.

Because of the "soft" nature of some criteria, such as how well people "get along," most psychologists today recommend a focus on the best available criteria. This means focusing on those elements of performance that *best* (and perhaps quantitatively) describe satisfactory performance, recognizing that many criteria can be used. A sales manager will look first at a salesperson's "measurables," such as sales volume, gross sales, or net profits; then the manager will assess other variables that may be important, such as customer relations or co-worker communication. Other measurable criteria might include a keyboarder's number of words or characters typed, a bank teller's number of shortages, or a nursery worker's number of saplings planted.

The task of doing performance appraisal requires objective measures whenever possible. But managers often compare individuals with one another, rank employees from best to worst, or rate employees in groups such as the top 10 percent, the next 20 percent, and so on. Such ratings may help differentiate employees, but they fall short of fairness in a variety of areas. What about workers evaluated by different supervisors, one of them "easy" and the other demanding? What if subjective, "soft" criteria such as camaraderie and friendliness with management are used? Might that discriminate against ethnic minorities and women, who don't necessarily have easy access to or common personal interests with management? (*Experiencing Psychology* considers the legal implications of job discrimination.)

You can see that even when objective measures are used, certain problems can be associated with them; these include leniency, central tendency, halo effects, and reliability. Some raters always judge people with *leniency*, giving them higher evaluations than they may deserve. The rater simply may want to be liked, or he or she may want to avoid confrontation or even to have the employee's positive evaluation reflect well on himself or herself. In addition, some raters always judge people "about average," giving them a *central* rating. These raters are unwilling to rank people very high or very low but give "safe" judgments that are unlikely to raise eyebrows. *Halo effects* in job performance evaluations occur when a rater is unable to objectively and independently distinguish between the many conceptually discrete parts of a job. Thus, a strong first impression or strong work on one part of a job may lead to a good rating on later work or on other parts of a job—regardless of the quality or quantity of later or different work. *Reliability* refers to the consistency of observations. Good raters consistently rate similar work in similar ways; many others, however, deviate in rating from one occasion to the next and from one employee to the next based on events that are hard to quantify, such as a worker's unique ability to work well in a team.

Many companies require periodic evaluations, but reluctant managers do them as infrequently as possible, and sometimes in a cursory manner. They often evaluate everybody about the same—average, or perhaps very good, which may leave employees feeling unappreciated.

Motivation of Job Performance

I/O psychologists help people work together in organizations; they work at understanding the emotional and social needs of employees, and they help organizations motivate management and workers. One obvious motivator is the fact that people need money to live. But both employers and psychologists know that different people are motivated by different things. Monetary rewards are important, of course—but so is praise for success. Such values are very much culturally determined; the value placed on hard work varies from culture to culture. Some cultures stress a person's duties to contribute to society; others stress a person's right to meaningful work; still others stress a person's need for happiness at work. I/O psychologists study especially carefully the impact of rewards and success within the context of culture.

When Hofstede (1983) examined attitudes in more than 50 countries, he found that organizations and culture varied on four main dimensions. *Power distance* is the extent to which there is a rigid hierarchy, or pecking order, in a company, limiting

experiencing psychology

The Law and I/O Psychology— A Dynamic Tension

The Canadian Charter of Rights and Freedoms holds that it is illegal to discriminate against individuals or groups of people on the basis of race, gender, or disability. Systematic discrimination is said to occur when any group or groups protected under the Charter are adversely affected by employment practices (Cronshaw, 1991). Supreme Court decisions have taken this further (*Bhinder v. CN Rail*, 1985; *O'Malley v. Simpson-Sears*, 1985), indicating that these provisions apply not only to direct discrimination (e.g., refusal to hire someone because she is a woman) but to indirect discrimination as well (e.g., the establishment of or a change in business practices that unintentionally adversely affects a protected group, such as the way Sunday store openings might affect persons with particular religious views). At a minimum, employers are required to demonstrate that their hiring and job performance criteria reflect bona fide occupational qualifications (BFOQs). It should come as no surprise that I/O psychologists are often called in to ensure that the guidelines used to select and promote employees are based on truly job-related knowledge and skills, or BFOQs.

I/O psychologists may be hired as expert witnesses by individuals who file suit against employers; in this capacity, they help the aggrieved individuals establish that employers engaged in bias, discrimination, and/or unfair practices. They sometimes assert that the validity of a particular employment criterion (such as attractiveness and youthfulness for flight attendants) is questionable. Of course, employers hire their own expert witnesses. In court, these I/O psychologists testify to the validity, reliability, and predictability of various tests and selection procedures.

In addition to concern over direct and indirect discrimination, the Supreme Court rulings also require that employers make reasonable accommodations for employees who have disabilities but are otherwise qualified to perform various jobs. That is, for potential or current employees who may fall short of a job requirement that has been properly identified as a BFOQ, employers may be expected to try to make accommodations in order to make the job more accessible. This can be a simple matter of making the office and equipment (e.g., desks) wheelchair accessible or it can be a more complex issue. As expert witnesses in these legal cases, I/O psychologists help the courts answer questions like these: What exactly is a disability? (Is an employee with attention deficit/hyperactivity disorder (ADHD) "disabled"?) What exactly is a reasonable accommodation? (Should such an employee be given extended deadlines?) What tests should be used to decide if an employee is disabled? (Who says the employee has ADHD? Is he or she "self-diagnosed"?) What if psychologists and medical doctors disagree about a person's disability?

Psychologists who are willing and qualified to act as expert witnesses are in high demand. And there is a dynamic and healthy tension between the law and psychology—with lawyers wanting psychologists to be more precise and psychologists wanting lawyers to show that they understand the complexity of human functioning. Psychological science has much to offer individuals, employers, and the courts. Like medical diagnoses, legal judgments are sometimes less precise than either employers or employees would like. With each passing year, however, psychological research is helping to sharpen the decision-making rules and to bring legal criteria into focus. ■

employees' independence of action. *Uncertainty avoidance* is a lack of tolerance for ambiguity or uncertainty in the workplace, which may be found in risk-averse countries such as Japan. Cultures varied in the extent to which they valued *individualism* as opposed to the collective good of the organization. Finally, Hofstede found that emphasis on work goals as opposed to interpersonal goals, a trait that he labelled

masculinity, also varied from culture to culture. Not surprisingly, Hofstede found that most Western companies fostered a combination he called independent individualism; Asian companies fostered collectivism; and some other societies fostered unique combinations. Israel, for instance, fosters dependent collectivism (high power distance, low individualism). These cultural values will affect people's needs and goals, what they value, what they consider equitable, and how they can be managed most effectively.

In Western culture, job performance generally is affected by *intrinsically motivated behaviour*—behaviour engaged in strictly because it brings pleasure. (We examined intrinsic and extrinsic motivation in Chapters 5 and 9.) Recall that when intrinsically motivated behaviours are constantly reinforced with direct external rewards (such as money), productivity often drops. Money often is not that important to job performance. A well-paid plumber may find plumbing work tedious and unfulfilling, whereas a lower-paid clerical worker who finds the job important and challenging will perform well and be given increased responsibilities. With the help of I/O psychologists' theoretical work, employers can find ways to motivate employees to be more productive (and thus to provide companies with more profits).

Goal-setting theory: A theory that asserts that setting specific, clear, attainable goals for a given task will lead to better performance.

Expectancy theories: Theories that suggest that a worker's effort and desire to maintain goal-directed behaviour (to work) is determined by expectancies regarding the outcomes of that work.

Need and Goal-Setting Theory. As we saw in Chapter 9, drive theory suggests that people are motivated to work towards a goal because of primary needs and drives—often physiological, such as the needs for food or shelter. But human beings also have desires and needs that are much more complex than the basic ones addressed by drive theory. Workers often will perform difficult tasks for long hours, not for pay or for food or for praise, but merely to reach a goal or to compare their present performance with new performance. Mountain climbers tackle a new peak "because it's there." **Goal-setting theory** asserts that setting specific, clear, attainable goals for a given task will lead to better performance. In running or biking, for example, you challenge yourself to run or ride harder and longer—not to break records for your age group, but to meet artificial goals that you have set for yourself.

Goal-setting theory states that goals work best when they are somewhat challenging but attainable and personally agreed to by a worker. Goals work especially well when they enhance a worker's sense of self-esteem or self-efficacy. For example, if a sales manager and her staff agree to a 50 percent increase in annual sales, rather than an unrealistic 200 percent increase, chances are that the sales staff will perform well (see Figure 17.1).

Goal-setting theory can account for some work behaviours, but it cannot explain why people will work on projects for years, at low pay, or under difficult conditions. More fully developed expectancy theories take the next step forward—explaining the motivation for this type of performance.

Expectancy Theories. A successful employer–employee relationship relies on many factors beyond economic motivation. **Expectancy theories**, which we discussed in Chapter 9, suggest that a worker's effort and desire to maintain goal-directed behaviour (in other words, to work) is determined by expectations regarding the outcomes of that work.

FIGURE 17.1
Drive Theory versus Goal-Setting Theory

DRIVE THEORY

Basic drives and motivation → Performance → Basic needs are met.

GOAL-SETTING THEORY

Specific, challenging but attainable, and agreed-to goals → Performance → Self-esteem and self-efficacy are enhanced.

One expectancy theory, proposed by Victor Vroom (1964), suggests that both motivation and ability determine job performance. Vroom's proposal is considered an expectancy theory because it states that motivation is determined by what people expect to experience in performing a task—a rewarding outcome or a frustrating one. According to Vroom, a person first must have the willingness and the ability to perform the task; without that, the experience will be frustrating and thus non-motivating. Given willingness and ability, Vroom's theory holds that motivation results from a three-part equation made up of expectancy, instrumentality, and valence. *Expectancy* is the belief that hard or extra work will lead to good or improved performance; *instrumentality* refers to a worker's belief that good performance will be rewarded; and *valence* refers to the value placed on the rewards that are offered. A person who is awarded a big raise but later gets the cold shoulder from co-workers because of it may then give the raise lower valence.

Edward Lawler and Lyman Porter (1967) modified and expanded on Vroom's theory. They contended that ability, effort, *and* role perceptions determine performance—the ways people believe they should be doing their jobs (see Figure 17.2). These researchers believed that workers must fully understand the nature of their positions and all that is required of them. Too often, people fail not because of lack of effort or ability, but because they do not know what is expected of them or how to achieve a sense of control or power in the organization (Ragins & Sundstrom, 1989). For example, an employee may burn a great deal of midnight oil, but if he or she has misread what it really takes to succeed in the organization, actual performance may be low.

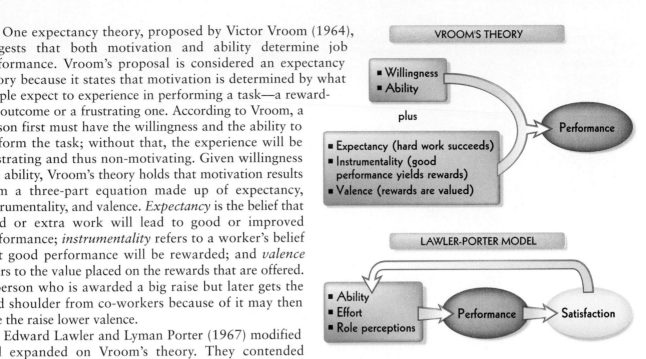

FIGURE 17.2
Expectancy Theories

Today, researchers claim that the motivation to work can be explained more by integrative theories that focus on goals, experiences, and thoughts (Locke & Latham, 1990a). Locke and Latham (1990b) assert that if a high challenge is accompanied by high expectations for success, then high performance is likely; however, employees also must be committed to the goals of the company and be open to feedback. Success is also based on effort, persistence, and specific task strategies. When people are given incentives, when they think their contributions are important, and when the effort required of them is not excessive, productivity will be high (Shepperd, 1993). When performance is high, job satisfaction is likely; this in turn facilitates commitment to the organization and its goals.

Equity Theory. Being treated fairly is a prime concern for almost everyone. People want to be compensated for their work, to earn as much as they can, and most feel that they are worth more than they are paid. As radio personality and author Garrison Keillor implied when he described the inhabitants of Lake Wobegon, most people feel that they are "above average." But what happens when people feel that they are being treated unfairly?

In I/O psychology, **equity theory** asserts that what people bring to a work situation should be balanced by what they receive compared with other workers; thus, workers' input (what they bring or do) should be balanced by their compensation (what they receive). If input and compensation are not balanced, people will adjust their work level and potentially their job satisfaction accordingly. According to equity theories, each individual privately weighs the balance between input and compensation and compares this ratio to other people's input/compensation ratio. When the ratios are similar, people are relatively happy. Thus, if a colleague's workloads and talent are compensated at a certain level, and other workers are similarly compensated, their ratios are about equal.

Equity theory: In I/O psychology, the theory that suggests that what people bring to a work situation should be balanced by what they receive compared with other workers; thus, input should be balanced by compensation, or rewards, or workers will adjust their work level and potentially their job satisfaction accordingly.

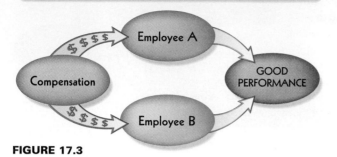

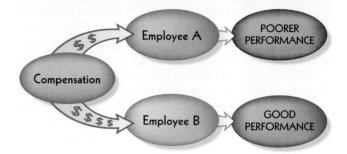

If two employees receive equal compensation for similar performance levels, they will tend to continue to exert the same effort.

In contrast, if two employees who exert the same effort and show comparable levels of performance receive unequal compensation, the employee who receives the lower reward is likely to exert less effort. His or her performance may suffer.

FIGURE 17.3
Equity Theory

But what if a person feels that his or her ratio is way out of balance? In such cases (especially in cases of underpayment) people may slow down their work behaviour and gripe and groan, and the quality of work often decreases (see Figure 17.3). If inequities exist, people will choose one of several alternatives to alter the situation (Berg, 1991; Greenberg, 1990; Summers & Hendrix, 1991). Hellriegel and Slocum (1992) assert that people have choices when they feel that an inequity exists:

- They can increase their inputs to justify higher rewards (when they feel over-rewarded).
- They can decrease their inputs to compensate for low rewards.
- They can change their rewards through legal actions, illegal actions (stealing company assets), or leaving early.
- They can distort reality by rationalizing inequities, and thus feel better.
- They can quit.

There are hidden costs of inequity in pay and benefits. When Greenberg (1990) examined employee theft rates in manufacturing plants after pay cuts, he found higher rates of theft than before pay reductions. When supervisors explained the basis for pay cuts to workers, feelings became less bruised, ratios were not perceived as being so out of kilter, and the theft rate decreased. A key finding of this study was that when management explains the nature of pay shifts, the perception of inequity is minimized.

Self-efficacy and Work. How well you believe that you will be able to execute a series of actions required to deal with a situation is your self-efficacy. People who view themselves as having high degrees of self-efficacy turn out to do better at work than others. This turns out to be especially true for easier tasks. When tasks are especially complicated or difficult, even people with a great deal of confidence don't do well (Stajkovic & Luthans, 1998). This leads researchers to some practical suggestions for employers: Managers should provide accurate descriptions of work to be performed; employees should be given clues as to what techniques should be used to complete tasks; employers should provide tasks that employees can accomplish to enhance worker self-efficacy; and contingencies and rewards should be timed to enhance a worker's self-efficacy. In the end, goals—their content and form—and the rewards associated with them, when well formed, can act to enhance self-efficacy and performance (Audia et al., 1996; Locke, 1996; Latham, Daghighi, & Locke, 1997).

Motivation Management: Three Approaches. Recognizing the complexity of motivation management, I/O psychologists have developed three basic approaches to motivation in the workplace: paternalistic, behavioural, and participatory. The fundamental idea of the *paternalistic approach* to motivation is that a company takes care of its employees' needs and desires in a fatherly manner. Early in the twentieth century, this approach was common in the mining companies and lumber and paper mills in the west, which provided housing, schools, recreation, and churches for employees. This approach is common today in some Japanese companies, which promote lifelong employment and support employees' needs, from recreation to drug rehabilitation. Nevertheless, such approaches are contrary to many Western psychologists' views on behaviour. Instrumental (operant) conditioning studies show that for a behaviour (such as work) to be established and maintained—at least in Western cultures—reinforcement must be contingent on performance. In a paternalistic system all employees, productive as well as nonproductive, are given reinforcement if they fulfil their roles as workers. Reinforcement without the need for performance does not encourage people to work hard, as equity theory predicts.

Behavioural approaches to motivation assume that people will work only if they receive tangible rewards for specific task performance. Examples include paying a factory worker by the piece and a typist by the page. In such a system, hard-working employees obtain more rewards—commissions, salary increases, bonuses, and so on—because they produce more; but little attention is paid to the emotional needs of workers. In the end, goal-setting theory and, to some extent, expectancy theory predict that this situation will not work.

The *participatory approach* to motivation is based on the belief that individuals who have a say in the decisions that affect their lives are motivated to work harder and smarter. Participation, it is argued, provides a setting in which managers and employees can exchange information to solve problems (Tjosvold, 1987). Supporters of this approach believe that a sense of competence and self-determination is likely to increase individuals' levels of motivation (Deci, 1975). *Quality circles* (such as the one shown in the photo), in which workers at all levels meet to discuss ways to improve product quality and promote excellence, constitute one technique employers use to involve workers in the management process (Matsui & Onglatco, 1990).

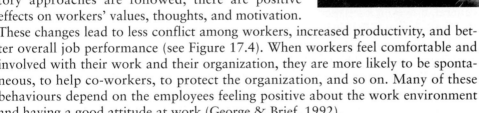

Many variables affect the success of participatory programs: the work setting, the individuals involved, the kinds of decisions to be made, and the hiring policies, for example. When truly participatory approaches are followed, there are positive effects on workers' values, thoughts, and motivation. These changes lead to less conflict among workers, increased productivity, and better overall job performance (see Figure 17.4). When workers feel comfortable and involved with their work and their organization, they are more likely to be spontaneous, to help co-workers, to protect the organization, and so on. Many of these behaviours depend on the employees feeling positive about the work environment and having a good attitude at work (George & Brief, 1992).

Job Satisfaction

If you have positive view of your abilities in life and feel competent and in control (at least most of the time) chances are good that you will like your job and that you will feel satisfied (Judge et al., 1998). It is important to realize that job satisfaction is different from job motivation. Motivation (the internal conditions that direct a person to act) is always shown in behaviour; job satisfaction (a person's attitude about the work and workplace) may not be shown in behaviour. A tired, bored, and

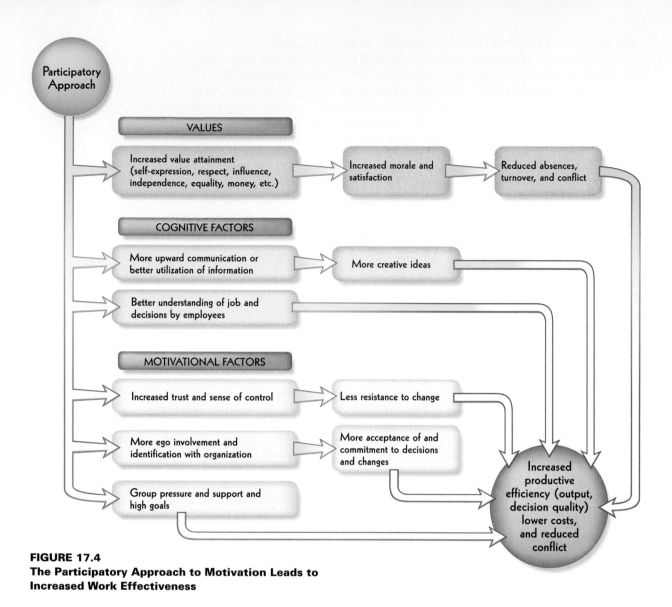

FIGURE 17.4
The Participatory Approach to Motivation Leads to
Increased Work Effectiveness

overworked electrician may feel discouraged and angry—and may even hate her job—but still be motivated to work. Her motivation may stem from the high pay she receives, from her obligation to complete a job, or from some other source. Thus, although her job satisfaction is low, it does not affect her performance. In general, however, a satisfied worker is a high-performing worker who will remain in the organization. This is why I/O psychologists seek to identify the sources of job satisfaction.

There are probably more sources of job satisfaction than we can list here, but they tend to cluster in five basic categories. These categories, as well as examples of each, are summarized in Table 17.1. They are the work itself, the perceived rewards of the work (which we just discussed), the quality of supervision, the support of co-workers, and the work setting. The overall level of satisfaction depends on the extent to which people feel that their expectations for satisfaction are matched by their actual satisfaction. The closeness of that match, in turn, depends on various aspects of a job. People can be pleased or dissatisfied about hours, pay, client contact, and promotion opportunities, among other things (Algera, 1990). People have standards for comparison that determine the extent to which they feel they are doing well or poorly. As we saw earlier, in the discussion of equity theory, one of those standards is fairness; when people believe that decisions, evaluations, and resource allocations are made fairly, their job satisfaction tends to be high. This finding is true for both men and women in many different settings (Witt & Nye, 1992).

Table 17.1 Key Factors Related to Job Satisfaction

Area	Factors
The work itself	The work is interesting.
	The work is perceived to be challenging.
	There are opportunities to apply one's own judgment.
	There is some degree of autonomy.
Perceived rewards	There is adequate recognition.
	The pay is adequate and equitable.
	The work contributes to self-esteem and self-efficacy.
	There are opportunities for advancement.
Quality of supervision	Supervisors offer encouragement, support, and help (Huebner, 1994).
Support from co-workers	There are opportunities to interact socially and in teams.
	Co-workers are supportive and compatible.
The work setting	There is job security.
	The work environment is viewed positively (it is seen as pleasant, attractive, and comfortable).
	There are opportunities to influence company policy and procedures.
	Adequate information and equipment are available.

Leadership

The Borg, in the popular television series *Star Trek*, tells its enemies that "resistance is futile." The Borg tries not to lead, but to dominate. In organizations large and small leaders try to persuade, encourage, and inspire. They try to build cohesion and goal-oriented teamwork. In every organization, some individuals emerge as *leaders*—people who influence other people's behaviour towards the attainment of agreed-upon goals. But there is no "right" type of leader; in fact, leadership styles fluctuate widely in popularity from autocratic leaders who might say "My way or the highway" to leaders who are democratic and might say "Let's decide this together."

Informal leaders may emerge spontaneously in any group, or higher management may choose them formally. Leaders are expected to help further the purposes of their organization. Thus, one of their primary roles is to persuade and motivate employees to perform at a high level. It is important to note, however, that not all managers are leaders; nor are all leaders managers. What makes for truly effective leadership is thus important but not clearly understood, so it should be no surprise that I/O psychologists have studied it intensively.

In some ways we all know a great deal about leadership; in other ways, we can see daily that our national leaders are often quite fallible, make mistakes, and fail to lead effectively. Can we choose a good leader? Can we forecast leadership? Why do some leaders succeed and others fail? The study of leadership has gone through three major phases, each with a characteristic focus: traits, behaviours, or situations. The right combination of these elements ultimately describes an effective leader.

Trait Theories of Leadership. The specific personality traits of individual organizational leaders were studied intensively in the early 1950s and are receiving increased attention again. This research tries to isolate the characteristics that make individuals good or poor leaders; for example, are good leaders assertive, directive, or authoritarian? But the trait approach troubles some researchers. Leaders cannot be universally characterized by traits such as assertiveness, self-confidence, or drive. Many business leaders are assertive, but many others are not. In fact, individual differences among leaders are extreme. Although an individual leader's personality traits will tell psychologists something about leadership, the differences among leaders tend to be greater than the similarities. One reason that studies are unable to find a common denominator is that each leader and each organization has different goals. Today, researchers also recognize that a key, and sometimes defining, trait of effective business leaders is *flexibility*—the ability to adapt to a rapidly changing workplace, organization, and global economy. Other key traits are intelligence, maturity, inner motivation, and being employee-focused.

Leadership Behaviours. Another focus of research in leadership is specific leadership behaviours. Many research studies try to find characteristic ways in which leaders interact with other members of their organizations. Some of the pioneering work on leadership was done at the University of Michigan's Institute for Social Research. The Michigan studies (as they are often called) found that business leaders tend to be either employee-oriented or task-oriented. Whether a leader is employee-oriented or task-oriented has to do with how the leader chooses to influence behaviour. An employee-oriented leader acts so as to maintain and enhance individual employees' feelings of self-worth or self-esteem. Such leaders try to empower employees and co-workers and make them feel valued and important. A task-oriented leader focuses on getting the job done efficiently and quickly, with as little effort as possible.

Leadership styles are sometimes related to gender, with women being more employee-oriented and men being more task-oriented (Eagly & Johnson, 1990). Recent studies show that the gender of the leader and of the followers has other important effects. For example, female leaders or managers tend to be evaluated as positively as their male counterparts. However, when they behave in stereotypically male ways, they are devalued—especially if the evaluators are men (Eagly, Makhijani, & Klonsky, 1992).

Further research has confirmed that behavioural differences among leaders are great and that a leader's behaviour is determined by personal traits, by overall orientation (employee or task), and sometimes by the group of people being led. Some groups of individuals have characteristics that demand an employee orientation on the leader's part. For example, an underpaid, overworked, but dedicated social worker may have a great need for self-esteem, feel that his work is worthwhile, but also know that he is underpaid. A supervisor must motivate this person not with authoritarian task-oriented directions but with concern for his need for self-worth. Highly paid executives, however, may be more easily motivated by a task-oriented approach, because they recognize that their salaries reflect their higher levels of creativity and productivity. Job performance, job satisfaction, and the way a worker is treated are closely related. In motivating workers, leaders must consider their own personal traits, the various possible behaviours they might use to influence others, and the conditions in which they and their co-workers work.

Situational Leadership Theory Many researchers have shifted from investigating leader behaviour to investigating the *situations* in which these behaviours are performed. Some situations lend themselves to leadership, and even to specific forms of leadership; others call for little leadership. Thus, a warm, friendly, employee-oriented leader (or supervisor) is generally very useful for a group of service workers. But if the organization encounters financial trouble and its workers must be laid off, with the supervisor having no control over who is let go, the climate of uncertainty may undermine the usefulness of the warm and friendly approach. To continue functioning, the organization then may have to find a task-oriented leader who is trusted for his or her integrity and fairness.

Theories of Leadership Effectiveness. A complex interplay of factors determines the most effective style of leadership for different situations, even within one organization. Effective leaders simply may be those who are best at perceiving the goals and needs of their organization and fitting their style to those needs. Two major theories that try to account for leadership effectiveness are the *Fiedler contingency model* and *Vroom's leadership model.*

Fred Fiedler (1964, 1974) developed a contingency model of leadership that acknowledges that traits, behaviours, and situations can vary among individuals and over time and that effective leadership is contingent on all of these factors. Fiedler's model assumes that there are numerous possible situations in which leaders may find themselves. Relationships between leaders and followers can be good or bad, tasks for the organization can be structured (or routine) or unstructured (or complex), and the leader's power can be weak or strong. A leader is obviously in a favourable position if he or she has good relations with employees, has a task that is structured, and is in a position of power. Fiedler developed scales for rating leadership ability and effectiveness and correlated them with the various possible situations. His results show that employee-oriented leaders have the best overall functioning, and that leaders who are task-oriented can have very effective organizations, but only in extremely favourable circumstances.

The key element of Fiedler's theory is that leaders can change their behaviour according to the situation in which they find themselves and adopt the most effective leadership approach possible for that situation. Fiedler made a great inferential leap in assuming that a combination of factors affects leaders' behaviour. Ultimately, his approach may not explain leadership, but it provides a solid theory with practical implications.

Unlike Fiedler, Vroom and his colleagues Yetton and Jago focused on the various ways in which leaders may make decisions in organizations. In this leader-participation model, Vroom laid out a flow chart for determining the amount of advice a leader should seek out, depending on the task to be accomplished. A leader can make an authoritarian decision and simply announce it; a leader can present a problem, solicit advice, and then make the final decision; or a leader can allow other people to make the decision. As a leader's use of authority increases, the freedom of others in the group decreases. That is, when a manager makes a decision and announces it, subordinates and co-workers have little freedom of choice; this style of leadership is called *boss-centred* (Vroom, 1974; Vroom & Yetton, 1973; Vroom & Jago, 1995). According to Vroom's view, each time a decision is to be made, managers or leaders can ask themselves a series of questions to arrive at the best possible leadership approach for the situation.

The strength of Vroom's model is that it recognizes that leaders have options—that they can choose how to behave in light of their own previous experiences and knowledge and on the basis of situations or conditions (Vroom, 1997). Vroom's model has received some research support, but its practical implications in the workplace have not been evaluated systematically. Like Fiedler's model, it emphasizes the important role of situational variables in determining which leadership approach is most appropriate to a situation.

Transformational Leadership. If one person took an organization or company and provided it with direction, a new vision, and a sense of purpose, that person would be considered a first-rate leader. Such leaders are hard to find, but occasionally someone emerges who is considered to be charismatic, having extraordinary effects on followers. These leaders are often called **transformational leaders;** they provide inspiration, intellectual stimulation, and individual care to followers and are able to draw extra creativity and effort out of organization members (Bass, 1985, 1990, 1997). Often such individuals do not have formal authority based on their position; because of their personality, style, and interpersonal skills, however,

Transformational leader: A charismatic leader who inspires and provides intellectual stimulation to recreate an organization.

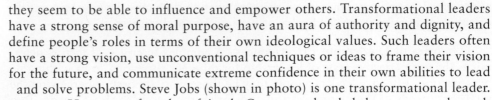

they seem to be able to influence and empower others. Transformational leaders have a strong sense of moral purpose, have an aura of authority and dignity, and define people's roles in terms of their own ideological values. Such leaders often have a strong vision, use unconventional techniques or ideas to frame their vision for the future, and communicate extreme confidence in their own abilities to lead and solve problems. Steve Jobs (shown in photo) is one transformational leader. He was co-founder of Apple Computer, has led the company through good and bad times, has never lacked confidence, and has always inspired commitment and loyalty in employees.

Transformational leaders often take advantage of organizational weaknesses and create opportunities to recreate, or transform, an organization and its employees or constituents. This occurs when the charismatic leader can distinguish the forest from the trees well enough to give individuals help and the courage to reach and achieve heretofore unthought-of goals. Such leaders are often able to create a willingness on the part of employees to go along with their ideas and a reluctance to criticize their ideas or them by creating situations that allow them to be seen as charismatic—such individuals can manage impressions well (Gardner & Avolio, 1998). When such an individual operates within the context of an organization, the organization often becomes something new. The members of the organization adopt new values, ideas, and ways of operating (Howell & Avolio, 1993; Sosik, Kahai, & Avolio, 1998). When new values are adopted, new levels of performance are often expected.

Transformational leadership is hard to create and generally is seen as competing with traditional values in organizations that focus on profits, personnel, productivity, and cost efficiency. Transformational leaders, many feel, are born, not made, and are individually unique. But contrary arguments are made by some researchers, who assert that transformational skills can be learned (Hackman & Johnson, 1991) and that men and women are both quite capable of being effective transformational leaders (Hackman et al., 1992).

Psychologists' knowledge of how people influence and manage others has grown dramatically. Researchers now know that effective leadership depends not only on personal traits and on specific techniques or behaviours, but also on the situation. Workers may exaggerate the leadership effectiveness of a boss if their environment is productive and they are happy (Shamir, 1992). Thus, leadership, workers' perceptions of leadership, and motivation are interrelated.

So what constitutes effective leadership? Although the research is complex and not unanimous there are several widely agreed-upon ideas (Bass, 1998; McGill & Slocum, 1998; Ross & Offermann, 1997):

- Know the job and be pragmatic in decision making
- Be an active leader—passive leadership is not effective
- Set solid personnel selection policies—good selection procedures help establish a favourable working situation

Focus

Review

◆ What are the goals of selection procedures and training efforts in today's workplace? pp. 604–607

◆ Identify and differentiate three approaches to motivation management. pp. 612–613

◆ Describe the key elements of transformational leadership. pp. 617–618

Think Critically

◆ Many jobs today require more cognitive than physical skills. What implications does this have for motivating employees?

◆ Many companies have relaxed their dress codes to allow more casual modes of dress. If you were running a large multinational corporation, what would your stance on workplace dress codes be? Why?

◆ How can leaders meet the goals of their organizations and at the same time attempt to be transformational leaders, creating new and different organizations? Are these goals mutually contradictory?

- Act in ways consistent with the organization's vision—this builds strong organizations
- Foster listening among all levels of employees
- Create an organization that allows for choices
- Be sensitive to worker motivation, satisfaction, and performance—be nurturing

Through carefully conducted I/O research, psychologists can help organizations more effectively meet their own goals by seeking out effective leaders who can persuade, motivate, build confidence, and create a better workplace with more satisfied workers and stockholders (Hogan, Curphy, & Hogan, 1994).

Human Factors and Ergonomics

W hen those of us old enough to remember what banking was like before automated teller machines were put in use stand at an ATM, we often recall how frustrating it used to be wait in line for 10 minutes to see a teller. At first, banks designed more efficient, roped-off waiting "stream" lines and even electronic client directing systems. Now we can bank at our convenience through a machine. In addition, by phone or Internet we can check our balance, move money between accounts, and pay bills—all rather easily. Applied psychologists who study human factors have played an important role in streamlining banking experiences as well as many other day-to-day routines. Donald Norman, a psychologist who has studied applied issues, wrote a best-selling book that is worth a look: *Design of Everyday Things* (1990). Entertaining and enlightening reading, it focuses on how clever machines are making life easier.

Human factors is the study of the relationship of human beings to machines and to workplaces and other environments. A human factors psychologist might focus on the creation of health-care products for use by the handicapped, on the design of cooking utensils or educational products, on the interaction of cellphone use and driving, or on the interaction of robots and people. The photos show various controls that adjust automobile seats. As you can see, not all are equally well designed. From a human factors view, the controls in photo (b) are the most effective; those in photo (d) are the least effective. Most human factors research focuses on the work environment, especially in the areas of efficiency and safety.

Efficiency

In the work environment, researchers have examined workers' ability to operate machines effectively. Much of this research centres on **ergonomics**—the study of the

(a)

(b)

(c)

(d)

fit between human anatomy or physiology, the demands of a particular task or piece of equipment, and the environment in which the task occurs. Human factors researchers seek to develop person–machine interfaces that minimize frustration and errors, maximize output, and are reliable. Such researchers have focused on studying machines and interfaces to ensure that speed and accuracy of work are optimized and that workplaces minimize fatigue and stress (Sanders & McCormick, 1993).

A key difference between a human factors researcher and an I/O psychologist is that the I/O researcher might examine what can be done to the human being to change his or her behaviour to improve efficiency. A human factors researcher, on the other hand, will look at what can be changed about the machine, computer, or interface. It is often easier to change a machine than to change a human being!

In the early part of the twentieth century, working with machinery meant reading dials, turning wheels, and lifting equipment. Human factors researchers then focused on creating machine–human interfaces that required as little energy as possible and resulted in as few errors as possible on the part of the machine operator. Today, working with machinery often means operating a computer, monitoring computer-controlled devices, programming equipment, and working in teams with other highly skilled employees. To a great extent, *controlling* equipment, rather than operating it, has become a focus of human factors research. If equipment is to be properly controlled, dials, computer screens, and display devices have to be designed to minimize errors. For example, a pilot must be able to read a computer screen accurately, under all possible conditions, in order to land a plane safely; a nuclear power plant operator must be able to read the temperature of nuclear devices. The design of computer display screens thus has dominated recent research in human factors (Howell, 1993).

Computer displays are everywhere. You often type at a computer, pay a restaurant cheque at a computer-controlled cash register, and bank at ATMs. Well-designed machines and computer interfaces minimize errors; but the ability to create good interfaces depends on knowledge of how human beings see, manipulate, and interact with the machine. This means studying perception, human information processing, and complex decision making. The ATM is an example of an interface that has been studied well by human factors researchers. Most banks have ATMs that are easy to operate. But the ATM at a bank next door may have a confusing, gaudy interface, and many users can be observed to kick the machine, curse, and lose their cards. Usually the human factors psychologist can take the credit for a well-designed interface that minimizes errors, confusion, and angry customers.

Computer screens are important, but displays are only one part of the study of human factors. Workers are also increasingly dependent on one another to get a task done in today's workplace, so there has been increased emphasis on social factors in the workplace. For example, researchers are studying interactions of pilots and navigators in the cockpit, in addition to the instrumentation displays they use.

Many jobs are complex and require advanced technology. In industries such as auto manufacturing, for instance, robotic equipment has been programmed to do many tasks that human beings once did. These devices must be designed effectively to duplicate the abilities of human beings. Much of the work of robotics engineers is dedicated to making sure that robots are both effective and safe.

Even the tools of carpenters, tailors, and technicians can be designed using the principles of human factors. For example, what is the best weight for a hammer? How tall should a drill press be? Can the design of sewing machines, computers, and robotic controls take into account the size of an operator's hand? Today, Apple Computer ships keyboards that have been designed to be easy to type on, to minimize typing errors, and to reduce carpal tunnel syndrome. These keyboards are split in the centre, with the two parts angled in different directions. The human factors psychologists at Apple are convinced that they have designed a keyboard that meets the important human factors considerations of accuracy, productivity, and safety.

Safety

Human factors research can provide a work environment that is not only efficient but also safe. Many industrial accidents occur despite attempts to protect workers' safety; human factors research can help reduce accidents through design improvements. Human factors psychologists also can help estimate how quickly people become fatigued and lose accuracy and then can design work schedules that optimize the safe use of equipment—especially of potentially dangerous equipment. Such psychologists can help promote safety through programs that improve people's attitudes about safety and therefore promote safer work behaviour. Only when workers believe that safety is valued and personally desirable are they likely to make safety-promoting changes.

It is often easier to design a safe, or nearly safe, work environment than to influence workers to work safely. Researchers classify efforts to design safe work environments in three categories (Sanders & McCormick, 1993). *Exclusion designs* make it impossible for a specific error to occur; *prevention designs* make it difficult though not impossible for an error to happen; and *fail-safe designs* do not reduce the likelihood of an accident, but lessen its consequences should it occur. For a nuclear power plant, human factors psychologists might develop prevention designs that greatly decrease the likelihood of a nuclear accident (or so they hope). In efforts to ensure safe work environments, governments invoke legislation that establishes standards for health and safety in the workplace and that act as prevention designs. These fall short of exclusion designs, of course, because establishing standards is easier than enforcing them. Workers must accept safety standards before they can be effective, and the government does not have an adequate staff to regulate, enforce, or inspect all places of business.

Research in an array of other subdisciplines in psychology helps to establish and maintain workplace safety. *Perceptual research* investigates the light levels that are appropriate for reading computer screens. Which colour is most easily seen in the dark? (Yellow.) Is it easier to see white letters on a dark background, or the reverse? (White letters on dark backgrounds are easier to see.) *Environmental research* (which we will examine in more detail later in this chapter) has focused on efficiency and safety when looking at variables such as temperature and noise. When temperature or noise is too high, performance decreases. Moderate, comfortable temperatures and machine-related noise levels that are not too distracting improve not only efficiency but also safety. Environmental research also reveals that signs and warnings help motivate people to follow regulations. Specific instructions that are personalized for a user—for example, using that person's name as part of the instructions—work better still. If the user has to do something before using a machine, such as remove a warning label, labels are especially effective (Duffy, Kalsher, & Wogalter, 1993). Even if people can attend to specific warnings about equipment safety and even if they are given clear directions, incentives and proper reinforcements must be put into play to ensure compliance. This is the domain of learning and social psychologists who study how reinforcements and social influence can be used to induce worthwhile and helpful behaviours.

Warnings, labels, and compliance techniques are all helpful in establishing safety. These efforts constitute a form of outreach that has been successful in improving the efficiency and safety of the workplace.

Focus

Review

◆ What is an effective technique to ensure that people will take safety measures when using equipment? p. 621

Think Critically

◆ Why do you think some businesses have been slow to adopt safety measures? What can psychologists do to help convince business leaders that it is in their best interest to improve safety?

Psychology and the Law

I n the workplace, as elsewhere, the laws that govern society help regulate both public and private behaviour. Among other things, laws determine how people make fair hiring or firing decisions and how old individuals have to be to work in the first place. To some extent, laws determine whom people can marry and when. People's thoughts and behaviours shape laws, and laws in turn shape people's behaviours; there is a reciprocal relationship in which each affects the other. The interface between the law and psychology is thus as complex as are people and the legal system.

The interaction between the fields of psychology and law has greatly increased over the past few decades in overlapping areas. *Legal psychology* is the field that conducts empirical research on psychological issues important to the legal system, such as eyewitness accuracy, police selection, decision making by juries, and legal assumptions about human behaviour relevant to the rights of defendants, victims, children, and mental patients. *Forensic psychology* focuses on legally relevant clinical areas where psychologists act as expert witnesses and consultants, as in the insanity defence, competence to stand trial, and commitment to mental hospitals. Forensic psychologists might help a judge decide which parent should have custody of the children or evaluate the victim of an accident to determine if he or she endured psychological or neurological damage. In criminal cases, forensic psychologists might evaluate a defendant's mental competence to stand trial. Some forensic psychologists counsel inmates; others counsel the victims of crimes and help them prepare to testify, cope with emotional distress, and resume their normal activities. Third, *psychological jurisprudence* is the study of efforts to develop a philosophy of law and justice based on psychological values.

Psychologists play several roles in the legal system: researchers, policy or program evaluators, advocates, and expert witnesses. As an area of research, psychology and law is concerned both with looking at legal issues from a psychological perspective (e.g., how juries decide cases) and with looking at psychological questions in a legal context (how jurors assign blame or responsibility for a crime). As *researchers*, they help determine why individuals behave in ways that are unacceptable to society. For instance, psychologists do basic research on intelligence, personality, mathematical ability, and the role of genetics in determining aggressiveness, to name just a few areas. This basic research often helps solve some very practical problems. For example, some psychologists develop tests to determine who is mentally ill and who is capable of standing trial, as well as tests to evaluate truthfulness and integrity among defendants and witnesses. Other psychologists look for the causes of aggressiveness in order to develop programs to avert it among accused criminals and to help convicted criminals channel their aggressive energy productively.

Psychologists often serve as *policy or program evaluators*, who help governments and other institutions determine whether various policies, agencies, or programs actually work. For example, psychologists interpret what remedial education has accomplished and whether IQ testing has been valid. When legislators wonder whether early intervention programs (designed to assist children in "at risk" family settings) are making a difference, they turn to psychologists. When new laws calling for equal educational opportunities for the handicapped were being considered, lawyers and judges turned to psychologists for insight into how well various programs might work.

Psychologists are also often asked to be *advocates* for individuals and society, helping to shape social policy in such areas as minority, remedial, and gifted education. When provincial and federal governments seek to trim budgets of social programs affecting children, they turn to psychologists to ascertain what the impact for the future might be. Boards of education consult psychologists to determine how best to assist exceptional students. Psychologists advise government agencies at all levels on how to help those who suffer post-traumatic stress after a flood, ice storm, or other disaster and on how to respond more effectively to such disasters in the future.

Finally, psychologists often serve as *expert witnesses*, bringing their knowledge to the courts as consultants. They do not try to address legal issues directly or to make the ultimate decisions for the courts. Psychologists help the courts in their area of competence—psychology. Psychologists often have been asked to determine who is a good eyewitness (we examined this topic in Chapter 6). They also address specific questions like these: Is this person insane? What are the implications of a divorce on this child? Is this person competent to stand trial?

Psychologists can help determine whether there was any link between a person's mental state or problem and a crime that occurred. From a legal standpoint, a person who deliberately plans a crime is more accountable than one who commits one accidentally. In many jurisdictions, when an accused person is convicted of a serious crime, a jury can judge the person "guilty, but mentally ill." This verdict is seen by many as a reasonable alternative because it reduces the frequency of findings of "not guilty by reason of insanity" (which many find unsatisfying), encourages treatment for the seriously mentally ill, and takes a potentially dangerous offender off the street.

There is, of course, an uneasy alliance between the legal and the psychological professions (Melton et al., 1987). Lawyers assert that psychology is an inexact, or "fuzzy," science and that psychologists should not be allowed to testify as expert witnesses. Psychologists argue that lawyers always want simple answers to complicated human questions and insist on seeking facts even when theories may best describe the truth. In the area of child custody, for example, psychologists are asked to testify in a divorce settlement as to who would be the best custodian of the children and what the psychological consequences of living with one parent or the other will be for a child. But because the legal system is adversarial, each side is likely to have a psychologist testifying that the children will do best with the parent who hired him or her. In fact, there may be no right or wrong answer in some cases. The fact is that answers to various legal questions are not always clear and definitive—this is especially true when psychologists look at environmental issues.

Environmental Psychology

In a small community near Calgary, a rainstorm caused a sewage holding pond to overflow into the local water system and into a small lake nearby. Children occasionally swim in this lake, and people regularly catch fish there. The reaction of the neighbourhood was swift; people became alarmed about their health and welfare. Signs went up warning people to stay away from the lake. The phone lines hummed, the press was brought in, and the local environmental control agency sprang into action. In the end, the spill turned out to be very localized, the levels of toxins were low, and no one was hurt. From an applied psychologist's point of view, however, the mobilization of the residents in the neighbourhood was classic. People became empowered, discussions ensued, and people were energized. Individuals who had never met one another started sharing ideas, and people who had never given much thought to sewage treatment systems became knowledgeable and outspoken on the subject.

A particular group of applied psychologists, known as environmental psychologists, study how physical settings such as people's homes and neighbourhoods affect behaviour. They are interested in issues such as the effects of crowding, how personal space can be changed to meet changing needs, and group reactions to environmental threats. These psychologists examine not only whole neighbourhoods but also smaller groups. **Environmental psychology** is the study of how physical settings affect human behaviour and how people change their environment, often to make it more comfortable and acceptable. Environmental psychologists focus on human interactions with the environment; they recognize that people are affected by the

Environmental psychology: The study of how physical settings affect human behaviour and how people change their environment.

environment in which they live, work, and play and that the environment is affected by human behaviour. Today, the field of environmental psychology has expanded to embrace the idea that human beings affect and to a great extent can control environmental quality for future generations. Behavioural interventions are now being designed to preserve and protect the environment (e.g., Dwyer et al., 1993; Porter, Leeming, & Dwyer, 1995). Because of the large number of variables that enter into studies in environmental psychology, the field has become multidisciplinary, encompassing research from many other fields, such as architecture, geography, and sociology (Stokols, 1995).

Environmental psychologists often conduct studies and consult for institutions, such as governments, schools, hospitals, churches, and museums. For example, consider the design of a nursing station in a hospital. The station is the centre of activity on each floor, and in traditional hospital floor plans it usually is placed at the junction of two long corridors. An alternative is to place it at the hub of a wheel-like arrangement of rooms (a radial design). Most of the patient rooms then will be closer to the nursing station, and nurses can reach them faster and more efficiently. When Trites and his colleagues (1970) investigated worker satisfaction with different hospital designs, they found a distinct preference for the radial design. That result led to the redesign of many hospital floors (Proshansky & O'Hanlon, 1977) with positive results (Ortega, 1991). The truth is that the work space of a hospital or any semi-public space is crucial. When museums are redesigned to allow for great interactivity, multisensory stimulation, and dynamic displays visitors are more immersed in exhibits—again, design affects how people use and appreciate space (Harvey et al., 1998).

Environmental Variables

The environment includes not only the shape of a building, the layout of a hospital floor or a dormitory, or the arrangement of buildings in a housing development or shopping mall. It also includes variables such as furniture and fixtures, climate, noise level, and the number of people per square metre. Environmental psychologists study the relationships among the many variables. Whether a room is perceived as crowded, for example, depends not only on the number of people in it but also on the room's size and shape, furniture layout, ceiling height, number of windows, wall colours, and lighting—as well as on the time of day (Devlin, 1992). Researchers who look at global environmental systems such as cities, communities, and neighbourhoods must consider all of these variables and more. Three of the environmental variables that are easiest to control in order to promote people's well-being are temperature, noise, and environmental toxins.

Temperature. Very hot or very cold climates can cause behavioural effects that range from annoyance to inability to function. Construction workers in Canada's north, for example, would never survive the winter without proper shelter, heating, and warm clothes; and workers in the southern United States would be far less productive without air conditioning during the summer.

Environmental variables that impair work performance are considered to be stressors. As we saw in Chapter 14, a **stressor** is a stimulus that affects an organism in physically or psychologically injurious ways and usually elicits feelings such as anxiety, tension, and physiological arousal. Temperature can be a stressor that affects many behaviours, including academic performance, driving an automobile, and being attracted to others. In general, performance is optimal at moderate temperatures and becomes progressively worse at high or low temperatures.

When the temperature rises and people become uncomfortable, they are more likely to make risky decisions and to behave erratically and less likely to be accurate (Kudoh et al., 1991). Research shows that as temperature rises (up to a point where *any* activity is too much given the heat), aggressive feelings and aggression increase (Anderson, Anderson, & Deuser, 1996). In hotter regions of the world, people show

Stressor: A stimulus that affects an organism in physically or psychologically injurious ways and usually elicits feelings such as anxiety, tension, and physiological arousal.

more aggression; hotter years, months, and days all have been associated with more aggressive behaviours, such as murders, riots, and wife beatings (C. A. Anderson, 1989). Laboratory research on temperature can never be identical to situations in a real-life setting; therefore, ongoing field-based work is likely to provide better evidence about the exact nature of a relationship between heat and aggression (Anderson & Anderson, 1998; Anderson & DeNeve, 1992).

Crowding: The perception that one's space is too limited.

Noise. Another environmental variable that often affects human behaviour is *noise*—unwanted sound. Noise is a stressor that can overstimulate people—they become uncommonly aroused—and often leads to poor work performance and social functioning.

Some noises are almost always present: the buzzing of fluorescent lights, the humming of refrigerators, the banging of doors as they open or close, the chirping of birds, the sounds of moving cars, and the murmur of people talking. Although some of these sounds may be unwanted, they are usually not too disruptive; nor are they stressors. They rarely raise levels of arousal or interfere with daily activities.

However, an unpredictable and intermittent noise of moderate intensity, such as a train whistle, can impair performance on tasks that involve sustained attention or memory. And if noise raises physiological arousal to very high levels, it may impair performance in general and even cause hearing damage (see Chapter 3). Thus, noise acts as a stressor when it interferes with communication, raises physiological arousal, or is so loud that it causes pain. More commonly, noise simply interferes with the ability to concentrate, learn, and remember—thus, it induces stress (Evans, Hygge, & Bullinger, 1995).

Environmental Toxins (Pollutants). As you drive into a congested city such as Windsor, Toronto, or New York, it is distressing to see how the skyline is at once beautiful and polluted with airborne toxins. These toxins include an array of chemicals and substances such as carbon monoxide and sulphur that fill the air from automobiles and from the burning of high-sulphur coal and oil in industrial cities. Nearly any airborne substance, whether an industry-based chemical or a naturally occurring substance such as pollen, can trigger respiratory problems and result in deleterious work performance and health consequences. Airborne toxins, which are often deeply breathed and absorbed by the lungs, can impair motor tasks that involve reaction time, as well as affect long-term health; for example, even in cities that meet federal standards for clean air, the risk of premature death is 3 to 8 percent higher than in the cleanest areas.

Crowding

Prisons are places where crowding can become a very serious issue, as more and more prisoners are held in a fixed amount of space. A key environmental variable that has a profound impact on individual and group behaviour is simply the number of people that are around. In some situations that involve many people, you may feel closed in and crowded. In other situations, the excitement of a crowd may be exhilarating. It generally is not the size of a space or the number of people that causes you to feel crowded; rather, **crowding** is the *perception* that your space is too limited. Thus, crowding is a psychological state. One person may feel crowded and uncomfortable in a mall filled with Christmas shoppers; someone else may feel that the throngs create a happy holiday ambiance. When people feel crowded their sense of well-being is threatened and day-to-day behaviours are affected (Fuller et al., 1996).

Personal Space. Both social density and spatial density affect crowding. *Social density* is the number of people in a given space; *spatial density* is the amount of space allocated to a fixed number of people. For example, in an empty theatre a person might feel lonely; but in a full, or even half-full, theatre the person might feel crowded (social density). In contrast, eight people may feel comfortable in a large modern elevator, but the same eight people might feel intolerably cramped in a small old-fashioned elevator (spatial density). Researchers must be careful to separate the variables of social and spatial density (Baum, 1987).

In 1973 Valins and Baum conducted a study on the effects of architectural design in dormitories. The dormitories were of two designs: (1) corridors with long hallways, 2 people per room, 34 people per floor, and a shared bathroom and lounge; or (2) suites, with 4 or 6 students sharing a bathroom and lounge, and several suites per floor (see Figure 17.5). The actual square footage per student was about the same in both types of dormitories, but 67 percent of corridor residents found their living space crowded, compared with only 25 percent of suite residents. Corridor residents reported too many people on their floor and too many unwanted interactions. Valins and Baum (1973) concluded that corridor designs promoted "excessive social interaction and that such interaction is associated with the experience of crowding" (p. 249).

If some dormitories produce feelings of crowding, as Valins and Baum have suggested, these feelings should be evident in people's behaviour. In a classic study, Bickman and colleagues (1973) compared the helping behaviour shown by students living in housing of different densities. They used a measure called the *lost-letter technique*, in which unmailed letters were purposely dropped in dormitory corridors. They reasoned that someone finding the letter would assume that a person in the dormitory had dropped it by mistake on the way to the mailbox.

The dependent variable was the number of "lost" letters that were subsequently mailed. The independent variable was the density of housing. The experiment involved high-density dormitories (high-rise, 22-storey towers, each housing more than 500 students), medium-density dorms (4- to 7-storey buildings, each housing about 165 students), and low-density dorms (2- to 4-storey buildings, each housing about 58 students). Letters were left unobtrusively in areas near stairwells and elevators, with no more than one letter per corridor. The letters were addressed, sealed, and stamped but had no return address.

The results showed that helping behaviour was 63 percent in high-density dorms, 87 percent in medium-density dorms, and 100 percent in low-density dorms. And when questionnaires were distributed to the students in the various dorms, the answers generally reflected attitudes related to the kind of housing in which the students lived. For example, students in high-density dorms reported feeling less trust,

FIGURE 17.5
The Psychological Effects of Architectural Design
A corridor dorm and a suite have different psychological effects on students, even when actual space per student is about the same. Valins and Baum reported that students living in corridor dorms complained about being crowded more than students living in suites did.

(Based on Valins & Baum, 1973.)

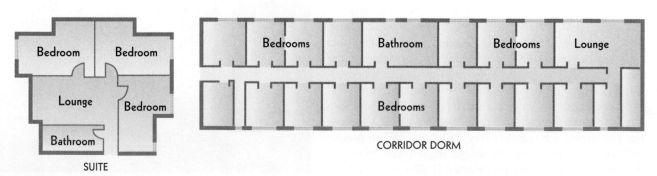

cooperativeness, and responsibility than did students in the lower-density dorms. The researchers concluded that students living in the high-density dormitories behaved in a less socially responsible manner towards other dormitory residents. Baum believes that in situations of high density, people feel stressed, out of control, and crowded. All of this contributes to potential problems in situations of high density—for example, in prisons (Fleming, Baum, & Weiss, 1987).

Although many of the effects of crowding are not consistent across all situations or populations, certain effects seem to be universal. In high-density situations, people feel stressed and sometimes overaroused (Ruback, Pandey, & Begum, 1997). They may feel alone or anonymous, and they may withdraw from the situation. They may become apathetic, may exhibit impaired task performance, and even may become hostile (Malik & Batra, 1998). Maintaining a sense of control and of personal space seems to be a crucial variable (Evans, Lepore, Shejwal, & Palsane, 1998; Morgan & Stewart, 1998).

Personal Space and Culture. It may be that to help assert their individuality and maintain a sense of personal control, human beings generally try to establish appropriate degrees of personal space. **Personal space** is the area or invisible boundary around an individual that the person considers private. Encroachment on that space causes displeasure and often withdrawal.

The size of your personal space can change, depending on the situation and the people near you. For example, you may walk arm in arm with a family member, but you will avoid physical contact with a stranger. You may stand close to a friend and whisper in his ear, but you will keep a certain distance from an elevator operator or a store clerk.

Anthropologist Edward Hall (1966) suggested that personal space is a mechanism by which people communicate with others. He proposed that people adhere to established norms of personal space that are learned in childhood. Hall also observed that the use of personal space varies from culture to culture. In Canada and the United States, especially in suburban and rural areas, people are used to large homes and generous personal space. In Japan, on the other hand, where there is little space available per person, people are used to small homes that provide little personal space. In general, Western cultures insist on a fair amount of space for people, reserving proximity for intimacy and close friends, while Arab cultures allow much smaller distances between strangers (Rustemli, 1991).

To explain the concept of personal space, Hall classified four *spatial zones*, or distances, used in social interactions with other people. The distances are intimate, personal, social, and public. An *intimate distance* (from 0 to 45 centimetres) is reserved for people who have great familiarity with one another. This space is acceptable for comforting someone who is hurt, for lovers, for physicians, and for athletes. The closeness enables a person to hold another person, examine the other's hair and eyes, and hear the other's breath. An acceptable distance for close friends and everyday interactions is *personal distance* (45 centimetres to 1.2 metres). This space is used for most social interactions. At 45 to 60 centimetres, someone might tell a secret to a close friend. At 60 centimetres, people can walk and talk together. At 60 centimetres to 1.2 metres, a person can maintain good contact with a co-worker without seeming too personal or too impersonal. *Social distance* (1.2 to 3.6 metres) is used for business and for interactions with strangers. At 1.2 to 1.8 metres, people are close enough to communicate their ideas effectively but far enough away to remain separated. Physical barriers, such as a desk to separate a clerk, receptionist, or boss from the people with whom the person interacts, may control personal space in the social zone. *Public distance* (3.6 to 7.5 metres or more) minimizes personal contact. This is the distance at which politicians speak at lunch clubs, teachers instruct classes of students, and

actors and musicians perform. Public distance is sufficiently great to eliminate personal interaction between individuals and their audiences.

Of course, determining personal space is a tricky endeavour, and researchers are trying to sort out distance estimations (Zakay, Hayduk, & Tsal, 1992) for adults and children (Roques et al., 1997) and for men and women (Idehen, 1997). Figure 17.6 presents generally accepted estimates of the spaces people use when seated and standing.

Territoriality. If you have ever lived in a dormitory you may have experienced a lack of privacy, and the less personal space you had, the more stressful you may have found that dormitory (Sinha & Mukherjee, 1996). Irwin Altman (1975) has suggested that the key to understanding why people feel crowded and need personal space is privacy. **Privacy** is the result of the process of controlling boundaries between people so that access is limited. Everyone needs privacy. According to Altman, privacy allows people to develop and nurture a sense of self. Without it, people feel they have no control over who and what can intrude on them. This sense of helplessness can lead to low self-esteem and poor social adaptations. Understanding people's need for privacy is central to understanding the behaviour of human beings in their environment.

One way in which people maintain a sense of privacy is to change their immediate environment. When a teenage girl goes into a room and closes the door, she closes herself off from other people; she limits their access to her. The teenager has set up a boundary—a closed door—behind which she can do what she wants when she wants to. Similarly, two people may enter a room and close the door, thereby controlling other people's access to them.

Maintaining a sense of privacy is closely related to territoriality, another important aspect of many people's lives. **Territorial behaviour** is behaviour involved in establishing, maintaining, personalizing, and defending a delineated space. It helps regulate the exclusive use of a specific area by a person or a group of people by marking a space as a private area where intruders are not welcome. Homeowners put up fences and signs reading "No Trespassing," teenagers lock their bedroom doors, street gangs defend their turf, and nations wage war in defence of their national boundaries. Like personal space behaviours, territorial behaviours are privacy-regulating mechanisms.

FIGURE 17.6
People's Use of Personal Space When Seated and Standing

(Based on Altman & Vinsel, 1977.)

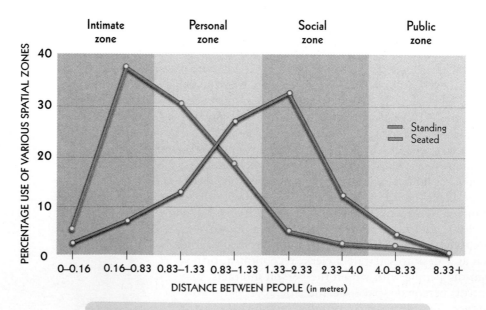

When standing, people use primarily the intimate and personal zones. When seated, people use primarily the social and personal zones.

Preserving the Environment

Territorial behaviour: Behaviour involved in establishing, maintaining, personalizing, and defending a delineated space.

Elementary school children often come home from special school programs reminding parents of the need to recycle, reuse, and cut back on waste. Starting at a young age, people are being encouraged to do their part to preserve this fragile planet. An emerging area of environmental research focuses on doing something to actually control people's behaviour in the environment. For example, research studies found that littering can be significantly reduced if instructions for proper disposal of objects are provided; the more specific the instructions, the less littering occurs (Geller, 1975; Geller, Witmer, & Tuso, 1977). But more important is integrating specific procedures with changing attitudes to increase pro-environmentalism (Geller, 1996).

What makes people want to preserve the environment? Aside from their children's reminders, what makes people want to conserve energy and reduce pollution by driving smaller, more fuel-efficient cars and investing in solar panels for their homes? Research on these issues has shown that tax laws that reward energy savings, signs about energy conservation, and new energy-saving equipment help people adopt more energy-saving behaviours. As with littering, when people are given specific energy-saving instructions and prompts, they are more likely to comply.

Some tremendous worldwide environmental problems must be solved. Geller (1989, 1992) suggests that information delivery and marketing principles be combined with behavioural analysis to solve problems such as preserving the earth's rain forests, managing waste, and conserving energy. First, environmentally beneficial ideas and behaviours must be advanced; this helps move people to at least intend to engage in such behaviours (Stasson & Fishbein, 1990). Products or ideas can be promoted as being affordable, accessible, easy to use, and desirable (Burn, 1991). Keeping in mind all of the means of attitude change that we discussed in Chapter 13, psychologists then must analyze the wants, needs, and perceptions of the people being targeted. After these steps have been taken, researchers should evaluate the results of efforts to change attitudes and behaviour to see whether the strategy has been effective. Geller claims that behavioural interventions combined with social marketing and policy strategies can provide an integrative program for environmental preservation (e.g., Geller, 1992). He also calls for a collaboration of social action research and scholarship to preserve the quality of the environment. Many cost-effective traditional interventions are still not as effective as they might be (Needleman & Geller, 1992). Once people stop being reinforced for recycling or other pro-environment behaviours, they often discontinue the behaviour; psychologists have to work at fostering long-term changes in behaviour. As William Dwyer and his colleagues assert (1993, p. 317): "Even the most effective techniques for the initiation of behavior change is of minimal importance unless that behavior can be maintained or if the intervention can remain in place for a long-period of time . . . behavioral scientists need to give much greater consideration to the development of lifelong behaviors that will help maintain environmental quality. Only then can behavior science meaningfully contribute to saving planet Earth."

Social change begins with individual change, and individuals can be assisted by healthier communities. Community psychologists, considered next, attempt to foster such changes.

Focus

Review

- How does each type of environmental stressor affect behaviour? pp. 624–625
- Describe the hypothesis and results of the lost-letter experiment. pp. 626–627
- What is the purpose of each of the four spatial zones that define personal space? pp. 627–628

Think Critically

- What are the implications of the study of environmental variables such as noise, temperature, and pollutants for architectural firms, heating and cooling companies, and window designers?
- How can people seek intimacy in their lives and still maintain personal space and a sense of territory and privacy?

Community Psychology

I f you live in a community that has faced a challenge before—unemployment, environmental spills, or the call to host the Olympic Games—you know that communities can be mobilized. They can take on a school board or vote mayors in or out of office, and they do so by pooling resources, volunteering, using their collective talent, and reaching out. Some communities are more proactive than others and seek to prevent problems before they occur. They toil on school problems and decaying sections of town and they lobby legislators for new funds for community centres. Psychologists today are working at prevention and consider it a part of psychology. They are looking not only at individuals but also at whole communities—they seek to influence individuals, families, and the entire social structure (Levine, 1998). They hope to help people develop resilience and a sense of purpose and nurture what is essential for survival and personal growth (Sonn & Fisher, 1998). Access to information, communication within a community, and a sense of social involvement are necessary for the work of these psychologists. *The Research Process* looks at the effect of the Internet on these kinds of variables.

To a certain extent this movement in psychology can be traced to the 1960s. In that decade, many psychologists recognized that individual therapy was at best imprecise and at worst inefficient for treating large numbers of people. Researchers and

the research process

The Internet and Social Well-being

A pproximately 40 percent of all Canadian households own a personal computer; nearly one-third of these have Internet access. Many scholars and business people feel that the Internet could change the lives of average citizens as much as the telephone did at the turn of the twentieth century and television did in the 1950s and 1960s. There is no doubt that the Internet is fast, inexpensive, immediate, and has transformed communication. But is it also changing our lives in harmful ways? Are people cutting themselves off from others as they hunker down, alone, over their terminals communicating with anonymous strangers or buying things or playing games through the telephone lines? Has it left people with fewer social contacts with others, seeking entertainment and

relationships through a medium that is asocial, potentially anonymous, and at a minimum a solitary activity?

Hypotheses. Robert Kraut and his colleagues (1998) have argued that the Internet is having enormous effects on society—they have outlined its strengths and potential weaknesses, its good and bad sides. It is entertaining, useful, and informative. It also can be too engrossing and a time waster, as well as inducing boredom. The Internet is still largely used for personal communication through electronic mail—e-mail. But what is at issue remains to be seen: Does it help build strong ties that strengthen relationships, or is it impersonal, anonymous, and often short and superficial? To examine this issue Kraut and colleagues (1998) collected longitudinal data to

examine the relationship between people's use of the Internet, their social involvement, and the consequences of Internet use on social involvement.

Method. The researchers studied 169 people who used the Internet. Participants came from diverse neighbourhoods in Pittsburgh, Pennsylvania, were over the age of 10, and lived in four school districts that were near each other (so some students knew each other and there was already some existing communication). Families were given computers, e-mail accounts, and access to the Internet and agreed to have their Internet usage tracked and to do a home interview.

Data Collection. Software automatically recorded the total

practitioners, as well as politicians, sought a more efficient and effective approach. Community psychology has emerged in response to a widespread desire for a more action-oriented approach to individual and social adjustment. **Community psychology** is a branch of psychology that seeks to reach out to society to provide services such as community mental health centres and especially to effect social change.

The general aims of community psychology are to strengthen existing social support networks and to stimulate the formation of new networks to meet new challenges (Gonzales et al., 1983). A key element is community involvement leading to social change. A church or synagogue group, for example, could mobilize its senior citizens for a foster grandparent program. A community psychologist might help a group develop better fire safety procedures in public housing. The focus of community psychology is often on solving applied behaviour problems. A key element of community psychology is **empowerment**—helping people in the community to enhance their existing skills and develop new skills, knowledge, and motivation so that they can gain control over their own lives (Rappaport, 1987). Community psychologists work in schools, churches, planning commissions, and prisons. They plan and set up programs for bringing psychological skills and knowledge into the community. Community psychologists work especially hard at prevention of psychological problems. This often comes in the form of developing neighbourhood organization to build cohesion and resilience to mental health problems (Wandersman & Nation, 1998). Prevention operates at three levels: primary, secondary, and tertiary.

> **Community psychology:** The branch of psychology that seeks to reach out to society to provide services such as community mental health centres and especially to effect social change.
>
> **Empowerment:** Helping people in the community to enhance their existing skills and develop new skills, knowledge, and motivation so that they can gain control over their own lives.

number of hours per week the participants accessed the Internet, the number of sites accessed on the Web each week, and the number of e-mail messages participants sent and received per week. The participants' social and psychological well-being was assessed via questionnaires when the study began and then at 12 and 24 months later. The questionnaire looked at social involvement, family communication, size of social network, size of distant social networks, and social support.

Results. Correlations between Internet use and various variables were calculated and results showed that teens used the Internet more than adults; whites and minorities used the Internet about the same amount. Greater use of the Internet was associated with declines in family communication. People from wealthier households expressed more loneliness with increased access to the Internet than did people from poorer ones, as did men compared to women, and minorities compared to whites.

People who used the Internet more reported more daily stress; more importantly, greater use of the Internet was associated with increased depression.

Discussion and Implications. Greater use of the Internet was associated with small but reliable increases in loneliness, declines in social involvement, and increases in depression. Kraut and colleagues assert that using the Internet adversely affects social involvement and psychological well-being. The researchers examined people during the first online activities; they acknowledge that whether the results would be the same at different points in their usage is not yet established. They make no claims that the Internet is bad—indeed, participants learned computer skills and it helped with homework. But is this worth the tradeoff?

The time people spent on the Internet displaced other social

activities, a finding that mirrors what has been frequently reported regarding television. It is not clear whether people are substituting poorer quality social relationships for better ones or vice versa. The new online relationships that participants formed were mostly superficial or supported existing friendships at school, work, or church. Can accessing the Internet be entertaining and useful, without causing disengagement from real life? Can psychologists help design Internet applications that enhance social interactions so as to benefit society? Can the Internet become a more social medium? ■

One focus of community psychology is *primary prevention*—reducing the risk of *new* cases of a disorder or counteracting harmful circumstances before they lead to maladjustment. Primary prevention usually targets groups rather than individuals. It may focus on an entire community, on mild-risk groups (such as children from families of low socioeconomic status), or on high-risk groups (such as children of schizophrenic parents). Community psychologists may establish drug prevention centres, safe houses for battered women, and suicide hotlines.

In response to growing public awareness of mental health problems, a special kind of primary prevention service agency—the *neighbourhood clinic*—came into being. Such clinics help communities cope with problems that may be created by mental illness, unemployment, and lack of education. Some clinics provide free, confidential treatment for such problems as drug addiction, alcoholism, and emotional and psychological disorders. They offer a variety of services, including partial hospitalization programs for people who require hospitalization during the day and outpatient care for people who live at home while receiving therapy. They also offer consultation, education programs, and lectures and literature on such topics as therapy, family planning, and drug rehabilitation.

Secondary prevention involves catching problems and identifying new cases in the early stages. Community psychologists offer secondary prevention services in *crisis intervention centres*, which help people deal with short-term stressful situations requiring immediate therapeutic attention. Often the crisis is a specific event; for example, a person may be contemplating suicide, or a woman may have been raped. The focus of crisis intervention is on the immediate circumstances, not on past experiences. Studies show that crisis intervention therapy can be especially effective (Sawicki, 1988), but one problem in evaluating such therapy is that a variety of techniques are used, making controlled comparisons difficult (Slaikeu, 1990).

Tertiary prevention focuses on the treatment of full-blown psychological problems. There is considerable overlap between secondary and tertiary prevention, as sometimes issues and problems that are presented as short term or in their early stages may have a long-standing basis. Community psychologists offer help to eliminate or reduce a problem as well as to strengthen existing family or community resources. Sometimes this help is an intervention to protect family members; other times, it consists of counselling, consulting with schools, or calling in other social service agencies. Again, the emphasis is on using existing community resources and empowering individuals to manage their own lives more effectively.

An important aim of community psychology is to serve all members of the community, including people who might not otherwise be able to afford the services of a psychotherapist or counsellor. They seek to develop a sense of community in individuals, which has a clear psychological benefit (Brodsky, 1996). Community psychologists are change-oriented. Because they believe that some social conditions and organizational procedures result in maladjusted individuals, they often advocate changes in community institutions and organizations. For example, they seek to improve the court system, develop programs to prevent drug use in schools, help energy conservation groups educate the public, consult with industry about reducing stress on the job, help religious organizations develop volunteer programs to aid the homeless, help hospitals set up preventive-medicine programs, and foster community involvement in educational issues.

Focus

Review

◆ Why did community psychology emerge, and what do community psychologists mean by *empowerment*? pp. 631–632

Think Critically

◆ Many community psychologists focus on helping groups of people, such as churches, neighbourhoods, schools, and even whole communities, to change. What is the role of community psychology with regards to individuals?

Educational Psychology

Educational psychology: The systematic application of psychological principles to learning and teaching.

A while ago, when the authors of this text were in school, students were grouped according to ability, but that ability was inferred only from the teacher's observations of classroom behaviour. Students who acted out in any way were assigned seats in the seventh row. Little attention was paid to those of us relegated to the seventh row.

Things have changed. Today, all teachers have undergraduate college degrees; most have advanced degrees. Teachers now must be trained not only in their content areas but also in sophisticated educational techniques. History teachers need to know history and how to teach it, as well as how to manage classrooms and help individual students meet their special challenges. And this is where educational psychology comes in.

Educational psychology is the systematic application of psychological principles to learning and teaching. Psychology has had a long tradition of studying learning principles; psychological researchers have thoroughly explored how people study, learn, and forget. Educators have long focused on instructional techniques and principles of classroom management. *Educational psychologists* bring these two disciplines together. They show how psychological ideas, methods, and theories can be applied to improve learning in individual students and in whole classrooms and to improve the process of teaching itself. In short, they help create better classroom managers (Fox, 1993). A distinction exists between educational psychologists and school psychologists. Although both share many similar concerns, educational psychologists are likely to focus on strategies to improve overall learning and classroom techniques. School psychologists are more likely to focus on interventions to affect individuals, on diagnoses of psychological and learning problems, and on consultations with parents and educators about an individual child's progress or plans.

Problems Studied by Educational Psychologists

Educational psychologists need to know a great deal about students to help promote effective teaching. For example, they seek to discover information about students' backgrounds, interests, abilities, and past learning and to understand how they interact with other students and other teachers and how they go about solving problems. Psychologists usually study these issues in the context of five areas of inquiry in order to put theory into practice. You will recognize these areas from earlier chapters, because educational psychologists apply the lessons of many psychological subdisciplines—from learning, to developmental psychology, to social psychology.

A key focus for educational psychologists is *developmental change*—how and when individuals develop physically, socially, and intellectually. In children these processes are rapid, change each year, and dramatically alter the ways a child or adolescent learns and interacts with teachers and other students.

Educational psychologists also study students' backgrounds to learn how *environmental conditions* can affect the learning process. Socioeconomic status is but one of those conditions; parental marital status, use of drugs in the home, and how learning is talked about at home are other important environmental factors.

Focus

Review

◆ What are the goals of and the problems studied by educational psychologists? pp. 633–634

Think Critically

◆ If you wanted to be a teacher, what do you think would be the most challenging part of ensuring effective instruction? How do you think that aspect of teaching would vary with the grade or the subject matter that you might teach?

◆ Many schools are moving towards the concept of block scheduling, in which two periods are joined to provide one long class. What are the advantages and/or disadvantages for effective instruction of block scheduling, compared with traditional classes of shorter duration?

Classroom learning styles are important to educational psychologists. These psychologists study *behavioural principles of learning* to ensure that the classroom has appropriate order, they study *cognitive processes* to learn how students learn and process new information, and they examine *social interactions* to find out how students are influenced by others and how they can be influenced in positive ways.

Putting Theory into Practice

Studying the principles of psychology is obviously a key prerequisite of effective classroom technique. But what are effective classroom techniques? Educational psychologists try to bridge the gap between theory and practice by developing approaches to learning and instruction that optimize student outcomes. For example, educational psychologists have focused on developing individualized educational plans to personalize instruction; they work to develop mastery learning—breaking learning down into a series of discrete steps in which all students can gain competence. They also foster immediate feedback and seek to establish clearly defined objectives and to develop effective classroom management techniques (as described in *Experiencing Psychology*).

Educational psychologists are both theoreticians and practitioners. They try to implement instructional techniques in innovative ways that have measurable outcomes. What if a student acts out in class by verbally abusing another child? There

experiencing psychology

Classroom Management

There is a difference between the amount of time allocated to a class and the amount of time students are actually engaged in learning. Both time allocation and management of engaged time are key issues for teachers. Establishing clear classroom rules and pacing a class effectively are important. When teachers who are modern and "reform-minded" participate in development programs to enhance classroom effectiveness, the result is usually quite positive for students (Stipek et al., 1998).

Time Allocation. Because teachers have such small amounts of time with students, they must manage allocated time effectively. How much time is actually spent on learning? In many elementary schools only about 60 percent of classroom time is actually spent on

the task at hand (Karweit & Slavin, 1981). Researchers have found that carefully dividing up the allocated class time is key. Other recommendations are to avoid late starts and early finishes to class periods. Late starts signal to students that the lesson is not of importance. This leads to further late starts by students and a general lackadaisical attitude. A teacher should avoid interruptions at all costs, as they break a lesson's momentum and steal substantial time from engaged learning. When students are actively engaged with learning, they are said to be *on task*. To encourage on-task behaviours, effective teachers minimize time spent on recurring activities by ensuring smooth and efficient handling of routine procedures. Cooperative learning, with children working in teams, facilitates achievement and on-task time (Ross,

Haimes, & Hoagaboam-Gray, 1998). Finally, efficient teachers minimize time spent on discipline by quickly and efficiently imposing penalties in private and then seeking to reestablish a positive relationship with the offender (Weinstein & Mignano, 1993).

Engaged Time. If time is well allocated, then students' on-task time is more likely to be well spent. Effective teachers try to maintain momentum and smoothness of instruction by setting up a meaningful sequence of instructional ideas. Managing transitions from one topic to the next helps keep students engaged and focused.

Maintaining an entire class's focus is also an important task. Letting students know that the teacher is aware of the activities of the class keeps students on task; praising students for their good

are dozens of things an instructor can do—and such situations happen throughout the day. Should a teacher *scold* the child, *ignore* the child, *banish* the child to the school office, *punish* the child for classroom misbehaviour, or *instruct* the child on respect for peers? The answers lie in psychological principles: Scolding is punishment; ignoring is another form of punishment; banishment is a form of time-out—but instruction tries to focus on positive future behaviours. Research in each of these areas, plus a little common sense and knowledge of children, makes for effective teaching.

Sport psychology: The systematic application of psychological principles to sports.

Sport Psychology

I magine lining up a shot—any kind of shot will do. You picture the ball, you think about its final destination, you visualize its trajectory. You shoot. When golfers such as Greg Norman or Mike Weir, basketball players such as Vince Carter, or quarterbacks such as Doug Flutie prepare to take their shots, they usually imagine them first. In using mental imagery, they are using principles of sport psychology.

Sport psychology is the systematic application of psychological principles in sports. Sport psychologists, like any psychologists, recognize that behaviour (in this

work turns out to be a key variable (Craft, Alber, & Heward, 1998). Instructors who can juggle many tasks at one time and who can work well with both individuals and small groups help ensure effective on-task instruction (Charles, 1985). Teachers who make the basics clear, monitor work in progress, and give frequent feedback are more effective in engaging students.

Classroom Rules. When instructors start the year with a clear set of guidelines for students, in which students are systematically introduced to the procedures and teachers' expectations, on-task and engaged student behaviours are more likely to occur. When rules are limited in number and clear, they are far more likely to be easily enforced. In addition, when students are asked to help establish ground rules, such as not talking without raising one's hand, offenders know that they are breaking their own rules, not arbitrary regulations. Educational psychologists assert that it is necessary to "let the punishment fit the crime" (Notterman & Drewry, 1993), that students themselves may be the best judges of appropriate

punishments, and that students can be helpers in the process of reducing disruptions (Arceneaux & Murdock, 1998).

Pacing. The tempo of a class is like the tempo of a symphony. A conductor does not want the musicians to play too quickly or with too much enthusiasm; engaging concerts, like good classes, use silences effectively. Phrases and ideas are not repeated too often, and the voice of the band, or the teacher, needs to change often to keep attention. The pace needs to be varied—short segments are more likely to hold attention than long ones.

Pacing is determined by the nature of the students, the material to be covered, and the instructor's own personal style. But combined with classroom rules and effective allocation of time to ensure on-task behaviour, pacing is an important element of effective instruction.

Each of these four elements—time allocation,

engaged time, classroom rules, and pacing—helps establish effective instruction. There are other important tactics, too, of course: summarizing, using feedback, encouraging student interaction, and even planning seating arrangements. All of these topics are part of the discipline of educational psychology. Each has been explored in depth by learning researchers, classroom teachers, and educational psychologists. ■

case, athletic performance) is affected by the individual athlete, the athlete's team, the team leader or coach, and the environment in which these individuals interact. The characteristics of athlete, coach, and environment are each multidimensional; people, their own personal characteristics, how they interact with others, and how the environment affects them are all influenced by years of past events, relationships, and successes or failures. Nevertheless, sport psychologists have tried to bring some order to the study of athletic performance. Sport psychologists study the behaviours associated with sports in the traditional ways that psychologists go about things: Some do basic research in sports; others take an educational role, teaching about sport psychology; still others are applied practitioners who help athletes overcome obstacles to achieve their highest potential. Practitioners need to be trained in sports and psychology to work in this area. There exist a whole range of sports behaviours that researchers consider appropriate for study and research, education, and intervention. Among the most important are the topics we will consider here: motivation, activation and arousal, anxiety and performance, and intervention strategies (Cox, Qiu, & Liu, 1993).

Motivation

If there were simple answers to explain what motivates an athlete—what factors energize, direct, and sustain athletic performance—then the task for sport psychologists, and especially for an athlete's coach, would be dramatically different. But athletic performance is exceedingly complicated. According to one researcher, it takes at least four levels of analysis to understand what motivates a person to perform a sport well (Roberts, 1992):

- *What is the goal?* Is the person seeking competitive abilities or merely mastery of a sport? Is the goal learning to play squash at a national level of competition, or is the goal to have a friendly game in which the athlete knows the rules, feels competent, and has fun playing? Based on such recognition of personal goals, the athlete must then accept goals set by a coach.

- *Is the motivational climate set by friends, parents, and coaches geared towards competition or mastery?* When the climate is geared towards mastery, the athlete's energy level is usually much lower, and so is anxiety.

- *How does the athlete perceive his or her abilities—as high, low, or not relevant?* When people have a strong self-concept of their abilities, they do better in sports. As we saw in Chapter 12, when people have a positive sense of self-efficacy, they do much better at a task.

- *Is the athlete's achievement behaviour adaptive or maladaptive?* Does the athlete set realistic goals and practice schedules and follow training routines, or does the athlete engage in self-defeating behaviours?

To a great extent, this four-step analysis of motivation looks at what energizes and sustains an athlete in sports. But a person who seeks to understand sport psychology must recognize that human beings are not always rational or goal-directed and do not always behave consistently. Their health, love life, family situation, and financial status, to name just a few variables, affect people's behaviour.

Consider how attribution theory might help explain motivations in sports (see p. 460 for a review of attribution theory). If a person attributes his or her failure to a lack of personal ability, this is likely to be detrimental to future motivation and performance. To test this hypothesis, Miserandino (1998) trained members of a boys' high-school basketball team to revise their attributions about their performance so that they were more facilitative and motivational. Half of the participants received feedback about shooting performance and were encouraged to attribute any performance to a lack of effort rather than to a lack of ability. The remaining participants received feedback on shooting technique only, with no attributions provided. After a four-week training period, the boys in the attributional group showed more mastery and greater improvement in their shooting. Attributions about the whys of behaviour make a difference.

In the end, enhancing motivation through attribution may be important, but it is only part of a more complex picture. In various sports, high achievers also:

- Set realistic goals
- Announce goals to others
- Chart progress towards goals
- Vary workout regimes
- Take days off so as to avoid burnout and boredom
- Have workout partners
- Try to keep their sport activity fun

The complexity of these situations makes the study of sport psychology resistant to easy explanations, but also more exciting. Researchers have so much to learn, especially about the energizing of behaviour through activation and arousal, our next topic.

Activation and Arousal

In our study of motivation in Chapter 9, we saw that, given moderate levels of arousal and moderately difficult tasks, as arousal increased, performance also increased. Arousal generally is viewed as stimulation and excitement—a performance enhancer (for example, a goalie's performance in the Stanley Cup playoffs often can be better than in the regular season). But excessive levels of arousal are associated with poor performance. Yerkes and Dodson characterized such a learning curve as an inverted U (see page 296 for a review of the Yerkes–Dodson law). One need not be a psychologist to recognize that when people are extremely frightened, aroused, or activated, performance suffers. This is certainly true in athletics; dozens of research studies have shown that being activated and aroused increases athletic performance—but only up to a point.

The inverted U–shape relationship for arousal and performance is not always orderly, however, especially in sports situations that involve a heavy level of cognitive activity, such as quarterbacking in football or catching in baseball. Researchers know that for every increase in a person's arousal, a corresponding increase (or decrease) in performance is not necessarily evident. Sometimes a small increase in arousal can push some people "over the top" to acute anxiety and poor performance. Young children are less affected by pressure; older children, in contrast, think about options ("My teammate at second base doesn't catch very well, so it makes more sense to throw to first") and are more affected by pressure (French, Spurgeon, & Nevett, 1995). How then is arousal distinct from anxiety?

Anxiety and Performance

In any sport, it is never good to prepare excessively either physiologically or psychologically—such overtraining can lead to serious anxiety (Kreider, Andrew, & O'Toole, 1998). When an athlete is fearful, tense, and apprehensive and such feelings are associated with arousal, the athlete is suffering from anxiety. Some people, including athletes, feel this way most of the time—trait personality theorists would say that such people have a strong or dominant anxiety trait. A whole range of tests has been developed to measure anxiety in athletes and to discern whether anxiety is related to specific events or is a general trait in a given athlete.

Unlike weekend or casual sports enthusiasts, competitive athletes often reach their peak of anxiety significantly before an athletic event begins, and their highest levels of anxiety may disappear immediately before the event. As they step up to the plate, hoop, skating rink, or scrimmage line, professional athletes often become cool, collected, and in control. Three hours earlier they may have felt overwhelmed by their arousal and fear, but when they have to perform, their anxiety is gone.

If this relationship between anxiety and performance were tidy, psychologists wouldn't fret about precompetitive anxiety. But, like so many other psychological phenomena, anxiety is related to other aspects of an athlete's performance and life. If an athlete's arousal exceeds the level needed for effective performance, anxiety can take over. Similarly, an underaroused athlete also may become anxious and stay anxious throughout an event. So arousal and anxiety are closely related and hard to separate. But separation can be achieved through good intervention strategies.

Intervention Strategies

When a person's level of anxiety is sufficiently high that arousal leads to lower performance, interventions can be put in place to help relieve anxiety and arousal. Stress management approaches, described in Chapter 14, have proved to be effective. There is a broad array of such anxiety-reducing techniques.

One widely used technique is *progressive relaxation*, in which athletes are taught to relax slowly and progressively as time passes. Individual muscle relaxation, with progressively deeper muscle-group relaxation, is the goal. Typical steps are suggestions to relax the limbs, to feel heaviness or warmth in the arms and legs, to feel a reduced heart rate, and to sense coolness on the forehead.

Hypnosis, the state encouraging uncritical acceptance of suggestions, has been used widely to help athletes achieve deep relaxation, as well as to help them focus their energy and attention. Closely associated with hypnosis is instruction in *meditation* to help an athlete relax and gain control of his or her focus. The technique of meditation is to focus energy and attention on a single thought, idea, sound, or object. (Hypnosis and meditation can help athletes relax and focus, of course, but they will never make a bad athlete into a good one.) Closely associated are the physical and mental techniques involved in yoga. Practitioners claim that yoga is capable of causing profound physiological and psychological changes. Head coach Phil Jackson of the Chicago Bulls made his team go to mandatory sessions a couple of years ago and it seemed to work!

Using *mental imagery* to promote relaxation has been shown to be worthwhile in many sports activities (Overby, 1990), and when mental imagery is combined with other relaxation strategies, the results have proved especially effective (Murphy & Jowdy, 1992). As described earlier, athletes also use mental imagery to "psych up," or practise for a sports activity in their thoughts (Murphy, 1990).

Cognitive interventions that focus on changing thought patterns about a sport, an event, abilities, or strategies have been especially helpful (Boutcher, 1992). Cognitive strategies often focus on educational issues in the sport in combination with training in relaxation, such as thinking calm thoughts just before a pole vault. Cognitive interventions may teach athletes to think positively, to block out distractions, and to focus on the one part of their body that is crucial in their sport.

Focus

Review

◆ Identify four levels of analysis needed for an understanding of motivation in sports. p. 636

Think Critically

◆ Sport psychologists seek to enhance athletes' performance by improving their physical and emotional condition and their motivation. Does such behaviour management raise any ethical problems for sport psychologists?

Summary and Review

Industrial/Organizational Psychology

What is I/O psychology?

- *Industrial/organizational (I/O) psychology* is the study of how individual behaviour is affected by the work environment, by co-workers, and by organizational practices. It can be divided into four broad areas: human resources psychology, motivation of job performance, job satisfaction, and leadership. p. 602

What are the goals of job analyses, selection procedures, and training efforts in today's workplace?

- The functional job analysis and the position analysis questionnaire are instruments that have been developed by I/O psychologists for *job analyses*. All such analyses have a similar goal: Employers need to ensure that jobs are appropriate and have the correct scope. Two of the key tasks of an I/O psychologist are to balance the scope and complexity of jobs and to help employers create jobs that will be motivating. pp. 603–604

- Selection procedures have the basic goal of predicting the success of job candidates to help an employer determine which candidates to hire and which to reject. Application forms, interviews, samples of work, and tests are some of the instruments used in selection. Training is the process by which organizations systematically teach employees skills to improve their job performance. pp. 604–607

What is a performance appraisal?

- *Performance appraisal* is the process whereby a supervisor periodically evaluates the job-relevant strengths and weaknesses of subordinates. The problem with performance appraisals is that they often are done inaccurately by people with few skills in evaluation and with few diagnostic aids. Multiple performance criteria must enter into an appraisal. pp. 607–608

How have psychologists tried to help managers motivate workers?

- I/O psychologists help employers find ways to motivate employees to be more productive. *Goal-setting theory* asserts that setting specific, clear, attainable goals for a given task will lead to better performance. p. 610

- *Expectancy theories* assert that both motivation and ability determine performance. Vroom suggests further that work motivation is determined by expectancy (the belief that hard or extra work will lead to good or improved performance), instrumentality (the belief that good performance will be rewarded), and valence (the value put on rewards that are offered). Lawler and Porter contended that performance is determined by motivation, ability, and role perceptions—the ways people believe they should be doing their jobs. pp. 610–611

How have psychologists analyzed worker performance and job satisfaction?

- The view that what people bring to a work situation should be balanced by what they receive there compared with others is captured in *equity theory*. Thus, workers' input (what they bring or do) should be balanced by the rewards they receive. If input is not balanced with compensation, people will adjust their work input accordingly. p. 611–612

- I/O psychologists have developed three basic approaches to motivation management: paternalistic, behavioural, and participatory. pp. 612–613

- There are many sources of job satisfaction, including the work itself, the perceived rewards of the work, the quality of supervision, the support of co-workers, and the work setting. In the end, the overall level of satisfaction depends on the extent to which people feel that their expectations for satisfaction are matched by their actual satisfaction. pp. 613–615

What makes a good leader?

- A leader is a person who influences other people's behaviour towards the attainment of agreed-upon goals. Business leaders can be employee-oriented or task-oriented; the context of the situation or the organization is a key determinant of which type of leader will be more effective. *Transformational leaders*—charismatic leaders who inspire and provide intellectual stimulation—create opportunities to transform an organization, often by empowering employees. pp. 615–619

KEY TERMS
applied psychology, p. 602; industrial/organizational (I/O) psychology, p. 602; job analyses, p. 603; performance appraisal, p. 607; goal-setting theory, p. 610; expectancy theories, p. 610; equity theory, p. 611; transformational leader, p. 617

Human Factors and Ergonomics

Describe the field of human factors and ergonomics.

- *Human factors* is the study of the relationship of human beings to machines and to workplaces and other environments. *Ergonomics* is the study of the fit between human anatomy or physiology, the demands of a particular task or piece of equipment, and the environment in which the task occurs. Human factors research can provide a work environment that is not only efficient but also safe. Warnings, labels, and compliance techniques are all helpful in improving safety. pp. 619–621

KEY TERMS
human factors, p. 619; ergonomics, p. 619

Psychology and the Law

What key roles do psychologists play in the legal system?

- As researchers, psychologists help determine why individuals behave in ways that are unacceptable to society. Psychologists also act as policy or program evaluators, helping governments and other institutions determine whether various policies, agencies, or programs actually work. Psychologists work as advocates for individuals and society, helping shape social policy in such areas as minority, remedial, and gifted education. Finally, psychologists often serve as expert witnesses, bringing their knowledge to the courts as consultants. pp. 622–623

Environmental Psychology

What do environmental psychologists study?

■ *Environmental psychology* is the study of how physical settings and aspects of the environment affect human behaviour, as well as how people can change their environment to meet their psychological needs. *Crowding* is the perception that one's space is too limited. Social density is the number of people in a given space, while spatial density is the amount of space allocated to a fixed number of people. *Personal space*, as defined by Hall, is the immediate area around an individual that the person considers private. Four spatial zones, or distances, in social interactions in the United States are intimate, personal, social, and public. pp. 623–629

KEY TERMS
environmental psychology, p. 623; stressor, p. 624; crowding, p. 625; personal space, p. 627; privacy, p. 628; territorial behaviour, p. 629

Community Psychology

Why did community psychology emerge, and what do community psychologists mean by empowerment?

■ *Community psychology* seeks to reach out to society to provide psychological services to people who might not otherwise receive them. The general aims of community psychologists are to empower people and to use three levels of prevention strategies to help ward off, treat, or stop psychological problems in the community. *Empowerment* refers to helping people to enhance existing skills and develop new skills, knowledge, and motivation so that they can gain control over their own lives. pp. 630–632

KEY TERMS
community psychology, p. 631; empowerment, p. 631

Educational Psychology

What are the goals of and problems studied by an educational psychologist?

■ *Educational psychology* is the systematic application of psychological principles to learning and teaching. To help create effective teaching, educational psychologists seek to discover information about students' backgrounds, interests, abilities, and past learning; about how they interact with other students and other teachers; and about how they go about solving problems. Key areas for educational psychologists are developmental changes—how and when individuals grow physically, socially, and intellectually. Educational psychologists study students' backgrounds to learn how

environmental conditions affect the learning process. Classroom learning styles are also important to educational psychologists. Both time allocation and management of engaged time are key issues for effective teachers. pp. 633–635

KEY TERM
educational psychology, p. 633

Sport Psychology

What is sport psychology?

■ *Sport psychology* is the systematic application of psychological principles in sports. Sport psychologists recognize that athletic performance is affected by the athlete, the team leader or coach, and the environment. Sport psychologists study issues such as arousal and performance and have found an inverted U–shape relationship between arousal and performance; but researchers know that as arousal increases, performance may or may not increase or decrease smoothly. pp. 635–637

What occurs when an athlete is anxious?

■ When an athlete is fearful, tense, and apprehensive and such feelings are associated with arousal, the athlete is suffering from anxiety. When anxiety is too high and arousal lowers performance, interventions can help lower arousal and relieve anxiety. pp. 637–638

KEY TERM
sport psychology, p. 635

Weblinks

The Leadership Challenge
www.perc.net/Background.HTML
Work through this simulation to test your leadership skills.

The Society for Industrial and Organizational Psychology
www.siop.org/
This comprehensive Web site provides links and information relevant to industrial and organizational psychology.

High Performance Team
rampages.onramp.net/~bodwell/home.htm
Coaching, high performance team concepts, team building and how all three can be used in the corporate world are discussed at this home page.

Exercise and Sport Psychology
www.psyc.unt.edu/apadiv47/
Learn how to become a sport psychologist, the purpose and goals of the organization, and how to become a member at this site.

Sport Psychology with Karlene Sugarman
www.psychwww.com/sports/index.htm
This Web site features essays on mental training and peak performance for athletes.

Human Factors and Ergonomics Society
hfes.org/
This Web site contains information about the society, its member services, and its activities. The organization is concerned with "characteristics of human beings that are applicable to the design of systems and devices of all kinds."

Current Trends in Environmental Psychology
www.ucm.es/info/Psyap/iaap/evans.htm
Gary Evans of Cornell University wrote this essay about the state of environmental psychology today.

Appendix

Statistical Methods

Scientific progress is in many ways directly linked to researchers' ability to measure and quantify data. **Statistics** is the branch of mathematics that deals with collecting, classifying, and analyzing data. To rule out coincidence and to try to discover and understand the true causes of behaviour, psychologists carefully study behaviour and sometimes control the variables in experiments (topics discussed in detail in Chapter 1), then use statistics to describe, summarize, and present results. These methods and procedures for analyzing data are the topics of this appendix.

Descriptive Statistics

R esearchers use statistics to evaluate and organize data. Specifically, they use **descriptive statistics**—procedures used to summarize, condense, and describe sets of data. For example, your professors use descriptive statistics to interpret exam results. A statistical description of a 100-point midterm exam may show that 10 percent of a class scored more than 60 points, 70 percent scored between 40 and 60 points, and 20 percent scored fewer than 40 points. On the basis of this statistical description, the professor might conclude that the test was exceptionally difficult and might arrange the grades so that anyone who earned 61 points or more received an A. But before inferences can be drawn or grades can be arranged, the data from a research study must be organized in a meaningful way.

Statistics: The branch of mathematics that deals with collecting, classifying, and analyzing data.

Descriptive statistics: A general set of procedures used to summarize, condense, and describe sets of data.

Frequency distribution: A chart or array of scores, usually arranged from the highest to the lowest, showing the number of instances for each score.

Frequency polygon: A graph of a frequency distribution that shows the number of instances of obtained scores, usually with the data points connected by straight lines.

Organizing Data: Frequency Distributions

When psychologists do research, they often produce large amounts of data that must be assessed. Suppose a social psychologist asked parents to monitor the number of hours their children watch television. The parents might report between 0 and 20 hours of television watching a week. Here is a list of the actual number of hours of television watched by 100 children in a particular week:

11	18	5	9	6	20
9	7	15	3	6	11
6	1	10	3	4	4
8	8	9	10	13	12
16	1	15	9	4	3
10	5	6	12	8	2
14	12	6	9	8	12
10	7	3	14	13	7
10	17	11	13	16	7
15	11	9	11	16	8
14	7	10	10	12	8
11	1	12	7	6	0
19	18	9	8	2	5
9	14	7	10	9	2
10	4	13	8	5	4
9	8	5	17	15	17
5	13	10	11		

The first step in making these numbers meaningful is to arrange them in a chart or array, organized from the highest to the lowest, showing the number of times each number occurs; this type of organization is known as a **frequency distribution**. As the frequency distribution in Table A.1 shows, 10 children were reported to have watched 9 hours of television in a week—a greater number of children than watched any other number of hours.

Researchers often construct graphs from the data in frequency distributions. Such graphs, called **frequency polygons**, show the range of possible results or scores (for example, numbers of hours of TV watching) on the horizontal axis, or *abscissa*, and the frequency of each score (for example, the number of children who watched television for each number of hours) on the vertical axis, or *ordinate*. Figure A.1 is a frequency polygon of the data from the frequency distribution in Table A.1. Straight lines connect the data points.

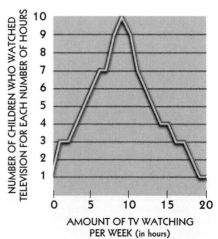

FIGURE A.1
A Frequency Polygon Showing Hours of Television Watched in a Week by 100 Children

TABLE A.1 A Frequency Distribution of the Number of Hours of Television Watched in a Week by 100 Children

Note that few individuals score very high or very low—most score in the middle range.

Number of Hours of Television Watched	Individuals Watching Each Number of Hours	Total Number of Individuals Watching
0	|	1
1	|||	3
2	|||	3
3	||||	4
4	|||||	5
5	||||||	6
6	|||||||	7
7	||||||||	8
8	|||||||||	9
9	||||||||||	10
10	|||||||||	9
11	|||||||	7
12	||||||	6
13	|||||	5
14	||||	4
15	||||	4
16	|||	3
17	|||	3
18	||	2
19	|	1
20	|	1
		100

Measures of Central Tendency

 A descriptive statistic that tells which result or score best represents an entire set of scores is a **measure of central tendency**. It is used to summarize and condense data. Also, because almost every group has members who score higher or lower than the rest of the group, researchers often use a measure of central tendency to describe the group *as a whole*.

People often use the word *average* in a casual way to describe a variety of commonalities or tendencies. A woman asks a clerk to help her find a sweater for her "average-sized" husband. The owner of a new sedan boasts that his car "averages" 15 kilometres to a litre of gasoline. A doctor tells her patient that his serum cholesterol level is "average" because it falls halfway between low and high measurements. In each of these cases, the person is using *average* to depict a type of norm, and others understand what the person means, even though not all of these examples are technically "averages." As another example, consider this statement: Men are taller than women. Because you know that some women are taller than some men, you assume that the statement means: *On the average*, men are taller than women. In other words, comparing the heights of all of the men and all of the women in the world would show that, *on the average*, men are taller.

Let's look more closely at three measures of central tendency: mean (arithmetic average), mode, and median.

Measure of central tendency: A descriptive statistic that tells which result or score best represents an entire set of scores.

Mean. How could a researcher investigate the truth of the statement that men are taller than women? One step towards answering this question would be to measure the heights of thousands of men and women, taking a careful sample from each country, race, and age group. The researcher then could calculate the average heights of the men and the women in the sample and plot the results on a graph. Table A.2 lists height data from a small sample of men and women. For each group, the heights of the men or women were measured, added together, and divided by the number of people in the group. The resulting number is the **mean**, or *arithmetic average* (in this case, of the heights of men or women in the group). The mean is the most frequently used measure of central tendency.

Mode. Another statistic used to describe the central tendency of a set of data is the mode. The **mode** is the most frequently observed data point. Table A.3 plots the frequencies of different heights for all of the heights in Table A.2. It shows, for example, that only one person is 58 inches tall, three people are 79 inches tall, and more people are 70 inches tall than any other single height. The mode of the heights of this group is therefore 70 inches.

Median. The **median** is the 50-percent point: Half of the observations (or scores) fall above it and the other half fall below it. Table A.4 (see page 647) arranges all of the heights for men and women given in Table A.2 from lowest to highest. It shows that half of the heights fall above 68 inches and half fall below 68 inches. The median of the data set, therefore, is 68 inches. You probably have read news reports that refer to medians, for example: "According to Statistics Canada,

Mean: The measure of central tendency that is calculated by dividing the sum of the scores by the total number of scores. Also known as the *arithmetic average*.

Mode: The measure of central tendency that is the most frequently observed data point.

Median: The measure of central tendency that is the data point having 50 percent of all the observations (scores) above it and 50 percent below it.

TABLE A.2   Calculation for Mean Height for 20 Men and 20 Women

Men	Height (in inches)	Women	Height (in inches)
Davis	62	Leona	58
Baird	62	Golde	59
Jason	64	Marcy	61
Ross	67	Mickey	64
David	68	Sharon	64
Cary	68	Rozzy	66
Mark	69	Bonnie	66
Evan	70	Dianne	66
Michael	70	Cheryl	66
Davey	70	Carol	67
Steven	70	Iris	67
Morry	70	Nancy	67
Alan	70	Theresa	67
Bernie	70	Sylvia	67
Lester	70	Jay	68
Al	70	Linda	68
Arnold	73	Elizabeth	71
Andrew	79	Jesse	75
Corey	79	Gabrielle	76
Stephen	79	Sarah	77
Total height	**1400**	*Total height*	**1340**

Mean: $\dfrac{\Sigma S}{N} = \dfrac{1400}{20} = 70$ inches   Mean: $\dfrac{\Sigma S}{N} = \dfrac{1340}{20} = 67$ inches

Note: ΣS means add up the scores; N means number of scores.

TABLE A.3 The Mode for Men's and Women's Heights

The mode is 70 inches, the most frequently observed height.

Height (in inches)	Number of Individuals of Each Height
58	I
59	I
60	
61	I
62	II
63	
64	II
65	
66	IIIII
67	IIIIII
68	IIII
69	
70	IIIIIII Mode
71	I
72	
73	I
74	I
75	I
76	I
77	I
78	
79	III

the median family income in Canada rose to $36 000 this year." What this means is that half of Canadian families earned more than this amount and half earned less.

Table A.5 (see page 648) presents a set of data from an experiment on memory. The scores are the numbers of correctly recalled items. There are three groups of participants: a control group, which received no special treatment; one experimental group, which received task-motivating instructions (such as think hard, focus your attention); and a second experimental group, which was hypnotized and told under hypnosis that its members would have better recall. The results of the study show that the task-motivated group did slightly worse than the control group: its mean was 10.3 words recalled, compared with the control group's mean of 10.6. But the hypnosis group did better, recalling 15.4 words on average, compared with the control group's average recall of 10.6 words— a difference of 4.8 words. Hypnosis therefore *seemed* to have a positive effect on memory. But let's look at it another way before coming to that conclusion.

The medians for the control group and the task-motivated group were equal: 10.5 words. The difference between the medians of the control group and the hypnosis group was 4 words. Hypnosis still seems to have a positive effect, but the median difference (4 words) is smaller than the mean difference (4.8 words) because the median discounts very high and very low scores. For example, if you get a test score of 0 after obtaining five other scores whose average is about 70, the sixth score will drop that *average* substantially; averaging in a sixth score of 60 would not have as large an impact. But with a median, a single extreme score (such as 0 or 120) would count the same. With a sample as small as this one, where a single score can have a big impact, the median is often a better measure of central tendency.

The mean, mode, and median are descriptive statistics that measure central tendency. Each tells researchers something about the average (or typical) person or item being scored. Sometimes the mean, the mode, and the median are the same number; but more often, enough variability exists (one very tall or very short person in a group of height measurements, for example) for each central tendency measure to yield a slightly different result and to be used for different purposes. In a country where most of the people were poor and a few people were very rich the mean income would suggest that everyone was middle class, the mode would suggest that there was practically no wealth in the country at all, while the median might indicate that a more equitable distribution of resources would benefit most citizens.

Measures of Variability

A measure of central tendency is a single number that describes a hypothetical "average." In real life, however, people do not always reflect the central tendency. Consequently, knowing how an average person or item scores is more useful when accompanied by knowledge of how the scores in the group are distributed relative to one another. If you know that the mean of a group of numbers is 150, you still do not know how widely dispersed are the scores that were averaged to calculate that mean. In other words, in your psychology class the mean on your final examination may be 150, and though you may have scored 170 (above the mean), you still do not know how much you can celebrate. Are there few others above your score? If there are many others, how much better than you did they do?

A statistic that describes the extent to which scores in a distribution differ from one another is called a *measure of variability*. **Variability** is the extent to which scores differ from one another, especially the extent to which they differ from the mean. If all scores obtained are the same, no variability exists; this, however, is unlikely to occur. It is more usual that, in any group of people being tested or measured in some way, personal and situational characteristics will cause some to score high and some to score low. If researchers know the extent of the variability, they can estimate the extent to which subjects differ from the mean, or "average," subject. Two important and useful measures of variability are range and standard deviation.

Range. The **range** shows the spread of scores in a distribution; it is calculated by subtracting the lowest score from the highest score. If the lowest score on a test is 20 points and the highest is 85, the range is 65 points. In this example, whether the mean is 45, 65, or 74 points, the range remains 65; that is, there is a 65-point spread from the lowest score to the highest.

The range is a relatively crude measure of the extent to which subjects vary within a group. In a group of 100 students, for example, the mean score might be 80, and nearly all of the students might have scored within 10 points of that mean. But if the lowest score is 20 and the highest is 85, the range will be 65. More precise measures of the spread of scores within a group are available, however. They indicate how scores are distributed as well as the extent of their spread.

Standard Deviation. Consider a reaction-time study that measures how fast people press a button when a light flashes. The following list gives the number of milliseconds it took each of 30 randomly chosen tenth-grade students to press the button when the light flashed; clearly, the reaction times vary.

450	490	500	610	520	470
480	492	585	462	600	490
740	700	595	500	493	495
498	455	510	470	480	540
710	722	575	490	495	570

If you were told only that the mean reaction time was 540 milliseconds, you might assume that 540 was the best estimate of how long it takes a tenth-grade student to respond to the light. But, of course, not everyone took 540 milliseconds; some took more time and some took less. Psychologists say that the data were variable, or that variability existed.

TABLE A.4 The Median of Men's and Women's Heights

The median is the height in the middle of the range of heights measured—half of the heights are above the median and half are below it.

Height (in inches)
58
59
61
62
62
64
64
66
66
66
66
66
67
67
67
67
67
67
68
68 — Median
68
68
70
70
70
70
70
70
70
70
70
71
73
74
75
76
77
79
79
79

TABLE A.5 Calculations of Mean and Median Memory Scores for Three Groups (with 10 People in Each Group)

Person	Scores of Control Group	Scores of Task-Motivated Group	Scores of Hypnosis Group
1	10	11	16
2	12	13	14
3	14	14	16
4	10	12	12
5	11	12	10
6	9	8	9
7	5	10	15
8	12	5	12
9	16	10	18
10	7	8	32
Total	106	103	154
Mean	10.6	10.3	15.4
Median	10.5	10.5	14.5

Control Group (scores are reordered lowest to highest)

$$\text{Mean} = \frac{5 + 7 + 9 + 10 + 10 + 11 + 12 + 12 + 14 + 16}{10} = \frac{106}{10} = 10.6$$

Median = 5 7 9 10 $\boxed{10\ 11}$ 12 12 14 16
$$\downarrow$$
$$10.5$$

The point at which half the scores fall above and half the scores fall below is 10.5; that is, 10.5 is the median.

Task-Motivated Group (scores are reordered lowest to highest)

$$\text{Mean} = \frac{5 + 8 + 8 + 10 + 10 + 11 + 12 + 12 + 13 + 14}{10} = \frac{103}{10} = 10.3$$

Median = 5 8 8 10 $\boxed{10\ 11}$ 12 12 13 14
$$\downarrow$$
$$10.5$$

The point at which half the scores fall above and half the scores fall below is 10.5; that is, 10.5 is the median.

Hypnosis (scores are reordered lowest to highest)

$$\text{Mean} = \frac{9 + 10 + 12 + 12 + 14 + 15 + 16 + 16 + 18 + 32}{10} = \frac{154}{10} = 15.4$$

Median = 9 10 12 12 $\boxed{14\ 15}$ 16 16 18 32
$$\downarrow$$
$$14.5$$

The point at which half the scores fall above and half the scores fall below is 14.5; that is, 14.5 is the median.

Variability: The extent to which scores differ from one another, especially the extent to which they differ from the mean.

Range: A measure of variability that describes the spread between the highest and the lowest scores in a distribution.

Standard deviation: A descriptive statistic that measures the variability of data from the mean of the sample.

To find out how much variability exists among data, and to quantify it in a meaningful manner, researchers need to know the standard deviation. A **standard deviation** is a descriptive statistic that measures the variability of data from the mean of the sample—that is, the extent to which each score differs from the mean. The calculations for a standard deviation are shown in Table A.6. Here is the general procedure: First, subtract the mean from each score and then square that difference. Next, add up the squared differences and divide by the number of scores minus 1. (For a small sample, to get a better estimate of the sample's standard deviation, researchers typically divide by 1 less than the number of scores.) Last, take the square root of the answer. You have now calculated a standard deviation.

TABLE A.6 Computation of the Standard Deviation for a Small Distribution of Scores

Score	Score – Mean	(Score – Mean)^2
10	10 – 6 = 4	16
10	10 – 6 = 4	16
10	10 – 6 = 4	16
5	5 – 6 = –1	1
4	4 – 6 = –2	4
4	4 – 6 = –2	4
4	4 – 6 = –2	4
1	1 – 6 = –5	25
48		86

Standard deviation = $\sqrt{\dfrac{\Sigma(X-\overline{X})^2}{N-1}}$, where Σ means "sum up," X is a score, $\overline{X}$ is the mean of the scores, and N is the number of scores.

Sum of scores = 48.

$\overline{X}$ = sum of scores ÷ 8 = 6.

Sum of squared differences from mean = 86.

Average of square differences from mean (dividing by the number of scores – 1) = 86 ÷ 7 = 12.3.

Square root of average square difference from the mean = 3.5.

Standard deviation = 3.5.

A standard deviation gives information about all of the members of a group, not just an average member. Knowing the standard deviation—that is, the variability associated with a mean—enables a researcher to make more accurate predictions. Table A.7 shows the reaction times for two groups of participants responding to a light. The mean is the same for both groups; but group 1 shows a large degree of variability, while group 2 shows little variability. The standard deviation (the estimate of variability) for group 1 participants will be substantially higher than that for group 2 participants because the scores differ from the mean much more in the first group than in the second. Since the standard deviation for subjects in group 2 is small, a researcher can more confidently predict that any one individual in that group will respond to the light in about 555 milliseconds (the mean response time). However, the researcher cannot confidently make the same prediction for individuals in group 1, since that group's standard deviation is high.

> **Normal distribution:** The approximately expected distribution of scores when a sample is drawn from a large population, drawn as a frequency polygon that often takes the form of a bell-shaped curve. Also known as a *normal curve.*

The Normal Distribution

When a large number of scores are involved, a frequency polygon often takes the form of a bell-shaped curve; this curve depicts the **normal distribution**, or *normal curve*. Normal distributions usually have a few scores at each extreme and progressively more scores towards the middle. Height, for example, is approximately normally distributed: More people are of average height than are very tall or very short (see

TABLE A.7 Reaction Times, Mean Reaction Times, and Standard Deviations for Responses to a Light

Group 1 shows a wider range of scores and thus great variability. Group 2, in contrast, shows a narrow range of scores and little variability.

Times for Group 1 (in milliseconds)	Times for Group 2 (in milliseconds)
380	530
400	535
410	540
420	545
470	550
480	560
500	565
720	570
840	575
935	580
Mean = 555	Mean = 555
Standard deviation = 197	Standard deviation = 17

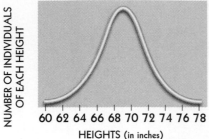

FIGURE A.2
A Normal Curve for Height
A normal curve for height shows that many more people are of average height than are at the extremes.

Figure A.2). Weights, shoe sizes, IQs, and scores on psychology exams also tend to be normally distributed.

Characteristics of a Normal Curve. A normal curve has certain characteristics. The mean, mode, and median are assumed to be the same; the distribution of scores around that central point is symmetrical; also, most individuals have a score that occurs within 6 standard deviations—3 above the mean and 3 below it (see Figure A.3).

To explain this phenomenon, Figure A.4 shows a normal curve for test scores. The mean is 50, and the standard deviation is 10 points. Note how each increment of 10 points above or below the mean accounts for fewer and fewer individuals. Scores between 50 and 60 account for 34.13 percent of those tested; scores between 60 and 70 account for 13.59 percent; and scores above 70 account for under 2.5 percent. The sum of these percentages (34.13 + 13.59 + 2.14 + 0.13) represents 50 percent of the scores.

When you know the mean and the standard deviation of a set of data, you can estimate where an individual in the sample population stands relative to others. In Figure A.5, for example, Dennis is 74 inches tall. His height is 1 standard deviation above the mean, which means that he is taller than 84 percent of the population (0.13 + 2.14 + 13.59 + 34.13 + 34.13 = 84.12 percent). Rob, who is 66 inches tall, is taller than only 16 percent of the population. His height is 1 standard deviation below the mean.

FIGURE A.3
Percentages of Population for a Normal Curve

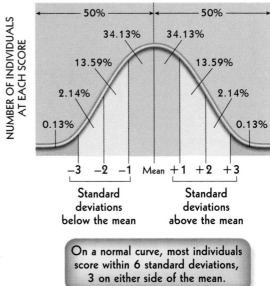

On a normal curve, most individuals score within 6 standard deviations, 3 on either side of the mean.

FIGURE A.4
A Normal Curve with a Standard Deviation of 10 Points

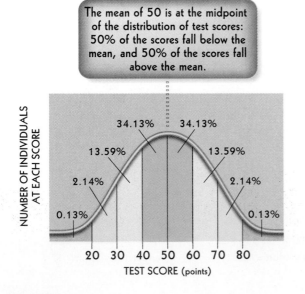

The mean of 50 is at the midpoint of the distribution of test scores: 50% of the scores fall below the mean, and 50% of the scores fall above the mean.

FIGURE A.5
A Normal Curve with a Mean of 70 and a Standard Deviation of 4 Inches
On this normal curve, Dennis's height of 74 inches is 1 standard deviation above the mean height of 70 inches. Rob's height is 66 inches, which is 1 standard deviation below the mean.

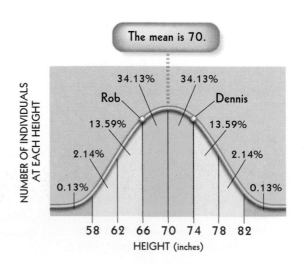

The mean is 70.

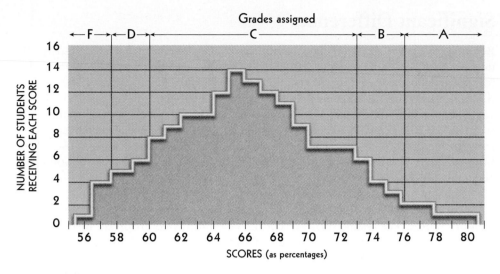

FIGURE A.6
Grading on a Sliding Scale
To calculate grades on a sliding scale, instructors often draw a graph like this one, showing the number of individuals who received each score. They then figure out the cutoff points for assigning letter grades (A, B, C, D, and F).

Normal Curves: A Practical Example. Your grade on an examination is often determined by how other members of your class do on the exam. This is what instructors mean when they say that a grade is on a "sliding scale" or a "curve." If the average student in a class answers only 50 percent of the questions correctly, a student who answers 70 percent correctly has done a good job. But if the average student scores 85 percent, then someone who scores only 70 percent has not done so well.

Before they assign grades on a sliding scale, testing services and instructors generally plot the test results on a graph in order to calculate a mean. They then inspect the scores and "slide the scale" to an appropriate level. Figure A.6 shows the scores achieved and grades assigned on a calculus test. The average score is 65 percent; the instructor decides to give students who score 65 percent a C, those who do better an A or a B, and those who do worse a D or an F.

Inferential Statistics and Correlation

C onfidence in predictions turns out to be a key issue for statisticians; they want to be as sure as possible that the mean of a group (sample) actually represents the mean of the larger population that the group represents. This concern is important because researchers want to be able to tell whether a difference between a control group and an experimental group is due to experimental manipulations, to extraneous variables, or to one or two deviant scores. It turns out that many of the manipulations and controls that researchers devise are necessary if they wish to make sound inferences, the topic we will consider next.

Researchers use inferential statistics in making decisions about data. **Inferential statistics** are procedures used to reach reasonable conclusions (generalizations) about larger populations from small samples of data. There are usually two issues to be explored: First, does the mean of a sample (a small group of people) actually reflect the mean of the larger population? Second, is a difference found between two means (for example, between the mean for a control group and the mean for an experimental group) a real and useful or important difference, or is it a result of chance?

Inferential statistics:
Procedures used to reach reasonable conclusions (generalizations) about larger populations from small samples of data.

Significant Differences

Psychologists hope to find a **significant difference**—a difference that is statistically unlikely to have occurred because of chance alone and thus is more likely to be due to the experimental conditions. To find a significant difference, a researcher shows that a performance difference between two or more groups is not a result of chance variations and can be repeated experimentally. Generally, psychologists assume that a difference is statistically significant if the likelihood of its occurring by chance is less than 5 percent—that is, it would occur by chance less than 5 out of 100 times. But many researchers assume a difference is significant only if the likelihood of its occurring by chance is less than 1 percent.

It is sometimes difficult to decide whether a difference is significant. Let's go back to Table A.5 (see page 648), where calculations were performed for a set of memory scores. The results showed that the task-motivated group recalled no more words, on average, than the control group did (in fact, 0.3 fewer words). The hypnosis group recalled 4.8 more words, on average, than the control group. Since the hypnosis group did better than the control group, can the researcher conclude that hypnosis is a beneficial memory aid? Did the hypnosis group do *significantly* better than the control group? Was a 4.8-word difference significant? It is easy to see that if the recall difference between the two groups had been 10 words, and if the variability within each group had been very small, the difference would be considered significant. Similarly, a 1- or 2-word difference would not be considered significant if the variability within each group was large. In the present case, a 4.8-word difference was not significant; the scores were highly variable, and only a small sample of people was used. When scores are variable (widely dispersed), both statistical analysts and researchers are unlikely to view a small difference between two groups as significant or important. (See Figure A.7 for an illustration of this point.)

Even if statistically significant differences are obtained, it would be ideal to be able to repeat an experiment and obtain the same results. Repeating an experiment to verify a result is called *replicating* the experiment. If the results of a replicated experiment remain the same, a researcher generally will say that the observed difference between the two groups is important.

FIGURE A.7
The Possible Outcomes of Experiments Whose Means Are Identical
In the first graph, the observed scores all cluster around the means—there is little variability. The difference between the means in the first graph is therefore likely to be significant. The means in the second graph (although identical to the ones in the first graph) are unlikely to be deemed significantly different—the scores are too widely distributed. Here, there is too much variability; the means may be affected by extreme scores. Thus, a scientist is less likely to accept these means as different from one another.

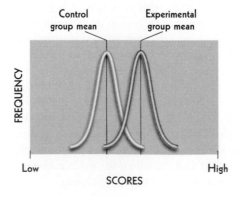

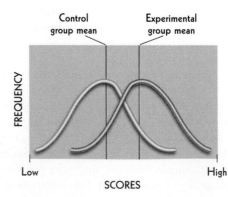

Correlation

Correlation coefficient: A number that expresses the degree and direction of a relationship between two variables, ranging from -1 (a perfect negative correlation) to +1 (a perfect positive correlation).

For many reasons, it is sometimes impractical or impossible to collect experimental data for control groups or experimental groups or to do research that involves manipulations of an experimental variable. Sometimes a researcher wants to compare data that were gathered by others in different kinds of surveys and questionnaires, for instance. In such cases, the researcher may calculate correlations.

A correlation exists when an increase in the value of one variable is regularly accompanied by an increase or a decrease in the value of a second variable. The degree and direction of relationship between two variables is expressed by a numerical value called the **correlation coefficient**. Correlation coefficients range from -1, through 0, to +1. Any correlation coefficient greater or less than 0, regardless of its sign, indicates that the variables *are* somehow related. When two variables are perfectly correlated, they are said to have a correlation coefficient of +1 or -1. A perfect correlation occurs when knowing the value of one variable allows a researcher to predict *precisely* the value of the second; this is, of course, a rare occurrence in psychological research.

Most variables are not perfectly correlated. One example of imperfectly correlated variables is the incidence of schizophrenia in children of schizophrenic parents. Research shows that if a parent is schizophrenic, the likelihood that his or her child will be schizophrenic increases sharply. Thus, there is a correlation between parents' and children's rates of schizophrenia. But this correlation is not perfect; that is, not every child born to a schizophrenic parent will develop the disorder. Because of this imperfect correlation, psychologists conclude that genetics is only one of several contributing factors in the development of the disorder.

Before calculating a correlation coefficient, researchers often plot, or graph, the data that they obtain in a scatter plot. A *scatter plot* is a diagram of data points that shows the relationship between two variables. An individual's score on one variable is measured on the horizontal axis, or *x* axis; the score on the second variable is measured on the vertical axis or *y* axis. Thus, a scatter plot might show 10 individuals' heights and weights; for each person, there is a height and weight pair. For example, in Figure A.8(a) the first person's height may be 6 feet and weight may be 170 pounds; a dot is made on the graph at the point where 6 feet on the *x* axis and

FIGURE A.8
Three Types of Correlation: A Summary
(a) In a positive correlation, an increase in one variable is associated with an increase in the other variable. (b) In a negative correlation, an increase in one variable is associated with a decrease in the other variable. (c) No correlation exists when changes in one variable are not associated in any systematic way with changes in the other variable.

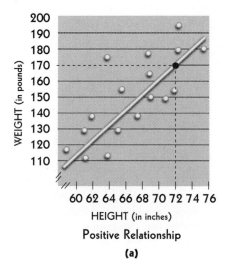

Positive Relationship

(a)

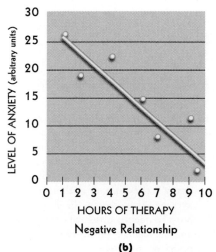

Negative Relationship

(b)

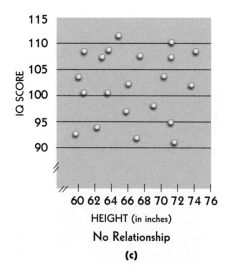

No Relationship

(c)

170 pounds on the y axis intersect. Plotting all 10 points in this way gives a graphic sense of the extent to which these two variables are related. Tall people do tend to weigh more than short people in general, and when height/weight data are plotted, the graph usually shows that as height increases, so does weight (at least most of the time).

When one variable shows an increase in value and a second also shows an increase, the two variables are said to be positively related, and the relationship is known as a *positive correlation*. Height and weight show a positive correlation: Generally, as height increases, so does weight. Although knowing a person's height does not allow one to predict his or her weight precisely, the scatter plot in Figure A.8(a) shows a positive direction overall—upward and to the right. These two variables have a correlation coefficient of about 0.65, which in most studies is considered to reflect a reasonably strong relationship.

On the other hand, if one variable decreases as the other increases, the variables are said to be negatively correlated, and the relationship is known as a *negative correlation*. For example, the relationship between the number of hours of therapy and the extent of anxiety shows a negative correlation; see Figure A.8(b). As the number of hours of therapy increases, anxiety decreases. The scatter plot shows a corresponding movement downward and to the right. These two variables have a negative correlation of about -0.6 or -0.7.

A correlation coefficient of +0.7 is no stronger than one of -0.7. That is, the plus or minus sign changes the *direction*, not the strength, of a relationship. The strength is shown by the number: The larger the number, the greater the strength of the correlation. A correlation coefficient of -0.8 is stronger than one of +0.7; a correlation coefficient of +0.6 is stronger than one of -0.5.

Some variables show absolutely no correlation; absence of correlation is expressed by a correlation coefficient of 0 (or close to 0, such as between +0.05 and −0.05). Figure A.8(c) plots data for IQ and height. The figure shows no pattern in the scatter plot and no correlation between IQ and height; the two variables are said to have a correlation coefficient of 0.

As we saw in Chapter 1, a correlation in no way implies a cause-and-effect relationship. A correlation between two variables simply indicates that if there is an increase in one variable, there probably will be an increase or decrease in the other variable. It is only through experimental studies that researchers can make cause-and-effect statements. Many of the studies reported in this text are correlational, but far more are experimental. Whenever possible, researchers wish to draw causal inferences.

Summary and Review

Descriptive Statistics

How do descriptive statistics help researchers organize data?

■ Researchers use *descriptive statistics* to summarize, condense, and describe sets of data. A *frequency distribution* is a way of organizing data to show the number of times each item occurs; the graphic version of a frequency distribution is a *frequency polygon*. p. 643

How are measures of central tendency used?

■ *Measures of central tendency* are descriptive statistics that indicate which single score best represents an entire set of scores. The most frequently used measure of central tendency is the *mean*, or arithmetic average. Also used are the *mode*, or most frequently observed data point, and the *median*, the 50-percent point. pp. 644–646

What is a measure of variability?

■ A measure of *variability* is any statistic that describes the extent to which scores in a distribution differ from one another. One such measure, the *range*, shows the spread of scores in a distribution. Another measure of variability, the *standard deviation*, shows the extent to which individual scores in a distribution vary from the mean. pp. 646–649

What are the key characteristics of a normal distribution?

■ The mean, mode, and median of a *normal distribution*, or normal curve, are generally assumed to be the same, and the distribution of scores around that central point is symmetrical. pp. 649–651

KEY TERMS

statistics, p. 643; descriptive statistics, p. 643; frequency distribution, p. 643; frequency polygon, p. 643; measure of central tendency, p. 644; mean, p. 645; mode, p. 645; median, p. 645; variability, p. 648; range, p. 648; standard deviation, p. 648; normal distribution, p. 649

Inferential Statistics and Correlation

What is the role of inferential statistics?

■ Researchers use *inferential statistics* to determine whether two or more groups differ from one another and whether the difference is a result of chance. A *significant difference* is one that most likely did not occur by chance and that can be repeated experimentally with similar groups of people. Repeating an experiment to verify a result is called replicating the experiment. pp. 651–652

What are the essential characteristics of a correlation coefficient?

■ The *correlation coefficient* expresses the degree of relationship between two variables. When two variables are perfectly correlated, they are said to have a correlation coefficient of 1. A plus or minus sign in front of the correlation coefficient indicates the direction, not the strength, of a correlation relationship. The strength is shown by the number: The larger the number, the greater the strength of the correlation. pp. 653–654

Compare correlational and experimental studies with regard to cause and effect.

■ Correlational studies make no statements about cause and effect. They simply show that if there is an increase in one variable, there probably will be an increase or decrease in another variable. Only through experimental studies can researchers make cause-and-effect statements. p. 654

KEY TERMS

inferential statistics, p. 651; significant difference, p. 652; correlation coefficient, p. 653

Glossary

Abnormal behaviour: Behaviour characterized as atypical, socially unacceptable, distressing, maladaptive, and/or the result of distorted cognitions.

Abnormal psychology: The field of psychology concerned with the assessment, treatment, and prevention of maladaptive behaviour.

Absolute threshold: The statistically determined minimum level of stimulation necessary to excite a perceptual system.

Accommodation: (1) In development, according to Piaget, the process of modifying previously developed schemes to adapt them to new experiences; (2) in perception, the change in the shape of the lens of the eye to keep an object in focus on the retina when the object is moved closer to or farther away from the observer.

Action potential: An electrical current sent down the axon of a neuron, initiated in an all-or-none fashion by a rapid reversal of the electrical balance of the cell membrane. Also known as *spike discharge*.

Actor–observer effect: The tendency to attribute the behaviour of others to dispositional causes but to attribute one's own behaviour to situational causes.

Addictive drug: A drug that causes a compulsive physiological need and that, when withheld, produces withdrawal symptoms.

Adolescence [add-oh-LESS-sense]: The period extending from the onset of puberty to early adulthood.

Affect: A person's emotional responses.

Afferent neurons: Neurons that send messages to the spinal cord and brain.

Ageism: Prejudice against the elderly and the discrimination that follows from it.

Aggression: Any behaviour designed to harm another person or thing.

Agnosia: An inability to recognize a sensory stimulus that should be recognizable (because all normal perceptual processes are intact and there is no verbal, memory, or intellectual impairment).

Agonist [AG-oh-nist]: Chemical that mimics the actions of a neurotransmitter, usually by occupying receptor sites and facilitating neurochemical transfers.

Agoraphobia [AG-or-uh-FOE-bee-uh]: An anxiety disorder characterized by fear and avoidance of being alone or isolated in open and public places from which escape might be difficult or embarrassing.

Alcoholic: A problem drinker who also has both a physiological and a psychological need to consume alcohol and to experience its effects.

Algorithm [AL-go-rith-um]: A simple, precise, and exhaustive problem-solving procedure that follows a set of rules to implement a step-by-step analysis, as in working out a math problem.

Allele [A-leel]: Each member of a pair of genes, which occupies a particular place on a paired chromosome.

All-or-none: Either at full strength or not at all; a principle by which neurons fire.

Altruism [AL-true-ism]: Behaviours that benefit other people and for which there is no discernible extrinsic reward, recognition, or appreciation.

Alzheimer's disease [ALTZ-hy-merz]: A chronic and progressive disorder of the brain that is the most common cause of degenerative dementia.

Amnesia [am-NEE-zhuh]: Inability to remember information (typically all events within a specific period) usually due to physiological trauma.

Amplitude: The total energy of a sound wave, which determines the loudness of a sound. Also known as *intensity*.

Anal stage: Freud's second stage of personality development, about age two to age three, during which children learn to control the immediate gratification they obtain through defecation and become responsive to the demands of society

Androgynous: Having both stereotypically male and stereotypically female characteristics.

Anorexia nervosa [an-uh-REX-see-uh ner-VOH-suh]: An eating disorder characterized by an intense fear of becoming obese, dramatic weight loss, concern about weight, disturbances in body image, and an obstinate and wilful refusal to eat.

Antagonist: Chemical that opposes the actions of a neurotransmitter, usually by preventing the neurotransmitter from occupying a receptor site.

Anterograde amnesia: Loss of memory for events and experiences that occurred after the amnesia-causing event.

Antisocial personality disorder: A personality disorder characterized by egocentricity, behaviour that is irresponsible and that violates the rights of other people (lying, theft, delinquency, and other violations of social rules), a lack of guilt feelings, an inability to understand other people, and a lack of fear of punishment.

Anxiety: A generalized feeling of fear and apprehension that may be related to a particular event or object and is often accompanied by increased physiological arousal.

Applied psychology: The branch of psychology that uses psychological principles to help solve practical problems of everyday living.

Approach–approach conflict: Conflict that results from having to choose between two equally attractive alternatives or goals.

Approach–avoidance conflict: Conflict that results from having to choose an alternative or goal that has both attractive and repellent aspects.

Archetypes [AR-ki-types]: In Jung's theory, emotionally charged ideas and images that have rich meaning and symbolism and are contained within a person's unconscious.

Arousal: Activation of the central nervous system, the autonomic nervous system, and the muscles and glands; according to some motivational theorists, organisms seek to maintain optimal levels of arousal by actively varying their exposure to arousing stimuli.

Assessment: The process of evaluating individual differences among human beings by techniques such as tests, interviews, observations, and recordings of physiological processes.

Assimilation: According to Piaget, the process by which a person absorbs new ideas and experiences and incorporates them into existing schemes.

Attachment: The strong emotional tie that a person develops towards significant others.

Attitudes: Long-lasting patterns of feelings and beliefs about other people, ideas, or objects that are based in a person's past experiences, shape his or her future behaviour, are evaluative in nature, and serve certain functions.

Attribution: The process by which a person infers other people's motives and intentions by observing their behaviour.

Autonomic nervous system [au-toe-NOM-ick]: The part of the peripheral nervous system that controls the vital and automatic processes of the body, such as heart rate, digestion, blood pressure, and functioning of internal organs.

Aversive counterconditioning: A counterconditioning technique in which an aversive or noxious stimulus is paired with a stimulus that elicits an undesired behaviour so that the client will adopt a new, more worthwhile behaviour in response to the familiar stimulus and thus cease the undesired behaviour.

Avoidance–avoidance conflict: Conflict that results from having to choose between two equally distasteful alternatives or goals.

Axon: A thin, elongated process that leads from the neuron cell body and serves to transmit signals from the cell body through the axon terminal to adjacent neurons, muscles, or glands.

Babinski reflex: A reflex in which a newborn projects its toes outward and up when the soles of its feet are touched.

Backwards search: A heuristic procedure in which a problem solver works backwards from the goal or endpoint to the current position, both to analyze the problem and to reduce the steps needed to get from the current position to the goal.

Behaviour therapy: A therapy based on the application of learning principles to human behaviour that focuses on changing overt behaviours rather than on understanding subjective feelings, unconscious processes, or motivations. Also known as *behaviour modification*.

Behaviourism: The school of psychological thought that rejects the study of the contents of consciousness and focuses on describing and measuring only that which is observable directly or through assessment instruments.

Binocular depth cues: Any visual cue for depth perception that requires the use of both eyes.

Biofeedback: A technique by which individuals can monitor and learn to control the involuntary activity of some of the body's organs and functions.

Biological perspective: The school of psychological thought that examines psychological issues based on how heredity and biological structures affect mental processes and behaviour and that focuses on how physical mechanisms affect emotions, feelings, thoughts, desires, and sensory experiences. Also known as the *neuroscience perspective*.

Bipolar disorder: A mood disorder characterized by vacillation between two extremes, mania and depression; originally known as manic–depressive disorders.

Body language: Communication of information through body positions and gestures.

Bonding: A special process of emotional attachment that may occur between parents and babies in the minutes and hours immediately after birth.

Brain: The part of the central nervous system that is located in the skull and that regulates, monitors, processes, and guides other nervous system activity.

Brainstorming: A problem-solving technique that involves considering all possible solutions without making initial evaluative judgments.

Brightness: The lightness or darkness of reflected light, determined in large part by the light's intensity.

Bulimia nervosa [boo-LEE-me-uh ner-VOH-suh]: An eating disorder characterized by repeated episodes of binge eating (and a fear of not being able to stop eating) followed by purging.

Burnout: A state of emotional and physical exhaustion, lowered productivity, and feelings of isolation, often caused by work-related pressures.

Bystander apathy: The unwillingness of witnesses to an event to help, an effect that increases when there are more observers.

Case study: A method of interviewing participants to gain information about their background, including data on factors such as childhood, family, education, and social and sexual interactions.

Catatonic type of schizophrenia [CAT-uh-TONN-ick]: A major type of schizophrenia, characterized by displays of excited or violent motor activity or by stupor (in which the individual is mute, negative, and basically unresponsive).

Categorical speech perception: The ability to discriminate sounds that belong to the same phonemic class.

Central nervous system: One of the two major parts of the nervous system, consisting of the brain and the spinal cord.

Cerebellum [seh-rah-BELL-um]: A large structure that is attached to the back surface of the brain stem and that influences balance, coordination, and movement.

Child abuse: Physical, emotional, or sexual mistreatment of children.

Chromosome: A strand of DNA in the nuclei of all cells, which carries genetic information.

Chunks: Manageable and meaningful units of information that can be easily encoded, stored, and retrieved.

Circadian rhythms [sir-KAY-dee-an]: Internally generated patterns of body functions, including hormonal signals, sleep, blood pressure, and temperature regulation, that have an approximate 24-hour cycle and occur even when normal day and night cues are removed.

Classical conditioning: A conditioning process in which an originally neutral stimulus, by repeated pairing with a stimulus that normally elicits a response, comes to elicit a similar or identical response. Also known as *Pavlovian conditioning*.

Client-centred therapy: An insight therapy, developed by Carl Rogers, that seeks to help people evaluate the world and themselves from their own perspective by providing them with a nondirective environment and unconditional positive regard. Also known as *person-centred therapy*.

Clinical psychologist: A mental health practitioner who views behaviour and mental processes from a psychological perspective and who uses research-based knowledge to treat persons with serious emotional or behavioural problems or to do research into the causes of behaviour.

Cognitive dissonance [COG-nuh-tiv DIS-uh-nins]: The state of discomfort that results when a discrepancy exists between two or more of a person's beliefs or between a person's beliefs and overt behaviour.

Cognitive psychology: The study of the overlapping fields of learning, perception, memory, and thought, with a special emphasis on how people attend to, acquire, transform, store, and retrieve knowledge.

Cognitive theory: In motivation, an explanation of behaviour that asserts that people are actively and regularly involved in determining their own goals and the means of achieving them.

Collective unconscious: In Jung's dream theory, a storehouse of primitive ideas and images in the unconscious that is inherited from one's ancestors; these inherited ideas and images, called *archetypes*, are emotionally charged and rich in meaning and symbolism.

Colour blindness: The inability to perceive different hues.

Community psychology: The branch of psychology that seeks to reach out to society to provide services such as community mental health centres and especially to effect social change.

Concept: A mental category used to classify an event or object according to a common property.

Concordance rate: The degree to which a condition or trait is shared by two or more individuals or groups.

Concrete operational stage: Piaget's third stage of cognitive development (lasting from approximately age 6 or 7 to age 11 or 12), during which the child develops the ability to understand constant factors in the environment, rules, and higher-order symbolism.

Conditioned response: A response elicited by a conditioned stimulus.

Conditioned stimulus: A neutral stimulus that, through repeated association with an unconditioned stimulus, begins to elicit a conditioned response.

Conditioning: A systematic procedure through which associations and responses to specific stimuli are learned.

Conduction deafness: Deafness resulting from interference with the transmission of sound to the neural mechanism of the inner ear.

Conflict: The emotional state or condition in which a person has to make difficult decisions about two or more competing motives, behaviours, or impulses.

Conformity: People's tendency to change attitudes or behaviours to be consistent with other people or with social norms.

Conscious: Freud's first level of awareness, consisting of the thoughts, feelings, and actions of which people are aware.

Consciousness: The general state of being aware of and responsive to events in the environment, including one's own mental processes.

Conservation: The ability to recognize that perceptual changes (such as the "shape" of a liquid put in a different container) may not indicate that an underlying quality has changed (for example, the liquid still has the same weight, substance, or volume).

Consolidation [kon-SOL-ih-DAY-shun]: The evolution of a temporary neural circuit into a more permanent circuit.

Control group: In an experiment, the comparison group—the group of participants tested on the dependent variable in the same way as the experimental group but for whom the treatment is not given.

Convergence: The movement of the eyes towards each other to keep visual input at corresponding points on the retinas as an object moves closer to the observer.

Convergent thinking: In problem solving, the process of narrowing down choices and alternatives to arrive at a suitable answer.

Conversion disorder: A somatoform disorder characterized by the loss or alteration of physical functioning for no apparent physiological reason.

Convolutions: Characteristic folds in the tissues of the cerebral hemispheres and the overlying cortex.

Coping: The process by which a person takes some action to manage, master, tolerate, reduce, or minimize environmental or internal demands that cause or might cause stress and that will tax the individual's inner resources.

Coping skills: The techniques people use to deal with changing situations and stress.

Correlation coefficient: A number that expresses the degree and direction of a relationship between two variables, ranging from −1 (a perfect negative correlation) to +1 (a perfect positive correlation).

Cortex: The convoluted, or furrowed, exterior covering of the brain's hemispheres, which is about two millimetres thick, consists of six thin layers of nerve cells, and traditionally is divided into a series of lobes, or areas, each with characteristic structures; thought to be involved in both sensory interpretation and complex thought processes.

Counterconditioning: A process of reconditioning in which a person is taught a new, more adaptive response to a familiar stimulus.

Creativity: The ability to develop original, novel, and appropriate responses to a problem, to break out of functional fixedness.

Crowding: The perception that one's space is too limited.

CT (computerized tomography) scans: Computer-assisted X-ray images of the brain (or any area of the body) in three dimensions—essentially a computerized series of X-rays that show photographic slices of part of the brain or body.

Dark adaptation: Increased sensitivity to light in a dark environment; when a person moves from a light environment to a dark one, chemicals in the rods and cones regenerate and return to their inactive state, and light sensitivity increases.

Debriefing: Informing participants about the true nature of an experiment after its completion.

Decay: Loss of information from memory as a result of disuse and the passage of time.

Decentration: Understanding the concept of perspective or point of view and thus being able to recognize other people's feelings, ideas, and viewpoints.

Decision making: Assessing and choosing among alternatives.

Declarative memory: Memory for specific facts.

Deep structure: The underlying meaning of a sentence.

Defence mechanism: An unconscious way of reducing anxiety by distorting perceptions of reality.

Deindividuation: The process by which individuals in a group lose their self-awareness and concern with evaluation and may engage in antinormative behaviour.

Delusions: False beliefs that are inconsistent with reality, held despite evidence that negates them, and may induce feelings of guilt, shame, and persecution.

Demand characteristics: Elements of a study situation that might set things up in a specific way or tip off a participant as to the purpose of the study and perhaps thereby elicit specific behaviour from the participant.

Dementia: A long-standing impairment of mental functioning and global cognitive abilities in otherwise alert individuals, causing memory loss and related symptoms.

Dendrites: Thin, bushy, widely branching fibres extending from the neuron cell body that receive signals from neighbouring neurons and carry them back to the cell body.

Denial: A defence mechanism by which people directly refuse to accept reality or to recognize the true source of their anxiety.

Dependent variable: The variable in a controlled experiment that is expected to change because of the manipulation of the independent variable.

Depressive disorders: A general category of mood disorders in which people on a day-to-day basis show extreme and persistent sadness, despair, and loss of interest in life's usual activities.

Descriptive statistics: A general set of procedures used to summarize, condense, and describe sets of data.

Developmental psychology: The study of the lifelong, age-related processes of change in the physical, cognitive, emotional, and social domains of functioning; such changes are rooted in biological mechanisms that are genetically controlled as well as in social interactions

Deviation IQ: A standard IQ test score for which the mean and variability remain constant at all ages.

Diabetes mellitus [mel-LIGHT-us]: A condition in which too little insulin is produced, causing sugar to be insufficiently transported out of the blood and into body cells.

Dichromats [DIE-kroe-MATZ]: People who can distinguish only two of the three basic hues.

Discrimination: Behaviour targeted at individuals or groups with the aim of holding them apart and treating them differently.

Disorganized type of schizophrenia: A major type of schizophrenia, characterized by severely disturbed thought processes, frequent incoherence, delusions, and inappropriate affect.

Dissociative amnesia: A dissociative disorder characterized by the sudden and extensive inability to recall important personal information, too extensive to be explained by ordinary forgetfulness.

Dissociative disorders: Disorders characterized by a sudden but temporary alteration in consciousness, identity, sensory/motor behaviour, or memory.

Dissociative identity disorder: A dissociative disorder characterized by the existence within an individual of two or more distinct personalities, each of which is dominant at particular times and directs the individual's behaviour at those times.

Divergent thinking: In problem solving, widening the range of possibilities and expanding the options for solutions.

Double bind: A situation in which an individual is given two different and inconsistent messages.

Double-blind technique: Research technique in which neither the experimenter nor the participants know who is in the control or the experimental group.

Dream: A state of consciousness that occurs during sleep and is usually accompanied by vivid visual, tactile, or auditory imagery.

Dream analysis: A psychoanalytic technique in which a patient's dreams are interpreted and used to provide insight into the individual's unconscious motivations.

Drive: An internal aroused condition that directs an organism to satisfy physiological needs.

Drive theory: An explanation of behaviour that assumes that an organism is motivated to act because of a need to attain, reestablish, balance, or maintain some goal that helps with the survival of the organism or the species.

Drug: Any chemical substance that alters normal biological processes.

Eating disorders: Psychological disorders characterized by gross disturbances in eating behaviour and in the way individuals respond to food.

Eclecticism [ek-LECK-ti-sizm]: In psychology, a combination of theories, facts, or techniques; the practice of using whatever clinical and counselling techniques are appropriate for an individual client rather than relying exclusively on the techniques of one school of psychology.

Educational psychology: The systematic application of psychological principles to learning and teaching.

Efferent neurons: Neurons that send messages from the brain and spinal cord to other structures in the body.

Ego: In Freud's theory, the part of personality that seeks to satisfy the individual's instinctual needs in accordance with reality.

Egocentrism [ee-go-SENT-rism]: The inability to understand the role that perspective can play in a situation; self-centredness.

Elaboration likelihood model: A theory suggesting that there are two routes to attitude change: central, which focuses on thoughtful, elaborative considerations, and peripheral, which focuses on less careful, more emotional, and even superficial considerations.

Elaborative rehearsal: Involves repetition and analysis, in which the stimulus may be associated with other events and further processed; elaboration links a stimulus to other information.

Electroconvulsive therapy (ECT) [eel-ECK-tro-con-VUL-siv]: A treatment for severe mental illness in which a brief application of electricity to the head is used to produce a generalized seizure (convulsion). Also known as *shock treatment*.

Electroencephalogram (EEG) [eel-ECK-tro-en-SEFF-uh-low-gram]: Record of electrical brain-wave patterns obtained through electrodes placed on the scalp.

Embryo [EM-bree-o]: The prenatal organism from implantation to the eighth week following conception.

Emotion: A subjective response (feeling), usually accompanied by a physiological change, which is often interpreted by an individual and then readies the individual for some action that is associated with a change in behaviour.

Empowerment: Helping people in the community to enhance their existing skills and develop new skills, knowledge, and motivation so that they can gain control over their own lives.

Encoding: The organizing of information so that the nervous system can process it.

Encoding specificity principle: The notion that the effectiveness of a specific retrieval cue depends on how well it matches up with the originally encoded information.

Encounter group: A group of people who meet to learn more about their feelings, behaviour, and interactions.

Endocrine glands [END-oh-krin]: Ductless glands that secrete hormones directly into the bloodstream, rather than through a specific duct, or opening, into a target organ.

Endorphins [en-DOR-finz]: Painkillers produced naturally in the brain and pituitary gland.

Environmental psychology: The study of how physical settings affect human behaviour and how people change their environment.

Episodic memory [ep-ih-SAH-dick]: Memory for specific events, objects, and situations that are usually personally relevant.

Equity theory: (1) In social psychology, the theory that people attempt to maintain stable and consistent interpersonal relationships in which the ratio of members' contributions is balanced; (2) in I/O psychology, the theory that suggests that what people bring to a work situation should be balanced by what they receive compared with other workers; thus, input should be balanced by compensation, or rewards, or workers will adjust their work level and potentially their job satisfaction accordingly.

Ergonomics: The study of the fit between human anatomy or physiology, the demands of a particular task or piece of equipment, and the environment in which the task occurs.

Ethics: Rules of proper and acceptable conduct that investigators use to guide psychological research; these rules concern the treatment of animals, the rights of human beings, and the responsibilities of investigators.

Evolutionary psychology: The psychological perspective that seeks to explain and predict behaviours by analyzing how specific behaviours, over the course of many generations, have led to adaptations that allow the species to survive; it assumes that behaviours that help organisms adapt, be fit, and survive will be passed on to successive generations through a greater chance of reproduction.

Excitement phase: The first phase of the sexual response cycle, during which there are initial increases in heart rate, blood pressure, and respiration.

Expectancy theories: (1) Explanations of behaviour that focus on people's expectations of success in reaching a goal and their need for achievement as energizing factors; (2) in applied psychology, theories that suggest that a worker's effort and desire to maintain goal-directed behaviour (to work) is determined by expectancies regarding the outcomes of that work.

Experiment: Procedure in which a researcher systematically manipulates and observes elements of a situation in order to answer a question and, usually, to test hypotheses and make inferences about cause and effect.

Experimental group: In an experiment, a group of participants to whom a treatment is given.

Explicit memory: Conscious memory that a person is aware of, such as a memory of a word in a list or an event that occurred in the past.

Extinction [egg-STINK-shun]: (1) In classical conditioning, the process through which not presenting the unconditioned stimulus gradually reduces the probability of a conditioned response; (2) in operant conditioning, the process by which the probability of an organism's emitting a conditioned response is reduced when reinforcement no longer follows the response.

Extrinsic motivation [ecks-TRINZ-ick]: Motivation supplied by rewards that come from the external environment.

Factor analysis: A statistical procedure designed to discover the independent elements (factors) in any set of data.

Family therapy: Therapy in which two or more people who are committed to each other's well-being are treated at once in an effort to change the ways in which they interact.

Fetus [FEET-us]: The prenatal organism from the eighth week following conception until birth.

Fixation: An excessive attachment to some person or object that was appropriate only at an earlier stage of development.

Fixed-interval schedule: A reinforcement schedule in which a reinforcer (reward) is delivered after a specified interval of time, provided that the required response occurs at least once after the interval.

Fixed-ratio schedule: A reinforcement schedule in which a reinforcer (reward) is delivered after a specified number of responses has occurred.

fMRI (functional magnetic resonance imaging): Imaging technique that can locate where the brain processes certain functions. A patient performs a particular task while the imaging is taking place. Brain areas responsible for this task will show an increase in metabolism (blood flow) that ultimately will lead to a signal change in the MRI image.

Forebrain: The largest, most complicated, and most advanced organizationally and functionally of the three divisions of the brain, with many interrelated parts: the thalamus and hypothalamus, the limbic system, the basal ganglia and corpus callosum, and the cortex.

Formal operational stage: Piaget's fourth and final stage of cognitive development (beginning at about age 12), during which the individual can think hypothetically, can consider all future possibilities, and is capable of deductive logic.

Fraternal twins: Double births that occur when two sperm fertilize two ova; fraternal twins are no more or less genetically alike than non-twin siblings.

Free association: A psychoanalytic technique in which a person reports to the therapist his or her thoughts and feelings as they occur, regardless of how trivial, illogical, or objectionable their content may appear.

Free-floating anxiety: Persistent anxiety not clearly related to any specific object or situation, accompanied by a sense of impending doom.

Frequency: In sound waves, a measure of the number of times a complete change in air pressure occurs per unit of time; expressed in hertz (Hz), or cycles per second.

Frequency distribution: A chart or array of scores, usually arranged from the highest to the lowest, showing the number of instances for each score.

Frequency polygon: A graph of a frequency distribution that shows the number of instances of obtained scores, usually with the data points connected by straight lines.

Frustration: The emotional state or condition that results when a goal—work, family, or personal—is thwarted or blocked.

Fulfilment: In Rogers's personality theory, an inborn tendency directing people towards actualizing their essential nature and thus attaining their potential.

Functional fixedness: The inability to see that an object can have a function other than its stated or usual one.

Functionalism: The school of psychological thought (an outgrowth of structuralism) that was concerned with how and why the conscious mind works; its main aim was to know how the contents of consciousness functioned and worked together.

Fundamental attribution error: The tendency to attribute other people's behaviour to dispositional (internal) causes rather than situational (external) causes.

Gender identity: A person's sense of being male or female.

Gender role stereotypes: Beliefs about gender-based behaviours that are strongly expected, regulated, and reinforced by society.

Gender roles: The full range of behaviours generally associated with one's gender, which help one establish who one is. Also known as *sex roles.*

Gender schema theory: The theory that children and adolescents use gender as an organizing theme to classify and interpret their perceptions about the world.

Gender stereotype: An expectation of specific patterns of behaviour—overly simple, often wrong, and often negative ideas about traits and attitudes—based on gender.

Gene: The unit of hereditary transmission carried in chromosomes and consisting of DNA and protein.

Generalized anxiety disorder: An anxiety disorder characterized by persistent anxiety on more days than not for at least six months, sometimes with autonomic hyperactivity, apprehension, problems with motor tension, and difficulty in concentrating.

Genetics: The study of heredity, the biological transmission of traits and characteristics from parents to offspring.

Genital stage [JEN-it-ul]: Freud's last stage of personality development, from the onset of puberty through adulthood, during which the sexual conflicts of childhood resurface (at puberty) and are often resolved (during adolescence).

Gestalt psychology [gesh-TALT]: The school of psychological thought that argued that behaviour cannot be studied in parts but must be viewed as a whole; the focus was on the unity of perception and thinking.

Gestalt therapy [gesh-TALT]: An insight therapy that emphasizes the importance of a person's being aware of current feelings and situations.

Goal-setting theory: A theory that asserts that setting specific, clear, attainable goals for a given task will lead to better performance.

Grammar: The linguistic description of how a language functions, especially the rules and patterns used for generating appropriate and comprehensible sentences.

Grasping reflex: A reflex in which a newborn vigorously grasps any object touching its palm or fingers or placed in its hand.

Group: Two or more individuals who are loosely or cohesively related and who share some common characteristics and goals.

Group polarization: Exaggeration of individuals' pre-existing attitudes as a result of group discussion.

Group therapy: A psychotherapeutic process in which several people meet as a group with a therapist.

Groupthink: The tendency of people in a group to seek agreement with one another when reaching a decision, usually prematurely.

Hallucinations [ha-LOOSE-in-AY-shuns]: Compelling perceptual (visual, tactile, olfactory, or auditory) experiences without a real physical stimulus.

Halo effect: The tendency for one particular or outstanding characteristic of an individual (or a group) to influence the evaluation of other characteristics.

Hawthorne effect: The finding, based on early research studies at the Hawthorne industrial plant, that people behave differently (usually better) when they know they are being observed.

Health psychology: Subfield concerned with the use of psychological ideas and principles in health enhancement, illness prevention, diagnosis and treatment of disease, and rehabilitation processes.

Heritability: The proportion of a trait's variation in a population of individuals that is genetically determined.

Heuristics [hyoo-RISS-ticks]: Sets of strategies that act as guidelines, not strict rules and procedures, for discovery-oriented problem solving.

Higher-order conditioning: A process by which a neutral stimulus takes on conditioned properties through pairing with a conditioned stimulus.

Hindbrain: The most primitive, organizationally, of the three functional divisions of the brain, consisting of the medulla, reticular formation, pons, and cerebellum.

Homeostasis: A tendency to attempt to maintain a constant state of inner stability or balance.

Hormones: Chemicals produced by endocrine glands that regulate the activities of specific organs or cells.

Hue: The psychological property of light referred to as colour and determined by the wavelength reflected from an object.

Human factors: The study of the relationship of human beings to machines and to workplaces and other environments.

Humanistic psychology: The school of psychological thought that emphasizes the uniqueness of each human being and the idea that human beings have free will to determine their destiny.

Humanistic theory: An explanation of behaviour that emphasizes the entirety of life rather than individual components of behaviour; focuses on human dignity, individual choice, and self-worth.

Hyperopic [HY-per-OP-ick]: Having trouble seeing things that are close but able to see objects at a distance. Also known as *farsighted.*

Hypnosis: An altered state of consciousness brought about by procedures that may induce a trance.

Hypochondriasis [hy-po-kon-DRY-a-sis]: A somatoform disorder characterized by an inordinate preoccupation with health and illness, coupled with excessive anxiety about disease.

Hypoglycemia [hi-po-gly-SEE-me-uh]: A condition in which overproduction of insulin results in a very low blood sugar level.

Hypothalamus: A relatively small structure of the forebrain, lying just below the thalamus, that acts through its connections with the rest of the forebrain and the midbrain and affects many complex behaviours, such as eating, drinking, and sexual activity.

Hypothesis: Tentative statement or idea expressing a causal relationship between two events or variables that are to be evaluated in a research study.

Id: In Freud's theory, the source of a person's instinctual energy, which works mainly through the pleasure principle.

Ideal self: The self that a person ideally would like to be.

Identical twins: Double births that occur when a zygote splits into two identical cells, which then separate and develop independently; identical twins have exactly the same genetic make-up.

Illusion: A perception of a physical stimulus that differs from measurable reality and normal expectations about its appearance.

Imagery: The creation or recreation of a mental picture of a sensory or perceptual experience.

Imaginary audience: A cognitive distortion experienced by adolescents, in which they see themselves as "on stage," with an imaginary audience always watching them.

Implicit memory: Memory for information or events a person is not aware of; considered an almost unconscious process, implicit memory occurs almost automatically.

Impression formation: The process by which a person uses the behaviour and appearance of others to infer their internal states and intentions.

Independent variable: The variable in a controlled experiment that the experimenter directly and purposely manipulates to see how the variables under study will be affected.

Industrial/organizational (I/O) psychology: The study of how individual behaviour is affected by the work environment, by co-workers, and by organizational practices.

Inferential statistics: Procedures used to reach reasonable conclusions (generalizations) about larger populations from small samples of data.

Informed consent: The agreement of participants expressed through a signed document that indicates that they understand the nature of their participation in upcoming research and have been fully informed of the general nature of the research, its goals, and its methods.

Insight therapy: Therapy that attempts to discover relationships between unconscious motivations and current abnormal behaviour in order to change that behaviour.

Insomnia: A prolonged inability to sleep.

Insulin: A hormone produced by the pancreas; facilitates the transport of sugar from the blood into body cells, where it is metabolized.

Intelligence: The overall capacity of the individual to act purposefully, to think rationally, and to deal effectively with the environment.

Interference: The suppression of one bit of information by another received either earlier or later or the confusion of the two pieces of information.

Interpersonal attraction: The tendency of one person to evaluate another person (or a symbol or image of another person) in a positive way.

Interpretation: In Freud's theory, the technique of providing a context, meaning, or cause of a specific idea, feeling, or set of behaviours; the process of tying a set of behaviours to its unconscious determinant.

Interview: A face-to-face meeting in which a series of standardized questions are used to gather detailed information.

Intimacy: A state of being or feeling in which each person is willing to self-disclose and to express important feelings and information to the other person; such behaviours are usually reciprocated.

Intrinsic motivation [in-TRINZ-ick]: Motivation that leads to behaviours engaged in for no apparent reward except the pleasure and satisfaction of the activity itself.

Introspection: Description and analysis by a person of what he or she is thinking and feeling. Also known as *self-examination*.

Job analyses: Careful descriptions of the various tasks and activities that are required for employees to do their jobs, along with the necessary knowledge, skills, and abilities; such analyses describe what gets done and how it gets done.

Kinesthesis [kin-iss-THEE-sis]: The awareness aroused by movements of the muscles, tendons, and joints.

Language: A system of symbols, usually words, that convey meaning; in addition, it also has rules for combining symbols to generate an infinite number of messages.

Latency stage [LAY-ten-see]: Freud's fourth stage of personality development, from about age seven until puberty, during which sexual urges are inactive.

Latent content: The deeper meaning of a dream, usually involving symbolism, hidden content, and repressed or obscured ideas and wishes.

Latent learning: Learning that occurs in the absence of any direct reinforcement and that is not necessarily demonstrated in any observable behaviour, though it has the potential to be exhibited.

Law of Prägnanz [PREG-nants]: The Gestalt principle that when items or stimuli *can* be grouped together and seen as a whole, they *will* be.

Learned helplessness: The behaviour of giving up or not responding, exhibited by people or animals who have learned that rewards and punishments are not contingent on behaviour.

Learning: A relatively permanent change in an organism that occurs as a result of experiences in the environment.

Levels-of-processing approach: A memory theory that suggests that the brain processes and encodes information in different ways, to different extents, and at different levels, depending on the degree of analysis.

Libido [lih-BEE-doe]: In Freud's theory, the instinctual (and sexual) life force that, working on the pleasure principle and seeking immediate gratification, energizes the id.

Light: The portion of the electromagnetic spectrum visible to the eye.

Limbic system: An interconnected group of structures (including parts of the cortex, thalamus, and hypothalamus) located deep within the temporal lobe and involved in emotions, memory, social behaviour, and brain disorders such as epilepsy; within the limbic system are the hippocampus and the amygdala.

Linguistics [ling-GWIS-ticks]: The study of language structure and language change, including speech sounds, meaning, and grammar.

Logic: The system or principles of reasoning used to reach valid conclusions or inferences.

Long-term memory: The storage mechanism that keeps a relatively permanent record of information.

Lucid dream [LOO-sid]: A dream in which the person is aware of dreaming while it is happening.

Mainstreaming: The integration of all children with special needs into regular classroom settings, whenever appropriate, with the support of special education services.

Maintenance rehearsal: The repetition of information with little or no interpretation.

Major depressive disorder: A depressive disorder characterized by loss of interest in almost all of life's usual activities; a sad, hopeless, or discouraged mood; sleep disturbance; loss of appetite; loss of energy; and feelings of unworthiness and guilt.

Manifest content: The overt story line, characters, and setting of a dream—the obvious, clearly discernible events of the dream.

Mean: The measure of central tendency that is calculated by dividing the sum of the scores by the total number of scores. Also known as the *arithmetic average*.

Means–ends analysis: A heuristic procedure in which the problem solver tries to move closer to a solution by comparing the current situation with the desired goal and determining the most efficient way to get from one to the other.

Measure of central tendency: A descriptive statistic that tells which result or score best represents an entire set of scores.

Median: The measure of central tendency that is the data point having 50 percent of all the observations (scores) above it and 50 percent below it.

Meditation: A state of consciousness induced by a variety of techniques and characterized by concentration, restriction of incoming stimuli, and deep relaxation to produce a sense of detachment.

Medulla [meh-DUH-lah]: The most primitive and lowest portion of the hindbrain; controls basic bodily functions such as breathing.

Memory: The ability to remember past events, images, ideas, or previously learned information or skills; the storage system that allows for retention and retrieval of previously learned information.

Memory span: The limited number of items that can be reproduced easily after presentation to short-term memory, usually confined to one or two chunks of information.

Mental retardation: Below-average intellectual functioning, as measured on an IQ test, accompanied by substantial limitations in functioning that originate before age 18.

Midbrain: The second level of the three organizational structures of the brain; receives afferent signals from other parts of the brain and from the spinal cord, interprets the signals, and either relays the information to a more complex part of the brain or causes the body to act at once; considered important in the regulation of movement.

Mode: The measure of central tendency that is the most frequently observed data point.

Model: A guideline, perspective, or approach derived from data in one field and used to help describe data in another field.

Monochromats [MON-o-kroe-MATZ]: People who cannot perceive any colour, usually because their retinas contain only rods.

Monocular depth cues [mah-NAHK-you-ler]: Depth cues that do not depend on the use of both eyes.

Morality: A system of learned attitudes about social practices, institutions, and individual behaviour that allows a person to evaluate situations and behaviour as being right or wrong, good or bad.

Moro reflex: A reflex in which a newborn stretches out its arms and legs and cries in response to a loud noise or a sudden, unexpected change in the environment.

Morpheme [MORE-feem]: A basic unit of meaning in a language.

Motivation: Any condition, although usually an internal one, that can be inferred to initiate, activate, or maintain an organism's goal-directed behaviour.

Motive: A specific (usually internal) condition, typically involving some form of arousal that directs an organism's behaviour towards a goal.

MRI (magnetic resonance imaging): Imaging technique that uses magnetic fields instead of X-rays and has great clarity and resolution. MRIs can distinguish brain parts as small as one or two millimetres and can penetrate bone, making them particularly useful for diagnosing cartilage and bone marrow problems and tissue damage.

Myopic [my-OP-ick]: Able to see things that are close but having trouble seeing objects at a distance. Also known as *nearsighted*.

Naturalistic observation: Careful and objective observation of events from a distance, without observer intervention.

Nature: An individual's genetically inherited characteristics.

Need: A state of physiological imbalance usually accompanied by arousal.

Need for achievement: A social need that directs people to strive constantly for excellence and success.

Negative punishment: A form of punishment in which a pleasant stimulus is taken away in an effort to decrease an undesirable behaviour.

Negative reinforcement: Removal of an aversive stimulus after a particular response to increase the likelihood that the response will recur.

Neo-Freudians: Personality theorists who have proposed variations on the basic ideas of Freud, usually attributing a greater influence to cultural and interpersonal factors than Freud did.

Nervous system: The structures and organs that act as the communication system for the body allowing all behaviour and mental processes to take place.

Neuromodulator: Chemical substance that functions to increase or decrease the sensitivity of widely distributed neurons to the specific effects of neurotransmitters.

Neuron [NYER-on]: The basic unit (a single cell) of the nervous system comprising dendrites, which receive neural signals; a cell body, which generates electrical signals; and an axon, which transmits neural signals. Also known as a *nerve cell*.

Neurotransmitter [NYER-oh-TRANS-mitt-er]: Chemical substance that resides in the axon terminals and within synaptic vesicles and that, when released, moves across the synaptic space and binds to a receptor site on adjacent neurons.

Nondirective therapy: A form of therapy in which the client determines the direction of therapy while the therapist remains permissive, almost passive, and accepts totally the client's feelings and behaviour.

Non-rapid eye movement (NREM) sleep: Four distinct stages of sleep during which no rapid eye movements occur.

Nonverbal communication: Information provided by cues or actions that involve movements of the body, especially the face.

Normal curve: A bell-shaped graphic representation of data arranged to show what percentage of the population falls under each part of the curve.

Normal distribution: The approximately expected distribution of scores when a sample is drawn from a large population, drawn as a frequency polygon that often takes the form of a bell-shaped curve. Also known as a *normal curve*.

Norms: The scores and corresponding percentile ranks of a large and representative sample of individuals from the population for which a test was designed.

Nurture: The sum of the experiences an individual has in the environment.

Obedience: Compliance with the orders of another person or a group of people.

Observational learning theory: A theory that suggests that organisms learn new responses by observing the behaviour of a model and then imitating it. Also known as *social learning theory*.

Obsessive–compulsive disorder: An anxiety disorder characterized by persistent and uncontrollable thoughts and irrational beliefs (obsessions) that cause performance of intrusive and inappropriate compulsive rituals that interfere with daily life.

Oedipus complex [ED-i-pus]: Occurring during the phallic stage, feelings of rivalry with the parent of the same sex and love of the parent of the opposite sex, ultimately resolved through identification with the parent of the same sex; in girls this process is called the *Electra complex*.

Olfaction [ole-FAK-shun]: The sense of smell.

Operant conditioning [OP-er-ant]: Conditioning in which the probability that an organism will emit a response is increased or decreased by the subsequent delivery of a reinforcer or punisher. Also known as *instrumental conditioning*.

Operational definition: Definition of a variable in terms of the set of methods or procedures used to measure or study that variable.

Opiate: A drug with pain-relieving and sedative properties that is addictive and produces tolerance.

Opponent-process theory: The theory, proposed by Herring, that colour is coded by stimulation of three types of paired receptors; each pair of receptors is assumed to operate in an antagonistic way so that stimulation by a given wavelength produces excitation of one receptor of the pair and inhibition of the other receptor.

Optic chiasm [KI-azm]: The point at which half of the optic nerve fibres from each eye cross over and project to the other side of the brain.

Oral stage: Freud's first stage of personality development, from birth to about age two, during which infants obtain gratification primarily through the mouth.

Orgasm phase: The third phase of the sexual response cycle, during which autonomic nervous system activity reaches its peak and muscle contractions occur throughout the body, but especially in the genital area, in spasms.

Overjustification effect: The decrease in likelihood that an intrinsically motivated task, after having been extrinsically rewarded, will be performed when the reward is no longer given.

Parallel distributed processing (PDP): Conception of the brain as being organized in neural networks, with many operations taking place simultaneously and at many locations.

Paranoid type of schizophrenia [PAIR-uh-noid]: A major type of schizophrenia, characterized by hallucinations and delusions of persecution or grandeur (or both), and sometimes irrational jealousy.

Parasympathetic nervous system [PAIR-uh-sim-puh-THET-ick]: The part of the autonomic nervous system that controls the ongoing maintenance processes of the body, such as heart rate, digestion, and blood pressure.

Participant: Individual who takes part in an experiment and whose behaviour is observed for research data collection. Also known as a *subject*.

Percentile score: A score indicating what percentage of the test population obtained a lower score.

Perception: The process whereby an organism selects and interprets sensory input so that it acquires meaning.

Performance appraisal: The process by which a supervisor periodically evaluates the job-relevant strengths and weaknesses of subordinates.

Peripheral nervous system [puh-RIF-er-al]: The part of the nervous system that carries information to and from the central nervous system through a network of spinal and cranial nerves.

Personal fable: A cognitive distortion experienced by adolescents, in which they believe they are so special and unique that other people cannot understand them and risky behaviours will not harm them.

Personal space: The area or invisible boundary around an individual that the person considers private.

Personality: A set of relatively enduring behavioural characteristics and internal predispositions that describe how a person reacts to the environment.

Personality disorders: Disorders characterized by inflexible and long-standing maladaptive ways of dealing with the environment that typically cause stress and/or social or occupational difficulties.

PET (positron emission tomography): Imaging technique that uses radioactive markers injected into the bloodstream to enable researchers to observe metabolic activity by recording glucose use taking place in the brain; measures local variations in cerebral blood flow, which is correlated with mental activity.

Phallic stage [FAL-ick]: Freud's third stage of personality development, about age three to age seven, during which children obtain gratification primarily from the genitals.

Phobic disorders: Anxiety disorders characterized by excessive, unreasonable, and irrational fear of, and consequent attempt to avoid, specific objects or situations.

Phoneme [FOE-neem]: A basic unit of sound in a language.

Phonology: The study of the patterns and distribution of speech sounds in a language and the tacit rules for their pronunciation.

Photoreceptors: The light-sensitive cells in the retina: rods and cones.

Pitch: The psychological experience that corresponds with the frequency of an auditory stimulus. Also known as *tone*.

Pituitary gland [pit-YOU-ih-tare-ee]: The body's master gland located at the base of the brain and closely linked to the hypothalamus; regulates the actions of other endocrine glands; major function is the control of growth hormones.

Placebo effect [pluh-SEE-bo]: A therapeutic change that occurs as a result of a person's expectations of change rather than as a result of any specific treatment.

Placenta [pluh-SENT-uh]: A mass of tissue in the uterus that acts as the life-support system for the fetus by supplying oxygen, food, and antibodies and by eliminating wastes—all by way of the mother's bloodstream.

Plateau phase: The second phase of the sexual response cycle, during which the sexual partners are preparing for orgasm, autonomic nervous system activity increases, and there is further vasocongestion.

Pons: A structure of the hindbrain that connects with the medulla and the cerebellum, provides a link with the rest of the brain, and is involved in sleep.

Positive punishment: A form of punishment in which an unpleasant stimulus is added in an effort to decrease an undesirable behaviour.

Positive reinforcement: Presentation of a rewarding or pleasant stimulus after a particular response, to increase the likelihood that the response will recur.

Post-traumatic stress disorder (PTSD): A mental disorder that may become evident after a person has undergone severe stress caused by some type of disaster; common symptoms include vivid, intrusive recollections or re-experiences of the traumatic event and occasional lapses of normal consciousness.

Preconscious: Freud's second level of awareness, consisting of mental activities of which people can become aware if they closely attend to them.

Prejudice: Negative evaluation of an entire group of people, typically based on unfavourable (often incorrect) ideas or stereotypes about the group.

Preoperational stage: Piaget's second stage of cognitive development (lasting from about age two to age six or seven), during which initial symbolic thought is developed.

Pressure: The emotional state or condition resulting from the real or imagined expectations of others for certain behaviours or results.

Prevalence: The percentage of a population displaying a disorder during any specified period.

Primacy effect: The more accurate recall of items presented first in a series.

Primary punisher: Any stimulus or event that is naturally painful or aversive to an organism.

Primary reinforcer: A reinforcer (such as food, water, or the termination of pain) that has survival value for an organism; thus, its value does not have to be learned.

Privacy: The result of the process of controlling the boundaries between people so that access is limited.

Proactive coping: Taking action in advance of a potentially stressful situation to prevent it, modify it, or prepare for it before it occurs.

Proactive interference [pro-AK-tiv]: Decrease in accurate recall of information as a result of the effects of previously learned or presented information. Also known as *proactive inhibition*.

Problem solving: The behaviour of individuals when confronted with a situation or task that requires insight or determination of some unknown elements.

Procedural memory: Memory for the perceptual, motor, and cognitive skills required to complete complex tasks.

Projection: A defence mechanism by which people attribute their own undesirable traits to others.

Projective tests: Personality-assessing devices or instruments in which examinees are shown a standard set of ambiguous stimuli and asked to respond in an unrestricted manner.

Prosocial behaviour: Behaviour that benefits someone else or society but that generally offers no obvious benefit to the person performing it and that may even involve some personal risk or sacrifice.

Prototype: An abstraction of a pattern, object, or idea stored in memory, against which similar patterns are evaluated to see how closely they resemble each other; it is the best example of a class of items.

Psychedelic: A consciousness-altering drug that affects moods, thoughts, memory, judgment, and perception and that is usually self-administered for the purpose of producing these results.

Psychiatrist: A physician (medical doctor) specializing in the treatment of patients with emotional disorders.

Psychic determinism [SYE-kick]: A psychoanalytic assumption that all feelings, thoughts, actions, and gestures have a purpose and are determined by past actions or events.

Psychoactive drug [SYE-koh-AK-tiv]: A drug that alters behaviour, thoughts, or emotions by altering biochemical reactions in the nervous system, thereby affecting consciousness.

Psychoanalysis [SYE-ko-uh-NAL-uh-sis]: A lengthy insight therapy developed by Freud that aims at uncovering conflicts and unconscious impulses through special techniques, including free association, dream analysis, and transference.

Psychoanalyst: A psychiatrist or, occasionally, a non-medical practitioner who has studied the technique of psychoanalysis and uses it to treat people with emotional problems.

Psychoanalytic approach [SYE-ko-an-uh-LIT-ick]: The school of psychological thought developed by Freud, which assumes that psychological maladjustment is a consequence of anxiety resulting from unresolved conflicts and forces of which a person may be unaware; includes the therapeutic technique known as *psychoanalysis*.

Psychodrama [SYF-ko-drama]: A group therapy procedure in which members act out their situations, feelings, and roles.

Psychodynamically based therapies [SYE-ko-dye-NAM-ick-lee]: Therapies based loosely on Freud's psychoanalytic theory, using a part of that approach but rejecting or modifying some of its elements.

Psycholinguistics: The study of how language is acquired, perceived, understood, and produced.

Psychological dependence: A compelling desire to use a drug, along with an inability to inhibit that desire.

Psychologist: A professional who studies behaviour and uses behavioural principles in scientific research or in applied settings.

Psychology: The science of behaviour and mental processes.

Psychoneuroimmunology (PNI) [SYE-ko-NEW-ro-IM-you-NOLL-oh-gee]: The study of how psychological processes and the nervous system affect, and in turn are affected by, the body's natural defence system—the immune system.

Psychophysics [SYE-co-FIZ-icks]: The subfield that focuses on the relationship between physical stimuli and people's conscious experience of them.

Psychostimulant: A drug that in low to moderate doses increases alertness, reduces fatigue, and elevates mood.

Psychosurgery: Brain surgery used in the past to alleviate symptoms of serious mental disorders.

Psychotherapy [SYE-ko-THER-uh-pee]: The treatment of emotional or behavioural problems through psychological techniques.

Psychotic [sye-KOT-ick]: Suffering from a loss of contact with reality that is wide-ranging and interferes with their ability to meet the ordinary demands of life.

Puberty [PEW-burr-tee]: The period during which the reproductive system matures; it begins with an increase in production of sex hormones and occurs at (and signals) the end of childhood.

Punishment: The process of presenting an undesirable or noxious stimulus, or removing a desirable stimulus, to decrease the probability that a particular preceding response will recur.

Questionnaire: A printed form with questions, usually given to a large group of people; used by researchers to gather a substantial amount of data in a short time. Also known as a *survey*.

Range: A measure of variability that describes the spread between the highest and the lowest scores in a distribution.

Rape: Forcible sexual assault on an unwilling partner, usually a woman.

Rapid eye movement (REM) sleep: Stage of sleep characterized by high-frequency, low-voltage brain-wave activity, rapid and systematic eye movements, and dreams.

Rational–emotive therapy: A cognitive behaviour therapy that emphasizes the importance of logical, rational thought processes.

Rationalization: A defence mechanism by which people reinterpret undesirable feelings or behaviour to make them appear acceptable.

Raw score: A test score that has not been transformed or converted in any way.

Reactance: A pattern of feelings and subsequent behaviours aimed at reestablishing a sense of freedom when there is an inconsistency between a person's self-image as being free to choose and the person's realization that someone is trying to force him or her to choose a particular alternative.

Reaction formation: A defence mechanism by which people adopt behaviours opposite to their true feelings.

Reasoning: The purposeful process by which people generate logical and coherent ideas, evaluate situations, and reach conclusions.

Recency effect: The more accurate recall of items presented last in a series.

Receptive fields: The areas of the retina that, when stimulated, produce a change in the firing of cells in the visual system.

Reflex: An involuntary, automatic behaviour that occurs in response to a stimulus without prior learning and usually shows little variability from instance to instance.

Refractory period: The recovery period of a neuron after it fires, during which it cannot fire again; this period allows the neuron to reestablish electrical balance with its surroundings.

Rehearsal: The process of verbalizing, thinking about, or otherwise acting on or transforming information in order to keep it active in memory.

Reinforcer: Any event that increases the probability of a recurrence of the response that preceded it.

Reliability: A test's ability to yield the same or similar scores for the same individual through repeated testing.

Representative sample: A sample of individuals who match the population with whom they are to be compared on key variables such as socioeconomic status and age.

Repression: A defence mechanism by which people block anxiety-provoking thoughts and feelings from conscious awareness and push them into the unconscious.

Residual type of schizophrenia: A schizophrenic disorder in which the patient exhibits inappropriate affect, illogical thinking, and/or eccentric behaviour but generally remain in touch with reality.

Resilience: The extent to which people are flexible, are less easily impaired by events, and respond adaptively to external or internal demands.

Resistance: In psychoanalysis, an unwillingness to cooperate by which a patient signals a reluctance to provide the therapist with information or to help the therapist understand or interpret a situation.

Resolution phase: The fourth phase of the sexual response cycle, during which the body naturally returns after orgasm to its resting, or normal, state.

Reticular formation [reh-TICK-you-lar]: Extending out from the medulla, a latticelike network of neurons that directly controls a person's state of arousal, waking, and sleeping, as well as other bodily functions.

Retinal disparity: The slight difference between the visual images projected on the two retinas.

Retrieval: The process by which stored information is recovered from memory.

Retroactive interference [RET-ro-AK-tiv]: Decrease in accurate recall of information as a result of the subsequent presentation of different information. Also known as *retroactive inhibition*.

Retrograde amnesia [RET-ro-grade]: Loss of memory for events and experiences that occurred in a period preceding the amnesia-causing event.

Rooting reflex: A reflex in which a newborn turns its head towards a mild stimulus that touches its lips or cheek.

Saccades [sack-ADZ]: Rapid voluntary movements of the eyes, to focus on different points.

Sample: A group of participants who are assumed to be representative of the population about which an inference is being made.

Saturation: The depth of hue of reflected light, as determined by the homogeneity of the wavelengths contained in the light. Also known as *purity*.

Schema [SKEEM-uh]: A conceptual framework that organizes information and makes sense of the world by laying out a structure in which events can be encoded.

Scheme: In Piaget's view, a specific mental structure; an organized way of interacting with the environment and experiencing it.

Schizophrenic disorders [SKIT-soh-FREN-ick]: A group of disorders characterized by a loss of contact with reality and by deterioration of social and intellectual functioning.

Scientific method: In psychology, the techniques used to discover knowledge about human behaviour and mental processes; in experimentation, the scientific method involves stating the problem, developing hypotheses, designing a study, collecting and analyzing data (which often includes manipulating some part of the environment to better understand what conditions can lead to a behaviour or phenomenon), replicating results, and drawing conclusions and reporting results.

Secondary punisher: A neutral stimulus with no intrinsic negative effect on an organism that acquires punishment value through repeated pairing with a primary punisher.

Secondary reinforcer: A neutral stimulus that has no intrinsic value for an organism initially but that can become rewarding when linked with a primary reinforcer.

Secondary sex characteristics: The genetically determined physical features that differentiate the sexes; they are not directly involved with reproduction, but help distinguish men from women.

Sedative–hypnotic: A drug that relaxes and calms people and, in higher doses, induces sleep.

Self: In Rogers's theory of personality, the perceptions individuals have of themselves and of their relationships to other people and to various aspects of life.

Self-actualization: The fundamental human need to strive to fulfil one's potential; thus, a state of motivation according to Maslow. From a humanist's view, a final level of psychological development in which a person attempts to minimize ill health, function fully, have a superior perception of reality, and feel a strong sense of self-acceptance.

Self-efficacy: A person's belief about whether he or she can successfully engage in and execute a specific behaviour.

Self-fulfilling prophecy: The unwitting creation by a researcher of a situation that leads to specific prophesied results.

Self-monitoring: An assessment procedure in which a person systematically counts and records the frequency and duration of his or her own specific behaviours.

Self-perception theory: An approach to attitude formation in which people are assumed to infer their attitudes based on observations of their own behaviour.

Self-serving bias: People's tendency to evaluate their own positive behaviours as being due to their own internal traits and characteristics, but to blame their failures and shortcomings on external, situational factors.

Semantic memory: Memory for ideas, rules, and general concepts about the world.

Semantics [se-MAN-ticks]: The analysis of the meaning of language, especially of individual words.

Sensation: The process in which the sense organ receptor cells are stimulated and relay their initial information to higher brain centres for further processing.

Sensorimotor stage: The first of Piaget's four stages of cognitive development (covering roughly the first two years of life), during which the child begins to interact with the environment and the rudiments of memory are established.

Sensorineural deafness [sen-so-ree-NEW-ruhl]: Deafness resulting from damage to the cochlea, the auditory nerve, or higher auditory processing centres.

Sensory memory: The mechanism that performs initial encoding and brief storage of stimuli. Also known as the *sensory register*.

Shape constancy: The ability to recognize a shape despite changes in the orientation or angle from which it is viewed.

Shaping: A gradual training of an organism to give the proper responses through selective reinforcement of behaviours as they approach the desired response.

Short-term working memory: The storage mechanism that temporarily holds current or recently attended-to information for immediate or short term use and that is composed of several subsystems: a component to encode and rehearse auditory information, a visual–spatial "scratch pad," and a central processing mechanism, or executive, that balances and controls information flow.

Shyness: Extreme anxiety in individuals who are socially reticent and often overly concerned with how they appear to others, often leading to avoidance of social situations.

Signal detection theory: The theory that holds that an observer's perception is dependent on the intensity of a stimulus, on the observer's motivation, on the criteria he or she sets up, and on the "noise" that is present.

Significant difference: In an experiment, a difference that is unlikely to have occurred because of chance alone and is most likely due to the systematic manipulation of the independent variable.

Size constancy: The ability of the perceptual system to recognize that an object remains constant in size regardless of its distance from the observer or the size of its image on the retina.

Skinner box: Named by others for its developer, B. F. Skinner, a box that contains a responding mechanism (usually a lever) capable of delivering a consequence, often a reinforcer, to an organism.

Sleep: Non-waking state of consciousness characterized by general unresponsiveness to the environment and general physical immobility.

Smooth pursuit movements: Automatic, smooth eye movements that follow a moving stimulus.

Social categorization: The process of dividing the world into "in" and "out" groups.

Social cognition: The thought processes involved in making sense of events, other people, oneself, and the world in general by analyzing and interpreting them.

Social facilitation: Change in performance that occurs when people believe they are in the presence of other people.

Social influence: The way in which one or more people alter the attitudes or behaviour of others.

Social loafing: A decrease in productivity that occurs when an individual works in a group instead of alone.

Social need: An aroused condition that directs people towards establishing feelings about themselves and others and towards establishing and maintaining relationships.

Social phobia [FOE-bee-uh]: An anxiety disorder characterized by fear of, and a desire to avoid, situations in which the person might be exposed to scrutiny by others and might behave in an embarrassing or humiliating way.

Social psychology: The study of how individuals influence and are influenced by the thoughts, feelings, and behaviours of other people.

Social support: The comfort, recognition, approval, and encouragement available from other people, including friends, family, members of organizations, and co-workers.

Sociobiology: A theory based on the premise that even day-to-day behaviours are determined by the process of natural selection—that social behaviours that contribute to the survival of a species are passed on genetically from one generation to the next and account for the mechanisms producing behaviours such as altruism.

Somatic nervous system [so-MAT-ick]: The part of the peripheral nervous system that carries information to skeletal muscles and thereby affects bodily movement; it controls voluntary, conscious sensory and motor functions.

Somatization disorder: A somatoform disorder characterized by recurrent and multiple physical complaints of several years' duration for which medical attention has been ineffective.

Somatoform disorders [so-MAT-oh-form]: Disorders characterized by real physical symptoms not under voluntary control and for which no apparent physical cause exists.

Sound: The psychological experience that occurs when changes in air pressure take place at the receptive organ for hearing; the resulting tones, or sounds, vary in frequency and amplitude.

Specific phobia: An anxiety disorder characterized by irrational and persistent fear of a specific object or situation, along with a compelling desire to avoid it.

Spinal cord: The portion of the central nervous system that is contained within the spinal column and transmits signals from the senses to the brain, controls reflexive responses, and conveys signals from the brain to the muscles and glands.

Split-brain patients: People whose corpus callosum, which normally connects the two cerebral hemispheres, has been surgically severed.

Spontaneous recovery: Recurrence of an extinguished conditioned response following a rest period.

Sport psychology: The systematic application of psychological principles to sports.

Standard deviation: A descriptive statistic that measures the variability of data from the mean of the sample.

Standard score: A score that expresses an individual's position relative to those of others based on the mean score and how scores are distributed around it.

Standardization: The process of developing uniform procedures for administering and scoring a test and for establishing norms.

State-dependent learning: The tendency to recall information learned in a particular physiological state most accurately when one is again in that physiological state.

Statistics: The branch of mathematics that deals with collecting, classifying, and analyzing data.

Stereotypes: Fixed, overly simple, often incorrect, and often negative ideas about traits, attitudes, and behaviours attributed to groups of people.

Stimulus control: Occurs when a particular stimulus comes to indicate that a contingency is in place in one situation but not in another.

Stimulus discrimination: Process by which an organism learns to respond only to a specific reinforced stimulus and not to other irrelevant stimuli.

Stimulus generalization: Occurrence of a conditioned response with a stimulus that is similar but not identical to the original conditioned stimulus.

Storage: The process of maintaining or keeping information readily available; it also refers to the locations of memory, which researchers call "memory stores."

Stress: A nonspecific, often global response to real or imagined challenges or threats; it is an emotional response, a result (a person must view a situation as stressful for it to be stressful).

Stress inoculation [in-OK-you-LAY-shun]: The procedure of giving people realistic warnings, recommendations, and reassurances to help them prepare for and cope with impending dangers or losses.

Stressor: An environmental stimulus that affects an organism in physically or psychologically injurious ways, usually producing anxiety, tension, and physiological arousal.

Structuralism: The school of psychological thought that considered the organized structure of immediate, conscious experience to be the proper subject matter of psychology.

Subgoal analysis: A heuristic procedure in which a task is broken down into smaller, more manageable steps, each of which has a subgoal.

Sublimation [sub-li-MAY-shun]: A defence mechanism by which socially unacceptable impulses are redirected into acceptable ones.

Subliminal perception: Perception below the threshold of awareness.

Substance abuser: A person who overuses and relies on drugs to deal with stress and anxiety.

Sucking reflex: A reflex in which a newborn makes sucking motions when presented with a stimulus to the lips, such as a nipple.

Superego [super-EE-go]: In Freud's theory, the moral aspect of mental functioning, comprising the ego ideal (what a person would ideally like to be) and the conscience, and taught by parents and society.

Superstitious behaviour: Behaviour learned through coincidental association with reinforcement.

Surface structure: The organization of a sentence that is closest to its written or spoken form.

Syllogism [SILL-oh-jiz-um]: A sequence of statements, or premises (usually two), followed by a conclusion; the task is to decide whether the conclusion is warranted.

Sympathetic nervous system: The part of the autonomic nervous system that becomes most active in response to emergency situations; it calls up bodily resources as needed for major energy expenditures.

Symptom substitution: The appearance of one overt symptom to replace another that has been eliminated by treatment.

Synapse [SIN-apps]: The microscopically small space between the axon terminals of one neuron and the receptor sites of another neuron.

Syntax [SIN-tacks]: The way that words and groups of words combine to form phrases, clauses, and sentences.

Systematic desensitization: A three-stage counterconditioning procedure in which people are taught to relax when presented with stimuli that formerly elicited anxiety.

Temperament: Early-emerging and long-lasting individual differences in the intensity and especially the quality of a person's emotional reactions.

Teratogen [ter-AT-oh-jen]: A substance that can produce developmental malformations (birth defects) during the prenatal period.

Territorial behaviour: Behaviour involved in establishing, maintaining, personalizing, and defending a delineated space.

Thalamus: A large structure of the forebrain that acts primarily as a routing station to send information to other parts of the brain but probably also performs some interpretive functions; nearly all sensory information proceeds through the thalamus.

Thanatology: The study of the psychological and medical aspects of death and dying.

Theory: In psychology, a collection of interrelated ideas and facts put forward to describe, explain, and predict behaviour and mental processes.

Time-out: A punishment procedure in which a person is physically removed from sources of reinforcement in order to decrease the occurrence of undesired behaviours.

Token economy: An operant conditioning procedure in which individuals who engage in appropriate behaviour receive tokens that they can exchange for desirable items or activities.

Tolerance: Progressive insensitivity to repeated use of a specific drug in the same dosage and at the same frequency of use.

Trait: Any readily identifiable stable quality that characterizes the way in which an individual differs from other individuals.

Transduction: The process by which a perceptual system analyzes stimuli and converts them into electrical impulses. Also known as *coding*.

Transfer-appropriate processing: Initial processing of information that is similar in modality or type to the processing necessary in the retrieval task.

Transference: A psychoanalytic phenomenon in which a therapist becomes the object of a patient's emotional attitudes about an important person in the patient's life, such as a parent.

Transformational grammar: An approach to the study of language that assumes that each sentence has both a surface structure and a deep structure.

Transformational leader: A charismatic leader who inspires and provides intellectual stimulation to recreate an organization.

Trichromatic theory [try-kroe-MAT-ick]: The visual theory, stated by Young and Helmholtz, that all colours can be made by mixing three basic colours: red, green, and blue. Also known as the *Young–Helmholtz theory*.

Trichromats [TRY-kroe-MATZ]: People who can perceive all three primary colours and thus who can distinguish any colour.

Type A behaviour: Behaviour characterized by competitiveness, impatience, hostility, and constant efforts to do more in less time.

Type B behaviour: Behaviour characterized by more calmness, more patience, and less hurrying than that of Type A individuals.

Types: Categories of personality in which broad collections of traits are loosely tied together and interrelated.

Unconditioned response: An unlearned or involuntary response to an unconditioned stimulus.

Unconditioned stimulus: A stimulus that normally produces a measurable involuntary response.

Unconscious: Freud's third level of awareness, consisting of mental activities beneath people's normal awareness.

Unconscious motivation: A psychoanalytic assumption that behaviour is determined by desires, goals, and internal states buried deep within the unconscious, of which an individual is unaware.

Undifferentiated type of schizophrenia: A schizophrenic disorder characterized by a mixture of symptoms, but that does not fit neatly into the diagnostic criteria of other categories.

Validity: The ability of a test to measure only what it is supposed to measure and to predict only what it is supposed to predict.

Variability: The extent to which scores differ from one another, especially the extent to which they differ from the mean.

Variable: Condition or characteristic of a situation or person that is subject to change (that varies) within or across situations or individuals.

Variable-interval schedule: A reinforcement schedule in which a reinforcer (reward) is delivered after predetermined but varying intervals of time, provided that the required response occurs at least once after each interval.

Variable-ratio schedule: A reinforcement schedule in which a reinforcer (reward) is delivered after a predetermined but variable number of responses has occurred.

Vasocongestion: In the sexual response cycle, engorgement of the blood vessels, particularly in the genital area, due to increased blood flow.

Vestibular eye movements: Reflexive eye movements that compensate for head or body movement.

Vestibular sense [ves-TIB-you-ler]: The sense of bodily orientation and postural adjustment.

Visual cortex: The most important area of the brain's occipital lobe, which receives information from the lateral geniculate nucleus. Also known as the *striate cortex*.

Vulnerability: A person's diminished ability to deal with demanding life events.

Withdrawal symptoms: Physiological reactions that occur when an addictive drug is no longer administered to an addict.

Working through: In psychoanalysis, the repetitive cycle of interpretation, resistance to interpretation, and transference.

Zygote [ZEYE-goat]: A fertilized egg.

References

Abbott, L. F., Varela, J. A., Sen, K., & Nelson, S. B. (1997). Synaptic depression and cortical gain control. *Science, 275,* 220–224.

Abdullaev, Y. G., & Posner, M. I. (1998). Event-related brain potential imaging of semantic encoding during processing single words. *Neuroimage, 7*(1), 1–13.

Abed, F. (1991). Cultural influences on visual scanning patterns. *Journal of Cross-Cultural Psychology, 22,* 525–534.

Abel, T., Martin, K. C., Bartsch, D., & Kandel, E. R. (1998). Memory suppressor genes: Inhibitory constraints on the storage of long-term memory. *Science, 279,* 338–341.

Abelson, R. P. (1988). Conviction. *American Psychologist, 43,* 267–276.

Aboud, R. E., & Mendelson, M. J. (1998). Determinants of friendship selection and quality: Developmental perspectives. In W. M. Bukowski et al. (Eds.), *The company they keep: Friendship in childhood and adolescence.* New York: Cambridge University Press.

Abramowitz, J. S. (1998). Does cognitive-behavioral therapy cure obsessive-compulsive disorder? A meta-analytic evaluation of clinical significance. *Behavior Therapy, 29,* 339–355.

Abrams, M., & Ellis, A. (1994). Stress management and counselling: Rational emotive behaviour therapy in the treatment of stress. *British Journal of Guidance and Counselling, 22,* 39–50.

Abramson, L. Y., Metalsky, G. I., & Alloy, L. B. (1989). Hopelessness depression: A theory-based subtype of depression. *Psychological Review, 96,* 358–372.

Abravanel, E., & DeYong, N. G. (1997). Exploring the roles of peer and adult video models for infant imitations. *Journal of Genetic Psychology, 158*(2), 133–150.

Acker, J. R. (1993). A different agenda: The Supreme Court, empirical research evidence, and capital punishment decisions, 1986–1989. *Law & Society Review, 27*(1), 65–88.

Adelmann, P. K., Antonucci, T. C., Crohan, S. E., & Coleman, L. M. (1989). Empty nest, cohort, and employment in the well-being of midlife women. *Sex Roles, 20,* 173–190.

Ader, R., & Cohen, N. (1985). CNS-immune system interactions: Conditioning phenomena. *Behavioral and Brain Sciences, 8*(3), 379–426.

Ader, R., & Cohen, N. (1993). Psychoneuroimmunology: Conditioning and stress. *Annual Review of Psychology, 44,* 53–85.

Adler, A. (1969). *The science of living.* Garden City, NY: Anchor Books. (Original work published 1929.)

Adorno, T., Frenkel-Brunswick, E., Levinson, D., & Sanford, R. (1950). *The authoritarian personality.* New York: Harper & Row.

Aganoff, J. A., & Boyle, G. J. (1994). Aerobic exercise, mood states and menstrual cycle symptoms. *Journal of Psychosomatic Research, 38,* 183–192.

Agne, K. J. (1999). Caring: The way of the master teacher. In R. P. Lipka, T. M. Brinthaupt, et al. (Eds.), *The role of self in teacher development. SUNY series, studying the self* (pp. 165–188). Albany: State University of New York Press.

Agnew, H. W., Jr., & Webb, W. B. (1973). The influence of time course variable on REM sleep. *Bulletin of the Psychonomic Society, 2,* 131–133.

Agras, W. S. (1992). Some structural changes that might facilitate the development of behavioral medicine. *Journal of Consulting and Clinical Psychology, 4,* 499–509.

Aiello, J. R., & Kolb, K. J. (1995). Electronic performance monitoring and social context: Impact on productivity and stress. *Journal of Applied Psychology, 80,* 339–353.

Aiken, L. R. (1985). *Dying, death, and bereavement.* Boston: Allyn & Bacon.

Aiken, L. R. (1988). *Psychological testing and assessment* (6th ed). Boston: Allyn & Bacon.

Aikens, J. E., Wallander, J. L., Bell, D. S. H., & Cole, J. A. (1992). Daily stress variability, learned resourcefulness, regimen adherence, and metabolic control in type I diabetes mellitus: Evaluation of a path model. *Journal of Consulting and Clinical Psychology, 60,* 113–118.

Ainsworth, M. D. S. (1979). Infant-mother attachment. *American Psychologist, 34,* 932–937.

Ainsworth, M. S., Blehar, M. C., Waters, E., & Wall, S. (1978). *Patterns of attachment: A psychological study of the strange situation.* Hillsdale, NJ: Lawrence Erlbaum.

Ajdukovic, M., & Ajdukovic, D. (1998). Impact of displacement on the psychological well-being of refugee children. *International Review of Psychiatry, 10*(3), 186–195.

Akbarian, S., Kim, J. J., Potkin, S. G., Hagman, J. O., Tafazzoli, A., Bunney, W. E., Jr., & Jones, E. G. (1995). Gene expression for glutamic acid decarboxylase is reduced without loss of neurons in prefrontal cortex of schizophrenics. *Archives of General Psychiatry, 52,* 258–266.

Aldag, R. J., & Fuller, S. R. (1993). Beyond fiasco: A reappraisal of the groupthink phenomenon and a new model of group decision processes. *Psychological Bulletin, 113,* 533–552.

Algera, J. A. (1990). The job characteristics model of work motivation revisited. In U. Kleinbeck, H. Quast, H. Thierry, & H. Hacker (Eds.), *Work motivation.* Hillsdale, NJ: Erlbaum.

Al-Issa, I. (1982). Does culture make a difference in psychotherapy? In I. Al-Issa (Ed.), *Culture and psychopathology.* Baltimore: University Park Press.

Alivisatos, B., & Petrides, M. (1997). Functional activation of the human brain during mental rotation. *Neuropsychologia, 35*(2), 111–118.

Alkon, D. L. (1989, July). Memory storage and neural systems. *Scientific American,* 42–50.

Allen, B. P. (1995). Gender stereotypes are not accurate: A replication of Martin (1987) using diagnostic vs. self-report and behavioral criteria. *Sex Roles, 32*(9/10), 583–586.

Allen, G. L. (1981). A developmental perspective on the effects of "subdividing" macrospatial experience. *Journal of Experimental Psychology: Human Learning and Memory, 7,* 120–132.

Allen, G. L. (1987). Cognitive influences on the acquisition of route knowledge in children and adults. In P. Ellen & C. Thinus-Blanc (Eds.), *Cognitive processes and spatial orientation in animal and man: Vol. 2. Neurophysiology and developmental aspects.* Boston: Martinus Nijhoff.

Allen, K. E., Turner, K. D., & Everett, P. M. (1970). A behavior modification classroom for Head Start children with problem behaviors. *Exceptional Children, 37,* 119–127.

Allgood-Merten, B., Lewinsohn, P. M., & Hops, H. (1990). Sex differences and adolescent depression. *Journal of Abnormal Psychology, 99,* 55–63.

Allgulander, C. (1994). Suicide and mortality patterns in anxiety neurosis and depressive neurosis. *Archives of General Psychiatry, 51,* 708–712.

Allgulander, C., Nowak, J., & Rice, J. P. (1990). Psychopathology and treatment of 30,344 twins in Sweden: I. The appropriateness of psychoactive drug treatment. *Acta Psychiatrica Scandinavica, 82*(6), 420–426.

Allington, R. L. (1981). Sensitivity to orthographic structure in educable mentally retarded children. *Contemporary Educational Psychology, 6,* 135–139.

Allison, T., Ginter, H., McCarthy, G., Nobre, A. C., Puce, A., Luby, M., & Spencer, D. D. (1994). Face recognition in human extrastriate cortex. *Journal of Neurophysiology, 71,* 821–825.

Allport, G. W. (1937). *Personality: A psychological interpretation.* New York: Holt.

Allport, G. W. (1979). *The nature of prejudice.* Cambridge, MA: Addison-Wesley. (Original work published 1954.)

Almagor, M., Tellegen, A., & Waller, N. G. (1995). The big seven model: A cross-cultural replication and further exploration of the basic dimensions of natural language trait descriptors. *Journal of Personality and Social Psychology, 69,* 300–307.

Altemeyer, B. (1988). *Enemies of freedom: Understanding right-wing authoritarianism*. San Francisco: Jossey-Bass.

Altman, F. (1998). Where is the "neuro" in psychoneuroimmunology? *Brain, Behavior, and Immunity, 11*(1), 1–8.

Altman, I. (1975). *The environment and social behavior*. Monterey, CA: Brooks/Cole.

Altman, I., & Vinsel, A. M. (1977). Personal space: An analysis of E. T. Hall's proxemics framework. In I. Altman, A. Rapoport, & J. F. Wohlwill (Eds.), *Human behavior and environment: Vol. 2. Advances in theory and research*. New York: Plenum.

Amaro, H. (1995). Love, sex, and power: Considering women's realities in HIV prevention. *American Psychologist, 50*, 437–447.

Ambady, N., & Rosenthal, R. (1993). Half a minute: Predicting teacher evaluations from thin slices of nonverbal behavior and physical attractiveness. *Journal of Personality and Social Psychology, 64*, 431–441.

American Association of University Women Educational Foundation. (1998). *Gender gaps: Where schools still fail our children* (Special Report). Washington, DC: Author.

American Association on Mental Retardation (1992). *Mental retardation*. Washington, DC: Author.

American Psychiatric Association (1994). *Diagnostic and statistical manual of mental disorders* (4th ed.) (DSM-IV). Washington, DC: Author.

American Psychiatric Association (1995). Practice guideline for psychiatric evaluation of adults. *American Journal of Psychiatry, 152*, 67–80.

American Psychological Association (1992). Ethical principles of psychologists and code of conduct. *American Psychologist, 47*, 1597–1611.

American Psychological Association (1993). Guidelines for providers of psychological services to ethnic, linguistic, and culturally diverse populations. *American Psychologist, 48*, 45–48.

American Psychological Association (1994). The Seville statement on violence. *American Psychologist, 49*, 845–846.

American Psychological Association (1995). *Demographic characteristics of APA members by membership status, 1993*. Washington, DC: Office of Demographic, Employment, and Educational Research, APA Education Directorate.

Ames, E. W. (1990). Spitz revisited: A trip to Romanian "orphanages." *Canadian Psychological Association Developmental Section Newsletter, 9*, 8–11.

Ames, E. W., & Carter, M. (1992). A study of Romanian orphanage children in Canada: Background, sample and procedure. *Canadian Psychology, 33*, 503.

Anderson, C. A. (1989). Temperature and aggression: Ubiquitous effects of heat on occurrence of human violence. *Psychological Bulletin, 106*, 74–96.

Anderson, C. A., & Anderson, K. B. (1998). Temperature and aggression: Paradox, controversy, and a (fairly) clear picture. In R. G. Geen, E. Donnerstein, et al. (Eds.), *Human aggression: Theories, research, and implications for social policy* (pp. 247–298). San Diego, CA: Academic Press, Inc.

Anderson, C. A., Anderson, K. B., & Deuser, W. E. (1996). Examining an affective aggression framework: Weapon and temperature effects on aggressive thoughts, affect, and attitudes. *Personality and Social Psychology Bulletin, 22*(4), 366–376.

Anderson, C. A., & DeNeve, K. M. (1992). Temperature, aggression, and the negative affect escape model. *Psychological Bulletin, 111*, 347–351.

Andreasen, N. C. (1997). Neuroimaging techniques in the investigation of schizophrenia. *Journal of Clinical Psychiatry Monograph Series, 15*(3), 16–19.

Angoff, W. H. (1988). The nature-nuture debate, aptitudes, and group differences. *American Psychologist, 43*, 713–720.

Annett, M. (1985). *Left, right, hand and brain: The right shift theory*. London: Erlbaum.

Anonymous (1994). Canadian study of health and aging: Study methods and prevalence of dementia. *Canadian Medical Association Journal, 150*(6), 899–913.

Antonuccio, D. O., Danton, W. G., & DeNelsky, G. Y. (1995). Psychotherapy versus medication for depression: Challenging the conventional wisdom with data. *Professional Psychology: Research and Practice, 26*, 574–585.

Apter, A., Galatzer, A., Beth-Halachmi, N., & Laron, Z. (1981). Self-image in adolescents with delayed puberty and growth retardation. *Journal of Youth and Adolescence, 10*, 501–505.

Apter, T. (1995). *Secret paths: Women in the new midlife*. New York: Norton.

Arango, V., Underwood, M. D., & Mann, J. J. (1992). Alterations in monoamine receptors in the brain of suicide victims. *Journal of Clinical Psychopharmacology, 12*, 8S-12S.

Arceneaux, M. C., & Murdock, J. Y. (1997). Peer prompting reduces disruptive vocalizations of a student with developmental disabilities in a general eighth-grade classroom. *Focus on Autism and Other Developmental Disabilities, 12*(3), 182–186.

Archer, J. (1996). Sex differences in social behavior: Are the social role and evolutionary explanations compatible? *American Psychologist, 51*(9), 909–917.

Arcus, D. (1994). Biological mechanisms and personality: Evidence from shy children. *Advances, 10*(4), 40–50.

Ariel, M., & Giora, R. (1992). Gender versus group-relation analysis of impositive speech acts. In K. Hall et al. (Eds.), *Locating power: Proceedings of the second Berkeley Women and Language Conference*. Berkeley: University of California Press.

Arkowitz, H. (1997). Integrative theories of therapy. In Wachtel, P. L., & Messer, S. B. (Eds.), *Theories of psychotherapy: Origins and evolution* (pp. 227–288). Washington, DC: American Psychological Association.

Arnon, R., & Kreitler, S. (1984). Effects of meaning training on overcoming functional fixedness. *Current Psychological Research and Reviews, 3*(4), 11–24.

Aron, A., & Aron, E. N. (1997). Self-expansion motivation and including other in the self. In S. Duck (Ed.), *Handbook of personal relationships: Theory, research and interventions*. Chichester, England: John Wiley & Sons, Inc.

Aronson, J., Quinn, D. M., & Spencer, S. J. (1998). Stereotype threat and the academic underperformance of minorities and women. In J. K. Swim, C. Stangor, et al. (Eds.). *Prejudice: The target's perspective* (pp. 83–103). San Diego, CA: Academic Press.

Arvey, R. D., & Campion, J. E. (1982). The employment interview: A summary and review of recent research. *Personnel Psychology, 35*, 281–322.

Asaad, G., & Shapiro, B. (1986). Hallucinations: Theoretical and clinical overview. *American Journal of Psychiatry, 143*, 1088–1097.

Asch, S. E. (1955, November). Opinions and social pressure. *Scientific American*, 31–35.

Asendorpf, J. B. (1989). Shyness as a final common pathway for two different kinds of inhibition. *Journal of Personality and Social Psychology, 57*, 481–492.

Ashcraft, M. H. (1989). *Human memory and cognition*. Glenview, IL: Scott, Foresman.

Aspinwall, L. G., & Taylor S. E. (1997). A stitch in time: Self-regulation and proactive coping. *Psychological Bulletin, 121*(3), 417–436.

Asthana, H. S., & Mandal, M. K. (1997). Hemiregional variations in facial expression of emotions. *British Journal of Psychology, 88*, 519–525.

Astington, J. (1999). What is theoretical about the child's theory of mind? A Vygotskian view of its development. In P. Lloyd, C. Fernhough, et al. (Eds.), *Lev Vygotsky: Critical assessments, future directions, Vol. IV* (pp. 401–418). New York: Routledge.

Atoum, A. O., & Farah, A. M. (1993). Social loafing and personal involvement among Jordanian college students. *The Journal of Social Psychology, 133*, 785–789.

Attie, I., & Brooks-Gunn, J. (1989). Development of eating problems in adolescent girls: A longitudinal study. *Developmental Psychology, 25*, 70–79.

Audia, G., Kristof-Brown, K. G., & Locke, E. A. (1996). Relationship of goals and micro-level work processes to performance on a multi-path manual task. *Journal of Applied Psychology, 81*(5), 483–497.

Ayllon, T., & Azrin, N. H. (1965). The measurement and reinforcement behavior of psychotics. *Journal of the Experimental Analysis of Behavior, 8*, 357–383.

Ayllon, T., & Haughton, E. (1964). Modification of symptomatic verbal behavior of mental patients. *Behavior Research and Therapy, 2*, 87–97.

Azrin, N. H., & Holtz, W. C. (1966). Punishment. In W. K. Honig (Ed.), *Operant behavior: Areas of research and application*. New York: Appleton-Century-Crofts.

Bachar, E. (1998). Psychotherapy—an active agent: Assessing the effectiveness of psychotherapy and its curative factors. *Israel Journal of Psychiatry and Related Sciences, 35*(2), 128–135.

Backman, L., & Lipinska, B. (1993). Monitoring of general knowledge: Evidence for preservation in early Alzheimer's disease. *Neuropsychologia, 31*, 335–345.

Backman, L., & Nilsson, L. G. (1996). Semantic memory functioning across the adult life span. *European Psychologist, 1*(1), 27–33.

Baddeley, A. (1994). The magical number seven: Still magic after all these years? *Psychological Review, 101*, 353–356.

Baddeley, A. D., & Hitch, G. (1974). Working memory. In G. Bower (Ed.), *Recent advances in learning and motivating* (Vol. 8). New York: Academic.

Baddeley, A. D., & Hitch, G. J. (1994). Developments in the concept of working memory. *Neuropsychology, 6*, 485–493.

Baddeley, A. D., & Longman, D. J. (1978). The influence of length and frequency of training session on the rate of learning to type. *Ergonomics, 21*(8), 627–635.

Bagely, C., & Tremblay, P. (1998). On the prevalence of homosexuality and bisexuality in a random community survey of 750 men aged 18 to 27. *Journal of Homosexuality, 36*(2), 1–18.

Bailey, W. C., & Perterson, R. D. (1999). Capital punishment, homicide, and deterrence: An assessment of the evidence and extension to female homicide. In M. D. Smith, M. Zahn, et al. (Eds.), *Homicide: A sourcebook of social research* (pp. 257–276). Thousand Oaks, CA: Sage Publications, Inc.

Baillargeon, R. (1994). How do infants learn about the physical world? *Current Directions in Psychological Science, 3*, 133–140.

Baillargeon, R. (1998). Infants' understanding of the physical world. In M. Sabourin, F. Craik, et al. (Eds.), *Advances in psychological science, Vol. II: Biological and cognitive aspects* (pp. 503–529). Hove, England: Psychology Press/Erlbaum, Taylor & Francis.

Baird, J. C., Wagner, M., & Fuld, K. (1990). A simple but powerful theory of the moon illusion. *Journal of Experimental Psychology: Human Perception and Performance, 16*, 675–677.

Baischer, W. (1995). Acupuncture in migraine: Long-term outcome and predicting factors. *Headache, 35*(8), 472–474.

Bak, M., Girvin, J. P., Hambrecht, F. T., Kufta, C. V., Loeb, G. E., & Schmidt, E. M. (1990). Visual sensations produced by intracortical microstimulation of the human occipital cortex. *Medical and Biological Engineering and Computing, 28*, 257–259.

Baker, C. (1993). The stress of settlement where there is no ethnocultural receiving community. In R. R. Masi, & L. L. Mensah (Eds.), *Health and cultures: Programs, services, and care*, Vol. 2. Oakville, ON: Mosaic Press.

Bala, N., Weiler, R., Copple, P., Smith, R., Hornick, J. P., & Paetsch, J. J. (1994). *A police reference manual on youth and violence*. Canadian Research Institute for Law and the Family and Solicitor General Canada.

Balay, J., & Shevrin, H. (1988). The subliminal psychodynamic activation method. *American Psychologist, 3*, 161–174.

Baldwin, D. R., Harris, S. M., & Chambliss, L. N. (1997). Stress and illness in adolescence: Issues of race and gender. *Adolescence, 32*(128), 839–853.

Baldwin, E. (1993). The case for animal research in psychology. *Journal of Social Issues, 49*, 121–131.

Ballen, W. (1997). Freud's views and the contemporary application of hypnosis: Enhancing therapy within a psychoanalytic framework. *Journal of Contemporary Psychotherapy, 27*(3), 201–214.

Baltes, P. B. (1987). Theoretical propositions of life-span developmental psychology: On the dynamics between growth and decline. *Developmental Psychology, 23*, 611–626.

Baltes, P. B. (1993). The aging mind: Potential and limits. *Gerontologist, 33*(5), 580–594.

Band, E. B., & Weisz, J. R. (1988). How to feel better when it feels bad: Children's perspectives on coping with everyday stress. *Developmental Psychology, 24*, 247–253.

Bandura, A. (1969). *Principles of behavior modification*. New York: Holt, Rinehart & Winston.

Bandura, A. (1977a). Self-efficacy: Toward a unifying theory of behavioral change. *Psychological Review, 84*, 191–215.

Bandura, A. (1977b). *Social learning theory*. Englewood Cliffs, NJ: Prentice-Hall.

Bandura, A. (1988). Self-regulation of motivation and action through goal systems. In V. Hamilton, G. H. Bower, & N. H. Frijda (Eds.), *Cognitive perspectives on emotion and motivation* (pp. 37–61). Dordrecht, Netherlands: Kluwer Academic.

Bandura, A. (1997). *Self-efficacy: The exercise of control*. New York: W. H. Freeman & Co.

Bandura, A., Blanchard, E. B., & Ritter, B. (1969). Relative efficacy of desensitization and modeling approaches for inducing behavioral, affective, and attitudinal changes. *Journal of Personality and Social Psychology, 13*, 173–199.

Bandura, A., Cioffi, D., Taylor, B., & Brouillard, M. E. (1988). Perceived self-efficacy in coping with cognitive stressors and opioid activation. *Journal of Personality and Social Psychology, 55*, 479–488.

Bandura, A., & Menlove, F. L. (1968). Factors determining vicarious extinction of avoidance through symbolic modeling. *Journal of Personality and Social Psychology, 8*, 99–108.

Bandura, A., Ross, D., & Ross, S. A. (1963). Imitation of film-mediated aggressive models. *Journal of Abnormal and Social Psychology, 66*, 3–11.

Bandura, A., & Walters, R. (1963). *Social learning and personality development*. New York: Holt, Rinehart & Winston.

Banich, M. T. (1995). Interhemispheric processing: Theoretical considerations and empirical approaches. In R. J. Davidson, K. Hugdahl, et al. (Eds.) *Brain asymmetry*. Cambridge, MA: MIT Press.

Barbaree, H. E., & Marshall, W. L. (1991). The role of male sexual arousal in rape: Six models. *Journal of Consulting and Clinical Psychology, 59*, 621–630.

Barbato, G., Barker, C., Bender, C., Giesen, H. A., & Wehr, T. A. (1994). Extended sleep in humans in 14 hour nights (LD 10:14): Relationship between REM density and spontaneous awakening. *Electroencephalography and Clinical Neurophysiology, 90*, 291–297.

Barber, J. (1991). The locksmith model: Accessing hypnotic responsiveness. In S. J. Lynn & J. W. Rhue (Eds.), *Theories of hypnosis: Current models and perspectives* (pp. 241–274). New York: Guilford Press.

Barber, J. P., & Ellman, J. (1996). Advances in short-term dynamic psychotherapy. *Current Opinion in Psychiatry, 9*, 188–192.

Barber, T. X., Spanos, N. P., & Chaves, J. F. (1974). *Hypnosis, imagination, and human potentialities*. New York: Pergamon.

Barbuto, J. E., Jr. (1997). Taking the charisma out of transformational leadership. *Journal of Social Behavior and Personality, 12*(3), 689–697.

Bard, P. (1934). Emotion: The neuro-humoral basis of emotional reactions. In C. Murchison (Ed.), *Handbook of general experimental psychology*. Worcester, MA: Clark University Press.

Bardon, J. I. (1983). Psychology applied to education: A specialty in search of an identity. *American Psychologist, 38*, 185–196.

Barinaga, M. (1998). Is apoptosis key in Alzheimer's disease? *Science, 281*, 1303–1304.

Baron, R. A. (1993). Interviewers' moods and evaluations of job applicants: The role of applicant qualifications. *Journal of Applied Social Psychology, 23*, 253–271.

Barondes, S. H. (1998). *Mood genes: Hunting for origins of mania and depression*. New York: W. H. Freeman.

Bar-Or, O., Foreyt, J., Bouchard, C., Brownell, K. D., Dietz, W. H., Ravussin, E., Salbe, A. D., Schwenger, S., St. Jeor, S., & Torun, B. (1998). Physical activity, genetic, and nutritional considerations in childhood weight management. *Medicine and Science in Sports and Exercise, 30*(1), 2–10.

Barrera, M., Li, S. A., & Chassin, L. (1993). Ethnic group differences in vulnerability to parental alcoholism and life stress: A study of Hispanic and non-Hispanic Caucasian adolescents. *American Journal of Community Psychology, 21*(1), 15–35.

Barrett, G. V., & Depinet, R. L. (1991). A reconsideration of testing for competence rather than for intelligence. *American Psychologist, 46*, 1012–1024.

Bartlett, F. C. (1932). *Remembering: A study in experimental and social psychology*. New York: Macmillan.

Bartoshuk, L. M., Duffy, V. B., & Miller, I. J. (1994, December). PTC/PROP taste: Anatomy, psychophysics, and sex effects. Paper presented at the Kirin International Symposium on Bitter Taste. *Physiology and Behavior, 56*(6), 1165–1171.

Bartoshuk, L. M., Duffy, V. B., Reed, D., & Williams, A. (1996). Supertasting, earaches and head injury: Genetics and pathology alter our taste worlds. *Neuroscience and Biobehavioral Reviews, 20*(1), 79–87.

Bashore, T. R., & Rapp, R. E. (1993). Are there alternatives to traditional polygraph procedures? *Psychological Bulletin, 113*, 3–22.

Bass, B. M. (1985). *Leadership and performance beyond expectations*. New York: Free Press.

Bass, B. M. (1990). From transactional to transformational leadership: Learning to share the vision. *Organizational Dynamics, 18*, 19–31.

Bass, B. M. (1997). Does the transactional–transformational leadership paradigm transcend organizational and national boundaries? *American Psychologist, 52*(2), 130–139.

Bass, B. M. (1998). *Transformational leadership: Industrial, military, and educational impact*. Mahwah, NJ: Lawrence Erlbaum Associates, Inc.

Bass, C., & Murphy, M. (1995). Somatoform and personality disorders: Syndromal comorbidity and overlapping developmental pathways. *Journal of Psychosomatic Research, 39*, 403–427.

Bates, E., & Elman, J. (1996). Learning rediscovered. *Science, 274*, 1849–1850.

Bates, J. E., Marvinney, D., Kelly, T., Dodge, K. A., Bennett, D. S., & Pettit, G. S. (1994). Child-care history and kindergarten adjustment. *Developmental Psychology, 30*, 690–700.

Bateson, G., Jackson, D. D., Haley, J., & Weakland, J. (1956). Toward a theory of schizophrenia. *Behavioral Science, 1*, 251–264.

Batson, C. D. (1990). How social an animal? *American Psychologist, 45*, 336–346.

Batson, C. D., Batson, J. G., Slingsby, J. K., Harrell, K. L., Peekna, H. M., & Todd, R. M. (1991). Empathic joy and the empathy-altruism hypothesis. *Journal of Personality and Social Psychology, 61*, 413–426.

Baum, A. (1987). Crowding. In D. Stokols & I. Altman (Eds.), *Handbook of environmental psychology*. New York: Wiley.

Baum, A., Grunberg, N. E., & Singer, J. E. (1992). Biochemical measurements in the study of emotion. *Psychological Science, 3*, 56–62.

Baumeister, R. F. (1990). Suicide as escape from self. *Psychological Review, 97*, 90–113.

Baumeister, R. F., Smart, L., & Boden, J. (1996). Relation of threatened egotism to violence and aggression: The dark side of high self-esteem. *Psychological Review, 103*(1), 5–33.

Baumeister, R. F., & Tice, D. M. (1985). Self-esteem and responses to success and failure: Subsequent performance and intrinsic motivation. *Journal of Personality, 53*, 450–467.

Bayley, N. (1969). Consistency and variability in the growth of intelligence from birth to eighteen years. *Journal of Genetic Psychology, 25*, 165–196.

Baynes, K., Eliassen, J. C., Lutsep, H. L., & Gazzaniga, M. S. (1998). Modular organization of cognitive systems masked by interhemispheric integration. *Science, 280*, 902–905.

Beaulieu, C., & Colonnier, M. (1988). Richness of environment affects the number of contacts formed by boutons containing flat vesicles but does not alter the number of these boutons per neuron. *Journal of Comparative Neurology, 274*(3), 347–356.

Beaulieu, C., & Colonnier, M. (1989). Number and size of neurons and synapses in the motor cortex of cats raised in different environmental complexities. *Journal of Comparative Neurology, 289*(1), 178–181.

Bechara, A., Tranel, D., Damasio, H., Adolphs, R., Rockland, C., & Damasio, A. R. (1995). Double dissociation of conditioning and declarative knowledge relative to the amygdala and hippocampus in humans. *Science, 269*, 1115–1118.

Beck, A. T. (1963). Thinking and depression: 1. Idiosyncratic content in cognitive distortions. *Archives of General Psychiatry, 9*, 324–333.

Beck, A. T. (1967). *Depression: Clinical, experimental, and theoretical aspects*. New York: Hober.

Beck, A. T. (1972). *Depression: Causes and treatment*. Philadelphia: University of Pennsylvania Press.

Beck, A. T. (1976). *Cognitive therapy and emotional disorders*. New York: International Universities Press.

Beck, A. T. (1991). Cognitive therapy. *American Psychologist, 46*, 368–375.

Beck, A. T., & Weishaar, M. (1989). Cognitive therapy. In A. Freeman, K. M. Simon, L. E. Beutler, & H. Arkowitz (Eds.), *Comprehensive handbook of cognitive therapy*. New York: Plenum.

Beck, J. (1966). Effects of orientation and of shape similarity on perceptual grouping. *Perception and Psychophysics, 1*, 311–312.

Beck, J. G., Stanley, M. A., Baldwin, L. E., Deagle, E. A., III, & Averill, P. M. (1994). Comparison of cognitive therapy and relaxation training for panic disorder. *Journal of Consulting and Clinical Psychology, 62*, 818–826.

Becker, M. H. (1993). A medical sociologist looks at health promotion. *Journal of Health and Social Behavior, 34*, 1–6.

Bee, H. L. (1987). *The journey of adulthood*. New York: Macmillan.

Begg, I. M., Needham, D. R., & Bookbinder, M. (1993). Do backward messages unconsciously affect listeners? No. *Canadian Journal of Experimental Psychology, 47*, 1–14.

Beidel, D. C., Turner, M. W., & Trager, K. N. (1994). Test anxiety and childhood anxiety disorders in African-American and white school children. *Journal of Anxiety Disorders, 8*, 169–179.

Beisteiner, R., Altenmuller, E., Lang, W., & Lindinger, G. (1994). Musicians processing music: Measurement of brain potentials with EEG. *European Journal of Cognitive Psychology, 6*(3), 311–327.

Beitel, A. H., & Parke, R. D. (1998). Paternal involvement in infancy: The role of maternal and paternal attitudes. *Journal of Family Psychology, 12*(2), 268–288.

Bekerian, D. A., & Bowers, J. M. (1983). Eyewitness testimony: Were we misled? *Journal of Experimental Psychology: Learning, Memory, and Cognition, 9*, 139–145.

Bekhtereva, N. P., Gilerovich, E. G., Gurchin, F. A., Lukin, V. A., et al. (1990). The first results of the use of embryonic nervous tissue transplantation for the treatment of Parkinsonism. *Ahurnal Nevropatologii i Psikhiatrii Imeni S-S-Korsakova, 90*(11), 10–13.

Belansky, E. S., & Boggiano, A. K. (1994). Predicting helping behaviors: The role of gender and instrumental/expressive self-schemata. *Sex Roles, 30*, 647–662.

Belenkey, M., Clinchy, B., Goldberger, N., & Tarule, M. (1988). *Women's ways of knowing*. New York: Basic Books.

Bell, B. E., & Loftus, E. F. (1989). Trivial persuasion in the courtroom: The power of (a few) minor details. *Journal of Personality and Social Psychology, 56*, 669–679.

Bell, S. T., Kuriloff, P. J., & Lottes, I. (1994). Understanding attributions of blame in stranger rape and date rape situations: An examination of gender, race, identification, and students' social perceptions of rape victims. *Journal of Applied Social Psychology, 24*(19), 1719–1734.

Belsky, J. (1990). Parental and nonparental child care and children's socioemotional development: A decade in review. *Journal of Marriage and the Family, 52*, 885–903.

Belsky, J. (1993). Etiology of child maltreatment: A developmental-ecological analysis. *Psychological Bulletin, 114*, 413–434.

Belsky, J., & Rovine, M. J. (1988). Nonmaternal care in the first year of life and the security of infant-parent attachment. *Child Development, 59*, 157–167.

Bem, D. J. (1972). Self-perception theory. In L. Berkowitz (Ed.), *Advances in experimental social psychology*. New York: Academic.

Bem, D. J. (1996). Exotic becomes erotic: A developmental theory of sexual orientation. *Psychological Review, 103*(2), 320–335.

Bem, S. L. (1985). Androgyny and gender schema theory: A conceptual and empirical integration. In T. B. Sonderegger (Ed.), *Nebraska symposium on motivation*. Lincoln: University of Nebraska Press.

Bem, S. L. (1993). *The lenses of gender*. New Haven, CT: Yale University Press.

Benbow, C. P., & Arjmand, O. (1990). Predictors of high academic achievement in mathematics and science by mathematically talented students: A longitudinal study. *Journal of Educational Psychology, 82*(3), 430–441.

Benet-Martinez, V., & Waller, N. G. (1997). Further evidence for the cross-cultural generality of the Big Seven Factor model: Indigenous and imported Spanish personality constructs. *Journal of Personality, 65*(3), 567–598.

Benjamin, L. T., Jr., Durkin, M., Link, M., Vestal, M., & Acord, J. (1992). Wundt's American doctoral students. *American Psychologist, 47*, 123–131.

Bentall, R. P. (1990). The illusion of reality: A review and integration of psychological research on hallucinations. *Psychological Bulletin, 107*, 82–95.

Berenbaum, S. A., & Snyder, E. (1995). Early hormonal influences on childhood sex-typed activity and playmate preferences: Implications for the development of sexual orientation. *Developmental Psychology, 3*, 31–42.

Berg, T. R. (1991). The importance of equity perception and job satisfaction in predicting employee intent to stay at television stations. *Group and Organizational Studies, 16*, 268–284.

Berhardt, P. C. (1997). Influences of serotonin and testosterone in aggression and dominance: Convergence with social psychology. *American Psychological Society, 6*(2), 44–48.

Berk, L. E. (1994). *Child development* (3rd. ed.). Boston: Allyn & Bacon.

Berkley, K. J. (1997). Sex differences in pain. *Behavioral and Brain Sciences, 20*(3), 371–380.

Berkowitz, L. (1964). *The effects of observing violence*. San Francisco: Freeman.

Berkowitz, L. (1989). Frustration-aggression hypothesis: Examination and reformulation. *Psychological Bulletin, 106*, 59–73.

Berkowitz, L. (1990). On the formation and regulation of anger and aggression. *American Psychologist, 45*, 494–503.

Berkowitz, L. (1993). Pain and aggression: Some findings and implications. *Motivation and Emotion, 17,* 277–294.

Berlin, B., & Kay, P. (1969). *Basic color terms: Their universality and evolution.* Berkeley: University of California Press.

Berlin, I. N. (1985). Prevention of adolescent suicide among some native American tribes. In S. C. Feinstein, M. Sugar, A. H. Esman, J. G. Looney, A. Z. Schwartzberg, & A. D. Sorosky (Eds.), *Annals of the American Society for Adolescent Psychiatry: Vol. 12, Adolescent psychiatry: Developmental and clinical studies.* Chicago: University of Chicago Press.

Berman, F. E., & Miner, J. B. (1985). Motivation to manage at the top executive level: A test of the hierarchic role-motivation theory. *Personnel Psychology, 38,* 377–391.

Bernal, G., & Berger, S. M. (1976). Vicarious eyelid conditioning. *Journal of Personality and Social Psychology, 34,* 62–68.

Berndt, T. J. (1992). Friendship and friends' influence in adolescence. *Psychological Science, 1,* 156–159.

Bernstein, D. & Ebbesen, E. (1978). Reinforcement and substitution in humans: A multiple-response analysis. *Journal of the Experimental Analysis of Behavior, 30,* 243–253.

Bernstein, I. L. (1988, September). What does learning have to do with weight loss and cancer? Paper presented at a science and public policy seminar sponsored by the Federation of Behavioral, Psychological, and Cognitive Sciences, Washington, DC.

Bernstein, I. L. (1991). Aversion conditioning in response to cancer and cancer treatment. *Clinical Psychology Review, 11*(2), 185–191.

Berridge, K. C., & Robinson, T. E. (1995). The mind of an addicted brain: Neural sensitization of wanting versus liking. *Current Directions in Psychological Science, 4,* 71–76.

Berry, D. S., & Landry, J. C. (1997). Facial maturity and daily social interaction. *Journal of Personality and Social Psychology, 72*(3), 570–580.

Berry, D. S., & Pennebaker, J. W. (1993). Nonverbal and verbal emotional expression and health. *Psychotherapy and Psychosomatics, 59,* 11–19.

Berscheid, E., Snyder, M., & Omoto, A. M. (1989). The relationship closeness inventory: Assessing the closeness of interpersonal relationships. *Journal of Personality and Social Psychology, 57,* 792–807.

Bertenthal, B. I., Campos, J. J., & Kermoian, R. (1994). An epigenetic perspective on the development of self-produced locomotion and its consequences. *Current Directions in Psychological Science, 3,* 140–145.

Best, C. T., & Queen, H. F. (1989). Baby, it's in your smile: Right hemiface bias in infant emotional expressions. *Developmental Psychology, 25,* 264–276.

Bettelheim, B. (1987). *A good enough parent: A book on child-rearing.* New York: Knopf.

Betz, N. E. (1992). Counseling uses of career self-efficacy theory. *Career Development Quarterly, 41*(1), 22–26.

Beutler, L. E., Williams, R. E., Wakefield, P. J., & Entwistle, S. R. (1995). Bridging scientist and practitioner perspectives in clinical psychology. *American Psychologist, 50,* 984–994.

Bexton, W. H., Heron, W., & Scott, T. H. (1954). Effects of decreased variation in the sensory environment. *Canadian Journal of Psychology, 8,* 70–76.

Bhatt, R. S. (1997). The interface between perception and cognition: Feature detection, visual pop-out effects, feature integration, and long-term memory in infancy. In C. Rovee-Collier & L. P. Lipsitt (Eds.), *Advances in infancy research.* Greenwich, CT: Ablex Publishing Corporation.

Bhinder and the Canadian Human Rights Commision vs. The Canadian National Railway (1985) 2 S.C.R. 561.

Bickerton, D. (1995). *Language and human behavior.* Seattle: University of Washington Press.

Bickman, L., Teger, A., Gabriele, T., McLaughlin, C., Berger, M., & Sunaday, E. (1973). Dormitory density and helping behavior. *Environment and Behavior, 5,* 465–466.

Binion, V. J. (1990). Psychological androgyny: A black female perspective. *Sex Roles, 22,* 487–507.

Biondi, M., & Zannino, L. G. (1997). Psychological stress, neuroimmunomodulation, and susceptibility to infectious diseases in animals and man: A review. *Psychotherapy and Psychosomatics, 66*(1), 3–26.

Bivens, J. A., & Berk, L. E. (1990). A longitudinal study of the development of elementary school children's private speech. *Merrill-Palmer Quarterly, 36,* 443–463.

Black, D. W., & Larson, C. L. (1999). *Bad boys, bad men: Confronting antisocial personality disorder.* New York: Oxford University Press.

Blagrove, M. (1996). Problems with the cognitive psychological modeling of dreaming. *The Journal of Mind and Behavior, 17,* 99–134.

Blakemore, C., & Cooper, G. F. (1970). Development of the brain depends on the visual environment. *Nature, 228,* 477–478.

Blanc-Garin, J., Fauré, S., & Sabio, P. (1993). Right hemisphere performance and competence in processing mental images in a case of partial interhemispheric disconnection. *Brain and Cognition, 22,* 118–133.

Blanchard, E. B., Appelbaum, K. A., Radnitz, C. L., Michultka, D., Morrill, B., Kirsch, C., Hillhouse, J., Evans, D. D., Guarnieri, P., Attanasio, V., Andrasik, F., Jaccard, J., & Dentinger, M. P. (1990). Placebo-controlled evaluation of abbreviated progressive muscle relaxation and of relaxation combined with cognitive therapy in the treatment of tension headache. *Journal of Consulting and Clinical Psychology, 58,* 210–215.

Bland, R. C., Newman, S. C., & Orn, H. (1988). Period prevalence of psychiatric disorders in Edmonton. *Acta Psychiatrica Scandinavia, 77* (Supp. 388), 33–42. © Munksgaard International Publishers Ltd. Copenhagen, Denmark.

Blatt, S. J. (1995). The destructiveness of perfectionism. *American Psychologist, 50,* 1003–1020.

Block, J., & Robins, R. W. (1993). A longitudinal study of consistency and change in self-esteem from early adolescence to early adulthood. *Child Development, 64,* 909–923.

Bloom, F. E. (1981, October). Neuropeptides. *Scientific American,* 148–168.

Bobo, L., & Kluegel, J. R. (1997). Status, ideology, and dimensions of whites' racial beliefs and attitudes: Progress and stagnation. In S. A. Tuch & J. K. Martin (Eds.), *Racial attitudes in the 1990s: Continuity and change.* Westport, CT: Praeger.

Bohannon, J. N., III (1988). Flashbulb memories for the space shuttle disaster: A tale of two theories. *Cognition, 29,* 179–196.

Boivin, D. B., Duffy, J. F., Kronauer, R. F., & Czeisler, C. A. (1996). Dose-response relationships for resetting of human circadian clock by light. *Nature, 379,* 540–542.

Bond, C. F., Jr., & Titus, L. J. (1983). Social facilitation: A meta-analysis of 241 studies. *Psychological Bulletin, 94,* 265–292.

Bond, R., & Smith, P. B. (1996). Culture and conformity: A meta-analysis of studies using Asch's (1952b, 1956) line judgement task. *Psychological Bulletin, 119,* 111–137.

Boninger, D. S., Brock, T. C., Cook, T. D., Gruder, C. L., & Romer, D. (1990). Discovery of reliable attitude change persistence resulting from a transmitter tuning set. *Psychological Science, 1,* 268–271.

Bonnet, M. H. (1980). Sleep, performance, and mood after the energy-expenditure equivalent of 40 hours of sleep deprivation. *Psychophysiology, 17,* 56–63.

Borg, E., & Counter, S. A. (1989, August). The middle-ear muscles. *Scientific American,* 74–80.

Borkenau, P., & Ostendorf, F. (1998). The Big Five as states: How useful is the five-factor model to describe intraindividual variations over time? *Journal of Research in Personality, 32*(2), 202–221.

Bornstein, M. H., Tal, J., Rahn, C., Galperin, C. Z., Pecheux, M. G., Lamour, M., Toda, S., Azuma, H., Ogino, M., & Tamis-Lemonda, C. S. (1992). Functional analysis of the contents of maternal speech to infants of 5 and 13 months in four cultures: Argentina, France, Japan, and the United States. *Developmental Psychology, 28,* 593–603.

Bornstein, R. F. (1989). Exposure and affect: Overview and meta-analysis of research, 1968–1987. *Psychological Bulletin, 106,* 265–289.

Bornstein, R. F. (1992). The dependent personality: Developmental, social, and clinical perspectives. *Psychological Bulletin, 112,* 3–23.

Boronat, C. B., & Logan, G. D. (1997). The role of attention in automatization: Does attention operate at encoding, or retrieval, or both? *Memory and Cognition, 25*(1), 36–46.

Borrie, R. A. (1991). The use of restricted environmental stimulation therapy in treating addictive behaviors. *International Journal of the Addictions, 25,* 995–1015.

Bosma, H., Richard, P., Siegrist, J., & Marmot, M. (1998). Two alternative job stress models and the risk of coronary heart disease. *American Journal of Public Health, 88*(1), 68–74.

Botschner, J. V. (1996). Reconsidering male friendships: A social-development perspective. In C. W. Tolman et al. (Eds.), *Problems of theoretical psychology.* North York, ON: Captus Press.

Botwin, M. D., Buss, D. M., & Shackelford, T. K. (1997). Personality and mate preferences: Five factors in mate selection and marital satisfaction. *Journal of Personality, 65*(1), 107–136.

Botwinick, J. (1984). *Aging and behavior: A comprehensive integration of research findings* (3rd ed.). New York: Springer-Verlag.

Bouchard, T. J., Jr. (1997). The genetics of personality. In K. Blum et al. (Eds.), *Handbook of psychiatric genetics*. Boca Raton, FL: CRC Press, Inc.

Bouchard, T. J., Jr., & Hur, Y. (1998). Genetic and environmental influences on the continuous scales of the Myers-Briggs Type Indicator: An analysis based on twins reared apart. *Journal of Personality, 66*(2), 135–147.

Bouchard, T. J., Jr., Lykken, D. T., McGue, M., Segal, N. L., & Tellegen, A. (1990). Sources of human psychological differences: The Minnesota study of twins reared apart. *Science, 250,* 223–228.

Bouchard, T. J., Jr., & McGue, M. (1981). Familial studies of intelligence: A review. *Science, 212,* 1055–1058.

Bourque, L. B. (1989). *Defining rape.* Durham, NC: Duke University Press.

Bourtchuladze, R., Frenguelli, B., Blendy, J., Cioffi, D., Schutz, G., & Silva, A. J. (1994). Deficient long-term memory in mice with a targeted mutation of the camp-responsive element-binding protein. *Cell, 79,* 59–68.

Boutcher, S. H. (1992). Attention and athletic performance: An integrated approach. In Thelma S. Horn (Ed.), *Advances in sport psychology* (pp. 251–265). Champaign, IL: Human Kinetics.

Bouton, M. E. (1994). Conditioning, remembering, and forgetting. *Journal of Experimental Psychology: Animal Behavior Processes, 20,* 219–231.

Bovbjerg, D. H., Redd, W. H., Jacobsen, P. B., Manne, S. L., Taylor, K. L., Surbone, A., Crown, J. P., Norton, L., Gilewski, T. A., Hudis, C. F., Reichman, B. S., Kaufman, R. J., Currie, V. E., & Hakes, T. B. (1992). An experimental analysis of classically conditioned nausea during cancer chemotherapy. *Psychosomatic Medicine, 54,* 623–637.

Bowden, E. M., & Beeman, M. J. (1998). Getting the right idea: Semantic activation in the right hemisphere may help solve insight problems. *American Psychological Society, 9*(6), 435–440.

Bower, G. H. (1981). Mood and memory. *American Psychologist, 36,* 126–148.

Bower, T. G. R. (1966, December). The visual world of infants. *Scientific American,* 80–92.

Bowers, K. S. (1979). Time distortion and hypnotic ability: Underestimating the duration of hypnosis. *Journal of Abnormal Psychology, 88,* 435–439.

Bowers, K. S. (1992). Imagination and dissociation in hypnotic responding. *International Journal of Clinical and Experimental Hypnosis, 40,* 253–275.

Bowers, K. S., Regehr, G., Balthazard, C., & Parker, K. (1990). Intuition in the context of discovery. *Cognitive Psychology, 22,* 72–110.

Bowlby, J. (1977). The making and breaking of affectional bonds: Etiology and psychopathology in the light of attachment theory. *British Journal of Psychiatry, 130,* 201–210.

Bowlby, J. (1988). *A secure base.* New York: Basic Books.

Bowring, M. A., & Kovacs, M. (1992). Difficulties in diagnosing manic disorders among children and adolescents. *Journal of the American Academy of Child and Adolescent Psychiatry, 31*(4), 611–614.

Boyd, B., & Wandersman, A. (1991). Predicting undergraduate condom use with the Fishbein and Ajzen and the Triandis attitude-behavior models: Implications for public health interventions. *Journal of Applied Social Psychology, 21,* 1810–1830.

Boynton, R. M. (1988). Color vision. *Annual Review of Psychology, 39,* 69–101.

Boysen, S. T., & Berntson, G. G. (1989). Numerical competence in a chimpanzee (Pan troglodytes). *Journal of Comparative Psychology, 103,* 23–31.

Boyum, L. A., & Parke, R. D. (1995). The role of family emotional expressiveness in the development of children's social competence. *Journal of Marriage and the Family, 57*(3), 593–608.

Brabeck, M. M., & Larned, A. G. (1997). What we do not know about women's ways of knowing. In M. R. Walsh (Ed.), *Women, men, and gender: Ongoing debates.* New Haven, CT: Yale University Press.

Bradley, B. P. (1990). Behavioural addictions: Common features and treatment implications. *British Journal of Addiction, 85,* 1417–1419.

Bradley, C. L., & Marcia, J. E. (1998). Generativity-stagnation: A five-category model. *Journal of Personality, 66*(1), 39–44.

Brainerd, C. J., Reyna, V. F., & Brandse, E. (1995). Are children's false memories more persistent than their true memories? *Psychological Science, 6,* 359–364.

Branden, N. (1980). *The psychology of romantic love.* Los Angeles: Tarcher.

Brannon, E. M., & Terrace, H. S. (1998). Ordering of the numerosities 1 to 9 by monkeys. *Science, 282,* 746–750.

Braun, A. R., Balkin, T. J., Wesensten, N. J., Gwadry, F., Carson, R. E., Varga, M., Baldwin, P., Belenky, G., & Herscovitch, P. (1998). Dissociated pattern of activity in visual cortices and their projections during human rapid eye movement sleep. *Science, 279,* 91–96.

Breedlove, S. M. (1997). Sex on the brain. *Nature, 389,* 801.

Brehm, J. W. (1966). *A theory of psychological reactance.* New York: Academic.

Brennen, K. A., & Shaver, P. R. (1995). Dimensions of adult attachment, affect regulation, and romantic relationship functioning. *Personality and Social Psychology Bulletin, 21,* 267–283.

Breton, J.-J., Valla, J-P., & Lambert, J. (1993). Industrial disaster and mental health of children and their parents. *Journal of the American Academy of Child and Adolescent Psychiatry, 32*(2), 438–445.

Bretschneider, J. G., & McCoy, N. L. (1988). Sexual interest and behavior in healthy 80- to 102-year-olds. *Archives of Sexual Behavior, 17,* 109–129.

Brewer, J. B., Zhao, Z., Desmond, J. E., Glover, G. H., & Gabrieli, J. D. (1998). Making memories: Brain activity that predicts how well visual experience will be remembered. *Science, 281,* 1185–1188.

Bridges, K. M. B. (1932). Emotional development in early infancy. *Child Development, 3,* 324–341.

Broadbent, D. E. (1958). *Perception and communication.* London: Pergamon.

Broberg, A. G., Wessels, H., Lamb, M. E., & Hwang, C. P. (1997). Effects of day care on the development of cognitive abilities in 8-year-olds: A longitudinal study. *Developmental Psychology, 33*(1), 62–69.

Brodsky, A. E. (1996). Resilient single mothers in risky neighborhoods: Negative psychological sense of community. *Journal of Community Psychology, 24*(4), 347–363.

Brody, E. M., Lawton, M. P., and Liebowitz, B. (1984). Senile dementia: Public policy and adequate institutional care. *American Journal of Public Health, 74,* 1381–1383.

Brody, G. H. (1998). Sibling relationship quality: Its causes and consequences. *Annual Review in Psychology, 49,* 1–24.

Brody, L. R. (1997). Gender and emotion: Beyond stereotypes. *Journal of Social Issues, 53*(2), 369–392.

Bronfenbrenner, U. (1979). *The ecology of human development.* Cambridge, MA: Harvard University Press.

Bronfenbrenner, U. (1989, September). Who cares for children? Invited address, UNESCO, Paris.

Bronson, G. W. (1997). The growth of visual capacity: Evidence from infant scanning patterns. In C. Rovee-Collier & L. P. Lipsitt (Eds.), *Advances in infancy research.* Greenwich, CT: Ablex Publishing Corporation.

Brooks-Gunn, J., & Furstenberg, F. F., Jr. (1989). Adolescent sexual behavior. *American Psychologist, 44,* 249–257.

Broughton, R. J. (1991). Field studies of sleep/wake patterns and performance: A laboratory experience. *Canadian Journal of Psychology, 45,* 240–253.

Brown, A. S. (1989). *How to increase your memory power.* Glenview, IL: Scott, Foresman.

Brown, G. M. (1994). Light, melatonin and the sleep-wake cycle. *Journal of Psychiatry & Neuroscience, 19,* 345–353.

Brown, K. W., & Moskowitz, D. S. (1998). Dynamic stability of behavior: The rhythms of our interpersonal lives. *Journal of Personality, 66*(1), 105–108.

Brown, L. M. (1998). Raising their voices: The politics of girls' anger. Cambridge, MA: Harvard University Press.

Brown, N. (1997). Context memory and the selection of frequency estimation strategies. *Journal of Experimental Psychology: Learning, Memory, and Cognition, 23*(4), 898–914.

Brown, R. (1970). The first sentences of child and chimpanzee. In R. Brown (Ed.), *Psycholinguistics: Selected papers.* New York: Free Press.

Brown, R., & Kulik, J. (1977). Flashbulb memories. *Cognition, 5,* 73–99.

Brown, T. A., & Barlow, D. H. (1995). Long-term outcome in cognitive-behavioral treatment of panic disorder: Clinical predictors and alternative strategies for assessment. *Journal of Consulting and Clinical Psychology, 63,* 754–765.

Browne, B. A. (1998). Gender stereotypes in advertising on children's television in the 1990s: A cross-national analysis. *Journal of Advertising, 27*(1), 83–96.

Bruch, M. A., Berko, E. H., & Haase, R. F. (1998). Shyness, masculine ideology, physical attractiveness, and emotional inexpressiveness: Testing a mediational model of men's interpersonal competence. *Journal of Counseling Psychology, 45*(1), 84–97.

Bruner, J. (1990). *Acts of meaning.* Cambridge, MA: Harvard University Press.

Bruner, J. (1997). Celebrating divergence: Piaget and Vygotsky. *Human Development, 40,* 63–73.

Bryant, R. A., & McConkey, K. M. (1989). Hypnotic blindness: A behavioral and experiential analysis. *Journal of Abnormal Psychology, 98,* 71–77.

Buchanan, C. M., Eccles, J. S., & Becker, J. B. (1992). Are adolescents the victims of raging hormones? Evidence for activational effects of hormones on moods and behavior at adolescence. *Psychological Bulletin, 111,* 62–107.

Buchsbaum, M. S., & Hazlett, E. A. (1997). Functional brain imaging and aging in schizophrenia. *Schizophrenia Research, 27*(2/3), 129–141.

Buchwald, A. M., & Rudick-Davis, D. (1993). The symptoms of major depression. *Journal of Abnormal Psychology, 102,* 197–205.

Buck, R., Losow, J. I., Murphy, M. M., & Costanzo, P. (1992). Social facilitation and inhibition of emotional expression and communication. *Journal of Personality and Social Psychology, 6,* 962–968.

Bukowski, W. M., Gauze, C., Hoza, B., & Newcomb, A. F. (1993). Differences and consistency between same-sex and other-sex peer relationships during early adolescence. *Developmental Psychology, 29,* 255–263.

Bulcroft, R. A., & Bulcroft, K. A. (1993). Race differences in attitudinal and motivational factors in the decision to marry. *Journal of Marriage and the Family, 55,* 338–355.

Bullock, W. A., & Gilliland, K. (1993). Eysenck's arousal theory of introversion-extraversion: A converging measures investigation. *Journal of Personality and Social Psychology, 64,* 113–123.

Bunge, V. P., & Levett, A. (1998). *Family violence in Canada: A statistical profile.* Ottawa: Minister responsible for Statistics Canada, Minister of Industry.

Burchinal, M., Lee, M., & Ramey, C. (1989). Type of day-care and preschool intellectual development in disadvantaged children. *Child Development, 60,* 128–137.

Burg, B., & Belmont, I. (1990). Mental abilities of children from different cultural backgrounds in Israel. *Journal of Cross-Cultural Psychology, 21,* 90–108.

Burger, J. M., & Hemans, L. T. (1988). Desire for control and the use of attribution processes. *Journal of Personality, 56,* 531–546.

Burman, B., Mednick, S. A., Machon, R. A., Parnas, J., & Schulsinger, F. (1987). Children at high risk for schizophrenia: Parent and offspring perceptions of family relationships. *Journal of Abnormal Psychology, 96,* 364–366.

Burn, S. M. (1991). Social psychology and the stimulation of recycling behaviors: The block leader approach. *Journal of Applied Social Psychology, 21,* 611–629.

Burnet, P. W., Eastwood, S. L., & Harrison, P. J. (1996). 5-HT-sub(1A) and 5-HT-sub(2A) receptor mRNAs and binding site densities are differentially altered in schizophrenia. *Neuropsychopharmacology, 15*(5), 442–455.

Bushman, B. J., & Baumeister, R. F. (1998). Threatened egotism, narcissism, self-esteem, and direct and displaced aggression: Does self-love or self-hate lead to violence? *Journal of Personality & Social Psychology, 75*(1), 219–229.

Bushman, B. J., & Geen, R. G. (1990). Role of cognitive-emotional mediators and individual differences in the effects of media violence on aggression. *Journal of Personality and Social Psychology, 58,* 156–163.

Buss, D. M. (1988). Love acts: The evolutionary biology of love. In R. J. Sternberg & M. L. Barnes (Eds.), *The psychology of love.* New Haven, CT: Yale University Press.

Buss, D. M. (1995). Psychological sex differences: Origins through sexual selection. *American Psychologist, 50,* 164–168.

Buss, D. M., Haselton, M. G., Shackelford, T. K., Bleske, A. L., & Wakefield, J. C. (1998). Adaptations, exaptations, and spandrels. *American Psychologist, 53*(5), 533–548.

Butcher, J. N., Graham, J. R., Dahlstrom, W. G., & Bowman, E. (1990). The MMPI-2 with college students. *Journal of Personality Assessment, 54,* 1–15.

Butcher, J. N., Lim, J., & Nezami, E. (1998). Objective study of abnormal personality in cross-cultural settings: The Minnesota Multiphasic Personality Inventory (MMPI-2). *Journal of Cross-Cultural Psychology, 29*(1), 189–211.

Butler, S. F., & Strupp, H. H. (1991). Psychodynamic psychotherapy. In M. Hersen, A. E. Kazdin, & A. S. Bellack (Eds.), *The clinical psychology handbook* (2nd ed.). New York; Pergamon.

Butterfield-Picard, H., & Magno, J. B. (1982). Hospice the adjective, not the noun: The future of a national priority. *American Psychologist, 37,* 1254–1259.

Byne, W. (1994, May). The biological evidence challenged. *Scientific American,* 50–55.

Byrne, A., & Byrne, D. G. (1993). The effect of exercise on depression, anxiety, and other mood states. *Journal of Psychosomatic Research, 37,* 565–574.

Cabeza, R., Kapur, S., Craik, F. I., McIntosh, A. R., Houle, S., & Tulving, E. (1997). Functional neuroanatomy of recall and recognition: A PET study of episodic memory. *Journal of Cognitive Neuroscience, 9*(2), 254–265.

Cabeza, R., & Nyberg, L. (1997). Imaging cognition: An empirical review of PET studies with normal subjects. *Journal of Cognitive Neuroscience, 9*(1), 1–26.

Cacioppo, J. T., Petty, R. E., Feinstein, J. A., & Jarvis, W. B. G. (1996). Dispositional differences in cognitive motivation: The life and times of individuals varying in need for cognition. *Psychological Bulletin, 119,* 197–253.

Cadoret, R. J., Yates, W. R., Troughton, E., Woodworth, G., & Stewart, M. A. (1995). Genetic-environmental interaction in the genesis of aggressivity and conduct disorders. *Archives of General Psychiatry, 52,* 916–924.

Caffarella, R. S., & Olson, S. K. (1993). Psychosocial development of women: A critical review of the literature. *Adult Education Quarterly, 43,* 125–151.

Cairns, R. B., & Cairns, B. D. (1994). *Lifelines and risks: Pathways of youth in our time.* Cambridge, England: Cambridge University Press.

Caldera, Y. M., Huston, A. C., & O'Brien, M. (1989). Social interactions and play patterns of parents and toddlers with feminine, masculine, and neutral toys. *Child Development, 109,* 70–76.

Call, V., Sprecher, S., & Schwartz, P. (1995). The incidence and frequency of marital sex in a national sample. *Journal of Marriage and the Family, 57*(3), 639–652.

Calvert, S. L. (1998). *Children's journeys through the information age.* New York: McGraw-Hill.

Calvin, W. H. (1996). *The cerebral code: Thinking a thought in the mosaics of the mind.* Cambridge, MA & London: The MIT Press.

Camara, W. J., & Schneider, D. L. (1994). Integrity tests: Facts and unresolved issues. *American Psychologist, 49,* 112–119.

Cameron, P., & Cameron, K. (1998). "Definitive" University of Chicago sex survey overestimated prevalence of homosexual identity. *Psychological Reports, 82*(3, Pt 1), 861–862.

Campbell, S. S., & Murphy, P. J. (1998). Extraocular circadian phototransduction in humans. *Science, 279,* 396–399.

Campfield, L. A., Smith, F. J., & Burn, P. (1998). Strategies and potential molecular targets for obesity treatment. *Science, 280,* 1383–1387.

Campion, M. A., Palmer, D. K., & Campion, J. E. (1998). Structuring employment interviews to improve reliability, validity, and users' reactions. *Current Directions in Psychological Science, 7*(3), 77–82.

Campis, L. B., Hebden-Curtis, C. J., & DeMaso, D. R. (1993). Developmental differences in detection and disclosure of sexual abuse. *Journal of the American Academy of Child and Adolescent Psychiatry, 32,* 920–924.

Camras, L. A., Oster, H., Campos, J. J., Miyake, K., & Bradshaw, D. (1992). Japanese and American infants' responses to arm restraint. *Developmental Psychology, 28,* 578–583.

Canada (1992). *Foetal alcohol syndrome: A preventable tragedy.* Ottawa: Standing Committee on Health and Welfare, Social Affairs, Seniors and the Status of Women.

Canadian Centre for Justice Statistics (1997). *Juristat: Canadian Crime Statistics, 18,* 11 (85–002–XPE).

Canadian Council on Animal Care (1989). *Ethics of animal investigation.* Ottawa.

Canadian Human Right Commission (1984). *Action Travail des Femmes vs. CN Rail* CHRR D 5: 2327.

Canadian Psychological Association (1991). *Canadian code of ethics for psychologists.* Old Chelsea, PQ: Canadian Psychological Association.

Canadian Study of Health and Aging Working Group (1994). Canadian study of health and aging: Study methods and prevalence of dementia. *Canadian Medical Association Journal, 150,* 899–913.

Canavan-Gumpert, D. (1977). Generating reward and cost orientations through praise and criticism. *Journal of Personality and Social Psychology, 35,* 501–513.

Cannon, T. D., & Marco, E. (1994). Structural brain abnormalities as indicators of vulnerability to schizophrenia. *Schizophrenia Bulletin, 20,* 89–102.

Cannon, T. D., Mednick, S. A., & Parnas, J. (1990). Antecedents of predominantly negative- and predominantly positive-symptom schizophrenia in a high-risk population. *Archives of General Psychiatry, 47*(7), 622–632.

Cannon, W. B. (1927). The James-Lange theory of emotion: A critical examination and an alternative theory. *American Journal of Psychology, 39,* 106–124.

Cannon-Bowers, J. A., & Salas, E. (1998). Team performance and training in complex environments: Recent findings from applied research. *American Psychological Society, 7*(3), 83–87.

Capaldi, D. M., Crosby, L., & Stoolmiller, M. (1996). Predicting the timing of first sexual intercourse for at-risk adolescent males. *Child Development, 67,* 344–359.

Carducci, B. J., & Stein, N. D. (1988, April). The personal and situational pervasiveness of shyness in college students: A nine-year comparison. Paper presented at the meeting of the Southeastern Psychological Association, New Orleans.

Carland, J. C., Carland, J. W., Ensley, M. D., & Stewart, H. W. (1994). The implications of cognition and learning styles for management education. *Management Learning, 25,* 413–431.

Carless, S. A. (1998). Gender differences in transformational leadership: An examination of superior, leader, and subordinate perspectives. *Sex Roles, 39*(11/12), 887–902.

Carli, L. L. (1997). Biology does not create gender differences in personality. In M. R. Walsh (Ed.), *Women, men, and gender: Ongoing debates.* New Haven, CT: Yale University Press.

Carlson, C. R., Gantz, F. P., & Masters, J. C. (1983). Adults' emotional states and recognition of emotion in young children. *Motivation and Emotion, 7,* 81–102.

Carpenter, P. A., Just, M. A., & Shell, P. (1990). What one intelligence test measures: A theoretical account of the processing in the Raven Progressive Matrices Test. *Psychological Review, 97*(3), 404–431.

Carr, M., Borkowski, J. G., & Maxwell, S. E. (1991). Motivational components of underachievement. *Developmental Psychology, 27,* 108–118.

Carton, J. S., & Nowicki, S. (1994). Antecedents of individual differences in locus of control of reinforcement: A critical review. *Genetic, Social, and General Psychology Monographs, 120*(1), 31–81.

Carton, J. S., Nowicki, S., & Balser, G. M. (1996). An observational study of antecedents of locus of control of reinforcement. *International Journal of Behavioral Development, 19*(1), 161–175.

Caruso, G. A. L., & Corsini, D. A. (1994). The prevalence of behavior problems among toddlers in child care. *Early Education and Development, 5,* 27–40.

Carver, C. S., & Scheier, M. F. (1990). Origins and functions of positive and negative affect: A control-process view. *Psychological Review, 97,* 19–35.

Casagrande, M., Violani, C., Lucidi, F., & Buttinelli, E. (1996). Variations in sleep mentation as a function of time of night. *International Journal of Neuroscience, 85*(1/2), 19–30.

Cascio, W. F. (1995). Whither industrial and organizational psychology in a changing world of work? *American Psychologist, 50,* 928–939.

Caspi, A., Elder, G. H., & Bem, D. J. (1988). Moving away from the world: Life-course patterns of shy children. *Developmental Psychology, 24,* 824–831.

Cassidy, J., & Berlin, L. J. (1994). The insecure/ambivalent pattern of attachment: Theory and research. *Child Development, 65,* 971–991.

Cattell, R. B. (1965). *The scientific analysis of personality.* Baltimore: Penguin.

Cavalier, A. R., Ferretti, R. P., & Hodges, A. E. (1997). Self-management within a classroom token economy for students with learning disabilities. *Research in Development Disabilities, 18*(3), 167–178.

Cavanagh, P., & Leclerc, Y. G. (1989). Shape from shadows. *Journal of Experimental Psychology: Human Perception and Performance, 15,* 3–27.

Ceci, S. J. (1991). How much does schooling influence general intelligence and its cognitive components? A reassessment of the evidence. *Developmental Psychology, 27,* 703–722.

Ceci, S. J., & Bruck, M. (1993). Suggestibility of the child witness: A historical review and synthesis. *Psychological Bulletin, 113,* 403–439.

Ceci, S. J., Rosenblum, T. B., & Kumpf, M. (1998). The shrinking gap between high- and low-scoring groups: Current trends and possible causes. In U. Neisser (Ed.), *The rising curve: Long-term gains in IQ*

and related measures (pp. 287–302). Washington, DC: American Psychological Association.

Ceci, S. J., & Williams, W. M. (1997). Schooling, intelligence, and income. *American Psychologist, 52*(10), 1051–1058.

Celuch, K., & Slama, M. (1995). Getting along and getting ahead as motives for self-presentation: Their impact on advertising effectiveness. *Journal of Applied Social Psychology, 25,* 1700–1713.

Centers for Disease Control and Prevention. (1996, September 27). CDS surveillance summaries. *Morbidity and Mortality Weekly Report, 45* (No. SS-4).

Cermak, L. S. (1975). *Improving your memory.* New York: Norton.

Chaiken, S., & Eagly, A. H. (1983). Communication modality as a determinant of persuasion: The role of communicator salience. *Journal of Personality and Social Psychology, 45,* 241–256.

Challis, G. B., & Stam, H. J. (1992). A longitudinal study of the development of anticipatory nausea and vomiting in cancer chemotherapy patients: The role of absorption and autonomic perception. *Health Psychology, 11*(3), 181–189.

Chalmers, D. J. (1996). *Conscious mind: In search of a fundamental theory.* New York: Oxford University Press.

Chamberlain, K., & Zika, S. (1990). The minor events approach to stress: Support for the use of daily hassles. *British Journal of Psychology, 81,* 469–481.

Chamberlain, K., & Zika, S. (1992). Religiosity, meaning in life, and psychological well-being. In J. F. Schumaker (Ed.), *Religion and mental health.* New York: Oxford University Press.

Chambless, D. L., & Hollon, S. D. (1998). Defining empirically supported therapies. *Journal of Consulting and Clinical Psychology, 66*(1), 7–18.

Chamizo, V. D., & Mackintosh, N. J. (1989). Latent learning and latent inhibition in maze discriminations. *Quarterly Journal of Experimental Psychology, 41B,* 21–31.

Chang, F. I. F., Isaacs, K. R., & Greenough, W. T. (1991). Synapse formation occurs in association with the induction of long-term potentiation in two-year-old rat hippocampus in vitro. *Neurobiology of Aging, 12,* 517–522.

Charles, C. M. (1985). *Building classroom discipline: From models to practice* (2nd ed.). New York: Longman.

Charles, G. (1991). Suicide intervention and prevention among northern Native youth. *Journal of Child and Youth Care, 6*(1), 11–17.

Chassin, L., Pillow, D. R., Curran, P. J., Molina, B. S. G., & Barrera, M., Jr. (1993). Relation of parental alcoholism to early adolescent substance use: A test of three mediating mechanisms. *Journal of Abnormal Psychology, 102,* 3–19.

Chaves, J. F., & Dworkin, S. F. (1997). Hypnotic control of pain: Historical perspectives and future prospects. *International Journal of Clinical and Experimental Hypnosis, 45*(4), 356–376.

Chen, H., & Lan, W. (1998). Adolescents' perception of their parents' academic expectations: Comparison of American, Chinese-American, and Chinese high school students. *Adolescence, 33*(130), 385.

Chen, X., Rubin, K. H., & Li, Z. (1995). Social functioning and adjustment in Chinese children: A longitudinal study. *Developmental Psychology, 31,* 531–539.

Cheng, A. T. A. (1995). Mental illness and suicide: A case-control study in East Taiwan. *Archives of General Psychiatry, 52,* 594–603.

Cheng, K., & Spetch, M. (1998). Mechanisms of landmark use in mammals and birds. In S. Healy (Ed.), *Spatial representation in animals.* New York: Oxford University Press.

Cherulnik, P. D., Turns, L. C., & Wilderman, S. K. (1990). Physical appearance and leadership: Exploring the role of appearance-based attribution in leader emergence. *Journal of Applied Social Psychology, 20,* 1530–1539.

Chia, E. K. F., & Jih, C. S. (1994). The effects of stereotyping on impression formation: Cross-cultural perspectives on viewing religious persons. *Journal of Psychology, 128*(5), 559–565.

Chidester, T. R. (1986). Problems in the study of interracial interaction: Pseudo-interracial dyad paradigm. *Journal of Personality and Social Psychology, 50,* 74–79.

Chodorow, N. (1978). *The reproduction of mothering: Psychoanalysis and the sociology of gender.* Berkeley, CA: University of California Press.

Choi, I., Nisbett, R. E., & Norenzayan, A. (1999). Causal attribution across cultures: Variation and universality. *Psychological Bulletin, 125*(1), 47–63.

Chomsky, N. (1957). *Syntactic structures.* The Hague, Netherlands: Mouton.

Chomsky, N. (1959). Review of B. F. Skinner's *Verbal Behavior. Language, 35,* 26–129.

Chomsky, N. (1986). *Knowledge of language: Its nature, origin, and use.* New York: Praeger.

Chomsky, N. (1990). On the nature, use and acquisition of language. In W. G. Lycan (Ed.), *Mind and cognition* (pp. 627–646). Oxford, England: Blackwell.

Chorney, M. J., Chorney, K., Seese, N., Owen, M. J., Daniels, J., McGuffin, P., Thompson, L. A., Detterman, D. K., Benbow, C., Lubinski, D., Eley, T., & Plomin, R. (1998). A quantitative trait locus associated with cognitive ability in children. *Psychological Science, 9*(3), 159–166.

Chorpita, B. F., & Barlow, D. H. (1998). The development of anxiety: The role of control in the early environment. *Psychological Bulletin, 124*(1), 3–21.

Christenfeld, N., Gerin, W., Linden, W., & Sanders, M. (1997). Social support effects on cardiovascular reactivity: Is a stranger as effective as a friend? *Psychosomatic Medicine, 59*(4), 388–398.

Chung, S. W., & Doh, H. S. (1997). Parental sociability, parenting behaviors, and shyness in children. [Korean]. *Korean Journal of Child Studies, 18*(2), 149–161.

Cialdini, R. B. (1993). *Influence* (3rd ed.). New York: HarperCollins.

Cialdini, R. B. (1994). Interpersonal influence. In S. Shavitt & T. C. Brock (Eds.), *Persuasion: Psychological insights and perspectives* (pp. 195–218). Boston: Allyn & Bacon.

Cialdini, R. B., Eisenberg, N., Green, B. L., Rhoads, K., & Bator, R. (1998). Undermining the undermining effect of reward on sustained interest. *Journal of Applied Social Psychology, 28*(3), 249–263.

Cialdini, R. B., Trost, M. R., & Newsom, J. T. (1995). Preference for consistency: The development of a valid measure and the discovery of surprising behavioral implications. *Journal of Personality and Social Psychology, 69*, 318–328.

Cicero, T. J. (1994). Effects of paternal exposure to alcohol on offspring development. *Alcohol Health and Research World, 18*, 37–41.

Clark, H. H. (1996). *Using language.* Cambridge, England: Cambridge University Press.

Clark, M. S., & Reis, H. T. (1988). Interpersonal processes in close relationships. *Annual Review of Psychology, 39*, 609–672.

Clarke-Stewart, A. (1973). Interactions between mothers and their young children: Characteristics and consequences. *Monographs of the Society for Research in Child Development, 38*.

Clarke-Stewart, A., Friedman, S., & Koch, J. B. (1985). *Child development: A topical approach.* New York: Wiley.

Clarkin, J. F., & Hull, J. W. (1991). The brief psychotherapies. In M. Hersen, A. E. Kazdin, & A. S. Bellack (Eds.), *The clinical psychology handbook* (2nd ed.). New York: Pergamon.

Claxton, G. (1975). Why can't we tickle ourselves. *Perceptual and Motor Skills, 41*(1), 335–338.

Claxton, R. P., & McIntyre, R. P. (1994). Empirical relationships between need for cognition and cognitive style: Implications for consumer psychology. *Psychological Reports, 74*, 723–732.

Clifton, R. K., Muir, D. W., Ashmead, D. H., & Clarkson, M. G. (1993). Is visually guided reaching in early infancy a myth? *Child Development, 64*, 1099–1110.

Coates, B., Pusser, H. E., & Goodman, I. (1976). The influence of "Sesame Street" and "Mister Rogers' Neighborhood" on children's social behavior in the preschool. *Child Development, 47*, 138–144.

Coffey, C. W., Weiner, R. D., Djang, W. T., Figiel, G. S., Soady, S. A. R., Patterson, L. J., Holt, P. D., Spritzer, C. E., & Wilinson, W. E. (1991). Brain anatomic effects of electroconvulsive therapy. *Archives of General Psychiatry, 48*, 1013–1021.

Cogan, J. C., Bhalla, S. K., Sefa-Dedeh, A., & Rothblum, E. D. (1996). A comparison study of United States and African students on perceptions of obesity and thinness. *Journal of Cross-Cultural Psychology, 27*(1), 98–113.

Cohen, R. J., Montague, P., Nathanson, L. S., & Swerdlik, M. E. (1988). *Psychological testing.* Mountain View, CA: Mayfield.

Cohen, S. (1996). Psychological stress, immunity, and upper respiratory infections. *Current Directions in Psychological Science, 5*(3), 86–90.

Cohen, S., Frank, E., Doyle, W. J., Skoner, D. P., Rabin, B. S., & Gwaltney, J. M., Jr. (1998). Types of stressors that increase susceptibility to the common cold in healthy adults. *Health Psychology, 17*(3), 214–223.

Cohen, S., Tyrrell, D. A. J., & Smith, A. P. (1991). Psychological stress and susceptibility to the common cold. *New England Journal of Medicine, 325*, 606–612.

Cohen, S., Tyrrell, D. A. J., & Smith, A. P. (1993). Negative life events, perceived stress, negative affect, and susceptibility to the common cold. *Journal of Personality and Social Psychology, 64*, 131–140.

Cohen, S., Tyrrell, D. A. J., & Smith, A. P. (1997). Psychological stress in humans and susceptibility to the common cold. In T. W. Miller et al. (Eds.), *Clinical disorders and stressful life events* (pp. 217–235). Madison, CT: International Universities Press, Inc.

Cohen, S., & Williamson, G. M. (1991). Stress and infectious disease in humans. *Psychological Bulletin, 109*, 5–24.

Cohn, D. A. (1990). Child-mother attachment of six-year-olds and social competence at school. *Child Development, 61*, 152–162.

Cohn, J. F., & Tronick, E. Z. (1983). Three-month-old infants' reaction to simulated maternal depression. *Child Development, 54*, 185–193.

Cohn, L. (1991). Sex differences in the course of personality development: A meta-analysis. *Psychological Bulletin, 109*, 252–266.

Cole, D. A. (1989). Psychopathology of adolescent suicide: Hopelessness, coping beliefs, and depression. *Journal of Abnormal Psychology, 98*, 248–255.

Coley, R. L., & Chase-Landsdale, P. L. (1998). Adolescent pregnancy and parenthood: Recent evidence and future directions. *American Psychologist, 53*(2), 152–166.

Collins, N. L., & Miller, L. C. (1994). Self-disclosure and liking: A meta-analytic review. *Psychological Bulletin, 116*, 457–475.

Colman, H., Babekura, J., & Lichtman, J. W. (1997). Alterations in synaptic strength preceding axon withdrawal. *Science, 275*, 356–361.

Colvin, C. R., & Block, J. (1994). Do positive illusions foster mental health? An examination of the Taylor and Brown formulation. *Psychological Bulletin, 116*, 3–20.

Comer, J. P. (1988, November). Educating poor minority children. *Scientific American*, 42–51.

Comuzzie, A. G., & Allison, D. B. (1998). The search for human obesity genes. *Science, 280*, 1374–1377.

Contrada, R. J. (1989). Type A behavior, personality hardiness, and cardiovascular responses to stress. *Journal of Personality and Social Psychology, 57*, 895–903.

Conway, M. A. (1991). In defense of everyday memory. *American Psychologist, 46*, 19–26.

Conway, M. A., Anderson, S. J., Larsen, S. F., Donnelly, C. M., McDaniel, M. A., McClelland, A. G. R., Rawles, R. E., & Logie, R. H. (1994). The formation of flashbulb memories. *Memory & Cognition, 22*, 326–343.

Conyers, L. M., Enright, M. S., & Strauser, D. R. (1998). Applying self-efficacy theory to counseling college students with disabilities. *Journal of Applied Rehabilitation Counseling, 29*(1), 25–30.

Cooper, M., Corrado, R., Karlberg, A. M., & Adams, L. P. (1992). Aboriginal suicide in British Columbia: An overview. *Canada's Mental Health, 40*(3), 19–23.

Coppola, D. M., & O'Connell, R. J. (1988). Behavioral responses of peripubertal female mice towards puberty-accelerating and puberty-delaying chemical signals. *Chemical Senses, 13*, 407–424.

Corbetta, M., Shulman, G. L., Miezin, F. M., & Petersen, S. E. (1995). Superior parietal cortex activation during spatial attention shifts and visual feature conjunction. *Science, 270*, 802–805.

Cordova, D. I., & Lepper, M. R. (1996). Intrinsic motivation and the process of learning: Beneficial effects of contextualization, personalization, and choice. *Journal of Educational Psychology, 88*(4), 715–730.

Coren, S. (1992). *The left-hander syndrome: The causes and consequences of left handedness.* New York: Vintage Books.

Coren, S. (1996). *Sleep thieves: An eye-opening exploration into the science and mysteries of sleep.* New York: The Free Press.

Coren, S., & Aks, D. J. (1990). Moon illusion in pictures: A multi-mechanism approach. *Journal of Experimental Psychology: Human Perception and Performance, 16*, 365–380.

Coren, S., & Porac, C. (1977). Fifty centuries of right-handedness: The historic record. *Science, 198*, 631–632.

Corina, D. P., Vaid, J., & Bellugi, U. (1992). The linguistic basis of left hemisphere specialization. *Science, 255*, 1258–1260.

Corkin, S. (1984). Lasting consequences of bilateral medial temporal lobectomy: Clinical course and experimental findings in H. M. *Seminar in Neurology, 4*, 249–259.

Cornell, E., Heth, C. D., & Rowat, W. L. (1992). Wayfinding by children and adults: Response to instructions to use look-back and retrace strategies. *Developmental Psychology, 28*(2), 328–336.

Coryell, W., Endicott, J., & Keller, M. (1992). Major depression in a nonclinical sample. *Archives of General Psychiatry, 49*, 117–125.

Costa, P. T., Jr., & McCrae, R. R. (1998). Trait theories of personality. In D. F. Barone, M. Hersen, et al. (Eds.), *Advanced personality. The Plenum series in social/clinical psychology* (pp. 103–121). New York: Plenum Press.

Costanzo, M. (1997). *Just revenge.* New York: St. Martin's Press.

Costanzo, M., Archer, D., Aronson, E., & Pettigrew, T. (1986). Energy conservation behavior: The difficult path from information to action. *American Psychologist, 41*, 521–528.

Courtney, S. M., Petit, L., Maisog, J. M., Ungerleider, L. G., & Haxby J. V. (1998). An area specialized for spatial working memory in human frontal cortex. *Science, 279*, 1347–1351.

Cowen, E. L. (1991). In pursuit of wellness. *American Psychologist, 46*, 404–408.

Cox, R. H., Qiu, Y., & Liu, Z. (1993). Overview of sport psychology. In R. N. Singer, M. Murphey, & L. K. Tennant (Eds.), *Handbook of research on sport psychology* (pp. 3–31). New York: Macmillan.

Craft, M. A., Alber, S. R., & Heward, W. L. (1998). Teaching elementary students with developmental disabilities to recruit teacher attention in a general education classroom: Effects on teacher praise and academic productivity. *Journal of Applied Behavior Analysis, 31*(3), 399–415.

Craik, F. I. (1994). Memory changes in normal aging. *Current Directions in Psychological Science, 3*, 155–158.

Craik, F. I. M., & Lockhart, R. S. (1972). Levels of processing: A framework for memory research. *Journal of Verbal Learning and Verbal Behavior, 11*, 671–784.

Craik, F. I. M., Moroz, T. M., Moscovitch, M., Stuss, D. T., Winocur, G., Tulving, E., & Kapur, S. (1999). In search of the self: A positron emission tomography study. *American Psychological Society, 10*(1), 26–34.

Crair, M. C., Gillespie, D. C., & Stryker, M. P. (1998). The role of visual experience in the development of columns in cat visual cortex. *Science, 279*, 565–570.

Crandall, C. S. (1994). Prejudice against fat people: Ideology and self-interest. *Journal of Personality and Social Psychology, 66*(5), 882–894.

Crandall, C. S., & Martinez, R. (1996). Culture, ideology, and anti-fat attitudes. *Personality and Social Psychology Bulletin, 22*(11), 1165–1176.

Crane, J. (1994). Exploding the myth of scientific support for the theory of black intellectual inferiority. *Journal of Black Psychology, 20*, 189–209.

Crave, J. (1998). It's a highschool, there must be gangs, right? *Cameron Chronicle: Collingwood's International Newspaper.* http://cses.scbe.on/gangs4.htm (accessed March 1999).

Crawford, C. B., & Anderson, J. L. (1989). Sociobiology. *American Psychologist, 44*, 1449–1459.

Crawford, H. J. (1994). Brain dynamics and hypnosis: Attentional and disattentional processes. *The International Journal of Clinical and Experimental Hypnosis, 42*, 204–232.

Crawford, M., & MacLeod, M. (1990). Gender in the college classroom: An assessment of the "chilly climate" for women. *Sex Roles, 23*, 101–122.

Crespi, T. D. (1988). Effectiveness of time-out: A comparison of psychiatric, correctional and day-treatment programs. *Adolescence, 23*, 805–811.

Crick, F., & Koch, C. (1998). Contraints on cortical and thalamic projections: The no-strong-loops hypothesis. *Nature, 391*(15), 245–250.

Crittenden, K. S., Fugita, S. S., Bae, H., Lamug, C. B., & Lin, C. (1992). A cross-cultural study of self-report depressive symptoms among college students. *Journal of Cross-Cultural Psychology, 23*, 163–178.

Cronan, T. A., Cruz, S. G., Arriaga, R. I., & Sarkin, A. J. (1996). The effects of a community-based literacy program on young children's language and conceptual development. *American Journal of Community Psychology, 24*(2), 251–272.

Cronan, T. A., Walen, H. R., & Cruz, S. G. (1994). The effects of community-based literacy training on Head Start parents. *Journal of Community Psychology, 22*, 248–258.

Cronell, E. H., Heth, C. D., and Broda, L. S. (1989). Children's wayfinding: Response to instructions to use environmental landmarks. *Developmental Psychology, 25*(5), 755–764.

Cronshaw, S. F. (1991). *Industrial psychology in Canada.* Waterloo, ON: North Waterloo Academic Press.

Cross, S. E., & Madson, L. (1997a). Elaboration of models of the self: Reply to Baumeister and Sommer (1997) and Martin and Ruble (1997). *Psychological Bulletin, 122*(1), 51–55.

Cross, S. E., & Madson, L. (1997b). Models of the self: Self-construals and gender. *Psychological Bulletin, 122*(1), 5–37.

Crowl, R. K., & MacGinitie, W. H. (1974). The influence of students' speech characteristics on teachers' evaluations of oral answers. *Journal of Educational Psychology, 66*, 304–308.

Crystal, D. S., Chen, C., Fuligni, A. J., Stevenson, H. W., Hsu, C., Ko, H., Kitamura, S., & Kimura, S. (1994). Psychological maladjustment and academic achievement: A cross-cultural study of Japanese, Chinese, and American high school students. *Child Development, 65*, 738–753.

Csikszentmihalyi, M. (1996). *Creativity: Flow and the psychology of discovery and invention.* New York: HarperCollins.

Csikszentmihalyi, M. (1997). *Finding flow: The psychology of engagement with everyday life.* New York: Basic Books.

Culbertson, F. M. (1997). Depression and gender: An international review. *American Psychologist, 52*(1), 25–31.

Cummings, N. A. (1986). The dismantling of our health system: Strategies for the survival of psychological practice. *American Psychologist, 41*, 426–431.

Cummings, N. A., Budman, S. H., & Lawrence, T. J. (1998). Efficient psychotherapy as a viable response to scarce resources and rationing of treatment. *Professional Psychology: Research and Practice, 29*(5), 460–469.

Cunningham, M. R., Barbee, A. P., & Pike, C. L. (1990). What do women want? Facialmetric assessment of multiple motives in the perception of male facial physical attractiveness. *Journal of Personality and Social Psychology, 59*, 61–72.

Curran, D. K. (1987). *Adolescent suicidal behavior.* Washington, DC: Hemisphere.

Czeisler, C. A., Johnson, M. P., Duffy, J. F., Brown, E. N., Ronda, J. M., & Kronauer, R. E. (1990). Exposure to bright light and darkness to treat physiologic maladaptation to night work. *New England Journal of Medicine, 322*, 1253–1259.

Dabul, A. J., Wosinska, W., Cialdini, R. B., Mandal, E., & Dion, R. W. (1997). Self-presentational modesty across cultures: The effects of gender and social context in the workplace. *Polish Psychological Bulletin, 28*(4), 295–306.

Dadds, M. R., Bovbjerg, D. H., Redd, W. H., & Cutmore, T. R. (1997). Imagery in human classical conditioning. *Psychological Bulletin, 122*(1), 89–103.

Dakof, G. A., & Taylor, S. E. (1990). Victims' perceptions of social support: What is helpful from whom? *Journal of Personality and Social Psychology, 58*, 80–89.

Damasio, A. R. (1994). *Descartes' error: Emotion, reason, and the human brain.* New York: Putnam.

Damasio, A. R., & Damasio, H. (1992, September). Brain and language. *Scientific American*, 89–95.

Damasio, A. R., Tranel, D., & Damasio, H. (1990). Face agnosia and the neural substrates of memory. *Annual Review of Neuroscience, 13*, 89–109.

Daniel, M. H. (1997). Intelligence testing. *American Psychologist, 52*(10), 1038–1045.

Daniels, D., & Plomin, R. (1985). Origins of individual differences in infant shyness. *Developmental Psychology, 21*, 118–121.

Danner, R., & Edwards, D. (1992). Life is movement: Exercise for the older adult. *Activities, Adaptation & Aging, 17*, 15–26.

Daum, I., Ackermann, H., Schugens, M. M., Reimold, C., Dichgans, J., & Birbaumer, N. (1993). The cerebellum and cognitive functions in humans. *Behavioral Neuroscience, 107*, 411–419.

Davies, M., Stankov, L., & Roberts, R. D. (1998). Emotional intelligence: In search of an elusive construct. *Journal of Personality and Social Psychology, 75*(4), 989–1015.

Davies, M. M. (1997). *Fake, fact, and fantasy: Children's interpretations of television reality.* Mahwah, NJ: Lawrence Erlbaum Associates, Inc.

Davis, D., & Padesky, C. (1989). Enhancing cognitive therapy with women. In A. Freeman, K. M. Simon, L. E. Beutler, & H. Arkowitz (Eds.), *Comprehensive handbook of cognitive therapy.* New York: Plenum.

Davis, K. E., & Todd, M. J. (1982). Friendship and love relationships. In K. E. Davis & M. J. Todd (Eds.), *Advances in descriptive psychology* (Vol. 2). Greenwich, CT: JAI.

Davis, N. S., & Thornburg, K. R. (1994). Child care: A synthesis of research. *Early Child Development and Care, 98*, 39–45.

Dawes, R. M. (1994). *House of cards: Psychology and psychotherapy built on myth.* New York: Free Press.

DeAngelis, T. (1988). In praise of rose-colored specs. *APA Monitor, 19*, 11.

Dearwater, S. R., Coben, J. H., Campbell, J. C., Nah, G., Glass, N., McLoughlin, E., & Bekemeier, B. (1998). Prevalence of intimate partner abuse in women treated at community hospital emergency departments. *Journal of the American Medical Association, 280*(5), 433–438.

DeBono, K. G. (1992). Pleasant scents and persuasion: An information processing approach. *Journal of Applied Social Psychology, 22,* 910–919.

DeCharms, R. C., Blake, D. T., & Merzenich, M. M. (1998). Optimizing sound features for cortical neurons. *Science, 280,* 1439–1443.

Deci, E. L. (1972). Effects of contingent and non-contingent rewards and controls on intrinsic motivation. *Organizational Behavior and Human Performance, 8,* 217–229.

Deci, E. L. (1975). *Intrinsic motivation.* New York: Plenum.

Decker, S. H., & Kohfeld, C. W. (1984). A deterrence study of the death penalty in Illinois, 1933–1980. *Journal of Criminal Justice, 12*(4), 367–377.

de Haan, M., & Nelson, C. A. (1997). Recognition of the mother's face by six-month-old infants: A neurobehavioral study. *Child Development, 68*(2), 187–210.

De Jongh, A., Muris, P., Ter Horst, G., & Duyx, M. P. M. A. (1995). Acquisition and maintenance of dental anxiety: The role of conditioning experiences and cognitive factors. *Behavior Research Theory, 33*(2), 205–210.

Delgado, P. L. C., Price, D. S., Aghajanian, L. H., Landis, G. K., & Heninger, G. R. (1990). Serotonin function and mechanism of antidepressant action: Reversal of antidepressant-induced remission by rapid depletion of plasma atryptophan. *Archives of General Psychiatry, 47,* 411–418.

DeLongis, A., Folkman, S., & Lazarus, R. S. (1988). The impact of daily stress on health and mood: Psychological and social resources as mediators. *Journal of Personality and Social Psychology, 54,* 486–495.

Dement, W. C., Greenberg, S., & Klein, R. (1966). The effect of partial REM sleep deprivation and delayed recovery. *Journal of Psychiatric Research, 4,* 141–152.

Dement, W. C., & Wolpert, E. A. (1958). The relation of eye movements, body motility, and external stimuli to dream content. *Journal of Experimental Psychology, 55,* 543–553.

DeNeve, K. M., & Cooper, H. (1998). The happy personality: A meta-analysis of 137 personality traits and subjective well-being. *Psychological Bulletin, 124*(2), 197–229.

Deniston, W. M., & Ramanaiah, N. V. (1993). California Psychological Inventory and the five-factor model of personality. *Psychological Reports, 73,* 491–496.

Denmark, F. I. (1994). Engendering psychology. *American Psychologist, 49,* 329–334.

Dennett, D. C. (1991). *Consciousness explained.* Boston: Little, Brown.

Dennett, D. C. (1996). *Kinds of minds: Toward an understanding of consciousness.* New York: Basic Books.

Dentan, R. K. (1968). *The Semai: A nonviolent people of Malaya.* New York: Holt, Rinehart & Winston.

DePaulo, B. M. (1992). Nonverbal behavior and self-presentation. *Psychological Bulletin, 111,* 230–243.

DePaulo, B. M., Dull, W. R., Greenberg, J. M., & Swaim, G. W. (1989). Are shy people reluctant to ask for help? *Journal of Personality and Social Psychology, 56,* 834–844.

DePaulo, P. J., & DePaulo, B. M. (1989). Can deception by salespersons and customers be detected through nonverbal behavioral cues? *Journal of Applied Social Psychology, 19,* 1552–1577.

Deregowski, J. B. (1980). Perception. In H. C. Triandis & J. W. Berry (Eds.), *Handbook of cross-cultural psychology: Vol. 3. Basic processes.* Boston: Allyn & Bacon.

Dershowitz, A. M. (1986). *Reversal of fortune: Inside the von Bulow case.* New York: Random House.

DeSantis, A., & Kayson, W. A. (1997). Defendants' characteristics of attractiveness, race, and sex and sentencing decisions. *Psychological Reports, 81,* 679–683.

D'Esposito, M., Zarahn, E., & Aguirre, G. K. (1999). Event-related functional MRI: Implications for cognitive psychology. *Psychological Bulletin, 125*(1), 155–164.

Detterman, D. K., & Thompson, L. A. (1997). What is so special about special education? *American Psychologist, 52*(10), 1082–1090.

DeValois, R. L., & Jacobs, G. H. (1968). Primate color vision. *Science, 162,* 533–540.

Devine, P. G. (1989). Stereotypes and prejudice: Their automatic and controlled components. *Journal of Personality and Social Psychology, 56*(1), 5–18.

de Vries, B., & Walker, L. J. (1986). Moral reasoning and attitudes toward capital punishment. *Developmental Psychology, 22*(4), 509–513.

Diehl, M., Willis, S. L., & Schaie, K. W. (1995). Everyday problem solving in older adults: Observational assessment and cognitive correlates. *Psychology and Aging, 10*(3), 478–491.

Diener, E. (1998). Subjective well-being and personality. In D. Barone (Ed.), *Advanced personality. The Plenum series in social/clinical psychology.* New York: Plenum Press.

Diener, E., & Diener, C. (1996). Most people are happy. *American Psychological Society, 7*(3), 181–185.

Diener, E., Lusk, R., DeFour, D., & Flax, R. (1980). Deindividuation: Effects of group size, density, number of observers, and group member similarity on self-consciousness and disinhibited behavior. *Journal of Personality and Social Psychology, 39,* 449–459.

Diener, E., Suh, E. M., Lucas, R. E., & Smith, H. L. (1999). Subjective well-being: Three decades of progress. *Psychological Bulletin, 125*(2), 276–302.

Dietvorst, T. F. (1978). Biofeedback assisted relaxation training with patients recovering from myocardial infarction. *Dissertation Abstracts International, 38,* 3389.

Dietz, T. L. (1998). An examination of violence and gender role portrayals in video games: Implications for gender socialization and aggressive behavior. *Sex Roles, 38*(5/6), 425–428.

DiGiuseppe, R. (1989). Cognitive therapy with children. In A. Freeman, K. M. Simon, L. E. Beutler, & H. Arkowitz (Eds.), *Comprehensive handbook of cognitive therapy.* New York: Plenum Press.

DiLalla, D. L., & Gottesman, I. I. (1995). Normal personality characteristics in identical twins discordant for schizophrenia. *Journal of Abnormal Psychology, 104,* 490–499.

DiLalla, L. F., & Gottesman, I. I. (1991). Biological and genetic contributors to violence: Wisdom's untold tale. *Psychological Bulletin, 109*(1), 125–129.

DiLalla, L. F., Thompson, L. A., Plomin, R., Phillips, K., Fagan, J. F., III, Haith, M. M., Cyphers, L. H., & Fulker, D. W. (1990). Infant predictors of preschool and adult IQ: A study of infant twins and their parents. *Development Psychology, 26,* 759–769.

DiMatteo, M. R., & DiNicola, D. D. (1982). *Achieving patient compliance: The psychology of the medical practitioner's role.* New York: Pergamon.

Dindia, K., & Allen, M. (1992). Sex differences in self-disclosure: A meta-analysis. *Psychological Bulletin, 112,* 106–124.

Dinges, N. G., & Hull, P. V. (1993). Personality, culture, and international studies. In D. Lieberman (Ed.), *Revealing the world: An interdisciplinary reader for international studies.* Dubuque, IA: Kendall-Hunt.

Dion, K., Dion, K., & Pak, A. W. (1992). Personality-based hardiness as a buffer for discrimination-related stress in members of Toronto's Chinese community. *Canadian Journal of Behavioural Science, 24*(4), 517–536.

Dion, K. K., Pak, A. W., & Dion, K. L. (1990). Stereotyping physical attractiveness. *Journal of Cross-Cultural Psychology, 21,* 158–179.

Dobson, K. S. (1989). A meta-analysis of the efficacy of cognitive therapy for depression. *Journal of Consulting and Clinical Psychology, 57,* 414–419.

Dobson, K. S., & Block, L. (1988). Historical and philosophical bases of the cognitive-behavioral therapies. In K. S. Dobson (Ed.), *Handbook of cognitive-behavioral therapies.* New York: Guilford.

Docherty, N. M., Hall, M. J., & Gordinier, S. W. (1998). Affective reactivity of speech in schizophrenia patients and their nonschizophrenic relatives. *Journal of Abnormal Psychology, 107*(3), 461–467.

Dohrenwend, B. P., & Shrout, P. E. (1985). "Hassles" in the conceptualization and measurement of life stress variables. *American Psychologist, 40,* 780–785.

Dolcini, M. M., Coates, T. J., Catania, J. A., Kegeles, S. M., & Hauck, W. W. (1995). Multiple sexual partners and their psychosocial correlates: The population-based AIDS in multiethnic neighborhoods (AMEN) study. *Health Psychology, 14,* 22–31.

Dollard, J., Doob, L. W., Miller, N. E., Mowrer, O. H., & Sears, R. R. (1939). *Frustration and aggression.* New Haven, CT: Yale University Press.

Dollins, A. B., Lynch, H. J., Wurtman, R. J., Deng, M. H., et al. (1993). Effects of illumination on human nocturnal serum melatonin levels and performance. *Physiology and Behavior, 53,* 153–160.

Donnelly, C. M., & McDaniel, M. A. (1993). Use of analogy in learning scientific concepts. *Journal of Experimental Psychology: Learning, Memory, and Cognition, 19,* 975–987.

Donovan, J. M. (1998). Brief couples therapy: Lessons from the history of brief individual treatment. *Psychotherapy: Theory, Research and Practice, 35*(1), 116–129.

Donson, N. (1999). Caring for day care: Models for early intervention and primary prevention. In T. B. Cohen, M. H. Etezady, et al. (Eds.), *The vulnerable child, Vol. 3* (pp. 181–212). Madison, CT: International Universities Press.

Doob, A. N., & McLaughlin, D. S. (1989). Ask and you shall be given: Request size and donations to a good cause. *Journal of Applied Social Psychology, 19*, 1049–1056.

Downey, G., & Coyne, J. C. (1990). Children of depressed parents: An integrative review. *Psychological Bulletin, 108*, 50–76.

Downey, V. W., & Landry, R. G. (1997). Self-reported sexual behaviours of high school juniors and seniors in North Dakota. *Psychological Reports, 80*(3, Pt. 2), 1357–1358.

Drennen, W. T., & Holden, E. W. (1984). Trait/set interactions in EMG biofeedback. *Psychological Reports, 54*, 843–849.

Dreyer, P. H. (1982). Sexuality during adolescence. In B. B. Wolman (Ed.), *Handbook of developmental psychology*. Englewood Cliffs, NJ: Prentice-Hall.

Dromi, E. (1997). Early lexical development. In M. Barerett (Ed.), *The development of language*. London: UCL.

Dryden, W., & Ellis, A. (1988). Rational-emotive therapy. In K. S. Dobson (Ed.), *Handbook of cognitive-behavioral therapies*. New York: Guilford.

Dubovsky, S. L., & Thomas, M. (1995). Beyond specificity: Effects of serotonin and serotonergic treatments on psychobiological dysfunction. *Journal of Psychosomatic Research, 39*, 429–444.

Duckitt, J. (1992). Psychology and prejudice. *American Psychologist, 47*, 1182–1193.

Duffy, R. D., Kalsher, M. J., & Wogalter, M. S. (1993). The effectiveness of an interactive warning in a realistic product-use situation. *Proceedings of the Human Factors and Ergonomics Society, 37th Annual Meeting*, 935–939.

Dunant, Y., & Israel, M. (1985, April). The release of acetylcholine. *Scientific American*, 58–83.

Dunbar, K. (1994). Concept discovery in the scientific domain. *Cognitive Science, 17*(3): 397–434.

Dunlosky, J., & Connor, L. T. (1997). Age differences in the allocation of study time account for age differences in memory performance. *Memory and Cognition, 25*(5), 691–700.

Dura, J. R., Stukenberg, K. W., & Kiecolt-Glaser, J. K. (1990). Chronic stress and depressive disorders in older adults. *Journal of Abnormal Psychology, 99*, 284–290.

Durex (1998). *Durex global sex survey*.

Dutton, D. G. (1998). *The abusive personality: Violence and control in intimate relationships*. New York: The Guilford Press.

Dweck, C. S. (1986). Motivational processes affecting learning: Special issue. Psychological science and education. *American Psychologist, 41*, 1040–1048.

Dweck, C. S., & Leggett, E. L. (1988). A socio-cognitive approach to motivation and personality. *Psychological Review, 95*, 256–273.

Dwyer, W. O., Leeming, F. C., Cobern, M. K., Porter, B. E., & Jackson, J. M. (1993). Critical review of behavioral interventions to preserve the environment: Research since 1980. *Environment and Behavior, 25*, 275–321.

Eacott, M. J., & Crawley, R. A. (1998). The offset of childhood amnesia: Memory for events that occurred before age 3. *Journal of Experimental Psychology: General, 127*(1), 22–33.

Eagly, A. H. (1992). Uneven progress: Social psychology and the study of attitudes. *Journal of Personality and Social Psychology, 63*, 693–710.

Eagly, A. H. (1995). The science and politics of comparing women and men. *American Psychologist, 50*, 145–158.

Eagly, A. H., Ashmore, R. D., Makhijani, M. G., & Longo, L. C. (1991). What is beautiful is good, but . . . : A meta-analytic review of research on the physical attractiveness stereotype. *Psychological Bulletin, 110*, 109–128.

Eagly, A. H., & Chaiken, S. (1993). *The psychology of attitudes*. Fort Worth, TX: Harcourt Brace Jovanovich.

Eagly, A. H., & Johnson, B. T. (1990). Gender and leadership style: A meta-analysis. *Psychological Bulletin, 108*, 233–256.

Eagly, A. H., Makhijani, M. G., & Klonsky, B. G. (1992). Gender and the evaluation of leaders: A meta-analysis. *Psychological Bulletin, 111*, 1, 3–22.

Eagly, A. H., & Steffen, V. J. (1986). Gender and aggressive behavior: A meta-analytic review of the social psychological literature. *Psychological Bulletin, 100*, 309–330.

Eaton, M. J., & Dembo, M. H. (1997). Differences in the motivational beliefs of Asian American and non-Asian students. *Journal of Educational Psychology, 89*(3), 433–440.

Eccles, J. S., Wigfield, A., Midgley, C., Reuman, D., Buchanan, C. M., Flanagan, C., & MacIver, D. (1993). Development during adolescence: The impact of stage-environment fit on young adolescents' experiences in schools and families. *American Psychologist, 48*, 90–101.

Edwards, D. C. (1999). *Motivation and emotion: Evolutionary, physiological, cognitive, and social influences*. London: Sage Publications.

Edwards, K. (1998). The face of time: Temporal cues in facial expressions of emotion. *American Psychological Society, 9*(4), 270–276.

Egeland, B., & Hiester, M. (1995). The long-term consequences of infant day-care and mother-infant attachment. *Child Development, 66*(2), 474–485.

Egeland, B., Jacobvitz, D., & Sroufe, L. A. (1988). Breaking the cycle of abuse. *Child Development, 59*, 1080–1088.

Eich, E. (1995). Searching for mood dependent memory. *Psychological Science, 6*, 67–75.

Eichenbaum, H. (1997). How does the brain organize memories? *Science, 277*, 330–332.

Eisenberg, N., Shepard, S. A., Faves, R. A., Murphy, B. C., & Guthrie, I. K. (1998). Shyness and children's emotionality, regulation, and coping: Contemporaneous, longitudinal, and across-context relations. *Child Development, 69*(3), 767–790.

Eisenberger, R., & Cameron, J. (1996). Detrimental effects of reward. *American Psychologist, 51*(11), 1153–1166.

Eisenman, R. (1993). Professor Anita Hill versus Judge Clarence Thomas: The view of students at a Southern university. *Bulletin of the Psychonomic Society, 31*, 179–180.

Ekman, P. (1992). Facial expressions of emotion: New findings, new questions. *Psychological Science, 3*, 34–38.

Ekman, P. (1993). Facial expression and emotion. *American Psychologist, 48*, 384–392.

Ekman, P. (1994). Strong evidence for universals in facial expressions: A reply to Russell's mistaken critique. *Psychological Bulletin, 115*, 268–287.

Ekman, P., Friesen, W. V., & O'Sullivan, M. (1988). Smiles when lying. *Journal of Personality and Social Psychology, 54*, 414–420.

Ekman, P., & Keltner, D. (1997). Universal facial expressions of emotion: An old controversy and new findings. In U. C. Segerstrale, P. Molnar, et al. (Eds.), *Noverbal communication: Where nature meets culture* (pp. 27–46). Mahwah, NJ: Lawrence Erlbaum Associates, Inc.

Elbert, T., Pantev, C., Wienbruch, C., Rockstroh, B., & Taub, E. (1995). Increased cortical representation of the fingers of the left hand in string players. *Science, 270*, 305–307.

Eley, T. C. (1997). General genes: A new theme in developmental psychopathology. *American Psychological Society, 6*(4), 90–95.

Elkind, D. (1981). Giant in the nursery—Jean Piaget. In E. M. Hetherington & R. D. Parke (Eds.), *Contemporary readings in child psychology* (2nd ed.). New York: McGraw-Hill.

Elkind, D., & Bowen, R. (1979). Imaginary audience behavior in children and adolescents. *Developmental Psychology, 15*(1), 38–44.

Elkins, L. E., & Peterson, C. (1993). Gender differences in best friendships. *Sex Roles, 29*, 497–508.

Elliot, A., & Devine, P. G. (1994). On the motivational nature of cognitive dissonance: Dissonance as psychological discomfort. *Journal of Personality and Social Psychology, 67*(3), 382–394.

Elliott, E. S., & Dweck, C. S. (1988). Goals: An approach to motivation and achievement. *Journal of Personality and Social Psychology, 54*, 5–12.

Elliott, R. (1987). *Litigating intelligence: IQ tests, special education, and social science in the courtroom*. Dover, MS: Auburn House.

Ellis, A. (1970). *The essence of rational psychotherapy: A comprehensive approach to treatment*. New York: Institute for Rational Living.

Ellis, A. (1988, August). The philosophical basis of rational-emotive therapy (RET). Paper presented at the 96th Annual Convention of the American Psychological Association, Atlanta.

Ellis, A. (1990). How can psychological treatment aim to be briefer and better? The rational-emotive approach to brief therapy. In J. K. Zeig & S. G. Gilligan (Eds.), *Brief therapy myths, methods, and metaphors*, New York: Brunner/Mazel.

Ellis, A. (1993). Reflections on rational-emotive therapy. *Journal of Consulting and Clinical Psychology, 61*, 199–201.

Ellis, A., & Harper, R. A. (1961). *A guide to rational living*. North Hollywood, CA: Wilshire.

Ellis, G. M. (1994). Acquaintance rape. *Perspectives in Psychiatric Care, 30*, 11–16.

Ellis, L. (1991). A synthesized (biosocial) theory of rape. *Journal of Consulting and Clinical Psychology, 59*, 631–642.

Ellis, R. J., & Oscar-Berman, M. (1989). Alcoholism, aging, and functional cerebral asymmetries. *Psychological Bulletin, 106,* 128–147.

Emde, R. N., Plomin, R., Robinson, J., Corley, R., DeFries, J., Fulker, D. W., Reznick, J. S., Campos, J., Kagan, J., & Zahn-Waxler, C. (1992). Temperament, emotion, and cognition at fourteen months: The MacArthur longitudinal twin study. *Child Development, 63,* 1437–1455.

Emery, R. E. (1989a). Family violence. *American Psychologist, 44,* 321–328.

Emery, R. E. (1989b, September 15). Family violence: Has science met its match? Edited transcript of a science and public policy seminar presented by the Federation of Behavioral, Psychological, and Cognitive Sciences in the Rayburn House Office Building, Washington, DC.

Engel, A. K., Konig, P., Kreiter, A. K., Schillen, T. B., & Singer, W. (1992). Temporal coding in the visual cortex: New vistas on integration in the nervous system. *Trends in Neurosciences, 15,* 218–226.

Erber, J. T., Caiola, M. A., Williams, M., & Prager, I. G. (1997). Age and forgetfulness: The effect of implicit priming. *Experimental Aging Research, 23*(1), 1–12.

Erel, O., & Burman, B. (1995). Interrelatedness of marital relations and parent-child relations: A meta-analytic review. *Psychological Bulletin, 118,* 108–132.

Ericsson, K. A., & Charness, N. (1994). Expert performance: Its structure and acquisition. *American Psychologist, 49,* 725–747.

Ericsson, K. A., Chase, W. G., & Faloon, S. (1980). Acquisition of a memory skill. *Science, 208,* 1181–1182.

Ericsson, K. A., Krampe, R. T., & Tesch-Römer, C. (1993). The role of deliberate practice in the acquisition of expert performance. *Psychological Review, 100,* 363–406.

Erikson, E. H. (1963). *Childhood and society* (2nd ed.). New York: Norton.

Erikson, E. H. (1968). *Identity: Youth and crisis.* New York: Norton.

Erlenmeyer-Kimling, L., & Jarvik, L. F. (1963). Genetics and intelligence: A review. *Science, 142,* 1477–1479.

Erngrund, K., Mantyla, T., & Nilsson, L. G. (1996). Adult age differences in source recall: A population based study. *Journals of Gerontology Series B Psychological Sciences and Social Sciences, 51B*(6), 335–345.

Eron, L. D. (1987). The development of aggressive behavior from the perspective of a developing behaviorism. *American Psychologist, 42,* 435–442.

Eron, L. D., & Huesmann, L. R. (1980). Adolescent aggression and television. *Annals of the New York Academy of Sciences, 347,* 319–331.

Eslinger, P. J., Grattan, L. M., Damasio, H., & Damasio, A. R. (1992). Developmental consequences of childhood frontal lobe damage. *Archives of Neurology, 49,* 764–769.

Esses, V. M., & Webster, C. D. (1988). Physical attractiveness, dangerousness, and the Canadian criminal code. *Journal of Applied Social Psychology, 18,* 1017–1031.

Estes, D. (1998). Young children's awareness of their mental activity: The case of mental rotation. *Child Development, 69*(5), 1345–1360.

Etaugh, C. (1980). Effects of nonmaternal care on children. *American Psychologist, 35,* 309–319.

Evans, D. A., Funkenstein, H. H., Albert, M. S., Scherr, P. A., Cook, N. R., Chown, M. J., Hebert, L. E., Hennekens, C. H., & Taylor, J. O. (1989). Prevalence of Alzheimer's disease in a community population of older persons. *Journal of the American Medical Association, 262,* 2551–2556.

Evans, G. W., Hygge, S., & Bullinger, M. (1995). Chronic noise and psychological stress. *Psychological Science, 6,* 333–338.

Evans, G. W., Lepore, S. J., Shejwal, B. R., & Palsane, M. N. (1998). Chronic residential crowding and children's well-being: An ecological perspective. *Child Development, 69*(6), 1514–1523.

Ewart, C. K. (1991). Social action theory for a public health psychology. *American Psychologist, 46,* 931–946.

Exner, J. E., Jr., Thomas, E. A., & Mason, B. (1985). Children's Rorschachs: Description and prediction. *Journal of Personality Assessment, 49,* 13–14.

Eyer, D. E. (1992). *Mother-infant bonding: A scientific fiction.* New Haven, CT: Yale University Press.

Eysenck, H. J. (1970). *The structure of human personality* (3rd ed.). London: Methuen.

Eysenck, H. J. (1995). *Genius: The natural history of creativity.* Cambridge, England: Cambridge University Press.

Eysenck, H. J. (1998). *A new look at intelligence.* London: Transaction Publishers.

Fagan, J. (1994). Correlates of maternal involvement in on-site and off-site day care centers. *Child and Youth Care Forum, 23,* 275–290.

Fagan, J. (1996). A preliminary study of low-income African American fathers' play interactions with their preschool-age children. *Journal of Black Psychology, 22*(1), 7–19.

Fagan, J. (1997). Patterns of mother and father involvement in day care. *Child and Youth Care Forum, 26*(2), 113–126.

Fagan, J., & Silverthorn, A. S. (1998). Research on communication by touch. In E. W. Smith (Ed.), *Touch in psychotherapy: Theory, research, and practice* (pp. 59–73). New York: The Guildford Press.

Fan, X., Chen, M., & Matsumoto, A. R. (1988). Gender differences in mathematics achievement: Findings from the National Longitudinal Study of 1988. *Journal of Experimental Education, 65*(3), 229–242.

Fang, H. (1996). Dopamine receptor studies in human postmortem brain by radioreceptor binding. *International Medical Journal, 3*(4), 265–272.

Fantz, R. L. (1961, May). The origin of form perception. *Scientific American,* 66–72.

Farah, M. J. (1990). *Visual agnosia: Disorders of object recognition and what they tell us about normal vision.* Cambridge, MA: MIT Press.

Farah, M. J., Levinson, K. L., & Klein, K. (1995). Face perception and within-category discrimination in prosopagnosia. *Neuropsychologia, 33*(6), 661–674.

Farah, M. J., O'Reilly, R. C., & Vecera, S. P. (1993). Dissociated overt and covert recognition as an emergent property of a lesioned neural network. *Psychological Review, 100*(4), 571–588.

Farah, M. J., Wilson, K. D., Drain, M., & Tanaka, J. N. (1998). What is special about face perception? *Psychological Review, 105*(3), 482–498.

Farrell, A. D., & Danish, S. J. (1993). Peer drug associations and emotional restraint: Causes or consequences of adolescents' drug use? *Journal of Consulting and Clinical Psychology, 61,* 327–334.

Farwell, L., & Wohlwend-Lloyd, R. (1998). Narcissistic processes: Optimistic expectations, favorable self-evaluations, and self-enhancing attributions. *Journal of Personality, 66*(1), 65–67.

Fazio, R. H. (1990). Multiple processes by which attitudes guide behavior: The MODE model as an integrative framework. In M. P. Zanna (Ed.), *Advances in experimental social psychology* (Vol. 23, pp. 75–109). San Diego: Academic.

Federation of Canadian Municipalities (1994). *Youth violence and youth gangs: Responding to community concerns.* Ottawa: Solicitor General and Department of Justice, Government of Canada.

Feeney, D. M. (1987). Human rights and animal welfare. *American Psychologist, 42,* 593–599.

Fehr, B., & Russell, J. A. (1991). The concept of love viewed from a prototype perspective. *Journal of Personality and Social Psychology, 60,* 425–438.

Feingold, A. (1988). Matching for attractiveness in romantic partners and same-sex friends: A meta-analysis and theoretical critique. *Psychological Bulletin, 104,* 226–235.

Feingold, A. (1992a). Gender differences in mate selection preferences: A test of the parental investment model. *Psychological Bulletin, 112,* 125–139.

Feingold, A. (1992b). Good-looking people are not what we think. *Psychological Bulletin, 111,* 304–341.

Feingold, A. (1993). Cognitive gender differences: A developmental perspective. *Sex Roles, 29,* 91–111.

Feingold, A. (1994). Gender differences in personality: A meta-analysis. *Psychological Bulletin, 116,* 429–456.

Feldman, L., Holowaty, P., Harvey, B., Rannie, K., Shortt, L., & Jamal, A. (1997). A comparison of the demographic, lifestyle, and sexual behaviour characteristics of virgin and non-virgin adolescents. *The Canadian Journal of Human Sexuality, 6*(3), 197–209.

Fenton, W. S., & McGlashan, T. H. Natural history of schizophrenia subtypes: II. Positive and negative symptoms and long-term course. *Archives of General Psychiatry, 48*(11), 978–986.

Fenwick, D. T. (1998). Managing space, energy and self: Junior high teachers' experiences of classroom management. *Teaching & Teacher Education, 14*(6), 619–631.

Fenwick, P., Donaldson, S., Gillies, L., Bushman, J., Fenton, G., Perry, I., Tilsley, C., & Serafinowicz, H. (1977). Metabolic and EEG changes during transcendental meditation. *Biological Psychology, 5,* 101–118.

Ferguson, G. A. (1993). Psychology in Canada 1939–1945. *Canadian Psychology, 33,* 2.

Fernandez, E., & Sheffield, J. (1996). Relative contributions of life events versus daily hassles to the frequency and intensity of headaches. *Headache, 36*(10), 595–602.

Fernandez, E., & Turk, D. C. (1992). Sensory and affective components of pain: Separation and synthesis. *Psychological Bulletin, 112,* 205–217.

Festinger, L. (1954). A theory of social comparison processes. *Human Relations, 7,* 117–140.

Festinger, L. (1957). *A theory of cognitive dissonance.* Evanston, IL: Row, Petersen.

Fiedler, F. E. (1964). A contingency model of leadership effectiveness. In L. Berkowitz (Ed.), *Advances in experimental social psychology* (Vol. 1). New York: Academic.

Fiedler, F. E. (1974). Personality, motivational systems, and behavior of high and low LPC persons. *Human Relations, 25,* 391–412.

Field, T. (1996). Attachment and separation in young children. *Annual Review of Psychology, 47,* 541–561.

Fine, A. (1986, August). Transplantation in the central nervous system. *Scientific American,* 52–67.

Fink, M. (1997). Prejudice against ECT: Competition with psychological philosophies as a contribution to its stigma. *Convulsive Therapy, 13*(4), 253–265.

Fischer, A. R., & Good, G. E. (1998). New directions for the study of gender role attitudes. *Psychology of Women Quarterly, 22,* 371–384.

Fischer, C. T. (1991). Phenomenological-existential psychotherapy. In M. Hersen, A. E. Kazdin, & A. S. Bellack (Eds.), *The clinical psychology handbook* (2nd ed.). New York: Pergamon.

Fischer, J., & Gochros, H. L. (1975). *Planned behavior change: Behavior modification in social work.* New York: Free Press.

Fisher, C. B., & Fyrberg, D. (1994). Participant partners: College students weigh the costs and benefits of deceptive research. *American Psychologist, 49,* 417–427.

Fisher, L., Ames, E. W., Chisholm, K., Savoie, L. (1997). Problems reported by parents of Romanian orphans adopted to British Columbia. *International Journal of Behavioral Development, 20*(1), 67–82.

Fisher, S. E., Vargha-Khadem, F., Watkins, K. E., Monaco, A. P., & Pembrey, M. E. (1998). Localisation of a gene implicated in severe speech and language disorder. *Nature Genetics, 18,* 168–170.

Fishman, D. B., & Franks, C. M. (1997). The conceptual evolution of behavior therapy. In P. L. Wachtel & S. B. Messer (Eds.), *Theories of psychotherapy: Origins and evolution* (pp. 131–180). Washington, DC: American Psychological Association.

Fiske, S. T. (1992). Thinking is for doing: Portraits of social cognition from daguerreotype to laserphoto. *Journal of Personality and Social Psychology, 63,* 877–889.

Fiske, S. T. (1998). Stereotyping, prejudice, and discrimination. In D. T. Gilbert et al. (Eds.), *The handbook of social psychology* (pp. 357–411). New York: McGraw-Hill.

Fitzgerald, L. F., & Osipow, S. H. (1986). An occupational analysis of counseling psychology. *American Psychologist, 41,* 535–544.

Flaskerud, J. H., & Hu, L. T. (1992). Relationship of ethnicity to psychiatric diagnosis. *Journal of Nervous and Mental Disease, 180,* 296–303.

Flavell, J. H. (1996). Piaget's legacy. *American Psychological Society, 7*(4), 200–203.

Flavell, J. H., Green, F. L., & Flavell, E. R. (1993). Children's understanding of the stream of consciousness. *Child Development, 64,* 387–398.

Flavell, J. H., Green, F. L., & Flavell, E. R. (1998). The mind has a mind of its own: Developing knowledge about mental uncontrollability. *Cognitive Development, 13,* 127–138.

Flavell, J. H., & Wellman, H. M. (1977). Metamemory. In R. V. Kail, Jr., & J. W. Hagen (Eds.), *Perspectives on the development of memory and cognition.* Hillsdale, NJ: Erlbaum.

Fleischman, D. A., Vaidya, C. J., Lange, K. L., & Gabrieli, J. D. E. (1997). A dissociation between perceptual explicit and implicit memory processes. *Brain & Cognition, 35*(1), 42–57.

Fleming, I., Baum, A., & Weiss, L. (1987). Social density and perceived control as mediators of crowding stress in high-density residential neighborhoods. *Journal of Personality and Social Psychology, 52,* 899–906.

Fleming, J. D. (1974, July). Field report: The state of the apes. *Psychology Today,* 31–46.

Flint, A. J., & Rifat, S. L. (1998). The treatment of psychotic depression in later life: A comparison of pharmacotherapy and ECT. *International Journal of Geriatric Psychiatry, 13*(1), 23–28.

Florence, S. L., Taub, H. B., & Kaas, J. H. (1998). Large-scale sprouting of cortical connections after peripheral injury in adult macaque monkeys. *Science, 282,* 1117–1120.

Flynn, J. R. (1987). Massive gains in 14 nations: What IQ tests really measure. *Psychological Bulletin, 101,* 171–191.

Flynn, J. R. (1998). IQ gains over time: Toward finding the causes. In U. Neisser (Ed.), *The rising curve: Long-term gains in IQ and related measures* (pp. 25–65). Washington, DC: American Psychological Association.

Flynn, J. R. (1999). Searching for justice: The discovery of IQ gains over time. *American Psychologist, 54*(1), 5–20.

Foa, E. B., & Riggs, D. S. (1995). Posttraumatic stress disorder following assault: Theoretical considerations and empirical findings. *Current Directions in Psychological Science, 4,* 61–65.

Ford, J. D., Chandler, P., Thacker, B., Greaves, D., Shaw, D., Sennhauser, S., & Schwartz, L. (1998). Family systems therapy after operation Desert Storm with European-theater veterans. *Journal of Marital and Family Therapy, 24*(2), 243–250.

Forgas, J. P. (1998). Asking nicely? The effects of mood on responding to more or less polite requests. *Personality and Social Psychology Bulletin, 24*(2), 173–185.

Forsythe, S. M. (1990). Effect of applicant's clothing on interviewer's decision to hire. *Journal of Applied Social Psychology, 20,* 1579–1595.

Fosshage, J. L. (1997). The organizing functions of dream mentation. *Contemporary Psychoanalysis, 33*(3), 429–458.

Foster, R. G. (1993). Photoreceptors and circadian systems. *Current Directions in Psychological Science, 2,* 34–39.

Foulkes, D. (1985). *Dreaming: A cognitive-psychological analysis.* Hillsdale, NJ: Lawrence Erlbaum.

Foulkes, D. (1990). Dreaming and consciousness. *European Journal of Cognitive Psychology, 2*(1), 39–55.

Foulkes, D. (1996). Dream research. *Sleep, 19*(8), 609–624.

Foulkes, D., & Kerr, N. H. (1994). Point of view in nocturnal dreaming. *Perceptual and Motor Skills, 78*(2), 690.

Foulkes, D., Meier, B., Strauch, I., & Kerr, N. H. (1993). Linguistic phenomena and language selection in the REM dreams of German-English bilinguals. *International Journal of Psychology, 28*(6), 871–891.

Fox, M. (1993). *Psychological perspectives in education.* New York: Cassell Educational.

Frable, D. E. (1989). Sex typing and gender ideology: Two facets of the individual's gender psychology that go together. *Journal of Personality and Social Psychology, 56,* 95–108.

Frank, M. G., & Ekman, P. (1997). The ability to detect deceit generalizes across different types of high-stake lies. *Journal of Personality and Social Psychology, 72*(6), 1429–1439.

Frank, M. G., Ekman, P., & Friesen, W. V. (1997). Behavioral markers and recognizability of the smile of enjoyment. In P. Ekman & E. L. Rosenberg (Eds.), *What the face reveals: Basic and applied studies of spontaneous expression using the Facial Action Coding System (FACS)* (pp. 217–242). New York: Oxford University Press.

Franko, D. L., & Erb, J. (1998). Managed care or mangled care? Treating eating disorders in the current healthcare climate. *Psychotherapy: Theory, Research and Practice, 35*(1), 43–53.

Frasure-Smith, N., Lesperance, F., & Talajic, M. (1993). Depression following myocardial infarction: Impact on 6-month survival. *Journal of the American Medical Association, 270,* 1819–1825.

Frasure-Smith, N., Lesperance, F., & Talajic, M. (1995). The impact of negative emotions on prognosis following myocardial infarction: Is it more than depression? *Health Psychology, 14,* 388–398.

Frasure-Smith, N., & Prince, R. (1989). Long-term follow-up of the ischemic heart disease life stress monitoring program. *Psychosomatic Medicine, 51,* 485–513.

Frederiksen, N. (1986). Toward a broader conception of human intelligence. *American Psychologist, 41,* 445–452.

French, K. E., Spurgeon, J. H., & Nevett, M. E. (1995). Expert-novice differences in cognitive and skill execution components of youth baseball performance. *Research Quarterly for Exercise and Sport, 66,* 194–201.

Freud, S. (1933). *New introductory lectures on psychoanalysis.* New York: Norton.

Freud, S. (1953). The interpretation of dreams. In J. Stachey (Ed.), *The standard edition of the complete psychological works of Sigmund*

Freud (Vols. 4 and 5). London: Hogarth. (Original work published 1900.)

Freud, S. (1966). *A general introduction to psychoanalysis* (J. Riviere, Trans.) New York: Washington Square. (Original work published 1920.)

Frezza, M., di Padova, C., Pozzato, G., Terpin, M., Baraona, E., & Lieber, C. S. (1990). High blood alcohol levels in women. *New England Journal of Medicine, 322*, 95–99.

Friedberg, F., & Jason, L. A. (1998). Understanding chronic fatigue syndrome: An empirical guide to assessment and treatment. *American Psychological Association, 17*, 266.

Friedman, M. (1996). *Type A behavior: Its diagnosis and treatment.* New York: Plenum Press.

Friedman, M., & Rosenman, R. H. (1974). *Type A behavior and your heart.* Greenwich, CT: Fawcett.

Friedman, S., Paradis, C. M., & Hatch, M. (1994). Characteristics of African-American and white patients with panic disorder and agoraphobia. *Hospital and Community Psychiatry, 45*, 798–803.

Friedman, W. J. (1993). Memory for the time of past events. *Psychological Bulletin, 113*, 44–66.

Frieze, I. H., Olson, J. E., & Russell, J. (1991). Attractiveness and income for men and women in management. *Journal of Applied Social Psychology, 21*, 1039–1057.

Fromm, E. (1956). *The art of loving.* New York: Harper & Row.

Fromme, K., Marlatt, G. A., Baer, J. S., & Kivlahan, D. R. (1994). The alcohol skills training program: A group intervention for young adult drinkers. *Journal of Substance Abuse Treatment, 11*, 143–154.

Fruzzetti, A. E., & Jacobson, N. S. (1991). Marital and family therapy. In M. Hersen, A. E. Kazdin, & A. S. Bellack (Eds.), *The clinical psychology handbook* (2nd ed.). New York: Pergamon.

Fuller, T. D., Edwards, J. N., Vorakitphokatorn, S., & Sermsri, S. (1996). Chronic stress and psychological well-being: Evidence from Thailand on household crowding. *Social Science and Medicine, 42*(2), 265–280.

Funder, D. C. (1995). On the accuracy of personality judgment: A realistic approach. *Psychological Review, 102*, 652–670.

Furby, L., Weinrott, M. R., & Blackshaw, L. (1989). Sex offender recidivism: A review. *Psychological Bulletin, 105*, 3–30.

Furstenberg, F. F., Jr., Brooks-Gunn, J., & Chase-Lansdale, L. (1989). Teenaged pregnancy and childbearing. *American Psychologist, 44*, 313–320.

Furstenberg, F. F., Jr., & Hughes, M. E. (1995). Social capital and successful development among at-risk youth. *Journal of Marriage and the Family, 57*(3), 580–592.

Gabrieli, J. D. E., Brewer, J. B., Desmond, J. E., & Glover, G. H. (1997). Separate neural bases of two fundamental memory processes in the human medial temporal lobe. *Science, 276*, 264–266.

Gaffan, E. A., Tsaousis, J., & Kemp-Wheeler, S. M. (1995). Researcher allegiance and meta-analysis: The case of cognitive therapy for depression. *Journal of Consulting and Clinical Psychology, 63*, 960–980.

Gaines, S. O., Jr., & Reed, E. S. (1995). Prejudice: From Allport to DuBois. *American Psychologist, 50*, 96–103.

Galambos, N. L. (1992). Parent-adolescent relations. *Current Directions, 1*, 146–149.

Galin, D. (1974). Implications for psychiatry of left and right cerebral specialization: A neurophysiological context for unconscious processes. *Archives of General Psychiatry, 31*, 572–583.

Gallup, G. G., Jr., & Suarez, S. D. (1985). Alternatives to the use of animals in psychological research. *American Psychologist, 40*, 1104–1111.

Gallwey, W. T. (1974). *The inner game of tennis.* New York: Random House.

Galotti, K. M. (1989). Approaches to studying formal and everyday reasoning. *Psychological Bulletin, 105*, 331–351.

Gannon, P. J., Holloway, R. L., Broadfield, D. C., & Braun, A. R. (1998). Asymmetry of chimpanzee planum temporale: Humanlike pattern of Wernicke's brain language area homolog. *Science, 279*, 220–222.

Garb, H. N., Florio, C. M., & Grove, W. M. (1998). The validity of the Rorschach and the Minnesota Multiphasic Personality Inventory: Results from meta-analyses. *American Psychological Society, 9*(5), 402–404.

Garbarino, J., Dubrow, N., Kostelny, K., & Pardo, C. (1992). *Children in danger: Coping with the consequences of community violence.* The Jossey-Bass social and behavioral science series and the Jossey-Bass education series. San Francisco, CA: Jossey-Bass Inc, Publishers.

Garcia, J., Gustavson, C. R., Kelly, D. J., & Sweeney, M. (1976). Preynlithium aversions: I. Coyotes and wolves. *Behavioral Biology, 16*, 61–72.

Garcia, J., & Koelling, R. A. (1971). The use of ionizing rays as a mammalian olfactory stimulus. In H. Autrum, R. Jung, W. R. Loewenstein, D. M. MacKay, & H. L. Teuber (Eds.), *Handbook of sensory physiology: Vol. 4. Chemical senses* (Pt. 1). New York: Springer-Verlag.

Gardner, H. (1983/1993). *Frames of mind: The theory of multiple intelligences.* New York: Basic Books.

Gardner, H. (1995). Multiple intelligences as a catalyst. *English Journal, 84*(8), 16–18.

Gardner, H. (1996). Personal communication.

Gardner, H., & Hatch, T. (1989). Multiple intelligences go to school: Educational implications of the theory of multiple intelligences. *Educational Researcher, 18*, 6.

Gardner, R. A., & Gardner, B. T. (1969). Teaching sign language to a chimp. *Science, 165*, 664–672.

Gardner, W., Scherer, D., & Tester, M. (1989). Asserting scientific authority: Cognitive development and adolescent legal rights. *American Psychologist, 6*, 895–902.

Gardner, W. L., & Avolio, B. J. (1998). The charismatic relationship: A dramaturgical perspective. *Academy of Management Review, 23*(1), 32–58.

Garfield, S. L. (1998). Some comments on empirically supported treatments. *Journal of Consulting and Clinical Psychology, 66*(1), 121–125.

Garfield, S. L., & Bergin, A. E. (1986). *Handbook of psychotherapy and behavior change* (3rd ed.). New York: Wiley.

Garfinkel, P. E., Lin, E., Goering, P., Spegg, C., et al. (1996). Purging and nonpurging forms of bulimia nervosa in a community sample. *International Journal of Eating Disorders, 20*(3), 231–238.

Garland, A. F., & Zigler, E. (1993). Adolescent suicide prevention. *American Psychologist, 48*, 169–182.

Garry, M. & Loftus, E. F. (1994). Pseudomemories without hypnosis. *The International Journal of Clinical and Experimental Hypnosis, 42*, 363–378.

Gazzaniga, M. S. (1983). Right hemisphere language following brain bisection: A 20-year perspective. *American Psychologist, 38*, 525–537.

Gazzaniga, M. S. (1989). Organization of the human brain. *Science, 245*, 947–952.

Ge, X., Conger, R. D., Cadoret, R. J., Neiderhiser, J. M., Yates, W., Troughton, E., et al. (1996). The developmental interface between nature and nurture: A mutual influence model of child antisocial behavior and parent behaviors. *Developmental Psychology, 32*(4), 574–589.

Ge, X., Conger, R. D., & Elder, G. H., Jr. (1996). Coming of age too early: Pubertal influences on girls' vulnerability to psychological distress. *Child Development, 67*(6), 3386–3400.

Geary, D. C. (1996). Biology, culture, and cross-national differences in mathematical ability. In R. J. Sternberg, T. Ben-Zeev, et al. (Eds.), *The nature of mathematical thinking. The studies in mathematical thinking and learning series* (pp. 145–171). Mahwah, NJ: Lawrence Erlbaum Associates, Inc.

Gebhardt, D. L., & Crump, C. E. (1990). Employee fitness and wellness programs in the workplace. *American Psychologist, 45*, 262–272.

Gedda, L. (1961). *Twins in history and science.* Springfield, IL: Charles C. Thomas.

Geen, R. G. (1991). Social motivation. *Annual Review of Psychology, 42*, 377–399.

Geller, E. S. (1975). Increasing desired waste disposals with instructions. *Man-Environment Systems, 5*, 125–128.

Geller, E. S. (1989). Applied behavior analysis and social marketing: An integration for environmental preservation. *Journal of Social Issues, 45*, 17–36.

Geller, E. S. (1992). It takes more than information to save energy. *American Psychologist, 47*, 814–815.

Geller, E. S. (1995). Integrating behaviorism and humanism for environmental protection. *Journal of Social Issues, 51*(4), 179–195.

Geller, E. S., Kalsher, M. J., Rudd, J. R., & Lehman, G. R. (1989). Promoting safety belt use on a university campus: An integration of commitment and incentive strategies. *Journal of Applied Social Psychology, 19*(1), 3–19.

Geller, E. S., Witmer, J. F., & Tuso, M. E. (1977). Environmental intervention for litter control. *Journal of Applied Psychology, 62*, 344–351.

George, J. M., & Brief, A. P. (1992). Feeling good—doing good: A conceptual analysis of the mood at work-organizational spontaneity relationship. *Psychological Bulletin, 112*, 310–329.

George, M. S., Ketter, T. A., & Post, R. M. (1993). SPECT and PET imaging in mood disorders. *Journal of Clinical Psychiatry, 54*, 6–13.

Gerber, L. (1994). Psychotherapy with southeast Asian refugees: Implications for treatment of Western patients. *American Journal of Psychotherapy, 48,* 280–293.

German, D. (1983). Analysis of word-finding disorders on the Kaufman Assessment Battery for Children (K-ABC). *Journal of Psychoeducational Assessment, 1,* 121–134.

Geschwind, N. (1972, April). Language and the brain. *Scientific American,* 76–83.

Gibson, E. J. (1992). How to think about perceptual learning: Twenty-five years later. In H. L. Pick, Jr., P. van den Broek, & D. C. Knill (Eds.), *Cognition: Conceptual and methodological issues* (pp. 215–238). Washington, DC: American Psychological Association.

Gibson, J. A. P., & Range, L. M. (1991). Are written reports of suicide and seeking help contagious? High schoolers' perceptions. *Journal of Applied Social Psychology, 21,* 1517–1523.

Gift, T. E., Strauss, J. S., Ritzler, B. A., Kokes, R. F., & Harder, D. W. (1980). How diagnostic concepts of schizophrenia differ. *Journal of Nervous and Mental Disease, 168,* 3–8.

Gilbert, R. K. (1988). The dynamics of inaction. *American Psychologist, 43,* 755–764.

Gillies, R. M., & Ashman, A. F. (1996). Teaching collaborative skills to primary school children in classroom-based work groups. *Learning and Instruction, 6*(3), 187–200.

Gilligan, C. (1982). *In a different voice: Psychological theory and women's development.* Cambridge, MA: Harvard University Press.

Gilligan, C. (1995). In a different voice: Women's conceptions of self and of morality. In B. Puka et al. (Eds.), *Caring voices and women's moral frames: Gilligan's view.* New York: Garland Publishing, Inc.

Gilligan, C. (1997). Remembering Iphigenia: Voice, resonance, and a talking cure. In B. Mark (Ed.), *The handbook of infant, child, and adolescent psychotherapy.* Northvale, NJ: Jason Aronson.

Glantz, M. D. (1989). Cognitive therapy with the elderly. In A. Freeman, K. M. Simon, L. E. Beutler, & H. Arkowitz (Eds.), *Comprehensive handbook of cognitive therapy.* New York: Plenum.

Glasgow, R. E., & Terborg, J. R. (1988). Occupational health promotion programs to reduce cardiovascular risk. *Journal of Consulting and Clinical Psychology, 56,* 365–373.

Gleaves, D. H. (1996). The sociocognitive model of dissociative identity disorder: A reexamination of the evidence. *Psychological Bulletin, 120,* 42–59.

Gleicher, F., & Petty, R. E. (1992). Expectations of reassurance influence the nature of fear-stimulated attitude change. *Journal of Experimental Social Psychology, 28*(1), 86–100.

Gleitman, H. (1985). Some trends in the study of cognition. In S. Koch, & D. E. Leary (Eds.), *A century of psychology as science.* New York: McGraw-Hill.

Glick, P., Diebold, J., Bailey-Wexner, B., & Zhu, L. (1997). The two faces of Adam: Ambivalent sexism and polarized attitudes toward women. *Personality and Social Psychology Bulletin, 23*(12), 1323–1334.

Glick, P., & Fiske, S. T. (1997). Hostile and benevolent sexism: Measuring ambivalent sexism toward women. *Psychology of Women Quarterly, 21*(1), 119–135.

Goldberger, N. (1997). Ways of knowing: Does gender matter? In M. R. Walsh (Ed.), *Women, men, and gender: Ongoing debates.* New Haven, CT: Yale University Press.

Goldfried, M. R., & Wolfe, B. E. (1996). Psychotherapy practice and research: Repairing a strained alliance. *American Psychologist, 51*(10), 1007–1016.

Goldfried, M. R., & Wolfe, B. E. (1998). Toward a more clinically valid approach to therapy research. *Journal of Consulting and Clinical Psychology, 66*(1), 143–150.

Golding, J., Rogers, I. S., & Emmett, P. M. (1997). Association between breast feeding, child development and behaviour. *Early Human Development, 49,* 175–184.

Golding, J. M., Potts, M. K., & Aneshensel, C. S. (1991). Stress exposure among Mexican Americans and non-Hispanic whites. *Journal of Community Psychology, 19,* 37–59.

Goldman, M. S., Brown, S. A., Christiansen, B. A., & Smith, G. T. (1991). Alcoholism and memory: Broadening the scope of alcohol-expectancy research. *Psychological Bulletin, 110,* 137–146.

Goleman, D. (1995). *Emotional intelligence.* New York: Bantam.

Gonzales, L. R., Hays, R. B., Bond, M. A., & Kelly, J. G. (1983). Community mental health. In M. Hersen, A. E. Kazdin, & A. S. Bellack (Eds.), *The clinical psychology handbook.* New York: Pergamon.

Gonzales, R. R., & Roll, S. (1985). Relationship between acculturation, cognitive style, and intelligence. *Journal of Cross-Cultural Psychology, 16,* 190–205.

Goodwin, R., & Tang, D. (1991). Preferences for friends and close relationship partners: A cross-cultural comparison. *Journal of Social Psychology, 131,* 579–581.

Gortmaker, S. L., Kagan, J., Caspi, A., & Silva, P. A. (1997). Daylength during pregnancy and shyness in children: Results from Northern and Southern hemispheres. *Developmental Psychobiology, 31*(2), 107–114.

Gostin, L. O. (1997). The legal regulation of smoking (and smokers): Public health or secular morality? In A. Brandt, P. Rozin, et al. (Eds.), *Morality and health* (pp. 331–357). New York: Routledge.

Gothard, K. M., Skaggs, W. E., Moore, K. M., & McNaughton, B. L. (1996). Binding of hippocampal CA1 neural activity to multiple reference frames in a landmark-based navigation task. *Journal of Neuroscience, 16*(2), 823–835.

Gottman, J. M., & Katz, L. F. (1989). Effects of marital discord on young children's peer interaction and health. *Developmental Psychology, 25,* 373–381.

Goulding, M. M. (1990). Getting the important work done fast: Contract plus redecision. In J. K. Zeig & S. G. Gilligan (Eds.), *Brief therapy myths, methods, and metaphors.* New York: Brunner/Mazel.

Graber, J. A., Lewinsohn, P. M., Seeley, J. R., & Brooks-Gunn, J. (1997). Is psychopathology associated with the timing of pubertal development? *Journal of the American Academy of Child and Adolescent Psychiatry, 36*(12), 1768–1776.

Grady, C. L., McIntosh, A. R., Horwitz, B., Maisog, J. M., Ungerleider, L. G., Mentis, M. J., Pietrini, P., Schapiro, M. B., & Haxby, J. V. (1995). Age-related reductions in human recognition memory due to impaired encoding. *Science, 269,* 218–220.

Graham, C. J., & Cleveland, E. (1995). Left-handedness as an injury risk factor in adolescents. *Journal of Adolescent Health, 16*(1), 50–52.

Graziano, M. S., Hu, X. T., & Gross, C. G. (1997). Coding the locations of objects in the dark. *Science, 277,* 239–240.

Graziano, M. S. A., & Gross, C. G. (1994). Mapping space with neurons. *Current Directions in Psychological Science, 3,* 164–167.

Greenberg, J. (1990). Employee theft as a reaction to underpayment inequity: The hidden cost of pay cuts. *Journal of Applied Psychology, 75,* 561–568.

Greenberg, J. (1998). Equity and workplace status: A field experiment. In S. Steven, S. Spencer, et al. (Eds.), *Readings in social psychology: The art and science of research* (p. 180). Boston: Houghton Mifflin.

Greenberg, R. P., Bornstein, R. F., Greenberg, M. D., Fisher, S., & Seymour, F. (1992). A meta-analysis of antidepressant outcome under "blinder" conditions. *Journal of Consulting and Clinical Psychology, 60,* 664–669.

Greene, K., & Rubin, D. L. (1991). Effects of gender inclusive/exclusive language in religious discourse. *Journal of Language and Social Psychology, 10*(2), 81–98.

Greenfield, P. M. (1997). You can't take it with you: Why ability assessments don't cross cultures. *American Psychologist, 52*(10), 1115–1124.

Greeno, C. G., & Wing, R. R. (1994). Stress-induced eating. *Psychological Bulletin, 115,* 444–464.

Greeno, J. G. (1989). A perspective on thinking. *American Psychologist, 44,* 134–141.

Greeno, J. G., and the Middle School Mathematics Through Applications Project Group. (1998). The situativity of knowing, learning, and research. *American Psychologist, 53*(1), 5–26.

Greenwald, A. G., Klinger, M. R., & Schuh, E. S. (1995). Activation by marginally perceptible ("subliminal") stimuli: Dissociation of unconscious from conscious cognition. *Journal of Experimental Psychology: General, 124*(1), 22–42.

Greer, S., & Brady, M. (1988). Natural killer cells: One possible link between cancer and the mind. *Stress Medicine, 4*(2), 105–111.

Griffeth, R. W., Vecchio, R. P., & Logan, J. W., Jr. (1989). Equity theory and interpersonal attraction. *Journal of Applied Psychology, 74,* 394–401.

Grilo, C. M., & Shiffman, S. (1994). Longitudinal investigation of the abstinence violation effect in binge eaters. *Journal of Consulting and Clinical Psychology, 62,* 611–619.

Gross, J. J., Fredrickson, B. L., & Levenson, R. W. (1994). The psychophysiology of crying. *Psychophysiology, 31,* 460–463.

Grossberg, S. (1995). The attentive brain. *American Scientist, 83,* 438–449.

Grossman, F. K., Pollack, W. S., & Golding, E. (1988). Fathers and children: Predicting the quality and quantity of fathering. *Developmental Psychology, 1,* 91–92.

Grunberg, L., Moore, S., & Greenberg, E. S. (1998). Work stress and problem alcohol behavior: A test of the spillover model. *Journal of Organizational Behavior, 19*(5), 487–502.

Guarnaccia, P. J. (1997). Social stress and psychological distress among Latinos in the United States. In I. Al-Ihsan et al. (Eds.), *Ethnicity, immigration, and psychopathology. The Plenum Series on stress and coping* (pp. 71–94). New York: Plenum Press.

Guerin, P. J., Jr., & Chabot, D. R. (1997). Development of family systems theory. In P. L. Wachtel & S. B. Messer (Eds.), *Theories of psychotherapy: Origins and evolution* (pp. 181–226). Washington, DC: American Psychological Association.

Guilford, J. P. (1967). *The nature of human intelligence.* New York: McGraw-Hill.

Gulevich, G., Dement, W., & Johnson, L. (1966). Psychiatric and EEG observations on a case of prolonged (264 hours) wakefulness. *Archives of General Psychiatry, 15,* 29–35.

Gulya, M., Rovee-Collier, C., Galluccio, L., & Wilk, A. (1998). Memory processing of a serial list by young infants. *American Psychological Society, 9*(4), 303–307.

Gunter, B., & Harrison, J. (1998). *Violence on television: An analysis of amount, nature, location and origin of violence in British programmes.* London: Routledge.

Gutierrez, P. M., & Silk, K. R. (1998). Prescription privileges for psychologists: A review of the psychological literature. *Professional Psychology: Research and Practice, 29*(3), 213–222.

Haaga, D. A. F., & Davison, G. C. (1993). An appraisal of rational-emotive therapy. *Journal of Consulting and Clinical Psychology, 61,* 215–220.

Haan, N., Millsap, R., & Hartka, E. (1986). As time goes by: Change and stability in personality over fifty years. *Psychology and Aging, 1,* 220–232.

Haber, R. N. (1979). Twenty years of haunting eidetic imagery: Where's the ghost? *Behavioral and Brain Sciences, 2,* 583–629.

Hackman, M. Z., Furniss, A. H., Hills, M. J., & Paterson, T. J. (1992). Perceptions of gender-role characteristics and transformational and transactional leadership behaviors. *Perceptual and Motor Skills, 75,* 311–319.

Hackman, M. Z., & Johnson, C. E. (1991). *Leadership: A communication perspective.* Prospect Heights, IL: Waveland.

Haddock, G., Zanna, M. P., & Esses, V. M. (1994). The (limited) role of trait-laden stereotypes in predicting attitudes toward native peoples. *British Journal of Social Psychology, 33,* 83–106.

Haith, M. M., & McCarty, M. E. (1990). Stability of visual expectations at 3.0 months of age. *Developmental Psychology, 26,* 68–74.

Hajek, P., & Belcher, M. (1991). Dreams of absent-minded transgression: An empirical study of a cognitive withdrawal symptom. *Journal of Abnormal Psychology, 100,* 487–491.

Hales, D. (1999). *Just like a woman: How gender science is redefining what makes us female.* New York: Bantam Books.

Halgren, E., Walter, R. D., Cherlow, A. G., & Crandall, P. H. (1978). Mental phenomena evoked by electrical stimulation of the human hippocampal formation and amygdala. *Brain, 101,* 83–117.

Hall, C. C. (1997). Cultural malpractice: The growing obsolescence of psychology with the changing U.S. population. *American Psychologist, 52*(6), 642–651.

Hall, E. T. (1966). *The hidden dimension.* Garden City, NY: Doubleday.

Hall, J. (1984). *Nonverbal sex differences: Communication accuracy and expressive style.* Baltimore: Johns Hopkins University Press.

Hall, S. M., Havassy, B. E., & Wasserman, D. A. (1991). Effects of commitment to abstinence, positive moods, stress, and coping on relapse to cocaine use. *Journal of Consulting and Clinical Psychology, 59,* 526–532.

Hallman, W. K., & Wandersman, A. H. (1992). Attribution of responsibility and individual and collective coping with environmental threats. *Journal of Social Issues, 48,* 101–118.

Halpern, D. F. (1986). *Sex differences in cognitive abilities.* Hillsdale, NJ: Erlbaum.

Halpern, D. F. (1997). Sex difference in intelligence. *American Psychologist, 52*(10), 1091–1102.

Halpern, D. F., & Coren, S. (1991). Handedness and life span (Letter to the editor). *New England Journal of Medicine, 324,* 998.

Halpern, D. F., & Coren, S. (1993). Left-handedness and life span: A reply to Harris. *Psychological Bulletin, 114*(2), 235–241.

Hamann, S. B., & Squire, L. R. (1995). On the acquisition of new declarative knowledge in amnesia. *Behavioral Neuroscience, 109,* 1027–1044.

Hamer, D., & Copeland, P. (1998). *Living with our genes: Why they matter more than you think.* New York: Doubleday.

Hamer, D. H., Hu, S., Magnuson, V. L., Hu, N., & Pattatucci, A. M. L. (1993). A linkage between DNA markers on the X chromosome and male sexual orientation. *Science, 261,* 321–327.

Hamilton, S., & Fagot, B. I. (1988). Chronic stress and coping styles: A comparison of male and female undergraduates. *Journal of Personality and Social Psychology, 5,* 819–823.

Hammond, D. L. (1980). The responding of normals, alcoholics, and psychopaths in a laboratory lie-detection experiment. Doctoral dissertation presented to the faculty of the California School of Professional Psychology.

Haney, C., Banks, W., & Zimbardo, P. (1973). Interpersonal dynamics in a simulated prison. *International Journal of Criminology and Penology, 1,* 69–97.

Haney, C., & Zimbardo, P. (1998). The past and future of U.S. prison policy: Twenty-five years after the Stanford Prison experiment. *American Psychologist, 53*(7), 709–727.

Hanson, C. L., Cigrang, J. A., Harris, M. A., Carle, D. L., Relyea, G., & Burghen, G. A. (1989). Coping styles in youths with insulin-dependent diabetes mellitus. *Journal of Consulting and Clinical Psychology, 57,* 644–651.

Hardy, P. A. J. (1995). Pain management in old age. *Reviews in Clinical Gerontology, 5*(3), 259–273.

Harkins, S. G., & Szymanski, K. (1988). Social loafing and self-evaluation with an objective standard. *Journal of Experimental Social Psychology, 24,* 354–365.

Harlow, H. F. (1962). The heterosexual affectional system in monkeys. *American Psychologist, 17,* 1–9.

Harlow, H. F., & Zimmerman, R. R. (1958). The development of affectional responses in infant monkeys. *Proceedings of the American Philosophic Society, 102,* 501–509.

Harms, T. (1994). Humanizing infant environments for group care. *Children's Environments, 11,* 155–167.

Harper, J. F., & Marshall, E. (1991). Adolescents' problems and their relationship to self-esteem. *Adolescence, 26,* 799–803.

Harris, C. R., & Christenfeld, N. (1997). Humor, tickle, and the Darwin-Hecker hypothesis. *Cognition and Emotion, 11*(1), 103–110.

Harris, J. R. (1995). Where is the child's environment? A group socialization theory of development. *Psychological Review, 102,* 458–489.

Harris, J. R. (1998). *The nurture assumption: Why children turn out the way they do.* New York: The Free Press.

Harris, K. M., & Morgan, S. P. (1991). Fathers, sons, and daughters: Differential paternal involvement in parenting. *Journal of Marriage and the Family, 53,* 531–544.

Harris, L. J. (1993). Do left-handers die sooner than right-handers? Commentary on Coren and Halpern's (1991) Left-handedness: A marker for decreased survival fitness. *Psychological Bulletin, 114*(2), 203–234.

Harris, M. B. (1994). Gender of subject and target as mediators of aggression. *Journal of Applied Social Psychology, 24,* 453–471.

Harris, M. B. (1996). Aggressive experiences and aggressiveness: Relationship to ethnicity, gender, and age. *Journal of Applied Social Psychology, 26*(10), 843–870.

Harris, M. B., & Knight-Bohnhoff, K. (1996). Gender and aggression: Personal aggressiveness. *Sex Roles, 35*(1/2), 27–42.

Harris, M. M., Gilbreath, B., & Sunday, J. A. (1998). A longitudinal examination of a merit pay system: Relationships among performance ratings, merit increases, and total pay increases. *Journal of Applied Psychology, 83*(5), 825–831.

Harris, V. A., & Katkin, E. S. (1975). Primary and secondary emotional behaviour: An analysis of the role of autonomic feedback on affect, arousal, and attribution. *Psychological Bulletin, 82,* 904–916.

Harrison, J. R., & Barabasz, A. F. (1991). Effects of restricted environmental stimulation therapy on the behavior of children with autism. *Child Study Journal, 21,* 153–166.

Harrison, Y., & Horne, J. A. (1996). Long-term extension to sleep—are we really chronically sleep deprived? *Psychophysiology, 33,* 22–30.

Hart, D. (1998). Can prototypes inform moral developmental theory? *Developmental Psychology, 34*(3), 420–423.

Hart, K. E. (1997). A moratorium on research using the Jenkins Activity Survey for Type A behavior? *Journal of Clinical Psychology, 53*(8), 905–907.

Hartmann, E. (1995). Making connections in a safe place: Is dreaming psychotherapy? *Dreaming, 5,* 213–228.

Hartmann, E. (1996). Outline for a theory on the nature and functions of dreaming. *Dreaming, 6,* 147–170.

Hartung, C. M., & Widiger, T. A. (1998). Gender differences in the diagnosis of mental disorders: Conclusions and controversies of the DSM-IV. *Psychological Bulletin, 123*(3), 260–278.

Hartup, W. W. (1989). Social relationships and their developmental significance. *American Psychologist, 44,* 120–126.

Hartup, W. W., & Stevens, N. (1997). Friendships and adaptation in the life course. *Psychological Bulletin, 121*(3), 355–370.

Harvey, E. (1999). Short-term and long-term effects of early parental employment on children of the National Longitudinal Survey of Youth. *Developmental Psychology, 35*(2), 445–459.

Harvey, M. L., Loomis, R. J., Bell, P. A., & Marino, M. (1998). The influence of museum exhibit design on immersion and psychological flow. *Environment and Behavior, 30*(5), 601–627.

Haskell, T. (1961). Toward a reference group theory of juvenile delinquency. *Social Problems, 8,* 220–230.

Haslam, N. (1997). Evidence that male sexual orientation is a matter of degree. *Journal of Personality and Social Psychology, 73*(4), 862–870.

Hauser, S. T., & Bowlds, M. K. (1990). Stress, coping, and adaptation. In S. S. Feldman & G. R. Elliott (Eds.), *At the threshold.* Cambridge, MA: Harvard University Press.

Hawkins, J. D., Catalano, R. F., & Miller, J. Y. (1992). Risk and protective factors for alcohol and other drug problems in adolescence and early adulthood: Implications for substance abuse prevention. *Psychological Bulletin, 112,* 64–105.

Hayflick, L. (1994). *How and why we age.* New York: Ballantine.

Hays, R. B. (1989). The day-to-day functioning of close versus casual friendships. *Journal of Social and Personal Relationships, 6,* 21–37.

Health Canada (1992). *Fetal alcohol syndrome: A preventable tragedy.* Ottawa: Standing Committee on Health and Welfare, Social Affairs, Seniors and the Status of Women.

Health Canada (1994). *Country paper Canada supplement.*

Health Canada (1994). *Suicide in Canada: Update of the report of the task force on suicide in Canada.* Ottawa: Mental Health Division, Health Services Directorate, Health Programs and Services Branch, Health Canada.

Health Canada (1996). *Heavily addicted smokers: Understanding the smoking behaviour and the factors that influence quitting among heavily addicted smokers.* Ottawa: Health Canada.

Health Canada (1998). *HIV and AIDS in Canada.* Surveillance report to June 30, 1998. Ottawa: Division of HIV/AIDS Surveillance, Bureau of HIV/AIDS, STD, and TB, LCDC, HPB, Health Canada.

Heath, A. C., & Martin, N. G. (1990). Psychoticism as a dimension of personality: A multivariate genetic test of Eysenck and Eysenck's psychoticism construct. *Journal of Personality and Social Psychology, 58,* 111–121.

Heatherton, T. F., & Baumeister, R. F. (1991). Binge eating as escape from self-awareness. *Psychological Bulletin, 100,* 86–108.

Hebb, D. O. (1949). *Organization of behavior.* New York: Wiley.

Hebb, D. O. (1955). Drives and the C. N. S. (conceptual nervous system). *Psychological Review, 62,* 243–254.

Hebb, D. O. (1972). *Textbook of psychology* (3rd ed.). Philadelphia: Saunders.

Heckler, M. M. (1985). Psychology in the public forum: The fight against Alzheimer's disease. *American Psychologist, 40,* 1240–1244.

Hedges, L. V., & Nowell, A. (1995). Sex differences in mental test scores, variability, and numbers of high-scoring individuals. *Science, 269,* 41–45.

Heeger, D. J. (1994). The representation of visual stimuli in the primary visual cortex. *Current Directions in Psychological Science, 3,* 159–163.

Heider, E. R. (1971). "Focal" color areas and the development of color names. *Developmental Psychology, 4,* 447–455.

Heider, E. R. (1972). Universals in color naming and memory. *Journal of Experimental Psychology, 93,* 10–21.

Heider, E. R., & Olivier, D. C. (1972). The structure of the color space in naming and memory for two languages, *Cognitive Psychology, 3,* 337–354.

Heider, K. G. (1991). *Landscapes of emotion: Lexical maps and scenarios of emotion terms in Indonesia.* Cambridge, England: Cambridge University Press.

Heider, K. G. (1994, March). An anthropologist discovers emotion in the New Guinea Highlands. Paper presented at the University of South Carolina Educational Foundation Research Award in Humanities and Social Sciences Lecture, Columbia, South Carolina.

Heilbrun, A. B., Jr., Wydra, D., & Friedberg, L. (1989). Parent identification and gender schema development. *Journal of Genetic Psychology, 150,* 293–299.

Heine, S. J., & Lehman, D. R. (1997a). The cultural construction of self-enhancement: An examination of group-serving biases. *Journal of Personality and Social Psychology, 72*(6), 1268–1283.

Heine, S. J., & Lehman, D. R. (1997b). Culture, dissonance, and self-affirmation. *Personality and Social Psychology Bulletin, 23*(4), 389–400.

Heinlein, R. (1961). *Stranger in a strange land.* New York: Putnam.

Hellriegel, D., & Slocum, J. (1992). *Management* (6th ed). Reading, MA: Addison-Wesley.

Hellstedt, J. C. (1995). Invisible players: A family systems model. In S. M. Murphy (Ed.), *Sport psychology interventions* (pp. 117–146). Champaign, IL: Human Kinetics.

Helman, C. (1992). Heart disease and the cultural construction of time. In R. Frankenberg et al. (Eds.), *Time, health and medicine* (pp. 31–55). London: Sage Publications, Inc.

Helmes, E., & Reddon, J. R. (1993). A perspective on developments in assessing psychopathology: A critical review of the MMPI and MMPI-2. *Psychological Bulletin, 113,* 453–471.

Helms, J. E. (1992). Why is there no study of cultural equivalence in standardized cognitive ability testing? *American Psychologist, 47,* 1083–1101.

Helson, R., & Moane, G. (1987). Personality change in women from college to midlife. *Journal of Personality and Social Psychology, 53,* 176–186.

Helson, R., & Picano, J. (1990). Is the traditional role bad for women? *Journal of Personality and Social Psychology, 59,* 311–320.

Helson, R., Stewart, A. J., & Ostrove, J. (1995). Identity in three cohorts of midlife women. *Journal of Personality and Social Psychology, 69,* 544–557.

Helweg-Larsen, M., & Collins, B. E. (1997). A social psychological perspective on the role of knowledge about AIDS in AIDS prevention. *American Psychological Society, 6*(2), 23–26.

Hendrick, C., & Hendrick, S. S. (1986). A theory and method of love. *Journal of Personality and Social Psychology, 50,* 392–402.

Herbert, T. B., & Cohen, S. (1993). Depression and immunity: A meta-analytic review. *Psychological Bulletin, 113,* 472–486.

Herbert, T. B., Cohen, S., Marsland, A. L., Bachen, E. A., et al. (1994). Cardiovascular reactivity and the course of immune response to an acute psychological stressor. *Psychosomatic Medicine, 56,* 337–344.

Herman, L. M., Kuczaj, S. A., & Holder, M. D. (1993). Responses to anomalous gestural sequences by a language-trained dolphin: Evidence for processing of semantic relations and syntactic information. *Journal of Experimental Psychology: General, 122*(2), 184–194.

Hermans, H. J. M., & Kempen, H. J. G. (1998). Moving cultures: The perilous problems of cultural dichotomies in a globalizing society. *American Psychologist, 53*(10), 1111–1120.

Herrnstein, R. J., & Murray, C. (1994). *The bell curve: Intelligence and class structure in American life.* New York: Free Press.

Herz, R. S., & Engen, T. (1996). Odor memory: Review and analysis. *Psychonomic Bulletin & Review, 3*(3), 300–313.

Hewlett, B. S., Lamb, M. E., Shannon, D., Leyendecker, B., & Schoelmerich, A. (1998). Culture and early infancy among central African foragers and farmers. *Developmental Psychology, 34*(4), 653–661.

Hewlett, S. A., & West, C. (1998). *The war against parents: What we can do for America's beleaguered moms and dads.* Boston: Houghton Mifflin.

Hildebrandt, K. A. (1983). Effect of facial expression variations on ratings of infant's physical attractiveness. *Developmental Psychology, 29,* 414–417.

Hilgard, E. R. (1965). *Hypnotic susceptibility.* New York: Harcourt, Brace & World.

Hilgard, E. R. (1994). Neodissociation theory. In S. J. Lynn, J. W. Rhue, et al. (Eds.), *Dissociation: Clinical and theoretical perspectives.* New York: Guilford Press.

Hill, J. O., & Peters, J. C. (1998). Environmental contributions to the obesity epidemic. *Science, 280,* 1371–1374.

Hilsman, R., & Garber, J. (1995). A test of the cognitive diathesis-stress model of depression in children: Academic stressors, attributional style, perceived competence, and control. *Journal of Personality and Social Psychology, 69,* 370–380.

Hines, D. (1997). Arguments for prescription privileges for psychologists. *American Psychologist, 52*(3), 270–271.

Hinton, G. (1992, September). How neural networks learn from experience. *Scientific American,* 145–151.

Hinton, G., Plaut, D. C., & Shallice, T. (1993, April). Simulating brain damage. *Scientific American*, 76–83.

Hirsch, H. V. B., & Spinelli, D. N. (1971). Modification of the distribution of receptive field orientation in cats by selective exposure during development. *Experimental Brain Research, 13*, 509–527.

Hirschfeld, R. M. A., Keller, M. B., Panico, S., Arons, B. S., Barlow, D., Davidoff, F., Endicott, J., Froom, J., Goldstein, M., Gorman, J. M., Guthrie, D., Marek, R. G., Maurer, T. A., Meyer, R., Phillips, K., Ross, J., Schwenk, T. L., Sharfstein, S. S., Thase, M. E., & Wyatt, R. J. (1997). The National Depressive and Manic Depressive Association consensus statement on the undertreatment of depression. *Journal of the American Medical Association, 277*(4), 333–340.

Hiscock, M., & Kinsbourne, M. (1987). Specialization of the cerebral hemispheres. *Learning Disabilities, 20*, 130–143.

Hobfoll, S. E. (1989). Conservation of resources: A new attempt at conceptualizing stress. *American Psychologist, 44*, 513–524.

Hobfoll, S. E., Spielberg, C. D., Breznitz, S., Figley, C., Folkman, S., Lepper-Green, B., Meichenbaum, D., Milgram, N. A., Sandler, I., Sarason, I., & Van der Kolk, B. (1991). War-related stress. *American Psychologist, 46*, 848–855.

Hobson, J. A. (1989). *Sleep.* New York: Freeman.

Hobson, J. A. (1994). *The chemistry of conscious states: How the brain changes its mind.* Boston: Little, Brown.

Hobson, J. A. (1996). *The chemistry of conscious states: Toward a unified model of the brain and the mind.* Boston: Little, Brown and Co.

Hobson, J. A., & McCarley, R. W. (1977). The brain as a dream state generator: An activation-synthesis of the dream process. *American Journal of Psychiatry, 134*, 1335–1348.

Hoffart, A. (1996). In vivo cognitive therapy of panic attacks. *Journal of Cognitive Psychotherapy, 10*(4), 281–289.

Hoffman, C., & Hurst, N. (1990). Gender stereotypes: Perception or rationalization? *Journal of Personality and Social Psychology, 58*, 197–208.

Hofstede, G. (1983). National cultures revisited. *Behavior Science Research, 18*, 285–305.

Hogan, R., Curphy, G. J., & Hogan, J. (1994). What we know about leadership: Effectiveness and personality. *American Psychologist, 49*, 493–504.

Hogan, R., Hogan, J., & Roberts, B. W. (1996). Personality measurement and employment decisions. *American Psychologist, 51*(5), 469–477.

Hogben, M. (1998). Factors moderating the effect of televised aggression on viewers. *Communication Research, 25*(2), 220–247.

Holder, M. D., Yirmiya, R., Garcia, J., & Raizer, J. (1989). Conditioned taste aversions are not readily disrupted by external excitation. *Behavioral Neuroscience, 103*, 605–611.

Holland, M. K. (1975). *Using psychology: Principles of behavior and your life.* Boston: Little, Brown.

Hollis, K. L. (1997). Contemporary research on Pavlovian conditioning: A "new" functional analysis. *American Psychologist, 52*(9), 956–965.

Hollister, J. M., Mednick, S. A., Brennan, P. A., & Cannon, T. D. (1994). Impaired autonomic nervous system habituation in those at genetic risk for schizophrenia. *Archives of General Psychiatry, 51*, 552–558.

Holloway, F. A. (1977). State-dependent retrieval based on time of day. In B. Ho, D. Chute, & D. Richards (Eds.), *Drug discrimination and state-dependent learning.* New York: Academic.

Holmes, D. S. (1984). Mediation and somatic arousal reduction. *American Psychologist, 39*, 1–10.

Holmes, T. H., & Rahe, R. H. (1967). The Social Readjustment Rating Scale. *Journal of Psychosomatic Research, 11*, 213–218.

Hom, H. L., Jr., & Arbuckle, B. (1988). Mood induction effects upon goal setting and performance in young children. *Motivation and Emotion, 12*, 113–122.

Honig, A. S., & Chung, M. (1989). Child-rearing practices of urban poor mothers of infants and three-year-olds in five cultures. *Child Development and Care, 50*, 75–97.

Honts, C. R. (1994). Psychophysiological detection of deception. *Current Directions in Psychological Science, 3*, 77–82.

Honts, C. R. (1996). Criterion development and validity of the CQT in field application. *Journal of General Psychology, 123*, 309–324.

Hood, B. M., Willen, J. D., & Driver, J. (1998). Adult's eyes trigger shifts of visual attention in human infants. *American Psychological Society, 9*(2), 131–134.

Hoosain, Z., & Roopnarine, J. L. (1994). African-American fathers' involvement with infants: Relationship to their functioning style, support, education, and income. *Infant Behavior and Development, 17*, 175–184.

Hopkins, W. D. (1997). Hemispheric specialization for local and global processing of hierarchical visual stimuli in chimpanzees (Pan troglodytes). *Neuropsychologia, 35*(3), 343–348.

Horne, J. (1988). *Why we sleep.* New York: Oxford University Press.

Horne, S. (1999). Domestic violence in Russia. *American Psychologist, 54*(1), 55–61.

Horney, K. (1937). *The neurotic personality of our time.* New York: Norton.

Hornstein, G. A. (1992). The return of the repressed. *American Psychologist, 47*, 254–263.

Hotamisligil, G. S., Johnson, R. S., Distel, R. J., Ellis, R., Papaioannou, V. E., & Spiegelman, B. M. (1996). Uncoupling of obesity from insulin resistance through a targeted mutation in aP2, the adipocyte fatty acid binding protein. *Science, 274*, 1377–1380.

Houde, J. F., & Jordan, M. I. (1998). Sensorimotor adaptation in speech production. *Science, 279*, 1213–1216.

Hovey, J. D. (1998). Acculturative stress, depression and suicidal ideation among Mexican-American adolescents: Implications for the development of suicide prevention programs in schools. *Psychological Reports, 83*(1), 249–250.

Howard, K. I., Kopta, S. M., Krause, M. S., & Orlinsky, D. E. (1986). The dose-effect relationships in psychotherapy. *American Psychologist, 41*, 159–164.

Howe, M. J. A., & Smith, J. (1988). Calendar calculating in "idiots savants": How do they do it? *British Journal of Psychology, 79*, 371–386.

Howe, N., & Jacobs, E. (1995). Child care research: A case for Canadian national standards. *Canadian Psychology, 36*(2), 131–148.

Howell, J. M., & Avolio, B. J. (1993). Transformational leadership, transactional leadership, locus of control, and support for innovation: Key predictors of consolidated-business-unit performance. *Journal of Applied Psychology, 78*, 891–902.

Howell, W. C. (1993). Engineering psychology in a changing world. *Annual Review of Psychology, 44*, 231–263.

Howes, C., Hamilton, C. E., & Philipsen, L. C. (1998). Stability and continuity of child-caregiver and child-peer relationships. *Child Development, 69*(2), 418–426.

Howes, C., Unger, O., & Seidner, L. B. (1989). Social pretend play in toddlers: Parallels with social play and with solitary pretend. *Child Development, 60*, 77–84.

Hoyt, I. P., Nadon, R., Register, P. A., Chorny, J., Fleeson, W., Grigorian, E. M., & Otto, L. (1989). Daydreaming, absorption, and hypnotizability. *The International Journal of Clinical and Experimental Hypnosis, 37*, 332–342.

Hudapaya, L. V. M. (1994). Four cases of supposed multiple personality disorder: Evidence of unjustified diagnoses. *Canadian Journal of Psychiatry, 39*, 247.

Hubel, D. H., & Wiesel, T. N. (1962). Receptive fields, binocular interaction, and functional architecture in the cat's visual cortex. *Journal of Physiology, 160*, 106–164.

Hudak, M. A. (1993). Gender schema theory revisited: Men's stereotypes of American women. *Sex Roles, 28*, 279–293.

Hudspeth, A. J. (1983, January). The hair cells of the inner ear. *Scientific American*, 54–73.

Huffcutt, A. I., & Roth, P. L. (1998). Racial group differences in employment interview evaluations. *Journal of Applied Psychology, 83*(2), 179–189.

Huffman, L. C., Bryan, Y. E., del Carmen, R., Pedersen, F. A., Doussard-Roosevelt, J. A., & Porges, S. W. (1998). Infant temperament and cardiac vagal tone: Assessments at twelve weeks of age. *Child Development, 69*(3), 624–635.

Hughes, C. F., Uhlmann, C., & Pennebaker, J. W. (1994). The body's response to processing emotional trauma: Linking verbal text with autonomic activity. *Journal of Personality, 62*, 564–585.

Hughes, S. L., & Neimeyer, R. A. (1993). Cognitive predictors of suicide risk among hospitalized psychiatric patients: A prospective study. *Death Studies, 17*, 103–124.

Humphreys, K. (1996). Clinical psychologists as psychotherapists: History, future, and alternatives. *American Psychologist, 51*, 190–197.

Hunt, E. B., & Agnoli, F. (1991). The Whorfian hypothesis: A cognitive psychology perspective. *Psychological Review, 98*, 377–389.

Hunt, M. (1974). *Sexual behavior in the 1970s.* New York: Dell.

Hurvich, L., & Jameson, D. (1974). Opponent processes as a model of neural organization. *American Psychologist, 30*, 88–102.

Huston, A. C., Donnerstein, E., Fairchild, H., Feshback, N. D., Katz, P. A., Murray, J. P., Rubinstein, E. A., Wilcox, B. L., & Zuckerman, D. (1992). *Big world, small screen.* Lincoln: University of Nebraska Press.

Hyde, J. S., Fennema, E., & Lamon, S. J. (1990). Gender differences in mathematics performance: A meta-analysis. *Psychological Bulletin, 107*, 139–155.

Hyde, J. S., & Linn, M. C. (1988). Gender differences in verbal ability: A meta-analysis. *Psychological Bulletin, 104*, 53–69.

Idehen, E. E. (1997). The influence of gender and space sharing history on the conceptions of privacy by undergraduates. *Ife Psychologia: An International Journal, 5*(1), 59–75.

Ilacqua, G. E. (1994). Migraine headaches: Coping efficacy of guided imagery training. *Headache, 34*, 99–102.

Ilgen, D. R. (1990). Health issues at work: Opportunities for industrial/organizational psychology. *American Psychologist, 45*, 273–283.

Ilgen, D. R. (1999). Teams embedded in organizations: Some implications. *American Psychologist, 54*(2), 129–139.

Ingbar, D. H., & Gee, J. B. L. (1985). Pathophysiology and treatment of sleep apnea. *Annual Review of Medicine, 36*, 369–395.

Ingraham, L. J., Kugelmass, S., Frenkel, E., Nathan, M., et al. (1995). Twenty-five-year followup of the Israeli High-Risk Study. *Schizophrenia Bulletin, 21*(2), 183–192.

Inhelder, B., & Piaget, J. (1958). *The growth of logical thinking from childhood to adolescence.* New York: Basic Books.

Inhoff, A. W., Morris, R., & Calabrese, J. (1986). Eye movements in skilled transcription typing. *Bulletin of the Psychonomic Society, 2*, 113–114.

Innes, J. M., & Young, R. F. (1975). The effect of presence of an audience, evaluation apprehension, and objective self-awareness on learning. *Journal of Experimental Social Psychology, 11*, 35–42.

Intraub, H. (1980). Presentation rate and the representation of briefly glimpsed pictures in memory. *Journal of Experimental Psychology: Human Learning and Memory, 6*, 1–12.

Intraub, H., Gottesman, C. V., & Bills, A. J. (1998). Effects of perceiving and imagining scenes on memory for pictures. *Journal of Experimental Psychology: Learning, Memory, and Cognition, 24*(1), 186–201.

Irwin, M., Smith, T. L., & Gillin, J. C. (1992). Electroencephalographic sleep and natural killer activity in depressed patients and control subjects. *Psychosomatic Medicine, 54*, 10–21.

Isaac, R. J., & Armat, V. C. (1990). *Madness in the streets: How psychiatry and the law abandoned the mentally ill.* New York: Free Press.

Isabella, R. A., Belsky, J., & von Eye, A. (1989). Origins of infant-mother attachment: An examination of interactional synchrony during the infant's first year. *Developmental Psychology, 25*, 12–21.

Ito, T. A., Larsen, J. T., Smith, N. K., & Cacioppo, J. T. (1998). Negative information weighs more heavily on the brain: The negativity bias in evaluative categorizations. *Journal of Personality and Social Psychology, 75*(4), 887–900.

Ito, T. A., Miller, N., & Pollock, V. E. (1996). Alcohol and aggression: A meta-analysis on the moderation effects of inhibitory cues, triggering events, and self-focused attention. *Psychological Bulletin, 120*(1), 60–82.

Iwata, B. A., Pace, G. M., Cowdery, G. E., & Miltenberger, R. G. (1994). What makes extinction work: An analysis of procedural form and function. *Journal of Applied Behavior Analysis, 27*, 131–144.

Izard, C. E. (1990). Facial expressions and the regulation of emotions. *Journal of Personality and Social Psychology, 58*(3), 487–498.

Izard, C. E. (1994). Innate and universal facial expressions: Evidence from developmental and cross-cultural research. *Psychological Bulletin, 115*, 288–299.

Izard, C. E. (1997). Emotions and facial expressions: A perspective from differential emotions theory. In J. A. Russell, J. M. Fernandez-Dols, et al. (Eds.), *The psychology of facial expression. Studies in emotion and social interaction, 2nd series* (pp. 57–77). New York: Cambridge University Press.

Izard, C. E., & Saxton, P. M. (1988). Emotions. In R. C. Atkinson, R. J. Herrnstein, G. Lindzey, & R. D. Luce (Eds.), *Stevens handbook of experimental psychology: Vol. 1. Perception and motivation.* New York: Wiley.

Izquierdo, I., & Medina, J. H. (1997). The biochemistry of memory formation and its regulation by hormones and neuromodulators. *Psychobiology, 25*(1), 1–9.

Jaccard, J., Helbig, D. W., Wan, C. K., Gutman, M. A., & Kritz-Silverstein, D. C. (1990). Individual differences in attitude-behavior consistency: The prediction of contraceptive behavior. *Journal of Applied Social Psychology, 20*, 575–617.

Jackson, J. M., & Latané, B. (1981). All alone in front of all those people: Stage fright as a function of number and type of co-performers and audience. *Journal of Personality and Social Psychology, 40*, 73–85.

Jackson, S. E., & Schuler, R. S. (1990). Human resource planning: Challenges for industrial/organizational psychologists. *American Psychologist, 45*, 223–239.

Jackson, S. E., & Schuler, R. S. (1995). Understanding human resource management in the context of organizations and their environments. *Annual Review of Psychology, 46*, 237–264.

Jacobs, B., Schall, M., & Scheibel, A. B. (1993). A quantitative dendritic analysis of Wernicke's area. II. Gender, hemispheric, and environmental factors. *Journal of Comprehensive Neurology, 237*, 97–111.

Jacobs, L., Berscheid, E., & Walster, E. (1971). Self-esteem and attraction. *Journal of Personality and Social Psychology, 17*, 84–91.

Jacobs, R. A. (1997). Nature, nurture, and the development of functional specializations: A computational approach. *Psychonomic Bulletin and Review, 4*(3), 299–309.

Jacobs, R. A., & Kosslyn, S. M. (1994). Encoding shape and spatial relations: The role of receptive field size in coordinating complementary representations. *Cognitive Science, 18*, 361–386.

Jacobson, N. S. (1991). Behavioral versus insight-oriented marital therapy: Labels can be misleading. *Journal of Consulting and Clinical Psychology, 59*, 142–145.

Jacobson, N. S., & Addis, M. E. (1993). Research on couples and couple therapy: What do we know? Where are we going? *Journal of Consulting and Clinical Psychology, 61*, 85–93.

Jacobson, N. S., & Hollon, S. D. (1996). Cognitive-behavior therapy versus pharmacotherapy. *Journal of Consulting and Clinical Psychology, 64*, 74–80.

Jacoby, L. L., Kelley, C., Brown, J., & Jasechko, J. (1989). Becoming famous overnight: Limits on the ability to avoid unconscious influences of the past. *Journal of Personality and Social Psychology, 56*, 326–338.

James, W. (1884). What is an emotion? *Mind, 9*, 188–205.

James, W. (1890). *Principles of psychology.* New York: Dover.

James, W. (1910). *The will to believe and other essays in popular philosophy.* London: Longmans, Green, and Co.

Jan, J. E., Espezel, H., & Appleton, R. E. (1994). The treatment of sleep disorders with melatonin. *Developmental Medicine and Child Neurology, 36*, 97–107.

Janis, I. L. (1982). *Groupthink* (2nd ed.). Boston: Houghton Mifflin.

Janis, I. L. (1983). The role of social support in adherence to stressful decisions. *American Psychologist, 38*, 142–160.

Janis, I. L. (1985). Stress inoculation in health care: Theory and research. In A. Monat & R. S. Lazarus (Eds.), *Stress and coping* (2nd ed.). New York: Columbia University Press.

Jansen, A. S. P., Nguyen, X. V., Karpitskiy, V., Mettenleiter, T. C., & Loewy, A. D. (1995). Central command neurons of the sympathetic nervous system: Basis of the fight-or-flight response. *Science, 270*, 644–646.

Jarrett, M. E., & Lethbridge, D. J. (1994). Looking forward, looking back: Women's experience with waning fertility during midlife. *Qualitative Health Research, 4*, 370–384.

Jason, L. A., Richman, J. A., Friedberg, F., Wagner, L., Taylor, R., & Jordan, K. M. (1997). Politics, science, and the emergence of a new disease: The case of chronic fatigue syndrome. *American Psychologist, 52*(9), 973–983.

Jaynes, J. (1976). *The origin of consciousness in the breakdown of the bicameral mind.* Boston: Houghton Mifflin.

Jazwinski, S. M. (1996). Longevity, genes, and aging. *Science, 273*, 54–59.

Jeanneret, R. P. (1992). Applications of job component/synthetic validity to construct validity. *Human Performance, 5*(1/2), 81–96.

Jenkins, G. D., Jr., Mitra, A., Gupta, N., & Shaw, J. D. (1998). Are financial incentives related to performance? A meta-analytic review of empirical research. *Journal of Applied Psychology, 83*(5), 777–787.

Jenkins, H. M., & Harrison, R. H. (1960). Effect of discrimination training on auditory generalization. *Journal of Experimental Psychology, 59*, 244–253.

Jennings, K. D., Curry, N. E., & Connors, R. (1986). Toddlers' social behaviors in dyads and groups. *Journal of Genetic Psychology, 147*, 515–528.

Jensen, A. R. (1969). How much can we boost IQ and scholastic achievement? *Harvard Educational Review, 39*, 1–123.

Jensen, A. R. (1970). Can we and should we study race differences? In J. Hellmuth (Ed.), *Disadvantaged child* (Vol. 3). New York: Brunner/Mazel.

Jensen, A. R. (1987). Psychometric g as a focus on concerted research effort. *Intelligence, 11,* 193–198.

Jensen, A. R., & Weng, L. J. (1994). What is a good g? *Intelligence, 18,* 231–258.

Job, R. F. S., & Barnes, B. W. (1995). Stress and consumption: Inescapable shock, neophobia, and quinine finickiness in rats. *Behavioral Neuroscience, 109,* 106–116.

John, E. R., Chesler, P., Bartlett, F., & Victor, I. (1968). Observational learning in cats. *Science, 159,* 1489–1491.

Johnsen, K., Espenes, G. A., & Gillard, S. (1998). The associations between Type A/B behavioural dimension and Type 2/4 personality patterns. *Personality and Individual Differences, 25(5),* 937–945.

Johnson, B. T., & Eagly, A. H. (1989). Effects of involvement on persuasion: A meta-analysis. *Psychological Bulletin, 106,* 290–314.

Johnson, D. L. (1997). Weight loss for women: Studies of smokers and nonsmokers using hypnosis and multi-component treatments with and without overt aversion. *Psychological Reports, 80(3, Pt. 1),* 931–933.

Johnson, F. W. (1991). Biological factors and psychometric intelligence: A review. *Genetic, Social, and General Psychology Monographs, 117,* 315–357.

Johnson, L. C., Slye, E. S., & Dement, W. (1965). Electroencephalographic and autonomic activity during and after prolonged sleep deprivation. *Psychosomatic Medicine, 27,* 415–423.

Johnson, S. H. (1998). Cerebral organization of motor imagery: Contralateral control of grip selection in mentally represented prehension. *American Psychological Society, 9(3),* 219–222.

Johnson, T. F. (1995). Aging well in contemporary society. *American Behavioral Scientist, 39(2),* 120–130.

Joiner, T. E., & Wagner, K. D. (1995). Attribution style and depression in children and adolescents: A meta-analytic review. *Clinical Psychology Review, 15(8),* 777–798.

Jones, E. G., & Pons, T. P. (1998). Thalamic and brainstem contributions to large-scale plasticity of primate somatosensory cortex. *Science, 282,* 1121–1125.

Jones, S. S., & Raag, T. (1989). Smile production in older infants: The importance of a social recipient for the facial signal. *Child Development, 60,* 811–818.

Jonides, J., Schumacher, E. H., Smith, E. E., & Lauber, E. J. (1997). Verbal working memory load affects regional brain activation as measured by PET. *Journal of Cognitive Neuroscience, 9(4),* 462–475.

Jorgensen, R. S., Johnson, B. T., Kolodziej, M. E., & Schreer, G. E. (1996). Elevated blood pressure and personality: A meta-analytic review. *Psychological Bulletin, 120(2),* 293–320.

Jorgensen, R. S., & Johnson, J. H. (1990). Contributors to the appraisal of major life changes: Gender, perceived controllability, sensation seeking, strain, and social support. *Journal of Applied Social Psychology, 20,* 1123–1138.

Joseph, J. A. (1992). The putative role of free radicals in the loss of neuronal functioning in senescence. *Integrative Physiological and Behavioral Science, 27(3),* 216–227.

Josephs, R. A., Markus, H. R., & Tafarodi, R. W. (1992). Gender and self-esteem. *Journal of Personality and Social Psychology, 63,* 391–402.

Judge, T. A., Locke, E. A., Durham, C. C., & Kluger, A. N. (1998). Dispositional effects on job and life satisfaction: The role of core evaluations. *Journal of Applied Psychology, 83(1),* 17–34.

Julien, R. M. (1995). *A primer of drug action: A concise, nontechnical guide to the actions, uses, and side effects of psychoactive drugs (7th ed.).* New York: W. H. Freeman & Co.

Jussim, L., Nelson, T. E., Manis, M., & Soffin, S. (1995). Prejudice, stereotypes, and labeling effects: Sources of bias in person perception. *Journal of Personality and Social Psychology, 68,* 228–246.

Just, M. A., Carpenter, P. A., Keller, T. A., Eddy, W. F., & Thulborn, K. R. (1996). Brain activation modulated by sentence comprehension. *Science, 274,* 114–116.

Kagan, B. L., Leskin, G., Haas, B., Wilkins, J., & Foy, D. (1999). Elevated lipid levels in Vietnam veterans with chronic posttraumatic stress disorders. *Biological Psychiatry, 45(3),* 374–377.

Kagan, J. (1997a). In the beginning: The contribution of temperament to personality development. *Modern Psychoanalysis, 22(2),* 145–155.

Kagan, J. (1997b). Temperament and the reactions to unfamiliarity. *Child Development, 68(1),* 139–143.

Kagan, J. (1998). *Three seductive ideas.* Cambridge, MA: Harvard University Press.

Kagan, J., Kearsley, R. B., & Zelazo, P. R. (1980). *Infancy: Its place in human development.* Cambridge, MA: Harvard University Press.

Kagan, J., Reznick, J. S., & Snidman, N. (1988). Biological bases of childhood shyness. *Science, 240,* 167–171.

Kagan, J., & Snidman, N. (1991). Infant predictors of inhibited and uninhibited profiles. *Psychological Science, 2,* 40–44.

Kahn, R. S., Davidson, M., & Davis, K. L. (1996). Dopamine and schizophrenia revisited. In S. J. Stanley et al. (Eds.), *Biology of schizophrenia and affective disease* (pp. 369–391). Washington, DC: American Psychiatric Press.

Kaitz, M., Lapidot, P., Bronner, R., & Eidelman, A. I. (1992). Parturient women can recognize their infants by touch. *Developmental Psychology, 28,* 35–39.

Kales, A., Tan, T. L., Kollar, E. J., Naithoh, P., Preson, T. A., & Malmstrom, E. J. (1970). Sleep patterns following 205 hours of sleep deprivation. *Psychosomatic Medicine, 32,* 189–200.

Kalichman, S. C., & Craig, M. E. (1991). Professional psychologists' decisions to report suspected child abuse: Clinician and situation influences. *Professional Psychology: Research and Practice, 22,* 84–89.

Kalichman, S. C., Szymanowski, D., McKee, G., Taylor, J., & Craig, M. E. (1989). Cluster analytically derived MMPI profile subgroups of incarcerated adult rapists. *Journal of Clinical Psychology, 45,* 149–155.

Kalick, S. M., Zebrowitz, L. A., Langlois, J. H., & Johnson, R. M. (1998). Does human facial attractiveness honestly advertise health? Longitudinal data on an evolutionary question. *Psychological Science, 9(1),* 8–13.

Kalimo, R., & Mejman, T. (1987). Psychological and behavioural responses to stress at work. In R. Kalimo, M. A. El-Batawi, & C. L. Cooper (Eds.), *Psychosocial factors at work and their relation to health.* Geneva: World Health Organization.

Kamarck, T., & Jennings, J. R. (1991). Biobehavioral factors in sudden cardiac death. *Psychological Bulletin, 109,* 42–75.

Kandel, E., & Abel, T. (1995). Neuropeptides, adenyl cyclase, and memory storage. *Science, 268,* 825–826.

Kanekar, S., Shaherwalla, A., Franco, B., Kunju, T., & Pinto, A. J. (1991). The acquaintance predicament of a rape victim. *Journal of Applied Social Psychology, 21,* 1524–1544.

Kanner, A. D., Coyne, J. C., Schaefer, C., & Lazarus, R. S. (1981). Comparison of two modes of stress measurement: Daily hassles and uplifts versus major life events. *Journal of Behavioral Medicine, 4,* 1–39.

Kaplan, C. A., & Simon, H. A. (1990). In search of insight. *Cognitive Psychology, 22,* 374–419.

Kapur, S., & Remington, G. (1996). Serotonin-dopamine interaction and its relevance to schizophrenia. *American Journal of Psychiatry, 153(4),* 466–476.

Karabenick, S. A., & Collins, E. J. (1997). Relation of perceived instructional goals and incentives to college students' use of learning strategies. *Journal of Experimental Education, 65(4),* 331–341.

Karau, S. J., & Williams, K. D. (1997). The effects of group cohesiveness on social loafing and social compensation. *Group Dynamics, 1(2),* 156–168.

Karniol, R., & Amir, A. (1997). Judging toy breakers: Gender stereotypes have devious effects on children. *Sex Roles, 36(3/4),* 195–205.

Karon, B. P., & Widener, A. (1998). Repressed memories: The real story. *Professional Psychology: Research and Practice, 29(5),* 482–487.

Karweit, N., & Slavin, R. E. (1981). Measurement and modeling choices in studies of time and learning. *American Educational Research Journal, 18,* 157–171.

Kashani, J. H., Reid, J. C., & Rosenberg, T. K. (1989). Levels of hopelessness in children and adolescents: A developmental perspective. *Journal of Consulting and Clinical Psychology, 57,* 496–499.

Kastmner, S., De Eerd, P., Desimone, R., & Ungerleider, L. G. (1998). Mechanisms of directed attention in the human extrastriate cortex as revealed by functional MRI. *Science, 282,* 108–111.

Katsuki, Y. (1961). Neutral mechanisms of auditory sensation in cats. In W. A. Rosenblith (Ed.), *Sensory communication.* Cambridge, MA: MIT Press.

Kaufman, A. S. (1983). Some questions and answers about the Kaufman Assessment Battery for Children (K-ABC). *Journal of Psychoeducational Assessment, 1,* 205–218.

Kaufman, A. S. (1990). *Assessing adolescent and adult intelligence.* Boston: Allyn & Bacon.

Kaye, K., Elkind, L., Goldberg, D., & Tytun, A. (1989). Birth outcomes for infants of drug abusing mothers. *New York State Journal of Medicine, 89(5),* 256–261.

Kazdin, A. E. (1991). Treatment research: The investigation and evaluation of psychotherapy. In M. Hersen, A. E. Kazdin, & A. S.

Bellack (Eds.), *The clinical psychology handbook* (2nd ed.). New York: Pergamon.

Kazdin, A. E., & Weisz, J. R. (1998). Identifying and developing empirically supported child and adolescent treatments. *Journal of Consulting and Clinical Psychology, 66*(1), 19–36.

Keane, T. M. (1998). Psychological effects of military combat. In B. P. Dohrenwend et al. (Eds.), *Adversity, stress, and psychopathology* (pp. 52–65). New York: Oxford University Press.

Kearney, C. A., & Silverman, W. K. (1998). A critical review of pharmacotherapy for youth with anxiety disorders: Things are not as they seem. *Journal of Anxiety Disorders, 12*(2), 83–102.

Keating, N. C. (1987). Reducing stress of farm men and women. *Family Relations: Journal of Applied Family and Child Studies, 36*(4), 358–363.

Kecklund, G., Akerstedt, T., & Lowden, A. (1997). Morning work: Effects of early rising on sleep and alertness. *Sleep, 20*(3), 215–223.

Keefe, K., & Berndt, T. J. (1996). Relations of friendship quality to self-esteem in early adolescence. *Journal of Early Adolescence, 16*(1), 110–129.

Keller, H. (1997). Evolutionary approaches. In J. W. Berry (Ed.), *Handbook of cross-cultural psychology, Vol. 1: Theory and method.* Boston: Allyn and Bacon.

Kelley, H. H. (1972). Attribution in social interaction. In E. E. Jones et al. (Eds.), *Attribution: Perceiving the causes of behavior.* Morristown, NJ: General Learning Press.

Kelley, H. H. (1973). Process of causal attribution. *American Psychologist, 28*, 107–128.

Kelley, H. H., Berscheid, E., Christensen, A., Harvey, J. H., Huston, T. L., et al. (1983). *Close relationships.* New York: Freeman.

Kelly, A. E., & McKillop, K. J. (1996). Consequences of revealing personal secrets. *Psychological Bulletin, 120*(3), 450–465.

Kelly, G. (1955). *The psychology of personal constructs.* New York: W. W. Norton.

Kelly, T. A., & Strupp, H. H. (1992). Patient and therapist values in psychotherapy: Perceived changes, assimilation, similarity, and outcome. *Journal of Consulting and Clinical Psychology, 60*, 34–40.

Keltner, D., & Buswell, B. N. (1997). Embarrassment: Its distinct form and appeasement functions. *Psychological Bulletin, 122*(3), 250–270.

Kempermann, G., Kuhn, H. G., & Gage, F. H. (1998). Experience-induced neurogenesis in the senescent dentate gyrus. *Journal of Neuroscience, 18*(9), 3206–3212.

Kendall, P. C. (1993). Cognitive-behavioral therapies with youth: Guiding theory, current status, and emerging developments. *Journal of Consulting and Clinical Psychology, 61*, 235–247.

Kendall, P. C., Krain, A., & Treadwell, K. R. H. (1999). Generalized anxiety disorder. In R. T. Ammerman, M. Hersen, et al. (Eds.), *Handbook of prescriptive treatments for children and adolescents* (2nd ed.) (pp. 155–171). Boston: Allyn & Bacon, Inc.

Kendall-Tackett, K. A., Williams, L. M., & Finkelhor, D. (1993). Impact of sexual abuse on children: A review and synthesis of recent empirical studies. *Psychological Bulletin, 113*(1), 164–180.

Kendler, K. S., Gruenberg, A. M., & Tsuang, M. T. (1985). Subtype stability in schizophrenia. *American Journal of Psychiatry, 142*(7), 827–832.

Kendler, K. S., Neale, M. C., Heath, A. C., Phil, D., et al. (1994). A twin-family study of alcoholism in women. *American Journal of Psychiatry, 151*, 707–715.

Kendler, K. S., Neale, M., Kessler, R., Heath, A., & Eaves, L. (1992). A population-based twin study of major depression in women. *Archives of General Psychiatry, 49*, 257–266.

Kendler, K. S., Neale, M., Kessler, R., Heath, A., & Eaves, L. (1993). A twin study of recent life events and difficulties. *Archives of General Psychiatry, 50*, 789–796.

Kendler, K. S., Neale, M., MacLean, C. J., Heath, A., Eaves, L., & Kessler, R. (1993). Smoking and major depression. *Archives of General Psychiatry, 50*, 36–43.

Kennell, J. H., Voos, D. K., & Klaus, M. H. (1979). Parent-infant bonding. In J. D. Osofsky (Ed.), *Handbook of infant development.* New York: Wiley.

Kerns, K. A. (1998). Individual differences in friendship quality: Links to child-mother attachment. In W. M. Bukowski et al. (Eds.), *The company they keep: Friendship in childhood and adolescence.* New York: Cambridge University Press.

Kerr, M., Lambert, W. W., & Bem, D. J. (1996). Life course sequelae of childhood shyness in Sweden: Comparison with the United States. *Developmental Psychology, 32*(6), 1100–1105.

Kerr, N., & Bruun, S. E. (1983). Dispensability of member effort and group motivation losses: Free-rider effects. *Journal of Personality and Social Psychology, 44*, 78–94.

Kessler, R. C., Kendler, K. S., Heath, A. C., Neale, M. C., & Eaves, L. J. (1992). Social support, depressed mood, and adjustment to stress: A genetic epidemiologic investigation. *Journal of Personality and Social Psychology, 62*, 257–272.

Kessler, R. C., Sonnega, A., Bromet, E., Hughes, M., & Nelson, C. B. (1995). Posttraumatic stress disorder in the National Comorbidity Survey. *Archives of General Psychiatry, 52*, 1048–1060.

Kettl, P. A., & Bixler, E. O. (1993). Alcohol and suicide in Alaskan Natives. *American Indian and Alaskan Mental Health Research, 5*(2), 34–45.

Kety, S. S., Wender, P. H., Jacobsen, B., Ingraham, L. J., Jansson, L., Faber, B., & Kinney, D. K. (1994). Mental illness in the biological and adoptive relatives of schizophrenic adoptees: Replication of the Copenhagen study in the rest of Denmark. *Archives of General Psychiatry, 51*, 442–455.

Kiecolt-Glaser, J. K., Page, G. G., Marucha, P. T., MacCallum, R. C., & Glaser, R. (1998). Psychological influences on surgical recovery: Perspectives from psychoneuroimmunology. *American Psychologist, 53*(11), 1209–1218.

Kier, C., & Lewis, C. (1997). Infant-mother attachment in separated and married families. *Journal of Divorce and Remarriage, 26*(3/4), 185–194.

Kihlstrom, J. F. (1998). Dissociations and dissociation theory in hypnosis: Comment on Kirsch and Lynn. *Psychological Bulletin, 123*(2), 186–191.

Kihlstrom, J. F., Barnhardt, T. M., & Tataryn, D. J. (1992). The psychological unconscious. *American Psychologist, 47*, 788–791.

Kikoski, J. F. (1998). Effective communication in the performance appraisal interview: Face-to-face communication for public managers in the culturally diverse workplace. *Public Personnel Management, 27*(4), 491–513.

Kilbourne, B. K. (1989). A cross-cultural investigation of the foot-in-the-door compliance induction procedure. *Journal of Cross-Cultural Psychology, 20*, 3–38.

Kilgard, M. P., & Merzenich, M. M. (1998). Cortical map reorganization enabled by nucleus basalis activity. *Science, 279*, 1714–1718.

Kim, J. J., & Fanselow, M. S. (1992). Modality-specific retrograde amnesia of fear. *Science, 256*, 675–677.

Kim, J. S., Bramlett, M. H., Wright, L. K., & Poon, L. W. (1998). Racial differences in health status and health behaviors of older adults. *Nursing Research, 47*(4), 243–250.

Kim, S. R. (1997). Relationships between young children's day care experience and their attachment relationships with parents and socioemotional behavior problems. *Korean Journal of Child Studies, 18*(2), 5–18.

Kimberg, D. Y., D'Esposito, M., & Farah, M. J. (1998). Cognitive functions in the prefrontal cortex—Working memory and executive control. *American Psychological Society, 6*(6), 185–192.

Kimmel, D. C. (1980). *Adulthood and aging: An interdisciplinary view* (2nd ed.). New York: Wiley.

Kimura, D. (1992, September). Sex difference in the brain. *Scientific American*, 119–125.

Kinder, D. R., & Sanders, L. M. (1996). *Divided by color: Racial politics and democratic ideals.* Chicago: The University of Chicago Press.

Kingstone, A., Enns, J. T., Mangun, G. R., & Gazzaniga, M. S. (1995). Guided visual search is a left-hemisphere process in split-brain patients. *American Psychological Society, 6*, 118–121.

Kinnunen, T., & Zamansky, H. S. (1996). Hypnotic amnesia and learning: A dissociation interpretation. *American Journal of Clinical Hypnosis, 38*(4), 247–253.

Kinsbourne, M. (1975). The ontogeny of cerebral dominance. In D. Aaronson & R. W. Rieber (Eds.), *Developmental Psycholinguistics and Communication Disorders. Annals of the New York Academy of Science, 263*, 244–250.

Kinsey, A. C., Pomeroy, W. B., & Martin, C. E. (1948). *Sexual behavior in the human male.* Philadelphia: W. B. Saunders.

Kinsey, A. C., Pomeroy, W. B., Martin, C. E., & Gebhard, P. H. (1953). *Sexual behavior in the human female.* Philadelphia: W. B. Saunders.

Kirkpatrick, K., & Wasserman, E. A. (1997). The what and the where of the pigeon's processing of complex visual stimuli. *Journal of Experimental Psychology: Animal Behavior Processes, 22*(1), 60–67.

Kirkpatrick. L. A. (1997). An attachment-theory approach to the psychology of religion. In B. Spilka et al. (Eds.), *The psychology of religion: Theoretical approaches.* Boulder, CO: Westview Press.

Kirmayer, L. J., Young, A., & Hayton, B. C. (1995). The cultural context of anxiety disorders. *Psychiatric Clinics of North America, 18*(3), 503–521.

Kirsch, I., & Lynn, S. J. (1995). The altered state of hypnosis: Changes in the theoretical landscape. *American Psychologist, 50*(10), 846–858.

Kirsch, I., & Lynn, S. J. (1998a). Dissociating the wheat from the chaff in theories of hypnosis: Reply to Kihlstrom and Woody and Sadler. *Psychological Bulletin, 123*(2), 198–202.

Kirsch, I., & Lynn, S. J. (1998b). Dissociation theories of hypnosis. *Psychological Bulletin, 123*(1), 100–115.

Kirsch, I., Montgomery, G., & Sapirstein, G. (1995). Hypnosis as an adjunct to cognitive-behavioral psychotherapy: A meta-analysis. *Journal of Consulting and Clinical Psychology, 63*, 214–220.

Kirsch, I., Silva, C. E., Comey, G., & Reed, S. (1995). A spectral analysis of cognitive and personality variables in hypnosis: Empirical disconfirmation of the two-factor model of hypnotic responding. *Journal of Personality and Social Psychology, 69*, 167–175.

Kirshnit, C. E., Richards, M. H., & Ham, M. (1988, August). Athletic participation and body-image during early adolescence. Paper presented at the 96th Annual Convention of the American Psychological Association, Atlanta.

Kitayama, S., & Burnstein, E. (1994). Social influence, persuasion, and group decision making. In S. Shavitt & T. C. Brock (Eds.), *Persuasion: Psychological insights and perspectives* (pp. 175–194). Boston: Allyn & Bacon.

Kitwood, T. (1990). *Concern for others*. New York: Routledge.

Kivilu, J. M., & Rogers, W. T. (1998). A multi level analysis of cultural experience and gender influences on causal attributions to perceived performance in mathematics. *British Journal of Educational Psychology, 68*(1), 25–37.

Klar, A. J. S. (1996). A single locus, RGHT, specifies preference for hand utilization in humans. *Cold Spring Harbor Symposium for Quantitative Biology, 61*, 59–65.

Klar, Y., & Giladi, E. E. (1997). No one in my group can be below the group's average: A robust positivity bias in favor of anonymous peers. *Journal of Personality and Social Psychology, 73*(5), 885–901.

Klaus, M. H., & Kennell, J. H. (1983). *Bonding: The beginnings of parent-infant attachment* (Rev. ed.). New York: New American Library.

Kleinke, C. L., Peterson, T. R., & Rutledge, T. R. (1998). Effects of self-generated facial expressions on mood. *Journal of Personality and Social Psychology, 74*(1), 272–279.

Kleinmuntz, B., & Szucko, J. J. (1984). Lie detection in ancient and modern times: A call for contemporary scientific study. *American Psychologist, 39*, 766–776.

Klesges, R. C., Isbell, T. R., & Klesges, L. M. (1992). Relationship between dietary restraint, energy intake, physical activity, and body weight: A prospective analysis. *Journal of Abnormal Psychology, 101*, 668–674.

Klingenspor, B. (1994). Gender identity and bulimic eating behavior. *Sex Roles, 31*, 407–432.

Klinger, M. R., & Greenwald, A. G. (1995). Unconscious priming of association judgments. *Journal of Experimental Psychology: Learning, Memory, and Cognition, 21*(3), 569–581.

Klonoff, E. A., Annechild, A., & Landrine, H. (1994). Predicting exercise adherence in women: The role of psychological and physiological factors. *Preventive Medicine, 23*, 257–262.

Klusman, L. E. (1998). Military health care providers' views on prescribing privileges for psychologists. *Professional Psychology: Research and Practice, 29*(3), 223–229.

Knee, C. R. (1998). Implicit theories of relationships: Assessment and prediction of romantic relationship initiation, coping, and longevity. *Journal of Personality and Social Psychology, 74*(2), 360–368.

Knight, G. P., Virdin, L. M., Ocampo, K. A., & Roosa, M. (1994). An examination of the cross-ethnic equivalence of measures of negative life events and mental health among Hispanic and Anglo-American children. *American Journal of Community Psychology, 22*(6), 767–783.

Knutson, J. F. (1995). Psychological characteristics of maltreated children: Putative risk factors and consequences. *Annual Review of Psychology, 46*, 401–431.

Knutson, J. F., & Selner, M. B. (1994). Punitive childhood experiences reported by young adults over a 10-year period. *Child Abuse and Neglect, 18*, 155–166.

Kochanska, G., & Thompson, R. A. (1997). The emergence and development of conscience in toddlerhood and early childhood. J. E. Grusec, L. Kuczynski, et al. (Eds.), *Parenting and children's*

internalization of values: A handbook of contemporary theory (pp. 53–77). New York: John Wiley and Sons.

Koehler, T., Kuhnt, K., & Richter, R. (1998). The role of life event stress in the pathogenesis of duodenal ulcer. *Stress Medicine, 14*(2), 121–124.

Kogut, D., Langley, T., & O'Neal, E. C. (1992). Gender role masculinity and angry aggression in women. *Sex Roles, 26*, 355–365.

Kohlberg, L. (1969). The cognitive-developmental approach to socialization. In D. A. Goslin (Ed.), *Handbook of socialization theory and research*. Chicago: Rand McNally.

Köhler, W. (1973). *The mentality of apes* (2nd ed.). New York: Liveright. (Original work published 1927.)

Kohn, A. (1993). *Punished by rewards: The trouble with gold stars, incentive plans, A's, praise, and other bribes*. Boston: Houghton Mifflin.

Kohout, J., Wicherski, M., & Cooney, B. (1992). *Characteristics of graduate departments of psychology: 1989–1990*. Washington, DC: Office of Demographic, Employment, and Educational Research, American Psychological Association.

Kolb, B. (1989). Brain development, plasticity, and behavior. *American Psychologist, 44*, 1203–1212.

Kolb, B., & Wishaw, I. Q. (1996). *Fundamentals of human neuropsychology*. New York: W. H. Freemen.

Koolstra, C. M., van der Voort, T. H., & van der Kamp, L. J. (1997). Television's impact on children's reading comprehension and decoding skills: A 3–year panel study. *Reading Research Quarterly, 32*(2), 128–152.

Kopp, C. B. (1989). Regulation of distress and negative emotions: A developmental view. *Developmental Psychology, 25*, 343–354.

Kopp, C. B., & Kaler, S. R. (1989). Risk in infancy: Origins and implications. *American Psychologist, 44*, 224–230.

Kopta, S. M., Howard, K. I., Lowry, J. L., & Beutler, L. E. (1994). Patterns of symptomatic recovery in psychotherapy. *Journal of Consulting and Clinical Psychology, 62*, 1009–1016.

Kopyov, O. V., Jacques, D., Lieberman, A., Duma, C. M., & Rogers, R. L. (1996). Clinical study of fetal mesencephalic intracerebral transplants for the treatment of Parkinson's disease. *Cell Transplantation, 5*(2), 327–337.

Kortenhaus, C. M., & Demarest, J. (1993). Gender role stereotyping in children's literature: An update. *Sex Roles, 28*, 219–232.

Koss, M. P. (1990). The women's mental health research agenda. *American Psychologist, 45*, 374–380.

Koss, M. P. (1993). Rape: Scope, impact, interventions, and public policy responses. *American Psychologist, 48*, 1062–1069.

Koss, M. P., Gidycz, C. A., & Wisniewski, N. (1987). The scope of rape: Incidence and prevalence of sexual aggression and victimization in a national sample of higher education students. *Journal of Consulting and Clinical Psychology, 55*, 162–170.

Kosslyn, S. M. (1975). Information representation in visual images. *Cognitive Psychology, 7*, 341–370.

Kosslyn, S. M. (1987). Seeing and imagining in the cerebral hemispheres: A computational approach. *Psychological Review, 94*, 148–175.

Koulack, D. (1991). *To catch a dream*. Albany: State University of New York Press.

Kozu, J. (1999). Domestic violence. *American Psychologist, 54*(1), 50–54.

Kozyk, J. C., Touyz, S. W., & Beumont, P. J. (1998). Is there a relationship between bulimia nervosa and hazardous alcohol use? *International Journal of Eating Disorders, 24*(1), 95–99.

Kramer, M. S., Cutler, N., Feighner, J., Shrivastava, R., Carman, J., Sramek, J. J., et al. (1998). Distinct mechanism for antidepressant activity by blockade of central substance P receptors. *Science, 281*, 1640–1644.

Krampe, R. T., & Ericsson, K. A. (1996). Maintaining excellence: Deliberate practice and elite performance in young and older pianists. *Journal of Experimental Psychology: General, 125*(4), 331–359.

Krantz, D. S., Contrada, R. J., Hill, D. R., & Friedler, E. (1988). Environmental stress and biobehavioral antecedents of coronary heart disease. *Journal of Consulting and Clinical Psychology, 56*, 333–341.

Krantz, D. S., Grunberg, N. E., & Baum, A. (1985). Health psychology. *Annual Review of Psychology, 36*, 349–383.

Kranzler, H. R., & Anton, R. F. (1994). Implications of recent neuropsychopharmacologic research for understanding the etiology and development of alcoholism. *Journal of Consulting and Clinical Psychology, 62*, 1116–1126.

Kranzler, J. H., & Jensen, A. R. (1991). The nature of psychometric g: Unitary process or a number of independent processes? *Intelligence, 15*, 397–422.

Kraut, R., Patterson, M., Lundmark, V., Kiesler, S., Mukopadhyay, T., & Scherlis, W. (1998). Internet paradox: A social technology that reduces social involvement and psychological well-being? *American Psychologist, 53*(9), 1017–1031.

Kreider, R. B., Fry, A. C., & O'Toole, M. L. (1998). Overtraining in sport. *International Journal of Sport Psychology, 27*(3), 269–285.

Krosnick, J. A. (1988). Attitude importance and attitude change. *Journal of Experimental Social Psychology, 24*, 240–255.

Krosnick, J. A., & Alwin, D. F. (1989). Aging and susceptibility to attitude change. *Journal of Personality and Social Psychology, 57*, 416–425.

Krosnick, J. A., Jussim, L. J., & Lynn, A. R. (1992). Subliminal conditioning of attitudes. *Personality and Social Psychology Bulletin, 18*(2), 152–162.

Kruley, P., Sciama, S. C., & Glenberg, A. M. (1994). On-line processing of textual illustrations in the visuospatial sketchpad: Evidence from dual-task studies. *Memory and Cognition, 22*, 261–272.

Kubey, R., & Csikszentmihalyi, M. (1990). *Television and the quality of life*. Hillsdale, NJ: Erlbaum.

Kübler-Ross, E. (1969). *On death and dying*. New York: Macmillan.

Kübler-Ross, E. (1975). *Death: The final stage of growth*. Englewood Cliffs, NJ: Prentice-Hall.

Kudoh, N., Tajima, H., Hatayama, T., Maruyama, K., Shoji, Y., Hayashi, T., & Nakanishi, M. (1991). Effects of room environment on human cognitive activities. *Tohoku Psychologica Folia, 50*, 45–54.

Kuhl, P. K., Andruski, J. E., Chistovich, I. A., Chistovich, L. A., Kozhevnikova, E. V., Ryskina, V. L., Stolyarova, E. I., Sundberg, U., & Lacerda, F. (1997). Cross-language analysis of phonetic units in language addressed to infants. *Science, 277*, 684–686.

Kuhl, P. K., Williams, K. A., Lacerda, F., Stevens, K. N., & Lindblom, B. (1992). Linguistic experience alters phonetic perception in infants by 6 months of age. *Science, 255*, 606–655.

Kuiper, N. A., & Martin, R. A. (1998). Laughter and stress in daily life: Relation to positive and negative affect. *Motivation and Emotion, 22*(2), 133–153.

Kutchins, H., & Kirk, S. A. (1997). *Making us crazy. DSM: The psychiatric bible and the creation of mental disorders*. New York: The Free Press.

Lachman, M. E., & James, J. B. (1997). *Multiple paths of midlife development. Studies on successful midlife development: The John D. and Catherine T. MacArthur Foundation series on mental health and development*. Chicago: The University of Chicago Press.

Lachman, M. E., & Weaver, S. L. (1998). Sociodemographic variations in the sense of control by domain: Findings from the MacArthur studies of midlife. *Psychology and Aging, 13*(4), 553–562.

Ladd, G. W. (1990). Having friends, keeping friends, making friends, and being liked by peers in the classroom: Predictors of children's early school adjustment? *Child Development, 61*, 1081–1100.

Laessle, R. G., Wurmser, H., & Pirke, K. M. (1996). A comparison of resting metabolic rate, self-rated food intake, growth hormone, and insulin levels in obese and nonobese preadolescents. *Physiology and Behavior, 61*(5), 725–729.

LaFerla, J. J., Anderson, D. L., & Schalch, D. S. (1978). Psychoendocrine response to sexual arousal in human males. *Psychosomatic Medicine, 40*, 166–172.

Lafferty, P., Beutler, L. E., & Crago, M. (1989). Differences between more and less effective psychotherapists: A study of select therapist variables. *Journal of Consulting and Clinical Psychology, 57*, 76–80.

Lahey, B. B., McNees, M. P., & McNees, M. C. (1973). Control of an obscene "verbal tic" through timeout in an elementary school classroom. *Journal of Applied Behavior Analysis, 6*, 101–104.

Lambert, A. J. (1995). Stereotypes and social judgment: The consequences of group variability. *Journal of Personality and Social Psychology, 68*, 388–403.

Landrine, H., Klonoff, E. A., & Brown-Collins, A. (1992). Cultural diversity and methodology in feminist psychology. *Psychology of Women Quarterly, 16*, 145–163.

Lang, P. J. (1994). The varieties of emotional experience: A meditation on James-Lange theory. *Psychological Review, 101*, 211–221.

Lange, C. G. (1922). *The emotions* (English translation). Baltimore: Williams & Wilkins. (Original work published 1885.)

Langer, E. J. (1989). *Mindfulness*. Reading, MA: Addison-Wesley.

Langer, E. J. (1992). Matters of mind: Mindfulness/mindlessness in perspective. *Consciousness and Cognition: An International Journal, 1*(4), 289–305.

Langer, E. J. (1993). A mindful education. *Educational Psychologist, 28*(1), 43–50.

Langer, E. J. (1997). *The power of mindful learning*. Reading, MA: Addison-Wesley.

Langlois, J. H., Ritter, J. M., Casey, R. J., & Sawin, D. B. (1995). Infant attractiveness predicts maternal behaviors and attitudes. *Developmental Psychology, 31*, 464–472.

Langlois, J. H., Ritter, J. M., Roggman, L. A., & Vaughn, L. S. (1991). Facial diversity and infant preferences for attractive faces. *Developmental Psychology, 27*, 79–84.

Langlois, J. H., Roggman, L. A., & Rieser-Danner, L. A. (1990). Infants' differential social responses to attractive and unattractive faces. *Developmental Psychology, 26*, 153–159.

Langman, B., & Cockburn, A. (1975). Sirhan's gun. *Harper's, 250*, 16–27.

Lapsley, D. K. (1993). Toward an integrated theory of adolescent ego development: The "new look" at adolescent egocentrism. *American Journal of Orthopsychiatry, 63*(4), 562–571.

Lapsley, D. K. (1996). *Moral psychology*. Boulder, CO: Westview.

Larrick, R. P., Morgan, J. N., & Nisbett, R. E. (1990). Teaching the use of cost-benefit reasoning in everyday life. *Psychological Science, 1*, 362–370.

Larson, R., & Ham, M. (1993). Stress and "storm and stress" in early adolescence: The relationship of negative events with dysphoric affect. *Developmental Psychology, 29*, 130–140.

Larson, R. W., Raffaelli, M., Richards, M. H., Ham, M., & Jewell, L. (1990). Ecology of depression in late childhood and early adolescence: A profile of daily states and activities. *Journal of Abnormal Psychology, 99*, 92–102.

Lassner, J. B., Matthews, K. A., & Stoney, C. M. (1994). Are cardiovascular reactors to asocial stress also reactors to social stress? *Journal of Personality and Social Psychology, 66*, 69–77.

Last, C. G., Hersen, M., Kazdin, A., Orvaschel, H., & Perrin, S. (1991). Anxiety disorders in children and their families. *Archives of General Psychiatry, 48*, 928–931.

Last, C. G., & Perrin, S. (1993). Anxiety disorders in African-American and white children. *Journal of Abnormal Child Psychology, 21*, 153–164.

Latané, B., & Darley, J. M. (1970). *The unresponsive bystander: Why doesn't he help?* New York: Meredith.

Latané, B., Williams, K., & Harkins, S. (1979). Many hands make light work: The causes and consequences of social loafing. *Journal of Personality and Social Psychology, 37*, 822–832.

Latham, G. P., Daghighi, S., & Locke, E. A. (1997). Implications of goal-setting theory for faculty motivation. In J. L. Bess et al. (Eds.), *Teaching well and liking it: Motivating faculty to teach effectively* (pp. 125–142). Baltimore, MD: Johns Hopkins University Press.

Laumann, E. O., Gagnon, J. H., Michael, R. T., & Michaels, S. (1994). *The social organization of sexuality: Sexual practices in the United States*. Chicago: The University of Chicago Press.

Laursen, B., Coy, K. C., & Collins, A. (1998). Reconsidering changes in parent-child conflict across adolescence: A meta-analysis. *Society for Research in Child Development, 69*(3), 817–832.

Lavie, P. (1996). *The enchanted world of sleep*. New Haven, CT and London: Yale University Press.

Lawler, E. E., & Porter, L. W. (1967). Antecedent attitudes of effective managerial performance. *Organizational Behavior and Human Performance, 2*, 122–142.

Lawler, J. J., & Elliot, R. (1996). Artificial intelligence in HRM: An experimental study of an expert system. *Journal of Management, 22*(1), 85–111.

Lazarus, A. A., & Fay, A. (1990). Brief psychotherapy: Tautology or oxymoron? In J. K. Zeig & S. G. Gilligan (Eds.), *Brief therapy myths, methods, and metaphors*. New York: Brunner/Mazel.

Lazarus, R. S. (1982). The psychology of stress and coping, with particular reference to Israel. In C. D. Spielberger, I. G. Sarason, & N. A. Milgram (Eds.), *Stress and anxiety* (Vol. 8). Washington, DC: Hemisphere.

Lazarus, R. S. (1984). The trivialization of distress. In B. L. Hammonds & C. J. Scheirer (Eds.), *Psychology and health: The master lecture series*. Washington, DC: American Psychological Association.

Lazarus, R. S. (1993). From psychological stress to the emotions: A history of changing outlooks. *Annual Review of Psychology, 44*, 1–21.

Lazarus, R. S., & Alfert, E. (1964). Short-circuiting of threat by experimentally altering cognitive appraisal. *Journal of Abnormal and Social Psychology, 69*, 195–205.

Lazarus, R. S., & DeLongis, A. (1983). Psychological stress and coping in aging. *American Psychologist, 38,* 245–254.

Leahey, T. H. (1992). The mythical revolutions of American psychology. *American Psychologist, 47,* 308–318.

Leaper, C., Anderson, K. J., & Sanders, P. (1998). Moderators of gender effects on parents' talk to their children: A meta-analysis. *Developmental Psychology, 34*(1), 3–27.

Lebow, J. L., & Gurman, A. S. (1995). Research assessing couple and family therapy. *Annual Review of Psychology, 46,* 27–57.

LeDoux, J. (1996). *The emotional brain: The mysterious underpinnings of emotional life.* New York: Simon and Schuster.

LeDoux, J. E. (1993). Emotional memory systems in the brain. *Behavioural Brain Research, 58,* 69–79.

LeDoux, J. E. (1995). Emotion: Clues from the brain. *Annual Review of Psychology, 46,* 209–235.

LeDoux, J. E., Romanski, L., & Xagoraris, A. (1989). Indelibility of subcortical emotional memories. *Journal of Cognitive Neuroscience, 1,* 238–243.

Lee, C., Ashford, S. J., & Bobko, P. (1990). Interactive effects of "Type A" behavior and perceived control on worker performance, job satisfaction, and somatic complaints. *Academy of Management Journal, 33,* 870–881.

Lefcourt, H. M. (1992). Durability and impact of the locus of control construct. *Psychological Bulletin, 112,* 411–414.

Lefcourt, H. M., & Davidson-Katz, K. (1991). Locus of control and health. In C. R. Snyder & D. R. Forsyth (Eds.), *Handbook of social and clinical psychology* (pp. 246–266). New York: Pergamon.

Lefcourt, H. M., & Thomas, S. (1998). Humor and stress revisited. In W. Ruch et al. (Eds.), *The sense of humor: Explorations of a personality characteristic. Humor research: 3* (pp. 179–202). Berlin: Walter De Gruyter.

Leffler, C. T., & Dembert, M. L. (1998). Posttraumatic stress symptoms among U.S. Navy divers recovering TWA Flight 800. *Journal of Nervous and Mental Disease, 186*(9), 574–577.

Lefkowitz, M. M., Eron, L. D., Walder, L. O., & Huesmann, L. R. (1977). *Growing up to be violent.* New York: Pergamon.

Leibowitz, H. W. (1971). Sensory, learned, and cognitive mechanisms of size perception. *Annals of the New York Academy of Sciences, 1988, 47* 62.

Leikin, R., & Zaslavsky, O. (1997). Facilitating student interactions in mathematics in a cooperative learning setting. *Journal for Research in Mathematics Education, 28*(3), 331–354.

Leinbach, M. D., Hort, B. E., & Fagot, B. I. (1997). Bears are for boys: Metaphorical associations in young children's gender stereotypes. *Cognitive Development, 12,* 107–130.

Leiner, H. C., Leiner, A. L., & Dow, R. S. (1986). Does the cerebellum contribute to mental skills? *Behavioral Neuroscience, 100,* 443–454.

Lenneberg, E. H. (1967). *Biological foundations of language.* New York: Wiley.

Leon, M. (1992). The neurobiology of filial learning. *Annual Review of Psychology, 43,* 377–399.

Leonard, B. E. (1987). Stress, the immune system and mental illness. *Stress Medicine, 3*(4), 257–258.

Leonard, C. M., Lombardino, L. J., Mercado, L. R., Browd, S. R., Breier, J. I., & Agee, O. F. (1996). Cerebral asymmetry and cognitive development in children: A magnetic resonance imaging study. *American Psychological Society, 7*(2), 89–95.

Leonard-Barton, D. (1981). The diffusion of active residential solar energy equipment in California. In A. Shama (Ed.), *Marketing solar energy innovations* (pp. 243–257). New York: Praeger.

Lepine, J. P., & Bouchez, S. (1998). Epidemiology of depression in the elderly. *International Clinical Psychopharmacology, 13*(Suppl. 5), S7–S12.

Lepper, M. R., & Greene, D. (1978). Overjustification research and beyond: Toward a means-end analysis of intrinsic motivation. In M. R. Lepper & D. Greene (Eds.), *The hidden cost of reward.* Hillsdale, NJ: Erlbaum.

Lesch, K. P., Bengel, D., Heils, A., Sabol, S. Z., Greenberg, B. D., Petri, S., Benjamin, J., Müller, C. R., Hamer, D. H., & Murphy, D. L. (1996). Association of anxiety-related traits with a polymorphism in the serotonin transporter gene regulatory region. *Science, 274,* 1527–1531.

Leserman, J., Petitto, J. M., Perkins, D. O., Folds, J. D., Golden, R. N., et al. (1997). Severe stress, depressive symptoms, and changes in lymphocyte subsets in human immunodeficiency virus-infected men. A 2–year follow-up study. *Archives of General Psychiatry, 54*(3), 279–285.

Lessard, N., Paré, M., Lepore, F., & Lassonde, M. (1998). Early-blind human subjects localize sound sources better than sighted subjects. *Nature, 395,* 278–280.

Lester, B. M & Dreher, M. (1989). Effects of marijuana use during pregnancy on newborn cry. *Child Development, 60*(4), 765–771.

LeVay, S. (1991). A difference in hypothalamic structure between heterosexual and homosexual men. *Science, 253,* 1034–1037.

LeVay, S., & Hamer, D. H. (1994, May). Evidence for a biological influence in male homosexuality. *Scientific American,* 44–49.

Levenson, R. W. (1992). Autonomic nervous system differences among emotions. *Psychological Science, 3,* 23–27.

Levenstein, S., Prantera, C., Varvo, V., & Arca, M. (1996). Long-term symptom patterns in duodenal ulcer: Psychosocial factors. *Journal of Psychosomatic Research, 41*(5), 465–472.

Levi, L. (1990). Occupational stress. *American Psychologist, 46,* 1142–1145.

Levin, D. J. (1990). *Alcoholism.* New York: Hemisphere.

Levin, J. S., & Taylor, R. J. (1997). Age differences in patterns and correlates of the frequency of prayer. *Gerontologist, 37*(1), 75–88.

Levine, E. L., Ash, R. A., Hall, H., & Sistrunk, F. (1983). Evaluation of job analysis methods by experienced job analysts. *Academy of Management Journal, 26,* 339–348.

Levine, J. A., Eberhardt, N. L., & Jensen, M. D. (1999). Role of nonexercise activity thermogenesis in resistance to fat gain in humans. *Science, 283,* 212–214.

Levine, M. (1998). Prevention and community. *American Journal of Community Psychology, 26*(2), 189–206.

LeVine, R. (1966). Sex roles and economic change in Africa. *Ethnology, 5,* 186–193.

Levine, R. L., & Stadtman, E. R. (1992). Oxidation of proteins during aging. *Generations, 16,* 39–42.

Levine, R. V., Martinez, T. S., Brase, G., & Sorenson, K. (1994). Helping in 36 U.S. cities. *Journal of Personality and Social Psychology, 67,* 69–82.

Levinson, D. J. (1978). *The seasons of a man's life.* New York: Knopf.

Levinson, D. J. (1980). Toward a conception of the adult life course. In N. J. Smelser & E. H. Erikson (Eds.), *Themes of work and love in adulthood.* Cambridge, MA: Harvard University Press.

Levinson, D. J. (1996). *The seasons of a woman's life.* New York: Alfred A. Knopf.

Levitt, M. J., Weber, R. A., Clark, M. C., & McDonnell, P. (1985). Reciprocity of exchange in toddler sharing behavior. *Developmental Psychology, 21,* 122–123.

Lewin, K. K. (1970). *Brief psychotherapy.* St. Louis, MO: Warren H. Green.

Lewinsohn, P. M. (1974). Classical and theoretical aspects of depression. In J. S. Calhoun, H. E. Adams, & K. M. Mitchell (Eds.), *Innovative treatment methods in psychopathology.* New York: Wiley Interscience.

Lewinsohn, P. M., Rohde, P., Klein, D. N., & Seeley, J. R. (1999). Natural course of adolescent major depressive disorder: I. Continuity into young adulthood. *Journal of the American Academy of Child and Adolescent Psychiatry, 38*(1), 56–63.

Lewinsohn, P. M., Rohde, P., Klein, D. N., Seeley, J. R., & Fischer, S. A. (1993). Age-cohort changes in the lifetime occurrence of depression and other mental disorders. *Journal of Abnormal Psychology, 102*(1), 110–120.

Lewinsohn, P. M., & Talkington, J. (1979). Studies on the measurement of unpleasant events and relations with depression. *Applied Psychological Measurement, 3,* 83–101.

Lewis, M. (1995). Self-conscious emotions. *American Scientist, 83,* 68–78.

Lewis, M. (1997). *Altering fate: Why the past does not predict the future.* New York: The Guilford Press.

Lewis, M. (1998). Altering fate: Why the past does not predict the future. *Psychological Inquiry, 9*(2), 105–108.

Lewis, M., & Feiring, C. (1989). Infant, mother, and mother-infant interaction behavior and subsequent attachment. *Child Development, 60,* 831–837.

Lidsky, T. I., Yablonski-Alter, E., Zuck, L. G., & Banerjee, S. P. (1997). Antipsychotic drug effects on glutamatergic activity. *Brain Research, 764*(1/2), 46–52.

Lidz, T. (1973). *The origin and treatment of schizophrenic disorders.* New York: Basic Books.

Liebrand, W. B. G., Messick, D. M., & Wolters, F. J. M. (1986). Why we are fairer than others: A cross-cultural replication and extension. *Journal of Experimental Social Psychology, 22,* 590–604.

Lilla, I., Szikriszt, E., Ortutay, J., Berecz, M., Gyoergy, F., & Attila, N. (1998). Psychological factors contributing to the development of coronary artery disease—a study of rigidity and the A-type behaviour pattern. *Psychiatria Hungarica, 13*(2), 169–180.

Lillo-Martin, D. (1997). The modular effects of sign language acquisition. In Marschark, M., Siple, P., et al. (Eds.), *Relations of language and thought* (pp. 62–109). New York: Oxford University Press.

Lilly, J. C. (1956). Mental effects of reduction of ordinary levels of physical stimuli in intact, healthy persons. *Psychiatric Research Reports, 5,* 1–28.

Linberg, M. A., Beggs, A. L., Chezik, D. D., & Ray, D. (1982). Flavor-toxicosis associations: Tests of three hypotheses of long delay learning. *Physiology and Behavior, 29,* 439–442.

Lindfors, O., Hannula, J., Aalber, V., Kaarento, K., Kaipainen, M., & Pylkkaenen, K. (1995). Assessment of the effectiveness of psychotherapy. *Psychiatria Fennica, 26,* 150–164.

Lindsay, D. S. (1993). Eyewitness suggestibility. *Current Directions in Psychological Science, 2,* 86–89.

Lindsey, K. P., & Paul, G. L. (1989). Involuntary commitments to public mental institutions: Issues involving the overrepresentation of blacks and assessment of relevant functioning. *Psychological Bulletin, 106,* 171–183.

Lindvall, O. (1991). Prospects of transplantation in human neurodegenerative diseases. *Trends in Neurosciences, 14,* 376–384.

Lindvall, O., Brundin, P., Widner, H., Rehncrona, S., Gustavi, B., Frackowiak, R., Leenders, K. L., Sawle, G., Rothwell, J. C., Marsden, C. D., & Bjorklund, A. (1990). Grafts of fetal dopamine neurons survive and improve motor function in Parkinson's disease. *Science, 247,* 374–577.

Linn, M. C., & Petersen, A. C. (1985). Emergence and characterization of sex differences in spatial ability: A meta-analysis. *Child Development, 56,* 1479–1498.

Lippincott, J. A., & Mierzwa, J. A. (1995). Propensity for seeking counseling services: A comparison of Asian and American undergraduates. *Journal of American College Health, 43*(5), 201–204.

Lips, H. (1994). Female powerlessness. In H. L. Radtke & H. J. Stam (Eds.), *Power/gender: Social relations in theory and practice.* London: Sage Publications.

Lipsey, M. W., & Wilson, D. B. (1993). The efficacy of psychological, educational, and behavioral treatment: Confirmation from meta-analysis. *American Psychologist, 48,* 1181–1209.

Livingstone, M. S., Rosen, G. D., Drislane, F. W., & Galaburda, A. M. (1991). Physiological and anatomical evidence for a magnocellular defect in developmental dyslexia. *Proceedings of the National Academy of Science, 88,* 7943–7947.

Livson, N., & Peskin, H. (1967). Prediction of adult psychological health in a longitudinal study. *Journal of Abnormal Psychology, 72*(6), 509–518.

Locher, P., Unger, R., Sociedade, P., & Wahl, J. (1993). At first glance: Accessibility of the physical attractiveness stereotype. *Sex Roles, 28,* 729–743.

Locke, E. A. (1996). Motivation through conscious goal setting. *Allied and Preventive Psychology, 5*(2), 117–124.

Locke, E. A., & Latham, G. P. (1990a). Work motivation: The high performance cycle. In U. Kleinbeck, H. Quast, H. Thierry, & H. Hacker (Eds.), *Work motivation.* Hillsdale, NJ: Erlbaum.

Locke, E. A., & Latham, G. P. (1990b). Work motivation and satisfaction: Light at the end of the tunnel. *Psychological Science, 1,* 240–246.

Loeber, R., & Stouthamer-Loeber, M. (1998). Development of juvenile aggression and violence: Some common misconceptions and controversies. *American Psychologist, 53*(2), 242–259.

Loehlin, J. C., McCrae, R. R., Costa, P. T., Jr., & John, O. P. Heritabilities of common and measure-specific components of the Big Five personality factors. *Journal of Research in Personality, 32*(4), 431–453.

Loewenstein, R. J. (1993). Dissociation, development, and the psychobiology of trauma. *Journal of the American Academy of Psychoanalysis, 21,* 581–603.

Loftus, E. F. (1979). The malleability of human memory. *American Scientist, 67,* 310–320.

Loftus, E. F. (1991). *Witness for the defense.* New York: St. Martin's.

Loftus, E. F. (1993). The reality of repressed memories. *American Psychologist, 48,* 518–537.

Loftus, E. F. (1997). Memory for a past that never was. *American Psychological Society, 6*(3), 60–65.

Lollis, S., Ross, H., & Leroux, L. (1996). An observational study of parents' socialization of moral orientation during sibling conflicts. *Merrill-Palmer Quarterly, 42,* 475–494.

Lombard, D. N., Lombard, T. N., & Winett, R. A. (1995). Walking to meet health guidelines: The effect of prompting frequency and prompt structure. *Health Psychology, 14,* 164–170.

Lore, R. K., & Schultz, L. A. (1993). Control of human aggression. *American Psychologist, 48,* 16–25.

Lorenz, F. O., Simons, R. L., & Conger, R. D. (1997). Married and recently divorced mothers' stressful events and distress: Tracing change across time. *Journal of Marriage and the Family, 59,* 219–232.

Lorenz, K. (1964). Ritualized fighting. In J. D. Carthy & F. J. Ebling (Eds.), *The natural history of aggression.* New York: Academic Press.

Lowe, M. R., Gleaves, D. H., & Murphy-Eberenz, K. P. (1998). The relation of dieting and bingeing in bulimia nervosa. *Journal of Abnormal Psychology, 107*(2), 263–271.

Lowell, E. L. (1952). The effect of need for achievement on learning and speed of performance. *Journal of Psychology, 33,* 31–40.

Lowenstein, R. J. (1993). Dissociation, development, and the psychobiology of trauma. *Journal of the American Academy of Psychoanalysis, 21*(4), 581–603.

Luborsky, L., Barber, J. P., & Crits-Christoph, P. (1990). Theory-based research for understanding the process of dynamic psychotherapy. *Journal of Consulting and Clinical Psychology, 58,* 281–287.

Lucidi, F., Devoto, A., Violani, C., Mastracci, P., & Bertini, M. (1997). Effects of different sleep duration on delta sleep in recovery nights. *Psychophysiology, 34,* 227–233.

Ludwick-Rosenthal, R., & Neufeld, W. J. (1988). Stress management during noxious medical procedures: An evaluative review of outcome studies. *Psychological Bulletin, 3,* 326–342.

Luecke-Aleksa, D., Anderson, D. R., Collins, P. A., & Schmitt, K. L. (1995). Gender constancy and television viewing. *Developmental Psychology, 31,* 773–780.

Luger, G. F., Bower, T. G. R., & Wishart, J. G. (1983). A model of the development of the early infant object concept. *Perception, 12,* 21–34.

Lundin, R. W. (1961). *Personality: An experimental approach.* New York: Macmillan.

Lundy, B., Field, T., McBride, C., Field, T., & Largie, S. (1998). Same-sex and opposite-sex best friend interactions among high school juniors and seniors. *Adolescence, 33*(130), 279–289.

Luria, A. R. (1968). *The mind of the mnemonist.* New York: Basic Books.

Luttrell, W. (1989). Working-class women's ways of knowing: Effects of gender, race, and class. *Sociology of Education, 62*(1), 33–46.

Luus, C. A. E., & Wells, G. L. (1994). The malleability of eyewitness confidence: Co-witness and perseverance effects. *Journal of Applied Psychology, 79,* 714–723.

Lykken, D., & Tellegen, A. (1996). Happiness is a stochastic phenomenon. *American Psychological Association, 7*(3), 186–189.

Lykken, D. T., McGue, M., Tellegen, A., & Bouchard, T. J., Jr. (1992). Emergenesis. *American Psychologist, 47,* 1565–1577.

Lynch, G., & Baudry, M. (1984). The biochemistry of memory: A new and specific hypothesis. *Science, 224,* 1057–1063.

Lynn, M., & Mynier, K. (1993). Effect of server posture on restaurant tipping. *Journal of Applied Social Psychology, 23,* 678–685.

Lynn, S. J. (1992). A non-state view of hypnotic involuntariness. *Contemporary Hypnosis, 9*(1), 21–27.

Lynn, S. J., Lock, T. G., Myers, B., & Payne, D. G. (1997). Recalling the unrecallable: Should hypnosis be used to recover memories in psychotherapy? *American Psychological Society, 6*(3), 79–83.

Lyons, M. J., Eisen, S. A., Goldberg, J., True, W., Lin, N., Meyer, J. M., Toomey, R., Faraone, S. V., Merla-Ramos, M., & Tsuang, M. T. (1998). A registry-based twin study of depression in men. *Archives of General Psychiatry, 55*(5), 468–472.

Lyons, M. J., True, W. R., Eisen, S. A., Goldberg, J., Meyer, J. M., Faraone, S. V., Eaves, L. J., & Tsuang, M. T. (1995). Differential heritability of adult and juvenile antisocial traits. *Archives of General Psychiatry, 52,* 906–915.

Lytton, H., & Romney, D. M. (1991). Parents' differential socialization of boys and girls: A meta-analysis. *Psychological Bulletin, 109,* 267–296.

Lyubomirsky, S., & Tucker, K. L. (1998). Implications of individual differences in subjective happiness for perceiving, interpreting, and thinking about life events. *Motivation and Emotion, 22*(2), 155–186.

Maas, J. B. (1998). *Power sleep.* New York: Villard.

Maccoby, E. E. (1988). Gender as a social category. *Developmental Psychology, 24,* 755–765.

Maccoby, E. E. (1998). *The two sexes: Growing up apart, coming together.* Cambridge, MA: Harvard University Press.

Mack, A., & Rock, I. (1998). *Inattentional blindness.* Cambridge, MA: The MIT Press.

MacKay, N. J., & Covell, D. (1997). The impact of women in advertisements on attitudes toward women. *Sex Roles, 36*(9/10), 573–576.

MacLeod, C. M. (1991). Half a century of research on the Stroop effect: An integrative review. *Psychological Bulletin, 109,* 163–203.

MacWhinney, B. (1998). Models of the emergence of language. *Annual Review of Psychology, 49,* 199–227.

Maddux, J. E. (1995). Self-efficacy theory: An introduction. In J. E. Maddux (Ed.), *Self-efficacy, adaptation, and adjustment: Theory, research, and application* (pp. 3–33). New York: Plenum.

Maddux, J. E., & Meier, L. J. (1995). Self-efficacy and depression. In J. E. Maddux (Ed.), *Self-efficacy, adaptation, and adjustment: Theory, research, and application* (pp. 143–169). New York: Plenum.

Madigan, M. F., Jr., Dale, J. A., & Cross, J. D. (1997). No respite during sleep: Heart-rate hyperreactivity to rapid eye movement sleep in angry men classified as Type A. *Perceptual and Motor Skills, 85* (3, Pt. 2), 1451–1454.

Madrazo, I., Drucken-Colin, R., Diaz, V., Martinez-Mata, J., Toress, C., & Becerril, J. J. (1987). Open microsurgical autograft of adrenal medulla to the right caudate nucleus in two patients with intractable Parkinson's disease. *New England Journal of Medicine, 316,* 831–834.

Magdol, L., Moffitt, T. E., Caspi, A., & Silva, P. A. (1998). Developmental antecedents of partner abuse: A prospective-longitudinal study. *Journal of Abnormal Psychology, 107*(3), 375–389.

Magolda, M. B. (1990). Gender differences in epistemological development. *Journal of College Student Development, 31,* 555–561.

Maguire, E. A., Burgess, N., Donnett, J. G., Frackowiak, R. S. J., Frith, C. D., & O'Keefe, J. (1998). Knowing where and getting there: A human navigation network. *Science, 280,* 921–924.

Mahoney, M. J. (1977). Reflections on the cognitive-learning trend in psychotherapy. *American Psychologist, 32,* 5–13.

Mahoney, M. J. (1993). Introduction to special section: Theoretical developments in the cognitive psychotherapies. *Journal of Consulting and Clinical Psychology, 61,* 187–193.

Mahrer, A. R., & Nadler, W. P. (1986). Good moments in psychotherapy: A preliminary review, a list, and some promising research avenues. *Journal of Consulting and Clinical Psychology, 54,* 10–15.

Maier, N. R. F., & Klee, J. B. (1941). Studies of abnormal behavior in the rat: 17. Guidance versus trial and error and their relation to convulsive tendencies. *Journal of Experimental Psychology, 29,* 380–389.

Maier, S. F., & Watkins, L. R. (1998). Cytokines for psychologists: Implications of bidirectional immune-to-brain communication for understanding behavior, mood, and cognition. *Psychological Review, 105*(1), 83–107.

Maier, S. F., Watkins, L. R., & Fleshner, M. (1994). Psychoneuroimmunology: The interface between behavior, brain, and immunity. *American Psychologist, 49,* 1004–1017.

Main, M., & Solomon, J. (1990). Procedures for identifying infants as disorganized/disoriented during the Ainsworth Strange Situation. In M. T. Greenberg, D. Cicchetti, et al. (Eds.), *Attachment in the preschool years: Theory, research, and intervention. The John D. and Catherine T. MacArthur Foundation series on mental health and development.* Chicago: University of Chicago Press.

Malamuth, N. M., & Sockloskie, R. J. (1991). Characteristics of aggressors against women: Testing a model using a national sample of college students. *Journal of Consulting and Clinical Psychology, 59,* 670–681.

Malik, A., & Batra, P. (1998). Effect of crowding on a complex task. *Journal of Personality and Clinical Studies, 13*(1/2), 87–91.

Mamelak, M. (1991). A model for narcolepsy. *Canadian Journal of Psychology, 45,* 194–220.

Mandler, J. M., & Johnson, N. S. (1977). Remembrance of things parsed: Story structure and recall. *Cognitive Psychology, 9*(1), 111–151.

Mangan, B. (1993). Dennett, consciousness, and the sorrows of functionalism. *Consciousness and Cognition, 2,* 1–17.

Manlove, J. (1998). The influence of high school dropout and school disengagement on the risk of school-age pregnancy. *Journal of Research on Adolescence, 8*(2), 187–220.

Mann, J. J., Malone, D. M., Diehl, D. J., P., J., Cooper, T. B., & Mintun, M. A. (1996). Demonstration in vivo of reduced serotonin reponsivity in the brain of untreated depressed patients. *American Journal of Psychiatry, 153*(2), 174–182.

Mann, J. J., Oquendo, M., Underwood, M. D., & Arango, V. (1999). The neurobiology of suicide risk: A review for the clinician. *Journal of Clinical Psychiatry, 60*(Suppl. 2), 7–11.

Mantzicopoulos, P. Y. (1997). The relationship of family variables to Head Start children's pre-academic competence. *Early Education & Development, 8*(4), 357–375.

Manuck, S. B., Cohen, S., Rabin, B. S., Muldoon, M. F., & Bachen, E. A. (1991). Individual differences in cellular immune response to stress. *Psychological Science, 2,* 111–115.

Manuck, S. B., Marsland, A. L., Kaplan, J. R., & Williams, J. K. (1995). The pathogenicity of behavior and its neuroendocrine mediation: An example from coronary artery disease. *Psychosomatic Medicine, 57,* 275–283.

Mao, Y., Moloughney, B. W., & Semenciw, R.W. (1992). Indian reserve and registered Indian mortality in Canada. *Canadian Journal of Public Health, 83*(5), 350–353.

March, J. S., Leonard, H. L., & Swedo, S. E. (1995). Obsessive-compulsive disorder. In J. S. March (Ed.), *Anxiety disorders in children and adolescents* (pp. 251–275). New York: Guilford.

Marcovitch, S., Goldberg, S., Handley-Derry, M., & MacGragor, D. (1994). *Recovery from early institutional care: Predictors of attachment and development for internationally adopted Romanian orphans.* Final report to Health Canada, Mental Health Division.

Marcus, G. F., Vijayan, S., Bandi, R., & Vishton, P. M. (1999). Rule learning by seven-month-old infants. *Science, 283,* 77–79.

Maris, R., & Silverman, M. M. (1995). *Suicide prevention: Toward the year 2000.* New York: Guilford.

Markow, T. M. (1992). Genetics and developmental stability: An integrative conjecture on aetiology and neurobiology of schizophrenia. *Psychological Medicine, 22,* 295–305.

Markowitsch, H. J., & Tulving, E. (1994). Cognitive processes and cerebral cortical fundi: Findings from positron-emission tomography studies. *Proceedings of the National Academy of Sciences of the United States of America, 91,* 10507–10511.

Marks, I. M. (1977). Clinical phenomena in search of laboratory models. In J. D. Maser & M. E. P. Seligman (Eds.), *Psychopathology experimental models.* San Francisco: Freeman.

Marks, I. M., et al. (1986). *Behavioral psychotherapy: Pocketbook of clinical management.* Bristol, England: John Wright.

Marks, W. B., Dobell, W. H., & MacNichol, J. R. (1964). The visual pigments of single primate cones. *Science, 142,* 1181–1183.

Marlatt, G. A., Larimer, M. E., Baer, J. S., & Quigley, L. A. (1993). Harm reduction for alcohol problems: Moving beyond the controlled drinking. *Behavior Therapy, 24,* 461–504.

Marschark, M., Yuille, J. C., Richman, C. L., & Hunt, R. R. (1987). The role of imagery in memory: On shared and distinctive information. *Psychological Bulletin, 102,* 28–41.

Marshall, G. N., Wortman, C. B., Vickers, R. R., Jr., Kusulas, J. W., & Hervig, L. K. (1994). The five-factor model of personality as a framework for personality-health research. *Journal of Personality and Social Psychology, 67,* 278–286.

Marshall, L. L., & Vitanza, S. A. (1994). Physical abuse in close relationships: Myths and realities. In A. L. Weber & J. H. Harvey (Eds.), *Perspectives on close relationships* (pp. 263–284). Boston: Allyn & Bacon.

Marshall, W. A., & Tanner, J. M. (1969). Variations in the pattern of pubertal changes in girls. *Archives of Disease in Childhood, 44,* 291–303.

Martin, C., Hill, K. K., & Welsh, R. (1998). Adolescent pregnancy, a stressful life event: Cause and consequence. In T. W. Miller et al. (Eds.), *Children of trauma: Stressful life events and their effects on children and adolescents.* Madison, CT: International Universities Press.

Martin, R., & Haroldson, S. (1977). Effect of vicarious punishment on stuttering frequency. *Journal of Speech and Hearing Research, 20,* 21–26.

Martindale, C., Hines, D., Mitchell, L., & Covello, E. (1984). EEG alpha asymmetry and creativity. *Personality and Individual Differences, 5*(1), 77–86.

Masia, C. L., & Chase, P. N. (1997). Vicarious learning revisited: A contemporary behavior analytic interpretation. *Journal of Behavior Therapy and Experimental Psychiatry, 28*(1), 41–51.

Maslow, A. H. (1962). *Toward a psychology of being.* New York: Van Nostrand.

Maslow, A. H. (1969). Toward a humanistic biology. *American Psychologist, 24,* 734–735.

Mason, C. A., & Sretavan, D. W. (1997). Glia, neurons, and axon pathfinding during optic chiasm development. *Current Opinion in Neurobiology, 7*(5), 647–653.

Masotto, C., & Racagni, G. (1995). Biological aspects of schizophrenia. *Rivista di Psichiatria, 30*(4), 34–46.

Masters, W. H., Johnson, V. E., & Kolodny, R. C. (1994). *Heterosexuality*. New York: HarperCollins.

Matarazzo, J. D. (1990). Psychological assessment versus psychological testing. *American Psychologist, 45,* 999–1017.

Mathews, F. (1990). *An exploratory typology of youth gangs in Metropolitan Toronto.* Toronto: Central Toronto Youth Services.

Mathews, F. (1993). *Youth gangs on youth gangs.* Ottawa: Minister of Supply and Services.

Maticka-Tyndale, E. (1997). Reducing the incidence of sexually transmitted disease through behavioural and social change. *Canadian Journal of Human Sexuality, 6*(2), 89–104.

Matsui, T., & Onglatco, M. L. U. (1990). Relationships between employee quality circle involvement and need fulfillment in work as moderated by work type: A compensatory or a spillover model? In U. Kleinbeck, H. Quast, H. Thierry, & H. Hacker (Eds.), *Work motivation.* Hillsdale, NJ: Erlbaum.

Matsumoto, D. (1994). *People: Psychology from a cultural perspective.* Pacific Grove, CA: Brooks/Cole.

Matsumoto, D. (1996). *Culture and psychology.* Pacific Grove, CA: Brooks/Cole.

Matsumoto, D., & Kudoh, T. (1993). American-Japanese cultural differences in attributions of personality based on smiles. *Journal of Nonverbal Behavior, 17,* 231–243.

Matthews, K. A. (1988). Coronary heart disease and Type A behaviors: Update on and alternative to the Booth-Kewley and Friedman (1987) quantitative review. *Psychological Bulletin, 104,* 373–380.

Matthies, H. (1989). Neurobiological aspects of learning and memory. *Annual Review of Psychology, 40,* 381–404.

Maunsell, J. H. R. (1995). The brain's visual world: Representation of visual targets in the cerebral cortex. *Science, 270,* 764–769.

Mayer, J. D., & Salovey, P. (1997). What is emotional intelligence? In P. Salovey & D. J. Sluyter (Eds.), *Emotional development and emotional intelligence.* New York: Basic Books.

McAuley, E., Duncan, T. E., & McElroy, M. (1989). Self-efficacy cognitions and causal attributions for children's motor performance: An exploratory investigation. *Journal of Genetic Psychology, 150,* 65–73.

McBride, A. B. (1990). Mental health effects of women's multiple roles. *American Psychologist, 45,* 381–384.

McCandliss, B. D., Posner, M. I., & Givón, T. (1997). Brain plasticity in learning visual words. *Cognitive Psychology, 33,* 88–110.

McCarty, D., Argeriou, M., Huebner, R. B., & Lubran, B. (1991). Alcoholism, drug abuse, and the homeless. *American Psychologist, 46,* 1139–1148.

McCaul, K. D., Jacobson, K., & Martinson, B. (1998). The effects of a state-wide media campaign on mammography screening. *Journal of Applied Social Psychology, 28*(6), 504–515.

McCauley, C. (1989). The nature of social influence in groupthink: Compliance and internalization. *Journal of Personality and Social Psychology, 57,* 250–260.

McClearn, G. E., Johansson, B., Berg, S., Pedersen, N. L., Ahern, F., Petrill, S. A., & Plomin, R. (1997). Substantial genetic influence on cognitive abilities in twins 80 or more years old. *Science, 276,* 1560–1563.

McClelland, D. C. (1958). Methods of measuring human motivation. In J. W. Atkinson (Ed.), *Motives in fantasy, action, and society.* Princeton, NJ: Van Nostrand.

McClelland, D. C. (1961). *The achieving society.* Princeton, NJ: Van Nostrand.

McClelland, D. C. (1986). Some reflections on the two psychologies of love. *Journal of Personality, 54,* 334–353.

McClelland, D. C. (1987). Characteristics of successful entrepreneurs. *The Journal of Creative Behavior, 21,* 219–233.

McClelland, J. L. (1994). The organization of memory: A parallel distributed processing perspective. *Revue Neurologique, 150*(8/9), 570–579.

McClelland, J. L., McNaughton, B. L., & O'Reilly, R. C. (1995). Why there are complementary learning systems in the hippocampus and neocortex: Insights from the successes and failures of connectionist models of learning and memory. *Psychological Review, 102*(3), 419–437.

McClintock, M. K. (1971). Menstrual synchrony and suppression. *Nature, 229,* 244–245.

McCloskey, M., Wible, C. G., & Cohen, N. J. (1988). Is there a special flashbulb-memory mechanism? *Journal of Experimental Psychology: General, 117,* 171–181.

McConahay, J. B., & Hough, J. C. (1976). Symbolic racism. *Journal of Social Issues, 32*(2), 23–45.

McConkey, K. M., & Kinoshita, S. (1988). The influence of hypnosis on memory after one day and one week. *Journal of Abnormal Psychology, 97,* 48–53.

McCormick, E. J., Jeanneret, P. R., & Mecham, R. C. (1972). A study of job characteristics and job dimensions as based on the Position Analysis Questionnaire (PAQ) [Monograph]. *Journal of Applied Psychology, 56,* 347–368.

McCormick, L., Nielsen, T., Ptito, M., & Hassainia, F. (1997). REM sleep dream mentation in right hemispherectomized patients. *Neuropsychologia, 35*(5), 695–701.

McCrady, B. S. (1994). Alcoholics anonymous and behavior therapy: Can habits be treated as diseases? Can diseases be treated as habits? *Journal of Consulting and Clinical Psychology, 62,* 1159–1166.

McCrae, R. R., & Costa, P. T., Jr. (1987). Validation of the five-factor model of personality across instruments and observers. *Journal of Personality and Social Psychology, 52,* 81–90.

McCrae, R. R., & Costa, P. T., Jr. (1990). *Personality in adulthood.* New York: Guilford.

McCrae, R. R., & Costa, P. T., Jr. (1994). The stability of personality: Observations and evaluations. *Current Directions in Psychological Science, 3,* 173–175.

McCrae, R. R., Costa, P. T., Jr., Del Pilar, G. H., Rolland, J. P., & Parker, W. D. (1998). Cross-cultural assessment of the five-factor model: The revised NEO personality inventory. *Journal of Cross-Cultural Psychology, 29*(1), 171–188.

McDermott, K., & Roediger, H. L. (1996). Exact and conceptual repetition dissociate conceptual memory tests: Problems for transfer-appropriate processing theory. *Canadian Journal of Experimental Psychology, 50*(1), 57–71.

McDonaugh, G. R. (1992). An examination of racial stereotypes: The differential effects of gender and social class on their content. Dissertation research, Purdue University, West Lafayette, Indiana.

McFall, M. E., Mackay, P. W., & Donovan, D. M. (1991). Combat-related PTSD and psychosocial adjustment problems among substance abusing veterans. *Journal of Nervous and Mental Disease, 179,* 33–38.

McGaugh, J. L. (1990). Significance and remembrance: The role of neuromodulatory systems. *Psychological Science, 1,* 15–25.

McGill, M. E., & Slocum, J. W., Jr. (1998). A little leadership, please? *Organizational Dynamics, 26*(3), 39–49.

McGinty, D., & Szymusiak, R. (1988). Neuronal unit activity patterns in behaving animals: Brainstem and limbic system. *Annual Review of Psychology, 39,* 135–168.

McGlynn, S. M. (1990). Behavioral approaches to neuropsychological rehabilitation. *Psychological Bulletin, 108,* 420–441.

McKeachie, W. J. (1988). Teaching thinking. *Update: National Center for Research to Improve Postsecondary Teaching and Learning, 2,* 1.

McKeachie, W. J., Pintrich, P. R., & Lin, Y. (1985). Learning to learn. In G. d'Ydewalle (Ed.), *Cognition, information processing, and motivation.* New York: Elsevier-North Holland.

McKelvie, S. J. (1984). Relationship between set and functional fixedness: A replication. *Perceptual and Motor Skills, 58*(3), 996–998.

McKenzie, B. E., Tootell, H. E., & Day, R. H. (1980). Development of visual size constancy during the 1st year of human infancy. *Developmental Psychology, 16,* 163–174.

McKenzie, D. (1997). *Canadian profile: Alcohol, tobacco, and other drugs.* Ottawa: Canadian Centre on Substance Abuse.

McLoyd, V. C. (1998). Socioeconomic disadvantage and child development. *American Psychologist, 53*(2), 185–204.

McLynn, F. (1997). *Carl Gustav Jung: A biography.* New York: St. Martin's Press.

McManus, I. C., & Bryden, M. P. (1991). Geschwind's theory of cerebral lateralization: Developing a formal, causal model. *Psychological Bulletin, 110,* 235–237.

McMinn, M. R., Lindsay, S. F., Hannum, L. E., & Troyer, P. K. (1990). Does sexist language reflect personal characteristics? *Sex Roles, 23,* 389–396.

McMinn, M. R., Troyer, P. K., Hannum, L. E., & Foster, J. D. (1991). Teaching nonsexist language to college students. *Journal of Experimental Education, 59,* 153–161.

McNally, R. J. (1994). Cognitive bias in panic disorder. *Current Directions in Psychological Science, 3,* 129–132.

McNally, R. J., Hornig, C. D., Otto, M. W., & Pollack, M. H. (1997). Selective encoding of threat in panic disorder: Application of a dual priming paradigm. *Behaviour Research and Therapy, 35*(6), 543–549.

McNeil, J. E., & Warrington, E. K. (1993). Prosopagnosia: A face-specific disorder. *The Quarterly Journal of Experimental Psychology, 46A*(1), 1–10.

McNeill, D. (1970). Explaining linguistic universals. In J. Morton (Ed.), *Biological and social factors in psycholinguistics*. London: Logos.

McReynolds, P. (1996). Lightner Witmer: A centennial tribute. *American Psychologist, 51*, 237–240.

McRoberts, C., Burlingame, G. M., & Hoag, M. J. (1998). Comparative efficacy of individual and group psychotherapy: A meta-analytic perspective. *Group Dynamics, 2*(2), 101–117.

Meadows, S. (1998). Children learning to think: Learning from others? Vygotskian theory and educational psychology. *Educational and Child Psychology, 15*(2), 6–13.

Mecklinger, A., & Muller, N. (1996). Dissociations in the processing of "what" and "where" information in working memory: An event-related potential analysis. *Journal of Cognitive Neuroscience, 8*(5), 453–473.

Medin, D. L. (1989). Concepts and conceptual structure. *American Psychologist, 44*, 1469–1481.

Mednick, S. A., Parnas, J., & Schulsinger, F. (1987). The Copenhagen high-risk project, 1962–1986. *Schizophrenia Bulletin, 13*, 485–495.

Meece, J. L., & Jones, G. (1996). Gender differences in motivation and strategy use in science: Are girls rote learners? *Journal of Research in Science Teaching, 33*(4), 393–406.

Meichenbaum, D. (1974). *Cognitive behavior modification*. Morristown, NJ: General Learning.

Meichenbaum, D. (1977). *Cognitive behavior modification*. New York: Plenum.

Meichenbaum, D., & Cameron, R. (1973). Training schizophrenics to talk to themselves: A means of developing attentional controls. *Behavior Therapy, 4*, 515–534.

Meinz, E. J., & Salthouse, T. A. (1997). The effects of age and experience on memory for visually presented music. *Journals of Gerontology Series B—Psychological Sciences and Social Sciences, 53B*(1), P60–P69.

Melton, G. B., Petrila, J., Poythress, N. G., & Slobogin, C. (1987). *Psychological evaluations for the courts*. New York: Guilford.

Melton, J. G. (1993). *Encyclopedia of American religions* (4th ed.). Detroit, MI: Gale Research, Inc.

Meltzoff, A. N. (1988). Imitation of televised models by infants. *Child Development, 59*, 1221–1229.

Meltzoff, A. N. (1996). The human infant as imitative generalist: A 20–year progress report on infant imitation with implications for comparative psychology. In C. M. Heyes et al. (Eds.), *Social learning in animals: The roots of culture*. San Diego, CA: Academic Press.

Melville, J. (1977). *Phobias and compulsions*. New York: Penguin.

Melzack, R. (1990, February). The tragedy of needless pain. *Scientific American*, 27–33.

Melzack, R. (1993). Pain: Past, present and future. *Canadian Journal of Experimental Psychology, 47*(4), 615–629.

Melzack, R., & Wall, P. D. (1970). Psychophysiology of pain. *International Anesthesiology Clinics, 8*, 3–34.

Mercer, R. T., Nichols, E. G., & Doyle, G. C. (1989). *Transitions in a woman's life* (Vol. 12). New York: Springer.

Merton, R. K. (1949). Merton's typology of prejudice and discrimination. In R. M. MacIver (Ed.), *Discrimination and national welfare*. New York: Harper & Row.

Merzenich, M. M., Jenkins, W. M., Johnston, P., Schreiner, C., Miller, S. L., & Tallal, P. (1996). Temporal processing deficits of language-learning impaired children ameliorated by training. *Science, 271*, 77–81.

Messer, S. B., & Wachtel, P. L. (1997). The contemporary psychotherapeutic landscape: Issues and prospects. In P. L. Wachtel & S. B. Messer, (Eds.), *Theories of psychotherapy: Origins and evolution* (pp. 1–27). Washington, DC: American Psychological Association.

Metcalfe, J., Funnell, M., & Gazzaniga, M. S. (1995). Right-hemisphere memory superiority: Studies of a split-brain patient. *Psychological Science, 6*, 157–164.

Meyer, R. G., & Salmon, P. (1988). *Abnormal psychology* (2nd ed.). Boston: Allyn & Bacon.

Meyers-Levy, J., & Maheswaran, D. (1991). Exploring differences in males' and females' processing strategies. *Journal of Consumer Research, 18*, 63–70.

Michael, R. T., Wadsworth, J., Feinleib, H., Johnson, A. M., Laumann, E. O., & Wellings, K. (1998). Private sexual behavior, public opinion, and public health policy related to sexually transmitted diseases: A U.S.-British comparison. *American Journal of Public Health, 88*(5), 749–754.

Middaugh, S. J. (1990). On clinical efficacy: Why biofeedback does—and does not—work. *Biofeedback and Self-Regulation, 15*, 191–208.

Middleton, B., Arendt, J., & Stone, B. M. (1997). Complex effects of melatonin on human circadian rhythms in constant dim light. *Journal of Biological Rhythms, 12*(5), 467–477.

Mikhailova, N. G., Zukhar, A. V., Loseva, E. V., & Ermakova, I. V. (1991). Influence of transplantation of embryonal brain tissue (early periods) on reactions of avoidance of artificial and zoosocial stimuli in rats. *Neuroscience and Behavioral Physiology, 21*, 34–37.

Miklowitz, D. J. (1994). Family risk indicators in schizophrenia. *Schizophrenia Bulletin, 20*, 137–150.

Milgram, S. (1963). Behavioral study of obedience. *Journal of Abnormal and Social Psychology, 67*, 371–378.

Milgram, S. (1965). Liberating effects of group pressure. *Journal of Personality and Social Psychology, 1*, 127–134.

Millar, M. G., & Millar, K. (1990). Attitude change as a function of attitude type and argument type. *Journal of Personality and Social Psychology, 39*, 217–228.

Millar, M. G., & Millar, K. (1995). Negative affective consequences of thinking about disease detection behaviors. *Health Psychology, 14*, 141–146.

Miller, A. H. (1998). Neuroendocrine and immune system interactions in stress and depression. *Psychiatric Clinics of North America, 21*(2), 443–463.

Miller, B. C., McCoy, J. K., Olson, T. D., & Wallace, C. M. (1986). Parental discipline and control attempts in relation to adolescent sexual attitudes and behavior. *Journal of Marriage and the Family, 48*(3), 503–512.

Miller, C. T., & Myers, A. M. (1998). Conpensating for prejudice: How heavyweight people (and others) control outcomes despite prejudice. In J. K. Swim & C. Stangor (Eds.), *Prejudice: The target's perspective* (pp. 191–218). San Diego, CA: Academic Press.

Miller, E. K., Erickson, C. A., & Desimone, R. (1996). Neural mechanisms of visual working memory in prefrontal cortex of the macaque. *Journal of Neuroscience, 16*(16), 5154–5167.

Miller, G. A. (1956). The magical number seven plus or minus two: Some limits on our capacity for processing information. *Psychological Review, 63*, 81–97.

Miller, G. A. (1965). Some preliminaries to psycholinguistics. *American Psychologist, 20*, 15–20.

Miller, K. F., & Baillargeon, R. (1990). Length and distance: Do preschoolers think that occlusion brings things together? *Developmental Psychology, 26*, 103–114.

Miller, L. C. (1990). Intimacy and liking: Mutual influence and the role of unique relationships. *Journal of Personality and Social Psychology, 59*, 50–60.

Miller, M. E., & Bowers, K. S. (1993). Hypnotic analgesia: Dissociated experience or dissociated control? *Journal of Abnormal Psychology, 102*, 29–38.

Miller, N. E. (1944). Experimental studies of conflict. In J. M. Hunt (Ed.), *Personality and behavioral disorders* (Vol. 1). New York: Ronald Press.

Miller, N. E. (1959). Liberalization of basic S-R concepts: Extensions to conflict behavior, motivation, and social learning. In S. Koch (Ed.), *Psychology: A study of a science* (Vol. 2). New York: McGraw-Hill.

Miller, N. E. (1969). Learning of visceral and glandular responses. *Science, 163*, 434–445.

Miller, P. F., Light, K. C., Bragdon, E. E., Ballenger, M. N., Herbst, M. C., Maixner, W., Hinderliter, A. L., Atkinson, S. S., Koch, G. G., & Sheps, D. S. (1993). Beta-endorphin response to exercise and mental stress in patients with ischemic heart disease. *Journal of Psychosomatic Research, 37*, 455–465.

Miller, P. H., & Aloise, P. A. (1989). Young children's understanding of the psychological causes of behavior: A review. *Child Development, 60*, 257–285.

Miller, R. P., Cosgrove, J. M., & Doke, L. (1990). Motivating adolescents to reduce their fines in a token economy. *Adolescence, 25*, 97–104.

Miller, T. Q., Turner, C. W., Tindale, R. S., Posavac, E. J., & Dugoni, B. L. (1991). Reasons for the trend toward null findings in research on Type A behavior. *Psychological Bulletin, 110*, 469–485.

Milner, B. (1966). Amnesia following operation on the temporal lobes. In C. W. M. Whitty & O. L. Zangwill (Eds.), *Amnesia*. London: Butterworth.

Milner, B., Corkin, S., & Teuber, H. L. (1968). Further analysis of hippocampal amnesic syndrome: 14–year follow-up study of H. M. *Neuropsychologia, 6*, 215–234.

Milner, J. S., & Chilamkurti, C. (1991). Physical child abuse perpetrator characteristics: A review of the literature. *Journal of Interpersonal Violence, 6*, 345–366.

Milner, P. M. (1989). A cell assembly theory of hippocampal amnesia. *Neuropsychologia, 27,* 23–30.

Milner, P. M. (1991). Brain stimulation reward: A review. *Canadian Journal of Psychology, 45,* 1–36.

Miranda, S. M. (1994). Avoidance of groupthink meeting management using group support systems. *Small Group Research, 25,* 105–136.

Mischel, W. (1979). On the interface of cognition and personality: Beyond the person-situation debate. *American Psychologist, 34,* 740–754.

Mischel, W. (1983). Alternatives in the pursuit of the predictability and consistency of persons: Stable data that yield unstable interpretations. *Journal of Personality, 51,* 578–604.

Mischel, W., & Grusec, J. E. (1966). Determinants of the rehearsal and transmission of neutral and averse behaviors. *Journal of Personality and Social Psychology, 3,* 197–205.

Miserandino, M. (1998). Attributional retraining as a method of improving athletic performance. *Journal of Sport Behavior, 21*(3), 286–297.

Mishima, K., Okawa, M., Hishikawa, Y., Hozumi, S., Hori, H., & Takahashi, K. (1994). Morning bright light therapy for sleep and behavior disorders in elderly patients with dementia. *Acta Psychiatrica Scandinavica, 89,* 1–7.

Mishler, E. G., & Waxler, N. E. (1968). Family interaction processes and schizophrenia: A review of current theories. In E. G. Mishler & N. E. Waxler (Eds.), *Family processes and schizophrenia.* New York: Science House.

Mitler, M. M., Miller, J. C., Lipsitz, J. J., & Walsh, J. K. (1997). The sleep of long-haul truck drivers. *New England Journal of Medicine, 337*(11), 755–761.

Mittmann, N., Herrmann, N., Einarson, T. R., Busto, U. E., Lanctot, K. L., Liu, B. A., Shulman, K. I., Silver, I. L., Naranjo, C. A., & Shear, N. H. (1997). The efficacy, safety and tolerability of antidepressants in late life depression: A meta-analysis. *Journal of Affective Disorders, 46*(3), 191–217.

Moncrieff, J. (1997). Lithium: Evidence reconsidered. *British Journal of Psychiatry, 171,* 113–119.

Monroe, S. M., & Simons, A. D. (1991). Diathesis-stress theories in the context of life stress research: Implications for the depressive disorders. *Psychological Bulletin, 110,* 406–425.

Monroe, S. M., Simons, A. D., & Thase, M. E. (1991). Onset of depression and time to treatment entry: Roles of life stress. *Journal of Consulting and Clinical Psychology, 59,* 566–573.

Monteith, M. J., Zuwerink, J. R., & Devine, P. G. (1994). Prejudice and prejudice reduction: Classic challenges, contemporary approaches. In P. G. Devine (Ed.), *Social cognition: Impact on social psychology.* San Diego, CA: Academic Press, Inc.

Montepare, J. M., & Zebrowitz-McArthur, L. (1988). Impressions of people created by age-related qualities of their gaits. *Journal of Personality and Social Psychology, 55,* 547–556.

Montgomery, S. A., & Kasper, S. (1998). Depression: A long-term illness and its treatment. *International Clinical Psychopharmacology, 13*(6), S23–S26.

Montgomery-St. Laurent, T., Fullenkamp, A. M., & Fischer, R. B. (1988). A role for the hamster's flank gland in heterosexual communication. *Physiology and Behavior, 44,* 759–762.

Moore, T. E. (1995). Subliminal self-help auditory tapes: An empirical test of perceptual consequences. *Canadian Journal of Behavioural Science, 27*(1), 9–20.

Moorehouse, M. J. (1991). Linking maternal employment patterns to mother-child activities and children's school competence. *Developmental Psychology, 27,* 295–303.

Moorhead, G., Ference, R., & Neck, C. P. (1991). Group decision fiascoes continue: Space shuttle challenger and a revised groupthink framework. *Human Relations, 44*(6), 539–550.

Morgan, C. A., III, Kingham, P., Nicolaou, A., & Southwick, S. M. (1998). Anniversary reactions in Gulf War veterans: A naturalistic inquiry 2 years after the Gulf War. *Journal of Traumatic Stress, 11*(1), 165–171.

Morgan, D. G., & Stewart, N. J. (1998). High versus low density special care units: Impact on the behaviour of elderly residents with dementia. *Canadian Journal on Aging, 17*(2), 143–165.

Morgan, W. P. (1992). Hypnosis and sport psychology. In J. Rhue, S. J. Lynn, & I. Kirsch (Eds.), *Handbook of clinical hypnosis.* Washington, DC: American Psychological Association.

Morin, C. M., Stone, J., McDonald, K., & Jones, S. (1994). Psychological management of insomnia: A clinical replication series with 100 patients. *Behavior Therapy, 25,* 291–309.

Morren, M. (1998). Hostility as a risk factor for coronary heart disease. *Psycholoog, 33*(3), 101–108.

Morris, C. D., Bransford, J. D., & Franks, J. J. (1977). Levels of processing versus transfer appropriate processing. *Journal of Verbal Learning and Verbal Behavior, 16*(5), 519–533.

Morris, M. W., & Peng, K. (1994). Culture and cause: American and Chinese attributions for social and physical events. *Journal of Personality and Social Psychology, 67,* 949–971.

Morrison, J. W., Ispa, J. M., & Thornburg, K. R. (1994). African American college students' psychosocial development as related to care arrangements during infancy. *Journal of Black Psychology, 20,* 418–429.

Moser, E. I., Krobert, K. A., Moser, M. B., & Morris, R. G. (1998). Impaired spatial learning after saturation of long-term potentiation. *Science, 281,* 2038–2042.

Moskowitz, B. A. (1978, November). The acquisition of language. *Scientific American,* 92–108.

Mount, M. K., Barrick, M. R., & Stewart, G. L. (1998). Five-factor model of personality and performance in jobs involving interpersonal interactions. *Human Performance, 11*(2/3), 145–165.

MRC, NSERC, and SSHRC (1998). *Tri-council policy statement: Ethical conduct for research involving humans.* Ottawa: MRC, NSERC, SSHRC.

Mroczek, D. K., & Kolarz, C. M. (1998). The effect of age on positive and negative affect: A developmental perspective on happiness. *Journal of Personality & Social Psychology, 75*(5), 1333–1349.

Mueser, K. T., Bellack, A. S., Morrison, R. L., & Wade, J. H. (1990). Gender, social competence, and symptomatology in schizophrenia: A longitudinal analysis. *Journal of Abnormal Psychology, 99,* 138–147.

Mukherjee, S., Sackeim, H. A., & Schnurr, D. B. (1994). Electroconvulsive therapy of acute manic episodes: A review. *American Journal of Psychiatry, 151,* 169–176.

Mullen, B., Anthony, T., Salas, E., & Driskell, J. E. (1994). Group cohesiveness and quality of decision making: An integration of tests of the groupthink hypothesis. *Small Group Research, 25,* 189–204.

Mullen, B., & Copper, C. (1994). The relation between group cohesiveness and performance: An integration. *Psychological Bulletin, 115,* 210–227.

Mulligan, N. W. (1996). The effects of perceptual interference at encoding on implicit memory, explicit memory, and memory for source. *Journal of Experimental Memory and Cognition, 22*(5), 1067–1087.

Mu–oz, R. F., Hollon, S. D., McGrath, E., Rehm, L. P., & VandenBos, G. R. (1994). On the AHCPR Depression in primary care guidelines: Further considerations for practitioners. *American Psychologist, 49,* 42–61.

Murachver, T., Pipe, M. E., Gordon, R., & Owens, J. L. (1996). Do, show, and tell: Children's event memories acquired through direct experience, observation, and stories. *Child Development, 67*(6), 3029–3044.

Murphy, C. M., & O'Farrell, T. J. (1996). Marital violence among alcoholics. *American Psychological Society, 5*(6), 183–186.

Murphy, G. E., Wetzel, R. D., Robins, E., & McEvoy, L. (1992). Multiple risk factors predict suicide in alcoholism. *Archives of General Psychiatry, 49,* 459–463.

Murphy, S. M. (1990). Models of imagery in sport psychology: A review. *Journal of Mental Imagery, 14,* 153–172.

Murphy, S. M., & Jowdy, D. P. (1992). Imagery and mental practice. In Thelma S. Horn (Ed.), *Advances in sport psychology* (pp. 221–250). Champaign, IL: Human Kinetics.

Murray, H. A. (1938). *Explorations in personality.* New York: Oxford University Press.

Murray, J. B. (1995). Evidence for acupuncture's analgesic effectiveness and proposals for the physiological mechanisms involved. *Journal of Psychology, 129*(4), 443–461.

Myers, D. G., & Diener, E. (1995). Who is happy? *Psychological Science, 6,* 10–19.

Myerson, J., Rank, M. R., Raines, F. Q., & Schnitzler, M. A. (1998). Race and general cognitive ability: The myth of diminishing returns to education. *American Psychological Society, 9*(2), 139–142.

Naar, R. (1990). Psychodrama in short-term psychotherapy. In R. A. Wells & V. J. Giannetti (Eds.), *Handbook of the brief psychotherapies.* New York: Plenum.

Nace, E. P. (1987). *The treatment of alcoholism.* New York: Brunner/Mazel.

Nakkab, S. (1997). Adolescent sexual activity. *International Journal of Mental Health, 26*(1), 23–34.

Narrow, W. E., Regier, D. A., & Rae, D. S. (1993). Use of services by persons with mental and addictive disorders: Findings from the National Institute of Mental Health Epidemiologic Catchment Area Program. *Archives of General Psychiatry, 50,* 95–107.

Nash, M. (1987). What, if anything, is regressed about hypnotic age regression? A review of the empirical literature. *Psychological Bulletin, 102,* 42–52.

Nash, R. A. (1996). The serotonin connection. *Journal of Orthomolecular Medicine, 11*(1), 35–44.

Nass, C., Moon, Y., Fogg, B. J., & Reeves, B. (1995). Can computer personalities be human personalities? *International Journal of Human Computer Studies, 43*(2), 223–239.

Nathan, B. R., & Tippins, N. (1990). The consequences of halo "error" in performance ratings: A field study of the moderating effect of halo on test validation results. *Journal of Applied Psychology, 75,* 290–296.

Nathan, P. E. (1988). The addictive personality is the behavior of the addict. *Journal of Consulting and Clinical Psychology, 56,* 183–188.

Nathan, P. E., & Skinstad, A. H. (1987). Outcomes of treatment for alcohol problems: Current methods, problems, and results. *Journal of Consulting and Clinical Psychology, 55,* 332–340.

Nathans, J. (1989, February). The genes for color vision. *Scientific American,* 42–49.

National Advisory Council on Aging (1997). How many people have hearing impairment? *Aging Vignettes, Number 88.* National Advisory Council on Aging.

National Council on Aging (1998, September 28). Half of older Americans report they are sexually active; 4 in 10 want more sex, says new survey. Washington, DC: NCOA [On-line press release]. Available Internet: <http://www.ncoa.org/press/sexsurvey.htm>

National Research Council Panel on Research on Child Abuse and Neglect, Commission on Behavioral and Social Sciences and Education (1993). *Understanding child abuse and neglect.* Washington, DC: National Academic Press.

Nauta, W. J. H., & Feirtag, M. (1986). *Fundamental neuroanatomy.* New York: Freeman.

Navon, D. (1990). How critical is the accuracy of an eyewitness's memory? Another look at the issue of lineup diagnosticity. *Journal of Applied Psychology, 75,* 506–510.

Neal, A. M., & Turner, S. M. (1991). Anxiety disorders research with African Americans: Current status. *Psychological Bulletin, 109,* 400–410.

Needleman, L. D., & Geller, E. S. (1992). Comparing interventions to motivate work-site collection of home-generated recyclables. *American Journal of Community Psychology, 20,* 775–785.

Neeham, A., Baillargeon, R., & Kaufman, L. (1997). Object segregation in infancy. *Advances in Infancy Research, 11,* 1–44.

Neisser, U. (1967). *Cognitive psychology.* Englewood Cliffs, NJ: Prentice-Hall.

Neisser, U. (1992). Two themes in the study of cognition. In H. L. Pick, Jr., P. van den Broek, & D. C. Knill (Eds.), *Cognition: Conceptual and methodological issues* (pp. 333–340). Washington, DC: American Psychological Association.

Neisser, U., Boodoo, G., Bouchard, T. J., Jr., Boykin, A. W., Brody, N., Ceci, S. J., Halpern, D. F., Loehlin, J. C., Perloff, R., Sternberg, R. J., & Urbina, S. (1996). Intelligence: Knowns and unknowns. *American Psychologist, 51,* 77–101.

Neitz, M. J. (1995). Feminist theory and religious experience. In R. W. Hood, Jr., et al. (Eds.), *Handbook of religious experience.* Birmingham, AL: Religious Education Press, Inc.

Nelson, B. A., & Stake, J. E. (1994). The Myers-Briggs type indicator personality dimensions and perceptions of quality of therapy relationships. *Psychotherapy, 31,* 449–455.

Nelson, D. L., McKinney, V. M., & Gee, N. R. (1998). Interpreting the influence of implicitly activated memories on recall and recognition. *Psychological Review, 105*(2), 299–324.

Nelson, K. (1993). The psychological and social origins of autobiographical memory. *Psychological Science, 4,* 7–14.

Nemeroff, C. B., Knight, D. L., Kirshnan, R. R., Slotkin, T. A., Bissette, G., Melville, M. L., & Blazer, D. G. (1988). Marked reduction in the number of platelet-tritiated imipramine binding sites in geriatric depression. *Archives of General Psychiatry, 45,* 919–923.

Nestler, E. J., & Aghajanian, G. K. (1997). Molecular and cellular basis of addiction. *Science, 278,* 58–63.

Neugarten, B. (1968). Adult personality: Toward a psychology of the life cycle. In B. Neugarten (Ed.), *Middle age and aging* (pp. 137–147). Chicago: University of Chicago Press.

Newcomb, A. F., & Bagwell, C. L. (1995). Children's friendship relations: A meta-analytic review. *Psychological Bulletin, 117,* 306–347.

Newcomb, M. D., & Bentler, P. M. (1989). Substance use and abuse among children and teenagers. *American Psychologist, 44,* 242–248.

Newcombe, N., & Huttenlocher, J. (1992). Children's early ability to solve perspective-taking problems. *Developmental Psychology, 28,* 635–643.

Newell, A., & Simon, H. A. (1972). *Human problem solving.* Englewood Cliffs, NJ: Prentice-Hall.

Newman, L. S., Duff, K. J., & Baumeister, R. F. (1997). A new look at defensive projection: Thought suppression, accessibility, and biased person perception. *Journal of Personality and Social Psychology, 72*(5), 980–1001.

NICHD Early Child Care Research Network (1997). The effects of infant child care on infant-mother attachment security: Results of the NICHD study of early child care. *Child Development, 68*(5), 860–879.

Niehoff, D. (1999). *The biology of violence: How understanding the brain, behavior, and environment can break the vicious circle of aggression.* New York: The Free Press.

Nigg, J. T., & Goldsmith, H. H. (1994). Genetics of personality disorders: Perspectives from personality and psychopathology research. *Psychological Bulletin, 115,* 346–380.

Nilsson, K. M. (1990). The effect of subject expectations of "hypnosis" upon vividness of visual imagery. *The International Journal of Clinical and Experimental Hypnosis, 38,* 17–24.

Nisbett, R. E. (1972). Hunger, obesity, and the ventromedial hypothalamus. *Psychological Review, 79,* 433–453.

Nolen-Hoeksema, S. (1994). An interactive model for the emergence of gender differences in depression in adolescence. *Journal of Research on Adolescence, 4*(4), 519–534.

Nolen-Hoeksema, S., & Girgus, J. S. (1994). The emergence of gender differences in depression during adolescence. *Psychological Bulletin, 115,* 424–443.

Norman, D. A. (1990). *Design of everyday things.* New York: Doubleday.

Norman, R. A., Tataranni, P. A., Pratley, R., Thompson, D. B., Hanson, R. L., Prochazka, M., Baier, L., Ehm, M. G., Sakul, H., Foroud, T., Garvey, W. T., Burns, D., Knowler, W. C., Bennett, P. H., Bogardus, C., & Ravussin, E. (1998). Autosomal genomic scan for loci linked to obesity and energy metabolism in Pima Indians. *American Journal of Human Genetics, 62*(3), 659–668.

Norris, J. (1989). Normative influence effects on sexual arousal to nonviolent sexually explicit material. *Journal of Applied Social Psychology, 19,* 341–352.

Noton, D., & Stark, L. (1971, June). Eye movements and visual perception. *Scientific American,* 35–44.

Notterman, J. M., & Drewry, H. N. (1993). *Psychology and education: Parallel and interactive approaches.* New York: Plenum.

Nyberg, L., Cabeza, R., & Tulving, E. (1996). PET studies of encoding and retrieval: The HERA model. *Psychonomic Bulletin and Review, 3*(2), 135–148.

Nyhuus, K. (1998). *Chasing ghosts: Asian organized crime investigation in Canada.* R.C.M.P.

O'Connor, F. L. (1998). The role of serotonin and dopamine in schizophrenia. *Journal of the American Psychiatric Nurses Association, 4*(4), S30–S34.

O'Donnell, C. R. (1995). Firearm deaths among children and youth. *American Psychologist, 50,* 771–776.

Ofshe, R. J., & Singer, M. T. (1994). Recovered-memory therapy and robust repression: Influence and pseudomemories. *The International Journal of Clinical and Experimental Hypnosis, 42,* 391–410.

Ogur, B. (1986). Long day's journey into night: Women and prescription drug abuse. *Women and Health, 11,* 99–115.

Okuda-Ashitaka, E., Minami, T., Tachibana, S., Yosihara, Y., Nishiuchi, Y., Kimura, T., & Ito, S. (1998). Nocistatin, a peptide that blocks nociceptin action in pain transmission. *Nature, 392,* 286–289.

Olds, J. (1955). Physiological mechanisms of reward. *Nebraska Symposium on Motivation, 3,* 73–139.

Olds, J. (1969). The central nervous system and the reinforcement of behavior. *American Psychologist, 24,* 114–132.

Olds, J., & Milner, P. (1954). Positive reinforcement produced by electrical stimulation of septal area and other regions of rat brain. *Journal of Comparative and Physiological Psychology, 47,* 419–427.

O'Leary, A. (1990). Stress, emotion, and human immune function. *Psychological Bulletin, 108,* 363–382.

O'Leary, K. D., Barling, J., Arias, I., Rosenbaum, A., Malone, J., & Tyree, A. (1989). Prevalence and stability of physical aggression between spouses: A longitudinal analysis. *Journal of Consulting and Clinical Psychology, 57,* 263–268.

Olio, K. A. (1994). Truth in memory. *American Psychologist, 49,* 442–443.

Olivardia, R., Pope, H. G., Jr., Mangweth, B., & Hudson, J. L. (1995). Eating disorders in college men. *American Journal of Psychiatry, 152,* 1279–1283.

Oliver, M. B., & Hyde, J. S. (1993). Gender differences in sexuality: A meta-analysis. *Psychological Bulletin, 114,* 29–51.

Olson, B., & Douglas, W. (1997). The family on television: Evaluation of gender roles in situation comedy. *Sex Roles, 36*(5/6), 409–427.

Olson, E. (1994). Female voices of aggression in Tonga. *Sex Roles, 30,* 237–248.

Ontario Human Rights Commision and O'Malley (Vincent) vs. Simpson-Sears (1985) 2 S.C.R. 536.

Ornstein, R. (1997). *The right mind: Making sense of the hemisphere.* New York: Harcourt Brace and Company.

Ornstein, R. E. (1976). A science of consciousness. In P. R. Lee, R. E. Ornstein, D. Galin, A. Deikman, & C. T. Tart (Eds.), *Symposium on consciousness* (San Francisco, 1974). New York: Viking.

Ornstein, R. E. (1977). *The psychology of consciousness* (2nd ed.). New York: Harcourt Brace Jovanovich.

Ortega-Andeane, A. P. (1989). User participation in an environmental evaluation in the remodeling of hospital facilities. *Revista Mexicana de Psycologia, 6*(1), 45–54.

Osborne, J. W. (1997). Race and academic disidentification. *Journal of Educational Psychology, 89*(4), 728–735.

Osofsky, J. D. (1995). The effects of exposure to violence on young children. *American Psychologist, 50,* 782–788.

Ostbye, T., & Cross, E. (1995). Net economic costs of dementia in Canada. *Canadian Medical Association Journal, 151*(10), 1457–1464.

Ottati, V., Fishbein, M., & Middlestadt, S. E. (1988). Determinants of voters' beliefs about the candidates' stands on the issues: The role of evaluative bias heuristics and the candidates' expressed message. *Journal of Personality and Social Psychology, 55,* 517–529.

Overby, L. Y. (1990). A comparison of novice and experienced dancers' imagery ability. *Journal of Mental Imagery, 14,* 173–184.

Overmier, J. B. Learned helplessness: State of stasis of the art? In M. Sabourin, F. Craik, et al. (Eds.), *Advances in psychological science, Vol. 2: Biological and cognitive aspects* (pp. 301–315). Hove, England: Psychology Press/Erlbaum Taylor & Francis.

Overmier, J. B., & Gahtan, E. (1998). Psychoneuroimmunology: The final hurdle. *Integrative Physiological and Behavioral Science, 33*(2), 137–140.

Owen, A. M., Evans, A. C., & Petrides, M. (1996). Evidence for a two-stage model of spatial working memory processing within the lateral frontal cortex: A positron emission tomography study. *Cerebral Cortex, 6*(1) 31–38.

Pagano, R. W., Rose, R. M., Stivers, R. M., & Warrenburg, S. (1976). Sleep during transcendental meditation. *Science, 191,* 308–310.

Paikoff, R. L., & Brooks-Gunn, J. (1991). Do parent-child relationships change during puberty? *Psychological Bulletin, 110,* 47–66.

Paivio, A. (1971). *Imagery and verbal processes.* New York: Holt, Rinehart & Winston.

Palinkas, L. A., Russell, J., Downs, M. A., & Petterson, J. S. (1992). Ethnic differences in stress, coping, and depressive symptoms after the Exxon Valdez oil spill. *Journal of Nervous and Mental Disease, 180,* 287–295.

Paloutzian, R. F. (1996). *Invitation to the psychology of religion.* Boston: Allyn and Bacon.

Paloutzian, R. F., & Ellison, C. W. (1991). *Manual for the Spiritual Well-Being Scale.* Nyack, NY: Life Advance Inc.

Pantev, C., Oostenveld, R., Engelien, A., Ross, B., Roberts, L. E., & Hoke, M. (1998). Increased auditory critical representation in musicians. *Nature, 392,* 811–814.

Pantin, H. M., & Carver, C. S. (1982). Induced competence and the bystander effect. *Journal of Applied Social Psychology, 12,* 100–111.

Papini, M. R., & Bitterman, M. E. (1990). The role of contingency in classical conditioning. *Psychological Review, 97,* 396–403.

Paradis, C. M., Hatch, M., & Friedman, S. (1994). Anxiety disorders in African Americans: An update. *Journal of the National Medical Association, 86,* 609–612.

Park, H. S., Bauer, S. C., & Sullivan, L. M. (1998). Gender differences among top-performing elementary school students in mathematical ability. *Journal of Research and Development in Education, 31*(3), 133–141.

Parke, R. D. (1995). Fathers and families. In M. H. Bornstein (Ed.), *Handbook of parenting. Vol. III: Status and social conditions of parenting.* Mahwah, NJ: Lawrence Erlbaum Associates.

Parker, D. E. (1980, November). The vestibular apparatus. *Scientific American,* 118–135.

Parker, G., Roy, K., Hadzi-Pavlovic, D., & Pedic, F. (1992). Psychotic (delusional) depression: A meta-analysis of physical treatments. *Journal of Affective Disorders, 24,* 17–24.

Parker, L. E. (1993). When to fix it and when to leave: Relationships among perceived control, self-efficacy, dissent, and exit. *Journal of Applied Psychology, 78,* 949–959.

Parkin, A. J., Reid, T., & Russo, R. (1990). On the differential nature of implicit and explicit memory. *Memory and Cognition, 18,* 507–514.

Parrott, W. G., & Schulkin, J. (1993). Neuropsychology and the cognitive nature of the emotions. *Cognition and Emotion, 7,* 43–59.

Patrick, C. J. (1994). Emotion and psychopathy: Startling new insights. *Psychophysiology, 31,* 319–330.

Patrick, C. J., & Iacono, W. G. (1989). Psychopathy, threat, and polygraph test accuracy. *Journal of Applied Psychology, 74,* 347–355.

Pavlov, I. P. (1927). *Conditioned reflexes.* London: Oxford University Press.

Payne, D. G., Neuschatz, J. S., Lampinen, J. M., & Lynn, S. J. (1997). Compelling memory illusions: The characteristics of false memories. *American Psychological Society, 6*(3), 56–60.

Payne, J. W., Bettman, J. R., & Johnson, E. J. (1992). Behavioral decision research: A constructive processing perspective. *Annual Review of Psychology, 43,* 87–132.

Pearlmann, S. F. (1993). Late mid-life astonishment: Disruptions to identity and self-esteem. *Women and Therapy, 14,* 1–12.

Pedersen, D. M., & Wheeler, J. (1983). The Müller-Lyer illusion among Navajos. *Journal of Social Psychology, 121,* 3–6.

Pedersen, N. L., Plomin, R., & McClearn, G. E. (1994). Is there g beyond g? (Is there genetic influence on specific cognitive abilities independent of genetic influence on general cognitive ability?) *Intelligence, 18,* 133–143.

Pedersen, N. L., Plomin, R., Nesselroade, J. R., & McClearn, G. E. (1992). A quantitative genetic analysis of cognitive abilities during the second half of the life span. *Psychological Science, 3,* 346–353.

Pendergrast, M. (1997). Memo to Pope: Ask the real questions, please. *American Psychologist, 52,* 989–990.

Penfield, W. W. (1958). *The excitable cortex in conscious man.* Springfield, IL: Charles Thomas.

Penfield, W. W., & Jasper, H. (1954). *Epilepsy and the functional anatomy of the human brain.* Boston: Little, Brown.

Penfield, W. W., & Mathieson, G. (1974). Memory: Autopsy findings and comments on the role of hippocampus in experiential recall. *Archives of Neurology, 31,* 145–154.

Penfield, W. W., & Milner, B. (1958). Memory deficit produced by bilateral lesions in the hippocampal zone. *Archives of Neurological Psychiatry, 79,* 475–497.

Penfield, W. W., & Perot, P. (1963). The brain's record of auditory and visual experience. *Brain, 86,* 595–696.

Penn, D. L., Corrigan, P. W., Bentall, R. P., Racenstein, J. M., & Newman, L. (1997). Social cognition in schizophrenia. *Psychological Bulletin, 121*(1), 114–132.

Pepperberg, I. (1994). Numerical competence in an African gray parrot (*Psittacus erithacus*). *Journal of Comparative Psychology, 108*(1), 36–44.

Pepperberg, I., Brese, K .J., & Harris, B. J. (1991). Solitary play during acquisition of English vocalizations by an African Grey Parrot (*Psittacus erithacus*): Possible parallels with children's monologue speech. *Applied Psycholinguistics, 12*(2), 151–178.

Perkins, D. N., & Grotzer, T. A. (1997). Teaching intelligence. *American Psychologist, 52*(10), 1125–1133.

Perlin, M. L. (1996). The insanity defense: Deconstructing the myths and reconstructing the jurisprudence. In B. D. Sales & D. W. Shuman (Eds.), *Law, mental health, and mental disorder* (pp. 341–359). Pacific Grove, CA: Brooks/Cole Publishing Company.

Perlman, M., & Ross, H. (1997a). The benefits of parental intervention in children's disputes: An examination of concurrent changes in children's fighting styles. *Child Development, 68*(4), 690–700.

Perlman, M., & Ross, H. (1997b). Who's the boss? Parents' failed attempts to influence the outcomes of conflicts between their children. *Journal of Social and Personal Relationships, 14*(4), 463–480.

Perner, J., & Ruffman, T. (1995). Episodic memory and autonoetic consciousness: Developmental evidence and a theory of childhood amnesia. *Journal of Experimental Child Psychology, 59*(3), 516–548.

Perrett, D. I., Lee, K. J., Penton-Voak, I., Rowland, D., Yoshikawa, S., Burt, D. M., Henzi, S. P., Castles, D. L., & Akamatsu, S. (1998).

Effects of sexual dimorphism on facial attractiveness. *Nature, 394,* 884–887.

Persky, H. (1978). Plasma testosterone level and sexual behavior of couples. *Archives of Sexual Behavior, 7,* 157–173.

Persons, J. B., Thase, M. E., & Crits-Christoph, P. (1996). The role of psychotherapy in the treatment of depression. *Archives of General Psychiatry, 53,* 283–290.

Peselow, E. D., Sanfilipo, M. P., & Fieve, R. R. (1995). Relationship between hypomania and personality disorders before and after successful treatment. *American Journal of Psychiatry, 152,* 232–238.

Pesut, D. J. (1990). Creative thinking as a self-regulatory metacognitive process: A model for education, training and further research. *Journal of Creative Behavior, 24,* 105–110.

Peterson, C., & Seligman, M. E. P. (1984). Causal explanations as a risk factor for depression: Theory and evidence. *Psychological Review, 91,* 347–374.

Peterson, L. R., & Peterson, M. J. (1959). Short-term retention of individual verbal items. *Journal of Experimental Psychology, 58,* 193–198.

Petrill, S. A., Plomin, R., Berg, S., Johansoon, B., Pedersen, N. L., Ahern, F., & McClearn, G. E. (1998). The genetic and environmental relationship between general and specific cognitive abilities in twins age 80 and older. *Psychological Science, 9*(3), 183–189.

Pettigrew, T. F. (1997). The affective component of prejudice: Empirical support for the new view. In S. A. Tuch & J. K. Martin (Eds.), *Racial attitudes in the 1990s: Continuity and change* (pp. 76–90). New York: Praeger.

Pettigrew, T. F., Jackson, J. S., Brika, J. B., Lemaine, G., Meertens, R. W., Wagner, U., & Zick, A. (1998). Outgroup prejudice in Western Europe. In W. Stroebe, M. Hewstone, et al. (Eds.), *European Review of Social Psychology, Vol. 8.* (pp. 241–273). Chichester, England: John Wiley & Sons, Inc.

Petty, R. E., & Cacioppo, J. T. (1981). *Attitudes and persuasion: Classic and contemporary approaches.* Dubuque, IA: Wm. C. Brown.

Petty, R. E., & Cacioppo, J. T. (1985). The elaboration likelihood model of persuasion. In L. Berkowitz (Ed.), *Advances in experimental social psychology* (Vol. 19). New York: Academic.

Petty, R. E., Cacioppo, J. T., Strathman, A. J., & Priester, J. R. (1994). To think or not to think: Exploring two routes to persuasion. In S. Shavitt & T. C. Brock (Eds.), *Persuasion: Psychological insights and perspectives* (pp. 113–148). Boston: Allyn & Bacon.

Petty, R. E., Schumann, D. W., Richman, S. A., & Strathman, A. J. (1993). Positive mood and persuasion: Different roles for affect under high- and low-elaboration conditions. *Journal of Personality and Social Psychology, 64,* 5–20.

Pezdek, K., Finger, K., & Hodge, D. (1997). Planting false childhood memories: The role of event plausibility. *American Psychological Society, 8*(6), 437–441.

Pfister, H. P., & Muir, J. L. (1992). Prenatal exposure to predictable and unpredictable novelty stress and oxytocin treatment affects offspring development and behavior in rats. *International Journal of Neuroscience, 62,* 227–241.

Phares, V., & Compas, B. E. (1993). Fathers and developmental psychopathology. *Current Directions in Psychological Science, 2,* 162–165.

Phelps, J. A., Davis, J. O., & Schartz, K. M. (1997). Nature, nurture, and twin research strategies. *American Psychological Society, 6*(5), 117–120.

Phinney, J. S. (1996). When we talk about American ethnic groups, what do we mean? *American Psychologist, 51*(9), 918–927.

Piaget, J. (1932). *The moral judgment of the child.* London: Routledge & Kegan Paul.

Pinel, J. (1993). *Biopsychology.* Boston: Allyn and Bacon.

Pinker, S. (1997). *How the mind works.* New York: W. W. Norton & Company.

Pinsof, W. M., Wynne, L. C., & Hambright, A. B. (1996). The outcomes of couple and family therapy: Findings, conclusions, and recommendations. *Psychotherapy, 33*(2), 321–331.

Pion, G. M., Mednick, M. T., Astin, H. S., Hall, C. C., Kenkel, M. B., Keita, G. P., et al. (1996). The shifting gender composition of psychology: Trends and implications for the discipline. *American Psychologist, 51*(5), 509–528.

Pittam, J., Gallois, C., Iwawaki, S., & Kroonenberg, P. (1995). Australian and Japanese concepts of expressive behavior. *Journal of Cross-Cultural Psychology, 26,* 451–473.

Pittenger, D. J. (1997). Reconsidering the overjustification effect: A guide to critical resources. *Teaching of Psychology, 23*(4), 234–236.

Plante, T. G., Boccaccini, M., & Andersen, E. (1998). Attitudes concerning professional issues impacting psychotherapy practice among members of the American Board of Professional Psychology. *Psychotherapy: Theory, Research and Practice, 35*(1), 34–42.

Plath, Sylvia. (1971). *The bell jar.* New York: HarperCollins Publishers.

Plihal, W., & Born, J. (1997). Effects of early and late nocturnal sleep on declarative and procedural memory. *Journal of Cognitive Neuroscience, 9*(4), 534–547.

Plomin, R. (1989). Environment and genes: Determinants of behavior. *American Psychologist, 44,* 105–111.

Plomin, R. (1990). *Nature and nurture: An introduction to human behavioral genetics.* Pacific Grove, CA: Brooks/Cole.

Plomin, R. (1994a). *Genetics and experience: The interplay between nature and nurture.* Thousand Oaks, CA: Sage.

Plomin, R. (1994b). Nature, nurture, and social development. *Social Development, 3,* 37–53.

Plomin, R., Fulker, D. W., Corley, R., & DeFries, J. C. (1997). Nature, nurture, and cognitive development from 1 to 16 years: A parent-offspring adoption study. *Psychological Science, 8*(6), 442–447.

Plomin, R., Petrill, S. A., & Cutting, A. L. (1996). What genetic research on intelligence tells us about the environment. *Journal of Biosocial Science, 28*(4), 587–606.

Plomin, R., Reiss, D., Hetherington, E. M., & Howe, G. W. (1994). Nature and nurture: Genetic contributions to measures of the family environment. *Developmental Psychology, 30,* 32–43.

Plotkin, W. B. (1980). The role of attributions of responsibility in the facilitation of unusual experiential states during alpha training: An analysis of the biofeedback placebo effect. *Journal of Abnormal Psychology, 89,* 67–78.

Plous, S. (1996). Attitudes toward the use of animals in psychological research and education. *American Psychologist, 51*(11), 1167–1180.

Plutchik, R. (1980). *Emotion: A psychoevolutionary synthesis.* New York: Harper & Row.

Pollack, W. (1998). *Real boys: Rescuing our sons from the myths of boyhood.* New York: Random House.

Pomerantz, E. M., Chaiken, S., & Tordesillas, R. S. (1995). Attitude strength and resistance processes. *Journal of Personality and Social Psychology, 69,* 408–419.

Pomerleau, A., Bolduc, D., Malcuit, G., & Cossette, L. (1990). Pink or blue: Environmental gender stereotypes in the first two years of life. *Sex Roles, 22,* 359–367.

Poole, D. A., Lindsay, D. S., Memon, A., & Bull, R. (1995). Psychotherapy and the recovery of memories of childhood sexual abuse: U.S. and British practitioners' opinions, practices, and experiences. *Journal of Clinical and Consulting Psychology, 63,* 426–437.

Pope, K. S. (1996). Memory, abuse, science. *American Psychologist, 51*(9), 957–974.

Porter, B. E., Leeming, F. C., & Dwyer, W. O. (1995). Solid waste recovery: A review of behavioral programs to increase recycling. *Environment and Behavior, 27,* 122–152.

Posner, M. I., DiGirolamo, G. J., & Fernandez-Duque, D. (1997). Brain mechanisms of cognitive skills. *Conscious Cognition, 6*(2/3), 267–290.

Posner, M. I., & Mitchell, R. F. (1967). Chronometric analysis of classification. *Psychological Review, 74,* 392–409.

Posner, M. I., & Pavese, A. (1998). Anatomy of word and sentence meaning. *Proceedings of the National Academy of Sciences, 95*(3), 899–905.

Post, R. M., Frye, M. A., Dnicoff, K. D., Leverich, G. S., Kimbrell, T. A., & Dunn, R. T. (1998). Beyond lithium in the treatment of bipolar illness. *Neuropsychopharmacology, 19*(3), 206–219.

Postmes, T., & Spears, R. (1998). Deindividuation and antinormative behavior: A meta-analysis. *Psychological Bulletin, 123*(3), 238–259.

Powell, B., & Steelman, L. C. (1996). Bewitched, bothered and bewildering: The use and misuse of state SAT and ACT scores. *Harvard Educational Review, 66*(1), 27–59.

Powers, P. C., & Geen, R. G. (1972). Effects of the behavior and the perceived arousal of a model on instrumental aggression. *Journal of Personality and Social Psychology, 23,* 175–184.

Powers, S. I., Hauser, S. T., & Kilner, L. A. (1989). Adolescent mental health. *American Psychologist, 44,* 200–208.

Powley, T. L. (1977). The ventromedial hypothalamic syndrome, satiety, and a cephalic phase hypothesis. *Psychological Review, 84,* 89–126.

Pratarelli, M. E., & McIntyre, J. A. (1994). Effects of social loafing on word recognition. *Perceptual and Motor Skills, 78,* 455–464.

Prather, J. E., & Minkow, N. V. (1991). Prescription for despair: Women and psychotropic drugs. In N. Van Den Bergh et al. (Eds.) *Feminist perspectives on addictions* (pp. 87–99). New York: Springer Publishing Co.

Pratkanis, A. R., Eskenazi, J., & Greenwald, A. G. (1994). What you expect is what you believe (but not necessarily what you get): A test of the effectiveness of subliminal self-help audiotapes. *Basic and Applied Social Psychology, 15,* 251–276.

Prelow, H. M., & Guarnaccia, C. A. (1997). Ethnic and racial differences in life stress among high school adolescents. *Journal of Counseling and Development, 75*(6), 442–450.

Premack, D. (1962). Reversibility of the reinforcement relation. *Science, 136,* 255–257.

Premack, D. (1965). Reinforcement theory. In D. Levine (Ed.), *Nebraska Symposium on Motivation* (Vol. 13, pp. 123–180). Lincoln: University of Nebraska Press.

Premack, D. (1971). Language in chimpanzees? *Science, 172,* 808–822.

Prentice-Dunn, S. (1991). Half-baked idea: Deindividuation and the nonreactive assessment of self-awareness. *Contemporary Social Psychology, 15,* 16–17.

Prinz, R. J., & Miller, G. E. (1994). Family-based treatment for childhood antisocial behavior: Experimental influences on dropout and engagement. *Journal of Consulting and Clinical Psychology, 62,* 654–660.

Prinz, R. N., Vitiello, M. V., Raskind, M. A., & Thorphy, M. J. (1990). Geriatrics: Sleep disorders and aging. *New England Journal of Medicine, 323,* 520–526.

Proshansky, H. M., & O'Hanlon, T. (1977). Environmental psychology: Origins and development. In D. Stokols (Ed.), *Perspectives on environment and behavior: Theory, research, and application.* New York: Plenum.

Prudic, J., Sackeim, H. A., & Devanand, D. P. (1990). Medication resistance and clinical response to electroconvulsive therapy. *Psychiatry Research, 31,* 287–296.

Puffer, S. M. (1987). Prosocial behavior, noncompliant behavior, and work performance among commission salespeople. *Journal of Applied Psychology, 72,* 615–621.

Pugh, K. R., Shaywitz, B. A., Shaywitz, S. E., et al. (1997). Predicting reading in performance from neuroimaging profiles: The cerebral basis of phonological effects in printed word identification. *Journal of Experimental Psychology: Human Perception and Performance, 23*(2), 299–318.

Puigserver, P., Wu, Z., Park, C. W., Graves, R., Wright, M., & Spiegelman, B. M. (1998). A cold-inducible co-activator of nuclear receptors linked to adaptive thermogenesis. *Cell, 92,* 829–839.

Punamöki, R. L., & Joustie, M. (1998). The role of culture, violence, and personal factors affecting dream content. *Journal of Cross-Cultural Psychology, 29*(2), 320–342.

Putnam, F. W., & Carlson, E. B. (1998). Trauma, memory, and dissociation. *Progress in Psychiatry, 54,* 27–55.

Putnam, F. W., Guroff, J. J., Silberman, E. K., Barban, L., & Post, R. M. (1986). The clinical phenomenology of multiple personality disorder: Review of 100 recent cases. *Journal of Clinical Psychiatry, 47,* 285–293.

Putnam, W. H. (1979). Hypnosis and distortions in eyewitness memory. International *Journal of Clinical and Experimental Hypnosis, 27,* 437–448.

Quigley, B., Gaes, G. G., & Tedeschi, J. T. (1989). Does asking make a difference? Effects of initiator, possible gain, and risk on attributed altruism. *Journal of Social Psychology, 129,* 259–267.

Quilitch, H. R., & Risley, T. R. (1973). The effects of play materials on social play. *Journal of Applied Behavior Analysis, 6,* 573–578.

Rabizadeh, S., et al. (1993). Induction of apoptosis by the low affinity NGF receptor. *Science, 261,* 345–348.

Rachlin, H. (1995). Things that are private and things that are mental. In J. T. Todd & E. K. Morris (Eds.), *Modern perspectives on B. F. Skinner and contemporary behaviorism* (pp. 179–183). Westport, CT: Greenwood.

Rafaeli, A. (1989). When clerks meet customers: A test of variables related to emotional expressions on the job. *Journal of Applied Psychology, 74,* 385–393.

Ragins, B. R., & Sundstrom, E. (1989). Gender and power in organizations: A longitudinal perspective. *Psychological Bulletin, 105,* 51–88.

Rahe, R. H. (1989). Recent life change stress and psychological depression. In T. W. Miller (Ed.), *Stressful life events.* Madison, WI: International Universities Press.

Raisman, G., Morris, R. J., & Zhou, C. F. (1987). Specificity in the reinnervation of adult hippocampus by embryonic hippocampal transplants. In F. J. Seil, E. Herbert, & B. M. Carlson (Eds.), *Progress in brain research* (Vol. 71, pp. 325–333). New York: Elsevier.

Ramey, C. T., & Ramey, S. L. (1998). Early intervention and early experience. *American Psychologist, 53*(2), 109–120.

Rao, S. C., Rainer, G., & Miller, E. K. (1997). Integration of what and where in the primate prefrontal cortex. *Science, 276,* 821–824.

Rapcsak, S. Z., Polster, M. R., Comer, J. F., & Rubens, A. B. (1994). False recognition and misidentification of faces following right hemisphere damage. *Cortex, 30*(4), 565–583.

Rapee, R. (1986). Differential response to hyperventilation in panic disorder and generalized anxiety disorder. *Journal of Abnormal Psychology, 95,* 24–28.

Rappaport, J., (1987). Terms of empowerment/exemplars of prevention: Toward a theory for community psychology. *American Journal of Community Psychology, 2,* 121–148.

Raskin, D. C. (1986). The polygraph in 1986: Scientific, professional and legal issues surrounding application and acceptance of polygraph evidence. *Utah Law Review, 29,* 29–75.

Raskin, D. C., Barland, G. H., & Podlesny, J. A. (1978). *Validity and reliability of detection of deception.* Washington, DC: National Institute of Law Enforcement and Criminal Justice.

Raskin, D. C., & Hare, R. D. (1978). Psychopathy and detection of deception in a prison population. *Psychophysiology, 15,* 126–136.

Ravussin, E., Lillioja, S., Knowler, W. C., Christin, L., Freymond, D., Abbott, W. G. H., Boyce, V., Howard, B. V., & Bogardus, C. (1988). Reduced rate of energy expenditure as a risk factor for body-weight gain. *New England Journal of Medicine, 318,* 467–472.

Raymond, J. E., Ogden, N. A., Fagan, J. E., & Kaplan, B. J. (1988). Fixational instability and saccadic eye movements of dyslexic children with subtle cerebellar dysfunction. *American Journal of Optometry and Physiological Optics, 65,* 174–181.

Rayner, K. (1985). Eye movements and the perceptual span: Evidence for dyslexic typology. In G. T. Pavlidis, & D. F. Fisher (Eds.), *Dyslexia: Its neuropsychology and treatment.* New York: John Wiley and Sons.

Rayner, K. (1998). Eye movements in reading and information processing: 20 years of research. *Psychological Bulletin, 124*(3), 372–422.

Rayner, K., & Pollatsek, A. (1992). Eye movements and scene perception. *Canadian Journal of Psychology, 46,* 342–376.

Raz, S., & Raz, N. (1990). Structural brain abnormalities in the major psychoses: A quantitative review of the evidence from computerized imaging. *Psychological Bulletin, 208,* 93–108.

Ree, M. J., & Earles, J. A. (1992). Intelligence is the best predictor of job performance. *Current Directions in Psychological Science, 1,* 86–89.

Ree, M. J., Earles, J. A., & Teachout, M. S. (1994). Predicting job performance: Not much more than g. *Journal of Applied Psychology, 79,* 518–524.

Reed, C. F. (1984). Terrestrial passage theory of the moon illusion. *Journal of Experimental Psychology: General, 113,* 489–516.

Reichle, E. D., Pollatsek, A., Fisher, D. L., & Rayner, K. (1998). Toward a model of eye movement control in reading. *Psychological Review, 105*(1), 125–157.

Reiger, D. A., Boyd, J. H., Burke, J. D., Rae, D. S., Myers, J. K., Kramer, M., Robins, L. N., George, L. K., Karno, M., & Locke, B. Z. (1988). One-month prevalence of mental disorders in the United States. *Archives of General Psychiatry, 45,* 977–986.

Reis, H. T., & Shaver, P. (1988). Intimacy as an interpersonal process. In S. Duck (Ed.), *Handbook of personal relationships: Theory, relationships and interventions.* Chichester, England: Wiley.

Reisenzein, R. (1983). The Schachter theory of emotion: Two decades later. *Psychological Bulletin, 94,* 239–264.

Reiss, D. (1995). Genetic influence on family systems: Implications for development. *Journal of Marriage and the Family, 57,* 543–560.

Reiss, D. (1997). Mechanisms linking genetic and social influences in adolescent development: Beginnning a collaborative search. *American Psychological Society, 6*(4), 100–105.

Reiss, D., & Price, R. H. (1996). National research agenda for prevention research: The National Institute of Mental Health Report. *American Psychologist, 51*(11), 1109–1115.

Renault, B., Signoret, J. L., Debruille, B., Breton, F., & Bolgert, F. (1989). Brain potentials reveal covert facial recognition in prosopagnosia. *Neuropsychologica, 27,* 905–912.

Repetti, R. L., Matthews, K. A., & Waldron, I. (1989). Employment and women's health. *American Psychologist, 44,* 1394–1401.

Reppucci, N. D., & Haugaard, J. J. (1989). Prevention of child sexual abuse. *American Psychologist, 44,* 1266–1275.

Rescorla, R. A. (1977). Pavlovian 2nd-order conditioning: Some implications for instrumental behavior. In H. Davis & H. Herwit (Eds.), *Pavlovian-operant interactions*. Hillsdale, NJ: Erlbaum.

Rescorla, R. A. (1978). Some implications of a cognitive perspective on Pavlovian conditioning. In S. H. Hulse, H. Fowler, & W. Honig (Eds.), *Cognitive process in animal behavior*. Hillsdale, NJ: Erlbaum.

Rescorla, R. A. (1988). Pavlovian conditioning: It's not what you think it is. *American Psychologist, 43*, 151–160.

Resnick, M. D., Bearman, P. S., Blum, R. W., Bauman, K. E., Harris, K. M., Jones, J., Tabor, J., Beuhring, T., Sieving, R. E., Shew, M., Ireland, M., Bearinger, L. H., & Udry, R. (1997). Protecting adolescents from harm: Findings from the National Longitudinal Study on Adolescent Health. *Journal of the American Medical Association, 278*(10), 823–831.

Resnick, R. J. (1997). A brief history of practice—expanded. *American Psychologist, 52*(4), 463–468.

Resnick, S. M. (1992). Positron emission tomography in psychiatric illness. *Psychological Science, 1*, 92–98.

Restak, R. M. (1994). *The modular brain: How new discoveries in neuroscience are answering age-old questions about memory, free will, consciousness, and personal identity*. New York: Macmillan.

Restle, F. (1970). Moon illusion explained on the basis of relative size. *Science, 167*, 1092–1096.

Reynolds, C. F., Frank, E., Perel, J. M., Imber, S. D., Cornes, C., et al. (1999). Nortryptyline and interpersonal psychotherapy as maintenance therapies for recurrent major depression: A randomized controlled trial in patients older than 59 years. *Journal of the American Medical Association, 281*(1), 39–45.

Rhode, D. L. (1997). *Speaking of sex: The denial of gender inequality*. Cambridge, MA: Harvard University Press.

Rhodes, N., & Wood, W. (1992). Self-esteem and intelligence affect influenceability: The mediating role of message reception. *Psychological Bulletin, 111*, 156–171.

Rice, G., Anderson, C., Risch, N., & Ebers, G. (1999). Male homosexuality: Absence of linkage to microsatellite markers at Xq28. *Science, 284*, 665–667.

Richardson, J. T. E., & Zucco, G. M. (1989). Cognition and olfaction: A review. *Psychological Bulletin, 105*, 352–360.

Richie, B. E. (1996). Gender entrapment: An exploratory study. In A. J. Dan et al. (Eds.), *Reframing women's health: Multidisciplinary research and practice* (pp. 219–232). Thousand Oaks, CA: Sage Publications.

Richman, A. L., Miller, P. M., & LeVine, R. A. (1992). Cultural and educational variations in maternal responsiveness. *Developmental Psychology, 28*, 614–621.

Riehle, A., Grun, S., Diesmann, M., & Aertsen, A. (1997). Spike synchronization and rate modulation differentially involved in motor cortical function. *Science, 278*, 1950–1953.

Rifai, A. H., George, C. J., Stack, J. A., Mann, J. J., & Reynolds, C. F. (1994). Hopelessness in suicide attempters after acute treatment of major depression in late life. *American Journal of Psychiatry, 151*, 1687–1690.

Rifai, A. H., Reynolds, C. F., & Mann, J. J. (1992). Biology of elderly suicide. *Suicide and Life Threatening Behavior, 22*, 48–61.

Ring, K., Wallston, K., & Corey, M. (1970). Mode of debriefing as a factor affecting subjective reaction to a Milgram-type obedience experiment: An ethical inquiry. *Representative Research in Social Psychology, 1*, 67–88.

Rips, L. J. (1990). Reasoning. *Annual Review of Psychology, 41*, 321–353.

Ritter, J. M., & Langlois, J. H. (1988). The role of physical attractiveness in the observation of adult-child interactions: Eye of the beholder or behavioral reality? *Developmental Psychology, 24*, 254–263.

Robberson, M. R., & Rogers, R. W. (1988). Beyond fear appeals: Negative and positive persuasive appeals to health and self-esteem. *Journal of Applied Social Psychology, 18*, 277–287.

Robbins, M., & Meyer, D. (1970). Motivational control of retrograde amnesia. *Journal of Experimental Psychology, 84*, 220–225.

Roberts, A. H., Kewman, D. G., Mercier, L., & Hovell, M. (1993). The power of nonspecific effects in healing: Implications for psychosocial and biological treatments. *Clinical Psychology Review, 13*, 375–391.

Roberts, B. W. (1997). Plaster or plasticity: Are adult work experiences associated with personality change in women? *Journal of Personality, 65*(2), 205–229.

Roberts, G. C. (1992). *Motivation in sport and exercise: Conceptual constraints and convergence* (pp. 3–29). Champaign, IL: Human Kinetics.

Robinson, L. A., Berman, J. S., & Neimeyer, R. A. (1990). Psychotherapy for the treatment of depression: A comprehensive review of controlled outcome research. *Psychological Bulletin, 108*, 30–49.

Rock, I., & Palmer, S. (1990). The legacy of Gestalt psychology. *Scientific American, 263*(6), 84–90.

Rodin, J. (1981). Current status of the internal-external hypothesis for obesity: What went wrong? *American Psychologist, 36*, 361–372.

Rodin, J. (1986). Aging and health: Effects of the sense of control. *Science, 233*, 1271–1276.

Rodin, J., & Ickovics, J. R. (1990). Women's health. *American Psychologist, 45*, 1018–1034.

Rodin, J., & Salovey, P. (1989). Health psychology. *Annual Review of Psychology, 40*, 533–581.

Rodriguez, E., George, N., Lachaux, J. P., Martinerie, J., Renault, B., & Varela, F. J. (1999). Perception's shadow: Long-distance synchronization of human activity. *Nature, 397*, 430–433.

Roehrs, T., Timms, V., Zwyghuizen-Doorenbos, A., & Roth, T. (1989). Sleep extension in sleepy and alert normals. *Sleep, 12*, 449–457.

Rogers, C. R. (1951). *Client-centered therapy*. Boston: Houghton Mifflin.

Rogers, M., & Smith, K. H. (1993). Public perceptions of subliminal advertising: Why practitioners shouldn't ignore this issue. *Journal of Advertising Research, 33*(2), 10–18.

Rogoff, B., & Morelli, G. (1989). Perspectives on children's development from cultural psychology. *American Psychologist, 44*, 343–348.

Romano, S. T., & Bordieri, J. E. (1989). Physical attractiveness stereotypes and students' perceptions of college professors. *Psychological Reports, 64*, 1099–1102.

Romans, S. E., Martin, J. L., Anderson, J. C., Herbison, G. P., & Mullen, P. E. (1995). Sexual abuse in childhood and deliberate self-harm. *American Journal of Psychiatry, 152*, 1336–1342.

Roose, S. P., Glassman, A. H., Attia, E., & Woodring, S. (1994). Comparative efficacy of selective serotonin reuptake inhibitors and tricyclics in the treatment of melancholia. *American Journal of Psychiatry, 151*, 1735–1739.

Roques, P., Lambin, M., Jeunier, B., & Strayer, F. F. (1997). Multivariate analysis of personal space in a primary school classroom. *Enfance, 4*, 451–468.

Rorty, M., Yager, J., & Rossotto, E. (1994). Childhood sexual, physical, and psychological abuse in bulimia nervosa. *American Journal of Psychiatry, 151*, 1122–1126.

Rosch, E. (1973). Natural categories. *Cognitive Psychology, 4*, 328–350.

Rosch, E. (1978). Principles of categorization. In E. Rosch & B. B. Lloyd (Eds.), *Cognition and categorization* (pp. 27–48). Hillsdale, NJ: Erlbaum.

Rose, A. J., & Montemayor, R. (1994). The relationship between gender role orientation and perceived self-competency in male and female adolescents. *Sex Roles, 31*, 579–595.

Rose, S. A., & Feldman, J. F. (1995). Prediction of IQ and specific cognitive abilities at 11 years from infancy measures. *Developmental Psychology, 31*, 685–696.

Rose, S. D. (1991). The development and practice of group treatment. In M. Hersen, A. E. Kazdin, & A. S. Bellack (Eds.), *The clinical psychology handbook* (2nd ed.). New York: Pergamon.

Rosebush, P. A. (1998). Psychological intervention with military personnel in Rwanda. *Military Medicine, 163*(8), 559–563.

Rosenberg, H. (1993). Prediction of controlled drinking by alcoholics and problem drinkers. *Psychological Bulletin, 113*, 129–139.

Rosenberg, P. S. (1995). Scope of the AIDS epidemic in the United States. *Science, 270*, 1372–1375.

Rosenstock, I. M., & Kirscht, J. P. (1979). Why people seek health care. In G. C. Stone, F. Cohen, & N. E. Adler (Eds.), *Health psychology: A handbook*. San Francisco: Jossey-Bass.

Ross, C. A., & Davis, B. (1986). Suicide and parasuicide in a northern Canadian community. *Canadian Journal of Psychiatry, 31*, 331–334.

Ross, H. (1996). Negotiating principles of entitlement in sibling property disputes. *Developmental Psychology, 32*(2), 90–101.

Ross, H. S., & Lollis, S. P. (1987). Communication within infant social games. *Developmental Psychology, 2*, 241–248.

Ross, J. A., Haimes, D. H., & Hogaboam-Gray, A. (1998). Improving student helpfulness in cooperative learning groups. *Journal of Classroom Interaction, 31*(2), 13–22.

Ross, L., Bierbrauer, G., & Hoffman, S. (1976). The role of attribution processes in conformity and dissent. *American Psychologist, 31*, 148–157.

Ross, S. M., & Offermann, L. R. (1997). Transformational leaders: Measurement of personality attributes and work group performance. *Personality and Social Psychology Bulletin, 23*(10), 1078–1086.

Rothbart, M. K., Taylor, S. B., & Tucker, D. M. (1989). Right-sided facial asymmetry in infant emotional expression. *Neuropsychologia, 27,* 675–687.

Rothblum, E. D. (1990). Women and weight: Fad and fiction. *Journal of Psychology, 124*(1), 5–24.

Rothblum, E. D. (1992). Women and weight: An international perspective. In U. P. Gielen, L. L. Adler, et al. (Eds.), *Psychology in international perspective: 50 years of the International Council of Psychologists* (pp. 271–280). Amsterdam: Swets & Zeitlinger.

Rotter, J. B. (1990). Internal versus external control of reinforcement. *American Psychologist, 45,* 489–493.

Rowland, D. L., Greenleaf, W. J., Dorfman, L. J., & Davidson, J. M. (1993). Aging and sexual function in men. *Archives of Sexual Behavior, 22,* 545–558.

Rowland, N. E., Li, B. H., & Morien, A. (1996). Brain mechanisms and the physiology of feeding. In E. D. Capaldi et al. (Eds.), *Why we eat what we eat: The psychology of eating* (pp. 173–204). Washington, DC: American Psychological Association.

Roy, A., Neilsen, D., Rylander, G., Sarchiapone, M., & Segal, N. (1999). Genetics of suicide in depression. *Journal of Clinical Psychiatry, 60*(Suppl. 2), 12–17.

Roy, A., Segal, N. L., Ceterwall, B. S., & Robinette, C. D. (1991). Suicide in twins. *Archives of General Psychiatry, 48,* 29–32.

Ruback, R. B., Pandey, J., & Begum, H. A. (1997). Urban stressors in South Asia: Impact on male and female pedestrians in Delhi and Dhaka. *Journal of Cross-Cultural Psychology, 28*(1), 23–43.

Ruback, R. B., & Riad, J. K. (1994). The more (men), the less merry: Social density, social burden and social support. *Sex Roles, 30*(11/12), 743–763.

Ruchlin, H. S., & Morris, J. N. (1991). Impact of work on the quality of life in community-residing young elderly. *American Journal of Public Health, 81,* 498–500.

Rugg, M. D. (1996). Differential activation of the prefrontal cortex in successful and unsuccessful memory retrieval. *Brain, 119*(6) 2073–2083.

Ruggieri, V., Milizia, M., Sabatini, N., & Tosi, M. T. (1983). Body perception in relation to muscular tone at rest and tactile sensitivity. *Perceptual and Motor Skills, 56*(3), 799–806.

Rumbaugh, D. M., Gill, T. V., & Von Glaserfeld, E. D. (1973). Reading and sentence completion by a chimpanzee (Pan troglodytes). *Science, 182,* 731–733.

Rumbaugh, D. M., Savage-Rumbaugh, S., & Hegel, M. T. (1987). Summation in the chimpanzee (Pan troglodytes). *Journal of Experimental Psychology: Animal Behavior Processes, 13,* 107–115.

Rumiati, R. I., & Humphreys, G. W. (1997). Visual object agnosia without alexia or propagnosia: Arguments for separate knowledge stores. *Visual Cognition, 4*(2), 207–217.

Rummelhart, D. E., Hinton, G. E., & McClelland, J. L. (1986). A general framework for parrallel distributed processing. In J. L. McClelland, & D. E. Rummelhart (Eds.), *Parallel distributed processing: Explorations in the microstructure of cognition,* Vol. 1. Cambridge, MA: Bradford.

Rushton, P. (1988). Race differences in behaviour: A review and evolutionary analysis. *Personality and Individual Differences, 9*(6), 1009–1024.

Russell, J. A. (1994). Is there universal recognition of emotion from facial expression? A review of the cross-cultural studies. *Psychological Bulletin, 115,* 102–141.

Rustemli, A. (1991). Crowding effects of density and interpersonal distance. *The Journal of Social Psychology, 132,* 51–58.

Ryan, N. D., & Varma, D. (1998). Child and adolescent mood disorders: Experience with serotonin-based therapies. *Biological Psychiatry, 44*(5), 336–340.

Saffran, J., Aslin R., & Newport, E. (1996). Statistical learning by 8-month old infants. *Science, 274,* 1926–1928.

Sakata, S., Shinohara, J., Hori, T., & Sugimoto, S. (1995). Enhancement of randomness by flotation rest (restricted environmental stimulation technique). *Perceptual and Motor Skills, 80*(3, Pt. 1), 999–1010.

Sakitt, B., & Long, G. M. (1979). Cones determine subjective offset of a stimulus but rods determine total persistence. *Vision Research, 19,* 1439–1443.

Salminen, S., & Glad, T. (1992). The role of gender in helping behavior. *The Journal of Social Psychology, 132,* 131–133.

Salt, R. E. (1991). Affectionate touch between fathers and preadolescent sons. *Journal of Marriage and the Family, 53,* 545–554.

Salthouse, T. A. (1995). Selective influences of age and speed on associative memory. *American Journal of Psychology, 108,* 381–396.

Salthouse, T. A. (1999). Theories of cognition. In V. L. Bengtson, K. W. Schaie, et al. (Eds.), *Handbook of theories of aging* (pp. 196–208). New York: Springer Publishing Co.

Salzberg, H. C., & DePiano, F. A. (1980). Hypnotizability and task motivating suggestions: A further look at how they affect performance. *International Journal of Clinical and Experimental Hypnosis, 28,* 261–271.

Salzman, C. (1997). Update on the somatic treatment of depression in the older adult: Psychopharmacology and ECT. *Journal of Geriatric Psychiatry, 30*(2), 259–270.

Sanchez, J. I., & Fernandez, D. M. (1993). Acculturative stress among Hispanics: A bidimensional model of ethnic identification. *Journal of Applied Social Psychology, 23*(8), 654–668.

Sande, G. N., Goethals, G. R., & Radloff, C. E. (1988). Perceiving one's own traits and others: The multifaceted self. *Journal of Personality and Social Psychology, 54,* 13–20.

Sanders, G. S., & Simmons, W. L. (1983). Use of hypnosis to enhance eyewitness accuracy: Does it work? *Journal of Applied Psychology, 68,* 70–77.

Sanders, M. S., & McCormick, E. J. (1993). *Human factors in engineering and design* (7th ed.). New York: McGraw-Hill.

Sanders, R. J. (1985). Teaching apes to ape language: Explaining the imitative and nonimitative signing of a chimpanzee (Pan troglodytes). *Journal of Comparative Psychology, 99,* 197–210.

Santos, M. D., Leve, C., & Pratkanis, A. R. (1994). Hey buddy, can you spare seventeen cents? Mindful persuasion and the pique technique. *Journal of Applied Social Psychology, 224,* 755–764.

Sapp, M. (1996). Potential negative sequelae of hypnosis. *Australian Journal of Clinical Hypnotherapy and Hypnosis, 17*(2), 73–78.

Sarason, I. G., & Sarason, B. R. (1987). *Abnormal psychology: The problem of maladaptive behavior* (5th ed.). Englewood Cliffs, NJ: Prentice-Hall.

Sattler, J. M. (1992). *Assessment of children: Revised and updated* (3rd ed.). San Diego: Jerome M. Sattler.

Savage-Rumbaugh, S., Pate, J. L., Lawson, J., Smith, S. T., & Rosenbaum, S. (1983). Can a chimpanzee make a statement? *Journal of Experimental Psychology: General, 112,* 457–492.

Sawicki, S. (1988). Effective crisis intervention. *Adolescence, 23,* 83–88.

Saxe, L. (1994). Detection of deception: Polygraph and integrity tests. *Current Directions in Psychological Science, 3,* 69–73.

Scalaidhe, S. P., Wilson, F. A., & Goldman-Rakic, P. S. (1997). Areal segregation of face-processing neurons in prefrontal cortex. *Science, 278,* 1135–1138.

Scarr, S. (1998). American child care today. *American Psychologist, 53*(2), 95–108.

Scarr, S. & Eisenberg, M. (1993). Child care research: Issues, perspectives, and results. *Annual Review of Psychology, 44,* 613–644.

Scarr, S., Eisenberg, M., & Deater-Deckard, K. (1994). Measurement of quality in child care centers. *Early Childhood Research Quarterly, 9,* 131–151.

Scarr, S., Phillips, D., & McCartney, K. (1990). Facts, fantasies, and the future of child care in the United States. *Psychological Science, 1,* 26–35.

Scarr, S., & Weinberg, R. A. (1994). Educational and occupational achievements of brothers and sisters in adoptive and biologically related families. *Behavior-Genetics, 24*(4), 301–325.

Schachter, S., Goldman, R., & Gordon, A. (1968). Effects of fear, food deprivation, and obesity on eating. *Journal of Personality and Social Psychology, 10,* 91–97.

Schachter, S., & Singer, J. E. (1962). Cognitive, social, and physiological determinants of emotional state. *Psychological Review, 69,* 379–399.

Schacter, D. L. (1996). *Searching for memory: The brain, the mind, and the past.* New York: Basic Books.

Schacter, D. L. (1997). False recognition and the brain. *American Psychological Society, 6*(3), 65–70.

Schacter, D. L., Alpert, N. M., Savage, C. R., Rauch, S. L., & Albert, M. S. (1996). Conscious recollection and the human hippocampal formation: Evidence from positron emission tomography. *Proceedings of the National Academy of Sciences of the USA, 93,* 321–325.

Schacter, D. L., Kihlstrom, J. F., Kihlstrom, L. C., & Berren, M. B. (1989). Autobiographical memory in a case of multiple personality disorder. *Journal of Abnormal Psychology, 98,* 508–514.

Schafe, G. E., Sollars, S. I., & Bernstein, I. L. (1995). The CS-US interval and taste aversion learning: A brief look. *Behavioral Neuroscience, 109*(4), 799–802.

Schaie, K. W. (1993). The Seattle longitudinal studies of adult intelligence. *Current Directions in Psychological Science, 2,* 171–175.

Schaie, K. W. (1994). The course of adult intellectual development. *American Psychologist, 49,* 304–313.

Schaie, K. W., & Willis, S. L. (1986). *Adult development and aging* (2nd ed.). Boston: Little, Brown.

Schaller, M. (1991). Social categorization and the formation of group stereotypes: Further evidence for biased information processing in the perception of group-behavior correlations. *European Journal of Social Psychology, 21*(1), 25–35.

Schatzman, M. (1992). Freud: Who seduced whom? *New Scientist,* 34–37.

Schedlowski, M., Fluge, T., Richter, S., Tewes, U., Schmidt, R. W., et al. (1995). Beta-endorphin, but not substance P, is increased by acute stress in humans. *Psychoneuroendocrinology, 20*(1), 103–110.

Scheibel, A. B., Conrad, T., Perdue, S., Tomiyasu, U., & Wechsler, A. (1990). A quantitative study of dendrite complexity in selected areas of the human cerebral cortex. *Brain Cognition, 12,* 85–101.

Scheier, M. F., & Carver, C. S. (1993). On the power of positive thinking: The benefits of being optimistic. *Current Directions in Psychological Science, 2,* 26–30.

Schiff, M., Duyme, M., Dumaret, A., & Tomkiewicz, S. (1982). How much could we boost scholastic achievement and IQ scores? A direct answer from a French adoption study. *Cognition, 12,* 165–196.

Schiffman, H. R. (1990). *Sensation and perception: An integrated approach (3rd ed.).* New York: John Wiley & Sons.

Schiller, P. H. (1994). Area V4 of the primate visual cortex. *Current Directions in Psychological Science, 3,* 89–92.

Schinka, J. A., Dye, D. A., & Curtiss, G. (1997). Correspondence between five-factor and RIASEC models of personality. *Journal of Personality Assessment, 68*(2), 355–368.

Schlaug, G., Jöncke, L., Huang, Y., Staiger, J. F., & Steinmetz, H. (1995). Increased corpus callosum size in musicians. *Neuropsychologia, 33*(8), 1047–1055.

Schleifer, S. J., Keller, S. E., & Stein, M. (1987). Conjugal bereavement and immunity. *Israel Journal of Psychiatry and Related Sciences, 24*(1/2), 111–123.

Schmidt, D. F., & Boland, S. M. (1986). Structure of perceptions of older adults: Evidence for multiple stereotypes. *Psychology and Aging, 1,* 255–260.

Schmidt, F. L., & Hunter, J. E. (1998). The validity and utility of selection methods in personnel psychology: Practical and theoretical implications of 85 years of research findings. *Psychological Bulletin, 124*(2), 262–274.

Schmidt, F. L., Onex, D. S., & Hunter, J. E. (1992). Personnel selection. *Annual Review of Psychology, 43,* 627–670.

Schmidt, L. A., Fox, N. A., Rubin, K. H., & Sternberg, E. M. (1997). Behavioral and neuroendocrine responses in shy children. *Developmental Psychobiology, 30*(2), 127–140.

Schmidt, S. R. (1991). Can we have a distinctive theory of memory? *Memory and Cognition, 19,* 523–542.

Schmit, M. J., & Ryan, A. M. (1993). The big five in personnel selection: Factor structure in applicant and nonapplicant populations. *Journal of Applied Psychology, 78,* 966–974.

Schnur, E., Brooks-Gunn, J., & Shipman, V. C. (1992). Who attends programs serving poor children? The case of Head Start attendees and nonattendees. *Journal of Applied Developmental Psychology, 13,* 405–421.

Schoelmerich, A., Fracasso, M. P., Lamb, M. E., & Broberg, A. G. (1995). Interactional harmony at 7 and 10 months of age predicts security of attachment as measured by Q-sort ratings. *Social Development, 4*(1), 62–74.

Schooler, C., Neumann, E., Caplan, L. J., & Roberts, B. R. (1997). A time course analysis of Stroop interference and facilitation: Comparing normal individuals and individuals with schizophrenia. *Journal of Experimental Psychology: General, 126*(1), 19–36.

Schramke, C. J., & Bauer, R. M. (1997). State-dependent learning in older and younger adults. *Psychology and Aging, 12*(2), 255–262.

Schulberg, H. C., & Rush, A. J. (1994). Clinical practice guidelines for managing major depression in primary care practice: Implications for psychologists. *American Psychologist, 49,* 34–41.

Schusterman, R. J., & Gisiner, R. (1988). Artificial language comprehension in dolphins and sea lions: The essential cognitive skills. *Psychological Record, 38*(3), 311–348.

Schutte, N. S., Malouff, J. M., Post-Gorden, J. C., & Rodasta, A. L. (1988). Effects of playing video games on children's aggressive and other behaviors. *Journal of Applied Social Psychology, 18,* 454–460.

Schwartz, B., & Robbins, S. J. (1995). *Psychology of learning and behavior.* New York: Norton.

Schwartz, J. C., & Shaver, P. (1987). Emotions and emotion knowledge in interpersonal relations. *Advances in Personal Relationships, 1,* 197–241.

Schwartzman, A. E., Gold, D., Andres, D., Arbuckle, T. Y., & Chaikelson, J. (1987). Stability of intelligence: A 40-year follow-up. *Canadian Journal of Psychology, 41,* 244–256.

Schwarz-Stevens, K. S., & Cunningham, C. L. (1993). Pavlovian conditioning of heart rate and body temperature with morphine: Effects of CS duration. *Behavioral Neuroscience, 107,* 1039–1048.

Schweickert, R., & Boruff, B. (1986). Short-term memory capacity: Magic number or magic spell? *Journal of Experimental Psychology: Learning, Memory, and Cognition, 12,* 419–425.

Schweiger, U., Deuschle, M., Körner, A., Lammers, C. H., Schmider, J., Gotthardt, U., Holsboer, F., & Heuser, I. (1994). Low lumbar bone mineral density in patients with major depression. *American Journal of Psychiatry, 151,* 1691–1693.

Seamon, J. G., Luo, C. R., & Gallo, D. A. (1998). Creating false memories of words with or without recognition of list items. *American Psychological Society, 9*(1), 20–26.

Sears, D. O., & Kosterman, R. (1994). Mass media and political persuasion. In S. Shavitt & T. C. Brock (Eds.), *Persuasion: Psychological insights and perspectives* (pp. 251–278). Boston: Allyn & Bacon.

Segall, M. H., Lonner, W. J., & Berry, J. W. (1998). Cross-cultural psychology as a scholarly discipline: On the flowering of culture in behavioral research. *American Psychologist, 53*(10), 1101–1110.

Segerstrom, S. C., Taylor, S. D., Kemeny, M. F., & Fahey, J. L. (1998). Optimism is associated with mood, coping and immune change in response to stress. *Journal of Personality and Social Psychology, 74*(6), 1646–1655.

Seidenberg, M. S. (1997). Language acquisition and use: Learning and applying probabilistic constraints. *Science, 275,* 1599–1603.

Seif, M. N., & Atkins, A. L. (1979). Some defensive and cognitive aspects of phobias. *Journal of Abnormal Psychology, 88,* 42–51.

Sejnowski, T. J., Koch, C., & Churchland, P. S. (1988). Computational neuroscience. *Science, 24,* 1299–1306.

Seki, S. (1992). The visual image in mind and brain. *Scientific American, 267*(3), 68–76.

Selekman, M. D. (1993). Solution-oriented brief therapy with difficult adolescents. In S. Friedman (Ed.), *The new language of change: Constructive collaboration in psychotherapy* (pp. 138–157). New York: Guildford Press.

Seligman, M. E. P. (1975). *Helplessness.* San Francisco: Freeman.

Seligman, M. E. P. (1976). *Learned helplessness and depression in animals and humans.* Morristown, NJ: General Learning.

Seligman, M. E. P. (1988, August). *Learned helplessness.* G. Stanley Hall lecture at the American Psychological Association Convention, Atlanta.

Seligman, M. E. P. (1991). *Learned optimism.* New York: Knopf.

Seligman, M. E. P. (1995). The effectiveness of psychotherapy. *American Psychologist, 50,* 965–974.

Sell, M. A., Ray, G. E., & Lovelace, L. N. (1995). Preschool children's comprehension of a Sesame Street video tape: The effects of repeated viewing and previewing instructions. *Educational Technology Research and Development, 43*(3), 49–60.

Sell, R. L., Wells, J. A., & Wypij, D. (1995). The prevalence of homosexual behavior and attraction in the United States, the United Kingdom and France: Results of national population-based samples. *Archives of Sexual Behavior, 24,* 235–248.

Selye, H. (1956). *The stress of life.* New York: McGraw-Hill.

Selye, H. (1976). *Stress in health and disease.* London: Butterworth.

Sengel, R. A., & Lovallo, W. R. (1983). Effects of cueing on immediate and recent memory in schizophrenics. *Journal of Nervous and Mental Disease, 171,* 426–430.

Seudfeld, P., & Coren, S. (1989). Perceptual isolation, sensory deprivation, and rest: Moving introductory psychology texts out of the 1950s. *Canadian Psychology, 30*(1), 17–29.

Sevcik, R. A., & Savage-Rumbaugh, E. S. (1994). Language comprehension and use by great apes. *Language and Communication, 14,* 37–58.

Severiens, S., & Ten-Dam, G. (1997). Gender and gender identity differences in learning styles. *Educational Psychology, 17*(1/2), 79–93.

Shadish, W. R., Montgomery, L. M., Wilson, P., Wilson, M. R., Bright, I., & Okwumabua, T. (1993). Effects of family and marital psychotherapies: A meta-analysis. *Journal of Consulting and Clinical Psychology, 61,* 992–1002.

Shallice, T., Fletcher, P., Frith, C. D., Grasby, P., Frackowiak, R. S. J., & Dolan, R. J. (1994). Brain regions associated with acquisition and retrieval of verbal episodic memory. *Nature, 368*, 633–635.

Shamir, B. (1992). Attribution of influence and charisma to the leader: The romance of leadership revisited. *Journal of Applied Social Psychology, 22*, 386–407.

Shanab, M. E., & Yahya, K. A. (1978). A cross-cultural study of obedience. *Bulletin of the Psychonomic Society, 11*, 267–269.

Shapiro, D. A., Barkham, M., Rees, A., Hardy, G. E., Reynolds, S., & Startup, M. (1994). Effects of treatment duration and severity of depression on the effectiveness of cognitive-behavioral and psychodynamic-interpersonal psychotherapy. *Journal of Consulting and Clinical Psychology, 62*, 522–534.

Sharabany, R., Gershoni, R., & Hofman, J. E. (1981). Girlfriend, boyfriend: Age and sex differences in intimate friendship. *Developmental Psychology, 17*, 800–808.

Sharit, J., & Czajia, S. J. (1999). Performance of a computer-based troubleshooting task in the banking industry: Examining the effects of age, task experience, and cognitive abilities. *International Journal of Cognitive Ergonomics, 3*(1), 1–22.

Shatz, C. J. (1992, September). The developing brain. *Scientific American*, 61–67.

Shatz, M., & Gelman, R. (1973). The development of communication skills: Modifications in the speech of young children as a function of listener. *Monographs of the Society for Research in Child Development, 38* (2, Serial No. 152).

Shaw, G. M., Shapiro, R. Y., Lock, S., & Jacobs, L. R. (1998). Trends: Crime, the police, and civil liberties. *Public Opinion Quarterly*, 405–426.

Shaw, J. S., III, Bjork, R. A., & Handal, A. (1995). Retrieval-induced forgetting in an eyewitness-memory paradigm. *Psychonomic Bulletin and Review, 2*, 249–253.

Shaywitz, B. A., Shaywitz, S. E., Pugh, K. R., Constable, R. T., Skudlarski, P., Fulbright, R. K., Bronen, R. A., Fletcher, J. M., Shankweiler, D. P., Katz, L., & Gore, J. C. (1995). Sex differences in the functional organization of the brain for language. *Nature, 373*, 607–609.

Shaywitz, S. E. (1996). Dyslexia. *Scientific American, 275*(5), 98–104.

Shaywitz, S. E., Shaywitz, B. A., Pugh, K. R., Fullbright, R. K., & Constable, R. T. (1998). Functional disruption in the organization of the brain for reading in dyslexia. *Proceedings of the National Academy of Sciences, 95*(5), 2636–2641.

Shedler, J., & Block, J. (1990). Adolescent drug use and psychological health. *American Psychologist, 45*, 612–630.

Sheehan, P. W., & Tilden, J. (1983). Effects of suggestibility and hypnosis on accurate and distorted retrieval from memory. *Journal of Experimental Psychology: Learning, Memory and Cognition, 9*(2), 283–293.

Sheehy, G. (1995). *New passages: Mapping your life across time.* New York: Random House.

Sheehy, G. (1998). *Understanding men's passages: Discovering the new map of men's lives.* New York: Random House.

Sheeran, P., Abraham, C., & Orbell, S. (1999). Psychosocial correlates of heterosexual condom use: A meta-analysis. *Psychological Bulletin, 125*(1), 90–132.

Shefler, G., Dasberg, H., & Ben-Shakhar, G. (1995). A randomized controlled outcome and follow-up study of Mann's time-limited psychotherapy. *Journal of Consulting and Clinical Psychology, 63*, 585–593.

Shen, B., & McNaughton, B. L. (1996). Modeling the spontaneous reactivation of experience-specific hippocampal cell assemblies during sleep. *Hippocampus, 6*(6), 685–692.

Shepard, S., & Metzler, D. (1988). Mental rotation: Effects of dimensionality of objects and type of task. Journal of Experimental Psychology: *Human Perception and Performance, 14*, 3–11.

Shepperd, J. A. (1993). Productivity loss in performance groups: A motivation analysis. *Psychological Bulletin, 113*, 67–81.

Sher, L. (1998). The role of the immune system and infection in the effects of psychological factors on the cardiovascular system. *Canadian Journal of Psychiatry, 43*(9), 954–955.

Sheridan, M. S. (1985). Things that go beep in the night: Home monitoring for apnea. *Health and Social Work, 10*, 63–70.

Sherin, J. E., Shiromani, P. J., McCarley, R. W., & Saper, C. B. (1996). Activation of ventrolateral preoptic neurons during sleep. *Science, 271*, 216–219.

Sherman, M., & Key, C. B. (1932). The intelligence of isolated mountain children. *Child Development, 3*, 279–290.

Sherrington, R., Rogaev, E. I., Liang, Y., Rogaeva, E. A., Levesque, G., Ikeda, M., Chi, H., Lin, C., Li, G., Holman, K., Tsuda, T., Mar, L., Foncin, J. F., Bruni, A. C., Montesi, M. P., Sorbi, S., Rainero, I., Pinessi, L., Nee, L., Chumakov, I., Pollen, D., Brookes, A., Sanseau, P., Polinsky, R. J., Wasco, W., Da Silva, H. A. R., Haines, J. L., Pericak-Vance, M. A., Tanzi, R. E., Roses, A. D., Fraser, P. E., Rommens, J. M., & St. George-Hyslop, P. H. (1995). Cloning of a gene bearing missense mutations in early-onset familial Alzheimer's disease. *Nature, 375*, 754–760.

Shiffman, H. R. (1990). *Sensation and perception: An integrated approach*, 3rd ed. New York: John Wiley and Sons.

Shih, M., Pittinsky, T. L., & Ambady, N. (1999). Stereotype susceptibility: Identity salience and shifts in quantitative performance. *American Psychological Society, 10*(1), 80–81.

Shimamura, A. P., Berry, J. M., Mangels, J. A., Rusting, C. L., & Jurica, P. J. (1995). Memory and cognitive abilities in university professors: Evidence for successful aging. *Psychological Article, 6*, 271–277.

Shimamura, A. P., & Squire, L. R. (1986). Memory and metamemory: A study of the feeling-of-knowing phenomenon in amnesic patients. *Journal of Experimental Psychology: Learning, Memory, and Cognition, 12*, 452–460.

Shiner, R. L. (1998). How shall we speak of children's personalities in middle childhood? A preliminary taxonomy. *Psychological Bulletin, 124*(3), 308–332.

Shneidman, E. S. (1994). Clues to suicide, reconsidered. *Suicide and Life-Threatening Behavior, 24*, 395–397.

Shobe, K. K., & Kihlstrom, J. F. (1997). Is traumatic memory special? *Current Directions in Psychological Science, 6*(3), 70–74.

Shore, J. H., Vollmer, W. M., & Tatum, E. L. (1989). Community patterns of posttraumatic stress disorders. *Journal of Nervous and Mental Disease, 177*, 681–685.

Shum, M. S. (1998). The role of temporal landmarks in autobiographical memory processes. *Psychological Bulletin, 124*(3), 423–442.

Shute, V. J., Pellegrino, J. W., Hubert, L., & Reynolds, R. W. (1983). The relationship between androgen levels and human spatial abilities. *Bulletin of the Psychonomic Society, 21*, 465–468.

Si, G., Rethorst, S., & Willimczik, K. (1995). Causal attribution perception in sports achievement: A cross-cultural study on attributional concepts in Germany and China. *Journal of Cross-Cultural Psychology, 26*, 537–553.

Siegel, E. F. (1979). Control of phantom limb pain by hypnosis. *American Journal of Clinical Hypnosis, 21*, 285–286.

Siegel, J. M. (1990). Stressful life events and use of physician services among the elderly: The moderating role of pet ownership. *Journal of Personality and Social Psychology, 58*, 1081–1086.

Siegel, J. M., Aneshensel, C. S., Taub, B., Cantwell, D. P., & Driscoll, A. K. (1998). Adolescent depressed mood in a multiethnic sample. *Journal of Youth and Adolescence, 27*(4), 413–427.

Siegel, S. (1984). Pavlovian conditioning and heroin overdose: Reports by overdose victims. *Bulletin of the Psychonomic Society, 22*(5), 428–430.

Siegel, S. (1988). State dependent learning and morphine tolerance. *Behavioral Neuroscience, 102*, 228–232.

Siegel, S. (1990). Classical conditioning and opiate tolerance and withdrawal. In D. J. K. Balfour (Ed.), *Psychotropic drugs of abuse: International encyclopedia of pharmacology and theraputics*, section 130. Elmsford, NY: Pergamon Press.

Siegel, S., & Allan, L. G. (1996). The widespread influence of the Rescorla-Wagner model. *Psychonomic Bulletin and Review, 3*(3), 314–321.

Siegel, S., & MacCrae, J. (1984). Environmental specificity of tolerance. *Trends in Neurosciences, 7*(5), 140–143.

Sigelman, L. (1997). Blacks, whites, and the changing of the guard in black political leadership. In S. A. Tuch & J. K. Martin (Eds.), *Racial attitudes in the 1990s: Continuity and change.* Westport, CT: Praeger.

Sigman, M. (1995). Nutrition and child development: More food for thought. *Current Directions in Psychological Science, 4*, 52–55.

Silverman, B. G. (1992). Modeling and critiquing the confirmation bias in human reasoning. *IEEE Transactions on Systems, Man, and Cybernetics, 22*(5), 972–982.

Silverman, L. H. (1983). The subliminal psychodynamic activation method: Overview and comprehensive listing of studies. In J. Masling (Ed.), *Empirical studies of psychoanalytic theories* (Vol. 1, pp. 69–100). Hillsdale, NJ: Erlbaum.

Simons, A. D., Gordon, J. S., Monroe, S. M., & Thase, M. (1995). Toward an integration of psychologic, social, and biologic factors in depression. *Journal of Consulting and Clinical Psychology, 63*, 369–377.

Simonton, D. K. (1988). Age and outstanding achievement: What do we know after a century of research? *Psychological Bulletin, 104,* 251–267.

Simpson, J. A. (1990). Influence of attachment styles on romantic relationships. *Journal of Personality and Social Psychology, 59,* 971–980.

Singer, D. G., & Singer, J. L. (1990). *The house of make-believe.* Cambridge, MA: Harvard University Press.

Singer, L. M., Brodzinsky, D. M., Ramsay, D., Steir, M., & Waters, E. (1985). Mother-infant attachment in adoptive families. *Child Development, 56,* 1543–1551.

Singer, W. (1995). Development and plasticity of cortical processing architectures. *Science, 270,* 758–763.

Sinha, S. P., & Mukherjee, N. (1996). The effect of perceived cooperation on personal space requirements. *Journal of Social Psychology, 136*(5), 655–657.

Skaalvik, E. M., & Rankin, R. J. (1994). Gender differences in mathematics and verbal achievement, self-perception and motivation. *British Journal of Educational Psychology, 64,* 419–428.

Skinner, B. F. (1938). *The behavior of organisms.* New York: Appleton-Century-Crofts.

Skinner, B. F. (1948). Superstition in the pigeon. *Journal of Experimental Psychology, 38,* 168–172.

Skinner, B. F. (1988, June). Skinner joins aversives debate. *American Psychological Association APA Monitor,* 22.

Skinner, B. F. (1989). The origins of cognitive thought. *American Psychologist, 44,* 13–18.

Skoog, G., & Skoog, I. (1999). A 40–year follow-up of patients with obsessive-compulsive disorder. *Archives of General Psychiatry, 56,* 121–132.

Slaikeu, K. A. (1990). *Crisis intervention* (2nd ed.). Boston: Allyn & Bacon.

Smart, R., & Peterson, C. (1994). Stability versus transition in women's career development: A test of Levinson's theory. *Journal of Vocational Behavior, 45,* 241–260.

Smith, C. A. (1989). Dimensions of appraisal and physiological response in emotion. *Journal of Personality and Social Psychology, 56,* 339–353.

Smith, E. E. (1997). Working memory: A view from neuroimaging. *Cognitive Psychology, 33*(1), 5–42.

Smith, E. E., Jonides, J., Koeppe, R. A., & Awh, E. (1995). Spatial versus object working memory: PET investigations. *Journal of Cognitive Neuroscience, 7*(3), 337–356.

Smith, K. H., & Rogers, M. (1994). Effectiveness of subliminal messages in television commercials: Two experiments. *Journal of Applied Psychology, 79,* 866–874.

Smith, M. (1996). Aboriginal street gangs in Winnipeg. *Alberta Sweetgrass.* Edmonton.

Smith, M. C. (1983). Hypnotic memory enhancement of witnesses: Does it work? *Psychological Bulletin, 94,* 387–407.

Smith, M. L., Glass, G. V., & Miller, T. I. (1980). *The benefits of psychotherapy.* Baltimore: Johns Hopkins University Press.

Smith, S. L., Wilson, B. J., Kunkel, D., Linz, D., Potter, J., Colvin, C. M., & Donnerstein, E. (1998). *National television violence study. Volume III.* London: Sage Publications.

Smyser, A. A. (1982). Hospices: Their humanistic and economic value. *American Psychologist, 37,* 1260–1262.

Sneed, C. D., McCrae, R. R., & Funder, D. C. (1998). Lay conceptions of the five-factor model and its indicators. *Personality & Social Psychology Bulletin, 24*(2), 115–126.

Snelders, H. J., & Lea, S. E. (1996). Different kinds of work, different kinds of pay: An examination of the overjustification effect. *Journal of Socio-Economics, 25*(4), 517–535.

Sniderman, P. M., & Tetlock, P. E. (1986). Symbolic racism: Problems of motive attribution in political analysis. *Journal of Social Issues, 42*(2), 129–150.

Snowden, L. R., & Cheung, F. K. (1990). Use of inpatient mental health services by members of ethnic minority groups. *American Psychologist, 45,* 347–355.

Snyder, C. R., & Higgins, R. L. (1988). Excuses: Their effective role in the negotiation of reality. *Psychological Bulletin, 104,* 23–35.

Snyder, D. K., Wills, R. M., & Grady-Fletcher, A. (1991). Long-term effectiveness of behavioral versus insight-oriented marital therapy: A 4–year follow-up study. *Journal of Consulting and Clinical Psychology, 59,* 138–141.

Snyder, S. H. (1980). Brain peptides as neurotransmitters. *Science, 209,* 976–983.

Soares, J. C., & Mann, J. (1997). The functional neuroanatomy of mood disorders. *Journal of Psychiatric Research, 31*(4), 393–432.

Sobell, M. B., & Sobell, L. C. (1982). Controlled drinking: A concept coming of age. In K. R. Blanstein & J. Polivy (Eds.), *Self-control and self-modification of emotional behavior.* New York: Plenum.

Sogon, S., & Izard, C. (1987). Sex differences in emotion recognition by observing body movements: A case of American students. *Japanese Psychological Research, 29,* 89–93.

Solomon, G. F., Segerstrom, S. C., Grohr, P., Kemeny, M., & Fahey, J. (1997). Shaking up immunity: Psychological and immunologic changes after a natural disaster. *Psychosomatic Medicine, 59*(2), 114–127.

Solomon, P. R., Flynn, D., Mirak, J., Brett, M., Coslov, N., & Groccia, M. E. (1998). Five-year retention of the classically conditioned eyeblink response in young adult, middle-aged, and older humans. *Psychology and Aging, 13*(2), 186–192.

Solowij, N. (1998). *Cannabis and cognitive functioning.* Cambridge, England: Cambridge University Press.

Solso, R. L. (1979). *Cognitive psychology.* New York: Harcourt, Brace Jovanovich.

Sommers-Flanagan, R., Sommers-Flanagan, J., & Davis, B. (1993). What's happening on music television? A gender role content analysis. *Sex Roles, 28,* 745–754.

Sonn, C. C., & Fisher, A. T. (1998). Sense of community: Community resilient responses to oppression and change. *Journal of Community Psychology, 26*(5), 457–472.

Sorce, J. F., & Emde, R. N. (1981). Mother's presence is not enough: Effect of emotional availability on infant exploration. *Developmental Psychology, 17,* 737–745.

Sosik, J. J., Kahai, S. S., & Avolio, B. J. (1998). Transformational leadership and dimensions of creativity: Motivating idea generation in computer-mediated groups. *Creativity Research Journal, 11*(2), 111–121.

Southwick, S. M., & Yehuda, R. (1993). The interaction between pharmacotherapy and psychotherapy in the treatment of posttraumatic stress disorder. *American Journal of Psychotherapy, 47,* 404–410.

Spangler, W. D. (1992). Validity of questionnaire and TAT measures of need for achievement: Two meta-analyses. *Psychological Bulletin, 112,* 140–154.

Spanos, N. P. (1983). The hidden observer as an experimental creation. *Journal of Personal and Social Psychology, 44*(1), 170–176.

Spanos, N. P. (1991). A sociocognitive approach to hypnosis. In S. J. Lynn & J. W. Rhue (Eds.), *Theories of hypnosis: Current models and perspectives* (pp. 324–361). New York: Guilford Press.

Spears, R., & Haslam, S. A. (1997). Stereotyping and the burden of cognitive load. In R. Spears (Ed.), *The social psychology of stereotyping and group life.* Oxford, England: Blackwell Publishers, Inc.

Specker, S., de Zwaan, M., Raymond, N., & Mitchell, J. (1994). Psychopathology in subgroups of obese women with and without binge eating disorder. *Comprehensive Psychiatry, 35,* 185–190.

Sperling, G. (1960). The information available in brief visual presentations. *Psychological Monographs, 15,* 201–293.

Sperry, R. W. (1985). Consciousness, personal identity, and the divided brain. In D. F. Benson & E. Zaidel (Eds.), *The dual brain: Hemispheric specialization in humans* (pp. 11–26). New York: Guilford.

Speth, C., & Brown, R. (1990). Effects of college students' learning styles and gender on their test preparation strategies. *Applied Cognitive Psychology, 4,* 189–202.

Sporer, S. L. (1993). Eyewitness identification accuracy, confidence, and decision times in simultaneous and sequential lineups. *Journal of Applied Psychology, 78,* 22–33.

Sporer, S. L., Penrod, S., Read, D., & Cutler, B. (1995). Choosing, confidence, and accuracy: A meta-analysis of the confidence-accuracy relation in eyewitness identification studies. *Psychological Bulletin, 118,* 315–327.

Sprecher, S. (1999). "I love you more today than yesterday": Romantic partners' perceptions of changes in love and related affect over time. *Journal of Personality and Social Psychology, 76*(1), 46–53.

Sprecher, S., Aron, A., Hatfield, E., Cortese, A., Potapova, E., & Levitskaya, A. (1992, July). Love: American style, Russian style, and Japanese style. Paper presented at the Sixth International Conference on Personal Relationships, Orono, Maine.

Sprecher, S., Sullivan, Q., & Hatfield, E. (1994). Mate selection preferences: Gender differences examined in a national sample. *Journal of Personality and Social Psychology, 66,* 1074–1080.

Sprock, J., & Yoder, C. Y. (1997). Women and depression: An update on the report of the APA Task Force. *Sex Roles, 36*(5/6), 269–303.

Squire, L. R. (1987). *Memory and brain.* New York: Oxford University Press.

Srinivas, K. (1996). Size and reflection effects in priming: A test of transfer-appropriate processing. *Memory and Cognition, 24*(4), 441–452.

Stagner, R. (1988). *A history of psychological theories.* New York: Macmillan.

Stajkovic, A. D., & Luthans, F. (1998). Self-efficacy and work-related performance: A meta-analysis. *Psychological Bulletin, 124*(2), 240–261.

Stake, J. E. (1997). Integrating expressiveness and instrumentality in real-life settings: A new perspective on the benefits of androgyny. *Sex Roles, 37*(7/8), 541–564.

Standing, L. (1973). Learning 10,000 pictures. *Quarterly Journal of Experimental Psychology, 25,* 207–222.

Standing, L., Conezio, J., & Haber, R. N. (1970). Perception and memory for pictures: Single-trial learning of 2500 visual stimuli. *Psychonomic Science, 19*(2), 73–34.

Stark, R. (1997). A taxonomy of religious experience. In B. Spilka, D. N. McIntosh, et al. (Eds.), *The psychology of religion: Theoretical approaches* (pp. 209–221). Boulder, CO: Westview Press.

Starkey, P. (1992). The early development of numerical reasoning. *Cognition, 43*(2), 93–126.

Stasson, M., & Fishbein, M. (1990). The relation between perceived risk and preventive action: A within-subject analysis of perceived driving risk and intentions to wear seatbelts. *Journal of Applied Social Psychology, 20,* 1541–1557.

Staszewski, J. J. (1987). The psychological reality of retrieval structures: An investigation of expert knowledge (doctoral dissertation, Cornell University, 1987). *Dissertation Abstracts International, 48,* 2168B.

Staszewski, J. J. (1988). Skilled memory and expert mental calculation. In M. T. H. Chi, R. Glaser, & M. J. Farr (Eds.), *The nature of expertise.* Hillsdale, NJ: Erlbaum.

Statistics Canada (1995). Canadian Statistics—Prevalence of depression, by age and sex. http://www.statcan.ca/english/Pgdb/People/Health/health35.html.

Statistics Canada (1995). *National population health survey.* Ottawa: Statistics Canada.

Statistics Canada (1996). *CANSIM, Matrix 6367.* http://www.statcan.ca/english/Pgdb/People/population/demo10a.htm.

Statistics Canada (1996). *Catalogue no. 82–221–XDE.* Age-specific fertility rate table.

Statistics Canada (1998). Projected population by sex and age group, for Canada (based on population July 1, 1993), annual, in thousands. *Matrix 6900,* SDS 3602 STC (91–520).

Statistics Canada (1998). Single and multiple ethnic origin responses, 1996 Census. *Nation Tables, 1996 Census.*

Staub, E. (1996). Cultural-societal roots of violence. *American Psychologist, 51,* 117–132.

Steele, C. M. (1997). A threat in the air: How stereotypes shape intellectual identity and performance. *American Psychologist, 52*(6), 613–629.

Steele, C. M., & Aronson, J. (1995). Stereotype threat and the intellectual test performance of African Americans. *Journal of Personality and Social Psychology, 69,* 797–811.

Steele, C. M., & Josephs, R. A. (1990). Alcohol myopia. *American Psychologist, 45,* 921–933.

Stein, M. I. (1974). *Stimulating creativity.* New York: Academic.

Steinberg, L., Dornbusch, S. M., & Brown, B. B. (1992). Ethnic difference in adolescent achievement. *American Psychologist, 47,* 723–729.

Steinberg, L., Dornbusch, S. M., & Brown, B. B. (1993). Ethnic differences in adolescent achievement: An ecological perspective. *Annual Progress in Child Psychiatry and Child Development,* 528–543.

Steinberg, L., Lamborn, S. D., Darling, N., Mounts, N. S., & Dornbusch, S. M. (1994). Over-time changes in adjustment and competence among adolescents from authoritative, authoritarian, indulgent, and neglectful families. *Child Development, 65,* 754–770.

Steinberg, L., Lamborn, S. D., Dornbusch, S. M., & Darling, N. (1992). Impact of parenting practices on adolescent achievement: Authoritative parenting, school involvement, and encouragement to succeed. *Child Development, 63,* 1266–1281.

Steinberg, M. (1995). *Handbook for the assessment of dissociation: A clinical guide.* Washington, DC: American Psychiatric Press.

Steinberg, M., Cicchetti, D., Buchanan, J., Rakfeldt, J., & Rounsaville, B. (1994). Distinguishing between multiple personality disorder (dissociative identity disorder) and schizophrenia using the structured clinical interview for DSM-IV dissociative disorders. *Journal of Nervous and Mental Disease, 182,* 495–502.

Steiner, I. D. (1982). Heuristic models of groupthink. In M. Brandstatter, J. H. Davis, & G. Stocker-Kreichgauer (Eds.), *Group decision making.* New York: Academic.

Stephan, C. W., & Langlois, J. H. (1984). Baby beautiful: Adult attributions of infant competence as a function of infant attractiveness. *Child Development, 55,* 576–585.

Stephenson, J. S. (1985). *Death, grief, and mourning: Individual and social realities.* New York: Macmillan.

Steptoe, A., Kimbell, J., & Basford, P. (1998). Exercise and the experience and appraisal of daily stressors: A naturalistic study. *Journal of Behavioral Medicine, 21*(4), 363–374.

Stern, K., & McClintock, M. K. (1998). Regulation of ovulation by human pheromones. *Nature, 392,* 126–127.

Sternberg, R. J. (1984). The Kaufman Assessment Battery for Children: An information-processing analysis and critique. *Journal of Special Education, 18,* 269–279.

Sternberg, R. J. (1985). *Beyond IQ.* Cambridge, England: Cambridge University Press.

Sternberg, R. J. (1986a). *Intelligence applied: Understanding and increasing your intellectual skills.* New York: Harcourt Brace Jovanovich.

Sternberg, R. J. (1986b). A triangular theory of love. *Psychological Review, 93,* 119–135.

Sternberg, R. J. (1995). For whom the bell curve tolls: A review of The Bell Curve. *Psychological Science, 6,* 257–261.

Sternberg, R. J. (1997a). The concept of intelligence and its role in lifelong learning and success. *American Psychologist, 52*(10), 1030–1037.

Sternberg, R. J. (1997b). *Thinking styles.* Cambridge, England: Cambridge University Press.

Sternberg, R. J. (1998). A balance theory of wisdom. *Review of General Psychology, 2*(4), 347–365.

Sternberg, R. J., & Lubart, T. I. (1993). Creative giftedness: A multivariate investment approach. *Gifted Child Quarterly, 37*(1), 7–15.

Sternberg, R. J., & Lubart, T. I. (1996). Investing in creativity. *American Psychologist, 51*(7), 677–688.

Sternberg, R. J., & Wagner, R. K. (1993). The g-ocentric view of intelligence and job performance is wrong. *Current Directions in Psychological Science, 2,* 1–4.

Sternberg, R. J., Wagner, R. K., Williams, W. M., & Horvath, J. A. (1995). Testing common sense. *American Psychologist, 50,* 912–927.

Sternberg, R. J., & Williams, W. M. (1997). Does the Graduate Record Examination predict meaningful success in the graduate training of psychologists? *American Psychologist, 52*(6), 630–641.

Sterrett, E. A. (1998). Use of a job club to increase self-efficacy: A case study of return to work. *Journal of Employment Counseling, 35*(2), 69–78.

Stewart, A. J., & Ostrove, J. M. (1998). Women's personality in middle age: Gender, history, and midcourse corrections. *American Psychologist, 53*(11), 1185–1194.

Stewart, A. J., & Vandewater, E. A. (1998). The course of generativity. In D. P. McAdams, E. de St. Aubin, et al. (Eds.), *Generativity and adult development: How and why we care for the next generation* (pp. 75–100). Washington, DC: American Psychological Association.

Stigler, J. W., & Baranes, R. (1988). Culture and mathematics learning. In E. Rothkopf (Ed.), *Review of Research in Education, 15* (pp. 253–306). Washington, DC: American Educational Research Association.

Stilwell, B. M., Galvin, M. R., Kopta, S. M., & Padgett, R. J. (1998). Moral volition: The fifth and final domain leading to an integrated theory of conscience understanding. *Journal of the American Academy of Child and Adolescent Psychiatry, 37*(2), 202–210.

Stimpson, D., Jensen, L., & Neff, W. (1992). Cross-cultural gender differences in preference for a caring morality. *Journal of Social Psychology, 132,* 317–322.

Stipek, D., Givvin, K. B., Aslmon, J. M., & MacGyvers, V. L. (1998). Can a teacher intervention improve classroom practices and student motivation in mathematics? *Journal of Experimental Education, 66*(4), 319–337.

Stitzer, M. L. (1988). Drug abuse in methadone patients reduced when rewards/punishments clear. *Alcohol, Drug Abuse, and Mental Health, 14,* 1.

Stoff, D. M., & Cairns, R. B. (1996). *Aggression and violence: Genetic, neurobiological, and biosocial perspectives.* Mahwah, NJ: Lawrence Erlbaum Associates, Inc.

Stokols, D. (1995). The paradox of environmental psychology. *American Psychologist, 50,* 821–837.

Stoléru, S., Grégoire, M. C., Gérard, D., Decety, J., Lafarge, E., Cinotti, L., Lavenne, F., LeBars, D., Vernet-Maury, E., Rada, H., Collet, C., Mazoyer, B., Forest, M. G., Magnin, F., Spira, A., & Comar, D. (1999). Neuroanatomical correlates of visually evoked sexual arousal in human males. *Archives of Sexual Behavior, 28*(1), 1–19.

Stone, J., Perry, Z. W., & Darley, J. M. (1997). "White men can't jump": Evidence for the perceptual confirmation of racial stereotypes following a basketball game. *Basic and Applied Social Psychology, 19*(3), 291–306.

Stone, J., Wiegand, A. W., Cooper, J., & Aronson, E. (1997). When exemplification fails: Hypocrisy and the motive for self-integrity. *Journal of Personality and Social Psychology, 72*(1), 54–65.

Stone, M. H. (1980). *The borderline syndromes.* New York: McGraw-Hill.

Stone, V. E., Nisenon, L., Eliassen, J. C., & Gazzaniga, M. S. (1996). Left hemisphere representations of emotional facial expressions. *Neuropsychologia, 34*(1), 23–29.

Straube, E. R., & Oades, R. D. (1992). *Schizophrenia: Empirical research and findings.* San Diego: Academic Press, Inc.

Strayer, D. L, & Kramer, A. R. (1990). Attentional requirements of automatic and controlled processing. *Journal of Experimental Psychology: Learning, Memory, and Cognition, 16,* 67–82.

Streissguth, A. P., Barr, H. M., & Martin, D. C. (1983). Maternal alcohol use and neonatal habituation assessed with the Brazelton Scale. *Child Development, 54,* 1109–1118.

Streissguth, A. P., Barr, H. M., Sampson, P. D., Darby, B. L., & Martin, D. C. (1989). IQ at age 4 in relation to maternal alcohol use and smoking during pregnancy. *Developmental Psychology, 25,* 3–11.

Stretch, R. H. (1990). Post traumatic stress disorder and the Canadian Vietnam veteran. *Journal of Traumatic Stress, 3*(2), 239–254.

Stretch, R. H. (1991). Psychosocial readjustment of Canadian Vietnam veterans. *Journal of Consulting and Clinical Psychology, 59*(1), 188–189.

Strickland, B. R. (1992). Women and depression. *Psychological Science, 1,* 132–135.

Striegel-Moore, R. H., Silberstein, L. R., & Rodin, J. (1993). The social self in bulimia nervosa. Public self-consciousness, social anxiety, and perceived fraudulence. *Journal of Abnormal Psychology, 102*(2), 297–303.

Stringer, P. (1998). One night Vygotsky had a dream: "Children learning to think . . ." and implications for educational psychologists. *Educational and Child Psychology, 15*(2), 14–20.

Stritzke, W. G. K., Lang, A. R., & Patrick, C. J. (1996). Beyond stress and arousal: A reconceptualization of alcohol-emotion relations with reference to psychophysiological methods. *Psychological Bulletin, 120*(3), 376–395.

Stroop, J. R. (1935). Studies of interference in serial verbal reactions. *Journal of Experimental Psychology, 18,* 643–662.

Stuart, E. W., Shimp, T. A., & Engle, R. W. (1987). Classical conditioning of consumer attitudes: Four experiments in an advertising context. *Journal of Consumer Research, 14,* 334–349.

Sturges, J. S. (1994). Family dynamics. In J. L. Ronch, W. V. Ornum, & N. C. Stilwell (Eds.), *The counseling sourcebook: A practical reference on contemporary issues* (pp. 358–372). New York: Crossroad.

Styron, W. (1992). *Darkness visible: A memoir of madness.* New York: Vintage Books.

Suarez, E. C., & Williams, R. B. (1989). Situational determinants of cardiovascular and emotional reactivity in high and low hostile men. *Psychosomatic Medicine, 51,* 404–418.

Suddath, R. L, Christinson, G. W., Torrey, E. F., Casanova, M. F., & Weinberger, D. R. (1990). Anatomical abnormalities in the brains of monozygotic twins discordant for schizophrenia. *New England Journal of Medicine, 322,* 789–794.

Sue, S. (1988). Psychotherapeutic services for ethnic minorities. *American Psychologist, 43,* 301–308.

Suedfeld, P. (1990). Restricted environmental stimulation and smoking cessation: A 15–year progress report. *International Journal of the Addictions, 25,* 861–888.

Suedfeld, P., & Bruno, T. (1990). Flotation REST and imagery in the improvement of athletic performance. *Journal of Sport and Exercise Psychology, 12*(1), 82–85.

Suedfeld, P., Collier, D. E., & Hartnett, B. D. (1993). Enhancing perceptual-motor accuracy through flotation REST. *Sport Psychologist, 7*(2), 151–159.

Suedfeld, P., & Coren, S. (1989). Perceptual isolation, sensory deprivation, and rest: Moving introductory psychology texts out of the 1950s. *Canadian Psychology, 30*(1), 17–29.

Suedfeld, P., & Eich, E. (1995). Autobiographical memory and affect under conditions of reduced environmental stimulation. *Journal of Experimental Psychology, 15*(4), 321–326.

Suedfeld, P., & Schwartz, G. (1981). *Restricted environmental stimulation therapy (REST) as a treatment for autistic children.* Annual meeting of the American Psychological Association, Los Angeles, California.

Sullivan, M. J. L., Bishop, S. R., & Pivik, J. (1995). The pain catastrophizing scale: Development and validation. *Psychological Assessment, 7,* 524–532.

Sullivan, P. F., Bulik, C. M., Fear, J. L., & Pickering, A. (1998). Outcome of anorexia nervosa: A case-control study. *American Journal of Psychiatry, 155*(7), 939–946.

Sulloway, F. J. (1996). *Born to rebel: Birth order, family dynamics, and creative lives.* New York: Pantheon Books.

Suls, J., & Wan, C. K. (1989a). Effects of sensory and procedural information on coping with stressful medical procedures and pain: A meta-analysis. *Journal of Consulting and Clinical Psychology, 57,* 372–379.

Suls, J., & Wan, C. K. (1989b). The relation between Type A behavior and chronic emotional distress: A meta-analysis. *Journal of Personality and Social Psychology, 57,* 503–512.

Suls, J., & Wan, C. K. (1993). The relationship between trait hostility and cardiovascular reactivity: A quantitative review and analysis. *Psychophysiology, 30,* 615–626.

Summers, T. P., & Hendrix, W. H. (1991). Modeling the role of pay equity perceptions: A field study. *Journal of Occupational Psychology, 64,* 145–157.

Sun, L-C., & Roopnarine, J. L. (1996). Mother-infant, father-infant interaction and involvement in childcare and household labor among Taiwanese families. *Infant Behavior and Development, 19*(1), 121–129.

Sutker, P. B. & Allain, A. N. (1988). Issues in personality conceptualizations of addictive behaviors. *Journal of Consulting and Clinical Psychology, 56,* 172–182.

Sutker, P. B., Davis, J. M., Uddo, M., & Ditta, S. R. (1995). War zone stress, personal resources, and PTSD in Persian Gulf War returnees. *Journal of Abnormal Psychology, 104,* 444–452.

Suzuki, L. A., & Valencia, R. (1997). Race-ethnicity and measured intelligence: Educational implications. *American Psychologist, 52*(10), 1103–1114.

Swaab, D. F., & Hofman, M. A. (1995). Sexual differentiation of the human hypothalamus in relation to gender and sexual orientation. *Trends in Neuroscience, 18,* 264–270.

Swets, J. A. (1992). The science of choosing the right decision threshold in high-stakes diagnostics. *American Psychologist, 47,* 522–532.

Swim, J. K., Aikin, K. J., Hall, W. S., & Hunter, B. A. (1995). Sexism and racism: Old-fashioned and modern prejudices. *Journal of Personality and Social Psychology, 68,* 199–214.

Swim, J., Borgida, E., Maruyama, G., & Myers, D. G. (1989). Joan McKay versus John McKay: Do gender stereotypes bias evaluations? *Psychological Bulletin, 105,* 409–429.

Szasz, T. (1984). *The therapeutic state: Psychiatry in the mirror of current events* (p. 502). Buffalo, NY: Prometheus.

Szasz, T. (1987). *Insanity: The idea and its consequences.* New York: Wiley.

Szymanski, K., & Harkins, S. G. (1993). The effect of experimenter evaluation on self-evaluation within the social loafing paradigm. *Journal of Experimental Social Psychology, 29,* 268–286.

Tamminen, K. (1994). Religious experiences in childhood and adolescence: A view of religious development between the ages of 7 and 20. *International Journal for the Psychology of Religion, 4*(2), 61–85.

Tanda, G., Pontieri, F. E., & Di Chiara, G. (1997). Cannabinoid and heroin activation of mesolimbic dopamine transmission by a common μ1 opioid receptor mechanism. *Science, 276,* 2048–2049.

Tarter, R. E., & Vanyukov, M. (1994). Alcoholism: A development disorder. *Journal of Consulting and Clinical Psychology, 62*(6), 1096–1107.

Tataranni, P. A., Young, J. B., Bogardus, C., & Ravussin, E. (1997). A low sympathoadrenal activity is associated with body weight gain and development of central adiposity in Pima Indian men. *Obesity Research, 5*(4), 341–347.

Taubes, G. (1998). As obesity rates rise, experts struggle to explain why. *Science, 280,* 1367–1368.

Taylor, S. E., Repetti, R. L., & Seeman, T. (1997). Health psychology: What is an unhealthy environment and how does it get under the skin? In J. T. Spence, J. M. Darley, & D. J. Foss (Eds.), *Annual Review of Psychology, Vol. 48.* Palo Alto, CA: Annual Reviews, Inc.

Teevan, R. C., & McGhee, P. E. (1972). Childhood development of fear of failure motivation. *Journal of Personality and Social Psychology, 21,* 345–348.

Tempo, P. M., & Saito, A. (1996). Techniques of working with Japanese-American families. In G. Yeo, D. Gallagher-Thompson, et al. (Eds.), *Ethnicity and the dementias* (pp. 109–112). Washington, DC: Taylor & Francis.

Tennen, H., & Affleck, G. (1990). Blaming others for threatening events. *Psychological Bulletin, 108,* 209–232.

Tennov, D. (1981). *Love and limerance.* Briarcliffe Manor, NY: Stein & Day.

Terrace, H. S. (1979, November). How Nim Chimpski changed my mind. *Psychology Today,* 65–76.

Terrace, H. S. (1980). *Nim.* New York: Knopf.

Terrace, H. S. (1985). In the beginning was the "name." *American Psychologist, 40,* 1011–1028.

Teske, J. A. (1988). Seeing her looking at you: Acquaintance and variation in the judgment of gaze depth. *American Journal of Psychology, 101,* 239–257.

Tesser, A., & Beach, S. R. H. (1998). Life events, relationship quality, and depression: An investigation of judgment discontinuity in vivo. *Journal of Personality and Social Psychology, 74*(1), 36–52.

Thelen, E. (1994). Three-month-old infants can learn task-specific patterns of interlimb coordination. *Psychological Science, 5,* 280–285.

Theorell, T., Svensson, J., Knox, S., Waller, D., & Alvarez, M. (1986). Young men with high blood pressure report few recent life events. *Journal of Psychosomatic Research, 30,* 243–249.

Thomas, A., & Chess, S. (1977). *Temperament and development.* New York: Brunner/Mazel.

Thompson, R. F. (1991). Are memory traces localized or distributed? *Neuropsychologia, 29,* 571–582.

Thompson, R. F., & Krupa, D. J. (1994). Organization of memory traces in the mammalian brain. *Annual Review of Neuroscience, 17,* 519–549.

Thompson, S. C., Sobolew-Shubin, A., Galbraith, M. E., Schwankovsky, L., & Cruzen, D. (1993). Maintaining perceptions of control: Finding perceived control in low-control circumstances. *Journal of Personality and Social Psychology, 64,* 293–304.

Thompson, T. L., & Zerbinos, E. (1997). Television cartoons: Do children notice it's a boy's world? *Sex Roles, 37*(5/6), 415–432.

Thompson, V. A. (1996). Reasoning from false premises: The role of soundness in making logical deductions. *Canadian Journal of Experimental Psychology, 50*(3), 315–319.

Tice, D. M., & Baumeister, R. F. (1985). Masculinity inhibits helping in emergencies: Personality does predict the bystander effect. *Journal of Personality and Social Psychology, 49,* 420–428.

Tice, D. M., & Baumeister, R. F. (1997). Longitudinal study of procrastination performance, stress, and health: The costs and benefits of dawdling. *American Psychological Society, 8*(6), 454–458.

Tilley, A., & Warren, P. (1983). Retrieval from semantic memory at different times of day. *Journal of Experimental Psychology: Learning, Memory, and Cognition, 9,* 718–724.

Timberlake, W., & Farmer-Dougan, V. A. (1991). Reinforcement in applied settings: Figuring out ahead of time what will work. *Psychological Bulletin, 110,* 379–391.

Tjosvold, D. (1987). Participation: A close look at its dynamics. *Journal of Management, 13,* 739–750.

Tomoyasu, N., Bovbjerg, D. H., & Jacobsen, P. B. (1996). Conditioned reactions to cancer chemotherapy: Percent reinforcement predicts anticipatory nausea. *Physiology & Behavior, 59*(2), 273–276.

Torrey, E. F., Bowler, A. E., Taylor, E. H., & Gottesman, I. I. (1994). *Schizophrenia and manic-depressive disorder: The biological roots of mental illness as revealed by the Landmark study of identical twins.* New York: Basic Books.

Tovee, M. J., & Cohen-Tovee, E. M. (1993). The neural substrates of face processing models: A review. *Cognitive Neuropsychology, 10*(6), 505–528.

Tracy, J. A., Thompson, J. K., Krupa, D. J., & Thompson, R. F. (1998). Evidence of plasticity in the pontocerebellar conditioned stimulus pathway during classical conditioning of the eyeblink response in the rabbit. *Behavioral Neuroscience, 112*(2), 267–285.

Tracy, R. J., & Barker, C. H. (1994). A comparison of visual versus auditory imagery in predicting word recall. *Imagination, Cognition and Personality, 13,* 147–161.

Trappey, C. (1996). A meta-analysis of consumer choice and subliminal advertising. *Psychology and Marketing, 13*(5), 517–530.

Travis, C. B. (1988). *Women and health psychology: Biomedical issues.* Hillsdale, NJ: Erlbaum.

Trickett, P. K., & Putnam, F. W. (1993). Impact of child sexual abuse on females: Toward a developmental, psychobiological integration. *Psychological Science, 4,* 81–87.

Trickett, P. K., & Susman, E. J. (1988). Parental perceptions of child-rearing practices in physically abusive and nonabusive families. *Developmental Psychology, 24,* 270–276.

Trites, D., Galbraith, F. D., Sturdavent, M., & Leckwart, J. F. (1970). Influence of nursing-unit design on the activities and subjective feelings of nursing personnel. *Environment and Behavior, 2,* 203–234.

Tronick, E. Z. & Cohn, J. F. (1989). Infant-mother face-to-face interaction: Age and gender differences in coordination and the occurrence of miscoordination. *Child Development, 60,* 85–92.

Tronick, E. Z., Morelli, G. A., & Ivey, P. K. (1992). The Efe forager infant and toddler's pattern of social relationships: Multiple and simultaneous. *Developmental Psychology, 28,* 568–577.

True, W. R., Rice, J., Eisen, S. A., Heath, A. C., Goldberg, J., Lyons, M. J., & Nowak, J. (1993). A twin study of genetic and environmental contributions to liability for posttraumatic stress symptoms. *Archives of General Psychiatry, 50,* 257–264.

Trull, T. J., & Geary, D. C. (1997). Comparison of the Big-Five Factor structure across samples of Chinese and American adults. *Journal of Personality Assessment, 69*(2), 324–341.

Tryon, W. W. (1998). A neural network explanation of posttraumatic stress disorder. *Journal of Anxiety Disorders, 12*(4), 373–385.

Tsai, M., & Uemura, A. (1988). Asian Americans: The struggles, the conflicts, and the successes. In P. Bronstein & K. Quina (Eds.), *Teaching a psychology of people.* Washington, DC: American Psychological Association.

Tuckman, A. (1996). Isn't it about time psychologists were granted prescription privileges? *Psychotherapy in Private Practice, 15*(2), 1–14.

Tukali-Williams, J., & Carrillo, J. (1995). The impact of psychosocial stressors on African-American and Latino preschoolers. *Journal of the National Medical Association, 87*(7), 473–478.

Tulving, E. (1972). Episodic and semantic memory. In E. Tulving & W. Donaldson (Eds.), *Organization of memory.* New York: Academic Press.

Tulving, E. (1993). What is episodic memory? *Current Directions in Psychological Science, 2,* 67–70.

Tulving, E., Kapur, S., Craik, F. I. M., Moscovitch, M., & Houle, S. (1994). Hemispheric encoding/retrieval asymmetry in episodic memory: Positron emission tomography findings. *Proceedings of the National Academy of Sciences USA, 91,* 2016–2020.

Tulving, E., Schacter, D. L., & Stark, H. A. (1982). Priming effects in word fragment completion are independent of recognition memory. *Journal of Experimental Psychology: Learning, Memory, and Cognition, 8,* 336–342.

Turk, D. C., Meichenbaum, D., & Genest, M. (1983). *Pain and behavioral medicine: A cognitive-behavioral perspective.* New York: Guilford.

Turkheimer, E. (1991). Individual and group differences in adoption studies of IQ. *Psychological Bulletin, 110,* 392–405.

Tversky, A., & Kahneman, D. (1973). Availability: A heuristic for judging frequency and probability. *Cognitive Psychology, 4,* 207–232.

Twenge, J. M. (1997). Changes in masculine and feminine traits over time: A meta-analysis. *Sex Roles, 36*(5/6), 305–309.

Tyler, T. R., & Schuller, R. A. (1991). Aging and attitude change. *Journal of Personality and Social Psychology, 61*(5), 689–697.

Tziner, A., & Murphy, K. R. (1999). Additional eveidence of attitudinal influences in performance appraisal. *Journal of Business and Psychology, 13*(3), 407–419.

Uba, L. (1994). *Asian Americans: Personality patterns, identity, and mental health.* New York: Guilford.

Umberson, D., Wortman, C. B., & Kessler, R. C. (1992). Widowhood and depression: Explaining long-term gender differences in vulnerability. *Journal of Health and Social Behavior, 33,* 10–24.

Underwood, G. (1994). Subliminal perception on TV. *Nature, 370,* 103.

Unicef (1998). *The progress of nations.*

United States House of Representatives. (1997). *Road rage: Causes and dangers of aggressive driving*. The Subcommittee on Surface Transportation Hearing. (Press Release).

Ursano, R. J., Fullerton, C. S., Kao, T., & Bhartiya, V.R. (1995). Longitudinal assessment of posttraumatic stress disorder and depression after exposure to traumatic death. *Journal of Nervous and Mental Disease, 183,* 36–42.

U.S. Department of Labor. (1998). Equal pay: A thirty-five year perspective. Available World Wide Web: <www.dol.gov/dol/wb/>

Vahava, O., Morell, R., Lynch, E. D., Weiss, S., Kagan, M. E., Ahituv, N., et al. (1998). Mutation in transcription factor POU4F3 associated with inherited progressive hearing loss in humans. *Science, 279,* 1950–1954.

Vaillant, G. E., & Milofsky, E. S. (1982). The etiology of alcoholism: A prospective view. *American Psychologist, 37,* 494–503.

Valenstein, E. S. (1998). *Blaming the brain: The truth about drugs and mental health*. New York: The Free Press.

Valins, S. (1966). Cognitive effects of false heart-rate feedback. *Journal of Personality and Social Psychology, 4,* 400–408.

Valins, S., & Baum, A. (1973). Residential group size, social interaction, and crowding. *Environment and Behavior, 5,* 421–435.

Valkenburg, P. M., & van der Voort, T. H. A. (1994). Influence of TV on daydreaming and creative imagination: A review of research. *Psychological Bulletin, 116,* 316–339.

Vandell, D. L., Henderson, V. K., & Wilson, K. S. (1988). A longitudinal study of children with day-care experiences of varying quality. *Child Development, 59,* 1286–1292.

Van Flect, D. D., & Atwater, L. (1997). Gender-neutral names: Don't be so sure! *Sex Roles, 37*(1/2), 111–123.

Vargha-Khadem, F., Gadian, D. G., Watkins, K. E., Connelly, A., Van Paesschen, W., & Mishkin, M. (1997). Differential effects of early hippocampal pathology on episodic and semantic memory. *Science, 277,* 376–380.

Vartanian, L. R., & Powlishta, K. K. (1996). A longitudinal examination of the social cognitive foundations of adolescent egocentrism. *Journal of Early Adolescence, 16*(2), 157–178.

Veenhoven, R. (1993). *Happiness in nations*. Rotterdam, Netherlands: Risbo.

Veniegas, R. C., & Peplau, L. A. (1997). Power and the quality of same-sex friendships. *Psychology of Women Quarterly, 21*(2), 279–297.

Verhaeghen, P., & Salthouse, T. A. (1997). Meta-analyses of age-cognition relations in adulthood: Estimates of linear and nonlinear age effects and structural models. *Psychological Bulletin, 122*(3), 231–249.

Vernon, P. (1979). *Intelligence: Heredity and environment*. San Francisco: W. H. Freeman.

Vinar, O. (1997). An attempt to prevent the sequelae of the posttraumatic stress disorder: Experience from the 1997 flood in Moravia. *Homeostasis in Health and Disease, 38*(4), 165–168.

Vitiello, M. V. (1989). Unraveling sleep disorders of the aged. Paper presented at the annual meeting of the Association of Professional Sleep Societies, Washington, DC.

Von Senden, M. (1932). *Raum- und Gestaltauffassung bei operierten: Blindgeborernin vor und nach der Operation*. Leipzig, Germany: Barth.

Vroom, V. H. (1964). *Work and motivation*. New York: Wiley.

Vroom, V. H. (1974). A new look at managerial decision making. *Organizational Dynamics, 5,* 66–80.

Vroom, V. H. (1997). Can leaders learn to lead? In R. P. Vecchio et al. (Eds.), *Leadership: Understanding the dynamics of power and influence in organizations* (pp. 278–291). Notre Dame, IN: University of Notre Dame Press.

Vroom, V. H., & Jago, A. G. (1995). Situation effects and levels of analysis in the study of leader participation. *Leadership Quarterly, 6*(2), 169–181.

Vroom, V. H., & Yetton, P. W. (1973). *Leadership and decision-making*. Pittsburgh: University of Pittsburgh Press.

Vroon, P. (1997). *Smell: The secret seducer*. New York: Farrar, Straus & Giroux.

Vygotsky, L. S. (1962). *Thought and language* (E. Hanfmann & G. Vakar, Eds. and Trans.). Cambridge, MA: MIT Press. (Original work published in 1934.)

Vygotsky, L. S. (1978). *Mind in society: The development of higher mental processes*. Cambridge, MA: Harvard University Press. (Original works published 1930, 1933, and 1935.)

Wacholtz, E. (1996). Can we learn from the clinically significant face processing deficits prosopagnosia and Capgras delusion? *Neuropsychology Review, 6*(4), 203–257.

Waddington, J. L. (1993). Neurodynamics of abnormalities in cerebral metabolism and structure in schizophrenia. *Schizophrenia Bulletin, 19,* 55–69.

Wadsworth, J., McEwan, J., Johnson, A. M., Wellings, K., et al. (1995). Sexual health for women: Some findings of a large national survey discussed. *Sexual and Marital Therapy, 10*(2), 169–188.

Wagner, A. D., Schacter, D. L., Rotte, M., Koutstall, W., Maril, A., Dale, A. M., Rosen, B. R., & Buckner, R. L. (1998). Building memories: Remembering and forgetting of verbal experiences as predicted by brain activity. *Science, 281,* 1188–1192.

Wagner, R. K. (1997). Intelligence, training, and employment. *American Psychologist, 52*(10), 1059–1069.

Walker, E., Hoppes, E., Mednick, S., Emory, E., & Schulsinger, F. (1983). Environmental factors related to schizophrenia in psychophysiologically labile high-risk males. *Journal of Abnormal Psychology, 90,* 313–320.

Walker, E. A. (1989). Psychology and violence against women. *American Psychologist, 44,* 695–702.

Walker, J. L., Walker, L. S., & MacLennan, P. M. (1986). An informal look at farm stress. *Psychological Reports, 59,* 427–430.

Walker, L. E. (1999). Psychology and domestic violence around the world. *American Psychologist, 54*(1), 21–29.

Walker, L. J., & Pitts, R. C. (1998). Naturalistic conceptions of moral maturity. *Developmental Psychology, 34*(3), 403–419.

Walker, L. S., & Walker, J. L. (1987). Stressors and symptoms predictive of distress in farmers. *Family Relations: Journal of Applied Family and Child Studies, 36*(4), 374–378.

Walker-Andrews, A. S. (1986). Intermodal perception of expressive behaviors: Relation of eye and voice? *Developmental Psychology, 22,* 373–377.

Walker-Andrews, A. S. (1997). Infants' perception of expressive behavior: Differentiation of multimodal information. *Psychological Bulletin, 121*(3), 437–456.

Wallbaum, A. B., Rzewnicki, R., & Steele, H. (1991). Progressive muscle relaxation and restricted environmental stimulation therapy for chronic tension headache: A pilot study. *International Journal of Psychosomatics, 38,* Special Issue, 33–39.

Waller, N. G., & Shaver, P. R. (1994). The importance of nongenetic influences on romantic love styles: A twin-family study. *Psychological Science, 5,* 268–274.

Walsh, B. T., & Devlin, M. J. (1998). Eating disorders: Progress and problems. *Science, 280,* 1387–1390.

Walsh, V., & Cowey, A. (1998). Magnetic stimulation studies of visual cognition. *Trends in Cognitive Sciences, 2*(3), 103–110.

Walters, E. E., & Kendler, K. S. (1995). Anorexia nervosa and anorexic-like syndromes in a population-based female twin sample. *American Journal of Psychiatry, 152,* 64–67.

Walton, G. E., & Bower, T. G. R. (1993). Newborns form "prototypes" in less than 1 minute. *Psychological Science, 4,* 203–205.

Wampold, B. E., Monding, G. W., Moody, M., Stich, F., Benson, K., & Ahn, H. (1997). A meta-analysis of outcome studies comparing bona fide psychotherapies: Empirically, "all must have prizes." *Psychological Bulletin, 122*(3), 203–215.

Wandersman, A., & Nation, M. (1998). Urban neighborhoods and mental health: Psychological contributions to understanding toxicity, resilience, and interventions. *American Psychologist, 53*(6), 647–656.

Wandersman, A. H., & Hallman, W. K. (1993). Are people acting irrationally? *American Psychologist, 48,* 681–686.

Ware, R., Rytting, M., & Jenkins, D. (1994). The effect of stress on MBTI scores. *Journal of Psychological Type, 30,* 39–44.

Washton, A. M. (1989). *Cocaine addiction*. New York: Norton.

Watkins, M. J. (1990). Mediationism and the obfuscation of memory. *American Psychologist, 45,* 328–335.

Watson, J. B. (1924). *Behaviorism*. Chicago: University of Chicago Press.

Watson, J. B., & Rayner, R. (1920). Conditioned emotional reactions. *Journal of Experimental Psychology, 3,* 1–14.

Waxer, P. (1990). Cantonese versus Canadian evaluation of directive and non-directive therapy. *Canadian Journal of Counselling, 23*(3), 263–272.

Weaver, C. A., III (1993). Do you need a "flash" to form a flashbulb memory? *Journal of Experimental Psychology: General, 122,* 39–46.

Webb, W. B., & Agnew, H. W., Jr. (1975). The effects on subsequent sleep of an acute restriction of sleep length. *Psychophysiology, 12,* 367–370.

Webster, R. (1995). Why Freud was wrong: Sin, science, and psychoanalysis. New York: Basic Books.

Weidner, G., Friend, R., Ficarrotto, T. J., & Mendell, N. R. (1989). Hostility and cardiovascular reactivity to stress in women and men. *Psychosomatic Medicine, 51*, 36–45.

Weingartner, H. (1977). Human state-dependent learning. In B. T. Ho, D. Richards, & D. L. Chute (Eds.), *Drug discrimination and state-dependent learning*. New York: Academic.

Weingartner, H., Adefris, W., Eich, J. E., & Murphy, D. L. (1976). Encoding-imagery specificity in alcohol state-dependent learning. *Journal of Experimental Psychology, 2*, 83–87.

Weinstein, C. S., & Mignano, A. (1993). *Organizing the elementary school classroom: Lessons from research and practice*. New York: McGraw-Hill.

Weintraub, S. (1987). Risk factors in schizophrenia: The Stony Brook High-Risk Project. *Schizophrenia Bulletin, 13*, 439–443.

Weisfeld, G. E. (1993). The adaptive value of humor and laughter. *Ethology and Sociobiology, 14*(2), 141–169.

Weissman, M. M., Bland, R. C., Canino, G. J., Greewald, S., Hwu, H.-G., Joyce, P. R., Karam, E. G., Lee, C.-K., Lellouch, J., Lepine, J.-P., Newman, S. C., Rubio-Stipec, M., Wells, J. E., Wickramaratne, P. J., Wittchen, H.-U., & Yeh, E.-K. (1999). Prevalence of suicide ideation and suicide attempts in nine countries. *Psychological Medicine, 29*(1), 9–17.

Wells, G. L. (1993). What do we know about eyewitness identification? *American Psychologist, 48*, 553–571.

Wells, G. L., Luus, C. A. E., & Windschitl, P. D. (1994). Maximizing the utility of eyewitness identification evidence. *Current Directions in Psychological Science, 3*, 194–197.

Werker, J. F., & Pegg, J. E. (1992). Infant speech perception and phonological acquisition. In C. A. Ferguson, L. Menn, & C. Stoel-Gammon (Eds.), *Phonological development: Models, research, implications*. Timonium, MD: York Press.

Werker, J. F., & Tees, R. C. (1984). Cross-language speech perception: Evidence for perceptual reorganization during the first year of life. *Infant Behavior and Development, 7*, 49–63.

Werler, M. M., Mitchell, A. A., & Shapiro, M. B. (1989). The relation of aspirin use during the first trimester of pregnancy to congenital cardiac defects. *New England Journal of Medicine, 321*, 1639–1642.

Wessels, H., Lamb, M. E., Hwang, C. P., & Broberg, A. G. (1997). Personality development between 1 and 8 years of age in Swedish children with varying child care experience. *International Journal of Behavioral Development, 21*(4), 771–794.

Wessinger, C. M., Fendrich, R., & Gazzaniga, M. S. (1996). Islands of residual vision in hemianopic patients. *Journal of Cognitive Neuroscience, 9*(2), 203–221.

West, M. A. (1980). Meditation and the EEG. *Psychological Medicine, 10*, 369–375.

West, M. A. (1982). Meditation and self-awareness: Physiological and phenomenological approaches. In G. Underwood (Ed.), *Aspects of consciousness: Vol. 3. Awareness and self-awareness*. London: Academic.

West, R. L. (1996). An application of prefrontal cortex function theory to cognitive aging. *Psychological Bulletin, 120*(2), 272–292.

Wetter, D. W., Fiore, M. C., Gritz, E. R., Lando, H. A., Stitzer, M. L., Hassleblad, V., & Baker, T. B. (1998). The Agency for Health Care Policy and Research smoking cessation clinical practice guideline: Findings and implications for psychologists. *American Psychologist, 53*(6), 657–669.

Wexler, B. E., & Cicchetti, D. V. (1992). The outpatient treatment of depression. *Journal of Nervous and Mental Disease, 180*, 277–286.

Wheeler, M. A., Stuss, D. T., & Tulving, E. (1997). Toward a theory of episodic memory: The frontal and autonoetic consciousness. *Psychological Bulletin, 121*(3), 331–354.

Whicker, K. M., Bol, L., & Nunnery, J. A. (1997). Cooperative learning in the secondary mathematics classroom. *Journal of Educational Research, 91*(1), 42–48.

Whisman, M. A. (1993). Mediators and moderators of change in cognitive therapy of depression. *Psychological Bulletin, 114*, 248–265.

Whisman, M. A., & Kwon, P. (1993). Life stress and dysphoria: The role of self-esteem and hopelessness. *Journal of Personality and Social Psychology, 65*, 1054–1060.

White, N. M., & Milner, P. M. (1992). The psychobiology of reinforcers. *Annual Review of Psychology, 43*, 443–471.

Whorf, B. L. (1956). *Language, thought, and reality: Selected writings of Benjamin Lee Whorf* (J. B. Carroll, Ed.). New York: Wiley.

Widiger, T. A., Frances, A. J., Pincus, H. A., Davis, W. W., & First, M. B. (1991). Toward an empirical classification for the DSM-IV. *Journal of Abnormal Psychology, 100*, 280–288.

Wiebe, D. J. (1991). Hardiness and stress moderation: A test of proposed mechanisms. *Journal of Personality and Social Psychology, 60*, 89–99.

Wiggins, J. S., & Trapnell, P. D. (1992). Personality structure: The return of the Big Five. In S. R. Briggs, R. Hogan, & W. H. Jones (Eds.), *Handbook of personality psychology*. Orlando, FL: Academic.

Williams, C. D. (1959). Case report: The elimination of tantrum behavior by extinction procedures. *Journal of Abnormal and Social Psychology, 59*, 269.

Williams, K., Harkins, S., & Latané, B. (1981). Identifiability as a deterrent to social loafing: Two cheering experiments. *Journal of Personality and Social Psychology, 40*, 303–311.

Williams, K. E., Chambless, D. L., & Steketee, G. (1998). Behavioral treatment of obsessive-compulsive disorder in African Americans: Clinical issues. *Journal of Behavior Therapy and Experimental Psychiatry, 29*(2), 163–170.

Williams, K. J., Suls, J., Alliger, G. M., Learner, S. M., & Wan, C. K. (1991). Multiple role juggling and daily mood states in working mothers: An experience sampling study. *Journal of Applied Psychology, 76*, 664–674.

Williams, L. M. (1994). Recall of childhood trauma: A prospective study of women's memories of child sexual abuse. *Journal of Consulting and Clinical Psychology, 62*, 1167–1176.

Williams, R. L. (1989). *The trusting heart: Great news about Type A behavior*. New York: Random House.

Williams, S. L., Kinney, P. J., & Falbo, J. (1989). Generalization of therapeutic changes in agoraphobia: The role of perceived self-efficacy. *Journal of Consulting and Clinical Psychology, 57*, 436–442.

Williams, W. M., & Ceci, S. J. (1997). Are Americans becoming more or less alike? Trends in race, class, and ability differences in intelligence. *American Psychologist, 52*(11), 1226–1235.

Williamson, R. C. (1991). *Minority languages and bilingualism: Case studies in maintenance and shift*. Norwood, NJ: Ablex.

Willoughby, J. C., & Glidden, L. M. (1995). Fathers helping out: Shared child care and marital satisfaction of parents of children with disabilities. *American Journal on Mental Retardation, 99*, 399–406.

Wilson, D. A., & Sullivan, R. M. (1994). Neurobiology of associative learning in the neonate: Early olfactory learning. *Behavioral and Neural Biology, 61*, 1–18.

Wilson, E. O. (1975). *Sociobiology: A new synthesis*. Cambridge, MA: Harvard University Press.

Wilson, E. O. (1998). *Consilience: The unity of knowledge*. New York: Alfred A. Knopf.

Wilson, F. A. W., & Goldman-Rakie, P. S. (1994). Viewing preferences of rhesus monkeys related to memory for complex pictures, colours and faces. *Behavioral Brain Research, 60*, 79–89.

Wilson, K. D. (1998). Issues surrounding the cognitive neuroscience of obsessive-compulsive disorder. *Psychonomic Bulletin and Review, 5*(2), 161–172.

Wilson, M. A., & McNaughton, B. L. (1994). Reactivation of hippocampal ensemble memories during sleep. *Science, 265*, 676–679.

Wing, R. R., Epstein, L. H., Nowalk, M. P., & Lamparski, D. M. (1986). Behavioral self-regulation in the treatment of patients with diabetes mellitus. *Psychological Bulletin, 99*, 78–89.

Wink, P., & Helson, R. (1993). Personality change in women and their partners. *Journal of Personality and Social Psychology, 65*, 597–605.

Winner, E. (1997). Exceptionally high intelligence and schooling. *American Psychologist, 52*(10), 1070–1081.

Witt, L. A., & Nye, L. G. (1992). Gender and the relationship between perceived fairness of pay or promotion and job satisfaction. *Journal of Applied Psychology, 77*, 910–917.

Wittrock, M. C. (1987, August 29). The teaching of comprehension. Thorndike Award Address, 1987 American Psychological Association annual meeting, New York.

Wodak, R., & Benke, G. (1997). Gender as a sociolinguistic variable: New perspectives on variation studies. In F. Coulmas (Ed.), *The handbook of sociolinguistics*. Oxford, England: Blackwell.

Wolpe, J. (1958). *Psychotherapy by reciprocal inhibition*. Stanford, CA: Stanford University Press.

Wong, R. O. L., Chernjavsky, A., Smith, S. J., & Shatz, C. J. (1995). Early functional neural networks in the developing retina. *Nature, 374*, 716–718.

Wood, J. M., Bootzin, R. R., Rosenhan, D., Nolen-Hoeksema, S., & Jourden, F. (1992). Effects of the 1989 San Francisco earthquake on frequency and content of nightmares. *Journal of Abnormal Psychology, 101*, 219–224.

Wood, J. M., Nezworski, M. T., & Stejskal, W. J. (1996). The comprehensive system for the Rorschach: A critical examination. *American Psychological Society, 7*, 3–10.

Wood, N. L., & Cowan, N. (1995). The cocktail party phenomenon revisited: Attention and memory in the classic selective listening procedure of Cherry (1953). *Journal of Experimental Psychology: General, 124*, 243–262.

Wood, W., Wong, F. Y., & Chachere, J. G. (1991). Effects of media violence on viewers' aggression in unconstrained social interaction. *Psychological Bulletin, 109*, 371–383.

Woods, C. J. P. (1996). Gender differences in moral development and acquisition: A review of Kohlberg's and Gilligan's models of justice and care. *Social Behavior and Personality, 24*(4), 375–384.

Woods, S. C., Seely, R. J., Porte D. P., Jr., & Schwartz, M. W. (1998). Signals that regulate food intake and energy homeostasis. *Science, 280*, 1378–1383.

Woodward, W. R. (1982). The "discovery" of social behaviorism and social learning theory, 1870–1980. *American Psychologist, 37*, 396–410.

Woody, E., & Sadler, P. (1998). On reintegrating dissociated theories: Comment on Kirsch and Lynn. *Psychological Bulletin, 123*(2), 192–197.

Worling, J. R. (1995). Sexual abuse histories of adolescent male sex offenders: Differences on the basis of the age and the gender of their victims. *Journal of Abnormal Psychology, 104*, 610–613.

Wright, L. (1997). *Twins and what they tell us about who we are.* New York: John Wiley and Sons.

Wright, W. (1999). *Born that way: Genes, behavior, personality.* New York: Alfred A. Knopf.

Wundt, W. (1896). *Lectures on human and animal psychology.* New York: Macmillian.

Wyatt, G. E. (1994). The sociocultural relevance of sex research: Challenges for the 1990s and beyond. *American Psychologist, 49*, 748–754.

Wynn, K. (1992). Addition and subtraction by human infants. *Letters to Nature, 358*, 749–750.

Wynn-Dancy, L. M., & Gillam, R. B. (1997). Accessing long-term memory: Metacognitive strategies and strategic action in adolescents. *Topics in Language Disorders, 18*(1), 32–44.

Wynne, L. C., Cole, R. E., & Perkins, P. (1987). University of Rochester child and family study: Risk research in progress. *Schizophrenia Bulletin, 13*, 463–467.

Wyszecki, G., & Stiles, W. S. (1967). *Color science: Concepts and methods, quantitative data, and formulas.* New York: Wiley.

Yamamoto, J., Rhee, S., & Chang, D. S. (1994). Psychiatric disorders among elderly Koreans in the United States. *Community Mental Health Journal, 30*(1), 17–27.

Yarmey, D. (1994). Earwitness evidence: Memory for a perpetrator's voice. In D. F. Ross, & J. D. Read (Eds.), *Adult eyewitness testimony: Current trends and developments.* New York: Cambridge University Press.

Yehuda, R., Schmeidler, J., Wainberg, M., Binder-Brynes, K., & Duvdevani, T. (1998). Vulnerability to posttraumatic stress disorder in adult offspring of Holocaust survivors. *American Journal of Psychiatry, 155*(9), 1163–1171.

Yoken, C., & Berman, J. S. (1984). Does paying a fee for psychotherapy alter the effectiveness of treatment? *Journal of Consulting and Clinical Psychology, 52*, 254–260.

York, J. L., & Welte, J. W. (1994). Gender comparisons of alcohol consumption in alcoholic and nonalcoholic populations. *Journal of Studies on Alcohol, 55*, 743–750.

Young, T. J., & French, L. A. (1993). Suicide and social status among Native Americans. *Psychological Reports, 73*, 461–462.

Youngstedt, S. D., O'Connor, P. J., & Dishman, R. K. (1997). The effects of acute exercise on sleep: A quantitative synthesis. *Sleep, 20*(3), 203–214.

Yousif, Y., & Korte, C. (1995). Urbanization, culture, and helpfulness: Cross-cultural studies in England and the Sudan. *Journal of Cross-Cultural Psychology, 26*, 474–489.

Zaidel, E., Aboitiz, F., Clarke, J., Kaiser, D., & Matteson, R. (1995). Sex differences in interhemispheric relations for language. In F. L. Kitterle (Ed.), *Hemispheric communication: Mechanisms and models* (pp. 85–175). Hillsdale, NJ: Erlbaum.

Zajonc, R. B. (1965). Social facilitation. *Science, 149*, 269–274.

Zajonc, R. B. (1984). On the primacy of affect. *American Psychologist, 39*, 117–123.

Zajonc, R. B., Murphy, S. T., & Inglehart, M. (1989). Feeling and facial efference: Implications of the vascular theory of emotion. *Psychological Review, 96*, 395–416.

Zakay, D., Hayduk, L. A., & Tsal, Y. (1992). Personal space and distance misperception: Implications of a novel observation. *Bulletin of the Psychonomic Society, 30*, 33–35.

Zangwill, O. L., & Blakemore, C. (1972). Dyslexia: Reversal of eye movements during reading. *Neuropsychologia, 10*, 371–373.

Zaragoza, M. S., & Mitchell, K. J. (1996). Repeated exposure to suggestion and the creation of false memories. *American Psychological Society, 7*(5), 294–300.

Zarcone, T. J., Branch, M. N., Hughes, C. E., & Pennypacker, H. S. (1997). Key pecking during extinction after intermittent or continuous reinforcement as a function of the number of reinforcers delivered during training. *Journal of the Experimental Analysis of Behavior, 67*(1), 91–108.

Zeki, S. M. (1992). The functional organization of projections from striate to prestriate visual cortex in the rhesus monkey. In S. M. Kosslyn & R. A. Andersen, et al. (Eds.),. *Frontiers in cognitive neuroscience.* Cambridge, MA: MIT Press.

Zhang, F., Shogo, E., Cleary, L. J., Eskin, A., & Byrne, J. H. (1997). Role of transforming growth factor in long-term synaptic facilitation in Aplysia. *Science, 275*, 1318–1320.

Zigler, E. F. (1987). Formal schooling for four-year-olds? No. *American Psychologist, 42*, 254–260.

Zigler, E. F. (1994). Reshaping early childhood intervention to be a more effective weapon against poverty. *American Journal of Community Psychology, 22*, 37–47.

Zigler, E. F. (1999). Head Start is not child care. *American Psychologist, 54*(2), 142.

Zigler, E. F., & Hodapp, R. M. (1991). Behavioral functioning in individuals with mental retardation. *Annual Review of Psychology, 42*, 29–50.

Zins, J. E., & Barnett, D. W. (1983). The Kaufman Assessment Battery for Children and school achievement: A validity study. *Journal of Psychoeducational Assessment, 1*, 235–241.

Zitrin, C. M. (1981). Combined pharmacological and psychological treatment of phobias. In M. Navissakalian & D. H. Barlow (Eds.), *Phobias: Psychological and pharmacological treatments.* New York: Guilford.

Zlotnick, C., Elkin, I., & Shea, M. T. (1998). Does the gender of a patient or the gender of a therapist affect the treatment of patients with major depression? *Journal of Consulting and Clinical Psychology, 66*(4), 655–659.

Zola-Morgan, S., Squire, L. R., & Mishkin, M. (1982). The neuroanatomy of amnesia: Amygdala-hippocampus versus temporal stem. *Science, 218*, 1337–1339.

Zuber, J. A., Crott, H. W., & Werner, J. (1992). Choice shift and group polarization: An analysis of the status of arguments and social decision schemes. *Journal of Personality and Social Psychology, 62*, 50–61.

Zuckerman, M. (1969). Variables affecting deprivation results and hallucinations, reported sensations, and images. In J. P. Zubek (Ed.), *Sensory deprivation.* New York: Appleton-Century-Crofts.

Zuckerman, M. (1990). Some dubious premises in research and theory on racial differences. *American Psychologist, 45*, 1297–1303.

Zuckerman, M. (1999). *Vulnerability to psychopathology: A biosocial model.* Washington, DC: American Psychological Association.

Zuckerman, M., Kuhlman, D. M., Joireman, J., Teta, P., & Kraft, M. (1993). A comparison of three structural models for personality: The big three, the big five, and the alternative five. *Journal of Personality and Social Psychology, 65*, 757–768.

Name Index

Subject Index

self-perception and, 463
stress and, 504, 505
women's moral development
and, 354
See also African-Americans;
Asians
Dark adaptation, 84
Data, collection and analysis of,
7, 15
Date rape, 483
Dating, 487
Deafness, 101–02
Death, 399–02
hospice care and, 402–03
Debriefing, 19, 472
Decay (memory), 198, 201, 218
Decentration, 346
Deception, 19
Decibels, 98–99
Decision making, 241–43
barriers to, 243–44
Declarative memory, 204
Deep structure, 253–54
Defence mechanisms, 414, 572
Defence-oriented coping
strategies, 509
Deindividuation, 475
Delta waves, 124
Delusions, 543, 552
Demand characteristics, 11
Dementia, 399
Dendrite, 43, 44, 46, 169
Denial, 414
Dependence, 147
psychological, 138–39
Dependent personality disorder,
539
Dependent variable, 8–9
Depolarization, 44–45
Depression, 309, 387, 392, 455,
507, 518, 531, 541, 595
disorders and, 541–45
drug treatments for, 27
early attitudes towards,
26–27
genetics and, 544–45
monoamine theory of, 545
Prozac and, 595, 596
therapy and, 594
Depressive disorders, 541–45
causes of, 545–47
major, 542–45
suicide and, 547–51
Depth perception, 91–94
Dermis, 106
Design of Everyday Things
(Norman), 619
Determinism, reciprocal, 435
Developmental change, 633
Developmental psychologists, 25
Developmental psychology, 332
Deviation IQ, 272
Diabetes mellitus, 70, 180
*Diagnostic and Statistical
manual of mental disorders*
(DSM-IV), 528–31, 532,
536, 591
Diathesis-stress model, 547,
554
Dieting, 305–06
Difference threshold, 77
Differentiation, 336
Diffusion of responsibility, 474,
485
Disability, 17
Discrimination, 464, 609
employee selection and, 605

Disidentification, 463
Disorders, 522–58
anxiety, 532–33
child abuse and, 539–40
dissociative, 537–38
eating, 307–09
emotional, 552
mood, 541–49
new, 531
obsessive-compulsive,
534–36
perceptual 552
personality, 538–39
phobic, 533–34
prevention of, 568
schizophrenia, 551–58
sleep, 127–28
somatoform, 536–37
thought, 551–52
Disorganized type of
schizophrenia, 552–53
Dissociative amnesia, 537
Dissociative disorders, 537–38
Dissociative identity disorder,
537
Distributed practice, 216
Divergent thinking, 239
Diversity, 17, 22. *See also*
Culture; Gender
DNA, 39–41, 230
Domestic assault, 480–82
Door-in-the-face technique, 453
Dopamine, 46, 48, 67, 545, 595,
596
-seratonin interaction
hypothesis, 555
theory of schizophrenia, 555
Double bind, 557
Double-blind technique, 11
Dream(s), 124, 129–30
analysis, 570, 571–72
culture and, 132–33
lucid, 130
theories, 130–33
Drive, 295
Drive state, 295, 296
Drive theory, 610
of motivation, 295, 296,
297, 299, 302
of social facilitation, 473
Drug(s), 118
abuse, 138–47, 519
addictive, 138
antianxiety, 593–94
antidepressant, 594–96
antimania, 596
antipsychotic, 596–97
psychedelic, 146
psychoactive, 138
psychotropic, 593
table of, 597
Drug abuse, 138–47, 519
table of, 145
Drug therapy, 593–97
depression and, 594
DSM-IV. *See* Diagnostic and
statistical manual of mental
disorders
Dualism, 116–17
Duplicity theory of vision, 83
Dyslexia, 42, 40
Dysthymic disorder, 544–45

Ear, 99–100. *See also* Hearing
Eating
disorders, 307–09
neurobiology of, 304

over-, 303–08
Echoic storage, 199
Eclectic approach, 567
Eclectic model, of abnormal
behaviour, 528
Eclecticism, 33
Ecological systems theory, of
child development, 334
Educational psychologists, 24
Educational psychology, 633–35
EEG. *See* Electroencephalogram
Efferent neurons, 42, 43
Efficiency, 619–21
Ego, 410, 572–73
Ego analysts, 572
Egocentrism, 346, 362–63
adolescent, 379
Elaboration likelihood model,
452–54
Elaborative rehearsal, 200
Elavil, 544, 596
Electra complex, 413
Electrochemical processes, 44
Electroconvulsive shock therapy,
168, 209
Electroconvulsive therapy
(ECT), 592–93
Electroencephalogram (EEG),
58–59, 122, 250
Electroencephalography, 58–60
Electromagnetic spectrum, 81
Embryo, 336
Emotion(s), 316–21
Asian Canadians and, 565
body language and, 458–60
cognitive theories of, 324–26
defined, 318
development in children,
354–58
expressed, 557
facial expression and, 320
gender and, 322, 383–84
as intelligence, 269–70
lie detection and, 326–27
stress and, 499
theories of, 321–24
Emotional Brain, The (LeDoux),
324
Emotional development, in
adolescence 380–81
Emotional dimension, of
attitudes, 448–49
Emotional disorders, 552
Emotional Intelligence
(Goleman), 269
Emotional stability, 425
Empowerment, 631
Encoding specificity principle,
196
Encoding, 195, 196, 202, 202,
213, 224, 231
Encoding specificity principle,
208–09
Encoding strategies, 435
Encounter groups, 590
Endocrine glands, 67–71
Endorphins, 47, 108
Engineering psychologists, 24
Enkephalin, 108
Environment
crowding in, 625–28
intelligence and, 279–82
in prenatal development,
337–38
preserving, 629
schizophrenia and, 556–57
variables in, 624–25

Environmental conditions, 633
Environmental psychology,
623–29
Environmental research, 621
Environmental toxins, 625
Epidermis, 105
Epilepsy, 63, 204
Epinephrine, 50, 325, 545, 595
Episodic memory, 206–07
Equity theory, 488, 611–12
Ergonomics, 619–21
Erikson's psychological stages of
development, 367–71,
387–89
Erogenous zones, 411–12
Escape conditioning, 167
Espectancy theories, of
motivation, 298
Estradiol, 310
Estrogen, 69, 310
Ethics, research, 17–19
Ethnicity, bias, 15–16. *See also*
Culture
Evolutionary psychology, 32
Evolutionary theories, of
motivation, 294–95
Excitatory postsynaptic
potentials, 45
Excitement phase of sexual
response cycle, 311
Exclusion designs, 621
Exercise, 510, 513, 515, 518
Exhaustion stage, 501
Expectancies, 435
Expectancy effects, 10–11 , 611
Expectancy theory(ies), 302,
610–11
of motivation, 299
Experiential therapy, 576
Experiment(s), 8, 15
alternatives, 13–15
bias in, 15–17
control groups in, 8–9
correlation in, 11–12
evaluating, 12–13
operational definitions, 9
significant differences in,
9–10
sample size in, 9–10
successful, 10–11
variables, 8–9
See also Research; Scientific
method
Experimental group, 8–9
Experimental psychology, 23,
25–26
Expert witnesses, 623
Explicit memory, 203, 207–08
Expressed emotions, 557
External attribution, 460
Extinction, 158, 161, 176–77,
178
curve, 158
Extraneous variables, 9
Extraordinary memory, 210–11
Extrasensory perception (ESP),
110
Extrinsic motivation, 299
Extroversion, 425
Eye, 82–86
contact, 460
movements of, 86–87
See also Vision; Visual
system
Eyewitness testimony, 221–22
Eysenck's type theory of
personality, 424–25

PET. *See* Positron emission tomography
Phallic stage, 412–13
Phantom pain, 135
Phenomenological approaches, 419
Phenothiazines, 555
Pheromones, 104–05, 310
Phobic disorders, 533–34, 583
Phoneme, 251
Phonology, 249, 250–51
Photoreceptors, 82
Phrenologists, 57–58
Physical development
    in adolescence, 377–78
    in adulthood, 392–94
    in children, 332–71
    in infants, 64, 336–38, 339
Physiological psychologists, 25
Physiological reactions, 5
Physiological theories, of emotion, 321–24
Piaget's theory of moral development, 351–53
Pictorial memory, 218
Pitch, 62, 98
Pituitary gland, 52, 68–70
Place theories, 100–01
Placebo effect, 566
Placenta, 337
Placticity, of brain, 64, 65
Plaque, 400
Plasticity
    of behaviour, 33
    of personality, 430–31
Plateau phase of sexual response cycle, 311
Pleasure centres, 57
Pleasure principle, 410
Polarization, 44
Policy or program evaluators, 622
Pollutants, 625
Polydrug abusers, 139
Polygraph test, 326–27
Pons, 52, 54
Ponzo illusion, 94–95, 96
Position analysis questionnaire, 603
Positive instance, 234
Positive punishment, 171
Positive reinforcement, 167
Positron emission tomography (PET), 58, 59–60, 61, 197, 202, 250
Postconventional morality, 351–53
Posterior lobe, 70
Postsynaptic potential (PSP), 45
Post-traumatic stress disorder (PTSD), 506–08
Power distance, 608–09
Practice, 214–15, 216
    distributed, 216
    massed, 216
Pragmatics, 247
Precognition, 110
Preconscious, 409–10
Preconventional morality, 351–53
Predictive validity, 273
Prefrontal cortex, 202
Prefrontal lobotomy, 592
Prejudice, 464–67
    antifat, 467
    causes of, 465–66

reducing and eliminating, 466–67
    See also Bias; Discrimination
Premack principle, 169, 180
Premises, 241
Preoperational stage, 346–47
Press, 314
Pressure, 498–99
Prevalence, 528
Prevention
    designs, 621
    of mental disorders, 568
    primary, 632
Primacy effect, 211, 214
Primary prevention, 632
Primary punisher, 172
Primary reinforcer, 170
Principles of Psychology (James), 28, 32
Privacy, 628
Private speech, 349
Proactive coping, 511, 512
Proactive inhibition, 220
Proactive interference, 220
Probability, 242–43
Problem drinkers, 141–42
Problem solving, 235–36, 250
    barriers to, 236–38
    creative, 238–40
Procedural memory, 204
Procrastination, 506–07
Productive vocabulary, 249
Progressive relaxation, 638
Projection, 414
Projective tests, 440–41
Proprioceptive cues, 109
Prosocial behaviour, 482–85
Prospagnosia, 85
Prototype, 234, 246
Proximodistal trend, 339
Prozac, 535, 544, 594, 595, 596
Pschophysics, 77–78
Psychedelic drugs, 146
Psychiatrist, 20–21
Psychic determinism, 409
Psychoactive drug, 138
Psychoanalysis, 29, 570–73
Psychoanalyst, 21–22
Psychoanalytic approach, 29
Psychoanalytic theory(ies) (Freud), 408–09
    of child development, 333
    development of personality in, 411–13
    key concepts of, 409
    structures of consciousness and mind in, 409–11
    unresolved conflicts in, 413–15
Psychoanalytic, 437
Psychodrama, 589, 590
Psychodynamic model of abnormal behaviour, 526
Psychodynamic theory, suicide and, 548
Psychodynamic therapies, behaviour therapy compared to, 578
Psychodynamically based approaches, 567
Psychodynamically based therapies, 570–73, 574, 577, 584, 587
Psychogenic amnesia, 537
Psychokinesis, 110
Psycholinguistics, 249

Psychological dependence, 138–39
Psychological jurisprudence, 622
Psychologists, 20–22
    career as, 22
    clinical, 20
    confessions and, 19
    psychiatrists vs., 20–21
    psychoanalysts vs., 21–22
    roles of, 22
    types of, 24–26
Psychology, 4–5
    of being sick, 518–19
    careers in, 22
    cognitive, 230–34
    community, 630–32
    developmental, 332
    educational, 633–35
    environmental, 623–29
    experimental, 23, 25–26
    forensic, 622
    health, 513–20
    history of, 26–33
    legal, 622–23
    social, 448
    sport, 635–38
Psychoneuroimmunology (PNI), 513–15
Psychopharmacology, 47
Psychosexual stage theory of personality (Freud), 411–13
Psychosocial stages of development (Erikson), 367–71, 387–89
Psychostimulants, 144–46
Psychosurgery, 592–93
Psychotherapists, types of, 570
Psychotherapy integration, 567–68
Psychotherapy, 564. *See also* Therapy
Psychotic, 551
Psychoticism, 425
Puberty, 376, 377–78
Public distance, 627–28
Punisher, 165, 172
Punishment, 170–73, 580–81, 634–35
Pupil, 82
Purity (colour), 88

Quality circles, 613
Quality time, 368–69
Questionnaires, 13–14, 15

Random assignment, 9
Rage
    road, 494–98
    sham, 321
Rape, 483
Rapid eye movement (REM) sleep, 123–225
Ratio schedules, 174–76
Rational-emotive therapy, 585
Rationalization, 415, 509
Ravens' Progressive Matrices, 274
Raw score, 271, 276
Reactance, 457
Reaction formation, 414, 509–10
Reactive theory, 456–57
Reactivity, 505
Reality principle, 410
Reality testing, 543
Reasoning, 241
    formal, 241

Recency effect, 211, 214
Receptive fields, 84, 86
Receptive vocabulary, 249
Reciprocal determinism, 435
Recognition, 217
Reconstruction, 217–18
Reconstructive-script theory of flashbulb memory, 210
Referential naming, 257
Reflex, 153, 339–41
Refractory period
    of action potentials, 45
    in sexual response cycle, 311
Refractory period, 45
Rehearsal, 200, 201
Reinforcement, 167–70, 171, 172
    continuous, 174
    electrical brain stimulation as, 179
    negative, 167–68
    positive, 167
    schedules of, 174–76
    variables affecting, 173–78
Reinforcer, 165, 167, 579
    nature of, 168–70
    primary and secondary, 170
Relationship therapy, 590–91
Relationships, 486–91
Relaxation, 513, 638
    techniques, 510
Relearning, 215–16
Reliability
    of employees, 608
    of intelligence tests, 272–73
Religious personality type, 426
REM sleep, dreams and, 129
Repeatability, 12
Representative sample, 271
Representativeness, 458
Repression, 414
Research
    with animals, 17–18
    applied, 23–26
    cross-sectional research, 334–35
    deception in, 19
    ethics, 17–19
    longitudinal research, 334–35
    process, 8–17
    See also Experiments
Reserpine, 555
Residual/undifferentiated types, of schizophrenia, 554
Resilience, 509
Resistance, 572
Resistance stage, 501
Resolution phase of sexual response cycle, 311
REST. *See* Restricted environmental stimulation therapy
Restricted environmental stimulation therapy (REST), 80–81
Retention, 216–18
Reticular formation, 52, 54
Retina, 82, 84, 89
Retinal disparity, 93–94
Retrieval, 202, 213, 224, 231
    of information from memory, 206–08
    success and failure, 208–09
Retroactive inhibition, 220
Retroactive interference, 220
Retrograde amnesia, 223–24